TRAVEL, TOURISM, AND HOSPITALITY RESEARCH

TRAVEL, TOURISM, AND HOSPITALITY RESEARCH
A Handbook for Managers and Researchers

Second Edition

EDITORS

J.R. BRENT RITCHIE

University of Calgary
Calgary, Alberta, Canada

CHARLES R. GOELDNER

University of Colorado
Boulder, Colorado, USA

John Wiley & Sons, Inc.

New York   Chichester   Brisbane   Toronto   Singapore

This text is printed on acid-free paper.

Copyright © 1994 by John Wiley & Sons, Inc.

All rights reserved. Published simultaneously in Canada.

Reproduction or translation of any part of this work beyond
that permitted by Section 107 or 108 of the 1976 United
States Copyright Act without the permission of the copyright
owner is unlawful. Requests for permission or further
information should be addressed to the Permissions Department,
John Wiley & Sons, Inc.

This publication is designed to provide accurate and authoritative
information in regard to the subject matter covered. It is sold
with the understanding that the publisher is not engaged in
rendering professional services. If legal, accounting, medical,
psychological, or any other expert assistance is required, the
services of a competent professional person should be sought.
ADAPTED FROM A DECLARATION OF PRINCIPLES OF A
JOINT COMMITTEE OF THE AMERICAN BAR ASSOCIATION
AND PUBLISHERS.

Library of Congress Cataloging-in-Publication Data:

Travel, tourism, and hospitality research: a handbook for managers
   and researchers/edited by J.R. Brent Ritchie and Charles R.
   Goeldner.—2nd ed.
      p. cm.
   Includes index.
   ISBN: 0-471-58248-4 (acid-free)
   1. Tourist trade—Research.   I. Ritchie, J.R. Brent.
II. Goeldner, Charles R.
G155.A1T6578 1994
338.4'79104'072—dc20   93-17481
                                            CIP

ISBN:0-471-58248-4

CONTRIBUTORS

JAMES R. ABBEY   William F. Harrah College of Hotel Administration, University of Nevada, Las Vegas, Nevada

BRIAN H. ARCHER   Department of Management Studies for Tourism and Hotel Industries, University of Surrey, Guildford, Surrey, England

VERNON AZUCENAS   Assistant to the Executive Director, U.S. Travel Data Center, Washington, D.C.

JAY BEAMAN   Director, Socio-Economic Division, Parks Canada, Ottawa, Ontario

UEL BLANK   Professor Emeritus, University of Minnesota, Minneapolis, Minnesota

JOHN C. CANNON   Chief, Housing Surveys Branch, Demographic Surveys Division, Bureau of the Census, Washington, D.C.

CAROLYN CAREY   Strategic Planner, Marketing Department, Knott's Berry Farm, Buena Park, California

ROBIN A. CHADWICK   Formerly of Statistics Canada, Bath, Ontario

JOHN D. CLAXTON   Professor, Faculty of Commerce, University of British Columbia, Vancouver, British Columbia

SUZANNE D. COOK   Executive Director, U.S. Travel Data Center, Washington, D.C.

LOUISE CRANDALL   Corporate Planning Analyst, National Capital Commission, Ottawa, Ontario

GEOFFREY I. CROUCH   Associate Professor, Tourism and Hospitality Management, The University of Calgary, Calgary, Alberta

LAWRENCE F. CUNNINGHAM   Professor of Marketing and Transportation, University of Colorado, Denver, Colorado

THOMAS LEA DAVIDSON   Principal, Davidson-Peterson Associates, Inc., York, Maine

DAVID L. EDGELL, SR.   Director, Office of Policy and Planning, U.S. Travel and Tourism Administration, U.S. Department of Commerce, Washington, D.C.

RANDYL D. ELKIN   Chairman and Professor, Department of Industrial and Labor Relations, West Virginia University, Morgantown, West Virginia

MARK FENTON   Curtin University of Technology, Bentley WA, Australia

DOUGLAS C. FRECHTLING   Associate Professor of Tourism, George Washington University, Washington, D.C.

DONALD GETZ   Associate Professor, Tourism and Hospitality Management, The University of Calgary, Calgary, Alberta

CHARLES R. GOELDNER   Professor of Marketing and Tourism, University of Colorado, Boulder, Colorado

NELSON H.H. GRABURN   Department of Anthropology, University of California, Berkeley, California

CLARE A. GUNN   Professor Emeritus, Department of Recreation, Park, and Tourism Sciences, Texas A&M University, College Station, Texas

STEPHEN J. HIEMSTRA   Professor, Department of Restaurant, Hotel, Institutional and Tourism Management, Purdue University, West Lafayette, Indiana

FRED HURST   Port Authority of New York & New Jersey, New York, New York

MARTINUS J. KOSTERS   Member, Board of Directors, Netherlands Institute of Tourism and Transport Studies, Breda, The Netherlands

WILBUR F. LAPAGE   Director, Division of Parks and Recreation, State of New Hampshire, Concord, New Hampshire

ALAN A. LEW   Northern Arizona University, Flagstaff, Arizona

CARL K. LINK   Link Hospitality Consultants Ltd., Calgary, Alberta

TYRRELL G. MARRIS   Former Head of Research Services, British Tourist Authority and English Tourist Board. Tourism Research Consultant, London, England

GORDON H.G. MCDOUGALL   Professor, School of Business

and Economics, Wilfrid Laurier University, Waterloo, Ontario

SCOTT MEIS   Manager, Socio-Economic Division, Parks Canada, Ottawa, Ontario

LISLE S. MITCHELL   Professor, Department of Geography, University of South Carolina, Columbia, South Carolina

GEORGE H. MOELLER   Deputy Station Director, Pacific Northwest Research Station, U.S. Forest Service, Portland, Oregon

ROLAND S. MOORE   Department of Anthropology, University of California, Berkeley, California

HUGH MUNRO   Director, Laurier Trade Development Center, Wilfrid Laurier University, Waterloo, Ontario

ROBERT P. OLSON   University of Wisconsin-Stout, Menomonie, Wisconsin

PHILIP PEARCE   Head, Department of Tourism, James Cook University, North Queensland, Australia

RICHARD R. PERDUE   Professor of Marketing, Tourism Management Program, Boulder, Colorado

KAREN IDA PETERSON   Principal, Davidson-Peterson Associates, Inc., York, Maine

BARRY E. PITEGOFF   Tourism Research Administrator, Office of Marketing Research, Florida Division of Tourism, Tallahassee, Florida

ABRAHAM PIZAM   University of Central Florida, Orlando, Florida

STANLEY C. PLOG   Chairman and CEO, Plog Research, Inc., Reseda (Los Angeles), California

LINDA K. RICHTER   Associate Professor, Department of Political Science, Kansas State University, Manhattan, Kansas

J.R. BRENT RITCHIE   Chairman, World Tourism Education and Research Centre, The University of Calgary, Calgary, Alberta

RANDALL S. ROBERTS   Employee Relations Manager, Louie Glass Company, Inc., Weston, West Virginia

STUART N. ROBINSON   Stuart N. Robinson and Associates, Inc., Dallas, Texas

ILKKA A. RONKAINEN   Associate Professor of Marketing, School of Business Administration, Georgetown University, Washington, D.C.

JAMES M. ROVELSTAD   Director, Center for Survey & Marketing Research, University of Wisconsin-Parkside, Kenosha, Wisconsin

ELWOOD L. SHAFER   Professor of Environmental Management & Tourism, School of Hotel, Restaurant & Institutional Management, Pennsylvania State University, University Park, Pennsylvania

WILLIAM SIEGEL   President, Longwoods International Inc., Toronto, Ontario

GINGER SMITH   Senior International Policy Analyst, Office of Policy and Planning, U.S. Travel and Tourism Administration, U.S. Department of Commerce, Washington, D.C.

GORDON D. TAYLOR   Ottawa, Ontario

PETER W. WILLIAMS   Director, Centre for Tourism Policy and Research, Simon Fraser University, Burnaby, British Columbia

ED WOHLMUTH   The Art Institute of Philadelphia, Philadelphia, Pennsylvania

ARCH G. WOODSIDE   The Malcolm S. Woldenberg Professor of Marketing, Tulane University, New Orleans, Louisiana

DON WYNEGAR   Deputy Assistant Secretary, U.S. Travel and Tourism Administration, Washington, D.C.

WILLIAM ZIFF-LEVINE   Managing Director, Data Management Counsel, Inc., Radnor, Pennsylvania

DEDICATION

This book is dedicated to the Travel and Tourism Research Association (TTRA) and its objectives. It was TTRA's original encouragement and its professional and financial support that made the first edition of the Handbook possible.

TTRA's objectives are:

- To serve as an international forum for the exchange of ideas and information among travel and tourism researchers, marketers, planners, and managers.

- To encourage the professional development of travel and tourism researchers, marketers, planners, and managers.

- To facilitate global cooperation between producers and users of travel and tourism research.

- To foster the development of travel and tourism research and related curricula in institutes of higher education.

- To advocate the effective use of research in the decision-making process of professionals in the travel and tourism industry.

PREFACE

This Second Edition represents a modest yet significant revision of the Handbook, *Travel, Tourism, and Hospitality Research*. Because of the importance we ascribe to this publication, we would very much like to update its contents on a continuous, or at least a regular, basis. At the same time, due to the nature, size, and scope of the Handbook, one hesitates to undertake a costly revision of such a work more frequently than is necessary. Upon reflection, it is seen that many of the basic concepts, methods, and practices of good research in the field remain relatively stable over time. This reality tends to minimize the need for frequent or major revisions of the contents of a work such as this Handbook. Conversely, a field as dynamic as travel, tourism, and hospitality research is constantly evolving and growing. As a result of this process, ideas change, references become outdated, examples lose their relevance, older research methodologies are found wanting, and new research approaches emerge. Of equal if not greater importance is the fact that long-time contributors are being joined by younger colleagues, who bring new energy and fresh insights to the field.

Originally, as editors, we had naively hoped that the original edition of the Handbook might remain useful for perhaps up to 10 years. However, in as little as 4 years, it became evident that at least some revision of the material should be undertaken. The most obvious requirement for such revision was the need to update the references related to each chapter. While this need was more significant for certain chapters than for others, no topic area is exempt from the infusion of new ideas and new findings. As such, we asked all authors to review their material with a view to incorporating any new, relevant works that have appeared over the past several years. In most cases, we were successful in obtaining such reviews and necessary updates, although in a few we were not. In two instances, we were forced to drop chapters the material of which had clearly outlived its usefulness.

The second pressure for revision came from those who felt that particular topic areas had been overlooked or inadequately developed in the First Edition. In an attempt to respond to these views, we have added 11 new chapters. These chapters address three shortcomings of the First Edition. First, they focus upon the research needs of sectors that we were unable to include in the First Edition. Second, they expand upon our efforts to describe the unique research concepts, approaches, and methodologies of specific disciplines important to the study of tourism. Finally, the added chapters have allowed us to present a discussion of certain well-established research measures and techniques that were not covered in the First Edition.

The third and perhaps most compelling incentive to undertake the present revision was to provide an opportunity to introduce new ideas and new authors. In terms of new ideas, we have been able to introduce some important new research approaches; we have been able to further reflect the increasing emphasis on globalization that has occurred over the past decade; and we have been able to focus more extensively on the controversial area of research that seeks to evaluate the effectiveness of tourism advertising. In the process, we have had the good fortune of attracting 12 new authors to the already distinguished list of contributors.

Needless to say, our challenge as editors of this Second Edition was to strike the correct balance between the desire for stability and the need for change. On the one hand, we wished to maintain a proper respect for the substantial efforts of our original authors and associate editors. At the same time, we recognized the very real need to keep the contents of the Handbook up-to-date and relevant. The approach we have chosen was to retain as much of the original effort as possible while attempting to enhance its timeliness. Simultaneously, we have sought to selectively expand the topics covered by the Handbook.

We are hopeful that this modest revision of the initial Handbook will continue to find acceptance among our colleagues in both industry and academia. As in the First Edition, our goal remains one of producing a useful, high-quality reference document that reflects the integrity and knowledge of our authors and that makes a positive contribution to the development and well-being of the travel, tourism, and hospitality industry. This said, there is little doubt in our minds that the field will continue to evolve substantially over the next few years as still newer approaches emerge and as the size and capabilities of our research community are enhanced. As such, we fully anticipate that future editions could change substantially in terms of both content and structure. In this regard, we welcome comments from any and all of our colleagues as to the kinds of changes that would make the next edition of this Handbook even more valuable to them.

ACKNOWLEDGMENTS

While the preparation of this Second Edition was by its nature much less demanding than that of the initial version, we nevertheless continue to be indebted to many individuals and organizations for the success of this Handbook.

Again, as for the First Edition, we wish first and foremost to thank the authors for their cooperation and their contributions. With very few exceptions, these busy professionals responded promptly and efficiently to our requests for either revisions or new material. As a result, we have been able to prepare this Second Edition within a very tight time frame. Thus, for their positive support, for their enthusiasm, and, above all, for their quality contributions, we are most appreciative to each and every author whose work appears in this Handbook.

Although the associate editors played only a minor role in the preparation of this version, we wish to continue to acknowledge the pivotal role that they played in the development and the ongoing success of the Handbook. With this in mind, we would draw your attention to the list of associate editors and remind you of the valuable service they have provided in the past. We trust we will continue to merit their confidence and support in the future.

From a historical perspective, we wish to remind readers of the critical role that the Travel and Tourism Research Association (TTRA) played in giving life to the concept of the Handbook. Without the moral and financial support that nurtured the publication in its early phases of development, it is questionable whether or not our efforts to produce the Handbook would have succeeded. While TTRA no longer has a direct involvement in its preparation or production, we wish to acknowledge the ongoing emotional bond that we feel still exists between the Handbook and the Association. As editors, we believe that the entire tourism community owes a debt of gratitude to the Association and its membership for their critical early support of the Handbook project.

Finally, we would again like to express our sincere appreciation to the Faculty of Management at The University of Calgary for its financial and administrative support in the preparation of this Handbook. While less onerous than in the past, the demands of preparing this publication have continued to draw upon the goodwill and the resources of the Faculty on numerous occasions. In particular, we wish to acknowledge the contribution of a very committed and talented individual: Meghan Whitelaw, who coordinated and supervised the solicitation, editing, and completion of the manuscripts in a most efficient manner.

INTRODUCTION

In the short span of just under 50 years, the travel, tourism and hospitality industry has achieved international and national recognition of one of the major social and economic forces of our times. Despite this reality, those of us in the industry are well aware that the rapid growth of the industry which has occurred during this period has not always been matched by the development of a solid foundation or an infrastructure on which to sustain and enhance the industry's future. In particular, we are only too well aware that the information base on which decisions are being made in tourism throughout the world is fragile and, in many cases, simply unreliable.

The reasons for this situation are several. The very nature of the industry itself is, of course, a major factor. The large number of organizations involved in tourism and their relatively small size means that efforts to collect data from them and for them is both costly and time-consuming. This is in marked contrast to other major industries such as banking or automobile manufacturing where information is concentrated in the hands of a much smaller number of firms and where government regulations for reporting requirements greatly facilitate the development of reliable data bases.

The second factor is the nature of the travel experience itself and the difficulties that are inherent in understanding consumer behavior and expenditure patterns within this travel experience. As has been pointed out (Ritchie 1975),[1] research efforts in travel and tourism face a number of difficulties which are unique to the field and which go beyond the normal data collection concerns encountered in other fields. These difficulties decrease the reliability of our data, make it more costly to gather, make it more difficult to interpret, frequently render it out of date before it is reported, and often cause it to be non-relevant to management issues faced by individual users.

[1]Ritchie, J.R. Brent (1975), "Some Critical Aspects of Measurement Theory and Practice in Travel Research," *Journal of Travel Research* 14(1).

A third factor is perhaps less obvious but more pervasive. Because tourism is a relatively new industry, it has not had the opportunity to establish the educational infrastructure necessary to systematically attract and train its fair percentage of the best minds and most ambitious, most effective managers. Historically, individuals have entered the travel industry for a broad range of reasons, a great many of which have little to do with a conscious decision to pursue a professional career in the tourism industry. As a result of this lack of formal education for a career in the industry, there has been little perceived need for systematic research and information systems on which to base management decisions.

All this has changed dramatically over the last fifteen years. During this period, world competition in tourism has grown dramatically as more and more countries and regions realize both the desirability and the necessity of including tourism as a major component of their social and economic structure. During this period, the tourism industry has been gradually "getting its act together" by becoming a more cooperative and more coordinated force. In parallel, and on another front, progress has been made in developing research techniques which improve the reliability of travel and tourism data, thus enhancing our understanding of consumer behavior and consumer spending patterns in tourism. While much progress yet remains to be accomplished, there is little doubt that the level of sophistication in tourism research is much higher than it was and that there will be continued pressure for even more rigorous information gathering, analysis and interpretation systems.

Finally, the last decade in particular has seen very meaningful progress in the development of programs designed to enhance the education and training levels of those entering the industry, as well as those currently employed in it. Tourism has not, of course, yet achieved the funding or the prominence in education that has been attained by other sectors of the economy such as manufacturing or agriculture, but progress is being made. This progress, as it continues, will further fuel the demand for more and better research.

THE NEED FOR THE HANDBOOK

It was against this background that the preparation of the present Handbook was first undertaken in the early 1980s. At that time it was evident to the editors that while advances were being made, in the preparation of textbooks and other teaching materials for tourism at the level of introductory courses, little was being done to consolidate the rapidly expanding knowledge base related to research in the field of travel, tourism and hospitality. In the six years since the first edition of this Handbook was published in 1987, the situation in this regard has not changed dramatically.

As in the past, the reasons for this situation are several in number. Perhaps the most important is the diversity of the knowledge base and the difficulty facing any single individual who attempts to master the many skills involved. While the past several years have seen the emergence of outstanding examples of well focused research texts, efforts to provide a comprehensive overview and understanding of the total field of travel, tourism and hospitality research remain limited.

The second underlying cause was perhaps the failure of many to realize the extent of the strides which had been taken in the field of travel/tourism/hospitality research in recent years and the perception that existing journals adequately captured available knowledge. In retrospect, this view appears to suffer from two shortcomings. First, as many are aware, the number of publications in travel, tourism and hospitality research has increased substantially over the past fifteen to twenty years. The pioneering *Journal of Travel Research* and *Journal of Leisure Research* have long been recognized. Over the years they have been complemented by the now well established publications such as the *Annals of Tourism Research, Leisure Sciences, Tourism Management, Hospitality Management* and *Leisure and Society* to name only a few. The ongoing vitality and growth of the field continues to be reflected in the emergence and growing reputations of still newer journals such as the *Journal of Travel* and *Tourism Marketing* and the recently published *World Travel and Tourism Review*.

Finally, there has been a failure to take into account much of the valuable work and the many research skills which exist outside of the framework tapped by formal publications. This is particularly true in the field of travel and tourism where, because of the lack of a formal research training system, individuals and firms have been forced to develop their own capabilities and research approaches. Certain of these individuals and firms have made major contributions to both research thinking and to the development of specific techniques in the field.

Given all of the above factors, it was felt that the most effective and most appropriate response was to prepare a research oriented handbook which would draw upon the knowledge and skills found among both educators and practitioners. The goal of the editors was to identify for each topic included in the Handbook, that individual judged by his/her peers to possess the most expertise in relation to each of the defined topics. This was done, and in most cases, we believe we have succeeded by various means to convince leading experts in various aspects of travel and tourism research to provide us with the benefits of their knowledge and experience.

PHILOSOPHY AND ORIENTATION OF THE HANDBOOK

From the very beginning, the philosophy and orientation of the editors has been to develop a major reference book which will be of use to:

1. Managers in tourism who have a need to use research as a means of providing information for improving their managerial effectiveness.

2. Beginning researchers who require an overview of available research methods, in a single source combined with an associated basic bibliography, which will permit them to pursue more in-depth work when required.

It is also hoped that the Handbook will prove useful to more experienced researchers who have a developed expertise in a given area, but who may wish to refresh their memories or review research topics with which they have had little or no direct experience. Finally, it is hoped that the Handbook will also be found valuable for use in introductory courses in tourism research methods.

The above philosophy and orientation was communicated to prospective authors from the very beginning and has colored both the review process and the subsequent revising and editing of each chapter. It should be emphasized that this desire to achieve readability on the part of managers and beginning researchers was constantly balanced by an equally strong desire to maintain as much rigor as possible in each author's presentation. This balance was certainly not easy to achieve and each reader will undoubtedly come to his/her own conclusions concerning the extent to which the goal has been attained. Undoubtedly, our success in this area has varied. In particular, there will be cases where academic authors may not have achieved the managerial relevance some might desire. In others, practitioners may not have achieved the sophistication in presentation that an academic might desire. It is hoped, however, that readers will find that we have been able to achieve a reasonable mix and balance in this regard across the entire contents of the Handbook.

STRUCTURE AND CONTENTS OF THE HANDBOOK

Given the diversity of the tourism industry, it is not surprising that tourism research also contains numerous, complex elements. As such, a major task facing the editors was to decide upon what to conceptually include in the Handbook and how to structure the material eventually obtained. The first step in this process was to review existing literature in an attempt to identify various substantive and methodological topics addressed by previous researchers. As a result of this process, some 55 topics were identified and tentatively designated as a Handbook chapter for the first edition. Since the initial version of the Handbook contained only 43 chapters, we clearly did not succeed in covering all 55 topics (which were themselves not necessarily exhaustive). In certain cases, we were simply unable to identify an author who was capable or willing to prepare the chapter in question. In others, individuals found they were unable to complete the task due to a lack of available information or other personal reasons.

In this second edition, as explained in the Preface, we have attempted to make the Handbook more complete in several ways. First, we have added certain topics which were omitted in the first edition. Second, we have tried to identify and include additional topics, particularly those covering newer research approaches which have emerged over the past six years. Finally, we have undertaken to update the existing material where necessary and appropriate. In this regard, we have had to regretfully drop certain chapters from this second edition in cases where the material was obviously dated and the authors were unable to provide revised material. In a few selected cases, because of enduring nature of the content, we have retained certain chapters even though the authors were not able to review and revise them as we would have liked. The end result of this process is that this second edition contains a total of 52 chapters which have been structured into eight major parts.

Concerning this structure, there were clearly several models that might have been chosen. The manner in which the Handbook was finally structured was a reflection of the overall philosophy of the Handbook, current industry practices, existing academic orientations, and the desire to regroup items likely to appeal to a similar audience. As a result, the Handbook contains eight major parts.

Part One, entitled "A Managerial Perspective," has been designed to clearly emphasize that research must be viewed as a tool to assist management in improving the quality of planning and decision making. This approach reflects the philosophy of the Handbook and emphasizes that management must lead and direct the research process.

Part Two of the Handbook intentionally switches very quickly to a presentation of fundamental concepts and approaches for travel, tourism, and hospitality research. The point being made is, that while research must serve managerial purposes, it must also be conducted with rigor and from a sound conceptual and theoretical base.

As the reader moves into Part Three of the Handbook, he/she returns to a more managerial setting, albeit, the specialized world of the public sector. In this section of the Handbook, an effort has been made to provide insight and understanding concerning the nature and extent of research within national, regional and municipal tourism organizations. The purpose of Part Three is to demonstrate how research is used at each of these levels and to clarify the nature of information requirements for decision making at different levels of aggregation/disaggregation.

Parts Four and Five of the Handbook are intended to be distinct yet complementary. Part Four provides a view of tourism research as perceived from a disciplinary perspective. The intent here is to demonstrate and emphasize that tourism is a multidisciplinary field of study which draws extensively on a number of disciplinary roots for the great majority of its concepts and research methods. Unfortunately, the number of disciplines it was possible to cover was limited. Indeed, the treatment of all relevant disciplines would merit a book in itself. In contrast, Part Five reflects the practical structure of the tourism industry itself. In this case, it has been possible to obtain chapters covering the research needs of most important segments of tourism. Again, however, this coverage is not complete. For example, we were not able to obtain a chapter on research for the airline sector. Hopefully, such gaps will be rectified in the future.

The latter three parts of the Handbook focus on more specific research approaches and methods. Part Six contains material dealing with various aspects of estimating the impact of tourism on both the host community as well as the tourists themselves. Part Seven discusses the nature and application of some very specific planning and data collection techniques. Finally, Part Eight outlines some research approaches which are particularly applicable to various marketing tasks which are especially important in the field of tourism.

USING THE HANDBOOK

There are clearly a variety of ways in which a Handbook, containing as much material as the present one, might be used. The reader, however, should keep in mind that the present document has been prepared primarily to fulfill its main mission; that is, to provide a working reference book for managers using research and for beginning researchers. It is anticipated that for such applications individuals are unlikely to read the Handbook from cover to cover at a given point in time (as might be the case with a textbook). Rather, it is envisaged that users will selectively read chapters containing information having direct bearing on the particular issue or problem they are currently facing. Given this type of usage, the Handbook has been prepared so that each chapter can be read on its own. As such, no one chapter is entirely dependent on others in the Handbook. While an attempt has been made by the various authors to refer specifically to other chapters related to their discussion, we have intentionally permitted a fairly substantial amount of duplication and overlap where this was appropriate and where it facilitated the ease of use and understanding of a given chapter.

The second way in which we anticipate the Handbook will be used is as a textbook for tourism research courses and seminars. From a course perspective, students will clearly run into a certain amount of repetition when reading from cover to cover. It is our hope and indeed our belief that such repetition may prove highly beneficial from two perspectives. First, it should provide reinforcement of a number of important concepts. Second, it will provide the student with alternative perspectives on various topics which different authors felt to be important.

The use of the Handbook for specialized seminars roughly parallels its use as a working reference document. As such, the approach of preparing compartmentalized stand-alone chapters, we feel, makes the Handbook particularly appropriate for this type of application. However, in this regard, it is expected that instructors will probably want to provide participants with additional in-depth material, the identification of which is facilitated by the rather extensive bibliographies that most authors have provided.

J.R. BRENT RITCHIE
CHARLES R. GOELDNER

CONTENTS

CHAPTER 47   545
Improving Advertising
Conversion Studies

Arch G. Woodside

Ilkka A. Ronkainen

CHAPTER 48   559
Evaluating Tourism Advertising Campaigns:
Conversion vs. Advertising Tracking Studies

William Siegel

William Ziff-Levine

CHAPTER 49   565
Methods of Accountability Research
for Destination Marketing

Richard R. Perdue

Barry E. Pitegoff

CHAPTER 50   573
Evaluating the Effectiveness of Travel
Trade Shows and Other Tourism Sales-
Promotion Techniques

Abraham Pizam

CHAPTER 51   583
Guidelines for the Study of International
Tourism Demand Using Regression Analysis

Geoffrey I. Crouch

CHAPTER 52   597
Estimating the Potential of International
Markets

Don Wynegar

INDEX   607

TRAVEL, TOURISM, AND HOSPITALITY RESEARCH

Part One

A Managerial Perspective

This introductory section of the Handbook is intended to emphasize the fact that travel and tourism research must be viewed from a managerial as well as a technical perspective. It is a well-recognized truism that managers and researchers, in virtually all sectors of industry, experience some degree of difficulty in working together effectively. While the reasons for this situation are many and varied, part of the difficulty stems from a lack of understanding of each other's purposes and priorities. Recognizing this reality, an attempt has been made in the six chapters that comprise Part One of the Handbook to sensitize both managers and researchers (but particularly researchers) to the need for a managerial perspective in the planning, execution, and use of research.

Chapter 1 has been written by Clare Gunn, one of the most respected pioneers of travel and tourism research. In this chapter, entitled "A Perspective on the Purpose and Nature of Tourism Research Methods," Dr. Gunn positions the field by examining a number of key dimensions that are required for an understanding of the scope of research in tourism, the range of contributions that can be anticipated, and the complexities that must be dealt with in bringing together research from various sources and disciplines.

In contrast to Chapter 1, which has a philosophical and informational orientation, Chapter 2 attempts to provide both managers and researchers with an understanding of the various research approaches available and the manner in which each approach serves a different role in the overall managerial process. The author, Brent Ritchie, argues that the type of research method employed must reflect the level of decision making within an organization, the stage of the decision-making process for which research is conducted, and the functional problems being addressed by management. Based on this analytical framework, it is seen that information needs that are to be met by research can vary substantially within an organization. As a result, care must be taken to select a research approach that is appropriate to the data-collection task at hand.

Chapters 3 and 4 provide different yet complementary research approaches for senior policy makers and executives who are responsible for formulating frameworks and setting directions for overall tourism development. In his award-winning essay from the *Journal of Travel Research* (Chapter 3), Elwood Shafer outlines a process designed to focus the knowledge and energies of senior CEOs who must balance a range of social, economic, managerial, environmental, and political benefits against their associated costs when they are undertaking strategic planning for tourism. One particularly important aspect of Shafer's process is the manner in which it brings together quantitative information and qualitative judgments. Another is the way it facilitates the input of executive judgments while maintaining procedural rigor. In Chapter 4, Brent Ritchie describes a recently developed methodology for strategic planning within major tourism destinations such as a country or a large metropolitan region. This methodology, referred to as "Strategic Visioning," provides a systematic framework within which senior tourism officials can solicit and coordinate public and industry input so as to define and determine the kinds of developments that are judged to be effective in the marketplace while remaining responsive to the views of residents of the destination in question. This integrated, consensus-based process for the "crafting" of a destination vision emphasizes a proactive philosophy in strategic tourism planning that we believe will become increasingly important in the years to come.

In Chapter 5, Jay Beaman and Scott Meis address an important topic that is frequently overlooked in the travel and tourism research literature, namely "Managing the Research Function for Effective Policy Formulation and Decision Making." The authors contend that, to be effective, research managers must spend much of their time on two main activities, research planning and research coupling. Research planning involves establishing a process in which areas of research are identified and prioritized in the light of existing resources, in which appropriate research methods are selected, and in which research is monitored during execution and is evaluated for effectiveness upon completion. Research coupling, on the other hand, includes communication and organizational structuring activities directed towards stimulating and facilitating dialogue between researchers and user groups. It is perhaps this latter area that has been most severely neglected by all concerned in the execution and use of travel and tourism research. Hopefully, the suggestions made by Beaman and Meis will be acknowledged and acted upon by readers of this volume.

The final chapter in Part One reflects another strong trend that has emerged in tourism over the past several years. In Chapter 6, David Edgell and Ginger Smith address the reality of globalization and how this phenomenon is increasingly exerting an impact upon the tourism sector. More specifically, they discuss the manner in which international factors and events influence national and local tourism development and demonstrate the resulting need to explicitly integrate these factors into the policy-formulation process at all levels. The importance that the authors attach to technological and environmental factors when formulating tourism policy is of particular note. As well, readers will want to review the increasing influence that Edgell and Smith attribute to the growing number of international organizations having a direct interest in global tourism development.

In brief, it is hoped that these introductory chapters will serve to encourage a common perspective among managers and researchers with respect to the nature and roles of the research process as a vehicle for providing assistance for policy formulation and decision making in tourism. It is only through such a common perspective that research can be truly effective.

1

A Perspective on the Purpose and Nature of Tourism Research Methods

CLARE A. GUNN
Professor Emeritus
Department of Recreation, Park, and Tourism Sciences
Texas A&M University
College Station, Texas

Tourism research, while no substitute for superior management practices, provides objective, systematic, logical, and empirical foundations for such management. Tourism, because of its great complexity of social, environmental, and economic aspects, requires research input from many disciplines—marketing, behavior, geography, anthropology, business, history, political science, planning and design, futurism, and many others. While the scientific method is basic to virtually all research, the several disciplines have slightly different approaches important to tourism. The value of such research lies in better development, management, policy making, and education in this important and growing field.

Today, business people and governmental leaders the world over are increasingly recognizing that the phenomenon of tourism has already become a powerful economic and social force. Developing countries seek its rewards, and developed countries strive to protect market share. This comparatively new revelation is due largely to statistical research several decades ago that demonstrated that tourism produced incomes, jobs, and taxes. Without doubt, published data revealing these positive impacts stimulated both the public and private sectors to expand activity in developing and promoting tourism.

Research into other facets of tourism, however, has been much slower to develop. There may be several reasons for this. A *preoccupation with promotion* has tended to favor large funding for promotion and little for research. Individual parts of the field of tourism—airlines, hotels, food services, parks, highway transportation—have engaged in proprietary research for some time; but, the *protective nature of proprietary research*, not sharing findings with the public, has benefited only those sponsoring the research. Another reason may be the general lack of understanding of how *sweeping and complicated* the field of tourism really is. It is not just business; nor is it really an "industry." It involves

much more. And each part sees tourism from its own perspective, not as a whole. This has not changed greatly since Sales (1959), in the first seminal work on tourism, *Travel and Tourism Encyclopedia*, observed the lack of each element's understanding of its role in overall tourism. Finally, these and other causes have resulted in a general *lack of faith* in the power of enlightenment that properly designed research can produce.

The discussion in this chapter has two main objectives: (1) to reveal the breadth of research need in tourism and (2) to emphasize the opportunity for stimulating progress in tourism by involving many disciplines in research. The recent growth and diversity of tourism-research topics now reported in journals and the great increase in the number of tourism researchers bear testimony to greater application of research methods to issues and problems of tourism.

THE VARIETY OF TOURISM RESEARCH NEEDS

All three sectors of tourism decision makers could benefit from research findings in their respective roles. *Govern-*

ments, as prime developers of tourism infrastructure (water, waste, police, fire protection, and attractions), need facts for enlightened policies and action. Governments involved in parks, zoos, recreation areas, and historic sites need findings related to tourists who view and use these as attractions. *Commercial enterprise* needs the results from studies of traveler trends as well as factors contributing to better business success. *Nonprofit organizations* need greater information on their roles as developers and managers of important parts of tourism such as museums, festivals, events, and cultural attractions. All three sectors, faced with global growth of tourism, need better solutions to negative impacts—social, economic, and environmental.

Viewed from this perspective, it can be seen that tourism is an extremely complex phenomenon and that the issues and problems will not be solved by the traditional method of conventional wisdom. Experience may be a good teacher, but the field of tourism now demands the sophisticated research approaches that have proven so effective in other fields.

ROLE OF OBJECTIVE RESEARCH

Tourism knowledge today is building through a variety of means. Some means are more exacting than others. Some have been more popular than others. It may be useful at this point to paraphrase Kerlinger's (1986) identification of four ways of knowing, based on the earlier work of Buchler, Cohen, and Nagel.

First, tourism practitioners know certain things because of *tenacity*. Certain "rules of thumb," known by those in the several facets of tourism, are passed from one to another as truths merely because they are held as truths. For years, the rule of high occupancy, for example, has been the truth of hoteliers everywhere. Research, however, has demonstrated that many other factors in addition to occupancy can contribute to success and that even 100 percent occupancy may not necessarily prove profitable, especially if capital was overextended. Sometimes, beliefs of certain truths prevail in spite of new objective research that proves them wrong.

The second way of knowing is the method of *authority*. In some countries and in some aspects of tourism, certain tourism information is believed because it has been stated by an accepted authority. Even the courts recognize the strength of statements by experts. Such authority can come from several sources. It may come from public acceptance, from one who is reputed to have superior knowledge, or from governmental decree.

A third form of gaining tourism knowledge is by means of *intuition*. Certain information about tourism is accepted because it just seems right. Some beliefs, such as that tourism has no impact on resources or that tourism is always an economic good, are believed because they seem right to be believed. It "stands to reason" that these statements are correct.

The fourth way of gaining knowledge is through *science*, obtained by means of objective research. Built into this form of identifying information is one quality that does not appear in the others. This is the matter of questioning and systematic check. The others may produce, by chance, correct information, but there is no questioning or check upon its correctness. In scientific research, there are many points along the way of investigation that force critical examination. Objective research is systematic, logical, and empirical and can be replicated (Tuckman 1992). As a result, the information is more dependable. "By testing thoughts against reality, science helps to liberate inquiry from bias, prejudice, and just plain muddleheadedness" (Hoover 1976). It is in the context of science that many new truths of tourism are developing.

RESEARCH APPROACHES

For tourism, a few approaches used today are more popular than others, and they vary in how they are performed and what they can accomplish. Four approaches, not necessarily mutually exclusive, are described in the following discussion. Sometimes one, such as description, leads to another, such as testing. (See the Suggested Sources of Information for resource materials and examples of tourism research.)

TO DESCRIBE AND INVENTORY

One approach in tourism is merely to describe, not to prove new relationships or to demonstrate the value of new practices. While some scholars denigrate the value of descriptive research, tourism knowledge is in such a stage of infancy that descriptive research is valuable and necessary today. The many facets of the complicated phenomenon called tourism have not even been described adequately. Basic inventory and description are often helpful in decision making also.

Individual tourism businesses of some portions of Texas, for example, have long recognized the value of tourism to them and to their areas. However, this knowledge was not generally known nor accepted by other businesses or agencies. The state of Texas contracted the U.S. Travel Data Center to obtain descriptive data for all counties. These data included expenditures, taxes paid, employment generated, and payrolls generated by travel. As a result of these research findings, several counties were surprised to discover the great importance of travel and stepped up their efforts to provide better service and to organize more formal efforts to promote tourism.

Throughout the United States, State Comprehensive Outdoor Recreation Plans employ descriptive research to inventory recreational facilities. These reports catalog items important to tourism, such as campgrounds, picnic facilities, playgrounds, swimming areas, golf courses, boating areas, and other recreational development.

Also important to tourism are time-series descriptive studies, such as those prepared by the U.S. Bureau of the Census. Every five years, that agency prepares a census of travel and a census of selected services. These provide base data, important to both the public and the private sectors.

Individual tourism businesses regularly develop statistics on their operations. Data on rooms rented, revenues obtained, costs of maintenance, and other facts are determined to describe the characteristics of the business. Descriptive data on markets are commonly compiled. Descriptive studies about certain tourism businesses, such as camping (Bevins, LaPage, and Wilcox 1979), are being produced.

TO TEST

Experimental research, used for generations in scientific laboratories and field experiments, has application to tourism. It is especially useful in experimenting with changes in practices. It is more difficult but is sometimes used in testing physical development.

Food services, for example, may experiment with various menu combinations and portions before arriving at standardized menus and portion control. Maintenance managers may run experiments on the most cost-effective maintenance strategies and equipment for taking care of large properties. Airlines may run experiments on special price-destination packages. Advertisers may use experiments to obtain opinion response by varying content and presentation of advertising copy and illustrations before deciding upon advertising layout.

Experimental methods of research can be very productive for certain types of tourism research.

TO PREDICT, FORECAST

Of interest to many tourist businesses is increasing the ability to make forecasts. Decisions on the purchase of new generations of equipment, new sites, and new technology may rest on predictions of increased demand for a specific tourism service or product. One of the fundamental problems in forecasting is the lack of basic data. Descriptive research can provide this foundation. Another problem is assuming that the external factors of influence will remain the same in the future. It is one thing to obtain research data on the past but quite another to assume that new factors will not change their arrangement or importance in the future. Predictability and forecasting are more reliable in the physical sciences than in social science, the realm of tourism behavior. At present, there is an increasing amount of research on the factors that influence forecasting (Witt and Witt 1990). Research of these factors, relating psychological and social factors to the economics of tourism, is seen as a major need in the field of tourism.

TO MODEL, SIMULATE

One approach to research is to set up hypothetical situations, establish mathematical relationships between factors, and study controlled changes. In a way, this represents the creation of a scenario patterned after real-world situations. However, the scenario does not utilize measures of existing situations but rather assumptions of these situations. The modeling process forces the researcher to assume a set of

conditions and to state explicit relationships. When the data are assigned quantifiable language, the computer is able to assist greatly in making rapid calculations regarding the influence of changes in relationships.

Simulation and modeling have useful approaches in outdoor-recreation-demand studies. Some of the types used have been gravity models (relationships between origins and destinations), linear programming (optimal acquisition of resources), Acar model (policy regarding recreational opportunities), systems theory (recreational camping and boating), and comprehensive simulation modeling (state recreation plans) (Analysis 1977).

TOURISM REQUIRES MULTIDISCIPLINARY RESEARCH

Because of the great diversity of the many elements that make up tourism, problems are not resolved by only one research method. The breadth and complexity of tourism require the use of many methods, depending on the topic. The nature of the information needed should be emphasized, and then every principle, technique, and method most appropriate for resolving that need should be tapped. "No single discipline alone can accommodate, treat, or understand tourism; it can be studied only if disciplinary boundaries are crossed and if multidisciplinary perspectives are sought and formed," state Graburn and Jafari, editors of the special issue "Tourism Social Science," *Annals of Tourism Research* (1991).

The following discussion of some key disciplines and their special approaches to research is intended to guide the planner, developer, and manager of tourism into research methods most productive for the special needs of tourism today.

MARKETING

By far the most active discipline in tourism, marketing is an application of behavior, business, and economics with its own set of research approaches. Marketing research "is an *instrument* of decision making" (Wentz 1972). Therefore, it is an applied field directed toward a specific function within the firm. Wentz identifies five types of market research: market and sales, distribution, product, business-economics, and advertising.

Adapting the scientific method to marketing, secondary data searches and survey research methods are used most frequently. Both experimental and nonexperimental designs are employed. Churchill (1991) emphasizes that the design must stem from the problem and classifies research into three categories: exploratory research (discovery of ideas and insights), descriptive research (frequencies, trends in consumption), and causal research (cause-and-effect relationships).

Because the emphasis is the solution of a problem, marketing research follows generally the scientific method: formulation of the problem; determination of sources of information and the research design; preparation of data-collection forms; design of the sample and collection of the data; analysis and interpretation of the data; and preparation of the research report (Churchill 1991).

Within the study of marketing is a special subtopic—consumer behavior—that is very important to tourism. This topic has been the focus of scholars for several years, building upon the mix between psychology, sociology, and economics. Consumer behavior forms the foundation for much of marketing decision making. It also provides information and insight into social policy in consumer affairs, and it affords better information of direct value to the consumer (Kassarjian and Robertson 1973).

Consumer behavioral research could be classified into several emphases. One emphasis is that of consumer perception of brand, price, and the influences of levels of learning. Then, studies of motivation and personality are important as they relate to decisions to purchase. Of equal concern to marketers of tourism is research in attitude and attitude change. Tourism market-segmentation research has been directed often toward objectives of psychographics and consumer benefits. The main purpose of consumer behavior research is to try to explain why tourists do what they do. For forecasting behavior, Delphi technique and nominal-group technique are sometimes used (Calatone and Mazanec 1991:113).

BEHAVIOR

Psychology and sociology, while different disciplines, have for years provided research insight into human behavior and how it is organized. Research techniques are increasingly employed to provide information and explanation of what activity takes place, as well as how, when, and where. The more difficult question of why it takes place continues to stimulate probing into factors influencing behavior, such as psychographic studies in tourism. Since tourism is dependent upon people's propensity, habits, and desires, behavioral research is a major element in building new knowledge and solving tourism problems.

In the behavioral sciences, two basic approaches—experimental and nonexperimental (Kerlinger 1986)—are made in utilizing the scientific method. The desire is to engage in experimental research whenever possible—whenever important variables can be manipulated, such as changes in management practice, room type, or transport vehicles. Other variables, however, are less amenable to manipulation, such as religious values, honesty, taste and esthetics, and many others. The process of behavioral research often uses methods of survey research and again follows the basic steps of the scientific method: (1) defining the problem, (2) identifying hypotheses, (3) selecting methodology, (4) collecting data, (5) analyzing data, and (6) presenting results and conclusions.

Leisure and recreation studies have often used techniques to measure optimal arousal—the level of mental stimulation at which performance, learning, or feelings are maximized (Smith and Godbey 1991:95). An area of cognitive psychological study has been applied to the use of maps (Pearce and

Stringer 1991:140). Because tourism is often in social context, techniques of social psychological research are sometimes used, such as for cultural shock of tourism. Studies in environmental psychology have been directed toward visitor imagery and crowding.

BUSINESS

Business, as a discipline, increasingly recognizes the value of research, and, therefore, the business sector of tourism has much to gain from research. Emory (1980) identifies four areas of research interest by business. First are those research studies that *report*, basically in statistical form. The research design may be simple but the products may be very valuable to management for decision making. Second, business research is often *description*, including comparisons and relationships beyond mere reporting. By adding certain facts and assumptions, a third form of research, that of *prediction*, is performed. Finally, when *explanation* of the forces that account for the phenomenon is included, usually more sophisticated research is required.

Frequently, the term *research and development* is associated with business. Actually, while some experimental and survey research methods are utilized, this is more directly in the area of technology—the handling of engineering and technology problems. In business, operations research usually emphasizes production and goods handling. However, in actual business organization, it may become merged with marketing research and research and development departments.

According to Gearing et al. (1976), operations research in tourism is closely allied to economic analysis but places greater emphasis on decision-making situations that arise from real life. Operations research involves three steps: (1) structuring into a mathematical model, (2) exploring systematic procedures, and (3) developing solutions with optimal values.

Adaptation of the scientific method to business research often results in the following research process: (1) exploration of the situation, (2) development of research design, (3) collection of data, and (4) analysis and interpretation of results (Emory 1980). The two most frequent research designs used in business are experimental and simulation.

Often economic analysis of tourism is used for benefit-cost study, multiplier analysis, demand studies, and optimal development levels. Another important use of economic analysis is the study of governmental intervention into business activity, such as for subsidies.

HISTORY

History, previously preoccupied with chronological documentation, has increasingly applied scientific methods to describe and explain the past. The discipline of history is making many valuable inputs to tourism. Documentation of the past development and growth of the many facets of tourism provide the context for evaluation of today's tourism. Case histories of tourist businesses and tourist destination areas contribute to tourism decision making today.

Greatly expanding historical restoration and interpretation, as tourist attractions, demand accurate research of past events and details of sites and architecture. Modern tourists require increasingly sophisticated description and presentation of historic places.

Historical research is performed for the same purpose as other research—to gain new understandings. By learning more about the past, the present is clarified. Historical research, however, is somewhat more difficult because evidence is of the past. Benjamin (1991) states that there are two basic forms of evidence: primary and secondary. Primary evidence includes the statements of those who actually participated in past events. These may be found in newspapers, diaries, notebooks, letters, minutes, interviews, and other forms of first-hand knowledge of the event. Audio- and videotapes, photographs, and artifacts are primary evidence. Secondary evidence includes the findings of those who did not witness the events but investigated primary evidence. History articles and books usually represent secondary evidence.

All historians face problems of reliability of evidence. Questions of bias, accuracy, and even fraudulence must be given critical review. Several years ago, Hockett (1949) identified three key steps of criticism: (1) external criticism (determination of circumstances attending the production of a document, question of original form of document); (2) internal criticism (positive, negative); and (3) determinable facts (allusions, contemporary statements, cross-check of statements, fit). Tests of consistency and corroboration are important.

Historical research can contribute much to the development and understanding of tourism, not only through documentation of the past but also through identification of attraction potential. According to Turner and Wall (1991), needed by historians is research that links findings to issues of the day, especially the social milieu.

GEOGRAPHY

Few disciplines are as closely related to tourism as is geography. Around the world, all tourism is developed on the land and its special characteristics. *Geography* is defined as "the science concerned with the spatial location, distribution, pattern, and organization of human activities on land and space." Certainly, the discipline of geography has much to contribute toward the understanding of traveler origins and destinations and their relationships. Research has also been focused on the relationship between geographic factors and preferred zones of development (Gunn 1972; Miossec 1977; Getz 1986; Fagence 1990). Mitchell and Murphy (1991) suggest that there is need for greater cooperative research of tourism by geographers and social scientists.

Basically, geographers employ the fundamental rules and procedures of scientific research. Generally, their research can be divided into two categories—predictive and explanatory. Geographers have expressed interest in tourism for several reasons: spatial distribution, landscape conservation, impact of mass tourism, role in economic geography, tourism as an export, and cultural aspects.

Recently, many geographers, such as Van Doren (1982), Pearce (1986), and Fagence (1990), have produced studies and models that help explain spatial relationships of tourism. Their findings can be of great assistance to policymakers of tourism, guiding tourism in directions that protect resources and produce economic gains.

Special applications of the scientific method for geographic studies of tourism have included input-output analysis, catastrophe theory, expansion method, and spatial modeling.

ANTHROPOLOGY

The field of anthropology, because it is the science of man and culture, has many applications to tourism. Whereas other disciplines are more specific, anthropology seeks to identify, describe, and explain holistically the many manifestations of mankind.

The most conspicuous subdivision of anthropology related to tourism is that of archeology, providing information and sites of great value as tourist attractions. Of equal value to tourism is sociocultural anthropology, which studies human social and cultural life. Two other subdivisions of anthropology, biological (physical) and linguistic, may have potential contributions to make. Anthropology utilizes both exploratory descriptive study and hypothesis-testing research. Descriptive studies, often using participant observation and informal interviewing as tools, frequently provide foundations for more highly focused hypothesis testing later on. Hypothesis testing is basically scientific research methodology, but for anthropology may be directed along one or more of four paradigms: (1) pretest-posttest, (2) static-group comparison, (3) nonequivalent control group, and (4) control group (Brim and Spain 1974).

"Anthropology has important contributions to offer to the study of tourism, especially through a neo-traditional approach that includes the basic ethnography and its national character variant, as well as the acculturation model and the awareness that tourism is only one element in culture change" (Smith 1980). More recently, Smith (1992) stated: "In summary, anthropologists, with their sensitivity to ethnic and minority cultures, their knowledge of cultural conservation, and their concern for directing cultural change into beneficial channels, should find interesting and rewarding employment in government, in visitor and convention bureaus, as guides and interpreters, and as consultants to governments and industry."

Nash and Smith (1991) emphasize that the field of anthropology will in the future provide greater insight into the forces that generate tourism, the transactions between cultures, and the consequences of tourism development.

POLITICAL SCIENCE

Increasingly, tourism is being recognized as having important political implications. Developed countries seek new policies to protect and maintain present levels of tourism, and developing countries promote policies of tourism expansion. Less well known is political science research and the opportunity it holds for tourism.

The basic tenets of the scientific method are followed in political science research. However, the nature of the field requires special problem identification along three lines: "(1) simple description of the phenomenon, (2) relational analysis of various aspects of the phenomenon, or (3) causal interpretation of the phenomenon, its antecedents and its consequents" (Leege and Francis 1974). In general, the research designs of social science are used, but political science studies for tourism may use a wide range of methods depending on the context. In some cases, true experimental design is appropriate, whereas in other instances, less rigorous designs may be used.

Matthews and Richter (1991) predict greater involvement of political science research in tourism. Needed is greater study of government's involvement, roles, and implications for tourism. The identification of tenets of tourism policy presents many challenges for study. The education and training of leaders and specialists in tourism increasingly need the results of political science research. International law and politics deserve greater attention.

PLANNING AND DESIGN

Planning and design (urban and regional planning, architecture, landscape architecture, engineering, interior design) are distinct professions with many subdivisions. Yet they have some common elements, such as creating new physical environments for human use—in this case, tourism. Today, all these professions are seeking new and better data upon which to base their plans and creative designs. This research is not along any common lines of strategy but generally reflects the scientific method by seeking objective information and solution to problems.

In the field of land-use and landscape-analysis, for example, many techniques are being experimented with. These include aerial photography, hand graphics, and computer techniques of inventorying and evaluating physical land factors of importance to planners of recreation and tourism development, such as Geographic Information Systems (GIS) (Gunn and Larsen 1988). Occasionally, studies are made of developed facilities to gain insight into how well the designed environment functions were planned.

Challenges in tourism planning require deeper research of the roles of official urban planning and zoning. Because civic officials determine much of a city's physical and economic growth, these decisions deserve greater research study for adaptation to tourism. As So (1988) points out, planning requires research of legal parameters, political implications, social impacts, intergovernmental relationships, and esthetic and environmental impacts.

FUTURISM

Although traditionalists may scoff at the notion of futurism as a distinct discipline, the field has risen to the level of considerable importance and relevance to tourism. Philosophers, scientists, technicians, and planners have joined in making insightful studies of trends, not necessarily to predict but to identify future possibilities. *Futuristics* can be defined as "applied history" (Cornish 1977).

Emerging among the futurists are many approaches toward gaining insight into the future. Some key approaches, used with varying degrees of success, are: (1) trend extrapolation, (2) scenarios, (3) use of experts (Delphi technique), and (4) models, games, and simulation. Already, several worldwide organizations and future-oriented research institutes have been organized and are producing research studies. Tourism, extremely vulnerable to many factors of the future, may look more and more to the works of these scientists involved in future-oriented research.

Futurists are identifying key trend factors that can influence major changes in tourism in the future (Godbey 1989); for example, it is predicted for the United States that over 64 percent of the population will be over the age of 65 by 2030. They predict also that increased quality of life, public-private cooperation, cultural exchange, and greater personal service will gain in importance for tourism in the future.

INPUT FROM OTHER DISCIPLINES

The complexity of tourism demands research input from many disciplines. The areas discussed above are merely a start on a long list of disciplines applicable to the development of new information for tourism or to the solution of tourism problems.

Leisure and recreation studies are building a distinct area of interest with special research approaches and literature involving very important aspects of tourism. Park and resource management research, involving land use as well as behavior, has direct bearing on tourism. Engineering research is a vital component of many businesses directly related to tourism products and equipment. The field of communications is frequently identified as a distinct discipline and is having tremendous impact on many elements of tourism. Wildlife, fisheries, and forestry are often considered discreet disciplines, and their research has direct bearing on tourism, especially in the planning and management of attractions. Probably the greatest amount of outdoor-recreation research in the United States has been sponsored by the several experiment stations of the U.S. Department of Agriculture, Forest Service. Marine engineering and oceanography, with their many concerns over coastal development, are important to coastal tourism. The field of law is of increasing importance to the many facets of tourism everywhere. Medicine, health, and nutrition are at the very foundation of many concepts of personal fitness and use of leisure. The leisure implications of veterinary medicine are great, including the control of pet disease and management of zoos as tourist attractions. And, of course, studies in tourism economics are needed in order to go beyond the impact of the firm.

CONCLUSION

More and more, the many social, environmental, and cultural, as well as economic, implications of tourism are being recognized. Even this brief review of a few disciplines demonstrates current and potential input of varied research that is valuable to tourism. Future businesses, organizations, educational institutions, and governments have the opportunity of harnessing many ways of gaining new knowledge and solutions to problems of tourism.

While the several disciplines appear to utilize different research approaches, there is more fundamental similarity than difference. Throughout, the basic aim is to perform objective, systematic, logical, and substantive research. Specific problem-solving research is becoming an integral part of many tourist-oriented businesses. At the same time, universally applicable research is increasingly assisting nations, states, provinces, cities, organizations, and educational institutions in gaining greater insight into tourism.

Techniques and methodologies vary somewhat across disciplines, but all seem to desire quantifiable methods whenever applicable. For some topics, it is sufficient to have the opinions of key leaders or specialists. However, more generalizable research, applicable to large masses of population, requires representative sampling designs. Tourism does not have a long history of research, and as such, descriptive and exploratory studies are providing worthwhile data.

The main conclusion is that tourism is a complex phenomenon, and, therefore, the research of tourism must utilize all the disciplinary approaches that will be most useful in solving problems and in providing new information. Because tourism is multidisciplinary, solutions to problems will increasingly require cooperation and collaboration of researchers from several disciplines. Problems of land use and planning will require team research from market analysts and geographers as well as planners. Historians, anthropologists, and sociologists can combine efforts to study means of alleviating culture shock from tourism development. Engineers, planners, and consumer behaviorists could combine efforts to improve transportation and travel information techniques. Research from wildlife, forestry, and water-resource specialists can assist in solving issues centered on attraction development of natural resources. These and many other combinations of disciplines will need to be created in order to address and provide solutions to needed tourism planning, development, and management issues in the future.

SUGGESTED SOURCES OF INFORMATION

The following sources are a sampling of research studies relating to the several disciplines. Further contact with the separate disciplines or agencies supporting such disciplinary research should provide other titles of interest.

GENERAL

Goeldner, Charles R. (1975), "Where to Find Travel Research Facts," *Journal of Travel Research* 13(4), 1–6.

Graburn, Nelson H.H., and Jafar Jafari, eds (1991), "Tourism Social Science," Special Issue, *Annals of Tourism Research* 18(1).

Hoover, Kenneth R. (1976), *The Elements of Social Scientific Thinking,* New York: St. Martin's Press.

U.S. Department of Commerce (1978), *Identifying Traveler Markets, Research Methodologies,* U.S. Travel Service, Washington, D.C.: U.S. Government Printing Office.

Ontario Research Council (1977), *Analysis Methods and Techniques for Recreation Research and Leisure Studies,* Ottawa, Canada: Environment Canada.

Sales, H. Pearce (1959), *Travel and Tourism Encyclopedia,* London: Blandford Press.

Tuckman, Brace W. (1992), *Conducting Educational Research,* New York: Harcourt Brace Jovanovich, Inc.

Witt, Christine A., and Stephen F. Witt (1990), "Appraising an Econometric Forecasting Model," *Journal of Travel Research* 28(3), 30–34.

MARKETING

Calatone, Roger J., and Josef A. Mazanec (1991), "Marketing Management and Tourism," *Annals of Tourism Research* 18(1), 101–119.

Churchill, Gilbert A., Jr. (1991), *Marketing Research: Methodological Foundations,* 5th ed., Hinsdale, IL: Dryden Press.

Kassarjian, Harold H., and Thomas S. Robertson (1973), *Perspectives in Consumer Behavior,* Glenview, IL: Scott Foresman.

Parasuraman, A. (1991), *Marketing Research,* 2nd ed., Reading, MA: Addison-Wesley Publishing Co.

Rao, S.R., et al. (1992), "Activity Preferences and Trip-Planning Behavior of the U.S. Outboard Pleasure Travel Market," *Journal of Travel Research* 30(3), 3–12.

Wentz, Walter B. (1972), *Marketing Research: Management and Methods,* New York: Harper & Row.

BEHAVIOR

Fakeye, Paul G., and John R. Crompton (1991), "Image Differences Between Prospective, First-Time, and Repeat Visitors to the Lower Rio Grande Valley," *Journal of Travel Research* 30(1), 10–16.

Gitelson, Richard J., and Deborah L. Kerstetter (1990), "The Relationship Between Sociodemographic Variables, Benefits Sought and Subsequent Vacation Behavior: A Case Study." *Journal of Travel Research* 28(3), 24–29.

Kerlinger, Fred H. (1986), *Foundations of Behavior Research,* 3rd. ed., New York: Holt, Rinehart & Winston.

Lawson, Rob (1991), "Patterns of Tourist Expenditure and Types of Vacation Across the Family Life Cycle," *Journal of Travel Research* 9(2), 543–563.

Nickerson, Norma P., and Gary D. Ellis (1991), "Traveler Types and Activation Theory: A Comparison of Two Models," *Journal of Travel Research* 29(3), 26–31.

and Activation Theory: A Comparison of Two Models," *Journal of Travel Research* 29(3), 26–31.

Pearce, Philip L., and Peter F. Stringer (1991), "Psychology and Tourism," *Annals of Tourism Research* 18(1), 136–154.

Smith, Stephen L.J., and Geoffrey C. Godbey (1991), "Leisure, Recreation, and Tourism," *Annals of Tourism Research* 18(l), 85–100.

BUSINESS

Bevins, Malcolm I., Wilbur F. LaPage, and Daniel P. Wilcox (1979), *The Campground Industry*, Technical Report NE-53, Broomall, Pennsylvania: Northeastern Forest Experiment Station, U.S. Forest Service.

Braun, Bradley M. (1992), "The Economic Contributions of Conventions: The Case of Orlando, Florida," *Journal of Travel Research* 30(3), 32–37.

Emory, C. William (1980), *Business Research Methods*, Homewood, IL: Richard D. Irwin, Inc.

Gearing, Charles E., William W. Swart, and Turgot Var (1976), *Planning for Tourism Development*, New York: Praeger.

Musselman, Vernon A., and Eugene H. Hughes (1973), *Introduction to Modern Business: Analysis and Interpretation*, 6th ed., Englewood Cliffs, NJ: Prentice-Hall.

Survey of the Labor Situation in the Accommodation and Food Services Sector of the Alberta Tourism Industry (1974), Prepared by Underwood, McLellan and Assoc., Calgary, Alberta, Canada: Travel Alberta.

HISTORY

Benjamin, Jules R. (1991), *A Student's Guide to History*, 5th ed., New York: St. Martin's Press.

Casson, Lionel (1971), "After 2,000 Years Tours Have Changed but Not Tourism," *Smithsonian* 2(6), 53–59.

Hockett, Homer Carey (1949), *Introduction to Research in American History*, 2nd ed., New York: Macmillan.

King, Doris Elizabeth (1957), "The First-Class Hotel and the Age of the Common Man, "*The Journal of Southern History* 23(2), 173–188.

Shafer, Robert J. (1969), *A Guide to Historical Method*, Homewood, IL: Dorsey Press.

Turner, John, and Geoffrey Wall (1991), "History and Tourism," *Annals of Tourism Research* 18(1), 71–83.

GEOGRAPHY

Fagence, Michael (1990), "Geographically-Referenced Planning Strategies to Resolve Potential Conflict Between Environmental Values and Commercial Interests in Tourism Development in Environmentally Sensitive Areas," *Journal of Environmental Management* 31, 1–18.

Getz, D. (1986) "Models in Tourism Planning: Towards Integration of Theory and Practice," *Tourism Management* 7(1), 21–32.

Gunn, Clare A. (1972), *Vacationscape: Designing Tourist Regions*, Austin: University of Texas.

Miossec, J.M. (1977), "Un Modele de L'Espace Touristique," *L'Espace Geographique* 6(1), 41–48.

Mitchell, Lisle S., and Peter E. Murphy (1991), "Geography and Tourism," *Annals of Tourism Research* 18(1), 57–70.

Pearce, Douglas (1986), *Tourism Today—A Geographical Analysis*, London: Longman.

Van Doren, C.S., and Larry Gustke (1982), "Spatial Analysis of the U.S. Lodging Industry: 1963–1977," *Annals of Tourism Research* 9(2), 543–563.

ANTHROPOLOGY

Brim, John A., and David H. Spain (1974), *Research Design in Anthropology*, New York.

Long, Veronica H. (1992), "Tourism Development, Conservation, and Anthropology," *Practicing Anthropology* 14(2), 14–17.

Nash, Dennison, and Valene L. Smith (1991), "Anthropology and Tourism," *Annals of Tourism Research* 18(1), 12–25.

Nolan, Mary Lee, and Sidney Nolan (1989), *Christian Pilgrimage in Modern Western Europe*, Chapel Hill: University of North Carolina Press.

Pelto, Peretti J., and Gretel H. Pelto (1978), *Anthropological Research*, 2nd ed., London: Cambridge University Press.

Smith, Valene L. (1980), "Anthropology and Tourism," *Annals of Tourism Research* 7(1), 13–33.

Smith, Valene L. (1992), "Managing Tourism in the 1990s and Beyond," *Practicing Anthropology* 14(2), 3–4.

POLITICAL SCIENCE

Campbell, D.T., and J.C. Stanley (1966), *Experimental and Quasi-Experimental Designs for Research*, Chicago: Rand McNally.

Jenkins, C.L. (1980), "Tourism Policies in Developing Countries: A Critique," *Tourism Management* 1(1), 22–29.

Leege, David C., and Wayne L. Francis (1974), *Political Research*, New York: Basic Books.

Matthews, Harry G., and Linda K. Richter (1991), "Political Science and Tourism," *Annals of Tourism Research* 18(1), 120–135.

Pearce, Douglas G. (1992), "Tourism and the European Regional Development Funds: The First Fourteen Years," *Journal of Travel Research* 30(3), 44–55.

Richter, Linda K. (1983), "Tourism Politics and Political Science—A Case of Not Too Benign Neglect," *Annals of Tourism Research* 10(3), 313–335.

PLANNING AND DESIGN

Baud-Bovy, Manual, and F. Lawson (1977), *Tourism and Recreation Development*, London: Architectural Press.

Gunn, Clare A. (1988), *Tourism Planning*, 2nd ed., New York: Taylor and Francis.

Gunn, Clare A. (1988a), "Small Town and Rural Tourism Planning," Chapter 15 in *Integrated Rural Planning and Development*, Floyd Dykeman, ed., Sackville, N.B., Canada: Mount Allison University.

Gunn, Clare A. (1988b), *Vacationscape: Designing Tourist Regions*, 2nd ed., New York: Van Nostrand Reinhold.

Gunn, Clare A., and Terry A. Larsen (1988), *Tourism Potential—Aided by Computer Cartography*, Aix-en-Provence, France: Centre des Hautes Etudes Touristiques.

Walter, P. (1986), "The Meaning of Zoning in the Management of Natural Resources," *Journal of Environmental Management* 22, 331–343.

So, Frank S., ed. (1988), *The Practice of Local Government Planning*, Washington, D.C.: International City Management Association.

FUTURISM

Cornish, Edward (1977), *The Study of the Future*, Washington, D.C.: The World Future Society.

Godbey, Geoffrey (1989), *The Future of Leisure Services: Thriving on Change*, State College, PA: Venture.

Kahn, Herman (1979), "Tourism and the Next Decade," presentation at the International Symposium: Tourism and the Next Decade, George Washington University, Washington, D.C., March 11–15, 1979.

Papson, Stephen (1979), "Tourism: World's Biggest Industry in the Twenty-First Century?" *The Futurist* 13(4), 249–257.

2

Roles of Research in Tourism Management

J.R. BRENT RITCHIE

Chairman,
World Tourism Education and Research Centre
The University of Calgary
Calgary, Alberta

*T*here are many different kinds of tourism research and an even greater number of research methods and techniques. This reality creates two major difficulties for the research professional; it creates confusion among managers as to the true nature of research, and it frequently leads to inappropriate research approaches being used in a given decision-making situation. This chapter attempts to clarify the roles of research as they relate to the field of tourism management. It stresses that, to be effective, research strategies must correspond to the nature and level of management decision.

The concept of research is diffuse and highly abused. While it is generally agreed that the term refers to some systematic form of investigation of a given topic, its true significance is seen to vary with both the area of application as well as the perceptions of different individuals within a given field. Archaeological research involving the unearthing of skeletons in remote regions of the world has only a vague conceptual relation to research designed to determine the optimal characteristics of a package tour. This comparison is not meant as a value judgment; in fact, the intention is quite the reverse. Each of these types of research has an important role to play within its proper context. The fact remains, however, that in each case the single word *research* describes a quite different reality. As a result, the term tends to lose its ability to communicate meaning; its significance becomes all too dangerously a function of the individual user rather than being one of objective group consensus.

Even within the more limited field of decision-oriented studies designed to improve the effectiveness of management actions in the field of tourism, the term *research* implies widely varying ideas. The current terminology describing management research abounds with a series of dichotomous expressions derived from a variety of the source disci-

plines upon which management research methods are based. These include: fundamental and applied, analytical and descriptive, exploratory and causal, empirical and theoretical, cross-sectional and longitudinal, short term and long term. Such terms—because of their number, interdependence, and generally vague definitions—often are confusing to the manager attempting to understand the nature and roles of research within the management process. They hinder the ability to see clearly the potential applications and contributions of research to the improvement of the manager's own effectiveness.

This discussion does not imply that the types of terminology just mentioned are irrelevant or useless. Employed in the proper context, such terms play a useful role in discussing and describing the research process. It remains true, however, that these terms have not always been constructed so as to explain or clarify the nature of various aspects of research as it applies to the management process.

This chapter is concerned with defining the roles and characteristics of the research process as it applies to tourism management decision making. The objective here is to provide a rational basis for classifying and describing different decision-oriented research needs using a framework based on three major dimensions directly related to the management process: the level of management activity; the stage of the management process; and the function of the management activity. The nature of these dimensions will be seen to substantially modify the nature of management information needs required for decision making. Because of these varying needs, it is essential that the appropriate type of research methodology and data-collection instrument be employed to satisfy each need.

Based on the proposed framework of research types and an understanding of their roles, limits, and corresponding methodologies, it is hoped tourism managers will be able to more effectively choose the type of information-gathering process most relevant to each particular decision-making situation.

RESEARCH AS AN INFORMATION SOURCE

Philip Kotler (1981) views the total information system of an organization as consisting of an internal information system composed of management accounting information; an external information system designed to monitor changing conditions in the organization's environment; and a research information system capable of providing in-depth studies pertaining to specific problems or situations. It is important for managers to realize that research should form an integral part of the overall information system related to their decision-making needs; otherwise, the risks of both missing and duplicating information are high.

It should be recognized that the composition of the internal, external, and research information subsystems is in constant evolution as the total system responds to different conditions both outside and within the organization. It might be decided, for example, that a specific type of information that has been gathered through a special research project and that has been found particularly useful should be collected on a regular basis and incorporated into either the internal or external information system, as the case may be. Similarly, it is possible that information currently collected on a continuous basis (such as the monitoring of tourist attitudes) may be judged too costly in comparison to its contribution to decision making. Data gathering in such instances might become the object of periodic research projects when it is deemed necessary.

In order to classify research functions within the context of management decision making, it is essential to identify the key variables that capture the fundamental nature of the dimensions and that can be considered to characterize the nature of the management process within an organization.

The model presented in this chapter proposes three major dimensions of the management process that it is felt can be usefully employed to define the nature of tourism-management information needs and to identify the types of research methodologies most appropriate for satisfying these needs. The dimensions shown in Figure 1 are defined as: stages of the management process; levels of management

activity within an organization; and functional areas of management activity.

STAGES OF THE MANAGEMENT PROCESS

The number and identity of the stages of the management process are by no means universally agreed upon by scholars in the field. For purposes of the discussion here, four stages (analysis, planning, execution, and control) will be retained as the components of Dimension One of the framework.

Analysis represents the initial stage of the management process in which executives are essentially interested in understanding the nature and scope of a given problem. Obviously, by its very nature, research has an important role to play in the analysis stage.

Planning, which flows logically from analysis and is often difficult to distinguish from it, may be viewed as the setting of objectives and the evaluation/choice of alternatives for meeting those objectives. Here again, formal research has a high potential contribution.

Execution of the selected course of action represents the translation of ideas into reality; the role of research may be considered less important at this stage. Despite this general component, there are occasions when the collection and monitoring of data during the implementation of a given action may be an essential part of the management information gathering process.

The *control* stage of the management process is the stage that attempts to measure the extent to which a given activity or action has achieved its original objectives. It is only recently that the potential contribution of research at this stage has been recognized. The contribution involves the returns to be derived from formal research methods in establishing and implementing performance measures that are both reliable and representative of reality. Perhaps more important, such methods provide a mechanism for systematically and objectively exploring the causes or reasons for the successes or failures resulting from management actions.

LEVELS OF MANAGEMENT ACTIVITY

The second dimension of the proposed research classification framework is based on the levels of management activity within an organization, as defined by Robert N. Anthony (1965). These levels are termed strategic, managerial, and operational. Each deals with a range of activities having distinct characteristics that reflect the nature of the management problems with which they deal.

Strategic activities concern long-term plans and policies that determine or change the character of an organization. The management-information needs related to this level of activity can generally be qualified as long-term or broad-scale indicators that measure critical elements of the economic, social, political, and technological environments having a potential impact on the organization. Naisbitt's (1982) review of megatrends affecting societal development is an example of such information.

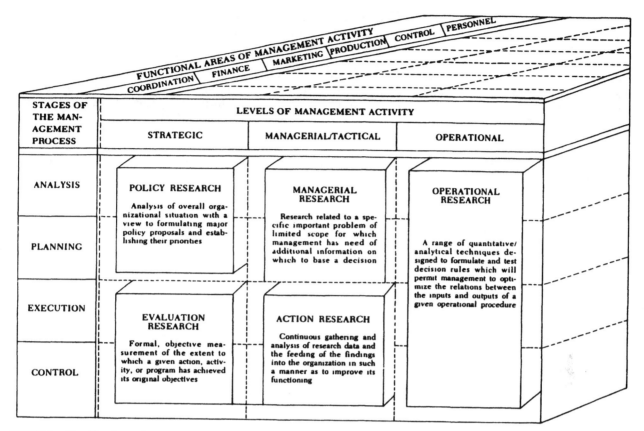

FIGURE 1   Classification of research methodologies according to the three dimensions of the management process.

Managerial or *tactical activities* involve those actions that are associated with the ongoing administration of the enterprise and that are carried on within the limits of objectives and policies defined at the strategic level. As such, the information needs of management at this level usually involve relatively well-defined data bearing directly on the solution of a given problem or decision.

Operational activities describe those specific transactions involved in carrying out the tasks required to achieve the variety of objectives defined at the management level. The management-information needs related to such tasks tend to be highly structured and recurring in nature.

FUNCTIONAL AREAS OF ACTIVITY

The previous two dimensions of the proposed framework for research classification have applied generally to an organization regardless of the different functional activities that it must execute. It is obvious that the nature of these functions also plays an important role in determining the information and research needs of management. Given this fact, the third dimension of the framework is seen to contain the following components: finance, marketing, production, control, personnel, and the general management function of coordination.

SOME ADDITIONAL DIMENSIONS

There exists a number of additional dimensions or criteria that might be used to classify tourism-management information and research needs. The distinction between internal and external information, for example, might be employed; and, similarly, the difference between fundamental and applied research is often used. However, the three dimensions that have been retained in the model are felt to be the most relevant and powerful with respect to their ability to capture the essence of the management process insofar as it relates to information and research needs. As such, only the perceived utility of the proposed framework will indicate whether the correct dimensions have been retained.

CLASSIFICATION OF MANAGEMENT RESEARCH

Based on the three previously defined dimensions of the management process, it is possible to identify within the framework five broad categories of research that are used in varying degrees by different management teams. These five categories, shown in Figure 1, are referred to as: operational research, managerial research, policy research, action research, and evaluation research.

Operational research consists primarily of a range of quantitative/analytical techniques designed to formulate and test decision rules that will permit management to optimize relations between the inputs and outputs of a given operational procedure. As such, it tends to arrive at programmed models prescribing the actions that are most efficient under a given set of circumstances. Because of the very applied nature of operations research, it tends to integrate all stages of the management process (as shown in Figure 1). Indeed, built-in feedback loops among different stages are a distinguishing feature of many operational-research models. Examples of such research in tourism would include studies to determine the optimal traffic flow within and through a major attraction or to establish decision rules for the setting of overbooking levels in a hotel (Toh 1985).

Managerial research covers a broad range of research types including those most commonly employed by management. Typically, such research deals with an important problem of limited scope for which management has need of additional information on which to base a decision. Examples of such studies include those concerning the market potential for a new attraction, the best approach for the implementation of a new accounting system, or feasibility study for a new hotel. In general, such research projects have one feature in common: they concern the seeking of solutions as to what should be done to solve a given problem and how to implement this solution. While there are exceptions, there are relatively few studies related to the control aspect of the management process, that is, studies that attempt to evaluate the degree of success of a given marketing activity, accounting system, or investment program. In brief, managerial research tends to be future and present oriented as opposed to taking an interest in the effectiveness of prior actions. This generalization is reflected in Figure 1.

Action research is the third broad category of approach suggested by the proposed framework (Whyte 1964). This form of research involves a continuous gathering and analyzing of research data during the normal ongoing operations of an organization or the execution of a specific management program and the simultaneous feeding of the results into the organization so as to change its model of functioning. As such, it is seen that action research is a continuing, task-oriented form of study designed to provide continuous feedback regarding the performance of a management activity and to improve that performance through direct forms of intervention suggested by the research findings. As shown in Figure 1, action research is considered to be a part of the tactical level of management activity; and, because of its continuous and recursive nature, it is carried out within both the execution and control stages of the management process.

Strategic research is a more recent phenomenon insofar as its recognition as a formal field of research is concerned. As such, it is less well defined and understood. Despite this situation, two major categories of strategic research can be identified. Policy research relates to the strategic analysis and planning activities of a tourism organization (Figure 1)

on the tourism system as a whole. It appears to be composed of three elements: research that studies how policy formulation occurs with a view to understanding and improving the process; research that is designed to analyze situations at the strategic level and to formulate overall policy proposals; and research that systematically evaluates the priorities to be accorded to conflicting/complementary policy alternatives (Bauer and Gergen 1968). Methodologies related to actual cases of strategic analysis and policy formulation range from various forms of decision theory to the expert-judgment-consensus approach commonly referred to as the Delphi Technique (see Chapter 39) and the Nominal Group Technique (see Chapter 42). Approaches to the ordering of the attractiveness of various policy options and studying the trade-offs among them have been referred to as priority analysis (Ritchie 1985).

The final portion of the conceptual framework pertains to the most recent application of formal research methodology that has been introduced into management research. *Evaluation research* can be viewed as the complement of policy research in which the objectives, strategies, and programs so derived are monitored both during and after their implementation (Figure 1) in order to determine their degree of success and failure as well as the underlying causes of their impact (Weiss 1972).

IMPLICATIONS OF THE RESEARCH CLASSIFICATION FRAMEWORK

The remainder of this chapter will compare the five research categories across five important attributes of the research process: the nature of the management situation to which the research methodology applies; the type of information/data required in each situation; the general nature of the research approach required for obtaining this data; the characteristics of the principal data-collection instruments used by the research approach; and, finally, the nature of the research output provided to management. This comparison is summarized in Table 1.

NATURE OF THE MANAGEMENT SITUATION

The three different dimensions of the management process give rise to at least five different types of decision-making situations and, consequently, a category of research appropriate to each situation. Column one of Table 1 is a brief restatement of the conditions defining policy, evaluation, managerial, action, and operational research and, as such, is intended to provide the logical link between the classification framework (Figure 1) and its implications concerning appropriate research characteristic (Table 1).

TYPE OF INFORMATION/DATA REQUIRED

Each of the five research categories has distinctly different data needs. Policy research requires primarily macro-level data related to the present values and anticipated trends of

TABLE 1 Implications of the Classification Framework Concerning Research Methods and Data Collection Frameworks

RESEARCH CATEGORY	NATURE OF THE MANAGEMENT SITUATION	TYPE OF INFORMATIONAL DATA REQUIRED	CHARACTERISTICS OF PRINCIPAL DATA COLLECTION METHODOLOGIES/ INSTRUMENTS	NATURE OF THE APPROPRIATE METHODS AND TECHNIQUES FOR EXTRACTING INFORMATION FROM THE DATA	NATURE OF RESEARCH OUTPUT FROM A MANAGEMENT PERSPECTIVE
Policy Research	Need to provide well-defined but broad guidelines that serve to establish priorities to direct the organization's activities	Macrodata related to present values and anticipated trends of major economic, social, technical, and political factors bearing on the organization's activities	Longitudinal/time series measures of major indicators; expert-judgment-consensus measures such as those provided by the Delphi methods; large-scale system stimulation such as that of econometric and industrial dynamics models	Methods that focus on predicting future conditions and their implications for the organization; methods for establishing priorities and trade-offs among alternative policies	Identification of key dimensions of future organizational priorities; recommendations concerning the nature of required action along each of these dimensions; priority levels for alternative actions/policies
Evaluation Research	Need to know the extent to which completed and continuing programs are performing as projected and to identify the major variables influencing the observed performance levels	Data related to the evaluation criteria chosen to represent the objective of a particular activity or program	Measures of program-utilization levels; measures of program-user-satisfaction levels; measures comparing program users to a nonuser control group; measures of the evolution of performance on evaluation criteria over time through panel methods	Methods for evaluating historical performance with respect to relatively ill-defined and often changing objectives and conditions	Identification of program strengths and weaknesses on an overall basis and within different user groups; understanding of factors influencing program success with a view towards recommendations for improvement
Management Tactical Research	Need to obtain an in-depth understanding with respect to specific management problems of limited scope; such problems are often related to a particular functional area	Descriptive information required to understand the key factors involved in a given problem situation; precise data that will permit in-depth analysis of a limited number of important variables influencing a particular situation	Technical and factual data bearing directly on the problem; measures of awareness, attitudes, and opinions; measures of effectiveness alternative actions; measures of behavior	Methods for extracting maximum from secondary data sources; survey research methods; experimentation methods for testing of alternatives; observational methods; model building	Background document or position paper with respect to the management situation; precise recommendations for management action to overcome a problem or take advantage of an opportunity

TABLE 1 *(Continued)*

Research Category	Nature of the Management Situation	Type of Informational Data Required	Characteristics of Principal Data Collection Methodologies/Instruments	Nature of the Appropriate Methods and Techniques for Extracting Information from the Data	Nature of Research Output from a Management Perspective
Action Research	Need to understand the functioning of ongoing operations and programs with a view to modifying the factors affecting these operations; subsequent monitoring of performance levels leads to repeated intervention so as to continually upgrade system performance	Continuous information related to the performance of an organization; behavioral data concerning the nature of interpersonal and intergroup relationships affecting organizational performance and satisfaction	Measures of organization or program performance; qualitative and quantitative measures of organizational structure and interpersonal/intergroup relations	Methods for identifying major organizational problems from performance measures; methods of intervention in organizational functioning designed to modify behavior or performance as it is occurring	Changes in the work environment; modification of the reward/punishment system related to performance; changes in organizational structure
Operational Research	Need to establish decision rules related to repetitive operations in order to reduce required level of management involvement and increase operating efficiency	Highly developed, reliable data pertaining to the performance of a very limited well-defined task	Measures indicating level and dispersion of variables describing task performance; such measures are often obtained through mechanical devices	Construction of analytical/quantitative models followed by attempts to validate and optimize the models	Decision rules prescribing required operational actions under all probable normal conditions; precisely defined "management by exception" task performance measures indicating when management is required to take corrective action

the major economic, social, technical, and political factors that have a present or potential bearing on tourism as a whole or on the success or failure of the activities of the individual tourism operator. Much of this data is available from government sources; some is available from the private sector; the remainder must be collected by the organization requiring it.

Evaluation research requires specific data related to the evaluation criteria chosen to represent the objective of a particular facility, activity or program. As such, there seldom exists readily available data that corresponds satisfactorily to the operational definitions of the criteria used to evaluate the program's performance. Therefore, such data must usually be collected within a specially designed project.

Management/tactical research also requires specific data relevant to a particular problem. Such data generally can be placed in one of two categories: descriptive information providing an overall understanding of the key factors involved in a given problem situation, or highly precise information used for in-depth analysis of a limited number of variables influencing a particular situation.

Similarly, the data required within the context of a given action-research project are directly related to the ongoing situation being studied. Specifically, the type of information needed pertains to both the performance of a given system or organization and the nature of interpersonal/intergroup relations that may affect organizational performance. It will be noted that, in some respects, there are similarities between the approach and information needs of action research and evaluation research; however, the differences are much more important. Action research strongly de-emphasizes evaluative aspects of performance measures and uses them only as guidelines to indicate problem areas and to take immediate corrective action.

Finally, operational research has highly precise information needs related to particular tasks within the organization. Such information must normally be measured using means that provide highly accurate, reliable, and timely data.

CHARACTERISTICS OF DATA-COLLECTION METHODOLOGIES/INSTRUMENTS

While it is conceptually easy to distinguish between a data-collection methodology and the techniques employed subsequently to extract information from this data, such a distinction becomes less pronounced in the actual practice of research. Accordingly, these two important items (see Table 1, columns 4 and 5) and their interactions will be discussed simultaneously.

Policy research employs at least three important types of measures as data sources. While varying widely in their nature, each of these serves as input to analytical techniques that focus on the prediction of future conditions and the implications of these conditions on the activities of the organization.

Longitudinal/time series measures of major indicators form one important source. The level of the data (international, national, regional) depends on the nature of the problem to be studied. Such data can usually be collected only on

a continuing basis with respect to economic, social, political, and technical phenomena of interest to a number of sectors of society. As such, they are limited in their ability to provide insight into very specific strategic questions. Thus, in order to complement such data, researchers in this field often employ the individual judgments of experts having knowledge related to the specific problem of interest. These individual judgments are then combined in a variety of ways in an attempt to reach a consensus opinion across experts. The Delphi Technique is one well-known version of the consensus approach in which the opinions of experts are obtained iteratively in order to focus on most probable future conditions.

A quite different approach to futures prediction involves large-scale system-simulation models designed to test the impact of alternative policy decisions on variables important to the organization. At least two important types of models can be identified: econometric models, based on input-output approaches to analysis; and simulation models, which focus on the interdependence (feedback) among the different components of large systems. The limitations of such models concern their ability to capture the complexity of reality, particularly with respect to factors that are more difficult to quantify (see Chapter 43).

Evaluation research may employ a variety of measures and data collection methods, depending on the research objective. In general, it should be kept in mind that the techniques used to analyze these data all have as their primary goal the evaluation of historical performance with respect to a program's or a firm's objectives, however ill-defined or shifting they may be.

The most traditional evaluative measure relates to various aspects of program- or facility-utilization levels; that is, simply, the number of individuals who have availed themselves of the service/activity/program in question. More recently, there has been a tendency to go beyond this simple accounting approach and to develop measures reflecting the satisfaction levels of users with respect to the entity being evaluated.

In order to increase the effectiveness of both utilization-rate and satisfaction-level measures in evaluation research, two additional types of measures are extremely valuable: measures that compare users to a non-user control group and measures that trace the evolution of performance over time. Given these additional measures, management is able to judge comparative performance as well as performance with respect to arbitrarily chosen standards.

Management/tactical research involves a range of methodologies designed to provide the information pertinent to a particular decision or problem. These approaches involve, at the simplest level, various aspects of information storage and retrieval designed to permit researchers to extract the maximum information from secondary-data sources (see Chapter 8). In parallel, there exists a number of primary-data-collection approaches that include survey research methods; techniques of laboratory or field experimentation designed to test the effectiveness of alternative courses of action; observational methods that furnish insight into human, organizational, or functional behavior under normal environmental conditions; and the simulation of subsystems of an organization.

The types of measures employed are correspondingly varied and include technical or factual data bearing directly on the problem; measures of awareness, attitudes, and opinions; measures of effectiveness of and reaction to alternative actions; and measures describing particular aspects of behavior that are relevant to the question at hand. In general, each of these has been the object of significant study and is relatively well understood.

Management action research requires as its basic data inputs a variety of quantitative and qualitative measures related to technical and human levels of performance and satisfaction. The distinguishing feature is the fact that these measures serve directly to define the nature of management intervention that will be made in an attempt to modify the behavior of the system in question. Specific examples of possible types of measures include measures of work flow, job satisfaction, the structure of an organization, the interpersonal/intergroup relations defined by the organization, and a range of indicators of organizational performance. Such measures need to be gathered within the framework of a continuing, on-site, data collection process that will permit immediate analysis and the rapid identification of major organizational problems. In addition, the analysis must be designed to suggest the immediate interventions necessary to overcome such problems.

Operational research, of course, represents the most limited scope of the research methods involving primarily the construction, validation, and optimization of analytical/quantitative models describing a particular operational task within the organization. However, it should be noted that operational research is not only "operations research" but may also involve other types of studies designed to improve a particular operational procedure. Examples might include personnel administration routines, purchasing practices, and shipping procedures.

Again, the required measures reflect the nature of the research problem and methodology. Such measures usually indicate the level and dispersion of variables describing the performance of a given task, be it by a machine or a human. Such measures must be taken systematically and with a high degree of reliability in order to permit the appropriate type of analysis. As a result, it is common for these measures to be obtained using mechanical devices such as counters, scales, cameras, and timers.

NATURE OF THE RESEARCH OUTPUT

The ultimate objective of the research is the information output designed to assist management to more effectively decide or act in a particular situation.

Policy research may be viewed as providing two principal types of output. The first of these can be summarized as the identification of key dimensions that underlie future organizational priorities and that are often referred to as policy options. Many policy research studies, because of the nature

of their mandate, provide only this first level of output. The second level involves going an important step further and providing recommendations concerning the priorities to be accorded to different policy options and the nature of the action required to implement the selection options.

Evaluation research also results in two possible types of output for management. The traditional output consists of an identification of facility/program strengths and weaknesses according to management-selected criteria within the user groups designated by program managers. As a complement to these objective measures of performances, management may also request researchers to provide them with varying degrees of understanding of the major factors that determine program success. Such understanding can serve as the basis of recommendations for program improvement.

Management/tactical research findings can be classified as either exploratory or definitive. Exploratory findings present management with an in-depth description and interpretation of available information related to the decision situation. Such information can be provided relatively quickly and permits management to make a more informed decision concerning whether action can be taken in the light of available knowledge and real-world competitive and time constraints. Should the collection of additional information be necessary and feasible, the exploratory research will have clearly specified these in-depth information needs. Definitive findings are the result of such in-depth research and should provide management with a clear understanding of the situation, followed by precise recommendation for actions to overcome the original problem or to take advantage of an opportunity.

Action research is designed to provide suggested courses of action that can be immediately implemented and the results of the implementation followed and studied. As such, the process is continuous and interactive. Types of action suggested by this type of research involve changes in the work environment to improve technical performance or human satisfaction, modification of the reward/punishment system related to performance, and changes in organizational structure designed to increase operating effectiveness.

Operational research provides management with precise answers to precise operational questions. These answers may take the form of explicit decision rules prescribing the required operational actions under all probable conditions. Alternatively, or in parallel, the research findings may be presented as precisely defined "management by exception" task-performance measures indicating when management is required to step in and take corrective action. In brief, such results consist of highly detailed instructions concerning "what to do, when to do it, how to do it" in relation to specific tasks within the organization.

CONCLUSION

This chapter, despite its treatment of the theoretical field of research, is not intended as an academic exercise. Rather, it is hoped that the discussion has served to support one very fundamental practical thesis. This thesis asserted that the wide range of problem situations within different levels and functions of an organization, as well as different stages of the management process, implies widely varying information needs for the effective solution of the problem situations. The logical result has been the appearance of different methodological approaches to data collection appropriate to each type of information need. Unfortunately, these fundamental distinctions have been little appreciated, leading to much confusion on the part of managers as to what research really is, what it can do to improve their effectiveness, and what its limits are as an aid to decision making.

It is hoped that the proposed framework for relating major research approaches to three important dimensions of the process of management has clarified to some extent the question as to the distinction among different categories of research methods and the type of decision situation to which each is most relevant. These distinctions among research and data-collection methods should not, however, obscure an important common characteristic and goal of all management research: an ability and desire to provide systematic and objective information for executive decision making that is timely, that is relevant, and that ultimately improves the effectiveness of the organization.

REFERENCES

Anthony, Robert (1965), *Planning and Control Systems: A Framework for Analyses*, Boston: Graduate School of Business Administration, Harvard University.

Bauer, A., and Kenneth J. Gergen (1968), *The Study of Policy Formulation*, New York: The Free Press.

Kotler, Philip (1972), *Marketing Management*, 2nd ed., Englewood Cliffs, NJ: Prentice-Hall, Inc.

Kotler, Philip (1981), *Marketing Management*, 4th ed., Englewood Cliffs, NJ: Prentice-Hall, Inc.

Naisbitt, John (1982), *Megatrends*, New York: Warner Books, Inc.

Ritchie, J.R. Brent (1976), "Priority Analysis: A Multiple Input Program Planning Approach," Working Paper, Université Laval, Quebec.

Ritchie, J.R. Brent (1985), "Tourism Education and Training in Canada; Principles for Development," *Global Village: Journal of the Canadian Hospitality Institute*, 13(4).

Toh, Rex S. (1985), "An Inventory Depletion Overbooking Model for the Hotel Industry," *Journal of Travel Research*, 23(4).

Weiss, Carol B. (1972), *Evaluation Research*, Englewood Cliffs, NJ: Prentice-Hall, Inc.

Whyte, William Foote, and Edith Lentz Hamilton (1964), *Action Research for Management*, Homewood, IL: Irwin, Inc.

3

A Decision Design for Tourism CEOs

ELWOOD L. SHAFER*

Professor of Environmental Management & Tourism
School of Hotel, Restaurant & Institutional Management
The Pennsylvania State University
University Park, Pennsylvania

A process is described for ranking a wide range of budget items in tourism planning and development activities when the anticipated combined social, economic, managerial, environmental, and political benefits of those items cannot be adequately described in economic terms and budgetary constraints do not permit funding all items under consideration. The process accounts for subjective judgment and contains a formal rigorous decision strategy that takes the place of intuition when qualitative and quantitative tourism values need to be evaluated.

What was the last major tourism management or planning decision you made where some of the benefits and costs of one or more of the items you were evaluating were either not readily quantifiable or easily accessible—and how did you make it? There is a good chance you collected a mountain of data, read it, studied it, paged through it, contemplated it, and then made your decision. But do you really know why you made the decision you did? Could you describe each of the specific factors you weighed in the decision-making process, and how much weight each of those factors carried? Very likely, the answer is "no." If so, don't feel badly. It just proves that you are not unlike most of the rest of us. So say the experts (Peters and Austin 1985; McCormack 1984; Naisbitt and Aburdene 1985). The literature is filled with examples of how tourism managers and planners and many other types of executives, when faced with a difficult, complex decision, traditionally gather information or appoint a committee to do it, or both (Austin 1986; Kahn et al. 1964; Richards and Greenlaw 1979). As a result, decision makers may be overwhelmed with data which is difficult to evaluate, or become mired in trade-off considerations as proponents push favorite ideas, programs, or options. When a decision is finally reached, it may be difficult to trace the process and discover why one item was chosen instead of another. There is no "audit trail." The process described in this article was developed and used originally by chief executive officers

(CEOs) to set priorities on a large number of research items involved in the National Resource Planning Act (USDA Forest Service 1983). The design's premise is that human judgment is indispensable to solve complex priority-setting problems. The solution is to use the perceived values and beliefs of CEOs responsible for making the final decision—thus insuring coherent decisions consistent with stated values. Since its conception, the design has been applied by a wide range of managers, negotiators, policy makers and analysts in a variety of decision-making situations related to tourism in government and industry (National Agricultural Research and Extension Users Advisory Board 1983 and 1984).

A TYPICAL EXAMPLE

The process is best described by sitting in on a typical meeting of a CEO and her or his staff where the process is being used. The purpose of the meeting could be to set priorities on a list of different public involvement options, tourism development opportunities, environmental impact alternatives, tourism development possibilities, or a complex combination of items in all of the above. The process applies equally as well to all of these and any other type of priority-setting situation where classic economic benefit-

*This article was originally pubished in the *Journal of Travel Research* 26(2), 1987. Permission to reprint is gratefully acknowledged.

cost analysis cannot be used to evaluate the combined social, economic, managerial, environmental, and political benefits of some, or all, of the items to be evaluated. Typical items to be evaluated, and quotations from participants in previous proprietary studies, are included in this hypothetical example to describe the process as realistically as possible.

SELECTING THE ITEMS TO BE EVALUATED

When the participants are asked to attend the meeting, the only information they are asked to bring is what is inside their heads. Once inside the conference room, they are literally sealed off until they make their decisions. Let us assume in this hypothetical example that the group has a specific number of dollars to invest over a certain period of years in the following 10 activities:

A. Purchase more water-related sports equipment
B. Improve hiking trails to scenic vistas
C. Restore historic landmarks on the property
D. Promote public relations efforts with local populations
E. Enlarge bar facilities
F. Acquire more land for future development
G. Increase marketing/advertising efforts
H. Send key personnel to graduate school management courses
I. Invest in ski area development at another location
J. Make major renovations in beach houses

COST CONSTRAINTS

The group cannot afford to invest in all 10 items. Some items can be evaluated in terms of economic benefit/cost analysis; some cannot. Which ones should the group go for? In this hypothetical example, the names of these items are not as important as the fact that they are very different in terms of the kinds of perceived benefits they eventually will provide or evoke in the minds of the meeting participants.

FACILITATORS ARE ESSENTIAL

Although their postures are relaxed, all eyes of the participants are riveted near one end of the conference table where a wall board is gradually being filled, by one of the group's facilitators, with definitions of the various terms that need to be positioned in order of priority. Two group facilitators, with backgrounds in decision analysis, play distinct roles in shepherding the participants through the tangle of possibilities, values, and risks the group is considering. Facilitator number one stands at the front, eliciting information, asking questions, responding to comments and objections from the table. Facilitator number two darts back and forth, taking copious notes and filling in on the board when needed. The facilitators are helping structure the definition of the items to be evaluated, along with each individual's description of perceived qualitative and quantitative benefits of the items.

The facilitators are essential to the success of the meeting. They are individuals who are able to think quickly and clearly on their feet in the midst of intense, people-oriented

situations; exhibit strong leadership skills; remain results-oriented; portray unusual self-confidence; and remain objective, dispassionate non-members of the decision-making group throughout the entire process. In effect, the facilitators act as praetorian guards, managing the entire process and making sure all players know what is required of them.

DETAILED DESCRIPTION OF ITEMS AND BENEFITS

Early in the discussion, one or more members of the group will point out: "This whole process depends entirely on how clearly we initially define the items to be evaluated and their respective benefits." A facilitator replies, "Exactly; that's why the group should be in agreement on this information before we take the next step."

"How specific should we be in trying to describe the perceived benefits of each item?" another member of the group asks. A facilitator responds, "Each of you has imperfect knowledge about the overall benefits of each item. Some benefits are difficult, and in some cases impossible, to define in a totally objective way. Try to describe the benefits of each item as best you can in terms of how you perceive the combined social, economic, managerial, environmental, and political benefits."

At the close of the first day's session, the facilitators leave the room with a briefcase full of notes to be edited and consolidated that evening for the next step the following day. Incidentally, this process may not require several days—it has been applied in actual situations that only require a few hours.

COMPARING ITEMS

The next morning, participants receive the edited material and a survey form (Table 1) for comparing the items—two at a time—in terms of their overall benefits. Now the facilitators begin to play a different role as they move about the room, coaching and assisting individuals as they complete the survey form.

Periodically, the facilitators will explain that this method for estimating any one item's value under these circumstances has been developed in a wide range of disciplines—including economics, political science, psychology, and sociology. Despite differences in approach, these methods tend to blend. Pair-wise comparisons—comparing all items, two at a time—may be used, for example, to derive an attitude scale for a psychologist (Edwards 1957; Thurston 1927; Torgerson 1958) or a utility scale for an economist (Sinden and Worrell 1979). In fact, the various disciplines often use different terms for the same things. Economists make the most use of these methods as value indicates for setting priorities in marketing strategy decisions.

COMPUTING BENEFIT SCORES FOR EACH ITEM

When all participants complete Table 1, which usually requires about 30 minutes for a 10-item exercise, they

TABLE 1   Survey Forms and Hypothetical Entries of How One Panelist Compared All Two-way Sets of Ten Items

	A Water sport equipment purchases	B Hiking trail improvement	C Historic landmarks restoration	D Public relations promotion	E Bar facilities enlargement	F Land acquisition	G Marketing effort increases	H Management training efforts	I Ski area investment	J Beach houses renovations
A. Water sports equipment purchases	X	1*	1	1	0	1	1	0	1	0
B. Hiking trail improvement		X	1	1	0	1	1	0	0	0
C. Historic landmarks restoration			X	1	0	0	1	0	0	0
D. Public relations promotion				X	0	0	0	0	0	0
E. Bar facilities enlargement					X	1	1	1	1	1
F. Land acquisition						X	1	0	0	0
G. Marketing effort increases							X	0	0	0
H. Management training efforts								X	1	0
I. Ski area investment									X	0
J. Beach houses renovations										X

*A "1" indicates the benefits of the column item were judged more favorable than the benefits of the row item. A "0" means just the opposite.

take a coffee break and the facilitators compute the benefit score for each item. Essentially, the proportion of times all respondents select each item over every other item provides the basic data for computing benefit scores (Table 2).

It is not unlikely at this point that one or more economists in the group will remark, "I believe calling the results of panel judgments 'benefits' is a misnomer. Benefits have a definite economic meaning—contribution to social welfare. In economics, quantified benefit estimation is imperfect, but the goal is to estimate total benefits generated, generally based on willingness to pay." A facilitator replies, "For many of the items being compared here, it may be impossible to describe the related benefits in pure economic terms. Remember, we have asked each of you to make judgment calls based on your perception of the total social, economic, managerial, environmental, and political benefits associated with each item. The challenge of comparing items two at a time is characterized by multiple criteria, both objective and subjective; an imperfect state of knowledge; and a plethora of relevant information that requires evaluation and rational choice under complexity, uncertainty, and risk. Thus, we are using the word 'benefits' in this exercise in a much broader context than that ordinarily used in economics."

COST ESTIMATES

Next, the group estimates the annual cost of each item. Cost estimates are made after the benefit scores are computed

because costs are independent of benefits and, therefore, should not influence perceptions of the related benefits. It is important that the group estimate the cost of each item before the facilitators report the benefit scores to the group. Costs are discounted to present worth—the money needed today in order to fund the item in total; the rate of interest is selected by the group. The total cost of all items in the hypothetical example is approximately $23 million—$8 million more than the group can afford to spend with a $15 million budget.

DEVELOPING CRITERION FOR DECISIONS

Using a benefit-only criterion, facilitators now list the 10 items on the wall board in order of their priority according to the initial benefit scores obtained from Table 2. Item B is first, A second, I third, etc. In a second, third, and fourth column, respectively, facilitators also record each of the item's benefit scores, the discounted costs, and the benefit-cost criterion values—the benefit score divided by its discounted cost (Table 3). Pointing to the board (Table 3), a facilitator explains, "Notice that if we had listed these items in column one in order of priority according to a benefit-cost criterion, rather than the way we have listed them here, item D would be first, H second, G third, and so on."

Inevitably at this stage a participant will ask, "If we only want to use the benefit-cost criterion for setting priorities, why even bother to record the benefit-only criterion data?" "Because we need to be aware of the magnitude of the difference if we reverted to benefit-only criterion for making

TABLE 2   Hypothetical Example of How Benefit Scores Were Calculated for Ten Items

	A Water sport equipment purchases	B Hiking trail improvement	C Historic landmarks restoration	D Public relations promotion	E Bar facilities enlargement	F Land acquisition	G Marketing effort increases	H Management training efforts	I Ski area investment	J Beach houses renovations	
	Proportion of times column effort was judged more favorable than row effort										
A. Water sports equipment purchases	0.00	0.70[a]	0.15	0.10	0.15	0.15	0.60	00.0	0.60	0.10	
B. Hiking trail improvement	0.30[b]	0.00	0.00	0.00	0.15	0.30	0.45	0.25	0.45	0.25	
C. Historic landmarks restoration	0.85	1.00	0.00	0.30	0.60	0.70	0.60	0.25	0.60	0.30	
D. Public relations promotion	0.90	1.00	0.70	0.00	0.85	0.70	0.75	0.55	0.75	0.85	
E. Bar facilities enlargement	0.85	0.85	0.40	0.15	0.00	0.55	0.60	0.40	0.75	0.60	
F. Land acquisition	0.85	0.70	0.30	0.30	0.45	0.00	0.75	0.30	0.60	0.55	
G. Marketing effort increases	0.40	0.55	0.40	0.25	0.40	0.25	0.00	0.25	0.55	0.25	
H. Management training efforts	1.00	0.75	0.75	0.45	0.60	0.70	0.75	0.00	0.75	0.70	
I. Ski area investment	0.40	0.55	0.40	0.25	0.25	0.40	0.45	0.25	0.00	0.25	
J. Beach houses renovations	0.90	0.75	0.70	0.15	0.40	0.45	0.75	0.30	0.75	0.00	
Totals	6.45	6.85	3.80	1.95	3.85	4.20	5.70	2.55	5.80	3.85	45.00
Benefit Scores	143[c]	152	84	43	86	93	127	57	129	86	1000.00

[a]Assume 10 panelists were used in this survey. We add the individual raw scores from the survey forms (for example, 1+1+0+1+1+0+1+1+1+0=7) and divide by the number of panelists (7/10=.70).

[b]The value in a cell to the left of the diagonal dash line is: 1.00 minus the corresponding pair-wise comparison value to the right of the diagonal. For example, the .30 in the first column, row two, is the result of 1.00-.70; the .70 being located in the second column, row one.

[c] $\frac{6.45}{45.00}$ x 1000 = 143 Multiplying by 1000 is a convenience to avoid the use of decimal points in the benefit scores.

decisions in a situation that involves qualitative as well as quantitative estimates of the benefits for the items involved," the facilitator answers.

The group takes a coffee break, and the facilitators use the data in Table 3 to cumulatively plot the costs and benefits of the 10 items in their order of priority: first, according to a benefit-only criterion; next, by the benefit-cost criterion (Figure 1).

The resulting diagram provides a design for decisions the group can use to examine the priorities of the 10 items under any budget constraint. As Figure 1 shows, the order of priority of the items along the benefit-cost criterion curve—or the decision curve—always provides the most benefits for a given budget. For example, since the group's total budget is $15 million, a program (on the benefit-cost curve) that contains items D, H, G, B, E, A, F, and C—with a total benefit score of 800—is preferred over a $15 million budget (on the benefit-only curve) with items B, A, I, G, and F—with a total benefit score of only 660.

FINE-TUNING THE PRIORITIES

Also at this point, one or more members of the group will comment, "Now that I understand how this whole process works, I'm not quite satisfied with the benefit scores we've assigned to each item. Can we go back and adjust them?" "Of course," a facilitator replies, "but we may not have to go back and compare the items two at a time again if we only want to make minor adjustments."

Pointing to the display board, the facilitator explains, "If we only wish to make minor corrections the only constraint is that, regardless of the number of adjustments we make in benefit scores, the sum of the benefit scores for all items must still only equal 1000—as we originally agreed on (Table 3). For example, if participants want to increase the benefit score of one item, they must reduce the value of another, or others, an equal amount. Up to this point, the system was designed to facilitate consensus as quickly as possible; now we can 'fine-tune' your perceptions of the benefit scores."

TABLE 3 Initial and Final Results, After Fine Tuning the Benefit Scores of the Ten Items

Ten Items		Initial Results			Final Results	
		Initial Benefit Score	Discounted Cost (Hundred Thousands)	Initial Benefit-Cost Criterion Value	Final Benefit Score	Final Benefit-Cost Criterion Value
B.	Hiking trail improvement	152	16	9.50	216	13.50
A.	Water sports equipment purchases	143	36	3.97	123	3.41
I.	Ski area investment	129	56	2.30	164	2.93
G.	Marketing effort increases	127	9	14.11	110	12.22
F.	Land acquisition	93	30	3.10	80	2.67
E.	Bar facility enlargement	86	20	4.30	74	2.11
J.	Beach houses renovations	86	35	2.46	74	2.11
C.	Historic landmarks restoration	84	26	3.23	72	2.77
H.	Management training efforts	57	2	28.50	49	24.50
D.	Public relations promotions	43	1	43.00	38	38.00
TOTALS		1000	231		1000	

During this period of adjusting benefit scores, facilitators record participants' comments that describe the additional benefits associated with those items that are assigned higher benefit scores.

THE FINAL DECISION

On the basis of participant suggestions, facilitators make final adjustments in benefit scores on the display board, recalculate final benefit-cost criterion values (Table 3), and plot the end results (Figure 2). Now, for a $15 million budget, for example, the most efficient budget program should

contain D, H, B, G, E, A, and I for a total benefit score of 800; rather than B, I, A, G, and F for a total score of 693.

CONCLUSION

This decision design for CEOs and their staffs facilitates consensus and serves the decision-making process primarily by enabling attention to be directed at different items in a complex priority-setting problem without losing sight of the interdependencies. Individual CEOs, managers, and planners may use the process without the aid of group consensus

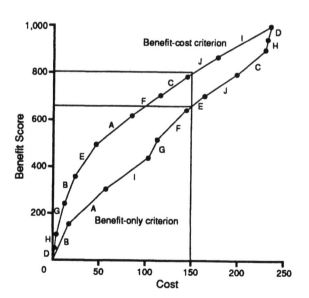

FIGURE 1 Benefit-cost versus Benefit-only Criterion: Initial Results

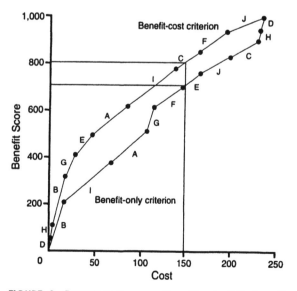

FIGURE 2 Benefit-cost versus Benefit-only Criterion: Final Comparisons

to discipline their own reasoning and to enhance communication among individuals at various levels of their organization. The process has been used effectively in tourism planning to communicate the basis for recommendations, to identify sources of disagreement, and to focus expertise on appropriate parts of decisions needing more attention. Because the process specifically focuses on policy or CEO decision options, results can be incorporated directly by lower management levels into planning and operating procedures. The process is not intended to stand on its own merits without, whenever possible, the benefits of additional information from other studies to improve the final priority-setting process within the constraints of a fixed budget.

This decision design recognizes that human judgment is indispensable to serious CEO decision making. With this realistic acceptance of human limitations, the potential for more balanced decision making emerges. The process takes exception to Shakespeare's optimistic assessment: "What a piece of work is man. How noble in reason, how infinite in faculties. . . ." Rather, the underlying pragmatic premise of the design is more closely related to the skepticism of Francis Bacon, who said, "We do ill to exalt the powers of the human mind, when we should seek out its proper helps." In the words of one of today's modern managers, "The qualities that make a good manager . . . come down to decisiveness. You can use the fanciest computers in the world and you can gather all the charts and numbers, but in the end you have to bring all your own information together, set up a timetable, and *act*" (Iacocca 1984). The decision design described above is intended to assist CEOs in taking that action.

REFERENCES

Austin, C. F. (1986), *Management's Self-Inflicted Wounds*, New York: Holt, Rinehart & Winston.

Edwards, A. L. (1957), *Techniques of Attitude Scale Construction*, New York: Appleton-Century-Crofts.

Iacocca, L. (1984), *Iacocca: An Autobiography*, New York: Bantam Books.

Kahn, R., D. M. Wolf, R. P. Quinn, J. D. Snoek, and R. A. Rosenthal (1964), *Organizational Stress: Studies in Role Conflict and Ambiguity*, New York: John Wiley & Sons, Inc.

McCormack, M. H. (1984), *What They Don't Teach You at Harvard Business School*, New York: Bantam Books.

Naisbitt, J., and P. Aburdene (1985), *Re-inventing the Corporation*, New York: Warner.

National Agricultural Research and Extension Users Advisory Board (1983), *Appraisal of the Proposed Budget for Food and Agricultural Sciences*, Washington, D.C.: USDA.

National Agricultural Research and Extension Users Advisory Board (1984), *New Directions for Science, Education, and Agriculture: Executive Summary* (AGR 101), Washington, D.C.: USDA.

Peters, T., and N. Austin (1985), *A Passion for Excellence*, New York: Random House.

Richards, M. D., and P. S. Greenlaw (1979), *Management Decisions and Behavior*, Homewood, IL: Richard D. Irwin, Inc.

Sinden, J. A., and A. C. Worrell (1979), *Unpriced Values—Decisions Without Market Prices*, New York: John Wiley & Sons, Inc.

Thurston, L. L. (1927), "A Law of Comparative Judgment," *Psychological Review*, 34, 278–286.

Torgerson, W. S. (1958), *Theory and Methods of Scaling*, New York: John Wiley & Sons, Inc.

USDA Forest Service (1983), *Draft Environmental Impact Statement: 1985–2030*, Washington, D.C.: Resources Planning Act Program Staff Report.

4

Crafting a Destination Vision[1]

J. R. BRENT RITCHIE[2]
Chairman,
World Tourism Education and Research Centre
The University of Calgary
Calgary, Alberta

The First International Tourism Policy Forum held at George Washington University concluded that:

"Resident responsive tourism is the watchword for tomorrow: community demands for active . participation in the setting of the tourism agenda and its priorities for tourism development and management cannot be ignored."

While this conclusion reflects lofty goals, it will have little meaning unless approaches to translating this concept into reality are developed. With this concern clearly in mind, the present essay describes a community-based process which had as its goal the crafting of a "Vision" for the long-term development of tourism of one particular destination. The process involved a task force of 18 committed citizens and industry leaders in the City of Calgary, Canada, for a period of over 12 months. After first establishing how tourism related to other opportunities for economic and social development, these Calgary residents subsequently focused their intellects and their energies on the "crafting" of a vision statement describing how they felt Calgary could and should develop as a tourism destination over the next 15 to 20 years. As well, they identified the major facilities, events, and programs that will be required to realize this vision. While perhaps grandiose in terms of its scope and ambition, the vision statement and the supporting action initiatives developed by the Task Force seek to build upon Calgary's ongoing commitment to tourism. Their ultimate goal, and that of the community as a whole, is to put in place the facilities, events, and programs required to make Calgary a major "Host, Consultant, and Educator to the World."

INTRODUCTION

One of the most compelling forces that has emerged in recent years is the desire of peoples all over the world to recapture control of the political processes that affect their daily lives. While the most dramatic examples of this movement have occurred in Central and Eastern Europe, equally important (although more subtle) manifestations of the same phenomenon are evident in other countries in Europe, in North America, and even in Asia. While the causes of this movement are many and varied, the end result is an increasing unwillingness on the part of educated and free peoples to bow to the unresponsive will of a few individuals for any extended period of time. One consequence of this movement has been a profound evolution of the socio-political ground rules that shape both policy formulation and decision making at all levels of society. As a result, societies in all parts of the globe have had to radically rethink and reshape the organizations and the processes that have traditionally been used to

[1]This article was first published in *Tourism Management* 14(5) 1993. Permission to reprint is gratefully acknowledged.
[2]The author wishes to express his appreciation to Lorn R. Sheehan for his assistance in support of the work on which this essay is based. As well, the invaluable contributions of the citizens of Calgary who participated in the work of the Task Force "Calgary: Host, Consultant, and Educator to the World" are gratefully acknowledged.

develop national policies and to implement supporting programs.

Tourism, as an important and integral part of the global social and economic fabric, has not escaped the pressures for change created by this metamorphosis of the democratic process. Increasingly, along with all important industry sectors, tourism is being critically assessed concerning its net contribution to the well-being of the community or region that it both serves and impacts. As part of this process, the residents of communities and regions affected by tourism are demanding to be involved in the decisions affecting their development. This reality was emphatically highlighted as one of the major conclusions of the First International Tourism Policy Forum held at George Washington University. To quote directly:

> Resident responsive tourism is the watchword for tomorrow: community demands for active participation in the setting of the tourism agenda and its priorities for tourism development and management cannot be ignored (Ritchie 1991).

In effect, the above conclusion from the Forum and its associated recommendations stressed the need for consultation involving the local community in all forms of tourism development. For interested readers, the entire section of the summary report discussing this conclusion is reproduced in Table 1.

It should be noted at this point that the idea of a community emphasis on tourism is not new (Murphy 1985). A number of other authors have pointed out the desirability of providing broad-based citizen input into tourism-related policy and development decisions (Keough 1990). As well, a range of approaches for obtaining consensus, or at least unbiased input into the decision-making process, has been developed and tested (Ritchie 1985 and 1988). However, none of these previous works has reflected the unanimous emphasis placed on meaningful citizen involvement by members of the Tourism Policy Forum. As such, it would appear that this strong desire for meaningful input into tourism-development decisions is a fairly recent reality.

LEVEL AND NATURE OF RESIDENT INPUT

Great care must be taken in identifying the kinds of input from community residents that are desirable and useful. This concern has three dimensions. First, the inputs and impact of citizens must be real; tokenism has no place in the new democratic processes that the public is demanding. Second, from a practical perspective, citizen input provided on a volunteer basis is a limited and valuable resource. As such, it can be obtained only in limited amounts and on periodic basis. Finally, in terms of content, it is acknowledged that the views that residents furnish represent nontechnical advice designed to provide direction concerning the nature and type of tourism development that the community wishes to sup-

TABLE 1   Conclusions from the International Tourism Policy Forum Concerning "Resident Responsive Tourism"

Resident responsive tourism is the watchword for tomorrow: community demands for active participation in the setting of the tourism agenda and its priorities for tourism development and management cannot be ignored.

For too long, much of the concern related to tourism development has been focused on the needs of the consumer of the tourism service. While in a competitive world this concern will continue to be of substantial importance, there is a strong and growing recognition that a greater balance needs to be struck in weighing the desires of visitors against the well-being of their hosts. There is a need to recognize that tourism must benefit the local community and that there must be broad-based participation in tourism development decisions at the community level. There is a realization that while tourism enhances community life, it can also threaten the well-being of residents as well as the values they hold.

Several policy recommendations emerged.

1. In general, there is a need to recognize that tourism development must be in harmony with the socio-cultural, ecological, heritage, goals, values, and aspirations of the host community.
2. Similarly, the economic benefits from tourism must be equitably accessible to all participants in the overall tourism process.
3. Creative approaches to foster host-country participation in the equity and ownership of tourism facilities and services must be developed. There is genuine concern that if host communities do not benefit from tourism, they will become alienated and reject tourism in all its forms. In this regard, there is particular concern with respect to Third World Countries and the need to optimize economic benefits from tourism—a recognition that this has not always been the case in the past.

In effect, these policy recommendations reflect a thematic need for consultation involving the local community in all forms of tourism development. In particular, there is a sensitivity to the cultural disparities that may exist between the host region and the visitors to this region. This results in the need to avoid the potential for social alienation on the part of host communities.

Source: Ritchie (1991)

port. Such input is not a version of professional or consulting advice pertaining to the implementation of strategies or plans on an ongoing basis. This role is the responsibility of professional managers.

Given this caveat, it becomes clear that the solicitation of resident input involves a process designed primarily to define the broad parameters within which tourism development should take place for a given destination or region. The intent of the process is to formulate a framework that provides the industry with broad guidelines as to the kinds of major facilities, events, and programs that residents find most consistent with their values and aspirations for the long-term development and well-being of the community. In traditional management terms, such a framework is often referred to as a "Long-Term Strategic Plan." More recently, the concept of "Visioning" or "Vision Management" has emerged.

STRATEGIC PLANNING AND VISIONING

While strategic planning and visioning are clearly related processes, there are some useful distinctions. Writings by Mintzberg and his colleagues in the field of strategic management provide some insights in this regard. As noted by Mintzberg (1990), the traditional approach to strategic planning (referred to as the "Design School" model) can be described as "prescriptive" in orientation. This terminology implies that strategy formation is viewed as a process of conceptual design, of formal planning and of analytical positioning. The essence of the Design School model is that it is by nature structured, logical, and somewhat mechanical. It emphasizes that strategy formation should be a controlled, conscious process of thought for which ultimate responsibility lies with the Chief Executive Officer of the entity involved in strategy development. The outcome of this process is a simple, unique, and explicit "best" strategy for a given situation.

At the other end of the spectrum is what Mintzberg defines as the "crafting" of strategy. Under this conceptualization, a strategy is a dynamic, evolving process in which strategies take form as a result of learning over a period of time—as opposed to being formulated at a fixed point in time. He emphasizes that the crafting of strategy reflects an ongoing iterative process of thinking and acting—and then thinking some more. One idea leads to another until a new pattern forms. As such, strategies can form as well as be formulated. A strategy can emerge in response to an evolving situation, or it can be brought about deliberately, through a process of formulation followed by implementation. Crafting strategy requires dedication, experience, involvement with the material, the personal touch, mastery of detail, a sense of harmony, and integration (Mintzberg 1987).

The process of "strategic visioning"—or simply "visioning"—like the crafting of strategy, is seen as a dynamic, interactive phenomenon (Westley and Mintzberg 1989). From a conceptual perspective, the process can be broken down into three distinct stages:

1. the envisioning of an image of a desired future organizational state that,
2. when effectively communicated to followers,
3. serves to empower those followers so they can enact the vision.

CRAFTING A TOURISM VISION

In traditional terms, the vision for an organization is provided by leaders, such as a Lee Iacocca, who "developed an agenda. . . . that included a bold *new vision* of what Chrysler could and should be" (Kotter 1988). Whether or not this model of the single, charismatic leader remains appropriate in a world of flat organizations, shared expertise, and networking is open to discussion. What is significant, however, is the importance of developing a vision for a given organization in relation to its particular mission. In the present context, the task is to establish a framework and a process by which to provide leadership to a community, a region, or a country in its efforts to formulate a vision as to what it can or should seek to become as a tourism destination.

In undertaking to craft a vision for a destination, it should be kept in mind that such a process is a new but important extension of the more common process of strategic planning in tourism (e.g., Gilbert 1990; Gunn 1988; Kaiser and Helber 1978). In extending the concept of visioning to tourism, it is found that three characteristics of the process need to be kept in mind when compared to its application in organizations such as the Chrysler Corporation.

1. The vision for a tourism destination must bring together the views of many organizations and individuals in the industry and the community. As such, the process is much more complex than that carried out within a single firm.

2. Because of the number and diversity of the stakeholders involved in the crafting of a destination vision for tourism, the value systems brought to the process can be greatly different, even to the point of being diametrically opposed. As such, the task of reaching consensus and obtaining endorsement of the destination vision is a challenging and often delicate task.

3. Compared to a firm, the vision developed for a destination tends to define the nature of extremely long-term major developments, many of which are relatively irreversible. While the choice of the right vision is critical for any entity, it is absolutely critical for a tourism destination as it will set in motion the development of facilities, events, and programs that will do much to define the very essence of that destination for years to come.

CRAFTING A TOURISM VISION FOR CALGARY

To this point, the discussion has focused on the nature of vision formulation in a very abstract way. Because of the relative newness of the concept, particularly in a tourism context, it was felt useful to review its origins so as to provide some basic insights into its purpose and characteristics.

In the remainder of this essay, attention turns to the application of the visioning process for a specific destination that has used the approach in an attempt to provide both direction and support for future tourism development. The destination in question is the City of Calgary, Canada—a city for which tourism is a major economic and social force. As previous studies have shown (Ritchie, Echtner, and Smith 1989), the destination is best known for three things, two of which are tourism oriented. These include the oil and gas industry, the annual Calgary Stampede, and the hosting of the 1988 Winter Olympic Games.

SOME BACKGROUND TO THE VISIONING PROCESS

Calgary is a rapidly developing city of some 750,000 residents. Its relatively isolated location just east of the Canadian Rocky Mountains in Western Canada has engendered a relatively strong feeling of the need for self-generated development initiatives. While clearly acknowledging that the quality of life enjoyed by its residents owes much to the oil and gas reserves with which the region is blessed, there is also a recognition of the need to plan for the future diversification of the economy. While this desire is driven primarily by economic motives, it also reflects a desire to develop a broader range of activities and interests for residents so as to make the city an even more vibrant and exciting place to live.

The success of the 1981 bid to host the XVth Winter Olympic Games represented the beginning of an important new phase in the city's history. From relative obscurity, Calgary achieved a level of international awareness that, at its height in 1988, made it nearly as well known as the three largest Canadian cities of Toronto, Montreal, and Vancouver (Ritchie and Smith 1991). Perhaps more important, the preparation for and actual hosting of this mega-event provided a unique opportunity for community development, both in economic and social terms (Ritchie 1989).

Recognizing that many of the benefits derived from the successful hosting of the Olympics would end as soon as the Games were over, community leaders sought to determine how best to capitalize on the reputation and the contacts generated by the event. Towards this end, just following the Games, community leaders called together over 100 residents of the city to address this issue. It is important to note that the community leaders directing this initiative included both the Mayor of Calgary and the President of the local Chamber of Commerce. This collaboration took place formally under the auspices of the Calgary Economic Development Authority (CEDA), a joint public/private sector entity reporting to both elected officials on the City Council and to the Board of Directors of the city's main business organization. While undoubtedly imperfect, this approach to public/private collaboration sought to ensure that the interests of city residents at large were represented, while at the same time involving the business community that, in the end, would be expected to implement many of the programs resulting from the strategic planning process.

The result of this initial meeting of residents from all segments of the community was the creation of a "Core Group" of 12 volunteer citizens whose formal mission was "... to develop a strategic plan that will positively influence the development of Calgary in directions that will strengthen our city as we know it today." Approximately one year later, after extensive deliberations, this Group released its report, which outlined a strategy for economic development for the city into the twenty-first century (CEDA 1989). This report was circulated widely and discussed extensively by residents of the city. In this way, every attempt was made to ensure

that members of the community were generally in agreement with the directions being proposed for the future development of the city. While it is indeed difficult to ascertain the extent to which the overall contents of the CEDA report were endorsed by all sectors of the community, local press coverage appeared to indicate general acceptance of the strategic direction being proposed.

Perhaps the most significant immediate outcome of the "Calgary ... Into the 21st Century" report was the creation of 10 ongoing Task Forces whose mandate was to further explore the opportunities identified by the Core Group. The specific focus of each of these Task Forces is summarized in Table 2. From a tourism standpoint, the most critical Task Force was that charged with the responsibility of attempting to establish Calgary as "Host, Consultant, and Educator to the World." While no doubt grandiose in its terminology, the mandate of this Task Force was to determine how the city could best build upon its fleeting international reputation from the Olympics, its legacy of sports facilities built for the Games, its proximity to the scenic Rocky Mountains, its world-class technical expertise in key sectors of the economy (notably oil and gas), and its situation as the most highly educated city in Canada in order to develop itself as a major international-travel destination.

HOST TO THE WORLD TASK FORCE

Using this general mandate as a starting point, the Task Force developed a more detailed mission statement within its formal Terms of Reference (Table 3). As seen from this table, the critical initial component of the mandate of the Task Force was:

to develop a vision concerning the kind of tourism destination it believes Calgary should become as we move into the 21st century. . . .

It is this initial part of the Task Force mandate, the development of a destination vision, that is the primary focus of the present discussion. This said, the reader should keep in mind the importance of the subsequent activities related to the implementation of the vision that was developed. While these implementation details will be noted only briefly, they

TABLE 2   Focus of the 10 Task Forces Established to Support the Economic Development of "Calgary . . . Into the 21st Century"

1. Capitalize on Free Trade
2. Modernize, Develop, and Expand Calgary's Existing Industries
3. Find New Economic Drivers—Diversification
4. Develop and Mobilize Our Human Potential
5. Increase Capital Availability
6. Establish Calgary as Host, Consultant, and Educator to the World
7. Internationalize and Respond to Globalization
8. Establish Calgary as the World's First Information Port
9. Enhance and Maintain Calgary's Enviable Quality of Life
10. Align to the 21st Century

**TABLE 3   Terms of Reference of Task Force #6
"Calgary . . . Host, Consultant, and Educator to the
World"**

The formal terms of reference defined the overall mandate of the
Task Force as being:

> *to develop a vision concerning the kind of tourism desti-
> nation it believes Calgary should become as we move
> into the 21st century in order to truly establish the city as
> a major host, consultant, and educator to the world. It
> should subsequently prioritize the major initiatives that
> will be essential to achieving this vision. Finally, it should
> recommend and initiate specific actions/implementation
> steps that will be required to translate the vision into
> reality.*

In seeking to fulfill this mandate, the Task Force set itself seven
specific tasks. These were:

1. To formulate, in a reasonable amount of detail, a *vision*
   describing the Calgary of the 21st Century as a tourism
   destination. This vision will define the kind of destination
   we want Calgary to be and the kind of people we are likely
   to attract if such a vision is realized.
2. To identify and prioritize the *major facilities* that it will be
   necessary to put in place over the next 20 years as Calgary
   moves to establish itself as the kind of host, consultant, and
   educator to the world defined by the above noted Vision
   Statement.
3. To identify and prioritize the development and/or enhancement of *major events* that are consistent with the Vision
   Statement and that will be necessary to realize it as we
   move into the 21st Century.
4. To identify critical aspects of the *support and educational/
   training infrastructure* that it will be necessary to develop/
   enhance as we move towards realizing the vision.
5. To provide concrete specifications of the image of *Calgary*
   that will be portrayed nationally and internationally so as to
   accurately, yet competitively, position Calgary in the markets it seeks to serve.
6. To provide useful *estimates of the amount of funding* likely
   to be required to implement initiatives related to the facilities, events, infrastructure, and other programs identified
   by the Task Force. As well, the issue of *possible sources of
   funding* should be addressed. If it is felt necessary, the Task
   Force may authorize additional feasibility studies to be
   undertaken where financial support for such studies can be
   successfully solicited.
7. To identify *organizations/individuals* who can be encouraged to assume responsibility and/or leadership in implementation and/or development of the various facilities,
   events, infrastructure, and programs deemed to be a priority by the Task Force.

are clearly important. Although discussion is minimal here,
they required a considerable amount of time and effort on the
part of Task Force members.

INTEGRATING TASK FORCE EFFORTS WITH THOSE OF EXISTING TOURISM ORGANIZATION

One obvious issue of significance that might be raised is the
potential for conflict between a short-term community stra-

tegic-planning group for tourism and those existing tourism-
related organizations that have had, and continue to have, a
very strong and ongoing involvement in the industry. In the
present case, this issue was dealt with very directly by asking
the local Convention and Visitor Bureau to assume a leadership role within the Task Force. In practical terms, this
involved inviting the Bureau to recommend a person to chair
the Task Force and convening the first meeting of the Task
Force at the offices of the Bureau. At the same time, the Core
Group took steps to ensure that membership on the Task
Force was not restricted to "industry insiders" only. The end
result was a larger Task Force (18 persons) than might have
been required from a strictly functional standpoint, but one
that did provide for broader community representation than
is often the case. In retrospect, it is felt (in the author's view)
that an even broader range of individuals from the community at large could have been incorporated into the process.
There are, however, practical limits to the size of the strategic planning group such as the present Task Force.

INTEGRATING TOURISM WITH OTHER SECTORS

Despite the importance that professionals in the field attach
to their sector, it is essential to keep in mind that tourism is
only one of several sources of income and employment
within most communities. As such, any effort that tends to
focus exclusively on the development of tourism for a destination must be concerned about the relationship of tourism
to other sectors. This concern was addressed by Task Force
#6 before undertaking the detailed work related to its man-
date through an examination of its relationship with the
mandates of the other nine Task Forces. In particular, it
noted its relationship with:

* The Internationalization and Globalization Task Force
(#7)—particularly that tourism will play an important role in
internationalizing Calgary businesses and other institutions.

* The Information Task Force (#8)—specifically that the
consulting and educational aspects of the "Host to the World"
mandate will rely heavily on efforts of this Task Force.

* The Human Resource Task Force (#4)—notably that
the educational dimension of Task Force #6 depends very
heavily on Human Resource Development. It was also
noted that this same dependency on Human Resources applied across several Task Forces.

PRINCIPLES UNDERLYING THE VISION

In the initial phases of their work, the 18 persons on the Task
Force attempted to establish a framework within which to
develop the vision for Calgary as a tourism destination. In
particular, considerable attention was devoted to identifying
principles on which to base development of the vision. These
principles are summarized in Table 4.

ELEMENTS OF THE VISION

Once the mandate of the Task Force and the principles on
which to base the process had been agreed to, attention then

TABLE 4   Principles Underlying the Vision of "Calgary . . . Host, Consultant, and Educator to the World"

- Developments related to the vision must always seek to ensure that Calgary and region residents are net beneficiaries (i.e., positive impacts must clearly outweigh any potential negative consequences).
- The vision should focus on initiatives that reflect our natural strengths, lifestyles, and heritage.
- The vision should incorporate and build upon the high quality of the natural, visual, and built environment enjoyed by Calgary and the surrounding regions.
- The vision should focus on significant themes and initiatives that will help position and develop Calgary as a major international destination and knowledge/education center.
- Although the concept of "host, consultant, and educator" is clearly applicable to all areas of excellence that Calgary enjoys, the vision proposes that we learn about the strategic combination of these areas through an initial focus on the oil and gas, agri-business, and tourism sectors. In brief, we will first strive for excellence as hosts, consultants, and educators in these areas.

TABLE 5   The Vision of Calgary as "Host, Consultant, and Educator to the World"

Calgary in the 21st century should be:

- A city that is safe, clean, attractive, and efficient, and whose priority is maintaining and enhancing its livability.
- A city that values and preserves the high quality and beauty of the natural environment, waterways, and setting with which it has been blessed.
- A city that reflects its proud and dynamic Western heritage and native cultures.
- A city that values and supports knowledge and education, particularly in those spheres upon which it depends for its well-being and development.
- A city that actively encourages and facilitates knowledge transfer between those who generate the knowledge and those who use it.
- A city that genuinely welcomes visitors from all parts of the world in an environment that encourages the exchange of insight and understanding while striving to create new personal and professional friendships.
- A city that values its cultural diversity and its artistic achievements.
- A city that thrives in all seasons—and that is, therefore, attractive to visitors at all times.
- A city that attracts attention and acclaim by providing first-class attractions and by hosting high-profile events that are of interest to its citizens.

focused on the primary goal of attempting to define a common vision as to what Calgary could and should look like as a tourism destination in some 15 to 20 years. As might be expected, this process required several sessions and a considerable amount of iterative reflection, reaction, and reformulation. As a result of this process, Task Force members agreed upon a series of nine statements that, in their totality, provided a composite picture as to how they envisage the Calgary of the future from a tourism perspective. These nine vision statements are given in Table 5.

An examination of this set of Vision Statements reveals that they fall into two general categories. The first category contains those that reflect some general values as to how the city should develop—almost without reference to tourism. The first two in particular fall into this category. It is important to keep in mind, however, that Task Force members insisted that such elements as overall livability of the city and environmental protection were indeed major tourism appeals. Furthermore, they insisted that if Calgary could not be maintained as a city that appealed to residents, it could not develop its attractiveness for others. The knowledgeable reader will immediately be able to provide examples as to exceptions regarding the generality of this assertion. Nevertheless, it was judged important by Calgary residents.

The second category of Vision Statements described more explicitly the key dimensions of the city's character on which tourism should build as Calgary enters the twenty-first century. It is believed that each of these Vision Statements fully respects the principle presented in Table 5.

Before leaving the Vision Statements, it should also be pointed out that the report of the Task Force contains a more extensive discussion concerning the manner in which members described and interpreted each statement. This information is available to those wishing a more detailed understanding of the process and its results (CEDA 1991).

REALIZING THE VISION

The definition of the nine Vision Statements and the subsequent elaboration of their specific meaning was viewed as fulfilling the first of the seven tasks contained in the overall mandate of Task Force #6 (see Table 2). As the next step in the total process outlined by the Terms of Reference, Task Force members subsequently focused their attention on efforts to both identify and prioritize the major facilities, events, and programs that it was felt would be necessary to put in place over the next 20 years if Calgary was indeed to establish itself as the kind of Host, Consultant, and Educator to the World defined by the composite Vision Statement.

With this goal in mind, the Task Force first generated a large number of possible initiatives and then selected a more limited set of higher priority items. The outcome of this process is shown visually in Figures 1, 2, and 3. These figures identify the specific Facilities (Figure 1), Events (Figure 2), and Programs (Figure 3) that members felt would contribute to the realization of each of the nine elements of the Vision. It should be noted that each of the figures contains Facilities, Events, or Programs that reflect:

- projects that are already in place and that require additional support to encourage evolution towards recognized international excellence;
- projects that have been proposed by others and that are currently under review; and
- suggested new projects that flow logically from the vision defined by the Task Force.

**A City that has the World-Class Facilities to Support
the Programs & Events Required to "Host the World"**

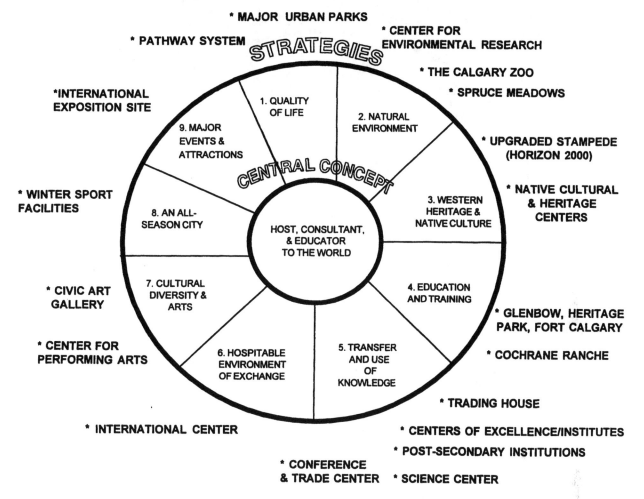

FIGURE 1 Facilities required to realize the vision.

While the individual facilities, events, and programs in Figures 1, 2, and 3 are by nature very specific to the community in question, a number do have characteristics that could be generalized to other settings. The important point to be emphasized, however, is that each of the various facilities, events, or programs bears a direct relation to one or more of the Vision Statements developed by members of the community.

Developing an Action Plan

While space does not allow discussion here, the final steps in the process defined by the "Task Force Terms of Reference" were to develop a relatively detailed action plan that specified, as far as possible, the organization(s) most appropriately responsible for undertaking each proposed initiative, the desired timing of various actions, and some preliminary estimate of the magnitude of the resources that would likely be required to develop a particular facility, event, or pro-

gram. Again, readers having an interest in the details are referred to the original documentation (CEDA 1991).

SOME OBSERVATIONS ON THE CRAFTING OF A TOURISM VISION

While one must be cautious not to exaggerate the significance of the present effort to develop a process for the crafting of a vision for tourism destinations, it is felt that the work does break some new ground. In the process of doing so, it is acknowledged that other cities have undertaken similar economic renewal initiatives (for example, Pittsburgh, Pennsylvania). However, most have not emphasized the visioning process in tourism to the extent of the present example. As well, it is recognized that certain things could certainly be done better—and hopefully will be in the future. Towards this end, a number of observations concerning the process may be of interest.

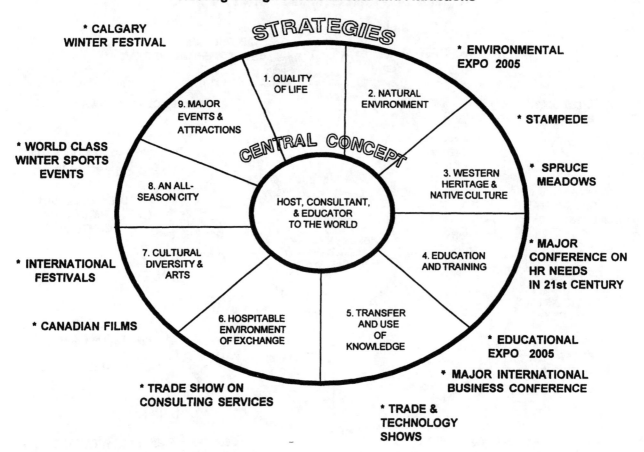

A City that Attracts Attention Through the Hosting of High-Profile Events and Attractions

* CALGARY WINTER FESTIVAL

* ENVIRONMENTAL EXPO 2005

* STAMPEDE

* WORLD CLASS WINTER SPORTS EVENTS

* SPRUCE MEADOWS

* INTERNATIONAL FESTIVALS

* MAJOR CONFERENCE ON HR NEEDS IN 21st CENTURY

* CANADIAN FILMS

* EDUCATIONAL EXPO 2005

* MAJOR INTERNATIONAL BUSINESS CONFERENCE

* TRADE SHOW ON CONSULTING SERVICES

* TRADE & TECHNOLOGY SHOWS

STRATEGIES

CENTRAL CONCEPT

1. QUALITY OF LIFE
2. NATURAL ENVIRONMENT
3. WESTERN HERITAGE & NATIVE CULTURE
4. EDUCATION AND TRAINING
5. TRANSFER AND USE OF KNOWLEDGE
6. HOSPITABLE ENVIRONMENT OF EXCHANGE
7. CULTURAL DIVERSITY & ARTS
8. AN ALL-SEASON CITY
9. MAJOR EVENTS & ATTRACTIONS

HOST, CONSULTANT, & EDUCATOR TO THE WORLD

FIGURE 2   Events required to realize the vision.

• **Where's the Beef?** In total, the Host to the World Task Force held 10 sessions over a period of 12 months. Readers may wish to note that, of these 10 meetings, the first four were devoted to the crafting of the actual Vision Statement—and that these sessions were by far the most challenging and the most stimulating. The remainder focused on identifying the details related to the specific initiatives and actions required to realize the vision. While these implementation sessions were acknowledged to be important, they did not generate the same level of energy—even electricity—that was associated with the crafting of the Vision Statement. The lesson to be retained is that making a vision operational requires a considerable amount of staff work. To ensure that this work occurs, it is important to start involving industry professionals and to start transferring ownership of the vision to them. In order for this to take place, it is advisable to have a number of these professionals as actively involved members of vision-crafting task forces. This said, care must be taken to ensure they do not dominate the process. Visioning is an exercise that must allow for genuine, broad-based, resident input.

• **Visions of Sugarplums, Gifts of Coal—Combining Intellect with Experience:** The process of "visioning" re-

quires a carefully balanced combination of creative, intellectual insights carefully sprinkled with flakes of reality derived from practical experience. Visioning is by nature a process designed to tap the imagination. As such, it is obviously essential that organizers include in the process a number of individuals who are prepared to explore new avenues, who are willing to reveal their true values, and who are prepared to dare to dream. This said, it must also be recognized that, while visions should challenge a community, they must also bear some relation to the ability of the destination to realize the vision. The challenge, of course, is to strike the right balance.

• **Camelot or Caracas?—Defining the Appropriate Unit of Analysis:** The example described in this essay focused on a well-defined metropolitan destination of moderate size. To a certain degree, because of Calgary's isolation, its fairly homogeneous value system, and its strong community focus, it might well qualify as one of the so-called emerging "city states." In this setting, the process of visioning was well received and appeared to work well. This said, it is fair to question whether or not the process is applicable to settings in which there is more diversity, greater land mass, or less

Programs To Develop and Support World-Class Leisure, Learning, and Business Opportunities to Serve Residents and Visitors Alike

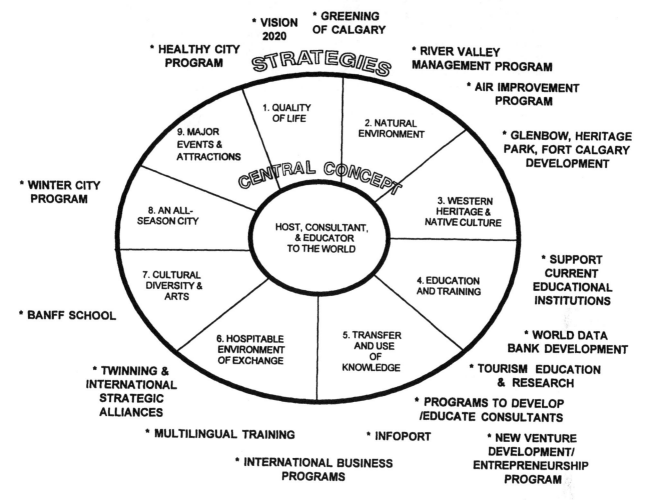

FIGURE 3 Programs required to realize the vision.

focused commitment; for example, a similar process of visioning is currently being carried out at the level of the entire Province of Alberta (in which Calgary is located). It remains to be seen whether or not this attempt to formulate a vision for a much larger area will be successful. Taken to yet another level, even more serious questions might be raised if one attempted to craft a vision for an entire country—particularly one as vast and diverse as Canada. The answers to these questions await further experience.

• **Maintaining Perspective:** While the visioning process is extremely important for all those involved in the development of a tourism destination, it is essential to recognize that tourism is not always the most critical or most valued component of a city's or region's overall economic development priorities. Thus, in addition to defining the vision, its advocates and supporters must also be prepared to deal with both apathy and resistance with respect to both the vision itself and the initiatives proposed for its realization. To the extent that

the Task Force that crafts the vision reflects the general views of the community, this concern will be minimized.

• **Patience Is Indeed a Virtue!** Visions are not realized overnight. As such, it is absolutely essential that, once the initial excitement has faded, there exists a true core of believers who are prepared to persist in efforts to transform wishes into reality. In this regard, it is usually a few key individuals who make the difference. At the same time, it must be recognized that an individual's circumstances change over time. As a consequence, if the vision is to be realized, it is also important to attempt to gain an ongoing commitment from those leading tourism organizations whose support is essential in the long term.

CONCLUSION

As stressed at the beginning of this essay, people around the world are attempting to achieve greater control over the decisions that affect their daily lives. While reality dictates that many forces that determine their well-being are beyond such control, this in no way minimizes the importance of attempting to do whatever is reasonably possible to shape the future in ways that increase the possibility that desirable futures will be realized. This essay has described one such attempt by residents of one very small corner of the world to define and influence how their tourism sector should develop over the next several decades. Whether or not the exercise will make any difference is still unclear. Whether or not the vision will be realized remains to be seen. At the very least, the process provided the residents of Calgary with some shared expectations concerning the kind of tourism development that seems appropriate for the place they call home.

REFERENCES

CEDA (1989), *Calgary...Into the 21st Century,* Calgary, Alberta: Calgary Economic Development Authority.

CEDA (1991), *Calgary: Host, Consultant & Educator to the World,* Calgary, Alberta: Calgary Economic Development Authority.

Gilbert, David (1990), "Strategic Market Planning for National Tourism," *The Tourist Review,* 1, 18–26.

Gunn, Clare A. (1988), *Tourism Planning,* New York: Taylor and Francis.

Kaiser, Charles, Jr., and Larry E. Helber (1978), *Tourism Planning and Development,* Boston: CBI Publishing Company, Inc.

Keough, Brian (1990), "Public Participation in Community Tourism Planning," *Annals of Tourism Research,* 17, 449–465.

Kotter, John P. (1988), *The Leadership Factor,* New York: The Free Press, 18–24.

Mintzberg, Henry (1987), "Crafting Strategy," *Harvard Business Review,* July–August, 66–75.

Mintzberg, Henry (1990), "The Design School: Reconsidering the Basic Premises of Strategic Management," *Strategic Management Journal,* 11, 171–95.

Murphy, Peter (1985), *Tourism: A Community Approach,* New York: Methuen, Inc.

Ritchie, J.R. Brent (1985), "Tourism Education and Training in Canada; Principles for Development," *Global Village: Journal of the Canadian Hospitality Institute,* 13(4).

Ritchie, J.R. Brent (1988), "Alternative Approaches to Teaching Tourism," Presented to the International Conference, *Teaching Tourism into the 1990's,* University of Surrey, U.K.

Ritchie, J.R. Brent (1989), "Promoting Calgary Through the Olympics: The Mega-Event as a Strategy for Community Development," in *Social Marketing,* Seymour H. Fine, Ed., Boston: Allyn and Bacon, 258–274.

Ritchie, J.R. Brent (1991), "Global Tourism Policy Issues: An Agenda for the 1990's," *World Travel and Tourism Review,* 1, 149–158.

Ritchie, J. R. Brent, and Brian Smith (1991), "The Impact of a Mega-Event on Host Region Awareness: A Longitudinal Study," *Journal of Travel Research,* 30(1), 3–10.

Ritchie, J.R. Brent, Charlotte M. Echtner, and Brian H. Smith (1989), "A Survey of the Views of Canadian Residents Concerning Calgary's Image as a Tourist Destination," Calgary, Alberta: World Tourism Education and Research Centre, University of Calgary.

Westley, Frances, and Henry Mintzberg (1989), "Visionary Leadership and Strategic Management," *Strategic Management Journal,* 10, 17–32.

5

Managing the Research Function for Effective Policy Formulation and Decision Making

JAY BEAMAN
Director

SCOTT MEIS
Manager

Socio-Economic Division
Parks Canada
Ottawa, Ontario

*T*his chapter deals with the problems of and solutions to managing applied social and economic research activities to support tourism policy formulation and tourism management activities. A supportive organizational context is identified as an important initial prerequisite. Specific necessary conditions in the organizational environment are discussed. Research management as a distinct activity is defined and two main subactivity components are delineated: research planning and research coupling. For each subactivity, the paper identifies and examines a further series of prescriptions for successful, effective, applied research management.

It has become fairly commonplace in the applied social science research field generally, and in tourism and recreation research specifically (Capstick and Riley 1977; Samuels 1973), to lament the lack of relevant information on planning and implementation decisions regarding facility development and the provision of services. It is also customary to bewail the lack of sufficient resources or time for sophisticated and elaborate studies concerning such complex decision-related issues as social carrying capacity and social and economic impacts. Indeed, several recent reviews have argued that most research and information generated in the field is relatively ineffective or irrelevant to applied decision-making processes (Driver and Knopf 1981; Rossi, Wright, and Wright 1978; Dimaggio and Useem 1980). It is much easier for academic observers, who write most of the critical literature, to identify weaknesses than to suggest possible corrective measures.

The most crucial recent advance in both applied social research and management information systems (MIS) has been the growing understanding of the need for active and careful management of the research and information systems processes (Schwarzbart 1979; Rossi et al. 1978). If the research process is not carefully managed, many problems arise that compromise the effectiveness and efficiency of the function. Experience has shown that the relevance and expected benefits and impact of most applied research and MIS projects have been greatly overestimated. On the other hand, time, labor requirements, and associated costs for such projects tend to be underestimated. This has led to bad feelings between management and the research and systems development groups, and it has also meant that most applied research was ineffective in organizational decision-making processes. In other cases, where researchers have attempted to make their work relevant, it has often been of low professional quality. Although these judgments are leveled at research and information systems development in the social and information sciences in general, an extensive review of the literature or thoughtful reflection is not necessary to realize that they are equally applicable to specific tourism research.

Applied research by its definition involves practical problem solving. The processes, however, by which research projects are defined, initiated, carried out, and successfully integrated into practical problem solving, decision making, and policy formation are not generally well understood. Experience and reviews of the rather diffuse literature indicate that certain series of prescriptions are essential for success. This paper identifies and specifies those prescriptions considered most important by the authors.

It is contended that the generally ineffective state of social research and MIS results from two basic conditions. In most cases, the organizational environment is not conducive to effective applied research. Secondly, the applied research and information-exchange processes are insufficiently or inappropriately managed. In addition, the effective utilization of applied social research in policy formulation and decision making depends on the combination of appropriate organizational conditions and careful management of the interface between the research and principal decision-making functions.

ORGANIZATIONAL PREREQUISITES FOR EFFECTIVE RESEARCH

It is often not recognized that several organizational factors outside a researcher's control are critical to effective research. A supportive organizational environment is one such external prerequisite. An appropriate organizational situation is essential if most of what is suggested is to be relevant to a researcher or research manager.

One can also identify four other important organizational prerequisites essential for the effective use of applied research as a decision-making aid. First, the presence of senior management support is needed to set the tone, style, and criteria for the use of research. Senior management is ultimately accountable for putting organizational structures and processes in place to facilitate research and its use. In other words, senior management must be committed to both specific and general research and recognize their importance in an effective research function leading to informed decision making. Furthermore, this commitment to research must be genuine and not done simply to create the appearance of an informed decision process. In practice, this means that senior management will use research findings, along with other decision inputs, when taking action.

A second organizational prerequisite is that the research function reports to a senior manager of sufficient authority to ensure that research results are considered, where relevant, in a given organizational issue or decision. In a nonsupportive organization, the reporting level of the research function is frequently low. As a consequence, the research unit's work

has no symbolic authority, and research is automatically considered as noninfluential. Ideally, the senior managers responsible for research must understand and, to some degree, approve of the "research" function. In general, they need not have a research background; however, critical senior managers associated with the research function must be able to recognize and explain the strengths and limitations of research to organizational equals and superiors.

Communication between the research function and organization decision makers at all levels comprises the third organizational prerequisite. If research results are to be relevant and timely, multiple formal and informal, direct and open channels of communication must exist between the researchers and the research users involved in decision-making processes. In the nonsupportive organization, formal communication paths between researchers and other functional decision makers are characteristically nonexistent or of dubious value.

A fourth and final organizational prerequisite for effective tourism research is the management of the research function itself. Someone must be designated to direct the research function and to be accountable, therefore, for the quality and effectiveness of the organization's research activities and its interface with other functions, professional quality and effectiveness. "Research management" is used here to describe that combination of processes, activities, skills, and attributes resulting in rational and efficient research that leads to sound organization decision-making goals and objectives.

These organizational prerequisites have received relatively little concentrated attention in the literature on applied social research, management, or management science, with the result that they are not generally well understood. The authors contend that, to be effective, research managers must spend much of their time on two main general activities: research planning and research coupling. Research planning activities include:

1. identifying potential areas for research support and establishing needs, rationales, and priorities for supporting these;
2. selecting appropriate research to support, given finite resources;
3. selecting the modes and resource levels for supporting such research;
4. reviewing research activities to see that they are well planned and that they remain "on track" throughout all stages of their execution;
5. assessing the successes and failures of research and appropriately modifying project selection, priority criteria, and resourcing.

Research coupling, on the other hand, includes communication and organizational structuring activities directed toward stimulating and facilitating dialogue between researchers and user groups. These communication processes should be two-way, involving users communicating their research and information needs to researchers, and researchers working with the research user to ensure appropriate applications of research results and effective and efficient research designs (Price 1969).

PLANNING AND RESOURCING PRESCRIPTIONS FOR THE RESEARCH MANAGER

Achieving a good research program involves much more than recognizing a number of "expressed user requirements" and responding to these according to a simple priority plan. Effective and efficient research management depends on substantial attention and importance being given to the process of research selection and planning (Price 1965; Price 1969). The selection of research problems can be difficult as there are few guidelines, many choices, high costs, high risks, and slow and uncertain results (Price 1969; Brooks 1967a). There are far more failures than successes.

It is possible to specify a set of managerial prescriptions for research planning and resourcing processes that can minimize the risks and ensure potential benefits.

IDENTIFYING AND SPECIFYING RESEARCH PROBLEMS

Particular care and attention must be given to identifying how the tourism policy maker or decision maker will use the results of the proposed research (Caplan et al. 1975b:10). Berg (1978:52) cites Weiss, who expands upon this point:

> Relevant research is research that answers the real question of persons participating in decisions. The pivotal phase in developing relevant research is framing the question. The most important choice is deciding whose questions.

While the user's input is critical for defining research problems, this input often lacks the logical rigor and specificity necessary to define research needs and, therefore, to provide an adequate basis for appropriate research. The importance of this aspect of relevance was specifically identified by Beaman (1976) as a weakness in early work in tourism research.

It should also be noted that many professionally trained but inexperienced applied researchers are not much better at defining appropriate research problems. Beaman has also identified the need for tourism-research programs that train researchers to define problems in terms not limited to (a) meeting vague information requests, (b) investigating "in-vogue" hypotheses, or (c) fitting all problems to a favored method.

As a consequence of poor research definition, studies of the use of government survey research in general (Rossi et al. 1978; Bernstein and Freeman 1975) and survey research relating to planning and management of arts and cultural activities in particular (Dimaggio and Useem 1980) have

indicated practically no correlation between research results and actual decisions.

The experience of government should serve as a cautionary note to anyone interested in implementing a sound research plan. Almost all surveys of people or businesses carried out either by or for Canadian and U.S. government departments are now subject to elaborate front-end research planning and review processes. The major weakness in these government control processes is their emphasis on sophisticated data collection, not on real needs. Whether proposed analyses to achieve applied objectives (i.e., decisions) as part of a research plan are valid is not easily subject to external review, as a client's statements that data are needed to plan or "evaluate" are usually not challenged or adequately verified. In practice, it is questionable if any organization can cope with such management-decision-related formal critiques across organizational units on a continuous basis. This process could probably be better handled through careful internal planning, coupling, and review or by periodic functional audits.

ESTABLISHING PRIORITIES

Establishing priorities is probably the second most critical issue for the research manager interested in effective research planning and management. The experienced research manager has no difficulty identifying numerous potential problems for study. As research is a costly, time-consuming, and highly uncertain process, the difficulty lies in deciding on which projects or programs to concentrate resources. A sustained focus on certain specific directions, programs, and projects is essential.

Determining research priorities is seldom simple. Initially, of course, some indications of appropriate priorities are given by senior management or through extra institutional direction regarding program needs. The research manager must then integrate projects with these needs. To do this, linkages between the current major program needs must be specified, the problems determined, and, finally, those research programs and projects that can address those problems with a reasonable probability of success arrived at (Ledley, Shaller, Rotolo, and Wilson 1967).

While such a process will provide a general set of priorities, it alone is insufficient for determining the specific priorities of any given time, program, or project. This requires that the manager also assess a number of other "softer" judgmental considerations. In the rest of this discussion, some of these other criteria are considered as independent prerequisites for effective research planning and resourcing. All, however, play an additional role as the secondary criteria in the manager's prioritization decisions.

SEARCHING FOR STANDARD RESPONSE MODES TO STRUCTURED PROBLEMS

The efficient research manager constantly searches for ways to attain more control over the work load by identifying standard problems and converting their solutions from expensive one-time research to more cost-efficient activities. Such activities may use existing data, established administrative routines, automated systems, or other management-science tools.

The important consideration in managing the research work load in terms of this objective is the extent to which decision-making needs are highly structured (Keen and Scott-Morton 1978). Simon (1960) used the terms *programmed* and *non-programmed* to differentiate between tasks having set rules or decision procedures and tasks that are one-time or require changing criteria with each recurrence. The point made by Keen and Scott-Morton is that highly structured problems can be routinized or automated while semistructured problems are not easily answered by routine research solutions. Unstructured problems can only be supported by new research activity, and then only partially at best (Keen and Scott-Morton 1978:11).

Based on analysis of various decision support systems (DSS), the appropriate research response can vary from developing clerical processes (Keen and Scott-Morton, 1978) to developing a database and associated analysis systems. DSS analysis may point to systematic solutions as alternatives to existing research approaches. Certainly, if analysis shows that structured decision making can be supported by cost-effective developments, these will have high priority for implementation.

While consistently attempting to convert decision-support responses from costly one-time research projects to routine information systems, the research manager must review routinized and automated "research," or Management Information Systems (MIS) functions, for their cost effectiveness. Since they are part of structured decision making, they require virtually fixed commitments of resources. Accordingly, the relevance of such work and the percentage of a budget committed to such activity should never be taken for granted.

TAILORING RESEARCH SCALE AND SCOPE TO USER'S DECISION REQUIREMENTS

In addition to considering the mode of research activity, the research manager must frequently determine a scope and scale for the research activity that will adequately satisfy the decision maker's needs. As noted earlier, the successful manager of tourism research and information systems has no shortage of problems and, in fact, is often besieged with requests, problems, and proposals. In order to make the most of resources, the research manager must be conscious of and skilled at determining the scale, scope, and precision of projects, and selecting the appropriate mode of response to each request.

The user's budget should not be the sole criterion dictating the elaborateness or precision of the research design. The level of aggregation, the scope, and the degree of accuracy of the required research results should also be included. These variables are frequently other aspects of the user's request. Three other attributes are the size of the user's

organization, the level of decision making being addressed, and the stage of the decision process concerned (Ritchie 1980:338–339).

Anthony (1965) and Ritchie (1980) have pointed out that the management level of users influences the level of decision making and, thus, the nature of the research or information systems required. In large organizations, top management generally has a strong interest in strategic planning that involves setting organizational objectives and formulating overall policies. Management control and tactical planning, largely carried out by middle management, are concerned with issues such as facility location, product development, and budget preparation. Operational planning and control focus on the use of existing facilities and resources to carry out activities effectively (Ritchie 1980). Information requirements differ at each of these levels of activity. Ritchie (1980:341) cites these differences as follows: "In general, strategic planning requires more outside information, less accuracy, and more summarization than tactical planning. Management control and planning tends to require more accurate, precise (problem-focused), and current data than strategic planning. Operations activities tend to use data in a less aggregate form than management control." These are only some of the more striking differences in the characteristics of information required by the different decision-making levels.

In a somewhat similar manner, the stage of the client's decision-making process affects the degree of rigor and precision required in the research response. Ritchie (1980), in discussing the developing of tourism information systems, cites an elaboration (Davis 1974) of Simon's (1960) three-stage decision-making model. The stages of the decision-making process are claimed to be (1) intelligence (problem recognition); (2) design (solution identification and analysis); and (3) choice (choice, implementation, and feedback).

Without careful management of these stages of the decision-making process, research resources can be wasted or communication failure can occur. Generally, the collected data have a level of detail not needed by the management involved, or the level of detail is such that further analysis by management is required to discern what is relevant and what is trivial.

One example of an inefficient decision-making process occurs frequently. Data collected for use as a basis for long-range forecasts or long-range market estimates often have a level of statistical accuracy that is irrelevant. Long-range futures estimated from these data are wasted because estimates with confidence limits of +25 percent, +50 percent or even +100 percent would be acceptable. Although this is only one example of ineffective, inefficient, or inept practices, it illustrates that an important key to effective and efficient research involves intelligently tailoring research activity to the client's needs.

MAINTAINING PROJECT FLEXIBILITY

While it is crucial to tailor research projects to satisfy the decision maker's specific requirements, it is nevertheless also desirable to strike a balance between obtaining information of specific relevance and information that is likely to be generally useful or useful in the longer run. In this way, the manager can continue to support a project should there be changes in the specific focus of the client's interest or the decision maker's needs during the life cycle of the project.

A balance of this sort can be struck if one first designs and rationalizes studies in terms of certain primary objectives relating to the specific needs of specific organizational clients. Then, at the same time, the studies are planned to satisfy certain secondary-information objectives relating to less specific, less clearly defined, or possible future needs. By mixing specific and general objectives, the work will remain relevant to some needs even if, by the time the research is completed, the client or the decision problem has changed.

MAINTAINING A WORK-LOAD MIX OF PROJECTS OF BOTH BROAD AND NARROW SCOPE

In addition to those project-specific planning actions described previously, the effective research manager must exercise care and judgment to ensure a mix of projects in the overall program of research activities. As part of this planning process, special consideration must often be given to the mix of broad phenomena, such as mass leisure trends, and the specific focal points within those fields. While an agency's research program should have a "center of gravity of interest" (Price 1966) that meets the needs of the agency it supports, at the same time, the distribution of projects must not be restricted by too narrow a definition of relevance. It should be recognized that areas of research, such as tourism and outdoor-recreation behavior, may have special importance to several "mission-oriented" organizations and that support of these areas by more than one organization or business can be important, not only to assure adequate research support in these vital areas, but also to provide an added basis for communication within the field (Price 1966:46). A mix of work of both broad and narrow scope is also justifiable, given the uncertainties in knowledge of tourism phenomena. Providing this mix ensures that the results of any particular study remain relevant even when new alternatives for projects are being considered or needs have changed in other ways.

MAINTAINING A MIX OF BOTH BASIC AND APPLIED RESEARCH

For research management to be effective in the long run, tourism-research managers must understand and successfully manage the interface between applied and basic social science research (Price 1966; Rossi et al. 1978). While the dividing line between these two types of research is by no means always clear, they can be differentiated by the purposes for which they are conducted. Applied research aids in the solution of real-world problems, while basic research enhances knowledge of a phenomenon. As Coleman (1973)

put it, applied research is "decision" oriented; basic research is "phenomena" or "discipline" oriented. In other words, one is technology, the other is science.

The common conceptual model has assumed a linear relationship between these two areas of science and technology. But a number of recent studies has shown that the relationship between these two areas of endeavor is fundamentally interactive: each field facilitates but does not produce developments in the other. More specifically, new science sustains further scientific development in the context of a permissive, ambient technology, while technological developments lead to still further technology in the context of a permissive, ambient science.

Phenomena-oriented research usually does not result directly in new and unexpected technological opportunities. Experience in observation of the effects of research results does not support the conventional model in which unique scientific events are followed in an orderly manner by applied research developments or new technology leads directly to new theory and conceptual development. Both need separate attention (Price 1968:42).

An example illustrates this point: When designing a tourist agency's research program, it would be a mistake to allocate the entire research budget to projects that support specific applied technological goals. Such a commitment would assume that the scientific or phenomena-oriented concerns would look after themselves or would follow directly from the applied studies. Any tourist organization that does only statistical analysis, survey design, and demand model research would end up with a mass of applied technology but little general knowledge and conceptual development. Some researchers, in fact, feel that this state of affairs characterizes tourism and outdoor-recreation studies in general (Coleman 1980; Stankey 1980). The unbalanced allocation of resources has three weaknesses: First, a broad, continuous flow of information is absent. Second, there is little opportunity to develop an increasingly sophisticated, general, field-wide handling of technological problems. Third, there is no development or elaboration of conceptual frameworks that integrate research findings and applications (Stankey 1980).

THE DECISION TO MAKE OR BUY RESEARCH

The successful and efficient tourism research manager must also control the mix between in-house research and that contracted out. Problems frequently occur that demand skills or expertise that are unavailable or that one cannot afford to keep on staff.

Appropriate decisions in this realm are important for several reasons. Well-chosen and judiciously applied contract research increases the manager's leverage on the work load. It can also reduce the risk associated with particularly tricky projects. Contracting is frequently the best approach when some of the following conditions apply:

1. Short-term needs for specialized knowledge and skills are beyond in-house capabilities.

2. There is a need for greater objectivity and a fresh view of problem identification and specification of research.
3. An assignment has to be performed promptly and on schedule to be relevant to the management decision-making process, but staff size or previous commitments limit the internal capability to respond in a timely fashion.
4. An independent researcher is able to state something that cannot be said by organization personnel because of policy, credibility, or political considerations.
5. Cost-saving advantages are possible by buying into syndicated research programs (Heit and Farrell 1978).
6. Contracting allows field work and analysis to be managed efficiently at peak and slack work periods, thereby preventing project backlogs (Forman and Bailey 1969).
7. The financial responsibility for the research needs to be shifted to the user from the in-house research unit (Forman and Bailey 1969). (This may allow the client to determine if the research is worth what it costs.)
8. Contract staff can compensate for the organization's inability to recruit competent in-house researchers because of some larger organizational problem such as a nonresponsive staffing function (Forman and Bailey 1969).
9. Theoretical, conceptual, or methodological development work is needed that cannot be justified as a priority for an in-house applied research unit but that can be funded (resourced) at a low level by contract (e.g., with universities).

While the research manager gains certain strategic or political advantages from contract research, it, too, has limitations. Among these are the following:

1. The problem at hand can require a period of extensive in-house education and orientation that makes an external approach inefficient (Forman and Bailey 1969).
2. The problem may be relatively unstructured and subject to many changes over the course of the project life cycle that make it incompatible with an agency's relatively rigid contracting procedures (Forman and Bailey 1969).
3. The problem may be sufficiently conducive to the development of programmed solutions that the tourism agency prefers to conduct the work, thereby gaining any educational benefits, in-house expertise, or standard solutions to the problem that may result from the research (Forman and Bailey 1969).
4. Buying research requires a set of skills and allocation of effort different from that required for conducting research itself. The skills and resources for this operation may be unavailable within the research unit at any given time (Heit and Farrell 1978).

RESEARCH-COUPLING PRESCRIPTIONS

As mentioned earlier, research coupling activities are done by the research manager to bridge the gap between the researcher and the client. Considerable general scientific literature now exists on this subject. In a review of this literature, Siedel (1982) observed that most of the prescriptions in this area can be subsumed under three different theories for effective information- and technology-transfer activities. He refers to these as (1) communication theories, (2) linkage theories, and (3) collaboration theories.

COMMUNICATION

Training for employee presentations, language use, and other communications aids are frequently mentioned as appropriate to the improved communication of research information. A number of writers, including Glaser et al. (1973), NIMH (1971), Caplan and Barton (1976), Berg (1978), Glaser and Taylor (1973), Paisley (1968), and Rosenblatt (1968) have commented on particular aspects of the report-packaging problem as a means of increasing the effectiveness of research results. Important aspects include simple language (NIMH 1971), good graphics (NIMH 1971), effective translation (Caplan and Barton 1976), targeting (Glaser et al. 1973; NIMH 1971:9; Rosenblatt 1968 and Paisley 1968), and personal contact (Glaser and Taylor 1973). In the final analysis, however, authors reviewing "packaging" or formatting of social science presentation usually concluded that presentation is not the critical factor in effective research use (Korobkin 1975:13–23). The crucial factor is linkage.

LINKAGE

While the general applied-science literature suggests that collaborative approaches are best for coupling with the research user, other linkage strategies appear to be most effective for allowing the research manager to maintain productive relations with researchers in the academic scientific community. In the field of tourism research and management, there are at least three distinctly different interest groups: researchers, users, and managers. The three interest groups are further separated by communities of cultures. Despite their differences, information can be passed back and forth if appropriate linkage structures are created. Such linkage structures include middlemen, advisory committees, opinion leaders, information-transfer specialists, conferences, travel symposia, and other information-transfer events.

Special events, symposia, advisory committees, and opinion leaders seem partially successful in bringing phenomena-oriented information problems to the attention of potential researchers. They do not, however, seem particularly successful with applied users (Siedel 1982). For them, the linkage theorists suggest the use of information-transfer specialists. It has been noted by several commentators that this is easier said than done. It is difficult to find people who can bridge the gap but are not producers or users themselves (Dror 1971; Frankel 1969:57).

THE COLLABORATIVE MODEL

The literature on coupling suggests that a collaborative approach remains the most important key to the effective application of research and technical information to decision processes (Siedel 1982; Driver and Knopf 1981). This approach involves structuring problem-solving situations so that research-information producers and users can work together to produce appropriate information plans, decisions, and actions. One important condition for such collaboration is that the policymaker or decisionmaker has to know what the problem is and what information should influence decisions on the problem, and has to understand that the formulation of a problem is essential to its solution because how it is defined determines what is done about it (Siedel 1982; Caplan, Morrison, and Stambaugh 1975).

Other conditions are also essential for successful collaboration. The policymaker and the researcher must have an understanding of the problems, policy issues, and required knowledge (Caplan et al. 1975). Finally, the researcher, in particular, must understand the limitations of his or her scientific contribution to the decision problem. This involves recognizing what contribution science or data-based knowledge will make as opposed to less objective non-research-based knowledge or intuition (Caplan et al. 1975).

This broad-based mutual understanding cannot be taken for granted. In fact, several observers have noted specifically that, initially, managers and researchers generally do not share this understanding. Duncan (1974:33), for example, comments that they often possess different values, particularly on their criteria of a good theory or finished product.

Both researchers and managers place considerable importance on practicality, usefulness, and applicability to specific problems in evaluating what is and what is not acceptable theory. However, researchers display more concern for empirical validity, while managers place considerable importance on profitability or the likelihood of payoffs in research efforts.

Furthermore, Driver and Knopf (1981) suggest that the two professions attract different personality types. Individuals attracted to research tend to be stimulated by mental games, like to work with abstract things, have a high degree of tolerance for uncertainty (unpredictability and ambiguity), and are not greatly bothered by the time required to solve a problem. Research reports often reflect these characteristics. Individuals attracted to the managerial profession, on the other hand, tend to be more "down to earth," and prefer to deal with more tangible matters. As a rule, managers have less interest in things that are uncertain, unpredictable, and abstract, and they need a clear-cut and familiar environment. For them, the solution to problems must usually be evident, and they tend to want immediate results from their efforts. Managers are described by researchers as not liking to read research reports or to hear what researchers have to say. While this can be the case in some instances, it could be that they require a certain manner of presentation. Certainly, managers do not want "iffy" statements or the conditional "maybe" and "perhaps" of many researchers. They are not interested in heavily qualified material. Instead, managers want clear-cut answers or specific, tangible steps

that they can take to resolve the problems they face on a daily basis.

It should also be stated that managers, under the constraints of time and daily pressures, frequently do not have the time to sufficiently study problems at hand. While their understanding can be intuitively sound, it is frequently quite difficult for them to articulate clearly what their managerial objectives are in a specific problem situation (Driver and Knopf 1981). In this regard, Driver and Knopf (1981) again argue that managers and researchers respond to markedly different professional recognition reward structures.

Collaboration has been proven to break down barriers. It also allows researchers and users to clarify their responsibilities and goals. Siedel (1974:22) writes:

Examining the results of over twenty studies supporting the collaboration theories, Glaser et al. (NIMH 1971:17) noted that increased relevance of information, mutual trust and education, and greater commitment to research results were products of collaboration between the researcher and the user.

But what, then, are the keys to good collaboration? There appear to be four: commitment, involvement, competence, and recognition of the other party's requirements (Siedel 1982). Both parties must meet the first three qualifications. In the case of the fourth, the manager must recognize the importance of specifying the problem in a manner that can be researched. In turn, the researcher must recognize that the user will make a decision with or without his or her help. In the end, the tourism manager must draw conclusions or take a position with respect to the decision problems in question. The researcher will rarely have the luxury of waiting until all the evidence is in before speaking.

SUMMARY AND CONCLUSION

The premise of this paper is that several factors can be identified to explain why tourism research has generally not been effectively applied. First, appropriate organizational conditions are usually not present. Prerequisites for successful research operations include senior-management support, sufficient reporting levels, direct channels of communication, and defined functional accountability.

Following these conditions, the research manager has to successfully master and manipulate two areas of activity: research planning and resourcing, and research coupling. Specific prescriptions have been offered for successful research planning and implementation: specifying the problem, priorization, standardizing solutions, scaling research to requirements, maintaining flexibility, mixing projects of different scope, mixing basic and applied work, and maintaining a mix of in-house and contractual research.

In the area of research coupling, the need for attention to three coupling activities was emphasized. These are communication techniques, linkage strategies, and collaboration.

Endeavoring to satisfy the organizational and planning

conditions described will help achieve the goal of improved research for more effective policy formulation and decision making in tourism.

REFERENCES

Anthony, Robert N. (1965), *Planning and Control Systems: A Framework for Analysis*, Boston, Division of Research, Graduate School of Business Administration, Harvard University.

Beaman, J. (1980), "Education for Tourism Research for the 1980's," Ottawa, Ontario: Socio-Economic Division, Program Co-ordination Branch, Parks Canada.

Beaman, J. (1978), "Leisure Research and Its Lack of Relevance to Planning Management and Policy Formulation: A Problem of Major Proportions," *Recreation Research Review*, 6(3), 18–25.

Berg, M.R. (1978), *The Use of Technology Assessment Studies in Policy-Making*, Ann Arbor: Center for Research on Utilization of Scientific Knowledge, Institute for Social Research, University of Michigan.

Bernstein, I.N., and H.F. Freeman (1975), *Academic and Entrepreneurial Research*, New York, Russell Sage.

Brooks, H. (1967a), "Applied Research: Definitions, Concept, Themes," *Applied Science and Technological Progress* (June), a report to the Committee on Science and Astronautics, U.S. House of Representatives, by National Academy of Sciences, Washington, D.C.: Government and Printing Office. 21–55.

Brooks, H. (1967b), "Science and the Allocation of Resources," *American Psychologist*, 22(March):3.

Caplan, Nathan S., and E. Barton (1976), *Social Indicators 1973: A Study of the Relationship Between the Power of Information and Utilization by Federal Executives*, Ann Arbor: Center for Research on Utilization of Scientific Knowledge, Institute for Social Research, University of Michigan.

Caplan, Nathan S., Andrea Morrison, and Russell J. Stambaugh (1975a), "The Use of Social Science Knowledge in Policy Decisions at the National Level: A Report to Respondents." Ann Arbor: Institute for Social Research, University of Michigan.

Caplan, Nathan S., et al. (1975b), *A Minimal Set of Conditions Necessary for the Utilization of Social Science Knowledge in Policy Formulation at the National Level*, prepared for the Conference on Social Values and Social Engineering, International Sociological Association, Ann Arbor: University of Michigan.

Capstick, Margaret, and Stuart Riley (1977), "Problems of Implementing Tourism Policy to Achieve Optimum Economic Impact," *Tourism as a Tool for Regional Development*, Edinburgh: Leisure Studies Association Conference.

Cohen, E. (1979), "Rethinking The Sociology of Tourism," *Annals of Tourism Research* 6(1), 18–35.

Coleman, J.S. (1973), "Problems on Conceptualization and Measurement in Studying Policy Impacts," *Public Policy Evaluation*, 19–40, Beverly Hills, CA: Sage Publications.

Davis, Gordon B. (1974), *Management Information Systems: Conceptual Foundations, Structure and Development*, New York: McGraw-Hill.

Dimaggio, P., and M. Useem (1980), "Small-scale Policy Research in the Arts," *Policy Analysis* 6(2), 187–209.

Driver, B.L., and R.C. Knopf (1981), "Some Thoughts on the Quality of Outdoor Recreation Research and Other Constraints on Its Application," *Social Research in National Parks and Wilderness Areas*, Atlanta, GA: USDI, National Park Service, Southeast Regional Office, 85–99.

Dror, Y. (1971), "Applied Social Science and Systems Analysis," *The Use and Abuse of Social Science*, New Brunswick, NJ: Transaction Books.

Duncan, W.J. (1974), "The Researcher and the Manager—Comparative View of the Need for Mutual Understanding," *Management Science* 20(8), 1157–1163.

Forman, Lewis W., and Earl L. Bailey (1969), *The Role and Organization of Marketing Research: A Survey*, New York: Conference Board.

Frankel, C. (1969), "Being In and Being Out," *The Public Interest* 17, 44–59.

Glaser, Edward M., and Samuel H. Taylor (1973), "Factors Influencing the Success of Applied Research," *American Psychologist* 28(2), 140–146.

Heit, M.J., and Farrell, R.P. (1978), "The Consultant-Client Process: Toward More Effective Research," *Recreation Research Review* 6(3, October).

Keen, Peter F., and Michael S. Scott-Morton (1978), *Decision Support Systems: An Organization Perspective*, Reading, MA: Addison-Wesley.

Korobkin, Barry J. (1975), *Images for Design: Communicating Social Science Research to Architects*. Cambridge, MA: Architecture Research Office, Harvard University.

Kotler, Philip (1976), *Marketing Management: Analysis, Planning and Control*, 3rd ed., Englewood Cliffs, NJ: Prentice-Hall.

Ledley, R.S., H.I. Shaller, L.S. Rotolo, and J.B. Wilson (1967), "Methodology to Aid Research Planning," *I.E.E.E. Transactions on Engineering Management* (June).

McFarlan, W. Franklin, Richard L. Nolan, and David P. Norton (1973), *Information Systems Administration*, New York: Holt, Rinehart & Winston.

Morton, J.A. (1967), "A Model of The Innovation Process," *Proceedings of a Conference on Technology Transfer and Innovation*, 1966, Washington, D.C.: National Science Foundation.

National Institute of Mental Health (NIMH) (1971), *Planning for Creative Change in Mental Health Services: A Distillation of Principles on Research Utilization* I and II, Washington D.C., Department of Health, Education and

Welfare and NIMH: DHEW Publication No.(HMS) 73–9148.

National Institute of Mental Health (1972), *Planning for Creative Change in Mental Health Services*, Rockville, MD: U.S. Government Printing Office.

Paisley, W.J. (1968), "Information Needs and Uses," *Annual Review of Information Science and Technology* 3, 1–30. Wiley Interscience.

Piore, E.R. (1969), "Science and Technology in Industry," *The Interaction of Science and Technology*, Urbana, Illinois: University of Illinois Press.

Price, D. (1965), "Is Technology Historically Independent of Science? A Study in Statistical Historiography," *Technology and Culture* 6(4, Fall), 553–568.

Price, W.J. (1966), "Concerning the Interaction Between Science and Technology," *OAR Research Review* 5(10, December)

Price, W.J. (1967), "Planning Phenomena-Oriented Research in AFOSR," *Planning Phenomena-Oriented Research in a Mission-Oriented Organization*, 12th Institute on Research Administration. The American University Center for Technology and Administration. Washington, D.C. April 24–27.

Price, W.J. (1969), "The Key Role of a Mission-Oriented Agency's Scientific Research Activities," *The Interaction of Science and Technology*, Urbana, Illinois: University of Illinois Press.

Quinn, James B., and R.M. Cavanaugh (1964), "Fundamental Research Can Be Planned: Excerpts from Studies," *Harvard Business Review* 42(January), 111–123.

Ritchie, J.R.B. (1976), "Marketing and Marketing Research in Tourism Management," *Management Problems in the Sphere of Tourism*, 26th Congress of Association internationale d'experts Scientifiques du tourisme, Bern, Switzerland: Editions Gurten.

Ritchie, J.R.B. (1980), "Tourism Management Information Systems—Conceptual and Operational Issues," *Tourism Marketing and Management Issues*, 337–355, Donald E. Hawkins et al. eds., Washington, D.C.: George Washington University.

Rosenblatt, A. (1968), "The Practitioner's Use and Evaluation of Research," *Social Work* 13, 57–59.

Rossi, Peter H., James D. Wright, and Sonia R. Wright (1978), "The Theory and Practice of Applied Social Research," *Evaluation Quarterly* 2(2), 171–191.

Rubenstein, A.A., and C.J. Haberstroh, eds. (1965), *Some Theories of Organization*, Homewood, IL: Richard D. Irwin, Inc.

Samuels, J.A. (1973), "Research to Help Plan the Future of a Seaside Resort," *The Marketing of Tourism and Other Services: Proceedings of the 12th Marketing Theory Seminar*, Lancaster, England: University of Lancaster.

Schwarzbart, G. (1979), "Recent Advances and Trends in the Design and Implementation of Management Information Systems," International Symposium on Information Systems, Terminology and Controlled Vocabularies, 1979, Hamburg, Germany/IUFRO Subject Group 6.03 Information Systems and Terminology. Hamburg, Kommissionsverlag, Buchhandlung M. Wiedebusch, 87–94.

Sherwin, C.W., and R.S. Isenson, R.S. (1967), "Project Hindsight," *Science* 156, (3782, June 23) 171–77.

Siedel, Andrew D. (1982), "Usable EBR: What Can We Learn from Other Fields?" *Knowledge for Design: Proceedings of the Thirteenth Conference of EDRA*, 16–25. College Park, MD: Environmental Design Research Association.

Simon, Herbert A. (1960), *The New Science of Management Decisions*, New York: Harper & Brothers.

Stankey, G.H. (1980), "Integrating Wildland Recreation Research into Decision Making: Pitfalls and Promises," *Symposium Proceedings: Applied Research for Parks and Recreation in the 1980's*, March 22, Victoria, British Columbia: Department of Geography, University of Victoria.

6

International Tourism Policy and Management

DAVID L. EDGELL, SR.

Acting Under Secretary for Travel and Tourism
Director, Office of Policy and Planning
U.S. Travel and Tourism Administration
U.S. Department of Commerce
Washington, D.C.

GINGER SMITH

Acting Director of Public Affairs
Office of the Under Secretary for Travel and Tourism
Senior International Policy Analyst
Office of Policy and Planning
U.S. Travel and Tourism Administration
U.S. Department of Commerce
Washington, D.C.

Worldwide tourism is an important activity of considerable economic, technological, sociocultural, and environmental significance. As a growth industry of increasing power and complexity in contemporary international relations, international tourism requires policy planning and management. This chapter is divided into five sections. The first presents an integrative model of international tourism policy as a framework for overall planning and management. The second section outlines several important tourism policy areas under the headings of economic, technological, sociocultural, and environmental issues. The third section addresses national and international influences on tourism policy including official codification of tourism policies, activities of government and nongovernment organizations, formation of alliances and coalitions, the role of bilateral tourism agreements, and international tourism constraints. The fourth summarizes the chapter, and the final part proposes policy recommendations.

The highest purpose of tourism policy is to integrate the economic, political, cultural, intellectual, and environmental benefits of tourism cohesively with people, destinations, and countries in order to improve the global quality of life and provide a foundation for peace and prosperity.
David L. Edgell, Sr.—*International Tourism Policy* 1990.

Conceptualizations of international tourism policy and management for the 1990s and the twenty-first century are embedded irrevocably in an international relations context characterized by rapid political and economic changes, technological and sociocultural transformations, and global environmental concerns. Activities of international and intergovernmental organizations and trends toward cross-sector alliances and coalitions in the tourism industry are influencing tourism policy formation at both national and international levels. Policy makers faced with present and future decisions on tourism issues will require a managerial framework for analyzing the appropriateness of alternative courses of action.

This chapter, therefore, first presents an integrative framework for analysis of tourism-policy decision making. Second, it addresses some important tourism-policy issues. Third, it examines key national and international influences on tourism policy. Fourth, it discusses constraints on international trade in tourism services, and, finally, it provides a summary, as well as some conclusions and recommendations for international tourism policy and management.

Communication and transportation technologies have revolutionized knowledge and the ability to travel. Regional crises—the Persian Gulf War, religio-political conflict, terrorism, and international and national economic recessions—all impose intermittent but nonetheless devastating "collateral damage" on tourism. Without international tourism policy and management, the long-term result may be increased constraints on international travel. In contrast, other measures indicate that the future is bright for increased international tourism. Worldwide population growth has been concomitant with increases in income and income distribution making travel accessible to more people of the world. Changing patterns of work habits and working conditions are influencing international business as well as leisure travel yielding greater participation in tourism for commercial and recreational purposes.

In its broadest sense, tourism encompasses all expenditures for goods and services by travelers. It includes purchases of transportation, lodging, meals, entertainment, souvenirs, refreshments, travel-agency and sightseeing tour services, and personal facilitative services. The full scope of international tourism, therefore, covers the production and distribution of goods and services of many interdependent industries.

Worldwide tourism is an important activity of considerable economic, technological, sociocultural, and environmental significance. As a growth industry of increasing power and complexity, tourism requires policy planning and management. For this reason, the 1990s may very well be heralded in future years as the seminal decade for the formation of national and international tourism policies. This places both the burden of opportunity as well as responsibility on the shoulders of today's policy makers, defined as those deciding on a present or future action or program based on specific goals and objectives from among alternatives and in light of given conditions. In today's complex world, the effects of such policies on the tourism industry will have far-reaching consequences for the many individuals, organizations, institutions, and governments engaged directly or indirectly in tourism activities.

To be optimistic about tourism's future importance and growth potential requires focusing attention on tourism's significance in overall international policy. In short, in the post-Cold War era, the definition of national and regional security is being recast from military into economic terms that acknowledge the importance of capital and information flows and of trade and investments, including trade in international tourism services. Thus, the future success of international tourism as a global industry will depend increasingly on the policies formulated by today's decision makers for managing its development, growth, and maturity. International tourism's inherent complexity and integration into contemporary international affairs is affecting an entire range of decision making at the heart of tourism policy and management. As a consequence, the tourism industry must prepare at the policy level for some difficult challenges confronting it over the next decade.

AN INTEGRATIVE TOURISM POLICY DECISION-MAKING MODEL

There has been little written about the process for making policy decisions in tourism. For most countries, the policy decisions regarding tourism in the past have focused on only two goals: (1) maximizing tourist arrivals and (2) improving the balance of payments through international tourism receipts. It is necessary today to recognize that on any given tourism issue, policy makers do not make decisions in a vacuum nor always in the same manner. Policy makers almost always have certain goals and objectives guiding them in the decision-making process. These also vary considerably from country to country. At the same time, there are numerous other considerations at national and international levels exerting influence on the decision-making process.

This chapter, therefore, focuses on aspects of economic, technological, sociocultural, and environmental tourism policy issues in an integrative decision-making framework. These tourism policy issues can be seen as part of the integrative model of international tourism policy and management illustrated in Figure 1 (Mowlana and Smith 1990). This model posits the international tourism infrastructure as the central hub in the interaction among tourism issue areas, international and national institutions, and governmental organizations comprising the international-relations policy field. There are other models and approaches that also illustrate the integrative nature of tourism policy decision-making concepts, but the telecommunications example discussed herein clearly demonstrates the multifaceted linkages so necessary in the conceptualization of international tourism policy and management. The model additionally provides a central role for telecommunications technologies as the energy source holding the tourism infrastructure together as a system and stimulating its growth. This model depicts a macrolevel view of international tourism policy and management as emerging areas in contemporary international relations, areas undergoing profound change as a result of the convergence of issues in contemporary international af-

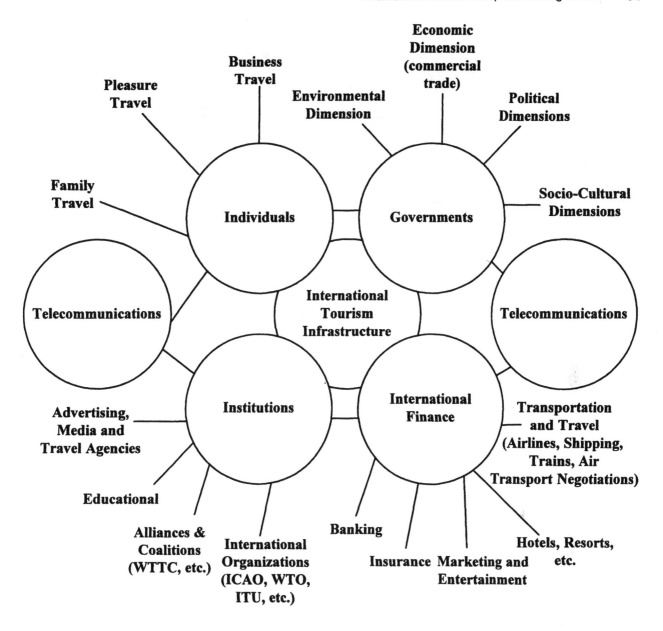

FIGURE 1 Integrative model of international policy and management.

fairs. A second international-tourism-policy-formation model developed by the Tourism Policy Forum (see Figure 2) provides a working diagram for analyzing specific tourism policy issues in the context of national and international influences on the tourism industry.

IMPORTANT TOURISM POLICY ISSUES

There are many important tourism policy issues that face today's decision makers and other issues that will become prominent over the next decade. This section, however, will describe four major issues: economic, technological, socio-cultural, and environmental.

ECONOMIC ISSUES

Today, tourism is indeed an activity of considerable economic importance throughout the entire world. This growing significance of tourism as a source of income and employment, and as a major factor in the balance of pay-

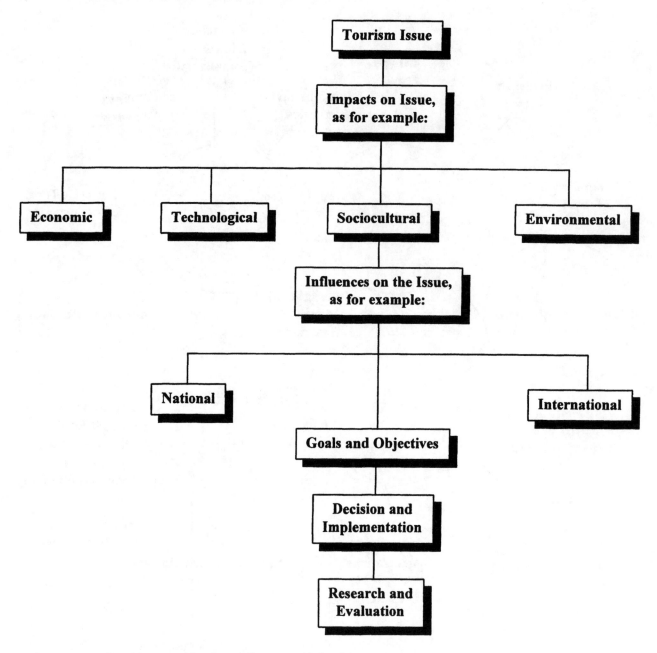

FIGURE 2   International tourism policy formulation: general diagram.

ments for many countries, has been attracting increasing attention from national government; regional, state, and local authorities; and others with an interest in economic development. A few brief statements compiled by the World Travel and Tourism Council and the World Tourism Organization suggest the importance of tourism from a worldwide perspective:

- Travel & Tourism is the world's largest industry and a major contributor to global economic development.
- Travel & Tourism (domestic and international travel expenditures) generates more than $2.5 trillion in gross output revenues, which is about 5.5 percent of the world's gross national product.
- Travel & Tourism employs more than 112 million people worldwide, or about 1 in 15 employees.
- Travel & Tourism invests more than $350 billion a year in new facilities and capital equipment, or 7.3 percent of worldwide capital investment.
- Travel & Tourism contributes $300 billion in direct, indirect, and personal taxes each year, more than 6 percent of total tax payments.
- Travel & Tourism provides more than $278 billion in world trade receipts.

- Travel & Tourism is growing faster than the world economy in terms of output, value added, capital investment, and employment.

Furthermore, an economic-multiplier effect operates within the tourism industry causing the expenditures for construction and maintenance of tourist and travel facilities and the establishment of accompanying services to be important stimuli for economic growth and development, especially for those countries with few natural resources and limited industrial capability. Because of tourism's integrative nature, half of every dollar, franc, yen, pound, or mark earned in tourism revenues is, in fact, returned to the global economy through the purchase of goods and services from other industries around the world.

Yet, as important as tourism is from an economic point of view, it continues to be relatively neglected as an important international-policy field. The economic benefits of tourism are often discussed but are seldom fully appreciated at the policy level. The economic-costs side of tourism, also, can no longer be ignored. Especially in developing nations, the negative impact is seen in economic leakages, low-paying employment and high employee turnover, rural to urban migration, local inflation, and the bypassing of trade in indigenous commodities through the importation of luxury tourism goods and services. In sum, tourism is and will continue to be the largest and fastest growing industry in the world today, strongly influencing the global balance of trade.

TECHNOLOGICAL ISSUES

Tremendous changes in communication technologies and transportation over the last two decades have elevated tourism into political, economic, financial, and cultural prominence as one of the world's most powerful agents in both national and global economic development. Supersonic passenger aircraft, overhead orbital satellite, undersea fiber optic cable, microwave, digital radio, facsimile, video, palmtop computer hardware, and voice- and data-transmission technologies represent only a few of the telecommunications innovations of the last several decades. Satellite ticket printers (STPs) and automatic teller machines (ATMs) are technologies more specialized for the tourism industry; however, most central to the technological development of tourism has been the advent of airline computerized-reservation-system (CRS) technology.

What began in 1964 as the lone and unsuccessful attempt of New York-based Telemex Reservation System to install an automated cathode-ray-tube (CRT) product in travel agency offices (costing $98) has become, in less than 30 years, a multi-billion-dollar global-information telecommunications industry. Between 1964 and 1975, the American Society of Travel Agents (ASTA) anchored negotiations among U.S. airlines to establish a national, multiaccess, jointly owned, computerized reservation system. On the eve of the common reservation system's formation in 1975, United Airlines abruptly withdrew from the joint talks claiming its ability to offer a cheaper system sooner by remaining independent;

and the airline carriers' scramble to develop sophisticated, innovatively customized, independent CRS began (Godwin 1983). By 1991, there were 12 major CRSs, five based in the United States (Sabre, Apollo, System One, Worldspan, and Pars P.R.) and seven in Europe and Asia (Abacus, Fantasia, Galileo, Amadeus, Gemini, GETS, and Infini).

Global connectivity of airline CRS networks in the 1990s, through joint ventures and multilink systems agreements between international air carriers, is raising CRS issues to the tourism policy-and-management-level. Information capabilities, strategic positioning, and financial leveraging effects derived from CRS ownership and control of global distribution networks are straining the limits of tourism policies originally designed for managing the booking of airline reservations for individual tourism consumers. In other words, as CRS technologies become more globally distributed, the implications of technological regulation-deregulation, standardization-innovation, and consolidation-divestiture increasingly become issues of concern at the policy-and-management level.

Covia Partnership's Apollo airline CRS, for example, second largest in the United States after American Airline's Sabre System, is a multinational partnership between United Airlines, British Airways, SwissAir, USAir, KLM Royal Dutch Airways, Alitalia, and Air Canada. Covia is structuring its research and development around CRS expansion outside traditional confines of the travel industry into systems integration and network management services for nontravel businesses dealing in high-volume transactions such as financial services (Mowlana and Smith 1991).

By 1983, the spread of cathode-ray-tube technologies and links with airline CRSs also had led to computerization of international hotel and car-rental chains and to the automation of the "back office" accounting functions of more than 2,000 travel agencies. One example, developed by THISCo, a multihotel corporation, is Ultraswitch—an electronic switch linking travel agents, via their airline CRS, directly to hotel computers. To date, over a dozen major international hotels and three of the five major U.S. computerized reservation systems have been connected, plus Amadeus, one of the two multinational European CRSs. Marketing agreements underway with Galileo, the second European system, plus the Asian CRS, Abacus, will complete Ultraswitch's global reach (Smith 1991).

Rapid advancements in CRS technologies today are providing for a myriad of new integrated electronic travel marketing systems for the use of governments, organizations, and individuals as both tourism providers and consumers. Systems exist today capable of establishing computerized data banks on services, prices, and individual consumers and of integrating reservations with payment transactions. Such systems offer consolidation of diverse groups of suppliers into a single marketing partnership providing enormous international tourism promotional advantage for national governments having CRS-technology access. Developments such as these are globalizing the impact of communication technologies on international tourism. One tangible result of the intensifying international competition for lucrative CRS market share is the addition of technology and international communication programs to the organizational structure of governmental and institutional travel-and-tourism divisions. Another, less tangible result has been intraindustry concern (from the U.S. Tour Operators Association, for example) that airline-owned CRSs discriminate against wholesalers, rural areas, land services, and other nonairline suppliers. Airline CRSs, therefore, are powerful capital and information-distribution networks for a growing international market in diversified tourism-related services and, as such, are presenting a complex and challenging technological-issue area for tourism policy and management today.

SOCIOCULTURAL ISSUES

It is clear that tourism, in a short period of time, has led to a closer association and mingling of people of different races, religions, and cultures. However, there is a growing concern that mass international tourism may have a detrimental impact on local cultures and customs or that a local area will distort its local festivals and ceremonies to "stage" spectacles for the benefit of international visitors. Thus, to some people, tourism leads to the disappearance of traditional human environments and replaces them with towers of artificial concrete, ideas, ethics, and morals, in effect, threatening the whole fabric of tradition and nature. In addition, there is concern that, as such distortions arise, the host and the guest become parts of separate worlds, which leads to even greater prejudices and misunderstandings. It is frequently mentioned, for example, that the attitude of the local population toward tourists is sometimes hostile due to the tourists' outlandish requirements for accommodations and services or due to the unreasonable wants and demands of a limited number of rude and arrogant visitors. Other problems cited include the fact that in many of the developing countries there is foreign ownership and management of tourist facilities, which may create the feeling that indigenous people perform only menial tasks. Tourism may be regarded as a threat to the indigenous culture and mores. There is often a perception that tourists are mainly responsible for the deterioration in standards of local arts and crafts as efforts are made to expand output to meet the tourist's demands. And, not infrequently, resort development has resulted in local people being denied access to their own beaches. All these factors can give rise to serious problems in the perception of tourists and, sometimes, to demands for limitations on the flow of visitors.

While certainly there are numerous incidents where tourism does have a negative impact on an area, this does not have to be the case. A carefully planned, well-organized tourist destination can benefit local residents through exposure to a variety of ideas, people, languages, and other cultural traits. It can add to the richness of resident experiences by stimulating an interest in the area's history through restoration and preservation of historical sites. Some of the cultural richness in the U.S. black communities, for example, is being revived as potential for tourism development. The revitalization of Harlem, New York, has made that commu-

nity a well-known destination for visitors from abroad. The myths, realities, folklore, and legacies of Harlem are becoming well known around the world. Harlem increasingly is being recognized both domestically and internationally for its rich cultural heritage, landmarks, museums, churches, parks, architectural structures, and varied night life.

Organized cultural-tourism development can provide opportunities for local people to learn more about themselves, thus increasing feelings of pride in their heritage and a heightened perception of their own self-worth. Residents of Mexico City, for example, speak with great pride about their Ballet Folklórico, their National Museum of Anthropology, and their Palace of Fine Arts. The Venezuelans speak longingly and affectionately about "la Feria de San Sebastian," a great festive event with cultural and other exciting celebrations that not only draw Venezuelan participation but also include foreign interest and visitation.

Even a highly localized heritage event such as "Cody Days," a festive occasion whereby the residents of Levenworth, Kansas, celebrate their historical link to William F. Cody—better known as "Buffalo Bill"—can be a positive cultural experience for nonresidents as well. And the local celebration of "Potomac Days Parade" in Potomac, Maryland, is an event that has grown into an international festival with people of many different heritages, ranging from Korea to Lithuania, showing off traditional clothes, food, and arts and crafts. These local celebrations started gradually and have grown into regular yearly celebrations to which both residents and visitors now look forward.

Tourism also can contribute to cultural revival. There are numerous examples where the demand by tourists for local arts and crafts has heightened the interest and maintained the skills of local artisans and craftsmen by providing an audience and market for their art. In the United States, a number of Indian ceremonies and dances owe much of their preservation to renewed interests in the revival and the teaching of the meaning of such traditions to the new generations. This preservation of cultural heritage, whether it be in local artifacts, historic sites, or religious rites, forms the heritage of an area or country. It is often this very uniqueness that is the primary tourism attraction. It is a contribution to the quality of life of both the residents and tourists, but it is often the tourists who provide the interest and economic means to preserve and maintain this cultural heritage.

In other words, the sociocultural aspects of an area can enrich tourism in general, and can provide unique opportunities for tourists to experience art, music, dance, food, literature, language, religion, and history different from their own. At the same time, tourists bring to the local area their own sociocultural manifestations, which can have positive or negative results depending on the way tourism is handled in the receiving country.

ENVIRONMENTAL ISSUES

Like the sociocultural dimension discussed above, the physical environment is another important area of interaction for tourism. The environment in which tourism interacts is broad in scope, including not only land, air, water, flora, and fauna, but also the man-made environment.

In brief, the environment in its broad definition is what attracts tourism in the first place. It may be the ecosystem, the wildlife, the rich archeological discoveries, the climate, or the culture that the tourist may have read about, seen in the movies or on the television screen, or been told about by a friend. The important note is that, whatever the environment, it must be protected as an inheritance for future generations of visitors.

There have been numerous recent happenings that suggest that tourists and the environment are not very compatible. Some tourists want souvenirs such as special corals, exotic rocks, or collections of sea shells. Others take samples of irreplaceable tundra or otherwise alter natural flora and fauna. Some people may chip off a piece of the Colosseum, or walk off with native artifacts, or otherwise desecrate important man-made objects of historical and artistic importance.

Today, people increasingly are concerned about all aspects of pollution, whether it be industrial, noise, population, visual, or tourism-development. Much evidence suggests that the development of tourism infrastructure and facilities generally has caused less physical environmental damage than have timber and mineral extractions or industrial plants. However, people continue to be concerned about tourism-development effects in an attempt to preserve the ecosystem and improve the quality of the environment. This recognition and protection has important benefits for the long-run health of the tourism industry. Without the protection of the scenic splendor that is often the very source of attraction to the tourist, the quality of tourism will deteriorate.

The challenge for tourism in the next quarter century, then, is to develop policy and management-planning strategies in support of investment in tourism facilities that improve rather than degrade the environment.

NATIONAL AND INTERNATIONAL INFLUENCES ON TOURISM POLICY

NATIONAL INFLUENCES

National involvement in tourism will vary from country to country. In many countries, the production of travel and tourism services, in fact, is both regulated and operated by the government. Mexico, for example, has had a national tourism policy at the executive level of government for over 40 years. In others, national tourism policy has been less institutionalized. The advent of economic, technological, sociocultural, and environmental issues affecting the tourism industry is influencing the national-tourism-policy-formation process. The United States, as a relative latecomer to the concept of a national tourism policy and management strategy, provides a good example.

After many years of consideration, in 1981 the U.S. Congress passed the National Tourism Policy Act. The Act, signed on October 16, 1981, by President Ronald Reagan,

established a national tourism policy, something that had occurred in most developed nations 30 years earlier. Key policy provisions of the Act included: (1) replacing the United States Travel Service with a new United States Travel and Tourism Administration; (2) broadening the goals and objectives to include greater international policy initiatives; (3) elevating the head of the agency from an Assistant Secretary of Commerce for Tourism to an Under Secretary of Commerce for Travel and Tourism; (4) establishing an interagency committee, the National Tourism Policy Council; and (5) creating a Travel and Tourism Advisory Board.

Additional policy goals of the Act included economic development of tourism, assurance of universal travel, stimulation of competition and of foreign travel to the United States through support for research and development, and upgrading the quality of tourism services. Sociocultural objectives included encouragement of educational values, stimulation of historic restoration, alignment of tourism policy with national energy and conservation policies, and harmonization of public-private development (Edgell 1982). Other broad national interests in tourism policy also were identified in the *National Tourism Policy Study: Final Report* (U.S. Senate 1978). Whether the policy objectives of the Act have been met over time is worthy of more detailed evaluation elsewhere. From a purely policy perspective, however, the creation of the Act was important because it recognized social and environmental issues as well as the importance of tourism to the economy.

The basic policy of the now decade-old U.S. Travel and Tourism Administration (USTTA) is to promote U.S. inbound tourism as an export. To accomplish this, the USTTA helps U.S. travel suppliers promote and sell products or services to foreign travel buyers at wholesale, retail, and consumer levels. This involves bringing potential wholesaler/operators or buyers together with U.S. suppliers, often via a travel-product-inspection visit. Additionally, USTTA helps make arrangements for U.S. suppliers who wish to go into the foreign marketplace to meet potential buyers at travel trade shows and through travel missions. Whatever the activity, the ultimate goal of USTTA is to act as a catalyst in assisting the private sector to increase America's share of the highly competitive international tourism market (Edgell 1984).

Although this promotional element of U.S. policy has become a reality, many other policy issues raised over the years are becoming increasingly important as tourism's national impact becomes more fully realized (Gunn 1983). Along these lines, advances in CRS technologies, for example, are raising the international profile of national tourism policies. The integration of diversified financial and information services, now available through CRS and other technologies, is opening new markets for international tourism for which national tourism policies and management are becoming prerequisites. In short, for national governments to remain competitive in the promotion of inbound tourism as an export, new policies addressing tourism's relationship to international issues in the areas of economic development, technological innovation, cultural identity, and environmental preservation must be devised.

INTERNATIONAL INFLUENCES

There are numerous intergovernmental and international bodies that become involved in worldwide tourism policies. This section first describes three such intergovernmental tourism organizations: the Organization of American States (OAS) Tourism Development Program, the Organization for Economic Cooperation and Development (OECD), and the World Tourism Organization (WTO). A second section outlines interactions among industry groups in the form of cross-sector alliances and coalitions, such as the Travel and Tourism Government Affairs Council, the World Travel and Tourism Council (WTTC), the "America. Yours to Discover." joint venture, and the "GO USA! . . . Travel Moves People!" coalition. Section three briefly points out the underlying importance of bilateral tourism agreements, and the final section discusses some contemporary constraints on international tourism.

Intergovernmental Organizations (IGOs)

There are at least eight intergovernmental organizations identified as being involved with international policy relating to problems and issues in tourism. Three principal organizations are the Organization of American States (OAS), Organization for Economic Cooperation and Development (OECD), and the World Tourism Organization (WTO). Following is a very brief description of the involvement of these organizations with international tourism.

Organization of American States (OAS)

The OAS, headquartered in Washington, D.C., currently is composed of the following countries: Antigua and Barbuda, Argentina, the Bahamas, Barbados, Bolivia, Brazil, Canada, Chile, Colombia, Costa Rica, Cuba, Dominica, Dominican Republic, Ecuador, El Salvador, Grenada, Guatemala, Haiti, Honduras, Jamaica, Mexico, Nicaragua, Panama, Paraguay, Peru, St. Kitts and Nevis, Saint Lucia, Saint Vincent and the Grenadines, Surinam, Trinidad and Tobago, United States, Uruguay, and Venezuela.

The principal policy bodies of the OAS tourism program are the Executive Committee (seven elected member nations that meet about once a year) and the Inter-American Travel Congress (which meets every three years and also includes invited observers from nonmember nations).

The OAS held its first Inter-American Travel Congress in San Francisco in 1939. Much of the significant work of the OAS in tourism was accomplished through its Tourism Development Program formed in 1970. The main functions were to assist member tourism sectors, support member-states' efforts to create appropriate conditions for increasing the flow of tourism to the region, provide broad policy advice on tourism issues, and coordinate with international bodies on tourism matters.

The OAS, over the years, has viewed tourism as having broad policy implications beyond the narrow economic benefits so important to most of the countries. Some of the important tourism matters dealt with included financing mechanisms, facilitation, statistics, and education and training. At a "special" meeting of the Inter-American Travel Congress in Rio de Janeiro, Brazil, on August 25, 1972, the OAS formulated the Declaration of Rio de Janeiro, an important document that relates tourism to some of the broader issues. This document was reinforced through the Declaration of Caracas at the XIII Inter-American Travel Congress, Caracas, Venezuela, September 24, 1977.

In addition, the OAS was an effective partner in the numerous activities prepared to celebrate, in 1992, the 500th Anniversary of the arrival of Christopher Columbus in the Western hemisphere. The planning for this event took place under the auspices of the "Quincentennial Commemoration of the Discovery of America: The Encounter of Two Worlds, and Opportunities of Tourism Promotion." In a recent reorganization of the OAS, the tourism programs have been integrated into the OAS' Department of Regional Development.

Organization for Economic Cooperation and Development (OECD)

The OECD, headquartered in Paris, is a forum for consultations and discussions by most of the industrialized countries on a broad range of economic issues. Through various committees and working groups, the OECD conducts studies and negotiations to solve trade and related problems and to coordinate its policies for purposes of other international negotiations. The OECD Tourism Committee reviews problems in international travel and tourism among member countries and publishes statistics and policy changes in a yearly publication entitled *Tourism Policy and International Tourism in OECD Member Countries*. A milestone was achieved in November 1985 when the OECD Council adopted a new instrument on international tourism policy that set forth principles aimed towards facilitation of tourism for the 24 member countries. It is a major attempt at reducing restrictions on tourism and setting in motion a process of liberalization.

World Tourism Organization (WTO)

The only worldwide (109 member countries in 1989) tourism organization is the World Tourism Organization (WTO), headquartered in Madrid. It was established formally on January 2, 1975. It provides a world clearinghouse for the collection, analysis, and dissemination of technical tourism information. It offers national tourism administrations and organizations the machinery for a multinational approach to international discussions and negotiations on tourism matters.

It includes more than 150 affiliate members (important private-sector companies) interested in international dialogue and implementation of worldwide conferences, seminars, and other means for focusing on important tourism-development issues and policies. WTO is also an implementing agency of technical assistance in tourism for the United Nations Development Program. WTO has an important Facilitation Committee whose aims are to propose measures to simplify entry and exit formalities, to report on existing governmental requirements or practices that may impede the development of international travel, and to develop a set of standards and recommended practices for a draft convention through passport, visa and health, and exchange control measures.

The WTO has conveyed its broad concerns for all aspects of tourism through a number of special documents. The most popular and most-often cited document is the Manila Declaration on World Tourism prepared during "The World Tourism Conference" held at Manila, Philippines, September 27–October 10, 1980, as sponsored by the WTO. Another important document is the Tourism Bill of Rights and Tourist Code. After several years of consideration and negotiations, the Tourism Bill of Rights and Tourism Code was adopted by the Sixth General Assembly of WTO in Sofia, Bulgaria, in September 1985. The most recent document of note is the Hague Declaration on Tourism. The Hague Declaration on Tourism was adopted during the "Inter-Parliamentary Conference on Tourism," April 10–14, 1989, jointly sponsored by the Inter-Parliamentary Union and the WTO.

While considerable progress has been made in utilizing tourism as an international policy tool for greater economic development and improved communications, cooperation, cultural understanding, and goodwill, there is much that remains to be accomplished. Barriers to international tourism continue to exist, and in some circumstances, have increased. And, while it may be overly optimistic to expect that the WTO's motto, "Tourism: Passport to Peace," will be shared by everyone, it is a step in the right direction—when peace prevails, tourism flourishes.

International Organizational Alliances and Coalitions

Travel and Tourism Government Affairs Council

(The following information on the Travel and Tourism Government Affairs Council is taken from the *10th Annual Tourism Industry Unity Dinner Program* as provided at the Washington Hilton Unity Dinner, February 5, 1992.)

The tourism industry for many years, and especially during periods of political, social, and economic crises, has formed associations or other similar bodies to exert collective influence on tourism policy and management. Twenty-nine travel organizations that represented every component of the enormous and diverse tourism industry met in Washington, D.C., on December 9, 1981, to consider a revolutionary shift in its heretofore heterogeneous approach to government relations. The meeting was prompted by the opportunities presented by two extraordinary events: the passage of the National Tourism Policy Act of 1981 and the decision of the U.S. Congressional Travel and Tourism Caucus Steering Committee to remain an official legislative service organization, requiring a drastic reduction in funding and staff support. These events led to the development of a proposal by the Travel Industry Association of America (TIA) to establish an industry-wide organization to provide the federal

government with information and expertise on matters of common interest and concern to the travel-and-tourism industry. The members of the new organization, initially called the Travel and Tourism Government Affairs Policy Council, unanimously adopted the following purposes:

1. To create an organized vehicle, under the existing TIA travel-and-tourism umbrella, with broad travel-industry representation, to relate effectively to the federal government;
2. To serve the on-going needs of the House and Senate Tourism Caucuses by providing industry input on matters of tourism concern and by developing a range of professional services such as issue research, policy recommendations, and information exchange;
3. To identify issues of common concern, to initiate programs and policies to influence federal government action, and to present industry views to the federal government;
4. To monitor federal government actions, to maintain linkages with federal government entities, and to develop programs and policies to respond to federal initiatives;
5. To develop consensus on issues of common travel-and-tourism-industry concern and on broad national issues that affect the economy generally in order to provide a national voice in federal government affairs;
6. To sponsor education and informational programs and to foster the exchange of ideas and information within the travel industry and between the industry and the federal government;
7. To assist organizations representing the Council in their individual government affairs activities and to promote industry-wide support on issues of concern to individual components of the industry whenever such assistance and/or support does not work to the detriment or competitive disadvantage of any other segment of the travel industry; and
8. To develop other federal government affairs programs or services that the industry, acting through the Council, may wish to develop and that would further the objectives of the travel industry in areas of common concern.

The Travel and Tourism Government Affairs Council now is recognized as one of the major official policy organizations representing the travel-and-tourism industry on government issues.

World Travel and Tourism Council (WTTC)

By the 1990s, in the face of regional political conflicts and recessionary national and international economies, the considerable resources and collective economic importance of international tourism needed harnessing in order to articulate its concerns to world leaders in a nation-state system. In April 1990, the World Travel and Tourism Council (WTTC) was founded, under the auspices of The American Express Company, as an action-oriented, public policy/lobbyist coalition on the transnational level. Comprised of nearly 50 chief executive officers (CEOs) of the world's leading travel-and-tourism corporations, the WTTC draws its strength from its high level executive homogeneity. The WTTC is financed by contributions from member companies and has an annual operating budget of $1.5 million. Its goal is to convince governments of the enormous economic contribution of travel and tourism, promote expansion of markets, and eliminate barriers to growth. With dual headquarters in Brussels and London, the WTTC represents one of the first attempts to unite diverse and powerful global corporations from within the industry in order to cope with the rising demands placed on tourism in a rapidly changing international environment.

"America. Yours to Discover."

International tourism is affected dramatically and adversely by every aspect and incident of political and economic instability. The slogan "America. Yours to Discover." was developed in 1991, representing a joint marketing and slogan-promotion campaign. This was sponsored in part by The American Express Company and produced by the U.S. Travel and Tourism Administration in key U.S. tourism markets abroad. The primary purpose of this campaign was to promote foreign travel to the United States in the face of a general crisis in world economic markets. Target markets for the promotional campaign were the prime sources for inbound travel to the United States—Japan, France, United Kingdom, Canada, Mexico, Germany, Australia, Italy, the Netherlands, and South America.

"GO USA!...Travel Moves People!"

The "GO USA! . . . Travel Moves People!" coalition was a public-awareness campaign conducted between March and July 1991 to offset the devastating effects on travel to and within the United States triggered by the Persian Gulf War. Specifically, campaign objectives included, first, countering wartime restrictions to business travel and increased corporate use of electronic alternatives such as facsimiles, videos, and computers; and, second, encouraging domestic leisure and foreign inbound travel to the United States. In this manner, the "GO USA!" campaign brought together in a unique heterogeneous alliance many local, national, and historically competing elements of the U.S. tourism industry. It was said, in fact, that the "GO USA!" campaign was the first time Hertz and Avis had ever agreed on anything. The "GO USA! . . . Travel Moves People!" campaign piggybacked overseas with the "America . . . Yours to Discover" campaign kickoffs.

Bilateral Tourism Agreements

The cross-sector alliance and coalition formation process evident in international tourism of the 1990s can be seen as a response to the transformation of economic power into political influence. Another important avenue for dealing with major policy concerns in this context is through bilateral tourism agreements. Usually, such agreements contain

provisions for cooperation in facilitation, research, and training. Most also attempt to reduce mutual constraints and barriers to travel, and some contain provisions calling for joint promotion and marketing. Bilateral tourism agreements have played central roles in "breaking the ice" for subsequent officially sanctioned bilateral free-trade and investment agreements between nations. The tourism agreement framework, in other words, has provided a working model, and indeed a model that works, for more all-encompassing intergovernmental agreements involving establishment of formal economic and political relationships. The 1989 U.S.-Venezuela tourism agreement framework, for example, provided the model for, first, the 1989 U.S.-Mexico tourism agreement and, shortly thereafter, in 1990, for the bilateral U.S.-Mexico Free Trade Agreement.

International Tourism Constraints

The value of the international travel market in the world would be greater were it not for a number of nontariff restrictions affecting travel-and-tourism services. Government regulations applicable to travel and to the business operations of tourism-related firms inhibit the expansion of international tourism. Over the last four decades, a structure of international rules on trade in goods has been negotiated. This has helped to bring about freer trade in merchandise, but there is no similar structure to facilitate trade in services.

The problems confronting trade in international tourism services in the world are many and varied. Some are peculiar to individual aspects of tourism, such as customs regulations, documentation formalities, and regulations affecting transport, lodging, and travel agencies. Others are more general in nature and apply to several aspects of tourism, such as market access and operation of subsidiary companies. Most of the problems do not lend themselves to quick solutions, particularly when actions are required by national legislatures or other deliberative bodies.

For travelers, and, consequently, for travel and tour businesses, another set of important issues are those that constitute disincentives to international tourism and to purchases by tourists while abroad. These include the difficulty of obtaining visa and passport approval, restrictive duty-free allowances for returning residents, and travel delays and inconveniences. Other important issues for international tourism are overly restrictive foreign exchange controls and limitations on the transfer of funds and repatriation of profits. Some examples of current impediments are mentioned in the following section.

There are nonmonetary types of obstacles, such as visas, that also impede tourism growth. Visas generally are issued freely for qualified temporary visitors, and other entry requirements are held to a minimum to avoid discouraging potential tourists. U.S. visa requirements, however, have been subject to much criticism from the travel industry. The United States requires that all foreign nationals (with the exception of those from Canada, the Bahamas, and United Kingdom nationals resident in Bermuda, the Cayman Islands, and the Turks and Caicos Islands and countries participating in the visa-waiver program) be in possession of a visa in order to enter the USA as a visitor. The difficulty of obtaining such visas acts as a deterrent to travel.

In general, there is a lack of information about tourism impediments. Few studies have been made to assess the effects on tourism businesses of restrictions or obstacles imposed by various governments. A recent Organization for Economic Cooperation and Development (OECD) survey found that the most numerous highly rated concerns among the countries responding were those impediments related to market access and the right of establishment. This reflects the importance of reaching customers in the country of residence in order to attract tourist and travel business. Without a local branch or subsidiary, travel agents, tour operators, airlines, and other tourist companies are unable to market their services adequately, thus placing them at a competitive disadvantage.

Over the years, a structure of internationally agreed-upon rules on trade in goods has been negotiated, and this structure has helped to bring about freer trade in merchandise; however, there is no similar structure to facilitate travel in services. In the absence of such a structure, many of the obstacles to trade in tourism have evolved.

Worldwide tourism has managed to grow despite the numerous and various impediments to travelers and travel businesses. Continued growth is projected, but few studies have been made of the higher level of international travel that could be attained in the absence of restrictive practices. Some increases, of course, only could be achieved on a limited bilateral level, and there are obvious limits to growth imposed by the limited purchasing power in some countries. Moreover, there is no assurance that new barriers will not be erected in individual countries in the future. The potential for government-imposed restrictions increases as economic conditions worsen and competition for tourist business sharpens.

Nearly all the problems discussed in this chapter have been addressed by governments in some way, either unilaterally, bilaterally, or multilaterally. However, the fact that many problems remain is an indication that further work is needed. Moreover, the relatively large number of international organizations with jurisdiction over limited aspects of tourism would seem to indicate that what is lacking is an overall plan with clear objectives and widespread general support by governments.

If the barriers can be eliminated or even reduced, that will mean freer trade-in-tourism, higher tourism receipts, more job opportunities, faster economic growth, greater consumer confidence, and, equally important, increased political stability and more peaceful progress toward national and international goals.

SUMMARY AND CONCLUSION

This chapter discussed the need for increased attention to international tourism policy and management in the face of the rapid changes occurring in contemporary international affairs. In an introductory way, it outlined a framework for a policy decision-making process and introduced tourism-policy issues in the areas of economics, technology, sociocultural factors, and the environment.

National and international influences on tourism policy also were examined. National influences included the passage of the U.S. National Tourism Policy Act and establishment of the U.S. Travel and Tourism Administration in 1981. International influences on tourism policy covered in the chapter included the role of intergovernmental organizations such as the Organization of American States, the Organization for Economic Cooperation and Development, and the World Tourism Organization. Recent trends towards cross-sector alliance and coalition formation in the international tourism industry were illustrated through discussions of the Travel and Tourism Government Affairs Council, the World Travel and Tourism Council, and the "America. Yours to Discover." and "GO USA! . . . Travel Moves People!" promotional campaigns. The chapter also examined the influential role of bilateral tourism agreements and international tourism constraints in the international interactions surrounding intergovernmental free-trade and investment agreements.

This chapter illustrates the diversity in the field of tourism-policy decision making. It suggests that the private sector, as well as government agencies, need to be aware of the increasing complexity and interdependence of economic, technological, sociocultural, and environmental factors usually associated with policy planning and management in tourism. The chapter suggests that policy in tourism can be aided by an integrated management approach.

In conclusion, the tourism-policy decision-making process must be guided by carefully planned policies, international in concept and interdisciplinary in approach and application. These policies must be developed based not only on economic benefits but also on the ideals and principles of human welfare and the quality of life. The decision maker in tourism must utilize policies that optimize economic, technological, sociocultural, and environmental forces for the benefit of broad-based, integrative, and increasingly global objectives. Following are some policy recommendations in these four central areas plus some suggestions regarding several other important and related issues, such as transportation, health and safety, and education and training, not directly addressed in this chapter.

POLICY RECOMMENDATIONS

1. IN THE AREA OF INTERNATIONAL POLITICAL ISSUES, IT SHOULD BE RECOGNIZED THAT:

• The opportunities that international travel and tourism provide for developing greater national and international understanding and goodwill cannot be measured, but tourism can develop the international context leading to a reduction of barriers to international tourism and, in so doing, develop an avenue for friendship and respect among nations.

• Impediments to travel such as travel allowance restrictions, foreign exchange, and visa restrictions will need to be reduced through political action by the respective countries imposing such impediments.

• Governments need to work more closely with intergovernmental organizations, such as the World Tourism Organization, or regional bodies to resolve important worldwide tourism issues.

• International tourism policy, as an extension of political objectives, must chart the course so that international leaders will recognize that tourism is an important tool leading toward a higher quality of life for mankind.

2. IN THE AREA OF ECONOMIC IMPACT OF INTERNATIONAL TOURISM, IT SHOULD BE RECOGNIZED THAT:

• There needs to be recognition that international tourism is not only one of the most important aspects of the world economy but also that it is growing more rapidly than most other areas of the international economy.

• In the future, more jobs and income will derive directly from international tourism.

• The growing significance of tourism as a major factor in the balance of payments for many countries will increasingly attract policy attention from national leaders and others with an interest in economic development.

3. IN THE AREA OF TECHNOLOGICAL TRANSFORMATION, ESPECIALLY ELECTRONIC MARKETING OF TOURISM SERVICES AND PRODUCTS, IT SHOULD BE RECOGNIZED THAT:

• The interests of countries whose tourism promotion offices do not have advanced computer technologies, such as airline CRSs, must be considered in the formation of national tourism policies by developed nations.

• In the competitive race over the next decade to establish innovative and sophisticated computerized data bases for national tourism industries, sources and allocations of funds must be recognized as ethical questions. Who pays? Who benefits?

• Criteria for selection of services and facilities to be included in electronic data bases must be unbiased and based on the objective of providing technological access to the greatest number of users.

• In terms of U.S. tourism policy and management, the U.S. Travel and Tourism Administration must work with other government agencies, private sector, and state and local entities to develop an electronic marketing strategy for the United States as a destination that addresses industry concerns that airline-owned CRSs sometimes discriminate against wholesalers, rural areas, land services, and other nonairline suppliers.

4. IN THE AREA OF SOCIOCULTURAL TRANSFORMATION, IT SHOULD BE RECOGNIZED THAT:

• International tourism provides an opportunity to increase knowledge and understanding between peoples of the world.

• Tourism development marketing and promotion will take into account the needs of local populations to maintain certain historic and local values.

• In the future, tourism development will take into consideration the importance of the preservation of cultural heritage and similar attributes of a country's culture in determining its international tourism policies and management.

5. IN THE AREA OF ENVIRONMENTAL ISSUES, IT SHOULD BE RECOGNIZED THAT:

• As tourism grows, there will be an increased sensitivity toward environmentally absorbing the movements of large numbers of people.

• The tourism concerns about pollution and deterioration of the environment will receive international recognition.

• Future decisions in international tourism will take into account that the development of tourism infrastructure and facilities must be compatible with the environment and the natural ecosystem in order to maintain a quality tourism product.

6. IN THE AREA OF PRESENT AND FUTURE CONCERNS FOR TRANSPORTATION, THAT THE FOLLOWING BE ADDRESSED:

• Concerns with respect to transportation accidents and fatalities.

• Terrorism issues in general, but particularly in transportation.

• The continued problems of congestion, especially on highways, in the skies, and at airports.

• A broad spectrum of concerns on pollution.

• A wide range of aviation issues through air-transport negotiations.

• New concerns resulting from changes in transportation technology such as high-speed "bullet" trains or hypersonic airplanes sometimes referred to as "scram-jets."

• Questions of expansion of airports, runways, and air-traffic-control systems.

• Issues such as providing essential transportation services to small cities and rural communities.

• City concerns for increased air access to more international destinations.

7. IN THE AREA OF EDUCATION AND TRAINING, IT SHOULD BE RECOGNIZED THAT:

• As tourism becomes a more important part of the economies of most countries of the world, there will need to be a highly educated and trained work force.

• Education and training as an international priority for tourism will dictate the need for greater attention by policy leaders and managers within governments.

• There will need to be greater numbers and higher quality texts and articles produced to address the many emerging tourism issues in the future development and management of international tourism.

8. IN THE AREA OF HEALTH AND SAFETY, IT SHOULD BE RECOGNIZED THAT:

• Health, security, and safety will continue to be important future tourism-policy issues for both national and international agendas.

• Tourism policies to combat sickness, crime, and accidents need to be formulated and implemented.

• World organizations and governmental authorities will need to be able to ensure the safety of visitors and the security of their belongings through preventive and protective measures.

• The tourism host communities must be able to afford the best possible conditions of hygiene and access to health services if they are to offer a quality tourism product.

REFERENCES

Ash, John, and Louis Turner (1976), *The Golden Hordes: International Tourism and the Pleasure Periphery*, New York: St. Martin's Press.

Edgell, David L., Sr. (1978), "International Tourism and Travel," in *International Business Prospects 1977–1999*, Howard F. Van Zandt, ed., Indianapolis: Bobbs-Merrill Educational Publishing. Book is based on "The ITT Key Issues Lecture Series," 1976–1977, University of Texas.

Edgell, David L., Sr. (1983), "Recent U.S. Tourism Policy Trends," *Journal of Tourism Management*, June, 121.

Edgell, David L., Sr. (1983), "Tourism and the Next 25 Years," *Travel Weekly*, June.

Edgell, David L., Sr. (1984), "U.S. Government Policy on International Tourism," *Journal of Tourism Management*, March.

Edgell, David L., Sr. (1990), *International Tourism Policy*, New York: Van Nostrand Reinhold.

Edgell, David L., Sr., Charles Gearing, Rodney Stiefbold, and William Swart (1976), "Public Policy Planning and Operation Research in the Tourism Sector," Joint ORSA/TIMS Conference, Miami Beach, Florida, November 3–6.

Edgell, David L., Sr., and Stephen A. Wandner (1977), "Tourism Statistical Information in Relation to Policy Decision Making." Paper presented at the Joint National Meeting of the Operations Research Society—The Institute of Management Sciences, Atlanta, Georgia, November 9.

Edwards, Anthony (1976), *International Tourism Development: Forecasts to 1985*, Special Report, London: Economic Intelligence Unit.

Gearing, Charles E., William Swart, and Turgut Var (1976), *Planning for Tourism Development: Quantitative Approaches*, New York: Praeger Publishers.

Gee, Chuck Y., Dexter J. L Choy, and James C. Makens (1984), *The Travel Industry*, Westport, Connecticut: AVI Publishing Company, Inc.

Godwin, Nadine (1983), "The Trade Was Automated after Years of Promises," in "Twenty-five Years of the Jet Age," *Travel Weekly's 25th Anniversary Issue* 42 (46), 100–102.

Gunn, Clare A. (1976), "Industry Fragmentation vs. Tourism Planning" (mimeograph).

Gunn, Clare A. (1983), "U.S. Tourism Policy Development," *Leisure Today*, April.

International Institute of Tourism Studies (1990), "Tourism Policy Forum: Background Papers," Washington, D.C.: George Washington University, October 1990.

Mowlana, Hamid, and Ginger Smith (1990), "Tourism, Telecommunications, and Transnational Banking: A Framework for Policy Analysis," in Frank Go and J.R. Brent Ritchie, eds., special edition, *Tourism Management* 11 (4), 315–324.

Mowlana, Hamid, and Ginger Smith (1991), "Tourism as International Relations: Linkages Between Telecommunications Technology and Transnational Banking," in *World Travel and Tourism Review: Indicators, Trends and Forecasts*, Vol. 1, Donald E. Hawkins and J.R. Brent Ritchie, eds., Wallingford, Oxon, UK: C.A.B. International.

McIntosh, Robert W. (1973), *Tourism Principles, Practices and Philosophies*, Columbus, Ohio: Grid, Inc.

Office of the United States Trade Representative (1983), *International Travel and Tourism*, May 18, Washington, D.C.

Richter, Linda K. (1983), "Tourism Politics and Political Science: A Case of Not So Benign Neglect," *Annals of Tourism Research* 10, 313–335.

Richter, Linda K. (1985), "Fragmented Politics of U.S. Tourism" *Tourism Management*, 6(3), 162–174.

Richter, Linda K. (1987), "The Political Dimensions of Tourism," in *Travel, Tourism, and Hospitality Research: A Handbook for Managers*, J.R. Brent Ritchie and Charles R. Goeldner, eds., New York: John Wiley & Sons, Inc.

Ritchie, J.R. Brent, and Charles R. Goeldner, eds. (1987), *Travel, Tourism, and Hospitality Research: A Handbook for Managers and Researchers*, New York: John Wiley & Sons, Inc.

Ritchie, J.R. Brent, and Donald E. Hawkins, eds. (1991), *World Travel and Tourism Review: Indicators, Trends and Fore-*

casts, Vol. 1, Wallingford, Oxon, UK: C.A.B. International.

Sharkansky, Ira, ed. (1970), *Policy Analysis in Political Science,* Chicago: Markham Publishing Company.

Smith, Ginger (1991), "Tourism, Telecommunications, and Transnational Banking: A Study in International Interactions," doctoral diss., 216–218, International Communication Program, School of International Service, The American University, Oxon, UK: C.A.B. International.

Smith, Valarie L., ed. (1977), *Hosts and Guests: The Anthropology of Tourism,* Philadelphia: University of Pennsylvania Press.

Tourism Policy Forum 1990, Institute for International Tourism Studies, George Washington University, Washington, D.C.

Turner, Louis, and John Ash (1975), *The Golden Hordes: International Tourism and the Pleasure Periphery,* London: Constable and Company.

United States Conference of Mayors (1978), *City Government, Tourism and Economic Development,* Atlanta, Georgia.

United States Senate, Committee on Commerce, Science and Transportation (1978), *National Tourism Policy Study: Final Report,* Washington, D.C.: U.S. Government Printing Office.

Williams, Roger M. (1980), "Will There Be Any Nice Places Left?" *Next,* September/October.

Part Two

Fundamentals of Travel and Tourism Research

This second part of the Handbook contains six chapters dealing with topics considered to be of fundamental importance to an understanding of research in the field of travel, tourism, and hospitality. The initial chapter has been authored by a long-time leader in the field of tourism statistics, Mr. Robin Chadwick. Its purpose is twofold. First, it is intended to facilitate the transition from the management orientation of Part One to the research emphasis of Part Two. Second, it has been prepared to provide a comprehensive and insightful review of the issues that need to be resolved to bring order to a complex and sometimes confused field of study. Formally entitled "Concepts, Definitions, and Measures Used in Travel and Tourism Research," this chapter first reviews alternative approaches that have been used both over time and within different geographical regions. More important, the chapter uses this review to delineate an updated and comprehensive framework for standardizing the concepts and definitions used by managers and researchers in the field.

The second chapter in Part Two also concerns a basic starting point for successful research. It has been prepared by Charles Goeldner of the University of Colorado and deals with sources of secondary information that are available in the field of travel, tourism, hospitality, and recreation. Dr. Goeldner categorizes and discusses these information sources under eight major headings: Indexing Services, Bibliographies, Data Bases and Documentation Centers, Periodicals, Trade and Professional Associations, Government, Yearbooks and other Annual Publications, and, finally, Major Books in the Field. This chapter highlights the fact that an extensive amount of research is readily available in a variety of well-documented sources. Traditionally, much of the available information in tourism in many countries has been assembled and disseminated by various government organizations at the international, national, state/provincial, and municipal levels. However, as pressures to shift to a more market-oriented economy have grown in recent years, so, too, have the number and variety of nongovernmental sources of research information. While the contents of this chapter are constantly subject to change over time, it nevertheless provides readers with a comprehensive overview of the various kinds and sources of travel and tourism research information that are available. Thus, while certain of the specific references may become dated with time, they are still quite indicative of available information and should serve as a useful starting point for interested researchers.

In Chapter 9, Abraham Pizam provides a comprehensive and rigorous overview of the steps involved in the planning and execution of research intended to provide management with valid, reliable, and cost-effective results. The reader will note that the author has made a very conscious attempt to provide an extremely practical framework for the planning of tourism research while at the same time ensuring that the need for rigor and attention to detail are not overlooked. In terms of content, the chapter identifies seven sequential steps into which a tourism research investigation may be divided. While these seven steps are applicable to research in many fields, the manner in which Dr. Pizam relates it to the field of tourism should make this chapter one that is referred to frequently by both managers and beginning researchers.

Chapter 10 has been prepared by another of the leading experts in the field of tourism. In this chapter, Brian Archer presents an insightful discussion concerning demand forecasting and estimation, a topic of considerable interest to virtually all individuals involved in either the management or the research aspects of the tourism industry. The chapter has been written in a manner designed to make it of value to even nontechnical readers. Its contents focus on criteria to be kept in mind when attempting to choose an appropriate forecasting method in relation to a particular information need. Discussion subsequently focuses upon the various quantitative forecasting techniques that are available and describes their individual characteristics and normal areas of application. Dr. Archer also includes a review of more qualitative approaches to forecasting that are frequently employed when the quality of data or the available time does not permit the development of more rigorous quantitative forecasting models. The chapter concludes with a brief discussion of some of the problems commonly encountered in travel forecasting.

The fifth chapter included in this section on fundamentals of travel and tourism research deals with the critical area of scaling and attitude measurement. Readers will be well aware that the field of travel and tourism research draws heavily upon survey methods that, in turn, rely extensively on the use of various scaling techniques to measure respondent perceptions and views concerning a broad range of topics. The chapter in question, which has been authored by Gordon McDougall and Hugh Munro, first provides a concise yet thorough review of the literature related to attitudes and their characteristics. It then examines a number of theoretical considerations related to scaling and discusses how these considerations are reflected in the development of specific types of scales commonly used in the field of travel and tourism research. The scales discussed include the Thurstone scale, the Lickert scale, and the Semantic Differential, as well as others. Following this conceptual discussion, the authors provide practical suggestions concerning the choice of an appropriate scale for a given research situation. This discussion is followed by a set of guidelines designed to assist individuals who find it necessary to undertake the construction of an attitude scale. Finally, the authors review several alternative approaches to attitude measurement and outline a number of special problems or issues that may arise in conducting attitude research in the travel and tourism area.

The concluding chapter in this section is entitled "Issues in Sampling and Sample Design—A Management Perspective." As the title implies, this chapter, authored by John Cannon of the U.S. Bureau of the Census, is intended to provide readers with a fundamental understanding of sampling in general, as well as particular sampling issues that pertain to the field of travel and tourism research. The initial section of the chapter includes a brief description of four basic sampling approaches and their advantages and disadvantages. Throughout the discussion, the author reminds the reader that nonsampling as well as sampling errors must be kept constantly in mind when assessing the value of different approaches to data collection. Following this conceptual part of the chapter, the focus of the discussion shifts towards the application of the various sampling methods discussed. The applications in question involve the National Travel Survey conducted by the U.S. Bureau of the Census and the Canadian Travel Survey conducted by Statistics Canada. It should be emphasized that in being asked to prepare this chapter, the author was requested to provide examples of broad-scale national surveys (such as those referred to above) since these form a common reference point and are extensively used by virtually all persons in the travel and tourism industry. At the same time, readers should keep in mind that the basic concepts of sampling that are discussed are applicable to much smaller surveys as well.

7

Concepts, Definitions, and Measures Used in Travel and Tourism Research

ROBIN A. CHADWICK*
Formerly of Statistics Canada
Bath, Ontario, Canada

*T*his chapter is intended to reflect the recent activities of the World Tourism Organization, its member countries, and researchers in reaching a common understanding regarding both the terminology and fundamental definitions of the area of human activity, business, and research known as travel and tourism. With the adoption of common standards and definitions, the discipline of travel and tourism is acquiring the basis for its development as a united body of thought. Furthermore, it can be expected to acquire credibility in the research community if it can explain itself clearly and consistently.

Various concepts of tourism are discussed; alternative terminologies and definitions for travelers and tourists are examined; a comprehensive classification of travelers is proposed; the idea of a travel and tourism industry is considered; broader aspects of tourism are noted; some aspects of trip characteristics are presented; and measures used in travel and tourism research are explained.

TRAVEL AND TOURISM

The term *travel and tourism* is used in this book to describe the field of research on human and business activities associated with one or more aspects of the temporary movement of persons away from their immediate home communities and daily work environments for business, pleasure, and personal reasons.

The "travel and tourism" approach represents a compromise between those who favor the use of one word over the other. Some current usage of these fundamental terms is given in Exhibit 1. In the last 20 years, a growing preference for the word *tourism* has been identified. The United States seems to be more reluctant than other English-speaking countries to give up the term travel.

It is common practice to use the two words *travel* and *tourism* either singly or in combination to describe three concepts:

1. The movement of people;
2. A sector of the economy or an industry;

3. A broad system of interacting relationships of people, their needs to travel outside their communities, and services that attempt to respond to these needs by supplying products.

THE MOVEMENT OF PEOPLE

The chapter will now look at the concept of the movement of people and the terminology and definitions applied by the World Tourism Organization and by the United States, Canada, the United Kingdom, and Australia. A comprehensive classification of travelers endeavors to reflect a consensus of current thought and practice.

THE WORLD TOURISM ORGANIZATION (WTO)

The International Conference on Travel and Tourism Statistics convened by WTO in Ottawa in 1991 reviewed, updated, and expanded upon the work of earlier international groups.

---

*The statements expressed are those of the author and do not necessarily represent the corporate viewpoint of Statistics Canada.

EXHIBIT 1   Travel and Tourism: Choosing the Term and Definition

Everyday usage:	*Tourist* and *tourism* mean pleasure travel.
Frechtling (1976):	"The term *tourist* has two strikes against it: it is too exclusive and pejorative in common parlance. *Travel* has one strike against it: it includes extraneous activity. On balance... I believe the term *traveler* is best for representing one who takes a trip."
Arthur D. Little, Inc. (1978) National Tourism Policy Study:	*Travel* and *tourism* treated as synonyms.
Mieczkowski (1990):	"The term *tourist* and later *tourism*, gained a wide approach and use. Although linguistically awkward as connected with the narrow meaning of the word *to tour*, it has been widely accepted because of its shortness, usefulness, grammatical flexibility (easy to form the noun and adjective), and similarity in all major languages."
International Organizations:	Tend to use the term *tourism* but have not dropped *travel* altogether. Examples: Tourism Committee of the Organization for Economic Co-operation and Development (OECD); the World Tourism Organization (WTO), but formerly the International Union of Official Travel Organizations (IUOTO); and note the Pacific Asia Travel Association (PATA), while it was the WTO that held an International Conference on Travel and Tourism Statistics in 1991.
Great Britain:	The term *tourism* seems to be becoming more popular. Example: name change from British Travel Association to British Tourist Authority in 1969 (Eagers 1979). On the other hand, the survey of the British on holiday, known as the British Tourism Survey Annual in the years 1985–88, has been called the British National Travel Survey (BNTS) since 1989. Meanwhile, the resident survey of tourism is known as the United Kingdom Tourism Survey, and the Department of Employment produces statistics on employment in tourism-related industries (British Tourist Authority).
United States:	In the 1970s, the term *travel* was preferred. Example: United States Travel Data Center. In the 1980s, there was more acceptance for the word *tourism*. Example: United States Travel Service 1977 study indicated "the public sector of tourism industry" preferred the term *travel* to *tourism*. A 1981 study indicated 33 states used *tourism* or *tourist* in their titles, while only 20 states used *travel*. In 1981, the National Tourism Policy Act established the United States Travel and Tourism Administration, replacing the U.S. Travel Service (Wynegar 1984).
Canada:	In all 12 provinces and territories, departments responsible for travel and tourism research and promotion were using the word *tourism* in their titles by 1982. In 1978, the Travel Industry Association of Canada became the Tourism Industry Association of Canada. The Canadian Tourism Research Institute was established in 1987 on the recommendation of the National Task Force on Tourism Data (1989).

The Ottawa Conference made some fundamental recommendations on definitions of *tourism, travelers, and tourists.*

Tourism: The activities of a person traveling outside his or her usual environment for less than a specified period of time and whose main purpose of travel is other than exercise of an activity remunerated from the place visited, where:

1. "usual environment" is intended to exclude trips within the area of usual residence and also frequent and regular trips between the domicile and the workplace and other community trips of a routine character;
2. "less than a specified period of time" is intended to exclude long-term migration; and
3. "exercise of an activity remunerated from the place visited" is intended to exclude only migration for temporary work.

International Tourism: Consists of *Inbound tourism*—visits to a country by non-residents and *Outbound tourism*—residents of a country visiting another country.

Internal Tourism: Residents of a country visiting their own country.

Domestic Tourism: Internal tourism plus inbound tourism (the tourism market of accommodation facilities and attractions within a country).

National Tourism: Internal tourism plus outbound tourism (the resident tourism market for travel agents and airlines).

Traveler Terminology for International Tourism (Internal Tourism)

Resident: A person is considered to be resident in a country (place) if that person has lived in that country (place) for at least twelve (six) consecutive months prior to his/her arrival in another country (place) for a period not exceeding one year (six months).

Visitor: A person who travels to a country other than that in which he/she has his/her usual residence and (a person residing in a country, who travels to a place that is within the country of residence, but) that is outside his/her usual environment for a period not exceeding one year (six months) and whose main purpose of visit is other than the exercise of an activity remunerated from within the country (place) visited.

Tourist	A visitor who spends at least one night in the country (place) visited.
Excursionist (Same-day visitor)	A visitor who leaves without spending a night in the country (place) visited.
Holiday-maker	A tourist who remains in a country (place) for more than a certain number of nights or days.
Short-term tourist	A tourist who travels for a period of time not exceeding the above limit but lasting more than 24 hours and involving at least one night's stay.

Main Purpose of Visit

1. Pleasure: leisure, culture, active sports, visits to friends and relatives, and so on;
2. Professional: meeting, mission, business;
3. Other purposes: study, health, transit, and so on.

UNITED STATES

The Western Council for Travel Research (1963) employed the term *visitor* and defined a *visit* as occurring every time a visitor entered the area under study. The definition of *tourist* used by the National Tourism Resources Review Commission (1973) was: "A *tourist* is one who travels away from home for a distance of at least 50 miles (one way) for business, pleasure, personal affairs, or any other purpose except to commute to work, whether he (she) stays overnight or returns the same day."

The National Travel Survey of the U.S. Travel Data Center (1992) reports on all round-trips with a one-way route mileage of 100 miles or more and, since 1984, on all trips involving one or more nights away from home, regardless of distance. Trips are included regardless of purpose, excluding only crews, students, military personnel on active duty, and commuters.

CANADA

In the series of quarterly household sample surveys, known as the Canadian Travel Survey, which commenced in 1978, trips qualifying for inclusion are similar to those covered in the National Travel Survey in the United States. The main difference is that in the Canadian survey, the lower limit for the one-way distance is 50 miles (80 km) instead of 100 miles (Statistics Canada 1990a). The 50-mile figure was a compromise satisfying concerns about problems of recalling shorter trips and about the possibility of the inclusion of trips completed entirely within the boundaries of a large metro-

politan area such as Toronto.

The determination of which length of trip to include in surveys of domestic travel has varied according to the purpose of the survey and the survey methodology employed. Whereas there is general agreement that commuting journeys and one-way trips should be excluded, qualifying distances vary. The Province of Ontario favors 25 miles (National Task Force on Tourism Data 1989:7).

In Canada's international travel surveys, the primary groups of travelers identified are nonresident travelers, resident travelers, and other travelers. Both nonresident and resident travelers include both same-day and business travelers. Commuters are included and are not distinguished from other same-day business travelers. Other travelers consist of immigrants, former residents, military personnel, and crews (Statistics Canada 1990b).

UNITED KINGDOM

The National Tourist Boards of England, Scotland, and Northern Ireland sponsor a continuous survey of internal tourism, the United Kingdom Tourism Survey (UKTS). It measures all trips away from home lasting one night or more, taken by residents for holidays, visits to friends and relatives (nonholiday), business, conferences, and most other purposes. In its findings, the UKTS distinguishes between holiday trips of short (one to three nights) and long (four or more nights) duration.

The International Passenger Survey collects information on both overseas travel by visitors to the United Kingdom and travel abroad by U.K. residents. It distinguishes five different types of visits: holiday independent, holiday inclusive, business, visits to friends and relatives, and miscellaneous (British Tourist Authority 1990).

AUSTRALIA

The Bureau of Industry Economics (1979) placed length-of-stay and distance-traveled constraints in its definition of *tourist* as follows: "A person visiting a location at least 40 km from his usual place of residence, for a period of at least 24 hours and not exceeding twelve months."

In supporting the use of the WTO definitions, the Australian Bureau of Statistics (1991) notes that the term "*usual environment* is somewhat vague." It states that "visits to tourist attractions by local residents should not be included" and that visits to second homes should be included only "where they are clearly for temporary recreational purposes."

A COMPREHENSIVE CLASSIFICATION OF TRAVELERS

The main types of travelers are indicated in Figure 1. It recognizes the fundamental distinction between residents and visitors and the interest of travel and tourism practitioners in the characteristics of nontravelers as well as of travelers. It also reflects the apparent consensus that business

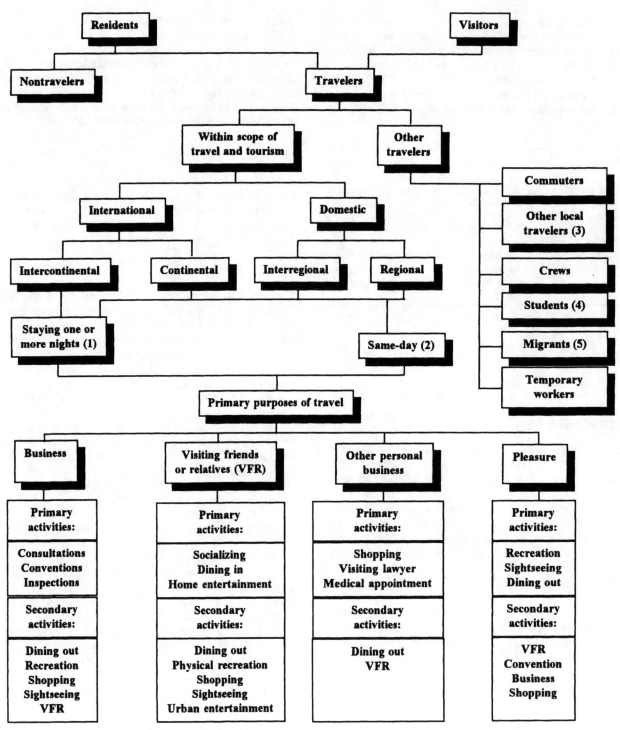

(1)   *Tourists* in international technical definitions.
(2)   *Excursionists* in international technical definitions.
(3)   Travelers whose trips are shorter than those that qualify for travel and tourism; e.g., under 50 miles (80 km) from home.
(4)   Students traveling between home and school only—other travel of students is within scope of travel and tourism.
(5)   All persons moving to a new place of residence including all one-way travelers, such as emigrants, immigrants, refugees, domestic migrants, and nomads.

FIGURE 1   Classification of travelers.

and same-day travel are both within the scope of travel and tourism. Some discussion of the topic appeared in *The Canadian Geographer* (Britton 1979; Mieczkowski 1981; Chadwick 1981).

Placed on the right side are some other types of travelers generally excluded from the area of interest, although included in some travel surveys. Foremost amongst these exclusions are "commuters," who, it seems to be unanimously agreed, fall outside the area of interest of the travel and tourism community. Other travelers generally excluded from studies on travel and tourism are those who undertake trips within the community, which, for convenience, are arbitrarily described as trips involving less than a specific one-way distance, such as 100 miles. These "other travelers" have been focused upon in the Nationwide Personal Transportation Surveys of 1969, 1977, 1983, and 1990 conducted by the U.S Department of Transportation (1991). The broad class of travelers categorized as "migrants," both international and domestic, is also commonly excluded from tourism or travel research. They are excluded on the grounds that their movement is not temporary, although they use the same facilities as other travelers, albeit in one direction, and frequently require temporary accommodation on reaching their destination. The real significance of migration to travel and tourism, however, is not in the one-way trip itself but in the long-run implications of a transplanted demand for travel and the creation of new travel destinations for separated friends and relatives. For observations on the significance of immigration on tourism, see Dunstan (1980) and Chadwick (1988; 1989; 1991).

Other groups of travelers are commonly excluded from travel and tourism studies because their travel is not affected by travel promotion, although they tend to compete for the same type of facilities and services. Students and temporary workers traveling purely for reasons of education or temporary employment are two leading examples. Another frequently excluded group consists of crews, although they can be regarded as special subsets of tourists and excursionists.

Of those travelers directly *within* the scope of travel and tourism, basic distinctions are made between those whose trips under study involve international travel and those whose trips are solely domestic and between those whose trips involve staying one or more nights and those whose trips are completed the same day. An additional meaningful division may also be made between those international travelers whose travel is between continents and those whose international travel is confined to countries in the same continent. In the case of the United States, the distinction is between trips to or from the neighboring countries of Canada and Mexico or elsewhere in the Americas and trips made to or from countries in Europe or other continents.

The same type of distinction may be made in domestic travel between interregional and regional. In the continental United States, there are nine major travel regions. These regions are: New England, Mid-Atlantic, South Atlantic, East North Central, West North Central, East South Central, West South Central, Mountain, and Pacific. Travel between any of the nine regions would be regarded as interregional and within one of the nine regions as regional. In Canada,

five major regions may be identified: Atlantic, Central, Prairies, West, and North. In practice, travel studies in Canada tend to show *interprovincial* data because of the large size of some provinces and the research-and-planning needs of each provincial department of tourism.

The purposes of travel identified in Figure 1 go beyond those traditionally accepted because of the growing evidence that "visits to friends and relatives" (VFR) are a basic travel motivation and a distinctive factor in marketing, accounting for a major proportion of travel. In any event, *primary purpose* is an arbitrary concept because many journeys are undertaken for a combination of reasons, such as "business and vacation" as recognized in the U.S. National Travel Survey (U.S. Travel Data Center 1992). See Appendix 1 for a summary of definitions for travelers.

TRIP CHARACTERISTICS

Surveys of travel and tourism are undertaken for a variety of reasons. The types of information they collect fall into four main categories: socioeconomic data on travelers; opinions and attitudes of travelers; geographic facts regarding origins, destinations, and places visited; and information about the characteristics of trips.

Trip characteristics are the most fundamental findings of travel surveys. They provide basic information on the "Why, When, What, and How" of travel, as distinct from the "Who and Where" covered by socioeconomic and geographical questions. Leading examples of trip characteristics are purpose of trip, mode of transportation, type of accommodation, and activities engaged in.

The "primary purposes for travel," or trip, listed in Figure 1 may be subdivided. The U.S. National Travel Surveys identify more specific purposes, such as conventions/meetings, as a subset under "business," and outdoor recreation and entertainment, under the heading of "pleasure." British statistics of international visits record "holiday inclusive tours" (i.e., package tours) separately from other pleasure travel described as "holiday independent visits" (British Tourist Authority 1990).

"Mode of transportation" can lead to a complex classification, although the main modes of general interest in North America are primarily commercial airplane and private automobile, with lesser interest shown in bus, rail, and water transportation. A further breakdown of commercial air travel of value to the travel trade and to travel, tourism, and transportation planners may be made between charter flight and scheduled flight. Depending upon the use to which the data can be put, automobile trips can be distinguished to identify the use of rental vehicles or vehicles equipped for camping, as is done in the U.S. National Travel Survey (U.S. National Travel Data Center 1992).

Several "types of overnight accommodation" exist, with regional and national variations. Despite pronounced differences between the types of accommodation found in different parts of the world, the OECD Tourism Committee distinction between main and supplementary types may be applied universally. The main types of commercial accommodation in North America are hotels and motels including specialized variations such as motor inns, motor hotels, resort hotels, and lodges. This basic accommodation stock is supplemented by campgrounds and trailer parks, bed and breakfast operations in private homes, rented condominiums and vacation homes, commercial cottages and cabins, and hostels. Most travel surveys also record nights spent by travelers in private accommodation facilities, including homes of friends or relatives and personally owned vacation homes.

"Activities engaged in" is an important trip characteristic but a difficult one on which to collect meaningful information because the frequency and duration of involvement cannot be readily assessed. Nevertheless, the Canadian Travel Survey (a household survey of residents) instituted an activities question in 1982. A compatible activities question was added to the mail-back exit/re-entry questionnaires of Canada's International Travel Surveys in 1990. This question currently identifies 15 different events and attractions on which to report attendance and seven specific outdoor recreational or sports activities in which to record participation (Statistics Canada 1990a).

UNITS OF MEASUREMENT IN SURVEYS OF TRAVEL AND TOURISM

The units of measurement are a function of the type of survey method or source that is selected. There are fundamentally only three different types of surveys used to collect information on the volume of travel and tourism:

- Household surveys collect information on the travel experience of individuals over a given recall period.
- Location surveys obtain counts of visitors or information from them about their current visitor trip.
- Business surveys mainly provide general information on travel and tourism business operations, but sometimes also collect traveler or visitor customer information.

HOUSEHOLD SURVEY MEASURES

From a household survey, it is possible to determine whether or not a person, or the members of a household, traveled over a given period of time. It is also possible to produce a count of *persons,* distinguishing between those who did not travel (*nontravelers*) and those who did travel (*travelers*), according to the definitions of *travel* employed in the survey. For the travelers, it is also possible to determine their *frequency of travel* and, thereby, produce counts of those who traveled once, twice, or more often during the survey period.

The survey period to which the frequency of travel applies depends upon the methodology of the survey. It may be impossible to produce data on frequency of travel over one whole calendar year even though the survey recall period is only three months. In the original U.S. National Travel Surveys (U.S. Bureau of the Census 1979), that problem was addressed by attempting to retain the same sample for each quarter of the calendar year. In the current U.S. National

Travel Survey, the sample changes each month, and, in the Canadian Travel Survey (CTS), the sample changes for every quarterly survey. Therefore, measures of frequency of travel are not readily available on an annual basis. In the CTS, an attempt has been made to overcome the problem by adding a question to pick up some trips by demanding a nine-month recall in addition to the regular three-month reporting.

To measure the volume of travel, it is necessary to collect information in such a way that it may be organized in units such as person-trips, household-trips, person- (or household-) nights, and person- (or household-) days. The basic unit, the *person-trip,* represents the travel from home and return to home of one person. In order to determine the volume of travel originating from households, the term *household-trip* is employed. When one person from a household travels alone, both one person-trip and one household-trip are scored; but if two persons from the household travel together the score is two person-trips and one household-trip. Sometimes the term *trip* is used alone, but it can be ambiguous if not defined.

Person-trips or household-trips are basic measures of travel volume, giving no indication of length or duration of stay or of likely impact upon the economy. A favored means of refining trip measurement is to take account of the length of time away in order to produce person-day or person-night measures. *Person-nights* are achieved simply by multiplying the number of travelers by the number of nights away. This is not necessarily fully reflected in the use of commercial accommodation because the majority of domestic tourists and many international tourists stay in the homes of friends or relatives.

Person-days are similar to person-nights and are arrived at by multiplying the number of travelers by the number of days away. For any one person-trip, there is generally regarded to be one more person-day than person-night. For same-day trips, the number of person-nights tallies zero and, therefore, person-night data can be misleading for researchers who want to include same-day travel in their studies. On the other hand, person-day data can be equally misleading for users interested only in travel involving overnight accommodation.

In addition to units of duration, there are units of distance. They are arrived at simply by multiplying the number of travelers by the number of units of distance each travels to produce *person-miles* or *person-kilometers.* Users should determine if such data are one-way or round-trip and straight-line or actual. Straight-line distances can be calculated from a computer program adjusted to trip distance, as in the U.S. National Travel Surveys, or simply derived from respondent estimates, as in the Canadian Travel Survey.

Perhaps the most useful travel-survey measurements, but also possibly the most difficult to record, are *expenditure data.* They can be estimated directly by respondents, as in the travel surveys of Statistics Canada, or developed from expenditure formulae applied to person-trip estimates, as calculated by the U.S. Travel Data Center. Information may be collected for each aspect of tourism service purchased, e.g., transportation, accommodation, food, recreation, entertainment, or retail goods. In practice, it is not easy for travelers to recall their expenditures or to itemize them, particularly in the case of packaged tours or business travel.

There are also a variety of conceptual questions to be raised on expenditure information, whether it is collected directly from respondents or estimated from travel volumes. These include such questions as: inclusion or not of travel-related expenditures incurred in anticipation of a trip, such as sports equipment, language lessons, and guidebooks; provision or not for a portion of the depreciation cost of major consumer durables used on the trip, such as a new automobile, a motor home, or a boat; the relevant calculation for the true cost of automobile usage on a trip, over and above fuel consumption; the appropriate geographical allocation of transportation expenses represented by fares paid to carriers; and the handling of certain day-to-day living costs that still would have been incurred in the home locality if the trip had not been taken.

LOCATION SURVEY MEASURES

Surveys taken at locations may be related to attendance at an event or attraction, to a count of passing travelers, or to users of a transportation facility. This family of survey types includes visitor surveys, entry and exit surveys, in-flight surveys, and highway counts. The survey information can all be collected at one particular time, or the survey can include a questionnaire to be returned later, as in the case of some surveys on travel between the United States and Canada (Statistics Canada 1990b).

The basic units for a location survey are different from those for household surveys because the information collected is normally related only to the one visit and may not even cover a whole trip. The resulting data, therefore, are recorded as *visits*, which are only approximately equal to person-trips. Using the example of travel across the United States-Canada border, it is quite possible for two or more visits to be made in the course of one trip. In fact, it is regular practice for United States residents traveling between the states of Michigan and New York to travel via southwestern Ontario in both directions on one trip. Likewise, automobile travelers from central Canada to both western and eastern provinces have the option of choosing between the Trans-Canada Highway and interstate highways or other routes in the United States.

For overseas (intercontinental) travel, counts of returning residents are very similar to overseas person-trip counts because multiple re-entries from overseas on the same trip are unlikely. On the other hand, a distinction has to be made between counts of re-entries of residents and numbers of visits of residents to overseas countries. This is because it is common for tourists to visit more than one country in the course of a trip. In the case of Canadian residents, for example, information is collected and published not only on re-entry from the United States and other countries, but also on numbers of visits to selected states of the United States and selected countries (Statistics Canada 1990c).

Location surveys are also a means of collecting expendi-

ture data. In some respects, this source of expenditure data might be expected to give more accurate results than household surveys because of the elimination of much of the recall problem. However, information collected from travelers is liable to be incomplete if they have to supply their answers under time pressures or in connection with customs declarations. In this respect, care is also required in distinguishing between expenditures made outside the country and expenditures made within it and whether or not both are reported in a survey. Care should also be taken to determine whether transportation expenditures relate to both domestic and foreign carriers.

BUSINESS SURVEY MEASURES

Surveys of businesses typically relate to a full financial year of operation, although more limited information may be available on a monthly basis. Examples of such businesses include hotels, restaurants, travel agencies, passenger transportation companies, and recreational attractions. Information collected from these sources normally consists primarily of receipts. It is frequently difficult to distinguish between receipts from travelers and from local residents. However, operators of businesses can be asked to give informed estimates of the breakdown of the sources of the receipts between local residents and visitors, between business travelers and pleasure travelers, and between visitors from other parts of Canada, from the United States, and from other countries. Other information can sometimes be obtained from businesses on such matters as their employees, their facilities, and even certain characteristics of their clients.

In North America, campgrounds and certain other accommodation establishments such as youth hostels may keep records in terms of numbers of visitors, person-nights, or party-nights. Campground data have to be particularly carefully scrutinized to determine the type of visitor units employed, the method of counting, and the definitions used. *Visitors* may be recorded in person-days or person-nights, or without regard to length of stay in terms of visits, number in party, or campsite registrations.

It is common practice for accommodation establishments in Europe to maintain a record of visitors according to their country of permanent residence and the number of nights that they stay. This type of information is not available in North America, although some information is produced on occupancy rates without regard to country of residence of visitors. Occupancy data in Europe tend to be based on beds occupied (OECD 1989), whereas in North America rooms or other units of accommodation are used.

Managers of events and attractions commonly count or estimate numbers of visits or visitors and sometimes arrange for special surveys to be conducted to determine the socioeconomic and geographical origin of their visitors. Examples of published data on these types of counts are to be found in reports of the U.S. Travel Data Center and of the English Tourist Board (British Tourist Authority 1990:58-61).

In North America, the passenger transportation companies producing the most complete origin and destination passenger data are the airlines, which have been required through the U.S. Department of Transportation (formerly the Civil Aeronautics Board) and the Statistics Act in Canada to supply this information from samples of used flight coupons from passengers on scheduled flights (Statistics Canada 1991a). A serious limitation of this type of ticket-based data is that it relates only to flows of passengers, with no identification of place or residence or even place of ticket purchase and with no demographic, social, or economic information whatsoever. The airport-origin information is not even an indicator of residence because origin may be either airport of commencement of outward segment of trip or airport of commencement of return segment of trip. For these data, the unit is the passenger or one-way trip. This means that it takes approximately two one-way airline trips, assuming air is used in both directions, to equate with one person-trip from a household survey.

Particular care needs to be taken of the use of the term *trip* in airline and airport activity statistics. It is sometimes used interchangeably with *leg* or *enplane*. In this case, if a person flies round-trip from New York to Los Angeles with a plane change in Chicago, there are four trips, compared to one person-trip in household surveys. In terms of airport arrivals and destinations, this same single person-trip might in fact acquire the status of eight trips if each airport arrival and departure is counted.

More complete information is available on the origin and destination of passengers on charter flights, both international and domestic (Statistics Canada 1991b). However, for charter airline passenger data, the unit of measurement is also the passenger or the one-way trip.

TRAVEL AND TOURISM INDUSTRY

The degree of acceptance given to the idea of a travel and tourism industry depends upon the nature of the definition of the word *industry* that is used. Macroeconomists who look at the overall picture of national economies are inclined to argue that tourism and travel do not comprise an industry because there is no distinct product or service that can be described. Furthermore, they argue that any attempt to account for travel and tourism is liable to lead to double counting because activities of all establishments are already allocated to existing industries. On the other hand, the very existence of the national trade associations, the Travel Industry Association of America and the Tourism Industry Association of Canada, clearly indicates that there is a sector of North American business that identifies itself as a travel or a tourism industry.

Government also began to recognize tourism as an industry in the 1970s. The *Report of the Tourism Sector Consultative Task Force* (Powell 1978) stated that:

Tourism is both an industry and a response to a social need: society's adoption of travel as part of a lifestyle. The industry does not have a discrete image like other industry sectors, partly because of its heterogeneity

and because many of its components are largely composed of small businesses, but it is pervasive across Canada. Its product includes all the elements that combine to form the tourism consumer's experience and exists to service his needs and expectations.

The definition of *tourism industry* used in the National Tourism Policy Study (U.S. Senate Committee on Commerce 1976) reads as follows:

The interrelated amalgamation of businesses and agencies which totally or in part provide the means of transport, goods, services, accommodations, and other facilities, programs, and resources for travel out of the home community for any purpose not related to local day-to-day activity.

A more concise definition is to be found in Leiper (1979):

The tourism industry consists of all those firms, organizations, and facilities which are intended to serve the specific needs and wants of tourists.

Leiper identified the main components of the industry as transportation, accommodation, food, and related services.

One of the clearest definitions coming from an international agency is to be found in a publication of the United Nations Conference on Trade and Development 1971:

The 'tourist sector' or 'tourist industry' . . . can be broadly conceived as representing the sum of those industrial and commercial activities producing goods and services wholly or mainly consumed by foreign visitors or by domestic tourists.

This United Nations source identified seven industrial areas that could be regarded as belonging, in different degrees, to the tourist sector, although for the most part not concerned exclusively with tourism. These were: accommodation, travel agents and tour operators, restaurants, passenger-transport enterprises, manufacturers of handicrafts and souvenirs designed for visitors and related outlets, establishments providing facilities for recreation and entertainment of visitors, and government agencies concerned with tourism. Of these seven, the United Nations source identified three areas that it considered were practical for the development of statistical series: accommodation, travel agents, and passenger-transport enterprises.

THE STANDARD INDUSTRIAL CLASSIFICATION

Most countries classify their industries in terms of those areas of production of goods and services that form a statistically meaningful and identifiable portion of their economies. Various attempts have been made to utilize these classifications to identify those segments applicable to tourism and travel.

Reference was made in the United Nations study of 1971 to the use of the International Standard Industrial Classification (ISIC) in order to identify some branches of tourist activity. It pointed out, however, the impracticality of using the ISIC to define the tourist industry because typically only part of the output of an SIC industry is sold to tourists. Similar conclusions have been reached by others who have attempted to use their national SICs as a basis for assessing the value of their tourism industries.

Steps have been taken at both national and international levels to overcome the problem. The latest revision of the ISIC (United Nations 1990) has two specialized annexes, each identifying the industrial activities related to a key sector of the world economy inadequately served by the traditional approach to the ISIC, Tourism and Energy. The industrial activities in the ISIC that relate to Tourism are presented here in the first column of Appendix 2.

In Canada, the National Task Force on Tourism Data (1989) developed the concept of tourism ratios, which reflect an estimate of the tourism content of industries with significant tourism components. The latest development of these tourism ratios (Chadwick 1992) is presented for each relevant three-digit Canadian SIC (Statistics Canada 1980) in the second column of Appendix 2. The Canadian SICs are grouped to match the ISIC groupings in the first column.

The United Kingdom publishes statistics on tourism-related industries defined by the U.K. SIC (British Tourist Authority 1991). Although these industries correspond to only two of the four groups in the ISIC, they are presented in the third column of Appendix 2. Apparently, Transport and Renting of Transport Equipment are not regarded as tourism-related industries by the United Kingdom authorities. To complete the picture, the approximate United States 1987 SIC equivalents to the ISIC annex on tourism are shown in the fourth column (United States, Executive Office of the President 1989).

The Australian Bureau of Statistics (1991) and the World Tourism Organization (1992) have taken the SIC definition of tourism a step further by developing proposals for classifications of tourism products and activities. Appendix 3 presents a tentative framework of main groups of tourism industries and compares it with the Australian and WTO proposals that influenced its construction.

The framework put forward in Appendix 3 also takes into account the advice of Lancetti (1991:15) to incorporate in the classification only those activities that, in producing goods and services for tourists, will or may be directly consumed by tourists. There are just seven industry groups in the framework, omitting several areas in the truly exhaustive Standard Industrial Classification of Activities (SICTA) proposed by WTO. The Lancetti guidelines justify omitting both manufacture of public-transportation vehicles (e.g., passenger airplanes) and construction of hotels, although the latter appear in the SICTA proposal.

In addition to following the Lancetti guidelines, the framework omits industries if they are providing products that are merely incidental to travel and that would in most cases be purchased by consumers even if they never left home; for example, food and pharmaceuticals. Also excluded are private accommodation and private vehicles on the grounds that private property does not belong in an industrial classification.

For any selection of tourism-related SICs, however carefully made, there are two major challenges: producing a relevant and accurate data source and identifying a realistic tourism component or ratio. Take passenger transportation as an example: Are all major elements covered, such as taxis and car rental? If so, is it possible to deduct for the out-of-scope aspects of these industries, such as commuter and shopping trips by taxi? And can truck rentals be separated from car rentals?

Commonly, individual businesses require a combination of traveler and local-resident support to ensure their continuing prosperity. Leiper (1991) described the case of the Summit Restaurant in Sydney, Australia, which, in a changing market, recognized a need to extend its promotion policy beyond advertising locally to contacting tour operators in order to tap the growing international market.

A SATELLITE ACCOUNT FOR TOURISM

A more sophisticated and, for some countries, a more practical approach to the measurement of tourism activity is the *satellite account* concept. Work progresses on a Tourism Satellite Account in Statistics Canada (1991a), and the World Tourism Organization (1991) is on record for supporting it, particularly for countries that already have an established System of National Accounts.

A Satellite Account for Tourism has the potential of identifying, within each industry, inputs and outputs of individual commodities relating to tourism. It would provide a more precise measure for a tourism industry than an arbitrary selection of SIC classes supported by incomplete data. It remains to be seen, however, how effective each of the two approaches can become.

TRAVEL AND TOURISM SYSTEMS

Systematic approaches to the study of travel and tourism have been developed by a number of researchers. A leader in this field is Gunn (1988), who has referred to the "functioning tourism system" involving five components: markets, attractions, services/facilities, transportation, and information promotion.

The travel and tourism system proposed in Figure 2 illustrates the concept of *people* requiring *services* in order to achieve certain *objectives*. When these *objectives* are located outside their community, of necessity they become *travelers* and require *services* available to those who travel. Thus, if residents of a northern community have the objective of a winter vacation in warm southern sunshine, they must travel outside their community by using transportation services, possibly a travel agent, and certainly accommodations, food, recreation, and entertainment services at their destination. Likewise, residents of a location with a warm, dry, winter

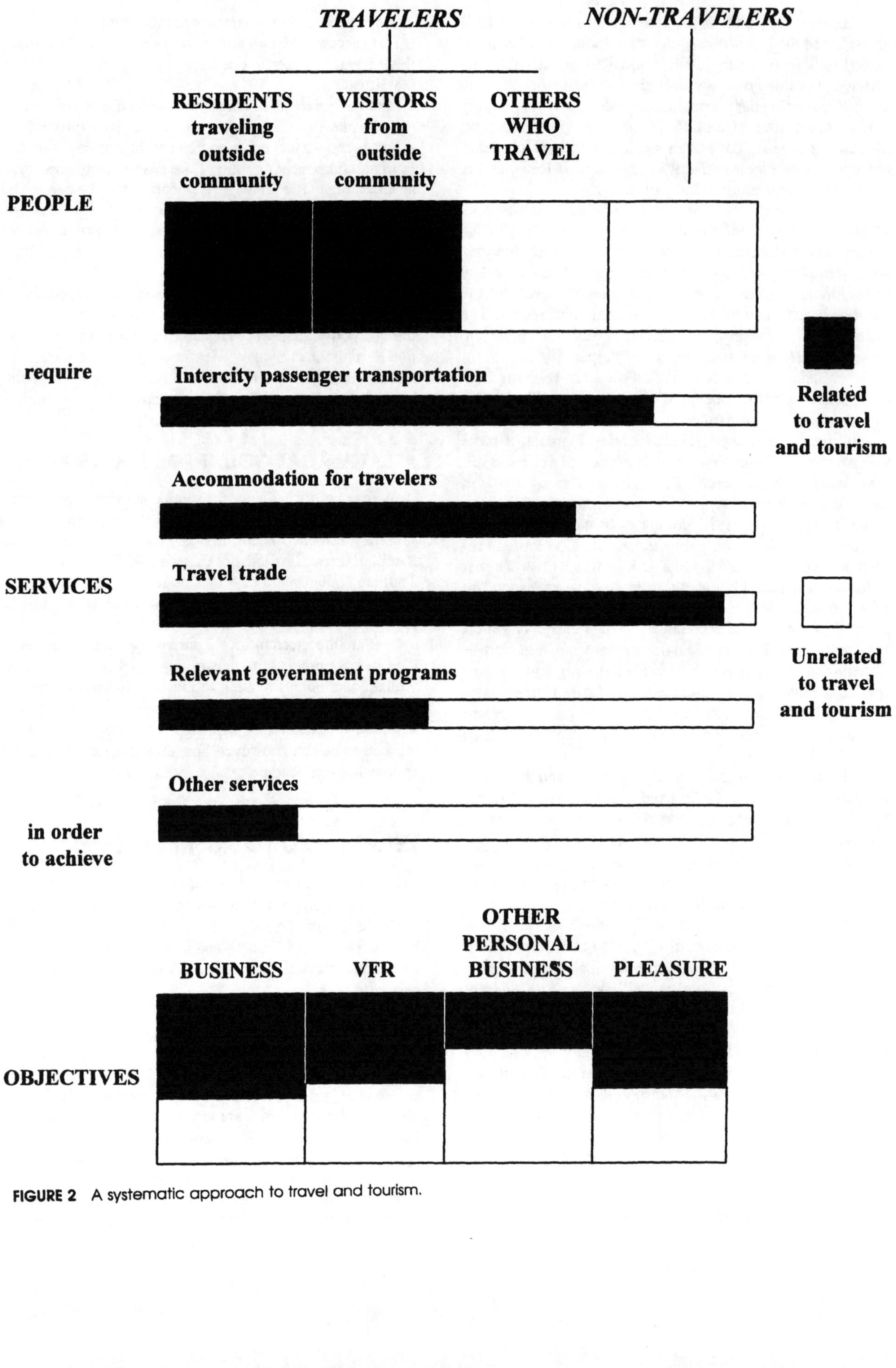

FIGURE 2   A systematic approach to travel and tourism.

location would require a similar package of services if their *objective* was a snow-skiing vacation.

Figure 2 indicates that some *travelers* qualify neither as *residents* traveling outside the community nor as *visitors* from other communities and are, therefore, designated as unrelated to *travel* and *tourism*. It also refers to those persons (*nontravelers*) who are not motivated to travel during the study period. Recognition is given to the main segments of the service industries relating to travel and tourism, pointing out that significant portions of each industry provide services unrelated to travel and tourism. It also recognizes that the four primary objectives of travelers can at times be fulfilled without indulging in travel. Most personal activity is accomplished within the home community. It can also be the location of many pleasurable activities, the place to socialize with those friends and relatives who live locally, and the venue for much business activity.

CONCLUSION

This chapter illustrates the trend toward the greater use of the word *tourism*, either alone or in combination with *travel*, to describe the area of program administration or research concerned with travel outside the community of residence. The conclusion is that, to minimize confusion, the term *travel and tourism* should be used.

The consensus of international and North American opinion seems to be that, despite certain arguments to the contrary, both same-day and business travel should be considered part of *travel and tourism*, while commuting and local travel of under 50 miles from home should be excluded. There seems to be general acceptance of the idea that crews, students, migrants, and temporary workers do not belong in the study of travel and tourism, although, like nontraveling residents, they do compete for use of certain travel and tourism facilities.

A classification of travelers and accompanying definitions are presented (Figure 1). Reference is made also to the classification of leading trip characteristics, such as purpose of trip, mode of transportation, type of accommodation, and activities. Units of measurement are discussed in terms of household, location, and business surveys.

Household surveys are shown to have a special ability to distinguish the characteristics of travelers from nontravelers, to determine the frequency of trips taken, and to determine aggregate volumes of travel in terms of person-trips, household-trips, and person-nights.

It is explained how the volume data collected in location surveys use the concept of the visit, which corresponds only roughly to the person-trip in household surveys. Business surveys are separately distinguished as sources for traveler statistics recorded in terms of visitors, passengers, and receipts, but typically cannot provide information on socioeconomic characteristics of travelers or on the overall characteristics of their trips.

It is concluded that there is a new general acceptance of travel and tourism as an industry or sector of the economy

reflected in the latest version of the International Standard Industrial Classification and the cooperation of central statistical agencies in the work of the WTO in developing the SICTA. National accounts statisticians continue to point out with some justification, however, that the recognition of tourism as an industry can lead to double counting because standard industrial classifications fully account for all elements of the economy without finding it necessary or appropriate to recognize tourism. For this reason, they are supporting the development of satellite accounts for important fields of industrial activity that cut across traditional lines of industry. Tourism is one example; others include Energy and Health.

For tourism, there is some consensus that there is a sector of the economy that includes accommodation, travel agents and tour operators (the travel trade), intercity passenger-transport enterprises, government agencies responsible for tourism programs and tourism facilities, and major elements of other businesses in the food service, entertainment, and recreational fields. Reference is made to tourism systems, and a fundamental conceptual approach is offered linking together *people* who require *services* outside their community of residence in order to achieve certain *objectives*.

REFERENCES

Australian Bureau of Statistics (1991), *Framework for the Collection and Publication of Tourism Statistics*, Canberra: Australian Bureau of Statistics.

British Tourist Authority (1990), *Digest of Tourist Statistics No. 14*, London: BTA/ETB Research Services.

Britton, R. (1979), "Some Notes on the Geography of Tourism," *The Canadian Geographer* 23 (Fall), 276–282.

Bureau of Industry Economics (1979), *Economic Significance of Tourism in Australia*, Canberra: Australian Government Publishing Service.

Chadwick, R. (1981), "Some Notes on the Geography of Tourism: Comments," *The Canadian Geographer* 25 (Summer).

Chadwick, R. (1988), "Immigrants in Canada . . . A Changing Picture," *Travel-log* 7(3), 9–10.

Chadwick, R. (1989), "People on the Move," *Travel-log* 8(2), 10.

Chadwick, R. (1991), "Immigration and International VFR Travel," *Travel-log*, 10(2), 8–9.

Chadwick, R. (1992), "Employment in the Tourism Industry," *Travel-log* 11(4).

Dunstan, P.J. (1980), "Tourism in Australia," *World Tourism* 154, 43–44.

Eagers, Derek (1979), "Development of Policies for Tourism and the Organization Structure," *British Tourism, Diagnosis and Prognosis, Conference Proceedings*, Farnborough, U.K.: The Tourism Society, 23–26.

Frechtling, Douglas C. (1976), "Proposed Standard Definitions and Classifications for Travel Research," *Marketing Travel and Tourism, Seventh Annual Conference Proceedings,* Boca Raton, FL: The Travel Research Association, 59–74.

Gunn, Clare A. (1988), *Tourism Planning*, 2nd ed., New York: Taylor and Francis.

Lancetti, Marco (1991), "A Conceptual Framework for the Development of a Set of International Classifications Concerning Tourism Activities," a discussion paper delivered at the *International Conference on Travel and Tourism Statistics*, Ottawa: WTO and Tourism Canada.

Leiper, Neil (1979), "The Framework of Tourism: Towards a Definition of Tourism and the Tourist Industry," *Annals of Tourism Research* 6(4), 390–407.

Leiper, Neil (1991), "Deflating Illusions of the Tourism Industry's Size," *New Horizons Conference Proceedings*, Calgary: The University of Calgary.

Little, Arthur D. (1978), *National Tourism Policy Study, Final Report*, Washington, D.C.: United States Congress.

Mieczkowski, Z. (1981), "Some Notes on the Geography of Tourism: Comments," *The Canadian Geographer* 25 (Summer).

Mieczkowski, Z. (1990), *World Trends in Tourism and Recreation*, New York: Peter Lang.

National Task Force on Tourism Data (1989), *Final Report*, Ottawa: Education, Culture and Tourism Division, Statistics Canada.

National Tourism Resources Review Commission (1973), *Destination U.S.A., Volume 2, Domestic Tourism*, Washington, D.C.: U.S. Government Printing Office.

OECD (1989), *National and International Tourism Statistics 1974–1985*, Paris: Organization for Economic Cooperation and Development.

Powell, John A. (1978), *Report of the Tourism Sector Consultative Task Force*, Ottawa: Department of Industry, Trade and Commerce.

Statistics Canada (1980), *Standard Industrial Classification Manual*, Ottawa: Statistics Canada.

Statistics Canada (1990a), *Domestic Travel, Canadians Traveling in Canada*, Cat. No. 87-504, Ottawa: Statistics Canada.

Statistics Canada (1990b), *The Redesigned International Travel Survey*, Ottawa: International Travel Section, Statistics Canada.

Statistics Canada (1990c), *International Travel*, Cat. No. 66-201, annual, Ottawa: Statistics Canada.

Statistics Canada (1991a), *Air Passenger Origin and Destination, Domestic*, Cat. No. 51-204, and *Air Passenger Origin and Destination, Canada-United States*, Cat. No. 51-205, two annual reports, Ottawa: Statistics Canada.

Statistics Canada (1991b), *Air Charter Statistics*, Cat. No. 51-207, annual, Ottawa : Statistics Canada.

United Nations (1990), *International Standard Industrial Classification of all Economic Activities*, 135–137, New York: United Nations.

United Nations Conference on Trade and Development (1971), "A Note on the 'Tourist Sector'," *Guidelines for Tourism Statistics*, 30, New York: United Nations.

United States, Executive Office of the President (1989), *Standard Industrial Classification Manual*, Washington, D.C.: U.S. Government Printing Office.

United States Bureau of the Census (1979), *National Travel Survey, Travel During 1977*, Washington, D.C.: U.S. Government Printing Office.

United States Department of Transportation (1991), *1990 Nationwide Personal Transportation Study, Early Results*, Washington, D.C.: U.S. Department of Transportation.

United States Senate Committee on Commerce (1976), *A Conceptual Basis for the National Tourism Policy Study*, Washington, D.C.: U.S. Government Printing Office.

United States Travel Data Center (1992), *1990–91 Winter Travel Market Report*, Washington, D.C.: U.S. Travel Data Center.

United States Travel Service (1977), *Analysis of Travel Definitions, Terminology and Research Needs Among States and Cities*, Washington, D.C.: U.S. Department of Commerce.

Western Council for Travel Research (1963), "Chapter II, Information Needed," *Standards for Traveler Studies*, Salt Lake City: University of Utah.

World Tourism Organization (1991), *Conference Resolutions, International Conference on Travel and Tourism Statistics, Ottawa*, Madrid: World Tourism Organization.

World Tourism Organization (1992), *Draft Standard International Classification of Tourism Activities* (SICTA) Rev. 2, Madrid: World Tourism Organization.

Wynegar, Don (1984), "USTTS Research: New Tools for International Tourism Marketing," *Travel Research: The Catalyst for Worldwide Tourism Planning, Fifteenth Annual Conference Proceedings*, 183–200, Philadelphia: Travel and Tourism Research Association.

APPENDIX 1   Definitions for Travelers (for a given area of study)

TRAVELERS are any persons who travel. For the purpose of any study, the within-scope traveler has to be more precisely defined according to the objectives of the study, the reference period, the geographical area of interest, and the practical restraints of the methodology employed.

VISITORS are travelers entering or traveling in the area under study, but resident outside the area under study.

RESIDENTS are persons living permanently (a term in itself subject to interpretation) within the boundaries of the study area, such as a city, region, province, country, or group of countries. A study may exclude Residents, deal with them exclusively, or take into account their travel only within the study area. In any event, it is normal, if they are included, to look at their travel separately from that of other Visitors.

NONTRAVELERS are those residents of an area who, over the reference period of a study, took no trip that qualified as travel.

TRAVELERS WITHIN SCOPE OF TRAVEL AND TOURISM are visitors or residents who travel for business, pleasure, and personal reasons beyond the limits of their local community and return to it.

INTERNAL (DOMESTIC) TRAVELERS are persons traveling within their country of residence.

INTERNATIONAL TRAVELERS are persons traveling outside their country of residence, including residents in the process of leaving their country of residence or in the process of returning from other countries.

SAME-DAY TRAVELERS (EXCURSIONISTS) are persons who travel without spending a night away from home.

ONE-OR-MORE-NIGHTS TRAVELERS (TOURISTS) are persons who travel and stay one or more nights away from home.

OTHER TRAVELERS outside the scope of travel and tourism are as follows:

- COMMUTERS are persons traveling to a regular place of work or education, provided that they do not stay overnight.

- OTHER LOCAL TRAVELERS are persons traveling within or close to the community in which they reside on trips which fall outside the distance, geographical boundary, or time-duration limits of the study, but who do not qualify as Commuters.

- STUDENTS are persons traveling in order to attend (or to return from) an educational establishment as students for a full academic year or more.

- CREWS are persons operating or providing service on a passenger or freight transportation vehicle, e.g., truck drivers and air crew, including airline attendants.

- MIGRANTS are persons on one-way journeys, changing their place of residence, including those without a home address, emigrants, immigrants, refugees and nomads, and others planning to stay away for more than one year, but excluding seasonal migrants such as retired persons moving to a warm climate for the winter season.

- TEMPORARY WORKERS are persons traveling to engage in temporary seasonal work, such as fruit picking.

APPENDIX 2 Standard Industrial Classification—Tourism-Related

International SIC 1990	Canadian SIC 1980 (Tourism Ratios)	United Kingdom SIC	United States SIC 1987 (Approx. Equiv.)
HOTELS AND RESTAURANTS			
5510 Hotels, camping sites, and other short-stay accommodation	911 Hotels, motels (86%) 913 Camping grounds (100%) 914 Recreation and vacation camps (100%)	665 Hotels and other tourist accommodation 667	7011 Hotels and motels 7033 Trailer parks and campsites 7032 Sporting and recreational camps
5520 Restaurants, bars, canteens	921 Food services (17%) 922 Taverns, bars, etc. (17%)	661 Restaurants, cafés, etc. 662 Public houses and bars 663 Night clubs and licensed clubs	5812 Eating places 5813 Drinking places
TRANSPORT			
6010 Transport via railways 6021 Other scheduled land transport 6022 Other nonscheduled land transport, including taxis (30%)	453 Railway transport (9%) 457 Public passenger transit (23%) 458 Other transportation		4011 Railroads, line-haul operating 4131 Intercity and rural bus 4142 Bus charter, except local 4111/9 Local and suburban 4121 Taxicabs
6110 Sea and coastal water 6120 Inland water 6210 Scheduled air transport 6220 Nonscheduled air transport 6304 Travel agencies/tour operators	454 Water transport (13%) 451 Air transport (85%) 996 Travel services (100%)		44881 Water transportation *42/9* of passengers 4512 Air transportation, scheduled 4522 Air transportation, nonscheduled
RENTING OF TRANSPORT EQUIPMENT			
7111 Land 7112 Water 7113 Air	922 Auto and truck rental (85%)		7514 Passenger car rental 7519 Utility trailer and recreational vehicle rental
RECREATIONAL, CULTURAL, AND SPORTING ACTIVITIES			
9219 Other entertainment (including amusement parks) 9231 Library and archives 9232 Museums, etc. 9233 Botanical and zoological gardens, etc. 9249 Other recreational activities	855 Museums and archives (47%) 963 Theatrical entertainment (47%) 964 Commercial spectator sports (47%) 965 Sports and recreation (47%) 966 Other amusement and recreation (47%)	977 Sports and other recreation, libraries, museums, and art galleries 979	7996 Amusement parks 8412 Museums and art galleries 8422 Aboreta and botanical or zoological gardens 7992 Public golf courses 7996/ Amusement and recreational 7999 services

APPENDIX 3   Proposed Main Groupings of Tourism Products and Activities

Author Recommendation	Australia (1990)		WTO SICTA (Second Revision 1992)	
ACCOMMODATION				
A. Commercial accommodation	211	Commercial accommodation	551	Hotel, camping sites, etc.
FOOD AND DRINK				
B. Food and drink	22	Food and drink	552	Restaurants, bars, and canteens
PASSENGER TRANSPORTATION				
C1. Air	234	Air transport		
C2. Road	231	Road transport	62	Air transport
C3. Water	233	Water transport	602	Land transport, nonrail
C4. Rail	232	Rail transport	61	Water transport
C5. Auto rental	(23123	Rental of private car, etc.)	601	Rail transport
			7111	Renting of land-transport equipment
TOURISM SERVICES				
D1. Travel agents	29	Package tours		
D2. Tour operators			6304-1	Travel agents
			6304-2	Tour operators, packagers, and wholesalers
D3. Guide services	(2354	Tour guide services)	6304-4	Guides
RECREATION AND LEISURE				
E1. Amusement (incl. amusement parks and gambling)	241	Entertainment		
E2. Cultural and heritage activities	242	Cultural affairs	921	Motion pictures, theaters, amusement parks, etc.
E3. Recreational participation	243	Sporting and recreational activities	923	Libraries, museums, and historical sites
E4. Commercial spectator sports			924	Sporting and other recreational activities
FINANCIAL ADMINISTRATION				
F1. Travel insurance	2351	Airport taxes, passport and visa charges		
F2. Currency exchange			65/66	Financial intermediation (including currency exchange and travel insurance)
F3. Credit cards	2352	Travel insurance		
	2353	Currency exchange, travelers cheques		
OTHER GOODS AND SERVICES (RETAIL)				
G1. Souvenirs	281	Souvenirs		
			5232-1	Retail sales—luggage and travel accessories
G2. Luggage and travel accessories	282	Clothes and luggage		
	283	Photographic goods	5239	Retail sales—outdoor-recreation equipment, photographic sales and services, gifts and souvenirs
G3. Recreation equipment				
G4. Photographic sales and service				

APPENDIX 3 *(continued)*

Author Recommendation	Australia (1990)		WTO SICTA (Second Revision 1992)	
RECOMMENDED FOR EXCLUSION				
Private accommodation	211	Private accommodation		(Not included)
Private vehicles	2313	Private vehicle operation and maintenance	50	Sale and maintenance of vehicles and fuels
Real estate activities	25	Business services	70	Real estate activities
Education/training	26	Education/training	80	Education
Public administration		(Not included)	75	Public administration and defence, etc.
Health and social services	27	Health	93	Health and social services
Construction		(Not included)	45	Construction of tourist facilities
Manufacturing (e.g., Aircraft and transportation objects)		(Not included)	D	(Manufacturing not included)
Food sales		(Under Food and Drink)	521/2	Food sales
International tourism bodies		(Not included)	9900/1	International tourism bodies
Rental of machinery & equipment (See C5 Auto rental) (Included in E3 recreational participation)		(Under Transport)	71	Rental of machinery & equipment
Wholesale (Services)		(Not included)	G	(See Wholesale and Retail)
Pharmaceutical sales		(Not included)	5231	Pharmaceutical sales

8

Travel and Tourism Information Sources

CHARLES R. GOELDNER
Professor of Marketing and Tourism
University of Colorado
Boulder, Colorado

This chapter presents a comprehensive list of sources of information available on tourism, travel, and hospitality. It is divided into eight sections: indexing services; bibliographies and finding guides; data bases and documentation centers; periodicals; trade and professional associations; government; yearbooks, annuals, and handbooks; and some final suggestions. A summary of the type of information in each source is also provided.

The number of sources of secondary information available on tourism, travel, and hospitality continues to grow. In the rapidly expanding, dynamic world of tourism, practitioners must know what information is available and where to find it. Information gathering requires a great deal of the tourism executives' time; yet little exists to guide them to the best sources of data for their particular concerns. Thus, this chapter provides a comprehensive list of the numerous sources along with a summary of the types of information available to each.

The chapter is organized into eight main categories: (1) Indexing Services, (2) Bibliographies and Finding Guides, (3) Data Bases and Documentation Centers, (4) Periodicals, (5) Trade and Professional Associations, (6) Government, (7) Yearbooks, Annuals, Handbooks, and Other Sources, and (8) Some Final Suggestions. The sources are arranged alphabetically within each heading.

Considerable effort has been made to make the list up-to-date and to give enough information to enable users who cannot find the information in their own library or public library to send requests to the sources indicated. Readers should be aware that names, addresses, and prices change frequently.

One of the biggest mistakes in travel and tourism research is to rush out and collect primary data without exhausting secondary source information. Only later do researchers discover they have duplicated previous research. Often, existing sources could have provided information to solve the problem for a fraction of the cost. Therefore, users should

exhaust secondary sources before turning to primary research for additional data.

In selecting sources of information, efforts have been made to (1) emphasize prime data, (2) list sources that can be used to locate more detailed data, and (3) keep the list brief enough to be actually read and used rather than just filed. Effective utilization can save money and hours of time and provide useful information that might otherwise be missed.

INDEXING SERVICES

Unfortunately, there is no one convenient heading under which you can look and automatically find travel research information listed. Travel research studies may be found under many headings. The most important subject heading in the indexes is "tourism" or "tourist trade." Examples of other headings that contain useful information are: travel, travel agents, vacations, transportation, tourist camps, motels, hotels, recreation, and national parks.

Business Periodicals Index (New York: H.W. Wilson, monthly except August). A cumulative subject index covering periodicals in the fields of accounting, marketing, finance, advertising, banking, and so on.

The Hospitality Index: An Index for the Hotel, Food Service and Travel Industries (Washington, D.C.: American Hotel and Motel Association, quarterly and annual), $99. This comprehensive data base comprising citations of articles, reports, and research from more than 40 different journals and periodicals has been published by the Consortium of Hospitality Research Information Services (CHRIS), a joint effort of Cornell University's School of Hotel Administration, the University of Wisconsin-Stout, and the Information Center of the American Hotel and Motel Association. Information contained in the published index is organized under more than 1,500 subject headings.

Lodging and Restaurant Index (West Lafayette, Indiana: Purdue University, annual). A periodical index of over 40 major journals of the hospitality industry.

Predicasts F & S Index Europe (Cleveland, Ohio: Predicasts, Inc., monthly). Devoted exclusively to Europe. Covers the European community, Scandinavia, other West European countries, the former Soviet Union, and other East European countries.

Predicasts F & S Index International (Cleveland, Ohio: Predicasts, Inc., monthly). Indexes articles from foreign publications. Information arranged by (1) industry and product, (2) country, and (3) company. Covers Canada, Latin America, Africa, Middle East, Oceania, and other Asian countries.

Predicasts F & S Index of Corporations and Industries (Cleveland, Ohio: Predicasts, Inc., weekly, quarterly, and annual cumulations). Indexes U.S. company, product, and industry information from articles in financial publications, business newspapers, trade magazines, and special reports. Includes foreign-company operations in the United States. Presented in two sections: (I) "Industries and Products," arranged by S.I.C. code, and (II) "Companies," arranged alphabetically.

Predicasts F & S Index United States (Cleveland, Ohio: Predicasts, Inc., weekly). Indexes articles from the United States and from foreign sources that may affect U.S. business.

Reader's Guide to Periodical Literature (New York: H.W. Wilson, semimonthly). An index of the contents of U.S. general magazines.

The Travel and Tourism Index (Laie, Hawaii: Brigham Young University Hawaii, quarterly). This quarterly index covers 47 travel and tourism publications. Annual subscription fee $40.

BIBLIOGRAPHIES AND FINDING GUIDES

Baretje, R. *Tourist Analysis Review* (Aix-en-Provence, France: Centre des Hautes Etudes Touristiques, Fondation Vasarely 1, Avenue Marcel Pagnol 13090, quarterly). This review, printed on 40 heavy-duty pages, gives complete references of studies and a short synopsis of their contents. Each issue analyzes 160 books or articles dealing with tourism.

Engass, Peter. *Tourism and the Travel Industry: An Information Sourcebook* (Phoenix, Arizona: Oryx Press, 1988),

152 pp. This bibliography lists and describes almost 900 books, journals, government publications, and proceedings dealing with domestic and international tourism.

Goeldner, C.R., and Karen Dicke. *Bibliography of Tourism and Travel Research Studies, Reports and Articles* (Boulder, Colorado: Business Research Division, College of Business, University of Colorado, 1980), 9 vols., 762 pp., complete set $60. This nine-volume bibliography is a research resource on travel, recreation, and tourism. Volume I, *Information Sources,* covers bibliographies, classics, books, directories, proceedings, list of travel and tourism trade and professional publications, list of U.S. travel and tourism associations, list of universities involved in travel and tourism research, list of U.S. travel contacts, selected list of Canadian travel contacts, and list of world travel contacts. Volume II, *Economics,* covers general economics, analysis, balance of payments, development, employment, expenditures, feasibility studies, impact, indicators and barometers, international economics, and economic multipliers. Volume III, *International Tourism,* covers general tourism; Africa; Asia and the Pacific; Canada; Central, Latin, and South America; Europe (excluding the United Kingdom); Middle East; and the United Kingdom. Volume IV, *Lodging,* covers general lodging, financial aspects, innovations, management, marketing and market research, statistics, and second-home development. Volume V, *Recreation,* covers general recreation, boating, camping, carrying capacity, demand, economics, forecasts, forests, hiking, hunting and fishing, land development, management, parks, planning, public input, research and research methodology, rural recreation, skiing, snowmobiling, sports, statistics, urban recreation, user studies, and water. Volume VI, *Transportation,* includes transportation—general and forecasts; air transportation—general, costs, commuters, deregulation, economics, fares, forecasts, international, passengers, planning, and statistics; highways and roads—bus, auto, and recreational vehicles; rail; water; and other. Volume VIII, *Advertising-Planning,* covers advertising and promotion, attitudes, business travel, clubs, conferences and conventions, education, energy, environmental impact, food service, forecasts, gambling, handicapped traveler, hospitality, leisure, management, and planning. Volume VIII, *Statistics-Visitors,* includes statistics, tourism research, travel agents, travel research methodology, vacations, and visitors. Volume IX, *Index,* includes several indexes to the material in Volumes I-VIII.

Herron, Nancy. *The Leisure Literature* (Englewood, Colorado: Libraries Unlimited, Inc., 1992), 181 pp., $28.50. This book endeavors to identify, describe, and organize into a usable format 283 reference sources that support research related to leisure. Contains an excellent section on travel and tourism.

The Hospitality Bibliography (Mineola, New York: Hospitality Valuation Services, 1991), 80 pp. This publication is a compilation of titles pertaining to the financial and real estate aspects of the hotel and restaurant industries. It is annotated.

Jafari, Jafar. "Tourism and the Social Sciences: A Bibliography," *Annals of Tourism Research* (Elmsford, New York: Pergamon Press) Vol. 6, No. 2 (1979), pp.149-194. The purpose of this bibliography is to bring together a selection of publications dealing with the study of tourism. This list of bibliographies is from 1970-1978.

Jafari, Jafar, and Dean Aaser. "Tourism as the Subject of Doctoral Dissertations," *Annals of Tourism Research* (Elmsford, New York: Pergamon Press) Vol. 15, No. 3 (1988), pp. 407-429. This article discusses tourism as a field of study and presents the results of a computer search of doctoral dissertations on tourism. The search resulted in 157 titles with a touristic focus written between 1951 and 1987. Titles, authors, and schools are given.

Jafari, Jafar, Philip Sawin, Christopher Gustafson, and Joseph Harrington. *Bibliographies on Tourism and Related Subjects: An Annotated Sourcebook* (Boulder, Colorado: Business Research Division, College of Business, University of Colorado, 1988), 81 pp., $25. This is a bibliography of bibliographies dealing with tourism and associated fields. There are 271 annotated entries, and information is arranged in three ways: (1) alphabetical listing, (2) author index, and (3) subject index. Also included is a listing of the tourism bibliographies available from the Centre des Hautes Etudes Touristiques in Aix-en-Provence, France.

Leisure, Recreation and Tourism Abstracts (formerly *Rural Recreation and Tourism Abstracts*). (Wallingford, Oxon, United Kingdom: C.A.B. International, quarterly). Annual subscription rate is $171. The abstracts, arranged by subject, provide short informative summaries of publications with full bibliographical details and often a symbol for locating the original documents.

Nixon, Judith. *Hotel and Restaurant Industries: An Information Sourcebook* (Phoenix, Arizona: Oryx Press, 1988), 240 pp. This bibliography is based primarily on the Consumer and Family Sciences Library at Purdue University, which has been specializing in hotel and restaurant materials for many years.

Pisarski, Alan. *An Inventory of Federal Travel and Tourism Related Information Sources* (Boulder, Colorado: Business Research Division, University of Colorado, 1985), 107 pp., $25. This inventory of existing federal data programs relevant to travel and tourism provides a comprehensive listing and description of pertinent government sources.

Pizam, A., and Z. Gu. *Journal of Travel Research Index and Abstracts, Volumes 6-24* (Boulder, Colorado: Business Research Division, College of Business, University of Colorado, 1988), 182 pp., $48. This is a comprehensive index and abstracts of the articles that have been published in the *Journal of Travel Research* and its predecessor, the *Travel Research Bulletin*. Articles indexed by author, title, subject, and destination outside the United States. *Journal of Travel Research Index and Abstracts, Volumes 25-26*, 1989, 39 pp; $18.

Recent Acquisitions (Ottawa, Ontario: Tourism Research and Data Centre, Tourism Canada, 235 Queen Street, K1A 0H6, monthly). This is a listing of publications received by the Tourism Reference and Documentation Centre of Tourism Canada.

Tourism and Vacation Travel: State and Local Government Planning (Springfield, Virginia: National Technical Information Service, U.S. Department of Commerce, May 1988), 50 pp., $40. Economic and socioeconomic aspects of vacation travel and tourism in various localities of the United States are documented. Most of these studies deal with the use of tourism for the economic development of local communities. Special attention is given to wilderness, coastal zone, lake, waterway, and Indian reservation areas. This updated bibliography covers the period 1970 to May 1988 and provides 175 citations.

Tourism: A Guide to Sources of Information (Edinburgh, United Kingdom: Capital Planning Information Ltd., 6 Castle Street, Edinburgh E112 3AT, Scotland, 1981), 73 pp. This publication gives a selected and evaluative listing of tourism literature primarily about the United Kingdom; however, it also includes some international sources.

"The Travel Research Bookshelf," *Journal of Travel Research* (Boulder, Colorado: Business Research Division, College of Business, University of Colorado). "The Travel Research Bookshelf," a regular feature of the quarterly *Journal of Travel Research*, is an annotated bibliography of current travel research materials. Sources and availability of materials are shown for each entry.

Whitlock, W., and R. Becker. *Nature-based Tourism: An Annotated Bibliography* (Clemson, South Carolina: Clemson University, 1991), $40. Containing over 300 citations, this bibliography includes author, geographical, and subject indices. Approximately 150 subjects are referenced.

DATA BASES AND DOCUMENTATION CENTERS

Several data bases containing travel and tourism information are available now. One of the quickest ways of finding information is to conduct a computer search of these data bases. Some data bases available are listed below. For a comprehensive list of data bases and documentation centers, check the final entry in this section.

ABI/INFORM, 620 South Third Street, Louisville, Kentucky 40202; (800) 626-2823. A computerized data base of business information for the most current five years. It consists of abstracts and indexes to business articles contained in more than 800 different journals.

AVIATION LINK, BACK Information Services, 65 High Ridge Road, Suite 346, Stamford, Connecticut 06905; (800) 446-2225. Computerized information service on almost all facets of the airline industry. Data base includes information from the International Air Transport Association, U.S. Department of Transportation, Association of European Airlines, Official Airlines Guide, and other sources.

CENTRE DES HAUTES ETUDES TOURISTIQUES, Fondation Vasarely 1, Avenue Marcel Pagnol, 13090, Aix-en-Provence, France. This center maintains a comprehensive collection of the world literature on tourism, which has now been computerized. The Centre has been publishing since 1964 in the collection *Etudes et Memoires*, which is a reference book of all studies in tourism. The 25 volumes issued to date have recorded over 36,500 documents. The Centre also publishes *Touristic Analysis Review* every quarter. Rene Baretje heads the Centre and requests that everyone send him complimentary copies of their tourism studies.

DIALOG, Information Services, Inc., 3460 Hillview Avenue, Palo Alto, California 94304; (415) 858-2700. Included in DIALOG are the C.A.B. Abstracts, a comprehensive file of the 26 journals published by Commonwealth Agricultural Bureaux in England. C.A.B. Abstracts include a subfile entitled "Leisure, Recreation and Tourism Abstracts." Subject areas covered in LRTA are leisure, recreation, and tourism; natural resources; tourism; recreation activities and facilities; culture and entertainment; and home and neighborhood activities.

INFORMATION CENTER, American Hotel and Motel Association, 1201 New York Avenue, Washington, D.C. 20005; (202) 289-3100. Contains information on more than 1,300 subjects related to hotel/motel operation. Divided into two divisions, the five-year files (information printed in the last five years) and "historical" files; information is provided on 30 major subject categories. There is a charge for services.

INFOTRAC, California: Information Access, Inc. (monthly laser disc). A self-contained periodical reference system. Indexes over 900 business-related journals and regional publications. Covers current three years on laser disc.

PAIS on CD-ROM (New York, New York: Public Affairs Information Service, PAIS Inc.). This data base indexes journal articles, books, and government publications pertaining to business, economics, political science, law, public administration, and other social sciences.

PERIODICAL ABSTRACTS ONDISC (Ann Arbor, Michigan: University of Michigan). This is an index to articles in over 300 general-interest periodicals, covering such topics as current events, health, business, science, arts, and entertainment. It began in January 1988 and is updated quarterly.

SIRLS, Faculty of Human Kinetics and Leisure Studies, University of Waterloo, Waterloo, Ontario, Canada N2L 3G1; (519) 885-1211, EXT 2560. A computerized, bibliographical data base and documentation center in the areas of leisure, sport, recreation, play, games, and dance. More than 12,000 citations are listed at the present time, and the system is accessible from external institutions.

TOURISM RESEARCH AND DOCUMENTATION CENTRE (TRDC), 3rd Floor West, 235 Queen Street, Ottawa, Ontario K1A 0H6, Canada; (613) 954-3943. The center maintains the most comprehensive collection of tourism-related information in Canada. The holdings of more than 5,000 books and documents include research papers, statistics, surveys, analyses, journals, conference proceedings, speeches, proposals, feasibility studies, legislation, guidebooks, bibliographies, and more. Information on this material is held in a data bank that can be accessed by TRDC staff or by the users of remote terminals in other parts of the country.

The computer system at TRDC is a bilingual bibliographic information storage and retrieval system that allows users to search the holdings using 1,500 key words or "descriptors." Information is classified into eight major sectors: transportation, accommodation, conventions, hospitality services, events and attractions, recreational activities and facilities, education, and tourist-related enterprises. The descriptors can be used singly or in combination to produce the information required. Searches can be undertaken, for instance, by subject, author, sponsor, date, document type, geography, or various combinations of these. The information has been compiled to assist the industry and officers of Tourism Canada; however, it is also available to the general public.

TRAVEL REFERENCE CENTER, Business Research Division, Campus Box 420, University of Colorado, Boulder, Colorado 80309; (303) 492-5056. The reference center was established in 1969 to assist the travel industry in finding information sources and to provide a facility to house a comprehensive collection of travel studies. The center now comprises the largest collection of travel, tourism, and recreation research studies available at any one place in the United States. The present collection numbers over 10,000 documents and is growing daily. The collection was computerized in 1985, and the center can do literature searches using more than 900 descriptors. The cost for a literature search is $50.

THE WORLD DIRECTORY OF DOCUMENTATION RESOURCES AND SYSTEMS FOR THE TRAVEL AND TOURISM SECTOR. (Madrid: World Tourism Organization), 200 pp., 1991, $30. Contains information on more than 100 national and international tourism information centers. Included are libraries, documentation centers, and computerized documentation data bases. Published in English, French, and Spanish.

PERIODICALS

The following are periodicals that contain travel research information.

Annals of Tourism Research (Elmsford, New York: Pergamon Press, quarterly), $225 per year.

ASTA Agency Management Magazine (Greensboro, North Carolina: Pace Communications Inc.), subscription fee: free for U.S. and Canadian members; $36 a year for nonmembers in the United States, $55 elsewhere.

The Cornell Hotel and Restaurant Administration Quarterly (Ithaca, New York: School of Hotel Administration, Cornell University, six issues per year), $62 for individuals; $95 for institutions.

Courier (Lexington, Kentucky: National Tour Association, monthly), $36 a year.

Hospitality and Tourism Educator (Washington, D.C.: Council on Hotel, Restaurant, and Institutional Education, quarterly), $35 a year in United States, $45 international.

Hospitality Directions: Forecasts and Analyses for the Hospitality Industry (New York: Coopers and Lybrand, quarterly), $295 a year.

Hospitality Research Journal (Washington, D.C.: Council on Hotel, Restaurant, and Institutional Education, three times a year), $50 a year in the United States.

Hotel and Motel Management (Duluth, Minnesota: Edgell Communications, 18 times per year), $35 a year in United States, $60 in Canada, $110 elsewhere; single copy $3 in United States, $5 in Canada, $10 elsewhere.

Hotels: The International Magazine of the Hotel and Restaurant Industry (Des Plaines, Illinois: Cahners, 12 times a year), $64.95 a year in United States, $96.25 in Canada, $89.95 in Mexico, $119.95 surface mail or $189.95 air mail elsewhere.

The Hotel Valuation Journal (Mineola, New York: Hospitality Valuation Services, Inc.), $125 annual subscription.

International Journal of Hospitality Management (Elmsford, New York: Pergamon Press, quarterly), $235 a year.

International Tourism Reports (London: The Economist Intelligence Unit, quarterly), $470 a year.

International Visitor (New York: International Visitor Publishing, Inc., 10 issues a year), $78.50 a year.

Journal of Hospitality and Leisure Marketing (Binghamton, New York: Haworth Press, Inc., quarterly), $24 a year individuals, $32 institutions, and $48 libraries.

Journal of Leisure Research (Alexandria, Virginia: National Recreation and Park Association, quarterly), member: $25 a year in United States, $28 a year elsewhere; nonmember: $40 a year in United States, $43 a year elsewhere. Single copy $10 domestic and $12 foreign.

Journal of Travel and Tourism Marketing (Binghamton, New York: Haworth Press, Inc., quarterly), $18 a year individuals, $24 institutions, and $32 libraries.

Journal of Travel Research (Boulder, Colorado: Business Research Division, College of Business, University of Colorado, quarterly), free to members of the Travel and Tourism

Research Association; nonmembers $82.50 a year in United States, $87.50 in Canada and Mexico, $97.50 elsewhere.

Leisure Sciences (Washington, D.C.: Taylor & Francis, quarterly), $99 a year institutions, $55 individuals.

Lodging (New York: American Hotel Association Directory Corporation, monthly except August), members $22 a year, nonmembers $35.

Meetings and Conventions (Secaucus, New Jersey: Reed Travel Group, monthly), $65 a year in United States, $95 elsewhere; single copy $20 in the United States, $25 elsewhere.

Revue de Tourism—The Tourist Review—Zeitschrift für Fremdenverkehr (St. Gallen, Switzerland: AIEST, Varnbuelstrasse 19, CH-9000 St. Gallen, quarterly), 52.00 Sfr.

Tour and Travel News (Manhasset, New York: CMP Publications Inc., weekly), $75 a year in United States and Canada, $125 in Mexico and Central America, $135 in Europe, $135 in South America, and $150 in Asia and Africa.

Tourism Management (Oxford, United Kingdom: Butterworth-Heinemann Ltd., quarterly), £136.00 a year in United States, single copy £40.00.

Tourism Recreation Research (Indira Nagar, Lucknow, India: Centre for Tourism Research, semiannually), $75 a year.

The Travel Agent (New York: American Traveler Division, Capital Cities ABC, Inc., weekly), $79 in United States, $149 elsewhere.

Travel & Tourism Analyst (London: The Economist Intelligence Unit, 6 times a year), $910 a year in North America.

Travel-log (Ottawa: Statistics Canada, quarterly), annual subscription fee: $42 in Canada, US $50 in United States, US $59 elsewhere.

Travel Printout (Washington, D.C.: U.S. Travel Data Center, monthly), $75 in United States, $80 elsewhere.

Travel Trade (New York: Travel Trade Publications, weekly), $10 a year in United States, $13 in Canada, $25 elsewhere.

Travel Weekly (Secaucus, New Jersey: Reed Travel Group, twice weekly), $26 a year in United States and Canada; single copy $1.

Visions in Leisure and Business (Bowling Green, Ohio: Appalachian Associates, quarterly), $25 a year individual, and $45 institutions in United States, $40 a year individuals and $80 institutions elsewhere.

There are also many other periodicals and journals dealing with the travel field. The sources for locating these are:

Business Publications Rates and Data, 3 volumes.

(Wilmette, Illinois: Standard Rate and Data Service, monthly). A listing of more than 5,244 U.S. and 170 international business, trade, and technical publications.

1992-1993 Travel Media Directory (Washington, D.C.: Travel Industry Association America, annual). A listing of some 1,200 key editorial and advertising contacts at travel, trade, and consumer publications in more than 40 countries.

Ulrich's International Periodicals Directory, 3 volumes. (New York: R.R. Bowker, annual). Includes entries for more than 108,590 in-print periodicals published throughout the world.

TRADE AND PROFESSIONAL ASSOCIATIONS

Many trade and professional associations publish valuable data on the travel industry. Examples are:

Association Internationale d'Experts Scientifiques du Tourism (AIEST), Varnbuelstrasse 19, CH-9000, St. Gallen, Switzerland. AIEST is composed primarily of academicians interested in tourism research and teaching. It publishes the *Tourist Review* and annual proceedings of its meetings.

Pacific Asia Travel Association (PATA), Telesis Tower, Suite 1750, 1 Montgomery Street, San Francisco, California 94104. It publishes the *PATA Annual Statistical Report* and other publications and holds research seminars.

Travel and Tourism Research Association (TTRA), 10200 West 44th Avenue, Suite 304, Wheat Ridge, Colorado 80033. It helps sponsor the *Journal of Travel Research* and publishes proceedings.

Travel Industry Association of America, Two Lafayette Center, 1133 21st Street NW, Washington, D.C. 20036. It has a publication program that includes special reports and newsletters.

The World Tourism Organization (WTO), Capitan Haya, 42, E-28020, Madrid, Spain. One of the main tasks of the WTO is to give members continuing information on tourism and its influence on the social, economic, and cultural life of nations. It offers a number of publications and educational programs. A publications list can be received by writing the organization.

Some other associations are the Tourism Industry Association of Canada, 130 Albert Street, Suite 1016, Ottawa, Ontario, Canada; Air Transport Association of America, 1301 Pennsylvania Avenue, NW, Washington, D.C. 20006; International Air Transport Association, IATA Building, 2000 Peel Street, Montreal, Quebec, Canada H3A 2R4; American Hotel and Motel Association, 1201 New York Avenue NW, Washington, D.C. 20005; International Association of Amusement Parks and Attractions, 1448 Duke Street, Alexandria, Virginia 22302; International Association of Convention

and Visitors Bureaus, P.O. Box 758, Champaign, Illinois 61820; Association of Travel Marketing Executives, P.O. Box 43563, Washington, D.C. 20010; American Society of Travel Agents, 1101 King Street, Alexandria, Virginia 22314; National Tour Association, P.O. Box 3071, 546 East Main Street, Lexington, Kentucky 40596; Institute of Certified Travel Agents, 148 Linden Street, P.O. Box 82-56, Wellesley, Massachusetts 02181; National Recreation and Park Association, 3101 Park Center Drive, Alexandria, Virginia 22302.

If you are in doubt about trade associations in the field, you can check:

Encyclopedia of Associations: 1993, 27th ed. (Detroit, Michigan: Gale Research, 1992), Volume I, *National Organizations of the United States,* 3,645 pp.; Volume 2, *Geographic and Executive Indexes,* 958 pp.; Volume 3, *Supplement, International Organizations,* Part I and Part II, 1992, 2,344 pp. A guide to over 23,000 national and international organizations.

GOVERNMENT

Probably no group collects more information on the tourism industry than government agencies. The government agencies vary according to the objectives of the particular country and, in most cases, the degree of importance of the tourism sector. Generally, the following public agencies are involved in travel and tourism research activities: (1) ministries of tourism; (2) undersecretarial or underministerial tourism organizations; (3) specific government organizations for travel and tourism; (4) statistical agencies for collection, analysis, and publication of data related to travel and tourism, such as Statistics Canada and U.S. Bureau of the Census; and (5) state or provincial tourism organizations.

Most government travel organizations are members of the World Tourism Organization (WTO), Capitan Haya, 42, E-28020, Madrid, Spain. Researchers can write for a list of members and associate members.

The major U.S. government tourism development organization is the U.S. Travel and Tourism Administration, Department of Commerce, Washington, D.C. 20230. An inventory of federal agencies by Pisarski is listed in this chapter's second section: Bibliographies and Finding Guides.

Selected examples of useful government publications in the travel field include:

1991 Annual Abstract National Park Service (Denver, Colorado: National Park Service), 37 pp., 1992. This report provides visit data to national parks.

Canadian Travel Survey: 1988 (Ottawa: Statistics Canada; Travel, Tourism and Recreation Section; quarterly). This report provides statistics on travel by Canadians on trips of 80 kilometers or more with destinations in Canada. Information is provided on who the travelers are, why they traveled, when they traveled, how they traveled, where they stayed, how much they spent, and what they did. A general summary of the travel situation in Canada is given and the importance of domestic travel is demonstrated.

The Impact of the Threat of Terrorism and the Recession on the Travel and Tourism Industry (United States Congress; House Committee on Small Business; Subcommittee on Procurement, Tourism, and Rural Development). This is the hearing before the Subcommittee on Procurement, Tourism, and Rural Development of the Committee on Small Business, House of Representatives, One Hundred Second Congress, first session, Washington, D.C., March 7, 1991.

Importance of Scenic Byways to Travel and Tourism (United States Congress; Senate Committee on Commerce, Science, and Transportation; Subcommittee on Foreign Commerce and Tourism). This is a hearing before the subcommittee on Foreign Commerce and Tourism of the Committee on Commerce, Science, and Transportation, United States Senate, One Hundred First Congress, first session, April 14, 1989.

In-Flight Survey of International Air Travelers (Washington, D.C.: U.S. Department of Commerce, U.S. Travel and Tourism Administration, annual, $400). The in-flight survey provides a comprehensive consumer-marketing data base on international travel to and from the United States, including travelers' residence, purpose of trip, port of entry, multiple destinations visited, duration of stay, type of lodging, information sources used, means of booking, use of package trips, domestic transportation, demographics, and expenditure categories. Two reports are available: (1) "Overseas Visitors to the United States" and (2) "United States Travelers to Overseas Countries." Reports can be purchased separately for $200 each. Quarterly reports are available on a special-request basis.

National Tourism Policy Study—Final Report (Washington, D.C.: Committee on Commerce, Science and Transportation, U.S. Senate, 1979), 361 pp. This report by Arthur D. Little, Inc., presents the findings of the final phase of the *National Tourism Policy Study*. It was designed to develop a proposed national tourism policy for the United States; to define appropriate roles for the federal government, the states, cities, private industry, and consumers in carrying out, supporting, and contributing to the national tourism policy; and to recommend organizational programmatic and legislative strategies for implementing the proposed national tourism policy.

A Strategic Look at the Travel and Tourism Industry (Washington, D.C.: U.S. Department of Commerce, U.S. Travel and Tourism Administration, 1989). The report discusses the following topics concerning the tourist trade: planning assumptions; the external environment; U.S. competitive position in the world tourism market; tourism market opportunities for the United States; constraints confronting the U.S. tourism industry; and barriers to international trade in tourism.

Touriscope: International Travel 1987 (Ottawa: Statistics Canada, 1988). The report presents significant trends on travelers to Canada and on Canadians traveling abroad.

Tourism in Canada, A Statistical Digest, 1988 (Ottawa: Statistics Canada, 1988). The report is full of current facts and figures on the demand and supply sides of tourism. Issues that are vital to the tourism industry are presented by experts.

User Friendly Facts: A Resource Book 1992. (Washington, D.C.: U.S. Travel and Tourism Administration), 135 pp., 1992, $50. This provides a bibliography of USTTA publications and a quick reference on international data available from USTTA.

YEARBOOKS, ANNUALS, HANDBOOKS, AND OTHER SOURCES

The 1990-91 Economic Review of Travel in America (Washington, D.C.: U.S. Travel Data Center, annual), $60. This annual report on the role of travel and tourism in the American economy reviews the economic contributions of travel away from home, developments in the travel industry, and the effects of economic changes on travel and tourism.

1992 Travel Agency Survey (Secaucus, New Jersey: Reed Travel Group, 1992), 126 pp. This 1992 Louis Harris Survey presents the findings of the 11th comprehensive study of the travel agency business. It updates information obtained in previous studies on the dimensions and scope of the travel agency market and on the sources and components of agency business. Like previous studies, this study also describes the importance of various criteria influencing travel agents' choices of air carriers, hotels, cruise ships, car rental agencies, and package tours for their clients. The August 13, 1992, issue of *Travel Weekly* (Vol. 51, No. 65) is the Louis Harris study issue.

1993 Outlook for Travel and Tourism (Washington, D.C.: U.S. Travel Data Center), approximately 150 pp., annual, $125. Proceedings of the 18th annual Travel Outlook Forum.

Air Transport (Washington, D.C.: Air Transport Association of America, annual). This official annual report to the U.S. scheduled airline industry contains historical and current statistical data on the industry.

The Annual Review of Travel 1992 (New York: American Express Related Service Company, annual), 98 pp., $25. This book contains the seven winning essays of the 1992 American Express Review of Travel International Essay Competition.

Compendium of Tourism Statistics, 11th Edition (1991) (Madrid: World Tourism Organization), 230 pp., $25. Annual digest of basic tourism statistics. First part: Country tables (170 countries and territories) containing the following categories of data: Movements, Transport, Motivations, Accommodation, and Tourism and the Economy; data cover the period 1985-1989. Second part: background information on international tourist arrivals and receipts at world and regional levels based on tourism series 1985-1990. Available in English, French, and Spanish.

Discover America 2000 (Washington, D.C.: U.S. Travel Data Center, 1989), 80 pp. This gives the implications of America's changing demographics and attitudes on the U.S. travel industry.

The Meeting Market 1992 (Secaucas, New Jersey: Reed Travel Group, 1992), 138 pp., $250. This report gives dimensions, expenditures, and characteristics of the off-premise meetings market. The size of the total meetings market is estimated at $38.7 billion.

PATA Annual Statistical Report (San Francisco: Pacific Asia Travel Association), $70 to members, $100 to nonmembers. This report presents visitor-arrival statistics and other relevant data reported by PATA member governments. The report gives visitor-arrival data for the individual countries by nationality of residence and mode of travel. Selected market sources of visitors to the Pacific area are given, along with data on accommodations, length of stay, visitor expenditures, and national-tourist-organization budgets.

Tourism Policy and International Tourism in OECD Member Countries (Paris: The Organization for Economic Cooperation and Development, annual). This is an annual report on tourism statistics in Australia, Austria, Belgium, Canada, Denmark, Finland, France, Germany, Greece, Iceland, Ireland, Italy, Japan, Luxembourg, the Netherlands, New Zealand, Norway, Portugal, Spain, Sweden, Switzerland, Turkey, the United Kingdom, and the United States.

Tourism to the Year 2000: Qualitative Aspects Affecting Global Growth (Madrid: World Tourism Organization, 1991), 42 pp., $15. The executive summary of a major WTO study. Includes an inventory of variables likely to affect tourism development over the 1990s. Available in English, French, and Spanish.

Tourism Works for America (Washington, D.C.: National Travel and Tourism Awareness Council, 1991), $50. This reports magnitude of travel and tourism industry in United States: $327.3 billion in 1990.

Travel Industry World Yearbook: The Big Picture–1991 (Rye, New York: Child and Waters, annual), $79 in the United States, $88 foreign airmail. This annual issue presents a compact up-to-date review of the latest happenings in the world of tourism.

Travel Market Close-up: National Travel Survey Tabulations (Washington, D.C.: U.S. Travel Data Center, quarterly and annual). In March 1979, the U.S. Travel Data Center began conducting a monthly *National Travel Survey*. Since that time, quarterly and annual summaries of the results have been published to provide researchers with timely, consistent, and relevant data on major trends in U.S. travel activity.

Travel Trends in the United States and Canada (Boulder, Colorado: Business Research Division, University of Colo-

rado, 1984), 262 pp., $45. This document provides statistics on visits to recreation areas, numbers of tourists, tourist expenditures, length of stay and size of party, economic impact of tourism, tourism-related employment, mode of transportation used, tourism advertising, passport statistics, international travel, foreign visitor arrivals, travel costs, and highlights from national travel surveys. Data has been compiled from 260 sources.

Trends in Travel and Tourism Advertising Expenditures in United States Measured Media (New York: Ogilvy and Mather, 1992), various paging, $100. Annual volume that reports on advertising spending in U.S. media by U.S. or foreign-flag airlines, by states or other domestic destinations, by foreign countries and destinations, and by cruise lines.

World Air Transport Statistics (Montreal: International Air Transport Association, annual). This is an annual compilation of facts and figures illustrated with numerous graphs and charts, representing the most up-to-date and complete source of data on the air transport industry.

World Travel and Tourism Review: Indicators, Trends, and Issues, Volume 2, 1992 (Wallingford, Oxon, U.K.: C.A.B. International, annual), 310 pp., $170. Part I provides a comprehensive overview of the most pertinent indicators of travel and tourism activity; Part II contains market and industry trends; and Part III contains special reports featuring education, training, and human-resource issues.

Yearbook of Tourism Statistics (Madrid: World Tourism Organization), approximately 1,000 pp., 1991, $60, two-volume set of global tourism statistics. Volume I (1990) covers world and regional totals for arrivals, overnight stays, receipts and expenditures, accommodation capacity, and domestic tourism. Volume II (1990) provides statistics for 150 countries. Published in English, French, and Spanish.

SOME FINAL SUGGESTIONS

This section provides information on the U.S. Travel Data Center and identifies some well-known books and reports on travel research.

U.S. Travel Data Center, Two Lafayette Center, 1133 21st Street NW, Washington, D.C. 20036, was organized early in 1973 as a nonprofit corporation dedicated to serving the travel-research needs of the industry and nation. Today, the Data Center is the focal point of a multitude of efforts to measure and understand the travel activities of Americans and of foreign visitors to this country. In some instances, the Data Center gathers, analyzes, and disseminates statistical data published by other recognized research organizations. In other cases, the Data Center collects original data for analysis and publication. Selected programs of the Data Center are (1) National Travel Survey, (2) Impact of Travel on State Economies, (3) Survey of State Travel Offices, (4) Travel Price Index, and (5) Annual Travel Outlook Forum. A catalog of its publications is available and can be obtained by writing to the center.

American Outdoors: The Legacy, The Challenge (Washington, D.C.: Island Press, 1987), 426 pp. This volume is the final report of the President's Commission on Americans Outdoors. The report makes an important contribution to our understanding of the nation's outdoor-recreation needs and resources.

Edgell, David. *International Tourism Policy* (New York: Van Nostrand Reinhold, 1990), 204 pp., $45.95. This book examines global tourism policy issues, discusses economic considerations, and covers emerging cultural developments.

Fridgen, Joseph. *Dimensions of Tourism* (East Lansing, Michigan: Educational Institute of the American Hotel and Motel Association, 1991), 361 pp. This book discusses the historical, psychological, social and cultural, international, economic, environmental, and managerial dimensions of tourism.

Gartrell, Richard. *Destination Marketing for Convention and Visitor Bureaus* (Dubuque, Iowa: Kendall Hunt, 1988), 336 pp., $29.95. This text provides theoretical and practical guidelines to marketing a destination, management of a convention bureau, and developing convention and visitor marketing programs.

Gee, Chuck Y. *Resort Development and Management, 2nd Edition* (East Lansing, Michigan: The Educational Institute of the American Hotel and Motel Association, 1988). This updates information about such important topics as the master planning of resort destinations, writing environment-impact statements, designing recreational and sports facilities, managing the resort investment, and technological changes influencing the future of the resort industry.

Gee, Chuck Y., Dexter J.L. Choy, and James C. Makens. *The Travel Industry* (New York: Van Nostrand Reinhold, 1989), 352 pp., $34.95. The emphasis in this text is on introducing concepts about travel as an industry. It provides a basic understanding of travel and tourism and provides insights into the development and operations of the various components of the travel industry.

Getz, Donald. *Festivals, Special Events and Tourism* (New York: Van Nostrand Reinhold, 1991), 374 pp., $39.95. This book covers systematic planning, development, and marketing strategies for promoting special events as tourism attractions and as image builders for destination areas.

Gunn, Clare A. *Tourism Planning* (New York: Taylor & Francis, 1988), 356 pp. This text takes a human-ecology approach and describes opportunities, on the state and regional scale, for greater expansion of tourism without damage to our delicate natural resources. The book provides a unique framework for understanding and regrouping the complicated elements that make up tourism. By relating planning to tourism, constructive guides for the future are offered.

Gunn, Clare A. *Vacationscope: Designing Tourist Regions* (New York: Van Nostrand Reinhold Company, 1988), 208 pp. This volume is a sourcebook of theory, new ideas, and real-world examples for designers, tourism developers, promoters, and students.

Howell, David W. *Passport: An Introduction to the Travel and Tourism Industry* (Cincinnati: South-Western Publishing Co., 1993), 436 pp. The book is designed to help readers understand the roles played by various components of the travel and tourism industry and to help them decide which of the many different careers would best suit them.

Krippendorf, Jost. *The Holiday Makers* (London: William Heinemann, Ltd., 1987), 160 pp. This book analyzes the different forms of tourism, examines the effects on various countries and their people, and outlines positive steps to reconcile people's holiday requirements with the world's economic and social structures.

McIntosh, Robert W., and Charles Goeldner. *Tourism: Principles, Practices, Philosophies* (New York: John Wiley & Sons, Inc., 1990), 534 pp., $37.95. The sixth edition of this classic introduction to tourism provides a broad global perspective with emphasis on planning and developing tourism. It investigates the cultural, economic, sociological, and psychological aspects of tourism. The book is divided into five parts: Understanding Tourism: Its Nature, History, and Organization; Motivation for Travel and Choosing Travel Products; Tourism Supply, Demand, Economics, and Development; Essentials of Tourism Marketing and Research; and Tourism Practices and Prospects.

Mill, Robert C., and Alastair M. Morrison. *The Tourism System* (Englewood Cliffs, New Jersey: Prentice-Hall, 1992), 506 pp. This book presents a comprehensive systems view of tourism, stressing the interrelationships and interdependencies of its various elements. The authors cover all aspects from a marketing point of view and describe how tourism works.

Pearce, Douglas. *Tourist Development* (New York: John Wiley & Sons, Inc., 1989), 341 pp. The general focus of this book is the way tourism develops and the economic and social effects of that development on the community, local economy, region, or country.

Plog, Stanley. *Leisure Travel* (New York: John Wiley & Sons, Inc., 1991), 244 pp. This book presents an overview of the leisure-travel market and follows with a psychologically based allocentrism-psychocentrism framework for understanding why people do or do not travel, the different types of vacations they take, their expectations, and sources of dissatisfaction.

Powers, Thomas F. *Introduction to Management in the Hospitality Industry* (New York: John Wiley & Sons, Inc., 1992), 634 pp. This book covers the hospitality industry. It discusses the management problems of institutions that offer shelter or food or both to people away from their homes.

Shriver, Stephen J. *Managing Quality Services* (East Lansing, Michigan: The Educational Institute of the American Hotel and Motel Association, 1988). This book defines quality assurance as a management system that ensures the consistent delivery of products and services. Quality assurance enables managers, supervisors, and employees to increase the profitability and productivity operation by solving problems and developing performance standards.

Smith, Valene. *Hosts and Guests, The Anthropology of Tourism* (Philadelphia: University of Pennsylvania Press, 1989), 341 pp. This second edition is a unique collection of essays on the profound cultural impact of tourism in societies ranging from the American Southwest to Tonga to Alaska to Iran.

Tourism's Top Twenty (Boulder, Colorado: Business Research Division, University of Colorado, 1992), approximately 118 pp., $50. This book, compiled in cooperation with the U.S. Travel Data Center, Washington, D.C., provides facts and figures on travel, tourism recreation, and leisure. Information is presented primarily for the United States; however, there is some coverage of world tourism. It provides fast facts on a wide array of tourism-related subjects, including advertising, airlines, attractions, expenditures, hotels and resorts, recreation, world travel, and travel statistics. Sources are given for each table, and complete addresses for the sources are provided in an appendix. A subject index is also included for ease in locating information. Available from the U.S. Travel Data Center, 2 Lafayette Center, 1133 21st Street, NW, Washington, D.C. 20036.

Witt, Stephen, and Luiz Moutinho. *Tourism Marketing and Management Handbook* (Hertfordshire, United Kingdom: Prentice Hall International, 1989), 656 pp. This handbook provides a comprehensive business and academic reference source related to the most crucial issues in tourism marketing and management. Over 100 tourism-topic entries are included.

The WTTC Report, Travel and Tourism: The World's Largest Industry (New York: World Travel and Tourism Council, 1992), approximately 50 pp., $200 for hardcopy or $95 per disk. This report examines the economic contribution of the travel and tourism industry to the world and national economies.

9

Planning a Tourism Research Investigation

ABRAHAM PIZAM
University of Central Florida
Orlando, Florida

This chapter outlines the sequential steps that are involved in carrying out a tourism research investigation. The emphasis is upon the need for careful planning throughout the process in order to ensure valid, reliable, and cost-effective results.

RESEARCH PLANNING—FOR WHAT PURPOSES?

The objective of tourism research is to provide information that will assist tourism managers in making decisions. Tourism research is an investigative process that can be distinguished from other forms of investigations by three unique requirements: objectivity, reproducibility, and systematization (Brown 1980).

Objectivity requires an approach that is independent of the researcher's personal view with respect to the answers to the problems under investigation. Reproducibility is a procedure that ensures that other researchers could duplicate the research and obtain the same results. Finally, systematization, the most important of the three research-investigation requirements, needs each step to be planned so that it will yield what is necessary at the next step. Systematization organizes the research process into sequential and interdependent steps that have to be specified and planned in advance. In other words, *systematization* in research is synonymous with *planning of research*. Therefore, no investigation can fulfill the three requirements of a research investigation unless it is properly planned in advance.

Many inexperienced researchers have logged hundreds of man-hours and thousands of dollars in the actual collection of data, only to find later that the data was not in the appropriate form for data analysis nor were the variables and concepts operationally defined. This would not have happened had those researchers systematized their investigation by planning each step in advance.

Investigators divide the research process into a series of steps. While the number of such steps and their names vary from one individual to another, the recognition of a sequence is universal.

As can be seen from Figure 1, this discussion divides the tourism research investigation into the following seven sequential steps:

A. Formulation of research problem
B. Review of related research
C. Definition of concepts, variables, and hypotheses
D. Selection of research design
E. Selection of data collection technique
F. Selection of subjects
G. Planning of data processing and analysis

FORMULATION OF RESEARCH PROBLEM

Every research investigation starts with the identification and selection of a research topic. The general topic of study may be suggested by some *practical* concern or by some *scientific* or *intellectual* interest.

In tourism, a wide variety of *practical* concerns may present topics for research. Basically, these can be divided into three categories:

1. Provision of information for decision making on the

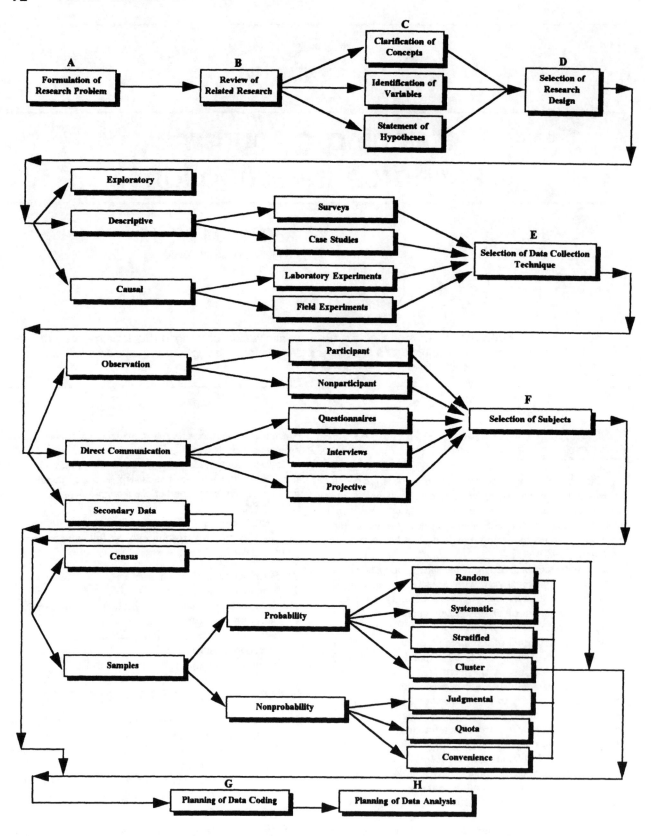

FIGURE 1   Steps in planning a tourism research investigation.

need for some new or enlarged facilities or services. Included in this category are: feasibility studies (hotels, restaurants), marketing studies for new tourism products or services, physical- and land-resources studies, and the like.

2. Provision of information concerning the probable consequences of various courses of action for deciding among proposed alternatives; for example, an airline may need to know which promotional fare would be more popular and profitable: an APEX or a back-to-back charter.

3. Prediction of some future course of events in order to plan appropriate action; for example, the impact of gasoline rationing on tourism expenditures in the city of Boston.

Scientific or *intellectual* interests may suggest an equally wide range of topics for research. Here, the selection of the topic may arise (a) from a concern with some social problem (tourist-related environmental pollution, tourist-induced inflation, tourist-inspired cultural change, etc.), (b) from an interest in some general theme or area of behavior (tourist motivation, destination attitudes change, expenditure patterns, etc.), or (c) from some body of theory (economic theory, psychoanalytic theory, etc.).

The major difference between topics suggested by *practical concern* and those dictated by *scientific interests* is that the latter are less likely to involve the study of a specific situation primarily for the sake of knowledge about that particular situation (Selltiz, Wrightsman, and Cook 1976: 26-27).

The topic selected should be of such scope that not all aspects of the problem can be investigated simultaneously. Too often, novice investigators select a topic that is too vast or too vague to study meaningfully. If the magnitude of the topic is such that it cannot be handled in one single study, the topic should be divided into a number of subtopics that can be dealt with in separate studies.

Before the investigator can select data-collection and data-analysis procedures, he or she needs to formulate *a specific scientific problem* that can be investigated. A scientific problem is an interrogative sentence or statement that asks what

relation exists between two or more variables; for example, what is the relation between disposable income and propensity to travel internationally among North American residents? The answer is what is being sought in the research (Kerlinger 1973:17). As has been said by Albert Einstein and L. Infeld (1938), "The formulation of a problem is far more often essential than its solution."

Therefore, the second step in the planning of a tourism research investigation is to discover a problem in need of solution. "A problem well defined is a problem half solved," says an old maxim. Only when the problem has been clearly defined and the objectives of the research precisely stated can the planning of research investigation move to the next phase. In the statement of the problem, the investigator has to describe what it is he or she plans to investigate; for example, an investigator might be interested in: What is the relation between socioeconomic characteristics of a given population and its expenditures on touristic products? The general goals of this study would be to determine the relative importance of such socioeconomic characteristics as income, education, occupation, and geographic location on annual touristic expenditures.

Unfortunately, it is not always possible for a researcher to formulate a problem simply, clearly, and completely. He or she may often have only a rather vague or diffused notion of the problem. This difficulty, however, should not affect the necessity of formulating the problem, nor should it be used as a rationalization to avoid the formulation.

In the process of problem formulation, the investigator has to undertake several personal, social, and methodological considerations, such as the ones listed in Table 1.

REVIEW OF RELATED RESEARCH

Science is a systematically cumulative body of knowledge. Theories interrelate individual findings, making their implications more general and permitting generalization and transfer to new situations. No study starts *de novo*. In general, each study rests on earlier ones and provides a basis for future ones. Investigators that build their studies upon work

TABLE 1 Social, Personal, and Methodological Considerations in the Process of Problem Formulation

Social	*Personal*	*Methodological*
1. Contribution to the knowledge in the tourism field.	1. A genuine interest in the problem coupled with a lack of biases in it.	1. The problem should express a relation between two or more variables.
2. Practical value to practitioners and scientists in the tourism field.	2. Possession of the necessary skills, abilities, and background knowledge to study the problem.	2. The problem should be stated clearly and unambiguously in question form.
3. Originality—the investigation should not be a duplicate of another work that has been adequately done by someone else (Van Dalen and Meyer 1966, Ch. 7).	3. Access to the tools, equipment, and subjects necessary to conduct the investigation.	3. The problem should be such as to imply possibilities of empirical testing.
	4. Possession of time and financial resources to complete the investigation.	
	5. Access to adequate data.	
	6. Ability to muster administrative support, guidance, and cooperation for the conduct of the study.	

that has already been done have a better chance of contributing to knowledge than those who start anew. The more links that can be established between a given study and other studies or a body of theory, the greater the scientific contribution.

There are two main reasons for reviewing the general and research literature related to the research problem (Kerlinger 1973:696):

1. To explain and clarify the theoretical rationale of the problem.
2. To tell the reader what research has and has not been done on the problem.

In addition, the search for related literature may serve as one of the quickest and most economical ways to discover hypotheses. Unfortunately, being human, investigators want their ideas to be considered as original and unrelated to what others have done. Therefore, one often sees investigators "rediscovering America" or "reinventing the wheel" because they neglected to do the proper background research.

If the proposed study has a theoretical base, the investigator must be sure to relate it to the theory by formulating the research problem at a level sufficiently abstract. This will enable one to relate the findings of the present study to findings of other studies concerned with the same concept.

Even investigators who plan to conduct studies that arise from the need to answer practical questions are neither exempt from the need to search for background research nor from relating their study to others on a sufficiently abstract level. Suppose, for example, that an investigator is interested in a typical practical problem: Why is room occupancy at hotel X down? Doing the proper background research by analyzing published data and trade literature in both the tourism industry and others will quickly and clearly indicate whether the problem belongs to hotel X, the destination in which hotel X is located, the tourism industry as a whole, or the national economy.

In planning this section, the investigator should search and select those studies that provide a foundation for the proposed project and discuss these studies in sufficient detail to understand their relevance. The search may involve conceptual literature, trade literature, or published statistics. Since this search is usually slow and time consuming, valuable tools have been developed to assist the investigator in the search for relevant literature. These tools fall into three general categories: indexes, abstracts, and bibliographies. Listings of available resource materials are given in the previous chapter (Chapter 8), "Travel and Tourism Information Sources" by C. Goeldner.

Today, the application of computers has made literature search faster, more accurate, and more comprehensive. Nowadays, most university libraries as well as those of research institutions have a Computer Assisted Literature Search through which, for a certain fee, one can get a complete listing of published works accompanied by abstracts of each entry for a given defined subject. The searches are done

through a console terminal hooked up to the vendor via telephone lines. Currently there are three major vendors: Lockheed Dialogue System, Bibliographic Retrieval System (BRS), and System Development Corporation (SDC). Each of these offers access to a multitude of data bases. Unfortunately, many tourism periodicals are not included in any of the existing data bases. Nevertheless, the tourism investigator could still get significant assistance from tourism articles published in periodicals that *are* included, as well as in nontourism periodicals.

This author has found the following data bases to contain some tourism-related research literature:

> ABI—Inform
> American Doctoral Dissertations
> Comprehensive Dissertations Abstracts (CDI)
> Economics Abstracts International
> EIS-NON MAN (a directory of companies with specific information on nonmanufacturing firms)
> Environmental Psychology (ENVPSYCH)
> Information Retrieval System for the Sociology of Leisure & Sports (SIRLS)
> Information Service on Social Science Research (FORIS)
> Management Contents
> PREDICAST (Statistical Data Base)
> Psychological Abstracts
> Selective Cooperative Indexing of Management Periodicals (SCIMP)
> Social Science Data Base
> Social Science Information System (SSIS)
> Social Science Citation Index (SSCI)
> Sociological Abstracts

Most of the above data bases are restricted to the last 10 years. However, since citations of current works refer to past ones, the significant past literature has rapidly become well mapped. For a complete listing of all available data bases, consult the latest issue of *Directory of Online Databases* (published quarterly), Santa Monica, California: Cuadra Associates, Inc.

In the process of literature search, it is advisable, if possible, to include studies currently under way that are likely to overlap the proposed project. In the United States, the Science Information Exchange of the Smithsonian Institution in Washington, D. C., maintains a record of all projects currently funded through the U.S. federal branches of the government and the larger foundations. Since this service is computerized, custom searches can be made on request for a fee.

CONCEPTS, VARIABLES, AND HYPOTHESES

Once the review of the relevant research literature has been completed, the next logical step in the design of research projects is to develop and define concepts, variables, and hypotheses. As can be seen in Figure 2, concepts, variables, and hypotheses are the linking pins between theory and empirical tests.

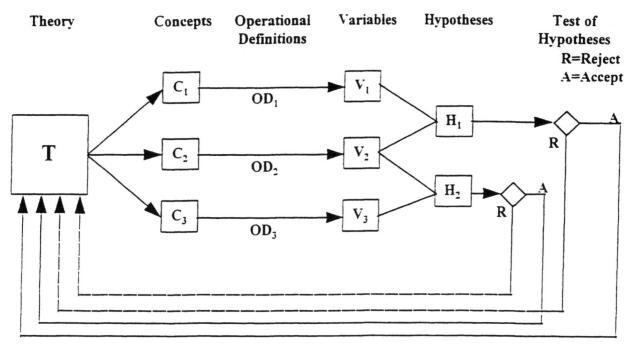

FIGURE 2 The relationship among theory, concepts, variables, and hypotheses.

Concepts

The basic components of theory are concepts and variables, which are related in propositions called postulates, theorems, or hypotheses. Sets of propositions in turn may be interrelated to form theories. Concepts are terms that refer to the characteristics of events, situations, groups, and individuals that are studied (Selltiz, Wrightsman, and Cook 1976:16).

Concepts may be impossible to observe directly, such as *justice* or *love*, or they may have referents that are readily observable, such as *a tree* or *a table* (Bailey 1978:33).

The explication of theory involves the use of concepts that are nominally defined. Nominal definitions of concepts are those definitions frequently found in dictionaries; for example, the nominal definition of the concept *wealthy* is "having large possessions of lands, goods, money, or securities" (Webster 1963:2589).

To test a theory or proposition, the nominally defined concepts must be put to an empirical test. This requires their operational definition. Operational definitions are nothing more than nominal definitions quantified (Black and Champion 1976:182-183); for example, the author's operational definition of *wealthy people* is "people having assets in excess of $1,000,000."

Operational definitions enable researchers to identify the presence or absence of a given concept in a person, group, or event; for instance, to know whether or not a concept such as *well-traveled tourist* is a characteristic of a given person, the researcher must first define what the empirical characteristics of the concept *well-traveled tourist* are. A *well-traveled tourist* may be operationally defined as "a person who has traveled for the last five years at least once a year to a destination 500 miles or more away from his permanent residence."

Variables

Concepts that have been operationally defined become variables. *Variables* can be defined as "relational units of analysis that can assume any one of a number of designated sets of values" (Black and Champion 1976:34) or "properties that take on different values—a symbol to which numerals or values are assigned" (Kerlinger 1973:29-30). Examples of variables used in tourism research are: age, sex, income, education, trip expenditure, miles driven on vacation, and so on.

Variables have several qualities central to any scientific explanation:

1. They represent features that are changeable.
2. They can assume any one of a designated set of values.
3. They can be arranged in a certain time order with respect to each other, enhancing the prospects for asserting cause-effect relations among them (Black and Champion 1976:14).

Variables can be classified in at least three possible ways: (1) according to their relationships with each other, (2) according to the research design, and (3) according to their level of measurement.

Relationships with Each Other

Under this category variables can be divided into four types: independent, dependent, intervening, and control.

• *Independent* variables are so called because they are "independent" of the outcome itself; instead they are presumed to affect or influence the outcome. Sometimes they are referred to as *predictor* variables.

• *Dependent* variables are so called because they are "dependent" on the independent variables. They are presumed to be the effect of the independent variables. Dependent variables sometimes are referred to as *criterion* variables.

• *Intervening* variables are variables that come between the independent and the dependent variables. Intervening variables are sometimes referred to as *moderating* variables.

• *Control* variables are so called because they need to be held constant, or randomized, so that their effects are neutralized or compensated.

Research Design

In experimental design, the variables that are manipulated are called active variables (e.g., exposure to media), and the variables that are measured are called attribute variables (e.g., selection of tourist destination for yearly vacation).

Level of Measurement

Under this category, variables can be categorized as either *discrete* or *continuous*.

• *Discrete*, or *categorical*, variables are those variables that have a set of finite or fixed values. In such variables, there are two or more subsets of the set of objects being measured. All the members of the subset are considered the same, and all are assigned the same name and the same value. When a value is assigned to such a variable, it serves merely as a label or means of identification. Examples of such variables are religion (Protestant, Catholic, Jew, Muslim, other), occupation (physician, lawyer, dentist, and so on), sex (male, female). These variables are sometimes referred to as *nominal* or *polytomies*.

• *Continuous* variables have no separate and distinct categories; rather, there is continuum that represents gradually greater and greater amounts of the characteristic or quality. On such variables, subjects can differ among themselves by very large amounts or by infinitely small degrees. To provide descriptions of subjects, intervals representing equal amounts or degrees of the property are arbitrarily "marked off" along a scale. Height is one such variable, which can be marked off in inches or centimeters. In actual practice, the quantitative description assigned to a subject is never precise, but rather an approximation. If the measuring device is crude, the intervals may be few and broad. If the measuring device is more refined, the continuum can be marked off into a large number of narrow intervals, thereby providing much more precise descriptions. As the categories increase in number and become narrower and narrower, a true continuum is approached (Ghiselli, Campbell, and Zedeck 1981:25-26).

The specified relations between variables are expressed hypotheses.

Hypotheses

A hypothesis is a proposition that is stated in testable form and that predicts a particular relation between two or more variables. It is a tentative statement about things that the investigator wishes to support or to refute. Consider, for example, a possible relationship between age and preferred touristic activity. If it is assumed that some relationship exists between these two variables, then the form of the relationship must be stated; for example, H_a—"The older the tourist is, the less active will be his/her preferred touristic activities."

As stated earlier, hypotheses are important, indispensable, and powerful tools of scientific research. They are powerful because they appear in the form of predictions: if X, then Y. Even when hypotheses are not confirmed, they have power. Negative findings are sometimes as important as positive ones, since they cut down the total universe of ignorance and sometimes point out fruitful further hypotheses and lines of investigation (Kerlinger 1973:26).

Hypotheses can express relationships between variables in three different ways: *univariate*, *bivariate*, and *multivariate*. A *univariate* hypothesis is one that discusses a single variable; for example, "Tourism expenditures for the United States will increase between 1980 and 2000." A *bivariate* hypothesis is one that expresses the relationship between two variables—usually one dependent and one independent; for example, "The higher the number of English-speaking residents in a generating country, the higher is the propensity of those residents to travel to the United States." Finally, a hypothesis relating more than two variables is called a *multivariate*; for example, "The higher the proportion of English-speaking residents in a generating country (X_1) and the higher their disposable income (X_2), the higher will be the propensity of those residents to travel to the U.S. (Y_1)."

Hypotheses are usually stated in two forms: *null* hypotheses and *research* hypotheses. The *null* hypothesis (H_0) is the hypothesis of "no relationship" or "no difference"—it is the one actually tested statistically. It is set up for possible rejection and is an arbitrary convention, hypothesizing that any relation or difference in the findings is due to chance or sampling error (Isaac and Michael 1971:142).

The *research* hypothesis (H_a) states the expectations of the investigator in positive terms. The probability that one dependent variable has multiple causes (independent variables) is always greater than the probability that it is caused by a single independent variable; for example, the dependent variable "tourist expenditures" (Y_1) is likely to be influenced not only by disposable income (X_1) but also by occupation (X_2), education (X_3), exposure to media (X_4), and so on. Following this, if a hypothesis—X_1—was disproved (in other words, the X_1 null hypothesis was not rejected), it would be discarded in favor of other rival hypotheses—X_2, X_3, X_4—predicting the dependent variable Y_1. From this point of view, the task of scientific research is not confirming research hypotheses. Rather, it is rejecting the null hypotheses.

Even when one has rejected a null hypothesis, the corresponding research hypothesis has not been *fully* confirmed yet. All that it means is that the corresponding research hypothesis has *possibly* been supported. It cannot be fully supported as long as there are rival hypotheses that have not been disconfirmed. This logic leads one to the conclusion that hypotheses can only be discarded (Blalock and Blalock 1968:390).

RESEARCH DESIGN

Once the concepts, variables, and hypotheses have been formulated and stated, investigators need to consider their research design. A research design is a form of a carefully developed and controlled plan to carry the research investigation. It indicates what steps will be taken and in what sequence. A research design's major purpose is to ensure that the study will (1) be relevant to the problem and (2) employ economic procedures (Churchill 1978:46).

Types of Research Designs

Research designs can be categorized into three main types: exploratory, descriptive, and causal.

Exploratory Designs

Exploratory designs serve primarily to acquaint the investigator with the characteristics of the research problem. Studies using this design can have one or more of the following purposes (Selltiz, Wrightsman, and Cook 1976:90):

1. Formulation of problem for more precise investigation at a later date.
2. Generation of hypotheses for further study.
3. Familiarization with the problem.
4. Clarification of concepts, etc.

As can be seen from the above, the common denominator for all of these purposes is discovery of ideas and insights. Therefore, exploratory studies are usually flexible enough to permit consideration of all aspects of the research problem. It is important to point out that exploratory designs, in comparison with descriptive or causal designs, "seek relations" rather than "predict relations."

Consider, for example, the question of "Future Energy Impact on the Tourism Industry in the United States." Since the problem is too vague to be stated in hypotheses and statistically tested, one needs to conduct first an exploratory study that will clarify the concepts, define them, and generate specific hypotheses. More specifically, it is necessary to define and analyze the types of impacts (perceived or objective, economic or social), the individual or units impacted (tourists of types I_1—I_n, tourist enterprises of types K_1—K_n, destinations of types J_1—J_n, etc.), the manifestation of the impact and its measurement, and so on. An exploratory study concerned with this problem could probably be based on the 1979 summer gasoline shortage in the United States; such a study will help to formulate the problem for a more precise investigation at a later stage.

Descriptive Designs

Descriptive designs are used when the objective is systematic description, factually and accurately, of facts and characteristics of a given population or area of interest. In such designs, the investigator measures the subjects of interest as they exist naturally. Descriptive designs are used for one or more of the following purposes (Churchill 1978:53-54):

1. To describe the characteristics of certain groups (e.g., the sociodemographic characteristics of big spenders in U.S. tourism vs. little spenders).

2. To estimate the proportion of people in a specified population who behave in a certain way.

3. To make specific predictions or discover relations and interactions among variables (e.g., disposable income is positively associated with annual tourist expenditures).

Descriptive designs include all forms of research except experimental and historical, and they are not limited to any one method of data collection. Such designs cannot be used to establish causality. They can, however, provide investigators with a vast amount of information that will enable them to construct experimental designs that will permit determination of causality. Kerlinger (1973:379) refers to this type of design as Ex-Post Facto design and defines it as "systematic empirical inquiry in which the scientist does not have direct control of independent variables because their manifestations have already occurred or because they are inherently not manipulable." A descriptive design has several major weaknesses (Kerlinger 1973:390): (1) the inability to manipulate independent variables; (2) the lack of power to randomize; and (3) the risk of improper interpretation. In other words, it lacks rigid control measures. Despite its weaknesses, the majority of tourism research is conducted using this design because, in tourism, as in most other social sciences, the problems do not lend themselves to experimental design.

The two major types of descriptive designs are *surveys* and *case studies*.

Surveys are studies of large and small populations conducted by selecting and studying samples from the population to discover the relative incidence, distribution, and interrelations of variables (Kerlinger 1973:410). Sample surveys are conducted when the study of the population is impossible, difficult, or costly. Surveys have the following advantages compared to other designs:

1. Flexibility in choosing data collection techniques (e.g., mail questionnaire, interview, telephone interviews, etc.).
2. Possibility of generalization to the whole population and other similar populations.
3. Relative low cost per subject or unit of analysis.
4. Ability to collect large amounts of information.
5. High accuracy of results.

On the other hand, surveys have some serious weaknesses, such as shallow penetration, time-consuming, no control over individual responses (misconceptions, misunderstandings, etc.), and, in the case of attitudinal surveys, unstable reflections of the attitudes (attitudes may change very frequently and may be affected by many exogenous variables).

Survey-samples studies are very commonly used in the tourism industry. Two well-known examples of such surveys in the United States are the National Travel Survey, conducted by the Bureau of the Census as a part of the Census Transportation, and the Consumer Expenditures Survey, also conducted by the Bureau of the Census.

Case studies are thorough examinations of specific social settings or particular aspects of social settings (Black and Champion 1976:90). They constitute in-depth investigations of a given social unit resulting in a complete, well-organized picture of that unit (Isaac and Michael 1971:20). The major characteristic of case studies is that they usually examine a small number of units (sometimes even one) across a large number of variables, for example, a study of the personnel practices in one airline.

Case studies have the following advantages over other types of research designs (Black and Champion 1976:91):

1. They are flexible with respect to data-collection methods used.
2. They may be conducted in practically any kind of social setting.
3. They are inexpensive.

In addition, they can be useful for obtaining background information for planning major investigations and can serve as hypotheses generators. In other words, they can be used as economical substitutes to exploratory studies.

On the other hand, case studies have the following grave limitations: limited generalizability, time consuming, and vulnerable to subjective biases. In tourism, case studies have been used primarily by anthropologists who favor this method over any other.

Causal Designs

In the social sciences, as in natural sciences, the only viable way to determine causality among variables is by using an experimental design. Experimental design is a highly controlled method of attempting to demonstrate the existence of causal relationship between one or more independent variables and one or more dependent variables. In experimental design, the investigator has complete control over introduction of independent variables. In addition, he or she has control over the environment in which the experiment is conducted and over the composition of the experimental and control groups by random assignment of subjects. The experimental design offers the following advantages over any other research design: (1) establishes causality; (2) offers the best opportunity in control; and (3) provides the opportunity for studying change over time. Conversely, its greatest weaknesses are that it takes place in an artificial environment and that the experimenter's expectations can affect the results of the experiment (Bailey 1978:192-194). Experiments can be divided into two major types: laboratory and field.

A *laboratory experiment* is a research study in which the variance of all possible influential independent variables not pertinent to the immediate problem of investigation is kept at a minimum. This is done by isolating the research in a physical situation apart from the routine of ordinary living and by manipulating one or more independent variables under rigorously specified, operationalized, and controlled situations (Kerlinger 1973:398). Consider, for example, the following hypothetical laboratory experimental design set up for the purpose of determining the causal relationship between exposure to certain information and choice of tourist destination: A test facility resembling a travel agency is set up in which various similar destinations are displayed. The experimenter selects a group of subjects and randomly assigns them to two different groups: one that is exposed to information (experimental group) and one that is not exposed (control). Each subject is then given a free coupon to select a travel of their choice. Given the proper handling of the control over the destination selection and the subject's assignment, this design can determine the causal effect of information exposure over destination selection.

In *field experiments*, the behavior under examination takes place in its natural setting. The researcher exerts experimental control through matching rather than by physical means (Cox 1979:154-155). In addition, the experimenter can compare a situation in which the causal variable is present with another in which it is not and, from this, infer causality. Consider, for example, the hypothetical question of determining the impact of different packaging on destination selection using a field experiment design. The experimenter selects three travel agencies with clienteles that have been statistically matched, each agency offering a different package for the same destination while holding control (matching) over exogenous variables such as cost, number of days, and season of the year, among others. Any statistically significant difference in selection among the three agencies could be attributed to (caused by) the packaging.

In tourism, experimentation in both lab and field is most often avoided in the belief that subjects do not behave naturally under analysis. Except for a small group of tourism marketing researchers, all others—sociologists, psychologists, economists, recreationists, geographers, anthropologists, etc.—have neglected the experimental design. As Blalock and Blalock (1968:333) suggest, this is a grave error undertaken by most social scientists, for the experimental method can be a necessary and valuable tool in the study of social phenomena.

DATA COLLECTION TECHNIQUES

The purpose of the various data collection techniques is to produce trustworthy evidence that is relevant to the research question being asked (Selltiz, Wrightsman, and Cook 1976:161). The instruments used to collect the data are usually acceptable definitions of the important variables and have proper measurement characteristics.

Essentially, there are three means of collecting data. First, data can be obtained by the investigator observing the phenomena. Second, data can be obtained by the investigator or his or her agents communicating directly with the subjects. Third, data can be obtained from secondary sources, that has been collected for another purpose. Each of these three categories can be further broken down in specific techniques. The remainder of this section will discuss the specific techniques within each category and analyze their appropriate use.

Observation

Observation can be defined as "the process of watching and listening to other persons' behavior over time without controlling or manipulating it and recording findings in ways that permit some degree of analytical interpretation" (Black and Champion 1976:330). Observation is a primary technique for collecting data on nonverbal behavior, and it is used when it is important to understand dynamic behavioral processes in natural settings. This technique is not concerned with what a respondent places on paper or says in an interview, but deals with the behavior of persons (Pelegrino 1979). Observational methods are used for the following purposes (Selltiz, Wrightsman, and Cook 1976:255):

1. When there is a need to describe behavioral patterns (e.g., tourists' behavior in a disco).
2. When the research phenomenon cannot be investigated in the laboratory (e.g., mass behavior).
3. When there is a need to describe ongoing behavior as it occurs (e.g., dining in a restaurant).

Observational methods have the following advantages over other data collection techniques: they (a) are superior to any other data collection method for the study of nonverbal behavior, (b) take place in a natural setting, and (c) enable the study of phenomena or subjects over a much longer time period than other methods.

On the other hand, they have some disadvantages, too, such as: (a) lack of control over the environment and possible extraneous contamination; (b) difficulty in quantifying; (c) usually restricted to small samples, which makes generalization very difficult; and (d) possibility of objections and lack of cooperation from subjects due to lack of anonymity (Bailey 1978:217-218).

There are two major types of observational methods: participant observation and nonparticipant observation. In the *participant observation*, the investigator is a part of the natural setting in which the observation is being made, but the investigator's role as a researcher is not known to other participants; for example, an investigator joins a Caribbean cruise as a tourist and, while on board, observes tourists' behavior. In the *nonparticipant observation*, the investigator observes the behavior of others in a natural setting but is not an actual participant in the behavior being examined. The investigator's role as outside member and investigator is known to all participants; for example, a fully dressed investigator observes and records tourists' behavior on a beach.

In the tourism research field, the observation method is not very popular and is mostly used by anthropologists who study either tourists' behavior or the local residents' reaction to the tourism phenomenon.

Techniques for Direct Communication with Subjects

Within this category, three specific techniques will be analyzed: the questionnaire, the interview, and projective methods.

Questionnaires

The questionnaire is a pencil-and-paper measurement instrument used when data is collected by means of self-reporting techniques (Cox 1979:192). Questionnaires are either mailed or handed face-to-face to the respondents and filled out by them without any help from the investigator. In questionnaires, the information obtained is limited to the written responses of respondents to prearranged questions (Selltiz, Wrightsman, and Cook 1976:294). All questionnaires perform at least two functions: (1) description of individual or group characteristics and (2) measurement of individual and/or group variables such as values, attitudes, opinions, and so on (Black and Champion 1976:380). Four classes of questions normally appear on survey questionnaires: demographics, behavior, knowledge, and attitude. While the last three types may be specific to an investigator's particular survey, the demographics questions should be worded according to common conventions. Such wordings can be found in various polls such as the Gallup Poll, the CBS-*New York Times* Poll, and the Public Opinion Quarterly to name a few. The most important goal of a questionnaire is to provide complete, valid, and reliable information from respondents (Bailey 1978:132). Questionnaires may be classified according to (1) type of response required and (2) type of questionnaire administration (Black and Champion 1976:383-389).

Type of Response Required

Responses to questionnaires may be (a) fixed, (b) open-ended, or (c) a combination of fixed and open-ended. The following is an example of one question asked in an open-ended format and in a fixed format.

Open-ended—Please state below the major reason for your visit to this destination. _____
_____
_____

Fixed—What is the major reason for your visit to this destination?
　　Please select one category only.

1. Visit friends and relatives
2. Recreation
3. Business
4. Sightseeing
5. Health
6. Other (please specify) _____
_____

Type of Questionnaire Administration

Questionnaires can be administered in two ways: (a) by mail and (b) in person.

a. Mailed questionnaires are administered by mailing to designated subjects a form with instructions for completing it, a cover letter explaining the purpose of the study, and a self-addressed, stamped envelope for the return of the questionnaire.
b. In person, questionnaires are handed by an investigator or his or her agents to the respondents, who are asked to complete the questionnaire in the investigator's presence and return it.

Questionnaires have the following advantages over other data collection techniques:

1. Are relatively inexpensive.
2. Require almost no skills to administer.
3. Assure respondents' anonymity (if properly designed).
4. Can be administered to a large number of respondents simultaneously.
5. Can be sent through the mail.
6. Eliminate interviewer bias.
7. Enable standardization and uniformity.

On the other hand, questionnaires have some disadvantages too, the major ones being that they:

1. Have a low response rate (with mailed questionnaires, it is not unusual to have a response rate as low as 20%).
2. Are restricted to verbal behavior.
3. Lack control over the research setting (Bailey 1978:156; Selltiz, Wrightsman, and Cook 1976:296).

Interviews

A research interview is a face-to-face interpersonal role situation in which one person, the interviewer, asks a person being interviewed, the respondent, questions designed to obtain answers pertinent to the research problem (Kerlinger 1973:481).

In research, interviews are used either as the major means of data collection or as a supplement for other methods. In addition, they can be used as exploratory devices to help identify variables and relations and to generate hypotheses. Interviews can be classified into two major types according to the degree to which they are structured: unstructured and structured.

Unstructured interviews are a free form of conversation in which the interviewer probes the general nature of the problem he is interested in, and asks the interviewee questions about it. It is a flexible form in which the content of the questions, their sequence, and their wording are left to the discretion of the interviewer.

Structured interviews, on the other hand, are more uniform and rigid. In this type of interview the questions, their sequence, and the wording are fixed. The interviewer usually reads the questions from interview schedules that have been previously prepared (Black and Champion 1976:364-368; Kerlinger 1973:481).

The interview has the following advantages over other data collection techniques:

1. Permits greater depth and probing.
2. Often has a higher response rate than questionnaires.
3. Provides information on nonverbal behavior.
4. Enables control over the environment in which it is conducted.
5. Enables spontaneity.
6. Provides greater sensitivity to misunderstanding by respondents.
7. More appropriate for revealing information about feelings and emotions regarding different subjects.

On the other hand, it also has the following disadvantages:

1. Very costly.
2. Time consuming.
3. Prone to interviewer personal bias.
4. Usually lacking in anonymity.
5. Inconvenient.
6. Contaminated by the eagerness of the respondent to please the interviewer (Bailey 1978:157-159; Selltiz, Wrightsman, and Cook 1976:296-297; Isaac and Michael 1971:96).

The interview technique is used extensively in tourism research.

Projective Methods

Projective methods are any one of a number of specific tests wherein a subject is presented with a visual or audio stimulus and is asked to respond. In this situation, the response is not taken at face value but is viewed as a clue to the subject's private interpretation of the stimulus or of his or her self or world. This is an indirect data collection technique since it avoids direct questions about the topic of interest and even disguises it.

Implicit in the use of projective methods is the assumption that the way an individual organizes a relatively unstructured stimulus (e.g., interprets a picture) reflects the basic trends in his or her perceptions of the world and his or her response to it (Selltiz, Wrightsman, and Cook 1976:333).

Projective methods are used in cases in which subjects may be unwilling or unable to discuss controversial topics, to reveal intimate information about themselves, or to express their undesirable attitudes and opinions.

One of the most frequently used projective techniques is the Rorschach Inkblot Test, consisting of a series of inkblots. The subject is asked to describe what he or she sees in each inkblot. Another technique is the Thematic Apperception Test (TAT): the subject is confronted with a series of pictures and asked to tell a story about each. Other tests include word association, sentence completion, figure drawing, and so on. For a comprehensive listing of projective methods, as well as other psychological tests, please consult: Buros, O.

(ed.), *The Mental Measurements Yearbook*, Highland Park, NJ: Gryphon; and/or Buros, O. (ed.), *Tests in Print*, Highland Park, NJ: Gryphon.

The use of projective techniques in tourism research is relatively scarce and restricted to psychologists and some marketing researchers. This is quite unfortunate since the techniques have a valuable potential in the field of tourism motivation. The present author demonstrates in class the utility of projective methods by use of the following experiential exercises. Students are shown pictures of two destinations—one, Daytona Beach, Florida (or Club Mediterranean in Martinique), and the other, Miami Beach (or the Catskill Mountains, New York)—and asked to describe the type of tourist who goes to each. The Daytona Beach (or Martinique) tourist is usually described as a young, well-to-do, educated, energetic, and creative individual, while the Miami (or Catskills) tourist is described as an elderly, lazy, insecure, unintelligent, and boring New York resident. These findings can be used to interpret the image college students have of these destinations.

Secondary Data

Secondary data are data gathered not for the immediate study at hand but for some other purpose. Secondary data can be obtained from either private sources or public sources.

Private sources of secondary data include both personal documents and published materials of various companies, voluntary organizations, research organizations, and other societies.

Public sources include data archives (e.g., Social Science Data Archives) and governmental data (e.g., U.S. Census, Census of Transportation, Consumer Expenditures Survey). Many of the above listed sources, especially the public ones, contain statistical data on socioeconomic demographic characteristics of samples and populations and are readily available for public use. For more information on this topic, see Chapter 8, "Travel and Tourism Information Sources."

The use of already collected data has the advantage of being low in cost (or often free), and no time is required to collect it. On the other hand, it may not fit perfectly for the research problem as defined and, in many cases, may be out of date (Churchill 1978:128-129).

No matter which of the data collection techniques is used, an investigator has the responsibility to analyze the validity, reliability, and sensitivity of his or her instruments before using them. *Validity* is the degree to which the instrument predicts a criterion; for example, if a questionnaire is developed to measure residents' attitudes towards tourism, validity in that case will be the extent to which people's scores on the questionnaire will correspond to their "true" attitude towards tourism. This type of validity is referred to as criterion-related validity and is the most important of all validities. Other types of validity include content validity construct, validity, and face validity. *Reliability* is the extent to which a measure gives consistent results. It is the accuracy or precision of a measuring instrument. A reliable instrument will tend to elicit the same results each time it is applied

under the same circumstances; for example, a reliable test intended to measure "touristic innovativeness" should produce similar results when administered repeatedly to the same group of subjects under the same conditions. *Sensitivity* is the extent to which an instrument is capable of making distinctions fine enough for the purpose it serves; for instance, an instrument intended to measure a tourist's satisfaction with a destination should be sensitive enough to measure not only "satisfied" or "dissatisfied," but also the degree of satisfaction or dissatisfaction (e.g., a five-point scale, 1 indicating complete dissatisfaction, 5 complete satisfaction, and 3 a neutral reaction).

SELECTION OF SUBJECTS

Once the data collection techniques have been selected, the next step in the research process is to select those elements from which the information will be collected. One way of doing this would be by studying all elements within the population (a census); another way would be to collect information from a portion of the population by taking a sample of it. The term *population* as it is used in this context does not refer only to individuals—it refers to entire groups having some common characteristics. These groups may be objects, materials, individuals, organizations, states, countries, and so on. The sum total of all the groups (or units of analysis) is a population (Bailey 1978:69).

Ideally, one would want to study the entire population. Often, however, it is impossible or infeasible to do this, and, therefore, one must settle for a sample. A sample is a portion of elements taken from a population (Black and Champion 1976:265). It is a proportion of the population and is considered to be representative of that population (Kerlinger 1973:118). A sample is always viewed as an approximation of the whole (population) rather than as a whole in itself.

There are four major advantages of using samples rather than populations (Pelegrino 1979:74):

1. Is less expensive.
2. Enables speedier processing of data and presentation of results.
3. Can secure more information per dollar from one investigation.
4. Enables accuracy with known precision, which may be specified in advance and calculated from the sample itself.

Types of Sampling Procedures

Sampling procedures can be divided into two major types: probability and nonprobability.

Probability Sampling

In probability sampling, each element of the population has a known nonzero chance of being included in the sample (Churchill 1978:299). Probability samples can be subdivided into four specific techniques: simple random sampling; systematic sampling; stratified sampling; and cluster sampling.

• *Simple random sampling* is the best known form of probability sampling. It is a method of drawing a sample of a population so that each element of the population will have an equal chance of being included (Kerlinger 1973:118).

• *Systematic sampling* is a probability sampling procedure involving the selection of successive sampling units at a specified interval throughout the sample (Cox 1979:272). Systematic sampling is one of the most convenient forms of probability sampling, certainly the most popular, and often a good approximation of random sampling.

• *Stratified sampling* is a probability sampling technique that is distinguished by the following two-step procedure (Churchill 1978:317):

1. The population is divided into mutually exclusive and exhaustive subsets.
2. A random sample of elements is chosen from each subset.

Stratified sampling can be done by using two or more variables simultaneously (e.g., gender and education: Male College Educated/Female College Educated; Male High School Educated/Female High School Educated; Male Elementary School Educated/Female Elementary School Educated).

Stratified samples can be either proportionate or disproportionate. Proportionate stratified samples have specified characteristics in exact proportion to the way in which those same characteristics are distributed in the population (e.g., 50% males, 50% females). In disproportionate samples, the substrata are not necessarily distributed according to the proportionate distribution in the population from which they were drawn (e.g., 30% males, 70% females).

• *Cluster sampling* is a simple random sample in which each sampling unit is a collection or cluster of elements (Bailey 1978:80). In this type of sample, individuals are not selected at random. Rather the sampling unit is a "bunch" or cluster of elements (Pelegrino 1979:326). Cluster sampling involves the following steps (Churchill 1978:326):

1. The population is divided into mutually exclusive and exhaustive subsets.
2. A random sample of the subsets is selected.
3. All the population elements in the selected subsets are used in the sample.

Cluster samples can be single-stage or multistage, in which case steps 1 and 2 are repeated as many times as is necessary and then step 3 is performed.

Nonprobability Sampling

Nonprobability samples are those samples that provide no basis for estimating how closely the sample characteristics approximate the characteristics of the population from which the sample was obtained (Black and Champion 1976:267). Since nonprobability sampling does not depend upon chance as a selection procedure, the researcher cannot properly con-

trol the probability of a unit being included in the sample and, therefore, cannot claim representativeness of the population. This is a serious and major weakness of this sampling type. However, as stated by Kerlinger (1973:129), this weakness can be mitigated, to some extent, by using knowledge, expertise, and care in selecting samples.

Nonprobability samples can be divided into three major techniques: judgmental sampling; quota sampling; and convenience sampling.

• Judgmental sampling, or purposive sampling, is a sampling procedure in which the representativeness of the sample is based on an evaluation by the researcher or some other "expert" (Cox 1979:369). In this case, the researcher uses "expert" judgment as to which respondents to choose, and picks only those who meet the purpose of the study. This judgment is a deliberate effort to obtain representativeness by including "presumably typical" population elements in the sample (Kerlinger 1973:129).

• Quota sampling is an attempt to ensure that the sample is representative by selecting elements in such a way that the proportion of the sample elements possessing a certain characteristic is approximately the same as the proportion in the population (Churchill 1978:303). Quota sampling derives its name from the practice of assigning quotas, or a proportion of sample units, for interviewers (Kerlinger 1973:129).

• Convenience sampling is a procedure in which representativeness of the sample is sacrificed for the sake of ease in obtaining the sample (Cox 1979:268). In this sampling method, the investigator chooses the closest units as respondents. Convenience sampling is undoubtedly the weakest form of sampling but, unfortunately, the most frequently used. The basic problem with this technique is that certain elements have a very high probability of being included in the sample, while others have none. Thus, the sample becomes unrepresentative, inconsistent, and biased (Cox 1979:268).

For more information on samples and sampling techniques, see Chapter 12 "Issues in Sampling and Sample Design—A Managerial Perspective."

DATA PROCESSING AND INFORMATION ANALYSIS

The last two steps in a tourism research investigation that need to be planned before the actual execution of the study are data processing and information analysis.

Data processing is an operation on data to achieve a desired result. It involves the conversion or reduction of the collected information to a form that will permit statistical tabulation, ease of storage, and access for future use (Selltiz, Wrightsman, and Cook 1976:434). Data processing can be done either manually or with the aid of the computer. To prepare the data for proper processing, the investigator needs to code the data. The process of coding involves the translation of the data into symbolic form by using numbers to represent the information. Coding is performed at the conclusion of the data collection. However, the planning and development of the coding scheme are done at the time the research instrument is developed. The coding scheme, or coding manual, is an outline that describes what is coded and how it is to be coded.

If the processing is to be done by computer, then the investigator needs to plan and develop not only a coding scheme but also a means of converting the data that permits it to be analyzed, stored, and retrieved by the computer (i.e., magnetic tapes, disks).

The purpose of *information analysis* is to summarize the completed data collected in such a manner that it yields answers to the research questions. Like data processing, information analysis is conducted after the information has been collected; however, the planning for analysis should be done in the earlier stage of the investigation. This planning scheme should specify the various forms of tabulation anticipated and the kind of statistical analysis of data that is to be performed.

Once the data processing and information analysis plans have been completed, the process of planning a tourism research investigation is terminated. What remains to do is the actual collection of data, its processing and analysis, and the interpretation and drawing of inferences.

In summary, what this chapter has attempted to achieve is a presentation of the sequential steps in the conduct of a tourism research investigation. These steps, as stated previously, need to be planned well in advance of their execution to assure valid, reliable, and cost-effective results.

Those readers who would be interested to learn more about social science research methodology are advised to look into some of the publications and manuals mentioned in the references.

REFERENCES

Aaker, David A., and George S. Day (1990), *Marketing Research*, 4th ed., New York: John Wiley & Sons, Inc.

Adams, Gerald R., and Jay D. Schvaneveldt (1985), *Understanding Research Methods*, New York: Longman.

Bailey, Kenneth D. (1978), *Methods of Social Research*, New York: Free Press.

Bailey, Kenneth D. (1982), *Methods of Social Research*, 2nd ed., New York: Free Press.

Balsley, Howard L., and Vernon T. Clover (1988), *Research for Business Decisions: Business Research Methods*, 4th ed., Columbus, OH: Publishing Horizons.

Black, James A., and Dean J. Champion (1976), *Methods and Issues in Social Research*, New York: John Wiley & Sons, Inc.

Blalock, Hubert M.J. (1982), *Conceptualization and Measurement in Social Sciences*, Beverly Hills, CA: Sage Publications.

Blalock, Hubert M.J. and Ann B. Blalock (1968), *Methodology in Social Research*, New York: McGraw-Hill.

Bordens, Kenneth S., and Bruce B. Abbott (1988), *Research*

Design and Methods: A Process Approach, Mountain View, CA: Mayfield Publishing Co.

Boyd, Harper W., Jr., Ralph Westfall, and Stanley F. Stasch (1989), *Marketing Research: Text and Cases,* 7th ed., Homewood, IL: Richard D. Irwin, Inc.

Breen, George E., and Albert B. Blankenship (1989), *Do-It-Yourself Marketing Research,* 3rd ed., New York: McGraw Hill.

Brown, Francis E. (1980), *Marketing Research: A Structure for Decision Making,* Reading, MA: Addison Wesley.

Churchill, Gilbert A., Jr. (1987), *Marketing Research: Methodological Foundations,* 4th ed., Chicago: Dryden Press.

Cox, Eli P., III (1979), *Marketing Research—Information for Decision Making,* New York: Harper & Row.

Einstein, Albert, and L. Infeld (1938), *The Evolution of Physics,* New York: Simon & Schuster.

Ferber, Robert, ed. (1978), *Readings in Survey Research,* Chicago: American Marketing Association.

Galtung, Johan (1967), *Theory and Methods of Social Research,* New York: Columbia University Press.

Ghiselli, Edwin E., John P. Campbell, and Sheldon Zedeck (1981), *Measurement Theory for the Behavioral Sciences,* San Francisco: W. H. Freeman & Co.

Green, Paul E., Donald S. Tull, and Gerald Albaum (1988), *Research for Marketing Decisions,* 5th ed., Englewood Cliffs, NJ: Prentice Hall.

Hakim, Catherine (1987), *Research Design,* London: Allen and Unwin.

Isaac, Stephen, and William B. Michael (1971), *Handbook in Research and Evaluation,* San Diego, CA: Edits Publishers.

Isaac. Stephen, and William B. Michael (1981), *Handbook in Research and Evaluation,* 2nd ed., San Diego, CA: Edits Publishers.

Jorgensen, Danny L. (1989), *Participant Observation,* Newbury Park: Sage Publications.

Kerlinger, Fred N. (1973), *Foundations of Behavioral Research,* 2nd ed., New York: Holt, Rinehart & Winston.

Kerlinger, Fred N. (1986), *Foundations of Behavioral Research,* 3rd ed., New York: Holt, Rinehart & Winston.

Kidder, Louise H. (1981), *Selltiz Wrightsman and Cook's Research Methods in Social Relations,* 4th ed., New York: Holt, Rinehart & Winston.

Kress, George (1988), *Marketing Research,* 3rd ed., Englewood Cliffs, NJ: Prentice Hall.

Leavitt, Fred (1991), *Research Methods for Behavioral Scientists,* Dubuque, Iowa: Wm. C. Brown.

Miles, Matthew B., and A. Michael Huberman (1984), *Qualitative Data Analysis,* Newbury Park, MA: Sage Publications.

Miller, Delbert C. (1970), *Handbook of Research Design and Social Measurement,* 2nd ed., New York: David McKay Co.

Miller, Delbert C. (1983), *Handbook of Research Design and Social Measurement,* 4th ed., New York: Longman.

Neale, John M., and Robert M. Liebert (1986), *Science and Behavior: An Introduction to Methods of Research,* 3rd ed., Englewood Cliffs, NJ: Prentice Hall.

Peterson, Robert A. (1988), *Marketing Research,* 2nd ed., Plano, Texas: Business Publications.

Pelegrino, Donald A. (1979), *Research Methods for Recreation and Leisure,* Dubuque, Iowa: William C. Brown Co.

Selltiz, Claire, Lawrence S. Wrightsman, and Stuart W. Cook (1976), *Research Methods for Social Relations,* 3rd ed., New York: Holt, Rinehart & Winston.

Stewart, David W. (1984), *Secondary Research: Information Sources and Methods,* Beverly Hills, CA: Sage Publications.

Van Dalen, D.B., and W.J. Meyer (1966), *Understanding Educational Research,* New York: McGraw-Hill.

Webster, Noah (1963), *Webster's Third New International Dictionary,* Springfield, MA.: C. & C. Merriam Publishing Co.

Weiers, Ronald M. (1988), *Marketing Research,* 2nd ed., Englewood Cliffs, NJ: Prentice Hall.

Yin, Robert K. (1984), *Case Studies Research: Design and Methods,* Beverly Hills, CA: Sage Publications.

Zikmund, William G. (1985), *Exploring Marketing Research,* 2nd ed., Chicago: Dryden Press.

10

Demand Forecasting and Estimation

BRIAN ARCHER
Department of Management Studies for Tourism
and Hotel Industries
University of Surrey
Guildford, Surrey, England

In economic terms, demand can be defined as the quantity of a product or service that people are willing and able to buy during a given period of time. In consequence, demand forecasting is the art of predicting the level of demand that might occur at some future time or period of time. This chapter describes the strengths, weaknesses, and limitations of the principal forecasting methods and their applicability in the field of tourism and travel. Sections of the chapter deal with the need for forecasting, the problems faced by forecasters, and forecasting as an aid to management decision making.

THE NEED FOR FORECASTING

Since the future is not predetermined, no forecast can guarantee complete accuracy. The aim of demand forecasting, therefore, is to predict the *most probable* level of demand that is likely to occur in the light of known circumstances or, when alternative policies are proposed, to show what different levels of demand may be achieved.

Forecasting should be an essential element in the process of management. No manager can avoid the need for some form of forecasting: a manager must plan for the future in order to minimize the risk of failure or, more optimistically, to maximize the possibilities of success. In order to plan, the manager must use forecasts. Forecasts will always be made, whether by guesswork, teamwork, or the use of complex models, and the accuracy of the forecasts will affect the quality of the management decision.

Forecasts are needed for marketing, production, and financial planning. Top-management needs demand forecasts for implementing long-term objectives; lower echelons of management require forecasts to plan their activities over a more limited horizon. In the tourism industry, in common with most other service sectors, the need to forecast accurately is especially acute because of the perishable nature of the product. Unfilled airline seats and unused hotel rooms cannot be stockpiled, and demand must be anticipated and even manipulated.

CHOICE OF METHOD

The question that should be asked is not whether to forecast, but how to forecast. The method chosen, the amount of detail provided, the frequency of the need for forecasts, and the time horizon of the forecasts vary according to the differing requirements of managers in different parts of the industry. In every case, however, it is essential that a forecast should:

• Provide the information required by managers
• Cover the specified time periods for which the forecast is needed
• Be of sufficient quality for its purpose

Within these constraints, several factors govern the approach adopted and influence the choice of method or combination of methods employed.

FACTORS GOVERNING THE CHOICE OF METHOD

The Purpose of the Forecast

The objectives of forecasts vary widely and, in order to select a suitable method, forecasters need to know the amount of detail required by managers and in what form it is useful; for example, tourism demand can be forecast by market area, by market segment, by region, by month, by season, or by some combination of these.

The Time Period for Which the Forecast Is Required and the Degree of Accuracy Which Is Needed

Different methods are used to make short-, medium-, and long-term forecasts and, in order to choose an appropriate method, forecasters need to know the time horizon required by policymakers and planners.

Short-term demand forecasts (up to two or three years) are normally built up from the available detail, but, in the longer run, the emphasis is often placed on forecasting overall levels of demand and then breaking these down into their main segments. The former approach is called "bottom-up" forecasting and the latter "top-down."

Other things being equal, the more distant the forecast's time horizon, the lower is the degree of accuracy attainable. Even so, the accuracy of long-term forecasts can be much improved if appropriate methods are used.

The Availability of Information

The choice of appropriate forecasting methods is constrained by the reliability and accuracy of the information available as well as the time horizon of the forecast. However rigorous the forecasting method, the results are unlikely to be accurate if the basic data are suspect or contain biases that cannot be removed. In such cases and also where insufficient data are obtainable, mathematical and econometric forecasting techniques should give way to more qualitative methods.

The Forecasting Environment

The multivariate nature of the factors affecting tourism demand makes analysis very difficult and renders forecasts liable to various forms of error. This is particularly true in the case of long-term forecasts, and, in such cases, it is important that the approach adopted should take into account the many economic, social, political, technological, and competitive factors that may affect future demand.

The Cost of Producing Forecasts

The costs of establishing and operating different forecasting methods vary widely. For some purposes, the simplest and cheapest methods can provide adequate results. To meet other needs, highly sophisticated computer models with an exhaustive appetite for expensively acquired data are essential. In general terms, forecasters should choose the simplest, least expensive method that is capable of providing all the information needed by managers.

FORECASTING METHODS

Mathematical, econometric, or other quantitative methods can be used to analyze and generate data, or the qualitative opinions of experts can be used to predict future demand. Perhaps the most successful approaches are those that involve both quantitative and qualitative analyses. Rarely,

however, is such a comprehensive approach adopted, although the forecasting methods used by some of the more progressive airlines and national tourist boards go some way towards meeting this ideal.

QUANTITATIVE TECHNIQUES

Three types of quantitative techniques are available—univariate, causal, and systems models—although some of the more sophisticated models incorporate elements of each. Univariate models are based upon the premise that what has happened in the past has some relevance for the future. They ignore the determinants of demand per se and assume that the effects of causal factors are already implicit in the past data of the variable to be forecast. Forecasts are obtained by analyzing movements in the data and extrapolating these forward into the future. In consequence, although they may provide accurate forecasts, they give no reasons for the predictions. Causal models, on the other hand, take into account the principal factors influencing demand and analyze their separate effects upon the variable under consideration. Forecasts are made by calculating the impact on demand of predicted changes in causal factors such as income levels, relative prices, and the cost of travel. Systems models describe the operation of systems and/or economies and can be used to assess the effects of changes in demand on their operation.

Univariate Models

All of the approaches described in this section are *univariate*; that is, they are concerned solely with the statistical analysis of past data for the variable to be forecast. Such models are available in varying degrees of sophistication from simple trend extrapolation to highly complex mathematical algorithms, involving the analysis and projection of individual components of the data.

Simple Trend Projection

In cases where the data exhibit great regularity, forecasts can be obtained merely by extrapolating the principal trends. The most common relationships are linear, exponential, and cyclical, and the objective is to project these curves forward into the future. Since it is unrealistic to expect these relationships to hold for more than a limited period, simple trend projection is suitable only for very short-term forecasting.

One variant of trend projection, however, known because of its shape as an S-curve, is used in some industries for long-term forecasting. This technique is used to analyze past demand over a period of several years and, on the basis of the mathematical relationship disclosed, to forecast by making various assumptions about the future growth path of demand. Because of the heroic nature of the assumptions that have to be made, the technique should be regarded as no more than a useful aid to forecasting, and its results in isolation should be treated with extreme caution. It can be used, however, as an adjunct to several of the qualitative approaches described later in this chapter.

Arithmetic Moving Averages

Another naive technique that can produce usable results is to base the forecast on an arithmetic moving average of previous data. In essence, the data for previous years, months, or seasons are added together and divided by the number of observations to give an average figure. When the next observation becomes available, the oldest in the sequence is dropped, the new one is included, and a new average is calculated. Unfortunately, the presence of linear or cyclical trends in the data causes the moving average to lag behind the movement of the data. Although methods exist to ameliorate the effects of such lags, the technique in its simplest forms is not accurate enough to produce reliable forecasts.

Decomposition Analysis

A more sophisticated use of moving averages is to break down (decompose) the main components in the time series and to analyze each of these mathematically. The task is to identify each of the principal components—seasonal variations, secular trends, and irregular fluctuations—and to produce formulae that describe their interrelationships. Forecasts are produced by applying moving averages, where relevant, to each of the data series. The forecasts are updated by including new data as soon as they become available. This approach can be used with any tourism data that exhibit sufficient regularity.

Perhaps the most successful application of this technique in the field of tourism is the work of Baron (1975) in Israel, who forecasts tourist arrivals, foreign currency earnings from tourists, the demand for bed-nights in hotels, and the numbers of residents departing.

Because moving averages inevitably lag behind movements of the data, decomposition analysis is not an appropriate technique to use when substantial changes are taking place in the data.

Exponential Smoothing

Moving averages, however, can be estimated exponentially as well as arithmetically. In such cases, the object is to produce a weighted moving average of past data with the weights assigned in geometric progression so that the heaviest weights are given to the most recent data and past data are discounted more heavily. As in the case of arithmetic moving averages, the data are then extrapolated into the future to produce a forecast.

If, however, the time series data contains trends, a simple, or single, exponential smoothing model is not appropriate. The effect of trends can be identified by the use of a double exponential smoothing model, for example, Brown's model (1963), which produces forecasts containing both a constant-level term and a linear-trend term. If in addition, however, the data contains seasonal factors, an alternative double exponential smoothing model, such as the Holt-Winters method

(Holt 1957 and Winters 1960) or the program STAMP, can be used to forecast these seasonal effects as well as the constant-level term and the linear-trend term.

Largely because of the assumptions of compound growth inherent in geometric progressions, exponential smoothing is not suitable for medium- or long-term forecasting. Although in isolation it is infrequently used as a forecasting technique, it forms an intrinsic element in the Box-Jenkins approach in the following paragraphs.

Autoregressive Models

It is quite common in time series for there to be a strong relationship between the data for any one time period and the corresponding data for the preceding time period. Indeed, many simple and naive forecasting models are based upon this observation. More rigorous forecasts, however, can be produced by the use of stepwise autoregressive models. The technique involves the use of a stepwise regression model, which adds data for past years one at a time into the calculation until no further data is statistically significant. The aim is to select only the minimum set of data necessary to produce a forecast and to omit data that is statistically insignificant. Such models are very flexible and, unlike many forecasting methods, can be used in cases where the trends are nonlinear.

Box-Jenkins Method I

The time series approach developed by George Box and Gwilym Jenkins (1970) is a highly sophisticated technique that is relatively inexpensive to use.

Basically the approach is (1) to identify the form of model that expresses relatively well the relationships between the values of a series of data through time, and then (2) to use the model to calculate numerical values for these relationships. Unlike other mathematical forecasting methods, therefore, the model is purpose-built to fit the data. In addition, a systematic process is used to allow identification, estimation, and diagnostic checking.

The technique can provide short- and medium-term forecasts as accurately as most causal approaches. An interesting example of the degree of accuracy attainable with this method can be seen in a study of tourism in Hawaii (Guerts and Ibrahim 1975). Their 24-month forecast of tourist arrivals in the state was shown to have an average forecast error of only 3.5 percent—a level of accuracy that would be very acceptable for any causal model.

In its simplest forms, the Box-Jenkins method is univariate; that is, it is concerned with the extrapolation of a time series of data based on its own movements through time. It can be used to predict when, but not why, demand may change and in consequence, it cannot be used to assess the impact of changes in any of the factors that influence demand. Yet Box and Jenkins themselves (1970:337-420) showed how the model can be adapted to take some causal factors into account (see Box-Jenkins Method II following). It is in this latter form that the technique provides a bridge between simple univariate time series analysis and the causal approaches described below.

Causal Models

Causal models involve the analysis of data for other variables considered to be related to the one under consideration and the use of these to forecast demand for the variable of interest. The approaches vary in sophistication from the use of simple indicators and surveys to the application of complex mathematical and econometric techniques.

Indicators

A simplistic causal approach is to study an individual or a combination of time series data for other economic activities to forecast tourist arrivals, without using a modeling approach. If it were possible to identify one or more time series that always gave correct indications of tourism demand, there would be no need to use more sophisticated forecasting techniques. Unfortunately, the factors governing tourism demand are very complex, and it would be unusual if all indicators (or barometers) gave the same signal at the same time. Hence, although indicators are a useful aid to forecasting for predicting the direction of changes and turnabouts in activity, alone they cannot achieve the degree of accuracy attainable by using more rigorous approaches.

Box-Jenkins Method II

Although normally used in its univariate form, more sophisticated versions of the Box-Jenkins method involve the use of a transfer function, which takes into account the movement through time of another variable or variables thought to affect the one of concern.

Thus, for example, forecasts can be made of tourist arrivals at a particular destination country by relating tourist arrivals to movements in real incomes per capita in the tourists' countries of origin. (It may prove necessary, however, to use time lags to allow the effect of the changes in income to be reflected in the arrivals data.)

An interesting application of this method is a study of tourist arrivals in Puerto Rico (Wandner and Van Erden 1979), where forecasts were obtained by relating the time series data for tourist arrivals to changing levels of unemployment in New York, the principal origin area.

It is in its transfer function form that the Box-Jenkins method offers its most effective medium-term alternative to econometric model building.

Market Analysis

Surveys—of tourists, potential tourists, or business establishments—are perhaps the most popular form of market analysis. Although not strictly a quantitative method, surveys can provide valuable data and useful insight into potential demand. Unfortunately, surveys aimed at discovering the future intentions of tourists are rarely accurate: apart from the normal difficulties of obtaining a representative sample when the potential tourists are numerous and difficult to locate, tourists rarely plan their holidays more than one year ahead, and, for most, the planning horizon, at least as far as a particular destination is concerned, is even shorter.

Nevertheless, for very-short-term forecasts, surveys can yield valuable information. The Austrian National Tourist Office (Schulmeister 1973), for example, carries out surveys of tourism managers and hotel owners in selected areas of the country at the beginning of winter and summer to discover their expectations for the coming season. The results are then grossed-up to give representative figures for the whole of the country.

Because of the inherent weaknesses and limitations of survey techniques, however, it is unrealistic to use the results of such surveys for medium- or long-term forecasts. There are, however, three other forms of market analysis. One of these, Sales Force Estimates, is considered later as a qualitative technique. The other two are described here.

Market study: The first of these, used by the Port Authority of New York and New Jersey, is a method of relating the travel patterns of various sectors of the population to their principal socio-economic characteristics. Basically, the population of the area under consideration is divided into cells classified by age, education, occupation, and income. Demand forecasts are made by first estimating population growth in each of these cells and then calculating the resultant number of trips (by multiplying the number of people in each cell by the percentage of those who take vacations). The estimates for each cell are then added and adjusted for any elements not covered in the survey to produce totals for future years.

The main weakness of this approach, however, is that it cannot take into account the effects of changes in the principal variables that affect demand, for example, an increase or decrease in fares. Nevertheless, it is a useful method of identifying the segments of the market that generate most travel.

Market share analysis: Market share analysis is particularly useful in forecasting tourism demand for a new destination or facility for which no past data is available. The approach is (1) to forecast the growth of demand in the whole market segment in which the new destination is competing and then (2) to assess the new destination's future share in the market.

The first stage is to identify the past and present proportions of total travel from the principal origin areas to the types of destination that are likely to compete with the new destination (in terms of the nature of its attractions, distance, and price). Second, quantitative techniques, such as trend projections, regression, and so on, are used to forecast the growth of the identified market segment. Third, the new destination's market share is measured. This can be assessed by dividing the market between the competing destinations on the basis of various subjective assumptions. A more realistic approach, however, is to develop a Market Potential Ranking Index. First, each destination is compared in terms of its cost, attractions, facilities, ease of access, and image. A points system is allotted for each factor, and the scores are weighted according to the relative importance of each element in attracting or repelling vacationers. Once suitable adjustments have been applied to allow for the relative maturity of each of the competing destinations and for their possible competitive reactions to the entry of the new destination, a trend curve can be drawn to show the new destination's movement towards maturity.

Despite its popularity, however, the approach is unlikely to achieve a high degree of accuracy and needs the support of other forecasting methods.

The Clawson Technique

In its basic form, the Clawson technique is a mechanistic method of calculating future demand for a facility based upon past usage. The approach, developed by Marion Clawson (1966) from earlier work by H. Hotelling, involves the construction of a demand curve that shows the number of visitors in relation to increases in the price charged.

In its simplest form, the approach contains some weaknesses and limitations, but later refinements have included the addition of further explanatory variables. More sophisticated versions of the model involve the use of multivariable regression analysis and bear little resemblance to the original model.

Multivariable Regression Demand Analysis

Multivariable regression analysis is the most popular causal technique used for demand forecasting. A survey of business establishments in Britain (Turner 1974), for example, showed that the approach is used widely in the manufacturing and service sectors. In the field of tourism and travel, regression analysis is used regularly by airlines, aircraft companies, and tourism researchers. A survey carried out among participants at the 1986 "Tourism in the 1990s" Conference (Witt and Witt 1992) revealed that multivariable regression analysis was used by tourist offices, government departments, consultants, practitioners, and academics and was used as frequently as moving averages and exponential smoothing—the most popular of the univariate methods.

The essence of the approach is the formulation and testing of a hypothesis. Typically, the basic model states that the demand for tourism to a particular area is a function of factors such as the levels of income of the tourists, the costs of travel from the tourists' homes to the destination, relative price levels in the two countries or regions (that is, origin and destination) and in alternative destinations, and, in the case of international tourism, the currency exchange rates.

Data for each of these variables are fed into a computerized model to calculate the part played by each of the explanatory factors in influencing demand. Forecasts are obtained by estimating the expected future values of each of the explanatory variables and running these into the regression model to produce a predicted future level of demand.

The approach is most suitable for short- and medium-term forecasting. For more than about four years ahead, it is no longer realistic to assume that the existing relationships between variables will remain constant, and the use of other techniques should yield more accurate forecasts.

Spatial Models

Spatial models postulate some basic relationship to explain the flow of traffic between specified places. In their simplest form—gravity models—the movement of traffic is stated to be directly proportional to the population of each region and inversely proportional to the distance apart of the origins and destinations.

More complex models incorporate a number of additional variables to explain the movement of traffic. Some of these variables relate to the propensity of an area to generate travel; others are concerned with the factors that attract visitors to the particular destination. Thus, for example, the variables that generate travel from an origin area, in addition to the size of its population, are likely to include the level and distribution of income and the age composition, education levels, social structure, and so on, of the population. The factors that attract visitors to a particular destination, in addition to the size of its population, include the physical attractiveness of the area compared with alternatives, as well as its climate, historical heritage, cultural factors, and so on. The travel constraints imposed by distance are often more appropriately expressed in terms of the costs and/or time involved in travel.

A distinction is sometimes drawn between trip-generation models, which explain the propensity of an area or several areas to generate travel, and trip-distribution models, which explain the flow of visitors to a particular destination or several destinations. In practice, more accurate demand forecasts can be achieved by constructing a model specifically for the type of forecast required. If, for example, the aim is to forecast tourist demand to a particular region, the model should include variables to explain the propensity of each origin area to generate travel, plus variables to describe the attractiveness of the particular destination area in relation to its competitors. Travel time and/or travel costs should be included as a constraint. Such models closely resemble multivariable demand models, and estimates are often computed by the same technique—least squares.

Spatial models have a wide application and have been used by tourism researchers to predict the future spatial demand for international tourism, to analyze the flow of tourists between particular countries and regions, to estimate the future demand for recreational and tourist facilities, and to examine how the demand for tourism is affected by highway improvements and increases in fares. The principal difference between spatial models and multivariable demand models lies more in their initial formulation than in their application.

Growth Scenario Model

A growth scenario model was used by the Bureau of Management Consulting to provide long-term forecasts for the Canadian Government Office of Tourism (Bureau of Management Consulting 1975a). The technique concentrates on the implications of growth trends rather than on providing an exact explanation of particular behavior patterns. The aim is to quantify and project the variables thought to affect tourism and, in the process, to determine which socioeconomic variables are most important in altering tourism demand. When data is inadequate for regression analysis, the technique offers a relatively efficient and inexpensive alternative.

Almost Ideal Demand System (AIDS)

The AIDS model is a functional model for the representation of consumer preferences using a system of demand equations, thereby linking economic theory to econometric application. In essence, it is a three-stage process of producing a forecast. The first stage involves the allocation of consumer expenditure (in each of the origin countries) into the proportions likely to be spent on each group of goods, with tourism identified as one of the groups. The second stage is concerned with the allocation of tourism expenditure into domestic and international, with the latter broken down into regions and subregions. The final phase involves the allocation of tourism expenditure to particular destination countries.

Whereas the AIDS model has a very sound foundation in demand theory, in practice, it is extremely difficult to acquire adequate reliable data to operate the model in its entirety. An extremely useful account of the model and its application is given by T.C. Syriopoulos (1990).

Systems Models

Systems Dynamics

Systems dynamics involves the construction of large-scale computerized mathematical models to simulate the behavior of a system in response to internal and external changes. In common with most other complex mathematical techniques, the approach is useful for forecasting only as long as the relationships expressed in the formulae remain constant. Once these alter, the forecast loses its accuracy.

Input-Output Analysis

Input-output analysis is a matrix technique used to analyze the structure of an economic system and to assess the impact of changes. Although not a suitable technique to use for tourism demand forecasting, it provides a useful method of assessing the economic effects of changes in demand and, in particular, the repercussive impact of such changes on sales, output, income, and employment in the area concerned.

QUALITATIVE TECHNIQUES

There are three situations in which qualitative methods are preferable to quantitative ones. These occur when:

- Data are insufficient or are known to be unreliable.
- It is not possible to construct a suitable numerical model.
- Time is insufficient to initiate and operate a quantitative analysis.

Qualitative methods range from hunches and managerial inspiration at one end of the scale to carefully structured attempts to gather and amalgamate the opinions of many experts at the other end. Qualitative forecasts are particularly suitable for long-term forecasting when changes of a large and unprecedented nature may be expected.

Simplistic Approaches

Executive Opinion

"Seat of the pants" forecasting, based upon a lengthy practical experience of the tourism business, is still widely used in the private sector. Indeed, at the microlevel, for example, in deciding whether or not to construct a new restaurant at a particular location, entrepreneurial flair can sometimes forecast demand as accurately as, or even more accurately than, the most rigorous econometric techniques.

Even so, it is more usual nowadays for chief executives to seek the views of other members of their organizations in order to broaden the base of the forecast and to reduce its subjectivity. Unless such discussions are structured, however, the process can deteriorate into a guessing game.

Sales Force Estimates

One of the most popular methods of demand forecasting in many industries is to analyze and then amalgamate the forecasts of salesmen and sales managers. In the travel and tourism industry, the equivalent method is to bring together the predictions of travel agents, tour operators, and others.

Whilst such forecasts benefit from the specialized knowledge and experience of those involved in selling the service, they merely shift the onus for forecasting onto people with insufficient knowledge or understanding of the factors involved in demand forecasting. Such forecasts are unlikely to be very accurate for more than a season ahead.

Technological Forecasting

Technological forecasting does not necessarily imply forecasts of technological changes. The term is used to define the prediction of the feasible and/or desirable characteristics of demand performance in the light of long-term changes, especially future technologies. Such approaches attempt to show what is possible, what is expected, and what is desirable.

Such forecasts can be exploratory or normative. Exploratory forecasts attempt either to generate new information about future structures and levels of demand or to simulate the outcome of expected events. Essentially, they are used to broaden management's knowledge of what levels of future demand may be expected. The most frequently used exploratory forecasts include Delphi Studies, Morphological Analysis, Scenario Writing, and Cross-Impact Analysis, in addition to S-Curve Analysis mentioned earlier in this chapter.

Normative forecasts are concerned also with generating new information or simulating the outcome of events, but such forecasts are made within the context of achieving certain objectives. Usually, the aim of such forecasts is to identify critical turning points and linkages and to show what steps can be taken to achieve the desired objectives. In addition to the exploratory techniques already mentioned, normative methods include Relevance Trees and Decision Analysis.

Delphi Studies

Details of this technique can be found elsewhere in this Handbook and in the principal literature (Linstone and Turoff 1975). The Delphi Technique is gaining in popularity in the tourism and travel industry: studies have been made by airframe manufacturers and trade associations (IATA 1977), tourist boards (D'Amore 1976), and various other research organizations (Dyck and Emery 1970; Shafer, Moeller, and Getty 1974).

Morphological Analysis

The aim of morphological analysis is to structure the existing information in an orderly manner in order to identify the possible outcome of events. To forecast demand, the first stage is to identify the most important variables. This is normally carried out intuitively. Second, each of the variables is considered in turn to assess its possible magnitude and effects. Third, each of them is placed in a multidimensional matrix (called a morphological box) to assess its interactions on demand. This process provides an indication of various attainable levels of demand under varying assumptions about the performance of each variable. Last, an estimation is made of the most desirable level of demand in relation to the variables at work, and an assessment is made of how this level might be achieved. In common with most qualitative approaches, morphological analysis lacks rigor unless it is supported by numerical analysis, but it can form a valuable input into group forecasting discussions such as the Delphi technique.

Scenarios

A *scenario* is an outline of a situation that could develop given the known facts and trends. A hypothetical sequence of events is described showing how demand is likely to be affected by various causal factors. The scenario focuses attention both on the variables that affect demand and on the decision points that occur, in order to indicate what action can be taken to influence the level of demand at each stage. By such means, a number of scenarios can provide a series of alternative strategies for achieving, modifying, or altering the forecast.

Scenario writing is not so much a forecasting technique as a method of clarifying the issues involved. As such, it can form a valuable input to group forecasting approaches such as Delphi.

Cross-Impact Analysis

Cross-impact analysis is a method of studying the interdependence of the factors that affect forecasting. The methodology is based upon an analysis of the probabilities attached to the occurrence and magnitude of each of a number of interdependent events and their relationships to each other. A matrix is constructed to show these relationships and to indicate the direction and strength of the impact that one occurrence would have upon the probability of others taking place. The data are obtained by asking panelists to give a scaled rating to the likely occurrence of each event and to the event's impact on others under various circumstances.

The technique is not a forecasting method per se but a way of examining the issues involved. It gives managers an insight into the sensitivities and interrelationships between different policy options.

Relevance Trees

This is another method of plotting and comparing alternative paths to a goal and, at the same time, identifying areas where more research is needed. Basically, the approach is to construct a matrix that shows the alternative means by which a goal can be achieved matched against the criteria that can affect its realization. Numerical weightings are applied subjectively to both the alternatives and the criteria in order to decide the most suitable path to take.

Although the technique has been used in other areas of forecasting, it has not yet found wide acceptance in tourism circles.

PROBLEMS IN TOURISM AND TRAVEL FORECASTING

The level of accuracy tolerable in any forecast depends upon:

- The use to which the forecast will be put and the nature of any decisions that have to be made.
- The nature of the product being forecasted—tourism demand is more variable in some parts of the world than in others.
- The length of the forecast horizon—the degree of uncertainty is greater in long-term forecasting.
- The coverage of the forecast—greater accuracy can normally be achieved in predicting demand for an entire sector than for a particular subgroup.

Inaccuracies in a forecast can result from any one or combination of five different factors:

- An inappropriate model may have been used.
- A valid model may have been used incorrectly.
- Errors may exist in the calculation of the relationships within the model.
- Significant variables affecting demand may have been omitted from consideration.
- The data used to produce the prediction may have been inadequate or inappropriate for the type of forecast required.

There are several tests available to evaluate both the data and the model, one of which is Theil's U Statistic (Theil 1965), which can be used to compare, among other things, the past performance of the model during the estimation period with the observed changes during that period.

Much work has been undertaken during the 1980s and early 1990s to assess the forecasting accuracy of several quantitative models. Particularly notable has been the work of S.F. Witt and C.A. Witt (1992). On the basis of tests carried out using a variety of quantitative techniques, the Witts concluded that ". . . the relative forecasting accuracy of the various techniques differ considerably according to the *measure* of accuracy chosen. . . ." (Witt and Witt 1991). For short-term forecasting, where no major changes occur or are expected in the data, naive time series analysis performs as well as or even better than more complex modeling techniques. Autoregressive models also outperform more complex techniques in cases where no changes are expected in trends. If, however, forecasting accuracy is defined in terms of trend-change error, then econometric forecasting techniques are often more appropriate.

Like many other social science phenomena, the determinants of travel and tourism demand are often difficult to identify and quantify. In the first place, the motives governing individuals' decisions to travel are very complex and often subjective and irrational. In recent years, a number of researchers have devoted considerable effort to the analysis of such motivations (see, for example, Woodside, Ronkainen, and Reid 1977).

Among the principal factors affecting tourism demand, though not in any order of importance, are changes in (1) income levels and income distribution, (2) the quantity of leisure time and its distribution, (3) educational levels, acting through consumer tastes and travel preferences, (4) the size of population in the origin areas, (5) the level of urbanization in the origin area, (6) travel costs, (7) the relative price levels in competing destinations, (8) exchange rates, (9) the relative prices of other goods and services that compete for the tourist dollar, (10) communication networks and the speed of travel, and (11) other socioeconomic factors, including the age and occupational distributions of the populations in the origin areas. A very useful analysis of these factors is given in a recent World Tourism Organization Discussion Paper (World Tourism Organization 1990).

Fortunately, many of these determinants change relatively slowly through time and for short- and medium-term forecasting, their effects can be largely ignored. In the long run, however, their influence may be important and should be taken into account when making forecasts.

The demand for tourist services is subject also to many external factors that can cause major shifts in demand from one destination to another. Perhaps the most potent of these are political and social unrest in the destination countries, although temporary problems can be caused by supply constraints or travel bottlenecks. The long-term effects of such factors are often difficult to forecast.

The difficulties inherent in forecasting tourism demand are compounded by the lack of adequate data. Tourism data are in general much inferior to those for other sectors. Despite the efforts made by several international bodies, no unifying data system exists, and data from different countries and regions are difficult to compare. In consequence, forecasters are often compelled to carry out expensive surveys to gather data to feed into their models. In such cases, it is essential that sufficient funds are made available to support the necessary data collection.

FORECASTING AND MANAGEMENT DECISIONS

Forecasting should be an essential element in the process of management.

NATIONAL TOURIST ORGANIZATIONS

National tourist organizations (NTOs) need short- and medium-term forecasts to plan their marketing strategy and to take other measures to reduce potential peaking and improve all-year occupancy rates. Such forecasts can also alert NTOs to likely shifts in the type of visitor and so enable plans to be made in time to cope with changes in the type of tourist services required and also to shape demand through promotion and marketing.

Long-term forecasts are required to plan in detail for the long-run development of the tourism industry. Such forecasts can be used to identify future infrastructure needs (new airport facilities, roads, utilities, etc.), to estimate future accommodation needs and related requirements and their mix, and to calculate future labor requirements and training needs.

In addition, long-term demand forecasts enable estimates to be made of future foreign exchange earnings, the contribution that tourism might make to national income, and the social and cultural impact that tourism might have on the country.

TOURIST AND TRAVEL OPERATORS

Airlines, tour operators, hotel companies, and other business organizations require forecasts to plan their strategy and operations. Short-term forecasts of traffic flows, occupancy rates, and visitor spending are important ingredients in the planning of marketing strategies, pricing policy, revenue targets, cash flow positions, stock requirements, and labor-force needs. Medium-term forecasts provide essential data for the timing of new operations and services, the planning of future budgets, and the assessment of personnel and training needs.

Long-term forecasts are needed to determine the future direction and strategy of the organization and to plan capital expenditure in the light of any major market or supply changes revealed by the forecast or to be initiated after a study of alternative possibilities.

British Airways, for example, uses weekly forecasts to compare the prevailing situation with previous target figures, quarterly forecasts to relate traffic flows to the prevailing economic environment, fiscal (or budgetary) forecasts to enable aircraft and market resources to be allocated in an optimum manner, development forecasts (from two to seven years ahead) to examine the overall market situation in order to plan routes and the size of its fleet most effectively, and speculative forecasts (over seven years ahead) to examine new products and market areas.

REFERENCES

Archer, Brian H. (1976), *Demand Forecasting in Tourism*, Cardiff: University of Wales Press.

Archer, Brian H. (1980), "Forecasting Demand: Quantitative and Intuitive Techniques," *Tourism Management* 1 (March), 5–12.

Baron, Raymond R. (1975), *Seasonality in Tourism*, London: Economist Intelligence Unit Ltd.

Box, George E.P., and Gwilym M. Jenkins (1970), *Time Series Analysis: Forecasting and Control*, San Francisco: Holden-Day.

Brodie, R.J., and C.A. De Kluyver (1987), "A Comparison of the Short-Term Forecasting Accuracy of Econometric and Naive Extrapolation Models of Market Share, "*International Journal of Forecasting* 3, 423–437.

Brown, R.G. (1963), *Smoothing, Forecasting and Prediction*, London: Prentice Hall.

Bureau of Management Consulting (1975a), *Methodology for Long-Range Projections of Tourism Demand*, Ottawa: Department of Supply and Services.

Bureau of Management Consulting (1975b), *Tourism Impact Model*, Ottawa: Canadian Government Office of Tourism.

Calantone, R.J., C.A. Di Benedetto, and D. Bojanic (1987), "A Comprehensive Review of the Tourism Forecasting Literature," *Journal of Travel Research* XXVI, 2 (Fall), 28–39.

Canadian Government Office of Tourism (1977), *Methodology for Short-Term Forecasts of Tourism Flows*, Ottawa: Economic Research Section, Policy Planning and Industry Relations Branch.

Clawson, Marion (1966), *Economics of Outdoor Recreation*, Baltimore, MD: Johns Hopkins Press.

D'Amore, L.J. (1976), "The Significance of Tourism to Canada," *The Business Quarterly* 3 (Autumn), 27–35.

Duke, K.E. (1981), "Survey of Travel Forecasting Techniques," *Looking Ahead: Proceedings of the 8th Annual Travel Research Seminar, PATA*, Christchurch, New Zealand.

Dyck, J.J., and G.J. Emery (1970), *Social Future of Alberta 1970–2005*, Edmonton, Alberta: Human Resources Research Council of Alberta.

Fritz, R.G., C. Brandon and J. Xander (1984), "Combining Time-Series and Econometric Forecasts of Tourism Activity," *Annals of Tourism Research* 11, 219–229.

Guerts, Michael D. (1982), "Forecasting the Hawaii Tourist Market," *Journal of Travel Research* 21 (1), 18–21.

Guerts, Michael D., and I.B. Ibrahim (1975), "Comparing the Box-Jenkins Approach with the Exponentially Smoothed Forecasting Model to Hawaii Tourists," *Journal of Marketing Research* 12 (May), 182–188.

Holt, C.C. (1957), *Forecasting Seasonal and Trends by Exponentially Weighted Moving Averages*, Pittsburgh, PA: Carnegie Institute of Technology Research Paper.

International Air Transport Association (1977), *IATA Regional Passenger Traffic Forecasts 1976–1982 Scheduled International Services*, Geneva, Switzerland: International Research Division.

Kliman, M.L. (1981), "A Quantitative Analysis of Canadian Overseas Tourism," *Transportation Research* 15A (6), 487–497.

Linstone, Harold A., and Murray Turoff, eds (1975), *The Delphi Technique*, Reading, MA: Addison-Wesley.

Makindakis, Spyros, and Steven C. Wheelwright (1978), *Forecasting Methods and Applications*, New York: John Wiley & Sons, Inc.

Martin, C.A., and S.F. Witt (1989a), "Accuracy of Econometric Forecasts of Tourism," *Annals of Tourism Research* 16(3), 407–428.

Martin, C.A. and S.F. Witt (1989b), "Forecasting Tourism Demand: A Comparison of the Accuracy of Several Quantitative Models," *International Journal of Forecasting* 5(1), 7–19.

Means, C.A., and R. Avila (1986), "Econometric Analysis and Forecasts of U.S. International Travel: Using the New TRAM Model," *World Travel Overview 1986/87*, 90–107.

O'Hagan, J.W., and M.J. Harrison (1984), "Market Share of U.S. Travel Expenditure in Europe: An Econometric Analysis," *Applied Economics* 16, 919–931.

Ostergaard, P. (1974), *A Geographically-Oriented Marketing Model of Automobile Tourist Flows from the United States to Canada*, Ottawa: Canadian Government Office of Tourism.

Schulmeister, Stephen (1973), *Erhebung zur kurzfristigen Prognose des Fremdenwerkehrs in Osterreich*, Vienna: Osterrichisches Institut fur Wirtschaftsforschung.

Schulmeister, Stephen (1979), *Tourism and the Business Cycle*, Vienna: Austrian Institute for Economic Research.

Shafer E.L., G.H. Moeller and R.E. Getty (1974), *Future Leisure Environments*, Upper Darby, Penn.: USDA Forest Service.

Syriopoulos, T.C. (1990), *Modelling Tourism Demand for Medi-*

terranean Countries, Ph.D. thesis (unpublished), University of Kent at Canterbury, England.

Taylor, Gordon D., and Peter H. Chan (1976), "An Approach to Forecasting Tourism Future," in *Forecasting in Tourism and Outdoor Recreation*, TTRA Canada, Art Chapter National Conference, Montreal, Quebec: L.J. D'Amore and Associates Ltd.

Theil, H. (1965), *Economic Forecasts and Policies*, Amsterdam, The Netherlands: North Holland.

Turner, John (1974), *Forecasting Practices in British Industry*, Leighton Buzzard, England: Surrey University Press.

Uysel, M., and J.L. Crompton (1985), "An Overview of Approaches Used to Forecast Tourism Demand," *Journal of Travel Research* XXIII (4), 7–15.

Van Doorn, J.W.M. (1984), "Tourism Forecasting and the Policy Maker: criteria for usefulness," *Tourism Management* 5(1), 24–39.

Wandner, Stephen A., and James D. Van Erden (1979), "Estimating the Demand for International Tourism Using Time Series Analysis," a paper presented at the International Symposium: Tourism in the Next Decade, Washington, D.C., 13 March 1979.

Wanhill, Stephen R.C. (1980), "Methods of Forecasting Demand," in *Managerial Economics for Hotel Operation*, Richard Kotas, ed., London: Surrey University Press.

White, K.J. (1982), *The Demand for International Travel: A System-Wide Analysis for U.S. Travel to Europe*, Discussion Paper, 82–88, University of British Columbia, Canada.

White, K.J. (1985), "An International Travel Demand Model: US Travel to Western Europe," *Annals of Travel Research* 12 (4), 529–545.

Winters, P.R. (1960), "Forecasting Sales by Exponentially Weighted Moving Averages," *Management Science* 6, 324–342.

Witt, S.F., and C.A. Witt (1991), "Tourism Forecasting: error magnitude, direction of change error, and trend change error," *Journal of Travel Research*, XXX (2), 26–33.

Witt, S.F., and C.A. Witt (1992), *Modelling and Forecasting Demand in Tourism*, London: Academic Press.

Woodside, Arch D., Ilka Ronkainen, and David M. Reid (1977), "Measurement and Utilization of the Evoked Set as a Travel Marketing Variable," in *The 80s: Its Impact on Travel and Tourism Marketing*, TTRA Eighth Annual Conference Proceedings, Salt Lake City, Bureau of Economic and Business Research, University of Utah.

World Tourism Organization (1990), *Tourism to the Year 2000: Qualitative Aspects Affecting Global Growth*, Discussion Paper, Madrid: World Tourism Organization.

11

Scaling and Attitude Measurement in Travel and Tourism Research

GORDON H.G. MCDOUGALL
Professor
School of Business and Economics
Wilfrid Laurier University
Waterloo, Ontario

HUGH MUNRO
Director
Laurier Trade Development Center
Wilfrid Laurier University
Waterloo, Ontario

The purpose of this chapter is to provide a review of the basic scaling and attitude measurement techniques and their potential in tourism research. The review first discusses attitudes, their components, and their characteristics. Next, the main scaling/attitude measurement techniques are outlined, and the advantages and disadvantages of each technique are considered. Subsequently, some of the unique aspects of measuring attitudes in the tourism/travel domain are presented, and examples of attitude measurement in tourism management decisions discussed. Finally, some conclusions concerning attitudes and travel research are drawn.

A primary reason for measuring attitudes is to gain an understanding of the reasons *why* people behave the way they do. Knowledge of people's feelings and beliefs, what they consider important in making choice decisions, the major benefits they are seeking when they select one alternative over another, all of these facts can aid managers in the design and implementation of effective marketing programs. To illustrate, attitude measurement has been used to:

- Shed useful light on the attitudes of tourists toward national parks as vacation destinations (Mayo 1975).
- Identify the perceptions held by potential visitors about various tourist-recreation regions (Hunt 1975).
- Provide, through vacation lifestyle dimensions, a better understanding of the major vacation orientations that different households assume (Perreault, Darden, and Darden 1977).

- Determine potential visitors' perceptions of a country and its regions (Ritchie and Sheridan 1988).

This type of information can help in selecting target markets for promotional campaigns and in the positioning of resort areas. Clearly, attitude research has a wide range of applications because of the insights offered into people's behavior.

The purpose of this paper is to provide a review of the basic scaling and attitude measurement techniques and their potential in travel and tourism research. The review will begin with a discussion of attitudes, their components, and their characteristics. Next, the main scaling/attitude measurement techniques will be outlined, and the advantages and disadvantages of each technique will be considered. Following this, some of the unique aspects of measuring attitudes in the tourism/travel domain will be presented, and then examples of attitude measurement in tourism management decisions will be discussed. Finally, some conclusions concerning attitudes and travel research will be drawn.

ATTITUDES

While *attitude* has been defined in a variety of ways, most definitions contain some reference to an enduring predisposition towards a particular aspect of one's environment. This predisposition can be reflected in the way one thinks, feels, and behaves with respect to that aspect. One's attitude towards foreign travel would be reflected in one's beliefs, feelings, and behavioral orientations with respect to foreign travel. In this section, the discussion focuses on the structure of attitudes, some of their important characteristics, and the attitude-behavior relationship.

COMPONENTS OF AN ATTITUDE

In an attempt to capture the multifaceted nature of attitude, many researchers have conceptualized attitudes as being structured of three components: (1) a cognitive component, (2) an affective component, and (3) a behavioral component. A discussion of each of these components and their interrelationships follows.

Cognitive Component

The cognitive component consists of the individual's beliefs and knowledge about a particular object, or the manner in which the object is perceived. For any object of interest, it is likely that an individual will possess a number of beliefs or perceptions; for example, an individual might perceive a particular tourist resort as (1) being relatively inexpensive, (2) offering a number of entertainment options, (3) having a variety of lodging and dining facilities, and (4) being extremely popular among the younger tourists. Each of these beliefs may be viewed as representing the individual's current knowledge of a characteristic, or attribute, of the particular tourist facility. Collectively, these beliefs or perceptions constitute the cognitive component of the individual's attitude towards that resort.

It is conceivable that an individual could possess certain beliefs about a particular tourist area without ever having visited the resort. The beliefs or perceptions could have been formulated through reading about the facility and/or through discussions with friends. As an individual gains more knowledge about a particular object or place and, in particular, when that knowledge has been acquired through personal experience (e.g., the individual actually visits the area), the structure of beliefs becomes more established and organized. In addition, certain beliefs about the characteristics of a particular object or place are likely to assume more importance than others. Some conceptualizations of attitudes explicitly incorporate the differences in importance that individuals place on the various beliefs they hold (Ajzen and Fishbein 1980); for example, preferences for vacation desti-

nations have been related to the perceptions of those destinations through importance ratings (Goodrich 1978). The issues surrounding importance measures are addressed in a subsequent section of the chapter.

Affective Component

An individual's feelings of like or dislike for a particular object or place constitute the affective component of an attitude. An individual may state that he or she dislikes a particular tourist facility, which tends to reflect his or her overall evaluation of the facility. It is likely that if the individual were to elaborate, evaluations of specific characteristics associated with the facility would surface. The individual might state that the lodging and dining facilities were too expensive and/or that the facility was too crowded for his or her liking. Collectively, the evaluation of specific characteristics associated with a particular object or place will contribute to an overall evaluation (i.e., like or dislike) of that object or place. Traditionally, a measure of this overall evaluation has served as a surrogate for one's attitude.

Behavioral Component

The behavioral component of an attitude reflects the action taken or the expressed intent to act with respect to a particular object or place. Continuing with the example of a tourist facility, an individual's actual visit to the facility or an expressed intent to vacation there would constitute the behavioral component of that individual's attitude. In most instances, the behavioral dimension is oriented towards the overall object or place, as opposed to being specific to a particular characteristic or attribute. It is highly likely that the multifaceted nature of many travel-and-tourism related activities would contribute to situations in which an individual could exhibit behavior related to specific aspects of a facility.

The three components of an attitude are expected to be related in a consistent manner. An individual's beliefs about or perceptions of a particular attitude object should be consistent with his or her evaluation of that object. The behavior exhibited towards that object should also be consistent with the other elements of the attitude structure. It is this latter relationship that has created much of the controversy surrounding the utility of attitude measurement. This issue is given special attention in a subsequent discussion on the attitude-behavior relationship.

Not all researchers are proponents of conceptualizing an attitude as being structured of three components. Some theorists feel that the dispositional characteristics of attitudes are captured in measures of belief (Fishbein and Ajzen 1975) and/or belief and affect (Heberlein 1973). Others perceive little utility in differentiating among any of the attitude components (McGuire 1969). Despite these alternative positions, sufficient support and interest exist in examining all three components of an attitude (Bagozzi 1978). An investigation that compared travel agents and their clients utilized all three components (Michie and Sullivan 1990).

SOME IMPORTANT CHARACTERISTICS OF ATTITUDES

The complex nature of individuals contributes to their possessing many attitudes related to various aspects of their environment. As such, it is useful for both managerial decision-making and research purposes to distinguish the types of attitudes that an individual can possess. The following discussion highlights some of the more important characteristics of attitudes.

The first important distinction with respect to attitudes is their level of specificity. Attitudes can range from being very general or global in nature to being very specific to a particular object, place, or event. This distinction has important implications for the approach adopted for attitude measurement. Measurement of an individual's general attitude toward leisure would likely have to incorporate a wide variety of related beliefs, feelings, and behaviors. Support for this is found in the work of Neulinger and Breit (1971) who identified five relatively independent dimensions in the leisure domain that they feel capture a person's general attitude toward leisure. The items used to generate the five dimensions were similar in nature to the psychographic measures employed by Perreault et al. (1977) in their classification of vacation life-styles. However, in measuring an individual's attitude toward a particular event, the domain is more clearly defined, and the items can be tied to specific beliefs, feelings, and behaviors related to that event. An example of such an approach is provided in Crompton's study of Mexico as a vacation destination (1979).

It is quite common for researchers to employ measures of general attitudes, interests, and opinions (i.e., life-style items like those of Wells 1974) in conjunction with demographic factors in an attempt to profile those with specific attitudes towards a particular object, event, or situation. Woodside and Pitts (1976) have used this technique in the travel and tourism domain.

Another important consideration is how closely the attitudes are linked to a person's underlying value system. The connection between an individual's personal values and attitudes is referred to as *centrality*. A strong link between a positive attitude towards foreign travel and personal values on being independent, broad-minded, and imaginative would contribute to a fairly central attitude. Researchers have found that since values are relatively stable, the more central the attitude, the more difficult it is to change (Eagley and Himmelfarb 1978).

The last distinction relates to the intensity of the attitude, or how strongly the individual feels. The intensity of an individual's feelings is determined by the affective component of an attitude. Like centrality, the more intense (i.e., strongly held) an attitude, the more difficult it is to change. Researchers and managers can gain valuable insights into the potential for attitude change by assessing the centrality and intensity of an attitude.

THE ATTITUDE-BEHAVIOR RELATIONSHIP

A key factor underlying the widespread use of the attitude construct is the assumption that there exists a consistent relationship between attitudes and behavior and that an understanding of a person's attitudes will permit an understanding and accurate prediction of his or her behavior.[1] Although the validity of this assumption has been questioned (Calder and Ross 1973), there is empirical evidence that does demonstrate a strong relationship between attitudes and behavior (Kelman 1974). Further support for this relationship with respect to the cognitive, affective, and behavioral components of attitudes towards leisure is provided in the work by Ragheb and Beard (1982). The apparent consensus among researchers is that attitudes are generally good predictors of behavior but that factors exist that can affect the strength of this relationship.

The question facing researchers is, therefore, no longer whether an individual's attitudes can be used to predict his overt behavior, but when. The task is to specify those variables which determine whether an observed attitude-behavior relationship will be relatively strong or weak (Regan and Fazio 1977:30).

The following are some of the major factors that have been found to influence the attitude-behavior relationship:

1. The degree of correspondence in the measures of attitude and behavior entities (Ajzen and Fishbein 1977).
2. The extent to which behavior is influenced by situational factors (Belk 1975).
3. The importance an individual places on complying with the norms established by relevant others (Snyder and Tanke 1976).
4. The relevance or importance of an attitude (Houston and Rothschild 1978).
5. The manner in which an attitude is formed (Regan and Fazio 1977; Olson and Mitchell 1975).
6. The degree of confidence associated with an attitude (Fazio and Zanna 1978; Smith and Swinyard 1983).

The above findings suggest that researchers and practitioners should be concerned with more than simply measuring attitudes and should attempt to explore their derivation, their many dimensions, and their importance to those who hold them. In addition, to fully understand the relative role of attitudes in shaping behavior, it would be useful to incorporate some of the relevant situational factors. This is likely to be particularly insightful in the travel and tourism domain where such forces are known to be operant.

---

[1]The sequence in the relationship among beliefs, feelings, and behavior can also be reversed. Behavior may lead to changes in the affective and cognitive components of attitude as a result of learning (Olson and Mitchell 1975) and self-perception or dissonance effects (Scott 1978; Cummings and Venkatesan 1976).

PROPERTIES OF SCALES

Prior to the discussion of attitude measurement techniques, a brief review of the properties of scales will be outlined. It is important to understand the scale properties attained with any survey instrument because both statistical techniques and interpretation are dependent upon the level of measurement.

Measurement, in its broadest sense, is the assignment of numerals to objects, according to some specified rule (Garner and Creelman 1970). The numerals represent a particular kind of scale, and care is required in determining which scale properties are applicable. The issue is to determine the properties of the attribute itself and then ensure that the numerals are assigned so that they properly reflect the properties of the attributes. Further, good measurement occurs when the properties of the scale employed are consistent with the phenomenon being measured. The four major properties of scales, referred to as levels of measurement, are briefly reviewed in this section.

NOMINAL SCALES

At the lowest level, numbers are used to classify objects, people, or characteristics. People are classified as males or females, and areas are classified as countries, states, or cities. The formal property of nominal scales is that classes or groups are assigned to a set of mutually exclusive subclasses. The only relationship involved is that of equivalence; members of any one subclass must be identified on the property being scaled. Statistics that may be used to describe, summarize, or understand nominal data include the mode, frequency, and, in most cases, chi-square. The appropriate statistical tests are nonparametric (Seigal 1956).

ORDINAL SCALES

An ordinal scale requires objects in one category to be described in relation to those in another category; that is, one category relative to another category can be described as being more popular, greater than, or more difficult. Ranking of vacation destinations in terms of choice (first, second, third) provides an ordinal scale. In this case, statistics such as the median and percentiles can be used to determine the most popular vacation destination. What cannot be determined is how much more or less popular a particular destination is in comparison to other measured destinations. While the appropriate statistical tests for ordinal scales are nonparametric, in practice this constraint is often violated.

INTERVAL SCALES

When the distances between any two numbers on the scale are of known size, then an interval scale has been achieved. Interval scales have a constant unit of measurement, although the units as well as the zero point on the scale are arbitrary. If people are asked to what extent they agree or disagree with a particular attitude statement (e.g., "Westerners are very friendly people") and seven response categories are provided (e.g., *strongly agree* to *strongly disagree*), it is frequently assumed that the level of agreement can be measured in intervals. In this example, it would be assumed that the interval between *strongly agree* and *strongly disagree* can be measured. The most important aspect of obtaining interval-scale data is that parametric statistical tests can be used that are more powerful than nonparametric tests. All of the "traditional" statistics, such as the mean, standard deviation, and product-moment correlations, can be used with interval scales.

RATIO SCALES

Scales that have a zero point as their origin are ratio scales. In a ratio scale, the ratio of any two scale points is independent of the unit of measure. Thus, a ratio scale can determine that one unit is twice as large as another unit. Examples of ratio scales are sales, income, and age. Attitude measurement techniques seldom, if ever, achieve a ratio scale.

THE ISSUES

The importance of determining the level of measurement of a scale is that the appropriate statistical techniques must be *matched* to the measurement level. In simple terms, parametric tests cannot be used on nominal or ordinal scales, whereas both parametric and nonparametric tests can be used with interval and ratio scales. This issue is particularly relevant in the field of attitude measurement because it is frequently assumed that the measures have interval properties, an assumption that may be incorrect (Seigal 1956:26). The use of inappropriate statistical techniques and the resultant misinterpretation of the analysis and incorrect conclusions have been well documented (Adams, Fagot, and Robinson 1965; Churchill 1991). Unfortunately, reasonable and clear-cut guidelines for addressing these issues have not been established.

ATTITUDE MEASUREMENT SCALES

Assuming the decision has been made to identify consumer attitudes towards some particular object (e.g., vacation destination) or activity (e.g., leisure), the researcher must decide what type of attitude measurement technique to use. This section of the paper will briefly review the major scales used to measure attitudes. Then some of the issues raised in terms of attitude measurement will be discussed.

In selecting a particular attitude scale, it should be noted that each has strengths and weaknesses, and most techniques can be adapted to measurement of the attitude components. What follows is a brief description of the well-known attitude measurement techniques. An illustration of each scale is provided in Table 1.

THURSTONE SCALE

The Thurstone scale, also referred to as the "equal-appearing interval scale," is designed to obtain a score that will identify

TABLE 1   Examples of Scales

Thurstone Scale

	Agree	Disagree
The primary purpose of a vacation should be rest and relaxation.	____	____
Any vacation spot I visit will have a quiet beach.	____	____

Likert Scale

	Strongly Agree	Agree	Neither Agree Nor Disagree	Disagree	Strongly Disagree
I like to relax when I am on vacation.	____	____	____	____	____
I look for a quiet beach when I'm on vacation.	____	____	____	____	____

Semantic Differential Scale

The "vacation site" is:

relaxing:_____:not relaxing
quiet:_____:noisy

Stapel Scale

The "vacation site" is:

	+3		+3
	+2		+2
	+1		+1
Relaxing	−1	Quiet	−1
	−2		−2
	−3		−3

Comparative Rating Scale

Compared to "vacation site A," "vacation site B" is:

Very Quiet	Neither Quiet Nor Noisy	Very Noisy
☐	☐	☐

Constant-Sum Scale

Please divide 100 points among the following characteristics so that the division reflects the relative importance to you in the selection of a vacation site.

Relaxing	____
Quiet	____
Sporting activities	____
Night life	____

a person's position on a scale reflecting a particular attitude. The scale is developed in two stages (Thurstone 1970). The first stage requires the collection of a large pool of statements (up to 100) related to the attitude under consideration. This pool is given to a sample of judges who sort each item into one of eleven categories that they consider to be at equal intervals ranging from extremely unfavorable through neutral to extremely favorable. The average value of the item (statement) is determined by its position in the category. In the second stage, items for which judges exhibit little agree-

ment as to their position are discarded. The final scale contains between 10 and 20 items whose scale values are more or less equally spaced along the scale in terms of favorability; and it has the properties of an interval scale. The scale is then administered to respondents by asking each individual to check those statements with which he or she agrees, and the attitude score is obtained by calculating the median or mean scale value of the items checked; for example, a person who agreed with four statements whose scale values were 1.4, 2.3, 3.6, and 4.2 would have a mean attitude score of 2.9.

Because the Thurstone scale requires a two-stage process that can be time-consuming and expensive, its use in attitude measurement has been limited. However, once the scale has been constructed, it is easy to administer and requires a minimum of instruction. An interesting application of a modified Thurstone scale (Case V) dealt with the touristic benefits sought by a group of international travelers (Goodrich 1977a). The eleven benefits were ranked on seven-point importance scales, and the results provided the opportunity to compare the relative importance or preference ordering of a set of stimuli (in this case, the benefits).

LIKERT SCALE

The Likert scale, also referred to as the "summated ratings" scale, requires respondents to indicate a degree of agreement or disagreement with a set of statements (items) concerning a particular attitude object. Frequently, respondents are asked to check the extent to which they agree or disagree with each item in terms of a five-point scale that is defined by the labels *agree strongly, agree, undecided, disagree,* and *disagree strongly* (Likert 1970). The items to be included in the scale are selected from a large pool that is usually generated by the researcher. This pool is administered to a sample of respondents representative of the population under study. The next step is to perform an item analysis to determine if each item discriminates between people with positive and negative attitudes. The respondents can be divided into two groups (frequently defined as the 25 percent of respondents with the most favorable total score and the 25 percent with the most unfavorable score), and a "good" item can be defined as one for which the mean scores for the two groups are very different. Simply put, item analysis is to select from a pool of statements the ones that discriminate between groups.

The final set of 10 to 20 statements are then administered to a sample of the population under investigation. The score for an individual is the total or the average (mean) of the statement scores where "1" can represent "strongly agree" and "5" can represent "strongly disagree." An individual who "strongly agreed" with all statements on a five-statement scale would receive a total score of 5 or a mean score of 1.

This scale is popular for measuring attitudes because it is relatively easy to construct and administer. Its drawbacks include a concern that the scale does not have interval properties. Likert scales, or variations of the scale, have been widely used in travel and tourism research to identify such things as: the psychographic correlates of national parks attractiveness (Mayo 1975), the important psychographic dimensions of vacation life-styles (Perrault, Darden, and Darden 1977), the relationship between leisure activities and need satisfaction (Tinsley and Kass 1978), and the images of a specific destination held by nonvisitors and visitors (Fakeye and Crompton 1991). Two of these studies provide a reasonable amount of detail on the methods used to construct the scale (Perrault, Darden, and Darden 1977; Tinsley and Kass 1978).[2]

[2] For a comparison of the Likert scale and the Thurstone scale, see Seiler and Hough, 1970, pp. 159–173.

The Likert scale has been frequently used in a modified fashion to collect information on a wide range of attitude dimensions including psychographics (Wells 1974) and activities-interests-opinions (Wells and Tigert 1971). In fact, the proliferation of Likert-type scales has sometimes created some confusion as to what constitutes a Likert scale. Researchers have taken considerable latitude with these scales, and the reliability of some scales has been questioned (Wells 1975; Mehrota and Wells 1977).

SEMANTIC DIFFERENTIAL

The semantic differential consists of a set of bipolar adjectives, such as good-bad and strong-weak, that can be used to measure respondents' attitudes towards organizations, brands, stores, activities, vacation destinations, and so on. Normally, respondents are asked to rate an attitude object on a series of five- or seven-point scales anchored at each end by bipolar adjectives or phrases (Osgood, Suci, and Tannenbaum 1957).

In using this technique, care must be given to ensure that the adjectives or phrases used are meaningful and important to the respondents. Further, the negative poles and positive poles should be alternated between the right and left sides to avoid a response tendency, or the "halo effect," which may occur when all favorable (or unfavorable) poles are on one side and the respondent simply checks off one side of the scale. The main drawback to the semantic differential scale is that it may not have interval properties, although researchers often assume that it has interval properties when in many instances it does not.

Semantic differentials have been widely used because of their ease of construction and descriptive capabilities. In the travel and tourism area, semantic differentials have been used to measure the images that potential visitors have of various tourist-recreation regions (Hunt 1975) and measure the role of attitudes in recreationists' choice decision (Murphy 1975), and as a partial validation of the wilderness scale (Heberlein 1973). Examples of how semantic differential scales and Likert scales could be used to measure the attitude components are provided in Table 2. Some concern has been expressed with the use of a semantic differential scale in image measurement of tourist-recreation areas because it limits respondents' answers to given dimensions, and comparisons of several tourist-attracting regions through the use of many semantic differential scales may be a cumbersome task (Goodrich 1977b).

OTHER ATTITUDE MEASUREMENT SCALES

A number of other scales exist for the measurement of attitudes, many of which are modifications of the aforementioned scales. The Stapel scale is a simplified version of the semantic differential scale (Stapel 1968), and the itemized rating scale is a modification of the Likert scale (Churchill 1991, Ch. 9). A comparison of the semantic differential scale, the Stapel scale, and the Likert scale concluded that there were no marked differences with respect to measure

TABLE 2   Examples of Scales to Measure Attitude Components

EXAMPLES OF TRUE OR MODIFIED SEMANTIC DIFFERENTIAL SCALES

Knowledge

• Attribute beliefs—This vacation site is:

very relaxing --- not relaxing at all

Affect or liking

• Overall preference—I would consider this vacation site as:

not appealing --- ideal destination

• Specific attributes—In choosing a vacation site, relaxation is:

very important --- not important at all

EXAMPLES OF TRUE OR MODIFIED LIKERT SCALES

Knowledge

• Attribute beliefs—

	SA	A	NA ND	D	SD
This vacation site is very relaxing:	—	—	—	—	—

Affect or liking

• Overall preference—

I think this vacation site is an ideal destination: — — — — —

• Specific attributes—

Relaxation is an important consideration
in the vacation site I choose: — — — — —

Action

• Intentions—

I will definitely take my vacation at Site A this year: — — — — —

validation (Menezes and Elbert 1979). The Guttman scale was designed to determine whether a set of beliefs or intentions can be rank-ordered along a single dimension (Guttman 1970). Comparative rating scales are designed to determine the relative position of various attributes in relation to each other (Churchill 1991, Ch. 9).

CHOOSING A SCALE

Researchers have a range of choices regarding which scale they could choose to measure attitudes. In deciding on a particular scale, a number of criteria must be considered, including the properties of the scale, which were discussed in an earlier section. A second criteria is the number of items/statements to be used in the scale. Generally speaking, the Likert scale and the semantic differential scale are suitable for relatively large numbers of items/statements. A third criteria is the importance of reliability and validity. These items will be discussed in the next section. A final criteria is the method of interviewing (e.g., telephone, mail, personal interview), which will influence the type of scale used.

As well, there are some technical considerations, including the extent of the category description, treatment of respondent uncertainty or ignorance, balance of favorable and unfavorable categories, and whether comparison judgment is

required. These considerations, as well as some guidelines in choosing a scale (Table 3), are discussed by Aaker and Day (1990).

CONSTRUCTING A SCALE

There are three basic approaches to constructing an attitude scale. The first, and easiest, is to select a scale that has been previously developed and tested by others. This approach has the obvious advantages of using a scale that is reliable and valid. Further, the results can be compared to prior research with the potential of generalizing the results to larger settings. The major drawback is that, depending on the purpose of the research, there may be no scale that fits the present situation. A number of scales have been developed in the travel and tourism area including: psychographic or activities-interest-opinion scales (Mayo 1975; Perreault, Darden, and Darden 1977), wilderness scales (Heberlein 1973), attitude towards leisure scales (Neulinger and Breit 1971), leisure activity scales (Ritchie 1975a), traveler's attitude scales (Thompson and Troncalli 1974), and travel motivations (Fisher and Price 1991). A review of these and related studies can provide an inventory of existing attitude scales.

The second approach is to develop a scale by either modifying an existing scale or introducing a new set of items. This

TABLE 3 Appropriate Applications of Various Attitude Scales

	TYPE OF SCALE				
ATTITUDE COMPONENT	ITEMIZED-CATEGORY	RANK-ORDER	CONSTANT-SUM	LIKERT	SEMANTIC DIFFERENTIAL
Knowledge					
awareness	..				
attribute beliefs	..	.		.	..
attribute importance	..	.	..	.	
Affect or liking					
overall preferences	..	.	..	.	.
specific attributes	..	.	.	.	..
Action					
intentions	..	.	..	.	

.. = very appropriate   . = sometimes appropriate
Source: Aaker and Day (1990), 293.

approach is appropriate when the research objective is relatively simple and straightforward, when further research in the area is unlikely, and when there are time pressures to complete the study. In this type of situation, selecting one of the basic measurement techniques, designing the scale items, and conducting a pretest to determine the usefulness of each item in providing a distribution of responses should be sufficient in developing the scale.

The third approach is to develop a new scale that is valid and reliable. In this situation, the research objective would likely entail some long-term strategy. The approach offered here has been developed by Ragheb and Beard (1982), Churchill (1979), Antil and Bennett (1979), and Peter (1979). It involves eight steps and is appropriate when designing a scale using multiple items. The eight steps, illustrated in Table 4, will be discussed in turn.

Specify Domain of Construct

The first step requires a relatively precise definition of the construct (i.e., attitude) that states what is to be included *and* excluded. In establishing the domain, there is no substitute for a thorough literature search. The end product of the literature search should be an operational definition of the construct. Unfortunately, few examples of well-defined, operational constructs are available in the travel and tourism area. One exception is the leisure attitude construct developed by Ragheb and Beard (1982).

Generate Sample of Items

The purpose of this step is to generate items that measure the defined attitude/construct. The available techniques include:

TABLE 4 Procedure for Developing Better Scales

STEP	RECOMMENDED COEFFICIENTS OR TECHNIQUES
1. Specify domain of construct.	Literature search
2. Generate sample of items.	Literature search Experience survey Insight-stimulating examples Critical incidents Focus groups
3. Collect data.	
4. Purify measure.	Coefficient alpha Factor analysis
5. Collect data.	
6. Assess reliabilty.	Coefficient alpha Split-half reliability
7. Assess validity.	Multitrait-multimethod matrix Criterion validity
8. Develop norms.	Average and other statistics summarizing distribution of scores

Source: Churchill (1979), 66.

literature searches, experience surveys, insight-stimulating examples, critical incidents, and focus groups (Selltiz, Wrightsman, and Cook 1976). The literature search should offer some existing scales that can be used as a starting point. Focus group or open-ended interviews with some experienced subjects (e.g., campers, frequent travelers) can lead to further ideas and items (Hollender 1977). An interesting example of item generation was reported by Abbey (1979) in preparing a life-style scale in a study of the design of package travel tours. In this case, the researcher reviewed the literature to identify vacation life-style dimensions that were consistent with the theoretical framework employed. Then the research literature that employed life-style variables was reviewed. Third, discussions were held with travel agents and tour organizers to gain some practical insights. Finally, tour specialists were asked to review the proposed instrument in terms of appropriate questions.

After a large number of items have been generated, item editing should occur. Items that are redundant, ambiguous, or not clearly positive or negative should either be rephrased or eliminated. The remaining items can then be pretested.

Collect Data

A convenience sample can be used in the pretest as long as the attitude/construct has some relevancy for the respondent. Because the purpose of this step is to develop the scale, most sampling issues (e.g., representative sample) are not relevant.

Purify Measure

Two analytic techniques are useful in establishing acceptable levels of reliability and validity (Antil and Bennett 1979). Factor analysis can be used to identify those items that are highly correlated with one another on any single dimension and also to divide the data into a number of dimensions. The investigator may be more certain of what underlying dimensions the scale is actually measuring. Because of the number of "garbage items" at this stage, factor analysis should probably not be used in a confirmatory fashion (Churchill 1979).

Item analysis is used to determine the internal consistency of a set of items, thereby increasing the reliability of the scale. The measure, coefficient alpha (Cronbach 1951), is the most commonly accepted formula for assessing the reliability of a measurement scale with multipoint items (Peter 1979). Of interest here is obtaining a "high" alpha (Nunnally 1967) for the scale *and* ensuring that the item-to-total correlations are also high. Item reduction can be accomplished by eliminating items with low item-to-total correlations (Antil and Bennett 1979) and recalculating alpha. In an excellent meta-analysis of published marketing studies that examined reliability and validity issues, Peter and Churchill (1986) reported an average reliability value of 0.75 for the studies, thus suggesting a minimum target alpha for researchers.

A fair amount of iteration is likely to occur in this step,

depending on the results obtained (Churchill 1979). In the best case, a satisfactory alpha is obtained, and further testing of the scale can occur. In the worst case, an unsatisfactory alpha is obtained, and the researcher must return to steps 1 and 2 and repeat the process.

Collect New Data and Assess Reliability

Assuming a satisfactory alpha is obtained, the revised scale is tested with a new sample of respondents. The item-analysis procedure is repeated, and, at this time, factor analysis can aid in "purifying" the scale. During this step, the researcher is also interested in reducing the number of items in the scale without reducing the reliability. Shorter scales are normally preferred because they reduce respondent fatigue and allow for the inclusion of other measures in the questionnaire.

Further pretesting of the reduced, revised scale may also be appropriate. In this case, the data should be collected from a representative sample or a sample of the target population. Of interest here is ensuring that the reliability of the scale remains high. As well as testing for internal consistency, two other measures of reliability can be used, test—retest and alternative forms (Peter 1979), although some questions have been raised about the use of test—retest in this context (Churchill 1979).

Assess Validity

The prior steps should result in a measure that has content or face validity and is reliable. At issue is whether the measure has construct validity, that is, the purpose is to validate the theory underlying the measure or scale (Bohrnstedt 1970). To establish the construct validity of measure, one must determine (1) the extent to which the measure correlates with other measures designed to measure the same thing (i.e., convergent validity), (2) the extent to which the measure correlates with other measures from which it should differ (i.e., discriminant validity), and (3) whether the measure behaves as expected (i.e., nomological validity) (Churchill 1979).

Two well-known methods for examining convergent and discriminant validity are Campbell and Fiske's multitrait-multimethod approach (1970) and the analysis of covariance structures (LISREL) approach (e.g., Bagozzi 1978). In addition, an alternative to LISREL has been suggested (the Browne model), which assumes that the effect of method on trait is multiplicative rather than additive (Browne 1984). Assessing nomological validity involves examining relationships between measures purported to assess different, but conceptually related, constructs (Peter 1981); for example, one reasonable approach in dealing with the expected behavior is to compare the results obtained on the scale from a sample of "normal" respondents and an "interest" group. A wilderness scale could be validated by comparing the results for "average" people with a group who belong to the Sierra Club.

Peter and Churchill (1986) found and offered the following pattern in testing for reliability and validity:

Reliability values should be largest because they represent the correlation of measures with themselves (e.g., average values of 0.75).

Convergent validity values should be second largest because they represent the correlation between two different measures purported to measure the same construct (e.g., average values of 0.57).

Nomological validity values should be third largest because they represent the correlation between different, conceptually related constructs (e.g., average values of 0.29).

Discriminant validity values should be the smallest because they represent the relationship between theoretically unrelated constructs (e.g., average values of 0.22).

Develop Norms

In some cases, it may be desirable to develop norms for scales (Churchill 1979). This step requires obtaining measures on relatively large numbers of representative respondents and can only be justified if the scale is to be widely used (e.g., personality measures, intelligence tests).

Summary

It is apparent that the development of a "good" scale requires considerable effort and expertise. While individual researchers may wish to avoid or eliminate some of the steps, it should be recognized that the emerging attitude-measurement literature in the travel and tourism area will only progress through the development of reliable, valid scales. To quote Frechtling, "This body of knowledge . . . about travel behavior that allows us a clear view of its structure and consequences . . . can only be developed through the painstaking process of building on the research of others in examining behavior and attitudes" (1979:2).

ALTERNATIVE APPROACHES TO ATTITUDE MEASUREMENT

MULTIDIMENSIONAL SCALING

The techniques discussed thus far involve the explicit specification of attributes or characteristics about an attitude object. It is assumed that the information provided by having respondents evaluate alternatives on these prespecified characteristics (i.e., assessing their beliefs) will provide valuable insights into their attitudes towards those alternatives. One concern in using this approach is the extent to which the characteristics specified accurately reflect the evaluative dimensions that the respondents would employ if the choice were theirs. A technique that alleviates this problem is mul-

tidimensional scaling.[3] Individuals are asked to rate alternatives on the basis of perceived similarity to one another. They are not told which criteria to use to determine similarity. A multidimensional scaling computer program converts the similarity data into distances on a map with a small number of dimensions so that similar alternatives are close together. An example of a map generated via multidimensional scaling is provided in Figure 1.

The program determines the underlying dimensionality to individuals' similarity judgments and the position of alternatives on each of those dimensions. The interpretation of the resulting dimensions is based on an understanding of the characteristics of those alternatives that are located close together on the map. In Figure 1, the activities: gardening, handicrafts, and reading, for example, are located very close to one another on the top end of the vertical dimension; similarly, playing bridge, bowling, and snowmobiling are located close to one another but on the opposite end of the vertical dimension. The author, based on the positioning of the various activities, subjectively labeled this vertical dimension as reflecting the extent to which an activity is an individual or group event.

The technique also lends itself to assessing individuals' preferences. This is accomplished by having individuals include an "ideal" alternative and rate its similarity to the other alternatives. The distance between each alternative and the ideal alternative is then used to generate preferences. The results can be generated on an aggregate basis or for one individual. An example of multidimensional scaling in the travel and tourism domain is the mapping of consumers' visitation patterns of tourist attractions (Fodness 1990).

The major advantages of such an approach are that it provides an overall structure of the various alternatives as the individuals perceive them (i.e., a perceptual map) and that it eliminates the risk of specifying evaluative characteristics that may not be relevant for individuals. One limitation is that researchers must interpret the dimensions generated, although this could be facilitated with the collection of additional data on the characteristics (i.e., attributes) of the alternatives. Other limitations of the approach and of the semantic differential approach as compared to free elicitation (e.g., open-ended questions) for tourism image assessment is provided by Reilly (1990).

CONSTANT-SUM SCALE

The importance that individuals place on certain characteristics when evaluating alternatives poses another issue for attitude measurement. As previously discussed, the importance of certain beliefs or characteristics can be assessed directly via a rating or ranking procedure. Another variation is to employ the constant-sum scale (briefly discussed earlier), which asks respondents to allocate a fixed number of points (e.g., 100) to each characteristic in proportion to their relative importance. One difficulty with many approaches is

[3]For a more detailed discussion of multidimensional scaling, see Shepard, Romney, and Nerlove, Volumes I and II (1972).

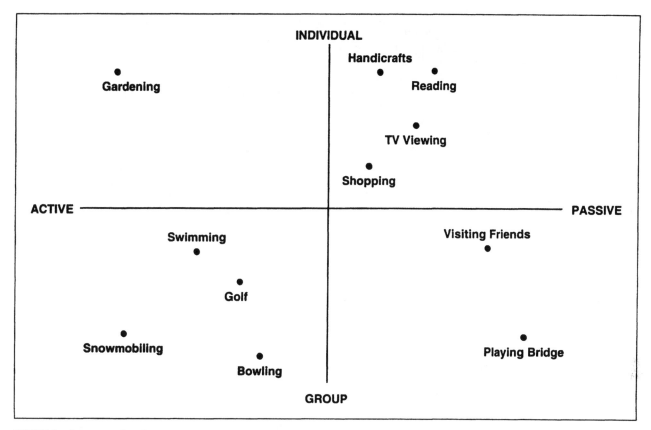

FIGURE 1 An example of a perceptual map generated by multidimensional scaling.
Source: This illustration is adapted from J. R. B. Ritchie (1975a), "On the Derivation of Leisure Activity Types: A Perceptual Mapping Approach, " *Journal of Leisure Research* 7(2) 128–140.

their failure to indicate those characteristics that are determinant in consumers' evaluation processes; for example, an attribute or characteristic can be considered important by consumers, but the alternatives may not be perceived as being different with respect to that characteristic. That characteristic is likely to be given less weight in the evaluation process than those that are not only perceived to be important but also can be used to differentiate among alternatives (i.e., determinant). These determinant characteristics are more relevant in that they provide greater insights into consumers' evaluations and choice processes.

An additional limitation in assessing importance through rating approaches is that the characteristics are considered independently. This tends to contribute to respondents rating many characteristics as being important and reduces the ability to distinguish among those that are considered more important than others. This weakness is alleviated to some extent when the constant-sum scale is employed.

CONJOINT ANALYSIS

Conjoint analysis, an indirect approach to assessing attribute importance, offers a means for addressing the limitations discussed above. The technique involves the trade-off of alternatives having characteristics that are varied in system-

atic ways. Based on respondents' preferences for the various alternative profiles, inferences are made about the underlying value systems or importance of characteristics. A detailed discussion of conjoint analysis is contained in Chapter 44 of this book, and those interested are referred to that chapter (Claxton 1993).

SPECIAL CONSIDERATIONS

There are a number of problems/issues that may arise in conducting attitude research in the travel and tourism area. The researcher might review these concerns to see if they are applicable for a particular situation. The following five issues are worthy of mention.

THE MULTIFACETED AND MULTIATTRIBUTE DIMENSIONS OF VACATIONS

Unlike even relatively complex products that usually have a known and definable set of dimensions, vacation destinations can offer a large number of possible dimensions that may be difficult for the researcher to identify. While respondents' attitudes toward the benefits of various vacation destinations can be measured, the motivations for a particular site may range from esoteric (e.g., escape from realism) to mundane (e.g., visit an aunt), and the perceptions of a site may vary depending on the distance the respondent is from that site (Scott, Schewe, and Frederick 1978). Further, the variations in these motivations may lead to subject responses that are not comparable. Researchers in the travel/leisure area must take care to construct scenarios that are factually explicit in order that measured differences in attitudes are referring to the same, rather than different, concepts (Ritchie 1975b). Simply put, when one measures attitudes towards products, usually the important factors/dimensions can be identified through a consumer-based approach. When one measures attitudes towards vacation destinations, even a consumer-based approach may lead to an incomplete list or a large list that may be unmanageable in a survey.

THE HIGH-INVOLVEMENT JOINT DECISION

The vacation-decision process can typically be described as one that involves active information search, that is fairly long, and that involves, to some degree, all members of the household (Ritchie and Filiatrault 1980; Nichols and Snepenger 1988). This type of decision process implies that attitudes towards various vacation destinations may be well structured and may be easily measured but that they also may change as additional information is obtained. Further, the measurement problem is complicated because it is likely to be a joint decision and it may be necessary to interview both the male and the female heads of households (Ritchie 1975b).

TIME BETWEEN PURCHASES

For most consumers, vacations are an annual event. This infrequent decision (as opposed to repetitive decisions) can create some problems. A weak relationship between attitudes and behavior, for example, may surface unless this time element is reflected in the measures employed.

THE REPEAT-PURCHASE DISCONTINUITY

When consumers purchase a product and then experience it through use, they will tend to purchase the same brand again if satisfaction levels are acceptable. High satisfaction with a particular vacation may not lead to a repeat purchase of that vacation site. Because many consumers want similar but *new* experiences with vacations, the destinations vary each year. The problem with respect to attitude measurement is that while consumers may be highly satisfied and have very favorable images of the destination they visited last year, they will not visit it again. Consequently, the attitude-behavior intention link is not present. Researchers need to be cognizant of this fact.

PERCEIVED RISK AND TRAVEL

It appears likely that, because a vacation choice may be a high perceived-risk decision, risk may operate as a moderating variable between attitudes and intended behavior; that is, consumers with a high tolerance for risk are more likely to

"go where their attitudes take them," whereas those with a low tolerance for risk are likely to return to familiar spots, even if another, new destination is preferred.

ATTITUDE RESEARCH AND TOURISM MANAGEMENT

The primary reason for using attitude research in tourism management is to gain an understanding of *why* and *how* people make travel decisions. This understanding enables managers to more effectively market their particular transportation or destination modes. The following examples illustrate how attitude research can lead to more effective marketing.

IDENTIFYING CONSUMER BENEFITS

The foundation of any successful marketing campaign, be it for soap or sailing, is a thorough understanding of the consumer benefits that can be satisfied by the offered product or service. Knowledge of these benefits assists in segmentation, positioning, and strategy. A service or facility can be successfully positioned in the marketplace by offering benefits that are important to a particular customer group and yet different from those benefits offered by competitors. With respect to vacation destinations, because they frequently can satisfy a multitude of needs, attitude measurement can help determine the importance or rank-order of the benefits for various segments. An interesting illustration of the determination of benefits (e.g., sightseeing opportunities, camping opportunities) through the use of factor analysis is provided by Crask (1981).

Establishing Segments and Target Selection

A critical aspect of any marketing plan is the identification of various segments and the selection of some of these segments for a focused marketing strategy. Psychographic or life-style research has been particularly useful in identifying segments such as the "budget vacationers" and the "adventurers" (Perreault, Darden, and Darden 1977). As well, the appeal of various tourist-attracting attributes by segment can be identified (Davis and Sternquist 1987). It is likely that a particular tourist facility will not be able to effectively service the desires of all customers. However, a clear understanding of the attitudes of the various customer groups will assist in identifying viable market segments in terms of potential revenue or heavy use and permit an effective channeling of resources in appealing to those segments.

DESIGNING MARKETING STRATEGIES

The essence of marketing strategy is the matching of the firm's product/service offering with some target segments. In this context, vacation destinations can be matched to selected consumer travel segments. A strategy is then designed to cement this match; for example, a tourist service or facility may be developed or modified such that it offers those characteristics desired by a particular group of consumers. Research has shown that tour travelers prefer tours designed with vacation life-style, as opposed to demographic, information, and this data can be used to design strategies that are compatible with the motivations, attitudes, and opinions of tour travelers (Abbey 1979).

IMPLEMENTING THE MARKETING MIX

The final step in the marketing process is to design a specific marketing program (e.g., advertising) to encourage the selected segments to visit/vacation at a particular destination. In the tourism domain, the major component of the marketing mix is usually advertising, and attitude research can be useful in identifying the salient attributes (to the consumer) of the program. Promotional efforts can then be directed at reinforcing favorable attitudes or altering consumers' perceptions such that more favorable attitudes will be formed. Examples of the various advertising strategies that can stem from a knowledge of consumers' attitudes is offered in a framework provided by Boyd, Ray, and Strong (1972). A practical illustration of the implementation of a promotional strategy is the decision of the Michigan Travel Bureau to increase advertising in high-potential geographic markets based on vacation-preference types (Bryant and Morrison 1980).

CONCLUSIONS

An important aspect of understanding and predicting human behavior is the study of attitudes, that is, the knowledge, feelings, and behavioral components individuals have with respect to some object or activity. With this understanding, the probability of designing effective marketing programs is greatly enhanced. This is particularly true in the travel and tourism domain where knowledge of consumers' attitudes towards leisure, travel, and vacation destinations can assist in preparing successful strategies.

The measurement of attitudes requires an understanding of what constitutes an attitude and what possible relationships may exist between attitudes and behavior in various situations. Further, it is important to appreciate what attitude measurement technique is appropriate given a particular research project. Within the travel and tourism domain, these issues can be addressed by ensuring that the attitude constructs under consideration are well defined and that the possible linkages between attitudes and behavior have been carefully documented. While some unique problems exist in measuring attitudes in the travel and tourism domain, they can be overcome. The major requirements are expertise and a knowledge of the field of investigation and of the attitudes to be studied.

The attitude measurement in the travel and tourism area has offered and continues to offer considerable potential. As a maturing field, it is now appropriate to spend more effort on the construction of reliable and valid attitudes scales, an objective that this paper has attempted to accomplish.

REFERENCES

Aaker, D.A., and G.S. Day (1990), *Marketing Research*, 4th ed., New York: John Wiley & Sons, Inc.

Abbey, J.R. (1979), "Does Life-Style Profiling Work?" *Journal of Travel Research* 17 (3) (Summer), 8–14.

Adams, E.W., R.F. Fagot, and R.E. Robinson (1965), "A Theory of Appropriate Statistics," *Psychometrika* 30, 99–127.

Ajzen, I., and M. Fishbein (1977), "Attitude-Behavior Relations: A Theoretical Analysis and Review of Empirical Research," *Psychological Bulletin* 84 (5), 888–918.

Ajzen, I., and M. Fishbein, (1980), *Understanding Attitudes and Predicting Social Behavior*, Englewood Cliffs, NJ: Prentice-Hall.

Antil, J.H. and P.D. Bennett (1979), "Construction and Validation of a Scale to Measure Socially Responsible Consumption Behavior," in *The Conserver Society*, K.E. Henion, and T.C. Kinnear, eds., 51–68, Chicago: American Marketing Association.

Bagozzi, R.P. (1978), "The Construct Validity of the Affective, Behavioral, and Cognitive Components of Attitudes by Analysis of Co-variance Structures," *Multivariate Behavioral Research* 13, 9–31.

Belk, R.W. (1975), "Situational Variables and Consumer Behavior," *Journal of Consumer Research* 1 (2) (December), 157–164.

Bohrnsted, G.W. (1970), "Reliability and Validity Assessment in Attitude Measurement," in *Attitude Measurement*, G.F. Summers ed., 80–99, Chicago: Rand McNally and Company.

Boyd, H.W., M.L. Ray, and E.C. Strong (1972), "An Attitudinal Framework for Advertising Strategy," *Journal of Marketing* 36, 27–33.

Browne, Michael W. (1984), "The Decomposition of Multitrait—Multimethod Matrices," *British Journal of Mathematical and Statistical Psychology* 37 (May), 1–21.

Bryant, B.E., and A.J. Morrison (1980), "Travel Market Segmentation and the Implementation of Market Strategies," *Journal of Travel Research* 18 (Winter), 2–7.

Calder, B.J., and M. Ross (1973), *Attitudes and Behavior*, Morristown, NJ: Learning Press.

Campbell, D.T., and D.W. Fiske (1970), "Convergent and Discriminant Validation by the Multitrait-Multimethod Matrix," in *Attitude Measurement*, G.F. Summers ed., 100–124, Chicago: Rand McNally & Company.

Churchill, G.A., Jr. (1979), "A Paradigm for Developing Better Measures of Marketing Constructs," *Journal of Marketing Research* 16 (February), 64–73.

Churchill, G.A., Jr. (1991), *Marketing Research: Methodological Foundations*, 5th ed., Chicago: Dryden Press.

Claxton, J.D. (1993), "Conjoint Analysis in Travel Research: A Manager's Guide," in *Travel, Tourism and Hospitality Research*, 2nd ed., J.R.B. Ritchie and C.R. Goeldner, eds., New York: John Wiley & Sons.

Crask, M.R. (1981), "Segmenting the Vacationer Market: Identifying the Vacation Preferences, Demographics, and Magazine Readership of Each Group," *Journal of Travel Research* 19 (Fall), 29–34.

Crompton, J.L. (1979), "An Assessment of the Image of Mexico as a Vacation Destination and the Influence of Geographical Location Upon That Image," *Journal of Travel Research* 17 (Spring), 18–23.

Cronbach, L.J. (1951), "Coefficient Alpha and the Internal Structure of Tests," *Psychometrika* 16 (September), 297–334.

Cummings, W.H., and M. Vankatesan, M. (1976), "Cognitive Dissonance and Consumer Behavior: A Review of the Evidence," *Journal of Marketing Research* 13 (3), 303–308.

Davis, B.D., and B. Sternquist (1987), "Appealing to the Elusive Tourist: An Attribute Cluster Strategy," *Journal of Travel Research* 26 (Spring), 25–31.

Eagley, A.H., and S. Himmelfarb (1978), "Attitudes and Opinions," *Annual Review of Psychology*, 517–554.

Fakeye, P.C., and J.L. Crompton (1991), "Image Differences Between Prospective, First-Time, and Repeat Visitors to the Lower Rio Grande Valley," *Journal of Travel Research* 30 (Fall), 10–16.

Fazio, R.H., and M.P. Zanna (1978), "On the Predictive Validity of Attitudes: The Roles of Direct Experience and Confidence," *Journal of Personality* 46 (June), 228–243.

Fishbein, M., and I. Ajzen (1975), *Belief, Attitude, Intention and Behavior: An Introduction to Theory and Research*, Reading, MA: Addison-Wesley.

Fisher, R.J., and L.L. Price (1991), "International Pleasure Travel Motivations and Post-Vacation Cultural Attitude Change," *Journal of Leisure Research* 23 (3), 193–208.

Fodness, Dale (1990), "Consumer Perceptions of Tourist Attractions," *Journal of Travel Research* 29 (Spring), 3–9.

Frechtling, D.C. (1979), "What's Wrong With Travel Research, *The Travel Research Association Proceedings*,1–3, University of Utah.

Garner, W.R., and C.D. Creelman (1970), "Problems and Methods of Psychological Scaling," in *Attitude Measurement*, G.F. Summers ed., 42–79, Chicago: Rand McNally & Company.

Goodrich, J.N. (1977a), "Benefit Bundle Analysis: An Empirical Study of International Travelers," *Journal of Travel Research* 16 (Fall), 6–9.

Goodrich, J.N. (1977b) "Differences in Perceived Similarity of Tourism Regions: A Spatial Analysis," *Journal of Travel Research* 16 (Summer), 10–13.

Goodrich, J.N. (1978), "The Relationship Between Preferences for and Perceptions of Vacation Destinations: Application of a Choice Model," *Journal of Travel Research* 17 (Fall), 8–13.

Guttman, L. (1970), "A Basis for Scaling Qualitative Data," in *Attitude Measurement*, G.F. Summers ed., 187–202, Chicago: Rand McNally & Company.

Heberlein, T.A. (1973), "Social Psychological Assumptions of User Attitude Surveys: The Case of the Wilderness Scale," *Journal of Leisure Research* 5 (Summer), 18–33.

Hollender, J.W. (1977), "Motivational Dimensions of the Camping Experience," *Journal of Leisure Research* 9 (2) 133–141.

Houston, M.J., and M.L. Rothschild (1978), "Conceptual and Methodological Perspectives on Involvement," in *Research Frontiers in Marketing: Dialogues and Directions*, S.C. Jain ed., A.M.A. Educators Proceedings.

Hunt, J.D. (1975), "Image as a Factor on Tourism Development," *Journal of Travel Research* 13 (Winter), 1–7.

Kelman, H.C. (1974), "Attitudes Are Alive and Well and Gainfully Employed in the Sphere of Action," *American Psychologist* 29, 310–324.

Likert, R. (1970), "A Technique for the Measurement of Attitudes," in *Attitude Measurement*, G.F. Summers ed., 149–158, Chicago: Rand McNally & Company.

Mayo, E. (1975), "Tourism and the National Parks: A Psychographic and Attitudinal Study," *Journal of Travel Research* 14 (Summer), 14–18.

McGuire, W.J. (1969), "The Nature of Attitudes and Attitude Change," in G. Lindsey and E. Aronson eds., *The Handbook of Social Psychology*, Vol III, 2nd ed., 136–171, Reading, MA: Addison-Wesley.

Mehorta, S., and W.D. Wells (1977), "Psychographics and Buyer Behavior: Theory and Recent Empirical Findings, in *Consumer and Industrial Buying Behavior*, A.G. Woodside et al. eds., 49–65, New York: North-Holland.

Menezes, D., and N.F. Elbert (1979), "Alternative Semantic Scaling Formats for Measuring Store Image: An Evaluation," *Journal of Marketing Research* 16 (February), 80–87.

Michie, D.A., and G.L. Sullivan (1990), "The Role(s) of the International Travel Agent in the Travel Decision Process of Client Families," *Journal of Travel Research* 29 (Fall), 30–38.

Murphy, P.E. (1975), "The Role of Attitude in the Choice Decisions of Recreational Boaters," *Journal of Leisure Research* 7 (3), 216–224.

Neulinger, J., and M. Breit (1971), "Attitude Dimensions of Leisure: A Replication Study," *Journal of Leisure Research* 3 (Fall), 108–115.

Nichols, C.M., and D.J. Snepenger (1988), "Family Decision Making and Tourism Behavior and Attitudes," *Journal of Travel Research* 27 (Spring), 2–6.

Nunnally, J.C. (1967), *Psychometric Theory*, New York: McGraw-Hill Book Company.

Olson, J.C., and A.A. Mitchell (1975), "The Process of Attitude Acquisition: The Value of a Developmental Approach to Consumer Attitude Research," in *Advances in Consumer Research: Vol. II*, Mary J. Schlinger ed., 249–264, Chicago: Association for Consumer Research.

Osgood, C.E., G. Suci, and P. Tannenbaum (1957), *The Measurement of Meaning*, Urbana, IL: University of Illinois Press.

Perreault, W.D., D.K. Darden, and W.R. Darden (1977), "A Psychographic Classification of Vacation Life Styles," *Journal of Leisure Research* 8 (3), 208–224.

Peter, J.P. (1979), "Reliability: A Review of Psychometric Basics and Recent Marketing Practices," *Journal of Marketing Research* 16 (February), 6–17.

Peter, J.P. (1981), "Construct Validity: A Review of Basic Issues and Marketing Practices," *Journal of Marketing Research* 18, (May), 133–145.

Peter, J.P., and G.A. Churchill Jr. (1986), "Relationships Among Research Design Choices and Psychometric Properties of Rating Scales: A Meta-Analysis," *Journal of Marketing Research* 23 (February), 1–10.

Ragheb, M.J., and J.G. Beard (1982), "Measuring Leisure Attitudes," *Journal of Leisure Research* 14 (2), 155–167.

Regan, D.T., and R.H. Fazio (1977), "On the Consistency Between Attitudes and Behavior: Look to the Method of Attitude Formation," *Journal of Experimental Social Psychology* 13, 28–45.

Reilly, M.D. (1990), "Free Elicitation of Descriptive Adjectives for Tourism Image Assessment," *Journal of Travel Research* 29 (Spring), 21–26.

Ritchie, J.R.B. (1975a), "On the Derivation of Leisure Activity Types: A Perceptual Mapping Approach," *Journal of Leisure Research* 7 (2), 128–140.

Ritchie, J.R.B. (1975b), "Some Critical Aspects of Measurement Theory and Practice in Travel Research," *Journal of Travel Research* 13 (Spring), 1–10.

Ritchie, J.R.B., and P. Filiatrault (1980), "Family Vacation Decision-Making—A Replication and Extension," *Journal of Travel Research* 18 (Spring), 3–14.

Ritchie, J.R.B., and M. Sheridan (1988), "Developing an Integrated Framework for Tourism Demand in Canada," *Journal of Travel Research* 27 (Summer), 3–9.

Scott, C.A. (1978), "Self-Perception Processes in Consumer Behavior: Interpreting One's Own Experiences," in *Advances in Consumer Research*, Vol. V., H. Keith Hunt ed., Association for Consumer Research.

Scott, D.R., C.D. Schewe, and D.G. Frederick (1978), "A Multi-Brand/Multi-Attribute Model of Tourist State Choice," *Journal of Travel Research* 16 (Summer), 23–29.

Seigal, S. (1956), *Nonparametric Statistics for the Behavioral Sciences*, New York: McGraw-Hill.

Seiler, L.H., and R.L. Hough (1970), "Empirical Comparisons of the Thurstone and Likert Techniques," in *Attitude Measurement*, G.F. Summers ed., 159–173, Chicago: Rand McNally and Company.

Selltiz, C., L.S. Wrightsman, and S.W. Cook (1976), *Research Methods in Social Relations*, 3rd ed., New York: Holt Rinehart, and Winston.

Shephard, R.N., K.A. Romney, and S.B. Nerlove (1972), *Multidimensional Scaling: Theory and Applications in the Behavioral Sciences, Volumes I and II*, New York: Seminar Press, Inc.

Smith, R.E., and W.R. Swinyard (1983), "Attitude-Behavior Consistency: The Impact of Product Trial Versus Advertising," *Journal of Marketing Research* 20 (August), 257–267.

Snyder, M., and E.D. Tanke (1976), "Behavior and Attitude: Some People are More Consistent than Others," *Journal of Personality* 44, 501–517.

Stapel, J. (1968), "Predictive Attitudes," in *Attitude Research on the Rocks*, L. Adler and I. Crespi eds., 96–115, Chicago: American Marketing Association.

Thompson, J.R., and M.T. Troncalli (1974), "A Psychographic Study of Tennessee Welcome Center Visitors," *The Travel Research Association Proceedings*, Salt Lake City, 46–51.

Thurstone, L.L. (1970), "Attitudes Can Be Measured," in *Attitude Measurement*, G.F. Summers ed., 127–141, Chicago: Rand McNally & Company.

Tinsley, H.E.A., and R.A. Kass (1978), "Leisure Activities and Need Satisfaction: A Replication and Extension," *Journal of Leisure Research* 10 (3), 191–202.

Wells, W.D. (1974), *Life Styles and Psychographics*, Chicago: American Marketing Association.

Wells, W.D. (1975), "Psychographics: A Critical Review," *Journal of Marketing Research* 12 (May), 196–213.

Wells, W.D., and Tigert, D.J. (1971), "Activities, Interests, and Opinions," *Journal of Advertising Research*, 11 (August), 79–85.

Woodside, A.G., and R.E. Pitts (1976), "Effects of Consumer Life Styles, Demographics, and Travel Activities on Foreign and Domestic Travel Behavior," *Journal of Travel Research* 14 (Winter), 13–15.

12

Issues in Sampling and Sample Design— A Managerial Perspective

JOHN C. CANNON*

Chief, Housing Surveys Branch
Demographic Surveys Division
Bureau of the Census
Washington, D.C.

*T*his chapter briefly describes four basic samples and their advantages and disadvantages. Also included is a summary of sampling and nonsampling errors and issues a manager should consider in selecting a sample design. The chapter ends with illustrations on bringing these variables together to select a sample plan.

The development of sampling theory and the acceptance of sample survey results has made it possible for persons who make decisions to have the ability to collect information relatively quickly and inexpensively and to use that information in their decision making. Managers and government officials involved in the travel and tourism industry are among those taking advantage of this. Service industries such as airlines and hotel/motel chains conduct surveys to learn about their customers and how they can improve their service. State and local government agencies use data from surveys to determine the impact of tourism on their economy and how best to use their advertising dollar. The federal government uses survey data to measure the levels of travel and the tourism economy at different intervals of time. Such information is used to help in planning to meet current and future needs in these and related areas, such as transportation. Indeed, taking surveys has become a relatively common practice and may, in some instances, be the standard response when information is needed.

IS A SURVEY NECESSARY?

Surveys are a good way of obtaining accurate information quickly and relatively inexpensively. However, there may be other alternatives that are cheaper, quicker, and more accurate. In many cases, the information needed may already be available. There is a great deal of information that has been published or is otherwise accessible to the public. Before undertaking the expense of a survey, a cost-conscious manager should make the effort to see if someone else, perhaps even someone inside his or her own organization, has already acquired the information. In other cases, a business's or organization's administrative or sales records may provide the data required. A summary of these records, or even a sample of the records, could provide the manager with the quick, reliable data that is needed at little or no cost.

In those instances when the information needed is not available from other sources or administrative records, a manager should ask whether the data needed is important enough to justify the expense of conducting a survey to collect it. Can the manager make do with the information that is available or rely on common sense to come up with the answer being sought? If the decision is that a survey is necessary, then there are several decisions left to be made. The remaining part of this chapter will focus on some basic issues in sampling and sample design.

*The author gratefully acknowledges the assistance of Dennis J. Schwanz, Chief, Longitudinal Surveys Branch, Statistical Methods Division, Bureau of the Census, in preparing the technical sections of this chapter.

TYPES OF SAMPLES

Basically, sampling describes the activity of selecting a few from the total and using characteristics of the few to estimate the characteristics of the total. How the selection of the few is done largely determines the accuracy of the estimates derived from the sample. There are several different types of sampling and various options that can be employed to enhance the quality of each. Books have been written describing various sampling methods, the mathematical proof of the theory, and their advantages and disadvantages. What will be attempted in the next few pages is to briefly summarize the major types of samples and their good and bad points so that the manager will at least have a starting point in considering what type of sample and sample design is needed. An attempt will be made to do this simply and without being overly technical. Those interested in a detailed, technical explanation of sampling should refer to any of the several complete books written by experts in this field. Four such books are mentioned at the end of this chapter.

SIMPLE RANDOM SAMPLING AND SYSTEMATIC SAMPLING

Simple random sampling is basically a sampling method in which each possible combination of persons/establishments/houses, or whatever, that exist in the area of interest (the *universe* for the study) has the same chance, or probability, of being selected as every other combination. It is the base on which some other types of sampling are built. In this method, a number is assigned serially to every unit in the universe, and then the sample is chosen by drawing numbers out of a hat or a fishbowl or by using a random-number table.

Simple random sampling is one of the purest forms of selecting a sample. Sometimes the size of the universe, and sample, make sample selection using this method an overly burdensome task. An alternative is systematic sampling. Using this method requires that first a list of all units in the universe is created. Once the list is completed, the sample is drawn by selecting one out of every so many on the list in a predetermined, systematic fashion. The selection is made by dividing the number of units in the universe by the sample size. The result of this calculation provides the interval between units that are selected; for example, if the number of units in the universe is 100 and the sample size is 10, the sample is selected by taking 1 out of every 10 units on the list. The proper procedure, continuing with this sample, would be to randomly select a number between 1 and 10 as a random start and then select every 10th unit on the list.

Systematic sampling may sometimes be confused with simple random sampling. The difference between the two methods is that while in simple random sampling every possible combination of units in the universe is possible, in using systematic sampling only certain combinations are possible. If a sample of two units out of a universe of four (A, B, C, D) was needed, under systematic sampling only the combinations of A and C, or B and D would be possible (start with the first or second on the list and take every second unit). In simple random sampling, a token to represent each unit is placed in a hat and two are selected as the sample. In this fashion, every combination is possible (A-B, A-C, A-D, B-C, B-D, C-D).

For systematic sampling to be an acceptable alternative to simple random sampling, the list must be arranged in a nearly random order. If there is a suspicion of any regularity in the sequence of the listing that could conform to the sampling interval, systematic sampling should be avoided. Suppose the manager of a 100-unit hotel, for example, wanted to select a sample of 10 units and interview the occupants of those units to learn more about the characteristics of the hotel guests. The manager selected the sample by listing all the hotel rooms in room-number order and then drawing a 1 in 10 sample. In many cases, this would be no problem. In this case, however, all the rooms with numbers ending in "0" are luxury suites that rent for rates that are very much higher than usual, while all the rooms with numbers ending in "5" are very small, inexpensive rooms that can sleep only one person. Depending on what the random start was, the manager could have a sample of all luxury suites, a sample of all one-person rooms, or a sample that included neither. Although using a simple random sampling method could have a similar result, in this situation, systematic sampling guarantees that the sample will not be representative as long as the list is arranged by room number.

As long as the list is arranged properly, systematic sampling is a simple, straightforward way of scientifically selecting an approximately random sample. If a list is readily available or can be made up with little effort and there is nothing unique about certain elements within the universe that would affect the objectives of the surveys, systematic sampling would be the cheapest and the easiest. There are disadvantages in addition to the one regarding the arrangement of the list. One possible disadvantage is the development of a complete list of elements in the universe. The effort required to develop a complete list of attendees at a travel conference who did not require registration or other similar means of check-in would probably be quite great and, in all likelihood, would be more than that effort required to do the survey once the list was made. Another disadvantage is revealed if the uniqueness of a few elements within the universe has a direct impact on the objectives of the study. Using a travel conference as an example, suppose the objective of the study was to estimate the amount of money participants expended to attend the conference. In this example, most of the attendees come from the surrounding area and, therefore, spend little for transportation or lodging; a relative few attendees travel long distances and, therefore, spent large amounts to attend the conference. Depending on the luck of the draw, the estimate might be too low (if the sample includes too many "locals") or too high (if the sample contains a disproportionate share of the "big spenders"). Although this can happen with any type of sample, there are ways of controlling this by using some form of stratification, which will be discussed later.

Another disadvantage to systematic sampling occurs if

the universe is widely dispersed, either geographically or over a period of time, the disadvantage being mainly one of expense rather than survey quality. To list all persons or addresses in a large geographic area or to record all occurrences (such as arrivals at bus stations) throughout a long period of time in order to develop a sample universe can be very time-consuming and costly. Cost is also a problem if personal interviews are required and the sample is spread evenly throughout the entire geographic area. The use of mail and telephone surveys makes geographic dispersion a less serious problem.

STRATIFIED RANDOM SAMPLING

Stratified random sampling is similar to systematic sampling, and it overcomes one of the disadvantages of the latter, while introducing another possible disadvantage. Stratification means (1) separating the universe into small groups of units so that the units within each group have similar characteristics, (2) making each of the groups as dissimilar as possible, and (3) placing the units within each group together on a list before selecting the sample. Again using the attendees at the travel conference as an example, by placing all the "big spenders" together on a list and all the "locals" together on a list, a stratified sample method would then provide a relatively proportionate sample from each of the two groups in attendance. Stratification overcomes the problem of uniqueness of certain elements within the universe but does require a prior knowledge of key characteristics of the elements. It would be hard to implement a stratification if knowledge about the elements in the universe was unavailable to the sampler. Another disadvantage in using stratification is that if the interest is in several somewhat unrelated characteristics, stratifying using just one or two of the characteristics might damage the study of the unstratified characteristics. The problem may be that by stratifying on one characteristic, the randomness of the distribution of another characteristic on the list is destroyed.

CLUSTER SAMPLING

Cluster sampling is used to overcome the cost problems of geographic dispersion or to reduce the size of the list one needs to develop or work with in selecting a sample. In cluster sampling, the universe is divided into distinct geographic areas, such as Census enumeration districts, townships, or counties. In the case of mail or telephone surveys, the area might be determined by ZIP code boundaries or by telephone area codes or exchanges. By first selecting a sample of areas and then selecting a sample of elements within the sample areas, the number of areas that must be contacted is reduced, and the number of sample cases is concentrated in fewer geographic areas. This is also known as two-stage sampling. At each stage, the sample is selected randomly or systematically.

The method has cost advantages if the universe to be covered is households, businesses, or persons that are scattered throughout a large geographic area, particularly if the

area must first be canvassed to create a list of eligible elements, such as addresses. In the case where lists exist, such as commercial address lists, telephone directories, or randomly generated telephone numbers, clustering would reduce the size of the list to more manageable, and efficient, proportions. While cost is the major advantage to cluster sampling, it also usually produces a larger sampling error; that is, the estimate obtained is not likely to be as reliable. The reliability of a cluster sample is affected by the composition of the clusters. If the members within clusters are very similar in respect to the characteristic of interest, then the cluster sample would have a larger sampling error or would be less reliable than a simple random sample of the same size. Conversely, if the members within clusters are relatively dissimilar in respect to this characteristic, then the cluster sample would be as reliable or more reliable than a simple random sample of the same size. In other words, the situations that result in an efficient stratified sample make for inefficient cluster sampling. The more alike that units are within a cluster, the better the results will be if the cluster is used as a group in stratified sampling and the worse the results will be if the cluster is used in a cluster sample.

Nonetheless, for a fixed budget, use of cluster sampling may increase the sample size above the number the same budget would allow for simple random sampling. If the increase in sample size more than compensates for the increase in sampling error resulting from the use of a cluster sample, then there will be a net gain in the reliability of the data.

QUOTA SAMPLING

This method of sampling requires the enumerators to interview a fixed number of elements with certain characteristics; that is, a quota is established for the number and type of elements to be selected. Selecting a sample in this fashion is simple, insures that elements with selected characteristics are represented, and, in certain instances, may be the only way that a sample of the population can be drawn. The quota is usually established based on known characteristics of the universe. Using the travel conference again as an example, if the purpose of the study is to determine the amount of money spent to attend the conference, and the length of travel required to attend the conference for each of the attendees is known, the attendees could be divided into groups based on length of travel. The interviewers would then be given a list of names in each group and instructed to interview a set number of persons in each group so that a representative sample is selected. The interviewers, armed with their lists, would then proceed to interview those persons on the list that were cooperative and easiest to contact. Those persons who refuse to be interviewed or who are consistently moving about are less likely to be included in the universe.

The major disadvantage of quota sampling is that the selection of the persons to be interviewed is not based on a random or systematic selection but on the accessibility and cooperativeness of those responding. For this reason, the chances that the sample is truly representative are less than with other sampling methods. Continuing with the travel conference example, if the people who were interviewed were easy to contact because they were spending their evenings in their rooms reading a book and eating a sandwich while those persons who were difficult to contact were spending their evenings out dining, barhopping, and attending shows, the estimate of expenditures derived from the sample would not be accurate.

There are times when using a quota is the only reasonable way to select a sample. This is particularly true when it is extremely difficult, if not impossible, to list and identify all the potential elements in the universe. A resort might want to brag about the size of fish available in its fishing area. Since most people would not go to the trouble of catching all the fish in the water to select a sample of fish to weigh, a quota sample would permit a catch of a selected number of the different types of fish available to serve as the sample for estimating average fish size.

APPLYING THESE METHODS

Up to this point, each of the sample types has been discussed individually. In large surveys, two or more of these methods may be used in combination to select the sample. Three such surveys selected as examples are:

1. The 1977 National Travel Survey (NTS) conducted by the U.S. Bureau of the Census.
2. The Canadian Travel Survey (CTS) conducted by Statistics Canada.
3. The 1980 U.S. Travel Data Center National Travel Survey (NTS).

THE 1977 NTS

The sample used for the 1977 NTS was addresses that had previously been in the Census Bureau's Current Population Survey (CPS) or in the Bureau's Quarterly Household Survey (QHS). Since the cost of selecting a large national sample of addresses is extremely high, many surveys done by the Bureau of the Census use samples of addresses that were included in earlier surveys or combine surveys so they are conducted during the same visit to an address. Both the CPS and the QHS samples are selected using the same methodology.

The CPS design and methodology are described in detail in Technical Paper 40, which is mentioned in the list of reference materials at the end of this chapter. A brief overview of the CPS design shows that first the United States was divided into Primary Sampling Units (PSUs), which are made up, for the most part, of one or more counties within the same census region. Certain guidelines are imposed to provide minimum-population and maximum-land-area limits.

Once this was done, the next step was to group the PSUs into several strata (stratification). This grouping (stratification) was carried out in such a way that PSUs with similar demographic and economic characteristics were put together

to form many homogeneous strata of approximately the same population size. The number of strata was determined by variance and cost considerations. One PSU was selected from each stratum to be in the sample. This was done by ordering the PSUs by population, selecting a random number between 1 and the total population size of the stratum, and then finding in which PSU that number falls on the list (systematic sampling). Those PSUs with the largest populations (the major metropolitan areas) were each put into their own stratum so that they would be included in the sample with certainty.

After the sample PSU within the strata is selected, sample areas within the PSU are selected. The land area in each PSU is divided into several enumeration districts (EDs). The EDs are listed in a prescribed manner based on land use and geographic proximity. A measure of size is calculated for each ED. A random start is selected, and a systematic sample of EDs is drawn using the measure of size. Within the EDs, one or more groups of four addresses (cluster sampling) are selected to be interviewed.

THE CTS

The Canadian Travel Survey is really a series of quarterly surveys that is done in conjunction with the Canadian Labour Force Survey (LFS). A detailed description of the methodology used in selecting the sample for the LFS has been published and is included in the list of reference materials at the end of this chapter.

In the LFS, each of the 10 provinces included in the survey are divided into economic regions (ERs) that consist of geographically contiguous areas of similar economic structure. These ERs are the primary strata (stratification) from which a sample is drawn. Each of the ERs is then further divided (stratified) into two major groups—self-representing units (SRUs), which primarily consist of cities and other large concentrations of population and non-self-representing units (NSRUs), which consist of areas outside SRUs. Further stratification is done within the SRUs and NSRUs. The last strata is made up of one or more groups of households called clusters. A sample of clusters is selected from each group. This is done by randomly arranging the clusters on a list with each cluster assigned a value that reflects the number of households in the cluster. Clusters are then selected, based on the assigned values, using systematic sampling principles. A sample of households is selected from each cluster using systematic sampling.

In the CTS, a further sampling was done to select only one person in the household to interview. This selection was made using simple random sampling.

THE 1980 NTS

Although the sample selected for the 1980 NTS conducted for the U.S. Travel Data Center consisted of telephone numbers instead of addresses, the sample methodology is still similar to those of the 1977 NTS and the CTS. Essentially the sample for the 1980 NTS was selected by first dividing (stratifying) the United States into the eight travel regions. Counties in each of the eight regions were then placed into one of two groups, Standard Metropolitan Statistical Areas (SMSA) and non-SMSA areas. The SMSAs in each region were assigned on a list in order of population. A systematic sample of SMSAs was selected in each of the eight travel regions. In the non-SMSA strata, the states, and counties within the states, were arranged in a prescribed manner, and a systematic sample of counties was drawn. In both the SMSA and non-SMSA strata, systematic sampling was used to select Minor Civil Divisions (MCDs) within the selected SMSAs or non-SMSA counties. Systematic sampling was then used to select telephone numbers from the largest telephone book containing the MCD. The numbers selected were the base for the survey sample, with adjustments made to represent nonlisted telephone numbers in the sample. A more complete description of the sample methodology is included in the Technical Description of the survey, which is referenced in the list of materials at the end of this chapter.

SAMPLING AND NONSAMPLING ERRORS

There are two basic types of errors in any sample survey. One type of error is associated with the fact that the sample used was only one of a large number of possible same-size samples that could have been selected. Each sample selected would give a different estimate of the characteristics being measured. The variability of the estimates among all the possible samples is called the sampling error. The measure of this sampling error is commonly referred to as the standard error. When the results of a survey are announced and the estimate is given with the modifying statement something like, "This estimate is subject to a 3 percent error either way," the 3 percent is the calculated standard error on the estimate. This is a measure of the statistical reliability of survey estimates. The estimates of the standard error should be provided along with the results of any survey. Formulae for calculating standard errors are presented in the appendix.

The sample estimate and its estimated standard error enable one to construct interval estimates such that the interval includes the average result of all possible samples with a known probability. If all possible samples were selected, and each of these samples was surveyed under essentially the same general conditions, and an estimate and its estimated standard error were calculated for each sample, then:

1. Approximately 68 percent of the intervals from 1 standard error below the estimate to 1 standard error above the estimate would include the average result of all possible samples.

2. Approximately 90 percent of the intervals from 1.6 standard errors below the estimate to 1.6 standard errors above the estimate would include the average result of all possible samples.

3. Approximately 95 percent of the intervals from 2 stan-

dard errors below the estimate to 2 standard errors above the estimate would include the average result of all possible samples.

The average result of all possible samples either is or is not contained in any particular computed interval. However, for a particular sample, one can say with specified confidence that the average result of all possible samples is included in the constructed interval.

In some cases, the standard error may be just as important to the manager as the survey estimate itself. An estimate that has a great deal of variability, or error, associated with it should be used with much caution, particularly if a modest change in the estimate could affect the future of the business. Two major factors that determine the size of the sampling error are the sample size and the proportion of the universe that has the characteristic being measured. Usually the larger the sample size, the smaller the sampling error. As can be seen by reviewing the standard error formulae in the appendix, however, because the standard error is a function of a square root, doubling the sample size does not result in a comparable decrease in the sample error. The proportional representation of a characteristic in the universe affects the size of the error in relation to the size of the estimate. A characteristic with a small proportion of the population will usually have a smaller absolute range of error than a characteristic with a large proportion. The characteristic with the large proportion, however, will have a relatively narrower margin of sampling error and, therefore, theoretically be a better estimate.

To illustrate, a characteristic is estimated to take place in 5,000 cases in a universe of 100,000, and the sampling error is 2,500, or 50 percent of the estimate. If the characteristic took place in 50,000 cases in the universe of 100,000, the sampling error could be 5,000, which in absolute terms is larger than the 2,500, but in relative terms, is only 10 percent of the cases and, therefore, much smaller.

The second type of error is nonsampling error. There are many possible sources of nonsampling error, including those created by poorly worded questions, not obtaining interviews for every sample unit, inadequate coverage of the universe in selecting a sample, and errors made in the processing of the data. Regardless of how well a sample is selected, the results of the survey are not going to be accurate if the questions are not properly phrased. Perhaps one of the most common phrasing problems is designing questions that assume a prior fact. The question "Have you stopped beating your spouse?" assumes the respondent did beat the spouse. If the only answers allowed to this question are "Yes" and "No," the respondent who never beat the spouse is unable to answer. Likewise, if a representative sample of 100 is drawn but only 50 interviews are obtained, and the 50 that were not interviewed had different characteristics than the interviewed 50, the results are not representative of the entire universe because only a portion of the sample was interviewed. While it is nearly impossible to interview every unit selected, the higher the percentage of noninterviews, the more likely it is that the results will not be truly representative of the universe.

Selecting a sample from an inadequate or incomplete sample list can also create problems. Most everyone is aware that to select a sample of an area by using a telephone book would exclude those units without telephones and those units with unlisted telephone numbers. When situations like this occur, the sample is said to have a bias; that is, some elements in the universe have no chance of selection and, therefore, the estimate is not based on a sample that would be expected to reflect accurately the population in the universe.

ISSUES TO BE CONSIDERED IN SELECTING A SAMPLE DESIGN

The first part of the chapter briefly discussed the basic types of sample-selection methodologies. This section will briefly discuss what issues should be considered in selecting the appropriate sampling method.

In deciding on a sampling plan, the first thing a manager should consider is the type of information needed, that is, what is the major reason a survey is being considered. As mentioned earlier, in some cases, the information needed can only be obtained by conducting a survey; the next thing to be considered, then, is who to interview. Depending on the information needed, there may be many different sources from which a sample can be selected. These sources are referred to as sample frames. Examples of sample frames include:

1. All households or persons living in a defined geographic area, such as a city, county, or state.
2. All business establishments in a defined geographic area.
3. Membership lists of organizations.
4. Persons using a specific facility or service, such as guests registered at a hotel, persons in an airplane, or persons visiting an amusement park.

In choosing the best, or most efficient, sample frame, several points must be considered.

THE TYPE OF INFORMATION NEEDED

The required information is the major factor in making any decisions regarding survey or sample design. There have been too many instances when the primary goal of the survey got lost when side issues were introduced. When this occurred, too often the result was an unsatisfactory performance in achieving what really was the purpose of the survey.

In selecting a sample frame, the individuals or businesses in the frame must have the information being sought. It would do little good to survey a group of hotel owners to find out how many times rental cars were used. Hotel owners could, by reviewing their records, tell how many nights people spent in their establishments and possibly where the people came from. Surveying hotel owners could also report how many hotel owners use rental cars. However, except in

rare situations, hotel owners do not have information on the number of times rental cars were used.

In cases where several possible sample frames could provide the key information, secondary information needs should be considered. Returning to the example on use of rental cars, suppose there is also a need for information about the number of times a rental car user rents a car during the course of a year. Among the possible sample frames for determining rental-car usage would be: 1) a sample of rental-car agencies, or 2) a sample of the general population. By surveying rental-car agencies, an estimate could be obtained on the use of rental cars. However, unless the rental-car agencies would release the names and addresses of their customers, it would probably be very difficult, if not impossible, to determine the number of times each rental-car user rented a car during a year. All other things being equal, a survey of the general population would seem to be the best way to get an estimate on the number of times rental cars were used *and* the number of times a rental-car user rents a car during the course of a year.

When reviewing the information required, a related point that should be considered is whether the sample design and collection plan chosen will provide the information needed. In some cases, it may not. Continuing with the rental-car example, assume the purpose of the survey is to provide an estimate on the number of persons who rent cars and the number of times they rent cars during the course of a year. This is no problem in a general-population survey if the reference period for the question is one year; that is, "Did you rent a car at any time in the past year?" However, in many cases, surveys have a much shorter reference period, such as one month or three months, so that events, such as trips, are still relatively fresh in the respondent's mind.

Combining or linking the results of monthly or quarterly surveys to provide estimates for a longer time period, such as a year, is usually a simple matter of adding the results together until the time period desired is obtained. However, this approach does not work when the purpose is to determine participation rates or the frequency with which people participate unless the same people are interviewed throughout the time period. To estimate how many different persons rented a car during a year, a participation rate, by adding the results of four quarterly surveys, will result in an overestimate because it is possible that at least some of the people who rented a car in the first quarter also rented a car in one or more of the subsequent quarters. If exactly the same people are interviewed for each of the four quarters, the car-rental participation rate can be determined by matching each person's report for the four quarters, summing the persons who reported renting a car at least once, and comparing that to the total number of persons in the sample.

The information in Table 1 helps illustrate this point. The sample consists of four persons, A, B, C, and D. They were interviewed quarterly and asked to report whether or not they used a rental car on a trip taken during the quarter. Their responses were as follows:

The sum of the four quarterly-participation rates is 150 percent, an obviously incorrect number. The true participa-

TABLE 1 Persons Who Rented Cars by Interview Period

	INTERVIEW PERIOD			
PERSON	1ST QTR	2ND QTR	3RD QTR	4TH QTR
A	Y	Y	Y	Y
B	N	N	Y	N
C	N	Y	N	N
D	N	N	N	N
Quarterly Participation Rate	25%	50%	50%	25%

tion rate is 75 percent since three out of the four people in the sample rented a car at least once during the four quarters. A similar method would be used to estimate how many times during a year a rental-car user rents a car, or the frequency of use.

If the sample changes from quarter to quarter, an accurate estimate of participation and frequency over a time period longer than the survey reference period cannot be obtained because a person's past and/or future behavior can change. Determining a person's behavior for an entire year based on three-months' experience can be subject to a great deal of error. Likewise, estimates obtained by other means, such as matching persons with similar characteristics, would only be as good as the extent to which the matching characteristics determine participation and frequency.

THE STATISTICAL RELIABILITY (OR QUALITY) OF THE DATA NEEDED

The major point or question here is how reliable the data needs to be: how confident of the data the manager needs to be in order to make a decision based on the results. As was stated previously, any type of sample survey has a margin of sampling error associated with it. The error is there because only a sample of the population was surveyed instead of everyone. By adjusting the size and the way in which the sample is selected, the desired statistical reliability of the data can be approximately determined before interviewing begins. Formulae are given in the appendix for determining the sample size needed to achieve a specific level of reliability. Here again, it is important to remember the major reason the survey is being conducted. If the main data need is an estimate of the number of times rental cars were used, then the type of sample and sample size should be designed to provide this estimate at the desired level of precision. It is a waste of resources to develop a sample design and require a sample size to provide an estimate of the number of times blue carpet was requested when renting a car if that is not one of the key data items required in the survey.

In deciding on the quality needed from a survey, a manager must keep in mind the purpose for which the data is needed. Some surveys are taken so that the results may be used as a promotional tool. The manager of Smith Island may take a survey, for example, to determine the number of guests on his or her island and the other neighboring (com-

peting) islands. If the results show that there are more guests on his or her island, then the next promotional literature may headline the fact that a survey indicated "More people come to Smith Island than any other island along the coast. There must be a reason." A survey of this type does not really need to have a large sample or a small degree of sampling error in the estimate. All it needs is the right results and some foundation in acceptable survey practices so that no one can seriously question the manager's integrity. In situations such as this, the statistical reliability of the data should not be much of a deciding factor.

Another use made of survey results is for marketing purposes. When an individual or organization is planning to introduce a new product or service, a marketing study (survey) is sometimes conducted to determine how this new product or service will be received. The statistical reliability of the data for these purposes would probably strongly depend on the amount of money being invested.

If the manager of the Jones Hotel on Smith Island notices that many of the guests are eating dinner at other establishments, he or she may decide that the problem is that the Jones Hotel restaurant does not have a salad bar. To verify that the addition of a salad bar would increase his or her restaurant business, the manager may decide to take a "survey" of the hotel guests. Assuming the cost of establishing and maintaining a salad bar is not prohibitively expensive, the owner may do no more than ask (survey) a few of the guests if the addition of a salad bar would entice them to eat dinner at the hotel restaurant. If the guests say "yes," the manager builds the salad bar. If they say "no," he or she thinks of something else—or decides the sample was no good and builds the salad bar anyway. In this example, obviously the statistical reliability was not a factor. Of course, the manager could have conducted the survey more scientifically by preselecting the occupants of certain rooms during certain days during certain months and reviewing the results before making the decision. This manager, probably correctly, figured that it was not worth the effort and could find out what he or she wanted to know by asking a few of the guests.

A decision by the Jones Hotel to buy the adjoining swamp land and build a championship golf course would (should) be based on a much more sophisticated approach. The manager would need to develop an estimate of the additional business the golf course would produce and then determine whether the additional business would cover the cost of developing and maintaining the course and providing a satisfactory profit. It would seem the precision of the estimate would have to be fairly good. A decision based on an estimate that could be off by 50 percent could mean financial disaster. If the manager's decision on investing funds for the golf course is to be based in part on the survey results, then the statistical reliability, or quality, of the data needs to be high.

A third reason for taking a survey is to gather information for general planning or policy making. In these situations, the quality requirements of the survey are usually rather high since estimates that are off by 50 percent have little practical value, and common sense will usually reach the same conclusions at a fraction of the cost. Because of the general purpose of such a survey, it is rather large in scope and serves many uses. Such surveys are usually conducted periodically to measure trends or changes and, in some instances, to see if a change in policy or practice had the desired impact. To measure all but the most radical changes requires a fairly reliable estimate. Many businesses can measure change by reviewing records or measuring sales. General planning surveys are usually undertaken by government agencies or private organizations who need to study or service a wide range of activities or interests.

RESOURCES REQUIRED OR AVAILABLE

Once it has been determined what information is needed and what degree of statistical reliability (quality) is required, the next step is to develop an estimate of the resources required to complete the job. Included as "resources" are money, staff, and time.

If the type of information required at an acceptable level of statistical reliability can only be obtained at a cost way beyond the money available, other alternatives have to be explored; for example, increased funding; reducing the reliability requirements; collecting the information from another, or existing, source; or deciding that the information was not really needed anyway. A manager should be aware of the options available if funds are not adequate. There are also instances where funds are secured first and then the planning begins involving the goal of the survey and the quality required, but this approach can be very inefficient. A manager should also be on the lookout for situations in which the objectives of the survey can be met without spending all the money available. Why spend more money than is necessary just so better statistical reliability and/or additional information can be collected even though there is no need for the better reliability or no plans for using the data? The availability of staff must also be considered. If it is decided to undertake a survey, the staff should have both the time and the skills necessary to complete the survey, or the manager must be willing to pay someone else to do part or all of the work. Staff time is not only a consideration in conducting a survey but also in analyzing and using the results. A survey that produces a great deal of valuable information really is of little use if no one has the time to make use of it.

Time is another resource that is important. If the data

needed at the quality level determined will not be available until two years after it is needed, then the data will not be of use. Likewise, if it will take four months to prepare the materials necessary to begin the survey but the time period or situation to be surveyed is only one month away, the manager must decide if the preparation time can be shortened, if the time period can be rescheduled, or if the survey should be conducted at all. In many cases surveys that require a high degree of sophistication and/or a high level of quality cannot be successfully conducted by arbitrarily reducing the preparation time. Inevitably, a key factor is overlooked or done incorrectly, which delays completion of the survey or makes the results less useful. The situation illustrated by the phrase "Do you want it right or do you want it Tuesday?" is not unique. Every manager has had to make this decision. If it appears that the manager will be faced with this sort of decision after reviewing the timing for the survey operation and the answer would be "Tuesday," the manager should consider other survey alternatives, including the possibility of canceling the survey.

SELECTING A SAMPLE— AN ILLUSTRATION

The remaining part of the chapter will provide an illustration of selecting a sample plan and determining the sample size. The manager of the Jones Hotel on Smith Island will be used as an example.

SELECTING A SAMPLE PLAN

Suppose that the manager wants to learn more about the guests' satisfaction with the hotel and future plans for visiting the island so that improvements in hotel services and marketing plans can be determined. Since the hotel's records do not have this information, a survey seems to be the only way.

Who should the manager interview? He or she could take a sample of households in the United States plus a sample of tourists visiting the United States from other countries and ask questions of those that stayed at the hotel. This obviously is very expensive and inefficient when a sample could be drawn from the hotel records. After some thought, the manager decides that the sample should consist of persons who have stayed at the hotel during the past year. Persons who last stayed at the hotel more than one year ago may not be aware of the changes that were made during that period. The manager also decides not to select the sample from current or future guests because that will lengthen the time needed to collect the data (waiting for future guests), and the manager wants the people surveyed to have time to reflect on their experience.

The next step is to decide which of the four basic sample types to use. Using simple random or systematic sampling would mean compiling a list and then selecting one out of every so many. A possible problem with this approach is that the manager wants the sample to adequately represent the out-of-state tourists. A simple random or systematic sample might underestimate this relatively small but important segment of the hotel's business.

A stratified random sample would ensure that the out-of-state tourist segment was adequately represented. The manager could stratify on these characteristics because the registration cards provide home address and purpose of trip, but this would require extra effort and time in preparing the survey list.

Because the manager decides to conduct the survey by mail, the advantages of cluster sampling do not apply. The manager realizes that the cost of mailing to addresses spread throughout the world is not prohibitive enough to warrant the extra effort involved to select the sample and to adjust for the somewhat higher sampling error that is associated with cluster sampling.

The manager also considers quota sampling but decides against it because he or she does not have enough demographic information about the guests to adequately control the sample to the point where there would be confidence in the results.

CHOOSING THE SAMPLE

The manager has decided to use systematic random sampling to select the sample of guests. The list is compiled in the order in which the guests' cards were found in the files. This did not result in any unusual ordering of the list. The final list of all guests in the past year contained 15,000 names. The major goal of the survey is to determine whether or not the guest was satisfied with the hotel during his or her last visit. Because no earlier surveys or studies on this subject were done, the manager uses Formula 1.B in the Appendix to calculate the sample size. To use this formula, the manager must approximate the number of people on the list that would be dissatisfied and how reliable an estimate is needed. Although the manager believes (hopes) the number of dissatisfied guests is very small, he or she decides to take no chances and assumes that half (7,500) were dissatisfied. A 50-50 split would provide for the maximum sample size. The manager also wants to have enough confidence in the survey results so that the final survey estimate would be, according to sampling theory, within a range of 10 percent of the true measure 68 times out of 100. A range of 10 percent on a survey estimate of 7,500 translates into a standard error of 750. Using these numbers, the manager determines that a sample size of 100 is needed.

$$\frac{(7,500)(7,500)}{(750)^2} = \frac{56,250,000}{562,500} = 100$$

Since there are 15,000 names on the list, the manager will select a sample of 1 in every 150. Using a random-number table, the manager picks a number between 1 and 150 as a starting point and then selects every 150th person on the list for inclusion in the sample.

STANDARD ERROR CALCULATION

To illustrate the calculation of a standard error from the survey results, assume the manager has collected the information for all 100 sample persons. The results showed that 96 out of the 100 in sample were satisfied—X is the number of satisfied sample persons. The manager determines that X' (an estimate of the number of satisfied guests if a complete census of the 15,000 were taken) is 14,400 by using $X' = (N/n) \times X$, a part of Formula 3 for determining the standard error (see Appendix).

$$X' = \frac{N}{n} X = X' = \frac{15,000}{100} 96$$

$$X' = 14,400$$

To determine how reliable that estimate (X') is, the manager computes the standard error for X' by using Formula 3 and finds it to be 294, to the nearest whole number.

Standard error

for $\quad X' = \sqrt{(15,000)^2 (0.9933) \left(\frac{3.84}{9,900} \right)} = 294.428$

This means that the 68 percent confidence interval would be 14,400 ± 294, or from 14,106 to 14,694, and that the 95 percent confidence interval would be 14,400 ± 2(294), or 14,400 ± 588, or from 13,812 to 14,988. Thus, the manager concludes that the average estimate derived from all possible samples of satisfied guests lies within the interval from 13,812 to 14,988 with 95 percent confidence.

APPENDIX—FORMULAE

FORMULAE FOR DETERMINING THE SAMPLE SIZE NEEDED TO ACHIEVE A SPECIFIC LEVEL OF RELIABILITY

1. Simple Random Sampling and Systematic Sampling

A. If a sample survey was previously conducted for which a standard error estimate is available for the characteristic of interest in your survey, then the formula for determining the sample size needed to achieve a specific level of reliability for this characteristic of interest is as follows:

Let: x = the characteristic of interest

σ_x = the standard error for the characteristic of interest as calculated from the previously conducted sample survey

n = the sample size of the previously conducted survey

$\sigma_x^I =$ the standard error for the characteristic of interest that you hope to achieve in your survey (i.e., the specific level of reliability)

$n' =$ the sample size needed for your survey to achieve the specific level of reliability

$$n^I = \left(\frac{\sigma_x}{\sigma'_x}\right)^2 n$$

Note that this formula assumes that both surveys (i.e., the previously conducted survey and your planned survey) utilized simple random samples or systematic samples selected from randomized orderings of the universe (i.e., approximately simple random samples). If the sample size n' calculated using the above formula is large relative to the universe size N, the sample size that should actually be used (n'') is as follows:

$$n'' = \frac{n'}{1 + \frac{n'}{N}}$$

B. If a standard error estimate of your characteristic of interest is *not* available from a previously conducted survey, then the formula for determining the sample size needed to achieve a specific level of reliability for the characteristic of interest is as follows:

Let: $X =$ your characteristic of interest

$N =$ the size of the universe

$\sigma_x =$ the standard error for the characteristic of interest that you hope to achieve in your survey (i.e., the specific level of reliability)

$n =$ the sample size needed for your survey to achieve the specific level of reliability

$$n = \frac{X(N-X)}{\sigma_X^2}$$

Note that this formula assumes that your planned survey will employ a simple random sample or a systematic sample selected from a randomized ordering of the universe (i.e., an approximate simple random sample) and that the characteristic of interest is a type of characteristic that can be expressed as a proportion (p) of the universe. If your characteristic of interest is a proportion of the universe, then the sample size formula would be as follows:

$$n = \frac{p(1-p)}{\sigma_p^2}$$

where:

$$P = \frac{X}{N} = \text{the proportion that is your characteristic of interest}$$

If the sample size, n, calculated using the above formulae is large relative to the universe size, then the sample that should actually be used, n^1, is as follows:

$$n^1 = \frac{n}{1 + \frac{n}{N}}$$

2. Stratified Random Sampling

A. Proportional allocation Using proportional allocation, the sample is allocated to each strata using the following formula:

$$n_h = \frac{N_h}{N} n$$

where $N =$ the universe size

$N_h =$ the universe size in the hth stratum

$n =$ the sample size

$n_h =$ the sample size in the hth stratum

If you plan to use proportional allocation, then the formula for determining the sample size needed to achieve a specific level of reliability for the characteristic of interest is as follows:

$$n = \frac{N \sum_{h=1}^{L} N_h S_{hx}^2}{\sigma_x^2}$$

where $x =$ the characteristic of interest

$L =$ the number of strata

$N =$ the universe size

$N_h =$ the universe size for the hth stratum

$n =$ the sample size

$\sigma_x =$ the standard error for the characteristic of interest that you hope to achieve in your survey (i.e., the specific level of reliability)

$S_{hx}^2 =$ the within-strata variation in the hth stratum for the characteristic of interest

$$S_{hx}^2 = \frac{\sum_{i=1}^{N_h}\left(X_{hi} - \frac{X_h}{N_h}\right)^2}{N_h - 1}$$

If data are not available from which an estimate of S_{hx}^2 can be made, then it can be approximated by the following:

$$S_{h_1}^2 = X_h (N_h - X_h)$$

If the sample size, n, calculated using the above formula is large relative to the universe size, then the sample size that should actually be used, n^1, is as follows:

$$n^1 = \frac{n}{1 + \frac{n}{N}}$$

B. Optimum allocation Using optimum allocation, the sample is allocated to each strata using the following formula:

$$n_h = \frac{N_h S_{hx}}{\sum_{h=1}^{L} N_h S_{hx}} n$$

where
- x = the characteristic of interest
- L = the number of strata
- n = the sample size
- n_h = the sample size in the hth stratum
- S_{hx} = the square root of the within-strata variation in the hth stratum for the characteristic of interest

$$S_{hx} = \sqrt{\frac{\sum_{i=1}^{N_h}\left(X_{hi} - \frac{X_h}{N_h}\right)^2}{N_h - 1}}$$

If you plan to use optimum allocation, then the formula for determining the sample size needed to achieve a specific level of reliability for the characteristic of interest is as follows:

$$n = \frac{\left(\sum_{h=1}^{L} N_h S_{hx}\right)^2}{\sigma_x^2}$$

where σ_x = the standard error for the characteristic of that you hope to achieve in your survey (i.e., the specific level of reliability)

If data are not available from which an estimate of S_{hx} can be made, then it can be approximated by the following:

$$S_{hx} = \sqrt{X_h (N_h - X_h)}$$

If the sample size, n, calculated using the above formula is large relative to the universe size, then the sample size that should actually be used, n^1, is as follows:

$$n^1 = \frac{n}{1 + \left(\dfrac{\sum_{h=1}^{L} N_h S_{hx}^2}{\sigma_x^2}\right)}$$

FORMULAE FOR CALCULATING STANDARD ERRORS OF SAMPLE ESTIMATES

3. Systematic Sample

Notation:

- n = the sample size
- N = the universe size
- X = the characteristic of interest
- X_i = the estimate of characteristic X for the ith sample case

$$X = \sum_{i=1}^{n} X_i = \text{the sum of the estimates of characteristic } X \text{ for the } n \text{ sample cases}$$

$$X' = \frac{N}{n} X = \text{the sample estimate of characteristic } X \text{ for the universe}$$

Standard Error of X''

$$= \sqrt{\frac{N^2\left(1 - \frac{n}{N}\right)\sum_{i=1}^{n}\left(X_i - \frac{X}{n}\right)^2}{n(n-1)}}$$

(This formula assumes that the systematic sample was selected from an ordering of the universe which was essentially random with respect to the items being measured.)

4. Stratified Simple Random Sample

Notation:

- L = the number of strata

N = the universe size
N_h = the universe size in the hth stratum
n = the sample size
n_h = the sample size in the hth stratum
X_{hi} = the estimate of characteristic X for the ith sample case in the hth stratum

$$X_h = \sum_{i=1}^{n_h} X_{hi} = \text{the sum of the estimates of characteristic } X \text{ for the } n_{th} \text{ sample cases of the } h_{th} \text{ stratum}$$

$$X' = \sum_{h=1}^{L} \frac{N_h}{n_h} X_h = \text{the sample estimate of characteristic } X \text{ for the universe}$$

Standard Error
of X'

$$= \sqrt{\sum_{h=1}^{L} N_h{}^2 \left(1 - \frac{n_h}{N_h}\right) \frac{\sum_{i=1}^{n_h} \left(X_{hi} - \frac{X_h}{n_h}\right)^2}{n_h(n_h - 1)}}$$

5. Cluster Sample

Notation:

N = the universe size
n = the sample size
m = the number of clusters in the sample
X_i = the estimate of characteristic X for the ith sample cluster

$$X = \sum_{i=1}^{m} X_i = \text{the sum of the estimates of characteristic } X \text{ for the } m \text{ sample clusters}$$

$$X' = \frac{N}{n} X = \text{the sample estimate of characteristic } X \text{ for the universe}$$

Standard Error
of X'

$$= \sqrt{N^2 \left(1 - \frac{n}{N}\right) \sum_{i=1}^{m} \frac{m\left(X_i - \frac{X}{m}\right)^2}{(n^2)(m-1)}}$$

(This formula is only appropriate if each of the n sample cases has the same probability of being in the sample.)

Quota Sample

A quota sample is basically a stratified sample with a non-random selection of the sample within the strata. Consequently, standard error formulae cannot readily be applied with confidence to the results of quota samples.

REFERENCES

The purpose of this chapter was to discuss briefly and simply basic issues in sampling and sample design. There are several books that contain one or more chapters that discuss those points in greater detail without going too deeply into sampling theory. These books should be available in most of the larger public and university libraries. Although certainly not a complete listing, among the books that may be referenced are:

Bowen, Earl K. (1960), *Statistics with Applications in Management and Economics*, Homewood, IL: Richard D. Irwin, Inc.

Cochran, William G. (1953), *Sampling Techniques*, New York: John Wiley & Sons, Inc.

Hansen, Morris H., William W. Hurwitz, and William G. Madow (1953), *Sample Survey Methods and Theory—Volume 1, Methods and Applications*, New York: John Wiley & Sons, Inc.

Yates, Frank (1960), *Sampling Methods for Censuses and Surveys*, New York: Hafner.

For more complete information on the methodology used by the U.S. Bureau of the Census, Statistics Canada, and the U.S. Travel Data Center in their surveys, refer to:

Methodology of the Canadian Labour Force Survey, Catalogue 71–526 Occasional (1977), Statistics Canada.

1980 National Travel Survey Monthly Report, Technical Description, A-1 (1980), U.S. Travel Data Center.

The Current Population Survey—Design and Methodology, Technical Paper 40 (1978), U.S. Bureau of the Census.

Finding references to articles and other types of publications that describe specific sample designs used in travel and tourism surveys is much harder. Most articles discuss the results and uses made of the surveys and devote little, if any, space describing the sample design. TTRA members and others who have access to the Journal of Travel Research and/or the materials in the Travel Reference Center in the Business Research Division at the University of Colorado in Boulder, Colorado, should find references to survey sample designs as part of articles in results of surveys and survey methodology.

A review of the proceedings of past TTRA annual conferences indicates a wide range of papers that had some discussion on sample plans. Among the papers were:

Ditmars, Earl E., and William H. Troxel (1978), "Usage of Consumer Sentiment Indices," *The Travel Research Association—Ninth Annual Conference Proceedings*, 9–12.

Fredericks, Alan (1976), "Marketing Through Travel Agents," *The Travel Research Association—Seventh Annual Conference Proceedings*, 27–30.

Funk, Deborah (1978), "National Tourism Policy Study: A Description of the Survey Research Components," *The*

Travel Research Association—Ninth Annual Conference Proceedings, 197–204.

Gilbert, Hamlin M. (1978), "Focus on Travel," *The Travel Research Association—Ninth Annual Conference Proceedings*, 71–75.

Gilbert, Sandy (1977), "The Car Rental Market in the '80's," *The Travel Research Association—Eighth Annual Conference Proceedings*, 53–56.

Goodrich, Jonathan N. (1978), "Qualitative Travel Research: A Study with American Express," *The Travel Research Association—Ninth Annual Conference Proceedings*, 87–93.

Hogenauer, Alan K. (1978), "The Research and Marketing Jigsaw Puzzle: Making the Pieces Fit," *The Travel Research Association—Ninth Annual Conference Proceedings*, 197–204.

Marzella, Dennis A., Samuel S. Shapiro, and George R. Conrade (1977), "How to Develop a Marketing Information Subsystem for a Tourist Destination," *The Travel Research Association—Seventh Annual Conference Proceedings*, 91–98.

Standish, Theodore C. (1978), "How the Computer Views the Family Vacation Travel Market," *The Travel Research Association—Ninth Annual Conference Proceedings*, 77–80.

Woodside, Arch G., William H. Motes, and David Reid (1978), "Profiling Inquirers from Magazine Advertising and its Implication for Value Assessment: An Initial Evaluation," *The Travel Research Association—Ninth Annual Conference Proceedings*, 81–83.

Part Three

National, Regional, and Municipal Perspectives

This third section of the Handbook provides an overview of the manner in which travel and tourism research is viewed by the national, regional, and municipal organizations responsible for tourism at each of these levels. Chapter 13 by Gordon Taylor examines the role of research within a national tourist organization (NTO). Mr. Taylor has extensive experience as a researcher in government, and the contents of his chapter clearly emphasize that NTO research must be planned and managed in relation to the major functions of the organization. In doing so, he emphasizes that the tourism system, and thus tourism research, operates within more general economic, physical, cultural, political, and social environments to which it must be related—and that the kind of research conducted by an NTO must reflect this fact. Having made this point, Mr. Taylor goes on to describe the various types of research that are commonly conducted by a national tourist organization and how these research outputs are used for program planning, market development, and the monitoring of tourism industry operations. Finally, Mr. Taylor briefly considers various alternative organizational arrangements that are possible within an NTO for the conduct of research.

As a complement to Chapter 13, included in this section is another perspective on the nature and role of research in national tourist organizations. In this case, Martinus Kosters provides an overview of the kinds of research conducted within NTOs in major European countries. There is a particular emphasis on the kinds of difficulties encountered when several countries are jointly involved in the collection and use of tourism data. In terms of the chapter's specific contents, Dr. Kosters first reviews the major activities pursued by various national tourist organizations, particularly those in a position to have offices in foreign countries. He then examines the forces that lead NTOs to undertake research, as well as those factors that determine the manner in which that research is conducted. The major emphasis is upon reviewing various kinds of research approaches and their relative costs in relation to the information needs of the NTO and the resources that are available to it. The chapter concludes by providing readers with considerable insight into the manner in which the European Travel Commission was created as a means of facilitating collaborative research and marketing among various countries in Europe. It is particularly interesting to note Kosters' comment that "although to a certain extent the NTOs are competitors, cooperation appears to be possible and even necessary."

In Chapter 15, Suzanne Cook and Vernon Azucenas of the United States Travel Data Center present an overview of research programs conducted by state and provincial travel offices. In the discussion, Cook and Azucenas provide information concerning the current level of state and provincial involvement in tourism as reflected by overall budgets as well as direct expenditures on research and then examine the factors that should be taken into account when establishing the research priorities of a particular state or provincial travel office. The authors subsequently present a detailed review of the types of research commonly conducted by state and provincial travel offices. These research types fall into five broad categories defined as Impact Analysis, Market Analysis, Evaluation Research, the Identification of Travel/Tourism Resources, and the Monitoring of Travel Activity. The chapter concludes by reviewing the major steps to be taken and the issues to be considered in establishing a comprehensive research program within a state or provincial travel office.

A frequently neglected level of research, namely, the municipal level, is the object of review and discussion in Chapter 16. This chapter, which is authored by Uel Blank, acknowledges that urban tourism research is among the most misunderstood and underestimated of all tourism types. The purpose of this chapter, then, is to clarify the nature of urban tourism research and to provide some insights into the very detailed kinds of research activities that are required at the municipal level. In examining this chapter, readers will become aware that, while the type of research conducted in urban areas may be conceptually similar to that carried out at the state or provincial level, it often differs substantially with respect to the level of funding available, the degree of sophistication involved, the attitudes towards research which surround it, and the availability of qualified personnel to execute it. With this in mind, the author goes on to identify the specific types of research that are particularly applicable at the municipal level. Dr. Blank then focuses extensively on the priority that he believes should be accorded to research on the overall impact of tourism on urban areas. In doing so, he emphasizes the importance of obtaining multiple measures of tourism impacts from various sources so as to enhance the reliability and credibility of the results. Subsequently, Dr. Blank emphasizes the need to put the research information that has been assembled into use and provides some suggestions for bringing this about. He concludes by briefly describing a number of recent examples of urban tourism studies. In reviewing this chapter, the reader will gain a renewed respect for the complexity of the data and the sophistication of the research required to truly understand tourism at the municipal level.

13

Research in National Tourist Organizations

GORDON D. TAYLOR
Ottawa, Ontario

*R*esearch must be related to the basic roles of an organization, and it must provide analysis and the interpretation of analysis keyed to the main functions of the agency. The research must be grounded on a comprehensive data bank that develops out of periodic and consistent data-gathering processes.

The objective of this chapter is to develop a basic outline for operation of a research function within national tourist organizations. While the emphasis throughout the paper will be on national tourist organizations, the principles would apply equally well to agencies with related functions at the state, provincial, regional, county, and local government levels. As the functions and responsibilities of individual national tourism organizations will vary from country to country, the approach that has been developed in this chapter is conceptual. The adaptation of the concept to any individual agency will depend, of course, upon the specific responsibilities of that agency and the role that it occupies within a particular governmental structure.

FUNCTIONS OF A NATIONAL TOURIST ORGANIZATION

The structure and functions of a national tourist organization (NTO) vary widely depending upon the political, economic, social, and cultural backgrounds of a particular country. The size of the country and the importance of tourism to the national economy are also important factors in determining the structure and functions. Thus, national tourist organizations can and do range from large to small organizations with a few or many responsibilities. The nature of the research required will be as varied as are the organizations themselves.

In spite of these apparent differences, it is possible to develop a basic structure for research in NTOs. This structure is based on the assumption that there is a good deal of commonality in these offices, and, on this basis, the major research requirements can be described.

Two basic roles are generally assigned to national tourist organizations:

A. A responsibility for the development of tourism markets

B. A responsibility for the development of tourism products

These two elements of tourism cannot be seen conceptually as distinct entities as one is dependent upon the other, although in many organizations they are separated for administrative purposes. If the basic elements of the marketing mix are price, product, promotion, and place, the rationale for treating the two elements as a single entity should be clear. Thus, there is little logic in developing a research activity that reflects such a dichotomy; hence, in thinking through the research needs of a national tourist organization, it would appear that there are four functions of the agency that can be articulated:

A. Strategic and policy planning
B. Program planning for marketing and development
C. Market and product analysis
D. Special projects

It is around these functions that research must be developed.

Consequently, the research needs of each of these functions will be outlined in succeeding sections. It must be recognized that the needs of each of these functions cannot be placed in discrete compartments; there will be areas of overlap between them. The broad thrust of interest for each one, however, should be clear. An attempt will be made to outline the information needs of each of these functions and to propose a system for determining the research activities that will be required as responses to these needs. In addition, a structural outline for a research organization will be suggested.

The research carried out in a national tourist organization must be viewed as applied. Studies must be designed, conducted, and interpreted to meet the ongoing planning and operational needs of the organization. These studies, in addition, constitute a resource that should be used for more basic and academic research. While individual researchers within an NTO may extend their interest beyond the very applied environment of the workplace, the theoretical research so needed in tourism must come primarily from other researchers. A key responsibility of the NTO is to make access to its data files relatively easy in order to foster other legitimate research interests.

RESEARCH OBJECTIVES

The research activity must be planned and managed in relation to the major functions of the organization. A basic set of guidelines has been developed to assist in the determination of the needs and for the design of the responsive activities.

These guidelines are:

A. Establish an information base to be anchored on periodic and consistent surveys that will supply tourism intelligence on a regular basis.
B. Provide projectable information on tourism needs for marketing and development planning.
C. Develop the analytical capacity required to interpret research findings for decision-making purposes.
D. Develop a research capability to deal with specific problems that are not of a recurring nature.

All of the research activity should be based on the intent of these guidelines.

STRATEGIC AND POLICY PLANNING

The needs of strategic and policy planning will be evident in all of the research areas that will be specified. There are, however, some broadly based specific requirements that can be identified. These broad subjects relate to the total environment in which tourism operates and to the significance and importance of tourism in the country concerned.

THE ENVIRONMENT

Tourism operates within an environment that has a great deal of effect upon it, but over which tourism has little or no control, although it does have impacts back upon the environment. First-level-research needs must be directed toward understanding the relationships that exist between tourism and the environment within which it operates. The nature of the relationships is shown in Figure 1.

Thus, tourism operates within an economic, physical/cultural, political, and social environment that strongly influences it, but over which it exerts little or no control. Tourism also impacts, to a greater or lesser degree, upon the elements.

Economic

There is no doubt that the state of the economy in the country concerned (and in the countries seen as major markets for its tourism products) has a profound influence on tourism. This influence is particularly important to the flow of travelers into and out of the country, as well as within, and upon the development of the tourism plant. Economic conditions in all countries are measured, documented, and analyzed by many public and private agencies. The national tourist organization needs to ensure a consistent receipt of the pertinent studies and documentation that are provided by the appropriate agencies.

The economic data that will need to be analyzed should include such facts as disposable income, gross national product, unemployment rates, exchange rates, Travel and Consumer Price Indexes, interest rates, taxes, and so on. The analytical role is to determine how each of the elements taken individually and in combination influence tourism and to establish trends so that these influences can be monitored over time. The key to this activity is a regular reporting system that transmits the analytical results to management.

Physical and Cultural

The physical and cultural resources of a country provide its prime tourism assets. Tourism's concern must be with the preservation of the quality of the physical and cultural environment and with the monitoring of the effects of tourism development upon that environment. Research's role should be concentrated in the conceptualization, verification, and institution of appropriate monitoring devices so that any existing or potential deterioration in the environ-

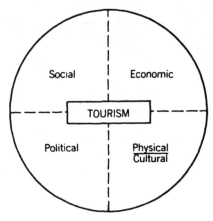

FIGURE 1 The environment.

ment can be quickly identified and remedial action proposed and carried out. Research must also be concerned with the identification and assessment of these elements as prime tourism attractions.

Political

Tourism operates within a political system, and it will be influenced by a variety of political decisions made from time to time. The role of the national tourist organization in this area should be to develop estimates of the probable outcome of the effects on tourism of political decisions and to attempt to influence the decisions in order to optimize tourism benefits to its nationals. It should also prepare recommendations for policy changes in order to ensure orderly growth of tourism within the national economy. Research must be one of the prime sources of the data and analytical techniques required for policy work.

Social

A wide range of social elements influences the development and performance of tourism. Such factors as population growth, population distribution, aging, urbanization, migration, social attitudes, and values can be taken as illustrative of the many items that could be listed. The analysis of these data must be directed towards determining the influence each factor, taken individually or in combination, has on tourism.

Most social factors are measured, documented, and analyzed by a variety of public and private agencies. As with the economic sector, the ongoing receipt of surveys and reports prepared by other agencies is essential. The critical research role is the interpretation of the findings into touristic terms and the onward transmission of the analytical results to management.

Thus, one of the key elements of a research plan must be to ensure the receipt of data pertaining to the economic, physical and cultural, political, and social environment of the country itself and of the countries that now and in the future will constitute the major markets for its tourism. The data received must be analyzed and interpreted in order to assist in the understanding of the environment in which tourism must operate. The research role in this area is primarily analysis and interpretation, and not data collection per se.

SIGNIFICANCE AND IMPORTANCE OF TOURISM

Tourism reacts back upon the environment, and the dynamics of this reaction are of concern to strategic and policy planners. Examples of the research needs in this area are described in the following paragraphs.

Impacts of Tourism

Tourism through the movement of people, the concentration of these people in popular tourist areas, and the expenditures related to this movement and concentration have important impacts upon the economic, social, physical and cultural,

and political environments. Some of the key economic impacts are employment, income generation, tax generation, and induced investment. The research role is to determine what these impacts are and to analyze changes in the impacts over time. Another research task is to determine the share of business for which tourism is responsible in a wide variety of business establishments. This latter role is vital if the true impacts of tourism are to be measured and if the industry is to be defined in a satisfactory manner. Very few business establishments receive all of their revenue from tourism. The proportion that tourism contributes will depend upon the type of business and its location.

The introduction of tourists into an area can have both positive and negative social effects. It is necessary to understand what these impacts are, both upon the visitors and the residents and upon the social relationships between the two groups. In the case of positive impacts, it is necessary to know what they are and how to reinforce them. It is also necessary to understand the causes of negative impact and how to recognize that they are occurring in order to develop plans for ameliorization or elimination.

The concentration of tourists in particular places can lead to detrimental physical and cultural environmental effects. The research interest must be in what the effects are, how they are caused, and what corrective action can be proposed and in monitoring the results of any such action. Too severe negative impacts in any of the above areas can also have profound political effects.

Tourism's Role in the National Economy

While tourism's role in the national economy is closely related to any study of economic impacts, it does present a separate macroeconomic case. In the total economy, there must be an understanding of tourism's contribution to, or share of, the gross domestic product, of tourism's role in the international balance of payments, and of its importance as an earner of foreign exchange.

The performance and competitiveness of the tourism industry at both the micro- and macroeconomic levels must be studied. In essence, it is important to examine the profitability of the individual enterprises. There must also be concern for the output of the tourism industry relative to the traditional inputs of land, labor, and capital and of comparing these outputs with those of other economic sectors and with the tourism industry in countries known to be competitive in the tourism market place.

Trends

Trends and the implications of them in terms of the numbers of tourists and in the tourism products available need to be developed over time. Trend data play an important role in understanding what has happened and in developing forecasts for the future.

Market Share

A constant monitoring of market share both domestically and internationally should be instituted. Particular concern must be directed toward the country's share of total world tourism and toward how the market share is moving in relation to those countries seen as major competitors. The same concern must lead to tracking the share obtained from each of the major tourist-origin countries and, where possible, of the major market segments within those countries.

PROGRAM PLANNING

The tourism industry should have two, major, ongoing program-planning activities based upon medium- and short-term time frames:

A. Market development plans for appropriate markets
B. Industry development plans

There must be a strong research activity relating to the specific tourism information requirements of these two functions. Although the emphasis will differ, both activities have needs for information relative to:

A. Travel, travelers, and potential travelers
B. The tourism plant
C. The linkages between travelers and the tourism plant

There are research needs relative to each, and there is a requirement for the development of an analytical framework to provide the essential relationships among the three data sets.

The relationship between the market needs and the available product, for example, is essential for market and development planning. In this type of analysis, it will be necessary to develop a technique that will describe how well the market needs are met by the product available in various geographic areas. The market, for this analysis, will be described in terms of the facilities required by all relevant segments in order to achieve the tourism experience sought. The product will be described in terms of geographic areas. The basic approach is outlined in Figure 2.

The specific techniques that will be used will have to be developed, but the necessity of this type of analysis must be kept in mind when determining data needs for both the market and product.

MARKET AND PRODUCT ANALYSIS

In addition to the broad needs outlined under strategic, policy, and program planning, there are specific needs for information related to the market and to the product.

MARKET

In the market area, there is a need for analysis and information on the traveler, on travel, and on the dynamics of the market. Within the traveler and travel data sets, information is required for each market and for potential markets of interest to the country on the following subjects:

1. Who
2. When
3. Where
4. What
5. How
6. Why
7. Expenditure

The outlines of the data set can be shown diagrammatically, as in Figure 3.

The research needs relative to the dynamics of the market would include such topics as:

1. Trends, forecasts
2. Growth segments
3. Attitudes and motivations to travel and to travel to the particular country
4. Consumer satisfaction
5. Leisure time: changes in activity preferences

PRODUCT

On the product side, data and analysis are required on each of the following six main sectors of the national tourism industry:

1. Transportation
2. Accommodation
3. Food and beverage
4. Recreation, entertainment, sports, and cultural facilities
5. Tourism-related retail trade
6. Scenic areas, parks, and historic attractions

The information needs relative to each sector of the plant would include:

1. Type
2. Quantity
3. Location
4. Quality
5. Utilization
6. Trends, forecasts
7. Potential

The relationship between the two sets of data required about the product can be illustrated. Figure 4 indicates that for each of the industry sectors, all of the items in the list headed "Data Elements for Tourism Plant" would be needed.

In addition to defining the specific items that will be required in this data collection process, a number of related problems must be solved. For all of the sectors of the tourism plant except transportation, the elements have a fixed location in geographic space. Transportation is both spatial and linear in nature. Terminal facilities such as airports, railway and bus stations, and ship terminals are fixed in space; the transportation network linking them is linear. It is also subject to frequent, often seasonal, changes in frequency and capacity.

In order to meet the spatial requirements of this type of

Market Segments \ Geographic Areas	A	B	C	D	E	F	G
1							
2							
3							
4							

FIGURE 2   Market/product analysis.

Data \ Market	Domestic	International	
		A	B
Who			
When			
Where			
What			
How			
Why			
Expenditure			

FIGURE 3   Data elements for tourism markets.

Sector \ Details	Type	Quantity	Location	Quality	Utilization	Trends/ Forecasts	Potential
Transportation							
Accommodation							
Food Service Beverage Service							
Recreation Entertainment Sports Cultural							
Retail Trade							
Scenic Areas/Parks Historical							

FIGURE 4   Data elements for tourism plant.

inventory, a geographical designation system will be required. The key to establishing such a system will be the smallest geographic area for which data will be required.

ACTIVITY SPECIFIC

The results of the proposed periodic and consistent surveys cannot be expected to meet all of the research needs of the organization. Special problems that require specific solutions will occasionally arise. The research capability to deal with these problems must be developed. In addition, certain activities will have their special needs for study from time to time.

The types of activities covered by this topic would include:

A. Advertising pre- and post-test of creative concepts and communication themes
B. Special market studies, such as the ski market or weekend market
C. Local market data in terms of a specific origin or destination
D. Site location, for tourism development
E. Feasibility of specific marketing, development, and data-collection projects

Many other topics that would be of particular interest to an individual organization could be added. The main concern in this paper is with information that is a common requirement to many agencies. Hence, specific and special needs are really beyond its purview, but the necessity of recognizing these needs and of developing the capability to deal with them is important.

Each study in this section would have to be designed, executed and analyzed to meet the specific objective established at the time it was required. This situation would apply to the listed activities A, B, and C. Insofar as D and E are concerned, attention must be paid to collecting and collating data in such a way that they can be used as inputs to specific studies that will usually be carried out by other divisions or outside agencies.

TOURISM DATA BASE

The review of the data needs that have been outlined in the past four sections leads to the conclusion that the requirements can be encompassed within the framework of a comprehensive tourism data base. This data base would constitute an element, albeit a major one, of an overall tourism information base.

A description of such an information base is beyond the scope of this paper. The concern of a research group is restricted to the data portion of such a system. Three different types of data are required to meet the needs of the functions that were discussed, namely, strategic and policy planning, program planning, market and product analysis, and activity specific research. These data, which are de-

scribed in detail in the following paragraphs, should be thought of as constituting the fundamental inputs to a tourism data base. They can be grouped into three broad classes:

A. Data relative to travel and traveler
B. Data relative to the operation of the tourism industry
C. Data relative to the physical facilities available for tourism

The more precise requirements under each of these headings will be spelled out in the course of this section.

DATA RELATIVE TO TRAVEL AND TRAVELERS

More specific details about the general requirements for data relative to travel and travelers are outlined in this section, along with an outline of an assessment technique for reviewing the availability of data for any market.

Basic information on the market would consist of the following data sets:

Who:
a. Demographic characteristics such as age, income, education, occupation, marital status, sex, place and type of residence

When:
a. The time that the trip actually takes place based either on start or end date, usually expressed in terms of month or quarter
b. The length of time that a trip actually lasts, usually expressed in nights

Where:
a. The destination of the trip, expressed in terms of a locality, region, province, country, or continent
b. The origin of the trip, also expressed in terms of a locality, region, province, country, or continent
c. The trip routing collected

What:
a. The purpose of the trip
b. The activities during a trip
c. The use of specific tourism services

How:
a. The mode of transportation
b. The type of accommodation
c. The use of travel agents and packages

Why:
a. Benefits sought from and gained through travel
b. Travel as part of life-style
c. Attitudes and motivations to travel
d. Attitudes and perceptions toward the tourism product offered and/or experienced

Expenditure:
a. Expenditures by purpose incurred while traveling, such as transportation, accommodation, food and beverage, entertainment and recreation

These seven main elements constitute the key market parts of a tourism information base. For each of the items listed, a specific definition is required.

When the main data elements are identified and defined, the next step is to determine, by means of a careful analysis of existing data, how well the data needs are being met. This review will identify the existing data and the source of those data and will highlight the need for any additional data. Revisions of existing data-collection procedures or the development of new ones are then possible.

The basic layout for the review procedure is outlined in Figure 5. In actual practice, the process will be more complicated than Figure 5 might indicate. Each of the subelements under a main element would need to be outlined in detail, and the extent of data availability carefully worked out. On the basis of this type of review, the adequacy of existing data can be judged, and new or modified data collection procedures can be instituted to fill the gaps. The detailed review sheet is shown in Figure 6.

DATA RELATIVE TO THE OPERATION OF THE TOURISM INDUSTRY

Central Statistical Agencies usually collect and disseminate a great deal of data directly relative to the operation of the tourism industry. The basic problem in the use of these data is the lack of a clearly defined tourism industry within standard industrial classifications (SIC) (see Chapter 7).

The types of data that should be available from the Central Statistical Agency are the essential operational ones, for example, labor utilization and/or employment, economic, and financial. These data are necessary for such analyses as

cost/price competitiveness, capital growth, manpower utilization, profitability, financial solvency, economic impact, and interindustry comparisons. It is necessary with regard to these data to determine how tourism is treated within the standard industrial classification and to work out, ideally, a clearly defined tourism sector.

DATA RELATIVE TO THE PHYSICAL FACILITIES AVAILABLE FOR TOURISM

The operational data sets described in the previous section do not constitute an inventory of the tourism plant, but they do provide essential data. The definition and establishment of a complete tourism-plant inventory that would be useful for development, planning, marketing, and policy decisions is a very complex problem. Experience elsewhere with comprehensive inventories is that they are expensive in terms of personnel and money, and, too frequently, the output does not justify the expense.

The broad data requirements for a tourism plant inventory were outlined in Figure 4. The plant inventory requirement should be spelled out in the same detail as that established for market data. If a plant inventory does not exist, there are several key steps that should be undertaken before such a data collection procedure is contemplated. The first and most important step is to determine who the users of the inventory will be and to what uses the data will be put. Until these two facts are known, it is not possible to proceed to the next two steps: determine the basic data elements and the level of detail to be included in such an inventory, and define the level of areal disaggregation needed.

In addition to an inventory of the physical plant available,

	Availability of Data		
	Markets of Interest		
Data Element	Domestic	Country A	Country B
Who: (a)			
When: (a)			
(b)			
Where: (a)			
(b)			
(c)			
What: (a)			
(b)			
(c)			
How: (a)			
(b)			
(c)			
Why: (a)			
(b)			
(c)			
(d)			
Expenditure: (a)			

FIGURE 5 General market data review.

Data Subelement	Markets of Interest		
	Domestic	Country A	Country B

WHO
  Demographic Characteristics
    Age
    Income
    Education
    Occupation
    Market status
    Sex
    Type of community
    Ownership of
      recreational artifacts			

FIGURE 6   General market data review.

it is also necessary to inventory the physical resource base available. A procedure similar to that outlined for the plant inventory would need to be followed.

RESEARCH ORGANIZATION

There are two factors that must be considered with regard to the organization that is needed in order to carry out the research functions that have been described. The first of these factors relates to the location of the research group within the total organization; the second deals with the internal structure of the group.

Research is clearly a staff function and, as such, should not be located within a line branch. The head of research should have direct access to the senior decision makers and should report to the senior officer of the organization. In this way, the research needs of the whole organization can be handled by a single research unit, and the implications of results from a study done, say, for marketing can be brought to the attention of development. As a result, the research can be done more effectively and more efficiently.

Within the research unit itself, there are a number of options for internal organization. A first option is that the unit can be organized along functional lines, that is, research management, data collection, data analysis and interpretation, and information dissemination. The advantage of this structure is that it permits the development of specialists in the different research functions; the disadvantage is that an individual researcher is never involved in a study from beginning to end. As a result, there is probably a lack of pride in the completion of a finished product because the study will have passed from one officer to another as the need for specialization changed during the life of a study.

A second option is to structure the research unit along the same lines as the total organization, that is, a market research unit, a development research unit, and so on. While this structure allows the development of specialization along specific subject-matter lines, it can lead to a myopic view of research and a real tendency to miss the relevancy of findings from market research for development and from both for the policy planning.

A preferred structure would be to use a project team approach. Under this system, a project team would be set up for each study, and the team would remain in existence for the life of the project. Project teams would vary in size and duration depending upon the scope of the particular research study. At any one time, a single research officer could be involved in several teams.

The type of research organization that will best suit the needs of any specific NTO will depend upon the size of the research budget and the number of person years available. In a small research unit, an informal structure on a project basis would probably be used. In a larger organization, a more formal structure would be needed, but, within this formal setting, a project system of operation would still offer the best approach to carrying out the research function.

CONCLUSION

The research needs of a national tourist organization are complex and interrelated. A basic criteria in the establishment and operation of a research activity within an NTO must be that the needs of the user are paramount. Total data needs and the appropriate analysis of those data should be identified clearly at the outset. Each research activity should then be judged on its contribution to the total needs. The second criteria is that the research studies should be both consistent and periodic. Priority in the assignment of resources should be to studies that fulfill the second criteria. A third key consideration is that emphasis should be placed on analysis and interpretation rather than on data collection. Restraint must be exercised to collect only those data that are essential.

It is also a responsibility of the research group to ensure that the analyzed and interpreted data are presented to the users in a clear, understandable manner. When several studies are used as sources of information, the results should be integrated before presentation in order to avoid any confusion by the recipients.

14

Tourism Research in European National Tourist Organizations

MARTINUS J. KOSTERS
Member, Board of Directors
Netherlands Institute of Tourism and Transport Studies
Breda, The Netherlands

*T*his chapter deals with the current, general research of national tourist organizations (NTOs) in Europe. There are many differences between the various countries and their respective NTOs. Various types of research are being conducted, from a simple desk research to the more sophisticated and expensive types of field research. There is a significant collaboration of 24 NTOs in the European Travel Commission.

When discussing Europe, one must bear in mind that Europe is not a political unity—it is a continent. It comprises over 30 sovereign nations. There is no tourism policy covering the entire region. In this respect, there is hardly a tourism policy in the European Economic Community (EEC), although there is a department for tourism at Brussels (D.G. XXIII). Indeed, several countries do not even have a specific, national tourism policy. When a country does have a policy in the form of a written manual, then it is, generally speaking, more a platform for practical operations than a thorough philosophy with short- and long-term priorities.

Every country has its own national tourist organization (NTO). Each of the 24 Western European countries has an NTO either in the form of a private organization with some government influence, like Austria, the Netherlands, Germany, Switzerland, and the United Kingdom, or an NTO as a part of the government system itself, like Belgium, France, and Spain. In either case, every NTO has the statutory obligation to stimulate tourism to the NTO's country in favor of the private tourist industry involved. In the seven Eastern European countries (Bulgaria, Yugoslavia, Czechoslovakia, Poland, Hungary, Romania, and Albania), NTOs are always part of both the national government systems and of the tourist industry in their countries, but this situation may change in the coming years. In those seven countries, each NTO promotes only the packages for its own organization.

Traveling for pleasure there is often restricted or forbidden in some areas.

As the political structure of every nation varies, the statutory task and the organization of every NTO varies from country to country as well. There is no uniform structural framework within which the NTO fits; it may be a section of a ministry, commissariat, or commission, or a section of a board or council or even a corporation. However, some main elements can be identified in the different packages of the many NTOs, and these common activities will be outlined before attention is focused on the research field.

WHAT IS AN NTO?

A national tourist organization is a country's official organization that is responsible for the development of promotion, research, and marketing of tourism of its country. Every NTO has at its disposal a complete inventory of the country's tourist attractions and facilities. It develops marketing plans for selected tourist markets abroad in cooperation with, or sometimes without, the interested private travel and accommodation industry and organizations. The same applies to domestic tourism, but, within this context, that is of minor importance. The NTO is preeminently the organization that should attempt to coordinate the tourism promotion plans of the country. For a good and alert policy, the NTO needs offices in the foreign markets. Such offices form an extension of the NTO in a specific market.

Here, an important observation should be made before discussing certain issues in detail. When a marketing organization makes proposals to adapt or to reshape a given tourist product, it is not self-evident that the industry will follow this advice. The NTO and the industry are different bodies (except in the Eastern European countries), and, consequently, the views of the partners may differ. When the process of the producing, marketing, and selling of services is in the hands of one agency, there should be at least a good internal discussion why the advice of the marketing department is ignored.

Dependent on the national policy in tourism, every country formulates its own goals for the NTO. As a result, organization structures of NTOs differ. In order to illustrate this, two organization charts of two NTOs are presented here as examples. Figure 1 is of the Austrian Osterreichisches Fremdenverkehrswerbung (OFVW) at Vienna, and Figure 2 is of the Dutch National Bureau voor Toerisme (NBT) at The Hague. Both NTOs do promote their respective countries, but, as modern NTOs, they also favor research. In addition, the Dutch NTO has a task for product development.

THE CHANGING PACKAGES OF ACTIVITIES OF NTOS

In all Western European countries, tourism is not completely left to the initiative of the private sector, not even in countries with a relatively free economy. While the degree of state intervention varies from country to country, the respective governments do intervene in the activities of their NTOs in order to stimulate incoming tourism (and also domestic tourism).

Basically, two types of NTO activities are well known:

(1) tourist information and (2) tourist promotion. Both activities are directed straight at the consumer, for example, the foreign tourist. Until the 1970s, these functions were the main activities. Subsequently, the more progressive NTOs started to organize campaigns to influence travel organizations and carriers to encourage tours to the country involved or to increase the number of tours. This is a more direct approach to the consumer because the travel organization develops its own consumer-oriented promotion campaigns for its travel program. When a certain country receives considerable attention in such a program, the NTO has succeeded in obtaining free publicity using the travel organization. In certain cases, the NTO agrees to pay the travel organizations for the promotional support provided.

PROMOTIONAL ACTIVITIES AIMED AT FOREIGN CONSUMERS

Broadly speaking, for a very passive NTO, a post-office box and a telephone number in the home country are enough to help a consumer with information about tourism. But for potential foreign tourists seeking information, it is clearly not a desirable situation to have to telephone another country, especially when the tourists do not speak the language of that country. Besides, it is a rather expensive way of communication. As a result, the majority of active NTOs establish offices in the capitals or big cities of those countries that represent potential tourist markets. Sometimes they have more than one office in a particular market. It is obvious that the decisions to establish operating offices abroad are primarily influenced by budgetary concerns.

When an NTO decides to establish an office in a foreign country, they have to decide on the city and its location in that city. In the past, the European NTOs have always sought to occupy street-level premises in the main streets of the capitals and big cities. Such an office was seen as a suitable point of distribution for tourist literature to the public in the

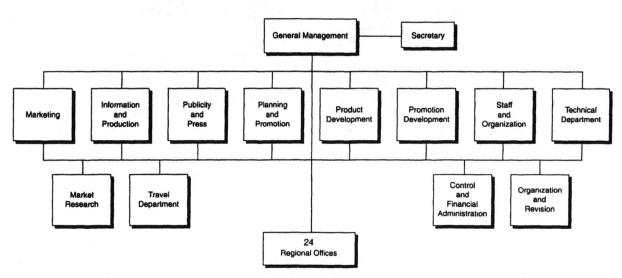

FIGURE 1   Organizational structure of the Austrian NTO OFVW 1991.

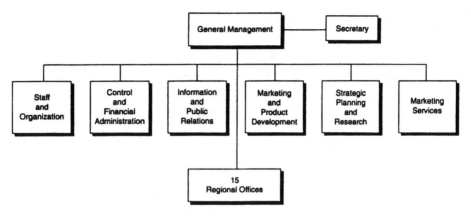

FIGURE 2 Organizational structure of Dutch NTO NBT 1992.

main shopping areas. Some NTOs, however, have recognized that this is an expensive formula and question its effectiveness. These NTOs have realized that their main purpose is to service the providers of tourist services—for that part of their job, they do not require an office in a busy street. Consequently, they have gradually moved to other locations in the same town. However, this decision remains an important concern: whether to go for the prestigious, expensive street-level premises downtown or select more modest off-street premises.

CONSUMER-ORIENTED ACTIVITIES

The main objective of promotional activities is to inform the public about the NTO's home country. By mail, this is a time-consuming and expensive operation, but it should be expected that some people will write for information. For many people, it is a problem to write at all, but, in a foreign language, it is very difficult. Therefore, the NTO needs staff who have command of the languages of the prime tourist markets. Much the same holds for clients' inquiries by telephone, but it is somewhat easier to help them and, generally, more effective. Consequently, it is important to have an office in the target market. If there is an office, it will always be possible to respond to potential clients. Besides, a wide range of printed matter should be available, as well as multidimensional presentations. The NTO office can offer all these services irrespective of its location.

Depending on the promoting country and on the market, each NTO office should be supplied with tourist literature: general and specialized brochures about the country; information bulletins about the various accommodation facilities, food and drinks, and museums and tourist attractions; maps and communications; and specialized information about towns, provinces, and regions and about facilities for sporting activities like yachting, boating, fishing, and swimming.

Today, more and more tourism fairs or exhibitions for tourists are organized in Western Europe. The biggest exhibition in the world is the Internationale Tourist Borse (ITB) in Berlin, where more than 80 countries present themselves to the tourist trade and to hundreds of thousands of consumers. In diverse countries, several of these exhibitions are

regularly organized. NTOs are expected to participate in them, even when an NTO runs an office in the same town. The NTOs could attract other market segments at an exhibition. So, many NTOs have changed their priorities in favour of tourism exhibitions.

In conjunction with other bodies, an NTO sometimes organizes a special week in a city, for example, a Dutch week in New York City. Depending on the budget allocated for such an occasion and on the collaboration of various organizations, shops might offer Dutch products and establish window display units about Holland. Newspapers, magazines, and radio and television stations might provide information about Holland (not only tourist information); restaurants might serve Dutch food on their menus, and pubs might offer Dutch drinks. There might be concerts by Dutch orchestras, performances by Dutch groups, and exhibitions of Dutch folklore and art and of Dutch products in general. In other words, for a few days, a Dutch atmosphere would be created in the city so that everyone will experience it. Although this is not pure tourism promotion, it may result in a strong impact on tourism from New York to Holland in the near future.

The NTOs also play an important role in the dissemination of information to authors, journalists, and producers of tourist programs on radio and TV. NTOs seek to provide these people with regular issues of press releases—the bulletins containing topical information—photographic material, slides and films, documentation, and with assistance during visits. They may even organize trips for VIPs to the home country.

On special festive occasions, every NTO office is prepared to assist in presenting food and drinks from the home country or to place some typical gifts or presents at the disposal of organizers of public events so that the attention of many people can be focused on the country. NTOs always have colorful posters at their disposal. NTOs may offer special familiarization trips to their country if this provides much free publicity.

Every NTO is always engaged in advertising campaigns. While such campaigns take a substantial part of the budget, NTOs recognize the need to inform large segments of the population about the existence of their country with the goal of creating an increase in tourism demand. Very often, NTOs invite people to ask for more free information by filling out coupons.

TRADE-ORIENTED ACTIVITIES

The following activities are more or less part of the trade-oriented tasks of European NTOs.

1. NTOs offer visits to the travel trade in the target markets with concrete offers for package tours, suggestions for travel destinations, excursions, facilities, or joint promotional campaigns. However, one must be aware that wholesalers and carriers may attempt to play off NTOs against each other.

2. The most progressive NTOs organize workshops for the representatives of the travel trade in a particular country and for the representatives of the incoming tourist industry in their own country. The NTOs invite participants and provide the opportunity for bringing them together to do business face-to-face.

3. The NTO organizes study tours for managers of the interested travel trade, either to open up new markets or to acquaint the tour operator's sales staff with the various aspects of the product.

4. The NTO arranges seminars where the various representatives of the travel trade in a particular market meet the staff of the NTO, and its related organizations provide a suitable platform for the exchange of information about the many products, services, (potential) markets, and prices. The goal is to discuss how to improve the results for the next season or for the next year.

5. Every NTO attempts to inform its business contacts through current information and travel data. Most of the NTOs publish a special magazine or newsletter, often in the form of a monthly bulletin.

6. In addition, NTOs undertake direct mailings of up-to-date tourism literature to the managers of the travel industry.

7. On special occasions, NTOs organize cocktail parties or banquets for their most important business friends.

8. NTO offices stage information meetings for the sales staff of travel agencies at which slides, films, or multimedia presentations are used to familiarize the travel agents with the tourist product of the NTO's country. They also present awards to the top sellers of tours to their country.

9. The travel trade in every country now has its own trade press. So, NTOs are more inclined to advertise in its magazines and journals. It is easily understandable that the information in the travel press should be different from the information in the advertising campaigns directed at the consumers.

10. Some NTOs take a very active part in attracting incentive travel to their country. Sometimes they attract the entire staff of companies or factories for a tour. Much the same

holds for persuading international or national organizations to hold a congress or an exhibition in the NTO's country.

RELATIONS BETWEEN THE HEADQUARTERS AND THE OFFICE ABROAD

It is clear that there should be a good understanding between the headquarters in the home country and the offices in foreign markets. Strictly speaking, the office abroad is no more than an extension of the home office into a foreign market. In all cases, the offices abroad carry out many of the tasks mentioned before. In addition, they form important antennae for monitoring developments in the market in order to devise (with or without the home office) marketing strategies for the coming season or year. The headquarters in the home country should coordinate the activities of the offices abroad. Some NTOs maintain only a few offices. However, the bigger NTOs, such as Austria, Great Britain, France, and Germany, have over 20.

The office abroad should provide the home office with market information. Conversely, the home office has to supply the office abroad with up-to-date tourist information and literature in the various languages. A progressive NTO should formulate both a long term program every three to five years, and yearly a marketing plan in cooperation with the managers of the offices abroad.

RESEARCH

In nearly every type of industry and in individual enterprises, research is considered of vital importance, but, oddly enough, not in tourism. However, the situation is now improving. The better tourism businesses have now incorporated research as a regular part of their operations. So do some NTOs; but there exist appreciable differences among a number of European NTOs. Only a few countries carry out very comprehensive research programs. For others, it is still a matter of either implementing a different management philosophy or of providing a bigger budget before research can be carried out.

It is by no means necessary for the NTO to undertake its own research. An NTO may collaborate in a research project with one or more interested private companies. It is obvious that research cooperation between the NTO and the flag carrier(s) should be feasible. On the other hand, it is also possible that several NTOs can combine their research activities. More will be said about this in the section on the European Travel Commission.

In the following sections, various types of research done by European NTOs will be analyzed. So far, the techniques and results of research have been very modest, with a few notable exceptions. Nearly all countries, however, possess professional research teams in the form of the national bureaus of statistics or distinguished tourism research specialists. So there exist possibilities for an NTO to farm out research to these specialists when the specialists required are not on the NTO's staff.

DESK RESEARCH

The least demanding type of research that an organization like an NTO can carry out is some desk research. This implies that an NTO should have at least one or two specialist staff members at the headquarters who gather information and collect data on tourism research carried out by others. These data can be obtained in the first instance from the national bureau of statistics and from private companies offering research results.

In addition to information from its own country, every NTO should collect relevant information from other countries. Within this context, it is interesting to mention that only a few countries like Great Britain, The Netherlands, Germany, France, Sweden, Switzerland, and Austria yearly provide data on the tourist behavior of both their inhabitants (i.e., on domestic and outgoing tourism) and incoming tourists. In these countries, the official bodies undertake very accurate research into the holiday patterns and holiday behaviors of their population through questionnaires administered to people selected by a representative, random sample of the whole population. In these questionnaires, the respondents are asked to provide information about the number of holiday trips made in a particular year; the destinations inside and outside the country; the means of transport, type of accommodation, and duration of each holiday trip; the period of the year; the expenditure; the booking period; and the type of holidays. In addition, there are questions about personal characteristics such as sex, age, marital status, family composition, income, profession, education, place of residence, and about personal belongings like car, travel trailer, second home, yacht, or boat.

It is regretful that such research is not done systematically in every European country, although a few countries like Belgium, France, Sweden, Norway, and Denmark do it periodically. Some countries, like Great Britain, The Netherlands, and Germany, have typologies of holiday-makers at their disposal, and sometimes of non-holiday-makers, too.

An important difference between Europe and North America regarding this type of research is the fact that in Europe, holidays are defined in terms of *nights away from home*, and in North America, the emphasis is on *geographical displacement*, which makes it completely impossible to compare between the two continents. In Europe, a holiday is defined as a period of at least five consecutive days spent for recreational reasons outside the place where one normally lives and works. It is clear that, for their own desk research, NTOs are very interested in the results of the previously mentioned form of research of the other European countries.

Nearly all countries gather data about tourism, as is evidenced by the annual reports published by the Organization for Economic Cooperation and Development (OECD, Paris) and the World Tourism Organization (WTO, Madrid). In doing so, most countries collect the following types of statistical information:

A. Volume statistics—counting arrivals at the borders, arrivals in the various forms of accommodation, the number of bednights and the number of visits
B. Expenditure statistics—measuring the expenditures at the destination of the journey and the exchange of money by the banks
C. Tourism characteristics—providing information on the profile and behavior of holiday-makers, participants in short duration trips, and daytrippers

In fact, Great Britain is the only European country with a complete range of statistics on an annual basis. In this respect, the insular character of the country is important. For instance, the officials can count every visitor because the number of the country's points of entry is limited. No other European country possesses anything like the Home Office Immigration Statistics. Besides, each year Great Britain carries out the International Passenger Survey, a sample survey designed to obtain information about travel to and from Great Britain.

Very few Western European countries have such reliable frontier information. The Benelux countries do not have such statistics at all. These examples show that an NTO desk researcher has to gather several statistics, which very often measure different things so that making comparisons is a rather laborious task. This lack of a universal research methodology in Europe and the completely different systems used in North America make desk research complicated, but not impossible.

The NTO researcher has to combine the previously mentioned relevant statistical information with the information gathered from incidental research, from the offices abroad, from articles in newspapers and magazines, from statements made by tourism managers, and so on. In this way, the European NTOs can do at least some research. The more dynamic and progressive NTOs present the information they gather in annual publications for the travel trade in the home country. With the help of the results of this desk research, an NTO can formulate its promotional campaign—it might increase its promotional activities aimed, for instance, at countries from which the number of tourists is decreasing; conversely, it could decrease its activities in markets that keep generating massive tourism flows to the NTO's country. However, if the results of the desk research are not sufficient to develop policies, field research is needed.

FIELD RESEARCH

Since field research is very expensive, the average NTO only rarely has the opportunity to commission a comprehensive research in a given country. Conversely, every NTO likes to get, periodically, up-to-date information about every one of its important markets. This implies that each year several studies are needed. It may be worthwhile for an NTO to combine its research on a specific market with another interested NTO so that they can share the costs. A later discussion will cover what the European NTOs are currently doing in this area.

In what type of field research might an NTO be interested? To answer this question, it is useful to distinguish between quantitative and qualitative research. Although a clear distinction cannot be made, quantitative research may be viewed as research that is mainly interested in describing a market with respect to such features as the number of visitors, their origin and destination, the amount of money spent, and so on. Qualitative research can be described as research that is mainly interested in such factors as the motives, attitudes, and images that form the basis of human behavior.

Quantitative Research

As has already been mentioned, every NTO needs quantitative information on the target markets, but it is often difficult to gather this information. In every country, however, there are now research agencies specializing in quantitative research through so-called *omnibus surveys*. These agencies use groups of consumers that are representative of the population in a country (the so-called *panels*). At weekly, monthly, or bimonthly intervals, the members of these panels answer a list of questions on a broad range of topics that are dictated by an agency's clients—various industries, sellers, suppliers, and advertisers who cannot afford separate research for their products under certain circumstances. For each client, the agency includes a few questions about his "problem" in the questionnaire that is filled out by the panels. Thus, each client participating in the omnibus survey can ask some questions, depending on the client's budget and problem.

Of course, the entire survey in a particular week may be carried out for a single client. It is very attractive for an NTO, especially for the NTO offices abroad, to participate in such an omnibus survey. It is cheap and very fast. Within a few weeks, it is possible to have the information required. On the other hand, since the research is based on a few questions, the scope of the answers provided is limited. Thus, an NTO should be very clear about its objectives, and the questions included in the omnibus survey should be phrased very precisely and unambiguously.

An omnibus survey is not the only way to gather quantitative information, but it has been dealt with here because this approach is well known and very popular. In fact, all the preceding types of desk and field research provide quantitative information, but they tend to be much more expensive and require more preparation.

Market Research

Currently, the European NTOs recognize the importance of their marketing function. Thus, it is worthwhile to consider which market segments in a particular country should be covered and how. Through image research, the NTO obtains general information for its campaigns. With the aid of field research among special target groups, like car owners, anglers, teenagers, families with pre-school-age children, families with post-school-age children, elderly people, owners of travel trailers, rail travelers, amateur photographers, and the like, the NTO can gain in-depth information on how to approach each market segment.

The type of research that an NTO wants to carry out is determined by the information that is needed. If the NTO has a good team of researchers, it is not impossible for the NTO to carry out the field research under its own direction with the help of interviewers; but that is more an exception than a rule. In general, it is advisable to employ a local research agency in the target market. If necessary, there is always the possibility that the specialized research agency carries out the field work, with the NTO staff evaluating the results and drawing the conclusions.

What is needed for this type of field research is a random sample of the target group. If the group is organized, for example, members of unions or associations, it will not be so difficult to obtain the addresses for the sample. However, if the target group is not organized, it may be much more difficult to do a field research.

Depending on the situation, a choice has to be made as to the approach of the target group, that is, through a home interview, a mailed questionnaire, or a telephone interview. Each of these techniques has its advantages and disadvantages. It is the task of the NTO's research department to determine how many respondents are needed with regard to the accuracy required and to formulate the projects. When the data of the field research have been compiled, it is again the task of the NTO researchers to interpret the results and to identify their implications for the design of marketing campaigns.

Effectiveness of Campaigns

It is clear from the foregoing that an NTO in Europe has to perform many tasks. Not every task is difficult, but, as the task becomes more important or more complicated, the NTO should undertake to design and evaluate its own campaigns and efforts. A commercial company either within or outside the field of tourism can measure the effects of specific extra efforts in the short term. However, for a promotion organization, this is much more complex. It is nearly impossible to measure the real effect of a campaign because it is spread among thousands of companies.

Even when there are positive results for a specific firm, it is extremely difficult to ascribe them to the NTO's campaign. Consequently, every NTO has serious problems with the feedback from its own industry. The NTO would like to hear that its campaigns are successful, but the industry often states that the results, if any, are only of marginal importance. Therefore, the NTO's research department should do follow-up studies of the results of its promotional efforts.

As a rule, an NTO does not possess the funds for carrying out such research. It could be done by the NTO itself, but it would be better to employ a specialized research agency as previously described. When the NTO does not properly monitor its own activities, it is unlikely that it will optimize its results with its relatively small and limited budget. Again, this is a matter of priorities. Reliable advertising agencies always include research on the results of a campaign as part of their services. Why should an NTO not do so? In the past, much money has been wasted through a lack of critical assessment of an NTO's own activities.

Coupon Research

A relatively easy and inexpensive type of research is the information an NTO can obtain from coupons included in advertisements in journals and magazines. Consumers are invited to return the coupons in order to receive information on topics mentioned in the advertisement. Through codes on the coupons, the NTO can check which journal or magazine provides a good return. It should be noted that the NTO can farm out the servicing of returns to specialized agencies.

If the NTO wants to obtain specific information through a coupon-reply system, a few additional questions may be inserted besides those asking for name, address, and place of residence. This is important for those managers of the offices abroad who have to step up their campaigns in their respective countries. Mostly, they cannot afford a full-time research professional on their staff. When the NTO engages an ongoing coupon reply system, it can gather quite a lot of useful information and improve the effects of its campaigns.

QUALITATIVE RESEARCH

Besides quantitative information, every organization needs qualitative information about the market. Image research is a good example of qualitative information.

Through the research agency, an NTO can have at its disposal focus groups of 5–12 people, representative of a specific market segment, who will discuss special topics with the help of experts of the research firm; for example, a country like Spain is heavily dependent on charter flights with tourists from the northern European countries and Great Britain. As a result of steadily increasing fuel prices, the prices of package tours to Spain have increased considerably since the beginning of the 1980s. So, the authorities in Spain will be worried about the future. Will the tourists keep coming despite the price increases? Will they opt for other modes of transportation and other destinations? Will they travel to foreign destinations each year? These are basic questions that can be discussed with focus groups. The members of the group can react to each other. When different groups, independently from each other, have discussed the same items, the experts can analyze the responses. The findings of such research may be insufficient or contradictory. In the latter case, the principal can do hardly anything with the information received. However, a focus group interview may also serve as a starting point for a more comprehensive research with a random sample of the population and questionnaires.

Image Research

For each NTO, it is important to know how to approach a particular market. Although a good local manager of the office abroad will be generally aware of consumer atti-

tudes within the local market, the manager and his or her advisers may only have knowledge of several segments of the total market. Field research among a cross section of the population on the basis of a questionnaire is, without any doubt, a suitable means to diminish these risks. With this information, an NTO can learn how people perceive its country; what they like and dislike and why; whether they want to go there or not; how long and where they prefer to stay and what they want to visit; how much time and how much money they are willing to spend; the way they like to travel; and so on.

It is very important for an NTO to know how a foreigner perceives its country; for example, in Germany, The Netherlands (as a small but leading industrial country in the world) still has the image of being an agricultural country of cattle and of tulips. Although these factors are correct, the Dutch prefer to emphasize different aspects. The same applies to other results of the above image survey: the Dutch population is very tolerant and open-minded, business-oriented, and many-sided. The Germans criticize Dutch cleanliness and traffic behavior. These opinions were mainly based on the experiences of German users of Dutch camping grounds, summer houses, and pensions, but not on the experiences of hotel guests. So the Dutch NTO concluded that Holland attracts mainly the lower paid segments of the German tourist market. The well-to-do tourists prefer destinations farther away from home. Average holiday duration was 20 days, and average expenditure per head per holiday was substantially lower than the average amount spent by Germans in other European destinations.

The Dutch tourism authorities were slightly surprised that the sandy beaches along the North Sea coast and the many small, old towns with their outstanding architectural beauty were hardly mentioned. In other words, the German consumers were attracted by attractions other than those the Dutch tourist industry in Holland has emphasized in its promotional campaigns.

On the basis of the findings of such (expensive) market research, it is possible to incorporate different items in promotion campaigns. Clearly, it still remains important to sell the tulip fields and the windmills, although many a Dutchman believes that this is not the right picture of the country. Many are even reluctant to continue to promote tourism by focusing on these traditional images. However, they ignore the fact that potential consumers search for information in which they are interested and not always what experts believe is good for them.

When a country has carried out an image survey in diverse countries, it is very interesting to notice how the impressions of the country involved as perceived by tourists from these countries will differ. A country should then emphasize different aspects in its campaigns in the respective markets.

OTHER TYPES OF RESEARCH

The NTO has to do research in each market in which it is going to conduct a campaign. As the European NTOs organize several forms of campaigns in different markets, an NTO has to engage in several forms of research. The most important types of research have been discussed, but there are some other relevant types of research.

Participation

When an NTO wants to test new posters or designs for campaigns, it is useful to submit them to a couple of panels in collaboration with the staff of a particular NTO office. The staff can observe which design appeals most to people and why. In the same way, the NTO can learn how tourists behave and feel in a specific situation or on a certain location. Through observation and participation, much can be learned as to the approach of people in such a situation or how to lure people to a tourist attraction.

Photographs and Pictures

When an NTO is interested in the behavior of groups of tourists, pictures of a situation may be a great help in analyzing a situation.

Letters

Every NTO receives letters with questions or complaints. Although it is a special group of people that writes letters, the NTO can learn from the remarks or complaints. Together with the information obtained during seminars and the evaluation of business contacts, the research department can process this information for the marketing department.

Various Research Possibilities

Every NTO has incidental possibilities for research because of cooperation with private companies intending to do research in a particular market. A less important, but quite interesting, type of research is that done by students of a university or institute of higher education. They may study a special problem in which the NTO is interested (e.g., in the form of a thesis). For the students, it is very stimulating to do research for the benefit of an organization like an NTO. For the NTO, it is an inexpensive form of research, although some of its experts have to spend some time supervising the students. As well, since students are not experienced researchers, there is always the risk of failure.

To conclude, it should be emphasized that research is not a goal in itself, but it is a cornerstone (and not the only one) of a successful NTO policy. Broadly speaking, it must be concluded that in Europe, some NTO management teams are less and others more research oriented.

THE EUROPEAN TRAVEL COMMISSION

As was indicated before, cooperation among NTOs in research and marketing, and also an exchange of distinct information, can be a great help and save operating costs. In 1948,

the European NTOs founded the European Travel Commission (ETC). There are 24 members now. (For a complete list of the members with their respective addresses, see the Appendix.) The ETC is a nonprofit organization that derives its direct support solely from the funds supplied by its members. In the ETC, the NTOs join their forces in research and marketing related to overseas markets, notably, the United States, Japan, and Canada. The ETC fulfills several other functions as well, but they will not be discussed here.

The current objectives of the ETC are:

- To promote greater visitor traffic in and to Europe, particularly from the United States, Canada, and Japan
- To foster international tourism cooperation in Europe
- To facilitate among members the exchange of information on tourism development projects and marketing techniques
- To undertake or to commission appropriate travel research

For these purposes, the ETC has a small executive unit for coordination, support, and initiation of actions not otherwise covered. The full commission is comprised of the chief executives of the member NTOs. They have set up a steering committee and several specialist committees, for example, for marketing, research, and environment. The ETC has operation groups established in the United States (New York City) and Japan (Tokyo).

THE ROLE OF THE RESEARCH COMMITTEE

Given the goals of this Handbook, the role of the research committee is important. Its functions are:

- To outline a research strategy in accordance with the Commission's policy and marketing needs
- To undertake and/or to commission research as requested by the Marketing Committee
- To recommend and, where approved, to undertake and/or to commission other research
- To gather information on relevant research projects undertaken by other organizations and to update ETC research material
- To monitor the use of research undertaken by or on behalf of the Commission

Several interesting research studies have been published in the more than 40 years of existence of the ETC. It should be clear that an active ETC is currently of vital interest to the European NTOs, perhaps more than in the past, now that research and marketing form the basis for the policies of the modern European NTOs. Although to a certain extent the NTOs are competitors, cooperation appears to be possible and even necessary!

CONCLUSION

This chapter has attempted to highlight the important functions of the European NTOs with regard to research. The

Eastern European NTOs are mentioned pro memoria because of their different task and their political involvement in the past.

It has been shown that the Western European NTOs have focused on two types of activities: consumer promotion and trade-oriented promotion. Both approaches contain many small-scale activities. In order to operate successfully, the NTO should effectively monitor its operations. Consequently, research is a cornerstone, especially now as tourism professionals in Europe begin to recognize the importance of research-and-marketing techniques.

This chapter has briefly indicated which types of research are done, or can be done, by NTOs. As NTOs are competitors in several markets, there appears no urgent need for cooperation. Nevertheless, the 24 Western European NTOs cooperate harmoniously in the ETC. The weak financial position of the majority of the NTOs has forced them to cooperate and made the ETC a real success in terms of collaboration and research activities in the overseas markets.

REFERENCES

Bukart, John, and S. Medlik (1974), *Tourism, Past, Present and Future*, London: Heinemann.

ETC Secretariat, (1979), *The European Travel Commission Handbook*, Dublin: ETC.

Fremdenverkehrs Wirtshapt (FVW), *Changing Structures of the National "Marketing Departments,"* English supplement, March 1992, Hamburg.

International Tourism Quarterly, No. 3, 1976, special article *"The Role and Functions of a National Tourist Office,"* London: No. 3, 1983, National Tourist Offices, the role and functions of an NTO abroad.

Kosters, Martinus (1979), *Holland and Tourism in the Next Decade*, International Symposium—Tourism in the Next Decade, George Washington University, Washington, D.C.

Kosters, Martinus (1985), *Focus op Toerisme*, Den Haag: Vuga.

Organization for Economic Cooperation and Development (1984), *Tourism Policy and International Tourism in OECD Member Countries 1979–1983*, Paris: Organization for Economic Cooperation and Development (OECD).

Wahab, Salah, Jack Crampon, and Louis Rothfield (1976), *Tourism Marketing*, London: Tourism International Press.

World Tourism Organization (1983), *World Tourism Statistics*, Madrid: World Tourism Organization (WTO).

World Tourism Organization (1980a), *Budgets of National Tourism Administrations 1977–1979*, Madrid.

World Tourism Organization (1980b), *Role and Structure of National Tourism Administrations*, Madrid.

APPENDIX List of Members of the European Travel Commission (ETC)

Secretariat ETC: Rue Linois 2, 75015 Paris, France

COUNTRY	NAME OF ORGANIZATION	ADDRESS
Austria Autriche	Osterreich Werbung	Margaretenstrasse 1 1040 Wien IV
Belgium Belgique	Vlaams comm.-gen. voor Toerisme + Office de Promotion du Tourisme	Grasmarkt 61 1000 Brussels
Cyprus Chypre	Cyprus Tourism Organization	Theodotou Street 18, Zena Building P.O. Box 4535 Nicosia
Denmark Danemark	Danmarks Turistrad	Vesterbrogade 6D 1620 Copenhagen V
Finland Finlande	Finnish Tourist Board	P.O. Box 625 Töölönkatu 11 SF—00101 Helsinki
France France	Maison de la France	8 avenue de l'Opéra 75001 Paris
Germany Allemagne	Deutsche Zentrale für Toerismus	Beethovenstrasse 69 D-6000 Frankfurt (Main) 1
Greece Grece	National Tourist Organization of Greece	2 Amerikis Street Athens 105 64
Hungary Hongrie	Hungarian Tourist Board	1051 Budapest Vigado U.6. 1387 Budapest P.O. Box 11

APPENDIX *(continued)*

COUNTRY	NAME OF ORGANIZATION	ADDRESS
Iceland Islande	Iceland Tourist Board	Laikjargata 3 101 Reykjavik
Ireland Irlande	Bord Failte Eireann	Baggott Street Bridge, Dublin 2
Italy Italie	Direttore Generale ENIT	Via Marghera 00185 Roma
Luxembourg Luxembourg	Office National du Tourisme	Boîte postale 1001 L-1010 Luxembourg
Malta Malte	National Tourism Organization	280 Republic Street Valletta
Monaco Monaco	Dep. Tourism and Congresses Principaute de Monaco	Boulevard de Moulins 2a Monte Carlo
The Netherlands Pays Bas	Netherlands Board of Tourism	Vlietweg 15 2266 KA P.O. Box 458 2260 MG Leidschendam
Norway Norvege	NORTRA Norwegian Tourist Board	Langkaia 1 Box 499 Sentrum N 0105 Oslo 1
Portugal Portugal	Istituto de Promoçao Turistica	Rue Alexandre Herculano 15-4 1200—Lisboa
Spain Espagne	Turespana	Castello 115 28006 Madrid
Sweden Suede	Swedish Tourist Board	Sverigehuset Kungstradgarden, Box 7473 S-10392 Stockholm
Switzerland Suisse	Swiss National Tourist Office	Bellariastrasse 38 DH 8027 Zürich
Turkey Turquie	Ministry of Tourism	Sehit Adem Yavuz Sokak, 10 Kizilay, Ankara
United Kingdom Royaume Uni	British Tourist Authority	24 Grosvenor Gardens London SW1W OET
Yugoslavia Yougoslavie	Foreign Economic Relations	Dept. of International Tourism Omladinskih Brigada 1 11070 Belgrade
	Turisticki savez Jugoslavije	Mose Pijade 8/IV 11001 Belgrade

15

Research in State
and Provincial Travel Offices

SUZANNE D. COOK
Executive Director

VERNON AZUCENAS
Assistant to the Executive Director
U.S. Travel Data Center
Washington, D.C.

As an overview of research programs conducted by state and provincial travel offices, this chapter provides summaries and analyses of research needs and objectives of travel offices, as well as the major research techniques used. It is designed to explore the range of current research activities, rather than to provide detailed descriptions of any particular type of research.

STATE AND PROVINCIAL ROLE IN TRAVEL PROMOTION AND DEVELOPMENT

Each state, province, and territory in the United States and Canada has an agency for travel promotion and development. In some states (Alaska, Hawaii, South Carolina, Texas) and Washington, D.C., other state agencies work in conjunction with the state travel office to implement parts of their programs.

The breadth of responsibilities and perspectives encompassed by state and provincial travel offices is unmatched by the private sector and provides a vital supplement to private promotion efforts. The primary function of these travel offices is to develop and implement marketing programs, integrating all of the facilities of the state or province to yield the most effective use of their marketing budgets. Travel-office budgets for travel promotion and development directly contribute to economic expansion by increasing traveler expenditures, which in turn produce new jobs, personal income, and tax receipts for all levels of government.

Further, state and provincial travel offices play a unique and vital role in affecting the terms of this growth by encouraging cooperation among industry sectors, providing assistance to the private sector in terms of travel marketing and development, and attending to planning and quality control. In addition, travel offices represent the views of both travel-related businesses and consumers in discussions of policies or regulations that might affect the industry.

State and provincial travel offices also provide important information services to the traveling consumer, unavailable anywhere else. Finally, increasingly these agencies are fulfilling a primary leadership role in destination-related research. In this capacity, they provide information that private-sector organizations within their state or province need to develop their own investment and marketing strategies.

CURRENT LEVELS OF STATE AND PROVINCIAL INVOLVEMENT

OVERALL PROGRAMS AND BUDGETS

In fiscal year 1991–1992, travel office budgets in the United States totaled $343 million, or approximately $6.9 million per state. Individual budgets vary widely, however, and range from a high of $26.8 million to a low of $808,000 (U.S. Travel Data Center 1992a). Provincial travel office budgets

165

averaged $20.9 million in 1991-92. This average is skewed significantly, however, by one province's budget of over $111 million. Nevertheless, six out of eight provinces responding to this question in a recent survey reported budgets exceeding $5 million (U.S. Travel Data Center 1992b).

Travel offices conduct a variety of programs, including advertising, promotion, provision of information to consumers, operation of highway welcome centers, participation in travel shows, package-tour development, education and training, and research. In most cases, advertising and other promotional activities represent the largest portion of the travel office budget.

RESEARCH PROGRAMS

The mean research budget for state travel offices in 1991–1992 was $122,300, representing about 1.8 percent of the average total budget. Research tends to enjoy a somewhat higher priority among provincial travel offices than among those in the United States. Reflecting generally higher total budgets, travel offices in Canada tend to have substantially higher research budgets, which averaged $507,200 in 1991–1992. Again, this number is skewed by one province's research budget of nearly $1.6 million. Six out of the nine provinces responding to this question, however, reported research budgets in excess of $200,000.

Research staffs also tend to be larger in Canadian provincial travel offices, averaging 5.1 full-time and 3.0 part-time staff members per office. All 10 provinces responding to this question reported at least one full-time research staff member. In the United States, one or more staff members are currently dedicated to research in 42 states and the District of Columbia. However, in only 14 of these states does the staff member have research as a full-time responsibility. On the average, state travel offices employ 1.5 full-time and 0.6 part-time people in research.

In a special survey conducted among state and provincial travel offices by the U.S. Travel Data Center (1992b), respondents were asked to rate, on a scale from 1 (not at all important) to 5 (extremely important), the importance of research in formulating travel promotion and development programs. In the United States, 82 percent of all respondents rated the importance of research as 4 or 5 (mean = 4.2). In Canada, 78 percent gave research a 4 or a 5 (mean = 4.1).

Research is essential to the effective planning and operation of any travel office program. Research is required to set goals for the travel office and to establish measurable objectives that can later be used to evaluate the effectiveness of various promotional and development programs. Research is vital to assessing the strengths and weaknesses of the state's or province's tourism products and services and to designing programs that capitalize on those strengths while improving or minimizing the weaknesses. Research is also critical to determining target audiences for marketing programs. Finally, sound research reduces risk—the risk of wasting advertising and other marketing funds or of actually reducing the net economic benefits of tourism to a state or province through overdevelopment (Davidson and Wiethaupt 1989; Frechtling 1991).

While funding for research tends to be limited, particularly in the United States, most travel officials recognize its value and attempt to maximize their research efforts by cooperating with other groups and making use of techniques that generate the greatest amount of accurate data in the most cost-effective way. The remainder of this chapter discusses the research activities of state and provincial travel offices in detail.

RESEARCH NEEDS AT THE STATE AND PROVINCIAL LEVEL

The size and sophistication of research programs vary considerably among travel offices in the United States and Canada and depend significantly on monetary and other resources available, as well as on the duration of time the research program has been in place.

The goal of travel offices should be to develop a carefully planned program of phased, or sequential, research projects. Establishment of research priorities should be based on a thorough analysis of the research needs of the particular state or provincial travel office and of the citizens and private sector that it serves. Such an analysis should take into consideration the following types of factors.

EXISTING DATA

A careful review of research conducted in the past by the travel office and other existing data sources should be one of the first steps in defining research needs. Travel and tourism research is conducted by a variety of public and private organizations. Agencies of the federal government conduct major research efforts related to travel and tourism, the results of which are available to the public. Examples include the United States Travel and Tourism Administration (USTTA), the U.S. Bureau of the Census, Tourism Canada, and Statistics Canada.

USTTA, in addition to regular reports based on its *Inflight Survey of International Air Travelers* (1992a) and other marketing research studies, also offers subscriptions for quarterly *USTTA Updates and Information Alerts* (1992b). Similarly, Tourism Canada publishes a monthly annotated bibliography of industry media and other reports entitled *The Tourism Intelligence Bulletin* (1992). *Travelog*, published quarterly by Statistics Canada, also presents concise summaries of research related to the Canadian inbound and outbound markets (1992).

Travel research is also frequently conducted by colleges and universities, private consulting firms, and travel-related companies. The Travel and Tourism Research Association is an excellent resource for travel researchers and marketers to learn about relevant research in the public domain. Its quarterly *Journal of Travel Research* includes a section entitled "Travel Research Bookshelf," which summarizes several new sources of information in each issue (1992). The editor of this journal, Charles R. Goeldner, also maintains, at the University of Colorado at Boulder, one of the largest collections of travel research and marketing materials available anywhere.

In addition, the U.S. Travel Data Center provides extensive research on the U.S. domestic travel market and also disseminates research on international travel conducted by USTTA and the European Travel Intelligence Center. Further, the Data Center periodically announces the release of new reports in the "Discoveries" column of its monthly newsletter, *Travel Printout* (1992c), and maintains a library of travel research materials for use by its members.

In Canada, a similar organization known as the Canadian Tourism Research Institute, located at The Conference Board of Canada, publishes a number of reports containing analysis of the Canadian tourism industry. Its monthly publication, *Exclusive* (1992a), is designed to provide tourism forecasts and keep tourism executives informed of the prospects for the industry.

For a more detailed review of travel and tourism information sources, see Charles Goeldner's discussion of the topic in Chapter 8.

MAJOR USERS

Knowledge of the most important users of research is also vital in determining research needs and in setting priorities. Users of state or provincial travel research, in addition to the travel office itself, might include other state or provincial agencies, primary tourism-serving businesses (e.g., hotels and attractions), secondary businesses (e.g., those businesses supplying primary tourism-serving businesses), travel industry associations, educational institutions, and citizens' associations. Based on potential users' requirements, the travel office can more effectively establish acceptable definitions, define the types of data to be collected, and design specific research projects to provide the necessary information.

IMPORTANCE OF TRAVEL AND TOURISM TO THE ECONOMY

The importance of the travel industry to the overall economy varies widely among different areas in the United States and Canada. Areas highly dependent on the travel industry as a source of jobs, for example, may consider economic impact studies and market research, designed to provide information useful in maintaining or increasing their market share, to be most important. Areas with less developed travel industries may place a higher priority on research designed to document current levels of investment in the industry, to compile inventories of travel and tourism resources, and to identify geographic areas having potential for growth and new target markets for travel promotion.

Related to this factor is the level of support for the travel industry among the citizens and legislature of the state or province.

LEVEL OF CITIZEN AND LEGISLATIVE SUPPORT

It has been shown that states having active citizen, executive, and legislative support are most likely to succeed in their travel promotion programs. Further, there is evidence that states using economic impact research as justification for larger promotional budgets have been most successful in gaining such support (The Council of State Governments 1979).

The present level of support for tourism in a particular state or province is, therefore, likely to be seriously considered when determining research needs and priorities. Areas suffering from a lack of citizen and legislative support might be wise to direct at least part of their resources to the documentation of travel and tourism's importance through economic impact research.

THE IMPORTANCE OF VARIOUS TYPES OF TRAVEL

The types of travel viewed by officials to be the most important to their state or province will, in large part, determine the content covered by research and the definitions used.

The U.S. Travel Data Center's survey indicates that nonresident motor-vehicle travel is judged to be the most important type of travel by the majority of the state and provincial travel offices responding. Respondents also agree that they have the greatest need for research in this area and tend to limit their definitions of travel and to design their research programs accordingly.

OTHER CONSIDERATIONS

There are a number of other factors that should be considered in determining research needs and priorities. Every state or province has a different product to market, problems to identify and resolve, and opportunities for growth and development.

Travel offices currently share a number of common problems, such as the depressing effects of recession on domestic travel activity. Other problems, however, may be more unique. Smaller or more isolated states and provinces often suffer from inadequate investments in travel-related businesses and underdeveloped infrastructure. A larger, more tourism-dependent state or province, on the other hand, may experience the opposite type of problem, that of overdevelopment, and may need to deal with reconciling continued growth with the needs of its citizens. Research projects should be designed to address those problems of most critical concern.

Finally, to be most effective, a research program should be developed in conjunction with other major programs conducted by the state or provincial travel office. The typical travel office has a variety of responsibilities, the most important of which is the marketing and promotion of the state or province as a travel destination in an effort to maximize the economic and social benefits of tourism for its citizens. Research is not its primary function and should not be considered an end in and of itself. Research is important only to the extent that it provides data that are helpful in achieving the travel office's primary goals. To be most effective, research must be based on a thorough assessment of the needs of the particular state or province. This assessment should consider the types of factors discussed above. Once research needs are determined and available resources are considered, objectives may be determined and specific research projects designed.

TYPES OF RESEARCH CONDUCTED BY STATE AND PROVINCIAL TRAVEL OFFICES

During the spring and early summer of 1992, the U.S. Travel Data Center conducted a survey among all state and provincial travel offices to collect information on their research programs. Thirty-nine states in the United States and ten provinces and territories in Canada responded.

Respondents were asked to indicate the frequency with which they conduct a variety of types of research. The results of this survey, summarized in Tables 1 and 2, supplemented by information from a number of other sources, suggest that the types of research most often conducted by travel offices fall into the following major categories:

1. Impact analysis
2. Market analysis
3. Evaluation research
4. Identification of travel and tourism resources
5. Monitoring travel activity over time

Tables 1 and 2 show that research programs in the United States emphasize somewhat different projects than those conducted by Canadian provinces. State travel offices tend to stress research on the economic benefits of travel and tourism development, as well as studies of current and potential markets and evaluation research.

Among offices in both the United States and Canada, market and evaluation research provides the basis for a system of monitoring travel activity over time. In addition, 29 percent of state travel offices and 44 percent of provincial travel offices responding to the survey indicated having conducted, at one time or another, special studies in response to particular situational and transient difficulties, such as the recession or the Persian Gulf crisis. The least frequently conducted types of research include environmental and societal impact studies.

Market and evaluation research are also popular among Canadian travel offices, but impact studies are conducted less frequently than in the United States. Canadian programs are more likely to include research to identify travel and tourism resources, reflecting the current concern with development in many of the provinces. Forecasting research is also more common in provincial travel offices.

IMPACT ANALYSIS

Impact analysis refers to the broad category of research designed to measure the positive and negative economic, psychological, environmental, and social effects of travel and tourism activity (The Ontario Research Council on Leisure 1977:93-108).

As state and provincial tourism promotional budgets (which are funded predominately from state/provincial and local tax bases) have grown, they have gained increasing exposure and scrutiny among legislators and their constituencies. In order to justify their existing budgets, not to mention any desired increase, tourism officials are being asked with more frequency to document the benefits and costs of their promotional efforts, as well as to show how these benefits and costs accrue to the state/province or local communities.

Economic impact studies have become very popular vehicles for illustrating the benefits of travel and tourism. These studies are used to educate legislators, other economic development officials, and the general public about tourism benefits. Economic impact studies are also important policy and planning tools that aid both public and private travel promoters in setting goals and objectives for their programs and in determining where to focus their promotional efforts.

Such studies are also used to evaluate the effectiveness of promotional programs and, if standardized measures are used, to compare the results of promotional programs to other programs within a state or in other regions. Trends can be tracked, and changes in the industries related to travel and tourism can be monitored. Changes in consumer tastes and preferences can also be identified by monitoring spending and travel patterns over time. Information from such studies can also be used to assist travel and tourism developers in determining the feasibility of and site selection for transportation, accommodation, and amusement and recreation facilities (Fleming and Toepper 1990).

Economic impact studies vary greatly in the methodological approaches utilized, as well as in the level of information yielded. Sources of data most frequently used by U.S. and Canadian travel offices in conducting economic impact research are:

1. State/provincial and national data on travel-related businesses
2. Surveys of travel-related businesses
3. Estimates from expenditure and economic impact models
4. Expenditure surveys with travelers

Travel offices in both the United States and Canada rely heavily on data generated by other state or provincial government agencies, the federal government, and other national organizations. State or provincial revenue departments are a major source of sales, receipts, and tax-revenue data for travel-related industries at the retail level. Employment and wage/salary data for the same industries may be obtained from state and provincial employment security offices. On the federal level, economic censuses conducted in the United States by the Bureau of the Census and in Canada by Statistics Canada provide national data on sales and receipts of individual industries, available on a state/province and county regional basis. Approximately 70 percent of both state and provincial travel offices report using these secondary data sources annually to measure economic impact.

TABLE 1   Types of Research Conducted in the United States

TYPE AND RANK OF IMPORTANCE	UNITED STATES				
	% OF STATES CONDUCTING	CONDUCTING ANNUALLY	CONDUCTING 2–3 YEARS	CONDUCTING PERIODICALLY	DO NOT CONDUCT
1. Impact Analysis:					
1. Economic Impact: Use of Economic Impact Models	97	65	16	16	3
2 Economic Impact: Use of Secondary Data	89	71	9	9	11
3. Economic Impact: Expenditure Surveys with Visitors	84	43	11	30	16
4. Psychological Impact	68	16	22	30	32
5. Social Impact	29	0	5	24	71
6. Environmental Impact	18	0	3	16	82
2. Market Analysis:					
1. Image/Awareness Studies of State	92	23	33	36	8
2. Travel Barometer	87	74	3	10	13
3. Surveys at Information Centers, etc.	84	34	8	42	16
Telephone Surveys with Travelers at Home	84	43	8	32	16
4. Mail Surveys with Travelers at Home	71	34	8	29	29
5. Research on the Motor Coach Tour Market	68	27	8	32	32
Psychological Studies of Traveler Motivation/Behavior	68	16	21	32	32
6. Exit Survey	42	13	11	18	58
7. Special Events Research	39	11	0	29	61
8. Specific Research on International Visitors	33	10	5	18	67
9. Self-Administered Mail-Back Diaries	32	13	0	18	68
Specific Research on Rural Tourism	32	13	0	18	68
3. Evaluation Research:					
1. Inquiry Tracking and Analysis	97	87	0	11	3
2. Pre/Post Advertising Effectiveness Studies	82	32	8	42	18
3. Coupon Conversion Studies by Mail	66	29	16	21	34
4. Pretests of Alternative Advertisements, Media, and Exposure Times	63	24	5	34	37
Coupon Conversion Studies by Telephone	63	26	13	24	37
5. Evaluation of Matching Grants Programs	41	24	6	12	59
4. Identification of Travel and Tourism Resources:					
1. Compile Inventories on Business Establishments	89	63	3	24	11
2. Feasibility Studies of Various Development Programs	49	3	8	38	51
3. Identification of Areas in Need of Investment in Travel Related Infrastructure/Facilities	49	11	11	27	51
4. Identification of Investment Opportunities	32	11	2	19	68
5. Monitoring Travel Activity Over Time:					
1. Research to Support Strategic/Master Plan	80	17	14	49	20
2. Studies of Competitive Destinations	47	14	6	28	53
3. Analysis of Effects of Situational and Transient Factors	29	6	6	18	71
4. Forecasting Research	26	9	0	18	74

n = 35–39 states responded. Source: U.S. Travel Data Center

TABLE 2 Types of Research Conducted in Canada

TYPE AND RANK OF IMPORTANCE	% OF PROVINCES CONDUCTING	CANADA			
		CONDUCTING ANNUALLY	CONDUCTING 2-3 YEARS	CONDUCTING PERIODICALLY	DO NOT CONDUCT
1. Impact Analysis:					
1. Economic Impact: Expenditure					
Surveys with Visitors	90	0	50	40	10
Economic Impact: Use of Secondary Data	90	70	10	10	10
2. Psychological Impact	80	0	20	60	20
3. Economic Impact: Use of Economic Impact Models	70	30	10	30	30
4. Environmental Impact	50	0	0	50	50
5. Social Impact	40	0	0	40	60
2. Market Analysis:					
1. Travel Barometer	90	80	0	10	10
Exit Survey	90	10	10	70	10
Image/Awareness Studies of Province	90	10	20	60	10
2. Surveys at Information Centers, etc.	80	30	10	40	20
Specific Research on International Visitors	80	20	30	30	20
Special Events Research	80	10	10	60	20
Telephone Surveys with Travelers at Home	80	20	10	50	20
3. Research on the Motor Coach Tour Market	70	20	0	50	30
Psychological Studies of Traveler Motivation/Behavior	70	10	30	30	30
4. Mail Surveys with Travelers at Home	60	10	20	30	40
5. Specific Research on Rural Tourism	30	0	0	30	70
6. Self-Administered Mail-Back Diaries	10	0	0	10	90
3. Evaluation Research:					
1. Pre/Post Advertising Effectiveness Studies	90	30	10	50	10
2. Pretests of Alternative Advertisements, Media, and Exposure Times	90	30	10	50	10
Inquiry Tracking and Analysis	90	60	10	20	10
3. Coupon Conversion Studies by Mail	80	10	40	30	20
Coupon Conversion Studies by Telephone	80	30	20	30	20
4. Evaluation of Matching Grants Programs	67	22	0	44	33
4. Identification of Travel and Tourism Resources:					
1. Compile Inventories on Business Establishments	90	70	0	20	10
Identification of Areas in Need of Investment in Travel Related Infrastructure/Facilities	90	30	10	50	10
Feasibility Studies of Various Development Programs	90	0	10	80	10
2. Identification of Investment Opportunities	80	50	0	30	20
5. Monitoring Travel Activity Over Time:					
1. Research to Support Strategic/Master Plan	88	13	13	63	13
2. Studies of Competitive Destinations	63	0	13	50	38
3. Forecasting Research	60	30	0	30	40
4. Analysis of Effects of Situational and Transient Factors	44	11	0	33	56

n = 8–10 provinces responded. Source: U.S. Travel Data Center

In addition to the prevalent use of secondary data, many travel offices also conduct primary research, usually involving surveys. Some travel offices survey travel-related businesses directly to collect the economic data described. This method, however, is generally considered to be quite unreliable because operators of many travel-related businesses cannot accurately estimate the percentage of those purchasing their goods and services who are travelers versus local residents (Fleming and Toepper 1990).

Surveys are also frequently conducted with the traveling consumer, often to collect information on expenditure patterns. Such surveys are conducted annually by 43 percent of all state travel offices. None of the provincial travel offices conduct expenditure surveys annually; however, 50 percent do so every two to three years.

Expenditure surveys may be conducted in a variety of ways. The exit survey, employing personal interviews with travelers as they leave the state or province, is a common method used at least periodically by many state and provincial travel offices. Surveys are also frequently conducted at various locations in the state or province, such as highway welcome/information centers. Travelers are also surveyed by mail or telephone after they have returned home.

The major problem with the types of expenditure surveys just discussed is one of recall. An alternative method involves the use of self-administered, mail-back expenditure diaries distributed to travelers as they enter the area. The most significant problem with this method is the relatively low response rate achieved and the resulting problem of nonresponse bias. For a more detailed review of expenditure surveys, see Douglas Frechtling's discussion of the topic in Chapter 32.

Surveys can provide estimates of travel expenditures within a state or province, but they cannot measure the traveler-generated benefits that accrue to economic areas in the form of payroll, employment, and taxes. Models have been developed to estimate these economic benefits. Nearly all of the travel offices in the United States (97 percent) use modeling procedures to estimate economic impact; 65 percent do so annually. In Canada, while 70 percent of the provincial travel offices report using travel economic impact models, only 30 percent do so annually.

In general, there are two types of modeling approaches that have been developed to estimate economic benefits. One approach estimates impacts of state/provincial subregions (county/city) and aggregates these results upwards to estimate the statewide or provincewide impact. The other approach estimates the statewide/provincewide impacts first and then disaggregates the results down to estimate subregions (Fleming and Toepper 1990).

Probably the best known disaggregated model is the Travel Economic Impact Model (TEIM), developed by the U.S. Travel Data Center in 1975 and revised in 1990. This model uses secondary data to provide annual estimates of travel expenditures and travel-generated employment, payroll, and federal, state, and local tax receipts for each of the 50 states and the District of Columbia, as well as a large number of individual counties. The TEIM also incorporates data from the Regional Input-Output Modeling System (RIMS II) program of the Bureau of Economic Analysis to provide estimates of the secondary economic impacts (i.e., indirect and induced) of travel and tourism spending at the national, state, and local levels (U.S. Travel Data Center 1992d). A similar model has been developed for Canada and is known as the Canadian Tourism Impact Model. For a more detailed review of the measurement of economic benefits of travel and tourism, see Chapter 32.

Most of the economic impact studies that have been conducted at the state or provincial level to date have dealt almost exclusively with economic benefits. But there may also be negative economic impacts associated with travel and tourism, including fiscal costs (e.g., the construction and maintenance costs of providing tourism-related facilities and services, such as parks, visitor information centers, police and fire protection, etc.) and life-quality costs (e.g., crowding, increasing prices). Somewhat less obvious are the opportunity costs of tourism development; that is, the money invested by government in tourism-related activities could have been spent for other purposes (e.g., environmental clean-up programs). Only by estimating both the economic benefits and the costs of tourism development in a state or province can it be determined whether tourism is good for an area and should, therefore, be encouraged. However, most economic impact studies currently being conducted do not attempt to measure the economic and social costs of tourism development because of the inherent difficulties in doing so. See Fleming and Toepper (1990) and Douglas Frechtling's discussion in Chapter 33 for recommended approaches.

Other types of impact analysis are conducted much less frequently. Among these, psychological impact research tends to be the most popular, with 80 percent of provincial travel offices and 68 percent of state travel offices reporting conducting such research at least periodically. Only a minority of travel offices, however, do so annually. Psychological impact research covers a wide variety of phenomena concerning human values. Most often, it addresses the effect of the travel experience on the emotional well-being of individuals and estimates the degree of satisfaction derived by travelers within the state or province. Also included in this type of research are studies of the attitudes of residents toward visitors, as well as evaluation of how the presence of visitors in the community may both positively and negatively affect residents of that community. An excellent example of this type of research is Pizam's (1978) study of the social costs of travel and tourism development in Cape Cod, Massachusetts. Since this seminal study in 1978, a number of other studies dealing with the social and psychological effects of tourism on a local community have been conducted (see, for example, Caneday and Zeiger 1991; Long, Perdue, and Allen 1990; Allen, Long, Perdue, and Kieselbach 1988).

The other two major types of research in this category include environmental and societal impact research. Environmental impact studies assess the effects of travel-industry development on the natural system of the state or province and are useful in selecting appropriate sites for development of particular facilities and in determining which of a number of types of development would be least detrimental to the environment of a particular area. Currently, half of the Canadian travel offices but only 18 percent of state travel offices report ever conducting this kind of research. Given the growing interest in and concern about the environment and the new emphasis on sustainable tourism development, it may be expected that environmental impact research will increase in the future. However, many have noted that the research tools required to define, measure, and evaluate sustainable tourism are currently not available and that their development should be a top priority within the travel industry (Cook, Stewart, and Repass 1992; Taylor and Stanley 1991).

Research on societal impacts assesses the influence of travel and tourism upon the society as a whole. It may include the evaluation of economic, psychological, and environmental impacts, as well as the interrelationship among all three. Forty percent of provincial travel offices and 29 percent of state travel offices indicate that they conduct social impact analysis at least periodically.

MARKET ANALYSIS

The second major objective of state and provincial travel office research is to identify and describe current and potential markets. Such research provides guidance for the development of new facilities and markets, creates a foundation on which to base attractive and effective marketing and promotional programs, guides the selection and application of an appropriate marketing mix (i.e., product, price, place, and promotion), and is necessary for evaluating the success of such programs. Data produced through market analysis are also often used in other research projects, such as economic impact analysis.

Market research studies collect information concerning the number of travelers in the state or province, as well as data on major traveler characteristics, such as origin and socioeconomic characteristics, and trip characteristics, such as mode of transportation, duration of stay, and overnight accommodations used. Such data also allow for market segmentation, the division of the overall market into groups that share common characteristics. Possible segmentation variables includes geographic, trip purpose, individual and/or household demographics, behavioral (e.g., frequency of trip, trip characteristics), and psychographics.

Sources of data most frequently used by travel offices when conducting marketing research are:

1. State/provincial and national data on travel-related activities
2. National/regional travel surveys
3. Counts of visitors at public/private parks, attractions, welcome/information centers, and exit/entry points
4. Surveys conducted with travelers at home
5. State/provincial and national data on demographic and socioeconomic characteristics of current and potential markets

Most travel offices make extensive use of secondary data produced by governmental agencies, associations, and private organizations to measure current levels of travel-related activities within their jurisdiction and describe its characteristics. Information on travel markets is also produced through consumer surveys conducted by agencies of the federal government and other national organizations.

In Canada, for example, a Canadian Travel Survey has been conducted on a quarterly basis every other year since 1979. The survey is conducted by Statistics Canada as a supplement to the Labour Force Survey and is funded by Tourism Canada. Provinces share the cost of increasing the sample size to provide province-level data. The survey provides detailed information on travel by Canadians available at the provincial and, in some cases, subprovincial or "tourist region" level (Statistics Canada 1991).

In the United States, the U.S. Travel and Tourism Administration (USTTA) conducts a basic research program to collect and publish data on international tourism in terms of travel volume, receipts, and expenditures. In 1982, the USTTA implemented a quarterly *In-flight Survey of International Air Travelers* to and from the United States (1992a). Extensive market segmentation analyses include breakdowns by U.S. regions visited. States and cities may contract for profiles of their visitors. Data from this survey has also been used in the U.S. Travel Data Center's Travel Economic Impact Model to estimate foreign-visitor expenditures and the payroll income, employment, and tax revenue generated for each state. Since 1979, the U.S. Travel Data Center has been conducting a monthly National Travel Survey (1992e). Quarterly and annual summaries of the data collected, tabulated on a regional basis, are used by many travel offices to supplement other secondary data and primary research efforts. In addition, some states receive custom tabulations of the data, while others use the survey as a vehicle for collecting additional state-specific information for use in their marketing and promotion programs.

The majority of states and provinces also conduct original research to estimate the size and characteristics of their markets. Most commonly, counting procedures are employed at areas such as highway welcome/information centers, parks, and attractions to obtain estimates of visitor volume. These data are usually compiled in a Travel Barometer, released on a monthly, quarterly, and/or annual basis. In Canada, 80 percent of provincial travel offices compile Travel Barometers at least annually, as do 74 percent of travel offices in the United States.

Most states and provinces also periodically survey visitors on-site to collect information on origins, demographics, trip characteristics, expenditures, and, in some cases, attitudinal data as well. About one-third of travel offices in both the United States and Canada report conducting such surveys on an annual basis. Respondents are also frequently asked for their names and addresses, thus producing a list of actual travelers in the state or province who may then be contacted in follow-up surveys. While such an approach is cost-effective and relatively easy to administer, there is always the concern that visitors to particular areas or facilities may be different in a number of ways from those who do not visit and, thus, may not be representative of the total market. A study by Cadez and Hunt (1978), for example, found significant differences between visitor-center stoppers and non-stoppers, particularly with regard to expenditures, duration, and purpose of trip.

Exit surveys are another popular way to collect market data, especially in Canada. Ninety percent of provincial travel offices and 42 percent of state travel offices periodically conduct exit surveys, usually on main highways or in air, bus, or rail terminals, but very few do so on an annual basis. Personal interviews are generally conducted, although in some cases mail-back questionnaires are distributed to be completed and returned later by respondents. A variation of this approach, the in-flight survey, is used rarely, although it is popular in states like Hawaii that are highly dependent on air arrivals. Major airlines utilize this approach extensively, as does the USTTA.

Most travel offices also conduct telephone or mail surveys with travelers at their places of residence. State travel offices are more likely to do so on an annual basis than travel offices in Canada. Studies of this type usually focus on nonresident travel, although a few of the travel offices have in recent years conducted domestic travel surveys of their residents. An example of this type of study is the *Ontario Travel Monitor* (Ontario Ministry of Tourism 1992). *Guidelines for Tourism Statistics* contains useful guidelines and suggestions for conducting survey research (World Tourism Organization 1988).

The U.S. Travel Data Center survey asked about a number of traveler segments that have attracted greater research attention in recent years. The survey found that approximately 70 percent of both the state and provincial travel offices responding have conducted research on the motor coach tour market, and about 33 percent have done so with regard to rural tourism. Research on international visitors and special events appears to be more common in Canada, with 80 percent of the travel offices reporting at least periodic research on both of these segments. In the United States, only about 33 percent of the travel offices conduct such research.

The research methodologies just described provide the following types of data: counts of travelers that may be used to estimate total demand; descriptive data on trip characteristics, such as duration, mode of transportation, purpose of trip, accommodations used, and expenditures; and information on traveler characteristics, such as origin and socioeconomic characteristics. From these data, traveler profiles are compiled.

Traveler profiles may also include other types of information, such as psychographic data. Psychographic research attempts to identify characteristics of consumers that may affect their response to various products, advertising, and promotional efforts. The variables most frequently investigated include personality characteristics, such as self-concept and values; life-style data, which deal with time and

monetary allocations of individual consumers; measures of attitudes, interests, and opinions (often known as AIOs); and the benefits sought from travel. More than two-thirds of the travel offices in both the United States and Canada report conducting psychological studies of traveler motivation and behavior at least periodically. Rebecca Piirto's recently published book entitled *Beyond Mind Games* (1991) and Stanley Plog's discussion in Chapter 18 provide a number of examples of this type of analysis in marketing research.

Other types of psychologically-oriented market research include investigations of the informational needs of travelers and assessments of the usefulness of informational materials currently produced by the travel office, user evaluations of facilities and services, and studies of how visitors view the state/province as a travel destination. Less frequently conducted are studies designed to study psychological processes such as motivation, how travel decisions are made, and constraints on travel.

Federal offices in the United States and Canada have begun in recent years to cooperate on the conduct of psychologically oriented travel research. USTTA and Tourism Canada, for the last several years, have conducted surveys in a number of countries. Known as the *Pleasure Travel Markets to North America* studies, their research determines the U.S. and Canadian market share of travelers from each of these countries. These surveys are also designed to estimate the size of the potential market for travel to the United States and Canada and to identify sources of information used and levels of awareness of specific U.S. and Canadian destinations among respondents. Further, the relative importance of various touristic attributes and the relative ratings of the United States and Canada against competing destinations for each attribute are measured to gain better insight into long-haul pleasure-travel motivations. The most recent studies completed were for France (1991), Germany (1991), and Canada (1992).

Many travel researchers believe that states and provinces, in their leadership role, should be conducting more basic research, thus helping to advance the state of research technology. It has been argued that if travel research is to advance beyond its present level of development, a shift from research that collects only macrolevel, descriptive data to research in which microlevel and more psychologically oriented data are included as well is essential (Ritchie 1975).

The types of market research discussed are all used to determine primary travel markets for the state or province. Market analysis also involves identification of new markets and estimation of their potential. As in analysis of existing markets, potential markets are frequently segmented by geographic area. Information on residents of those areas is then collected through the use of secondary data, such as that produced by the U.S. Bureau of the Census or Statistics Canada, and special household surveys. The demographic, psychographic, and travel characteristics of present and potential markets may then be compared in an attempt to identify those markets having the most potential for producing travel to the state or province.

PROGRAM EVALUATION

Evaluation research consists of the measurement of the degree to which the stated goals of a specific marketing or other program are being or were achieved. The focus of evaluation research is on change (i.e, the increase in destination awareness, the increase in visitation, and so on) that can be attributed to the promotional campaign being studied. In addition to being a measure of performance, evaluation research is also very useful in reviewing the adequacy of these goals and provides essential guidance for future promotional efforts (Perdue and Pitegoff 1990; Davidson and Wiethaupt 1990).

Evaluation research has assumed a much more prominent position in the tourism industry in the last few years. This reflects the growing pressures on marketing decision makers to justify budget requests and to effectively place available promotional resources. Accountability measures of effectiveness provide a means to communicate the benefits of the program to those who provided the monetary and staff resources to implement the destination marketing efforts. Measuring the performance of a promotional program is also required to make informed decisions about whether the entire program or individual components should be continued, modified, or eliminated (Davidson and Wiethaupt 1990; Burke and Lindblom 1989).

The research projects previously discussed all become part of the travel office's evaluation research program. Continuing data on the volume and characteristics of travelers to the state or province or to particular facilities and areas provide information useful in monitoring the effectiveness of various marketing strategies over time and suggest ways to increase market share. Impact analysis allows travel officials to demonstrate, in meaningful and understandable terms, the importance of their programs and to provide quantitative measures of the success of the various programs. Psychological studies provide information useful in evaluating current information programs, such as distribution of literature to consumers.

A number of other types of research are also routinely conducted as part of a travel office's evaluation research program. A major component of many evaluation research programs is advertising research. Advertising typically represents one of the largest items in the travel office budget. For fiscal year 1991-1992, the average state travel office's domestic advertising budget was nearly $2.4 million out of an average total budget of nearly $6.9 million. In addition, 41 states spent an average of $365,700 per state on foreign promotion and advertising. It is not surprising, therefore, that travel offices place advertising evaluation among their top research priorities (U.S. Travel Data Center 1992a).

Advertising research is conducted for a variety of purposes. These include investigation of the need for advertising, identification of specific ads and media most likely to be successful, and measurement of the effectiveness of advertising campaigns in terms of inquiries generated, changes in consumer awareness, visitor volume, and/or travel-related sales.

The types of advertising evaluation research most frequently conducted by state and provincial travel offices are:

1. Inquiry tracking and analysis
2. Conversion studies
3. Pre- and post-advertising studies to measure impact of advertising on awareness and attitudes
4. Pretests of alternative advertisements, media, and/or exposure time

Among state and provincial travel offices, one of the primary objectives of advertising is to generate requests for information packages that have been prepared by the state or province. These direct response marketing strategies are usually dependent on an inquiry-fulfillment-referral process. The inquiry is often in the form of a coupon or a reader-response card (which involves the respondent indicating which of the advertisers in the publication are of interest) that has been returned, a telephone call, or some combination of these. The fulfillment component involves the internal processing of the inquiries and sending the requested materials to respondents. These materials usually include publications that provide photographs and information designed to influence decision making about travel destinations. The referral component involves providing the list of inquirers to a sales force or to tourism businesses who use the list to follow up with either a sales pitch or additional promotional materials (Burke and Lindblom 1989).

Marketing objectives of a direct-response marketing campaign may include (1) generating inquiries, (2) creating a list of new leads, (3) introducing alternatives to those already planning to visit so that they will extend their length of stay or visit more or different places, (4) renewing interest in those who have visited in the past, and (5) convincing inquirers to visit the destination that is being promoted. These campaigns may also have other more general objectives such as building awareness, creating a positive image, or influencing consumer expectations and perceptions. The objectives of the campaign will influence the type and scope of the evaluation techniques used. These evaluation techniques should be determined and designed while developing the promotional campaign, and not after. A recent article by Burke and Lindblom provides some guidance in doing this (1989).

The majority of travel offices in both the United States and Canada are now involved in inquiry tracking and analysis. In the United States, 87 percent do so annually, while only 60 percent of provincial travel offices report having annual inquiry tracking and analysis programs.

This tracking usually involves the creation of a computerized data base that can include some or all of the following information: the name, address, and telephone number of each inquirer; the media source that influenced the inquirer to respond; the planned date of travel; preferred activities; lodging types; travel party characteristics; and whether the inquirer is a return visitor. This data base can be used to design cost-efficient direct-response campaigns in the future; to identify different target markets and to communicate to them through specially designed promotional materials; and to segment the inquiry list to make it a more effective promotional tool.

An inquiry-tracking data base is also essential in helping to evaluate a particular advertising campaign by monitoring the rate at which various advertising placements are generating inquiries. Regular tracking allows the marketer to make informed decisions as to whether to rerun or cancel an advertisement, extend the time the advertisement is to run, and so on. Analysis of inquiries by source allows for the evaluation of the relative performance of the various components of the program.

Although information about the rate and quality of inquiries is important, marketers are also interested in the proportion of inquirers who actually visit their destination and in which media placements appear to have been most effective in influencing inquirer decisions. Conversion studies are a frequently used method of investigating these questions.

Over the last several years, inquiry-conversion research has become the dominant accountability research tool for evaluating media advertising. It can also be used to determine if the advertising is reaching its target market. Finally, inquiry-conversion research can assess the quality of the travel information packet and its contribution to visitor satisfaction (Perdue and Pitegoff 1990).

Conversion studies usually involve surveys of those requesting information from the state or province to determine their attitudes and behavior since requesting the information. Two-thirds of the travel offices in the United States report conducting conversion studies by mail, with 29 percent doing so annually. A similar percentage (63 percent) say they conduct conversion studies by telephone, with 26 percent conducting these annually. Canadian travel offices appear somewhat more likely to conduct conversion studies, with 80 percent each reporting conducting these by mail and by telephone. Only 30 percent, however, conduct telephone-conversion studies annually, and 10 percent conduct mail-conversion studies at least once a year.

While the actual methodology used to conduct coupon-conversion studies varies widely among travel offices, the primary measure of interest is the *conversion rate*, an estimate of the number of people who saw the ad and converted this perception into an actual visit (Burke and Gitelson 1990; Muha 1976).

Conversion-rate estimates can be used in conjunction with information on the cost of particular advertising campaigns to determine the cost per conversion, a measure useful in comparing the relative effectiveness of different advertisements and use of different media. A number of other ratios are commonly calculated and are discussed by James Burke (1989; 1990).

Additional data usually collected through conversion studies include demographic and trip characteristics, and in some cases expenditure data, useful in comparing the effectiveness of an advertising campaign across various market segments. These data are also frequently used in some general market analysis.

In recent years, several authors have criticized inquiry-conversion assumptions (i.e., that the information provided was directly responsible for converting the inquirer into a visitor), primarily on the basis that most people have already

decided to visit the destination area prior to requesting the information packet, as well as aspects of the research methodologies used. It is well known that conversion studies conducted by mail, for example, may produce biased results. Experience has shown that inquirers who subsequently visited the state or province advertised have a higher propensity to respond to a conversion survey than those who did not visit. This can result in a highly inflated conversion rate. It has been recommended that to minimize this problem, telephone surveys or mail surveys, with several follow-up mailings and increasing incentives, be used whenever possible (Hunt and Dalton 1983; Burke and Lindblom 1989; Burke and Gitelson 1990).

Regardless of the limitations of and potential difficulties with conversion research, if appropriate care is taken with regard to study design, analysis, and interpretation, the conversion study can provide useful diagnostic information to destination marketers and to those approving marketing budgets.

In addition to generating inquiries, media advertising usually has one or more of the following additional goals: (1) increasing the awareness of consumers in the target market of the destination, (2) improving the destination's image, (3) motivating new tourists to visit the destination, (4) reminding previous tourists to return to the destination, and (5) informing consumers about changes in the destination tourism product (Perdue and Pitegoff 1990; Siegel and Ziff-Levine 1990). While conversion studies may be able to measure the effectiveness of an advertising campaign with regard to some of these objectives, an alternative method—that of the advertising tracking study—may be more appropriate.

Advertising tracking studies typically have a preadvertising wave consisting of interview questionnaires conducted with a large, representative sample of respondents within the advertising campaign's intended target market(s), and conducted immediately prior to the launch of the campaign. As well, there is a post-advertising wave consisting of the same interview questionnaire administered to a large, representative sample of respondents drawn from the same target group immediately after the campaign.

Advertising tracking studies are usually conducted by telephone and include a set of core measures covering some or all of the following: advertising awareness (unaided and aided), source of advertising awareness, brand awareness (unaided and aided destinations), message recall, main-point communication recall, campaign diagnostics, destination image, motivation (intentions to visit), behavior (actual visit), and demographics. Comparison of pre/post differences in these measures are used to evaluate the campaign. Great care, however, is needed in interpreting results as any number of other factors, besides the advertising itself, may have caused the differences noted. To help account for such changes in these measures, advertising tracking studies also often include a control group—another market where advertising of the destination is not scheduled—to which pre/post results may be compared (Siegel and Ziff-Levine 1990).

In the United States, 82 percent of the state travel offices report conducting pre/post advertising studies at least periodically, with 32 percent doing so annually. All of the provincial travel offices responding to the survey reported that they conduct this type of research, although only 30 percent do so on an annual basis.

The majority of state and provincial travel offices also at least periodically conduct pretests of alternative advertisements, media schedules, and exposure times prior to launching major advertising campaigns. This allows for the measurement of the relative effectiveness of a number of different ads, different media, and a number of other variables such as exposure times. Travel-related companies with large budgets use this method continuously to design the most effective advertising programs possible. Among Canadian offices, 90 percent report conducting this type of research at least periodically, while 30 percent do so annually. The incidence of this type of research is slightly lower in state travel offices, with 82 percent ever conducting but only 32 percent doing each year.

Next to media advertising, the operation of interstate welcome/information centers is the second highest expense of most state travel offices. These centers distribute information to visitors as they enter the state with the goals of (1) encouraging them to extend their stay in the state, (2) encouraging them to expand their list of tourism products enjoyed at the destination, and (3) enhancing their satisfaction with their visit to the state. Previously, this article has discussed the types of research conducted with visitors to information centers. On-site surveys with visitors to information centers, however, do not provide an adequate evaluative measure of the effectiveness of information centers in achieving many of their goals. One difficulty with such research as a measure of the effectiveness of information centers is, for example, that the measurement occurs usually prior to the visit to the state. Thus, while such surveys provide reliable data on the characteristics of information centers' visitors and their plans, they cannot provide accurate information on the effects of the information center on respondents' visits to the state.

One way to overcome this difficulty is to distribute survey cards at information centers, asking visitors to complete and return them at the end of their stay. Florida has experience with this procedure, offering a state pin in exchange for return of the questionnaire. Nonresponse bias is an obvious difficulty with this approach. An alternative approach to evaluating information centers would be to include questions in the on-site survey regarding planned length of stay and intended activities at the time of the information center visit. A follow-up telephone or mail survey could then be conducted to determine actual length of stay and activities to evaluate the influence of the information-center visit and materials provided at that time (Perdue and Pitegoff 1990).

Evaluation research has increasingly come under attack in recent years. Legislators and corporate leaders are becoming increasingly suspicious of claims of grandiose returns-on-investment accruing from marketing programs. Recognizing the need for industry guidelines and standards to help offset these criticisms, the USTTA convened a U.S. Depart-

ment of Commerce Task Force on Accountability Research. The work of this Task Force appeared in a five-part series of articles in the *Journal of Travel Research* (Wynegar 1989).

IDENTIFICATION OF TRAVEL AND TOURISM RESOURCES

Another major objective of research among state and provincial travel offices is to describe the travel and tourism product by compiling an inventory of travel-related business establishments; natural, scenic, and cultural attractions; and special events within the state or province.

Nearly all states and provinces have compiled, at some point, such inventories and about two-thirds of all offices in both countries do so on an annual basis. An example of an inventory of travel and tourism resources is contained in the *Utah Tourism Study* (U.S. Travel Data Center 1987). Guidelines for preparing such an inventory are provided in Part II of Volume II of the series of publications entitled *Tourism USA* (University of Missouri 1978:31-41).

From a travel and tourism resource inventory, geographic and industry areas suffering from lack of investment may be identified. Areas heavily involved in planning and development, particularly in Canada, are active in this area of research and conduct a number of studies to identify investment opportunities, assess development potential, and examine the feasibility of various development programs.

Research on the travel and tourism plant is crucial to the formulation of comprehensive development plans, to securing further investment and locating geographic and industry areas suffering from lack of investment, and to identifying travel industry sectors that might benefit most from cooperative advertising and promotional efforts.

MONITORING TRAVEL ACTIVITY OVER TIME

A final objective of state and provincial travel research is to continually monitor travel activity in an effort to determine how the travel product and markets, economic and other impacts of travel on the state or province, and effectiveness of travel office programs change over time.

In some respects, the monitoring objective is similar to evaluation research, in both purpose and data requirements. Much of the information collected through a travel office's market and economic research program may be used in conjunction with other readily available information to analyze the effects of a number of situational and transient factors, such as adverse weather conditions or weak economic conditions, on travel demand and impact. In some cases, however, additional research, designed to address previously unresearched areas, may be needed.

Some other types of research most frequently conducted by travel offices include:

1. Research to support strategic/master plans
2. Studies of competitive destinations
3. Studies of effects of external factors, such as recession
4. Forecasting studies

Eighty-eight percent of provincial travel offices and 80 percent of state travel offices report conducting research to support strategic/master plans.

Nearly half of the state travel offices in the United States and two-thirds of those in Canada report at least periodically conducting studies of competitive destinations. While none of the offices in Canada conduct such research annually, 14 percent of the state travel offices report that they do.

Investigations of the effects of situational and transient difficulties, such as the effects of higher prices and recession, are conducted at least periodically by 44 percent of all provincial travel offices but only by 29 percent of state travel offices.

Forecasting studies are another type of research falling most logically within this group. Research of this type attempts to project what the future holds for travel and tourism in the state or province based on a number of different scenarios. While 60 percent of Canadian travel offices have, on occasion, conducted forecasting research, only 26 percent of state travel offices report ever doing so. Many of these, however, rely on the work of other government, industry, and academic groups; for example, the U.S. Travel Data Center annually prepares a *Summer Vacation Travel Forecast* (1992f). Another approach to forecasting future travel activity involves the measurement and analysis of intentions to travel. Currently, the Travel Industry Association of America, through the Data Center, conducts seasonal surveys of travel intentions called the *Travelometer* (1992). Similarly, the Canadian Tourism Research Institute publishes quarterly and biannual forecasts such as *Tourism in Perspective* and *Travel Market Outlook* (1992b).

For the last 17 years, the U.S. Travel Data Center has also conducted an annual Travel Outlook Forum, which is cosponsored by the Travel and Tourism Research Association, during which experts from a variety of travel industry sectors, including regional, state, and local destinations, provide forecasts for the coming year. These forecasts are also published in a full proceedings, which is distributed to and used by many state travel offices in planning their future marketing programs (1992g). Similarly, the Canadian Travel Research Institute also conducts the Tourism Outlook Conference and Tourism Marketing Trends Conference for the Canadian travel industry.

A travel monitoring system should be, therefore, the basic goal of a travel office's research department. Through creative use of data produced through other projects, in addition to studies designed to meet special needs, a travel office can develop such a system, which will help ensure the success of its marketing and promotion programs.

DEVELOPMENT OF A COMPREHENSIVE TRAVEL RESEARCH PROGRAM

This chapter has focused on the research needs and objectives of state and provincial travel offices and on the major

techniques used to conduct research. To summarize the major points, this section reviews major steps to be taken and issues to be considered in establishing a comprehensive travel research program.

ASSESS RESEARCH NEEDS

Before implementing any changes in an existing research program or establishing a new one, the research needs of the particular state or province should be reviewed and discussed with other members of the travel office staff, as well as all potential users of the data to be produced. Two major elements to be considered in such an analysis include the requirements of other data users and the present level and usefulness of research conducted by the travel office. A thorough review of available data sources, many of which are discussed in this chapter, as well as discussions with officials from other travel offices, should also be part of this assessment process. Other factors, such as the current contribution of the travel industry to the state/provincial economy and the level of support given the industry by citizens and legislators, should also be considered.

CONSIDER LIMITATIONS

State and provincial travel offices currently face a number of difficulties in developing a comprehensive travel research program. The U.S. Travel Data Center's recent survey of travel office research activities asked respondents to rate the seriousness of a number of obstacles facing travel officials in developing such a program. The results are shown in Table 3.

Among travel offices in both the United States and in Canada, the most serious problem perceived by officials involves limited resources, both in terms of funding and staff. Approximately 80 percent of both groups responded that budget constraints and limited staff and time resources are very or extremely serious problems.

If money is available to conduct research but staff members are not, the travel office might consider contracting with an outside organization, such as a university, research center, or consulting firm, with known expertise in the field of travel and tourism research.

Nearly half of the travel officials in both Canada and the United States who responded to the survey believe that the complexity of factors affecting the travel industry today is a very/extremely serious difficulty in designing a comprehensive program. Situations such as an economic recession, which may be a major deterrent to travel one year, may be replaced the next year by some other problem requiring specialized research.

Respondents appear to be less concerned with the research methodologies and data sources available today, although most reported minor problems and suggested that there is room for improvement. Most officials, however, indicated that they have the computer technology and facilities needed to conduct research and that they have experienced little problem with lack of cooperation from

TABLE 3 Seriousness of Obstacles Facing Travel Officials

		PERCENTAGE	
		U.S.	CANADA
1.	Budgets constraints	79%	80%
2.	Limited staff/time	78	78
3.	Complexity of factors affecting travel industry	43	44
4.	Lack of workable data collection system	32	33
5.	Lack of cooperation from other segments of travel industry	24	30
6.	Inadequacy of travel data sources	24	0
7.	Lack of research training among staff	21	20
8.	Inadequacy of travel research methods	18	0
9.	Lack of computer technology/facilities	11	10

other segments of the travel industry in their states or provinces.

When designing a research program, such limitations should be seriously considered. The needs analysis will help determine which research projects should be conducted, while a review of available resources for such projects will suggest how much research can realistically be undertaken.

ESTABLISH PRIORITIES

A comprehensive program of continuing travel research is necessarily an ambitious project. The ultimate goal should be the development, over time, of a research program that includes the five types of research discussed in this chapter, conducted on a continuing and consistent basis. Most importantly, the program should be designed to complement and to provide data necessary to the effective implementation of other travel office programs. It is doubtful that any state or provincial travel office can implement all elements of such a program immediately, given current research budgets. By considering available resources in conjunction with a thorough needs assessment, travel officials should be able to determine priorities for the various types of research discussed. Douglas Frechtling's recent paper *Proposed Work Program for Tourism Marketing and Economic Statistics*, while dealing primarily with research at the national and international level, provides some useful guidance on the development of such a "phased" program of research (1991).

Further, as each research project is being designed, those involved should consider methods of collecting data that will be useful to other types of analyses and continue to look for opportunities to expand their research activities.

INVESTIGATE ALTERNATIVES

Cooperation and creative use of research are two important ways that travel offices can expand their research programs substantially without incurring additional expenditures. Many travel offices cooperate with other organizations, such as universities, regional travel councils, tourism associations, and other state/provincial agencies, as well as companies in the private sector, on travel research programs. This is particularly true in the United States, where research budgets

tend to be substantially smaller than among provincial travel offices.

MONITOR RESEARCH PROGRAMS

Finally, if possible, at least one staff member should be assigned to research as a full-time responsibility. This individual would be responsible for monitoring the program, reviewing the quality of the information being produced, and assessing its usefulness to others in both the travel office and travel industry at large in marketing the state or province effectively as a travel destination.

It is also recommended that a research advisory committee, made up of major users of the research conducted by the travel office, be established to meet once a year to set program priorities for the following year. According to the U.S. Travel Data Center survey, today only 17 percent of travel offices in the United States, but 40 percent of travel offices in Canada, have such a research advisory committee. While new projects may be proposed to address newly emerging problems or opportunities, it is important that the basic types of research discussed in this chapter continue to be conducted regularly to provide a data base of market, economic impact, and other types of information necessary to the effective operations of the travel office.

Research in state and provincial travel offices has often been a neglected part of the overall program. This chapter has attempted to provide an overview of the current levels of research at the state and provincial level, to suggest those areas most important for inclusion in a comprehensive travel research program, and to offer some guidelines in the establishment of such a program.

It is hoped that as travel officials learn more about the research activities of other offices and become increasingly aware of the value of a continuing and consistent research program, such programs will grow and increase in sophistication in the future.

REFERENCES

Allen, Lawrence R., Patrick T. Long, Richard R. Perdue, and
Scott Kieselbach (1988), "The Impact of Tourism Devel-

opment on Residents' Perceptions of Community Life," *Journal of Travel Research* 27 (Summer), 16–21.

Burke, James F., and Richard Gitelson (1990), "Conversion Studies: Assumptions, Applications, Accuracy and Abuse," *Journal of Travel Research* 28 (Winter), 46–51.

Burke, James F., and Lisa A. Lindblom (1989), "Strategies for Evaluating Direct Response Tourism Marketing," *Journal of Travel Research* 28 (Fall), 33–37.

Cadez, Gary, and John D. Hunt (1978), *A Comparison between Port-of-Entry Visitor Center Users and Nonusers*, Logan, Utah: Institute for Outdoor Recreation and Tourism, Utah State University.

Canadian Tourism Research Institute (1992a, Monthly), *Exclusive*, Ottawa, Canada: Canadian Tourism Research Institute.

Canadian Tourism Research Institute (1992b, Quarterly), *Tourism in Perspective, and Travel Market Outlook*, Ottawa, Canada: Canadian Tourism Research Institute.

Caneday, Lowell, and Jeffrey Zeiger (1991), "The Social, Economic, and Environmental Costs of Tourism to a Gaming Community as Perceived by its Residents," *Journal of Travel Research* 30 (Fall), 45–48.

Cook, Suzanne D., Elizabeth M. Stewart, and Kelly Repass (1992), *Tourism and the Environment*, commissioned by the Discover America Implementation Task Force, Washington, D.C.: Travel Industry Association of America.

Council of State Governments, The (1979), *Tourism: State Structure, Organization and Support: A Technical Study*, Washington, D.C.: U.S. Government Printing Office.

Davidson, Thomas Lea, and Warren B. Wiethaupt (1989), "Accountability Marketing Research: An Increasingly Vital Tool for Travel Marketers," *Journal of Travel Research* 27 (Spring), 42–45.

Fleming, William R., and Lorin Toepper (1990), "Economic Impact Studies: Relating the Positive and Negative Impacts to Tourism Development," *Journal of Travel Research* 29 (Summer), 35–42.

Frechtling, Douglas C. (1991), *A Proposed Work Program for Tourism Marketing and Economic Statistics*, Presentation to the International Conference on Travel and Tourism Statistics, Ottawa, Canada, June 25–28, 1991.

Hunt, J., and M. Dalton (1983), "Comparing Mail and Telephone for Conducting Coupon Conversion Studies," *Journal of Travel Research* 21 (Winter), 16–18.

Long, Patrick T., Richard Perdue, and Lawrence Allen (1990), "Rural Resident Tourism Perceptions and Attitudes by Community Level of Tourism," *Journal of Travel Research* 28 (Winter), 3–9.

Muha, Steve (1976), *Evaluating Travel Advertising: A Survey of Existing Studies*, Washington, D.C.: U.S. Travel Data Center.

Ontario Ministry of Tourism (1992), *Ontario Travel Monitor*, Toronto: Ontario Ministry of Tourism.

Ontario Research Council on Leisure, The (1977), *Analysis, Methods and Techniques for Recreation and Leisure Studies*, Ottawa: Environment Canada.

Perdue, Richard R., and Barry E. Pitegoff (1990), "Methods of Accountability Research for Destination Marketing," *Journal of Travel Research* 28 (Spring), 45–49.

Piirto, Rebecca (1991). *Beyond Mind Games*, Ithaca, NY: American Demographics Books.

Pizam, Abraham (1978), "Tourism's Impact: The Social Costs to the Destination Community as Perceived by Its Residents," *Journal of Travel Research* 16 (Spring) 8–12.

Ritchie, J.R. Brent (1975), "Some Critical Aspects of Measurement Theory and Practice in Research," *Journal of Travel Research* 14 (Spring), 1–10.

Siegel, William, and William Ziff-Levine (1990), "Evaluating Tourism Advertising Campaigns: Conversion Vs. Advertising Tracking Studies," *Journal of Travel Research* 28 (Winter), 51–55.

Statistics Canada (1992, Quarterly), *Travelog*, Ottawa: Statistics Canada.

Statistics Canada (1991), *Touriscope: Domestic Travel, Canadians Traveling in Canada 1990*, Ottawa: Statistics Canada.

Taylor, Gordon D., and Dick Stanley (1991), *Tourism, Sustainable Development and the Environment: An Agenda and Code of Practice for Research*, Travel and Tourism Research Association, Canadian Chapter.

Travel and Tourism Research Association (1992, quarterly), *Journal of Travel Research*, Boulder, CO: Travel and Tourism Research Association.

Travel Industry Association of America (1992, quarterly), *Travelometer*, Washington, D.C.: Travel Industry Association of America (Conducted by the U.S. Travel Data Center).

Tourism Canada (1992, Monthly), *The Tourism Intelligence Bulletin*, Ottawa: Tourism Canada.

U.S. Travel and Tourism Administration (1992a), *In-flight Survey of International Air Travelers: Overseas Travelers to the United States, January-December 1991*, Washington, D.C.: U.S. Travel and Tourism Administration.

U.S. Travel and Tourism Administration (1992b, Quarterly), *USTTA Updates and Information Alerts*, Washington, D.C.: U.S. Travel and Tourism Administration.

U.S. Travel and Tourism Administration (1991, 1992), *Pleasure Travel Markets to North America for France, Germany, and Canada*, Washington, D.C.: U.S. Travel and Tourism Administration.

U.S. Travel Data Center (1992a), *1991–92 Survey of State Travel Offices*, Washington, D.C.: U.S. Travel Data Center.

U.S. Travel Data Center (1992b), *Survey of State/Provincial Travel Office Research Programs*, unpublished study, Washington, D.C.: U.S. Travel Data Center.

U.S. Travel Data Center (1992c, monthly), *Travel Printout*, Washington, D.C.: U.S. Travel Data Center

U.S. Travel Data Center (1992d), *Impact of Travel on State Economies 1990*, Washington, D.C.: U.S. Travel Data Center.

U.S. Travel Data Center (1992e), *1991 National Travel Survey Full Year Report*, Washington, D.C.: U.S. Travel Data Center.

U.S. Travel Data Center (1992f), *1992 Summer Vacation Travel Forecast*, Washington, D.C.: U.S. Travel Data Center.

U.S. Travel Data Center (1992g), *1992 Outlook for Travel and Tourism*, Washington, D.C.: U.S. Travel Data Center.

U.S. Travel Data Center; Dan Jones & Associates, Inc.; Bureau of Economic and Business Research, University of Utah; RL Associates; Grant & Associates, Inc. (1987), *The Utah Tourism Study*, prepared for the Utah Travel Council and the Salt Lake Convention and Visitors Bureau.

University of Missouri (1978), *Tourism USA*, Washington, D.C.: U.S. Government Tourism Printing Office.

World Tourism Organization (1988), *Guidelines for Tourism Statistics*, Madrid, Spain: World Tourism Organization.

Wynegar, Don (1989), "U.S. Department of Commerce Task Force on Accountability Research," *Journal of Travel Research* 27 (Spring), 41–42.

16

Research on Urban Tourism Destinations

UEL BLANK

Professor Emeritus
University of Minnesota
Minneapolis, Minnesota

*E*very city has tourism, but relatively few cities have definitive information about the nature of their tourism industry. This chapter treats the approaches to and techniques for conducting urban-area tourism research. The several types of applicable research and the objectives that can be achieved with each are discussed. The most detailed treatment is given to overall impact and market studies as a major step toward improved understanding of urban tourism.

The discussion gives attention to the need for teamwork in urban tourism research. A team effort is needed to adequately conduct the research work; of equal importance, teamwork involving governmental and private industry leadership is essential to making full use of research findings for improving the community's tourism industry.

WHY RESEARCH THE URBAN AREA'S TOURISM INDUSTRY?

Most citizens are aware that tourists visit their city. Despite this awareness, when considering procedures for economic development, most city fathers give little more than lip service to tourism as an industry. Instead, other industry types, particularly manufacturing, are typically given the major attention. Urban tourism suffers from long-standing underestimation and misunderstanding. How, in the present day, when economic segments appear to be carefully analyzed, can such oversights occur?

• Restrictive tourism definitions cause much urban tourism to be simply overlooked. Many chambers of commerce, for example, appear only to consider convention travel as tourism. Conventions are highly visible and important; but convention travel often constitutes less than one-tenth of a city's total tourism. Often overlooked are visitors to friends and relatives, nonconvention business travelers, and those traveling on personal business.

• Regularly used economic data series lack a comprehensive tourism component. The Standard Industrial Classifications (SICs) of the U. S. Census of Business show few sectors that can be recognized as tourism. SIC 70, lodging places, is one of the few. Instead, urban tourism is the sum of fractional parts from a large number of different SICs. Nearly every sector offering services or goods at retail contributes to tourism.

• The diverse and heterogeneous nature of urban tourism makes it difficult to measure comprehensively and accurately.

These reasons are in addition, and partly related, to the long-standing problem that service sectors such as tourism have in being recognized as an industry. Services suffer particularly in contrast to manufacturing operations that produce a tangible, physical product. For this reason, it is worth reviewing urban tourism's nature and its outputs to the community.

THE ROLE AND NATURE OF URBAN TOURISM

Every city has a tourism industry; this is the first and most important fact about urban tourism. Tourism is or can be an important generator of profits, employment, rents, and tax return in the same manner as other economic activities. Systematic attention to tourism development can pay off in terms of these economic benefits.

Many states realize a greater return from tourists to urban areas than from all other tourism destinations. In addition, the tourism to many cities continues to grow rapidly; for example, travelers to New Orleans are reported to have increased by almost three times in a recent 20-year period (Brooks 1990).

Laymen commonly equate vacation or pleasure travel with tourism, but urban tourism diverges markedly from this popular concept. Rather than being restricted to recreational travel to the casinos of Las Vegas or fun-in-the-sun in Florida, the tourism of most urban areas is complex and heterogeneous.

Why this complexity? Because cities are concentration points for human interaction, part of which involves tourists. As indicated in Table 1, the pattern of visitor interaction—their purposes for coming—differs greatly from one city to another.

The following factors help explain this complexity:

• Cities are, by definition, areas of high population density. Thus, travel to "visit friends and relatives" constitutes a major tourist sector in many cities.

• Most cities are major travel nodes. Nearly all owe their establishment and growth to an initial access advantage. Because cities are the focal points of highways, railroads, and air and water routes, most who travel any distance must go to a city whether they wish to or not.

• Manufacturing, trade, and finance concentrate in cities. The Seattle Primary Metropolitan Statistical Area (PMSA), for example, has 41 percent of the state of Washington's population, but it accounts for 52 percent of the value added in manufacture, 48 percent of the value of retail trade, and 75 percent of the value of wholesale trade. All of these activities require a flow of travel and people interaction. An adequate set of hospitality businesses is needed to service this travel. Thus, the tourism plant is essential to all components of the PMSA's economy.

• Just as commerce and industry concentrate in cities, so do all types of people services. These include health care, education, government, and headquarters for religious, industry, and other special interest groups and associations. In some cities, such as Rochester, Minnesota, health care is the primary tourist attraction; in many state capitals, government is the primary attractor.

• Cities offer a wide variety of cultural, artistic, and recreational experiences. This offering varies from opera performances to major sports; from art exhibits to nightclubs; and from historical interpretation to zoos. These are available not only to residents but also to the tourists attracted by them (Brown 1990; Kavanaugh 1991). Tourists' purchases of these services often make possible facilities and programs of a quality that the resident population could not otherwise afford.

Because of the rich variety of activities and attractions offered by cities, most travel to cities is multipurpose; that is, most travelers undertake more than one activity while there (Blank and Petkovich 1980). They usually have a major purpose, such as to make sales contacts, but they may also attend a sports event in the evening. The sport's schedule may even influence the timing of the travel. Thirty-three percent of travelers to Washington, D.C., report "work or convention" purposes for travel; but it may be hypothesized that a high proportion of these travelers also went to the theater and/or sightseeing in the nation's capital.

Patterns of overnight lodging vary widely among urban areas. For some purposes, travelers staying in hotels and motels may adequately define the tourist population. Usually, however, the tourist definition must be much wider. Studies in the Minneapolis-St. Paul PMSA have shown that those whose purpose for coming is to "visit friends," and who usually stay overnight with these friends, also generate a large volume of retail purchases in addition to participating in many other activities (Blank and Petkovich 1979). The city wishing to understand its total tourist impact will need to consider travelers staying overnight by all lodging forms. In addition, tourists not staying overnight may represent a component that, in the interests of defining the city's ability to attract travel, cannot be overlooked.

For most cities, travelers may come by a wide variety of travel modes. This is in contrast to some recreational destinations where one mode of travel may predominate. Cities grow because of travel access that usually includes all modes. Island locations such as Honolulu and Singapore are exceptions.

Urban tourism will be seen as complexly varied, with each city having a unique set of amenity attractions, hospi-

TABLE 1 Tourists to Selected SMSAs by Purpose for Travel (Percentage of Person-Trips) 1977

PURPOSE	ORLANDO, FLA.	INDIANAPOLIS, IND.	WILMINGTON, N.C.	PORTLAND, ORE.
Visit friends and relatives	18	38	27	29
Business/convention	12	30	10	30
Outdoor recreation	6	3	47	3
Entertainment/sightsee	53	8	10	13
Personal	5	13	2	17
Shopping	1	0	0	3
Other	5	8	4	5
	100	100	100	100

Source: 1977 U.S. Census of Travel

tality services, geographic market appeals, and travel systems. These factors may add to the difficulty of research in urban tourism, but proper investigation will reveal the rich tapestry of social and economic interaction of which a city's tourism consists.

ORGANIZING TO RESEARCH THE URBAN AREA'S TOURISM

This section reviews briefly some of the essential preliminary steps toward a productive urban-tourism research effort. A key step involves organizing a sponsoring and/or advisory group (Blank 1989). These groups should represent not only those specifically interested in tourism, but also those having a broad interest in the city's welfare. It is the sponsoring group's task to think through the research, provide needed guidelines and resources, and take leadership in putting findings to work.

SPONSORING GROUP RESPONSIBILITIES

The catalyst to a research effort usually starts with a question such as "What does tourism mean to our city?" or "How can our tourism industry be managed to advantage?" The sponsoring group's first and most important responsibility is to refine these questions, giving careful consideration to the general question "What do we want to know about our city's tourism?"

A first response to the last question may be "We need to know everything." Such a response is useless; no research or research series can yield all knowledge. The problem must be sharply defined and priorities established: What is the *most important* information needed *now*?

Closely related to refinement of the research problem or question are the definitions of *tourism* and *tourists*. Only the sponsoring group, or sponsors, can define a tourist because the definition must fit the research purposes. Too narrow a definition can cause problems. To avoid this, they might think, first, of *all nonresidents who enter their city* as tourists and, then, systematically eliminate each class of traveler that is *not* to be included. Commuters are usually excluded. Does this definition also exclude those living within 50 miles? 100 miles? Not staying overnight in commercial lodging? Traveling on business? In every case, the sponsors must think through the ramifications of each group that is not to be counted as a tourist: if those traveling on business are excluded, what about businesspeople who stay an extra day to attend a football game or a tennis match, or who attend a theatrical performance in the evening, or who are accompanied by a spouse? These are a limited sampling of the questions that must be raised in forming the definition of *tourists* to fit the sponsors' research purposes.

The sponsor must determine the scope and scale of the research. These, in turn, will be dictated by resource limitations, time limitations, and research purposes. The sponsor is responsible for securing money that is needed, and the amount of money available may set specific limits upon the research

project. Time limits come into play if data are needed within, for example, 6 months. In this case, it will not be possible to collect data over a 12-month period. It should be clear that the *scope* of the research effort requires equal attention as the *purposes* and *definitions*.

The sponsor is responsible for the accuracy of the research results. This responsibility may come as a surprise—but it is inescapable for the sponsor. This is true even if a professional is hired to conduct the actual research. It underscores the need to be familiar with other sections of this Handbook. The sponsor need not necessarily know a lot about statistical methods and probabilities, but it must be sure that these are known and applied properly by whomever designs and conducts the research. Sponsors must be able to evaluate procedures, oversee them, and be certain that they accomplish established research objectives.

Most importantly, the payoff! The sponsor must put the research findings to work: The findings must be made widely available and used to stimulate and help direct the development of the urban area's tourism industry (Blank 1989). For detailed suggestions, see the section of this chapter "Putting the Results to Work."

KINDS OF DATA: PRIMARY AND SECONDARY

Will the urban research require the gathering of primary data, or can the objectives be achieved by using only secondary data? Secondary data is that which has been gathered by someone else (Woodside, Pearce, and Wallo 1989) and especially that published by governmental agencies, such as the state department of economic development, or the U.S. Bureau of the Census. Secondary data has the advantage of costing much less than primary data, and much of it is readily available. Other sections of this Handbook discuss secondary sources for travel and tourism data.

Primary data is data that is gathered by the researchers themselves, and it can, thus, be tailored to fit specific research purposes. Unfortunately, primary-data collection is expensive and time-consuming, and, without expert direction, it may yield seriously misleading results.

Most urban tourism research projects require the use of both secondary and primary data. Most projects begin with a review of available, relevant secondary data. Information thus obtained is used to guide further research effort, including the collection of primary data. Despite its cost there are compelling reasons for gathering primary data about a city's tourism:

• Every city is unique. To know about a particular city's tourism, that city must be studied specifically. Table 1 illustrates the great variety among cities' tourism patterns.

• Primary data can be gathered to fit a sponsor's specific purposes. Every secondary data set has within it an implicit definition of the industry or population that it describes. Seldom will this definition fit specific purposes exactly.

• Specific information about the visitors to a city and their experiences there can best be gathered while they are on-site, or by focusing directly upon their visit to that city. Few secondary data sources provide this kind of information.

• Data collection provides a means of involving many others in the tourism development project. This participation alerts them to the effort and can assist their understanding, belief in, and active participation in constructive follow-up activities.

These factors can assist sponsors' thinking as they formulate research strategy.

TOURISM RESEARCH TYPES FOR URBAN AREAS

Table 2 summarizes examples of major tourism research types that are applicable to urban areas. The list is not fully inclusive and many variations, additions, and refinements are possible; the type or types of research employed must be adapted to the purposes and nature of the given city. Each type is discussed briefly below.

Urban Tourism Impact Research

Impact research is used to assess the scale, economic returns, overall markets, and economic segments involved in an area's tourism industry. When repeated it may be used to monitor progress. It may be of two kinds: The assessment of a single event or specific tourist type, such as convention-travel studies done by the International Association of Convention and Visitors Bureaus (IACVB); or, it may be an overall measurement of impacts and markets for an entire metropolitan area. Because fully comprehensive studies of urban tourism are relatively rare up until this time, detailed treatment is given to procedures for this research type in the next separate section.

Urban Marketing Research

Specialized market research can be used to estimate market potential for given facilities and services or to serve as a guide to kinds of facilities and services needed (Chon, Weaver, and Kim 1991). It can be used to help answer such questions as: What is the profit potential for added lodging? Can a major sports stadium, recreational park, or art museum attract sufficient paying users?

In another form, marketing research can determine the effectiveness of specific marketing promotional efforts (Laster 1990). Marketing research may also extend to study of other areas and activities to determine the extent and nature of competition or complementarity.

Tourism-Facility Management and Personnel-Training-Needs Research

Many cities are just beginning to become aware of their overall role as hosts to travelers. Research can help determine if tourists felt that they were welcomed and well treated. This information can help guide programs for "hosting train-ing" of the large and varied numbers of business establishments and employees that contact tourists.

Research of the patrons of individual businesses can indicate the extent to which their firms' personnel and services have yielded satisfaction. This, in turn, can guide improvements in management of the facility both for services offered and personnel training.

Researching Residents' Attitudes toward Tourism

Opening parts of this chapter expressed a view of widespread misunderstanding of the tourism industry. How widespread is this misunderstanding within a particular community, and what is its nature? Studies might investigate understandings of the man on the street, business managers, and retail employees. This information may indicate need for programs of educational awareness, and/or hosting training. Such research can closely complement studies of tourists and their satisfactions.

Questions treated may range from residents' knowledge of tourism's economic role in the economy and in their business, personal attitudes toward tourists, and family use of city amenities to the role of residents in hosting visitors, and their patterns of hosting treatment.

The City's Tourism Plant

Assessing the nature of a city's tourism facilities, services, and attractions could be viewed more as simple inventorying than as research. But in another view, this operation is the complement of visitor attitude and market research: What is there to attract and serve the visitor (National Technical Information Service 1990; Statistics Canada 1991)? The variety and volume of the urban tourism plant are astonishing. A Minneapolis-St. Paul investigation found over 8,000 different operations, sites, and organizations. These were distributed among 270 categories (Blank and Numerich 1969). The definitions, classifications, and search procedures required for this effort demand systematic knowledge of tourism as well as considerable ingenuity. Systematic knowledge about the urban tourism plant serves as one measure of impact, provides a basis for contact with managers having direct interest in tourism, is a necessary input into judgments about tourism service development, and is needed by information systems that answer travelers' questions.

RESEARCHING OVERALL IMPACT AND MARKETS

Research of overall tourism impact on urban areas is treated here in detail as a sequel to the opening thesis of this chapter: most urban tourism studies investigate only parts of the traveler pattern. Partial studies lead to widespread underestimation and misunderstanding of urban tourism. As a serious consequence, many urban leaders give the tourism industry less support than if its full role and scope were more clearly defined. Further, market studies, which must often be

TABLE 2 Types of Urban Tourism Research

Type		Objectives To:	Procedural Examples and Suggestions
I	*Impact* Overall Impact and Markets Dollars; Visitors	—Assess scale and value of city's tourism —Measure market types and/or industry segment —Monitor progress	—Include all tourism segments and all relevant industries —Cover a 12-month period —Multiple procedures required
	Single Event or Traveler Segment	—Assess scale or value of event or segment —Measure market types —Monitor progress	—Tally "registrations" where applicable —Contact a random sample of travelers during the event
II	*Marketing* Advertising Effectiveness	—Determine results from a specific marketing/promotional effort	—Track responses to ad —Household surveys of target areas (mail, telephone)
	Market Potential	—Determine target audience for marketing efforts —Provide guide to scale of market	—Use focus groups to guide —Household surveys of target areas (mail, telephone) —Survey predetermined travel types while in city, at home, or at business
III	*Development/Training Needs* Visitor Satisfaction and Image	—Guide development of facilities and services —Guide training programs for personnel	—Question, in person, a random sample of visitors using target services —Survey a sample who register at a given service (mail, telephone) —Marketing procedure may be adapted to this use, including focus groups
IV	*Resident* Citizens	—Determine citizen attitudes toward the tourism industry —Determine activities of residents in support of tourism	—Survey resident households (in person, mail, telephone) —Citizen focus groups
	Business Managers/Employees	—Determine understanding and attitude toward tourism —Determine positive attitudes toward tourism —Determine positive actions in support of tourism	—Survey business managers —Survey employees in selected business types
V	*Tourism Plant* Facilities/Services	—Prepare a definitive list of services available to tourists —Determine the physical scale and geographical distribution of tourism services —Determine the qualitative range of the tourism plant	—Gather by geographic jurisdiction; use telephone directories, association lists, brainstorming by knowledgeable people —Gather by industry and facility classes

limited in scope, are best undertaken in full knowledge of the total market. This knowledge can only be obtained by means of an overall study.

Researching the full scope of a city's tourism impact usually means conducting a coordinated set of research investigations. This procedure is dictated by the complex nature of urban tourism. There are a multiplicity of tourism segments that vary widely. Definitive information about many of these segments requires the complementary use of both secondary and primary data.

Usually a number of different procedures and questionnaires must be developed. Air travelers may require a different approach than automobile travelers. Often, more than one approach to a tourism segment is required in order to achieve adequate insights.

Wherever possible, a city should consider "boxing in" its estimate of tourism segments using all data sources that are available. Suppose, for example, that you are estimating total expenditures for lodging using data from a sample of travelers. Are there also estimates of city lodging revenues generated by sales tax collections and/or the Census of Business? These should be investigated and compared. Estimates from your research may be different. But, if this is the case, you must be able to explain *why* your estimate differs.

Even for those items of tourist expenditure that represent only a fraction of total sales, a test of reasonableness may be possible. Gasoline sales to tourists at filling stations, for example, may amount to only 10 to 15 percent of total gasoline sales. In this case, interviews with knowledgeable petroleum dealers may be helpful. Total gallons of gasoline sold in the area may be available from an agency licensing such sales. Restaurant and theater sales to tourists may be similarly checked. This procedure can sometimes help avoid major errors. One added caveat is in order: secondary sources of data may also be subject to error—sometimes large error. Again, data of a given activity from two different sources may not agree but there should be an explanation for the disagreement.

AN INDUSTRY SEGMENT APPROACH TO OVERALL IMPACT

A commonly used approach to overall impact measurement of urban area tourism is by industry segments. The procedure makes use of data of the Standard Industrial Classifications (SIC) of businesses that can be identified as making sales to tourists. The percentage of sales to tourists in each SIC group is multiplied by total sales, and the results from all of the groups summed to determine total dollar impact.

The SICs commonly used for this purpose are:

SIC 70	—Lodging
SIC 58	—Food and Beverage
SIC 55 and 75	—Automobile Transportation
SIC 78 and 79	—Entertainment
SIC 53, 54, and 56 to 59	—Retail Purchases

This method has the advantage of yielding a total impact estimate quickly and inexpensively. Usually the percentage of tourist sales in each class is obtained from studies in other cities or from general studies. This procedure poses a serious threat of inaccuracy, since the tourism pattern in each city is unique. The disadvantage can be overcome by conducting surveys in representative businesses in each classification to determine the actual percentage of sales made to tourists. To be fully accurate, the firms where tourists are surveyed need to be systematically selected, and the study must be conducted throughout a 12-month period.

While the previously listed SICs are usually the classes making most sales to tourists, actually every business selling goods or services at retail makes some tourist sales. These include health services, legal services, museums, and so on. In given situations, sales to tourists by classes such as those just mentioned may constitute a large proportion of total tourists' expenditures—the special case of Rochester, Minnesota, was previously noted.

Another limitation of the industry-segment approach is the lack of information about the market: Who are the tourists? Sometimes other secondary data are available to provide this information. Where tourists are interviewed directly to determine their proportion of purchases by industry classes, data about their characteristics can also be gathered.

HOUSEHOLD APPROACH TO OVERALL IMPACT

Household surveys made in a city's market area can yield some types of overall information about the city's tourism. It is exemplified by the data in Table 1, which was obtained from a national survey of households. Unfortunately, the U. S. Census of Travel has not been recently conducted, 1977 being the most recent. Thus, up-to-date information from this secondary source is not currently available.

Currently, proprietary research groups employ this method. It appears more useful for obtaining market information than for generating quantifiable impact data. Thus far, fully comprehensive impact studies have not used household surveys as the primary procedure; however, wherever available, information from this source can provide useful insights as a part of the total information input.

A TRAVELER APPROACH TO OVERALL IMPACT

This approach, in its most comprehensive form, consists of interviewing a sample of travelers while they are physically present in the study area. It offers potential for yielding the most complete data obtainable from one study about tourism dollars, activities, and market characteristics. But the method is difficult and expensive to use, and, because of its complexities, easily subject to errors.

This section treats the gathering of primary and secondary data about urban tourists by specific travel modes. These include air, bus, train, water, and auto/truck. In some cities with controlled means of access, this procedure may be used relatively easily. Heartland cities, which are freely accessible by automobile, will find its application more difficult. But, because of the comprehensive understanding of tourism thus obtainable, the approach merits serious attention by any urban area wishing to emphasize development of its tourism industry.

Table 3 lists the several travel modes. It gives suggestions for secondary-data sources and primary-data gathering procedures. The accompanying discussion expands on the outline in Table 3. Since most cities operate as year-round tourist attractors, data covering a 12-month period will be most accurate and will yield the most useful information.

Scheduled Air Flights

Scheduled air flights are perhaps the easiest type of transportation mode about which to collect usable primary and secondary data. The Federal Aviation Administration (FAA) requires airports to keep records on the number of passengers arriving and departing each day, and this information forms the basis for estimates of tourists. Unfortunately, this data does not include information about passenger origin or destination or whether the passenger is in the airport only to change planes. Sometimes surveys done by the local airport commission or by airlines provide information that can supplement the required data.

Primary data are easy to collect from passengers because departing passengers must pass through the boarding gate and most have free time before boarding to complete questionnaires. This procedure requires involving the local airport commission at the beginning of the study; they can contact all of the airlines to get permission to interview passengers. Interviewers can easily survey three or four flights in 2 to 3 ½ hours in a preselected random pattern. Experience suggests avoidance of three procedures: (1) do not put interviewers on the airplanes; (2) do not ask cabin attendants to distribute or collect questionnaires; and (3) avoid mail-back problems by having interviewers complete the questionnaire on the spot. Some airlines do collect in-flight infor-

TABLE 3   Researching Urban Travel Modes

Travel Mode	Examples of Secondary Data	Examples of Primary Data Methods
Scheduled Air	—Data of passenger arrivals and departures from airport management	—Interview passengers in boarding areas —Give mail-back diary on arrival while in baggage area
Charter Air	—Data of passenger arrivals and departures from airport management	—Interview passengers in boarding area (note: permission may be difficult to obtain)
Private Air (General Aviation)	—Takeoffs and landings from airport management	—Interview pilots (note: lack of schedule makes this difficult)
Scheduled Bus	—Bus arrivals and departures from bus company	—Interview passengers in boarding area
Charter Bus	—Data from U.S. Tour Operators Association and related groups	—Questionnaire to hotel sales manager —Questionnaire to tour operators
School Bus	—Limited useful data available	—Mail questionnaire to schools in travel range
Train	—Data of passenger arrivals and departures from Amtrak	—Interview passengers in boarding area —Give mail-back diary on arrival
Water	—Data from port authority Operational data from docks	—Questionnaire to commercial operations —Interview sample of water travelers at exit points
Auto	—Traffic origin-destination studies of Dept. of Transportation —Traffic-counter data and route volume estimates —Data of check-in points, customs, toll systems, and agricultural checks	—Stop random sample of in-bound travelers and give mail-back diary —Exit interviews of random sample of travelers —Interviews of auto travelers at gasoline stations
Truck	—Same as auto —Licenses, trucking operations data, Dept. of Transportation	—Same as auto —Mail questionnaire to trucking firms
Commercial Transportation Crews		—Questionnaire to sample of crew members —Questionnaire to transportation firms

mation on their own initiative. If available, this information can be helpful.

Charter Air Flights

Charter-air secondary data are similar to scheduled-air data and have similar shortcomings. Primary data collection, while also similar to scheduled air, is more difficult because corporations and institutions charter aircraft. Airlines are reluctant to give permission for interviewing unless the group renting the aircraft has also given permission.

Private Air Flights

Of all the transportation modes, private air (general aviation) may present the most difficulty in collection of dependable primary and secondary data. Information collected by the Federal Aviation Administration is limited to total takeoffs and landings, with no data on passengers. Occasionally, nationwide private air surveys are done by the federal government that can give useful estimates of local traffic. When no control tower is present at an airport, the total takeoffs and landings may be estimated by traffic counts from other comparable airports.

Primary data collection is expensive per questionnaire because of the nature of private air travel. Unscheduled flying times and small numbers per flight make the use of paid interviewing personnel questionable. A box of self-administered questionnaires for pilots has been found to work, in part. A possible, but not fully satisfactory, alternative is to use surveys from other locations, such as those done by the FAA, and extrapolate the findings to the local airport.

Scheduled Buses

Primary and secondary scheduled bus data is similar to scheduled air. Data on the number of bus arrivals and departures is available from the bus companies, and the interviewing of passengers is facilitated because of a common boarding area. One major problem is that there may be remote passenger pickups located in suburbs, and these passengers should be included in the data. A numbers adjustment can be made for this factor by noting the number of such remote stops and the percentage of tickets taken there.

Charter Buses

Charter buses present difficulties. Data are kept on the number of charter buses stopping at central terminals, but there is usually no prior notice of the stop. More serious, some buses do not stop at terminals, and there is no central record of their visit to the city. Two alternatives are suggested: (1) a survey of local hotel sales managers asking data of patrons arriving by tour bus and (2) surveys of firms chartering buses into the city.

School Buses

Many cities serving as the trading, cultural, and/or governmental center for a large hinterland will have a large number of visits by young people transported in school buses. Excellent response has been received to a one-page mail questionnaire to superintendents of school districts asking for this information.

Trains

Passenger trains are much like scheduled air flights and buses. Records of total passenger arrivals and departures are kept. All passengers must go through a boarding gate, and departure times are fixed. In areas where there is substantial commuting by train, the press of large numbers of passengers and dilution of tourist numbers by commuters may present special problems in data collection.

Autos

In most cities, auto travelers do not "check in" at any one point. This characteristic makes auto travelers difficult to interview. For this reason, considerably more attention is given here to gathering data about auto tourists than to other travel modes. Furthermore, auto tourists are the most important type by mode of travel for most cities; they commonly make up 70 to 95 percent of all tourist person-days. Auto travel is complex, and there is limited experience in comprehensive measurement of city auto visitors. But it is possible to design a procedure for a particular city, and the wealth of information obtained about auto tourists will make the effort worthwhile.

Estimates of total traffic flow on all highways into and out of the city are usually available from transportation authorities. The problem is to classify this traffic flow and obtain information from a representative sample of those who are classed as tourists.

The theoretically most accurate means of researching auto travelers is to interview a randomly selected sample of them just as they leave the border of the metropolitan area. The procedure is similar to that of highway department origin-destination (O-D) studies that are conducted at various points each year in most states and provinces. There are differences: surveys should be repeated on selected routes throughout the year—many O-D surveys are operated for only one day; only departing travelers need be interviewed; and the questionnaire is changed to gather information about the traveler's stops in the destination area. The questionnaire must be short. Many O-D surveys have a goal of holding motorists only three minutes. Any city contemplating a tourism study should discuss with the highway agency the existing highway travel data and the feasibility of gathering new data by O-D survey means (Blank 1982b).

Origin-destination type surveys have serious drawbacks that may prevent complete reliance upon them for auto/truck data. Among the difficulties are:

- O-D surveys are relatively expensive and require a substantial crew to operate.
- Weather causes problems: cold and snow in some cases, rain and heat in others.

- Highway safety may be one of the most serious difficulties with O-D sampling. Most traffic departs cities on high-speed freeways. In times of high-traffic flow, stopping a sample may be imprudent, and this could lead to serious gaps in the data.
- Limitations on the length of time that motorists can be held pose a problem in gathering detailed information. Only minimal, basic questions can be asked.
- Exit interviews have memory-bias problems with activity and expenditure reporting. Careful questionnaire construction and interviewer training can reduce this limitation.

Are there alternatives?—Yes, partially; but some O-D surveys at the area's border are highly desirable. Even a limited number of O-D surveys can serve as guides for adjusting other data. Further, there is no other way to get information about vehicular traffic that enters the area, passes through, and leaves without stopping at all. Precise data about the "pass-throughs" are of lesser importance than that of other traveler types. But a comprehensive understanding of an area's tourist appeal should include an estimate of those who are physically present but who do not feel that there is a sufficient attraction to make any kind of stop!

Other factors can provide surveying opportunities that can supplement and/or complement complete reliance upon O-D surveys include:

- Traffic departing some cities is regularly stopped: at toll bridges, toll tunnels, highway toll gates, and customs and quarantine stations. These locations may serve as well or even better than an O-D traffic station.

- Moving traffic surveys can fill in some of the information needed. In this procedure, traffic is classified from a visual vantage point without stopping it or making oral contact. Data thus obtained can sometimes be refined by operating an O-D station part of the time to learn the relationship between classifications made by eyeballing traffic and those made by actual measurements. Data recorded can include license plate origin, number of people in the vehicle, and apparent travel purpose.

- Highway vehicles do "check in" at one place—the gasoline stations. If the study area is sufficiently large so that motorists are likely to need to refuel within its boundary, questionnaires can be administered there in a manner similar to an O-D station. This procedure has been successfully used in a large MSA (Blank and Petkovich 1979). But there is one major problem: the resulting sample is a sample of vehicles that *stopped for gasoline*. It is not a sample of *all* vehicles. Adjustment must be made for this fact.

- Time limitations in holding traffic at O-D Stations have been partly solved by giving the motorist an additional longer questionnaire to be completed and mailed back. Mail-back questionnaires typically have low rates of return. Return rates can be greatly improved by incentive gifts. The gift can be given at the time the questionnaire is distributed, or, perhaps better, promised upon receipt of the completed questionnaire.

- Diaries are sometimes useful for getting further activity detail and for reducing memory problems of exit interviews. In this procedure, a sample of *incoming* traffic is stopped and given a diary to record activities and expenditures while in the destination area and then to mail back. Incentive gifts, as suggested in the previous item, can be used to improve completion rates. In addition, data from mail-back questionnaires and diaries can be partly adjusted with the use of data gathered when the respondent was contacted in person.

- Data from individuals who stop at information stations is often used in tourism analysis. It has the advantage of being easy to obtain. But information-station data about travelers can be seriously misleading since only certain kinds of travelers use these facilities. The most useful data thus generated is that of a numbers count—amounting to one kind of tourist index. Any other information station traveler data should be subjected to sophisticated adjustment, if it is used at all.

Trucks

Truckers are also tourists. They use hospitality services and participate in many recreational activities. Data can be gathered from them in the same manner as for other motorists when using O-D type procedures. Fuel-station data of heavy trucks may be unreliable because many trucks fill at base terminals. Mailing addresses of companies licensed to ship into an area can often be obtained from the Department of Transportation. Good response has been obtained with a short questionnaire mailed to a sample of these trucking firms.

Transportation Crews

By some definitions, transportation crews are not included as tourists. Each community must make that definitional decision, depending upon its own circumstances. Data about transportation crews can be obtained from the carrier firms. Individual crew members can usually be interviewed in the process of contacting passengers in the transportation terminals.

Water

Most cities in the world owe their initial locational advantage to access by water. Technological development in travel has reduced water travel to a minor factor for most cities. In cities served by commercial water travel, tourists using this travel mode may be measured in a manner similar to that used for air, bus, and train, working in cooperation with the port director and the travel company. Cities located on rivers having locks can often obtain useful information from the Army Corps of Engineers. A survey of public and private docking facilities may be needed to complement data from the suggested sources.

PUTTING THE RESULTS TO WORK

Possible uses of urban tourism data have been indicated in the foregoing. By way of summary they are:

• To *sell* the value of the community's tourism industry—so there is a wider base of ongoing support for tourism programs.

• To manage the marketing of tourism: gain insights into the range of the city's market segments and their relative importance; provide guidelines for marketing of specific governmental and private tourism facilities and/or experiences; evaluate the effectiveness of promotional programs; and guide the provision of information services to travelers.

• To manage the development of tourism services and facilities: develop needed private and governmental tourist-serving facilities; indicate training needs for service personnel who contact travelers; and upgrade the hosting of guests by all city residents.

At least two things must take place in order that the product of tourism research may be put to its best use:

• The information gathered must be accurate and relevant to intended purposes, and data treatment and display must be appropriate.

• Research findings must be disseminated to those who need it and can make use of it.

USE OF THE DATA DEPENDS UPON ITS USEFULNESS

Reliability and accuracy lead all other characteristics in rendering data useful. The more specifically that research findings fit the needs of potential users, the more likely they are to be used. Data concerning retail purchases by tourists, for example, will have specific value to retail merchants; characteristics of tourists who travel by bus will be more useful to bus firms than overall traveler characteristics; and theaters want to know which tourists attend cultural offerings.

The previous paragraph places responsibility upon research design for relevance. The tourists interviewed and the questions asked must effectively gather the needed information. Analysis of this data and the way that it is displayed must follow through so that relevant questions are answered:

• What is the overall impact upon the city's economy?
• How are the different business sectors impacted by tourists?
• How do seasonal patterns vary?
• What are the tourist segments according to behavior while in the city: activity patterns, lodging, length of stay, and expenditures?
• What are market segments according to tourists' characteristics: socioeconomic, demographic, travel patterns, and so on?

Providing answers to these and many other questions makes research findings useful.

SPREADING THE WORD BEGINS AT THE BEGINNING

The first step toward disseminating tourism research findings begins at the start of the project. Those who should

make use of the potential findings should be involved: as part of the sponsoring group; in an advisory capacity; to help generate funding; to cooperate in data gathering; and so on (Blank 1989).

Why this effort to achieve a wide involvement of the private and governmental leadership? First of all, because their advice and support are needed and a better research effort will result. Second, people tend to believe those things in which they have had an active part, and they are much more likely to make effective use of the research findings.

A SPECIFIC PROGRAM IS NEEDED FOR SPREADING THE WORD

Research findings that gather dust on the shelf do no good; nor can these findings be used by any agency or firm that does not know about them. The following paragraphs outline some methods of spreading the word:

• If the research effort extends over a period of time—for example, data is being collected for an entire 12-month period—interim reporting should be considered. Occasional news releases and a short, periodically issued newsletter reporting progress will help to sustain interest and help prospective users prepare to utilize the new information.

• Early in the analysis process, a workshop can be held with the steering committee or advisory group. This can include a review of findings to date and a probe of the meanings and implications for action. This procedure can not only inform the group but can take advantage of their insights and experience to guide the final analysis. If done with the latter objective clearly stated, such preliminary reporting will in no way compromise final conclusions that may vary from preliminary observations.

• There can be separate workshops with each of the agencies or kinds of firms that have representation in the advisory group. This makes possible a more focused discussion.

• Findings can be published in a report or in a series of reports. One may be a summary report. A longer report may provide more detailed information. Other reports may be written for special interest groups such as commercial lodging, food services, and retail stores. These printed reports provide ready reference for ongoing use.

• A media event can be held or a press release issued at the time when the findings are first available; this should attract community-wide attention to tourism's impact.

• The major media event should be followed up with news stories drawn from the research findings that are regularly released. These may not only be used by the media, but also in Chamber of Commerce, and similar, publications.

• A series of media shorts can be developed, each highlighting specific findings, and offered to radio and/or television as public service announcements (PSAs).

• A speakers bureau can be made available to clubs,

council groups, and so on, on the subject of tourism for the city.

• A videotape, slide show, or automated slide-tape that highlights research findings and tourism in the city can be made available to clubs and other groups seeking program materials.

The net result sought is to put information gained to work in the management of the city's tourism industry. The goal is to realize payoffs in terms of profits, employment, rents, and tax returns, and/or in terms of living amenities for residents of the city and the region.

FOLLOW-UP AND UPDATING

Research should be considered as an ongoing part of any city's tourism program. A single project is only the beginning. The better the tourism research project and the more it is discussed, more questions will be raised. What else needs to be known about marketing to specific tourist segments? What are the results from a given advertising effort? Has the employee training program improved the city's hosting abilities? What is the visitor's image of the new downtown mall? Or waterfront? Or airport?

Yesterday's research findings quickly become outdated due to the dynamic nature of most cities' tourism. How will these findings be updated? Often, annual updating can be done using secondary data series. Ongoing data series, such as air- and auto-traffic figures and retail sales, can be used to index year-to-year growth. But, over time, structural changes occur: in the ratio of auto to air travelers, the distribution of dollars spent, the patterns of overnight lodging, and other variables. These changes require repeating all or parts of the impact study every 5 to 10 years.

EXAMPLES OF URBAN TOURISM RESEARCH

Described briefly in the following paragraphs are examples of urban tourism research. These provide readers with suggestions about the range in research approaches and objectives.

All examples given here use basically valid procedures, but it should be noted that the part of the tourism spectrum defined and treated by these reports varies greatly. The range is from the IACVB studies, which include only tourists attending major conventions, to studies that attempt a fully comprehensive measurement. Treatment varies from straightforward reporting of findings to a full-fledged set of management recommendations.

1988 CONVENTION INCOME SURVEY

This is the most recent of the periodically conducted studies of guests at major conventions. Its focus is upon the United States, but it also has international dimensions. The primary purpose is to determine the dollar impact of these convention visitors. The studies are sponsored by the International Association of Convention and Visitors Bureaus (IACVB).

THE MAYOR'S TASK FORCE ON PUBLIC SUPPORT FOR CULTURAL ORGANIZATIONS IN METROPOLITAN MILWAUKEE (1990)

This report is based upon a 1988 survey of the impact of those attending cultural events upon the five-county area. The research also sought information about the extent of support for cultural activities. The project had a well-organized support group. Included is a set of eight goals for support and development of cultural activities.

1991 LAS VEGAS VISITOR PROFILE STUDY

These studies are ongoing and annually sponsored by the Las Vegas Convention and Visitors Authority. The procedure employed was to interview about 150 visitors per month. Interviews determine reasons for visiting, travel planning, trip characteristics and expenditures, gaming behavior, entertainment, and attitudinal and demographic information. Visitors are interviewed in or near casinos and hotels.

ASSESSMENT OF THE SOCIAL IMPACTS OF TOURISM ON FLAGSTAFF, ARIZONA (1990)

This study interviewed residents of Flagstaff, Arizona, to determine their image of the impacts of tourism upon their community. Differences in perceptions by socioeconomic characteristics of residents were noted, as well as between those employed in the hospitality industry and others. Impacts of tourism upon living quality were also determined.

1989 U.S. PLEASURE TRAVEL MARKET, CANADA'S PROGRESS AND CHALLENGES

This is a study of the U.S. traveler in Canada, sponsored by Tourism Canada. The U.S. vacation travelers in Canada are classified into four vacationing pattern types: touring, city, outdoors, and business/pleasure. The urban vacationers are described by personal characteristics, trip planning, traveling and lodging patterns, and activities and experiences while on vacation in Canada. The information was gathered by a mail questionnaire to households.

INVENTORY OF STUDIES CONDUCTED ON CANADIAN CITIES: VANCOUVER'S TOURISM PRODUCT (ALSO TORONTO AND MONTREAL) (1991)

These summaries of the three Canadian cities' tourism is presented in five categories: tourism context, tourism infrastructure and support services, cultural attractions, natural attractions, and events. Each study presents conclusions and recommendations.

TOURISM COMMUNITY DEVELOPMENT INITIATIVE: ECONOMIC IMPACT STUDY, NIAGARA FALLS (1988)

This study, commissioned by Tourism Canada, investigates the characteristics and economic impacts of the tourism industry upon Niagara Falls. Methods for gathering data include visitor exit interviews and a survey of the tourism industry. Included in the report are implications for tourism marketing and development.

DULUTH (MINNESOTA) TRAVEL INDUSTRY (1982)

This study is an example of primary reliance upon highway origin-destination procedures. A highway cordon line was maintained for two summer weeks. The relatively small size of the community (about 130,000) made this possible.

MINNEAPOLIS-ST. PAUL'S TRAVEL TOURISM (1979)

This study continues as one of the few examples of a fully comprehensive measurement of the tourism of a large metropolitan area (about 2 million). Its primary procedure was personal interview of travelers by all travel modes, while they were in the MSA. A number of special studies were used to supplement the primary-data-gathering procedure.

SPOKANE: 1979 VISITOR AND CONVENTION STUDY

This study provides an example of reliance upon secondary data to estimate visitor numbers and dollar impact. The principal data sources are Census of Travel Data and expenditure estimates of the U. S. Travel Data Center. Local tax data and hotel guest data are also used.

REFERENCES

Ballman, Gary, and Uel Blank (1982), *What Does Tourism Mean To Ely?*, Minneapolis: University of Minnesota.

Blank, Uel (1982a), *Life Style-Tourism Interrelationships of Minneapolis-St. Paul Residents*, Staff Paper P82–9, Minneapolis: Department of Agricultural and Applied Economics, University of Minnesota.

Blank, Uel (1982b), *Duluth-Superior's Travel Tourism Economy*, Staff Paper P82–14, Minneapolis: Department of Agricultural and Applied Economics, University of Minnesota.

Blank, Uel (1989), *The Community Tourism Industry Imperative*, State College, Pennsylvania: Venture Publishing, Inc.

Blank, Uel, and Elizabeth Numerich (1969), "Recreational Services and Facilities of the Twin Cities Metropolitan Area," Unpublished paper prepared for the Minneapolis-St. Paul Metropolitan Tourist Council.

Blank, Uel, and Michael Petkovich (1979), "The Metropolitan Area Tourist: A Comprehensive Analysis," *A Decade of Achievement, Proceedings TTRA*, 227–236.

Blank, Uel, and Michael Petkovich (1980), "The Metropolitan Area: A Multifaceted Travel Destination Complex," in *Tourism Planning and Development Issues*, D.E. Hawkins, E. L. Shafer, and J.M. Rovelstad, eds., 393–405, Washington, D.C., George Washington University.

Brooks, Jane (1990), "Community Impacts of Tourism: The Case of the New Orleans Vieux Carré," *The Tourism Connection, Proceedings TTRA*, pp. 135–139.

Brown, Martha (1990), *The Mayor's Task Force On Public Support For Cultural Organizations in Metropolitan Milwaukee*, Milwaukee, Wisconsin.

Chon, Kye-Sung, Pamela Weaver, and Chol Yong Kim (1991), "Marketing Your Community: Image Analysis In Norfolk," *The Cornell Hotel and Restaurant Administration Quarterly* 31(4), Ithaca, New York.

GLS Research (1992), *1991 Las Vegas Visitor Profile Study*, Las Vegas Convention and Visitors Authority.

Hospitality Valuation Services, Inc. (1988), *Market Supply and Demand Analysis of the Lodging Industry, San Antonio, Texas*, Mineola, New York.

Johnson, Dennis (1973), "A Market Analysis of the Lodging Industry in the Twin Cities Metropolitan Area," Unpublished M.S. thesis, Minneapolis: Department of Agricultural and Applied Economics, University of Minnesota.

Kavanaugh, Mary Beth (1991), "Tourism And The Arts In San Francisco: A Case Study," *Tourism: Building Credibility For A Credible Industry, Proceedings TTRA*, 399–401.

Kent, William, and Thomas Chestnutt (1991), "Underground Atlanta Resurrected and Revisited," *Journal of Travel Research* 29(4), 36–39.

Laster, Bruce (1990), "Greater Ft. Lauderdale: Profile of a Changing Destination Community," *The Tourism Connection, Proceedings, TTRA*, 143–145.

Laventhol & Horwath (1989), *1988 Convention Income Survey*, International Association of Convention and Visitor Bureaus, Champaign, Illinois.

Longwoods Research Group (1990), *1989 U. S. Pleasure Travel Market; Canada's Progress and Challenges*, Toronto: Tourism Canada.

National Technical Information Service (1990), *Airport System Capacity: Strategic Choices*, Springfield, Virginia.

Reed Travel Group (1991), *The Hotel & Travel Index 1990 U. S. Hotel Guest Study, Summary Report: Profile of U. S. Hotel Guests*, Secaucus, New Jersey.

Rose, Warren (1981), "The Measurement of Economic Impact of Tourism on Galveston, Texas: A Case Study," *Journal of Travel Research* 19(4), 13–11.

Schroeder, Tim, (1990), "Preliminary Assessment of the Social Impacts of Tourism on Flagstaff, Arizona," *Visions in Leisure and Business*, Appalachian Associates, Bowling Green, Ohio.

Somersan, Ayse (1979), *Spokane Economic Impact*, Madison, Wisconsin: Recreation Resources Center, University of Wisconsin.

Statistics Canada (1991), *Inventory of Studies Conducted on Canadian Cities, Overview: Montreal, Toronto, and Vancouver*, Ottawa, Ontario.

Tourism Canada (1988), *Tourism Community Development Initiative: Economic Impact Study Niagara Falls, Main Report*, Ottawa, Ontario.

Woodside, Arch, Bill Pearce, and Matt Wallo (1989), "Urban Tourism: An Analysis of Visitors to New Orleans and Competing Cities," *Journal of Travel Research* 17(3), 22–30.

Part Four

Some Disciplinary Perspectives

This part of the Handbook is intended to emphasize the fact that tourism is a multidisciplinary field of study. As such, it is essential that researchers be aware of, and utilize, the rich resource base available to them from the various basic disciplines. Because of the number of disciplines from which tourism research draws, it was not possible in this single publication to include chapters covering all possible fields. However, the five chapters that are included here represent some of the most important areas, both in terms of past development of tourism thought as well as some new and evolving directions.

Chapter 17, which has been authored by Lisle Mitchell, reviews research in tourism as viewed from the discipline of geography. In opening the chapter, Professor Mitchell first distinguishes how the geographer differs from other social scientists with respect to the study of the tourism phenomenon. He clearly points out that the geographer's bias is towards research that involves the study of place and space—the factors, forces, and processes that explain why a phenomenon is located where it is or why certain phenomena are distributed in a particular pattern in a specific region. Having defined this orientation, the author then presents a number of conceptual considerations pertaining to tourism research and certain fundamental constructs drawn from the field of geography. Following this discussion, Dr. Mitchell provides several examples in which general concepts from geography have been applied to the study of specific tourism situations. In providing these examples, particular importance is attributed to the concept of *linkage* as the concept necessary for the understanding of travel to and from recreation activity and participation in it. Subsequently, the author moves from reported examples of previous research to a discussion of other possible applications, particularly those having a managerial perspective.

The second chapter in this part is rooted in the field of psychology. This chapter, entitled "Developing and Using Psychographics in Tourism Research," was authored by Stanley Plog, who is widely recognized as one of the most insightful consultants in the travel and tourism field. In this chapter, Dr. Plog focuses on personality research as it applies to tourism and attempts to show how the underlying principles of personality/psychographic research can be effectively utilized in achieving a better understanding of tourists. The initial part of the chapter examines the uses of psychographic research in tourism and discusses its relationship to the field. It is emphasized that the purpose of psychographic research is to enable segmentation of the market into groups of people having different sets of motives and behaviors so that unique appeals can be developed for each of the separate groups. Having shown the relevance of psychographic research in tourism, the author subsequently provides a review of previous applications of pschychometrics in the field of travel and tourism. This brief section is followed by a much more extensive discussion on how to carry out psychographic research. Throughout, the emphasis is on presenting the concepts in a clear, understandable, and usable manner. At the same time, the author ensures that the reader remains aware of the psychological origin of the concepts discussed. The latter part of the chapter summarizes some of the common dimensions of psychographic findings that have been found to be of particular relevance to the field of tourism.

Chapter 19 focuses upon a discipline that, until recently, has received relatively little attention as a contributor to tourism thought. The discipline in question is that of political science. In

Chapter 19, Linda Richter provides a framework for examining some of the major political issues that increasingly affect tourism. Discussion in the chapter is presented from three main perspectives. The first is that of the host country, which must be concerned with balancing the positive and negative impacts of tourism. In the discussion related to this topic, Dr. Richter provides a thorough review of the broad range of political considerations that must be assessed in relation to tourism. The second political perspective addressed by the chapter is that of the country of origin of tourists. While the issues involved here are perhaps less substantial than issues raised in other parts of the book in terms of their potential repercussions on all segments of the population, they nevertheless represent an important range of political considerations that need to be evaluated by any country that permits its citizens to travel freely throughout the world. Finally, the chapter examines tourism from a number of international perspectives that have a political dimension to them. In particular, emphasis is placed on the role of the international corporation. While many of the issues involved go well beyond the field of tourism as such, the discussion nevertheless brings clearly into focus how international organizations function as the interface between host countries and countries that generate large numbers of tourists.

Chapter 20, by Nelson Graburn and Roland Moore, provides an anthropological perspective on tourism research. Prior to focusing on research in the field per se, the authors present a review of selected anthropological concepts and methods that are particularly relevant to the study of tourism. This review is complemented by a second review, which examines a number of alternative models that are helpful in gaining an understanding of tourism motivation from an anthropological viewpoint. The remainder of the chapter focuses heavily on a discussion of various examples of anthropological research on the impacts of tourism. As might be anticipated, there is a heavy emphasis in the field on the study of the social impacts of tourism, many of which have largely negative dimensions. Examples are given in the areas of ethnicity, situations of social inequality, the commoditization of art, and the interactions between hosts and guests. The chapter concludes with a brief discussion of the role that anthropologists can play in a consulting capacity. The authors emphasize that in order for the anthropologists' understanding of tourism to be of value in planning, their research expertise should be introduced early in the process.

The final chapter in Part Four represents a second contribution by Clare Gunn to this Handbook. Entitled "Environmental Design and Land Use," it presents a comparatively new and rapidly evolving area of tourism research. In this case, the disciplinary origin of the field is less well defined and, in fact, is still emerging. As such, Dr. Gunn's contribution will continue to receive considerable attention as the field develops. In terms of content, the chapter first reviews the recent rise in usage of the concept *sustainable development* as a replacement for the older term *conservation* and discusses its application to the field of tourism. Dr. Gunn emphasizes that sustainable development is achieved best by developers who understand that it is essential to their success rather than by government regulation. The second major topic addressed by this chapter is the nature of the major criteria employed in environmental design. In all, seven such criteria are identified and discussed. These include functional design and planning, market acceptance, owner rewards, relevance to transportation, resource protection, local community goals, and environmental decisionmakers. Having identified the design criteria that must be satisfied, Dr. Gunn then turns to an examination of the processes that must be put in place for effective environmental research and planning. A fundamental tenet of this section is the need for the *integrated planning* of tourism, a term that stresses a cooperative approach involving many constituencies, particularly local citizens and professionals. The chapter concludes with a brief discussion of three other environmental issues (the need for land-use regulation, the desirability of clustering, and the use of interpretive centers) and several principles that should be kept in mind for successful land-use planning in tourism.

17

Research on the Geography of Tourism

LISLE S. MITCHELL

Professor
Department of Geography
University of South Carolina
Columbia, South Carolina

*P*urposes of this chapter are: to discuss the interrelationships between the geographer and the manager; to distinguish between the approach of the geographer and other scientists who study tourism; to provide a definition of the geography of tourism; to outline some basic conceptual considerations of the geographic science; to illustrate a theoretical frame of reference by presenting examples of tourism geography research; and to offer some solutions to managerial problems based on geographic investigations.

Tourism, or traveling for pleasure, consists of two parts, one static and the other dynamic (Figure 1) (Matley 1976:2). The static aspect is a recreation experience that occurs at a desired site. The dynamic aspect is travel to and from the destination. This view of tourism is based on the relationship existing between population and environment (Figure 2). Population, or a selected segment of the population (i.e., tourists) interacts with physical and cultural environments during both phases of the tourism process. The travel phase is characterized by interaction along and through various landscapes (i.e., natural and cultural environments) utilizing appropriate transportation modes such as the automobile, airplane, or cruise ship (i.e., cultural environment) and in a particular social setting such as with relatives, friends, or neighbors, (i.e., cultural environment). Interaction also occurs at recreation sites that are user oriented (i.e., cultural environment) or resource oriented (i.e., physical environment) or that have an intermediate orientation (i.e., both environments) (Clawson and Knetsch 1966). This interaction may lead to beneficial results, such as satisfaction of hosts' and guests' desires, improvement of travel routes, construction of accommodation and entertainment facilities, and increased employment opportunities; or it may lead to harmful results, such as traffic congestion, air and water pollution, crime, utility shortages, and carrying-capacity problems.

It is the totality of the beneficial and harmful results of the interaction between population (i.e., hosts and guests) and

the environment (i.e., physical and cultural) that creates the context within which managers and geographers operate (Figure 3). The manager of an individual establishment is charged with the task of supervising the population-environment interaction. He or she is responsible for the planning and construction of facilities, for formulating recreation programs and activities, for the care and maintenance of facilities, for the safety of the patron, for internal circulation and parking, for wise land-use practices, for the securing of life and property, and for earning a profit or providing a public service. The geographer has the task of understanding the population-environment interaction and of developing conceptual models and tools that enable the manager to supervise more effectively and efficiently. The primary tasks of the manager and geographer, therefore, are to supervise and examine the interaction between population and environment.

The differences between managers and geographers are important, but the correspondence of needs is the rationale behind this chapter. A significant interrelationship exists between the two groups, and it is the purpose of this chapter to clarify the fundamental nature of geography. The procedures followed to achieve this goal are: first, to distinguish between the approaches of the geographer and of other social scientists to the study of tourism; second, to provide a definition of the *geography of tourism* and to outline some conceptual considerations; third, to present some research examples that illustrate the conceptual frames of reference;

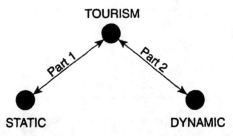

FIGURE 1 Tourism: dynamic and static aspects.

and fourth, to discuss some possible applications of geographic research to managerial problems.

THE GEOGRAPHIC APPROACH

Geographers and other disciplinary specialists who investigate tourism all study the same phenomena and collect data from the same sources. The difference between the approaches of various disciplines is explained by the unique perspectives out of which they operate. A discussion of nongeographic points of view is beyond the scope of this chapter, but special issues of the *Annals of Tourism Research* have extended explanations and examples of these perspectives (e.g., Geography, Vol. 6, No. 3, 1979; Sociology, Vol. 6, Nos. 1 and 2, 1979; Anthropology, Vol. 7, No. 1, 1980, and Vol. 10, No. 1, 1983; Management, Vol. 7, No. 3, 1980; Tourism Education, Vol. 8, No. 1, 1981; Economics, Vol. 9, No. 1, 1982, and Vol. 13, No. 1, 1986; Planning, Vol. 9, No. 3, 1982, and Vol. 17, No. 1, 1990; Political Science, Vol. 10, No. 3, 1983; Social Psychology, Vol. 11, No. 1, 1984; Economic Psychology, Vol. 13, No. 1, 1986; Anthropology and Sociology, Vol. 11, No. 3, 1984, Vol. 12, No. 1, 1985, and Vol. 13, No. 1, 1989; History and Geography, Vol. 12, No. 3, 1985; Methodology, Vol. 15, No. 1, 1988; and Social Science, Vol. 18, No. 1, 1991).

The geographer's bias is toward place and space. The geographer's fundamental question is—Where? He or she is interested in the factors, forces, or processes that explain why a phenomenon is located where it is or why certain phenomena are distributed in a particular pattern in a specific region on the Earth's surface. The tool that separates the geographer from other scientists is the map. Archival searches, computer applications, field investigations, inductive and deductive approaches, library research, and quantitative techniques are methodologies that are used by all investigators. Geographers, however, believe that an appropriate map or a series of maps provide insights into subject matter that can

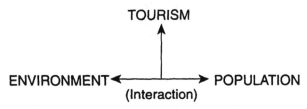

FIGURE 2 Environmental, population, tourism, interaction.

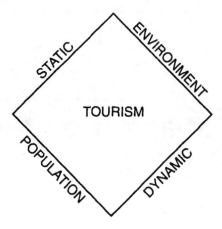

FIGURE 3 The geography of tourism.

be gained in no other way. Therefore, maps, various cartographic devices (i.e., spatial models), and the application of qualitative and quantitative methods to those maps and models, along with a spatial perspective, are the characteristics that distinguish the geographer from other scientists.

CONCEPTUAL CONSIDERATIONS

DEFINITION

In a special issue of the *Annals of Tourism Research, tourism geography* was defined as being ". . . concerned essentially . . . with the spatial expression of . . . the relationships and phenomena arising out of the journeys and temporary stays of people traveling primarily for leisure and recreational purposes" (Pearce 1979:248). This definition consists of five separate parts: (1) space or place; (2) relationships; (3) phenomena or facilities and activities; (4) travel; and (5) leisure or recreation. The geographer, therefore, views tourism within a spatial or place context. The geographer's bias pertains to specific site and situational characteristics of a particular area or region. In addition, the relationships of distinct activities and facilities are emphasized. The travel aspect of tourism implies the journey to a given location and the pleasurable experience engaged in at the destination and the return trip. Both phases, travel and activity, take place during leisure time and are of a recreational nature. It may be concluded that tourism geography is concerned with patterns of the use of leisure, in addition to travel, as it occurs in space. Tourism geographers observe, analyze, and explain the relationships of specific activities and facilities that are located in particular areas or regions. The geographer's view of tourist landscape may be examined through two simple models.

MODEL ONE

The first model consists of three basic ideas: demand, supply, and linkages (Ullman 1956:867-871). These ideas are analyzed from two perspectives: spatial and aspatial. *Tour-*

ism demand is defined as "an expressed but unattained desire to travel to some other place and to participate in some leisure or recreation activity or activities." Demand is a result of the complex interrelationships between personality, cultural values, and socioeconomic class of an individual or individuals. Comprehension of demand is difficult because the knowledge and perspective of potential tourists are subject to wide variation. Demand does not occur in a vacuum but rather exists in space and time. Individuals who demand tourist experiences reside at specific locations, and, if these locations are known, then it is possible to describe and analyze their spatial distribution. An understanding of demand or places of demand and the activity space of demanders is necessary to the comprehension of the tourism landscape.

Supply of tourist experiences is based on two principles: one is to provide a service (e.g., camping space or water and electricity) to the general public at little or no cost and the other is to earn a profit from providing goods (e.g., a meal or a motel room) or services (e.g., automobile repair or entertainment). Service and profit motives are the main reasons for the provision of tourism opportunities. Establishments that attempt to satisfy the needs and wants of the traveling consumer tend to locate in one of three places. The first is a position as close to the potential consumers as possible (i.e., major metropolitan areas). The second is a site on or near physical resources (i.e., a body of water, a scenic vista, or other natural feature), which serve as magnets to attract customers. The third is a position between places of demand and supply, usually along transportation routes and especially at major intersections (Clawson and Knetsch 1966).

Linkages are the connections between places of demand and places of supply. The most important association between those two places is complementarity. In other words, the desires of the demander, or potential tourist, should be satisfied by a place of supply, and purposes of the place of supply should be achieved by the demander's use of the facilities and programs provided. Consumption, or attendance rates, is a valid measure of complementarity. Consumption, however, cannot take place unless the places of demand and supply are linked by communication and transportation networks. Communications are necessary to provide potential tourists with information required to overcome the distance separating the places. Transportation routes are vital links between places of demand and supply, or origins and destinations, that enable consumption of tourism goods and services to occur. The tourism landscape has no meaning and no unity unless there are physical linkages between places.

MODEL TWO

The second model utilized by geographers to view the tourism landscape consists of three concepts: purpose, structure, and distribution. This model assumes that there is a fundamental purpose or rationale behind the decisions and actions of tourists and members of the tourism industry. It is believed that the spatial and aspatial aspects of purpose, structure, and distribution provide valuable insights into tourism (Lovingood and Mitchell 1978:33-34 and Mitchell 1991).

Purpose is defined to include an understanding of the reasons why an individual or group is interested in participating in a specific tourism experience or in providing tourism opportunities for others. The purpose of a tourism activity may be explained by physical, emotional, economic, or social needs and wants, and these factors are fundamental to the ideological and/or value systems that are the basis of rational decision making and planning.

Structure consists of two components: stratification and categorization. Stratification refers to formal and/or informal institutions, such as socioeconomic classes, that segregate individuals during the normal course of tourist events. Categorization refers to the classification of tourist facilities and activities into either functional groups (e.g., seaside resort as different from mountain skiing village) or a hierarchy of activities that differ more in degree than in kind (e.g., accommodation of varying quality and cost). Structure, therefore, is concerned with the organization of individuals and/or groups of tourists on the basis of some socioeconomic or other criteria in order to match their characteristics with the most appropriate destination, facility, or activity. It should be noted that structure and its components logically follow and are based on the value systems that are rudimentary to the idea of purpose.

The *distribution* of tourism sites and facilities may be described using several spatial measures. First, tourist attractions may be oriented toward the residence of tourists, the site of natural or cultural resources that are modified for tourist consumption, or a position that is intermediate between tourism and resource locations (Clawson and Knetsch 1966:36–40). Second, tourist establishments may be distributed in a concentrated, random, or uniform pattern. All tourist units have individual site and situational characteristics, and those spatial attributes reflect their unique purposes and structures. Accommodation, for example, is user oriented. The vast majority of hotels, motels, villas, and camp sites are located in or adjacent to metropolitan centers because potential consumers tend to agglomerate in such places and because urban areas, in and of themselves, are tourist attractions. On the other hand, some accommodation establishments are found at sites of physical resources (e.g., Mammoth Cave) or cultural resources (e.g., Las Vegas). Finally, some hotels and motels are distributed along major transport routes or at principal intersections and/or interchanges of those routes to take advantage of the traveling public's need for accommodation. These sites are selected to attract the largest possible clientele and to maximize profits, which is a basic purpose of management. This purpose influences the cost of rooms and other services, and costs stratify potential consumers into various groups to match the wide variance in the quality of accommodation. In summary, the distribution of hotels, motels, villas, and camp sites or any other tourist establishment is largely determined by its purpose and logically associated structure. Therefore, the concepts of purpose, structure, and distribution are inextricably interlocked and interrelated.

CONCEPTUAL MATRIX

These models may be used in a variety of ways as both provide interesting insights into tourism. Examples of applications of these schema will not be presented as they are beyond the scope of this chapter. The models may be placed, however, in a three-by-three matrix to serve as a guide to the geography of tourism (Figure 4). The placement of the elements of each scheme in this position results in some interesting associations. Each of the cells numbered 1 through 9 may be thought of as the intersection of two concepts:

Cell 1: Purpose—Place of Demand
Cell 2: Purpose—Place of Supply
Cell 3: Purpose—Linkage
Cell 4: Structure—Place of Demand
Cell 5: Structure—Place of Supply
Cell 6: Structure—Linkage
Cell 7: Distribution—Place of Demand
Cell 8: Distribution—Place of Supply
Cell 9: Distribution—Linkage

The connecting of the ideas of purpose and place of demand in Cell 1 might raise such questions as: What is the purpose of demand for a tourist experience? or What are the causes of demand for tourism? or What are the socioeconomic characteristics of potential tourists? These questions and others like them suggest the limits of the cell. Each cell could be considered in the same manner. For a detailed explanation of each of the nine cells, see Mitchell (1991).

The framework is logical and flexible enough to be used as a description of the present state of the geography of tourism, as a tool for the classification of tourism geography literature, and as a device for the formulation of research questions or the focusing of research efforts. While individual cells serve as a research concentration, it is also

possible to view combinations of rows or columns at a second level of application (Figure 4). The row entitled "Purpose," or Cells 1, 2, and 3, is concerned with ideology or human values; the row "Structure," or Cells 4, 5, and 6, pertains to activities, facilities, and institutions; and the row "Distribution," or Cells 7, 8, and 9, has a spatial or regional bias. The column "Demand," or Cells 1, 4, and 7, has a behavioral thrust; the column "Supply," or Cells 2, 5, and 8, centers on management or physical and cultural impacts; and the column "Linkage," or Cells 3, 6, and 9, concentrates on transportation, communication, interaction, and participation. The analysis of the matrix by row or by column, rather than by cell, produces a general combination of four interrelated ideas although one of these—the row or column title—is of primary concern. These procedures add to the versatility and utility of the matrix and broaden its scope beyond the apparent narrowness of the nine cells. For more complete coverage of these procedures, see Mitchell (1991).

In summary, the ideas contained in the two models form the basic elements of the matrix. The matrix, in turn, is utilized as a geographer's guide to the investigation of tourism. In the remainder of this chapter, relevant research examples and possible applications will be organized, with the matrix serving as a principal frame of reference.

RESEARCH EXAMPLES

Examples of geographic research will be presented by examining the columns of the matrix and focusing on the concepts of demand, supply, and linkage. The concepts of purpose, structure, and distribution will be incorporated in the discussion of each column. This organizational structure has been selected because the conceptual and factual findings in the literature are more easily arranged following this general approach.

		COMPLEMENTARITY			
		DEMAND Origin	**SUPPLY** Destination	**CONSUMPTION** Linkage	**DIRECTIVES**
LOCUNOMY	**PURPOSE** Intention Motivation	1	2	3	Ideology
	STRUCTURE Categorization Stratification	4	5	6	Activity Facility Institution
	DISTRIBUTION Site Situation	7	8	9	Environment
	DIRECTIVES	Perception Cognition Behavior	Management Resources Land Use	Interaction Transportation Participation	

FIGURE 4 Tourism matrix.

DEMAND AND PLACE OF DEMAND

Demand and consumption are often assumed to be the same, but they are, in fact, opposites. *Demand* is an individually felt want or desire, while *consumption* is an act of acquiring, participating, or utilizing (Mercer 1973). Demand, therefore, is a feeling, emotion, or belief, while consumption is an activity. The participation in a tourism experience (i.e., consumption) may satisfy an individual's tourism desire (i.e., need), but consumption of tourism activities is not the same as need for tourism activities. The significance of the distinction between demand and consumption will become clearer in the discussion of linkage.

Even though demand is an emotion, it exists in space like any other fact, and geographers have attempted to identify the factors that seem to explain demand for tourist experiences. According to Wolfe (1951), demand is influenced by physical factors, such as distance and access, and these factors have been verified by Laber (1969), Malamud (1973), Gurgel (1976), and Perdue (1986). Relative location among competing destinations has been found to strongly affect demand (Haahti 1986). Wolfe (1951) also notes the significance of sociological factors as predictors of demand. These factors are expanded upon by Mercer (1973) to include population size, age, income, mobility, and available leisure time. The supply of tourist activities stimulates demand, and, according to Demars (1979), the attractivity of tourism centers and market conditions are prominent explanatory variables. Likewise, Fesenmaier and Lieber (1988) found that demand is stimulated by diversified and compatible recreation activities. The quantity and quality of tourist resorts or complexes are important in understanding the rationale of tourist desires (Stanfield 1971). Market conditions, such as inflation, interest rates, employment, amount of expendable income, and available leisure time, have a significant effect on tourist needs.

Decisions pertaining to touring and recreation experiences are based on individual needs and values, and a logical attempt is made to maximize satisfaction and to minimize monetary and time costs (Stutz 1977). The decision-making process involves not only personal characteristics but the sources of information and degree of knowledge about alternative attractions and transportation facilities (Murphy 1979). Information and knowledge are collected from a number of sources that may be as simple and direct as word-of-mouth advertising or as complicated, indirect, and impersonal as a radio or television commercial. No matter what the source, an individual must decide between competing tourist establishments and alternative transportation modes. Not all tourist facilities are equally attractive, and those that project the best image have an obvious advantage (Murphy and Rosenbloom 1974). Likewise, not all sites have equal access, and such factors as natural and cultural barriers, transportation networks, and physical and psychological distance are important in explaining the selection of one tourist unit over another.

Demand for and decision processes pertaining to tourism are made at some place, usually the residence of the individual involved. It is well known that tourists and, thus, tourist demand are concentrated like the general population in central cities and surrounding suburbs (Wolfe 1951; Fussell 1965; Bell 1977; Wolfe 1978; Van Doren 1981; Mitchell 1984; and Blank and Petkovich 1987). The locational pattern of demand from activity to activity and from facility to facility is illustrated for beach activities by Fussell (1965), for state parks by Enger and Guest (1968), for second homes by Ragatz (1979), for camping facilities by Taylor and Knudson (1973), for ski resorts by Ewing and Kulka (1979), for urban cultural facilities by Wall and Sinnott (1980), and for rural festivals by Janiskee (1991).

Nevertheless, the spatial distribution of demand in both general and specific instances may be better understood if factors of demand (i.e., purpose) and decision-making processes (i.e., structure) as well as distribution are considered.

SUPPLY AND PLACE OF SUPPLY

The purpose of supply is seldom examined in the geographic literature because it is assumed that the provision of tourism services is the function of governmental agencies and the earning of profit is the goal of tourism corporations. Lovingood and Mitchell (1978), however, investigated the differences between public and private recreation units in Columbia, South Carolina. It was discovered that public agencies provide general recreation activities to the lower and middle classes as close and accessible to their residences as possible. Private concerns, on the other hand, offer relatively specialized facilities to the middle and upper economic classes at locations that are intermediate or resource oriented. Thus, the public and private tourism sectors tend to be complementary, and there is relatively little duplication of recreation opportunities.

Places of supply (i.e., structure) have been classified by Wolfe, Fussell, and Gunn. The major summer resorts of the province of Ontario, Canada, are grouped into three classes (Wolfe 1951). Three hundred seventy-nine resorts are included in 43 resort areas, 22 resort regions, and 10 recreational divisions. The classification scheme is based on contiguous regions, with physical and cultural factors used to delineate boundaries. The South Carolina coastal area is categorized by Fussell (1965) using a modified version of a system utilized by the Outdoor Recreation Resources Review Commission. Seven self-explanatory groups are listed: (1) high-density recreation areas, (2) general outdoor recreation areas, (3) natural environment areas, (4) unique natural areas, (5) primitive areas, (6) historic and cultural sites, and (7) low-density and high-cost recreation areas. Tourist regions or community-attraction complexes are divided into five elements by Gunn (1972): (1) a transport system linking a region or complex with its market (i.e., external transportation); (2) an entrance point or points where information and directions are dispensed (i.e., gateway); (3) an urban settlement that provides goods, services, facilities, and recreation attractions (i.e., community); (4) sites and facilities providing a wide variety of recreation opportunities (i.e., recreation clusters); and (5) a transit network connecting the gateway, community, and recreation clusters (i.e., internal circulation). These three classifications schemes—spatial, descriptive, and functional—are methodologically simple and relatively easy to apply to a managerial problem. However, a great deal of research needs to be conducted on the classification of places of supply, as indicated by dates of the examples cited.

The best known and most widely used system to explain the locational pattern of tourism enterprises is by nongeographers Clawson and Knetsch (1966:36–40). This system is based on the tendency of places of tourism supply to be oriented toward users, resources, or positions intermediate between population and resources. According to Christaller (1964), tourism is a peripheral activity, and most geographic studies tend to concentrate on resorts that focus on natural or cultural resources. Most of the studies cited in this chapter center on the resource-oriented locations: wilderness cottages (Wolfe 1951), the shoreline (Fussell 1965), coal mines (Deasy and Griess 1966), and caves (Wall 1978). However, urban studies have been conducted on user-oriented sites, such as Vancouver by Murphy (1979), on Canadian cities by Rajotte (1975), on recreation business districts by Stanfield and Rickert (1970), and on recreational boating by Heatwole and West (1982). The only article found specifically related to intermediate tourism places was by Eiselen (1945).

The investigation of supply and places of supply of tourism experiences is technically simple. Inventories of tourism activities, facilities, programs, and policies are conducted continuously, but the examination of the rationale of establishments, the classification of enterprises and their influence on consumption, and the location patterns of places and supply are seldom examined. Studies of tourism attractions, which were conducted in a context that excludes spatial considerations, are missing an important dimension that can provide valuable insights into serious operational problems.

LINKAGE

Clawson and Knetsch (1966) have identified five phases of a tourism experience: planning, travel to the site, participating in a recreation experience, the return trip, and the recollection of the total experience. Chubb and Chubb (1981) have greatly expanded this classification system into 11 phases. The planning, or decision-making, phase was discussed earlier, and the recollection, or recall, phase is beyond the scope of this chapter. However, travel to and from and participation in recreation activity are basic to the idea of linkage.

Connections between places of demand and supply are not made unless there is some degree of complementarity. In other words, a place of supply must provide some recreation good (i.e., a drink, meal, or novelty) or service (i.e., a room, activity, or program) that is desired by a tourist. The trip to a tourist attraction, engaging in recreation experiences, and the return trip are identified as consumption. Consumption is the satisfaction, at least to some extent, of a tourist demand (i.e., purpose). The examination of linkage from a geographic

perspective is concerned, therefore, with complementarity and the consumption of tourist goods and services and related concepts (Gunn 1972).

Wall (1978) compared the consumption patterns of a national park and a state park in Kentucky. The national park had approximately twice the attendance of the state park: 1,739,957 vs. 926,750. The national park was larger in size, had more recreation and travel facilities, and had a more central and accessible location than the state park; thus, the greater attractivity of the national park explains it larger attendance. To further explain the consumption pattern, Wall noted that the average distance traveled to the national park was greater than that of the state park, 302 vs. 108 miles, and that the percentage of out-of-state visitors was higher at the national park, 73.8 vs. 61.6 percent. This study demonstrates three spatial principles. First, consumption or attendance is positively correlated with attractivity and advertising, or the more attractive and better advertised tourist establishment is more likely to have greater attendance than less attractive facilities. Second, tourist sites may be classified on the basis of their attractivity. Third, tourists are willing to travel long distances to visit tourist sites that are highly attractive.

Changing interrelationships between transportation and accommodation on Vancouver Island were investigated by Nelson and Wall (1986). Evolutionary changes in transportation technology (i.e., type and route) greatly influenced the quantity and quality of accommodation on the island. Changes in railroad, steamship, and automobile transport, along with economic conditions, affected the number and type of accommodation facilities. A shift from a concentration of large, elegant hotels for the wealthy to self-catering camping accommodation for the less wealthy has been the long-term trend in Victoria. The automobile, with its inherent flexibility, has been the greatest impact on the type and distribution of accommodation on Vancouver Island and demonstrates the significance of linkages between origins and destinations.

Implications of the trader concept for spatial-choice modeling were examined by Perdue (1986). *Traders* are defined as individuals who make a choice between a closer, less attractive site and a further, more attractive site. Of 430 Texas recreation boaters surveyed, almost 48 percent were classified as traders. The recreation boaters were provided with a set of two lakes with differing travel distances and asked to state their travel preference. It was found that the 206 traders were more likely to trade off lake attractiveness for lake access than the 224 nontraders. Individual recreational boaters, classified as traders in this study, had a tendency to choose the convenience of easy access over the quality of the lake as their primary rationale for decision making. This finding indicates the importance of linkage to recreation and tourism consumption.

The linkages that directly bind place of demand to place of supply are communication and transportation networks. Indirect connections are related to the concept of complementarity (i.e., purpose) and are observed in: consumption patterns; classes of tourists (i.e., structure); hinterland sizes and shapes; minimum, mean, and maximum distances traveled; and explanatory factors like access, familiarity, and advertising (i.e., distribution).

POSSIBLE APPLICATIONS

The research needs of managers of tourism facilities are large, complex, and specific. Nevertheless, it is believed that the general geographic concepts and examples presented have value. It is assumed that managers who are responsible for the successful operation of a place or places of supply have a direct interest in the structure and location of places of demand, and the linkages between places of demand and supply. Furthermore, it is assumed that managers rationalize their decision-making processes and, therefore, are aware of the significance of their formal programs, activities, policies, and location characteristics.

This portion of the chapter will be organized around a manager's view of the conceptual framework and the research examples presented above. A manager must first consider the supply of tourism goods and services and the place of supply (i.e., the actual tourism establishment under consideration). In turn, demand, places of demand, and linkages are examined (Figure 5). A series of questions about supply, demand, and linkage considerations will be stated with regard to purpose, structure, and distribution to illustrate the implications of geography research for the tourism manager.

SUPPLY AND PLACE OF SUPPLY

Table 1 contains examples of the kinds of questions a manager might ask about the purpose, structure, and distributional characteristics of supply as related to his or her establishment. From a geographic perspective, the ability to provide goods and services to the traveling public centers on location and distribution. The location type, site, and situation within the local landscape and the position in relationship to potential patrons are fundamental to the purpose and the place of the establishment in the structure of the touristscape. The economic viability (i.e., the minimum number of patrons needed to earn a profit) of a business is directly related to location and distribution. Associated with

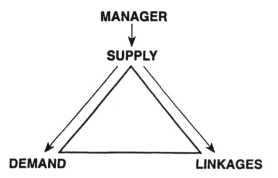

FIGURE 5 Manager's view—supply, demand, and linkages.

TABLE 1 Questions about Supply

Purpose
1. What is the minimum patronage needed to cover capital and operating costs?
2. What quantity and quality of facilities, activities, programs, policies, and promotions will attract the minimum patronage?
3. The market for this particular enterprise consists of what socioeconomic level?

Structure
1. What level of attraction is provided by this enterprise?
2. How does this enterprise fit into the surrounding businesses?
3. Which surrounding businesses are complementary, and which are competitive?

Distribution
1. What type of location does this establishment have: user, intermediate, or resource oriented?
2. Does this site have any locational advantages and/or liabilities?
3. What are the situational characteristics of this establishment in the local tourism landscape?

distribution and the economies of operation are the types of individual, family, or group to be served and the number and quality of attractions developed to entice potential patrons. Once the purpose is rationalized, concern for the facilities and programs to suit customers, the complementary and/or competitive nature of surrounding enterprises, and the existence of beneficial external institutions must be investigated.

Possible applications of geographic research to the questions of supply are fourfold. First, an analysis of the site would be useful to determine the most advantageous positioning of facilities and buildings and to ensure convenient and safe entrance and exit to the establishment. Second, an investigation into the situational relationship between the site and the potential market area is necessary to come to an understanding of the source regions of tourists. Third, a study of the functional association between the establishment and both complementary and competitive businesses is helpful to the comprehension of how the establishment fits into the tourist attractions surrounding the site. Fourth, an examination of the activities and facilities of an establishment is important to understanding the class of tourist served.

DEMAND AND PLACE OF DEMAND

Examples of general questions pertaining to the purpose, structure, and distributional aspects of demand are found in Table 2. Implications from geographic research suggest the following applications. First, an analysis of the spatial distribution can provide information about residential patterns. Tourist destinations can be classified as being distributed in a concentrated, uniform, or random fashion, and each distributional form needs to be approached utilizing different management strategies and tactics. Second, once the locational characteristics are known, a study of socioeconomic factors and personality profiles can result in better comprehension of tourist needs and wants. Finally, after the basic motives

TABLE 2   Questions about Demand

Purpose
1. What are the needs, motives, and values of potential patrons? What do they want, and what do they want to do?
2. How can tourists be attracted to this establishment?
3. How familiar are tourists with this establishment?

Structure
1. What are the socioeconomic characteristics of tourists who might be attracted to this establishment?
2. What is the personality profile of a typical individual or family who might be a potential patron?
3. What type of attraction is desired by potential patrons?

Distribution
1. Where do potential patrons reside?
2. Are there spatial concentrations of potential patrons?
3. Are there spatial voids of potential patrons?

and values of tourists are discovered, it is possible to develop methods to inform and lure them to a tourism attraction. All three of these approaches are closely interrelated and must be considered simultaneously, although systematically, to be effective.

LINKAGE

Questions about the linkages connecting places of supply and places of demand are found in Table 3. Geographically, the first concern is with the size and shape of the market area, the transportation networks utilized, and various distance measures of tourist travel. Therefore, the delimiting and demarcation of the market area and the analysis of related spatial concerns are of foremost importance. Second, but related to the first, is the examination of attendance records. Studies of past consumption are a key to understanding present and future trends. This is especially true when the records are viewed in the context of the state of the economy and when variables like fuel costs and/or availability are considered. In this light, an investigation of attendance in relation to the market area can be a valuable management

TABLE 3   Questions about Linkages

Purpose
1. How many patrons have been attracted in the past?
2. What are the possibilities of increasing consumption?
3. How do the economy and the fuel situation affect consumption?

Structure
1. What are the facility needs and skill abilities of the patrons?
2. What goods and services do patrons consume?
3. What individual or family types utilize the goods and services?

Distribution
1. What are the size and shape of the market area?
2. What transportation modes and routes are used to reach this establishment?
3. What is the minimum, maximum, and average distance traveled to reach this establishment?

tool. Third, and last, the on-site experiences of tourists should be evaluated. The socioeconomic-class level and skill abilities of the tourist to a large extent determine the kind of goods and services that are demanded and the type of consumption that will take place. Thus, an activity and facility analysis of tourist participation can be helpful in making management decisions.

SUMMARY

The geographer's bias toward space and place is reflected in the types of research carried out and the possible applications of methods and findings to the problems of tourism managers. The spatial connections between places of supply and places of demand are fundamental to the geographer. The study of consumption reflects the complementarity that exists between supply (i.e., managers) and demand (i.e., tourists) and demonstrates that distance and other physical and cultural barriers to travel have been overcome. The classification of attractions and the stratification of visitors illustrate the structure of the tourism system. The size and shape of the market area are directly related to both purpose and structure and are a product of the interconnecting transportation systems and the distance traveled by tourists.

A model of tourist space developed by Miossec (1976) synthesizes many of the concepts discussed in this chapter. The original article, unfortunately not formally translated into English at this date, considers four basic elements: resorts (i.e., supply), transportation networks (i.e., linkages), the behavior of tourists (i.e., demand and consumption), and the attitudes of local decision makers and population (i.e., purpose). The spatial model (Figure 6) incorporates the concepts of structure and distribution. Thus, this prototype, with its emphasis on space and place and the use of maps, provides imaginative insights into the evolutionary phases of the touristscape. Geographic research that is comprehensive, internally consistent, and logical, like this example, is of value to managers in three broad areas: (1) the solution of problems of market segmentation, classification schemes, carrying capacity, and spatial orientation (i.e., supply); (2) the distribution of tourists, decision-making processes, and matching the needs and wants of tourists with goods and services provided by tourist establishments (i.e., demand); and (3) to locate and determine the size and shape of the market area, to discover the major modes and routes of travel and estimate the minimum, mean, and maximum distances traveled, and to define the spatial thrust of advertising efforts (i.e., linkage).

CONCLUSION

Geographic investigations of tourism attractions do not have to be large or expensive. It is possible with the use of probability theory to draw a relatively small sample of data that is either readily available or easily obtained to produce findings of significant value to managers. Rigorous research

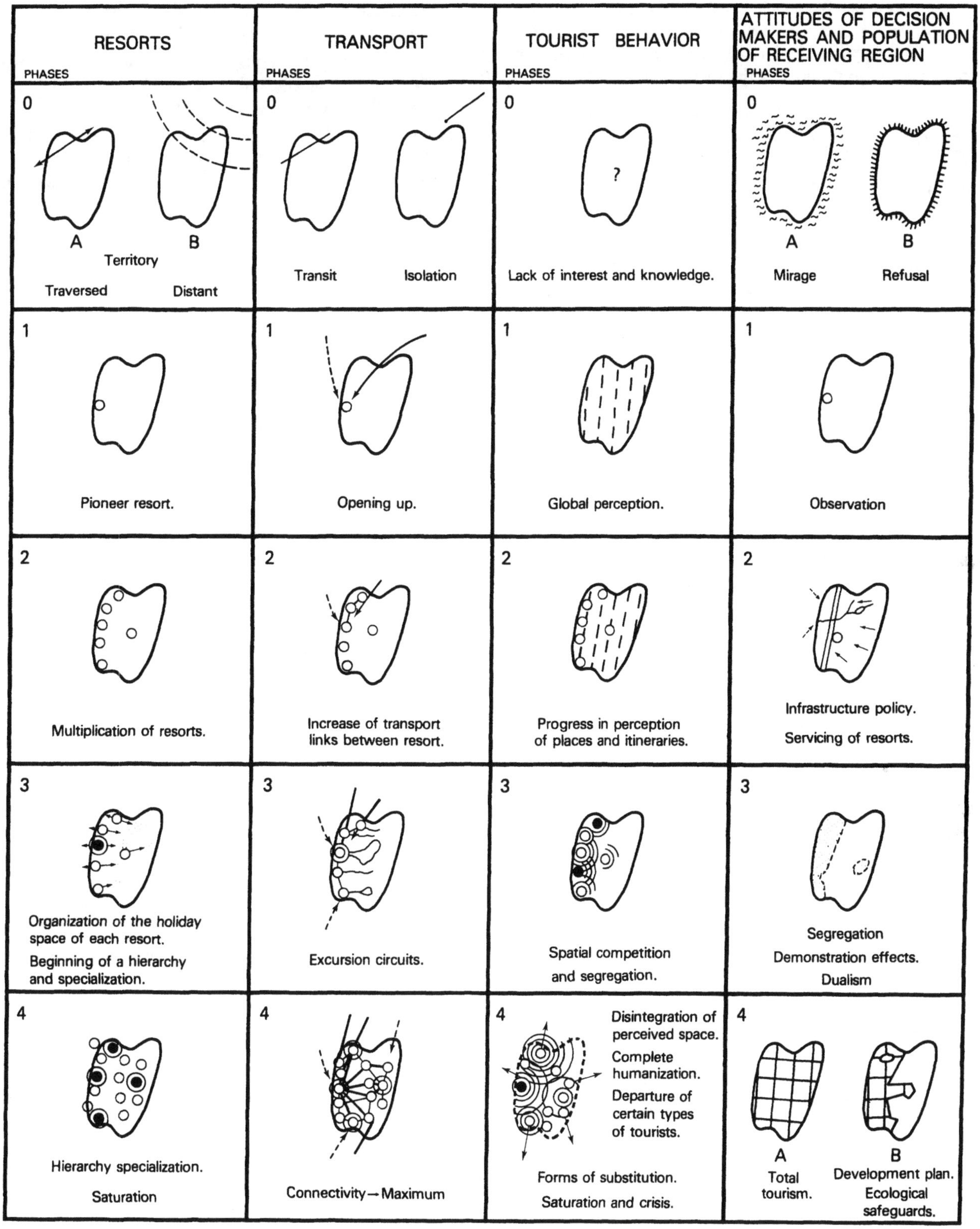

RESORTS	TRANSPORT	TOURIST BEHAVIOR	ATTITUDES OF DECISION MAKERS AND POPULATION OF RECEIVING REGION
PHASES	PHASES	PHASES	PHASES
0 A B Territory Traversed Distant	0 Transit Isolation	0 ? Lack of interest and knowledge.	0 A B Mirage Refusal
1 Pioneer resort.	1 Opening up.	1 Global perception.	1 Observation
2 Multiplication of resorts.	2 Increase of transport links between resort.	2 Progress in perception of places and itineraries.	2 Infrastructure policy. Servicing of resorts.
3 Organization of the holiday space of each resort. Beginning of a hierarchy and specialization.	3 Excursion circuits.	3 Spatial competition and segregation.	3 Segregation Demonstration effects. Dualism
4 Hierarchy specialization. Saturation	4 Connectivity → Maximum	4 — Disintegration of perceived space. Complete humanization. Departure of certain types of tourists. Forms of substitution. Saturation and crisis.	4 A B Total Development plan. tourism. Ecological safeguards.

FIGURE 6 A model of tourist space.

design based on fundamental managerial objectives, carefully collected data, and effective utilization of research methodology can result in useful spatial generalizations that are normally overlooked by the tourism industry.

REFERENCES

Annals of Tourism Research, various vols. and nos. (1979–1991).

Bell, Michael (1977), "The Spatial Distribution of Second Homes: A Modified Gravity Model," *Journal of Leisure Research*, Vol. 9, No. 3, 225–233.

Blank, Uel, and Michael D. Petkovich (1987), "Research on Urban Tourism Destinations," *Travel, Tourism, and Hospitality Research*, J. R. Brent Ritchie and Charles R. Goeldner, eds., New York: John Wiley & Sons, Inc., 165–177.

Christaller, Walter (1964), "Some Considerations of Tourism Location in Europe," *Papers, Regional Science Association*, 95–105.

Chubb, Michael, and Holly R. Chubb (1981), *One Third of Our Time*, New York: John Wiley & Sons, Inc., 230–235.

Clawson, Marion, and Jack L. Knetsch (1966), *Economic of Outdoor Recreation*, Baltimore, MD: Johns Hopkins Press.

Demars, Stanford (1979), "British Contribution to American Seaside Resorts," *Annals of Tourism Research*, Vol. 6, No. 3, 285–293.

Eiselen, Elizabeth (1945), "The Tourist Industry of a Modern Highway, US 16 in South Dakota," *Economic Geography*, Vol. 21, No. 3, 221–230.

Enger, Bruce M., and B. Ross Guest (1968), "The Response of a State Park to Demand for Recreation," *Professional Geographer*, Vol. 20, No. 3, 171–176.

Ewing, Gordon O., and Terrence Kulka (1979), "Revealed and Stated Preference Analysis of Ski Resort Attractiveness," *Journal of Leisure Sciences*, Vol. 2, No. 3, 249–275.

Fesenmaier, Daniel R., and Stanley R. Lieber (1988), "Outdoor Recreation Expenditures and the Effects of Spatial Structure," *Leisure Sciences*, Vol. 9, No. 1, 27–40.

Fussell, James R. (1965), "Recreation and the South Carolina Coast," *Southeastern Geographer*, Vol. 5, 48–56.

Gunn, Clare A. (1972), *Vacationscapes: Designing Tourist Regions*, Austin: Bureau of Business Research, the University of Texas.

Gurgel, Klaus D. (1976), "Travel Patterns of Canadian Visitors to the Mormon Cultural Hearth," *Canadian Geographer*, Vol. 4, 405–418.

Haahti, A.J. (1986), "Finland's Competitive Position as a Destination," *Annals of Tourism Research*, Vol. 13, No. 1, 11–35.

Heatwole, Charles A., and Niels C. West (1982), "Recreational-Boating Patterns and Water Surface Zoning," *Geographic Review*, Vol. 72, 304–311.

Janiskee, Robert L. (1991), "Rural Festivals in South Carolina," *Journal of Cultural Geography*, Vol. 11, No. 2, 31–43.

Laber, Gene (1969), "Determinants of International Travel Between Canada and the United States," *Geographical Analysis*, Vol. 1, No. 4, 329–336.

Lovingood, Paul E., Jr., and Lisle S. Mitchell (1978), "The Structure of Public and Private Recreation Systems: Columbia, South Carolina," *Journal of Leisure Research*, Vol. 10, 21–36.

Malamud, Bernard (1973), "Gravity Model Calibration of Tourist Travel to Las Vegas," *Journal of Leisure Research*, Vol. 5, No. 4, 23–33.

Matley, Ian M. (1976), *The Geography of International Tourism*, Washington, D.C.: Association of American Geographer, Resource Paper No. 76–1.

Mercer, David C. (1973), "The Concept of Recreation Need," *Journal of Leisure Research*, Vol. 5, No. 1, 37–50.

Mercer, David C. (1969), "The Geography of Leisure—A Contemporary Growth Point," *Geography*, Vol. 55, No. 3, 261–273.

Miossec, J. M. (1976), "Elements pour une Theorie de l'Espace Touristique," *Les Cahiers du Tourisme*, C-36, CHET, Aix-en-Provence.

Mitchell, Lisle S. (1984), "Tourism Research in the United States: A Geographic Perspective," *GeoJournal*, Vol. 9, No. 1, 5–15.

Mitchell, Lisle S. (1991), "A Conceptual Matrix for the Study of Tourism," *Les Cahiers du Tourisme*, C-N-146, CHET, Aix-en-Provence.

Murphy, Peter E. (1979), "Tourism in British Columbia: Metropolitan and Camping Visitors," *Annals of Tourism Research*, Vol. 6, No. 3, 294–306.

Murphy, Peter E., and Lorne Rosenbloom (1974), "Tourism: An Exercise in Spatial Search," *Canadian Geographer*, Vol. 18, No. 3, 201–210.

Nelson, R., and G. Wall (1986), "Transportation and Accommodation: Changing Interrelationships on Vancouver Island," *Annals of Tourism Research*, Vol. 13, No. 3, 239–250.

Pearce, Douglas (1979), "Towards a Geography of Tourism," *Annals of Tourism Research*, Vol. 6, No. 3, 245–272.

Perdue, Richard R. (1986), "Traders and Nontraders in Recreational Destination Choice," *Journal of Leisure Research*, Vol. 18, No. 1, 12–25.

Ragatz, Richard L. (1979), "Vacation Homes in the Northeastern United States: Seasonality in Population Distribution," *Annals of the Association of American Geographers*, Vol. 60, No. 3, 447–455.

Rajotte, Freda (1975), "The Different Travel Patterns and Spatial Framework of Recreation and Tourism," *Tourism as a Factor in National and Regional Development*, Peterborough, Canada: Trent University, Department of Geography, Occasional Paper 4, 43–52.

Stanfield, Charles A., Jr. (1971), "The Geography of Resorts:

Problems and Potentials," *Professional Geographer*, Vol. 23, No. 2, 164–166.

Stanfield, Charles A., Jr., and John E. Rickert (1970), "The Recreational Business District," *Journal of Leisure Research*, Vol. 2, No. 3, 213–225.

Stutz, Frederick P. (1977), "A Descriptive Model of Non-work Travel," *Yearbook Association of Pacific Geographers*, Vol. 39, 89–103.

Taylor, Charles E., and Douglas M. Knudson (1973), "Area Preferences of Midwestern Campers," *Journal of Leisure Research*, Vol. 5, No. 2, 39–48.

Ullman, Edward L. (1956), "The Role of Transportation and the Basis of Interaction," *Man's Role in Changing the Face of the Earth*, William L. Thomas, Jr., et al., eds., Chicago: The Chicago University Press, 862–880.

Van Doren, Carlton S. (1981), "Outdoor Recreation Trends in the 1980's: Implications for Society," *Journal of Travel Research*, Vol. 19, 3–10.

Wall, Geoffrey (1978), "Competition and Complementarity: A Study in Park Visitation," *International Journal of Environmental Studies*, Vol. 13, 35–41.

Wall, Geoffrey, and J. Sinnott (1980), "Urban Recreational and Cultural Facilities and Tourism Attractions," *Canadian Geographer*, Vol. 24, 50–59.

Wolfe, Roy I. (1952), "The Wasaga Beach: The Divorce from the Geographic Environment," *Canadian Geographer*, Vol. 1, No. 2, 57–65.

Wolfe, Roy I. (1978), "Vacation Homes and Social Indicators: Observations from Canadian Census Data," *Journal of Leisure Sciences*, Vol. 1, No. 4, 327–343.

Yu, Jih-Min (1981), "A Leisure Demand Projection Model," *Journal of Leisure Sciences*, Vol. 4, No. 2, 127–142.

18

Developing and Using Psychographics in Tourism Research

STANLEY C. PLOG

Chairman and CEO
Plog Research, Inc.
Reseda (Los Angeles), California

Demographics, although useful in travel research, does not explain underlying motivations for travel. Psychographics, in contrast, answers many important questions about the how, what, and why of travel, allowing travel marketers and developers to become more focused and effective in their efforts. This chapter describes the historical antecedents of contemporary psychographic research, offers examples of how it can be used effectively, and provides a framework for interested researchers to develop their own psychographic systems.

Frank Layden, the coach who built the Utah Jazz basketball team into a championship franchise, recalled the time when a college basketball player filled out an application to play with him. On the line where "church preference" was requested, he wrote "red brick."

Like the hapless applicant to Layden's team who missed the point that a church requires people and their beliefs to be a church, it is easy in the travel field to look only at the external characteristics of travelers. When researchers segment on the basis of age, income, sex, and marital status alone, they see only the bricks and mortar of behavior. Rather, they want to get inside the "building" and feel the living, breathing soul of its people. Psychographics provides that opportunity.

Although used infrequently in travel research in the past, interest in psychographics has been growing in recent years. More articles on the relationship of personality patterns and travel behavior are apparent over the last several years in the *Journal of Travel Research* than was true for much of *JTR*'s previous history. Psychographics has an important place in travel and tourism research. People of similar age, income, and occupation usually do not have the same travel interests. Far too often, many travel marketers attempt to target the same demographic customers. Typically, they seek persons with upper incomes, with a defined age profile (30 to 45 years, or 45 to 60 years, etc.), who travel frequently for

leisure (take one to three vacations more than 250 miles from home each year), and who reside in specific geographic areas (the "draw" areas for the destination, or cruise line, or hotel, etc.). This analysis leaves the target market too broadly defined, resulting in excessive advertising or promotional costs in trying to reach a relatively large audience. But, more important, what media should be selected and what message should be presented? Without a clear definition of the personality types and their travel preferences, the promotional message is likely to be poorly focused and unclear. Media choices can become scattered and not targeted, and the message may be off-target or diffuse.

Segmentation systems based on psychographic segments, when successful, produce clearly defined groupings of individuals with similar personalities, life-styles, and interest patterns. Thus, good psychographic research can immeasurably increase the effectiveness of a promotional campaign by:

- Targeting the appropriate audience
- Focusing the message on their psychological needs
- Selecting the appropriate media

A wild promise? No, not if the ground work has been done properly. The only "fly in the ointment" is that psychographic research takes more time and, therefore, also costs more. And, closer attention must be given to all phases

209

of the research in order to ensure a successful outcome. In this day of slimmed-down research budgets and short time schedules, unfortunately, few clients will dedicate a sufficient amount of either. But, the outcome is so valuable that the technique deserves consideration more often.

This paper will attempt to present the underlying principles of good personality/psychographic research as it applies to travel and tourism topics.

THE USES AND DEMANDS FOR PSYCHOGRAPHIC RESEARCH

Survey research grew up on demographics. From the time of its early beginnings, during the late 1920s and early 1930s, slicing the population into various categories by age, sex, income, occupation, area of residence, and so on, was common. It was an easy thing to do, quite useful for interpretation, and readily understood by all readers. This tendency has been so prevalent that it is intertwined in all research and marketing concepts to the point that print and broadcast media are now bought primarily on the basis of audience demographics.

Psychographics, as a newer field, has not had the time to make the same impact in research and marketing circles. And, unless standardization of terminology and concepts occurs, it may never realize its full potential. Psychographic research is being helped along, though, by an interesting turn of events. Demographic categories are far less predictive than they used to be. Just when prognosticators predicted the homogenization of the personal tastes and life-styles of the American public, because of the increasing influence of mass media, the realization has grown that people's tastes are now even more varied than ever before. So, there is the rise of niche marketing—going after small segments because these have become important. When researchers really want to get inside the skin of travelers—to understand why they select their special places to visit and how travel marketers can fulfill their needs—it is necessary to look beyond the standard approaches of the research industry.

Many uses exist for psychographics. Ideas occur almost spontaneously to anyone involved in the travel industry because they relate to critically important marketing questions such as, "I wonder what kind of person my customer really is?"; "Why did he or she buy (or not buy) my product (service)?"; "What motives should I appeal to in my advertising?"; "What kinds of media fit the life-style(s) of my target markets?"

Examples of psychographically relevant topics in travel/leisure research include:

• Destination development—clarifying the concept of a new, planned resort; the markets to be served; the services and amenities to be provided to visitors; and so on.

• Product positioning—focusing the primary message on the needs and psychology of the target audience. Much like automotive- and food-product companies, travel and leisure organizations must position their products and services to appeal to specific market segments.

• Destination positioning—refocusing the positioning of an existing destination to attract new customers. Usually, this task comes at a time of a declining tourism base and includes major improvements to the destination.

• Development of supporting services—determining which services are essential and which are optional for a travel-related company. Essential services must be included, while optional services should be considered only if they are not very costly or if they add to the overall marketability of the product.

• Advertising and promotion—focusing the message on the appropriate group of travelers. Their psychology, personal whims, motivations, and basic needs can be appealed to through highly targeted messages.

• Packaging—making certain that you not only have the right products and services, but that you have also packaged (presented) them appropriately. A destination may have all of the amenities, facilities, and activities desired by a group of travelers, but not be identified as such. Advertising can get the message out, but the concept must be presented in such a way that it fits the customer's perceived needs.

• Master planning—developing a master plan that protects, on a long-term basis, the inherent beauty and attractiveness of a destination, while still meeting the needs of travelers. This requirement is fundamental to all groups concerned with travel and tourism, such as visitors' associations, developers, hotels, airlines, and cruise ship companies.

DOES PERSONALITY RESEARCH RELATE TO TRAVEL AND TOURISM?

Since demographics, as a research tool, has held sway for so long—and it continues to be useful—the obvious question has to be answered. Is it necessary to know anything about personality, life-style, or other psychological variables to understand the growth and development of travel and tourism throughout the world? The answer is simple: researchers need to know basic demographics about tourist populations—the bricks and mortar of behavior. But, in today's world, there is not much to be said about people who travel after their income, age, and marital status have been defined.

The fact is that the butcher, the baker, and the candlestick maker—and the doctor, the lawyer, and the Indian chief—all may earn rather good incomes these days. They may live in the same neighborhood, shop at the same stores, go to the same church or temple, and have the same amount of money left over to take vacations. But there the similarity ends since they choose different destinations for vacations, different modes of transportation to get there, and participate in different activities after they arrive. The only way to find out about why they choose different vacation life-styles is to get inside their heads to determine what makes them tick. By definition, that means examining their psyches.

This task has come to be called psychographics—the

measurement of personality dimensions through a question-naire instrument. It has developed a somewhat tarnished name in recent years because the proselytizers of the field have often overpromised and underdelivered. Excessive claims about wondrous benefits of one psychographic system versus another have only proved that lots of researchers will jump on any bandwagon, if it seems to be moving.

In spite of these problems, a need exists to understand why different types of people travel (psychographics) and what they want to do when they get there (life-style). At Plog Research, the staff believes in it and also is committed to the idea that it can be done.

To accomplish these tasks, psychographic research requires segmenting the market into groups of people with different sets of motives and behaviors so that unique appeals can be developed for each of the separate groups.

A quick example will demonstrate the utility of psychographic research. As part of a major resort development, the owners of the property were planning to construct both golf and tennis facilities, but only one integrated clubhouse. Costs of construction would be less and, more important, it would allow them to emphasize the size of their recreational facilities in their promotional materials. On the surface, golfers and tennis players who travel are demographically very much alike. Their incomes are high; their occupational categories include a heavy representation of professionals and business executives; their age categories are similar; and they stay at destinations for about the same length of time. But, the research advised that there were major differences in personality structures and that cooperative facilities may not be the best route to go. In fact, there is an underlying hostility between the two groups of sports enthusiasts:

• Golfers play the game because of their social needs. The betting, constant ribbing, and 19th-hole camaraderie all demonstrate the heavy need for friendship (need for affiliation). Serious tennis players, however, often exhibit traits of social isolation. In a match, winning dominates their thoughts, and the game becomes a true competitive struggle (need for achievement). They restrict conversation between points, give few compliments, may argue over line calls, and after-match socializing and drinking are usually quite limited.

• Golfers like the good life. They eat more, drink more, stay up for shows at night, most often ride around the course in a golf cart, and generally spend more to have a good time at a destination. Tennis players, on the other hand, are more Spartan personality types. They eat less, skip much of the nighttime entertainment, go to bed earlier, utilize fewer of the amenities at a facility, and generally spend less while there. In short, golfers typically are more desirable as target markets for resorts because they are the bigger spenders.

The group of developers followed the advice, and golfers and tennis enthusiasts now coexist at the resort—with separate but equal facilities. Otherwise, they have limited contact with each other.

The utility of personality-based research becomes even more obvious when you examine the larger pieces that make up the tourism jigsaw puzzle. Different destination areas of the world attract different types of personalities. There is a whale of a difference in the psychology of someone who prefers a trip to China vs. someone who wants to go to the French Riviera. And, Miami attracts a very different set of travelers than individuals who seek out the Oregon coastline.

Understanding the basis of travel personalities, then, sets the stage for successful development of travel destinations—a critical task in a world in which there is an ever increasing number of travel possibilities and a finite number of travelers. Travel planners must target specific market segments and provide them with the experiences they want. And the framework for understanding must be plain, common, and simple, or the results will be impossible to implement.

PSYCHOGRAPHIC RESEARCH: A FOCUSED REVIEW

The antecedents of psychographic research are diverse, but meaningful. The field draws on a background deriving from personality research, sociology, marketing research, and segmentation statistics.

The contributions of sociology and marketing research are self-obvious and are not the subject of this chapter. Basically, the method for developing psychographic profiles must rely on questionnaire instruments. The skill of the researcher in designing well-constructed, easy-to-administer instruments to provide focused and meaningful data determines the ultimate usefulness of the psychographic scale(s). Questionnaire construction continues to be an art, not a science, although there are some general rules that can be followed.

Segmentation statistics are also utilized in most psychographic research projects. While techniques may vary, the typical approach includes:

• Employing factor analysis to determine the primary factors (psychographic types).
• Clarifying the cutting points between these factors by means of cluster analysis and/or discriminant function analysis.
• Utilizing regression statistics to determine which consumer behaviors can be predicted by each psychographic personality characteristic and to what degree.

Somewhat different orderings of the above sequence, and different statistics, are employed by various researchers (including the present author), depending upon the needs of the moment.

The more important topic, for the purpose of this chapter, relates to personality research and its historical antecedents. Although it is possible to follow the chain of psychographic investigations back to the foundations of scientific psychology in the laboratory of Helmholtz, the most important early contributions relate to the works and writings of Sigmund Freud. His psychoanalytic concepts explained a wide range of motives and behaviors (especially those that were unconscious). The influence of Freud extended far beyond psychoanalysis. All of the social sciences and much of popular literature were impacted by his conclusions, and market research followed suit. Motivational psychology was the latter-day result, which was prevalent as recently as the 1970s. Unfortunately, the fuzziness of the id, ego, and super-ego concepts and the dynamic interplay between the various psychosexual stages of development do not lend themselves to measurement through personality tests, let alone by means of questionnaires.

The real impetus to psychographics came from psychologists who developed basic, and still useful, personality tests. Their fundamental assertion, a necessary precondition for all psychographic research, is that self-report (answering questions) can be reliable and predictive of behavior. The Allport-Vernon Study of Values, for example, is still a useful conceptual tool for market researchers. The field was given an even greater lift, however, by Raymond B. Cattell, who used systematic research techniques and sophisticated statistics to develop his Trait Factor Theory of Personality and the Cattell Personality Scale to support his conclusions. Other powerful instruments followed, such as the Minnesota Multiphasic Personality Inventory (MMPI), the most widely used diagnostic test employed by clinicians, and the California Psychological Inventory (CPI), a more general measure of personality.

There are other instruments, some of which will be mentioned later in this chapter, but the important point is that these researchers paved the way for psychographic research. Not only did they show that personality factors can be measured reliably (test/retest reliability is very high for some of these instruments), but the method of test development set the stage for how psychographic instruments would be formulated.

Psychographic measurement, that is, using personality items to develop profiles of consumer types, is a young field. It has grown up approximately in the last 20 years. Except for a few early marketing books, which did not rely on data, such as Pierre Martineau's *Motivation in Advertising* (1957), the general focus has been to become research centered. The early studies tended to use standardized instruments to determine relationships between personality variables and buying behavior, such as the MMPI, CPI, and Allport-Vernon scales, and various measures of persuasibility and other more recent concepts, such as "yea saying" and "nay saying" (identified by Couch and Kenniston 1960) and dogmatism (Rokeach Scale). Most of these studies offered very few correlations (limited predictability to consumer choice for products) because the standardized instruments were developed for basic research purposes rather than for the more focused and limited needs of a market researcher. The discouragement was such that it led a veteran psychographic researcher to comment, "To summarize, then, I would say that the environment is so important in determining consumer behavior and the problems of measuring personality traits are so difficult to handle in consumer studies that personality traits may never have much value in consumer work" (Wells 1966:187–188). A few years later, however, his views had mellowed, and he now believes that personality/consumer behavior research shows utility in several areas (1975).

This early discouragement leading to more focused and tentative acceptance has been typical of other researchers (Yankelovich 1964, for example). The primary reason is that researchers are now developing scales that are more specific to the needs at hand. Thus, there is a greater likelihood that the personality characteristics measured will have some meaningful relationship to consumer behavior.

There are several authors whose works are useful to review by interested persons (the complete references are at the end of this chapter). These include:

- Elayn K. Bernay
- Joseph T. Plummer
- William D. Wells
- Douglas J. Tigert
- Ruth Ziff
- Harold H. Kassarjian
- Daniel Yankelovich
- William R. Darden

In addition, the American Marketing Association has supported the development of two useful reference documents, one on personality research in marketing (Bibliography Series No. 23) and the other on market segmentation (Bibliography Series No. 28). It must be remembered, however, that psychographics is a young field; the concepts employed often are conceptually elusive. As a result, demographics still dominates most advertising and marketing research—not that demographics predicts behavior very well (it doesn't!), but psychographics, by definition, has taken on a heavy assignment. Its fundamental task is to predict behavior, reliably and with utility, in areas where demographics has failed.

HOW TO DO PSYCHOGRAPHIC RESEARCH

George Burns once quipped, "You know you're getting old when you stoop down to tie your shoes and you wonder what else you can do while you're down there." And so it is with personality research. The field may not be old, but you better be prepared to do many things when you start psychographic research. A lot of effort can be devoted to developing a new personality-based classification system, but if it does not go well, your research neck gets chopped off. To forestall this uncomfortable possibility, a considerable amount of work must take place at several important stages.

Unlike demographic questions, there are no standard, commonly available psychographic approaches to tourism research, or to consumer goods research, or to automobile research or whatever. The common personality test produced by social-science publishing houses possess little direct relevance to travel and tourism, and, they are almost impossible to use in a research setting because they are too time-consuming or too personal or have prohibitions from being employed in all but psychiatric or counseling settings. In the end, a system developed by a researcher (or company) or a self-devised system will probably have to be used. Since the detailed features of many of the systems on the market (which also tend to be proprietary) cannot be adequately described, the following offers some principles for a self-directed program. Even if they are not attempting this task on their own, perhaps the researchers will be in a better position to evaluate the research provided to them by others. The author has tried to keep the explanations simple.

Two basic approaches to developing measures of personality exist: inductive and deductive. The inductive method, stated simply, derives from believing that two groups of people differ in their behavior—travel behavior, as an example. The researcher develops a large list of questions and items and administers them to each of these groups. Then, the items answered differently by the two groups are retained, and those that do not discriminate are discarded. It is pure empiricism because a large data base was utilized to produce the personality dimensions.

The method works! The MMPI was developed this way. Thousands of questions were administered to thousands of people who were diagnosed as exhibiting specific psychiatric symptoms. The discriminating items were assembled into a final instrument that measures symptomatologies and personality defense mechanisms in normal and not-so-normal people.

The success of the MMPI in psychiatric settings hides a fundamental flaw, however. And, it is a characteristic of almost all empirically derived instruments when applied to survey research projects (beyond the fact that researchers customarily are not concerned about the psychiatric diagnosis of tourist populations). It contains about 500 items and requires 45 minutes to 1 hour 15 minutes to complete. The respondent is not likely to be very cooperative when he or she is asked to answer additional questions about travel behavior. Empirically derived instruments also demonstrate a second flaw: questions often seem to be unrelated to the topic of discussion (travel) or are too sensitive ("Did you play spin-the-bottle as a child?").

There are additional problems of empirically derived tests that, although not as important in scope, contribute to the difficulty of using them in travel research settings. The potpourri of ill-selected and seemingly unrelated items that distinguish between different personality types frequently do not provide a way to interpret the multivariate-based personality dimensions that grow out of the research. How does one interpret dimensions that might be based on the fact that a given personality type likes to brush his teeth after every meal, hates exercise machines, and never allows a parking attendant to park his car? It is difficult to understand the personality "glue" that holds those items together, let alone relate them to other behaviors (as the propensity to take pleasure trips). The story is told, whether true or not, that Macy's department store in New York City developed a screening test to help them select better Christmas help. They finally discarded the instrument because wearing glasses was a negative indicator (poor risk) and liking brown shoes was a positive indicator.

The second approach to developing personality/psychographic dimensions is deductive. Postulate a personality dimension and then write questions to test that postulate. Support for the personality dimension comes when question answers fall in the predicted direction. If they do not, then scratch the takeoff and build a new launch pad. But, how strongly do the data have to fall in predicted directions to be valid? Although there are no hard-and-fast rules, one should expect to develop correlations of 0.25 or better for each item to the predicted behavior, with levels of 0.40 and above being much more acceptable. The total predictability and utility of the scale is higher, however, because the individual items contribute collectively to greater statistical power.

A number of personality tests have been developed this way. A theory of personality is translated into a relatively large number of questions on the basis of deducing how a given personality type would probably act or think in specific situations. Question items are retained or eliminated on the basis of how well they discriminate between groups and whether the discrimination is in the predicted direction.

The pitfalls of deductively derived psychographic dimensions in travel research center around the difficulty of being able to hypothesize or derive a relevant travel/tourism theory. Enormous sums of research dollars can be wasted testing out concepts that prove to be either invalid or, more likely, difficult to measure. Besides, if a researcher really understands the psychology of travel so well that he or she can easily develop a discriminating test, then perhaps they do not need research after all. They should just follow their hunches! Many resort developers and tour operators do, and they are quite successful. But, in a rapidly changing world, the question is whether their footwork will be fast enough to stay ahead of the variable needs of new traveling populations.

THE INDUCTIVE/DEDUCTIVE METHOD

An alternative exists. It grows out of the sound research practices and approaches followed, to some degree, by many researchers. It combines both inductive and deductive approaches to research. Efficient and cost-effective, it fits within the constraints of most projects—for both budget and time. The heavier emphasis is on the deductive side of the equation, but empirical, or inductive, reasoning is also a strong contributor to the final result.

The inductive portion of developing psychographic (personality) characteristics of travelers depends upon good qualitative research. A short example will help. In this case, the author offers research his company conducted—it follows the example, and, though not an attempt to convince anyone of the validity of what was done, it is an approach that has been used a number of times for travel studies and in consumer-product research.

We were given the task by 16 airline/travel companies to determine what could be done to broaden the base of the travel market, that is, to turn more nonflyers into flyers. Our early search of the literature pointed out that there was a hard core of the population that refused to fly, even when disposable income was sufficient and there were compelling reasons to fly. Obviously, the personal psychology of these people kept them from participating in experiences that others were enjoying, in spite of the fact that they were often severely inconvenienced by their unwillingness to travel by air. It could be fear of flying, unfamiliarity with flight, maintenance of old habits, and so on. Whatever the reason, we became convinced that there was a strong emotional core to the problem, and personality-based exploratory research was necessary.

We opted for in-depth, one-on-one, two-hour, psychologically based interviews with nonflyers who had median incomes above the national average. We structured an interview that looked at their current explanations for nonflying, the amount of traveling they did currently (and had done in the past), their early family experiences, and important life events.

During the interviews, the standard reason these nonflyers gave for not flying was, "I simply have not had any reason to fly." It was obvious that this innocuous statement covered over more important reasons.

Analyzing the transcripts of these interviews, we noticed a common pattern among nonflyers that included:

• "Territory boundness"—a tendency for these people to have traveled less throughout their lifetimes. They came from families that were not very venturesome, and this very conservative, cautious approach continued until today.

• "Generalized anxieties"—a strong feeling of insecurity in daily life, about one's job, regarding one's relationships to others, about personal skills and abilities, and so on. In short, these people were very uncertain of themselves, and they demonstrated a tendency to "wear their anxiety on their sleeves."

• A "sense of powerlessness"—a feeling that they have very little control over the fortunes and misfortunes that are likely to strike them during their lifetimes, and that they are likely to be victims of much of what is bad that can happen in life.

Because of the common tendency for these characteristics to appear in each nonflyer, we gave it a name—*Psychocentrism*. It refers to a person whose center of attention is focused on self-doubts and anxieties, rather than using this energy to venture out into the world to explore it.

At this point, the task became relatively easy. Some of these dimensions had the ring to them of the characteristics

described by David Riesman et al. in *The Lonely Crowd* (inner-directed vs. other-directed individuals) and by Julian Rotter in his Internal/External scale. The internalizer is an individual who is more self-confident, comfortable, and likely to do things his way. The externalizer looks for support and comfort from others and is much more cautious. Not all aspects of this dimension were covered in the ideas of Riesman and Rotter, and questions were written that focused more clearly on generalized anxieties and territory boundness.

The end result? It requires a maximum of eight questions to separate people on a continuum into different travel-personality groups, ranging from Psychocentric to Allocentric (a dimension developed to extend the scale to its polar opposite), leaving the vast majority of the questionnaire free to explore other topics necessary for travel studies. And, surprisingly, the dimension distributes along a bell-shaped curve rather well (Figure 1). We call these self-inhibited and anxious personality types "Psychocentrics." Their more venturesome and self-assured counterparts have been labeled "Allocentrics." The Allocentrics seek out more novel and unique destinations in the world. Psychocentrics, ultimately, are the last to visit—when an area has become over-commercialized and faces decay and decline.

The question is, then, does it work? If you fully understand the psychology of your travelers, then there is no reason why it should not (see Plog, *Leisure Travel: Making it a Growth Market...Again!*, 1991, for more complete explanation).

Based on this project, *Reader's Digest* put together a two-year advertising campaign of eight-page inserts in the *Digest* (sponsored by a select group of the original study sponsors). It focused on the psychology of these nontravelers to induce them to fly. By focusing on their fears and concerns and by using testimony of experts to provide the reasons why they should travel (for health, for job advancement, for a better marriage, for educational broadening, etc.), the needs and fears of these nontravelers were addressed. In a memorandum dated July 2, 1970, from Rene Isaac, Director of Adver-

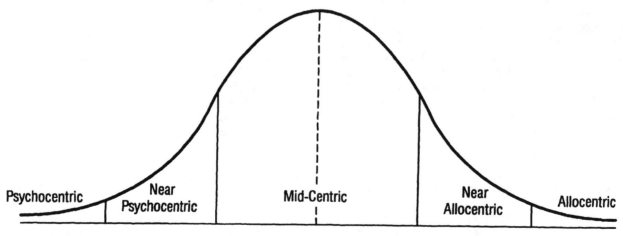

FIGURE 1   Distribution of psychographic segments.

tising Research for *Reader's Digest*, to all U.S. sales staff, he reported on an analysis of the Starch readership scores for the ad series, and indicated:

> *The readership scores, all of which are long test (multi-page) ads, are at least twice the average for the travel and resort category.*

The *Digest* was also given the "Discover America Award" for the best magazine travel promotion. A more complete description is contained in the book *Leisure Travel: Making it a Growth Market...Again!* (Plog 1991). And, various research studies have appeared testing its assumptions (Tarlow and Muehsam 1992; Nickerson and Ellis 1991).

THE SOURCES OF PSYCHOGRAPHIC AND LIFE-STYLE DIMENSIONS

The sources for dimensions may come from the use of qualitatively based research methods (in-depth interviews or focus groups) as was described earlier in this chapter, but this does not mean that all of the ideas have to be generated by the researcher. A rich source resides in the personality theories in the literature, concepts that have taken a lifetime to develop by their promulgators. Their concepts and ideas may not be directly related to travel, but sufficient relevance exists to make further examination and development quite fruitful. These researchers have developed tests that divide people into different personality types. Test items cannot be used in survey instruments without the express permission of the author (which normally will **not** be given), but the theoretic framework on which they are based is open for additional development by interested researchers.

As indicated earlier, the psychoanalytic-based theories of Freud and most of his disciples have proved to be of very little value in data-based research. Not only are the concepts loose and hard to pin down for research purposes, but the dimensions cannot be tied directly into advertising or promotional programs.

The concepts of the basic "needs" developed by Henry A. Murray, however, show much greater utility. These "needs" tend to show low intercorrelations, suggesting that they are relatively independent of each other, and they cover some psychological characteristics of people that are important in day-to-day social interactions (15 of the dimensions have been pulled together by Allen Edwards into a well-standardized test).

The following list of some of Murray's needs contains a few admittedly obscure dimensions, but others are very relevant. (In his lifetime of research, Murray altered the list at various times, expanding and contracting the items.)

An example of the utility of some of these dimensions is:

• Need for achievement—the desire to get ahead and be successful, especially to be competitive. It measures higher in persons who participate in competitive-sports vacations (tennis, hunting clubs, sailing regattas, handball, racquetball) or who are serious about jogging, distance running,

List of Murray's Needs

Abasement	Harm avoidance
Achievement	Intraception
Affiliation	Nurturance
Aggression	Order
Autonomy	Play
Counteraction	Rejection
Defendant	Sentience
Deference	Sex
Dominance	Succorance
Exhibition	Understanding

skiing, and other high-exercise activities that also demand skill coordination. A tennis-oriented resort facility should organize tournaments with prizes that clearly indicate that superb effort and achievement were necessary to win one of the trophies.

• Need for affiliation—the desire for friendship with others and to be with others in sociable settings. This dimension tends to be higher among golfers and others who like an easier and relaxed time on vacations, including heavy use of entertainment facilities, dining and restaurant facilities, and so on. Also, there is a preference for warm climates for vacations with the availability of a broader array of leisure-time activities and pursuits. The awards and prizes for a golf tournament can be more humorous and offbeat, and it is useful to have photos taken of all of the winners together to emphasize the camaraderie.

• Need for intraception—the desire to understand others, communicate with them, and have empathy for their problems, their position in life, and so on. This type of individual tends more to be inclined towards intellectual/historical/cultural trips that tour places to meet native/local people or to view and understand the significance of historical settings. Brochure material about these destinations should emphasize the common bond of all cultural groups, with a special emphasis on how people can learn more about themselves by interacting with different cultures.

• Need for succorance—the desire to be cared for, entertained, and provided for by others. Obviously, the dimension relates closely to types of vacations and destinations that provide more total care. Complete tour packages, with all ground arrangements provided, are reflective of the types of choices made by these people, as are cruise packages in warm-water areas such as the Caribbean, the Greek Islands, Mexico, and so on.

These few examples show the utility of some of the dimensions that can come from the Murray system of needs.

Other systems exist that also can provide useful help at various times. The depth psychology of Carl Gustav Jung has been translated into a very-easy-to-administer test—the Myers-Briggs. The test requires so little time that it can be administered in a survey research setting, and it is not obnoxious to respondents. The respondent indicates a preference between groups of words that are related to:

- Introversion
- Extraversion
- Sensing
- Intuition

- Thinking
- Feeling
- Judgment
- Perception

It can be very useful in a psychographic-based research setting. But, the interpretation of these dimensions requires the analyst to have a strong background in personality theory and clinical research. The task is not as difficult as it may seem since qualified people are available as consultants. The dimensions are useful for determining the types of people who are attracted to specific kinds of advertising or who like to participate in selected activities at destinations, or are useful generally in situations that require greater understanding of the psychology of travelers.

An excellent resource for still more general and special-purpose psychological tests is the current edition of the *Mental Measurements Yearbook*, edited by O.K. Buros.

THE COMMON DIMENSIONS OF PSYCHOGRAPHIC/PERSONALITY-RELATED TRAVEL RESEARCH

Unlike demographics, there are no standard psychographic categories or ways of defining people. Rather, the creative insight and inventiveness of the researcher develop the dimensions. Even if the questionnaire items contributing to the personality dimensions appear to be similar in two different survey instruments, the multivariate statistics involved may have been manipulated in somewhat different ways by the two researchers. Further, researchers may actually come up with fairly similar dimensions but may label them differently.

As it turns out, probably a limited number of psychographic/personality dimensions exist in travel research. These dimensions vary in clarity or may be recombined in various ways, but they cover about eight broad categories. These are listed here and, in each case, there typically is an opposite character type at the other end of the spectrum from the dimension.

- **Venturesomeness**—called by a variety of titles, primarily the type of individual who is more seeking and exploring. In terms of travel destinations, new products, or new marketing concepts, it is this individual who tends to be the first user.

- **Pleasure-seeking**—the type of person who desires a considerable amount of luxury and comfort in all aspects of travel (transportation carrier services, hotel services, entertainment and other activities, etc.).

- **Impulsivity**—the tendency to want to do something now. Very low on the ability to delay gratification, persons who measure high in this characteristic are more apt to live more for the moment and will be high spenders. Trip decisions are made quickly, at the last moment, and without much planning.

- **Self-confidence**—a characteristic growing out of some of the other variables, closely related to the willingness to do unique and very different things. Individuals who measure high in this characteristic typically select the unusual in tour destinations or activities at these destinations.

- **Planfulness**—an obvious reference to very systematic, planful characteristics in people. Individuals who measure high on this dimension not only think about and plan their trip well in advance, but will typically look more for bargains and prepackaged tour programs.

- **Masculinity**—sometimes called the traditional male role, defines the action-oriented man who seeks the outdoors (fishing, camping, hunting, field-and-stream pursuits) and engages in typical male-role activities around the home (working on cars, woodworking, and other crafts). This type of person is more likely to travel by car and take many things with him. Wives are often forced into going along with these interests, or they would take few vacations.

- **Intellectualism**—refers to that type of individual who not only possesses high brow interests (goes to plays, museums, and other cultural activities), but has a heavy orientation towards historical touring. Old cities, cultural events, and exploring the undiscovered antecedents of present-day societies are of prime interest to persons dominated by this characteristic.

- **People orientation**—a desire to get close to people through travel and to experience the many cultures of the world. The dimension includes a combination of sociability, lack of organization (frequently bordering on disorganization), unique venturesomeness, and some degree of impulsivity.

To summarize, dimensions and labels may look different than those described above, but they are likely to be reflective of many of these patterns.

THE QUESTION OF VALIDITY

Standardized tests commonly available through publishers have typically gone through a rigorous series of trials designed to measure their statistical reliability and validity. These measures of their quality and power are defined in the manuals that accompany each test.

The authors of these personality instruments have a luxury not available to the travel researcher. It may have required years of effort to develop the final standardized test instruments, but that amount of time and accompanying costs lie beyond the freedoms allowed most travel researchers, especially in today's slim-and-trim corporate environments. As a result, psychographic tests typically are devoid of research related to statistical reliability, and only the most cursory questions about statistical validity can be answered.

The ultimate dream in designing tests is to determine whether the instrument measures well on statistical tests of criterion validity. Job-performance tests are good examples of criterion validity since the instrument can take a sample of the behaviors required in a job situation (a typing test is a good measure of on-the-job performance for typists). Since personality is usually defined on the basis of a conceptual framework of a researcher, however, only a slight possibility exists to develop a measure of criterion validity. As a result, only two more indirect measures of validity seem feasible.

• Face validity—Do the items that measure each psychographic dimension appear to have some relationship to the dimension (i.e., on the "face of it," does it make sense)? When a researcher develops a questionnaire for a study, it may be necessary to accept the dimensions at the level of face validity since there is no way to know whether each item is predictive of the population it purports to measure.

• Construct validity—This concept refers to the idea that, when someone has developed a theory, it should be possible to predict, in advance, how different types of persons defined by the theory will answer questions related to their personality interests. Do travelers answer questions in the predicted directions? Correlational statistics define the interrelatedness of the items contributing to the different personality types. Construct validity is a well-accepted method for validating personality instruments, and it can and should be used in travel/leisure research.

CONCLUSION

The ultimate and most important question to ask after a study has been completed is whether the results have been put into practice. The task is to communicate their utility to persons who will have to implement the results—marketing executives, advertising directors, and creative types at ad agencies. At this point, by necessity, questions must be raised about the effectiveness of the researcher in communicating the findings to others and how willing the user is to learn everything possible about the new concept(s).

The big task is to ensure that the marketing department wants to follow through on the results. This can be best achieved by the researcher working closely with the end-user groups from start to finish: involving them in the formulation of the research, providing periodic progress reports, discussing problems as they arise, and working at selling the ideas after the project has been completed.

Psychographic research is not new, but it has become more sophisticated in recent years. Travel and leisure groups are attempting to become more adept at positioning their product and segmenting their markets to appeal to the right kinds of travelers. *National Geographic*, that great magazine with a long history of stimulating interest in travel and unique leisure pursuits, carried the tag line for many years after World War I (printed on each page of its advertising), "Mention the Geographic—it identifies you." The class and quality of the magazine, by implication, carry over to the person who reads it. That, too, is the message of much of today's travel advertising. If travelers mention where they have been, how they got there, or what they did while they were there, they have given others a mental picture of the kind of individual they are. They have presented a word picture of their own psychographic personality.

REFERENCES

Allport, Gordon W., Philip E. Vernon, and Gardner Lindzey (1960), *Study of Values*, 3rd ed., Boston, MA: Houghton-Mifflin.

Bernay, Elayn K. (1971), "Life Style Analysis as a Basis for Media Selection," in *Attitude Research Reaches New Heights*, C. King and D. Tigert, eds., 189–195, Chicago: American Marketing Association.

Buros, Oscar K. (1978), *The Eighth Mental Measurements Yearbook, Volume II*, High Park, NJ: The Gryphon Press.

California Psychological Inventory, Harrison G. Gough, Consulting Psychologists Press, Inc., 577 College Avenue, Palo Alto, California 94306.

Cattell, R.B. (1950), *Personality: A Systematic Theoretical and Factual Study*, New York: McGraw-Hill.

Cuch, A., and K. Kenniston (1960), "Yeasayers and Naysayers: Agreeing Response Set as a Personality Variable," *Journal of Abnormal Social Psychology*, 60 (March), 171–174.

Dahlstrom, Leon E. (1972), *An MMPI Handbook, Revised Edition: Volume I*, clinical interpretation, Minneapolis, MN: University of Minnesota Press.

Darden, William R. (1974), "Backward Profiling of Male Innovators," *Journal of Market Research* 11 (February), 79–85.

Darden, William R., and Fred D. Reynolds (1972), "Predicting Opinion Leadership for Men's Apparel Fashions," *Journal of Market Research* 9 (August), 324–328.

Edwards, A.L. (1967), *Edwards Personality Inventory Manual*, Chicago: Science Research Associates.

Freud, S. (1938), *The Basic Writings of Sigmund Freud*, A.A. Brill, ed., New York: Modern Library.

Isaac, Rene, "Memo to U.S. Sales Staff," *Reader's Digest*, July 2, 1970. Information provided to author by Anthony L. Antin, Vice-President, *Reader's Digest*.

Jung, C.G. (1968), *The Archetypes and the Collective Unconscious*, 2nd ed., translated by R.F.C. Hull, Bollingen Series XX, Princeton, NJ: Princeton University Press.

Kassarjian, Harold H. (1971), "Personality and Consumer Behavior: A Review," *Journal of Market Research* 8 (November), 409–418.

Martineau, Pierre (1957), *Motivation in Advertising*, New York: McGraw-Hill.

Minnesota Multiphasic Personality Inventory, Starke R. Hathaway and J. Charnley McKinley, Psychological Corporation, 304 East 45th Street, New York, New York 10017.

Murray, Henry A. (1938), *Explorations in Personality*, New York: John Wiley & Sons., Inc.

Myers-Briggs Type Indicator, Isabel B. Myers and Katharine C.

Briggs, Educational Testing Service, Suite 100, 17 Executive Park Drive, Atlanta, Georgia 30329.

Myers, Isabel B. (1962), *Manual for the Myers-Briggs Type Indicator*, Princeton, NJ: Educational Testing Service.

Nickerson, Norma Polovitz, and Gary D. Ellis (1991), "Traveler Types And Activation Theory: A Comparison Of Two Models," *Journal of Travel Research* XXIX, (3), 26–31.

Plog, Stanley C. (1991), *Leisure Travel: Making it a Growth Market...Again!*, New York: John Wiley & Sons, Inc.

Plummer, Joseph T. (1971), "Life Style and Advertising: Case Studies," in *American Marketing Association Proceedings*, 290–295.

Plummer, Joseph T. (1975), "Psychographics: What Can Go Right?" in *1974 Combined Proceedings*, R. Curhan, ed., 41–44, Chicago: American Marketing Association.

Riesman, David, Revel Denney and Nathan Glazer (1950), *The Lonely Crowd*, New Haven, CT: Yale University Press.

Rokeach, M. (1968), *Beliefs, Attitudes, and Values*, San Francisco: Jossey-Bass.

Rotter, J. (1966), "Generalized Expectancies for Internal versus External Control of Reinforcement," *Psychological Monographs* 80 (1, Whole No. 609).

Tarlow, Peter E., and Mitchell J. Muehsam (1992), "Turning the Theory of the Plog Model into Application: Some Initial Thoughts on Attracting International Tourists," paper presented at the annual meeting of the Travel & Tourism Research Association, Minneapolis, June 1992.

Tigert, Douglas J. (1974), "Life Style Analysis as a Basis for Media Selection," in *Life Style and Psychographics*, W.D. Wells, ed., 173–201, Chicago: American Marketing Association.

Wells, William D. (1966), "General Personality Tests and Consumer Behavior," in *On Knowing the Consumer*, J.W. Newman, ed., 187–189, New York: John Wiley & Sons, Inc.

Wells, William D. (1974), *Life Style and Psychographics*, Chicago: American Marketing Association.

Wells, William D. (1975), "Psychographics: A Critical Review," *Journal of Market Research* 12 (May), 196–312.

Wells, William D., and Arthur D. Beard (1973), "Personality and Consumer Behavior," in *Consumer Behavior: Theoretical Sources*, S. Ward and T.S. Robertson, eds., 141–199, Englewood Cliffs, NJ: Prentice-Hall.

Yankelovich, Daniel (1964), "New Criteria for Market Segmentation," *Harvard Business Review* (March/April), 83–90.

Ziff, Ruth (1971), "Psychographics for Market Segmentation," *Journal of Advertising Research*, 11(2), 3–9.

19

The Political Dimensions of Tourism

LINDA K. RICHTER
Associate Professor
Department of Political Science
Kansas State University
Manhattan, Kansas

*T*his chapter examines some of the major political issues affecting decision making on tourism at the international, national, and subnational levels. Special attention is given to those issues affecting developing nations. Because political science has neglected the study of tourism, the chapter also identifies where more research is particularly needed.

The numerous facets of political and legal decision making about tourism constitute an enormous topic. Directed as they are at so many nations and other political units, any discussion requires some conceptual simplification. The focus in this article is on the political aspects of tourism from the vantage points of key decision makers at the local, national, and international levels. The goal is to enable those in the industry and within policy-making circles to encourage the type of tourism likely to be politically and economically successful for both the entrepreneur and the host environment. This analysis sees tourism as *potentially* compatible with public and private interests (Richter 1991a, 1991b). To make that potentiality real and not just myth, both the industry specialists and those involved in broader questions of community, regional, and national planning have to appreciate the political and legal constraints upon one another.

The chapter is divided into three parts addressing the political issues as seen from (1) the *host country*, (2) the *country of tourist origin*, and (3) the *international arena*. Because of the immense variety that exists in political conditions globally, this chapter attempts only to suggest avenues of inquiry and to make recommendations for the reader's further research.

HOST COUNTRY PERSPECTIVES

Decision makers can expect governmental interest in tourism to be most uneven globally. Governmental involvement appears, however, to be a function of general patterns of industrial and commercial development (Young 1977; DeKadt 1979:32-33). If the government has been generally content to leave business development to the private sector, as in the United States, interest in the political and legal implications of tourism is likely to follow the industry's lead. This has led, in the United States and elsewhere, to rather haphazard and often conflicting regulations and direction. The efforts needed to secure a national tourism policy for the United States reflect both government's and industry's belated recognition of the confusion that has evolved (National Tourism Policy Study 1978; Creal 1980). Since the 1981 National Tourism Policy Act, the United States has enjoyed a dramatic surge in international tourism revenues to $51 billion in 1990, a balance-of-trade surplus in travel trade since 1989, and an unparalleled level of presidential interest and support under President Bush (Waters 1991:8). In 1991, the President had not only a personal meeting with some 200 leaders of the tourism industry, but also made the first presidential video inviting international visitors to the United States. State- and city-government budgets for tourism also soared in the 1980s, but the United States still has more control and direction of tourism policy in the private sector than is characteristic of most countries.

If the government is committed to elaborate national and regional planning, as in India and Mexico, then tourism planning will be part of that strategy (Richter and Richter 1985). For those governments centrally directed and where private ownership is severely restricted, such as in socialist states like Cuba and China, tourism will be under state control and presumably reflect national priorities in its pace and shape of development. Extensive political interest and regulation may also be dictated by the sudden emergence of the tourism industry as central to the nation's economy, as in Egypt, or as the result of particular political needs unrelated to tourism per se, as in the Philippines under President Marcos or in Spain under Fascism (Richter 1980a, 1989a; Pi-Sunyer 1979).

For those interested in the encouragement of national policies favoring travel and tourism generally, it is critical to recognize those *political* advantages and disadvantages national government decision makers need to weigh.

POLITICAL USES OF TOURISM

PRESTIGE AND POLITICAL LEGITIMACY

Tourist arrivals are a barometer not only of a nation's currency relative to other currencies but also of the reputation of the nation. Since tourism is critically dependent on law and order, tourist arrivals become a commentary on the political stability of the society and its desirability as a destination (Richter and Waugh 1991). Tourism to South Africa was, until recently, depressed by the regime's unpopular apartheid policies, while tourism to Haiti and Peru has been crippled by those nations' internal violence.

Specific propaganda objectives underlie many tourism programs in capitalist and communist nations alike. Cuba and China have historically designed tourism programs to attract clienteles targeted more for their influence than their pocketbooks (Schuchat 1979; Richter 1983b). Other tours cater to educators and students at bargain rates while admitting only those foreign individual travelers willing to pay handsomely for the trip.

Tourism development can be politically useful in countries attempting to overcome a vague or indifferent national image, to change political directions, or to overcome bad press internationally. Pakistan is a country that seized upon tourism as a priority vehicle in 1972 for all three of these reasons (Richter 1984a). The Philippines also sought to use tourism to legitimize martial law with specific promotions designed to defuse criticism of martial law, as with the slogan "Where Asia Wears A Smile" (Richter 1982).

Israel is a particular example of such links between foreign policy and tourism. Israel has garnered significant support for its policies toward its Arab neighbors by courting fundamentalist Christian tourism. Those on biblical tours of Israel are often receptive to excursions that stress identification of the modern secular Israel with the Israel of the *Bible*. So important is the interpretation of Israel to visitors that former Defense Secretary Moshe Dayan was quoted as saying, "It is easier for Arabs to become air force pilots than to become tourist guides," (Halsell 1986:126).

AID

Though one might quarrel with specific tourism decisions, the evidence suggests that rapid expansion of tourism under priority incentives has paid off as a *political* strategy in most developing nations. Countries with active tourism programs seem to attract more foreign aid, for example, than comparable countries without such programs (Young 1973). This relationship probably reflects the fact that most international tourists are from the major aid-giving nations.

Tourism destinations may also benefit disproportionately from international investment, but, at this juncture, existing research does not establish a distinct causal link between amount of tourism and amount of foreign investment. A probable explanation is that investment and aid are both a result of the political stability and government receptivity to foreign influence that also permit tourism to flourish. Such a political climate also has encouraged international lending institutions, like the World Bank and UNESCO, to become involved in tourism support in the past.

There is, however, increasing evidence of a waning of enthusiasm for such projects in international lending institutions. The World Bank, which provided nearly a half billion dollars in tourism-development aid over the 1970s, decided in 1979 to disband its tourism department. The Bank's affiliates, such as the International Finance Corporation, however, have continued to invest in tourism (Sturken 1980).

IMMIGRATION

Tourism has a largely unnoticed political potential for spurring immigration from other countries. Obviously, the tourist industry prefers the regular visitor, but it is a powerful inducement to some nations contemplating expanded tourism programs to think in terms of permanently enlarged tax bases from affluent and/or young skilled immigrants. Israel during the 1970s was particularly adept in utilizing tourism planning for the promotion of immigration (Stock 1977). Mexico and Costa Rica are two other countries that have benefited from an influx of resident aliens who came originally as tourists but have opted to retire there.

It should be noted, however, that immigration as a result of tourism is not an unmixed blessing. Often such individuals tend to be more affluent than the rest of the population. This may give them a disproportionate political and economic influence, which it is well for decision makers to anticipate.

Fear of impoverished individuals using tourism as a pretext for immigration has also encouraged countries like the United States to maintain stringent tourist visa requirements and to be especially concerned about the rising number of passport and visa forgeries (*Wichita Eagle*, March 8, 1992). Some of these concerns arise from stereotypes and are dysfunctional: fears of Indian poor, for example, immigrating to the United States keeps draconian visiting regulations in place; however, India's vast 800 million population has at least twice as many affluent potential visitors as the heavily promoted Japanese market!

POLITICAL AND CULTURAL SUPPORT

Host country governments appreciate tourism as a policy offering broad political discretion. Conditions for admission, duration of visit, rates of currency exchange, degree of freedom to travel internally, and, often, the conditions of accreditation for lodgings, restaurants, and tour and travel agencies are under the jurisdiction of some governmental level.

Not only can the government manipulate the entry, movement, and facilities of tourists, but even the most laissez-faire governments have great leverage in influencing the selective development of tourism. At one governmental level or another, they can determine the ground rules for most of the supportive infrastructure for the industry, such as airports, roads, port facilities, water and electric power, and often the timing and terms under which hotels, casinos, and transport are developed.

Government tourism policy represents a selective opportunity to assist depressed or politically troubled areas or areas of highest political priority (Richter 1980a; Chow 1980; Clarke 1981). Tourism may also help weakly integrated areas identify their interests more strongly with the national government.

The successful entrepreneur must be ready to demonstrate to those in government who make such decisions how the industry can assist the government in rewarding political priority areas (and individuals) through incentives for industry development with or without local involvement.

Getting information about the political regulations governing tourism usually varies in difficulty in inverse proportion to the ease with which private entrepreneurs can become involved. It may be easier, for example, to determine which level, department, office, and individuals make decisions about the tourism sector in a centrally controlled system, but it may require higher levels of executive commitment to get the original access or approval for tourism projects.

Even in countries where tourism is primarily privately owned and promoted, tourism can be profoundly influenced by government policy. Just as the industry can be affected by government policy, a well-developed tourism industry can be a powerful political ally to a government intent on expanding imports, developing transportation and communication linkages, attracting new businesses and cultural attractions, or launching a major campaign for crime control. The foreign exchange and domestic revenues from tourism will be important, but if it is an organized sector of the economy, its political clout may also add needed assistance to the government's policy proposals.

Governments have discovered that tourism may encourage secular and cosmopolitan attitudes while paradoxically providing a support base for the restoration and preservation of the most unique features of the traditional culture (Richter 1984b; McKean 1978; Gamper 1981; Swain 1978). Tourism may also help to make feasible expensive commitments to beautification, to pollution control, and to the arts (Stock 1977).

For many countries tourism represents an entree to international politics and regional cooperation. Southeast Asian nations, through the Association of South-East Asian nations (ASEAN), and countries like Switzerland, Iceland, Spain, and Bermuda are only a few of the many nations that have found it possible to build political strength from a tourism base.

POLITICAL PROBLEMS OF TOURISM

The political disadvantages of tourism are becoming increasingly salient to governments and travel specialists alike. The recognition of certain political problems is an entirely healthy development, however, entirely consistent with the long-range interests of the industry. Fortunately, with some care, many of the political liabilities can be anticipated and the problems correspondingly reduced.

Much of what follows may seem common sense to those interested in tourism. Yet it is seldom as obvious in concrete development proposals of the industry. Tourism, ironically, can do more damage to the industry and the societies in which it flourishes through myopic and thoughtless expansion than by lackluster and sluggish development (Richter 1980b; OECD 1980; Holden 1984a).

TOO NARROW A BASE

One of the foremost political disadvantages can result from an industry dependent on too narrow an economic clientele or too few countries of origin. Affluent tourists, for example, are notoriously fickle, and some of the more exotic and remote resorts are ill-suited to a switch to mass tourism. Countries may also discover belatedly that promotion efforts and geography may have resulted in a tourist industry perilously dependent on very few nations. Frequently Country A may discover, to its chagrin, that over one-third of its tourists are from Country B. This does not imply that the dependence is reciprocal. Country B's tourists may have a huge impact on Country A, yet outward tourist flow to Country A may represent only a tiny fraction of its outward-bound travelers. Asymmetrical vulnerability and commitment are common to tourism (Hoivik and Heiberg 1980).

Nations like Sri Lanka, Thailand, and the Philippines have experienced dramatic slumps in tourism as a result of shifts in the advice tourist-generating countries give to their citizens going abroad. The political frictions such situations engender between host country and country of origin have their own multiplier effect within the host country. The local travel industry feels abandoned by the government, and the government feels betrayed by those who sold tourism incentives, tax holidays, and major government involvement with the argument that tourism was a "sure thing." Diversification of facilities, attractions, and clienteles, which could reduce such political problems, is frequently mentioned but often is neglected in the actual planning and implementation stages (Richter 1989b).

LAND-USE CONTROVERSIES

Of course, success is not without its share of political headaches even when diversification is assured. Land-use disputes may be severe, especially in nations where land is scarce and land pressure from tourism is great. Typically, islands have the most intense land-use struggles. In many instances, the disputes pitting industry, conservationists, the travel industry, and residential interests against each other can be anticipated in detailed planning. Often, as a result, tourist design can mitigate power, water, pollution, and multiple-use disputes (Fukenaga 1976; Loukissas 1978). In Cancun, as in so many of the resort sites, the problems of land use are exacerbated by the type of development foisted on the arid environment. The demand for golf courses has led to over a dozen being constructed in this resort area from 1989 to 1991. These courses, with their need for irrigation and massive amounts of chemicals, threaten to cripple other sectors that need water and to pollute the ocean with the resulting chemical runoff.

INFLATION

Where tourism has increased rapidly and massively, there may be political fallout from the resultant inflation, including spiraling land prices; increased transport, housing, and food costs; and the boom-bust cycle of the construction industry. Case studies of the Philippines and the Seychelles illustrate the social and political havoc that can ensue (Richter 1980a; Franda 1979; Wilson 1979). By contrast, countries or regions developing gradually are able to digest tourism growth much more easily.

URBANIZATION

Tourism can also result in the problem of too much migration to some regions, as in parts of Hawaii, California, and the Pacific Northwest of the United States. In other societies, it is the movement of people from the countryside into the cities for tourism jobs that creates political problems. Such migration to the cities may offset the gains made in using tourism for regional development.

POOR ADVICE

It may appear obvious that the government and the industry consider some of the issues discussed in the preceding sections, but, unfortunately, many such political problems are never openly considered at all. The industry has erred in emphasizing marketing almost exclusively. Just as the industry may betray the tourist through misleading promotional materials, the industry frequently underestimates the problems that must be considered in its eagerness to sell potential destinations on the advantages of tourism development.

Many governments, especially in developing nations, either by ignorance, neglect, or inexperience, lack planning, personnel, or data independent of marketing biases (Richter 1985a, 1985b). Relatively few governments have staff or skills to monitor more than very crude tourism indexes like arrivals, bed-nights, surveys of tourist expenditures, and gross receipts (Richter 1983b). Rarely do governments, developed or developing, attempt *net* receipt figures, social impact studies, or systematic independent appraisals of market needs (Richter 1984b, 1985b). Surprisingly, the host country almost never attempts to assess the expectations or reactions of its own citizens (Hoivik and Heiberg 1980) to what have been described as "the most successful agents of change (short of political or military agents) active in the contemporary world" (Nunez 1978). Much more research attention needs to be directed here (Belisle and Hoy 1980).

POLITICAL OPPOSITION

It should not be surprising, then, that increasingly both local and national governments are discovering that their high-profile tourist industry, chosen for its economic and political promise some years earlier, has become a rallying point for the politically disgruntled in societies as varied as Hawaii, Thailand, and India.

Sometimes the tourist industry is controversial, as in the Philippines under President Marcos (1965-1986), because much of the tourism there was owned or controlled by those close to the discredited ruling elite. This caused resentment about the excessive attention given to tourism. In the Philippines, a rash of arson and bombing attacks was directed at the hotels. Efforts were made to embarrass the regime and disrupt tourism by threats and bombs directed at international tourism conclaves. Though the Philippine government moved swiftly to contain the political damage by offering travel agents and those affected free hospitality and travel, the political and economic costs were immense (Richter 1982, 1989a). Sniping incidents and robberies in Hawaii have been directed at tourists, who in some minds symbolize the ravishing of the islands with unsightly overconstruction and relentless inflation (Kent 1983; Governor's Conference on Tourism 1984).

Political opposition may also be a reaction to inadequate consideration of the type of tourism introduced and the prevailing cultural mores (O'Grady 1981; Powers 1986; Kincaid 1989; Holden 1984b). Some nations, like Singapore, are modern, strong, and geographically compact enough to restrict entry to the conventional tourist that the government wants. However, in other countries, traditional religious values are strong, whether Muslim, Christian, or Hindu, and the presence of leisured, often scantily clad tourists is a persistent affront to local sensibilities. That such cultural irritations have political import is abundantly clear in the political resurgence of conservative Christian and militant Islamic movements (Matthews 1978).

Entrepreneurs in Iran, Pakistan, and elsewhere have noted too late the change in political climate and, as a consequence, have found themselves without any leverage when the political order changes. In this way, enormous investments by government and by local and international bodies have been wasted, and prejudice against future tourism has been fanned (Richter 1983a; Laurie).

Failure to anticipate potential negative consequences of certain types of tourism in given societies leaves the government and the entire industry vulnerable to sabotage, and tourism is astoundingly easy to destroy. Having so many other alternative destinations, neither the tourist nor the marketing agent is likely to plot a trip anywhere that has a hint of insecurity (Richter and Waugh 1991).

Tourism is also vulnerable to the general political climate within the country and in nearby destinations. Violence in Sri Lanka in 1984 and 1985 and in Jamaica in 1976 and

1977, for example, crippled tourism despite the calm in tourist areas. Similarly, political upheavals in Uganda took a heavy toll on tourist trade in neighboring Kenya in the early 1970s and again in 1985.

Sabotage of tourism efforts may also take place from outside the host country. Disputes between important marketing agents and the government or local industry personnel may leave the host government with little leverage over the fate of international tourism to its own country (Turner 1976; Richter 1983a and 1989a).

SUBNATIONAL POLITICAL DIMENSIONS OF TOURISM

It is extremely difficult to generalize about research at the subnational level. Most have concentrated on the usefulness of or problems associated with using tourism as a tool for regional or local development. The perspective in such instances has been national. Studies of tourism from a regional or local perspective have been primarily case studies and have been investigated primarily by anthropologists and sociologists, rather than by political scientists (Belisle and Hoy 1980; Papson 1981). As a consequence, the issues raised have not usually focused on such political issues as power, control, legitimacy, support, and authority. Attempts to investigate the public-sector dimensions of subnational tourism in the United States suggest that this is an important level of analysis for future research (Richter 1984b, 1985a; Matthews and Richter 1991).

The following categories are by no means exhaustive but do suggest some political categories in which research has been and needs to be done to provide those in tourism management with some guidance at this level.

LEVEL AND SOURCE OF POLITICAL SUPPORT

Tourism, while ranking as one of the top three sources of revenue in 37 of the 50 states of the United States, is still erratically funded and almost whimsically developed in most parts of the country. State governments heavily dependent on tourism may consider tourism, as Hawaii did until 1981, simply as something to be controlled rather than aggressively fostered. However, *all* states are taking tourism promotion more and more seriously. States with a relatively small number of natural attractions may need to spend disproportionately more for tourism development and may have initially fewer political choices about the nature and type of tourism to attract. States like Alaska with enormous tourism potential, but far from major markets, may have to spend more than states like Kansas to attract fewer but still critical dollars (Waters 1991).

Political leadership is also an uncertain variable at the local level. Gubernatorial and mayoral candidates differ widely in their commitment to tourism, and they can be decisive in shaping responses to the industry (Richter 1984b; 1985e). Two outstanding studies highlight the importance of local elites: *White Town Drowsing* examines the efforts of

Hannibal, Missouri, to celebrate the 150th anniversary of Mark Twain's birth (Powers 1986); *A Sunny Place for Shady People* dissects the decision making that so influenced tourism policy for the Gold Coast of Australia (Jones 1986).

PACE AND CONTROL OF TOURISM DEVELOPMENT

The pace of development and the nature of its control is another dimension of the local political support for tourism. Little research has been conducted on these issues. What has been done suggests that tourism's development and impact have cyclical tendencies that cause the least disruption to community values when political power is dispersed fairly evenly (Peck and Lepie 1978).

Case studies of the 1982 World's Fair in Knoxville, Tennessee, and Asiad'82 in New Delhi confirm that, as with world fairs in general, such fairs characteristically represent a narrow elite initiative that can create severe political problems. These occur because of the speed with which a tourism infrastructure is developed, its typically short duration, and the havoc it entails for those caught in the housing squeeze and the inflationary spiral such sudden and massive development creates (Lin and Patnaik 1982). Other research suggests that the smaller and less diversified the city, the greater are the political traumas likely to be (Loukissas 1978).

TOURISM PROMOTION AND PLANNING

Regional multistate and intrastate organizations may also constitute political allies for the tourism industry. In some areas, these are wholly sponsored by the private sector, while in others, economic development agencies of several states develop regional promotions together. Such collaboration often acts as a spur for states to compete even as they cooperate for the tourist dollar.

Research on regional and multistate tourism development is scant indeed and is, as noted earlier, focused on the impact of tourism on the *region* rather than on the impact of regional politics and planning on *tourism*.

How important the latter can be has been demonstrated in the United States by the National Organization of Women and its boycott of states that did not ratify the Equal Rights Amendment. A significant percentage of the more than 200 professional organizations that supported the ERA refused to hold national or regional meetings in such major convention centers as Chicago, St. Louis, Kansas City, and Miami from 1977 to 1982. Losses of convention revenue were in the hundreds of millions of dollars to these tourism centers, even as other regions enjoyed expanded convention bookings as a result. Since this stratagem has been upheld by the courts as not being an illegal restraint of trade, the way is open for potential tourism revenue to be used as a political ploy. Recently, Arizona suffered major conference tourism consequences from its refusal to adopt the Martin Luther King's birthday as a state holiday. Arizona lost millions in tourism revenues as a result of a boycott by convention planners until the decision was reversed.

CHARACTERISTIC POLITICAL ISSUES INVOLVING TOURISM

Many political conflicts are generated over the type of tourism. Several states, like Kansas, have debated whether gambling, in the form of casino, state lotteries, racing, and so on, would attract enough tourism revenue to offset the potential increase in crime or social problems. Other states seeking to develop convention centers have had heated political controversies over liquor-by-the-drink. Hotel conference centers and airport taxes have been other political issues (Governor's Conference on Tourism 1984).

In other communities, the political tension has not been over how to develop or what type of tourism market should be targeted, but over whether tourism represents an industry compatible with certain rural or traditional life-styles. Often, the very hospitality of a community is perceived as threatened by tourism, the hospitality industry. The U.S. Travel and Tourism Administration had sought to address these issues by holding a series of regional rural-tourism conferences focused on responsible promotion of tourism and training of community leaders in tourism development.

Subnational research on the integration of tourism is critically needed. Some of the best available is focused on Hawaii, where traditional rural values have collided abruptly in the last generation with mass tourism (Fukenaga 1976; Chow 1980; Kent 1983). These studies document the relatively modest trickle down effect of either political or economic power—a chronic problem area sure to make tourism increasingly controversial in communities throughout the world. Studies on this topic focus on such settings as Catalan, Spain, coastal development in France, and communities within Canadian provinces (Clarke 1981, Papson 1981).

India, Canada, and other countries with fairly decentralized tourism programs have found that the advantages of federalism allow for flexible and varied responses to tourism locally, but the diffusion of political debate is certainly no political panacea, as U.S. tourism illustrates.

HOST-COUNTRY PERSPECTIVES OF THE DEVELOPING NATIONS

"International tourism is simultaneously the most promising, complex, and understudied industry impinging on the Third World" (Turner 1976:253). The 120-plus developing nations in the world experience most of the advantages and disadvantages of tourism development common throughout the world, but they also experience some political aspects that are peculiar to their underdevelopment.

Tourism receipts have been increasing rapidly among many nations in excess of other development sectors and at a rate that far exceeds tourism growth in developed countries. Such advances throughout the 1970s and 1980s, in the face of soaring fuel costs and economic uncertainties globally, made tourism look unusually attractive. Asia is a case in point. There, tourism receipts have grown 13 percent at a time when overall growth in the area has been 2 percent (Dannhorn 1979). But the picture may be misleading. Political conditions in Kampuchea, Uganda, Kenya, Barbados, Peru, Myanmar, Jamaica, Haiti, Iran, Afghanistan, Grenada, and Sri Lanka, for example, threatened tourism in those developing societies. Elsewhere, other developing nations most enamored with tourism had experienced it in mass form for less than a decade.

PROBLEMS OF PERCEIVED NEOCOLONIALISM

Neocolonial appearances may enrage nationalists and threaten a tourism backlash (Nash 1978). There may be, for example, a genuine sense of "relative deprivation" when nationals see leisured tourists spend in hours what may take them several months to earn (Blanton 1981). Moreover, such a "demonstration effect" by affluent tourists may spur political anger or unrealistic consumption demands that are costly in the very foreign exchange that tourism is supposed to generate (Karunatilake 1978; O'Grady 1981; Holden 1984a, 1984b).

Aggravating tensions are the very real possibilities that, in most parts of the developing world, the most frequent tourists will be from a new nation's former colonial master (Hoivik and Heiberg 1980). The superior wealth and power of the tourists relative to the citizens who will service their needs are made still more politically sensitive by the racial dimension. Most tourists are white; most residents of the developing world are not.

Neoimperialistic economic ownership and/or control of tourism facilities may also raise political issues for the government and its foreign investors (Center on Transnational Corporations 1982). In some small countries, the foreign tourism establishment may be the most powerful political force in the country. In Gambia, for example, there was no economic or political counterweight to the foreign-controlled hotels (Harrell-Bond 1978). Before the Seychelles even recognized the political dimensions of tourism, much of the land was in foreign hands (Franda 1979).

The degree of dependence a nation may experience has been suggested before in terms of the general importance of conservative political stability and accord with international marketing agents. All nations face such constraints, but the developing nation that has opted for tourism development is especially vulnerable. Such countries lack clout when, by intent or indifference, decisions are taken internationally that affect them. Consider, for example, Pan Am's decision to cut service to Antigua shortly before the peak winter season of 1975-1976. Subsequent airline bankruptcies in the United States in the 1980s and 1990s have illustrated the dependence of both developed and developing nations on multinational industries. Decisions by large tour operators to cancel large conventions or change itineraries may have similarly disastrous consequences for weak, undiversified economies. The collapse of Britain's largest tour operator, Court Line, for example, led to the closure in 1974 of 180 hotels in Majorca alone (Turner 1976).

HIRING

Colonial and/or racist patterns may also seem apparent in the filling of top industry positions with foreigners, while recruiting local people for primarily menial jobs. In some countries, particularly for international standard tourism, such decisions may be inevitable; in others, it is clearly the result of habit and convenience (Blanton 1981). Though the political elite may not pressure entrepreneurs on this issue of local hiring, it is clearly in the long-term political interest of government and investor to integrate local personnel at the top levels as soon as possible. By doing so, opposition to the industry can be defused on this issue. One apparently successful approach to this issue has been in Cyprus, where the legislature mandated the employment of local personnel in the tourist industry (DeKadt 1979).

Another response is also possible: bypass international standard tourism for more modest industry development. The *net* economic and political gains, not to mention the reduced likelihood of social and cultural problems, may easily offset the gains from more lavish approaches. Careful studies of Indonesian tourism development challenge the profitability of international standard tourism on several socioeconomic dimensions (Rodenburg 1980; Noronha 1979) and substantiate the results of other critics of international tourism elsewhere (Turner 1976; Matthews 1978; Wood 1984).

The bed-and-breakfast phenomenon in the United States in the 1980s; farm and ranch tourism in Australia, New Zealand, and France; and the new mandate of the U.S. Travel and Tourism Administration (USTTA) to promote rural tourism, all promote a type of tourism long on friendliness, hospitality, and in most cases, informality. Such tourism builds on local people, products, and services, which allows greater control of tourism and more local employment opportunities.

INTEGRATED OR ENCLAVE TOURISM

Though tourism is rarely a policy assumed under duress, this does not mean it is always chosen freely. For some nations, for example, Nepal or Fiji, the decision to permit tourism was less a result of enthusiasm for the industry than the absence of other more attractive development options. In such countries, as well as others, where local traditions are both an attraction for tourists and a potential basis for misunderstanding and where tourist dollars are needed desperately but their impact on society feared, the government decision makers must make some particularly important political decisions. Through failure to target desirable clienteles specifically, the government can lose control over a powerful social phenomenon and greatly reduce the industry's ability to contribute to the society.

Ideally, the government either (1) should insist that whatever elements are promoting the country design their promotions to attract clientele unlikely to be intrusive (the integrated option) or (2) should stipulate that facilities for tourists be well removed from the general population (the enclave option). Either decision has important political consequences. The integrated option generally means a very gradual development of tourism paced to the overall development of the country, where tourism's relationship to the society evolves with increased interaction. Particularly well suited may be religious or cultural tourism, where either the visitors share the nation's religious traditions or the visiting groups are small and relatively unobtrusive. They may be affluent, but their motivations for travel are more cultural than comfort oriented.

The enclave option, as found in the numerous "Club Med" resorts or in the large-scale developments in Tanzania, Indonesia, and the Maldives, reduces the social impact of tourism and its political consequences, but greatly restricts the diffusion of industry profits. Moreover, the elaborate infrastructure created for such developments can be used only by the tourists and actually reduces the amount of capital available for public facilities and transport (Enloe 1975; Richter and Richter 1985).

Despite the desirability of local participation in tourism and the advantage of gradual expansion of the industry with maximum diffusion, some governments may lack the luxury of options on this issue. Where major infrastructure like a new airport is required, "only rapid and large-scale development will earn a reasonable rate of return on the airport. Rather than choosing between slower and faster or dispersed and concentrated tourism, the choice may have to be between tourism and no tourism" (DeKadt 1979:27). Even in developed countries, communities reel under the impact of rash development following airport facilities for jumbo jets. Cairns, Australia, became a gateway to the Great Barrier Reef during the 1980s, and the transformation has been socially and ecologically troubling (Personal Interviews, February and March, 1987).

THE COUNTRY OF ORIGIN

POLITICAL ADVANTAGES OF OUTBOUND TRAVEL

Though countries prefer to keep their wealth at home, there are numerous advantages to national policies that permit orderly travel abroad and that do so without unduly restricting destinations.

Public Relations

The propaganda advantages are perhaps the clearest benefit that comes from nationals going abroad. This was articulated most forcefully in the 1984 slogan of the U.S. National Tourism Week, "Travel: The Perfect Freedom." It is difficult to argue the desirability of one's political system while curtailing the exit of citizens. Freedom of travel was, in fact, one of the most revealing controversies during the negotiation of the Helsinki Accords in 1975. The former Soviet Union was most reluctant to agree to such a provision and interpreted it narrowly. More common than outright bans on foreign travel are the stipulations that travelers take out only limited amounts of currency for foreign exchange.

The United States restricts somewhat the travel abroad of resident aliens seeking naturalization and prohibits citizens from going to specific countries. The United States, like many other countries, expands and contracts permission to travel to certain countries as a signal of normalization or worsening of political relations. In general, however, countries permit as much travel as they believe to be politically and economically feasible because of the negative connotation of restrictions.

Tourists abroad may have a positive demonstration effect. Their presence and behavior reflect their country's prosperity, culture, and values. The increase, for example, in Japanese tourism in the 1980s parallels the economic strength of the country. As a consequence, the travel industry as a whole has adjusted to the needs and tastes of this important clientele group.

In catering to the desires of powerful tourism clienteles, their home countries may benefit from expanded trade designed to import abroad products familiar to major tourist groups. Moreover, Country A's businesses may be more welcome in Country B if there is a flourishing tourist trade from A to B.

International Cooperation

Tourism is also an arena for regional and international cooperation, which may facilitate constructive exchanges on other thornier issues. Normalization of travel is often a very early issue in the repair of political relationships, and it can also be a base for multilateral efforts, as the ASEAN and other regional political associations have demonstrated. Collaboration on environmental problems and tourism development have been two policy areas on which Western and Eastern Europe have worked since 1989.

DISADVANTAGES OF OUTBOUND TRAVEL

There are any number of political problems associated with outbound international travel, but three of these illustrate the political constraints on decision makers: (1) currency flight, (2) political opposition attacks, and (3) citizens in trouble abroad.

Currency flight is a major disadvantage of outbound tourism. Strict customs regulations, limits on currency taken out of the country, and a requirement that the national carrier be used may help, but effective controls require more repression than most governments want to enforce. While currency flight is, at root, an economic issue, the decision of whether or how to confront it is political in nature.

Societies that have the most lenient travel policies will occasionally find that dissidents have been able to leave the country posing as tourists only to harass the government from some sanctuary abroad. However, there appears to be an inverse relationship between government policies allowing for easy exit and their abuse by critics.

A more serious problem is the danger that tourists will get involved in incidents abroad that may embarrass their own country (drug traffic, arms sales, prostitution) or that may endanger their lives, as in the kidnapping of Japanese tourists in the southern Philippines in the mid-1970s or the sporadic violence since then that has occurred in such destinations as Peru, Kenya, Israel, and Tibet.

Political instability may also threaten the lives of citizens abroad, or simple fraud in the sale of charters may provoke demands for government action on behalf of its stranded travelers; yet consulates have limited authority and funds to help nationals overseas.

WHAT TO DO: A MINI-MAX STRATEGY

From the home country's perspective, several steps are important for minimizing the political risks and maximizing the political advantages of nationals touring abroad.

It is important for governments to monitor political developments in tourist-belt areas and to encourage travel agencies and airlines to have tour leaders or individual travelers check with their embassies if local conditions are unsettled. Japan has always been very zealous about the safety of its tourists abroad, and, since the late 1980s, the United States routinely has had 30 to 40 country warnings of varying severity out at any given time. The United States also has a State Department hotline to alert citizens to dangers beyond the border!

Such actions are sometimes resented by the destination country as alarmist, by some governments as politically motivated (as Kenya, for example, which is given a more negative advisory than Mexico where there is much more violence against American tourists), and by some citizens as inadequate (as in the failure to warn passengers about threats to bomb the Pan Am plane that was destroyed over Lockerbie, Scotland). Travel agencies are often reluctant to say anything that might discourage travelers; but it is shortsighted for the industry to behave irresponsibly in this regard.

Tourists should also be informed of countries on their itinerary where their reading material may be confiscated or their customs check prolonged by their nationality or dress: *Playboy* and other "girlie" magazines are contraband in many, particularly non-Western, countries. Bibles, critical literary works, and even several pairs of jeans may be suspect in China. Stiff sentences under grim conditions are the norm in many countries for individuals found with even personal quantities of illegal drugs. Travelers in general should be urged to be especially careful if venturing to countries without consular treaties with their home country.

Female travelers should be advised that the Muslim nations, particularly in the Middle East and North Africa, have become increasingly conservative about dress, and there are many countries where local custom does not permit unescorted women access to points of historical, religious, or touristic interest. Both sexes should be aware that severe punishment is likely for those indulging in extramarital relations. Briefings and orientation sessions common to student tours may also be desirable in some form for charter groups, convention travelers, and standard business and government travelers (Holden 1984a).

The country of origin's best approach to reducing the negative political impact of external travel is to launch and encourage domestic tourism appropriate to the level and pattern of discretionary spending of the society. A developed country may offer a wide variety of facilities, while a developing country may prefer to focus on hotels or low-cost accommodations near religious shrines as a means of providing for economy mass travel. Domestic tourists may also be allowed preferential rates or certain exemptions from local bed or hotel taxes that foreigners must pay. Such steps encourage local tourism, improve profitability of establishments, reduce seasonality of establishments, and keep facilities from becoming dominated by outsiders. Hawaii's "kamaaina" rates are but one example.

To mitigate the economic impact of outbound travel, tourism promotion overseas is a must. Special tour packages like "America, Yours to Discover," Eurail Pass, and their equivalents in the British Isles, India, and elsewhere, are especially important for their ability to tap long-distance clienteles and to diffuse such tourists' expenditures. Too often, long-haul travel may leave only 10 percent of the tourist dollar at the destination (Turner 1976). Touring packages within the country or region improve the rate of return. Such promotions as "Holland on the House," which discounted travel and lodging for one day, also may be a successful means of attracting tourists for longer visits to countries often overlooked on grand tours.

Targeted nostalgia tours, like "Balikbayan" and "Reunion for Peace" in the Philippines and similar promotions in Korea and "Roots" tours in Africa, may also combine economic and political objectives to increase inbound tourism (Richter 1980a).

The most predictable though blunt approach to reducing outbound tourism and increasing arrivals almost overnight is the government decision to devalue the currency (Turner 1976). Whether it is a wise political or economic decision hinges particularly on the country's need to import items from abroad for tourism and other policy sectors.

INTERNATIONAL PERSPECTIVES

There is a scarcity of research on the politics of tourism generally and international politics in particular. Much of what has been done is not readily available. In this section, therefore, there will be a brief survey of the political issues that need to be addressed by various participants in the field of international tourism with suggestions for further research.

INTERNATIONAL CORPORATE PERSPECTIVE

Corporations have proved unusually adaptable in working with governments of every political persuasion in the development of tourism. Ideology has played surprisingly little role in initial access of a corporation to a country. French, Indian, and Swedish firms have built hotels in eastern Europe; the Austrians, Americans, and French have been active in Pakistan; Filipinos and Americans have been active in

Chinese tourism, while Japanese firms have supplied both transport and hotel expertise in Hawaii and the Philippines.

Ownership, leasing arrangements, and overall planning, however, are likely to reflect national attitudes toward external capital and expertise. It is hard to generalize about such matters because local sensibilities differ from area to area and regime to regime.

Outside of limited contractual agreements for noninvestment relationships, like consulting advice, market surveys, and tourism planning, corporations will want to consider carefully the likely political consequences of investment outside the home base. The following represent a general and by no means exhaustive checklist of some of the political factors to be considered from the corporate perspective.

Political Stability

Political stability is of the foremost importance to any investment, but it is of special consequence to tourism because of what is being sold: serenity, leisure, fun, and comfort. These can only be marketed under stable conditions. No destination has a monopoly on desirability that would encourage the level of risk-taking common to other investments.

To evaluate political stability is not easy, especially when one is dealing with national leaders interested in tourism and willing to offer liberal terms for investment. There are, however, a few techniques one may use.

First, in the United States, there are many consulting firms that specialize in political forecasting. The subject of risk analysis is a large and relatively unrefined one for the international-tourism entrepreneur. Broad studies focusing on the political forecast for a specific nation may not be very helpful for an investor concentrating on one segment of the market. Situations like agrarian unrest, which constitute hazards for Del Monte or United Fruit, may create genuine opportunities for tourism as the government searches for new avenues for garnering foreign exchanges (La Palombara 1982; Kobrin 1979; Laurie).

A second approach is to attempt to predict the security of an investment in terms of the pattern of outside capital flowing into a nation. If there is growth in investment, some travel industries conclude, the political situation is stable for tourism. No statistics are available that either confirm or refute that relationship. But such figures have been notoriously unreliable on occasion as a basis for prediction, as in Cuba, before the takeover by Fidel Castro set Cuban tourism back 30 years, or as in Iran in 1979. This approach also does not take into consideration the possibility that tourism itself may be the focus of political strife, as in Hawaii, Fiji, or the Philippines in recent years (Kent 1983; Richter 1982, 1989a).

A third barometer of political stability is the country's credit record. Heavy World Bank or International Monetary Fund loans are sometimes looked upon as an indicator of the country's overall political stability and credit worthiness. This indicator, however, is flawed by the fact that credit is just as easily a measure of political compatibility with the major creditor powers as it is a measure of de facto fiscal responsibility and political stability (Payer 1982).

Executive Commitment

Sophisticated political preplanning should employ more care. That it rarely does so is a serious defect. It is crucial to have a detailed understanding of the current leadership's commitment to tourism and any caveats it may have about the industry. In several countries, profitability and initial investments in luxury hotels, for example, were premised on the assumption that there would be casinos and supper clubs. A change in regimes in Pakistan and a misreading of executive sentiments in the Philippines changed all that, leaving the hotels in dire financial straits (Richter 1989a, 1984a).

It is also important to consult with likely leaders of the political opposition regarding their attitudes toward tourism. Their relative strength and their sentiments toward the tourist industry may influence the timing of investments, bargaining terms, or even the decision to invest at all. Jamaica, Grenada, and Nicaragua are three nations where just such sleuthing might have saved the industry considerable grief.

Government Experience with Foreign Investment

Other political cum economic considerations include the government's political actions toward outside capital. Indian hotel magnate Oberoi learned to his chagrin that Pakistan had expropriated five of his luxury hotels following the 1965 Indo-Pakistani war (*Asiaweek* 1980). Nationalization of tourist establishments in China, Cuba, and Vietnam is the exception, but, in numerous other countries, there have been policies of expropriating key industries. If tourism became central to such economies, they too might become targets for nationalization. In fact, investors are now recommended to anticipate such nationalization in the initial contracts drawn, thereby providing that "in the event of a dispute regarding compensation, recourse to international arbitration or other previously agreed upon dispute-settlement facilities may be had at the request of either party" (OECD Policy Statement 1981).

GOVERNMENT CONDITIONS OF INVESTMENT AND ACCESS

The availability of local or national capital and/or investment incentives is another area deserving intense political scrutiny. Even the poorest countries have concessions that can be made to encourage investment. Finding the most appropriate ones consistent with corporate and national objectives is important. Studies suggest that the countries, rather than the corporations, are likely to be poor bargainers (Center on Transnational Corporations 1982), but that does not mean that the corporation automatically gains in the long run from lopsided agreements. Developing terms of mutual interest may, in fact, mean more predictable gains from the venture than the shrewd corporate deal that soon leaves the host country disenchanted.

Leasing rather than buying land, for example, may be more advantageous to both sides than outright foreign ownership. For the corporation, it minimizes the commitment of locked-up capital and reduces the degree of vulnerability to the country's long-range political fortunes and/or changes in tourist tastes. At the same time, leasing can defuse national concerns about the extent of foreign ownership in the society, a factor of concern to nations as disparate as the United States and Fiji. Despite that logic, disputes between multinationals and host developing countries have generally been more severe where the corporations have no equity involved (Center on Transnational Corporations 1982).

Foreign airlines seeking routes or other agreements on air travel will need to negotiate with both the host country and the country of origin. Scheduling, the degree of reciprocity sought for the host country's national carrier, and other issues may involve not only economic issues but the relations among the host country, the country of origin, and often several other countries that may be involved in the routing.

In the United States, for example, despite deregulation, airlines need to deal with both houses of Congress, the Department of State, and even the President as in 1985 when President Reagan attempted to reduce tax deductions for business travel. In some less pluralistic countries, like the Philippines under President Marcos, certain key individuals, for example, the minister of tourism, may have almost total discretion about such matters.

Having specific contractual agreements does not prevent their abrogation, of course, in times of political tension. Many airlines will refuse to fly into countries at war or involved in great civil strife. In other instances, curtailment of flights between nations displeased with each other is a favorite government weapon. In late 1981, for example, President Reagan suspended Aeroflot flights to New York as a signal of his displeasure with Soviet influence in Poland, and other Western European countries followed suit after the USSR shot down a Korean civilian plane in 1983.

Much of the preceding discussion has focused on bilateral political negotiations. However, that does not include the usually inevitable regulations of the National Tourist Organization (NTO) with rules governing other levels of planning and negotiation with state, province, or city governments. Consulates or embassies are the best preliminary sources of legal and trade information. They will have addresses and titles of specific agencies charged with tourism information for investors.

POLITICAL LINKAGES

The entrepreneur and the host government are themselves politicking in the midst of a much larger web of political decision making that may make critical decisions for the industry in which their own participation may be peripheral at best. Consider, for example, the disastrous impact of world energy prices on tourism costs in the 1970s and the subsequent pressure for deregulation of transportation that was accepted by several of the nations most active in tourism. The 1991 Gulf War also dramatically altered travel and tourism patterns throughout the world.

In the United States, linkages between tourism and environmental, energy, tax, and employment policies are becoming especially salient as the government struggles to implement the broad objectives of its national tourism policy. To date, the federal response can be most charitably labeled *indecisive* (Borcover 1985).

Though the tourist industry prefers to see the government's commitment as proportionate to the industry's importance to the national economy, other scenarios are also reasonable. Is the responsibility for promotion in the face of lucrative returns on promotion necessarily the government's? Is there some optimal ratio of private to state to federal involvement? Do those lucrative returns from promotion constitute a subsidized bonanza for the tourist industry, or do the national balance of trade, tax revenues, and increased employment constitute a significant national interest that government should foster?

Moreover, is the stimulation of tourism consistent with the government's energy, conservation, and ecological needs, and what modifications are appropriate to meet national goals fairly vis-à-vis tourism and energy? Though specific national needs differ, the United States' effort to formulate a national tourism policy suggests a few of the most obvious political issues that the tourist industry and the government must continually negotiate. Even in less pluralistic countries, the political balance of tourism and other policies continues to be difficult.

INTERGOVERNMENTAL ORGANIZATIONS

Increasingly, international organizations have become involved in the planning, regulation, and pressure-group activities central to tourism politics. Also, what little monitoring of the industry has taken place has been done typically by a few academics and such international bodies as the World Bank, UNESCO, UNCTAD, the International Academy for the Study of Tourism, and the International Civil Aviation Organization (ICAO). Regional groups, like OECD, the OAS, ASEAN, and RCD countries, have also begun tentative efforts to facilitate and improve tourism, though the efforts have focused primarily on promotional and marketing concerns.

International tourism organizations are quite naturally preoccupied with the politics of tourism (with politics within the organizations sometimes almost as time-consuming as tourism issues per se). Of these, the World Tourism Organization (WTO) is the newest and most important of the hospitality-centered organizations. Formed in 1975 in response to increased governmental interest in tourism, it supplants its predecessor, the International Union of Official Travel Organizations. Unlike the IUOTO, which was nongovernmental, the WTO is intergovernmental in nature. Members include sovereign states, associate memberships of territories or groups of territories, and affiliate members that are international bodies involved in tourism.

The WTO is designed to be an operative rather than deliberative body helping members maximize benefits from tourism. It intends to function as a sort of global data bank assisting in tourism planning, and in identifying markets and funding possibilities for a wide range of tourism enterprises

(Henson 1979:194-196). It is primarily an informed cheerleader for the industry and for governments interested in tourism. It is an unlikely critic, though at its 1980 conference it did consider a variety of quasi-political issues (Gunn and Jafari 1980:478–487).

Regional tourism organizations, like the Pacific Area Travel Association (PATA) or the Caribbean Tourism Association (CTA), are also important in tourism politics. Like the American Society of Travel Agents (ASTA), these organizations are primarily interested in group or charter travel. Their perspective tends to weigh the interests of consumers more heavily than the impact on host communities, as revealed in the theme of one PATA convention, "The Consumer: The Only One that Really Matters!"

In the transportation sector of the industry, the most important international group is the International Air Transport Association (IATA), which regulates ticketing and fares of member airlines on a nongovernmental basis. Membership is voluntary, with the outstanding holdout being Icelandic Airlines.

CONCLUSION

The complexity of political and legal dimensions of tourism should not dismay or discourage decision makers. By anticipating the political and legal dimensions in preplanning, consultation, and contractual agreements, the potential for positive results from tourism is enhanced for all participants. Tourism *can* succeed if the political issues are directly confronted. As one journalist observed, "Tourism is like fire. It can cook your food or burn your house down" (Fox 1976:44).

It is beyond the scope of this short chapter to do much more than suggest the participants and the parameters of typical political issues that are emerging in the realm of tourism, but it can be expected that international organizations of global or regional scope will increasingly play important planning and lobbying functions in the shaping of tourism in various countries.

REFERENCES

Asiaweek, October 24, 1980.

Belisle, Francois J., and Don R. Hoy (1980), "The Perceived Impact of Tourism by Residents: A Case Study in Santa Marta, Colombia," *Annals of Tourism Research* 7 (1), 83–101.

Blanton, David (1981), "Tourism Training in Developing Countries: The Social and Cultural Dimension," *Annals of Tourism Research* 8 (1), 116–131.

Borcover, Alfred (1985), "Funding Cuts Imperial U.S. Tourism Agency at Inopportune Time," *The Atlanta Constitution*, May 12, 3–F.

Center on Transnational Corporations (1982), *Transnational Corporations in International Tourism*, New York: United Nations.

Chow, Willard T. (1980), "Integrating Tourism with Regional Development," *Annals of Tourism Research* 7 (4), 584–607.

Clarke, Alan (1981), "Coastal Development in France: Tourism as a Tool for Regional Development," *Annals of Tourism Research* 8 (3), 447–479.

Creal, James (1980), "A National Tourism Policy: Good Business for America," *National Journal* 10 (40), 1981.

Dannhorn, Robin (1979), "Asia's Tourism Catalyst," *Far Eastern Economic Review* (January 21), 36–37.

DeKadt, Emanuel (1979), *Tourism: Passport to Development?*, New York: Oxford University Press.

Enloe, Cynthia (1975), *The Politics of Pollution in a Comparative Perspective*, New York: McKay.

Fox, Morris (1976), "The Social Impact of Tourism: A Challenge to Researchers and Planners," in *A New Kind of Sugar*, Ben Finney and Karen Ann Watson, eds., 44, Honolulu: East-West Center Press.

Franda, Marcus (1979), "Quiet Turbulence in the Seychelles. Part 1. Tourism and Development," *American Universities Field Staff Reports*, No. 10.

Fukenaga, Lawrence (1976), "A New Sun in North Kohala: The Socioeconomic Impact of Tourism and Resort Development on a Rural Community in Hawaii," in *A New Kind of Sugar*, Ben Finney and Karen Ann Watson, eds., Honolulu: East-West Center Press.

Gamper, Josef (1981), "Tourism in Austria: A Case Study of the Influence of Tourism on Ethnic Relations," *Annals of Tourism Research* 8 (3), 432–446.

Governor's Conference on Tourism (1984), Honolulu, Hawaii, December, 11–12, 1984.

Gunn, Clare A., and Jafar Jafari (1980) "World Tourism Conference: An Intergovernmental Tourism Landmark," *Annals of Tourism Research* 7 (3), 478–487.

Halsell, Grace (1986), *Prophecy and Politics: Militant Evangelists on the Road to Nuclear War*, 126, Westport, CT: Lawrence Hill and Co.

Harrell-Bond, Barbara (1978), "A Window on an Outside World: Tourism as Development in the Gambia," *American Universities Field Staff Reports*, No. 19.

Henson, Edda (1979), "World Tourism Organization in Asia and the Pacific," *Fookien Times Yearbook*, Manila: Fookien Times Yearbook Co.

Hoivik, Tord, and Turid Heiberg (1980), "Center-Periphery Tourism and Self-reliance," *International Social Science Journal* 32 (November), 69–98.

Holden, Peter, ed. (1984a), *Alternative Tourism with a Focus on Asia*, Bangkok: Coalition on Third World Tourism.

Holden, Peter, ed. (1984b), *Contours*, Volume 1, Bangkok: Coalition on Third World Tourism.

Jones, M. (1986), *A Sunny Place for Shady People*, Sydney: Allen and Unwin.

Karunatilake, H.N.S. (1978), "Foreign Exchange Earnings from Tourism," in *The Role of Tourism in the Social and Economic Development of Sri Lanka*, no author given, Colombo: Social Science Research Center.

Kent, Noel (1983), *Hawaii: Islands under the Influence*, New York: Monthly Review.

Kincaid, Jamaica (1989), *A Small Place*, New York: Penguin.

Kobrin, Stephen J. (1979), "Political Risk: A Review and Reconsideration," *Journal of International Business Studies* (Spring/Summer), 67–80.

La Palombara, Joseph (1982), "Assessing the Political Environment for Business: A New Role for Political Scientists," *PS* (Spring) 180–187.

Laurie, Donald, "International Risk...Six Questions for the Concerned Executive," no publishing information.

Lin, Sharat G., and Nageshwar Patnaik (1982), "Migrant Labour at Asiad '82 Construction Sites in New Delhi," *Bulletin of Concerned Asian Scholars* 14 (3) July-September, 23–31.

Loukissas, Philippo J. (1978), "Tourism and Environment in Conflict: The Case of the Greek Island of Myconos," in *Tourism and Economic Change*, Valene L. Smith, ed., Williamsburg, VA: College of William and Mary.

Matthews, Harry G., and Linda K. Richter (1991), "Political Science and Tourism," *Annals of Tourism Research* 18 (1), 120–136.

Matthews, Harry (1978), *International Tourism: A Political and Social Analysis*, Cambridge: Schenkman.

McKean, P.F. (1978), "Towards a Theoretical Analysis of Tourism: Economic Dualism and Cultural Innovation in Bali," in *Hosts and Guests*, Valene L. Smith, ed., Oxford, England: Basil Blackwell.

Nash, Dennison (1978), "Tourism as a Form of Imperialism" in *Hosts and Guests*, Valene L. Smith, ed., Oxford, England: Basil Blackwell.

National Tourism Policy Study Final Report (1978) (April 21), Washington, D.C.: U.S. Government Printing Office.

Noronha, Raymond (1979), "Paradise Review: Tourism in Bali," in *Tourism: Passport to Development?*, Emanuel DeKadt, ed., New York: Oxford University Press.

Nunez, Theron (1978), "Touristic Studies in Anthropological Perspective," in *Hosts and Guests*, Valene L. Smith, ed., Oxford, England: Basil Blackwell.

O'Grady, Ronald (1981), *Third World Stopover*, Geneva: World Council of Churches.

Organization for Economic Cooperation and Development (1980), *The Impact of Tourism on the Environment*, Paris: OECD.

Organization for Economic Cooperation and Development (1981), *Tourism Policy Statement*, Paris: OECD.

Papson, Stephen (1981), "Spuriousness and Tourism: Politics of Two Canadian Provincial Governments," *Annals of Tourism Research* 8 (2), 220–235.

Payer, Cheryl (1982), *The World Bank: A Critical Analysis*, Monthly Review.

Peck, J.B., and A.S. Lepie (1978), "Tourism and Development in Three North Carolina Coastal Towns," in *Hosts and Guests*, Valene L. Smith, ed., Oxford, England: Basil Blackwell.

Pi-Sunyer, Oriol (1979), "The Politics of Tourism in Catalonia," *Mediterranean Studies*, 1 (2), 46–69.

Powers, Ron (1986), *White Town Drowsing*, New York: Penguin.

Richter, Linda K. (1980a), "The Political Uses of Tourism: A Philippine Case Study," *Journal of Developing Areas* 14 (January), 237–257.

Richter, Linda K. (1980b), "The Politics of Tourism: A Comparative Perspective," a paper presented at the Midwest Political Science Association meeting, Chicago.

Richter, Linda K. (1982), *Land Reform and Tourism Development: Policy-Making in the Philippines*, Cambridge, MA: Schenkman.

Richter, Linda K. (1983a), "Tourism and Political Science: A Case of Not So Benign Neglect," *Annals of Tourism Research Special Issue on Political Science* (October–December).

Richter, Linda K. (1983b), "The Political Implications of Chinese Tourism Policy," *Annals of Tourism Research* (October–December).

Richter, Linda K. (1984a), "The Potential and Pitfalls of Tourism Planning in Third World Countries: The Case of Pakistan," *Tourism Recreation Research* (March).

Richter, Linda K. (1984b), "The Politics of Tourism Development in the American States," a paper presented at the American Society for Public Administration meeting in Denver, Colorado, April 8–11.

Richter, Linda K. (1985a), "Tourism Development: Public Sector Careers for the 21st Century," a paper presented at the American Society for Public Administration meeting, Indianapolis, Indiana, March 25.

Richter, Linda K. (1985b), "State-Sponsored Tourism Development: A Growth Field for Public Administration?" *Public Administration Review*, November–December.

Richter, Linda K. (1989a), *The Politics of Tourism in Asia*, Honolulu: University of Hawaii Press.

Richter, Linda K. (1989b), "Bureaucracy and the Political Process: Two Case Studies of Tourism Development in Asia," in R.B. Jain, ed., *Bureaucratic Politics in the Third World*, New Delhi: Gitanjali Publishing House.

Richter, Linda K. (1991a), "Political Issues in Tourism Policy: A Forecast," in Donald E. Hawkins and J.R. Brent Ritchie, eds., *World Travel and Tourism Review*, Vol. 1, U.K.:C.A.B. International.

Richter, Linda K. (1991b), "The Search for Appropriate Tourism" in Tej Vir Singh, Valene L. Smith, Mary Fish, and Linda K. Richter, *Tourism Environment Nature, Culture, Economy*, India: Inter-India Publications.

Richter, Linda K., and William L. Richter (1985), "Policy Choices in South Asian Tourism Development," *Annals of Tourism Research* 12 (2).

Richter, Linda K. and William L. Waugh, Jr. (1991), "Terrorism and Tourism as Logical Companions," reprinted in *Managing Tourism*, 318–326, Oxford: Butterworth-Heinemann Ltd.

Rodenburg, Eric E. (1980), "The Effects of Scale in Economic Development: Tourism in Bali," *Annals of Tourism Research* (November), 177–196.

Schuchat, Molly (1979), "State Tourism in China and the USA," *Annals of Tourism Research* (November), 177–196.

Singh, Tej Vir (1989), *The Kulu Valley: Impact of Tourism Development in the Mountain Areas*, New Delhi: Himalayan Books.

Stock, Robert (1977), "Political and Social Contributions of International Tourism to the Development of Israel," *Annals of Tourism Research* (October/December).

Sturken, Barbara (1980), "The World Bank Well Runs Dry," *Travel Scene* (November), 14–15.

Swain, Margaret Byrne (1978), "Cuna Women and Ethnic Tourism: A Way to Persist and an Avenue to Change," in *Hosts and Guests*, Valene L. Smith, ed., Oxford, England: Basil Blackwell.

20

Anthropological Research on Tourism

NELSON H.H. GRABURN

ROLAND S. MOORE
Department of Anthropology
University of California
Berkeley, California

*T*his chapter examines tourism in relation to anthropological concepts of culture and society. It focuses on the functions of tourism within the tourists' home culture and on the social and cultural impacts of tourism on host regions. It pays special attention to the strengths and opportunities of anthropological research methods.

Anthropologists specialize in the study of the dynamics of human cultures and cross-cultural communication. Their subject matter includes annual and life-cycle events, such as rituals and vacations, as well as inter-cultural contacts, such as the impact and meanings of tourism for both hosts and guests. Anthropology has always been a comparative discipline. In the past, it specialized in research on far-off places and small-scale societies (now known as the Third and Fourth Worlds)(Graburn 1976), and, in recent years, studies of Europe and the Americas have also become prominent. Since about 1970, anthropologists have turned their attention to tourism, and many of the now classic case studies and theoretical formulations cited in this essay stem from the years after that.

ANTHROPOLOGICAL CONCEPTS AND METHODS

Two key concepts in anthropology are **culture** and **society**. E.B. Tylor (1871) originally defined culture as:

> *That complex whole which includes knowledge, belief, art, morals, law, custom and any other capabilities and habits acquired by man as a member of society.*

In the **functionalist** model, this comprehensive view of culture is elaborated to assert that cultures are interconnected wholes and that changes in any one part have consequences for all other parts. The study of cultural changes over the long term includes **evolutionary theory**, and the study of changes brought about by contact between different peoples was developed as **acculturation theory**. More recent approaches also consider the internal dynamics of human cultures—individuals in society and as members of groups, the interactions of those groups—and the cognitive aspects of culture—the languages and concepts with which people think, and the moral and political ideologies that are guides for action.

By *society* is meant organized systems of groups of people who conceive of themselves and can be analyzed as a discrete unit. The concepts of both culture and society are increasingly problematic in a world where extensive migration and tourism have blurred sociocultural boundaries; sometimes terms like "**creole**" cultures or the "**world** [sociocultural] **system**" are used.

In some ways, tourists resemble anthropologists—travelers who leave their home environment to learn things (MacCannell 1976). Indeed, at times, they are so like each other that a degree of rivalry or opposition develops (Errington and Gewertz 1989). This superficial resemblance refers to the major research strategy of anthropologists, the **ethnographic method**. Anthropologists, after much preparation, travel to a field site where they stay for a few months to a few years to immerse themselves in local communities. They not only learn the language(s), geography, and social norms of the society they study but, through **participant observation**, they join their hosts in their daily activities, learning the mundane details and motor skills of everyday life.

In addition to long-term fieldwork and participant observation, anthropologists share other research methods with the social sciences and humanities (Graburn and Jafari 1991). Historical, archival, and statistical analyses supplement direct observation. Studies of symbolic meanings and of local and national identities, using linguistic, psychological, and semiotic as well as textual analyses, are important in the analysis of advertising, motivation, representation, and cross-cultural understanding.

These distinctive research methods (see Pelto and Pelto 1978) have a number of consequences. Anthropological research is, at first, relatively slow and sometimes expensive as compared to quick site visits or the use of official records and statistics. Anthropologists often develop a strong sympathy or identity with their hosts/friends through a lifetime of repeated visits and may claim to represent "the natives' point of view." Above all, the anthropologist is a kind of translator, a person with a great depth of knowledge who is a bridge between the inside and outside of a culture, characteristics that can be used to advantage in tourism research.

THE ANTHROPOLOGY OF TOURISTS

TOURISM AND EVERYDAY LIFE— THE PUSH FACTORS

Anthropologists, like psychologists, sociologists, and other professionals, have studied the topic of tourist motivations and the place of tourism in people's lives. Anthropologists tend to take the broad view, examining the historical growth of tourism, tourism in relation to class, life-style, and nationality, and in relation to stages of the life cycle.

The **processual approach** uses the anthropological model of the structure and meaning of the passage of time in people's lives. All societies mark the passage of time through ritual and special events (Graburn 1983a, 1989; Nash and Smith 1991). This approach proposes that, in all societies, life is an alternating sequence of mundane (profane) and special (sacred, ritualized, feast) time periods (see Figure 1) and that the latter mark a break from the former while adding special meaning to life. The analyst must examine the relation between these two aspects of life and show how each form covaries with the other. Not all people travel in these "special, break periods," though tourists and pilgrims do; so "travel away from home" is a feature distinguishing tourism from most other leisure forms and must be explained in terms of the characteristics of the particular culture and society under study. Even the desire to travel is not enough without the necessary time, discretionary income, and cultural self-confidence (Graburn 1983a; Smith 1989).

Using the processual model, annual vacations are seen as analogous to or even as a kind of ritual of renewal (recreation) in the annual cycle, comparable to or coinciding with such holidays as Christmas, Easter, the summer solstice, Ramadan in Islam, or Oshogatsu (New Year) in Japan. More extended or special tourist excursions, for example, honeymoons, pre- or postcollege "drifter" tourism (Cohen 1973; Teas 1988), postdivorce and major-occupational-change breaks (Hastings 1988), or retirement cruises (Foster 1986), are analogous to traditional **rites of passage** (Van Gennep 1909) or intermittent pilgrimages (Turner and Turner 1978; Smith 1992) such as the Muslim *hajj* to Mecca or the Japanese *jingumaeri* to major Shinto shrines (Graburn 1983b).

Within every complex society, there are many population segments with different travel habits. Even in major industrial societies, such as the United States or the United Kingdom, 30 to 50% of the population never travels (i.e., never undertakes tourism) during their holiday breaks. These are generally blue collar or poor people (Campbell 1988) or the

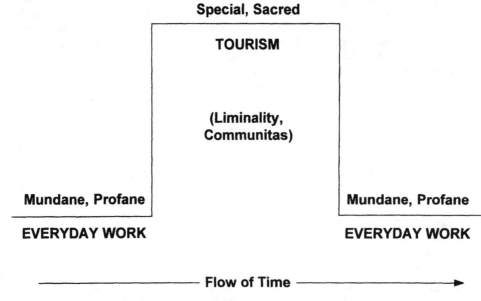

FIGURE 1   The processual model: Tourism as ritual (after Graburn 1989, p. 25; Leach 1961, p. 134).

sick, young, or very old. While the latter groups may have the desire but not the ability the travel (unassisted), the former may lack the discretionary income and, often, the cultural self-confidence to voluntarily leave their familiar environments. Nevertheless, the majority of the population may look down upon or pity those who have no opportunity or desire to travel.

Social scientists have segmented the majority who do travel into different types, often along a continuum (see Table 1).

Marxist-oriented scholars have explained these motivational factors as the result of alienation caused by the oppressive nature of people's lives in mid- and late-capitalism. MacCannell's seminal work (1976) starts with such an explanatory framework, but his main analysis, that modern tourism is a search for "authenticity" (see below), is actually compatible with the processual model, that is, that tourism is a search for the spiritually uplifting, the specially meaningful, or the historically significant in between periods of ordinary, workaday life.

More extreme Marxist interpretations (e.g., Kelly 1986) draw on "critical" and "post-modern" theory (Jameson 1991) to assert that tourism, as commoditized leisure, presents overpriced and unauthentic experiences and cheap souvenirs to an alienated population oppressed and bored in their menial jobs, bereft of spiritually meaningful lives. While this might have been true of the working classes in the nineteenth and early twentieth centuries and of the underclasses and disaffected youth today, it is overly simple and monocausal: one could also argue that (1) tourism existed in classical (pre-capitalist) Greek and Roman times, (2) tourism is (or was) also a major feature of late-Marxist societies, (3) it is much less characteristic of those with boring low-paid jobs than of the self-actuating upper-middle classes, and (4) not all tourism is so phenomenologically unfulfilling as these authors claim. As Campbell (1988) has shown so well, middle-

class intellectuals rarely subscribe to or understand the values and activities of the working classes they claim to represent. Moreover, the latter, knowing their "inferior" position, withhold vital information or "play the part" in order to get rid of the short-term researcher.

A CHANGE IS AS GOOD AS A REST— SYMBOLIC REVERSALS

Tourist motivation must also be explored in terms of what tourists travel toward. The processual model implies that, like traditional holidays, modern tourism supplies experience and meaning not so richly available in everyday life. Thus, tourist satisfactions and behavior always contain some opposites to or reversals of the normal or mundane (Leach 1961); during the vacation period, tourists are in a **liminal** (betwixt and between) status and may experience a heightened sense of life or reality, which results in a sense of shared **communitas**, or togetherness (Turner and Turner 1978). But, as Graburn (1983a) shows, the specific reversals that tourists seek—better weather, wide open scenery, "high" culture, freedom from routine, license to spend money or expand sexual mores, contacts with different people, and so on—are reflections of their culturally constructed conceptions of strictures of life at home; and the degree of spiritual communitas the tourists actually experience depends on the degree to which these changes meet their expectations and, as Cohen (1979a; see Table 1) posits, on the tourists' commitment to de-centering their temporary touristic lives away from the familiar.

Clear reversals (of climate, status, or milieu) may constitute the main theme of some tourist trips. Gottlieb (1983) focused on Americans' touristic reversals of their status position either to splurge or to slum. Urry (1991) pointed out that the ability to pursue a number of different themes in one trip, for example, to ski and visit historical cities or to play

TABLE 1 Classification of Types of Tourists

Smith 1989 [1977]	Cohen 1972	Cohen 1979a	Urry 1991
[Explorer]			
Elite		Existential (like pilgrims)	Romantic Gaze
Off Beat	Drifter	Experimental (drifters)	↑
Unusual	Explorer	Experiential (exploratory individuals)	
Incipient Mass	Individual Mass	Diversionary (looking for a change)	↓
Mass			Collective Gaze
	Organized Mass		
Charter		Recreational (Hedonists, SSSS)	

"peasant for a day" and then eat at a fancy restaurant, are more status enhancing than unimodal switches (see also Bourdieu 1984).

ATTRACTIONS AND GOALS— THE PULL FACTORS

Recent literature on tourism has debated the general nature of attractions. Smith (1989:4–6) has listed them empirically: Ethnic—Cultural—Historical—Environmental—Recreational; and Graburn, in the same volume (1989:32), tried to bring these discrete types into a culturally unified system (noting, of course, that more than one type can be indulged in a single tour). (See Figure 2.)

All of these types reflect the particular changes or reversals of stimulation sought in tourism. Almost by definition, touristic goals are something other than home environment experiences, and the nature of **otherness** itself has been much debated in anthropology. Authors such as Lowenthal (*The Past Is a Foreign Country*, 1985) remind readers that history is equally "other" and is a central component of many tourist attractions.

MacCannell (1976) tried to find "subterranean connections" between all these attractions: he claimed that "otherness" in nature, the past, or foreignness [nationality, ethnicity] are the places where modern man, the tourist, searches for the **authenticity** lacking in everyday alienated home or work lives. His corollary conclusion, shared by Barthes (1979) and other cultural critics, is that tourists are doomed to fail in this search because commercial tourism is dominated by "artificial" cultural productions erected or framed especially for tourist consumption. In the process of touristic development, distinctive local features are often exploited and elevated to an extent that they are greatly

exaggerated. MacCannell (1976) terms this transformation of objects and places into iconic tourist attractions **sight sacralization.**

While authenticity may well be sought by elite and exploratory tourists—whose commitment to meaning lies "out there" on Cohen's (1979a) continuum—other researchers (Mosher 1988; Campbell 1988) argue that this does not apply to those tourists who are less education/self-actualization minded. Cohen (1988) showed that educational level correlates strongly with tourists' concerns about authenticity. More purely recreational tourists, and those "post-tourists" (Urry 1990: 100) playfully aware of the "artificiality" of attractions, find satisfaction without the grim reckoning of authenticity in every experience.

An increasingly key factor in the tourist search is nostalgia, which is closely related to authenticity. That nostalgia motivates and attracts tourists can also be taken as evidence of dissatisfaction with modern life and of the search for simpler or more morally uplifting qualities in other places, times, or cultures. Nostalgia is now a powerful force not only in North America but especially in Europe (Lowenthal 1985; Horne 1984) and Japan (Graburn 1983b). The same criticism can be made of the centrality of nostalgia as a motivational force as of authenticity, that it only applies to the more educated, snobbish tourists.

TOURISTIC REPRESENTATIONS—BETWEEN THE TOURIST AND THE TARGET

Tourism is the commoditization of experience. Its products are mainly intangible: it is promised through representations such as brochures, advertisements, personal photographs, and movies; and its lasting effects are vindicated through word of mouth, photos and movies, and souvenirs. A variety

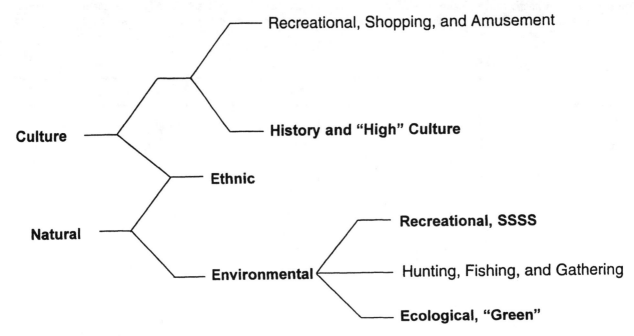

FIGURE 2 Types of tourism—attractions and motivations (after Graburn 1989:32).

of methods can be used to analyze the content and impact of these representations.

Visual anthropology focuses on postcards and photography (Albers and James 1988; Chalfen 1979) or even commercial movies (Bruner 1989) to analyze what is important for tourists to try to "capture" and what commercial imagemakers make available to them. A key category of "tangible proofs" is souvenirs; Graburn (1969, 1976, 1984) and Cohen (1993) examine the cultural as well as the economic negotiations by which producers assess their market and tourists assess the "truth value" of tourist arts. This **anthropology of material culture** coincides with tourism in the study of museums (Graburn 1977), which are one of the central locales of touristic representation and nostalgia.

A most important set of representations are brochures and advertisements, which have been the subject of research both for their impact and their probity. It is here that cultural critics, especially those of a late-Marxist persuasion, find ammunition for the claim that the commercial and political promoters of tourism perpetrate successful frauds on an unsuspecting and alienated public (Crick 1989). One important analytical tool is **semiotics**, which MacCannell (1989: 3) has defined as "A technical perspective for close analysis of the forms and processes of communication." Relating semiotics to modern consumption studies, Thurot and Thurot (1983) analyze the relation between class, status, and representation in advertisements generated by the French tourism industry. They show the production of a succession of "life style images" in the evolving competition for market segments.

Using a **sociolinguistic** variant of the method, Moeran (1983) analyzes the language of Japanese tourist advertising to show the use of key words like *heart*, *nature*, and *my* in the emerging trends appealing to Japanese youth; similarly, Cohen (1989) demonstrates how the image of "Primitive and Remote" was constructed to attract people to go trekking among the Hill Tribes of Thailand. Beer, in a more ambitious project, worked as a participant observer within the industry to show how Japanese tourist wholesalers construct the images, content, and pricing of tours to East and Southeast Asia.

ANTHROPOLOGICAL RESEARCH ON THE IMPACTS OF TOURISM

The comparative nature of anthropology is most clearly seen in studies of differences and similarities among cultures. Anthropologists may also compare aspects of one culture at two or, ideally, many more points in time in order to understand processes of cultural change. Changes in a culture are driven externally by long-term environmental changes and through contact with other cultures. Internally, change occurs through innovation and intracultural conflicts. Tourism is certainly a phenomenon that may promote both internal and external change. The process wherein members of one culture react to another culture with which they are in contact is called **acculturation**.

As a phenomenon found all over the world, tourism af-

fords anthropologists the opportunity to study different kinds of change, especially acculturation. Tourism also sets the scene for another area of interest to anthropologists: **intracultural variation**, that is, such differentiation within cultures as ethnicity, gender, class, and age. Anthropologists of tourism also study tourism's impacts on **expressive culture**, particularly the ethnic arts that become commodities for the tourist trade. One other research area within the anthropological study of tourism's impacts is the character of cross-cultural interaction and communication.

SOCIAL IMPACTS OF TOURISM

Anthropological studies of the impact of tourism on host societies have far outnumbered reports of research on the tourists themselves, following the traditional anthropological focus on communities and cultures that differ from those of the researchers. Several special issues of *Cultural Survival Quarterly* provide an overview of the negative impacts of tourism on indigenous peoples (Callimanopoulos 1982; Johnston 1990).

While tourism is not viewed as the primary agent of social change in many anthropological works, it has been the focus of increasing numbers of studies. As Greenwood (1989:181) points out, tourism is only one of a number of modernizing, westernizing, or simply disruptive forces in a complex and rapidly changing world.

Pioneering anthropological studies on the impact of tourism during the 1970s concluded that the advent of mass tourism is destructive to traditional ways of life. More recent studies have tended to present a more balanced view of tourism as a catalyst for both positive and negative social changes (Smith 1989).

Whereas economists tend to focus on the financial aspects of touristic development, anthropologists have carefully studied the social repercussions of such economic phenomena as occupational change, increased incomes, greater disparities in wealth between rich and poor, the upheaval of traditional status hierarchies as formerly lower-status individuals reap inordinate benefits from tourism, and the overall response of host populations to different phases of touristic development. Boissevain states that the attitudes of host peoples "tend to change, as their new tourist industry develops, from euphoria through apathy through hostility to overt antagonism" (cited in Benthall 1988:22).

Several studies have documented the decidedly negative effects of rapid touristic development on the Greek island of Mykonos (Loukissas 1978; Packer 1974; Stott 1978). The beautiful beaches and the distinctive whitewashed Cycladic architecture first drew elite international tourists and then a more diversified throng of drifter tourists, mass tourists, and even domestic tourists. The highly seasonal nature of tourism on Mykonos places a number of strains on the island and its residents. Loukissas and Stott pointed out the ways in which tourism was particularly taxing to the fragile island ecosystem. The depletion of fresh water and problems of garbage and sewage management are some of the most vivid environmental impacts from tourism.

In addition to heavily taxing the island's fragile eco-system, the seasonal arrival of large numbers of tourists has brought on negative social repercussions: increasing crime rates; the development of a "false authenticity"; weakening of ethical standards, such as adulteration of traditional forms of hospitality and communal work-parties; and the costly imitation of foreign styles of conspicuous consumption. Like Stott, Packer identified the following stress-points in the social world of Mykonos: "change in the physical appearance of town, in structural features, in occupational structure, in relations with outside sources of political power, in interpersonal relationships, and in cultural identity" (1974:20).

One of the most visible ways in which tourism may affect a community is through major increases in income. A dramatic example is the town of Medjugorje in Herzegovina. Prior to the breakup of Yugoslavia, Medjugorje was a center of international pilgrimage and group tours. According to Vukonic,

> . . . gross spatial disorder in the village and the negative ecological consequences around it . . . are the price to be paid for the individualistic way of thinking based on commercialization and profit making that have accompanied Medjugorje's fame as a place of pilgrimage. Great social change is also evident in the local population, of whom many have amassed fortunes from kitsch and poor service (1992:88–89).

Tourism has been reported to substantially widen the gap between generations. It may also alter the relationship between men and women; in many parts of the world, women are the innkeepers and merchants. In some cases, wives may bring more cash into their household economy than their husbands, as among the Kuna Indians of Panama (Swain 1989).

The sharp rise in real estate prices that accompanies the widespread recognition of a region's touristic potential is another way in which preexisting patterns of social relations may be disrupted. The establishment of ski lifts on Greece's Mount Parnassos, for example, enriched farmers who sold their low-yield legume fields to Athenians wishing to build ski villas. The concurrent soaring cost of buying or building housing in the region has meant that other families without such plots found it increasingly difficult to provide dowry housing for their daughters (Moore 1992).

ETHNICITY

Ethnicity is one of the most important forms of intra-cultural variation studied by anthropologists. In addition to the fact that hosts and guests often are of different ethnic backgrounds, different ethnic groups may be tied to different kinds of tourism jobs in multiethnic settings. In San Cristobal de las Casas in Southern Mexico, Maya Indians (whose colorful clothing and customs help attract tourists to the town in the first place) create handicrafts and souvenirs that are sold by street vendors, most of whom are also Maya. The

more lucrative hotels, restaurants, and shops are owned by members of the more powerful ladino ethnic group (van den Berghe 1992).

Gamper (1981) analyzes how the development of tourism affected ethnic relations between two villages in one mountain valley in Austria. Such distinct markers of ethnicity as language, dress, and architecture became less divisive as both villages grew wealthy from growing tourist outlays. For the first time in well over a century, villagers are finding marriage partners from outside of both their villages and their ethnic groups.

In some tourist settings, such as Santa Fe, New Mexico, the everpresent tourists may functionally constitute another ethnic group in a multiethnic community. Kemper terms such a situation a "tourist culture" (1978). Just as stereotypes of different ethnic groups govern many expectations and interactions in the United States, stereotypes of tourists, based upon their origin, form the basis of interactions between tourists and hosts in a number of settings. Brewer (1978) describes the phenomenal accuracy of Mexican shop-keepers in assaying the origin of their customers, who are then guided to the stereotype-appropriate section of their store based upon past dealings with similar people. Laxson (1991), in fact, found that interaction between Anglo tourists and the Native Americans they visited did not create greater understanding between the two groups but, instead, strengthened previously held stereotypes.

UNEQUAL RELATIONS ON LARGE AND SMALL SCALES

A theoretical perspective informing a significant number of writings in anthropology and other social sciences is **dependency theory,** which is the view that more powerful countries benefit unfairly in their economic relationships with poorer countries (Wallerstein 1974 is one of the progenitors of this approach). This view has been refined by anthropologist Eric Wolf (1982), who shifted the focus on how traditional societies have been drawn into these exploitative relationships. The relevance of dependency theory to the study of international tourism is clear; the idea of core regions exploiting peripheral areas is also applicable to many instances of domestic tourism. In line with this perspective, Schneider, Schneider, and Hansen (1972) refer to tourism in parts of southern Europe as an example of modernization without corresponding economic development.

The relationship of inequality between host and guest is played out at an intimate level in the co-occurrence of prostitution and tourism in many parts of the world. Anthropologists have written in particular about sex tourism in Southeast Asia (Cohen 1982). Apart from prostitution, sexual relations between hosts and guests often reflect the differences in power between the host and sending countries; Cohen (1971) reports how relatively powerless Arab shopkeepers in Israel gain satisfaction through the sexual conquest of well-off tourist women from Europe. This phenomenon has been widely reported elsewhere in the Mediterranean, in Africa, and in the Caribbean.

When local residents retain control over the rights to resources and have a hand in designing the touristic development (Gamper 1981; Moon 1989), they are far more likely to benefit from that development than when local involvement remains at the servant level.

ETHNIC AND TOURIST ARTS

Tourism has regenerated or revived indigenous arts in a number of cases studied by anthropologists. While the production of handicrafts is upheld as one of the best ways for groups without other industries to capitalize on their local culture, anthropologists have shown that the transformation of ethnic arts into tourist arts often can produce great changes in both the form and content of those arts.

In response to the needs and buying patterns of tourists, the alteration in form and size of traditional arts, such as miniaturization of ceramics or sculptures in order to fit them into suitcases, has been called **airport art** (Graburn 1967). Mass-produced replicas of ethnic arts are characteristic of the process of **trinketization** which often accompanies tourist development (Smith 1989:8).

Graburn (1976) introduced the idea that art in contact with other cultures will diverge into two forms: one for outsiders (for trade, but also for presentation of an image) and one for insiders (maintaining ethnic identity and values). The phenomenon of selling less detailed art to outsiders while retaining the finest for insider consumption is widespread; Lathrap mentions a similar situation wherein a Peruvian Shipibo potter reserved her finest work for herself (1976:204). The innovation-resisting Amish have in fact responded to demands of the tourist market in their production of quilts made for sale; however, quilts intended for their own homes employ the same designs that were used prior to the major onset of tourism (Boynton 1986).

Debates over the commercialization of art and culture in general persist in anthropology: Greenwood (1989) found that tourism **commoditized** the festival he studied, while McKean (1989) argues for the concept of **cultural involution**—tourism-inspired revivals of traditional aspects of culture. Boynton states that "As the demand for Amish quilts increases through the impact of tourism and art collectors, there is a definite increase in the number and variety of Amish quilts made. This may be termed 'cultural involution' in that there is an increased elaboration of established art forms and practices" (1986:464).

Some studies that note the deleterious effects of tourism on ethnic arts attributed the decline in standards to the uncritical buying patterns of the tourists. Such conclusions are widespread throughout the anthropological literature; however, the slightly less frequent observation should also be noted: that in some cases, tourism has revitalized some "moribund" crafts, as in Cyprus, Tunisia, and Malta (de Kadt 1979:69). The study of tourism's effects on local music traditions is young but reaches many of the same conclusions (Ishimori 1991).

INTERACTION BETWEEN HOST AND GUEST

The differences between the cultures of the sending and receiving countries may be very great. Local perception of economic inequalities between host and guest can be magnified by greater than average spending on the part of the visitors. The tourist "bubble" in which many mass tourists spend most of their time effectively insulates them from substantive contact with residents of the localities they visit (Nettekoven 1979). Some of these barriers to interaction may be erected by the hosts as well. In a small Vermont community, villagers resent the intrusions of the city dwellers who vacation there in large numbers, even though the community's economic well-being depends on tourism. The response of the natives is to exclude the vacationers from their decisions and activities as much as they can (Jordan 1980).

Language barriers frequently increase the social distance between many tourists and hosts. In a study on the relative social status accorded different languages in Thailand, Cohen and Cooper (1986) observed that Thai expected long-term, low-status foreigners to learn their language but made efforts to speak the touristic *lingua franca* of English to higher ranking tourists from the West. In the common situation where neither tourist nor host speaks the other's language well, bilingual tour guides gain a great deal of power from being able to control conversations between monolingual guests and hosts (Cohen 1985). Connelly-Kirch (1980) reported that Tongans would ridicule other Tongans working in the informal tourism sector. Not only were they mocked for having no other work options than the low prestige selling of handicrafts, but also for imitating English speakers.

Anthropologists have also described situations in which direct contact with the local residents is actively discouraged. In the 1970s, the Brazilian government, for example, established FUNAI shops to sell handicrafts created by Amazonian Indians. These shops were set up not only to encourage economic self-sufficiency but also to minimize contact between tourists and some of the native peoples (Aspelin 1977). In North America, as Buck (1977) observes, tourist brochures are part of a generalized pattern of focusing tourist attention on staged attractions rather than encouraging direct contact with residents of a destination region. An example is the way in which tourists are diverted from visiting Pennsylvania Amish farms (which do not particularly welcome their attention anyway) to such attractions as gigantic plastic replicas of Amish farmers or model villages (Buck 1977:201). Smith (1989) espouses the development of **model cultures** as a way to deflect tourist attention from host people's everyday lives.

ALTERNATIVE TOURISM

Tourism's negative impacts on the environment as well as on the lives of indigenous peoples are discussed in two issues of *Cultural Survival Quarterly* (Johnston 1990). Eco-, "green" or "soft-path" tourism has been touted as a solution to the environmental damage caused by tourist visits to ecologically sensitive areas.

This brings up the much-debated question of **alternative tourism**, the idea that the careful management of tourism flows and behavior can prevent possible negative environmental and sociocultural effects. Some have claimed that alternative tourism is the wave of the future, whereas others argue that it is merely the thin end of the wedge, opening the way for mass commercial tourism (Smith and Eadington 1992).

ANTHROPOLOGISTS AS CONSULTANTS

Ever since the 1970s when attention was drawn to the possible negative sociocultural impacts of tourism developments, anthropologists have been increasingly employed as consultants by various agencies in the world tourist system. Such often-confidential work usually does not result in easily available publications, and it has lower visibility than their research and teaching publications. Anthropologists have suffered in comparison to some other professions because of their confused public image (e.g., Are they mainly archaeologists, like "Indiana Jones," or "bones people," like the late Louis Leakey?) and because of their research foci on long-term ethnographic fieldwork and holistic analyses rather than on quick attention to narrow sectors.

Anthropologists have been involved in the study of both the operation of the tourism industry and its impacts: One of the authors (Graburn) has advised (1) Club Mediterranée about problems they had with the behavior of American tourists and with attracting and satisfying Japanese tourists, (2) Canadian Inuit (Eskimo) organizations on attracting and controlling tourists and selling them their arts, and (3) the Ecotourism Society in evaluating the environmental and social impacts of "green" tourism operators. Others have used their regional expertise in the planning and evaluation of tourist developments for corporations, local and national governments, and international agencies, such as the World Bank.

Anthropologists of tourism have a lot to offer to these agencies in terms of both their understanding of the world tourism system derived from their research and teaching efforts and their long-term regional contacts, with cultural and linguistic expertise. Anthropologists have a global outlook and may bring attention to tourism research in far-flung areas (e.g., Poland, *Problems of Tourism/Problemy Turystyki*; Spain, Aguirre Baztán 1988; or Japan, Ishimori 1991). With their holistic perspective, they can see the linkages between particular developments and other parts of the sociocultural system: they have shown, for instance, that local opposition to tourism may be a displacement of general anxiety about all kinds of change, focusing on visible outsiders, such as tourists and planners.

Unfortunately, anthropologists are too often brought in post hoc, that is, after things have already begun to go wrong, as with the first examples given above. They would be better used at the planning and training stages, as well as at the impact stage. Anthropologists are particularly valuable as coordinators between local peoples, whose interests they are bound to bear in mind, and agents of change; and they have been successful at avoiding unforeseen consequences to relatively powerless or voiceless local cultures and social systems (Smith 1980).

There are a number of ways that agencies can become acquainted with anthropological analyses of both the tourist system and of local impacts. The increasing literature on these topics can be found in major libraries and in such journals as the *Annals of Tourism Research*. For any particular region, expertise on sociocultural change can also be found in the many disciplinary and regional journals, as well as in the American Anthropological Association *Guide to Departments*. Organizations such as the International Academy for the Study of Tourism, the American Anthropological Association (Information Services Office), or the Royal Anthropological Institute are other important sources.

REFERENCES

Aguirre Baztán, Angel, ed. (1988), [Special issue "Estudios sobre Turismo"] *Antropologica* 4, Barcelona.

Albers, Patricia C., and William R. James (1988), "Travel Photography: a Methodological Approach," *Annals of Tourism Research*, 15(1), 134–63.

American Anthropological Association (updated annually), *A.A.A. Guide*, Washington, D.C.: American Anthropological Association.

Aspelin, Paul L. (1977), "The Anthropological Analysis of Tourism: Indirect Tourism and Political Economy in the Case of the Mamainde of Mato Grosso, Brazil," *Annals of Tourism Research*, 4(3), 135–160.

Barthes, Roland (1979), *The Eiffel Tower, and Other Mythologies*, New York: Hill and Wang.

Beer, Jenny, *The Packaging of Experience: Japanese Tours to Southeast Asia*, unpublished Ph.D. dissertation in anthropology, University of California, Berkeley, CA.

Benthall, Jonathan (1988), "The Anthropology of Tourism," *Anthropology Today* 4(3), 20–22.

Bourdieu, Pierre (1984), *Distinction: A Social Critique of the Judgment of Taste*, Cambridge, MA: Harvard University Press.

Boynton, Linda L. (1986), "The Effect of Tourism on Amish Quilting Design," *Annals of Tourism Research* 13(4), 451–465.

Brewer, Jeffery (1978), "Tourism, Business, and Ethnic Categories in a Mexican Town," in *Tourism and Behavior, Studies in Third World Societies 5*. Valene L. Smith, ed., 83–100, Williamsburg, VA: College of William and Mary.

Bruner, Edward M. (1989), "Of Cannibals, Tourists, and Ethnographers," *Cultural Anthropology* 4(4), 438–45.

Buck, Roy C. (1977), "The Ubiquitous Tourist Brochure: Explorations in Its Intended and Unintended Use," *Annals of Tourism Research* 4(4), 195–207.

Callimanopoulos, Dominique, ed. (1982), "The Tourist Trap:

Who's Getting Caught?," special issue of *Cultural Survival Quarterly*, 6(3).

Campbell, Robert (1988), "Busman's Holiday—or the Best Surprise Is No Surprise," *Kroeber Anthropological Society Papers*, 67–68, 12–19.

Chalfen, Richard M. (1979), "Photography's Role in Tourism," *Annals of Tourism Research* 6(4), 435–447.

Cohen, Erik (1971), "Arab Boys and Tourist Girls in a Mixed Jewish-Arab Community," *International Journal of Comparative Sociology*, 12(4), 217–233.

Cohen, Erik (1972), "Toward a Sociology of International Tourism," *Social Research* 39(1), 164–182.

Cohen, Erik (1973), "Nomads from Affluence: Notes on the Phenomenon of Drifter Tourism," *International Journal of Comparative Sociology*, 14(1–2), 89–103.

Cohen, Erik (1979a), "A Phenomenology of Tourist Experiences," *Sociology*, 13, 179–201.

Cohen, Erik (1979b), "Rethinking the Sociology of Tourism," *Annals of Tourism Research* 6(1), 18–35.

Cohen, Erik (1982), "Thai Girls and Farang Men," *Annals of Tourism Research* 9(3), 403–428.

Cohen, Erik (1985), "The Tourist Guide: The Origins, Structure and Dynamics of a Role," *Annals of Tourism Research* 12(1), 5–29.

Cohen, Erik (1988), "Authenticity and Commoditization in Tourism," *Annals of Tourism Research* 15(3), 371–386.

Cohen, Erik (1989), "'Primitive and Remote': Hill Tribe Trekking in Thailand," *Annals of Tourism Research* 16(1), 30–61.

Cohen, Erik, and Robert L. Cooper (1986), "Language and Tourism," *Annals of Tourism Research* 13(4), 533–563.

Cohen, Erik, ed. (1985), "Tourist Guides," special issue of *Annals of Tourism Research* 12(1).

Cohen, Erik, ed. (1993), "Tourist Arts," special issue of *Annals of Tourism Research* 20(1).

Connelly-Kirch, Debra (1980), "A Comment on Boundaries Between Work and Private Worlds," *Annals of Tourism Research* 7(4), 608–609.

Crick, Malcolm (1989), "Representations of International Tourism in the Social Sciences: Sun, Sex, Sights, Savings and Servility," in *Annual Review of Anthropology*, 307–344, Palo Alto, CA: Annual Reviews.

de Kadt, Emanuel, ed. (1979), *Tourism: Passport to Development?*, Oxford: Oxford University Press.

Errington, Frederick, and Deborah Gewertz (1989), "Tourism and Anthropology in a Post-Modern World," *Oceania*, 60(1), 37–54.

Foster, George M. (1986), "South Seas Cruise," *Annals of Tourism Research* 13(2), 215–238.

Gamper, Josef A. (1981), "Tourism in Austria: A Case Study of the Influence of Tourism on Ethnic Relations," *Annals of Tourism Research* 8(3), 432–446.

Gottlieb, Alma (1983), "Americans' Vacations," *Annals of Tourism Research* 9(2), 165–188.

Graburn, Nelson H. H. (1967), "The Eskimos and 'Airport Art,'" *Trans-action* (October), 28–33.

Graburn, Nelson H. H. (1969), "Art and Acculturative Processes," *International Social Science Journal*, 21, 457–468.

Graburn, Nelson H. H., ed. (1976), *Ethnic and Tourist Arts: Cultural Expressions from the Fourth World*, Berkeley, CA: University of California Press.

Graburn, Nelson H. H. (1977), "The Museum and the Visitor Experience," in *The Visitor and the Museum*, L. Draper, ed., Berkeley, CA: Lowie Museum [for Museum Educators, American Association of Museums].

Graburn, Nelson H. H. (1983a), "The Anthropology of Tourism," *Annals of Tourism Research* (Special Issue on Anthropology of Tourism), 10(1), 9–34.

Graburn, Nelson H. H. (1983b), *To Pray, Pay and Play: the Cultural Structure of Japanese Domestic Tourism*, Aix-en-Provence: Centre des Hautes Etudes Touristiques (Cahiers du Tourisme, B-26).

Graburn, Nelson H. H. (1984), "Evolution of Tourist Arts," *Annals of Tourism Research* 11, 393–419.

Graburn, Nelson H. H. (1989), "Tourism: The Sacred Journey," in *Hosts and Guests: The Anthropology of Tourism*, 2nd ed. [1st ed. 1977], Valene L. Smith, ed., 21–36, Philadelphia: University of Pennsylvania Press.

Graburn, Nelson H. H., and Jafar Jafari, eds. (1991), "Tourism Social Sciences," special issue of *Annals of Tourism Research* 18(1).

Greenwood, Davydd J. (1989), "Culture by the Pound: An Anthropological Perspective on Tourism as Cultural Commoditization," in *Hosts and Guests: The Anthropology of Tourism*, 2nd ed. [1st ed. 1977], Valene L. Smith, ed., 171–185, Philadelphia: University of Pennsylvania Press.

Hastings, Julie (1988), "Time out of Time," *Kroeber Anthropological Society Papers*, 67–68, 42–54.

Horne, Donald (1984), *The Great Museum: The Re-presentation of History*, London: Pluto.

Ishimori, Shuzo, ed. (1991), *Kanko to Ongaku [Tourism and Music]*, Tokyo: Shoseki.

Jameson, Frederic (1991), *Postmodernism, or, the Cultural Logic of Late Capitalism*, Durham, NC: Duke University Press.

Johnston, Barbara R., ed. (1990), "Breaking out of the Tourist Trap," special issues of *Cultural Survival Quarterly*, 14(1 and 2).

Jordan, James William (1980), "The Summer People and the Natives: Some Effects of Tourism in a Vermont Vacation Village," *Annals of Tourism Research* 7(1), 34–55.

Kelly, John (1986), "Commodification of Leisure: Trend or Tract," *Society and Leisure*, 9(2), 455–475.

Kemper, Robert Van (1978), "Tourism and Regional Development in Taos, New Mexico," in *Tourism and Economic Change, Studies in Third World Societies No. 6*, Valene Smith, ed., 89–103, Williamsburg, VA: William and Mary Press.

Lathrap, Donald W. (1976), "Shipibo Tourist Art," in *Ethnic and Tourist Arts: Cultural Expressions from the Fourth World,* Nelson H. H. Graburn, ed., 197–207, Berkeley, CA: University of California Press.

Laxson, Joan (1991), "How 'We' See 'Them': Tourism and Native Americans," *Annals of Tourism Research* 18(3), 365–391.

Leach, Edmund R. (1961), "Time and False Noses," *Rethinking Anthropology,* E. R. Leach, ed., 132–136, London: Athlone.

Loukissas, Philippos J. (1978), "Tourism and Environment in Conflict: The Case of the Greek Island of Myconos," in *Tourism and Behavior, Studies in Third World Societies 5,* Valene L. Smith, ed., 105–132, Williamsburg, VA: College of William and Mary.

Lowenthal, David (1985), *The Past Is a Foreign Country,* Cambridge: Cambridge University Press.

MacCannell, Dean (1976) [2nd ed. 1989], *The Tourist: A New Theory of the Leisure Class,* New York: Schocken Books.

MacCannell, Dean, ed. (1989), "Semiotics of Tourism," special issue of *Annals of Tourism Research* 16(1).

McKean, Philip F. (1989), "Towards a Theoretical Analysis of Tourism: Economic Dualism and Cultural Involution in Bali," in *Hosts and Guests: The Anthropology of Tourism,* 2nd ed., [1st ed. 1977], Valene L. Smith, ed., 119–138, Philadelphia: University of Pennsylvania Press.

Moeran, Brian (1983), "The Language of Japanese Tourism," *Annals of Tourism Research* 10(1), 93–108.

Moon, Okpyo (1989), *From Paddy Field to Ski Slope: The Revitalization of Tradition in Japanese Village Life,* Manchester: Manchester University Press.

Moore, Roland S. (1992), *From Shepherds to Shopkeepers: The Development of Tourism in a Central Greek Town,* unpublished Ph.D. dissertation in anthropology, University of California, Berkeley, CA.

Mosher, Maggie (1988), "A Case Study of Tourism in Chinese Peasant Society," *Kroeber Anthropological Society Papers,* 67–68, 55–61.

Nash, Dennison (1981), "Tourism as an Anthropological Subject," *Current Anthropology,* 22(5), 461–82.

Nash, Dennison, and Valene Smith (1991), "Anthropology and Tourism," *Annals of Tourism Research* 18(1), 12–25.

Nettekoven, Lothar (1979), "Mechanisms of Intercultural Interaction," in *Tourism: Passport to Development?,* Emanuel de Kadt, ed., 135–145, Oxford: Oxford University Press.

Packer, Lance V. (1974), *Tourism in the Small Community: A Cross-cultural Analysis of Developmental Change,* unpublished Ph.D. dissertation in anthropology, University of Oregon, Eugene, OR.

Pelto, Pertti H., and Gretel H. Pelto (1978), *Anthropological Research. The Structure of Inquiry,* New York: Cambridge University Press.

Schneider, Peter, Jane Schneider, and Edward Hansen (1972), Modernization and Development: The Role of Regional Elites and Noncorporate Groups in the European Mediterranean," *Comparative Studies in Society and History,* 14, 328–350.

Smith, Valene L. (1980), "Anthropology and Tourism: A Science-Industry Evaluation," *Annals of Tourism Research* 7, 13–33.

Smith, Valene L. (1989), "Introduction," in *Hosts and Guests: The Anthropology of Tourism,* 2nd ed. [1st ed. 1977], Valene L. Smith, ed., 1–14, Philadelphia: University of Pennsylvania Press.

Smith, Valene L., ed. (1989) [1st ed. 1977], *Hosts and Guests,* Philadelphia: University of Pennsylvania Press.

Smith, Valene L., ed. (1992), "Pilgrimage and Tourism," special issue of *Annals of Tourism Research* 19(1).

Smith, Valene L., and William Eadington, eds. (1992), *Tourism Alternatives: Perspectives on the Future of Tourism,* Philadelphia: University of Pennsylvania Press.

Stott, Margaret (1978), "Tourism in Mykonos: Some Social and Cultural Responses," *Mediterranean Studies,* 1(2), 72–90.

Swain, Margaret Byrne (1989), "Gender Roles in Indigenous Tourism: Kuna Mola, Kuna Yala, and Cultural Survival," in *Hosts and Guests: The Anthropology of Tourism,* 2nd ed. [1st ed. 1977], Valene L. Smith, ed., 83–104, Philadelphia: University of Pennsylvania Press.

Teas, Jane (1988), "'I'm Studying Monkeys; What Do You Do?' Youth and Travellers in Nepal," *Kroeber Anthropological Society Papers,* 67–68, 35–41.

Thurot, Jean-Marie, and Gaetane Thurot (1983), "Ideology of Class and Tourism: Confronting the Discourse of Advertising," *Annals of Tourism Research* 10(1):173–189.

Tsartas, Paris (1989), *Social and Economic Impacts of Touristic Development in the Cyclades, Particularly on the Islands of Ios and Serifos from 1950–1980,* Athens: National Center for Social Research [in Greek].

Turner, Victor, and Edith Turner (1978), *Image and Pilgrimage in Christian Culture,* Oxford: Basil Blackwell.

Tylor, E.B. (1871), *Primitive Culture: Researches into the Development of Mythology, Philosophy, Religion, Art and Custom,* London: John Murry, Ltd.

Urry, John (1990), *The Tourist Gaze,* London: Sage.

Van Gennep, Arnold (1909), *The Rites of Passage,* (trans. by M. Vizedom and G. Caffee), London: Routledge and Kegan Paul (1960 edition).

van den Berghe, Pierre L. (1992), "Tourism and the Ethnic Division of Labor," *Annals of Tourism Research* 19(2), 234–249.

Vukonic, Boris (1992), "Medjugorje's Religion and Tourism Connection," *Annals of Tourism Research* 19(1), 79–91.

Wallerstein, Immanuel (1974), *The Modern World-System: Capitalist Agriculture and the Origins of the European World-Economy in the Sixteenth Century,* New York: Academic Press.

Wolf, Eric (1982), *Europe and the People Without History,* Berkeley, CA: University of California Press.

Wulff, Robert A., and Shirley J. Fiske, eds. (1987), *Anthropological Praxis. Translating Knowledge into Action,* Boulder, CO: Westview Press.

21

Environmental Design and Land Use

CLARE A. GUNN
Professor Emeritus
Department of Recreation, Park, and Tourism Sciences
Texas A&M University
College Station, Texas

As a very important aspect of the supply side of tourism, environmental development, including the landscape and built environment, is a comparatively new topic of research. In the past, planners, designers, and owners relied more on skill, tradition, and experience than upon research for land design and use decisions. Increased concern over the built environment has come from more discriminating tourists, narrower margins of financial returns from tourism businesses, increased competition for land, and greater awareness of tourism's impact on the physical and aesthetic environment. The future portends even greater emphasis on issues of better environmental planning, design, and land use for tourism.

A fundamental peculiar to tourism is that it is anchored to place. Therefore, how environments are used and how places are designed are critical tourism issues. Placeness is a tourism fact of life, with many very important ramifications. As described by Vivien Stewart (1990), "Our perception of the landscape is based, not just on what we see, but what we know to be there." No industry or social activity has as great a relationship to land—the givens of resources and the cultural modifications made by man. All other production industries distribute products to customers quite some distance from the origin. Most consumers have no notion whatsoever regarding the source location of the vegetables they eat or the clothing they wear. The reverse, the absolutism of the placeness of the tourism product, is extremely powerful— the very heart of tourism. The enticement of traveling to some place away from home and the satisfactions derived from being in that other place are basic to all tourism. Therefore, how places are identified, planned, and designed for tourism is vital to the best fit with resources and all other land uses, as well as to the success of tourism.

When tourism's impact on the environment is placed in proper perspective as related to other land development, it pales by comparison. Worldwide, it is not tourism but other development that has been the major cause of environmental damage, as is well documented by the 1991 *Report of*

Progress Toward a Sustainable Society, produced by the Worldwatch Institute. Since the first Earth Day in 1970, as many as 200 million hectares of tree cover have been lost (Brown 1991). Deserts have expanded some 120 million hectares, usurping more land than is currently planted to crops in China. Water pollution continues to threaten all animal life. Farmers have lost an estimated 480 billion tons of topsoil. Carbon dioxide, the main greenhouse gas in the atmosphere, is now rising 0.4 percent a year. Air pollution is of health-threatening levels in hundreds of cities. The atmospheric ozone layer continues to thin. The number of plant and animal species is diminishing, and damage from acid rain is seen on every continent.

Dealing with these issues and tourism's contribution to environmental stress *are* the responsibility of everyone, including tourism's developers and managers. Because qualities of places mean everything to tourism's success, environmental degradation must be of concern to everyone involved in tourism. Fortunately, new policies, new planning concepts, and new management principles hold promise of developing tourism in a more rational and responsible manner. It is toward these goals that this chapter is directed. The major topics discussed are sustainable development, environmental design criteria and planning, and design concepts and processes.

SUSTAINABLE DEVELOPMENT

The term *sustainable development* is now replacing the older term *conservation*. This new concept implies that development and resource protection are compatible. It has been defined by Rees (1989):

> Sustainable development is positive socioeconomic change that does not undermine the ecological and social systems upon which communities and society are dependent. Its successful implementation requires integrated policy, planning, and social learning processes; its political viability depends on the full support of the people it affects through their governments, their social institutions, and their private activities.

APPLICATION TO TOURISM

Improved sustainable tourism may result from policies of better quality rather than growth. Many destinations contain sites with obsolescent or obsolete uses that could be converted to attractions with creative design and management. Taylor (1991:29) goes so far as to advocate that "a concept of demarketing may have to be developed as it becomes necessary to reduce rather than increase the number of visitors in an area." Another answer to environmental problems from mass tourism is better behavior by providers and their visitors. All of the nature-tour operators in the Queen Charlotte Islands in northern British Columbia and Alaska, for example, have agreed to a binding code of ethics (Falconer 1991:21). This self-regulation covers etiquette, wildlife observation, visiting archeological and historic sites, food gathering, garbage disposal, camping, and local cooperation.

Stanley (1991), in a summary of a conference on sustainable development for tourism, concluded that no one should expect to exercise rigid standards. Instead, he identified seven different threads for its accomplishment. First, sustainable development is *determined largely by what the stakeholders want it to be*—a wilderness or a resort. Second, it can be accomplished only when people have found mechanisms for *working together*. Third, environmental impact results from many forms of tourism other than only visiting natural resources that require *special planning for each tourism use*. Fourth, because most tourism businesses are small, they are unable to obtain the research results needed. Therefore, much *education on sustainable development* is needed. Fifth, research can demonstrate that *sustainable development pays*. Sixth, economic measures, such as willingness to pay and contingent value, can demonstrate the *real value of sustainable development*. And, finally, *a review of cases* where sustainable development is being achieved can be of help to other areas seeking this objective.

Sustainable development is achieved best not by governmental regulation but by developers who understand it is essential to their success. Today, a more sophisticated market is demanding clean air, water fit for recreation, non-

eroded and scenic landscapes, abundant wildlife, protected and restored historic sites, and safe environments for visits. It is not so much altruism as simple tourism economics that should encourage all tourism developers to advocate and practice sustainable tourism development.

LOW-IMPACT VERSUS HIGH-IMPACT TOURISM

In the past, governments, investors, and developers have tended to favor high-intensity and high-impact tourism development. For some time, this scale of development has met with reasonable success. It provided a large enough critical mass of visitors to make air access profitable. It concentrated infrastructure for greater efficiency. It met the needs of certain market segments. This type of development continues to have merit where the previous destination image was low.

However, experience has demonstrated several negative impacts from high-impact tourism. For one, the local cultural shock may be intense, especially where the norms of the visitors differ greatly from those of the local hosts. Second, concentrations of masses of visitors have frequently eroded the values and mores of the host areas, destroying ethnic integrity and tradition. Third, unplanned mass-tourism development has often damaged local natural resources—soil erosion, reduction of wildlife through habitat destruction, pollution of swimming beaches, elimination of native vegetation, and pollution of air from too many vehicles. Fourth, promises of economic improvement have not been realized because officials gave away tax incentives, and outside multinational firms made the investment and imported management and staff. Finally, for undeveloped countries, high-impact tourism has been disruptive of a traditional agricultural economy. Although many of these impacts can be reduced or ameliorated, high-impact tourism may need to be balanced with low-impact development.

By *low-impact* is meant a slower and more adaptive tourism development policy that is less disruptive of the local environment and economy. Each increment of growth can be evaluated and used as an experience foundation for a next step. Social, environmental, and economic costs can be assessed by the local population so that any negative tendencies can be dealt with before they grow into major issues. Native populations have the opportunity to choose tourist volumes depending on how they cope with tourism's impact. When local people plan, own, and manage tourist attractions and businesses, they are able to respond more rapidly to pending negative impacts than outsiders could. Finally, market trends are showing that there is a strong travel-market segment seeking less glitter and congestion and more quality of experience in travel destinations. But, low-impact tourism development still demands long-range planning so that each increment can become integrated into tourism as a whole.

ECOTOURISM

One current expression of sustainable tourism development is called *ecotourism*, again implying that resource protection and tourism development can be compatible. The ground swell of environmentalism has fostered a strong market segment interested in experiences at destinations important for their natural and cultural resources. And it has been used as a marketing ploy to cash in on a popular trend. Ecotourism is defined in several ways, ranging from low-volume use by highly specialized environmental travelers to larger volumes of tourists, often led by tour guides, interested in interpretive visitor centers near important resource areas. Again, resource protection is an essential planning and design criterion.

Stewart et al. (1990) emphasize the political environment relationship within ecotourism: "comprehensive ecosystem management implies some degree of mutual understanding and reciprocity across multiple sociopolitical systems." They state further that ecotourism planning and development require: "(1) integration of non-financial objectives, and (2) a planning process which encourages decision making encompassing entrepreneurs, land managers, host community, and interested tourists or visitors."

Ecotourism offers opportunity for financial support for resource protection from the proceeds of tourism (Ziffer 1989). Provided they are not diverted to general funds, visitor revenues in protected areas can be used to increase resource management. Entrance fees, donations, taxes on ancillary services or products, private investment, and land leases can be used to aid conservation.

Wight (1992) cites several cases in which ecotourism is stimulating greater collaborative interaction. The Association of Independent Tour Operators (AITD) has taken a joint initiative with Green Flag International to promote ecotourism and sustainable tourism development. She describes the case of Sobek Expeditions as providing a remarkably high amount of its proceeds (7.6–10%) to local conservation groups. Wight has identified important principles that should underlie the concept of ecotourism:

- Better understanding of the linkage and potentially symbiotic relationship between conservation and marketing
- Balance between environmental, or "green," marketing and industry commitment to environmentally responsible action
- Taking a supply management perspective that acknowledges resource values and accepts resource constraints and limits, as well as seizing resource-based opportunities
- Development of understanding and partnerships between host communities, governments, nongovernmental organizations, and the industry
- Greater discrimination in client selection by identifying market segments that better match the range of ecotourism products
- Development of formal or informal product and performance standards
- Promotion and acceptance of a tourist and operator code of ethics and of guidelines for responsible travel practices and behavior

A classic example of ecotourism is the profit-making Maho Bay Camps, located within the U.S. Virgin Islands National Park. This nature resort is designed with minimum intrusion to the native landscape and offers visitors intimate contact with local flora and fauna. According to the owner (Selengut 1992), the land rent for 1990, contributed to the national park for its use, was $217,000, even after netting a profit of 20 percent on the investment.

Ecotourism is demonstrating a new trend in low-key planning and design for a burgeoning travel market interested in the special qualities of place.

ENVIRONMENTAL DESIGN CRITERIA

If environments of the supply side of tourism are to be planned and designed to meet the needs of visitors, to support public and private development, and yet to perpetuate resource assets, what criteria must be followed? The following discussion identifies some of the main criteria that experience has demonstrated are important. These should offer the many developers and managers of tourism new opportunities for success as well as for avoiding environmental pitfalls.

FUNCTIONAL PLANNING AND DESIGN

For both developers and travelers, tourism should be planned and designed to function. But, such functioning has many dimensions, especially the following four.

First of all, tourism must function *as a system*. The only one who cuts across the results of decisions on tourism supply is the traveler. Perhaps, in some instances, all the hundreds of separate developments function well together, but mostly this is by chance, not by design. Because development is created and managed by such a great number of diverse public and private entities, needed are mechanisms for cooperation and even collaboration on decision making. All components of supply—attractions, services, transportation, information, promotion—must be integrated for tourism to function well for both visitors and developers.

All design must meet *structural criteria*. In an age of space shuttles and high technology, it seems redundant to stress the need for basic structural stability, and yet drives do erode, bridges do collapse, and sometimes hotel structural failures cause loss of life. Although the incidence of these problems is very low, these examples do point up the need for concern over structural functionalism. Legislation may be less in need than greater precision, professionalism, and conscientious responsibility on the part of all involved in environmental design. By and large, research and testing, as well as tightened regulation, now offer little excuse for error in structural design. Buildings, drainage systems, drives, walks, and landscapes must be designed and maintained to withstand wear and tear as well as climatic conditions that would cause structural failure or shorten the structure's life.

Another measure of design is that of *physical* function. By this is meant the capability of the designed environment, indoors and outdoors, to meet the physical needs of people, animals, automobiles, or any other units that will need to use the environment. For people-environments, designers need to be aware of the physical dimensions of the human body and how the various parts function (including the disabled and handicapped).

In spite of the availability of design reference data books, generally derived from research, designers still give tourists noisy and uncomfortable heat and cooling, airline seats with unreachable controls, signs and directions on highways and in buildings that are illegible or misleading, and lockers that cannot be reached by groups of short stature. In the landscape, the changing physical requirements of compact cars, recreation vehicles, tour buses, and large trucks must be considered in the site planning for overnight accommodations and food services for travelers. Owners and developers must continually insist upon efficient physical functional design for all their environments.

But environments can meet criteria of structural and physical needs and yet not fully satisfy the demands of tourism. How often one sees adjectives such as "comfortable," "pleasant," "beautiful," "luxurious," and "sparkling" in tourist promotional literature. These point up the need for a fourth category of criteria that all environments must meet—an *aesthetic* or *cultural* function. Drab, institutional, plain, and unexciting landscapes and buildings are not acceptable even though sometimes more economical to build.

For tourist appreciation, understanding, and enjoyment, architects, engineers, and landscape architects must design buildings, walks, drives, and overlooks with sensitivity to natural vistas and beauty. Sidestepping the engagement of creative and talented designers may appear to save money only to result in the later discovery that tourists patronize the better-designed competition. Some businesses, fearing decline in popularity of their design, regularly schedule remodeling of all exteriors and interiors.

Managers and designers of tourist environments need to consider all four functions—systematic, structural, physical, aesthetic—then develop new or remodel older lands and buildings for tourists.

MARKET ACCEPTANCE

Environmental design and land use for tourism has a market side as well as a resource side. Land use is a social attribution as well as an activity based on physical assets. What visitors want to see and do—and they are not all alike in their tastes and interests—makes a difference. The sorting out of market diversity and translating it into appropriately created environments is no easy task. It is complicated by several factors.

First, there is a great difference in *preference* of destination activities among travelers. Studies variously classify travelers by whether they like active physical challenge or passive spectatorism, historic sites or natural resource areas, entertainment or solitude, and many other ways of sorting out the activity interests. This is further complicated by the difference in trip purpose and different interest by the tourist at different times.

Second, *fad and fashion* are powerful variables and can

boom or break destinations. The capricious nature of some markets creates a volatile design and planning problem. Tourism activities grow out of culture's leisure patterns and, therefore, are extremely dynamic, not static. Early on, research of trends may be able to predict important ins or outs of travel trade.

Third, the vagaries of *transportation technology and cost* greatly influence the design and planning of destinations. Areas dependent upon automobile travel are subject to fluctuations of fuel cost, costs of vehicles, and changes of highways. They may also be affected by competitive fares of airlines, car rentals, and bus tours. Research of the comparative influence of transportation modes on travel can be valuable for all tourism destination management.

Fourth, some areas are blessed with *natural resource assets* in support of special activities much preferred by markets. No matter how much market analysis may suggest demand for winter sports, southern climes have difficulty in meeting this demand. Conversely, no matter how attractive some northern beaches may be, they cannot meet market demands for warm water, extended periods of sunshine, and high temperatures. Research of physical resource assets can assist managers in design and planning issues.

In addition to the above factors of market acceptance of designed tourism development, there is a *temporal* problem. For tourism, in which the product is fixed to place and has relatively high capital investment, this may mean a short life. Does the designer intentionally create flimsy environments that are to be flushed away after their usable life span? Can environments be designed with built-in flexibility that anticipates decline and, therefore, incorporates a chance for remodeling to meet new needs? Research has not yet provided adequate answers to these questions, but all managers must be aware of the anticipated life of built environments and must have contingency plans available for meeting the new needs. Many older resorts are meeting today's market needs with innovative programs and renovation.

OWNER REWARDS

Both public and private owners expect certain rewards from their ownership and management and resist modifications for someone else's objectives. Those groups standing outside owners, such as advocates of greater environmental protection, must be able to translate their ideologies through the existing system of land ownership and development.

For the *public sector* in tourism, the greatest role as an owner-developer is that of holding and managing vast acreage of resource assets, functioning primarily as attractions. In the United States, federal agencies alone own and manage 85 percent of all outdoor recreation lands (Domestic Tourism 1973:9), but considerable internal policy stress has developed because none of the agencies was originally given tourism as a significant function.

The rewards to the U.S. National Park Service are twofold: providing visitor experiences for many millions of visitors each year and protecting outstanding natural resource assets for the national long-range welfare. Fulfilling these objectives influences greatly its policies on design and land use. Throughout its history, much controversy has centered on the extent of providing for visitors and at the same time protecting the resource. This has resulted in much vacillation in land-use planning for the Service.

When one adds some 90 or more federal agencies to the hundreds of state, county, and city jurisdictions over lands used by tourists, the magnitude of governmental involvement in land development and use can be appreciated. How well cities have managed their infrastructure (water supply, waste disposal, streets, police, fire protection) can influence citizens' willingness to pay taxes for public services.

Rewards to the private *nonprofit sector* are prescribed by their individual organizational policies. Owners of the Alamo and Williamsburg, for example, seek to inspire in visitors a sense of national-heritage understanding and pride, as well as to restore and preserve important elements of national history. Much of the restoration of urban historic areas is motivated by altruistic rewards, while greatly influencing the storehouse of development, land use, and profit to local tourism businesses.

Rewards to the *free enterprise sector* are commonly considered to be profit making, but those in business quickly point out that this is not an exclusive reward. Much social responsibility is felt and carried out, not merely for altruistic objectives but in order to function properly as a business. According to Drucker (1975):

> There is no conflict between 'profit' and 'social responsibility.' To earn enough to cover the genuine costs which only the so-called 'profit can cover,' is economic and social responsibility—indeed it is the special social and economic responsibility of business. It is not the business that earns a profit adequate to its genuine costs of capital, to the risks of tomorrow and the needs of tomorrow's worker and pensioner that 'rips off' society. It is the business that fails to do so.

Profits cannot be an isolated goal, removed from service to tourists, protection of resources, or concern over social issues.

Regarding land use, all sectors are acting as brokers between visitors (with their preferences) and resources (with their intrinsic developable qualities). The more that research demonstrates the linkage between visitors and resources, the more that a closer balance between resource protection and use can be accomplished by all sectors. Their rewards are derived as much from visitor satisfactions as from other goals of the enterprise, public or private.

RELEVANCE TO TRANSPORTATION

An important criterion of environmental design for tourism—obvious but not well understood—is that of the relevance of transportation. This must be approached not only through the perception of the managers of the several modes (air, auto, rail, ship) but also through the perspective of the

traveler. Research is demonstrating time and again that travelers do not stray very far from main thoroughfares. Even wilderness users have been found to congregate primarily at points of access penetration. Instead of citing this as a frailty of visitors, managers would do well to accept it as a principle and adapt destination design and planning thereto.

This does not mean that strip development is inevitable. It merely means that a transportation system that provides convenient, dependable, and affordable linkage between access and all points of interest to the tourist is important. Modern home-to-destination modes are dominantly automobile, tour bus, RV, and plane. (Cruise ships today are more destination resorts than modes of transportation.)

At all exchange points (freeway exits, airports, bus depots), interconnecting modes—personal car, car rental, tour bus, tour ferry—become very important. At these points of intermodal connection, greater concern over integrated land use and information systems is needed. Research is showing that mastery of today's complicated regional airports is not for the infirm or fainthearted.

The planning and development of future destinations should depend more heavily on studies of passenger transportation preferences and behavior than they have in the past.

RESOURCE PROTECTION

Polarized advocacy positions between resource protectionists—even "preservationists"—and developers have clouded the issue of environmental protection and tourism. Environmentalism, and now sustainable development, has fostered greater awareness of the finite limits of natural resources.

Poorly understood is the overwhelming dependence of tourism upon natural and cultural resource assets. Instead of opposing moves for resource protection, tourism managers could well lend their support not only for the long-range goals of society but also for their own self-interest.

Natural resource foundations for tourism include *water and waterlife, vegetative cover, wildlife, topographic change, soils and geology, and climate and atmosphere.* An essential part of any tourism planning is research of the distribution, size, quality, and management trends governing these resources.

Of increasing importance are culture resources. For planning purposes, these can be identified as *prehistoric and archeological sites, historic sites and events, shrines, major works (outstanding engineering, technical, and scientific accomplishments), lore and legends, arts and crafts, ethnic and national customs, industries, institutions, and settlements.*

Critical is the design of places such that masses of visitors can be accommodated without erosion of these valuable and finite assets. Properly planned, tourism can foster the clarification and perpetuation of traditions and customs of special populations.

Much of the gap between tourist business management and resource protection is the lack of product definition. Hoteliers, for example, do not only provide lodging and food; they also provide a facility so that travelers can see and do something in the area. The attractions, largely depending on resource protection, are part of their product and deserve their support and protection for business success as well as long-range value to society.

COMMUNITY GOALS

Too often, tourism is taken out of the context of basic community interest, activity, and goal seeking. Since so much of tourism is directed to destination communities (even those resource assets in remote settings are served by local communities), it is necessary for tourism management to link all its efforts with the society, government, and traditions of cities. A polarized position such as that of Garland (1981:19), "Tourism is a spinoff industry. . . . It should never be permitted to influence land use in any fundamental way," forecloses constructive environmental design and planning for the good of the community as well as for tourism.

Behind the obvious facade of tourism businesses—hotels, gas stations, airlines—lies the infrastructure of tourism. Because most development for tourism takes place at cities, research study of the economic input-output regarding infrastructure is needed. Expanded tourism brings in new revenues, but it also requires more water, electricity, gas, waste disposal, streets, policing, fire protection, and even medical care. Communities should have knowledge of added infrastructure costs, as well as added returns, before deciding on a positive or negative tourism-development policy.

Because cities are where most people live, it is well for tourism management to be aware of what environmental development policies are important to local citizens. People value their cities because of their amenities.

Coincidentally, most of these are the same elements that attract visitors and provide them with satisfactions. Therefore, essential are the careful design, planning, and management that reduce conflict between visitor and resident as each competes for the same amenities. Much of this may be resolved if the tourism interests (chambers of commerce, hoteliers, restaurateurs) communicate with city councils and citizen organizations when urban decisions are being made. A proactive stance by tourism has greater opportunities than the present reactive position in most communities. While environmental designers and planners extol the virtue of diversity for all groups, they also recognize the need for constant managerial interplay that maintains diversity with a minimum of conflict.

ENVIRONMENTAL DECISION MAKERS

This discussion of environmental design and land use would not be complete without reference to the decision-makers. Popularly, professional planners and designers are considered to have a major role. They do in many instances, but research of this subject shows the important influence of several other segments. In fact, in today's complex environmental development process, it is not always easy to identify the true decision makers—those who most directly influence how land is to be used and how final development is to appear. Therefore, it is equally difficult to identify present policy, to guide better future policy, and to guide future research.

Certainly, *owners* do have a major influence, whether they be hotel corporations, marina entrepreneurs, historical societies, national resource-management agencies, or the individual with a cottage. For all land owners, public and private, certain owner objectives are very critical—speculation, specific business use, quasi-business use, tax reduction, social welfare, personal home. What actually is developed for tourists depends heavily upon the owner's intent, not only for the type of use but also the quality and quantity of use. For government agencies, most are bound to their legal administrative mandates but exercise considerable freedom in their own land-use policies within such mandates.

Today, *moneylenders* have a very strong influence on land use of tourism. Public and private financial sources have their own policies regarding land uses that they will and will not support. Moneylenders have great power and, in many instances, have stopped or changed drastically an owner's intended use of land. Private finance is often very restrictive, especially for what is conceived as high-risk development, such as for resorts and theme parks. Outside investors, while stimulating a local economy, frequently ignore local interests, resource values and traditions, and culture norms. When out of control, this can be devastating to resource foundations and societies, especially rural areas and small towns.

The *land development and construction industry* has a critical role in tourism land use. New methods and technology have reduced many limitations on environmental manipulation and building. But a most important control is the cost of construction. Many final decisions on uses of land and building design are dictated by how much the development would cost. Some land has never been developed for tourism because of this single factor. Especially in periods of inflation and recession, the availability and cost of labor and construction materials can dramatically influence decisions.

The *manager* of tourist lands frequently has an after-the-fact rather than a planning role in decision making on land use. Managers of parks, hotels, airports, campgrounds, and other tourist establishments have important design knowledge based upon experience. Frequently, however, they are brought into an active role only after most decisions on land use and design and even construction have been made by others. Hence, they face the dilemma of doing the best they can with the opportunities and constraints handed to them.

Perhaps the preceding review has shown that *designers and planners* do not have quite as much influence on decision making on land use as popularly believed. While it is true that professional designers and planners (architects, engineers, landscape architects, interior designers, urban planners) produce the concepts, sketch plans, working drawings and specifications for actual development of land, their freedom of choice is severely limited by other factors. Still, new environmental form and function, structure or landscape, are the realm of the creative designer.

One area of the designer-owner relationship needs to be emphasized. In most projects today, there is often a gap between the owner's land and the designer's understanding of what is to be done with the land. The designer, whose last few projects likely were each entirely different, expects the information on *what* is to be done to come from the owner. On the other hand, the owner, believing that he is hiring the expert to design his land, relies on the designer. Neither one fully realizes the need for deeper research of the problem—a study of the numbers of people, the level of market stratification, the seasons of intensity, tourism interests now and predicted, and many other program needs. The filling of this gap is becoming an important role of research by consulting firms.

Another important role of research, not being done very much today, is evaluation of design success after construction and use. Seldom are designers brought back in a research role to determine if the design really worked.

Finally, *publics* have entered into the process of land-use decision making in several ways. Many agencies and private organizations, either because of legislation or voluntarily, use public involvement during the land-use planning stage. Some publics have created specific organizations or worked through existing ones to lobby for legislation on land use. Many new rules and regulations on land use have been developed in recent years, from local to national levels, due to increased activity by private groups. An important public is the total of tourist users of developed land. Theirs is really the ultimate deciding factor regarding the success of design and land use.

Recently, greater emphasis in planning has been placed on clarifying commitment and objectives in earlier stages of tourism planning. Because tourism actors and stakeholders are so diverse and because of potential impact on local citizens, such public involvement, although essential, is very difficult to obtain. It is essential, right at the start of any tourism planning, that *all* constituency groups are involved.

Two processes that have proven helpful are brainstorming and Nominal Group Technique (NGT) (Crompton and Watt 1990). Brainstorming is an open meeting dialog among interested parties, whereas NGT ideas are generated individually without oral interaction. In both, the purpose is not to resolve problems but to bring many constituencies, even dissidents, into a common forum in order to generate ideas and give priority to concerns.

In order to obtain information on the perceived role of the San Antonio Convention and Visitors Bureau, for example, the NGT process involved 22 representatives of diverse interests in the city (Watt and Stribling 1990). The fields represented were:

banking
telephone service
biomedical research
electrical power
uniform, towel service
library

CVB advisory committee
water supplier
shopping center
Hispanic chamber of commerce
property management
hospital

international relation official consultants, accountants women's chamber of commerce small business advocate

This resulted in identifying as top roles: promotion, business growth, hospitality education, coordinate bookings, and image building. This process is equally applicable to planning for future tourism growth.

This review of decision making and decision makers in design and land use is intended merely to suggest the need for more and better research information on improvement both in the process and in the role of each sector.

PROCESSES

Throughout the discussion of environmental planning, design, and land use thus far, many solutions have been hinted at, even suggested. If better tourism environmental solutions are to be accomplished, what are some of the processes that can be employed? It is one thing to have noble goals, proper criteria, and decision makers with the right policies for environmental design and land use; it is quite another to make them work. The complexity of tourism, as described previously, suggests some of the problems of implementing desirable improvements in tourism development, but progress is being made, both on the research side and on the environmental design side.

Two aspects of environmental planning and design are especially critical. First, the so-called *elitist* approach, performed solely by professionals, is giving way to *integrated planning*. *Integrated planning* means a cooperative approach involving many constituencies, particularly local citizens and professionals. Even the traditional plan-implementation sequence is being replaced by introducing implementation factors at the very beginning of tourism planning. Unless there is an organization, agency, or individual committed to implementation at the very start, there is little likelihood of plans being acted upon.

For all tourism planning, representatives of all three sectors—government, nonprofit organizations, commercial enterprise—should be involved from the start. Other representatives of the area also should be involved. If, for example, environmentalists are not involved from the beginning, they may become polarized in opposition no matter how valuable and sustainable tourism may be if properly planned and managed. Often the weight of opinion is heavier than factual documentation. Conflicts of opinion should be resolved early so that they do not escalate into bitter issues preventing planning progress.

Second, essential to all tourism planning is fact-finding *research* on fundamentals of tourism development. Cursory knowledge of tourism planning can lead to conflict, degradation of resources, and disappointing tourism results. No matter whether at the regional, destination, or site scale, two sets of information should be obtained as foundation for planning: characteristics of travel markets and facts about the supply side. Unless these are well understood before expansion plans are laid, major errors can take place.

An example of successful tourism planning was the preventing of a major resort intrusion of the island of Moorea, Tahiti. A task force, sponsored by the Pacific Asia Travel Association and French Polynesia, studied market data and supply-side development of the island (Moorea 1990). It was concluded that the relatively low resort-hotel occupancy (50%) and market needs would not be met by allowing a major resort-golf complex to be established. Such a proposal would be damaging to the fragile environment of Opunohu Valley's natural and cultural (ancient Polynesian) resources. Instead, recommended were: placing the mountain and several beaches in national park status; adding visitor interpretive centers (cultural and natural), central sewage system, and tours and events based on resources; and tapping the growing ecotourism markets. These recommendations generally have been accepted, and the large resort-golf complex has been denied by a vote of the residents.

Nations, regions, destinations, and sites intended for tourism development need the early integration of all stakeholders and complete descriptive analysis of present resources and tourism status before major plans are created.

REGIONAL SCALE

Even though the planning steps for all scales—regional, destination, site—are similar, the processes at the macro scale need special emphasis. A project at the regional (national, state, provincial) scale should accomplish these objectives:

- Identification of destination zones of potential
- Solutions to constraints and issues
- Policies, organizational structures
- Integration with destination and site plans

Such a project can best be accomplished by a *task force* representing the public and private sectors and planning consultants. Generally, the following steps would be followed:

Setting Goals and Objectives

The best plans can be accomplished considering four overall goals: increased visitor satisfactions, improved business and economy, protection of resources, and integration into destination and local economy and quality of life. Specific objectives usually include guidelines for action, responsibilities of action organizations, and action strategies.

Research

Several sets of factors need to be studied. A description of *market* characteristics—preferences, segments, trends—is needed. A description of existing *supply* components is required including attractions, transportation, services, information and guidance, and promotion. This research step should also identify *constraints and issues* relevant to tourism development. Finally, a description of *agencies and organizations* and their roles in tourism should be completed. If this regional study is to identify zones of develop-

ment potential, research of *geographical factors* that can be mapped will be required. (Refer to Gunn 1988a for details of computer analysis.)

Synthesis

Before concepts and recommendations are prepared, the results of the research step need to be synthesized for their meaning. This step should involve all Task Force members to derive important conclusions as foundations for further steps.

Concepts

This is an ideation step whereby new concepts are presented, primarily by the professional planners but described for all constituencies to review. The model, illustrated in Figure 1, reduces the complicated makeup of a region into major planning components: circulation corridors, destination zones, access, and relationship to markets. Computerized GIS overlay systems, as illustrated in Figure 2, can aid in the discovery of destination zones with potential for tourism (Gunn and Larsen 1988). Figure 3 illustrates such zones for a portion of South Carolina (Gunn 1990).

Recommendations

The final step is the result of the earlier findings and concepts. Recommendation topics vary, but the following would be desirable:

1. Policy
2. Physical development
3. Program development
4. Objectives, strategies, responsibilities

   1. *Policy* recommendations at the regional scale would encompass primarily the governmental role. This should include: promotion, interagency cooperation, public-private cooperation, private-sector incentives, and needed regulatory action. New policy statements and agreements among private-sector tourism organizations would be desirable, such as goals of environmental planning, management, and protection.

   2. *Physical development* recommendations would include identification of zones of tourism potential and guidelines for their implementation. Based on the extent to which present supply meets market demand and resource support, new kinds of development would be identified, especially for attractions, services, and transportation. Recommendations for physical development at the regional scale would be generalized because plans will be executed primarily at the destination and site scales.

   3. *Program development* recommendations would include those needed to meet market needs—festivals, events, information and guidance, and promotion.

   4. *Objectives, strategies, and responsibilities* is the final step that defines specific objectives that need to be acted upon in order to correct deficiencies and to expand tourism devel-

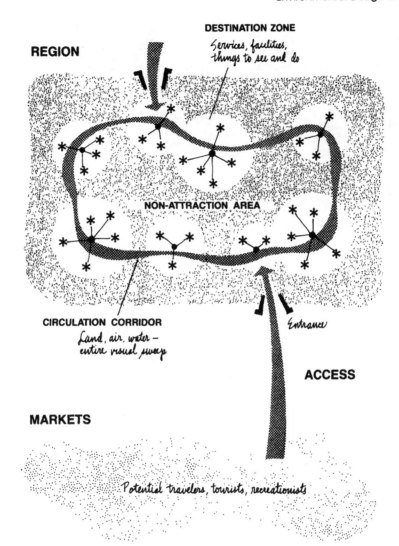

FIGURE 1 Conceptual model of a tourism region, illustrating spatial components of destination zones, circulation corridor, access, and relationship to markets. *Source:* Gunn, 1988b, p. 71.

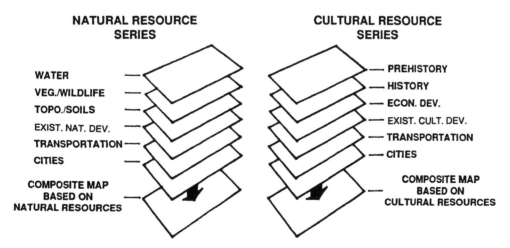

FIGURE 2 Map overlays used to produce composite maps illustrating potential destination zones based on natural and cultural resources.

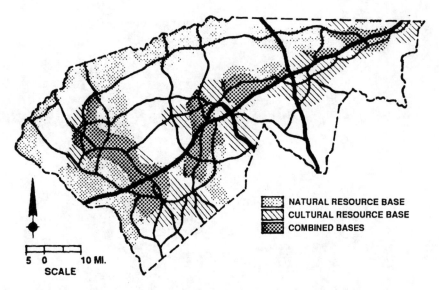

NATURAL RESOURCE BASE
CULTURAL RESOURCE BASE
COMBINED BASES

FIGURE 3 Potential destination zone interpretations for six counties in northwestern South Carolina. Map shows zones based on natural resources, cultural resources, and their combination.

opment throughout the region. For each objective, strategies for action required and the logical implementing agency to accept responsibility would be specified. Some of these recommendations would be specific at the regional level, implemented primarily by government, whereas generalized recommendations would be offered for further consideration at the destination and site scales.

DESTINATION SCALE

Although the term *destination* has many meanings, it is defined here as a travel target area, serviced by one or several communities, and containing several attraction complexes. For environmental planning purposes, a destination zone could be modeled as illustrated in Figure 4. The principal elements needing planning and development attention are: *attraction complexes, community, linkage* between community and attractions, and *access* from markets.

If potential destination zones were derived through regional study, they will have been influenced greatly by key geographic factors. This means that they will likely include many governmental jurisdictions. In the United States, for example, a zone would likely encompass several counties and townships, as well as cities and villages.

In many instances, cooperation and even collaboration on planning and development among several destination zones is required. Travel market patterns are of two types. Some market segments travel directly from place of origin to a single destination where all activity interests are fulfilled. The traditional resort vacation is typical of this pattern. Today, a very large segment of travel is directed toward a series of destinations in a touring circuit. Travelers interested in history, for example, may visit several communities and their historic sites on a tour. The physical and program planning required for touring-circuit versus long-stay at one destination is quite different.

The steps in a destination planning process are similar to those at the regional scale but are much more definitive. Following is a suggested sequence of planning steps for planning tourist destinations.

Focusing Commitment

Especially important at the destination scale is obtaining consensus and leadership for tourism planning and development. Unless a clear commitment to the goals and objectives of tourism development is made at the start, professional plans and guidelines are not likely to be implemented. As in the earlier discussion of processes, many constituency groups, not just primary tourist businesses, must work together for the betterment of tourism.

An example of formalizing planning at this level is the creation of a "Tourism Action Committee," as recommended in the *Community Tourism Action Plan Manual* (1988) developed in Alberta, Canada. Suggested members of the committee include representatives of:

Chamber of commerce	Economic Development Board
Hotel/motel operators	Service station operators
Restaurant operators	Historical society
Service clubs	Tourist zone reprsenatives
Sports groups	Municipal administration
Recreation board	Tourist attractions
Tourist event organizers	

Others, such as schools, industries, environmentalists, tour agencies, campground operators, and youth and church organizations, could add valuable input to all future tourism-destination planning. The purpose is to safeguard social, economic, and environmental qualities at the same time tourism is expanded or improved. In addition, the committee needs to engage planning professionals for overall guidance and execution of plans.

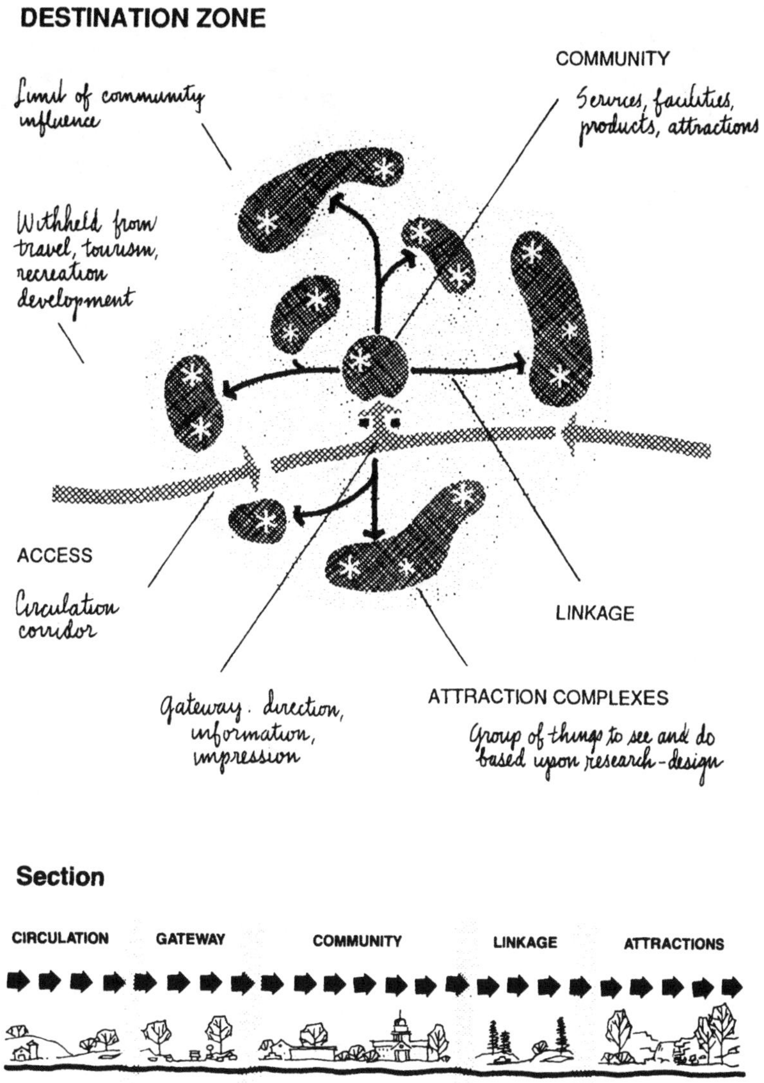

DESTINATION ZONE

COMMUNITY

Services, facilities, products, attractions

Limit of community influence

Withheld from travel, tourism, recreation development

ACCESS

Circulation corridor

Gateway. direction, information, impression

LINKAGE

ATTRACTION COMPLEXES

Group of things to see and do based upon research-design

Section

CIRCULATION   GATEWAY   COMMUNITY   LINKAGE   ATTRACTIONS

FIGURE 4 Model of geographic components of a destination zone: attraction complexes, community, linkage corridor between community and attractions, and access from major circulation corridor. *Source:* Gunn 1988b, p. 57.

Analyzing Markets

Destination market analysis is a refinement of generalized regional market studies. Both secondary data and new surveys should be utilized to obtain information on existing and potential travel markets. Helpful is discovery of these characteristics: activity interests, origins, seasonality, and classification of market segments.

Analyzing Supply Side

For most communities and their surrounding areas, little has been done to identify what has been developed on the tourism supply side and what resources have potential for further development. Key items of supply to be studied regarding present as well as potential status include:

Services—hotels, motels, restaurants, shops
Transportation—all modes, intermodal coordination
Attractions—physical developments, events
Information—descriptive literature, maps
Promotion—programs, effectiveness
Resource base—natural and cultural resources

Identifying Organizations, Roles

This step identifies the many public and private organizations and agencies that influence or have a role in planning, development, and management of tourism. Included should be:

Governmental agencies for parks, reserves, historic sites
Nonprofit organizations for parks, reserves, historic sites
Private travel, tourism, and hospitality organizations

Financial institutions, programs
Governmental planning and regulatory agencies

Identifying Constraints, Issues, Needs

By means of public forums, brainstorming sessions, or applications of NGT, all constraints inhibiting tourism should be identified. The need for enhancing tourism quality as well as quantity should be stressed. It is from these public-input processes that capacity concerns would be identified, such as: limits to water supply, waste disposal; street-capacity limits; park and recreation capacities; resource base limitations; financial constraints; obsolete or overlapping regulations; and transportation limitations.

Concepts for Supply Development

In conjunction with professional consultants (planners, landscape architects, tourism specialists), the committee should develop some basic concepts for each of the supply-side components. This step would reflect market segment demand and the special resource qualities of the destination. Concepts should be developed for each of the following:

Attractions
Services
Transportation
Information
Promotion

Recommendations

This final step encompasses the action needed to implement the concepts that have emerged from all of the earlier planning steps. What should be done, by whom, where, and when (short-range versus long-range)? Encompassed in these recommendations should be the following:

• Integration of Action—It is essential that tourism is integrated into all of the community and surrounding areas plans for social, economic, and environmental development. Tourism must not be treated superficially as only an overlay without incorporation into the life and breadth of the entire destination area.

• Solution to "Gaps" between Market Demand and Supply—Specific recommendations need to be made to identify changes in all supply-side development to meet travel-market trends.

• Solution to Constraints and Limitations—Detailed recommendations on solutions to capacity, environmental, societal, regulatory, organizational, financial, or other constraints must be offered.

• Policies on Growth and Sustainable Development—The committee should prepare policy statements that could be adopted by all public and private stakeholders in tourism. Such policy statements would identify roles, responsibilities, growth, resource protection, human resources, and integration with all facets of the community and surrounding areas.

• Implementation Follow-up—Built into all tourism planning must be clear identification of an implementation timetable and who is responsible for each step. Generally, priority should be given to the easier and least costly items that also demonstrate visible results. All new development should be made on an incremental basis to avoid stressful impact from change.

SITE SCALE

Today, with new understandings of tourism as a system, planning and design at the site scale can no longer be confined to an individual property. Planning decisions for hotels, restaurants, resorts, marinas, theme parks, visitor interpretive centers, and park areas have an external as well as an internal dimension. Each site influences, and is influenced by, many other sites. When this principle is practiced by owners-developers of sites, they will be more successful, not less. Developers can no longer ignore their impact on the environment, society, and economy of the area around their development. Conversely, when cooperating with external tourism decision makers, they can benefit because their "product" is not provided only on the site. Motloch (1991:269) has described this important relationship as follows:

By focusing on the piece, we make it more difficult to understand and apply ecological, physiological, and psychological interrelatedness to the management and design of systems. In the process, we create even larger crises, symptoms of the increased system breakdown that occur because the elements that we design aggregate over time to create systems that are not sustainable.

Most desirable for site developers and planners would be the situation whereby regional and destination plans and planning processes are already in place. A regional plan would have identified destination zones of greatest potential. Destination plans would have identified the needed improvement (on sites) in order to match market demand and utilize resource advantages. With this framework in place, site decisions already have considerable guidance. Sites can then be planned knowing that environmental capacities have been considered, access and transportation have been planned, public utilities (water supply, waste disposal, power) have been planned for tourism expansion, and the site is in proper geographical context for best success.

PROCESS

The site planning process, while similar to regional and destination scales, requires specific steps for best development for tourism. The steps could be generalized as the following five.

Program Agreement

By means of discussion between the owner (client) and professional planners/designers (landscape architects, architects, engineers), an agreement is reached on *what* is to be designed. This is a critical step because misunderstandings at this stage will prove detrimental throughout the process. For tourism sites, much discussion must take place to obtain not only the client's statements of intended development but also characteristics of the tourist market segment likely to visit the site. As stated by designer Motloch (1991), this is a cyclical process between client and designer.

Site Criteria, Selection, and Analysis

A common failure at this point is not to engage the designer in site selection. Certainly, the owner-developer must consider cost, availability, and other criteria, but the designer can assist by considering landform, buildability, and adjacent-site context. Certainly, as many alternate sites as possible should be considered. At this stage, generalized reactions to the suitability of the site for purposes intended can be obtained and discussed between designer and client.

A site analysis results in a detailed description and assessment of the physical characteristics of the site. Included are: topography, soil, geology, drainage, weather conditions, vegetation, and views. Existing development is identified: structures, pavements, sewage systems, and electrical power. Influences surrounding the site are described: shadowing from high-rise, access, adjacent land use, and visual and odor considerations (see Landphair and Motlock 1985).

Functional Relationships

With an understanding of site conditions, the designer collaborates with the client in discussing the needed functional relationships—which land use functions should go where and their interrelationships. This is an organizational spatial stage. The designer often uses sketch diagrams to model these relationships—building masses, circulation, plant masses, vistas, access. After much experimentation and discussion between client and designer, consensus is reached on a final composite relationship diagram.

It must be emphasized here that because this step forms the very foundation for the site design, external functional factors must be included. If it is to be a hotel, how will it relate to traveler activities in the area, how will it fit related development for visitor service (food, shopping, medical, touring), and how will it impact the environment? These and other external factors are as critical to success and resource protection as internal operation. The designer can act as a catalyst for bringing the client into agreement with outside public and private interests.

Design Concepts

At this stage, the collective talent, training, and experience of the designers and client are introduced. This is an ideation and creative stage. While observation of similar projects may help, there is a temptation by owners to copy too literally, resulting in homogenized tourism development. Instead, the unique characteristics of the site should be inte-

grated with the program for a special design concept. Motloch (1991) calls this "the coming together of idea, symbol, and sense of place."

Plans

Upon consensus of the design concept, detailed plans, specifications, and construction contract are prepared. These are the legal and detailed documents that assure the project will be constructed exactly as visualized by client and designer. In today's context, this final stage produces not only what the client desired but also what best fits the immediate and broader environmental setting.

OTHER ENVIRONMENTAL ISSUES
LAND-USE REGULATION

When governments cannot rely upon voluntary compliance with land-use guidelines or when land-use trends change, it may be necessary for governments to enact legislation, such as zoning regulations and building codes. Zoning action in the United States is vested in the power of government to intervene for protection of public health, safety, and welfare. Official governmental planning has been done primarily at the community level and consists of five types: comprehensive (land use), system (water, transportation), area (waterfronts, industrial districts), subsystems (sewer line), and site (fire station, park)(So 1988:15).

Detailed controls, such as building codes and zoning ordinances, must be preceded by a comprehensive plan that performs these functions (So 1988):

- The plan is an expression of what a community wants. It is a statement of goals, a listing of objectives, and a vision of what might be.
- The plan, once prepared, serves as a guide to decision making. It provides the means for guiding and influencing the many public and private decisions that create the future of the community.
- The plan, in some cases, may represent the fulfillment of a legal requirement. It may be a necessary obligation. Such a mandated plan can, of course, still fulfill the first two functions, but the fact that it is required adds a distinctive dimension to the planning process.

Environmental concerns in recent years have given rise to governmental requirements of *environmental impact statements* (EIS) directed primarily to government-funded and -directed projects. Thus far, in spite of documented accomplishments, the EIS process has not been incorporated into planning processes. Therefore, it is often seen by business as another bureaucratic obstacle. Wight (1991) recommends stronger integration of environmental assessment early in the planning and design process. She identifies these aspects:

- Building sound environmental principles into each stage of project design, from the outset.

- Early lead-in time for initiating assessment so that environmental management is integral to development.
- Assessment of project acceptability versus simply incorporating mitigation into project design.

CLUSTERING

A quick managerial response to increased wear and tear from too many visitors in one spot is dispersal. But now the problems of dispersal are beginning to show. Dispersal denies all the advantages of clustering, which is more functional from the standpoint of both visitors and services. As Balmer et al. (1977:3) have described, clustering has merit from several perspectives.

From a Development Perspective

The necessary infrastructure is much more efficient and certainly less costly in a developed area or where several developments are being planned. The viability of a new commercial tourism plant increases with the degree of travel and the size of the resident market. Experience has shown the marketing advantages of motels being located near other motels, food services near others, and other like groupings. Several developments from the same sector can create or ensure efficient use of necessary support services. The California coast plan, for example, "encourages the concentration of new development in those places that are already developed, so as to minimize resource damage, economize on public facilities and make non-automobile transportation possible" (Healy 1976:221).

From an Economic Perspective

Longer stays in the area, generated by a variety of attractions, boost revenues in accommodation and food service sectors of the local economy. Diversity, both within the tourism industry and in the way in which tourism complements existing industry, increases the economic stability of the community. A large and mixed tourism development will gradually create a skilled and reliable local labor pool. The more complete the local service (both to the tourist and to the services) the smaller the possibility of "leakage." The benefits (direct and indirect through the multiplier effect) to the primary impact area increase with the size and diversity of local tourism.

From a Social Perspective

The opportunity for increased interaction between the resident and the tourist is enhanced by greater concentration. Traditional customs may be reinforced in an area. Many facilities, even though designed for the tourists, will be available to the resident population (specialty restaurants, convention centers, museums, theme parks).

From an Environmental Perspective

Expansion of currently viable urban areas in tourism service centers is likely to alter rural and natural environments less than new development in those environments. Planners can become skilled in the direction of tourism to ensure that unique and sensitive areas are protected, that adequate design standards are maintained, and that all necessary support services have been planned for and provided. Intensive site development and use are easier to control and manage with consequent protection and preservation of secondary impact areas. Clustering prevents sprawl and general visual pollution of key natural features (primary attractions in themselves).

From a Promotional Perspective

The potential for packaging of diverse but complementary opportunities increases with the scale of local tourism investment. The possibilities of "themeing" to better convey the appeal of the area to the potential visitor are enhanced when a larger number of attractions and services exist. The synergistic effect of several attractions creates a natural ability to draw tourists over relatively large distances, thus increasing the market potential for each.

Clustering is an important principle for coastal tourism, very important in the United States and many other countries. The term *coast* implies a uniform linearity for great distances along the water's edge. Coastal tourism, however, functions primarily at nodes (see Lewis 1964 and Gunn 1988b). By designing for mass concentrations (meeting market needs for gregarious waterfront uses: beaches, festivals, marinas), better management, better control, and better guest satisfactions can be derived. Such concentration relieves the pressure on remote areas and provides greater solitude for the market segment desiring it.

CAUTIONS

While the principle of clustering has environmental design advantages for tourism, it can be abused.

The *location* of development clusters requires care in planning. As historic districts become more popular, the need for travel services increases. Clustering these services too close to the historic area can damage the image of a revered landscape and reduce its attraction value. Clustering of services too close to natural resource areas also creates problems. Frequently, resort hotels have been built too close to beaches that are subject to hurricanes and erosion. New service clusters should not be placed directly upon or too close to special natural resource features, such as has happened in national parks. It is better planning to place such clusters some distance away and shuttle people to the resource area where visitor use can be controlled. Certainly, this principle protects the aesthetic integrity of resource areas.

Planning of clusters must consider *capacity*. Although tourism planning must be dynamic and adjust to change, it must also recognize capacity limits. Regular monitoring is necessary to stimulate incremental planning that recognizes dangers of overuse. Three types of capacity levels need planning attention. *Environmental* capacity refers to the limits at which development begins to be destructive of environmental assets. *Social* capacity refers to the level at which people begin to feel uncomfortable among masses of visitors and begin to react to overcrowding. (This is not the same as density—to see only a few others on a wilderness trail may be considered over capacity, whereas thousands of others on a beach may be considered desirable by visitors.) *Managerial* capacity is critical. Too great a concentration of visitors in one area may be difficult to control and may introduce thievery, litter, vandalism, and public disturbance. Public- and private-sector developers need to plan only for a capacity for which they have funding and staff to manage.

Although clustering as a principle has merit, quality planning demands care and judgment in its application to each situation.

INTERPRETATIVE VISITOR CENTERS

A current planning solution to much of the environmental problem of mass visitors to natural and cultural resource areas is increased use of interpretive visitor centers. Already, museums, aquariums, and zoos are demonstrating the value of designing a major facility that interprets the resource but is not located directly upon it. Such a facility meets both market demand and need for protecting rare, fragile, and limited capacity resources.

Conceptually, a major interpretive facility for either cultural or natural-resource function can serve as a surrogate attraction. It can be designed for mass use, providing visitor satisfaction without disturbing the resource.

Functional design features of a major interpretive visitor center would include:

- Parking for cars, buses, RVs
- Center building: lobby, restrooms
  information desk
  exhibit rooms, interpretive displays
  auditorium for videos, lectures
  library, study rooms
  food service
  shops (books, crafts, souvenirs)
  theater (pageants)
  staff offices
- Area: trails for guided and self-guided tours
  outdoor exhibit areas
  special features (overlook towers)

CONCLUSIONS

With greater taste discrimination of travelers and greater recognition of the role and limits of resources, environmental design and land use have increased greatly in managerial concern. What was viewed as a simple and private function of a market economy is now known to be much more complex. It involves characteristics of places, markets, transportation, owners, local citizens, and many other aspects of community and national life.

Research does not adequately prove what must be one of the most profound truths of tourism—placeness, and all the

characteristics inherent in the location and development of tourism places. In many ways, tourism, the environment, and places are synonymous. All are important to tourists, to governments, to businesses, and to those concerned with perpetuating quality resource assets. The development and the promotion of the individuality of places may be tourism's greatest opportunity.

A few conclusions regarding environmental design and land use:

Planning tourism requires research. Reliance only on past tourism experience is insufficient foundation for today's planning and design needs. Communities, areas, and nations must have greater factual information upon which to make development decisions. Research is especially needed in market trends and resource (natural and cultural) characteristics.

Tourism planning succeeds only with commitment. Environmental planning for tourism requires full commitment before plans are laid. At the regional and destination scales, many constituencies are involved, all of whom must be committed to tourism planning. Such planning need not always be for growth but often for improved quality or for coordination with other planning and plans.

Environmental planning for tourism depends heavily on the private sector. Because success of the commercial sector is highly dependent upon tourists attracted by natural and cultural resource activities, environmental protection is in its self-interest. Needed are stronger voluntary organizational and individual movements and advocacy to resolve environmental issues.

Governmental roles need to be clarified. Although the tourism economy is derived primarily through the private commercial sector, governments are heavily involved everywhere. For effective planning, these governmental roles must be clarified—interagency coordination, prevention of overlap of functions (especially promotion), excessive regulation, support for research and education, and public-private cooperation.

Public involvement is essential to environmental planning for tourism. All constituencies, both those involved in tourism development and those impacted by it, must have input into planning at all stages. Professional designers and planners can make valuable input, but action takes place only by others. Various techniques—workshops, meetings, brainstorming, NGT—need to be employed at all planning stages. Only in this manner will plans be implemented and the several objectives accomplished with least social, environmental, and economic stress.

Planning for tourism requires integration of regional, destination, and site plans. Especially important for individual success and sustainable use of the environment is site development (hotels, parks, transportation) that is planned in relation to destinations and the entire region. Integration of planning at all levels, even though difficult, holds promise of fulfilling all tourism development goals and extending environmental values.

Environmental design and planning for tourism is cycli-

cal. Best planning is incremental, with each new phase building on the last. All tourism development is in flux at all times. Both short- and long-range plans need to be placed in this context of dynamic change. Physical development tends to be more permanent but is always under the influence of changing markets and other supply changes around it.

The best tourism planning involves innovation and creativity. Tourism planning processes require inspiration as well as information. Results from research should be incorporated in plans, but experience has already demonstrated that no amount of facts can guarantee good planning and design. Local citizens as well as designers have a wealth of ideas that must be unleashed on a regular basis if tourism is to adapt continuously to new conditions and new needs. All inhibitors to such creativity and innovation must be replaced by opportunities to freely investigate and experiment with new ideas and approaches.

REFERENCES

Balmer, Crapo & Associates (1977), *A Review of Existing Tourism Zones and Suggested Primary Tourism Destination Zones*, Ottawa: Canadian Government Office of Tourism.

Brown, Lester R. (1991), "The New World Order," Chapter 1 (3–20), *State of the World*, New York: W.W. Norton.

Community Tourism Action Plan Manual (1988), Edmonton, Alberta, Canada: Alberta Tourism.

Crompton, John L., and Carson E. Watt (1990), *How to Generate and Evaluate Ideas: A Guide to Brainstorming and Nominal Group Techniques*, College Station: Texas A&M University.

"Domestic Tourism: An Ambivalent Tourism Policy" (1973), *Destination USA* (4) 7–18, Washington, D.C.: U.S. Government Printing Office.

Drucker, Peter F. (1975), "The Delusion of Profits," *Wall Street Journal*, February 5, 10.

Falconer, Brian (1991), "Tourism and Sustainability: The Dream Realized," 21–26, *Tourism-Environment-Sustainable Development*, conference proceedings, TTRA Canada, Hull, Quebec, October 27–29.

Garland, Joseph E. (1981), "A New Englander Looks at Tourism," presentation, "Tourism and New England Seaports," June, *Livability Digest* 1 (1) (Fall), 18–19.

Gunn, Clare A. (1988a), *Tourism Planning*, 2nd ed., New York: Taylor & Francis.

Gunn, Clare A. (1988b), *Vacationscape: Designing Tourist Regions*, 2nd ed., New York: Van Nostrand Reinhold.

Gunn, Clare A., and Terry R. Larsen (1988), *Tourism Potential—Aided by Computer Cartography*, Aix-en-Provence, France: Centre des Hautes Etudes Touristiques.

Gunn, Clare A. (1990), *Upcountry South Carolina Guidelines for Tourism Development*, Clemson, SC: Clemson University.

Healy, Robert G. (1976), *Land Use and the States*, for Resources for the Future, Inc., Baltimore: Johns Hopkins University Press.

Landphair, Harlow, and John Motloch (1985), *Site Reconnaissance and Engineering: An Introduction for Architects, Landscape Architects and Planners*, New York: Elsevier.

Lewis, Philip (1964), "Quality Corridors for Wisconsin," *Landscape Architecture* 54 (2), 100–107.

Moorea, French Polynesia (1990), a report on "Managing the Balance Between Development and Conservation," Sydney, Australia: PATA.

Motloch, John L. (1991), *Introduction to Landscape Design*, New York: Van Nostrand Reinhold.

Rees, William E. (1989), "Defining Sustainable Development," *CHS Research Bulletin*, University of British Columbia (May), 3.

Selengut, Stanley (1992), "Forum on Ecotourism," *Landscape Architecture*, 82 (8).

So, Frank, ed. (1988), *The Practice of Local Government Planning*, Washington, D.C.: International City Management Association.

Stanley, Dick (1991), "Synthesis of Workshop Sessions," 116–118, *Tourism-Environment-Sustainable Development: An Agenda for Research*, conference proceedings, Ottawa: Canada Chapter, TTRA.

Stewart, Vivien (1990), "Editorial," *Historic Environment*, (7) 3–4, iv.

Stewart, William P., et al. (1990), "Sustainable Tourism Development: A Conceptual Framework," presentation, Third Symposium on Social Science in Resource Management, Texas A&M University.

Taylor, Gordon (1991), "Tourism and Sustainability: Impossible Dream or Essential Objective," 27–29, *Tourism-Environment-Sustainable Development*, conference proceedings, TTRA Canada, Hull, Quebec, October 27–29.

Watt, Carson E., and James C. Stribling (1990), *San Antonio Tourism Industry Information Needs*, College Station: Texas A&M University.

Wight, Pamela (1991), "Tourism-Recreation EIA's in Alberta: A Need for an Integrated Approach in Legislation, Environmental Assessment, and Development Planning," presentation, 12th International Seminar on Environmental Assessment and Management, July 13, University of Aberdeen, Scotland.

Wight, Pamela (1992), "Ecotourism: Ethics or Eco-Sell?" *Journal of Travel Research* (in process).

Ziffer, Karen A. (1989), *Ecotourism: The Uneasy Alliance*, Washington, D.C.: Conservation International.

Part Five

An Industry Sector Perspective

The contents of Part Five of the Handbook are structured from a perspective with which the majority of tourism managers will be most familiar, namely, by industry sector. In contrast to Part Four, which contains an academic orientation to the study of tourism, the chapters in the present section categorize research to reflect the way in which the tourism industry is generally perceived by the bulk of the population. Part Five also reflects the task-oriented concerns of individual managers who, not infrequently, view themselves as belonging to the lodging industry, the airline industry, the restaurant industry, the attractions industry and so on, rather than as part of the tourism industry.

This part of the Handbook is particularly enriched by the written views of several individuals who are actively involved in different sectors of the tourism business. As witness to this claim, Chapter 22 has been authored by Ed Wohlmuth, who has written and worked extensively in the field of travel retailing and wholesaling. Readers of this chapter, entitled "Research Needs of Travel Retailers and Wholesalers," very quickly become aware of both the author's knowledge of the field and his ability to present this knowledge in a stimulating manner. Mr. Wohlmuth starts his presentation by reminding readers of the rapid changes that are occurring in all facets of life and particularly in areas related to travel and tourism. This opening set of comments leads into a discussion of the nature of research in the real world. Flowing out of this discussion is Mr. Wohlmuth's very broad definition of *research* as "any activity that provides useful information." Having taken this perspective, the author then provides a number of very insightful and practical guidelines for determining what kind of research is most appropriate in a given situation and for carrying out that type of research. This general discussion of practical research is then directly related to the information needs of the travel agent and tour operator. The manner in which this is done is both entertaining and informative.

Chapter 23 addresses the operation and research needs of the convention and meetings sector of the travel and tourism industry. This chapter, which is authored by James Abbey and Carl Link, first describes the size and scope of the convention market and describes how it operates. Discussion in this area includes a review of the economic importance of conventions to a region and the manner in which associations and meeting planners choose the site for their activities. Subsequently, the authors provide insight into the issues faced by suppliers of convention and meeting facilities. Following this description of the functioning of this sector, Abbey and Link review the nature and extent of present research efforts in the convention industry. Their review includes studies conducted by industry associations, those reported in trade publications, and finally those carried out in an academic setting. The chapter concludes with an overview of future trends and research needs in the convention and meetings sector.

Chapter 24 again presents the perspective of an experienced manager. Authored by Carolyn Carey, this chapter reviews the research needs of operators in the attractions sector of the tourism industry. Ms. Carey's presentation makes several basic yet important distinctions. First, she distinguishes between the needs for ongoing research related to the monitoring of current performance of the attraction and the need for special research projects to deal with specific management concerns that may arise from time to time. The discussion also makes an important distinction between the manager's need to have information on present customers versus the need to acquire knowledge and understanding of individuals who currently do not patronize a particular event or attraction. Following this discussion at the micro level of the individual operator, Ms. Carey then turns to a review of the research needs of the events and attractions sector taken as an industry. Here, after pointing out some of the difficulties involved in undertaking industrywide research, the author reviews and categorizes the kinds of information that can be reasonably anticipated from a group of cooperating events and attractions. Ms. Carey draws upon her experience with the Southern California Attractions committee to provide an example of how one region addressed its needs for research information in this important industry sector.

The fourth chapter in this industry-oriented section provides a theoretical framework to guide research related to tourism attractions. Its contents provide an interesting and useful complement to the foregoing discussion. In Chapter 25, Alan Lew first discusses the framework that is based on three distinctively different research perspectives. The first of these perspectives focuses on the characteristics of the site, the second on the organizational nature of the attraction, while the third emphasizes the perceptions and experiences of tourists relative to the attraction. Professor Lew subsequently applies the framework to two specific areas of attraction-related research. The first of these involves regional planning studies in Greece; the second focuses on the area of attraction image studies. In both instances, the author attempts to demonstrate how the framework can be used to evaluate the basic research objectives of a study, to compare the research design of similar studies, and to examine the type, quantity, and quality of the data collected.

The research needs of the restaurant industry are addressed in Chapter 26. This chapter, authored by Robert Olson and Uel Blank, is again structured so as to provide guidelines for researching the operation of both the individual restaurant business and the restaurant industry taken collectively. Following an initial overview of the food service industry and its components, the authors identify the kinds of research that are appropriate to the individual restaurant operator. In doing so, the emphasis is upon information and analysis that provide the operator with measures of performance effectiveness or an indication of the profitability of a given market opportunity. The second part of this chapter provides a macro view of the overall research needs of the restaurant industry within a particular community, region, or country. The discussion here recognizes that different restaurant industry interests may vary widely and, therefore, that the kind of information to be gathered can be extremely diverse. Having recognized this situation, the authors go on to provide guidelines concerning the type of information appropriate to collect and how the required data can be gathered. Throughout, the emphasis is upon the assembling of information that is useful and that can be readily disseminated to interested restauranteurs. In this regard, a major ongoing consumer study sponsored by the National Restaurant Association is described.

The next two chapters in Part Five both deal with transportation-related research but from very different perspectives. In Chapter 27, Lawrence Cunningham discusses research related to personal transportation modes, while Stuart Robinson, in Chapter 28, examines research needs in two important common carrier modes, namely, intercity bus and rail transportation. The personal transportation chapter, by Professor Cunningham, first identifies priorities for research in the personal motor vehicle tourism area. The chapter then reviews statistics describing the personal motor vehicle tourist with a particular distinction being made between these tourists per se as compared to other travelers. This review is followed by a discussion of the various market segments that have been identified among personal motor vehicle tourists using a variety of segmentation criteria. Finally, the chapter examines a number of institutional issues that the author believes have inhibited research related to personal transportation modes. In particular, limited funding and the lack of overall research policies and direction at the international, federal, state, and local levels are cited as the major causes of present research inadequacy.

The Robinson chapter on research needs in the intercity bus and rail transportation industry takes a very different orientation from the previous chapter. It explains the responsibilities of selected managers within a corporation and specifies what information they need as well as how this information might be gathered. The chapter starts by reviewing regulatory policy in the intercity bus industry and its impact upon the functioning of that industry. Having clarified the rules of the game, Dr. Robinson identifies the responsibilities of marketing research in relation to the tasks facing senior management. As a means of presenting his case, Dr. Robinson describes how a market researcher can provide information that will help vice presidents in the areas of marketing, advertising, control, traffic operations, and passenger service.

Chaper 29, by Stephen Hiemstra, addresses a range of research issues related to one of the largest components of tourism, the lodging industry. In introducing the topic, Dr. Hiemstra first provides the reader with a number of industry statistics and trends that are essential to an understanding of research needs in the field. He then examines a selected number of research areas that are currently viewed as industry priorities. These include long-standing concerns such as the projection of future sales and employment levels by individual firms as well as industry groups. They also include issues that have attained greater visibility in recent days, notably research related to labor productivity, labor turnover, and the taxation of income from tips. Dr. Hiemstra subsequently focuses the discussion on a specific, detailed example of research designed to assess the impacts of room taxes on the industry. The chapter concludes with a discussion of methodological and data-collection issues related to three areas of great importance to the lodging industry in which the author believes additional work is required: yield management systems, market segmentation specifically tailored for the lodging sector, and assessment of the effectiveness of industry advertising.

The final chapter in this section is somewhat different from those previously discussed. Authored by Tyrrell Marris and entitled "Research Needs of Small Tourism Enterprises," Chapter 30 does deal with an industry sector but one that cuts across the traditional functional definitions employed by the previous chapters. This chapter has been included because the small tourism enterprise represents an important component of the tourism industry and because it does have very specialized information needs, particularly in light of the resources available to assemble that information. The contents of the chapter start from the premise that owners of small enterprises often do not realize that they are part of a wider tourism industry. They are often also unaware of their need for information and for research. Accordingly, Mr. Marris attempts to identify the various types of rather straightforward information that the small enterprise should have available to it. Subsequently, he provides guidance on how the small tourism operator can get started doing research by identifying readily available internal and external sources of information. Throughout, the emphasis is on describing approaches that can be pursued personally by the owner of a small operation. This orientation has two main advantages. First, it limits the resources required to gather information, and, perhaps more important, it ensures understanding and involvement on the part of the small tourism enterprise and its managers. The emphasis on simplicity and the provision of a typical questionnaire that might be used by a small enterprise make this chapter both unique and valuable to a large segment of the travel, tourism, and hospitality sector.

22

Research Needs of Travel Retailers and Wholesalers

ED WOHLMUTH
The Art Institute of Philadelphia
Philadelphia, Pennsylvania

*T*he travel retailer and wholesaler have research needs that parallel the general needs of all businesses, yet are unique unto themselves. As usual, a lack of money and time are thought to be the research barriers—as indeed for some companies they may be. But what is really missing is an understanding of the true nature of research and how it can be applied to the everyday world of selling travel. This chapter is recommended reading not only for travel agents and tour operators, but for anyone who would benefit from a practical knowledge of this phase of the industry.

PROLOGUE

Things change.

When this chapter was originally written, I owned a well-known Philadelphia travel agency and was in my second decade as a tour operator selling packages to other travel agents across North America. Although my outside writing and seminar activities were steadily increasing, my point of view was definitely that of a travel insider.

Today I'm an outsider. Now when I walk into a travel agency, it's to purchase an airline ticket from someone else. Looking around at the now ubiquitous computers, I have to remind myself that just a little over a decade ago, we were doing ten million retail dollars annually without a single PC. Wow. . ..

A quick personal update:

When a big competitor wanted my company as a prestige acquisition, I was handed a unique opportunity—to reinvent myself. I knew I wanted to teach more, but I had no idea I would end up in a college classroom with a full-time career teaching Marketing and Communications. I love it.

Where once my name would occasionally appear in *Travel Weekly*, today you're more likely to find it in an airport bookstore—on the front cover of the new mass-market paperback edition of my public speaking book.[1] A new book on personal communications is also on the way. The author will gladly autograph all purchases.

While *The Wall Street Journal* remains a daily constant, my travel-trade reading has been replaced by computer magazines and numerous marketing/presentations trade publications.

What hasn't changed is my constant fascination with everyday marketing—and market research—as it applies to selling anything from a designer sweater to a Hawaiian cruise. In redrafting this chapter, I'm struck by how much of the original still applies. There's been lots of updating, of course, but the original basics are still here. I think they're as valid today as ever, but you, my former travel colleagues, will have to be the final judge. It's a great pleasure to be with you again.

A CHANGING WORLD

As the travel distribution system enters the middle third of the decade of the 1990s, the winds of change blow everywhere.

To a degree unknown since World War II, political events are reshaping the world. Almost overnight, a once-charming Yugoslavia is battle scarred and out of bounds, while, from

---

[1] *The Overnight Guide to Public Speaking* by Ed Wohlmuth, NAL/DUTTON (Penguin USA), 1993.

the Berlin Wall to the Russian steppes, the iron curtain crumbles before our satellite-aided eyes. It's still too early to understand the full ramifications of the demise of the Soviet Union, but if we have truly entered an era of big-power peace in tandem with small-power wars, the effects on world tourism could be staggering.

No less significant are the associated and resulting economic changes. A major realignment in world economies—already well underway in the United States with the change from an industrial- to a service-based economy—will just be hastened by the decline of military/industrial needs. Meanwhile, deluxe hotels the world over are filled, not with American but with Japanese tourists.

Momentous as they are, however, these political and economic changes are only part of the total picture. A worldwide revolution in communications technology has also taken place and continues to reshape the world. Whether in the form of personal computers or fax machines, private satellite channels or portable cellular telephones, *Internet* or *CompuServe*, the twenty-first-century communications genie is out of the bottle—never to be stuffed back again!

Consider this one tourism-related event: An entire industry devoted to the manufacture, sale, and processing of home-movie film has vanished from the face of the Earth—totally replaced by a communications technology (the camcorder) largely unforeseen a decade or so ago. And that same new home-video technology is reshaping TV news broadcasts—even network entertainment shows—in ways also unforeseen just a few years ago.

Consider further: many thousands of people now go to the office by staying at home. We've entered the age of *telecommuting*, made possible by far-ranging company networks of personal computers and file-servers. In the scientific community, hundreds of meetings now take place using multimedia *teleconferencing*, combining large-screen computer images and interactive graphics. Yes, the live video image is still a little crude, but you can see and converse with colleagues thousands of miles away—and even edit their scientific papers line by line while they (sometimes ruefully) watch. What do these two examples have in common? They both eliminate a need to travel.

What does all this mean for the travel agent and wholesaler? For those who welcome and embrace the communications revolution, it means further opportunities to enlarge profit through greater efficiency of operation and maximum promotional/sales impact. The printed cruise-ship deck plan may soon be, for example, a relic of the past. *Virtual reality*, an exciting new combination of video and computer-driven graphics, will allow clients to don special electronic goggles and "walk around" not only inside a selection of staterooms, but inside the entire ship—without leaving the travel agency. Sound farfetched? It's being used right now to sell dream kitchens to Japanese homeowners.

On the consumer's side of the equation, such technologies may mean far different behavior and expectations. The lessons of automated teller machines, self-service gas pumps, and computerized discount brokerage services should not go unheeded. The modern consumer is a very adaptable animal,

shedding old habits and adopting new ones with great regularity. These days, many of us think nothing of obtaining our bank balances or seeing if a check has cleared with a few keypad punches on a touchtone phone. Travel is no more immune to these changes than any other product.

It would be a mistake, however, to assume that all patterns of travel purchase might change or that all industry units would have to change with them. Travel is the most complex of all consumer items—requiring, as it does, an expenditure of both time and money. For many, planning a vacation remains an intensely personal experience, frequently involving what psychologists call an emotional investment. Face-to-face counseling will certainly remain a staple of the travel industry for decades to come. But with which clients and for what types of travel?

It's going to require a high degree of insight into the future relationship between the travel client and the travel product. With these insights, those who wish to remain travel agents and tour operators in the traditional mold can promote their services to prospects looking for one-on-one counseling, while nearby competitors use the new technologies to seek clients who want the speed and efficiency of an electronic relationship. Either way, market research is the only sound basis on which such positioning and planning decisions can be made.

But what kind of research is either affordable or meaningful in the real world of travel agents and tour operators? Perhaps it's time to rethink the entire concept of research as it applies to this type of business.

THE REAL WORLD OF RESEARCH

Just over a decade ago, first in a front-page story in *The Wall Street Journal* and later in the bestseller *Megatrends*,[2] millions of readers learned of a unique service being offered to corporate America. Using a World War II-developed technique called *content analysis*, long-range trends in American life are identified via a method of deceptive simplicity: researchers scan the pages of hundreds of local newspapers and measure the amount of space editors devote to any particular topic. When one topic starts inheriting space formerly devoted to another topic, trends are deduced and a report is sent to corporate subscribers.

The existence of this service tells us a number of important things, not least of which being what it says about the word *research*. All too often, we tend to think of research in terms of fancy statistical models or extrapolations based on specially collected data, when the reality is frequently far different. A trend spotted in the back pages of local newspapers is no less important than a trend theorized through the interpretation of thousands of questionnaires.

When the end result is useful information, research can be ANY activity—from a series of short phone calls to years spent poring over vast amounts of technical data. It all de-

[2]*Megatrends: Ten New Directions Transforming Our Lives* by John Naisbitt, Warner Books, 1982.

pends on your needs, your resources, and how clever you are in turning seemingly ordinary facts and activities into important information.

But whatever it is, the research activity must be systematic. That's the second point raised by the content analysis method. Meaningful trends cannot be spotted by reading newspapers just now and then. To be valid, the chosen activity must be regular and consistent. That may sound like a time-consuming proposition, but it isn't. Regular activities lend themselves to great efficiency, simply because they are regular. You just concentrate on what's important and eliminate anything else.

Some people waste valuable time by reading every page of every trade journal. Not only is there the inevitable duplication of stories, but many items are either of questionable value or aren't relevant to current circumstances. Studies show that most people forget a third of what they read within 24 hours—and perhaps 85 percent of all new input within a week. With those kinds of negative odds, why read *anything* unless you absolutely must.

I use a far more efficient method: clip articles that may be of future use, but never read more than a paragraph or two until the information is actually needed. After they're cut out, I don't even sort them—the articles sit until needed in a general file of mixed topics. Sounds chaotic, but it's very efficient, and, in a pinch, I can assemble a complete file on almost any subject in a matter of minutes.

Point number three is that research does not require original material. We tend to think that it does because projects based on original data (such as TV network/print-media polling) tend to be highly publicized, and with good reason: the studies cost money and the sponsors want to get maximum mileage out of their investment. The projects you don't hear about are quietly conducted in-house by savvy agents and operators who are using data that already exists as a by-product of normal operations.

That's an important point: everything you need for a meaningful research program may be just a few feet away, in your sales or accounting data. The material may require organizing and sorting, but that's duck soup for even the smallest computer (later, we'll discuss using a PC to destination- or client-sort your mailing list without spending an extra dime on software). Are some new destinations getting hot? Are certain clients traveling more with their children? The keys to the future may lie just beneath the surface in your own sales figures.

And that brings us to point number four. The future almost always has its roots in what's happening now. Emerging trends are spotted by watching current—and sometimes quite ordinary—activity. While spending untold millions to unearth Soviet military secrets, Western intelligence agencies failed to see that the USSR itself was coming apart at the seams. The evidence was there for all to see—in every outdoor market and food store. In the travel industry, meaningful current events are not hotel openings and tour announcements. Regardless of whether the trip is for business or pleasure, what's meaningful is what clients want at the inquiry stage and how they react to what they get at the

delivery stage. The information is yours for the asking, but you do have to ask.

Finally, and inescapably, productive research does not demand large amounts of money. A simple methodology—clipping articles or mailing survey forms—can be operated on a very modest budget and can produce results worth many thousands of times the investment. By the same token, highly deceptive results can be obtained from expensive methods of data collection and interpretation. Success in research is not measured by the cost of the project but by the quality and usefulness of the information obtained.

What would you like to know? What do you need to know? And if you can obtain the answers to those questions, how can they be adapted into profitable, practical actions?

WHAT THE TRAVEL AGENT NEEDS TO KNOW

An old axiom says that a mark of true intelligence is knowing what you don't know, in other words, being able to identify the areas where your knowledge is deficient. In the world of business, however, that's only a portion of a larger truth: you must pinpoint the deficiency, know that you *need* the information, and be able to find an affordable source to provide it in a timely manner.

The great majority of travel business failures can be traced to managers who did not know what they needed to know. They were too overwhelmed by the routine, day-to-day details of running the business: reservations that hadn't cleared, documents that hadn't arrived, conflicts that hadn't been resolved, and so on. Add a constant barrage of payment problems, visits from sales reps, and relatives demanding Christmas reservations, and there wasn't room for anything else in the work week. In other words, the manager was indistinguishable from everyone else on the staff.

Staff members can afford to spend their time scurrying after hoary details, but the manager cannot. The future waits for no one, and it's the manager's responsibility to plan for it. But planning involves abstracts, and abstracts are difficult to grasp and veil the future in an impenetrable fog—while the small problems of the moment are highly visible, glowing with a seductive urgency.

To make the planning task just a bit less abstract and to demonstrate the importance of research to it, I've devised three small concepts. They're called *coming soon*, *today only*, and *starting tomorrow*.

COMING SOON

Coming soon is a very easy concept to grasp: your travel agency doesn't exist—yet. You've picked the location, signed the lease, and hired key personnel; but advertising, promotion, and operational details must still be decided. You have no clients. What do you need to know?

Before we get to the clients themselves, let's take a moment to consider what your agency will look like to outsiders. We live in a visually oriented society, where first—

and frequently lasting—impressions are formed by our eyes. What type of image do you want to convey? Fun? Adventure? Professionalism? Consider the visual effect of every item you'll have in your office. What do you picture as your ideal "look"?

Now examine your agency as it actually exists. Does it bear any resemblance to what you'd put together at the coming-soon stage of development? If not, you might want to make some changes, perhaps in inexpensive areas such as window displays and general tidiness. At the other extreme, you might consider bringing in an interior designer (not an interior decorator; they're different) to propose major changes in space utilization and office layout. Either way, you've performed an important management function by applying a simple planning concept.

Now let's get to the heart of the matter—your clientele. Since your location is already fixed, you'll have to deal with the demographics that exist in and around that area. What are they? Who are the people who live nearby? What levels of income and sophistication do the people represent? Your entire advertising and promotion program may hinge on what you find. Perhaps you'll discover that your location borders on several distinctly different neighborhoods, each suggesting a different marketing approach.

How about nearby businesses? What are they, and what type of workers do they employ? There are opportunities here in both vacation and business travel, but, to fully exploit either, you'll have to know the market. A thorough survey may produce a surprise or two: office buildings can hide many different types of enterprise.

What about the traffic pattern that flows past your door? What is it and where are people going? What are the transit routes? All of us fall into daily travel routines and become so familiar or bored with them that we fail to see changes taking place along the way. Many people who pass your door—on foot or in vehicles—may not know you're there; yet they represent solid sales potential.

Sound demographic research will expose your actual market potential and show how much of it still remains untapped. Once you've developed an accurate picture, compare it with what you thought all these years. Your entire plan for the future might be shaped by the simple process of taking a good look around.

The beauty of *coming soon* is that it sweeps away all the natural prejudices and misconceptions we build through years of doing business in a certain way. The type of client you see most frequently may not be representative of the true demographics of your area because your image or promotion is only appealing to a narrow slice of the market. Segmentation is fine, but not when it excludes potential customers. Perhaps you can build a solid framework of additional clients, people who will be loyal customers well into the future. You won't know until you do your research.

TODAY ONLY

The world is coming to an end in exactly 24 hours! I'll leave this evening's activities to your personal discretion; mean-

while you have one complete business day to prove you're the world's greatest travel-agency manager. What do you need to know?

There are two general measures of success in our society: profit and esteem. Since esteem is partly a function of financial success, we'll concentrate on profit—which, in turn, hinges on maximizing income and minimizing expense. Remember, you have just today. How can you maximize profit?

A quick walk through your office might reveal that your vacation counselors are working on limited-profit sales, only because they're the next ones in order of departure date. Which would you prefer they handle first, the upcoming quickie weekends or the deluxe cruises due to depart in several months? Either way, we'll credit you with earned commission as soon as the arrangements are completed (I know, I know, it's not the way your accountant wants income recorded, but when the world's coming to an end, who cares about accountants).

Did I hear you tell the staff to give priority to the cruise arrangements? If they move quickly, it might be possible to obtain the exact accommodations the clients want, rather than inferior offerings.

The next stop is your business-travel department and, as usual, the joint's jumping—every position busy with an incoming call. That's good: once again, we'll credit commission earnings as soon as each itinerary is completed. But what about that big pile of hotel vouchers waiting for commission collection follow-up? As you well know, some hotels won't pay a commission, but you won't know which ones until you try to collect. Worst of all, your staff members are using some of those very same hotels on today's bookings—and we'll have to deduct the deadbeats from today's income. The answer, of course, is maintaining an up-to-date list of commission-paying properties—as basic a research function as you'll ever encounter.

Finally, into the accounting department. Since every penny counts toward the day's profit, you're looking at the checking account for any excess balance that can be shifted to an interest-earning account—and you're comparing present yields with possible higher returns from T-bills, commercial paper, or even U.S. Savings Bonds (a very underrated, very safe investment).

As you can see, *today only* extends the familiar concept of the profit center by treating each day as if it were the last. By focusing on important planning considerations rather than routine details, overall profit is maximized and areas of deficient knowledge are quickly exposed.

STARTING TOMORROW

Years ago, a wise old real estate agent told me that the time to start looking for a new business location is the day you sign your present lease. *Starting tomorrow* is an extension of that logic.

Let's suppose your landlord has just served notice that your lease will not be renewed (there's no stopping progress: they're tearing down your building to make way for a new porno movie theater!). The big question is, do you want to remain in the general vicinity or move to a totally new location? Either way, you're forced to construct new quarters, so the expense will be about equal.

Our starting point is a big bonus provided by *coming soon*: you now know the complete demographics of your present location. You also know about an upcoming change—that porno palace isn't going to do anything good for the neighborhood. Even allowing for that, however, your immediate reaction is to concentrate on a nearby location, which will allow you to maintain your present clientele. On the other hand. . ..

A dynamite area, just begging for a new travel agency, may be just a few miles away. The real estate could be very reasonable, the demographics excellent, and the growth potential even better than your current location. Best of all, it could be close enough to be convenient for many of your present clients. But you're not sure—maybe you should stick to the old neighborhood.

There are three problems at work here. First, there's a natural tendency for all of us to want to stay within familiar territory (which, as you probably know, is the reason so many people want to be in their own cars when traveling). Second, most of us have only surface impressions of nearby areas where we don't live or work. And finally, most retail enterprises have no idea whether customer loyalty and satisfaction are really sufficient to bring present clients to a less-convenient new address.

Starting tomorrow requires you to do your long-range homework, first by knowing everything there is to know about your entire community, and second by knowing all there is to know about your clientele. There's help in both areas—and other areas we've covered in these examples—in the pages ahead. Meanwhile, *starting tomorrow* offers substantial rewards as a planning concept. It prepares for the unknown, helps solidify relocation or branch-office expansion possibilities, and avoids costly mistakes caused when sudden changes in the business climate yield inadequate planning time.

But enough of concepts: it's time to explore the research opportunities available in the real world of the travel agent.

PUTTING RESEARCH OPPORTUNITIES TO WORK

An incredible variety of research opportunities are available to the travel agency manager. They range from free or low-cost outside sources to in-house projects that can be devised and operated on modest budgets. The list presented here is by no means inclusive, but it does cover the major information areas explored earlier.

Because no two agency operations are ever identical, some of these sources may seem elementary to one manager and highly sophisticated to another. Whatever your initial reaction, I urge you to read this complete section. Many of these items can be adapted to more- or less-sophisticated uses, depending on your actual needs.

CENSUS BUREAU

The U.S. Bureau of the Census (Commerce Department) is the single most overlooked source of low-cost research information for the American small business operator. With offices located in many urban centers and with printed and microfiche extracts available at thousands of local libraries, the bureau can provide a wealth of vital information available from no other source.

From statistics compiled in the standard population census taken every 10 years (required by the U.S. Constitution to apportion the House of Representatives among the states), the bureau breaks down the demographics of the country by state, county, municipality, and even neighborhoods—providing personal income and life-style information on residents and family units. The information may appear complex, but a few minutes of instruction by bureau personnel or a knowledgeable real estate broker can provide important data for the travel agency manager.

The American population is changing, and it's important that you know how and why and how it's likely to affect future travel sales. With major advances in diagnostic medicine and geriatrics, and because women are marrying and bearing (fewer) children later in life, the country's population is growing older. For the first time in history, we now have more senior citizens than teenagers, and the shift is growing more pronounced with each passing year. Major merchandisers are paying close attention to these changes and are altering marketing promotions and products accordingly. Case in point: the jeans of Levi Strauss, Lee, and other major manufacturers are being cut more generously to accommodate an aging customer base. Meanwhile, some cruise lines—once interested solely in empty-nest older couples, widows, and widowers—are finding golden opportunities among the growing ranks of childless younger couples.

Another important demographic—the majority of women now in the work force—is having ramifications throughout the marketing world. The old concept of *time utility*, adding value to the merchandise by making items easier (therefore, faster) to buy at all hours, is changing the way both men and women shop. L.L. Bean has always been "open" 24 hours every day, but now they've been joined by countless other direct sellers. J.C. Penney now routinely promises merchandise delivery to your door in three working days. And some direct merchants are doing it even faster and making it even easier.

In travel agent and airline computer programs, client records of seating, meal, hotel, and car-rental preferences are no longer a fringe benefit—they're a necessity in a world of time-short people of both sexes. And the day is coming when travelers will order airline and hotel reservations as easily as millions of Parisians now order their daily groceries—with a couple of swipes at a little phone-coupled computer terminal. These trends and much more can be discerned from an intelligent reading of the census data.

In addition to population data, the Census Bureau also collects business data in a less-well-known study of commercial and transportation enterprises conducted every five years (in years ending 2 and 7). An examination of retail trade data for your community might indicate areas where other types of merchants are prospering and where branch-office expansion should be considered.

Conversely, areas can also be identified where stores are experiencing larger than normal downturns and where expansion or movement into the market should be avoided.

Business census data can also establish the number of travel agency (Standard Industrial Code 4722) locations in any geographic area. This, in turn, can easily be divided into the appropriate population figures to determine the per capita coverage of the average agency among various types of potential customers.

For further information on their many and varied services, contact the Data User Services Division, Bureau of the Census, Washington, D.C. 20233, or phone (301)763-4100.

Readers in other countries should investigate similar services provided by government or quasi-governmental agencies. Statistics Canada, for example, can give you access to population census figures developed every five years and available in numerous breakdowns and studies, again down to the neighborhood level. Like its counterpart in the United States, the agency charges a fee for special, custom-produced studies—which, in most cases, are worth every penny of the cost.

PRIVATE RESEARCH SERVICES

Private research companies, offering data collation and interpretation services, are located throughout the world. In addition to the long-term contracts usually offered to volume users, many services will also conduct specific, one-time projects, sometimes at modest fees. Thus, the agency manager who wants to consider all branch-office-expansion variables can usually contract with a nearby firm for such a service. At your local business library, consult the latest edition of *Bradford's Directory of Marketing Research Agencies* or *Consultants and Consulting Organizations*.

LOCAL PLANNING AUTHORITIES

Every community has a public agency that acts as a repository for zoning variances, building permits, and the like. Yet, to hear realtors tell it, these agencies are unlikely to be contacted by small business operators seeking to relocate or expand. The results are all too predictable: although it's on the public record for all to see, the chain's intention to build a large mall store comes as a total shock to the small operator who's just opened across the street. It happens all the time, and to travel agents no less than anyone else. Do your zoning research before signing any new lease. The minimal time involved is certainly worth it, in peace of mind if nothing else.

LOCAL BUSINESS AND LEGAL PUBLICATIONS

Every metropolitan area has at least one source of public information on bankruptcies, incorporations, real estate ac-

quisitions, and so on. Whether it's a legal newspaper or a chamber of commerce monthly journal, it should be on your regular reading list. In particular, look for trends that might affect your operation. Is your area losing business or industrial activity to another region? If so, why? Perhaps that all-important business client will be the next to go and is already looking for a new site elsewhere. Forewarned is forearmed. On the other hand, you might spot a potentially lucrative new account (by keeping a sharp eye on real estate transactions) before they've even arrived on the scene. This is basic research for every agency handling commercial accounts.

THE WALL STREET JOURNAL

The Wall Street Journal is America's single most important source of business news (and, not incidently, superb writing). It should be required reading for every manager, and, at some companies, it is. *Journal* articles profile industries and activities on the way up—as well as on the way down—and give numerous insights into the way business conducts itself on all levels. The Marketing section coverage of consumer trends and fads—now enhanced by data taken directly from store checkout scanners—is also unique.

The greatest value of daily reading, however, is that it's also where your business clients get their news, not only about their own industries, but about the travel business as well (the coverage of major airfare changes is especially frequent)—an important research source.

ON-LINE SERVICES AND ELECTRONIC BULLETIN BOARDS

With its almost unlimited ability to store complex information, the mainframe computer can act as a vast, electronic storehouse of data, providing millions of pieces of information on demand. Using such technology, thousands of on-line services are now available to modem-equipped (needed to make the phone connection) computer users both among the general public and in specific professions/industries. Dozens of data bases like *Dow Jones News/Retrieval*, for example, contain the full text or extracts of magazine, trade publication, and newspaper articles from around the country and around the world. *Lexis* and its big competitor *Westlaw* contain legal decisions and precedents from virtually every court in the land. *PR Newswire* will provide the complete text of almost any press release of importance. And, of course, *Eaasy Sabre, OAG Electronic Edition, Travel+Plus,* and others, provide on-line travel services.

The best-known suppliers of on-line services are companies like *CompuServe* (over a million subscribers), which provide a selection of many different data bases and special-interest "forums" (like the popular "Working from Home" forum), and *EasyNet*, which provides umbrella access to over 800 other data bases. To enter these and like services, one pays a monthly membership fee and frequently a per-minute or per-search charge.

At the other extreme are the tens of thousands (nobody knows exactly how many) of electronic bulletin board services (BBSs) being operated on personal computers (PCs) in people's homes or offices—the BBS is usually free, the only requirement being an interest in that BBS's targeted topics.

To make possible the easy exchange of information *between* bulletin boards or data bases, many hundreds are linked together in formal networks where access to one means access to all. Thus, travel agents and tour operators could get together to exchange worldwide information as easily as *Internet* users gain access to university and scientific computer systems throughout the hemisphere.

For a complete directory of who offers what among the mainframe services, see the *Directory of Online Data Bases* at your public or business library. For a list of all the BBSs in your area, access one and ask.

PUBLIC LIBRARY SERVICES

Librarians were among the first to recognize the on-line data base's vast power (along with its fearsome potential as a competitor), and most now tap into these resources with computers of their own. This enables your local library to offer a call-in information service to everyone—first-come, first-served. It's not only free, it's usually very fast (once you get through the busy signal, that is). Library computer operators not only know the relative strengths and weaknesses of the many data bases at their command, but they also know the (frequently arcane) search commands and can access the information with maximum speed. If you need research data or have a question but don't have access to a computer of your own, here's your answer. All it takes is a phone call.

SMALL BUSINESS ADMINISTRATION

The Small Business Administration (SBA) wasn't chartered just to make loans. It also assists small business operators with a wide variety of projects and problems. In addition to the staffs on hand at local offices throughout the United States, the SBA also maintains an extensive library of publications, many of which are free for the asking. Subjects covered include everything from locating or relocating your office to operating your own in-house research project.

The latest wrinkle at the administration is SBA On-Line (800-859-4636), their new electronic bulletin board. When it was first announced, the service started receiving over a thousand computer log-on's a day, and they've had to double (to 40) the number of incoming toll-free lines. If you don't have a computer, you can get further information on programs and booklets by calling 800-U-ASK-SBA or by writing Small Business Administration, Washington, D.C. 20416.

YOUR MAILING LIST

Whether it's computerized or on 3-by-5 cards, the company mailing list is a valuable research tool. It can not only tell you who your clients are and where they live and work, but where they've been going and where they want to go in the future (see Newsletter Feedback and Postdeparture Survey forms, both coming up).

One of the easiest ways to gain information from your list is to sort it by zip codes. You may see a definite pattern, with two or three zip-code areas providing the bulk of your clients. Door-to-door leaflet distribution (but not using people's mailboxes, which is illegal under U.S. postal laws) might be a natural outgrowth of such information.

Another excellent use of mailing lists is to classify singles and family units by ages and destination preferences—and here's where your PC can really pay for itself. Unknown to most users, the DOS operating system comes with a powerful "sort" command/filter, which can be used to assemble a targeted mailing at the push of a button. The secret is the command's ability to alphabetically sort any word or letter, or numerically sort numbers, as long as they appear in the same spot on each entry. Thus, typing an "A" in the first column before the name of every cruise client will enable you to instantly sort them out for a targeted promotion. Simply tell "sort" to sort the first column, and all the "A's" magically come to the top. Similarly, the second column can be used to identify travelers to Europe, the third column the Orient, and so on. And the same trick can be used periodically to see how destination preferences are changing from year to year.

NEWSLETTER FEEDBACK FORMS

Newsletters are an increasingly popular form of travel agency promotion that can yield even greater benefits when a customer feedback form is provided in each issue. Not only does this give clients a convenient method of asking for additional information on featured trips, but it can also provide a wealth of research data: articles found most appealing (don't be surprised if the gossip column about your staff is one of them), additional features they'd like included, where and when they'd like to vacation next, and so on.

Experience has shown that the most effective type of mail-back form is a lightweight postcard with the return address and return postage indicia preprinted on one side and a grouping of numbers representing responses on the other (i.e., "If you'd like more information on this destination, circle 99 on the reply card"). These forms are easy for clients to complete and mail (even easier when their name/address label on the newsletter is a peel-off sticker that they can attach to the mail-back form) and can present a wealth of information in compact form. Most users experience a far superior response rate when such forms are provided.

A word of caution, however: Don't use such a form if you can't instantly perform the necessary follow-up. Clients consider themselves to be your top priority and don't react kindly when requested information doesn't arrive by return mail. If you're temporarily out of the brochure, telling them so in a quick phone call will be greatly appreciated—and potentially save the sale.

POSTDEPARTURE SURVEY FORMS

When it comes to obtaining information from actual travelers, the travel agent occupies the catbird seat among all industry units. No other segment of the industry has such complete access to the total travel picture: from airport limousine to flights, to hotel or cruise accommodations. Sadly, this incredible resource is wasted by the great majority of agents.

The few agencies using postdeparture survey forms usually report phenomenal results. Not only are response rates very high (better than 60 percent when 3 percent is considered good on the average survey), but client loyalty and referrals almost always improve as a result. Why? Everyone loves to be asked his or her opinion, and the travel client more than most. It's a matter of ego, but it's also a matter of being appreciated—and the agency that sends such forms is expressing an interest in the welfare of the customer.

The work involved is minimal: the form can be included with the document delivery or, better yet, mailed to the client's home a few days after departure—a nice "welcome home" (which is what my cards always said on the outside) to greet the weary traveler. To ensure maximum response and client convenience, return postage is always provided.

In addition to the obvious benefit of quickly spotting substandard services and accommodations, the postdeparture form allows the agency to nip complaints—sometimes serious ones—in the proverbial bud. Recent studies show that many people don't communicate their complaints to the source, preferring, instead, the revenge of negative word-of-mouth comments to friends and family. The form puts an end to most of that. You may not be able to adjust the complaint to the client's complete satisfaction, but at least it's a positive start. After all, you took the time and trouble to ask how things went.

Once a complaint has been verified, the form can be used to back up refund claims with suppliers or to demonstrate to a sales rep that there's good cause for the downturn in sales coming from your agency. On the flip side of the coin, surveys help isolate habitual complainers, particularly with respect to group trips. When you have a bunch of written responses, it's much easier to prove that everyone did NOT think the food was rotten.

Finally, the forms can be used for market research, eliciting answers to questions like "Where would you like to travel next?" or "Would you consider a trip to DisneyWorld with children?"

As with everything used for research, the postdeparture form is a tool, a good one but still a tool. Obtaining the answers is only the first step along the road. You must know where you're going . . . and what you want to accomplish when you get there.

THE RESEARCH NEEDS OF WHOLESALERS

The unique need for both money and time in order to purchase the travel product makes the task of the tour operator especially difficult. It's not enough to know—if you can find out—what destinations prospective clients want to visit; you must also know when they want to go, how long they're willing to be away from home, and how far in advance

they're willing to make a commitment. Add to this the problems of contracting for sufficient but not excessive advance transport and lodging capacity, and the need to set attractive prices well before the selling season, and the tour operator's challenge becomes rather formidable. But one must start somewhere and, logically, it's with the destination.

TOURIST OFFICE AND PASSPORT STATISTICS

The tour operator in search of destination information can turn to two readily available sources: the U.S. State Department and individual destination tourist offices. In the first instance, statistics gathered from passport applications can show broad trends in demand, but only for those destinations requiring passports. There are three further limitations: the information is collected on a voluntary basis and is, therefore, incomplete; it only shows where people intend to go and not actual travel behavior; and it only applies to the trip for which the passport is first issued and not to future journeys using the same document.

Tourist office information, in many cases, is based on actual arrivals or statistically valid samples and can, therefore, be very helpful. In addition to highlighting by season the number of lodging room/nights sold—an indication of average length of stay—the data can also show state or country of origin, method of arrival, size of traveling/family unit, and other pertinent information. Depending on specific needs, tour operators can develop from the raw data sophisticated extrapolations based on cross-indexes of lodging/transport cost and/or indicators such as the consumer/price index or consumer confidence level.

It's another matter whether such data is totally valid as a predictor of the future. Political factors are sometimes impossible to foresee and, in a fleeting moment, can totally destroy the best efforts of even the most successful operators. The lessons of Yugoslavia should remain fresh in everyone's mind.

PROFESSIONAL TELEPHONE SURVEYS

Advances in computer-driven automated dialing—coupled with intense competition and technological advances among long-distance communications carriers—have made national or regional telephone surveys far more efficient and, thus, less expensive than ever. It is this method that is now exclusively used for polling by TV-network and print-media news organizations, with results frequently available in a matter of hours.

The real secret of success, however, is in the sample size: computerized selection programs can now produce statistically valid (plus/minus 3%) national results from under 2,000 calls. That's quite a trick, and there's no reason why tour operators can't get in on the action. The combination of a well-devised questionnaire and the right sample area could yield answers available nowhere else. Might there be interest in a Black Sea resort package? At what price and how long a flight would people be willing to endure? Is the lack of deluxe hotels a problem? How about the lack of people who speak English? In the hands of a competent survey team, such questions can be resolved at a cost that's degrees cheaper than printing and distributing a brochure for a program that doesn't sell.

POSTDEPARTURE SURVEY FORMS

The use of a postdeparture survey can be as valid for the wholesaler as it is for the travel agent. This is especially true for motorcoach-tour brokers, where the high percentage of repeat customers can produce meaningful future-planning data. Escorted tours also lend themselves especially well to this type of survey; but almost any kind of wholesale operation can gain valuable information from enroute or just-returned customers.

In addition to seeking passenger comments on transport, lodging, meals, and services, a number of firms seek demographic information on the clients themselves: occupation, marital status, home or condo ownership, special interests, and so on. To assist in future advertising and promotion, some surveys also ask for information on publications read regularly, TV and radio habits, and the method by which the customer first heard of the tour company.

A clever PR step, but one that's never gained wide usage, is sharing the data supplied by the customer with the travel agent who originated the booking. Not only does this make excellent promotional sense (it shows that the wholesaler cares about the agent's valuable clients), but the retailer also has the ability to follow up on any indication that the client might consider another of the operator's offerings—thus enhancing the possibility of added revenue for both parties.

NEGATIVE-FEEDBACK PROGRAM

A properly operated negative-feedback program can increase the conversion ratio on coupon- or 800-number-originated inquiries. At the end of each season, the operator's computer is asked to compile a list of people who requested literature but didn't buy one of the company's programs. A questionnaire is then mailed either to the entire list or to a representative sample.

The form begins by reminding the recipient that literature was requested and asks if it was received. Negative responses mean a problem either with fulfillment or brochure memorability. The respondent is then asked to check off any of a number of reasons why the program wasn't purchased: "Too expensive," "Too long," "Didn't include the features I wanted" (followed by a request to specify which features), "Took someone else's tour" (again followed by a request to specify), and so on.

One particularly important answer relates to the travel agent: "My agency recommended another program (which?)." A predominance of replies with this answer might indicate all sorts of problems at the retail level—some of which we'll cover shortly.

When eliciting negative feedback, there are three keys to success. First, the form must be perceived as nonthreatening and a genuine quest for information—as opposed to a sales ploy. This requires special attention to form design and wording. Second, the recipient must be convinced that cooperation will yield some personal benefit, perhaps in the form of an improved future offering from the operator. And finally, as encouragement to honestly answer financial questions, the respondent must be offered complete anonymity, if desired.

Used properly, a negative-feedback program can be an important part of in-house research, improving not only the quality and selection of literature and advertising but also the tour product itself.

WHAT THE WHOLESALER NEEDS TO KNOW ABOUT THE RETAILER

Show me a tour operator enjoying superior results with retailers, and I'll show you a management that has chosen to dig beneath surface impressions and prejudices to learn about the real world of the travel agent.

It's a complex world where the next client will want who-knows-what, where the list of destinations and travel products stretches almost to infinity, and where the smallest supplier slipup can cause the loss of a long-valued customer. It's a world where it's easy to become cynical about a supplier's intentions to deliver a quality product or, as with airline and hotel bumping, to deliver any product at all! Either way, it's the agent who loses.

It's against this background that the situation of the wholesaler must be viewed. To successfully reach the people who do the actual selling, the tour operator must penetrate the agent's daily profusion of last-minute problems, urgent phone calls, and endless sales pitches. And let's not forget the hourly airfare changes! The messages of savvy operators are getting through, however. It's all the proof one needs that point-of-sale research pays handsome dividends. The areas that beg scrutiny follow.

THE TRAVEL AGENT'S MAILBAG

Agents receive a huge volume of mail, most of it unsolicited. At smart retailers, the owner or a senior manager sorts the daily first-class mail for client and commission checks, confirmations, documents, and especially debit memos (a not infrequent tip-off of employee theft). Once that's done, the brochures and solicitations are set aside for separate action. What separate action? Many principals haven't the faintest idea, as is clearly demonstrated by the things they send.

The travel agent's mailbag is the point-of-entry into the retail marketplace. Successful principals know this and view each prospective promotion not as artwork pasted to ad agency cardboard, but as one of hundreds of promotional pieces that will arrive at the travel agency in a given week. Will it be read? Will the envelope even be opened? Real answers only come through valid, retail-level research.

THE AGENT'S LITERATURE FILE

Given a choice between a trip to an ASTA convention or a tour of a typical agent's literature files, the wise travel principal will choose the latter. Agency file drawers are where the action is. Bulk literature is the lifeblood of the travel agency business; without it, many vacation sales just wouldn't take place. Yet most principals have only a vague notion of how much literature to send and when—and even less notion of how the stuff should be designed. The result is thousands of lost sales for both retailer and wholesaler.

Here's a well-kept secret: In a properly designed travel brochure, the major features can be read upside-down! Why? Because when there's only one copy in the office (as is all too frequently the case), the literature must be placed on the agent's desk *facing the client*. If you're a wholesaler and didn't know that, you've just paid for the cost of this book, and then some.

But other bulk-literature design features are also important *and* revolve around the way agencies open, file, and retrieve current brochures—and the way they discard old ones (when they have time to do it, which isn't often). The well-designed brochure tells the agent everything he or she needs to know in a single glance: the destinations covered, whether a package or escorted tour is being offered, the dates of the season, and so on. How do you best do it? Perform your point-of-sale research; see what's being done, successfully and unsuccessfully, on the brochures of others.

A final point about layout: I work daily in the company of a faculty of top commercial artists, people of tremendous talent and creativity. They would be the first to tell you that on any project, the all-important concept—the overview—must come from you, and that you're making a big mistake when you leave literature design solely in the artists' hands. If you need the services of a top-flight art director, start by taking a walk together—to the literature rack of the nearest successful travel agency.

THE RESEARCH OF DIALOGUE

Most retail sales personnel are creatures of habit, recommending the known, predictable products and ignoring ev-

erything else. When wholesalers build brand loyalty with retailers, they're taking advantage of this potent, unseen force. Conversely, it's extremely difficult for a new tour operator to battle a long-established, highly regarded competitor.

A lot has been said and written about the use of override commissions to expand travel agent sales of various offerings—and extra bucks in the bank do make people—all people—sit up and take notice. But in a contest between overrides and happy clients, the latter always win, hands down. Satisfied clients are the agent's stock-in-trade, providing not only the higher profits of repeat business but the much needed bonus of personal referrals. In actuality, it's no contest; the agency that always opts for the override will not long remain a viable entity.

Some nearsighted principals may think of travel agents as order takers, but that's ego-driven drivel. The truth is that the agent faces the most difficult task in the entire industry: matching (frequently overblown) client expectations with the realities of the product. It's a business of constant compromise, and the task is made a hundred-fold more difficult by the exaggerated prose that permeates much travel literature. In this regard, the tour operator can be his or her own worst enemy.

These crucial factors—and many more—can be exposed by the tour operator who opens a meaningful, continuing dialogue with successful retailers. The sales call, meeting, or junket that's specifically designed to create information flow in both directions is as important a research activity as any on the face of the planet. "What do your clients want? Are we promising more than we can deliver? How can we create even happier customers for both of us?"

Basic questions. Find a face-to-face way to ask them. And *listen* to the answers.

23

The Convention and Meetings Sector— Its Operation and Research Needs

JAMES R. ABBEY
William F. Harrah College of Hotel Administration
University of Nevada
Las Vegas, Nevada

CARL K. LINK
Link Hospitality Consultants Ltd.
Calgary, Alberta

The income potential available through the convention and meetings market can significantly affect the economics of virtually every city and resort setting. The monies generated from convention delegates benefit the entire community and, for the most part, represent revenues beyond the normal cash flow. This chapter introduces the reader to how the convention market operates, the present research efforts of the industry, and the future research needs of this sector.

HOW THE CONVENTION MARKET OPERATES: ITS SIZE AND SCOPE

Travel is stimulated by a number of motivators. One of the most significant and fastest growing is the need to attend meetings and conventions. Business and professional persons travel throughout the year from their home base to attend meetings. The economic impact of these travelers, the amount of money spent, and their needs and wants are largely unexplored, despite their significance to the tourism industry.

The convention and meetings business is but one element of the tourism industry, but it is one of the healthiest and most growth oriented. Unlike the tourist who seeks varied dining experiences outside his lodging facility, conference participants normally meet, sleep, and eat under the same roof. Growth in convention, business, and meeting travel frequently increases during times when the pleasure-travel market is on the decline. The principal reason pleasure travel is outpaced by convention and meeting travel during difficult economic times is because a poor economy actually stimulates nondiscretionary travel activity by creating the need for more direct contact among business associates.

One commonly held misconception of this market is that all conventions are large gatherings of thousands of people. In reality, there are more small meetings than large. Research conducted by the industry trade publications estimates that 75 percent of all corporate meetings has fewer than 100 people in attendance. The fact that the majority of meetings never approach the 1,000 attendance figure is significant because the convention and meetings sector represents a market potential for virtually every tourist center and city.

WHAT CONVENTIONS MEAN TO A TOURISM AREA

Hotels, restaurants, visitors and convention centers, retail stores, theaters, museums, airlines, and local governments all rely heavily on the revenues generated from convention/trade-show sponsors and their delegates. Traditionally, the meetings market has been perceived as a major source of income for lodging establishments, but the delegates' expenditures are felt throughout the economy. The convention attendee not only spends dollars for lodging services but also contributes to local food-service operations, cultural and sporting activities, sightseeing and tourism attractions, and local stores and gift shops, as well as benefiting local transportation firms. Furthermore, the benefits to the city or tourism area are twofold: not only are additional jobs created, but the tax revenues of the community are also increased by the influx of convention attendees.

Results of Convention and Visitor Bureaus' Income Surveys reveal that the average delegate spends only from 32 percent to 38 percent of his convention dollar on hotel accommodation. The balance of attendees' expenditures—transportation, food and beverage, entertainment, shopping, exposition and trade-show services—ripple through the local and national economy.

Additional advantages accrue to the tourist area and local community through the meetings markets. Convention business can fill the gaps in slack months. Although *season* is often associated with the time of year, it also pertains to the day of the week. Peak season at downtown hotels, for example, typically extends from Monday to Thursday. At gaming destinations such as Las Vegas and Atlantic City, peak season is Friday and Saturday nights.

As Table 1 shows, most corporate meetings take place during the spring and fall season when most tourism areas are faced with seasonal shoulder periods.

Convention business can fill these soft periods. Second, group business is an excellent builder for repeat business. Through conventions, a large number of potential repeat visitors become acquainted with a tourism area. If they are treated well and are pleased, they will not only advertise with word of mouth, but will also likely visit the area on other occasions.

CONVENTION PURCHASING— THE BUYER'S VIEWPOINT

In assessing the research needs of the convention sector, it seems prudent to familiarize the reader with both the supply and the demand sides of the market, that is, from the buyers' and from the sellers' perspectives.

WHO HOLDS MEETINGS?

Several different buyer groups purchase convention services. Each group and each organization within these groups has needs that are not exactly identical. In fact, rarely does a single firm or organization have needs that are the same from one convention to the next.

In broad terms, the meetings market can be separated into two categories: association-type meetings and corporate or company meetings. Within each group, there are numerous further refinements. These additional types of meetings can be categorized as follows:

TABLE 1   Off-Premises Meetings by Season: Corporate Meetings

Winter (December, January, February)	19%
Spring (March, April, May)	33%
Summer (June, July, August)	20%
Fall (September, October, November)	28%

Source: Reprinted with permission from *Meetings & Conventions* (1992) ©1992 by Reed Travel Group

- Trade shows are often sponsored through a specific industry group and are not always accessible to the public. The Hannover Fair in Germany is the largest trade show in the world.
- Reunions are organized for social purposes and may involve military, social, or educational groups.
- Regional meetings are geographically confined to a specific location. The reason for keeping meetings in a particular region may be convenience, political expediency, or budget restraints.
- Events are typically public gatherings with an entertainment focus.

The most visible convention organizers are the many associations throughout the country—indeed, throughout the world because many of them are truly international. Associations vary in size and nature. They may be charitable, fraternal, educational, service, trade, union, or public organizations. Their scope ranges from small regional organizations through statewide associations to national and international ones. The meetings of trade associations are usually considered a lucrative form of the meeting business because their memberships are composed mostly of executives who have made it in business. It is a rare trade that does not have at least one association. The numerous associations in the professional and scientific fields also are inveterate meeting holders. Their subject range is wide and diverse, but they share a love for meetings and conferences.

Less visible, but of major importance, is the corporate meeting segment. Corporations have no need or desire to publicize their meetings, but meet they do. And often. They hold large meetings, small meetings, and middle-sized meetings. Insurance and appliance meeting planners frequently sponsor incentive trips for their top salespeople. Attending meetings is very definitely a part of business activity. Companies that stage meetings for dealers may deduct the cost of such events as business expenses. This has been a strong stimulant to meetings and conventions.

Figures 1 and 2 will help to put these two types of meeting segments in perspective. Figure 1 shows that, in terms of number of meetings, the corporate segment has an enormous 78.2 percent market share. Figure 2 reflects meeting expenditures by the two segments, showing that, while association meetings are fewer in number, their size generates expenditures that outdistance the corporate market.

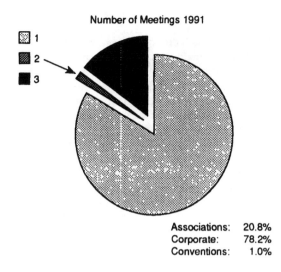

Number of Meetings 1991

Associations: 20.8%
Corporate: 78.2%
Conventions: 1.0%

FIGURE 1 Proportion of meetings held by type (1991).
Source: The Meetings Market 1992, *Meetings & Conventions 1992,* Reed Travel Group, a Division of Reed Publishing (USA) Inc.

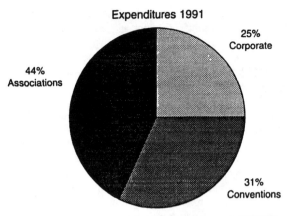

Expenditures 1991

25% Corporate

44% Associations

31% Conventions

Corporate: $ 8.7 Billion
Conventions: $11.0 Billion
Associations: $15.3 Billion

Associations: 43.7%; Corporate: 24.9%; and Conventions: 31.4%

FIGURE 2 Expenditures in dollars (1991).
Source: The Meetings Market 1992, *Meetings & Conventions 1992,* Reed Travel Group, a Dvision of Reed Publishing (USA) Inc.

When convention and meeting buyers select sites to hold sizable meetings, many factors become part of the decision-making process. Criteria for site selection include the amount of local support a group can expect from the host community. Obviously the number of sleeping rooms, banquet space, and the amount of exhibit space available in a host city are important to match supply capacity to the requirements of the convention group. But other factors become important variables for the convention buyer. These include hotel room rates, food costs, programming for spouses and children, and transportation; and sometimes the local climate is an important consideration.

Convention buyers and corporate planners often rank service at the destination, the hotel, and the convention center as the most important criteria for site-selection decision making. The availability of air service; number, size, and quality of meeting rooms; and cost of food and room rates are also top factors. *Successful Meetings* magazine found during a 1991 survey that a recent trend is for concern with site and hotel security. This is especially true for associations that house delegates in various parts of a host city.

Meeting News, a trade publication, has taken the lead in profiling the meeting planner. This publication has researched the demographic features of meeting planners, including gender, average income, educational background, years of experience in meeting planning, and the like.

THE SELLER'S PERSPECTIVE

Many different names are given to properties that house conventions. Facilities chosen by meeting planners include resort hotels, commercial hotels, suburban hotels, airport hotels, large motels and motor hotels, cruise ships, universities, condominium resorts, and specialized meeting centers.

The supply side of the convention industry is faced with two tasks in garnering the meeting and convention trade. The first and most obvious task is that of marketing and selling their community and facilities. The second is servicing the group by delivering what was promised. Securing a convention is only the beginning for the seller. Facilities should be much more concerned with how a convention goes out than with how it comes in.

OTHER SUPPLIERS IN THE MEETING INDUSTRY

Destination Management Companies

Since the growth of the meeting industry, several suppliers have evolved who cater to the needs of the meeting business.

Specialty operators called Destination Management Companies will coordinate transportation, speakers and entertainment programming (including theme parties), delegate and speaker accommodations, and numerous other details.

Destination Management Companies bill for their time and expertise by either charging the planner an hourly fee and expenses or by calculating a percentage markup on project activities.

PRESENT RESEARCH EFFORTS IN THE CONVENTION INDUSTRY

To date, limited research has been conducted in the convention and meetings area. The previous research that has been undertaken has been done by three different groups: (1) by the industry itself through meeting associations, (2) by trade publications within the convention field, and (3) by universities.

STUDIES CONDUCTED BY INDUSTRY ASSOCIATIONS

The International Association of Convention and Visitor Bureaus (IACVB) serves as a clearinghouse for the exchange of industry data, ideas, and information. It represents the major convention cities throughout the world and has 395 member bureaus worldwide. A computerized information network called the CINET© captures demographic and historical data on organizations holding meetings. The IACVB periodically conducts what they term a Convention Income Survey. The primary emphasis of its survey is to identify delegate expenditures.

The first such survey took place in 1948 with subsequent research conducted in 1956, 1966, 1973, 1979, 1985, 1986, and 1988. The first four studies were concerned only with delegate expenditure information. The 1979 survey, while collecting expenditure data, went beyond prior research efforts by collecting information on total travel-party expenditures and the convention-related expenditures of exhibitors, associations, and exposition service contractors. The 1986 survey covered 130 conventions and enjoyed a 49 percent response rate from 13,000 delegates who were surveyed.

The United States Travel Data Center designed the survey methodology and analyzed the data for the 1979 Convention Income Survey. The conventions sampled were chosen proportionately on the basis of four factors: (1) time of year, (2) scope (i.e., international, national, regional, or state), (3) whether exhibitors participated, and (4) attendance. The survey took place over the course of a year with 55 U.S. and two foreign cities participating.

Key results of the 1979 and 1985 IACVB surveys are summarized in Table 2. Convention attendees spent an average of $66.61 per day in 1979. This daily average rose to $125.66 in 1986. Of this, 38.4 percent was spent for hotel rooms and incidentals; 26.5 percent for food; and 10.9 percent at retail stores. For the 1986 survey year, figures show that spending on lodging increased to 50.9 percent, while

food and retail expenditures decreased to 23.4 percent and 7.6 percent, respectively.

The 1979 results indicate the average length of stay per delegate to be 3.8 nights and the average party size to be 2.4 persons. The average party size declined to 1.65 persons in 1986 according to IACVB figures.

Fifty-six percent used the airplane as the mode of transportation to the convention site, while 39 percent arrived by private car, truck, or recreational vehicle.

The value of the Convention Income Survey is that it allows the industry to assess its financial impact, size, and scope. It is designed to measure the monetary value of the convention business, thus allowing a community or host city to get a picture of how much convention/trade show attendees are worth to an area. The results of the 1979 Convention Income Survey provided a more comprehensive picture of the economic impact of conventions on city economics than were ever before available; however, certain limitations need to be noted.

First, the geographical coverage of the survey is restricted principally to the continental United States and cities with IACVB members and does not extend to rural areas outside the influence of local convention bureaus. Second, the survey obtains data on conventions, trade shows, conferences, and meetings, but does not cover incentive trips, combination business/incentive trips, or the nonoccupant delegate (a delegate who stays for only one day and does not utilize lodging facilities). Moreover, only out-of-town delegates are represented. Further, only city conventions are covered, excluding resort settings, which book considerable association convention business.

Third, because the 1979 survey is more comprehensive than earlier studies, comparative analysis across the board cannot be made. However, by isolating delegate expenditure information, comparisons can be made; for example, the 1985 survey results reveal a 65.1 percent increase in total delegate expenditures over 1979, and the average stay per delegate increased from 3.8 days to 4.0 days.

Over and above expenditures by individual delegates, considerable additional monies are committed to association, exhibitor, and exposition service contractors. In 1985, the total daily expenditure allocated to each professional

TABLE 2   Comparison of Delegate Spending—1979 and 1985

	ALL CONVENTIONS 1979*	ALL CONVENTIONS 1985*	INCREASE %
Average total expenditure per delegate	$253.96	$419.26	65.1%
Average daily expenditure per delegate	$66.61	$105.05	57.5%
Average length of stay per delegate	3.8	4.0	5.3%
Average travel-party size	2.4	2.5	4.2%

* Includes international data.
Source: International Association of Convention and Visitor Bureaus.

delegate by the IACVB totaled $660.57. An analysis of 1991 data collected by *Meetings & Conventions* indicated an average expenditure of $844.38 per attendee at convention and association meetings. Over the 6-year period from 1985 to 1991, this amounts to a 27.8 percent increase in daily delegate expenditure.

A final question of concern with the IACVB studies is whether they are truly income surveys. The IACVB derives its dollar data primarily from a survey of delegates' expenditures. Perhaps a truer measure of income would be derived from surveying the beneficiaries of convention business (i.e., hotels, restaurants, convention consultants, and the destination-area retail trade). In that case, the so-called multiplier effect should be calculated by economists to determine the cascading spillover impact of the convention trade on a city or tourism community.

The Hotel Sales and Marketing Association International, in a joint effort with the American Society of Association Executives in 1983, conducted a survey on association-meeting trends. In the survey, 396 executives from professional and trade associations were questioned on various issues concerning the meetings market, such as the lead time for annual convention planning, the size and scope of educational seminars, and the use of teleconferencing. The survey is divided into six sections: (1) annual conventions, (2) expositions, (3) educational seminars, (4) board and committee meetings, (5) teleconferencing, and (6) general classification information, with each section giving statistical information related to its topic.

TRADE PUBLICATION RESEARCH

Several of the trade journals in the meetings field survey their subscribers. The most up-to-date information on the dimensions of the off-premises meetings market comes from a comprehensive, biennial survey of the corporate and association subscribers of *Meetings & Conventions* magazine. The major aspects that are explored in this study are the number and types of meetings held, the dollar expenditures, the number of attendees, the number of days' duration of meetings, the lead time involved in planning meetings, the types of facilities used, the selection criteria used to choose destinations and facilities, the types of transportation used to and from and at the site of the meetings, and a profile of meeting planners' duties and responsibilities.

Because the sample is based on the magazine's circulation, the data contained in the report is not representative of the entire market. However, it is estimated by the research department of the publication that they reach virtually 100 percent of the associations that hold off-premises meetings and 70 percent of the corporations actively holding such meetings. The study includes trade shows.

Meetings & Conventions' 1983 survey of its subscribers showed the meetings and convention sector to be a $27.8 billion industry, while the 1991 survey projects a $35 billion figure. This figure does not include the incentive-travel market, which, according to industry observers, represented a $9.1 billion industry in 1991.

In contrast to the survey conducted by the IACVB, *Meetings & Conventions* explores the corporate market as well as associations. Of note in their 1991 "Meeting Market Study" is their finding that the corporate sector experienced a decline in attendance of 7 percent as compared to a study two years earlier. During the same time period, the convention sector saw a significant decline of 19 percent in delegate attendance. According to the 1983 *Meetings & Conventions* report, expenditures for corporate meetings were $6.4 billion. This figure then rose to $9.7 billion but dropped to $8.7 billion by 1991.

The North American recession that began in the late 1980s clearly has had an impact on the size of the average convention and on the number of exhibitors at convention sites. Groups are not spending money the way they did before, and expense control by corporations has become a survival tool more than ever. A long-term view of the convention and meeting sector, however, shows a 22 percent growth for all types of meetings between 1981 and 1991.

There were 1,031,400 meetings held in 1991, according to the latest *Meetings & Conventions* survey, with attendance exceeding 80 million people. The most frequently held type of corporate meeting was the training seminar, representing 24 percent of the total in 1983 and 27 percent of the total in 1991, followed by management meetings at 22 percent in 1983 and 1991.

Two other publications that conduct similar research of their readers are *Successful Meetings* and *Meeting News*. *Successful Meetings* magazine segments the corporate and the association markets and presents both the type and number of meetings held, attendance, length of meetings, and site-selection statistics.

RESEARCH STUDIES BY UNIVERSITIES

A few researchers have attempted to determine the manner in which the association and corporate groups select sites at which to hold their conventions. One of the most definitive studies on the site-selection process is the work done by Fortin and Ritchie titled *A Study of the Decision Process of North American Associations Concerning the Choice of a Convention Site* (1976). The study sampled all associations that were known to have held their conventions in Canada over a five-year period as identified by *Successful Meetings'* data bank. The specific objectives of the research were:

1. To obtain a descriptive understanding of the nature of the association convention site-selection process (length, timing, etc.).
2. To measure the relative importance of a range of factors thought to influence the choice of a convention site.
3. To identify the different elements or subdecisions of the site-selection decision process.
4. To measure the relative influence of different groups involved in site selection within and across different stages of the decision process.
5. To identify major segments of the association convention market based on association characteristics, factors

affecting site selection, and the structure of influence within the site-selection decision process.

The findings of this research study are too lengthy to discuss in this chapter, but the authors' conclusions and implications section is particularly noteworthy. The directions for future research suggested by this study include:

- A need to conduct a parallel study with the corporate meetings and the incentive-travel markets.
- A need to measure the extent to which market segments are willing to trade off various combinations of site benefits.
- A need to more extensively study the roles, utilization, and impact of different types of information and information sources on the site-selection process.
- A need to develop a methodology for assigning relative weights to the influence of site-selection benefits in the decision process.

McCleary (1977) conducted similar, though not nearly as extensive, research of the corporate-meetings market, a potentially strong source of business for lodging facilities. Therefore, research to determine which facilities and services should be offered is extremely important to the tourism industry.

The corporate-meetings market differs significantly from that of association meetings, having several unique characteristics that make it attractive:

- The majority of corporate meetings involve less than 65 persons; thus, smaller-lodging operators can capture a portion of this market.
- Because corporate meetings are smaller, lodging facilities can take several groups simultaneously and may use small meetings to fill in around larger conventions.
- Corporate groups tend to meet more frequently, are not tied to a north-south-east-west geographic pattern as are many associations, and tend to spread their meetings throughout the year. This allows the lodging operator to use the corporate market to fill shoulder periods.
- Corporate groups are generally better spenders, sometimes require fewer price concessions, and tend to utilize the other profit centers of the hotels, including the restaurants, lounges, and recreation areas.

McCleary's (1977) study was based on personal interviews with 15 corporate-meeting planners and a like number of marketing persons from meeting facilities. The meeting planners were interviewed first, to establish their needs and compare them with the marketer's perception of these needs. The meeting planner was also asked to complete a questionnaire, listing various attributes of meeting facilities. The final phase of the interview examined the decision process and criteria for site selection. Questions were structured to determine which factors affected satisfaction, as well as the negative aspects of a meeting facility.

McCleary's findings indicated that the decision process for selecting corporate-meeting sites is similar to the process for purchasing other industrial products. While multiple in-

fluences determine the corporate site decision, the major concerns for the planner were the meeting accommodations themselves, the supplier's staff, and location.

The Institute of Outdoor Recreation and Tourism at Utah State University conducted an image study of the Salt Lake Valley as a meeting site (Dalton 1978). The study was designed to gather information from national associations concerning their convention habits and needs and their perception of Salt Lake City as a potential convention site.

Based on interviews of over 140 associations, the Institute found that the hotel, the location of the host city, and the location of the convention facility were the three most positive qualities reported of the most recent convention site. The hotel was indicated by nearly one-quarter of the respondents. The climate, the hotel, and the convention facility itself were the three most reported, least positive qualities of the most recent site. Meeting facilities were reported as the single most important item to be considered when selecting a convention site. The location of the site and sleeping facilities followed.

In an article on research in the meetings market, Margaret Shaw and Ellen Mazukina (1984) cite three independent research studies. In 1981, Heidi Bloom undertook a comparative study of hotel operators' current marketing programs and meeting planners' criteria for hotel selection; in 1983, Robert Lewis completed a study of the incentive-travel market; and in 1984, Lisa Stavro and Thomas Beggs reported their findings of a study designed to identify the perceptions and motivations of meeting planners when booking meetings at hotels.

FUTURE TRENDS AND RESEARCH NEEDS

The convention and meetings market will continue to thrive as the need for communication within both associations and corporations increases in the years ahead. Several industry trends and their need for research are identified and discussed in this section.

INTERNATIONAL MARKET

Very little research has been undertaken of the characteristics, trends, and implications of international congress-type meetings. Therefore, little market planning data relevant to these visitors are available. One exception is the work done by the Danish Institute for Transport, Tourism, and Regional Science, which has done extensive research in the international convention field. The Institute, under the direction of Ejler Alkjaer, has conducted a number of studies on congress science including (1) feasibility studies and promotion plans for congress centers, (2) forecasts of the international congress business over 20-year periods, (3) global surveys of exhibitions and trade shows and their integration with congress activities, and (4) image research in congress tourism.

Researchers need to investigate the nature of this growing market and to segment out the convention traveler from the tour-and-travel international visitor. Possible areas to explore include: size of congress, visit duration, first-time visitors, sources of planners' information, the strengths and weaknesses of the area as a meeting site, services and needs of international congress delegates, activities in the host area, and spending patterns, as well as demographic characteristics profiling the meeting group. The role the convention and meetings market might play in a developing country would certainly be well-received research.

TELECONFERENCING

There is some evidence that communication facilities may soon be so advanced that there will be less need for people to gather in one room or even in the same city for a meeting. Savings in travel expense and, more importantly, in executive time are the real driving force for an ongoing revolution in electronic communications, with some of these communication services available today:

1. *Videoconferencing*—This electronic medium transmits the picture of the speaker, product, or explanatory graphics. Improvements in compressed video hardware provide high-quality videoconferencing. Two or more lines can be used to further enhance picture quality.

2. *Teleconferencing*—Ideas can be shared in real time with enhanced audio and graphics. Reservations for special transmission facilities are no longer necessary.

3. *Electronic data transfer*—Large amounts of data are moved between computers separated by long distances. Examples of use are the movement of inventory records, payroll logs, data-base updates, remote job entry and distributed data processing.

4. *Computer graphics*—These provide internationally distributed workstations with real-time access to remote data bases and powerful central computers for designing blueprints and manufacturing processes.

5. *Facsimile*—High-resolution Group IV facsimiles permit quick and accurate transmission of large documents. Transmission of color documents will be popular in the near future.

Video- and audio-teleconferencing are supported by most international telephone and communications companies. Users are demanding computer interfaces to their videoconferences and asking equipment vendors for the ability to simultaneous transmit data and video during conferences. Today's videoconference participants want a virtual meeting space with all the real-time computer support they would have during a face-to-face meeting.

Once videoconferences are digitized and transmitted over networks, they become computer applications. Videomail is an example of how videoconferencing is becoming a computer application.

On-demand, usage-sensitive service uses terrestrial and satellite facilities to establish a digital call between the United States, Canada, and a growing number of foreign locations. In the United States, subscribers to domestic services can use the same access line to dial up international locations in 18 countries. A popular application for videoconferencing is international sales meetings and market planning sessions. Through public teleconferencing networks and the U.S. Sprint *Meeting Channel*, for example, corporations can reach more than 260 videoconferencing rooms worldwide.

The impact of teleconferencing on future meetings raises a number of questions that should be answered by researchers. What is the attitude of convention delegates towards telecommunications as a substitute for attendance at meetings? What percentage of the business meetings can be conducted via telecommunications? Have video- and teleconferencing and other forms of electronic communication, in fact, enhanced travel and convention growth? Or will the knowledge worker of the twenty-first century prefer electronic interfacing to the discomfort of travel?

Words, body gestures, facial expressions, eye contact, and shared common space are all important ingredients in a successful meeting. Can teleconferencing overcome these benefits inherent in face-to-face communication?

Hotel chains such as Hyatt, Hilton, Marriott, and Holiday Inn have installed videoconferencing hardware in their convention hotels. Lodging operators, as well as meeting planners, have some unanswered questions on the effect of this technology. What has been the impact of teleconferencing on guest room sales? Have hotels increased their banquet and other meeting room business?

Research identifying the pros and cons of substituting telecommunications for actual attendance at meetings needs to be undertaken.

By 1993, business-travel revenue, including entertainment, will have grown to about $130 billion (up from $28 billion in 1980) according to the American Express Survey of Business Travel Management. Video- and teleconferencing will most likely benefit the small meeting environment. Some business travel in companies with video- and teleconference networks can be expected to be diverted. For the market as a whole, however, teleconferencing will likely promote domestic- and international-travel intentions.

NEGOTIATIONS AND CONTRACTS

On behalf of his organization, the average meeting planner typically negotiates and prepares more than 20 meetings per year. Professional planning for these meetings can become very technical and complex. For this reason, negotiations, including contracts, guarantees, and deposits, are one of the challenging subjects of the meeting business today. There are no universally accepted industry standards governing the use of contracts and cancellations. In the past, the convention and meetings industry could run fairly effectively on gentlemen's agreement, but the handshake is rapidly giving way to the formal contract. Issues of general importance, such as commitments for accommodation, food, and required meeting space, are usually captured on standard agreement documents or preprinted forms supplied by the hotel or convention venue.

Larger convention hotels and industry associations keep history records and profiles on association meetings. The

Professional Convention Management Association (PCMA) launched a data bank in 1992 that contains detailed records on 8,000 associations and their meeting characteristics.

For negotiating purposes, both the hotels and the association planner may want to maintain such historical data as room pickup (the ratio of forecasted to actual rooms taken by the delegates), food and beverage pickup, cancellation rate, and no-shows. All these factors relate to forecasted commitments at major conventions and association meetings. If this information is available, it can help both parties during the negotiating phase of a new contract. Hotels often assess a penalty to the convener if it does not use the forecasted convention block of guest rooms.

The possible protection of all parties if the group is not able to live up to its original forecast should be contemplated in legal contract agreements between groups and convention venues.

More serious difficulties can arise when planners find new owners and management at a previously selected convention hotel. These cases have happened in North America because of the uncertain climate in the real estate and hotel industry and its frequent changes in ownership and management. This has serious implications for a planned convention or meeting, and a planner must attempt to protect his organization with properly drafted documentation and sound legal advice.

As there is always potential for litigation and disputes between buyer and seller, the Convention Liaison Council in Washington, D.C., has set up an Alternative Dispute Resolution (ADR) program that is endorsed by its 24 member organizations. Some of the key organizations are:

- The Air Transport Association of America
- The American Hotel and Motel Association
- The American Society for Association Executives
- The International Association of Convention and Visitor Bureaus

The purpose of the ADR program is to promote equitable settlements of disputes between associations and suppliers. The ADR group assesses a fee for its service, and cases are heard by a three-member panel from the Convention and Exposition Industry. All hearings are held in Washington, D.C., and, unlike an arbitration procedure, decisions are not binding unless both parties agree.

What would be of value to the meetings industry is a study identifying policies regarding standard legal agreements presently employed. Questions that might be addressed include: What is the liability of the lodging facility or convention center if there is overbooking? What is the liability of the convener if committed hotel accommodation is not used? Is there a difference in the negotiating approach used by corporate meeting planners as contrasted with association planners? The impact of the written agreement on the meeting's industry has yet to be adequately researched.

IDENTIFICATION OF THE MEETING PLANNER

Future research efforts might be directed to the role and responsibilities of the meeting planner. *Meeting News*, a

publication for the industry, undertakes such a study through polling its readership each year. The 1991 research, for example, showed demographic data confirming a significant increase in female convention planners employed in this industry sector. In the most recent survey year, 75.8 percent of all association planners were female compared to a 1990 figure of 53.7 percent.

However, future research might track changes within this profession, might suggest appropriate guidelines and channels for career planning, and might identify academic programs and curriculums for developing the professional meetings manager.

Other areas for research might include profile studies of both corporate and association planners. Psychographics studies of meeting planners might be helpful in determining if there is a relationship between the decision maker's lifestyle and the site selected. Comparative studies exploring how the wants, needs, and benefits sought by the association meetings market differ from those of the corporate market would be valuable.

RESEARCH ON MEETING FACILITIES OF THE FUTURE

The design and layout of future conference facilities is an area in need of research. What will meeting rooms of the future look like? How will new technology, including closed circuit, satellite hookup, cable, and videoconferencing, affect the meeting facilities? Future meeting facilities will require sophistication and ingenuity in their physical design to accommodate customer demands.

How will changes in design alter management functions? It seems likely that the function rooms of the future will also require more sophisticated conference service departments as meeting planners' needs become more complex. Research exploring the future might confirm that hotel facilities will need to include high technology work areas for guests, television studios, and video- and computer-conferencing facilities. On the operational level, convention venue managers need to make use of advanced computer software in order to integrate reservations, sales, marketing, and profit-margin evaluation functions.

Research into the most appropriate meeting environment has, to date, been sketchy. What of lighting, acoustics, sight lines, and air circulation?

A conference-center building boom has begun in the early 1990s with convention centers around the world being constructed or expanded. Major facilities in the United States that provide from 500,000 square feet to over 1,000,000 square feet of exhibit and meeting space include the Georgia World Congress Center, The Los Angeles Exhibit & Convention Center, and the Las Vegas Convention Center. The RAI International Exhibition & Congress Center in Amsterdam, the Netherlands, also falls into this category of megasize meeting facility.

There has been a shift in types of facilities used for meetings since 1979. A comparison of survey data collected by *Meetings & Conventions* magazine in 1991 showed that, since 1979, resort and airport sites have been declining in popularity for the convention buyer, while the corporate meeting customer has a marked preference for urban and midtown meeting venues. As Table 3 shows, several non-traditional meeting facilities—cruise ships, gaming facilities, university-owned facilities, and condominium resorts—are becoming a factor in the market.

THE SOURCES OF INFORMATION USED BY MEETING PLANNERS

Tourism destinations and individual lodging operators devote considerable expense to communicating benefits to meeting planners in an attempt to influence the planner's site selection. Little is known about which sources of information meeting planners use in making their site decision. Fortin and Ritchie (1976) cite a need to study more extensively the impact of different types of information and information sources on the site-selection process. Researchers might address the role of various information sources: information secured from other meeting planners, hotel convention collateral material, advertisements in trade publications, and direct mail pieces. Identification of those sources that most strongly influence the choice decision would offer the marketer opportunities to increase the probability of securing convention-group business. A closely related research approach might be to identify the type of information sources used by particular types of meeting planners, that is, corporate versus association decision makers. Also, researchers might examine whether decision makers in the area of meeting planning see personal or external media sources of information as being more important.

IMPACT OF CONFERENCE CENTERS

Conference centers—once viewed as dreary, dormitory-like facilities—have altered their product-service mix and become direct competitors of lodging properties. The conference center concept was created at Tarrytown House Conference Center in Tarrytown, New York, and has proliferated to

locations throughout the country. The reason for the success of conference centers is founded upon their creation of a self-contained environment for learning. The hotel meeting frequently involves a series of separate purchases. Lodging, meals, audiovisual, and support services are often arranged with different firms. In contrast to this piecemeal purchase of a meeting, conference centers provide lodging, food and beverage, meeting rooms, and, most importantly, auxiliary support services for a single package price.

While there is no clear-cut method of determining whether a property meets the requirements of a conference center, the International Association of Conference Centers, formed in 1981, has established certain guidelines. To call itself a conference center, a property must consider meetings their priority business—they must do at least 60 percent of total volume in meetings. In addition, a conference center offers a total environment dedicated to meetings. The center's meeting rooms form the nucleus of the property. They are supported by lodging, food and beverage, and recreation. Often, but not always, the center is located in a quiet area—off the beaten path, yet close to a major city or airport. Another distinguishing mark of conference centers is the number and quality of conference service professionals that are in their employ. Most conference centers fall into one of four basic categories as to type: Executive, Resort, Corporate, and College/University.

While little research has been undertaken on this active sector of the meetings market, Laventhol & Horwath has annually, since 1976, prepared a statistical and financial profile of the executive conference center. This study is designed to define the type of facilities, style of operation, source of customers, and financial profile of the typical conference center. Data are secured from clients of Laventhol & Horwath. The establishments that provide data on operating results are those that are specifically designed and operated as executive conference centers. A significant limitation of this work is its narrow sample. Further, since there are differences in the composition of the sample from year to year, comparisons of studies are not possible.

TABLE 3 Corporate Meetings: Type of Facilities Used in 1991

Type of Facility	Number in Past Year	Percent of Total
Urban/Midtown hotels	304,000	32%
Suburban hotels	203,300	21
Resort hotels	131,100	14
Airport hotels	96,800	10
Privately owned conference centers	60,500	6
Suite hotels	42,400	4
Condominium resorts	11,300	1
University owned conference centers	8,900	1
Gaming facilities	7,500	1
Cruise ships	6,000	1
Other facilities	92,100	10
Total Meetings*	963,900	100%

*Includes trade shows.
Source: Reprinted with permission from *Meetings & Conventions* (1992) ©1992 by Reed Travel Group.

This rapidly growing sector is much in need of research. Research efforts identifying the wants and needs of the conference-center customer would be beneficial in marketing these facilities, as would attitude-and-awareness studies of the meeting planning industry. Image-and-perception studies should be undertaken as well.

Research efforts should be directed to determine the size, composition, and pace of development of the executive conference center market. Site-selection variables need to be explored, and choice models developed. The levels of audiovisual and program-support services required, as well as conference room design and flexibility, are areas that to date have not been researched.

SPOUSE ATTENDANCE AND CHILDREN

What part the spouse and, perhaps, children play in convention attendance is an area that has not been examined extensively. However, in recent years, more attendees have brought their spouses to meetings, according to industry surveys. According to *Meetings & Conventions*, the number of spouses at corporate meetings went up from 6,670,600 in 1989 to 6,739,600 in 1991, although the number of corporate meeting attendees had dropped during the same time period. At association meetings, spouse attendance increased from 2,714,000 in 1989 to 3,370,500 in 1991.

The International Association of Convention and Visitor Bureaus, in their 1991 convention income survey, shows average length of stay as 4.1 days per delegate. When compared to the 1979 figure from the same survey (3.8 days), it can be concluded that the trend is for more delegates to stay longer and perhaps bring their spouses. Society has changed and labor-force participation by spouses is still rising. As both the delegate and the spouse have less discretionary time, the opportunity to travel together provides for quality time. The recession of the late 1980s has given meeting attendees another reason to travel with their spouses: Difficult economic times have encouraged a number of people to take advantage of this inexpensive family vacation.

A reflection of stronger marketing practices by the convention industry can be seen in efforts to show the spouse a good time and provide stimulating programs that include entertainment and learning opportunities. In North America, hotels have created more children's programs to meet the demands of this audience. Delta Hotels in Canada, for example, started a children's center in a major city hotel as far back as 1977 in their Chelsea Inn property in Toronto.

Is it possible that convention attendance can be boosted by offering spouse and family programs specific to the wants and needs of spouses and children? What role do spouses and, possibly, children play in the convention decision process?

An intriguing question arises on the issue of children as decision makers. Children can be catalysts in motivating a family to visit an attraction, destination, or event. A worthwhile question to explore may be what specific activities and destination characteristics, including cultural opportunities would interest children, at a convention venue? In addition, the question as to the relative decision-making influence of

family members in general relative to convention attendance remains unexplored.

FOREIGN AND OFFSHORE MEETING TRENDS

There has been an ongoing trend to hold meetings in overseas locations and foreign countries, including Canada. Communications technology has made the 1990s the decade of global orientation and international sharing of knowledge; and the meeting and convention industry will be no exception to these developments.

Incentive-travel packagers were the first to hold meetings abroad. Sales and Management meetings conducted as part of an incentive trip abroad have the advantage of introducing staff in the host country to their North American peers. Discussions and information exchange on marketing and product issues with international colleagues benefit the North American corporation in a very competitive global environment. In addition, political reasons can be the rationale for holding meetings abroad. More companies hold meetings in proximity to international developments, such as the unification of the European community and the current transformation of former Soviet Union economies.

England, France, and Germany are considered the most attractive overseas locations as these countries possess an infrastructure favorable to the convention and meetings sector.

According to the *1992 Meetings Market Report* conducted by Market Probe International, Europe remains the most popular destination for overseas meetings. As Table 4 shows, the Caribbean has become a popular destination (44 percent of all offshore meetings), with Canada maintaining an almost 20 percent share of the 60,000 meetings held in foreign countries. Top cities and regions ranked in terms of destination popularity are as follows:

Canada: Toronto and Vancouver
Europe: London and Paris
Mexico: Cancun and Acapulco
Caribbean: U.S. Virgin Islands and Bahamas
Asia: Tokyo and Hong Kong

TABLE 4 Location of Meetings in Foreign Countries

Geographic Areas	Corporate Planners
Europe (net)	57%
Leading Countries:	
England	21%
France	14%
Germany	12%
Caribbean	44%
Hawaii	37%
Canada	19%
Mexico	14%
Asia	13%
Pacific	6%
(Base = 154)	

Source: Reprinted with permission from *Meetings & Conventions* (1992) ©1992 by Reed Travel Group.

South Pacific: Sydney and Brisbane
South America: Sao Paulo and Buenos Aires

It should be noted that no destinations in Eastern Europe or the former Soviet Union have made this list of top-ranked foreign destinations. As the transformation of the economies of these countries continues, more convention and meeting events will take place in this region. Western businesses will accelerate joint-venture and other business opportunities as several hundred million consumers in those countries will soon be ready to buy North American goods and services.

CONCLUSION

The conventions and meetings segment of the travel industry is substantial and growing at an increasing rate; for example, one source cites a 93 percent growth rate for the convention market between 1981 and 1991.

The International Association of Convention and Visitor Bureaus estimates that the association market segment generates an average of $150 each day to the host community (1991). Some economists have suggested the multiplier effect for the convention industry ranges from a factor of 3.0 to 5.0, which is a remarkable benefit for any host community.

In a more comprehensive study of both the association and corporate meetings industry, it was estimated that this market was approaching a value of $39 billion; and some sources predict the industry will reach $50 billion in the mid-1990s.

With a 1991 attendance of 82 million delegates, the market is enormous, yet it is also changing. New technology, the emerging importance of the specialized convention and exhibit suppliers, and the impact of communications technology are just some of the trends that promise to alter this segment of the tourism industry in the future.

Despite the importance of this market segment to both individual properties and host cities, little research has been undertaken on its structure and workings. This lack of information is a handicap to operating managers and tourism officials responsible for marketing and promoting their product and services. Moreover, the meeting and convention planners responsible for organizing and conducting effective meetings are equally affected.

While this lack of research is, on the one hand, a hindrance to the convention and meetings industry, it presents a promising opportunity for researchers. Convention and meeting research is, for the most part, an untapped market for researchers. Considerable work is needed to increase understanding of this important segment of the tourism industry.

REFERENCES

Alkjaer, Ejler (1976), "Images and Realities in Congress Tourism," *Journal of Travel Research* 14(Spring), 14–15.

Alkjaer, Ejler (1980), *The Congress Market of the 80's*, Copenhagen: Institute for Transport, Tourism and Regional Science.

Alkjaer, Ejler, and Jorn Eriksen (1967), *Location and Economic Consequences of International Congresses,* Copenhagen: Institute for Transport, Tourism and Regional Science.

American Express Survey of Business Travel Management (1992), Phoenix, Arizona

American Society of Association Executives (1980), *Convention Liaison Manual*, Washington, D.C.

American Society of Association Executives and Hotel Sales Marketing Association (1983), *Association Meeting Trends*, Washington, D.C.

Astroff, Milton, and James Abbey (1978), *Convention Sales and Services*, Dubuque, Iowa: Wm. C. Brown Publishing.

Bloom, Heidi (1981), "Marketing to Meeting Planners: What Works?" *Cornell Hotel and Restaurant Administration Quarterly*, 22(August), 45–50.

Convene: The Journal of the Professional Convention Management Association (1992), Birmingham, Alabama.

Chon, K. S., and Y. H. Huo (1992), Environment for future Conference Centers as perceived by conference center managers, in *Proceedings of the Convention/Expo Summit III*, 4–19, W.S. Roehl, ed., Las Vegas, Nevada: William F. Harrah College of Hotel Administration, University of Nevada, Las Vegas.

Dalton, Michael J. (1978), *The Image of the Salt Lake Valley Convention Analysis*, Institute of Outdoor Recreation and Tourism, Utah State University, Logan, Utah.

English Tourist Board (1974), *Report on a Survey of a Survey of Conference Venue Selection,* London.

Fortin, Paul A., and J. R. Brent Ritchie (1976), *A Study of the Decision Process of North American Associations Concerning the Choice of a Convention Site*, Quebec, Canada: Universite Laval.

Getz, Donald (1992), *Trends in Event Tourism—Growth Trends*, World Travel and Tourism Review Indicators, Trends and Issues, Volume 2, Wallingford, U.K.: CAB International.

Horwath and Horwath International (1984), *Worldwide Lodging Industry*, New York.

International Association of Convention and Visitor Bureaus (1978) (1983, Update) (1986), *Convention Income Survey*, Champaign, IL.

Jones, James (1979), *Meeting Management: A Professional Approach*, Stamford, CT: Bayard Publications.

Laventhol & Horwath (1982), *The Executive Conference Center: A Statistical and Financial Profile*, Philadelphia.

Lewis, Robert (1983), "The Incentive Travel Market: How to Reap Your Share," *Cornell Hotel and Restaurant Administration Quarterly* 24(May), 19–27.

McCleary, Ken W. (1977), "Factors Influencing the Marketing of Meeting Facilities: An Empirical Study of the Buying/Selling Relationship for Corporate Group Meetings," unpublished doctoral dissertation, Michigan State University, East Lansing, Michigan.

Meeting News (1980, 1992), *The Meeting Planner: An Emerging Specialist*, New York.

Meeting Planners International (1980), *Source Book for Meeting Planners: A Bibliography*, Middletown, Ohio.

Meetings & Conventions (1981, 1983, 1991, 1992), *Meetings Market Study*, New York: Ziff-Davis Publishing Company.

Oh, HaeMoon (1992), "Family Decision Making in Convention Participation," unpublished Master of Sciences thesis, William F. Harrah College of Hotel Administration, University of Nevada, Las Vegas, Nevada.

Pannell Kerr Forster (1984), *Trends in the Hotel Industry*, Houston.

Ritchie, J.R. Brent (1992), "New Realities, New Horizons. Leisure, Tourism and Society in the Third Millennium," *The American Express Annual Review of Travel*, New York, N.Y.

Shaw, Margaret, and Ellen Mazukina (1984), "The Meetings Market: Where the Research Is," *Hotel Sales Marketing Association Marketing Review*, (Fall), 27–30.

Stavro, Lisa, and Tom Beggs (1984), "Attributes of Significance a Priori and during the Meeting," published in the proceedings of the World Hospitality Congress II, March 25–28, Boston, MA.

Successful Meetings (1980, 1992), *Corporate and Association Meetings Market*, Philadelphia.

Weirich, Marguerite L. (1992), *Meetings and Conventions Management*, Albany, NY: Delmar Publishers.

MEETING INDUSTRY PERIODICALS

ASSOCIATION & SOCIETY MANAGER, Barrington Publications, 825 S. Barrington Avenue, Los Angeles, CA 90049

BUSINESS TRAVEL NEWS, CMP Publications, Inc., 600 Community Drive, Manhasset, NY 11030

CORPORATE MEETINGS & INCENTIVES, Edgell Communications, Inc., 7500 Old Oak Boulevard, Cleveland, OH 44130.

CORPORATE TRAVEL, Gralla Publications, 1515 Broadway, New York, NY 10036

INCENTIVE/MANAGING & MARKETING THROUGH MOTIVATION, Bill Communications, Inc., 633 Third Avenue, New York, NY 10017

INCENTIVE TRAVEL MANAGER, Barrington Publications, 825 S. Barrington Avenue, Los Angeles, CA 90049

INSURANCE CONFERENCE PLANNER, Bayard Publications, 1234 Summer Street, Stamford, CT 06905

MEDICAL MEETINGS, Medical Meetings, 20 Central Avenue, P.O. Box 700, Ayer, MA 01432

MEETING NEWS, Gralla Publications, 1515 Broadway, New York, NY 10036

MEETINGS & CONVENTIONS and INCENTIVE WORLD, Ziff-Davis Publishing Co., One Park Avenue, New York, NY 10016

SUCCESSFUL MEETINGS, Bill Communications, Inc., 633 Third Avenue, New York, NY 10017

MEETINGS & INCENTIVE TRAVEL, Southam Communications, Ltd., 1450 Don Mills Road, Ontario M3B2X7

RESORTS & INCENTIVES, Gralla Publications/United Newspapers Group, 1515 Broadway, New York, NY 10036

THE MEETING MANAGER, Meeting Planners International, 1950 Stemmons Freeway, Dallas, TX 75207

TOUR & TRAVEL NEWS, CMP Publications Inc., 600 Community Drive, Manhasset, NY 11030

ASSOCIATIONS

AMERICAN HOTEL & MOTEL ASSOCIATION (AH&MA), 1201 New York Avenue NW, Washington, D.C. 20005-3917

AMERICAN SOCIETY OF ASSOCIATION EXECUTIVES (ASAE), 1575 Eye Street NW, Washington, D.C. 20005

CONVENTION LIAISON COUNCIL (CLC), 1575 Eye Street NW, Washington, D.C. 20005

INTERNATIONAL ASSOCIATION OF CONVENTION & VISITORS BUREAUS (IACVB), P.O. Box 758, Champaign, IL 61820

INTERNATIONAL EXHIBITORS ASSOCIATION (IEA), 5103 B. Backlick Road, Annandale, VA 22003

MEETING PLANNERS INTERNATIONAL (MPI), 1950 Stemmons Freeway, Dallas, TX 75207

NATIONAL ASSOCIATION OF EXPOSITION MANAGERS (NAEM), 334 E. Garfield Road, Aurora, OH 44202

PROFESSIONAL CONVENTION MANAGEMENT ASSOCIATION (PCMA), 2027 First Avenue North, Suite 1007, Birmingham, AL 35203

SOCIETY OF COMPANY MEETING PLANNERS (SCMP), 2600 Garden Road, #208, Monterey, CA 93940

SOCIETY OF INCENTIVE TRAVEL EXECUTIVES (SITE), 271 Madison Avenue, New York, NY 10016

24

Research Needs for Developing Established Events and Attractions

CAROLYN CAREY

Strategic Planner
Marketing Department
Knott's Berry Farm
Buena Park, California

*E*vents and attractions, by their broadest definition, could encompass anything that attracts an audience by appealing to specific tastes or desires. In the context of travel and tourism, this broad spectrum becomes limited to that segment of the industry that is unique to specific geographic locations. An event has a limited duration, whereas an attraction is permanent.

This chapter covers the unique research needs for the marketing of established events and attractions. It covers analysis of customers and noncustomers and of continuous and special basis research requirements. The types of research described satisfy needs for ongoing marketing activities as well as for future planning at the individual and industrial level.

The research needs of events or attractions vary. This chapter will assume that the magnitude of the customer base can be estimated and that the event or attraction is established. Three main areas of concern are ongoing marketing research, special research studies, and joint research compiled by the events and attractions industry. The objective of research is to maximize attendance and/or profitability through product improvement, marketing strategy, and long-range planning.

Key factors that make this research unique are the joint and inseparable dependency on the resident and tourist population bases, the large array of competition for discretionary time and money, and the availability of a very large customer base at all times for research.

RESEARCH TECHNIQUES

Collection of historical data pertaining to existing customers is the first step in amassing information on events and attractions. Attendance and financial records provide valuable information about customer usage patterns. Correctly re-

corded data of this nature form a basis for future-attendance projections and trending analysis relating to such factors as length of stay, per capita spending, in-facility capabilities, ticketing structures, product improvement, and product component utilization. Along with appropriate additional secondary information, it also allows the multidimensional analysis of the effects of such external variables as weather, media exposure, economy, energy availability/cost, competitive activity, and airline deregulation.

Collection of secondary research data varies significantly with geographic location of the event and attraction and with government involvement. The geographic definition of the resident base for an event or attraction usually includes any household within an area that allows its members to visit the event or attraction and return home within one day. The nonresident or tourist base, therefore, includes anyone required to stay overnight in the area of the event or attraction in order to visit.

In most cases, the Bureau of the Census can provide all the secondary data required for the resident population, although, as the time since the last census increases, the availability of updated data becomes fragmented and dependent on private-sector updates. Data regarding the nonresident or tourist population is the major variable being entirely dependent on government involvement at a city, state, and national level. This involvement can range from extensive, as in the case of the State of Florida, to minimal, as in the case of the State of California. Where government involvement is extensive, the individual event or attraction can derive all the secondary data required for the quantitative demographic identification of the *noncustomer* within the nonresident or tourist base. Where government involvement is minimal, the individual event or attraction naturally has to identify an alternate source for their information. Their options are to subscribe to a national travel survey or to initiate the collection of primary data either on an individual basis or in conjunction with other events or attractions. Neither of these options are totally adequate because of the primary nature of their data, their exclusion of the foreign-tourist component for reasons of language, and their noncustomization to geographic designations.

Once all the existing secondary data are organized, the next step is to separate it by demographic component. The demographic components of greatest significance are geographic area of residence, age, race, sex, and customer party composition. In the case of larger events or attractions, primary or survey data must be collected. At this point, a decision has to be made as to whether primary data should be collected by interviewing or by self-administered questionnaires. Many variables will affect this decision but, where budgets permit, the use of a personal interview is preferable to ensure valid and maximum responses. Personal interviews also facilitate quality control and the use of open-end questioning and screening techniques.

In determining the best method of personal interviews, the decision is based upon whether customers or noncustomers are being questioned. Whenever possible, the use of interviewers who are on the payroll of the event or attraction is considered preferable when interviewing customers. This ensures maximum cooperation and conduct compatible with the standards of the event or attraction as well as complete familiarity with the event or attraction. When noncustomers are being interviewed, it is recommended that an outside supplier be utilized to conduct the data collection by whatever means they advise as appropriate. Telephone surveys will usually be recommended for the resident noncustomer and their visiting nonresident friends or relatives, whereas in-person surveys at hotels or airports will usually be recommended for the nonresident or tourist. An outside supplier is better equipped to collect this type of data by virtue of their access to WATTS Lines, experience with telephone techniques, access to a larger and experienced interviewer base, and ability to receive authorization for interviewing in public locations.

It is further recommended, in both situations, that the design and reporting of such a study should be handled by staff of the event or attraction for reasons of cost control, familiarity with the product, and feasibility of the recommendations.

ONGOING MARKETING RESEARCH

KNOWING YOUR CUSTOMER— QUANTITATIVE AND QUALITATIVE DATA REQUIRED

In conjunction with standard demographic data, other valuable customer-related data includes mode of transportation to the event or attraction, prior visiting patterns, reason for visit, awareness of the event or attraction geographic area, planning cycles, use of travel professionals or package tours, accommodation used, length of stay, and competitive visitations.

Qualitative information to be gathered from the customer about the visit to the event or attraction includes overall satisfaction; satisfaction with components such as food, merchandising, employees, or rides; satisfaction with aspects such as landscaping, cleanliness, signage, layout, or public announcements; pricing; intent to return; and best- and least-liked features. If budget and time permit, psychographic characteristics of the customer should also be collected to ensure usable qualitative data.

These data form the basis of a quality control system where the strengths and weaknesses of the product relative to customer psychographics as well as demographics can be carefully monitored to ensure maximum product perception and, therefore, to maximize word-of-mouth advertising and the repeat-visit factor. In collecting these data, the guidelines in Table 1 should be kept in mind.

KNOWING YOUR NONCUSTOMER— QUANTITATIVE AND QUALITATIVE DATA NEEDED

The opinions and values of the noncustomers are required to identify their profiles. The basic reason for identifying the noncustomers is to ascertain why they are not customers. The data are cross-referenced with demographic and geographic information. The data collection required to generate this type of information is fairly complex and costly, and the benefits must be carefully assessed. The following represents the type of information that would be generated while identifying reasons for noncustomer status: perception of the event or attraction and its components; perceptions towards competitive events or attractions; effects of competitive activity; patronage of competitive events or attractions; and psychographic evaluation of the noncustomer. Having compiled the reasons for the noncustomer status, directions for product improvement or marketing strategy will become apparent, and steps can be taken to broaden the customer base of the event or attraction.

QUANTITATIVE AND QUALITATIVE DATA NEEDED IN LONG-RANGE PLANNING

Long-range planning relies on historical and predictive demographic data. In most cases, resident population projec-

Table 1   Guidelines for Reliable Demographic Data

- Minimum sample size should be 2% of attendance during period of interest.
- Data collection schedule should coincide with every time-frame part of the period of interest.
- Schedule should coincide with peak and nonpeak periods—two-hour periods are recommended.
- To maximize the random nature of response, projectionable demographic data should not be collected with other survey data.
- Interviewers should address the party unit rather than individuals to avoid the bias of the male adult responding on behalf of the other party members.
- Design questionnaires to allow cross-tabulation of demographics.
- Weigh the raw data in relation to the actual attendance contributions during the day or day part it was collected.
- Customers are guests; sensitive demographics such as income or race should be avoided or collected by observation.

tions are available from Chambers of Commerce or private-sector industries such as banking or housing. Data regarding the nonresident or tourist population projections are available through some state governments or industry trade groups.

Additional qualitative data needed on a continuous basis for predictive reasons relate to the ways in which the product can be adapted to maximize the penetration of the available population bases by the event or attraction in the future.

Product improvements are usually undertaken to maximize resident attendance. Data relating to the product should, therefore, be collected from the resident customer and noncustomer of the event or attraction; but, for reasons of cost, it is recommended that as much preliminary data collection as possible be conducted at the event or attraction. Customer product improvements should be screened and rank-ordered by customers.

SPECIAL RESEARCH STUDIES

KNOWING YOUR CUSTOMER—QUANTITATIVE AND QUALITATIVE DATA NEEDED

Most events and attractions will have special periods where additional quantitative data becomes mandatory. Examples of such periods are: periods of paid advertising on behalf of the event or attraction; periods where additional product is offered on a temporary basis; and periods of promotional activity.

Secondary-data and secondary-information variables, such as paid media weights, admission discounts, attendance incentives, media derived from publicity or tie-ins with noncompetitive ventures, should be analyzed for the effect of the present event. The additional qualitative data required includes satisfaction with the additional product offering, reac-

tions to the various media campaigns, and reactions to the promotional activities. Such testing contributes in assessing the value of repeating the period of special activity and in maximizing attendance.

The next step is to relate this information to the demographic information collected during these special periods. Additional quantitative information required includes:

- The media through which the customer was informed about the event or attraction or its activities
- The specific station or newspaper causing the awareness
- The messages received through the media, generated on open-end basis
- The extent to which the media influenced the visit to the event or attraction
- In the case of nonresidents or tourists, whether the media exposure occurred before or after leaving home

Quantitative primary and secondary data of this type can serve to analyze inter- and intra-media effectiveness as a ratio of cost and awareness; incremental business as a function of temporary product additions; and the extent to which customers would have attended the event or attraction despite the special activities.

KNOWING YOUR NONCUSTOMER—QUANTITATIVE AND QUALITATIVE DATA NEEDED

Identification of the noncustomer in relationship to special periods, unlike the identification of the noncustomer on a continuous basis, cannot rely on data for the population bases as a whole. Again the resident and nonresident or tourist bases must be addressed directly, and the benefits to be derived from such a survey must be carefully considered relative to cost. Information generated from interviewing the noncustomer includes media impact on the entire population, demographics of the "aware" population, and the extent of media impact on the nonresponding regular-customer base.

The qualitative data can further serve to identify whether the product, the media, or some other factor contributed these strengths or weaknesses. Data of this type assists in determining the reasons for the response or non-response to a period of special activity, which, in the case of the quantitative data, essentially translates into what is commonly known in the consumer product industry as "Standard Advertising Testing."

QUANTITATIVE AND QUALITATIVE DATA NEEDED IN LONG-RANGE PLANNING

Additional data needed on a special basis for predictive reasons relate to the planning of media exposure and to the ways in which these periods of special activity can be adapted to maximize the penetration of the population bases by the event or attraction in the future. Special activities are usually undertaken by an event or attraction to maximize their resident attendance on the basis that the nonresident or tourist population would not be exposed to most of the periods of media or special activities. Although it relates only to the resident base, this research is further addressed for completeness.

Again, the needs from the resident and nonresident or tourist populations differ with quantitative data of this type only needed from the tourist population. Data relative to quantitative media planning are required from the tourist population to determine the extent to which the individual event or attraction needs to rely on national or even international awareness to secure a place in the itinerary of a tourist entering the geographic area of that event or attraction. Data of this type can only be collected on a national or international level and are naturally also extremely costly. Studies of this type can be of value on an industry basis and are discussed in the next section.

THE RESEARCH NEEDS OF THE EVENTS AND ATTRACTIONS INDUSTRY

The research needs of the events and attractions industry are equal to those required by individual events and attractions. However, unless the individual events and attractions are organized into a group, the amorphous nature of the industry precludes any research, needed or not. Under ideal conditions, the events and attractions industry could provide much of the information already described for its individual members, eliminating the duplication of effort. However, under the extremely competitive conditions, there is considerable resistance to sharing of information. When the information affords the vehicle for enhancement of the customer base and the industry as a whole, at the expense of other leisure-time industries, then there is a reason for cooperation. The following section describes the types of information that an organized industry could collect.

KNOWING YOUR INDUSTRY'S CUSTOMERS— QUANTITATIVE AND QUALITATIVE DATA REQUIREMENTS

The first step is to organize existing information about industry members. The organization does exist on a national level, but members are usually defined as those events and attractions within a geographic area. It is very significant to the industry to determine the strengths and weaknesses of their products as perceived by various market bases.

Availability of information depends upon the degree of cooperation and upon the publication of information for public relations or stockholder reports. Although it is doubtful that events and attractions will share all their individual data, they do have a mutual interest in determining how their products perform as an industry.

The nature of the data to be exchanged is usually limited to attendance rather than financial data. Any information of this type is extremely important in determining factors in-

cluding whether attendance shifts are isolated or industry-wide, in determining market share, external effects such as gasoline price, airline deregulation or climatic changes. As an example of close cooperation, the Southern California Attractions Industry exchanges the following data: daily percentage shifts in total attendance with the seven largest attractions participating, monthly and yearly percentage shifts in total attendance of all major attractions, and monthly and yearly shifts in market share for all major attractions. To implement this exchange, one attraction takes responsibility for the collection and dissemination of data, in this case Universal Studio Tours (Steinberg 1971-1981).

On a national level, the United States Amusement Park Marketing Association's major attractions, with exception of Disneyland and Disney World, exchange actual weekly attendance numbers. The Six Flags Corporation is responsible for this exchange (Delanoy 1972-1981).

The next step is to organize data by its demographic components. This exchange will probably only occur very informally on a local level and is dependent on availability of data as well as cooperation. The Southern California Attractions Industry, having close cooperation and available data, has set up a relatively formal exchange at one of six yearly meetings. Also, the Southern California Attractions Industry has organized itself to conduct simultaneous surveys to collect identical data two to three times a year with the objective of sharing the results. The data collected includes age of guest; geographic residence; party composition; media awareness; pattern of visits between member attractions; drive time to member attractions, arrival time and length of stay; nonresidents place of stay in Southern California; and questions relating to industry likes and dislikes.

This information is of significant value in planning the media message for joint media exposure. The data collection is controlled by Knott's Berry Farm; the data processing is undertaken by an outside supplier; and the report is issued on an individual and total basis to the participants (Carey 1972-1981). Although there are serious flaws with the collection techniques, these data become invaluable in determining strengths and weaknesses of individual attractions as well as the industry as a whole.

KNOWING YOUR INDUSTRY'S NONCUSTOMERS—QUANTITATIVE AND QUALITATIVE

Availability of quantitative data about nonresident or tourist population is dependent upon government involvement. In situations of minimal government involvement, events and attractions are usually very willing to cooperate in generating the data as it benefits them all individually as well as the entire industry.

Southern California has minimal government involvement in collecting tourist demographics, and, as well, there is no consensus as to the actual number of tourists arriving in the area in any one year. Even the nationally available data as issued by the U.S. Travel Data Center (*Travel Printout, National Travel Survey,* and *Quarterly Travel Trend*) do not assist in that it is infrequently collected, or reported too long after collection, or addresses the entire state of California, or addresses domestic arrivals only.

To overcome this problem, the Southern California Attractions Industry formed a committee in conjunction with the Greater Los Angeles Visitor and Conventions Bureau to initiate the collection of all available secondary data in an attempt to piece together a tourist count and profile (Baltin 1978-1980). The California State Office of Tourism, in fact, later took over this project (Bousseloub 1981). The following information is amassed and indexed: airport arrivals, hotel occupancy rates, attraction attendance, highway travel, and fuel sales.

This index, however, did not give an accurate estimate of tourist numbers, particularly those originating in the United States. In addition, it certainly did not give any indication of tourist demographics or projections for the future. The committee, therefore, decided to initiate its own primary data collection. It was decided that a statistically representative mail panel was the most economical and practical method of data collection in assessing tourism originating in the United States. This is the first time in this chapter, therefore, that research outside the geographic area of the event or attraction has been required. In the case of Southern California, a quantitative assessment of tourism was considered impossible for anyone other than the State Office of Tourism, due mainly to the great number of access highways into the state, which account for a large portion of its tourist entries. The information collected from the mail panel, however, not only allowed quantification of domestic travel to Southern California, but also the time of year of visit occurrence, composition of the tourist party, purpose of the visit, counties within Southern California visited, and future plans to visit Southern California (Haug 1978).

It was also decided by the committee that quantification of foreign tourism to Southern California would have to rely on airport arrival and Mexican-border-crossing information. This was acknowledged to be inaccurate in that it does not account for any foreign tourist passing through United States customs in any other state; nor does it account for non-Mexican foreign tourists arriving in Southern California by automobile, particularly Canadian nationals and those overseas residents arriving by air in another state. However, it was decided that, in conjunction with statistics issued by the United States Department of Commerce (1975-1981), the above data was the only cost-effective way to quantify foreign tourism into Southern California.

These tourist assessments, which were initiated in 1978, were repeated in a modified form in 1979 to determine the effects of the gasoline crisis on tourism in Southern California (Haug 1979). The study will be repeated in an expanded way in the future and should provide an invaluable base from which the individual event or attraction, as well as the industry, can determine its strengths and weaknesses relative to the available tourists.

Two pieces of information were still considered to be missing from this tourism assessment by some of the member events and attractions, so they independently sponsored

additional primary studies. It was considered extremely important by the member attractions, in planning for industry as well as individual media exposure outside their geographic area, to assess the extent to which the nonresident or potential tourist markets needed to be educated as to the existence of that event, attraction, or industry. It was the feeling of these attractions that with the extremely high costs involved in national or even international media exposure, the media message must address the majority of the population bases.

A mail panel was selected to address awareness for participating attractions on a national level on the basis that domestic tourists already in Southern California would clearly exhibit a higher level of awareness. The information collected allowed for quantification not only of awareness levels, but also of visiting history to the participating attractions, source of awareness, and future plans to visit the participating attractions (National Family Opinion, Inc. 1979).

This information became invaluable not only in the determination of media message but also in planning media placement, trade show participation, sales blitzes, publicity blitzes, and travel professional interaction. A second study was jointly sponsored to address the foreign or international tourist for similar reasons. However, the cost of such data collection outside the geographic area of the attraction is prohibitive. Interviewing was, therefore, conducted, with the acknowledged biases, at airport arrivals and departure terminals throughout California in the native language of the foreign tourist (Moore 1980).

The demographic and psychographic categories of the noncustomer are of interest in determining why these people do not become customers of the industry when they are in the neighborhood. Although it is doubtful that events and attractions will, in fact, share such individual data, they do have a mutual interest in expanding their industry's overall attendance base. The Southern California Attractions Industry occasionally conducts spot surveys at area motels and hotels to address this problem among the available tourist base with the objective of sharing data. There is no need for data of this type from the Southern California resident population as it is widely known that almost its entire population base frequents at least one attraction in a year.

IMPLEMENTATION OF THE RESEARCH NEEDS FOR EVENTS AND ATTRACTIONS

Most of the research described in this chapter is conducted on a regular basis by Knott's Berry Farm. This amount of research is considered appropriate for an attraction such as Knott's Berry Farm whose size, dependence on tourism, and location in a geographic area of minimal state involvement intensify these needs. In order to implement this amount of research, Knott's Berry Farm employs two research professionals and one clerical and three interviewing personnel on a full-time basis. With this staff, Knott's Berry Farm's dependence on outside suppliers and nonlabor budgets is minimal, despite it not being a member of a multipark corporation.

REFERENCES

Baltin, Bruce (1978–1981), *Southern California Tourism Index*, unpublished report, Pannell Kerr Forester, Los Angeles, CA.

Bousseloub, Tiffany (1980), *California Travel Index*, unpublished report, California State Office of Tourism, Los Angeles, CA.

Carey, Carolyn (1972–1981), *The Southern California Attractions Visitor Analysis*, unpublished report, Research Department, Knott's Berry Farm, Buena Park, CA.

Delanoy, George (1972–1981), *The United States Attractions Marketing Association Attendance Exchange*, unpublished report, Marketing Division, Six Flags Corporation, Los Angeles, CA.

Haug, Arne (1978), *Los Angeles/Southern California Vacationers Study*, unpublished report, Haug Associates, Inc., Los Angeles, CA.

Haug, Arne (1979), *Southern California Travel Patterns: A Non-resident Visitor Survey*, unpublished report, Haug Associates, Inc., Los Angeles, CA.

Moore, William (1980), *A Survey of International Vacationers in the State of California*, unpublished report, Tourmark, Ltd., Los Angeles, CA.

National Family Opinion, Inc. (1979), *Awareness Analysis of Selected Southern California Attractions*, unpublished report, National Family Opinion, Inc., San Francisco, CA.

Steinberg, Herbert (1971–1981), *The Southern California Attractions Leisure Time Index*, unpublished report, Marketing Division, Universal Studios Tour, Los Angeles, CA.

United States Department of Commerce (1971–1981), *Profile Sheets in Major USTS Markets*, Washington, D.C.

U.S. Travel Data Center (1974–1981), *National Travel Survey*, Washington, D.C.

U.S. Travel Data Center (Monthly Newsletter), *Travel Printout*, Washington, D.C.

U.S. Travel Data Center (1980), *Quarterly Travel Trends*, Washington, D.C.

25

A Framework of Tourist Attraction Research[1]

ALAN A. LEW
Northern Arizona University
Flagstaff, Arizona

*A*lthough tourist attractions are fundamental to the very existence of tourism, there have been few attempts to come to terms with the breadth of approaches that have been employed in their study. An examination of research methods used in the study of tourist attractions and the tourist attractiveness of places reveals that most studies can be classified into one or more of three general perspectives: the ideographic listing, the organization, and the tourist cognition of attractions. Each of these perspectives shares a distinct set of questions concerning the nature of the attractions, as expressed through the typologies used in their evaluation. At the same time, all three perspectives make comparisons based on the historical, locational, and various valuational aspects of attractions. This framework can be applied in the comparison and evaluation of tourist attraction related research.

THE TOURIST ATTRACTION

Without tourist attractions there would be no tourism (Gunn 1972:24). Without tourism there would be no tourist attractions. Although a tautology, such an argument still points to the fundamental importance of tourist attractions and the attractiveness of places to tourism. Efforts at specificity often reduce the simple concept of "tourist attraction" to exploitable "resources" (Ferrario 1976:4), marketable "products" (Wahab et al. 1976:38) and "images" (WTO 1980a; 1980b), or simply place "attributes" (Witter 1985:16) or "features" (Polacek and Aroch 1984:17). Most researchers, however, agree that attractions are the basic elements on which tourism is developed (Gunn 1979:48–73, 1980a; Lundberg 1980:33–40; Pearce 1981:30–2).

In essence, tourist attractions consist of all those elements of a "nonhome" place that draw discretionary travelers away from their homes. They usually include landscapes to observe, activities to participate in, and experiences to remember. Yet it can sometimes be difficult to differentiate between attractions and non-attractions. Transportation (e.g.,

cruise liners), accommodations (e.g., resorts), and other services (e.g., restaurants) can themselves take on the attributes of an attraction, further complicating the distinction between various segments of the tourism industry. At times, tourists themselves can even become attractions (MacCannell 1976:130–1).

MacCannell (1976:109) proposes that a phenomenon must have three components to be considered an attraction: a tourist, a site to be viewed, and a marker or image which makes the site significant. These criteria could enable virtually anything to become a tourist attraction. Thus, "attraction" in its widest context would include not only the historic sites, amusement parks, and spectacular scenery, which are normally associated with the word, but also the services and facilities which cater to the everyday needs of tourists. Also included would be the social institutions which form the basis for the very existence of human habitation. Non-entertainment oriented attractions have been variously referred to as "comfort attractions" (Lew 1986a:215), "conditional elements" (Jansen-Verbeke 1986:86), or have been categorized into "services and accommodations" (McIntosh and Goeldner

[1]This article was originally published in the *Annals of Tourism Research* 14(4), 1987, Pergamon Press Ltd., Oxford, England. Permission to reprint is gratefully acknowledged.

291

1984:11) or the nebulous "other" (Gunn 1979:58; Polacek and Aroch 1984:17).

Although the importance of tourist attractions is readily recognized, tourism researchers and theorists have yet to fully come to terms with the nature of attractions as phenomena both in the environment and in the mind (Gunn 1980a). An examination of some of the research related to tourist attractions reveals a consistent pattern of research questions and designs. The following discussion summarizes the range of approaches employed in the categorization of attractions, as revealed in recent tourism literature. The typologies, in part, reflect the nature of the various disciplines involved. However, in the least the review provides an initial step toward focusing on and understanding tourist attractions.

A COMPREHENSIVE FRAMEWORK

Research on tourist attractions has been undertaken from one or more of three broad perspectives: the ideographic definition and description of attraction types, the organization and development of attractions, and the cognitive perception and experience of tourist attractions by different groups. Each perspective addresses a shared concern for a particular feature of tourist attractions. The essence of a comprehensive framework for tourist attraction typologies and research is based on these three perspectives. It is appropriate to consider each as one aspect of a single body of knowledge.

By comparing the different typologies employed by researchers, it is also possible to identify general continua against which attraction characteristics have been measured. In the examples below the identification of attractions as being natural or social, reflecting separation or connectivity, or offering security or risk are the principal continua basic to the three perspectives. Further refinements of such measures are, of course, necessary for use in research. For example, the nature-social continuum includes a range of attraction types from wilderness to parks and zoos to cities. Together, the three research perspectives and their accompanying continua of attraction categories comprise a comprehensive framework for understanding the diversity of typologies used in research on tourist attractions. The examples provided for each of these perspectives will clarify their differences.

THE IDEOGRAPHIC PERSPECTIVE

Attraction typologies which focus on the ideographic perspective describe the concrete uniqueness of a site, rather than an abstract universal characteristic. At the most concrete level are those typologies in which specific attractions are individually identified by name (Neffler 1975:38; Pitts and Woodside 1986:21; Woodside et al. 1986:11). The listing of specific attractions by name is most often used in studies of small areas, such as cities, although exceptions exist (Machlis et al 1984:81). A list of places or countries as attractions is a variation of this approach (Goeldner et al 1975:95; Perdue and Gutske 1985:171; White 1985:534). Inasmuch as these can be further placed into general types,

named attractions are not further distinguished as a separate type of ideographic approach to this review.

By far, the most common attraction typologies are general ideographic descriptions of similar attraction types (Archer 1977:104; Christaller 1955; Goodrich 1978:4; Graburn 1977:27; Gunn, 1980:265; Lew 1986a:16; Matley 1976:5; Peters 1969:148-9; Smith 1977:2-3; Wahab et al. 1976:38-9). The use of Standard Industrial Codes (SIC) is an example of this approach (Frechtling 1976:69-71), although variations are significant. Attraction typologies for use in determining monetary flows normally use an ideographic approach, classifying attractions into different "expenditure types" (Archer 1977:104; Kreck 1985:28). Tourist guide books usually classify attractions under a combination of both specific and general categories (e.g., Liounis 1985).

Not all typologies are intended to cover the entire spectrum of attractions. Stores (Keown et al. 1984:27), restaurants (Smith 1985:588), accommodations (Price 1980:26), inner-city areas (Jansen-Verbeke 1986:86), spectator sports (Ritchie and Aitken 1985:30), participant sports (Fesenmaier 1985:19), outdoor recreation (Bryant and Morrison 1980:4), and cruiseship activities (Field et al. 1985:4) are examples of subcategories of ideographic attraction types.

When combined with data on location, preference, perception, or participation, ideographic attraction typologies have been further generalized through the use of multidimensional analysis, such as factor analysis (Bryant and Morrison 1980:4; Eitzel and Swensen 1981:30; Goodrich 1977b:8; Pizam et al 1978:319; Witter 1985:18) and multidimensional scaling (Goodrich 1977a:12; 1978:4-6; Haahti 1986:21-7; Pearce 1982:107-11; Perry 1975:119-24).

Among the more detailed and comprehensive examples of ideographic attraction listings are those developed by Ferrario (1976:111-14), Gearing et al (1976:93), Ritchie and Zinns (1978:256-7), the World Tourism Organization (1980a:6-17), and Shih (1986:8). Using Ritchie and Zinns as an example, at the most general level this classification includes natural beauty and climate; culture and social characteristics; sport, recreation, and educational facilities; shopping and commercial facilities; infrastructure; price levels; attitudes toward tourists; and accessibility. Each of these facets is divided into a long series of elements, which are further divided into features that were inanimate, those that expressed normal daily life activities, and those involving activities beyond normal. Using this list, the researchers administered surveys to public and private sector tourism professionals to ascertain which elements were most important to the tourist attractiveness of the Canadian province of Quebec.

Ritchie and Zinns' typology is typical of ideographic approaches. It allows an objective comparison of one destination with another in terms of attractions. Certain aspects, however, are missing in the typology. As with most ideographic typologies, limitations exist in the assessment of quality, management, and tourist motivation and preference for different attractions. Also lacking is an understanding of the spatial relationships between attractions. It might be possible to extrapolate some of these aspects from the less strictly ideographic categories related to price levels, local attitudes toward tourists, and accessibility. These aspects tend to be more organizational and cognitive than ideographic.

When attempting to incorporate organizational or cognitive perspectives, ideographic typologies frequently become more abstract. For example, Schmidt (1979:447-8) distinguished different types of attractions based on aspects which made them unique and therefore of interest to tourists. Schmidt initially divided attractions into five types, based on their geographical, social, cultural, technological, or divine emphasis. These basic ideographic categories were then further divided into those associated with: origins, transitions, extremes, and changes. This typology was devised to try and explain why certain places are particularly prone to attract tourists. While the approach moves a step closer to incorporating the cognitive features of a site, at the same time, it loses the readily identifiable image of the attraction which is provided by the more clearly ideographic approach of Ritchie and Zinns.

In general, the less abstract and the more concrete the research is, the more likely that it will incorporate an ideographic approach in the conceptualization of attractions. Every attraction has some tangible, material presence. It is the appreciation and understanding of this presence that the ideographic approach represents.

For the most part, researchers have attempted to develop comprehensive typologies in which every possible attraction could be classified. The diversity of classification schemes indicates a somewhat arbitrary methodology. A review of a number of ideographic typologies, however, indicates the most basic distinction employed to be that between attractions which are nature-oriented and those with a human orientation. This distinction, however, is only explicitly expressed in the typologies proposed by Perry (1975:119) and Graburn (1977:27), although it is also the basic dichotomy found in Gunn (1979:57-8). Most other ideographic typologies are based on this same distinction, but with the nature and human attractions divided up among several categories. This is particularly true of the human-oriented attractions which tend to dominate most ideographic schemes. For example, while Ritchie and Zinns cover the nature-oriented attractions in one category (Natural beauty and climate), the human-oriented attractions are divided into seven basic types.

One major difficulty some researchers encounter with a simple nature-human typology is in the classification of infrastructure and service facilities (e.g., Gunn 1979:57-8). While tourists use these facilities, they are not necessarily attracted to a specific location to see them. However, given the breadth of the definition of tourist attraction, as discussed above, such facilities do have value as attractions in that they contribute to the overall ambience of the tourist experience. Further, they are cultural manifestations and should, therefore, be included in the human-oriented attraction category.

A complete listing of the attraction categories used in the various ideographic typologies reviewed is shown in Table 1. These categories have been rearranged within the

nature-human continuum. The table only includes general categories of attractions. It does not include all of the specific terminology employed among the reviewed typologies due to the inordinate length of this list. Nine categories of attractions are indicated, based on a matrix of Nature, Human and Nature-Human Interface across the top, and General Environments, Specific Features, and Inclusive Environments along the side. The horizontal categories portray three discrete groupings along the nature-human continuum. Human intervention in nature and natural intrusions into human-built environments require further refinements of the fundamental nature-human dichotomy and are included in the Nature-Human Interface attraction categories. The three vertical groupings of categories indicate different levels of ideographic attractions. General Environments are broad in scope and often large in scale. They generally require little or no tourist involvement to exist. Specific Features are notably smaller in scale and often have clear connections to tourism, although they are sometimes peripheral to major tourist interests. The tourists themselves are passive in their involvement with specific features. Inclusive Environments are the principal attractions which draw tourists to a destination. They are inclusive in that they are environments in which tourists become completely absorbed in the attraction experience. All of the ideographic attractions examined in the literature fit within the typology proposed in Table 1.

THE ORGANIZATIONAL PERSPECTIVE

Ideographic approaches are the most frequent form of attraction typology encountered in tourism research. The organizational perspective is a different research approach which does not necessarily examine the attractions themselves, but rather focuses on their spatial, capacity, and temporal nature. In this approach, attraction typologies are developed to reflect these qualities.

Scale is the simplest basis for categorizing the spatial character of an attraction within an organizational perspective. Simple scale continuums are based on the size of the area which the attraction encompasses (Gunn 1972:40-42; Hills and Lundgren 1977:251-3; WTO 1980a:17). For example, a spatial hierarchy of attraction scale would progress from the smallest specific object within a site to entire countries and continents (Pearce 1982:99). Scale considerations can provide insight into the organization of tourist attractions, their relationship to other attractions, and the relationship of attraction images to attractions themselves. These considerations are important in the planning and marketing of tourism. Tourism marketers promote the images of specific, small-scale attractions (which are easier to sell) to create identifiers for larger attraction complexes (Lew 1987; MacCannell 1976:112; WTO 1980a). Planners are then faced with the problem of an over-concentration of demand at some tourist sites and under-utilization of others.

Characteristics associated with the spatial integration of attractions provide a more detailed understanding of the influence of scale. Several approaches have specifically intended to highlight the spatial integration of attractions, in-

TABLE 1   Composite Ideograph Tourist Attraction Typology

NATURE	NATURE-HUMAN INTERFACE	HUMAN

General Environment:
1 Panoramas
    Mountains
    Sea Coast
    Plain
    Arid
    Island
	4 Observational
	    Rural/Agriculture
	    Scientific Gardens
	        Animals (zoos)
	        Plants
	        Rocks & Archeology
		7 Settlement Infrastructure
		    Utility types
		    Settlement Morphology
		    Settlement Functions
		        Commerce
		            Retail
		            Finance
		        Institutions
		            Government
		            Education & Science
		            Religion
		        People
		            Way of Life
		            Ethnicity

Specific Features:
2 Landmarks
    Geological
    Biological
        Flora
        Fauna
    Hydrological
	5 Leisure Nature
	    Trails
	    Parks
	        Beach
	        Urban
	        Other
	    Resorts
		8 Tourist Infrastructure
		    Forms of Access
		        To and from a destination
		        Destination Tour Routes
		    Information & Receptivity
		    Basic Needs
		        Accommodations
		        Meals

Inclusive Environments:
3 Ecological
    Climate
    Sanctuaries
        National Parks
        Nature Reserve
	6 Participatory
	    Mountain Activities
	        Summer
	        Winter
	    Water Activities
	    Other Outdoor Activities
		9 Leisure Superstructure
		    Recreation Entertainment
		        Performances
		        Sporting Activities
		        Amusements
		    Culture, History & Art
		        Museums and Monuments
		        Performances
		        Festivals
		        Cuisine

Generalized from the following sources: Archer 1977:104; Bryant and Morrison 1980:4; Christaller 1955; Crompton 1979:20; Doyle et al. 1977:118–20; Eastlack 1982:28; Eitzel and Swensen 1981:30; Ferrario 1976:111–4; Gearing et al. 1976:93; Goodrich 1977a:12; 1977b:8; 1978:4; Graburn 1977:27; Gunn 1979:57–8; 1980b:265; Haddon 1960:287; Henshall and Roberts 1985:229–30; Hills and Lundgren 1977:258,261; Jansen-Verbeke 1986:86, 92; Kreck 1985:28; Lew 1986:16; Liounis 1985; Matley 1976:5; Machlis et al. 1984:80; Neffeler 1975:38; Peters 1969:148–9; Pizam et al. 1978:319–20; Polacek and Aroch 1984:17; Ritchie and Zinns 1978:256–7; Robinson 1976:41–3; Schmidt 1979:447–8; Shih 1986:8; Smith 1977:2–3; U.S. Department of Commerce 1981:33; Van Veen and Verhallen 1986:46; Wahab et al. 1976:38–9; Witter 1985:16; Woodside et al. 1986:10; WTO 1980a:6–17.

cluding Gunn's (1979:55, 1980b:265–6) distinction between "touring" and "destination" attractions and Pearce's (1981:16–9) "catalytic-integrated" dichotomy.

According to Gunn, touring attractions are aimed at travelers who are in transit and are characterized by short visits to many dispersed and poorly integrated destinations. They, therefore, tend to not be of the same quality of attractions as destinations with long-term and repeat visitor demands. As the name implies, destination attractions are usually major centers of tourism and are characterized by numerous tourist activities integrated around a central point. For a tourism planner, the primary considerations for touring attractions

are mobility and access, whereas destination planning centers on providing a mix that offers both variety and stimulation. While Pearce's dichotomy is based on the historical development and presence or lack of planning in resort communities, similar patterns of integrated (well planned) versus disjunctive (spontaneous, unplanned) spatial patterns arise.

Related to the spatial scale of an attraction is its capacity. The spatial size of an attraction, however, may have little relationship to its capacity to accommodate large numbers of tourists. In addition to relative desirability, factors which can affect the tourism capacity of an attraction include the availability of services (lodging, food, merchandise, entertainment, etc.); the fragility of the attraction; the level of education and technological development; and community and political support for tourism (Peck and Lepie 1977:160–1; Rodenberg 1980).

In addition to the spatial situation of an attraction, the concepts of permanence and change affect the organization and development of tourist attractions. This is seen in the distinction between "temporal" and "site" attractions (Lundberg 1980:38) and can have a significant impact on visitor flow patterns and infrastructure development. An attraction characterized by a year-round flow of visitors is generally better integrated into the local community than one with large seasonal fluctuations. Long-term and repeat visitors are also preferred over short-term, one-time visitors (Peck and Lepie 1977:160). In extreme situations, isolated special event attractions can place a serious burden on infrastructure capacities designed for fewer visitors (Lew 1985:9).

A listing of the attraction categories used in the various organizational typologies reviewed is shown in a matrix in Table 2. What these types of studies most fundamentally accentuate is the difference between the separation and connectivity of attractions. This dichotomy is applied to organizational typologies of both spatial (scale) and functional (integration, capacity, and temporal) nature. Along the side of the matrix are shown the different typologies focusing on spatial, capacity, and temporal aspects of attractions. Spatial typologies accentuate the spatial differences which exist between attractions developing in association with one an-

other. In terms of size, attractions that are smaller in scope tend toward greater separation and less connectivity. This does not apply, however, to the size of the attraction's market, where aspects of popularity (a cross-perspective measure) and renown (cognitive perspective) are more important. Capacity typologies, on the other hand, place principal emphasis on the internal organization of attraction. Temporal typologies focus on the organizational influence of time, both in terms of how long and when an attraction occurs and the time a visitor spends at the attraction.

THE COGNITIVE PERSPECTIVE

Studies of tourist perceptions and experiences of attractions constitute the third major approach to the study of tourist attractions. More so than with organizational perspectives, cognitive perspectives are sometimes found intermixed with ideographic categories, although in virtually all such cases the ideographic categories clearly predominate (Eastlack 1982:28; Henshall and Roberts 1985:229; Lickorish 1974:2; Neffeler 1975:36; Pearce 1982:107; Shih 1986:8; Wahabetal 1976:76).

Pearce defines a tourist place as "any place that fosters the feeling of being a tourist" (1982:98). One way that this feeling has been understood is through the juxtaposition of "outsideness" and "insideness" (Relph 1976:48–55). One of the goals of the tourist is to penetrate into the insideness or back region of the attraction in order to experience the au-

TABLE 2   Composite Organizational Tourist Attraction Typology

INDIVIDUAL/SEPARATION				COLLECTIVITY/CONNECTION
Spatial Features:				
Unstructured				Structured[l]
Catalytic				Integrated[g]
Unplanned infrastructure				Planned infrastructure[g]
Inaccessible/permit barrier				Accessible[a]
Isolated				Free entry[a]
Touring				Clustered[cdej]
Nucleus		Inviolate belt		Destination[de]
Remote	Rural		Suburban	Zone of enclosure[c]
Outside SMSA				Urban[c]
Local scale	Regional		National	Inside SMSA[b]
Building/site		Regional/local		International scale[m]
				Continents/countries[h]
Capacity Features:				
Craft tourism		Small industrial		Large industrial tourism[k]
Slow growth		Transient development		Rapid growth[i]
Small/low capacity		Medium		Large/high capacity[a]
Temporal Features:				
Event				Site[f]
Itinerant, Short-term				Resident, Long-term[i]
Single visitation				Multiple visitation[de]

Sources: [a] Ferrario 1976:195-7; [b] Goeldner et al. 1975:87; [c] Gunn 1972:40-2, 49-52; [d] Gunn 1979:55; [e] Gunn 1980b:265-6; [f] Lundberg 1980:38; [g] Pearce 1981:16-9; [h] Pearce 1982:99; [i] Peck and Lepie 1977:160-1; [j] Robinson 1976:42; [k] Rodenberg 1980; [l] Schmidt 1979:449; [m] WTO 1980a:17.

thenticity of a place (MacCannell 1976:94). For the tourist, some risk is required to take this leap into authenticity. The review of cognitive-oriented research typologies indicates that the degree to which tourists are willing and able to take such a risk is a major indicator of the general experiences offered by different types of attractions.

Every environment, not just tourist places, has elements of security and risk. This is, however, a useful distinction to begin with. Tourist places can further be distinguished by those which are primarily intended for tourists and those which are not designed for them (Schmidt 1979:449). Tourists are, by definition, outsiders and places which are primarily intended for them tend to focus on security and the minimization of risk. As such, these safe attractions frequently occur in a staged, unauthentic and highly structured environment where tourists primarily relate to the promoted or advertised image, rather than the direct experience of the site. MacCannell (1976:111) refers to this as "marker involvement" because the tourist is more interested in the label that is attached to the attraction than the attraction itself. Most historic sites, such as empty battlefields, are marker involvement types of attractions. Non-tourist oriented attractions involve greater risk, are less structured, and are generally more authentic. The tourists' interest is stimulated by the actual site itself. The experience in this situation is one of "sight involvement," or one where what is supposed to be seen does not interfere with what is seen and experienced. Outstanding natural landscapes and culturally unique places are examples where "sight involvement" often predominates over "marker involvement."

The categories common to studies oriented toward the perception and experience of tourist attractions are shown in Table 3. In addition to the Security-Risk continuum, along the top, these typologies have been divided into those that focus on general Tourist Activities, the general Attraction Character, and the individual Tourist Experience, along the side. The Participatory category of the ideographic typology (Table 1) appears to overlap somewhat with the Tourist Activities category presented here. For example, a "campground" is clearly an ideographic attraction; however, "camping" is more of an experience. Participation makes these attractions more than just sites to be observed. They remain ideographic, however, in that they do not attach a specific experience to the attraction. In theory, cognitive categories can be attached to any type of ideographic category (which further makes their intermixing with ideographic categories inappropriate).

The major difference between cognitive typologies focusing on Tourist Activities and those within the Tourist Experiences category is that the activity-oriented research tends to be primarily behavioral, while the experience-oriented research is approached from either behavioral or phenomenological perspectives. Mere preference for one type of attraction over another is not classified as being within the experiential perspective of this framework, but rather is a cross-perspective aspect.

The Attraction Character category refers to the general

perceptual nature of the attraction. How animated (staged) and how well-known (evoked set) an attraction is are included in this category. Related to an attraction's renown is the concept of market scale (Lundberg 1980:38), with internationally known attractions offering less risk in the tourist's itinerary planning than smaller market attractions.

CROSS-PERSPECTIVE MEASURES

Two ways of combining ideographic, organizational, and cognitive perspectives have been identified. These are the combining of complementary categories from different perspectives, and research measures which are common to all three perspectives.

The ideographic, organizational, and cognitive perspectives have useful application within their defined contexts. No single approach, however, is able to cover the entire range of research interests on tourist attractions. Ideographic approaches, with their detailed and lengthy descriptive categories, tend to be weak in shedding insight on the organizational and experiential aspects of attractions. More abstract organizational categorizations can get bogged down in the specificity of ideographic categories and the diversity of human experiences. Cognitive approaches do not adequately address the complementary and competitive nature of specific attractions, nor their spatial and temporal relationships. These shortcomings, however, are fully acceptable within the context of the research objectives of each approach, so long as they are recognized as such.

These differences do not preclude the combination of categories from different perspectives. Ideographic, organization, and cognitive approaches can even be quite complementary to one another. For example, the experience of an individual at an attraction can be highly influenced by its organization, with poor infrastructure, and low quality services causing experiences of difficulty and incomprehensibility. As discussed above, the ideographic approach, due to its fundamental nature, is the most frequently used in combination with another perspective. Further examination of such cross-perspective relationships offers a potential venue for developing a comprehensive typology of tourist attractions.

Other measures of attraction research are more distinctly cross-perspective in that they can be employed in any of the three approaches described above. However, they are not typologies. Three of these have been identified: historical, locational, and valuational measures. Historical measures compare one place at more than one point in time to determine trends and changes. Locational measures compare the same attraction categories at different locations. Valuational measures (the numeric rating of attractions) are obtained through visitor preference surveys, tourist attendance and usage rates, guidebook analysis, surveys of experts or professionals in the field, and economic expenditures and income (cf. Ferrario 1976; Lew 1986a). Whereas some form of valuation determination is included in most attraction research, historical and locational comparisons are limited to the research objectives of a particular study.

TABLE 3   Composite Cognitive Tourist Attraction Typology

SECURITY					RISK
Tourist Activities:					
Education[rh]		Exercise[r]			Exploration[r]
Place to talk[k]					Face-to-face meeting[h]
Guided tours					Unguided touring[p]
Passive[e]					Active[g]
Attraction Character:					
Contrived	Staged	Denial of authenticity			Authentic[b]
Especially animated		Inanimate			Normal daily life[n]
Evoked set		Inert set			Inept set[qs]
International/extended market		National		Regional	Local market[lst]
Tourism oriented					Non-tourism oriented[p]
Touristy					Authentic[g]
Structured/organized					Unstructured[p]
Front region					Back region[j]
Modern					Traditional/Antiquated[gt]
Heard a lot about/Important place[k]					Absence of other tourists[l]
Tourist Experiences:					
Expensive/luxury/quality/prestige[eht]		Economy/reasonable prices/ value for money[do]			Inexpensive/cheap[cklt]
Safe/sanitary[cer]		Different/getting away[dhk]			Escapism/freedom[r]
Pleasant/friendly[cdko]		Companionship[r]			Novelty[r]
Leisurely/restful/relaxing/quiet/homey[chkort]		Fun/swinging[kl]			Adventurous/wild/exciting[egklort]
Mass produced experience		Limited experience			Individual Experience[f]
Common/ordinary[gm]		Interesting[kl]			Unique[gm]
No role transformation					Role transformation[f]
Recreational	Diversionary	Experiential		Experimental	Existential[a]
Marker involvement					Sight involvement[j]
Familiar					Exotic[g]
Easy and quick/easy to tour[dgk]					Effort to tour[g]

Sources: [a] Cohen 1979a:183; [b] Cohen 1979b:26; [c] Crompton 1979:20; [d] Haahti 1986:15; [e] Henshall and Roberts 1985:229; [f] Kotler 1984:10; [g] Lew 1986b; [h] Lickorish 1974:2; [i] Lundberg 1980:38; [j] MacCannell 1976:92, 111–7; [k] Neffeler 1975:33–8; [l] Pearce 1982:107; [m] Piperoglou 1966:170; [n] Ritchie and Zinns 1978:257; [o] Shih 1986:8; [p] Schmidt 1979:449; [q] Thompson and Cooper 1979:24; [r] Wahab et al. 1976:76; [s] Woodside et al. 1977:123; [t] WTO 1980b:27.

APPLICATION OF THE FRAMEWORK TO PAST RESEARCH

The tourist attraction framework may be applied in several different ways. Its use in assessing the methodological approaches of selected tourist attraction studies is examined in depth here. The framework, used in this way, helps highlight the decisions which the researcher makes in formulating the research design. It also allows a better understanding of the relationship between different studies and of the utility of a single study within the context of the three perspectives.

For the sake of brevity, the examples chosen focus exclusively on two types of subject matter: national or regional planning, and image studies. These have been selected because each is a major area of tourism research. Although the examples were chosen arbitrarily, they do provide the opportunity to explore the applicability of the framework as an evaluative tool.

REGIONAL PLANNING STUDIES

Piperoglou (1966), in evaluating the tourist attractions of western Greece, undertook the following steps:

1. The definition of three main attraction types: "Ancient Greece," "picturesque villages and islands," and "sun and sea."
2. A survey of tourists to determine their preference for each attraction.
3. An evaluation of attractions to determine their "uniqueness."
4. The mapping of attractions to determine their proximity to access points within defined regions and to urban settlements of 50,000 or more people. Higher values were given to attractions with better accessibility.
5. Development priorities were assigned based on the overall value of each region.

The steps in Piperoglou's study respectively involved the following aspects of the tourist attraction framework:

1. A nature versus human attraction typology (Ideographic perspective, Panoramas, Leisure Nature, and Leisure Superstructure categories). Of the three attraction types employed in the study, "picturesque villages and islands" is the most natural and is of the Panoramas category (although the rural villages could also be of the Observational category). "Sun and sea" is essentially a reference to beaches and resorts and clearly of the Leisure Nature ideographic category, while "Ancient Greece" is the most social, falling within the Leisure Superstructure category.

2. An assessment of preference (Cross-Perspective, Valuation type). Tourist preference is one of the cross-perspective measures which can be applied to typologies based on any of the three perspectives. The survey used by Piperoglou resulted in an additional value given to the more popular of the attraction types.

3. An experience measure of "uniqueness" (Cognitive Perspective, Tourist Experience category). This evaluation was used to distinguish between individual attractions of the same attraction type, resulting in each attraction having its own numeric value.

4. Two spatial measures of clustering and accessibility (Organizational Perspective, Spatial Features). These measures were given the strongest value as each coincidence of more than one attraction type within a day's journey from a regional center raised the attraction value of that region by one power. Larger weights were given to regions with large urban centers, which implied better infrastructure and access.

5. A location comparison of regions (Cross-Perspective, Locational type).

Table 4 compares this study with the tourist attraction framework. It is apparent from this summary that Piperoglou's approach is well balanced, using typologies associated with all three perspectives. One measure (with three categories) is provided from the ideographic perspective. This measure actually encompasses several different categories from Table 1. One measure (with two categories) is from the cognitive perspective. Two measures, both spatial features, are from the organizational perspective (two categories each). In addition two measures are of the cross-perspective type. Although the study includes elements from all three perspectives, Piperoglou gave greater emphasis to the organizational measures, both in terms of having more of them and in the larger weighted values they received in determining regional attraction ratings. This is, therefore, primarily an organizational study.

In a similar evaluation of the tourist attractions of South Africa, Ferrario (1976) undertook the following approach:

1. Determination of 22 types of attractions (Ideographic Perspective, most categories). In addition, these were further divided into 51 classes, which were still further subdivided.

All of the nine categories of ideographic attractions were included.

2. Survey of tourist demand for the basic 22 types of attractions (Cross Perspective, Valuation type). Tourist demand here is the same as preference in Piperoglou's study above. It is essentially used to rank types of attractions.

3. Determination of the appeal or popularity of the attraction types (Cross-Perspective, Valuation type). This was based on the frequency that the type of attraction was mentioned in a number of tourist guide books. It was a form of expert judgment and provided a weighted value to the preferences obtained in the tourist survey.

4. A survey of expert opinions on the accessibility of specific attractions measured in terms of (a) Seasonality (Organizational Perspective, Temporal Feature); (b) Conservation (Organizational Perspective, Capacity Feature). This measure essentially related to the fragility of the attraction, or its ability to withstand large numbers of visitors; (c) Popularity (Cross-Perspective, Valuation type). This was based on visitation rates; (d) Accessibility to nearest town (Organizational Perspective, Spatial Feature); (e) Admission or permit requirements (Organizational Perspective, Spatial Feature); (f) Importance (Cross-Perspective, Valuation type). This was obtained by a subjective rating of the attraction as compared to other attractions of the same type.

5. The determination of the tourist potential (Cross-perspective, Valuation type) of 2,365 attractions based on a formula in which all the above measures were employed (Ferrario 1976:252–62). In a situation like this, numeric values allow the direct comparison of attraction categories based on different perspectives.

6. The mapping of these values and the introduction of a clustering weight (Organizational Perspective, Spatial Feature). Clusters of low potential attractions were valued lower than isolated, but major attractions. This weighting was based primarily on increasing the value of the number of foreign tourists to heavily visited attractions.

7. Determination of major attraction regions or clusters and suggestions for development (Cross-Perspective, Locational type). Regions were identified based on the comparative numeric values resulting from steps 5 and 6 above. These values do not represent attraction types, but do permit a comparison of the overall attractiveness of one place to another.

Table 5 summarizes the perspectives, categories and typologies employed in the South African study by Ferrario. This summary indicates that Ferrario's approach is a strong organizational study in that it uses at least one typology from each of the three categories associated with the organizational perspective. It is also apparent that Ferrario included a large number of cross-perspective valuation measures, although an effort was made to reduce the combined value of these valuation measures in the final formula. Pearce

TABLE 4   Piperoglou's Evaluation of Tourist Attractions in Western Greece

PERSPECTIVE AND CATEGORY	TYPOLOGY AND FORM OF EVALUATION
Ideographic:	
Panoramas, Leisure Nature, and Leisure Infrastructure	Ancient Greece—Picturesque Village—Sun and Sea (subjective expert evaluation)
Organizational:	
Spatial Features	Clustered—Dispersed (number of attraction types within 80 km. of a base point)
Spatial Features	Accessible—Isolated (presence of city of 50,000 or more in the region)
Cognitive:	
Tourist Experience	Unique—Common (subjective expert evaluation)
Cross-Perspective Measures:	
Valuation	Preference (tourist survey)
Locational	Regional Comparisons (mapping)

(1981:32) has pointed out that these valuation measures resulted in Ferrario's emphasizing well-established, existing tourist attractions.

The objective of Ferrario's study was similar to that of Piperoglou's, that is, to evaluate the future development potential of tourist attractions and attraction complexes. Both studies were primarily from an organizational perspective, although Ferrario's was more so, and both attempted "to reduce phenomenon of aesthetic or cultural significance to quantifiable magnitudes for purposes of comparative evaluation" (Piperoglou 1967:169). A comparison of the two studies shows how Ferrario's emphasis on the cross-perspective valuation measure associated with a very detailed listing of attractions types may have accentuated the existing tourist attractions, whereas Piperoglou's focus on spatial organizational features over popularity probably presented a better

evaluation of development prospects of unestablished areas. The emphasis on established attractions in Ferrario's study makes an implied policy judgment of expanding the existing tourism product rather than developing new ones.

ATTRACTION IMAGE STUDIES

Image is the most important aspect of a tourist attraction from a marketing point of view. It also has a major impact on the cognitive experience of an attraction. Britton (1979) has examined the themes used to advance the image of Third World countries as tourist destinations. Through inductive analysis of advertising for the Caribbean, six dominant themes were identified. These themes and their relationship to the proposed attraction framework, include:

1. Mythification and fantasy, in which places are por-

TABLE 5   Analysis of Ferrario's Evaluation of Tourist Attractions

PERSPECTIVE AND CATEGORY	TYPOLOGY AND FORM OF EVALUATION
Ideographic:	
All nine categories	Nature—Culture (22 types)
Organizational:	
Spatial Features	Dispersed—Clustered (mapped proximity)
Spatial Features	Isolated—Accessible (expert judgement)
Spatial Features	Controlled Access—Open Access (expert judgement)
Capacity Features	Low—High Carrying Capacity (expert judgement)
Temporal Features	Highly Seasonal—Year Round (expert judgement)
Cross-Perspective Measures:	
Valuation	Preference (tourist survey)
Valuation	Importance (expert judgement)
Valuation	Popularity (visitation rates and expert judgement)
Locational	Regional Comparisons (mapping)

trayed as paradises of the untouched and exotic (Ideographic Perspective, mostly Nature and Nature-Human Interface categories). Most of the ideographic categories can be manipulated to fit within this scheme, although urban oriented and lifestyle characteristics tend to be of the Romanticization theme, below. The Cognitive Perspective, (Attraction Character and Tourist Experience) is implied from emphasis on authenticity and the sense of escape associated with this classification.

2. Minimization of foreignness in places considered too "strange" and possibly uncomfortable for tourists (Cognitive Perspective, Tourist Experience). Advertisements often explicitly try to balance risk with security experiences, such as showing a photo of a luxury hotel next to one emphasizing the exoticness of a place.

3. Recreation, entertainment, and enjoyment, with little, if any, reference to cultural attractions (Ideographic Perspective, Participatory and Leisure Superstructure). The enjoyment aspect of this attraction type is of the Cognitive Perspective, Tourist Experience category, with considerable more emphasis on security than risk experiences.

4. Romanticization, of traditional (and often poverty stricken) lifestyles (Ideographic Perspective, Settlement Infrastructure). The Cognitive Perspective, Tourist Activity may be implied from this if the advertisement promotes a sense of exploration.

5. Placelessness, in which images are transferred from other, better known, attractions and associated with the advertised place, rather than using the place itself. This type of attraction is classified as being of the Cognitive Perspective, Attraction Character category because of its basis on well-known attractions.

6. Realistic portrayals of attractions (Ideographic Perspective, Settlement Infrastructure) are limited, but growing through efforts to stem some of the negative social impacts of Third World tourism. The Cognitive Perspective, Tourist Activity may be implied from this if the advertisement promotes a sense of education.

With the possible exception of "realistic portrayals," these themes all emphasize the security characteristics of the cognitive perspective (Table 3). They are often used in combination with one another in a single advertising effort, demonstrating the complex nature of attraction images. They are summarized in Table 6. Unlike the planning studies examined above, this study does not incorporate the organizational perspective in any way. The suggested attraction categories are a mix of ideographic and cognitive perspectives. In their definition, they are primarily ideographic. However, Britton also incorporates numerous implied cognitive perspectives within each type. Thus, analysis of the study reveals that travel advertisements have ideographic (Nature-Human) and cognitive (Security-Risk) aspects.

The final study to be analyzed is a publication by the World Tourism Organization (1980b) which outlines a re-

search method for developing national tourist attraction images. The WTO approach is directed principally at the identification and development of a national "brand image," that is, an image that readily evokes the name of the country in the visitor's mind. Examples of such brand images include the maple leaf for Canada and the Eiffel Tower for France. The approach, therefore, deals with countries as tourist products, rather than the variety of attractions within a country. The approach suggested in this report is:

1. An exhaustive analysis of reality, involving a survey of a country's strengths and weaknesses in six types of resources: natural environment; sociocultural environment; government support for tourism; infrastructure; economy; and tourism planning and resource management.

2. Determination of a suitable brand image. This is done through analysis of tourist motivations for visiting the country and through survey of selected groups to identify their images of the country.

3. Development and marketing of the new image or corrections to old images.

Using the framework to analyze the WTO approach to attraction images, the research steps are (see Table 7):

1. Division of attractions into ideographic types (Ideographic Perspective, most categories).

2. Valuation of natural and social attractions on a scale of "weak—unsure—strong" (Cross-Perspective, Valuation type). How this valuation is conducted is unclear, as the reader is referred to another WTO publication (1980b).

3. Assessment of attractions on an "expensive-inexpensive" scale (Cognitive Perspective, Tourist Experience). This is the economic section of the initial resource survey.

4. Assessment of the attractions on a "government support-antagonism" scale (Ideographic Perspective, Tourist Infrastructure). This is the government section of the resource survey.

5. Assessment of the attractions on a planned-unplanned scale (Organization Perspective, Spatial Feature). This is the planning and management section of the resource survey.

6. Assessment of attractions/resources on an "adequate-inadequate infrastructure" scale (Organizational Perspective, Spatial Feature). This is the infrastructure section of the resource survey.

7. Survey of target groups to determine motivation and preference for attraction types and characteristics. Preferences are of the Cross Perspective, Valuation type, while motivations fall within the Cognitive Perspective, Tourist Activities, and Experiences categories.

8. Assessment of attractions/resources on a "local-extended market" scale (Cognitive Perspective, Attraction Characteristic). This is an aspect of the brand imageability of the attractions and is based on their prominence.

TABLE 6   Analysis of Britton's Study of Third World Tourism Marketing Image

PERSPECTIVE AND CATEGORY[a]	TYPOLOGY AND FORM OF EVALUATION[a]
Ideographic:	
Nature, Nature-Human Interface	Mythification
Participatory, Leisure Superstructure	Recreation and Entertainment (combined)
Settlement Infrastructure	Romaniticized Tradition versus Realistic Portrayal
Cognitive:	
Tourist Experiences, Tourist Activities	Exploration—Escape—Education—Enjoyment—Familiar or Comfortable (implied in association with ideographic types)
Attraction Character	Authenticity (implied in association with mythification)
Attraction Character	Association with famous other places
Cross-Perspective:	
Locational	(comparisons of advertisements for different places)

[a] The ideographic and cognitive typologies are all based on the subjective evaluation of place portrayals.

While also based primarily on the cognitive perspective, the WTO approach differs from Britton's study in its incorporation of organizational perspective categories—a perspective ignored by Britton. The reason for this may be linked to the nature and function of the WTO as an organization composed of and working for government tourism bodies. Governments have a stronger interest in infrastruc-ture development and planning than does the private-sector advertising industry which Britton's study examined. Thus, not only is the framework reflective of research approaches, but it also appears to indicate different perspectives held by various segments of the tourism industry.

There is another difference between the WTO approach and all the other studies assessed here: WTO is not a research

TABLE 7   Analysis of the WTO's Publication on Tourist Images

PERSPECTIVE AND CATEGORY	TYPOLOGY AND FORM OF EVALUATION
Ideographic:	
Most Categories	Natural—Social—Cultural (general categories)
Tourist Infrastructure	Government Welcome—Antagonism toward tourism (expert judgement)
Organizational:	
Spatial Features	Planned—Unplanned (compared to competing attractions/countries)
Spatial Features	Adequate—Inadequate Infrastructure (compared to competing attractions/countries)
Cognitive:	
Tourist Experiences	Expensive—Inexpensive (compared to competing attractions/countries)
Tourist Experiences and Activities	Motivation (survey of selected groups)
Attraction Character	Local—Extended Market (unspecified)
Cross-Perspective Measures:	
Valuation	Strength of attraction image
Valuation	Preference for attractions among target tourist groups

project, but rather an outlined methodology intended to be employed by others. In addition to the steps outlined above, the report discusses considerations in marketing the defined image. Whether the methodology is effective in achieving its goals cannot be determined in the publication itself. This does not, however, limit the application of the tourist attraction research framework due to its specific focus on methodology.

DISCUSSION

The analysis of the attractions typologies employed in these four examples demonstrates the potential usefulness of the framework as a tool in research evaluation. As would be anticipated, the organizational emphasis of the two planning studies contrasted with the cognitive emphasis of the image studies. Ferrario's (1976) planning study, however, was found to be more comprehensive in its use of different types of organizational categories than that of Piperoglou. Ferrario's study was also found to have incorporated numerous cross-perspective valuation measures, which caused him to emphasize existing attractions more so than Piperoglou. The WTO image study involved a greater emphasis on organizational categories than did the study by Britton (1979), which was more purely cognitive in nature.

The strength of the framework as an evaluative tool lies in the three distinct typologies. They can be used to judge basic research objectives of relevant investigations, to compare the research designs of similar studies, and to examine the type, quantity, and quality of the data collected.

CONCLUSION

In addition to the applicability of the framework for the comparative evaluation of past research, it can also be applied in the formation of research objectives and research design. An understanding of alternative approaches to tourist attraction study will help ensure that the data collected will match the intended objective of the research.

While the framework appears to be consistent within the subject matter of tourist attractions, it also fits into the larger area of general tourism research. Mitchell (1979:239) proposed a frame-of-reference for tourism research. It divides tourist attraction research into nine basic components arranged in a matrix of Demand, Supply, and Linkages on one axis and Purpose, Structure, and Distribution on the other.

The tourist attraction framework suggested here fits into the Structure vector, with the ideographic perspective associated with the supply component, the organizational perspective associated to the linkages component, and the cognitive perspective related to the demand component. This further supports the value of the attraction framework in organizing research on tourist attractions. The tourist attraction framework provides insight into the relationship of attraction research to some of the fundamental questions of human existence. The relationship of the human environment to the natural environment, the tension between the human need for collective behavior and the need for inde-

pendence, and the psychic qualities of fear and security are shown to be basic concerns explored by tourist attraction research. The considerations of these relationships in and of themselves should improve one's appreciation of the depth of tourism research.

In the last analysis, the necessity of a comprehensive organization of tourist attraction typologies is an important issue. Places are different from one another and, it could be argued, attraction typologies must reflect this difference. This writer would not deny such to be the case. However, the review of tourist attraction research reveals such a high degree of consistency in the general categorization of attractions that surely some fundamental organization would be beneficial, if only to enable researchers to communicate in the same language. While the framework proposed here may appear inappropriate to some, it does offer a basis for further discussion on the nature of tourist attractions.

REFERENCES

Archer, B. (1977), "Input-Output Analysis: Its Strengths, Limitations and Weaknesses," in *The 80's—Its Impact on Travel and Tourism Marketing*, Eighth annual conference proceedings, The Travel Research Association, June 12–15, Scottsdale, Arizona, pp. 89–107. Salt Lake City: TTRA.

Britton, Robert (1979), "The Image of the Third World in Tourism Marketing" *Annals of Tourism Research* 6(3):318–29.

Bryant, B.E., and A.J. Morrison (1980), "Travel Market Segmentation and the Implementation of Market Strategies," *Journal of Travel Research* 18(3):2–11.

Christaller, Walter (1955), "Beitrage zu einer Geographie des Fremdenverkehrs," (Contributions to a Geography of Tourism), *Erdkunde* 9(1):1–19.

Cohen, Erik (1979a), "A Phenomenology of Tourist Experiences," *Sociology* 13:179–201.

Cohen, Erik (1979b), "Rethinking the Sociology of Tourism," *Annals of Tourism Research* 6(1):18–35.

Crompton, John L. (1979), "An Assessment of the Image of Mexico as a Vacation Destination and the Influence of Geographical Location Upon That Image," *Journal of Travel Research* 17(4):18–23.

Doyle, W.S., J. Pernica, and M. Stern (1977), "Some Technical Aspects of a Recent Study of Tourism in New York State," in *The 80's—Its Impact on Travel and Tourism Marketing*, Eighth annual conference proceedings, The Travel Research Association, June 12–15, Scottsdale, Arizona, pp. 109–120. Salt Lake City: TTRA.

Eastlack, J.O., Jr. (1982), "Applying a Package Goods Research Method to Tourism Marketing," *Journal of Travel Research* 20(4):25–29.

Eitzel, M.J., and P.R. Swensen (1981), "Taking the Mystery out of Travel and Tourism Investment Decisions," *Journal of Travel Research* 20(2):24–34.

Ferrario, Francesco (1976), "The Tourist Landscape: A Method of Evaluating Tourist Potential and its Application to South

Africa," Ph.D. dissertation, Department of Geography, University of California, Berkeley.

Ferrario, Francesco (1979), "The Evaluation of Tourist Resources: An Applied Methodology," *Journal of Travel Research* 17(3):18–22 and 17(4):24–30.

Fesenmaier, Daniel R. (1985), "Modeling Variation in Destination Patronage for Outdoor Recreation Activity," *Journal of Travel Research* 24(2):17–23.

Field, Donald R., Roger N. Clark, and Barbara A. Koth (1985), "Cruiseship Travel in Alaska: A Profile of Passengers," *Journal of Travel Research* 24(2):2–8.

Frechtling, D.C. (1976), "Proposed Standard Definitions and Classifications for Travel Research," in *Marketing Travel and Tourism*. Seventh annual conference proceedings, The Travel Research Association, June 20–23, Boca Raton, Florida, pp. 59–73. Salt Lake City: TTRA.

Gearing, Charles E., William W. Swart, and Turgut Var (1976), "Establishing a Measure of Touristic Attractiveness," in *Planning for Tourism Development*, Gearing, C.E., Swart, W.W. and Var T., eds. pp. 89–103. New York: Praeger.

Goeldner, C.R., K. Dicke, and Y. Sletta, eds. (1975), *Travel Trends in the United States and Canada*, 1975 edition. Boulder, Colorado: Business Research Division, University of Colorado.

Goodrich, J.N. (1977a), "Differences in Perceived Similarity of Tourism Regions: A Spatial Analysis," *Journal of Travel Research* 16(1):10–13.

Goodrich, J.N. (1977b), "Benefit Bundle Analysis: An Empirical Study of International Travelers," *Journal of Travel Research* 16(2):6–9.

Goodrich, J.N. (1978), "A New Approach to Image Analysis Through Multidimensional Scaling," *Journal of Travel Research* 16(3):3–7.

Graburn, N.H.H. (1977), "Tourism: The Sacred Journey," in *Hosts and Guests*, V. Smith, ed. pp. 17–31. University of Pennsylvania Press: Philadelphia.

Gunn, Clare A. (1972), *Vacationscape: Designing Tourist Regions*, Austin, Texas: Bureau of Business Research, University of Texas.

Gunn, Clare A. (1979), *Tourism Planning*, New York: Crane Russak.

Gunn, Clare A. (1980a), "Amendment to Leiper, The Framework of Tourism," *Annals of Tourism Research* 7:253–255.

Gunn, Clare A. (1980b), "An Approach to Regional Assessment of Tourism Development Potential," in *Tourism Planning and Development Issues*, D.E. Hawkins, E.L. Shafer and J.M. Rovelstad, eds. pp. 261–276. Washington: George Washington University.

Haahti, Antti J. (1986), "Finland's Competitive Position as a Destination," *Annals of Tourism Research* 13(1): 11–35.

Haddon, John (1960), "A View of Foreign Lands," *Geography* 45 (209) pt. 4:286–289.

Henshall, Brian D., and Rae Roberts (1985), "Comparative Assessment of Touristic Generating Markets for New Zealand," *Annals of Tourism Research* 12(2):219–238.

Hills, Theo L., and Jan Lundgren (1977), "The Impact of Tourism in the Caribbean: A Methodological Study," *Annals of Tourism Research* 4(5):248–267.

Jansen-Verbeke, Myriam (1986), "Inner-city Tourism: Resources, Tourists and Promoters," *Annals of Tourism Research* 13(1):79–100.

Keown, Charles, Laurence Jacobs, and Reginald Worthley (1984), "American Tourists' Perception of Retail Stores in 12 Selected Countries," *Journal of Travel Research* 22(3):26–30.

Kotler, Phillip (1984), "'Dream' Vacations, The Booming Market for Designed Experiences" *The Futurist* 18(5):7–13.

Kreck, Lothar A. (1985), "The Effect of the Across-the-Border Commerce of Canadian Tourists on the City of Spokane," *Journal of Travel Research* 24(1):27–31.

Lew, Alan A. (1985), "Bringing Tourists to Town," *Small Town* 16(1):4–10.

Lew, Alan A. (1986a), "Guidebook Singapore: The Spatial Organization of Urban Tourist Attractions," Ph.D. dissertation, Department of Geography, University of Oregon.

Lew, Alan A. (1986b), Tourist and Tourguide Perceptions of Tourist Attractions in Singapore. Paper presented at the annual meeting of the Association of American Geographers, Minneapolis, Minnesota, May 2–7, 1986.

Lew, Alan A. (1987), "The History, Policies and Social Impact of International Tourism in the People's Republic of China," *Asian Profile* 15(2):117–128.

Lickorish, L.J. (1974), "Travel Research Needs in Critical Times," in *The Contribution of Travel Research in a Year of Crisis*, Fifth annual conference proceedings, The Travel Research Association, September 8–11, Williamsburg, Virginia, pp. 1–3. Salt Lake City: TTRA.

Liounis, Audrey, ed. (1985), *Fodor's Arizona*, New York: Fodor's Travel Guides.

Lundberg, Donald E. (1980), *The Tourist Business*, (4th ed.). Boston: CBI.

MacCannell, Dean (1976), *The Tourist: A New Theory of the Leisure Class*, New York: Schocken Books.

Machlis, G.E., D.D. Field, and M.E. Van Every (1984), "A Sociological Look at the Japanese Tourist," in *On Interpretation: Sociology for Interpretation of Natural and Cultural Resources*, Machlis, G.E. and Field, D.R., eds. pp. 77–93. Corvallis, Oregon: Oregon State University Press.

Matley, Ian M. (1976), *The Geography of International Tourism*, Association of American Geographers, Resource Paper No. 76–1. Washington, D. C.

McIntosh, Robert W., and Charles R. Goeldner (1984), *Tourism: Principles, Practices, Philosophies* (4th ed.). New York: John Wiley.

Mitchell, Lisle (1979), "The Geography of Tourism," *Annals of Tourism Research* 6(3):235–244.

Neffeler, S.H. (1975), "Tourism in San Diego, The Research

Dimension," in *The Impact of Travel*, Sixth annual conference proceedings, The Travel Research Association, September 18–21, San Diego, California, pp. 33–38. Salt Lake City: TTRA.

Pearce, Douglas (1981), *Tourism Development*, New York: Longman.

Pearce, Phillip (1982), *The Social Psychology of Tourist Behavior*, Oxford: Pergamon.

Peck, John Gregory, and Alice Shear Lepie (1977), "Tourism Development in Three North Carolina Towns," in *Hosts and Guests: The Anthropology of Tourism*, V.L. Smith, ed. pp. 159–182. Philadelphia: University of Pennsylvania Press.

Perdue, Richard R., and Larry D. Gutske (1985), "Spatial Pattern of Leisure Travel by Trip Purpose," *Annals of Tourism Research* 12(2):167–180.

Perry, Michael (1975), "Planning and Evaluating Advertising Campaigns Related to Tourist Destinations," in *Management Science Applications to Leisure Time Operations*, Ladany, Shaul P., ed. pp. 116–123. New York: American Elsevier Publishing Co.

Peters, M. (1969), *International Tourism*, London: Hutchinson.

Piperoglou, John (1966), "Identification and Definition of Regions in Greek Tourist Planning," in Papers, Regional Science Association 18:169–76.

Pitts, Robert E., and Arch G. Woodside (1986), "Personal Values and Travel Decisions," *Journal of Travel Research* 25(1):20–25.

Pizam, Abraham, Yoram Neuman, and Arie Reichel (1978), "Dimensions of Tourist Satisfaction with a Destination Area," *Annals of Tourism Research* 5(3):314–322.

Polacek, Michal, and Rudolph Aroch (1984), "Analysis of Cultural Sights Attractiveness for Tourism," *The Tourist Review* 39(4):17–18.

Price, Richard L. (1980), "A Geography of Tourism: Settlement and Landscape on the Sardinian Littoral," Ph.D. dissertation, Department of Geography, University of Oregon.

Relph, Edward (1976), *Place and Placelessness*, London: Pion.

Ritchie, J.R. Brent, and Catherine E. Aitken (1985), "Olympulse II—Evolving Resident Attitudes Towards the 1988 Olympic Winter Games," *Journal of Travel Research* 23(3):28–33.

Ritchie, J.R. Brent, and Michael Zinns (1978), "Culture as a Determinant of the Attractiveness of a Tourism Region," *Annals of Tourism Research* 5(2):252–267.

Robinson, H.A. (1976), *A Geography of Tourism*, London: Macdonald & Evans.

Rodenburg, E. (1980), "The Effects of Scale on Economic Development: Tourism in Bali," *Annals of Tourism Research* 7(2):177–196.

Schmidt, Catherine (1979), "The Guided Tour," *Urban Life* 7(4):441–467.

Senior, Robert (1982), *The World Travel Market*, London: Euromonitor.

Shih, David (1986), "VALS As A Tool of Tourism Market Research: The Pennsylvania Experience," *Journal of Travel Research* 24(4):2–11.

Smith, Stephen L.J. (1985), "Location Patterns of Urban Restaurants," *Annals of Tourism Research* 1 2(4): 58 1602.

Smith, Valene L., ed. (1977), *Hosts and Guests: The Anthropology of Tourism*, Philadelphia: University of Pennsylvania Press.

Thompson, John R., and Phillip D. Cooper (1979), "Additional Evidence on the Limited Size of Evoked and Inept Sets of Travel Destinations," *Journal of Travel Research* 17(3):23–5.

U.S. Department of Commerce (1981), *Creating Economic Growth and Jobs Through Travel and Tourism*, Washington, D.C.: U.S. Department of Commerce, Economic Development Administration.

Van Veen, Walle M. Oppedijk, and Theo W.M. Verhallen (1986), "Vacation Market Segmentation: A Domain-Specific Value Approach," *Annals of Tourism Research* 13(1):37–58.

Wahab, Salah, L.J. Crampon, and L.M. Rothfield (1976), *Tourism Marketing: A Destination-Oriented Programme for the Marketing of International Tourism*, London: Tourism International Press.

White, Kenneth J. (1985), "An International Travel Demand Model: US Travel to Western Europe," *Annals of Tourism Research* 12(4):529–545.

Witter, Brenda Sternquist (1985), "Attitudes About a Resort Area: A Comparison of Tourist and Local Retailers," *Journal of Travel Research* 24(1):14–19.

Woodside, Arch G., Ellen M. Moore, Mark A. Bonn, and Donald G. Wizeman (1986), "Segmenting the Timeshare Resort Market," *Journal of Travel Research* 24(3):6–12.

Woodside, Arch G., Ilkka Ronkainen, and David M. Reid (1977), "Measurement and Utilization of the Evoked Set as a Travel Marketing Variable," in *The 80's—Its Impact on Travel and Tourism Marketing*. Eighth annual conference proceedings, The Travel Research Association, June 12–15, Scottsdale, Arizona, pp. 123–130. Salt Lake City: TTRA.

World Tourism Organization (1980a), *Evaluating Tourism Resources*. Madrid: WTO.

World Tourism Organization (1980b), *Tourist Images*, Madrid: WTO.

26

Research Needs
of the Restaurant Industry[1]

ROBERT P. OLSON
University of Wisconsin—Stout
Menomonie, Wisconsin

UEL BLANK
Professor Emeritus
University of Minnesota
Minneapolis, Minnesota

This chapter provides guidelines for researching the operation of an individual restaurant business or the restaurant industry of a community or region. Restaurants share much in common; hence, maximum use should be made of existing industry data. But every individual operation and each community's restaurant industry is unique and must be separately researched. Many of the procedures treated by other chapters in this Handbook are applicable. This chapter brings them into workable focus upon restaurants.

THE ROLE OF RESTAURANTS AND THE FOOD SERVICE INDUSTRY

Food service away from home is essential to tourism. In the Minnesota setting, 30 percent of restaurant sales overall are estimated to be made to tourists. This leaves 70 percent of sales to residents of the local community (Blank and Olson 1982). The proportions will differ in each state, in each community, and for each restaurant. In communities having a mixed economic base, a major part of the restaurant industry's output can be considered "industry support" (Blank 1982a). Most modern industry requires that individuals travel and work at a distance from home; thus, restaurants play a required supporting role in providing food for these individuals. In the Minnesota setting, the industry support role is estimated to make up 50 percent of total sales, composed partly of sales to business tourists and partly to residents engaged in work patterns.

Restaurants provide a complex output in performing the cited roles. In addition to food and beverage away from home, they provide convenience, communication settings, and a wide variety of outputs contributing to life's quality. Among the latter are entertainment/diversion; the sweetening of social and business interactions; and ambiences contributing to variety in living experiences.

In order to produce its output, each restaurant purchases inputs. It is through these purchases, or "backward linkages" to the community, that the restaurant industry contributes to the local economy. A major type of input is labor; hence, the restaurant industry is a major generator of jobs. The group of firms providing food and restaurant supplies has been found a substantial source of economic base in itself (Blank 1982b).

[1]**Editor's Note:** This chapter appeared in the first edition of the publication and is reprinted here without change as the authors were unable to revise it. While some information is dated, the fundamental concepts presented are still valid and useful, so the chapter was included. Readers seeking the latest information should contact the National Restaurant Association, 1200 Seventeenth Street, NW, Washington, D.C. 20036-3097, or call their Distribution Center and request such publications as "Restaurant Industry Operations Report: 1992," $39; "Food Service Numbers," (1992), $25.

Restaurants also support the community infrastructure through utility systems and local taxes.

Overall, the food service industry now provides about one-third of meals eaten in the United States. In addition to its scale, it exhibits a pattern of dynamic growth not only in overall output but in its employment pattern and in its service types. Table 1 shows a 10-year growth in dollar sales of all food of 165 percent; but "places of refreshment" increased sales by 472 percent. The latter corresponds roughly to short-order food operations. This growth indicates how important it is that those interested in the industry remain abreast of these developments.

DEFINITIONS: KNOW WHAT YOU ARE DEALING WITH!

Restaurants are part of an industry system, providing services to people away from home, that becomes progressively more general and broader as it moves from restaurants to food services to hospitality industry. Each of these is defined and discussed briefly in this section. A clear definition specifically applicable to each research situation should be devised by the research manager.

There can be and are many definitions for a *restaurant.* "A place where food is served" may be too broad. "A place that serves food to the public" is more restrictive and may be the appropriate one under some situations. If still too inclusive, how about "a place of business serving food to customers with inside dining"?

As travel-tourism related research is discussed in this chapter, a restaurant will be defined as an enterprise having the following attributes:

- A commercial operation
- Prepares and/or sells food (meals and snacks) to customers for consumption on premises (may also provide take-out service)
- Open to the general public and/or restricted clientele, such as members (element of choice on the part of the patron is a necessary but not sufficient consideration)
- Operates on a continuous basis (may close seasonally)

The term *food service* (or food and beverage service) is generally broader in scope than restaurant. It is often used to refer to "all operations serving food (and/or beverages) to people away from home." As such, a food service not only includes restaurants as was defined but also hospitals and nursing homes, various kinds of noncommercial institutional food services, and sometimes occasional food services such as that provided by a church.

The *hospitality industry* is often defined as "those businesses serving people away from home." The difference between hospitality and tourism is that in the case of the latter, the operations are specialized to serve people away from home (department stores may be a part of tourism but not hospitality) and a hospitality service may occur in the home area or work area. A restaurant illustrates the distinction—it is always a part of the hospitality industry, but only that part of sales to people away from their usual residence or work area can be considered tourism. There is no universal framework recognized by governmental agencies, practitioners, or academicians that defines precisely hospitality industry components. Despite this, the classification as an industry generally holds. A common reference is to the *hospitality service* industries—the plural form denoting a collection including food services, lodging services, resorts, recreation centers, festivals, camps, attractions, and related operations.

The *service* aspect applied to restaurants, food services, and hospitality operations suggests a conscious level of appeal or dedication to those away from home. It also suggests the absence of a tangible product for ownership or consumption. The meal one purchases is a "product" accompanied by "services" that are necessary, rendered, and utilized for the execution of the complete transaction.

RESEARCHING THE INDIVIDUAL RESTAURANT OPERATION

WHO NEEDS INFORMATION ABOUT A RESTAURANT?

People requiring restaurant information will range from the owner or manager to its suppliers of goods and services, the

Table 1 Growth of U.S. Food Service 1967 to 1977*

	1967	1977	PERCENT CHANGE
Sales			
Food ($ billion)	$23.8	$63.8	+ 165
All retail ($ billion)	310.2	723.1	+ 133
Employment			
Food (million)	2.4	4.1	+ 71
Employed U.S. (million)	74.4	90.5	+ 22
Places of Refreshment			
Sales ($ billion)	$3.4	$19.5	+ 472
Employment (thousands)	296	1157	+ 291

*Source: U.S. Census of Business 1967, 1977.

financial sector, governmental and regulatory agencies, the business community, various associations, and the general public. Each of these will host different views of both the restaurant industry and individual restaurants; hence, their research interests and needs will differ.

Managers, owners, and investors in a given restaurant need information to monitor ongoing operations and to guide potential improvements in markets and/or internal operations. Since each restaurant has a unique market and labor force, data from that individual operation or applying directly to it must be used in making decisions concerning marketing and operations.

MANAGER RESEARCH—MONITORING THE ONGOING OPERATION

Restaurant managers want to know how well the operation is doing in relation to:

- Previous time periods
- Comparable units classed by size, type, geographic location, and so on
- Industry standards or averages
- What may be possible or desirable

The comparisons could include such things as sales, market patterns, expenditures, productivity, energy usage, employee turnover, and many other enterprise-related questions.

A wealth of valuable data already exists in most, if not all, restaurants, and they should not be overlooked. It would be prudent to review existing records to determine if they are current, complete and accurate. In-house records should be organized to mesh with industry standards and norms so that meaningful comparisons can be made. Examples of restaurant records would be guest checks, sales records, banquet/group folios, accounting records and reports, production schedules, employee records, and purchase orders.

A number of questions needs to be asked. Probably the most important is, who is going to use the information and for what purpose? Others are:

- Are sales composed of food only, or is revenue from alcoholic beverages included?
- Are banquet and/or carry-away sales included, and should they be?
- Are guest checks used for all defined sales?
- Has the use of guest checks been consistently applied during the time period?
- Are there factors that inflate or deflate the average, such as lost or otherwise unaccounted for checks?
- Is a single guest check used for hundreds of people or dollars in group sales?
- Do units to which comparisons are to be made follow the same conventions?
- What is the accepted and preferred practice?

MANAGER RESEARCH—SALES, SALES POTENTIAL

Another major concern of the manager is sales or the operation's sales potential, the latter term being the per-

ceived share of the potential market. This *potential market* is defined as "the total expected sales in a given geographic area for a measured period of time." A manager might want to increase sales. Reliable information concerning the market would be necessary to make a determination as to who the potential customers are, how many they are, and where they are located, along with their principal characteristics.

It may seem that everyone is a potential customer because everyone eats. Such is not the case. It is important to be able to select out of the masses those with the inclination and resources to patronize a given restaurant. In planning sales and market research, the reader is referred to Part Two of the Handbook (especially Chapter 10) dealing with demand estimation.

CONDUCTING A STUDY TO ESTIMATE MARKET POTENTIAL

One approach is to arrive at a description or profile of present satisfied patrons and use this to locate others that are similar in critical attributes. It is usually necessary to conduct a survey or study of present customers to determine their important characteristics. Principal ones are age, sex, education, occupation, income, marital status, and location of residence and/or workplace.

Surveys provide original data and may be conducted on site by personal contact, via a mail-out-return instrument, or by telephone. Other ways of gathering information may be the use of a guest register, prize drawings, or redemption of incentive coupons.

Data are usually gathered with the aid of a formal questionnaire (or instrument) in which information such as residence (state, city, zip code), menu preference, mode of travel to the restaurant, distance traveled, frequency of patronage, frequency of eating out, and much more may be requested. The hazard, of course, is that a questionnaire that is too long, complex, or personal may not be answered and, in fact, be a turnoff. It is preferable to seek only the information that is necessary and immediately useful.

A survey is often a part of a larger research effort. Before undertaking a survey, all available information pertaining to the question should be gathered from secondary sources.

Since skills and finances are usually limited, it is important to employ all appropriate resources to accomplish the survey. These resources may include the restaurant's manager and staff, specialized research firms, and individual consultants for part or all of the project.

It is desirable to seek counsel and assistance from a variety of sources, such as other owners or managers, trade associations, chambers of commerce, professional groups, governmental agencies, faculty of colleges and universities, and Service Corps of Retired Executives (SCORE).

EXISTING DATA SOURCES

Before conducting a survey of a specific restaurant operation, there should be familiarity with existing sources of information. These are given in Table 2 of this chapter and in Chapter 8 by Goeldner, Travel and Tourism Information Sources.

Table 2   Sources of Existing Restaurant Industry Information

A.   UNITED STATES GOVERNMENT DATA AND RESEARCH METHODS SOURCES

DEPARTMENT	BUREAU	PUBLICATION	TYPE OF DATA
Commerce	Census	Census of Population	Population, income, employment
		Current Population Reports	Population, income
		Population Estimates	Population
		Census of Business: Retail, Wholesale, Manufacturers, Selected Services	Employment, sales, number of businesses
		County Business Patterns	Employment
		Retail Trade Reports	Sales
		Wholesale Trade Reports	Sales
		Statistical Abstract	Varied
	Economic Analysis	Survey of Current Businesses	Income, sales, employment
Labor	Labor Statistics	Employment and Earnings	Employment, income
		Area Trends in Employment and Unemployment	Employment
Treasury	Internal Revenue Service	Statistics of Income: Individuals, businesses	Income, sales, taxes
Agriculture	Agricultural Research Service	Marketing Research Reports	Operating costs, labor requirement; food consumption, equipment; utilization and other selected topics.

B.   CANADIAN GOVERNMENT DATA AND RESEARCH METHODS SOURCES

DEPARTMENT	BUREAU	PUBLICATION	TYPE OF DATA
Industry, Trade, and Commerce	Office of Tourism: Marketing Research, Policy Planning, and Coordination Division	Special Reports	Varied
		Travel Trends	Food and beverage expenditures
		Many others	Trip purpose and travel modes
			Varied and comprehensive
	Statistics Canada: User Services	Restaurant, Caterer & Taverns Industry Survey	Food and beverage sales
			Numbers and kinds of restaurants and other food services
		Urban Family Food Expenditure Survey	Family restaurant expenditures
		Travel, Tourism, and Outdoor Recreation	Travel economics
		Canadian Travel Survey	Socioeconomic data on travel
Agriculture Canada	Food Markets Analysis Division	Food Market Commentary	Updates on expenditures for restaurant food

C. STATE AND PROVINCIAL DATA AND RESEARCH METHODS SOURCES

TYPE OF DATA	POSSIBILITIES	POSSIBLE AGENCY NAMES
Population	Vital Statistics Population Reports Population Estimates	Health Department Department of Economic Development
Income	Economic Report Personal Income Per Capita Income	Department of Economics & Business Department of Administration Department of Revenue
Employment	Employment and Payroll Work Force Estimates Labor Market Statistics	Department of Employment Security Department of Human Resources Department of Manpower
Sales and Tax	Sales and Use Tax	Department of Revenue Department of Taxation Department of Treasury Department of Industry Department of Tourism Department of Travel

D. GOVERNMENT AND COMMUNITY DATA AND RESEARCH METHODS SOURCES

SOURCE	CONTACT	LOCATION
U.S. Department of Agriculture	Extension Service Statistical Reporting Service Agricultural Research Service	Washington, D.C.
Colleges and Universities	Cooperative Extension Service Faculty Researchers in business Schools and Economics Departments	Land grant universities State universities and colleges Community colleges
Libraries	Research librarian Electronic data librarian Professional journals Trade publications	Public and educational institution libraries

E. PRIVATE DATA AND RESEARCH METHODS SOURCES

ORGANIZATION TYPE	POSSIBLE TITLE	TYPE OF DATA
Accounting Firms	The Restaurant Industry (for city, region, or county) The International Restaurant	Numbers of operations, employees, total sales Trends in overall sales by type of operation Kinds of sales (food, beverages) Analysis of sales (per seat, per employee, etc.)
Publishing Firms	Magazine articles and reports of food services	Total sales, number of operations services Employment by firm categories or geographic regions Ranking by sales or number of operations
General Management and Restaurant Consultant Firms	Proprietary, may cover a wide range of topics, use only with permission.	May treat any type of restaurant industry and operating data
Professional and Trade Associations	Restaurant Association (national, state, local) Food Service Society Hospitality Association	May collect and disseminate member-ship and industry-wide data

Data from existing sources can often be used as a preliminary or partial guide to operation of a given restaurant. Study of these data can also indicate what is considered relevant by management experts. In making comparisons of data from a specific restaurant with data from other existing sources, it is important that the same kinds of observations are being compared. Thus, the implicit definitions contained in both sets of data must be well understood by the user.

PUTTING THE FINDINGS TO WORK

Data generated from research of a restaurant's operation does no good unless it is put to work. This is the payoff—what has been learned that can improve the restaurant's operation and marketing?

Use of the data depends, of course, upon the problem as originally defined. Problems could have been as widely different as efficiency of sales per employee, shrinkage of supplies, or employee turnover. Rather than treating all the possible range, one example illustrating use of information from market research will be discussed.

Market research would deal with some of the following questions.

Who Are the Present Customers?

Most restaurants, over time, have been able to appeal to and attract a relatively homogeneous clientele. This is an important ingredient to being successful. The purpose of conducting a survey is to develop a profile of present patronage.

Once a manager has a good understanding of who (by attributes) the customers are and that there will be no major change in the operation of the restaurant such as location, ambience, menu, services offered, and so on, it is possible to locate and measure the potential market.

Who Are the Potential Customers?

Potential customers can be defined as those persons in the population that are similar to present satisfied customers. This relationship underscores the importance of having a well-conducted survey based on a professionally designed survey instrument that accurately samples your present customers and their degree of satisfaction.

Fortunately, the important socioeconomic characteristics of the general population are readily available from a number of state and federal governmental sources, which are listed in Table 2. These data sources make it possible to determine how many persons with selected characteristics are to be found in a given geographic area, such as state, province, county, or even census tract.

How Can They Be Reached?

Knowing the size and location of the target group then begs the questions—How can I tell and sell them? There is no standard formula that can be applied to all situations in order to generate customers. Reaching potential customers with a marketing message will take a commitment of time, energy, and financial resources. The mix of these ingredients will vary depending upon, among other things, the marketing objectives, staff skills available, and funds to be dedicated.

Some of the ways to reach people are by radio, television, newspapers, other periodicals, speciality publications, direct mail, and handbills. Often, several approaches are necessary to realize expected results. It is wise to seek out professional assistance to design a marketing program.

Are There Enough Potential Customers?

One may find out, after conducting a survey and analyzing the population data, that there are too few persons of the type that you are seeking. It may not be possible to satisfactorily increase customer count even if a disproportionately large share of those available were attracted.

Should this be the case, it would probably be advisable to carve out a different niche in the market and appeal to a different and larger or more responsive clientele.

RESEARCHING THE RESTAURANT INDUSTRY

In many situations, information is needed about not just one restaurant but about the restaurant industry of a community or region.

PLANNING FOR RESTAURANT INDUSTRY RESEARCH

Research of a community's restaurant industry must begin with a full understanding of the research purposes and the possible limitations to which it may be subject. It is suggested that three specific, interrelated questions be addressed as part of the planning process.

Who wants to know about the restaurant industry, and what use do they plan for the information?   This question deals primarily with purpose—what questions are to be answered. The kinds of restaurant industry interests may vary widely and include such divergent groups as:

- Restaurant industry leadership having interests in showing overall economic impact upon the community
- Tourism development interests seeking information about tourism sales by the restaurants or seeking means for better service to tourists
- Potential investors investigating food service markets for the area and how well they are currently served
- Restaurant users needing to know what types and qualities of eating experiences are available
- Restaurant supply and service firms wanting to know the market for their services or products
- Those having interests in employment opportunities, labor needs, manpower training, and teenage employment
- Government agencies treating public health, and so on.

All of the above and many others are possible research interests. No one study can supply information needs of all of these. In order to be certain that essential questions are treated, it is necessary to carefully define purposes at the outset, and then redefine them as progress into the research process dictates. (It may be found, for example, that objectives must be scaled down in order to stay within cost limits.)

What is the applicable restaurant industry?

As purposes are defined, the industry to be studied will also be defined. One dimension is geographic: Is interest focused upon only a municipal neighborhood? A county? A Standard Metropolitan Statistical Area (SMSA)? An entire state/province? The way in which existing data are aggregated, as by county, may influence this decision. Another question is: What dimension concerning components of the food service industry is to be included? If, for example, the purpose is to estimate supply needs, it may be desirable to include not only commercial operations, but also in-plant feeders and not-for-profit institutional operations.

What data will be collected and how will this be done?

Having dealt with the "why" and "who," the "what" and "how" questions now involve the heart of the restaurant industry research process. The "what" and "how" require that one confront two issues: First, can secondary data (data collected and published by others) be used, or must primary data (data which one collects) be gathered? And second, will the actual research be contracted, or will it be done by the person wanting the information? In considering these and related issues of "what" and "how," another set of interrelated questions must be dealt with. These must be considered by the person or organization making the basic decisions about the research and authorizing it, whether or not the actual work is contracted to another individual or firm or carried out in-house.

• What specific questions require answers? The precise information needs must be spelled out. These, in turn, determine what data are useful and dictate the nature of any new (primary) data gathered.

• How much time is available? If results are needed within one month, there is usually not time to gather new data and already existing information must be used.

• How much money is available? Resources available, together with time constraints, will often dictate how extensive the research can be and whether or not it must be done in-house using staff resources.

• How accurate must the findings be? A first response might be that any study should discover the truth! In fact, all data have limitations to their accuracy. If sales trends are to be charted, they will require reasonably accurate, consistent data. On the other hand, estimates of demand for a new type of food offering may tolerate a modest margin of error.

• Does the information needed already exist? Needless time and effort can be spent gathering data or assembling it from partial sources when the job, or most of it, already has been done. In many studies, combinations of secondary and primary data are used.

EXISTING DATA SOURCES

The preceding question makes clear that any restaurant industry researcher must investigate fully the existing sources of information. Even in cases where primary data will be gathered, it is almost always necessary to use secondary data in the research design stages and to support and add further depth to primary research findings. Table 2 gives suggestions for sources of existing data that are specific to the restaurant industry. The reader should also consult Chapter 8 in Part Two of this Handbook.

Any data or conclusions about the restaurant industry from existing sources must be scrutinized for *relevance* and *accuracy* in deciding how to use it. Sometimes secondary restaurant industry data may be used as partial guides, even though it is not judged as fully relevant and/or accurate. *Relevance* as used here means "Are the definitions implied in the data compatible with the stated purposes and needs?" Every set of data has a built-in definition of *industry*, dependent upon how the information was collected:

• If a given state only licensed restaurants in communities of 2,500 or more, such a license list would contain few rural restaurants.

• Some restaurant lists include operations primarily serving alcoholic beverages. Do these types fit your needs?

• Many compilations may define a *motel with a restaurant* as either "lodging" or "food service" depending upon whichever sales figure is larger; then all sales from both categories are attributed to the one business *type*.

Accuracy can only be guaranteed by ensuring that proper statistical procedures were followed in getting the data and that the restaurant population of interest was sampled. In this step, the services of a statistician skilled in sampling and survey methods are a must. If a full picture of a city's restaurant industry is needed, it should be understood that this cannot be obtained simply from a few restaurants in the central business district or the managers present at a local restaurant association meeting. Neither of these represent well the full range of the city's restaurant industry, and conclusions from such a survey could be misleading.

CONDUCTING YOUR OWN SURVEY

Despite the wealth of data that are available about the restaurant industry, a decision to gather primary data might be made. There are a number of situations demanding this course:

• The restaurant industry of each community, state, or province is unique. A comprehensive description of a particular restaurant industry can only be obtained by gathering primary data.

• Specific qualitative data that is not elsewhere available might be needed, for example, the nature and composition of the restaurant work force—in studying the Minnesota food service industry, it was discovered that as much as one-fourth of the young people may have their first major employment experience in a restaurant.

Part Two, Chapter 9, goes into extensive detail on how to set up research. This is very applicable to restaurant industry research.

MARKET AND EMPLOYEE STUDIES

As noted above, restaurant market and employee studies may be carried out through the restaurants. Often the firms already have a substantial amount of information about their markets and/or employees. In addition, a sampling may be made of customers while they are in the restaurant. Employees may be interviewed in person while in the restaurant, or they may be interviewed at home, in person or by mail or telephone.

Market studies may also involve household surveys in the community, possibly combined with surveys of tourists (who, by definition, are not community residents).

Employee studies may also be conducted through household surveys. This is the origin of census of population employment data and of some labor/industry agency data.

PUTTING RESTAURANT INDUSTRY FINDINGS TO WORK

Time, effort, and money will have been invested in a study of a community's (city, county, state, province) restaurant industry. What use will be made of it? Of what value to the industry will it be?

Part of the usefulness depends upon how well the purposes have been defined, how accurate and usable the data are, and how good an analysis has been made of the data. These original perceived needs for the research should direct use of the improved information that is now on hand. Important uses include:

• Highlighting the value of the restaurant industry—such as in terms of sales dollars, employment, and contribution to community living. Improved understanding can contribute to general public relations, restaurant association membership support, and appropriate restaurant industry legislation.

• Helping in managing the industry and directing its development regarding:
—Developing new markets among restaurants, local firms, and community tourists
—Promotion needs and practices
—Types of restaurant services needed
—Employment needs and employment legislation
—Supply systems, financing, and business management aids
—The safeguarding of public health

SPREAD THE WORD

Assuming that purposes have adequately been set up and research properly executed, there is much more to be done; that is, it is necessary to get findings into the hands of those who can and will use them.

The first step toward getting the data into use started at the beginning—all of those who were expected to use the findings should have had a hand, or at least been represented, in setting up the purposes. They should have been updated regularly as progress was made and given opportunity to contribute to inputs of data. Finally, they should have been challenged to help interpret the data into usable terms. This requires major communications procedures—such as a newsletter (perhaps an existing one can be used) or regular reports at association meetings.

A report of the findings should be published at as early a date as possible. Consider a set of publications, each part covering a given special-interest item or each addressed to a specific audience. Use media to release some of the findings. Possibly a media event, such as a press conference, would be in order.

Perhaps the material can be used with managers and others in a workshop where it is combined with other inputs to help in management, legislative, and other decisions.

EXAMPLES OF FOOD SERVICE RESEARCH

CREST (Consumer Reports on Eating Share Trends) was initiated in 1974 by the National Restaurant Association (NRA) to learn about consumer attitude and behavior in the market place. These periodic studies gather data from national representative panels using mail surveys.

Some of the specific reports have dealt with topics such as:

• Consumer attitudes
• Life-style and economic issues
• Take-out purchases
• Meal/snack purchases
• Business traveler
• Coffee Shops
• Fast-food restaurants

Restaurant Operation Report is published annually on a cooperative basis by the National Restaurant Association (NRA) and Laventhol & Horwath, an international accounting firm.

Data presented are based on survey instruments sent to NRA members. Computation and analysis considers tenure of operation, type, location, sales, expenses, size, employment, and other characteristics.

The report is not intended to reflect standards, but rather present summaries that may be useful to managers as they consider their own enterprises.

Minnesota's Food Service Industry Study was conducted by the hospitality group of the Agricultural Extension Service, University of Minnesota. It was designed to be a comprehensive study of all regularly operating food services in Minnesota; thus, it covers not-for-profit as well as for-profit food operations. It was a mail survey to a sample of about one-third of all licensed establishments. About a 50 percent response rate was achieved. It gathered information about the types of operations, their age, size, employment, markets, advertising programs, and energy conserving programs. Data are aggregated by types and by Minnesota development regions and tourism regions.

The Food Service Industry Study of U.S. food service was conducted by the Marketing Economics Division, ERS, USDA. It was done by means of personal interviews with a national sample of 3,000 U.S. food service operations. It gathered overall data about sales by types. It especially concentrated upon kinds and quantities of food used by type and size of food service establishment.

Market Surveys of Individual Restaurants are conducted, on a limited basis, by the hospitality group at the University of Minnesota as a service to local restaurants.

They are done by means of a one-page questionnaire that is completed by patrons while they are in the restaurant. A predetermined number of questionnaires are distributed on a random pattern throughout an entire week. These may be handled by the waitresses, by the cashier, or by university students.

Data is tabulated and results prepared by students and staff of the university. Reports are released to the management of participating restaurants on a confidential basis.

REFERENCES

Anon. (1974), *Youth and the Meaning of Work*, Washington, D.C.: U.S. Department of Labor, Manpower Administration, Manpower Research Monograph No. 32.

Anon. (1976), *New Labor Force Projections to 1990*, Special Labor Force Report 197, BLS, U.S. Department of Labor.

Anon. (1980), *Food Market Commentary*, Food Markets Analysis Division, Agriculture Canada. Vol. 2, No. 1, March.

Anon. (1982), *Minnesota Analysis and Planning Newsletter*, Vol. 14, No. 1, University of Minnesota.

Anon. (1982), *Restaurants & Institutions Magazine*, Vol. 91, No. 1, (July 1): 36.

Blank, Uel (1982a), "Interrelationships of the Food Service Industry with the Community." *The Practice of Hospitality Management*, Westport, CT: AVI Publishing Company.

Blank, Uel, (1982b), *Minnesota's Food Service Industry Supply System*, Staff Paper P82–6, Department of Agriculture & Applied Economics, University of Minnesota.

Blank, Uel (1982c), *Life Style—Tourism Interrelationship of Minneapolis-St. Paul Residents*, Staff Paper 82, Department of Agriculture & Applied Economics, University of Minnesota, July.

Blank, Uel, and Robert Olson (1982), *The Food Service Industry—A Major Minnesota Economic Sector*, Staff Paper P82, Department of Agriculture & Applied Economics, University of Minnesota.

Drake, Willis (1982), "Back-to-Basics Job Creation Lesson Needed," *St. Paul Pioneer Press*, July 18, p. 4G.

Fay, Clifford T., Jr., Richard C. Rhoads and Robert L. Rosenblatt (1971), *Managerial Accounting for the Hospitality Service Industries*, Dubuque, Iowa: Wm. C. Brown.

Powers, Thomas F. (1979), *Introduction to Management in the Hospitality Industry*, New York: John Wiley & Sons, Inc.

Van Dress, Michael G. (1971), *The Food Service Industry: Type Quantity & Value of Foods Used*, Marketing Economics Division, Economics Research Service, USDA, Statistical Bulletin No. 476.

27

Tourism Research Needs in the Personal Transportation Modes: A 1990s Perspective

LAWRENCE F. CUNNINGHAM
Professor of Marketing and Transportation
University of Colorado
Denver, Colorado

This paper examines the research issues of personal motor vehicle tourism. It addresses the issues of determining the identity of the motor vehicle tourist, developing information and data bases about market segments of the personal motor vehicle tourist, exploring his/her planning and decision making, identifying the timing of personal motor vehicle tourist trips, uncovering data about trip habits, and investigating personal motor vehicle tourism research. There are also a number of institutional issues facing personal motor vehicle tourism researchers that inhibit their efforts. It also examines the role of private and public sector efforts to collect data necessary to answer these research issues. Furthermore, it examines the effectiveness of these data collection efforts.

INTRODUCTION

This chapter will seek to identify the major research issues and needs confronting researchers studying personal motor vehicle tourism. Personal forms of transportation appear most frequently in the highway mode but also include certain forms of water and air transportation. Personal forms of highway transportation include automobiles, recreational vehicles, motorcycles, and even bicycles. Personal water transportation forms include privately owned motorized boats and sailing vessels. Personal air transportation modes consist of privately owned aircraft that are used for private enjoyment or personal business.

Overall, privately owned autos and, to a more limited extent, recreational vehicles account for the majority of tourism expenditures by travelers using the personal transportation modes. In 1989, all forms of automotive tourism gener-

ated total expenditures of approximately $29 billion, surpassing the tourism-related expenditures of all other modes of transportation (Mina 1985; Cook 1992).[1]

In the context of this chapter, the term *personal motor vehicle* will encompass automobiles and recreational vehicles, but exclude other modes such as motorcycles, boats, and other segments having only minimal tourism-related impact.

CHAPTER SCOPE

Identifying future research needs in the personal motor vehicle tourism area requires a careful examination of work conducted by international, governmental, and private-sector organizations and agencies within the United States. Internationally, the chapter examines current research activi-

[1] In 1985, Nancy Mina of the U.S. Travel Data Center provided a figure of approximately $22 billion for all forms of automobile tourism expenditures in 1982. Being unable to duplicate that figure for 1989, the author took the original number and multiplied it by the Travel Price Index, compiled by the U.S. Travel Data Center, to arrive at an approximate estimate of $29 billion for 1989. In that same year, all automobile travel generated $50.5 billion in revenues, excluding hotel/motel receipts (Cook 1992).

Part Five   An Industry Sector Perspective

ties conducted by the United Nations, the Organization of Economic Cooperation and Development (OECD), and Canada and Mexico.

Domestically, the analysis examines research conducted by the U.S. Bureau of the Census, the U.S. Trade and Tourism Administration (formerly the U.S. Travel Service Organization), both branches of the U.S. Department of Commerce, and the U.S. Department of Transportation. It also carefully examines the research activities of private and nonprivate organizations such as the U.S. Travel Data Center, the Travel Industry Association of America (formerly the Discover America Travel Organization), and the American Automobile Association, among others.

In addition, the analysis also includes a review of current research needs and future research directions of state tourism offices and departments of transportation. It also examines the research activities and requirements of private-sector firms, such as hotels and car rental companies, and auxiliary services, such as magazines, advertising agencies, and consulting firms.

The fundamental questions posed are:

1. What are the priorities for research in personal motor vehicle tourism?
2. What major institutional issues inhibit addressing or attaining these research priorities?

PRIORITIES FOR RESEARCH ISSUES IN PERSONAL MOTOR VEHICLE TOURISM

WHO IS THE PERSONAL MOTOR VEHICLE TOURIST?

There are extensive federal, nonprofit, and private-sector data bases describing auto/truck and recreational vehicle (RV) trips and travel in terms of demographics and trip purpose. Some of the most effective data bases are available from the U.S. Travel Data Center and private consulting firms such as D.K. Shifflet and Associates, Ltd. Basically, the following trends emerge:

• Nearly 80 percent of auto travelers who undertook auto/truck trips had incomes less than $40,000 (U.S. Travel Data Center 1989).

• White travelers seemed to dominate auto/truck trips in proportions substantially in excess of normal population distributions (U.S. Bureau of the Census 1979).

• Trip-taking activity seemed to decline as individuals moved into older age categories. The results of a 1989 study, for example, indicate that individuals between 25 and 34 accounted for approximately 26 percent of all person-trips (a person-trip is one person taking one trip; a family of four traveling together would account for one trip and four person-trips), while individuals between 35 and 44 and between 45 and 54 accounted for 21 percent and 15 percent of all person-trips, respectively (U.S. Travel Data Center 1989).

• Auto trip-takers represented a lower proportion of noncollege graduates compared to trip-takers using other modes of transportation such as air, where college graduates were predominant. This seemed to be the case for both business and recreational travel (U.S. Travel Data Center 1989).

• Nonmarried and married individuals without children were responsible for a large percentage of family travel in terms of miles. Families with children between 16 and 22 years of age were also responsible for a substantial percentage of trip-taking (U.S. Travel Data Center 1989).

• Seventy-one percent of all travelers own their own homes (U.S. Travel Data Center 1989).

• The number of persons who typically undertook such trips alone constituted the largest percentage of trip-takers (U.S. Travel Data Center 1989). Of trips involving the use of personal motor vehicles, 76 percent were taken by two persons or less. Only 4 percent of these auto/truck/RV trip-takers included five or more travel companions (U.S. Travel Data Center 1989).

• Personal motor vehicle occupancy was higher for vacation travel than for any other trip purpose, standing at 2.11 persons per vehicle versus 1.37 persons per vehicle for business travel and 2.06 persons per vehicle for pleasure travel. As could be expected, the rate of vehicle occupancy increased as household income decreased and as size of the household expanded (U.S. Travel Data Center 1989).

But, these data describe a sample of all travelers, not the personal motor vehicle tourist in particular. Federal agencies, the U.S. Travel Data Center, and private consulting organizations have sought to maximize knowledge of the motor vehicle tourist by surveying travelers undertaking trips of 50 to 100 miles or more away from home. While understanding of the motor vehicle tourist has improved as a result of these efforts, additional work is required.

The key challenges for researchers in the public and private sectors are to develop research approaches that focus on the personal motor vehicle tourist and to develop a "richer" understanding of the individual(s). Market researchers recognized some years ago that it was impossible to predict potential purchasers based on demographic data. These researchers realized that greater predictability would likely ensue from a better understanding of the major facets of a purchaser's life-style, or psychographics. Psychographics is a technique utilized by market researchers to measure life-style. It involves measuring the activities, interests, and opinions (A.I.O.) of subjects (Westfall 1962).

Two basic types of A.I.O. questions or statements are used in psychographic research. One type, which is more common, employs general life-style items designed to ascertain the patterns of basic constructs that affect a person's activities and perceptual processes. These general statements provide market researchers with the opportunity to analyze an individual's overall perspective on satisfaction with life, family orientation, price vs. quality trade-offs, levels of self-esteem, and religious attitudes (Kotler 1991).

Psychographic research also seeks to measure activities, interests, and opinions that are product related. Specifically, it may request information on attitudes towards a product class, frequency of use of a product or service, media in which information is sought, and so on (Kotler 1991).

In the past five years, consulting firms specializing in travel behavior have launched major efforts to initiate and utilize psychographic and attitudinal approaches to understanding the motor vehicle tourist. Consulting firms enhance effectiveness of their primary data collection by linking their survey data to other demographic and psychographic data bases like PRIZM and VALS to supplement their own research. VALS classifies people into nine categories, based on the idea that, as people pass through developmental stages, their needs and attitudes change. PRIZM uses zip code areas and classifies people into 40 picturesque clusters, like "money and brains" and "shotguns and pickups" (Kotler 1991; Moore 1985).

While using these data bases helps to solve the problem of obtaining psychographic information, some researchers claim they are of limited use in automobile tourism. Many of those researchers claim the information they provide is not easily adaptable to the automobile tourist and inadequate to accurately determine psychographics and develop market segments (Mason 1992).

In conclusion, a richer understanding of the motor vehicle tourist is likely to result only when public-sector agencies at the federal, state, and local levels, as well as nonprofit and private-sector data bases, reflect a universe that more closely resembles the motor vehicle tourist and when researchers devote more attention to psychographic and attitudinal factors. Focusing on the correct universes in psychographic and attitudinal analyses will tell researchers more about who is the personal motor vehicle tourist. But, more importantly, proper focus will also enable researchers and users to more effectively target marketing resources.

WHAT ARE THE MAJOR MARKET SEGMENTS AMONG PERSONAL MOTOR VEHICLE TOURISTS?

Federal, national, and private-sector studies have provided an excellent working knowledge of personal motor vehicle travelers from an overall perspective. But, there is limited public knowledge regarding the various segments of motor vehicle tourists. Federal and state studies have made some progress in developing segmentation among motor vehicle tourists. Consulting firms specializing in this area, such as D.K. Shifflet and Associates, Ltd., have suggested they are able to perform a detailed segmentation analysis by linking their ongoing surveys to other data bases such as PRIZM and VALS. Limited information exists regarding which product attributes attract various segments; for example, recreational vehicle tourists might find different combinations of destinations, facilities, outdoor activities, and accessory services attractive, depending on their stage in life, marital status, number of children, hobbies, and ways in which they wish to spend their leisure time. Unfortunately, there is little empirical evidence beyond isolated studies to link these segments with product attributes.

This limited market segment information often impinges academic and business community research activities. However, some consulting firms have made their data bases available to academic institutions at reasonable rates; hence, academics may develop hypotheses using these data bases for subsequent use in field or laboratory settings. In the past five years, the business community has also enjoyed increasing access to data bases related to automobile tourism.

Besides limitations in the depth of secondary knowledge about market segments, business analysts will also find that using such information is somewhat awkward. In linking market segments to bundles of product attributes, for example, an analyst would be forced to use a "top-down" and "bottom-up" approach. He or she would descend through macrolevel data in an attempt to identify specific gaps in the information base as they relate to the research objective. At the same time, the analyst would have to piece together information on a segment or segments from several isolated and unrelated studies of microissues.

In the past few years, private-sector consulting firms dealing with tourism-related issues have made substantial progress in this area. These firms have the ability to link market segments with other demographic and psychographic data bases. But it is not clear whether they have the capability to further link the data bases to assessment of product attributes. Consequently, much of the awkwardness and legwork that market analysts traditionally faced is somewhat reduced. Undoubtedly, the inroads made by consulting firms have reduced the awkwardness of the research approach and the overall cost of identifying market segments in this area.

The development of this market opportunity for consulting firms is the direct result of federal government practice. Upon entering office, the Reagan administration announced its dramatic curtailment of data collection activities by government agencies in a number of areas, including tourism and tourism-related areas. Their argument was that the cost of data collection should be shifted to those who benefit. The impact of this philosophy was to limit the availability of data to the business and academic communities, as well as to government users. Of course, the availability of data not only benefited those who were willing to pay (businesses and academics undertaking consulting projects for private firms), but also those who could not necessarily pay but benefited from their availability (federal and state government users).

Unfortunately, the cost-shifting argument completely ignored two important facts. First, the ability of states to attract tourists often generated funds that reduced the level of federal assistance needed for such programs as employment training for the unskilled. Second, private-sector, university and state researchers may have not only lacked the capability, but also the statutory authority to collect or analyze data highly beneficial in understanding automobile tourism flows.

Clearly, at least for those who were willing to pay a high enough price, certain data was available on a project-by-project basis. Private consulting firms seem to have stepped into some of the gaps in federal data. For essentially the highest bidders, they are able to provide segmentation data on which decisions could be made for specific areas.

PLANNING AND DECISION MAKING

The first two potential research areas discussed in the preceding sections basically entailed an extension of existing research activities. A third area for future research involves how the automobile tourist goes about planning and making decisions about his or her trips. Existing data and knowledge on this subject, at least in terms of publicly available studies, are somewhat limited. Knowledge has been dependent upon specific tourism studies and general principles based on consumer behavior models developed by marketing theorists. While such studies have become more common recently, they are still somewhat limited. They seem to be either overbroad or too narrow to be useful. In short, knowledge is limited about how individuals go about planning their automobile tourism trips, outside of specific proprietary studies conducted by private consulting firms.

This lack of information is also partially the result of the minor role played by intermediaries in the planning and decision-making process of motor vehicle travelers. While tourists using other modes of transport often consult with a transport company representative or travel agent at some time in the decision-making process, the motor vehicle tourist usually plans his or her trip in private, with little assistance from intermediaries; for example, only 3 percent of all auto travelers consulted a travel agent, compared to 51 percent of all air travelers and 13 percent of all travelers (Cook 1992). This is unfortunate for researchers, because intermediaries often serve as a fertile ground for collecting primary data at reasonable costs.

Intermediaries sometimes used or contacted by personal motor vehicle tourists, which might be tapped by researchers, include state tourism officers, the American Automobile Association, and those conducting roadside surveys. But, such data should be treated with some suspicion, because those patronizing or responding to such intermediaries may prove to be members of self-selecting samples.

One area of focus is the role of family influence. Family influence constitutes an important element of planning and decision making in modern American society. But while the airline industry has made a major effort to understand family interaction and its influence on decisions related to airline trips, there is relatively little information available about the roles family members play in the decision-making process of personal motor vehicle tourists. *Better Homes and Gardens* recently completed a study that focused on how families make travel decisions and how far in advance they plan (Mason 1992). This issue has apparently also been explored by private consulting firms, but that information is not readily available.

Better Homes and Gardens research also indicates that one of the primary reasons for families taking trips is to reduce stress and "get away from it all." They also found that baby boomers prefer to take trips with children more than in

years past, but they have less time to take the trips. Thus, shorter trips are becoming more important (Mason 1992). How the aging of the baby boomers will affect automobile travel patterns is not yet clear (see "Discover America 2000: The Mature Market," U.S. Travel Data Center 1990a).

TIMING OF TRIPS

Knowledge regarding the timing of trips is rather basic and has evolved from federal and selected state data bases and the data bases of national nonprofit travel organizations. However, information on this topic also does exist in the private sector. Federal data suggests that 49 percent of all auto/truck trips of 100 miles or more occurred on weekends. Vacation trips accounted for approximately 50 percent of all trips (U.S. Travel Data Center 1989).

According to federal data bases and a recent *Better Homes and Gardens'* survey, summer months account for the bulk of personal motor vehicle tourism, especially auto trips. Studies indicate more vehicle miles were driven during the summer than any other season. But, more auto trips were taken during the spring. As could be expected, automobile travel was at its lowest point during the winter, both in terms of number and distances of trips (U.S. Travel Data Center 1989; Mason 1992).

Seasonality is still a problem in the area of automobile tourism. Publicly available data bases do not indicate which segments travel most heavily during the summer months, shoulder seasons, and winter periods. *Better Homes and Gardens'* information indicates that travel in the shoulder seasons accounts for 3 to 5 percentage points of that in the summer. Winter lags behind by 10 percentage points.

The key issue is to determine which segments prefer to vacation during seasons of the year other than summer. In many cases, the seasonality of personal motor vehicle tourism is dictated by inflexible job and school vacations. But, there are a tremendous number of market segments that have job-vacation flexibility and are not encumbered with the problem of school vacations. In essence, there is not enough knowledge about the primary factors that motivate these segments to take vacations during seasons other than the traditional summer vacation time. While seasonality segmentation is probably available in many private consulting studies, there is little evidence to suggest which are the important motivational factors.

Another problem for researchers in trip timing is the limited understanding of weekend trips. While much information exists about the purposes of weekend trips, it is difficult to define, for many activities, precise market segments by trip purpose. Market segments associated with sightseeing and visiting friends and relatives, for example, may prove virtually impossible to identify. On the other hand, it is usually possible to identify the market segments that patronize ski resorts on weekend trips. Some consulting firms claim the ability to define these segments, but the consulting firms contacted for this study refused to divulge specific results.

A final research issue in this area is the overall relationship between frequency and timing of trips. Several studies have investigated trip frequency, while other studies have considered trip timing; but few have sought to link the two variables in a comprehensive fashion. Consequently, there is a limited understanding of ways to exploit the trip timing of the frequent personal motor vehicle tourist, who represents the most lucrative market in automobile tourism.

TRIP HABITS

Traditionally, urban transportation planners have checked travel habits through such mechanisms as travel diaries. These mechanisms, combined with origin-destination surveys, enabled them to assess the nature and intent of trip-taking activities within urban areas.

Tourism researchers have used similar types of techniques to monitor travel habits of motor vehicle tourists. The task for these researchers is more difficult, however, because knowing the travel habits of the many diverse segments among personal motor vehicle tourists is so important.

From the perspective of expenditures, it is possible to identify how the motor vehicle traveler votes with his or her pocketbook for food and lodging. This technique, however, often fails to address several key issues. First, such studies, while they often include demographic profiles, frequently fail to develop a psychographic profile. Consequently, there is often an ill-defined linkage between trip habits and market segments. Second, while there is a good understanding of how the personal motor vehicle tourist spends his funds, there is little information regarding why the tourist decides to patronize particular types of food and lodging establishments. This issue is largely unaddressed in publicly available studies.

While at first glance this research issue may seem to be private sector in orientation, it also seems to have implications for the public sector. It seems to be important to federal planners charged with the responsibility of assessing the magnitude and types of facility needs on public lands, for example. It is also considerably important to state officials seeking to create incentives for constructing tourist superstructures, that is, hotels and restaurants. When capital is properly allocated, such investments will maximize spending from tourists in the state and, hence, tax revenues from tourism.

THE INTERNATIONAL ARENA

The interrelationship between personal transportation modes and tourism is receiving varying degrees of attention from various countries around the world. While most nations recognize the potential of tourism to generate export income, they are aware that, in the vast majority of cases, personal motor vehicle tourism contributes a relatively small proportion of tourism exports. From an individual nation's perspective, its stage of industrial, economic and road-infrastructure devel-

opment, and population density to a large extent determine the contribution to the nation's gross national product (GNP) made by tourism from the personal transportation modes. Needless to say, only nations with a substantial contribution may justify undertaking such research.

Interestingly, the importance of tourism generated by the personal transportation modes is also determined by qualitative factors. Worldwide traveling habits, for example, differ significantly from those in the United States. In no other country but the United States has the personal automobile achieved such a paramount societal, economic, and even cultural role. In addition, other nations with different population densities possess adequate transportation alternatives, which may affect the appeal of personal transportation modes for tourism. In France, for example, most employers and the government substantially subsidize vacation-travel costs, provided the elected transportation mode is the nationalized railroad.

These criteria limit the importance of personal motor vehicle tourism to a small number of advanced industrialized countries. These include the United States, Canada, certain Western European nations, and countries bordering such nations (e.g., Mexico). Likewise, personal motor vehicle tourism is also important to such international organizations as the OECD and the United Nations.

CANADA AND MEXICO

Canadian research in personal motor vehicle tourism offers some interesting similarities and contrasts with U.S. research. The most important federal Canadian effort is Statistics Canada. It provides, on a quarterly basis, statistics on personal motor vehicle tourism and various economic activities, including the number of U.S. visitors. Many of these statistics resemble those collected by the U.S. Census of Transportation and parallel U.S. Federal Highway Administration efforts in scope and content.

At the provincial level, research activities are varied and seem more numerous than those at the U.S. state level. All provinces seem to undertake some form of personal transportation research. Recently, Alberta completed a province-wide study on tourism in general, including automobiles. Generally, the research includes:

1. Origin-destination studies
2. Studies regarding levels and types of tourist spending within each province
3. Inventories of tourism resources
4. Evaluations of the psychographic profile of the automobile traveler (in some limited cases)

A major orientation of this research at both the federal and provincial level is analyzing U.S. traffic into Canada. Clearly, these tourist flows represent a sizable amount of export income.

For Mexico, the emphasis on U.S. traffic flows is accentuated. This is primarily because the economic impact of domestic personal transportation mode tourism is negligible, and export income (especially in U.S. dollars) has become a principal concern.

The history of Mexican personal transportation tourism research is short. In the past few years, Banamex and Confederacion Panamericana have begun to research this area in Mexico (Goeldner 1992); but the extent and content of these studies is not clear.

From a true international perspective, several organizations research the personal transportation modes in general and personal motor vehicle tourism in particular. Although the OECD does not undertake any tourism research, it does publish economic reports that include specific tourism statistics. Results of extraordinary research or experts' opinions regarding tourism are also frequently published. And while the United Nations and the World Bank have pursued some research in tourism-related areas, the bulk of their activities has little to do with personal motor vehicle tourism.

Certain key conclusions and issues arise from this rather cursory analysis of the international arena. First, research issues surrounding motor vehicle tourism primarily apply to a small handful of countries in North America and Europe. Unfortunately, the magnitude of tourism generated by the personal motor vehicle modes seems to be much larger in North America than in Europe. This is probably because the former has a limited alternative transportation infrastructure, for example, a well-developed train system.

Second, Mexico's and Canada's primary concern is with the impact of traffic flows from the United States because those interborder flows produce the bulk of tourism expenditures. As a consequence, the major challenges facing those two countries are to determine the precise impacts of domestic versus international motor vehicle tourism and to develop mechanisms to attract more tourists from the United States

In essence, the key international issue—attraction of more motor vehicle tourists—is not unlike the issue faced by various states, municipalities, and attractions within the United States itself.

INSTITUTIONAL FUNDING ISSUES

The majority of data collection and research activities in the area of personal motor vehicle tourism in the United States is undertaken by the Bureau of the Census, the Federal Highway Administration, the U.S. Travel and Tourism Administration, and the U.S. Travel Data Center.

The Census Bureau probably gathers the most data in the federal government. In particular, the National Travel Survey of the Census of Transportation provides information on the volume and characteristics of nonlocal auto/truck travel. Although the National Travel Survey may be relevant only as a source of macro-secondary data, it is essential because it provides comprehensive and timely data regarding the interrelationship between personal motor vehicle tourism and levels of economic activity.

The U.S. Travel and Tourism Administration (formerly the U.S. Travel Service) was a joint sponsor of the 1977 National Travel Survey. It provided each state with NTS

highlights for its jurisdiction but consisted only of a re-tabulation of existing data (U.S. Travel Service 1979). Because of funding cutbacks, that survey was not repeated until 1990.

The Federal Highway Administration's Nationwide Personal Transportation Study was a series of reports covering questions administered by the Bureau of the Census as part of the National Travel Program.

The U.S. Travel Data Center is an important, national, nonprofit organization conducting tourism research in a wide variety of areas, including motor vehicle tourism. It publishes numerous research studies particularly relevant to personal motor vehicle tourism. Some pertinent U.S. Travel Data Center reports are specified in the Appendix. The U.S. Travel Data Center also performs customized research services for members and nonmembers, for a fee. These services range from a travel economic impact model for local or state entities to access to the U.S. Travel Data Bank, which can provide a sound source of secondary data.

Unfortunately, the Reagan and Bush administrations radically changed the role of the actors in this equation. The objective of budget-cutting at the Bureau of the Census was to shift the cost of data collection to the private sector and data users themselves. But these cutbacks have led to the cancellation or postponement of critical data-gathering activities, including the National Travel Survey and the Nationwide Personal Transportation Study. The U.S. Travel Data Center tried to bridge this research gap with the Annual National Travel Survey; and, while the survey provides solid groundwork, there is no doubt that a more extensive basic data base would be helpful.

Other consulting firms have emerged to also assist with the development of critical information on travel in general and the automobile tourist in specific. D.K. Shifflet, for example, has developed a traveler data base known as DIRECTIONS, which surveys 30,000 households on a monthly basis. Substantial information is available in this data base, which was launched in 1986 and expanded in 1990.

LACK OF OVERALL RESEARCH POLICIES AND DIRECTION AT THE INTERNATIONAL, FEDERAL, STATE, AND LOCAL LEVELS

The lack of overall research policies and direction at the international, federal, state, and local levels can be attributed to the unique nature of personal transport. Privately owned vehicles are usually operated on publicly financed and provided rights-of-way (e.g., interstate highways in the United States). The actual routing of these vehicles is a function of individual decision.

The nature of the individual decision-making process has, to some extent, precluded private-sector firms from funding more research, although some firms engaged in activities that benefit from personal transportation, such as hotels, have attempted to estimate the interrelationship between their businesses and motor vehicle tourism. Nonetheless, public-sector entities have provided the majority of research funding for such activities.

Public-sector agencies need to understand the effects of motor vehicle tourism expenditures to ascertain the economic contribution of this form of tourism. But the wide geographic scope of motor vehicle tourism has prompted research activities by a multitude of nonprofit and public-sector agencies operating at various federal, state, and local levels.

Simply stated, the involvement of these nonprofit and public-sector organizations has created a fundamental research problem in analyzing the current knowledge and future direction for personal motor vehicle tourism research: a lack of coordination among research agencies. There is simply no master plan for research in the field, nor is there a functioning and active central coordinating agency or organization.

Research activities by federal agencies and national organizations have suffered from several policy and directional weaknesses. Federal agencies such as the Bureau of the Census and the Federal Highway Administration, for example, have primarily sought to develop data bases, some of which describe different characteristics of motor vehicle travelers and the utilization of their vehicles. However, there has been no consistent or comprehensive effort to analyze the implications of the data. In addition, federal agencies have failed to initiate research programs designed to expand knowledge of the interrelationships between personal motor vehicles and tourism.

According to the 1987–1988 *Survey of State Travel Offices* published by the U.S. Travel Data Center in 1989, most states are involved in monitoring traffic flows to and through their states. A significant number of them use traffic counts to determine attendance at public and private facilities. Many also monitor length of stay in the state, travel industry sales and receipts, levels of tourism expenditures, hotel occupancy, and travel-generated tax revenues and employment.

The parameters most often established in state surveys are demographic and parallel federal agency statistics in orientation. Nonetheless, these data, as they are published, form only a rudimentary basis for states to use as a tourism/travel marketing tool.

The gap in federal information pertaining to micro-origin-destination studies is partially filled by state research efforts. These market research studies are most often broken down by mode of transportation and, within the area of motor vehicle tourism, compile information such as trip and traveler characteristics, length of stay, and hotel facilities used. The research entities most often used by states for such studies are the U.S. Travel Data Center, consulting firms, and universities.

One criticism of most federal and state research is that it has generally overlooked the local level. This proved to be a serious flaw for local entities when ascertaining the true nature of the personal motor vehicle tourist. In the late 1980s, dwindling tax revenues forced many large states like California to substantially decrease, or cut altogether, automobile tourism studies. California abandoned a decentralized tourism promotion/research system that provided local political entities with study models to use when conducting

their own research. The consequences of the cutbacks so crippled the California research effort that substantial funds were recently appropriated for research at the state and local level.

This brief description of the research activities at the federal, national, state, and local levels serves to highlight the nature of the organizational problems affecting the relationships between such entities. There is no overall policy direction or guidance mechanism, for example, to provide a target at which these entities can aim. This is true in major activity areas such as economic research and/or psychographic data-base development. Hence, it is fair to say that there is little overall direction and coordination in personal motor vehicle tourism research conducted by either the public or private sector in the United States today.

To a large extent, the federal government must bear the burden of blame for this problem. It has the capability to initiate policies to guide research activities by both the public and private sectors. The most promising federal initiative that may affect automobile tourism research is the Intermodal Surface Transportation Efficiency Act of 1991, which mandates more extensive and organized collection of transportation-related statistics.

Organizational problems also plague the relationship between the public and private sectors in this area of research. The private sector has traditionally regarded research material as proprietary in nature. As a consequence, consulting firm clients are the prime beneficiary of both the findings and conclusions of the research and the methodological developments of the study.

Government has offered little incentive or assistance to ensure that nonproprietary or marginally proprietary research is circulated to academic, state government, or business community researchers. With encouragement and reimbursement, private industry might be willing to release parts of internal research documents to such researchers. Without such moral support and financial incentive, such sharing of information is highly unlikely.

Of course, there are other solutions to the organizational problems between the public and private sectors: Government is often aware of business-entity studies of specific personal motor vehicle tourism research areas. These areas, in many cases, also happen to hold high priority for state and federal researchers. Instead of bemoaning the fact that the private sector will not share the results, government agencies could share the costs with the private sector to facilitate the release and dissemination of selected research results. Both parties would share in the research results and enjoy lower costs.

CONCLUSION

There are a variety of research and institutional problems with tourism-related research in the personal transportation modes in general and personal motor vehicle tourism in particular.

One of the key research questions is "Who is the motor

vehicle tourist?" While there is some rudimentary knowledge about the automobile traveler, there is only limited knowledge about the motor vehicle tourist. But, in the past few years, some progress on this issue has been made by private-sector consulting firms. Identifying the automobile tourist is likely to occur only when federal and state research efforts are expanded beyond their traditional data-collection emphasis to include developing psychographic profiles for various market segments.

Another issue is the need to develop information and data bases regarding market segments of the personal motor vehicle tourist. Considerable progress has been made in this area.

The research areas of planning and decision making are extremely difficult topics because so little is known about them. The general lack of information is at least partially the result of the limited role intermediaries play in assisting the personal motor vehicle tourist in planning trips.

The timing of personal motor vehicle tourist trips is an important issue because the tourism superstructure must supply adequate capacity at the times tourists demand service. Federal data bases suggest that a great number of trips occur on weekends and during the summer months. But the key research issue here involves determining why individuals who can exercise great discretion in the timing of tourist trips choose off-peak times.

While there is at least some knowledge of when and how the personal motor vehicle tourist spends his or her money when traveling, there is little information in publicly available research regarding why he or she decides to patronize particular types of food and lodging establishments. This issue seems to have importance for both private- and public-sector entities in their planning of facility needs.

Internationally, there is limited interest in personal motor vehicle tourism. Only a handful of countries, such as the United States, Canada, Mexico, and several of the more advanced industrialized countries of Europe, conduct and are interested in such research. The United States and Canada seem to have fairly well-developed programs. But the U.S. program seems to suffer from lack of policy and direction, while the Canadian program devotes substantial attention to border flows.

A number of institutional issues seem to affect the ability of researchers to adequately address the research issues identified. One such issue is limited funding of federal and state data-collection efforts related to automobile tourism. While the U.S. Travel Data Center has sought to bridge some of the gap, its coverage is less comprehensive and more costly for users.

REFERENCES

Asim, Ruth H. (1974), *Purpose of Automobile Trips and Travel*, 1969–70 Nationwide Personal Transportation Study Report No. 10, U.S. Department of Transportation, Washington, D.C.: U.S. Government Printing Office.

Asim, Ruth H. (1982), *Rural vs. Urban Travel*, 1977 Nation-

wide Personal Transportation Study Report No. 8, U.S. Department of Transportation, Washington, D.C.: U.S. Government Printing Office.

Asim, Ruth H., and Paul V. Sverci (1974), *Automobile Ownership*, 1969–70 Nationwide Personal Transportation Study Report No. 11, U.S. Department of Transportation, Washington, D.C.: U.S. Government Printing Office.

Bar-On, Ray (1989), *Travel and Tourism Data, A Comprehensive Research Handbook on the World Travel Industry*, New York: Oryx Press.

Belden Associates (1978), *Identifying Traveler Market Research Methodologies*, Washington, D.C.: U.S. Government Printing Office.

Better Homes and Gardens (1976), *Pleasure/Vacation Travel*, New York: Meredith Corporation Publishing Group.

Better Homes and Gardens (1979), *The Highlights: Comparison of Consumers Opinion on Gas, June 1979 vs. September 1979*, New York: Meredith Corporation Publishing Group.

Bousseloub, Tiffany (1983), Travel Research Director California, Telephone interview 12/21/92.

Bryan, William R. (1981), "Improved Mileage, Discretionary Income and Travel for Pleasure," *Journal of Travel Research*, 20(Summer), 28–29.

Cadez, Gary, and John D. Hund (1978), *A Comparison between Port of Entry Visitor Center Users and Non-users*, Logan, Utah: Institute for Outdoor Recreation and Tourism, Utah State University.

Cook, Suzanne (1992), Executive Director, U.S. Travel Data Center, Telephone interview 8/11/92.

Corsi, Thomas M., and Milton E. Harvey (1979), "Changes in Vacation Travel in Response to Motor Fuel Shortage and Higher Prices," *Journal of Travel Research* (Spring), 7–11.

Curtin, Richard T. (1980), *The RV Consumer*, Chantilly, VA: Recreation Vehicle Industry Association, University of Michigan Survey Research Center.

Energy Research and Development Administration (1977), *Transportation Energy Data Book*, Washington, D.C.: U.S. Government Printing Office.

Erdman, Ron (1992), Market Research Analyst, U.S. Tourism Administration, Telephone interview 7/28/92.

EC Info (February 1981), *European Documentation*, Brussels, Belgium: European Communities Information Commission.

EC Info (November 1982), *European File*, Brussels, Belgium: European Communities Information Commission.

Frechtling, Doug (1992), Visiting Professor, George Washington University, Telephone interview 8/5/92.

Goeldner, C.R. (1992), Director, Travel Reference Center, University of Colorado, Interview 7/17/92.

Goeldner, C.R., and Karen Dicke (1980), *Bibliography and Tourism and Travel Research Studies Reports and Articles*, Boulder, Colorado: University of Colorado and the Travel Research Association.

Goley, Beatrice T., Geraldine Brown, and Elizabeth Samson (1972), *Study of Household Travel Patterns in the U.S.*, 1969–70 Nationwide Personal Transportation Study Report No. 7, U.S. Department of Transportation, Washington, D.C.: U.S. Government Printing Office.

Hartung, Melita (1983), Research Staff AAA, Telephone interview 3/2/83.

Hebert, Richard (1992), Managing Director, Public Affairs, AAA, Washington, D.C., Telephone interview 8/12/92.

United States Intermodal Surface Transportation Efficiency Act of 1990.

Kotler, Philip (1991), *Marketing Management: Analysis, Planning, Implementation, and Control*, Englewood Cliffs, NJ: Prentice-Hall.

Kuzmyak, Richard J. (1980a), *Characteristics of Licensed Drivers and Their Travel*, 1977 Nationwide Personal Transportation Study Report No. 1, U.S. Department of Transportation, Washington, D.C.: U.S. Government Printing Office.

Kuzmyak, Richard J. (1980b), *Purposes of Vehicle Trips and Travel*, 1977 Nationwide Personal Transportation Study Report No. 2, U.S. Department of Transportation, Washington, D.C.: U.S. Government Printing Office.

Kuzmyak, Richard J. (1981a), *Household Vehicle Utilization*, 1969–70 Nationwide Personal Transportation Study Report No. 5, U.S. Department of Transportation, Washington, D.C.: U.S. Government Printing Office.

Kuzmyak, Richard J. (1981b), *Vehicle Occupancy*, 1977 Nationwide Personal Transportation Study Report No. 6, U.S. Department of Transportation, Washington, D.C.: U.S. Government Printing Office.

Mason, Peter (1992), *Better Homes and Gardens*, New York, Telephone interview 8/28/92.

Mina, Nancy (1985), U.S. Travel Data Center, Telephone interview 4/29/85.

Moore, Thomas (1985), "Different Strokes, Different Folks," *Fortune*, September 16, 1985.

OECD (1981), *Tourism Policy and International Tourism in OECD Member Countries*, Paris, France: OCDE/OECD.

OECD (June 1982), *The Future of the Use of the Car*, ECMT Roundtable 55, 56, 57. Paris, France: OCDE/OECD.

Randill, Alice, Helen Greenhalgh, and Elizabeth Samson (1973), *Modes of Transportation and Personal Characteristics of Tripmakers*, 1969–70 Nationwide Personal Transportation Study Report No. 9, U.S. Department of Transportation, Washington, D.C.: U.S. Government Printing Office.

Roskin, Mark E. (1980), *Purposes of Vehicle Trips and Travel*, 1977 Nationwide Personal Transportation Study Report No. 3, U.S. Department of Transportation, Washington, D.C.: U.S. Government Printing Office.

Siegel, Bill (1992), Longwoods International, Toronto, Canada, Telephone interview 8/14/92.

Skidmore, Sereta (1992), Menlo Consultants, Telephone interview 8/11/92.

Stevens, Blair (1992), Director General, Research, Tourism Canada, Ottawa, Ontario, Telephone interview 8/4/92.

Strate, Harry E. (1972a), *Automobile Occupancy*, 1969–70 Nationwide Personal Transportation Study Report No. 1, U.S. Department of Transportation, Washington, D.C.: U.S. Government Printing Office.

Strate, Harry E. (1972b), *Annual Miles of Auto Trips and Travel*, 1960–70 Nationwide Personal Transportation Study Report No. 2, U.S. Department of Transportation, Washington, D.C.: U.S. Government Printing Office.

Strate, Harry E. (1972c), *Seasonal Variations of Automobile Trips and Travel*, 1969–70 Nationwide Personal Transportation Study Report No. 3, U.S. Department of Transportation, Washington, D.C.: U.S. Government Printing Office.

Transportation Research Board (1992), *Data For Decisions: Requirements for National Transportation Policy Making*, Washington, D.C.: Transportation Research Board.

U.S. Bureau of the Census (1979), *1977 Census of Transportation, National Travel Survey, Travel During 1977*, Washington, D.C.: U.S. Government Printing Office.

U.S. Bureau of Outdoor Recreation (1973), *Outdoor Recreation—A Legacy for America*, U.S. Department of the Interior, Washington, D.C.: U.S. Government Printing Office.

U.S. Travel Data Center (1977), *1977 Travel Outlook Forum Proceedings*, 86–90, Address by James J. Gibson, Marketing Director, 3M National Advertising Company, Washington, D.C.: U.S. Travel Data Center.

U.S. Travel Data Center (1978a), *Travel Data Locator Index*, 2nd ed., Washington, D.C.: U.S. Travel Data Center.

U.S. Travel Data Center (1978b), *1977 National Travel Expenditure Study*, Washington, D.C.: U.S. Travel Data Center.

U.S. Travel Data Center (1978c), *1978 Travel Outlook Forum Proceedings*, 93–102, Address by James A. Imwold, Marketing Operations Manager, 3M National Advertising Company, Washington, D.C.: U.S. Travel Data Center.

U.S. Travel Data Center (1979), *1979 Travel Outlook Forum Proceedings*, 93–101, Address by Robert C. Olney, Vice President and General Manager, 3M National Advertising Company, Washington, D.C.: U.S. Travel Data Center.

U.S. Travel Data Center (1980a), *1979–80 Quarterly Travel Trends*, Washington, D.C.: U.S. Travel Data Center.

U.S. Travel Data Center (1980b), *1980 Economic Report of Travel in America*, Washington, D.C.: U.S. Travel Data Center.

U.S. Travel Data Center (1980c), *1979 National Travel Expenditure Study*, Washington, D.C.: U.S. Travel Data Center.

U.S. Travel Data Center (1980d), *1979 National Travel Barometer Quarterly*, Washington, D.C.: U.S. Travel Data Center.

U.S. Travel Data Center (1980e), *The 1979 Gasoline Shortage: Lessons for the Travel Industry*, Washington, D.C.: U.S. Travel Data Center.

U.S. Travel Data Center (1980f), *1980 Travel Outlook Forum Proceedings*, 83–91, Address by Gregg P. Ganschaw, National Manager of Publications, Marketing & Travel Market Research, 3M National Advertising Company, Washington, D.C.: U.S. Travel Data Center.

U.S. Travel Data Center (1981a), *1980 National Travel Survey: Full Year Report*, Washington, D.C.: U.S. Travel Data Center.

U.S. Travel Data Center (1981b), *1981–82 Survey of State Travel Offices*, Washington, D.C.: U.S. Travel Data Center.

U.S. Travel Data Center (1981c), *1981 Travel Outlook Forum Proceedings*, 95–105, Address by Gregg Ganschaw, Director of Marketing, Color Arts, Inc., Washington, D.C.: U.S. Travel Data Center.

U.S. Travel Data Center (1982a), *1982 Outlook for Travel and Tourism*, 97–105, Address by Gregg Ganschaw, Vice President of Marketing, Color Arts, Inc., Washington, D.C.: U.S. Travel Data Center.

U.S. Travel Data Center (1982b), *1981–82 Economic Report on Travel in America*, Washington, D.C.: U.S. Travel Data Center.

U.S. Travel Data Center (1982c), *1982 Travel Outlook for Travel and Tourism*, Address by Barbara Wickliffe, Director, Best Western International Advertising Division, Washington, D.C.: U.S. Travel Data Center.

U.S. Travel Data Center (1983a), *Monthly Travel Printout*, Washington, D.C.: U.S. Travel Data Center.

U.S. Travel Data Center (1983b), *Monthly Travel Price Index*, Washington, D.C.: U.S. Travel Data Center.

U.S. Travel Data Center (1983c), *The Economic Review of Travel in America*, Washington, D.C.: U.S. Travel Data Center.

U.S. Travel Data Center (1984), *1983 Full Year Report: National Travel Survey*, Washington, D.C.: U.S. Travel Data Center.

U.S. Travel Data Center (1986), *1985 Full Year Report: National Travel Survey*, Washington, D.C.: U.S. Travel Data Center.

U.S. Travel Data Center (1989), *Survey of State Travel Offices 1987–1988*, Washington, D.C.: U.S. Travel Data Center.

U.S. Travel Data Center (1990a), *Discover America 2000: The Mature Market*, Washington, D.C.: Travel Industry Association of America.

U.S. Travel Data Center (1990b), *1989 Travel Market Close-Up: National Travel Survey Tabulations*, Washington, D.C.: U.S. Travel Data Center.

U.S. Travel Data Center (1990c), *The 1989–90 Economic Review of Travel In America*, Washington, D.C.: U.S. Travel Data Center.

U.S. Travel Data Center (1990d), *1989 Travel Executive Briefing*, Washington, D.C.: U.S. Travel Data Center.

U.S. Travel Data Center (1990e), *Weekend Travel: America's Growing Trend*, Washington, D.C.: U.S. Travel Data Center.

U.S. Travel Data Center (1991a), *Impact of Travel on State Economies 1989*, Washington, D.C.: U.S. Travel Data Center.

U.S. Travel Data Center (1991b), *1992 Outlook for Travel and Tourism*, Washington, D.C.: U.S. Travel Data Center.

U.S. Travel Service (1977), *Analysis of Travel Definitions, Terminology and Research Needs among States and Cities*, Washington, D.C.: U.S. Travel Service.

U.S. Travel Service (1979), *1977 National Travel Survey Highlights for Each State*, Washington, D.C.: U.S. Travel Service.

Wassenaar, Dirk J. (1981), *California Visitor Impact Model*, Sacramento, CA: California Office of Tourism Department of Economics and Business Development, San Jose State University.

Waters, Somerset R. (1991), *The Big Picture*, New York: Child & Waters.

Weil, Susan (1992), U.S. Travel Data Center, Telephone interview 8/5/92.

Westfall, Ralph (1962), "Psychological Factors in Predicting Product Choice," *Journal of Marketing*, April 1962.

Wickliffe, Barbara (1983), Director Market & Research Advertising Division, Best Western International Hotels, Telephone interview 3/1/83.

Worby, Tim (1983), VP Market Research, Hertz Rent-A-Car, Telephone interview, 3/22/83.

World Bank (annual), *Urban Transport*, Sector Policy Paper, Washington, D.C.: World Bank Publications.

Zimmerman, Carol (1981), *A Life Cycle of Travel by the American Family*, 1969–70 Nationwide Personal Transportation Study Report No. 7, U.S. Department of Transportation, Washington, D.C.: U.S. Government Printing Office.

3M National Advertising Company (1970a), *Greater Nags Head*

Chamber of Commerce Visitors Study, Argo, IL: 3M National Advertising Company.

3M National Advertising Company (1970b), *Impulse Travel Changing Trends in Auto Vacation Travel*, Argo, IL: 3M National Advertising Company.

3M National Advertising Company (1972), *Psychographics of the Auto Traveler*, Argo, IL: 3M National Advertising Company.

28

Research Needs in the Intercity Bus and Rail Transportation Industry

STUART N. ROBINSON[1]

Stuart N. Robinson and Associates, Inc.
Dallas, Texas

This chapter describes the travel information needs of managers in rail and bus companies. It explains the responsibilities for selected managers within the corporation, and it specifies what information they need. Special emphasis is given to the unique aspects of marketing within the limitations of federal and state regulations.

The needs of five managers are discussed. The Vice-President of Passenger Marketing needs information that will help price tickets and travel services, develop and evaluate marketing promotions, and forecast passenger miles, passenger revenues, and profits. The Vice-President of Advertising needs research support for testing advertising copy, developing media plans, and tracking advertising. The Marketing Controller needs help in evaluating the costs-benefits of marketing programs. The information requirements of the Vice-President of Passenger Service focus on receiving ratings of passenger service on a timely basis, and the Vice-President of Traffic and Operations needs to be kept appraised of changes in preferred origins and destinations.

Marketing intercity rail and bus travel is different from marketing other types of transportation and travel for two reasons. First, this industry is regulated by the government, and second, both the rail and bus market are dominated by one major competitor. This chapter describes how these influences determine the research needs in this industry and defines the functions of the market research staff in a transportation company. This chapter also predominately addresses the intercity bus industry since it operates in a more competitive market than intercity rail. Most everything described about the bus market, however, is relevant, if not directly parallel, to the rail market except when noted otherwise.

REGULATION

The intercity bus industry is regulated by the Interstate Commerce Commission (ICC) and by various state regulatory agencies. Under these authorities, the ICC must approve all fare increases and decreases before they are implemented. This prevents bus companies from making unfair profits by taking advantage of the public need for transportation. In so doing, it establishes transportation as a public right. This regulatory procedure, however, also makes it possible for all transportation companies to discover when a bus company plans to increase or decrease its fares before those fares go into effect. It would be like Macy's calling Gimbel's on Tuesday and saying, "Hey, on Saturday we're selling men's suits for $50." Well, come Saturday, Gimbel's will surely have a $49 suit sale. Needless to say, this makes developing pricing strategies for bus companies a challenge.

Another form of control under government regulation is route authority. Under government regulation, a bus company has to be granted authority to provide service between two cities. This forces bus companies to satisfy public needs first, before they expand into routes for the sole purpose of

[1]The author would like to acknowledge the efforts of Mr. Terry L. Case and Miss Karyn Heemann in the preparation of this manuscript, which could not have been completed without their help.

increasing profits. One may ask, if the industry is so regulated, why is it that some routes are served by only one company? If a service already exists between two cities, a bus company must first demonstrate that there is a need for additional service before it can be granted authority. Meanwhile, the company already providing the service will attempt to demonstrate that there is no need for additional service. This usually leads to lengthy and expensive litigation, which is prohibitive for most small companies. As a result, a large number of communities are served by only one major bus company. This limitation makes developing service strategies and route analysis for bus companies even more challenging than establishing fares.

COMPETITION

People are rarely surprised to find out that one company has dominated the intercity bus industry for over 40 years. That company is named Greyhound. However, people are usually astonished when they find out that Greyhound's share of class I, regular route, intercity passenger miles and passenger operating revenues is over 60 percent (American Bus Association 1978). Even under classical airline regulation, four or five trunk airlines together had a national market share about what Greyhound alone holds in the bus industry today. United Airlines was the largest with about 20 percent of the market, yet the #1 transportation company in the United States is handling more passengers than all the largest airlines combined. This overwhelming position held by one company makes market research and marketing for the other bus companies a continuous, uphill struggle and for Greyhound, somewhat unique.

The rail industry is influenced by both regulation and competition in a similar manner. Intercity rail is controlled by government agencies and the market is dominated by one company—Amtrak.

MARKET RESEARCH RESPONSIBILITIES

With a clearer understanding of the rules of the game, the reader has a basis for appreciating the research needs of the intercity bus company. The dynamic nature of the intercity bus market requires all companies to develop marketing plans in an atmosphere of considerable uncertainty, and these plans must be flexible enough to adapt quickly to a constantly changing market. The major responsibility of the corporate market research department, therefore, is to help senior managers develop strategies that can be changed and modified at a moment's notice.

Most of the time, senior managers do not realize they lack the information they need to make a management decision until it is time to make the decision. The market analyst who has a complete understanding of the function and responsibilities of the senior managers he or she supports, eventually learns to anticipate their needs for information quickly and to satisfy their requests completely. This approach is very dif-

ferent from the classical problem-solving mode of providing market information after someone in the company asks a question. To be efficient and cost-effective, the market research department must act, not just react; plan, not just respond.

The following examples will demonstrate this need. Each example will show a senior manager, inside or outside of the marketing department, who needs information and is looking to the market research department to supply it. The senior manager's function and the inherent stresses of the job are briefly described, along with ways a market researcher can provide information that will help the manager complete his or her tasks.

VICE-PRESIDENT OF MARKETING

One of the major responsibilities of the Vice-President of Marketing is to develop a pricing strategy. He or she usually asks the market research staff to develop a price/volume curve. The curve will usually look something like the one shown in Figure 1, which shows travel volume decreasing as ticket prices increase. This curve, however, is limited because it predicts tendency to purchase under the most simplistic and static conditions. It does not consider competitive pricing; it does not consider changes in the economy; and it does not consider changes in consumer motivation that are not related to price. Worse yet, however, is that no one seems to care. Most senior managers have learned to accept these deficiencies especially when they need the information right away. This complacency is also the result of market researchers, who find these curves easier to present to naive managers than something more complicated and harder to explain or sell.

The demands of planning in a regulated market require a price/volume curve that incorporates market dynamics, like the graph in Figure 2. It not only shows how volume varies

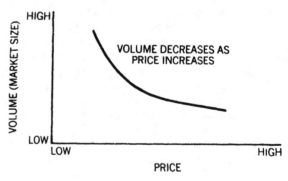

Weaknesses	Does Not Consider
Simplistic	Competitive Pricing
	Complexities of Buying Decision
Static	Shifts in Economy
	Changes in Consumer Motivation

FIGURE 1   V.P. marketing price/volume curve. *Source:* Stuart N. Robinson and Associates, Inc., 1980.

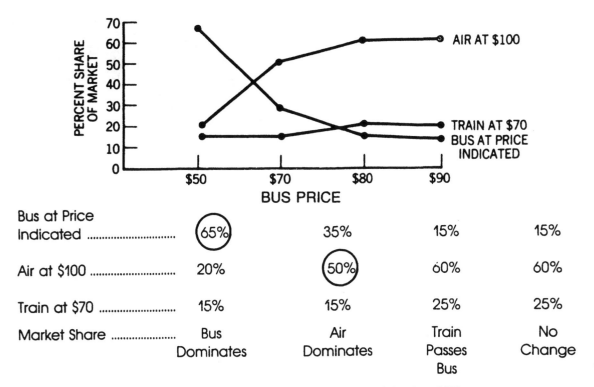

Bus at Price				
Indicated	(65%)	35%	15%	15%
Air at $100	20%	(50%)	60%	60%
Train at $70	15%	15%	25%	25%
Market Share	Bus Dominates	Air Dominates	Train Passes Bus	No Change

FIGURE 2   Dynamic price/volume curve. *Source:* Stuart N. Robinson and Associates, Inc., 1980.

with price, but also predicts how this price/volume relationship is affected by competitive pricing. It describes the relationship between fares for air, bus, and train between two cities. The air fare stays constant at $100 and the train fare stays constant at $70; but the bus fare is allowed to vary from $50 to $90. The graph shows that at $50 the bus can capture 65% of the market, but at $90 loses substantial market share to airlines and at $80 loses market share to trains. Other price/volume relationships can be estimated considering the effects of various external influences like the price of gasoline or the rate of inflation.

The methodology to generate these types of price/volume curves most often incorporates conjoint measurement or trade-off analysis procedures, which are described elsewhere in this book. The research project needed to develop these curves requires more time and funds than most. It can easily cost $50,000 per project and require a minimum of three months to complete. The pricing information they generate, however, can be retabulated every time the competitive environment changes.

VICE-PRESIDENT OF ADVERTISING

Most ad directors come up with a new ad campaign at the mere suggestion of a new fare or a change in route structure. They need guidance that will direct and focus their apparent unlimited creativity. They do not need ideas and ad copy, and they will not cooperate or support market research analysts who forget their role as researchers and try to develop ad campaigns.

Ad-tracking studies monitor the effects of advertising on a number of measures. They relay the consumer feedback that provides the guidance an advertising manager needs to continually fine tune his advertising.

Most often, ad-tracking data are collected via telephone interviews and the results are reported in percent of total people interviewed. The percent of people who are aware of the advertising without being prompted is called *unaided ad awareness*; the percent who were aware of the advertising after being prompted is called *aided awareness*. The assumption is that increases in ad awareness reflect increases in advertising effectiveness or the successful communication of advertising messages.

Figure 3 shows how ad awareness of one bus company increased as a result of its advertising campaign. It shows that most increases followed campaigns that were aired on both national and local (spot) television, as opposed to either national or local television. It does not indicate the effects of changing the messages of the advertising or the effects of the competitive advertising. Both are important factors that must also be monitored.

Finally, advertising effectiveness can be evaluated using a number of performance measures. Ad campaigns will often show positive performance on one measure and negative on another. Research managers should report performance on a number of measures and recommend corrective actions on each.

To expect advertising to increase sales *directly* is asking quite a lot. Some people will not see the ads, some will see one or two exposures, but no more. More will not pay

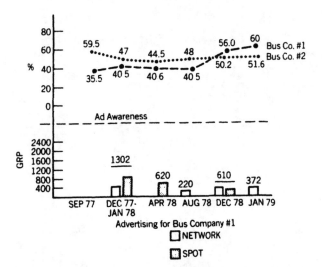

FIGURE 3 Ad awareness total sample. *Source:* Stuart N. Robinson and Associates, Inc., 1980.

attention, even though they see the ad, and even more will not remember what they were. Still more people will not learn the message well enough to recall at a later point in time, and fewer will be prompted to change their minds about service. Finally, even fewer will actually modify their habits and, thereby, increase sales. A complete performance evaluation should track all these measures. Only when each effect is measured over time will it be known what modifications increase sales as well as promote attention or communicate information.

MARKETING CONTROLLER

The Marketing Controller must develop long-range travel forecasts, detailed financial analyses of a competitor's financial status, and regional market analyses to help determine

priorities with regard to market expansion. By far, the most critical information that a researcher can provide a marketing controller is that which will help to perform a costs-benefits analysis of marketing promotions. The main difficulty in performing a costs-benefits analysis is that, in most instances, the benefits cannot be clearly identified. Market research must operationally define and measure the individual items identified under the "benefits" column so the market controller can assign a cost to each.

Costs-benefits analyses also require teamwork. Here, management techniques that promote cooperation and cooperative task orientation are very useful. Many of these can be found in management texts (Drucker 1974) as well as in various industrial psychology and social-organizational psychology textbooks (Siegel 1969 and Whyte 1969).

VICE-PRESIDENT OF TRAFFIC OPERATIONS

Traffic managers make sure that the buses are where the people are when they are needed. Without expertise, there would be utter chaos. The major difficulty in determining the demand and profitability of different routes arises from the complex nature of a transportation system where profit on one route is dependent on volume from another. This means that routes must be considered as a network, not just as independent routes linked together. Figure 4 provides an example of a transportation network analysis. It shows a hypothetical bus line from the small community of Elkin, Maryland, to Wilmington, Delaware, continuing on to Philadelphia, Pennsylvania. On a typical bus run, 10 people ride the full route from Elkin to Philadelphia, 2 ride only the Elkin-Wilmington segment, and 20 ride the Wilmington-Philadelphia segment. If the route segments are viewed separately, the Elkin-Wilmington segment with just 12 passengers looks unprofitable, while the Wilmington-Philadelphia segment with 30 passengers seems considerably more lucrative. Yet, if the bus company were to drop its Elkin-Wilmington service, it would risk losing the 10 passengers

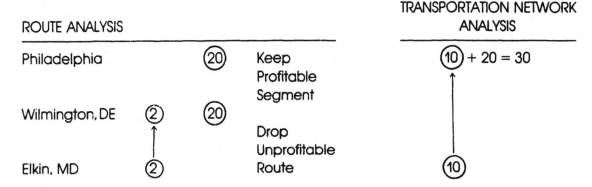

FIGURE 4 Transportation network analysis. *Source:* Stuart N. Robinson and Associates, Inc., 1980.

on the Wilmington-Philadelphia run who embarked in Elkin. Because they would have to find alternative service from Elkin to Wilmington to catch the bus there, these passengers would be inclined to switch modes for the entire trip. The Wilmington-Philadelphia segment would be left with only 20 passengers, which at best would be only marginally profitable.

VICE-PRESIDENT OF PASSENGER SERVICE

The Vice-President of Passenger Service must establish which customer services are most important. He has to satisfy everyone and needs guidance as to who needs what, when, and how. He has a variety of service options readily available, but, without priorities, he can rarely utilize this potential. When inadequately supported by the market research department, he knows too little too late and never has enough people to sell tickets when demand increases.

He is often faced with questions such as, "Should this schedule leave five minutes early to attract 12 more passengers from our competitor's terminal across the street, or should it be held up 12 minutes for thorough cleaning?" "Should we dump the johns at 3:00 in the morning at Bugtussle, Iowa, or schedule a late-and-long dinner stop the night before?" Such priorities can only be made with the benefit of passenger-preference data. But the data alone are not enough. As with the price/volume curves discussed earlier, this preference information must be collected and ana-

lyzed in such a way that it remains a source of information that will be as good tomorrow as it is today. This information should suggest a set of recommendations based on current passenger preferences. However, when the market expands or new fares are introduced, the same passenger responses need to be retabulated in light of the new priorities that address the new marketing environment. It should be kept in mind that the market changes too often to implement new research projects, even if the research funds were available, which they are not.

This situation calls for another trade-off analysis that shows how much one service is specifically desired relative to a set of other services. Each preference is given a specific value and, since these scores are developed on a linear scale, they may be added, combined, or subtracted from each other at will.

Figure 5 shows what services can be compromised with the least effect on passenger satisfaction. It indicates that a manager can make arrivals less convenient if he keeps his buses clean and departures convenient. If this is not possible, then his next best option is to keep his buses clean, arrival times convenient, and make his departures less convenient.

MARKET RESEARCH MANAGEMENT

In each case described above, the solutions presented were always flexible and adaptable to change. Price/volume curves

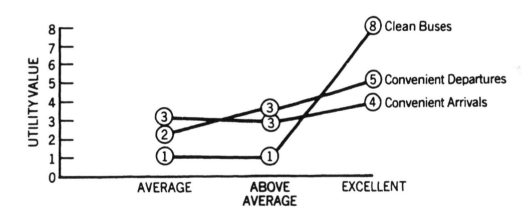

Optimum Service	Clean Buses	Convenient Departures	Convenient Arrivals	
1st Trade-off	Excellent	Excellent	Excellent	
	8 +	5 +	4	= 17
2nd Trade-off	Excellent	Excellent	Above Average	
	8 +	5 +	3	= 16
3rd Trade-off	Excellent	Above Average	Excellent	
	8 +	3 +	4	= 15

FIGURE 5 Service trade-offs. *Source:* Stuart N. Robinson and Associates, Inc., 1980.

considered the changing competitive prices; ad tracking guided and helped course correct advertising; route analyses considered transportation systems as networks; and service strategies considered the changing preferences.

Flexibility is easiest to maintain if a systems approach is used that establishes ongoing, continuous data-collection systems that allow periodic market analysis. More importantly, such systems allow a periodic analysis and can update the information anytime the market dynamics require. Once established, these systems prove to be more cost-effective than research on an as-needed basis.

Table 1 gives some examples of these transportation systems. It indicates that on-board passenger surveys, advertising evaluations, origin-destination studies (ticket studies), and secondary-source literature reviews are the four primary market-information systems.

THE FUTURE

As the deregulation of the intercity bus industry receives more and more attention, the removal of route and price regulation by the Interstate Commerce Commission and by state regulatory agencies becomes inevitable. This will mark the beginning of a whole new ball game. Companies will introduce new fares and establish new routes whenever and wherever they want. The market research department that is most flexible under a regulated market will provide the best support to its company after the industry has been deregulated.

REFERENCES

American Bus Association (1978), America's Number One Passenger Transportation Service, Washington, D.C.

Drucker, Peter F. (1974), Management: Tasks, Responsibilities, Practices, New York: Harper & Row Publishers Inc.

Marketing Support Services (1980), Marketing Research Study, Unpublished in-house report, Dallas, Texas.

Siegel, Laurence (1969), Industrial Psychology, Georgetown, Ontario: Irwin-Dorsey Limited.

Whyte, William Goote (1969), Organizational Behavior-Theory and Applications, Georgetown, Ontario: Irwin-Dorsey Limited.

Table 1   Projects for Transportation Companies and Travel Organizations

1   On-Board Passenger Surveys

Objective— To measure passenger preferences, attitudes, characteristics and travel habits.
  Purpose— Develop and track national marketing, advertising, and media plans on a yearly basis.
Procedure— One to three administrations per year.

2   Ad-Tracking Studies

Objective— Monitor consumer awareness of TV advertising and of corporate image.
  Purpose— Evaluate effectiveness of advertising and advertising agency performance and modify when appropriate.
Procedure— One to five telephone polls a year.

3   Ad Pretesting

Objective— Pretest rough copy of newsprint, magazine, radio, and TV ads.
  Purpose— Modify early versions in order to maximize communication effectiveness.
Procedure— Administered on an as-needed basis.

4   Sales Analysis and Forecasts

Objective— Track and analyze sales on a monthly basis, make yearly sales forecasts, and modify monthly.
  Purpose— Identify or predict weak sales areas or seasons, and recommend marketing strategies to counter them.
Procedure— One to four times a year.

5   Schedule Analysis

Objective— Track and analyze passenger volume on all schedules between all origins and destinations in the system.
  Purpose— Weed out small revenue producers, and provide more transportation to big revenue producers.
Procedure—(Same as with sales analysis).

6   Advertising Analysis

Objective— Evaluate the effects of advertising on sales.
  Purpose— Evaluate and judge the performance of the advertising agency.
Procedure— Costs-benefits analysis weighing ad costs versus sales generated.

TABLE 1 *(continued)*

7   Energy Reports

Objective— Monitor extent and effects of energy crisis and nationwide gasoline shortages.
  Purpose— Modify operations accordingly.
Procedure— Monthly reports.

8   Competitive Reports

Objective— Monitor activities, marketing, financial condition, and advertising of all major competitors.
  Purpose— Alter marketing and promotions to match or better competition.
Procedure— Monthly reports.

9   Market Intelligence Reports

(same as competitive reports but for market/industry information)

10   Public Opinion Polls on Deregulation

Objective— Measure change in opinion after public is informed as to the advantages of deregulating the transportation industry
      through PR.
  Purpose— Support deregulation efforts focused on state legislation.
Procedure— Administered as needed.

11   Site Analysis

Objective— Evaluate pros and cons of alternative sites for new terminals relative to their potential.
  Purpose— Support deregulation efforts focused on state legislation.
Procedure— Adminstered as needed.

12   Special Travel Studies

Objective— To measure changes in travel habits as a result of gasoline shortage, competitive discounts, economy, etc.
  Purpose— Predict extent of sales increases due to gasoline shortages, and recommend modifications to market and advertising
      plans.
Procedure— Monthly reports.

13   Seasonality

Objective— To determine when sales go up consistently and when they go down consistently each year.
  Purpose— Identify trends in sales so that media plans can support both low and high sales periods accordingly.
Procedure— Monthly reports.

14   Market Segmentation Study

Objective— Identify major target market segments.
  Purpose— Develop target marketing plans.
Procedure— Factor analysis, perceptual mapping, and multidimensional scaling of psychographic, behavioral, and attitudinal data.
      Quarterly reports.

15   Promotion Evaluations

Objective— Evaluate effectiveness of promotions to increase sales.
  Purpose— Modify or cancel current marketing promotions.
Procedure— Administered as needed.

16   Secondary-Source Reports

Objective— Compile, evaluate, and report on all available current secondary-source information of the travel or transportation
      industry.
  Purpose— Continuous market information data base.
Procedure— Monthly.

Table 1 *(continued)*

17 Media Planning

Objective— To identify who (passenger characteristics) reads, listens to, or watches which newspapers, magazines, radio stations, or TV shows.

Purpose— Develop media plan.

Procedure— Administered on a quarterly basis.

18 Origin-Destination Reports

Objective— To determine who goes where, when, etc.

Purpose— Modify old routes and establish new routes.

Procedure— Administered on a monthly basis.

19 New Service Concept Evaluations

Objective— Develop new services to customers.

Purpose— Identify needs of passengers not being adequately satisfied, and develop services that provide better satisfaction.

Procedure— Administered on an as-needed basis.

Source: Marketing Support Services, Inc., 1980.

29

Research Needs of the Lodging Industry

STEPHEN J. HIEMSTRA
Professor
Department of Restaurant, Hotel, Institutional,
  and Tourism Management
Purdue University
West Lafayette, Indiana

The purposes of this chapter are threefold: (1) to identify some of the major marketing issues facing the lodging industry that are in need of research, (2) to provide selected research findings as a case study, and (3) to discuss some methodological issues related to conducting marketing research.

Examples will be given of selected research results conducted recently by the author in an effort to analyze some of the current issues of the day. The perspective will be to present research findings not as the definitive resolution of problems addressed, but rather as examples upon which others can build.

Other issues will be identified as researchable questions about which little is known, at least in the published literature. Suggested research approaches sometimes will be given. First, however, selected major trends affecting the industry will be discussed briefly as a way of focusing on relevant research issues.

INTRODUCTION

The lodging industry is a major industry with a wide scope of marketing and related problems, many of them begging for solution. The 1990–1991 recession has shown once again how dependent the industry is on the general level of economic activity in the country. Recently, it has become fashionable for all segments of the industry—even the most luxurious—to discount rooms and to compete on the basis of price. Whether or not this practice makes economic sense depends upon the nature of the price elasticity of market demand that they face. But, unfortunately, there is little published research on the nature of these elasticities.

Another analytical marketing activity that has recently gained in stature has been the adoption of yield management in the determination of room prices. However, the success or failure of yield management also depends on the level and changes in the price elasticity of demand for lodging services over time.

A short time ago, the lodging industry perceived itself facing an employee shortage due to a reduction in birth rates during the 1960s and 1970s. The shortfall in demand during the 1990–1991 recession has allayed these concerns, but they may return when demand accelerates. A contributing problem is the trend of an increasing employees-per-room number and the declining level of labor productivity facing the lodging industry.

Other marketing issues involve: (1) an assessment of the impacts on the industry of room taxes that have been increasing dramatically over most parts of the United States and elsewhere, (2) the nature of market segmentation and the proliferation of products offered, (3) projections of sales to the year 2000 and beyond, (4) the importance of advertising and promotion in stimulating sales, and (5) the impacts on the market of the dramatic changes in structure and organization of the lodging industry, including the increase in franchising and the growing importance of chains in relation to independents and management companies relative to owner management.

TRENDS IN THE LODGING INDUSTRY

NUMBER OF ROOMS

The number of rooms in the lodging industry has increased dramatically during the past decade and continues to increase (Figure 1). In 1991, there were 44 percent more rooms in the industry than 10 years earlier. Between 1982 and 1987, the annual rate of growth was 4 to 5 percent each year. These growth rates slowed considerably late in the decade to the rate of 1.6 percent in 1991.

Much has been written about the reasons for these increases. One important factor has simply been the strong demand for lodging away from home due to the strong economy during much of the 1980s. But other factors included the stimulative financial structures, such as limited partnerships; the wave of leveraged buy-outs and other mergers and acquisitions; and income tax incentives for quick write-offs of depreciation prior to the Tax Reform Act of 1986. Other factors include the desire to reposition assets in growing or more profitable segments of the market, such as all-suites properties and extended-stay facilities.

Regardless of the reasons for the increased size of the industry, its rapid growth reduced occupancy rates and squeezed profits when the economy moved into recession in 1990. That result was not surprising in the sense that the lodging industry is typically quite sensitive to trends in the general economy (Figure 2). In real terms, the lodging industry normally accounts for slightly less than 1.0 percent of the gross national product (GNP) (Gomes 1986). However, the increase in number of rooms exceeded population growth, which typically has shown a stable relationship over time. In properties of more than 25 rooms, the number of rooms per 100 population reached nearly 1.2 in 1990, whereas historically, this relationship has remained quite stable between 0.8 and 1.0 (Figure 3).

NUMBER OF EMPLOYEES

The increasing number of rooms in the industry has resulted in a strong demand for employees. In fact, the number of employees in the industry has been growing more rapidly

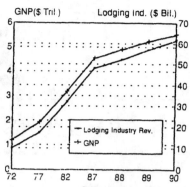

FIGURE 2 Lodging industry and GNP, 1972–1990 (current dollars).

than has the number of rooms over the past two decades, despite vigorous growth of the economy segment of the industry. In properties of more than 125 rooms, the number of employees per room peaked at 0.54 in 1989, compared with only 0.43 in 1970 (Figure 4).

Consequently, the projected shortfall in the labor force threatened to dry up the pool of new entrants into the industry in the 1980s and 1990s. In turn, these concerns resulted in increased wages; a focus on attracting females, handicapped, and older workers; and concern for reducing the large labor turnover (Hiemstra 1987, 1990).

Aside from the upturn in number of rooms in the industry, reasons for the increases in employment included the move toward increasing service levels, but also included a faltering trend in labor productivity. The Index of Labor Productivity, published by the Bureau of Labor Statistics for the lodging industry, in 1990 was down a sharp 5 percent from the previous year and down 16 percent from the peak year of 1984 (Figure 5). In addition, there has been a trend toward a reduced number of hours worked per week, which results in a need for a larger number of employees.

ROOM RATES

Room rates in the lodging industry (CPI, Lodging-while-out-of-Town) over time have increased more rapidly than has the

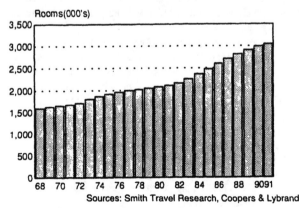

FIGURE 1 Number of rooms in the lodging industry (1,000), 1968–1991.

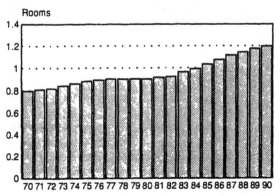

FIGURE 3 Rooms per 100 population, 1970–1990.

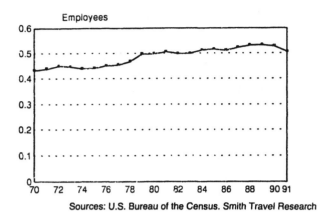

Sources: U.S. Bureau of the Census. Smith Travel Research

FIGURE 4   Employees per room, 1970–1991.

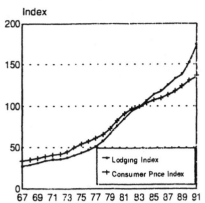

Source: CPI Detailed Report

FIGURE 6   Consumer price index vs. lodging while out of town index, 1967–1991 (1982–1984=100).

overall Consumer Price Index (CPI), based on data from the Bureau of Labor Statistics (BLS) (Figure 6). This trend was particularly strong during the expansion of the 1980s. During the recession of 1990–1991, however, average room rates stabilized even more than had other consumer prices, according to room rates published by Smith Travel Services (STR) (1992).[1] During January–June 1992, average rates were up only 0.6 percent from the same period of 1991 according to STR data.

These trends raise research questions about the trade-off between price changes and number of rooms rented, particularly during times of recession when incomes are also falling. Price increases that exceed general price increases in the economy will be expected to result in fewer rooms rented, but increases in income are expected to result in more rooms rented. These relationships are compounded by increasing

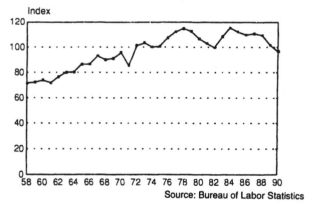

Source: Bureau of Labor Statistics

FIGURE 5   Labor productivity index, 1958–1990 (1982=100).

[1]The data published by BLS for Lodging away from Home are not consistent with data from Smith Travel Research (STR). The BLS data are based on prices for specified rooms in a select sample of lodging establishments deemed to serve nonbusiness travelers, which is less than one-half of the industry, whereas the STR data are average daily rates from all rooms from a large sample of all lodging establishments.

room taxes added to room rates, discussed in the following section.

PROJECTIONS OF SALES AND EMPLOYMENT

SALES PROJECTIONS

One of the most common marketing research problems involves projections of sales by individual companies as well as industry groups. Company sales can be projected in many ways, but most of them involve assessment of historical trends in an organized fashion. Four factors need to be explicitly controlled in developing sales trends: (1) number of establishments, (2) inflation, (3) seasonality, and (4) revenue from sales other than rooms.

It is desirable, at least for internal purposes, to separate sales of existing establishments over the projected period from those that are added over time through either purchase or internal growth. Sales from new establishments should be projected independently but, of course, will be greatly affected by strategic decisions regarding growth rates rather than market forces. Similarly, sales from food service and other profit centers should be projected independently from that of rooms. Nationally, about 58 percent of industry sales are from rooms alone, but the percentage will vary considerably for those with no food service (Hiemstra 1987).

The purpose of adjusting for inflation is to abstract from changes in the value of the dollar. This is accomplished by computing real prices, that is, by dividing revenue by an index of general consumer price increases (first, converted to ratio form), usually by use of the Consumer Price Index (U.S. City Average, Urban Areas, all items) (BLS 1991a). Room rates may increase more or less rapidly than inflation by either adding to the value received by the guests, either actual or perceived, or by providing additional services at the same or lower prices. Any such changes in room rates will be reflected in the resulting real prices calculated. Thus, trends in real room revenue may differ from that of the number of rooms rented.

Allowing for seasonality is imperative in assessing monthly or quarterly trends because of the wide variation in rooms rented by most establishments. This is easily accomplished by limiting comparisons to changes from the same months or quarters during the previous one or two years. For longer-term trends, it may be necessary to calculate the seasonal pattern in the data. This can be accomplished by computing an annual average over a period of one to five years and calculating each quarter's or each month's data as a ratio of this average. Seasonally adjusted data can then be computed by dividing original revenues by its corresponding ratio of seasonality.

A more precise method, using multiple regression analysis, is to introduce a "dummy," or indicator, variable into the regression model for each time period involved, less one; that is, for quarterly data, 3 dummy variables are needed, and for monthly data, 11 dummy variables are needed. The coefficient for quarter 1 provides, for example, a measure of the seasonal difference between that quarter and the fourth quarter omitted in the model.

EMPLOYMENT PROJECTIONS

Employment projections can be derived from sales projections by computing employee/sales ratios over time for either individual companies or industry totals, and then multiplying these ratios by projected sales. These ratios have increased over time for the industry in total, as noted earlier. But, for an individual company, these ratios may be quite stable. In fact, these ratios are quite useful to calculate for management purposes because of the ramifications for assessing changes in labor productivity itself. Increases may consciously be occurring due to the intention of increasing service levels, but unintended increases may portend lack of management control.

The BLS routinely computes long-term employment projections; the latest is for the year 2005 (1991c). It is based on previous trends and economic data through 1990. The U.S. lodging industry employed 1,649,000 people in 1990, which was up by 84 percent over that of 898,000 in 1975, 15 years earlier.[2] Over the next 15 years, employment is expected to increase to 2,174,000, an increase of 32 percent, for an annual compounded growth rate of 1.9 percent. While this growth rate has slowed considerably, it still well exceeds that of 1.2 percent for the entire United States. These projections assume the civilian labor force grows by a similar amount, 1.3 percent. Disposable personal income is projected to grow by 1.5 percent in real terms over this period.

While the BLS projection involves use of a complex statistical model with many variables, one can easily do a simple projection with fewer variables and arrive at similar results; for example, a study published in 1987 developed the following projections model using annual time-series, multiple regression analysis of data for 1970–1986 (Hiemstra):

[2]These figures omit unpaid family workers and self-employed entrepreneurs, which would add an estimated 56 percent to the above totals for paid employees.

$$E = -1247.87 + 0.25\ R + 0.37\ I + 14.93\ P$$
$$(-5.4)\quad (3.6)\quad\ \ (6.0)\quad\ \ (2.5)$$

where E equals employment in the lodging industry
            R equals number of rooms in the lodging industry
            I equals real disposable income
            P equals percentage of total revenue from rooms

Adjusted $R^2 = 0.991$; t statistics are shown in parentheses.

This model projects employment in the lodging industry of 2.0 million in the year 2000, for an annual rate of increase of 2.6 percent. The BLS projection at that time was for 1.97 million and a 2.5 percent rate of growth.

The model shows an income elasticity of 0.81, which means that a 1 percent increase in real disposable income would be expected to be associated with an increase of 0.81 percent in the number of employees in the lodging industry. As noted earlier, BLS is projecting real-income growth of 1.5 percent to the year 2005, which would contribute importantly (1.2 percent) to the employment projection. The rooms elasticity was computed at 0.58, which means that a 1 percent increase in number of rooms would be expected to be associated with an increase of 0.58 percent increase in number of employees.

LABOR ISSUES

PRODUCTIVITY

The Bureau of Labor Statistics defines labor productivity as output per unit of labor input. It is measured for each industry, in index form, as the index of output for that industry divided by the index of labor inputs (computed as ratios) (BLS 1983, 1985). Number of employees is converted to man-hours to avoid the problem of varying amounts of part-time employment over time. Output is measured in terms of real dollars of sales (that is, actual dollars deflated by a price index).

Lagging productivity of labor has been one of the pervading problems facing the lodging industry (Figure 5). Only fragmentary research is available to understand the nature and causes of this problem. Its importance is easily dismissed in noting that the amount of labor input itself is one of the more useful measures of service provided by different segments of the industry (Gomes 1987). The problem expresses itself in the upward trend noted in number of employees per room (Figure 4), but that trend ignores the perceived industry trend toward providing more real service along with lodging away from home. On the other hand, the viability of the budget sector with its limited service suggests that at least some parts of the industry are moving in the opposite direction. The subject requires research to clarify the confusing situation and to provide policy guidance to the industry.

Stable or even declining labor productivity is a common

phenomena of the service industry, including food service, in part due to the crude methods of measurement necessarily employed by BLS (1983). Man-hours may not be the best way to measure labor inputs in the service industry for which service is the essence of the business; the quality of an hour of labor is not necessarily consistent over time. Output trends rely heavily on sales revenues deflated by prices indexes, which themselves are not always carefully constructed (see footnote 1).

There are no measures of the productivity of capital (or Multifactors, which include capital and labor) for the lodging industry, as there are for other private business and the manufacturing sectors of the economy (BLS 1991b).

LABOR TURNOVER

Labor-turnover rates are known to be quite high in the lodging industry and, in fact, in most service industries, including food service. Few studies have quantified these rates, but one study based on a national sample of lodging properties measured labor turnover in 1987 at 105 percent for hourly employees and 46 percent for salaried employees (Hiemstra 1987).

High rates of labor turnover and low rates of productivity growth both exacerbate the labor shortage likely to again face the lodging industry as soon as it recovers more fully from the 1990–1991 recession; the unemployment rate was still increasing into mid-1992. Research clarifying recent trends in turnover rates and factors contributing to the perceived high rates is needed for making employment policy decisions affecting the lodging industry.

SOCIAL SECURITY ON TIPS

Since passage of the 1986 Tax Reform Act, Social Security payments must be paid by employers on tips received by employees in the restaurant and lodging industries, even if those tips have not been collected or verified by the employers. This onerous obligation poses undue burden on the industry in the form of collection and accounting burdens and increased labor costs. Little solid information is available on the magnitude of tips received by various types of employees and the cost of this new obligation. Research is needed to assess the magnitude of the problem to the industry for policy purposes.

A related 1986 income tax issue affecting both the lodging and restaurant industries, but unrelated to employment, is the provision that only 80 percent of the cost of business or entertainment meals are deductible by guests for business purposes. Unpublished research suggests that this tax provision has been an important factor in the declining relative importance in the atmosphere sector of food service, of which hotel dining rooms are an important part. Future research needs to be conducted to verify these findings. This issue is an important policy question because of continuing legislative proposals to change the 80-percent rate to a lower level.

ASSESSMENT OF IMPACTS OF ROOM TAXES

DEMAND ANALYSIS

Taxes targeted to away-from-home lodging have been on the increase. According to one study conducted for the American Hotel & Motel Association, room taxes averaged 9.8 percent nationally in spring 1990, including both lodging specific and general sales taxes (Ismail and Hiemstra 1991). Many state and local areas now levy double-digit tax rates. About one-half of the proceeds were found to be used for purposes other than assisting the lodging industry.

Since ad valorem taxes must be paid by the guests, tax increases combined with normal room-rate increases will serve to dampen or reduce the demand for rooms over time. The research questions are to measure the extent of this adverse impact on the industry and to determine the incidence of those taxes, that is, the extent to which room taxes are ultimately borne indirectly by the lodging industry in the form of reduced demand for rooms rather than by the guests that initially must pay them.

A recent study of these questions found that a 10 percent increase in real prices, due either to an increase in room rates or taxes on those rooms, was associated with a 4.4 percent drop in number of rooms rented (Hiemstra and Ismail 1992a, 1992b). The negative impact was found to vary by size of property, from 0.9 to 7.8 percent (Table 1) (Hiemstra and Ismail 1991). By level of room rates charged, the elasticity varied from 3.4 to 6.7 percent.

This study was based on cross-sectional analysis of a national sample of about 375 hotels owned or operated by members of the American Hotel & Motel Association (AH&MA). Since room taxes average about 10 percent of sales in the United States, they account for a loss in demand of about 4.4 percent, on average. These figures translate into a drop in U.S. occupancy rates averaging 3 percent, other things equal. Applying the varying elasticities by number of rooms and room-rate groups in Table 1 gives the varying impacts of a 10 percent room tax shown in Table 2.

Another study, in Hawaii, indicated a stronger adverse impact of room taxes on rooms rented than did the study for AH&MA (Fujii, Khaled and Mak 1985; Mak 1988). That study indicated that the impact on room rentals was about −1.0 percent for every increase in real room rates of 1 percent. The study employed use of a sophisticated model called the Almost Ideal Demand System (AIDS) using time-series data (1961–1980) in the form of budget shares.

Another early study, by Laventhol & Horwath (L&H), estimated the elasticity of demand for room sales at −0.6 in one model based on time-series data (Greenberg 1986). A second model in the same paper measured the elasticity at −0.2 using a cross-sectional model explaining hotel occupancy rates, based on L&H data.

Further study of this important question is warranted for several reasons: (1) Room taxes continue to increase dramatically, and it is important for policy purposes to know the

Table 1   Price Elasticity of Demand for Lodging, by Number of Rooms and Room Rate Segments

| ROOM RATES | NUMBER OF ROOMS | | | | |
	1–150	151–300	301–600	> 600	AVERAGE
< $40.00	–4.0	–1.9	–0.8	N.A.	–3.4
$40.00–$74.99	–6.8	–2.8	–1.6	–0.7	–3.8
$75.00–$99.99	–9.1	–4.4	–1.8	–1.0	–3.8
≥ $100.00	N.A.	–7.2	–3.4	–1.0	–6.7
Average	–7.8	–3.8	–2.1	–0.9	–4.4

Source: Hiemstra and Ismail 1992a.

impacts on the industry. (2) Extant studies show a rather wide range in degree of impacts, in part because of the divergent techniques used, for example, the use of time-series versus cross-sectional data. (3) The same models used to measure tax impacts can be used to assess price-quantity demand relationships explaining room rentals in relation to changes in room rates regardless of taxes. This information also is critical to development of yield management models discussed later.

The preceding studies measure only the adverse impacts of room taxes on the lodging industry. It is also known that some of these taxes, estimated at approximately one-half of the total, have some beneficial impacts on the lodging industry. They are often used to build convention centers, support local Convention and Visitor Bureaus, or advertise travel or tourism attractions. However, the significance of these positive tax impacts has not been measured statistically. A beginning in conducting research with this objective would be to concentrate on assessing the beneficial impacts of travel advertising and promotion, discussed later.

SUPPLY MODELS

The question of room-tax incidence requires the calculation of the price elasticity of supply as well as the price elasticity of demand, because it is the relationship of these two measures (plus the level of the tax itself) that determines the sharing of the tax burden (Mak 1988). The Fujii, Khaled, and Mak study (1985) measured the supply elasticity at 2.0 and concluded that about two-thirds of the hotel room tax in

Hawaii would be passed on to visitors in the form of higher room rates. The remaining one-third of the tax would be absorbed indirectly by the hotel industry.

The Hiemstra and Ismail study of the entire United States measured the supply elasticity to be higher, at 2.7, and the demand elasticity to be lower than did the Hawaiian researchers (1992a, 1992b). Hiemstra and Ismail concluded that nearly seven-eighths of the tax would be paid by guests and only one-eighth paid indirectly by the industry in the long run.

Supply elasticities are more difficult to estimate than are demand elasticities, largely because of the long-run nature of the relationships. Research is continuing at Purdue University to refine these estimates using simultaneous equations, particularly in view of the 1986 and later changes in tax and depreciation laws, as well as the recent 1990–1991 recession. It would be useful to the industry if several other researchers would either verify or modify the above results.

YIELD MANAGEMENT SYSTEMS

PRINCIPLES INVOLVED

Yield management systems are attempts to systematically apply economic principles in setting hotel and motel room rates. They also involve recognition of the essence of market segmentation, both among different classes of guests and over time. These systems result in considerable variation in room rates actually charged. However, in some sense, they

Table 2   Impacts of a 10 Percent Room Tax on Occupancy Rates for the Lodging Industry, by Number of Rooms and Room Rate Segments

| ROOM RATES | NUMBER OF ROOMS | | | | |
	1–150	151–300	301–600	> 600	AVERAGE
< $40.00	–2.7	–1.3	–0.5	N.A.	–2.3
$40.00–$74.99	–4.3	–1.9	–1.1	–0.6	–2.5
$75.00–$99.99	–6.8	–3.0	–1.4	–0.7	–2.7
≥ $100.00	N.A.	–5.1	–2.6	–0.8	–4.8
Average	–5.4	–2.6	–1.5	–0.7	–3.1

Source: Hiemstra and Ismail 1992a.

only systematize variations in rates charged by sharp desk clerks who vary rates in relation to supply and demand on an ad hoc basis. In concept, yield management is akin to the systems used in setting fares by the airlines and to the menu management systems used in setting joint prices by food service operations.

The fundamental concepts involved in the development of a yield management system include: (1) changes in price elasticities of demand over time for rental of a given room for a given day; (2) differing time horizons and consequent price elasticities between business- and pleasure-traveler segments; (3) recognition of different demands associated with different days of the week, different seasons of the year, and different types of rooms; and (4) joint products or services provided (i.e., length of stay, banquet and other food service required, etc.). Articles by Kimes (1989) and Relihan (1989) discuss some of these concepts.

It is well known that many of these factors affect demand for room rates. Pleasure travelers tend to book early, while business travelers tend to book late; and they expect these differences to be reflected in prices paid. Weekend guests expect to receive lower rates than during the week because of the different purposes served. Similarly, out-of-season resort rooms are expected to be lower than those at peak season due to differing demands. Long-staying guests may expect a free night at the end of the week. Large groups expect to receive a reduction of price or complimentary meeting rooms in recognition of economies of scale.

NEEDED RESEARCH

The types of research problems are twofold: (1) lack of the fundamental price-quantity data quantifying these interrelated demands for use in building the models, and (2) development of the complex computer systems that can mesh together the various components involved, on a timely enough basis and in simplified form for quick, management decision making. The problems are compounded because of the variations known to exist among individual properties, even those under common ownership and management. They relate to differences in occupancy rates, location, types of guests, service provided, and so on.

Only sketchy data are available, at least publicly, to satisfy the voluminous need for these various demand relationships. Some of the background kinds of information needed to understand the problems can be found in Jeffrey and Hubbard (1988) and Wilensky and Buttle (1988). Presumably, many of the existing yield management systems involve "rules of thumb," or ranges in data, rather than actual measurements of the price-elasticity data needed. Others are internally generated by the usual requirement for data histories to individualize a yield management system. However, these systems are proprietary and, therefore, not available either for public scrutiny or even for clients who likely do not understand all of the internal assumptions in the system. The user can only hope and judge by experience whether the true demand relationships are embodied in their own system.

MARKET SEGMENTATION

PRINCIPLES INVOLVED

There is a large amount of literature on the importance of market segmentation as a sound principle of marketing (Frank, Massy, and Wind 1972). However, there are wide differences in the bases upon which to develop the actual segments. Early studies tended to segment markets on the basis of geographic or demographic characteristics. More sophisticated studies pointed to the usefulness of benefit segmentation or psychographic segmentation because of their focus on customer preferences (Dhalla and Mahatoo 1976). While the latter approaches have merit, they may not all encompass the fundamental principles underlying successful market segmentation, which are rooted in the economics of marketing.

The objective of market segmentation is to capture as much as possible of the complete area under a given market-demand curve. This objective is accomplished by subdividing a market into components that satisfy individual customers more precisely than could a mass market. In the process, sellers must be able to raise prices more than commensurately with cost increases, that is, the segments must have different price elasticities of demand to make the procedure worthwhile.

Economists call this process *first-degree price discrimination*. Under perfect competition, a price is set at the single market-clearing level that maximizes profits. But, in the process, there typically will be customers that would be willing to pay higher rates for a small quantity of product. This area under the demand curve and above marginal cost is commonly called *consumer surplus*. A necessary condition for success is that the segments have differing price elasticities of demand.

A second condition for successful market segmentation is that the segments are capable of separating targeted customers, to avoid profitable arbitrage in buying low from one segment and selling high to another. The airline industry segments its business and pleasure customers by requiring advance purchase and staying over a Saturday night, which business people are unable or loath to do. It is not as simple for the lodging industry, particularly during economically stressful times such as 1990–1992. Some business people and pleasure travelers stray from the lodging segments in which they are targeted, but specialized services try to prevent such overlap.

A third condition of success of market segmentation is that profits from the various segments exceed the costs of differentiating the segments. Market segmentation normally is costly, and, therefore, only if sufficiently different demand elasticities exist will it pay to segment.

RESEARCH NEEDS

The lodging industry in recent years has been segmenting its market extensively by tailoring its product more finely to meet perceived customer demands. The one-size-fits-all approach to mass merchandising by Holiday Inn, Ramada, Howard Johnson, Best Western, and other early entrants have largely given way to economy, midpriced, and upscale segments. These segments themselves have proliferated into luxury economy and other distinctions. In addition, all-suites and extended-stay segments have been added, among others.

The research problem is that these segments have not all been developed through use of sound marketing and economic principles, and some of them have experienced severe marketing problems during the recent recession. Courtyard and a few other entries are notable exceptions in having been well researched prior to development (Wind, Green, Shifflet, and Scarbrough 1989). Segmentation research is difficult and costly to perform, particularly ex ante. It may involve application of multiple regression, conjoint analysis, cluster analysis, discriminate analysis, or multivariate statistical techniques, and often several of them in the same study. Early studies of conjoint analysis, which involve measuring trade-offs useful in developing meaningful segments, can be found in Green, Goldberg, and Montegayor (1981) and Goldberg, Green, and Wind (1984).

ADVERTISEMENT AND PROMOTION

Assessing the effectiveness of advertising must rank as the single most underresearched area for the lodging industry, as well as for many other industries. The industry spends over one billion dollars per year on advertising and promotions on the faith that it is having a positive impact on sales, without having hard information to support the decision. There likely is some pickup in sales, based on an anecdotal information, but whether the level of advertising is justified, or possibly short of that needed, is usually not empirically established. More often, if advertising does not seem to pay, the prescription is that one needs to change advertising agencies or change the message, but to continue advertising at the same rate.

Further, most of the research monies that are allocated to advertising research are used for designing future messages rather than evaluating effectiveness of previous advertisements. While future planning is useful research activity, it does not take the place of measuring effectiveness.

Reasons for the lack of advertising evaluation research, or at least its availability, include the difficulty of conducting such research and often the proprietary nature of the findings. Internal company studies are unlikely to be published.

It was mentioned earlier that substantial sums of money collected from room taxes are used for promoting travel, but there are no known studies to indicate the impacts of these expenditures on the lodging industry in terms of additional rooms rented to justify these expenditures. In this case, public rather than private funds are involved.

The type of research useful for this purpose would be to obtain baseline data related to hotel occupancy rates in selected areas that are planning major advertising campaigns.

Periodic and postadvertising measurements would be taken of similar occupancy rates along with data related to types and expenditures on advertising. Related economic and seasonality information would need to be collected to adjust for factors that are responsible for observed changes. In addition, similar areas used as control groups should be monitored during the same periods to adjust for any outside influences.

Individual companies are in the best position to conduct similar types of research related to their own advertising campaigns, because of the availability of their own sales data and ability to control advertisement expenditures. Advertisement campaigns can be targeted to selected areas of the country, thus, allowing control groups to be monitored during the same period. One such published study measured magazine advertising impacts on sales of alcoholic beverages, in cooperation with *Sports Illustrated* and *Time*, which carried their ads. This carefully designed study was able to measure the sales impacts of given brands of product attributable to related advertisements (Hinkle and Stineman 1984).

SUMMARY AND CONCLUSION

This chapter has stressed the need for selected types of research—mainly related to marketing issues—of concern to the lodging industry. In the process, some of the major trends related to the industry have been discussed. The areas of research, without implying rank-order priorities, included the following general activities:

- Projections of sales and employment
- Labor productivity and labor turnover
- Supply and demand for lodging services
- Yield management
- Market segmentation
- Advertisement and promotion

Data problems are greater and more difficult to resolve than is methodology of analysis. Industry-aggregate data is often available from secondary sources from such organizations as Bureau of Labor Statistics and U.S. Department of Commerce. Selected data series are available also from Pannell Kerr Forster, Smith Travel Research, and other proprietary sources. However, often these data series are of limited duration and consistency over time. The major data problems usually relate to lack of sufficient detail for analysis of such important issues as effective market segmentation, advertising effectiveness, rates of labor turnover, and factors related to yield management.

The industry needs an advocate, such as the American Hotel & Motel Association, that would see its role as the collector and depository for basic data related to the industry for use in conducting a wide variety of meaningful research. AH&MA sees the need for research—and has supported many research activities—but to date has failed to commit the necessary resources related to primary-data collection.

REFERENCES

Bureau of Labor Statistics (BLS)(1983), U.S. Department of Labor, "Concepts and Measures of Productivity," *A BLS Reader on Productivity*, Washington, D.C.: Superintendent of Documents, Bul. 2171, June.

Bureau of Labor Statistics (BLS)(1985), *Productivity Measures for Selected Industries, 1958–84*. Washington, D.C.: Superintendent of Documents, Bul. 2256.

Bureau of Labor Statistics (BLS)(1991a), "Productivity By Industry," *News*, Annual issues, February.

Bureau of Labor Statistics (BLS)(1991b), "Multifactor Productivity Measures, 1990," *News*, August 29.

Bureau of Labor Statistics (BLS)(1991c), "Outlook: 1990–2005, Industry Output and Job Growth Continues Slow Into Next Century," *Monthly Labor Review* 114(11): 45–63, Washington, D.C.: Superintendent of Documents.

Bureau of Labor Statistics (BLS)(1991d), "CPI for All Urban Consumers (CPI-U)-Analysis," Annual data, December issues.

Dhalla, N.K., and W.H. Mahatoo (1976), "Expanding the Scope of Segmentation Research," *Journal of Marketing* 40(April): 34–41.

Frank, R.E., W.F. Massy, and Y. Wind (1972), *Market Segmentation*, Englewood Cliffs, NJ: Prentice-Hall.

Fujii, E., M. Khaled, and J. Mak (1985), "The Exportability of Hotel Occupancy and Other Tourist Taxes," *National Tax Journal* 38: 169–77.

Goldberg, S.M., P.E. Green, and Y. Wind (1984), "Conjoint Analysis of Price Premiums for Hotel Amenities," *Journal of Business* 57(1, part 2): S111–132.

Gomes, A.J. (1986), *Hospitality in Transition*, Washington, D.C.: American Hotel & Motel Association.

Gomes, A.J. (1987), *The Optimum Size and Nature of New Hotel Development in the Caribbean*, Washington, D.C.: General Secretariat, Organization of American States.

Green, P.E., S.M. Goldberg, and M. Montemayor (1981), "A Hybrid Utility Estimation Model for Conjoint Analysis," *Journal of Marketing* 45(Winter): 33–41.

Greenburg, C. (1986), "The U.S. Lodging Industry—Today and Tomorrow," *U.S. Lodging Industry, 1985*, Philadelphia: Laventhol & Horwath.

Hiemstra, S.J. (1987), *Analysis and Future Needs of Human Resources Used in the Lodging Industry* (November), Washington, D.C.: American Hotel & Motel Association (AH&MA).

Hiemstra, S.J. (1990), "Employment Policies and Practices in the Lodging Industry," *International Journal of Hospitality Management*, Special issue, 9(3): 207–221, Strategic Management in the Hospitality Industry. Oxford, England: Pergamon Press.

Hiemstra, S.J., and J.A. Ismail (1991), *Impacts of Room Taxes on the Lodging Industry*, Washington, D.C.: American Hotel & Motel Association, March.

Hiemstra, S.J., and J.A. Ismail (1992a), "Analysis of Room Taxes Levied on the Lodging Industry," *Journal of Travel Research* 31(1, Summer): 42–49.

Hiemstra, S.J., and J.A. Ismail (1992b), "Room Taxes—There is No Free Lunch," *The Cornell Hotel and Restaurant Administration Quarterly* 33(5): 84–89.

Hinkle, C.L., and E.F. Stineman (1984), "Time Inc./Seagram," *Cases in Marketing Management: Issues for the 1980s*, Englewood Cliffs, NJ: Prentice-Hall.

Ismail, J., and S.J. Hiemstra (1991), "Room Taxes—A Growing Burden on the Industry," *The Bottomline*, Austin, Texas: Journal of International Association of Hospitality Accountants, 6(2, April/May): 20–21, 27.

Jeffrey, D., and N.J. Hubbard (1988), "Temporal Dimensions and Regional Patterns of Hotel Occupancy Performance in England: a Time Series Analysis of Midweek and Weekend Occupancy Rates in 266 Hotels, in 1984 and 1985," *International Journal of Hospitality Management* 7(1): 63–80.

Kimes, S.E. (1989), "The Basics of Yield Management," *The Cornell Hotel and Restaurant Administration Quarterly* 30(3, November): 14–22.

Mak, J. (1988), "Taxing Hotel Room Rentals in the U.S.," *Journal of Travel Research* 27(Summer): 10–15.

Pannell Kerr Forster, *Trends in the Hotel Industry*, Various years, Houston, TX: P.O. Box 60808 AMF.

Relihan, W.J. (1989), "The Yield-Management Approach to Hotel-Room Pricing," *The Cornell Hotel and Restaurant Administration Quarterly* 30(1, May): 40–45.

Smith Travel Research (1992), *Lodging Outlook*, Monthly issues through June, Gallatin, TN: P.O. Box 659.

Wilensky, L., and F. Buttle (1988), "A Multivariate Analysis of Hotel Benefit Bundles and Choice Trade-Offs," *International Journal of Hospitality Management* 7(1): 29–41.

Wind, J., P.E. Green, D. Shifflet, and M. Scarbrough (1989), "Courtyard by Marriott: Designing a Hotel Facility with Consumer-Based Marketing Models," *Interfaces* 19(1, Jan.–Feb.): 25–47.

30

Research Needs of Small Tourism Enterprises

TYRRELL MARRIS*
Tourism Research Consultant
London, Great Britain

*T*his chapter concentrates on market research for the small enterprise working in tourism. Market research attempts to find out about the enterprise's customers: who they are, what they want from the enterprise, and whether what they bought seemed fair value for money. A small enterprise is lucky to be directly in touch with its customers; market research really should take advantage of that and help turn the owner's hunches or guestimates into valid insights or sound estimates. The aim has been to condense within one chapter just enough ideas, knowledge, and simplified techniques to interest the reader and yet require few resources to turn the information to practical use.

Small enterprises need market research information just as large ones do: there is much the small enterprises can do to help themselves. The published sources of tourism statistics provide a context for the small enterprises' own comparable researches. Because small enterprises are in close touch with their customers, there are realistic ways to achieve their own surveys, which are described herein. They can proceed step by step, learning from the most useful results of previous research.

For simplicity, this chapter will refer to the *enterprise* as the best single name to describe a business, or company, or whatever. The *owner* will be the main decision maker, who might in fact be a manager or partner. Also, the owner of the enterprise will be nominated a *he*: in many small enterprises, the owner might equally be a she or that sometimes most successful combination of wife and husband.

There is no easy definition of *small*. It really means, in this context, the size enterprise that has not the resources to have its own research department, nor the finances to buy much custom-designed research from outside agencies. So, are such enterprises helpless when they need research? This chapter aims to show that, on the contrary, there is much research that the owner can have to help him.

WHO IS IN TOURISM?

An enterprise that is small in size can still think big. The owner, who will usually be the manager, too, can very well think of the wider possibilities of the industry of which his own enterprise is a small part.

Owners of small enterprises might not realize that they are part of the wider tourism industry. Hoteliers or campsite operators probably do realize this because they sell lodgings for the night; but they need also to realize that most tourists want something to do during the day. And vice versa, owners of other enterprises are often more deeply in the tourism industry than they realize: for instance, archeological sites, boutiques, cafes, discos, exhibitions, fishing lakes, golf courses, hairdressers, information centers, and many more, right through the alphabet to yacht marinas and zoos.

Because the tourist wants a great variety of things to do and see, owners of all those enterprises are directly contributing to the customer's satisfaction. The customer does not see the enterprises as competing—to him or her, they are largely complementary. That even applies to very similar enterprises: if most of the restaurants in a town are to be found in one area, that is often a much greater inducement to

*The author thanks the English Tourist Board, of which he was formerly an Assistant Director and head of research, for use of the Board's many published sources. The opinions and advice given here are the author's own, without implied or expressed agreement by the Board.

having a meal out than any individual place would be on its own. The sense of excitement and entertainment in such an area can add to everybody's enjoyment and, hence, to increased sales. As a group, restaurants complement each other.

Anyone planning to start a new enterprise can easily research his best location by going to see where existing tourist attractions are. Location is known to be crucial, and that will be reflected in site values. Simple observation of where tourists stay, eat, have fun, or conduct business, and how they travel can help the new owner choose the best site he can afford. A good way for an owner to observe is to be a tourist himself, in and around the area he has in mind, imagining where other tourists would want to find the service he plans to offer. Remember to make your observations at various times of day, on various days of the week, and, if possible, during different seasons of the year.

WHO NEEDS RESEARCH?

Wherever an enterprise's sales depend on the general market of consumers, it needs market research to aid its other skills and energies. Many vast business enterprises choose to spend enormously on market research because they cannot be directly in touch with their millions of customers by any other means. But in tourism, many sales are made directly to the customer. That is especially true of small tourism enterprises. Also, what a small enterprise sells is not like an extensively advertised branded item. Small tourist enterprises sell something uniquely their own: their motel at this particular site; their composition of fish menus; their pony treks on these ranges; this style of hand-thrown pottery; and so on.

Because these tourist attractions or facilities or services are so unique, it is wise to research what the market wants so as to understand their customers' special needs. It is dangerous to rely on guesswork or tradition. This chapter on market research means to interest, in particular, those who provide accommodation or food or special goods or entertainment or stimulus or relaxation to the tourist—and who would like to do it better.

Small enterprises need much the same customer information as big enterprises. A small enterprise has the advantage of much closer contact between the owner and the customers than do the big businesses. But small or big, the aim is the same: to discover what makes a happy customer who is likely to come back for more. It is necessary to identify customers in a systematic way. A good way is for the owner to write what he already knows about present customers under headings relevant to the enterprise, for instance:

- What they do at or buy from the enterprise
- The proportion of customers on vacation, on business, on social trips
- Their sex, age, and party size and if children are included
- Spending pattern and income
- Duration of stay
- Frequency of visit

- Mode of travel
- Where they come from
- How they found out about the enterprise
- What attracts them to the enterprise, to the locality.

Having done that, the owner should ask himself: "Do I really know, or am I guessing?" His research is just starting.

STARTING TO RESEARCH: INTERNAL SOURCES

Some of those headings will be more important to his type of business than other headings will. If the owner detects an information gap that is obviously important to him and his customers, then he should fill it if possible. Widespread, thorough, custom-designed surveys cannot be afforded by small enterprises, but previously published market surveys can be useful for filling gaps. They need not be expensive to buy or borrow. An example of relevance to vacation farms, typical small tourist enterprises, is the research of Pizam and Pokela (1980). Researches of that sort might be located through local reference libraries. More likely, the owner will need to consider other sources. His own financial records will be a good starting point. Charles Goeldner in Chapter 8, *Travel and Tourism Information Sources*, discusses possible secondary sources extensively.

The owner can use his financial records to make simple calculations such as spending/customer or spending/day. Seasonal variations or weekend-versus-weekday comparisons can be revealing. Some calculations might seem promising but impossible to do because the records are not kept in suitable form. A way to improve the usefulness of financial records is to contrive simple coding of the paper or ink color used on payment slips. Where sales records are computerized, it could be possible to code transactions by that means. Thus, different types of customer, or times of day, or categories of sales can be picked out for special analysis. All this will help to identify the largest revenue-earning aspects of the enterprise.

Where customers came from and how they knew about the enterprise are other questions needing other sorts of research. A hotel, for instance, has the opportunity to modify slightly its advertising in each media used so as to identify the sources of its visitors. Potential tourists can be invited to write for the hotel brochure using differently coded coupons in each advertisement to identify different media. It is simple to see, from the codes of coupons returned, whether local or national newspapers are attracting more potential customers. In the same way, alternative layout or wording of advertisements can be tested for pulling power. Ronkainen and Woodside, in Chapter 47, cover conversion studies more extensively.

An occasional refinement of those methods is to make the same tests but to base them on actual sales attributable to the advertisement, rather than on returned coupons, which are only potential sales. It might be helpful to concentrate on those coupons that do convert into immediate sales if the hotel is advertising a short-period offer—for instance, a spring price reduction. But generally, advertising has a longer-term aim, not just to create a sale here and now; so the simple return of a coupon with its consequent opportunity to mail a brochure or other follow-up literature to the potential customer may usually be taken as a valid test.

Calculations of the interval between when advertisements are published and when and how many replies are received will help to appraise how best to time promotional activity. The location of replies will help pinpoint how far afield to go. The style of the media generating replies to advertisements also tells something of the style and tastes of customers.

STARTING TO RESEARCH: EXTERNAL SOURCES

None of the research methods so far described will have done much to answer questions about why the customers chose the particular enterprise, or the general locality, or why they chose to come away from their hearth, home, and television set to spend their time and money as tourists. Well-informed opinions of the owner can be a good starting point for finding answers, but opinions need to be tested. Preconceived ideas can mislead or overlook new opportunities.

A good test is, first, to use the observation method. Looking at and listening to the enterprise's customers is informative. Doing the same in competitive and complementary enterprises adds a new dimension to that information. The time and location of other enterprises' advertising, opening and closing times, peak and off-peak pricing are all revealing to the owner of a small enterprise. A question for an owner to consider is whether to do the same as others or to deliberately choose a different policy for his enterprise.

The importance of recognizing the complementary nature of tourism enterprises was stressed above. That has a relevance to probing the why questions about customers' tastes and choices. Owners of the local restaurant, the general store, and the camping site will find they have many customers in common. By exchanging ideas and opinions and concrete statistical facts about their enterprises, each owner can gain entirely new insights into why tourists come in the first place and what makes them happy to stay and what might bring them back.

The second readily available source of external research is published statistical information. Local tourism statistics are published by various town, state, provincial, or regional bodies or by their national and regional tourist offices. Local tourism information often comes from national surveys the results of which have been broken down to provide statistics for smaller parts of the country. There are many such surveys in tourist destinations with highly developed economies and established research agencies. Examples are:

- The National Travel Survey (U.S. Travel Data Center), which has been made monthly since 1979 and which

covers trips of 100 miles or more (one way)
- The Canadian Travel Survey (Canadian Government Office of Tourism) which has been made quarterly since 1978 and which covers trips of 50 miles or more
- The United Kingdom Tourism Survey (English, Northern Ireland, Scottish and Wales Tourist Boards), which in various forms has been made monthly since 1972 and which covers trips of any distance of 24 hours duration or more
- The statistical publications of many other government bodies or statistical services such as those of Statistics Canada and United States Travel Service (see list of references)
- Hotel occupancy surveys (see below)
- Surveys of visits to tourist attractions

The sources of a selection of tourism surveys are given in the references section at the end of the chapter. A feature of many such surveys, which makes them appealing to small tourism enterprises, is that the results are inexpensive or freely published. Usually they are frequent enough for the owner to compare his business trends with national and local trends.

More rarely, collections of many tourism statistics from several sources are available for particular areas. An example is the Tourism Regional Fact Sheets (English Tourist Board), which are usually published yearly. They are digests of regional information on the volume and value of tourism, its origin and season, the demographic characteristics of tourists, the main tourist destinations, the use of accommodation, the occupancy of hotels, and visitors to particular attractions. A reading list is included, so that the owner of any enterprise can see where to look for more detailed facts and figures.

A very comprehensive source of tourism statistics for the North American market is the updated edition of *Travel Trends* in the United States and Canada (Goeldner and Dicke 1984). It is a compendium—rather than a digest—of a great range of statistical sources and, likewise, includes a listing of where and from whom one can find more detailed facts. Local libraries might have or get it for reference.

The major tourist bodies often publish books or booklets to advise small enterprises. They can give the owner ideas for research and practical information that saves having to do so much of his own research. It might not always be obvious to which bodies one should go for information. Seeking such bodies and investing in stamps or telephone calls to find what they have to help the small tourism enterprise is part of the research process. An obvious source of advice is the local tourist board or office. Less obvious, but useful for general statistics, are the yearbooks published by the World Tourism Organization.

DOING YOUR OWN RESEARCH

When the owner has seen what data can be gleaned from analysis of his own internal records, when he has carefully

The owner, however, may well decide it is worth paying a little to have the work done by a specialist.

examined competitive or complementary enterprises, and when he has sought out what can be had from other local sources and from bodies promoting tourism, there will be a pile of research facts to consider. The character and seasonality and so forth of the enterprise's custom can be compared with past and recent trends for similar localities or types of tourist. But such comparisons are difficult if there are still large gaps in knowledge about the enterprise's own customers.

The owner may now use simple surveys to fill the gaps. The way to do that with the full rigor of a professional market research survey is explained in countless books; however, they will presumably take more time to read and resources to apply than the small enterprise can afford. There are three other possible methods described below. The first two are just simplified versions of the full survey; they can never be as good as the real thing. But, on the principle that half a loaf is better than no bread at all, they do offer a realistic solution to the owner's need for better knowledge. Other sections of this book go into more detail on how to develop and administer survey methods.

FIRST: DO-IT-YOURSELF QUESTIONS

When there are just a few bits of marketing information needed, it can be simple and reliable to ask brief questions of only a hundred or so customers. The method requires talking to those particular customers in a more deliberate and controlled way than usual. The owner and other staff must all do this in the same way, noting customers' answers in a form that is easy to add up. Also, there has to be an impartial way of selecting customers to avoid the risk of not getting a fair answer because only the more approachable ones have been questioned.

An owner might need to know more about repeat customers, for example. So for one week, at the start of each month, the person served nearest to the hour is asked: "Is this the first time we have served you here or have you come before? If before, how often?" Immediately afterwards, the answer is noted down. Naturally, those questions will be preceded and followed by the normal courtesies of conversation (but avoiding opening remarks that could influence the answer). Such a survey is designed to give rough and ready information. It need continue only long enough to show a fairly steady proportion of repeat/first-time customers—or any other topic chosen for survey.

SECOND: DO-IT-YOURSELF MINI-SURVEY

When an enterprise needs a range of market information, the owner will need to use a more formal way to get it. Seldom will he or his staff have the time to ask customers all the necessary questions, and it is unlikely that he will have the skill to conduct formal interviews: that calls for a personality and training not normally found amongst owners. The way to get the information will be by means of a questionnaire filled in by the customers themselves. Postal return of questionnaires is both inefficient and subject to unknown bias, response rates below 50 percent being likely. So it is best

personally to ask the selected customers to complete and return the forms near the end of their visit, but before they are in such a hurry to leave that they will not answer all the questions before they do leave. Where the customer spends only a short time at the enterprise—for instance, at a restaurant—the questionnaire has to be correspondingly shorter and, therefore, quicker to complete.

People approached the right way at the right time can feel that it is a compliment to be asked their opinions. It matters that the questionnaire is given to selected customers personally, by the owner or responsible staff, making clear that there is a special need for that customer's response: "I/The manager would really value *your* response, madam/sir." And that is indeed true because, when a carefully written questionnaire is necessary, it becomes very important that customers are selected properly. Customers coming at different times or for different reasons need to be included; for example, questionnaires might be given to one member of all parties leaving on a Monday in one week, on a Tuesday the next week, and so on; any practicable customer-selection method that is impartial is valid.

Ideally, one particular member of a party of customers should be instructed to fill in the questionnaire, but, without experienced interviewers, that is unrealistic for a small enterprise. Anyway, in such circumstances, a good questionnaire can be so interesting that many members of the party will want to help complete it—even if dad or the boss or the person paying the bill has the final say.

An example of a questionnaire including a range of questions suitable for a small enterprise is shown in Appendix 1. Some questions are more suitable for lodgings, and some are more suitable for meals. The owner must take care to ask just those questions from which the information is needed and cut out everything unnecessary or irrelevant to the customers.

The limit on the number of questionnaires issued is most likely to be set by the ability of the owner to add up and analyze all the answers returned. Although the process is straightforward, it is bound to be time consuming. As a rule of thumb, experience shows that more than 100 completed questionnaires are necessary to establish roughly valid answers, but more than 300 are unnecessary for a first mini-survey. It is always possible to make repeat surveys to examine, say, other topics or other seasons of the year.

Assuming that there are between 100 and 200 questionnaires to tabulate, results are obtained by adding up the number of checks in the answer "boxes" and simply expressing the number as a percentage of all responses. Where the questionnaire asks for written answers, it is surprisingly easy to thumb through them to get a first impression of frequent types of written reply. The owner then lists typical replies and allocates the actual written answers accordingly, always being conscientious about extending the list rather than forcing a particular reply where it does not really fit.

The adding up and percentaging is aided by a small electronic calculator. Everyone will find his own best method: it needs a clear day, a clear head, and plenty of paper and pencils. As an alternative to his own or his staff's efforts, the owner might find a local high school willing to help with tabulating answers (but not with interviewing or similar jobs—student labor needs too much supervision).

When main findings have emerged, it might be worth breaking down some answers for different types of customers such as vacation/business, repeat/first-time, local/distant, origin, and so on. Without a programmed computer, it is a laborious process, so only a few breakdowns should be attempted at any time. The simplest method is to deal the questionnaire forms into piles, for instance: single adults/ adults with child(ren)/ adults only, and then retabulate the three separate types of customer.

THIRD: OCCUPANCY SURVEY

The third possible method of research that is easily applied to a small enterprise providing accommodation is the occupancy survey. The advantages of this are three:

• Information is obtained that has obvious practical value for the day-to-day management of the enterprise.

• Partly because of the first advantage, existing methods of record keeping will probably need little modification to make the survey possible.

• There are occupancy-survey results published freely, or at small cost, for many countries.

The essence of the occupancy survey is that it gives an accurate record of how fully the enterprise's accommodation is used. Daily, weekly, or monthly figures can be calculated, of which the last are the most frequently published. The ability to compare the enterprise's own monthly performance with the average for similar enterprises in the same locality, or of the same type, is invaluable. Some of the many published sources are given as references at the end of the chapter. If there is no readily available published source for a locality, but there is a strong desire amongst the industry for information, then a local association of owners can organize its own survey. To ensure proper confidentiality of individual figures, the occupancy returns necessary for the survey should be sent to some reliable third party, such as a firm of accountants, for monthly addition and issue.

The form on which occupancy should be recorded for a small hotel is shown in Appendix 2, together with an example of the arithmetic needed to calculate (1) average room occupancy, (2) average bed occupancy, and (3) duration of stay. All three pieces of information can be revealing: If occupancy of beds is below average, the cause might be that guests are staying a shorter-than-average duration at the hotel, rather than that there are fewer-than-average arrivals. If stays are short, perhaps there is too little to keep the guests amused in or near the hotel. Alternatively, if arrivals are below average, there might be too little to attract guests in the first place. The full diagnosis of what the trouble is and, therefore, what should be done will depend on a variety of factors. Undoubtedly, having sound information on which to base the diagnosis is a vital starting point for marketing action.

CONCLUSION

The information needs of a small enterprise are very like those of a large one. The disadvantage is that small enterprises lack the resources of time and money to buy their own custom-made research services. The advantage is that the owner and his family or staff are so much closer to their customers that do-it-yourself research is a real possibility for small enterprises. They need market research to keep in touch with their customers' needs.

Starting to research requires that the owner recognizes the sort of industry in which he works. Many other small enterprises must be regarded as complementary to the total experience a tourist is buying. Observing the enterprises of other owners and exchanging information with them about customers is the start of research. An oversensitivity to the competition is a mental barrier to be discarded: much mutual benefit can be had from cooperation.

There are various simple calculations possible, using the enterprise's own financial records, that can pinpoint the greater or lesser revenue-earning aspects of the business. Slight changes to methods of record keeping can make the financial records more adaptable to such calculations.

Before embarking on more elaborate methods of do-it-yourself research, the owner should see what is published about tourism in his locality or for his type of enterprise. Specialist libraries, tourist bodies, and other professionals might be available to help that search. In some areas, there might be a danger of being swamped by all that is available; in others, there might be almost nothing useful. Some attempt needs to be made to look for and use what information is already available.

The small enterprise can do its own research both to fill gaps of knowledge and to get information comparable to what is published. It is quite practical for the owner to question his customers in an effective, structured way so as to improve his knowledge. The resulting market survey, for such it is, can range from one or two questions asked informally of 50 customers to a dozen questions on a printed questionnaire given to 200 or so customers. A step-by-step approach is wisest, so that more elaborate methods are not tried until the simpler ones have been achieved. Amongst the simplest, and most useful for enterprises offering accommodation, are occupancy surveys.

Market research for small tourism enterprises aims to help them, like larger tourism enterprises, to provide customers with satisfaction. When outlining research ways and means, it is possible to mention only a few of the results that might come out of research and the ways those results are applicable to meeting customers' needs. Many owners of small enterprises, until they have experience of research, will have little preconceived knowledge of how much they could be helped by surveys. They will be well advised to enter into research gradually, always assessing which previous results have been valuable to them before getting any more. Equally, they are well advised to not reject research as a complicated irrelevance, but to welcome it as a greatly useful possibility.

REFERENCES

Some sources of national tourism surveys that include useful breakdown of the statistics are as follows:

Australian Government Tourist Bureau (Canberra City, Australia) for results of the *Domestic Tourism Monitor*, and so on.

Bahamas Ministry of Tourism (Nassau, Bahamas) for its annual report.

Belgium: Westvlaa/ms Ekonomisch Studiebureau (Brugge, Belgium) for their annual survey of Belgian holiday taking.

Bermuda Department of Tourism (Hamilton, Bermuda) for its tourism statistics.

Bord Failte Iran (Dublin, Irish Republic).

Canadian Government Office of Tourism or Statistics Canada (Ottawa, Canada) for their many publications.

Denmark Statistics (Copenhagen, Denmark) for their *Statistical News*, and so on.

English Tourist Board (London, England) for the *United Kingdom Tourism Survey* and *Regional Fact Sheets*, and so on.

Finnish Tourist Board (Finland) for the twice yearly statistical publications.

France: Institut National de la Statistique et des Etudes Economiques (Paris, France) for its annual survey of French holiday taking.

Germany: Studienkreis fur Tourismus (Starnberg, Germany) for the annual *Deutsche Reiseanalyse*.

Hawaii Visitors Bureau (Honolulu, Hawaii) for its annual research report.

Japan National Tourist Organization (Tokyo, Japan) for its yearly statistical analyses.

Kenya Ministry of Finance and Economic Planning (Nairobi, Kenya) for its *Statistical Digest*.

Netherlands Central Bureau of Statistics (Voorburg, Holland) for the annual survey of Dutch holiday taking.

Pacific Area Travel Association (San Francisco, U.S.A.) for its annual reports.

Spanish Ministry of Tourism Information (Madrid, Spain) for its yearly statistics.

Switzerland: Institute for Tourism and Transport (St. Gallen, Switzerland) for travel market surveys.

U.S. Travel Data Center (Washington, D.C., U.S.A.) for *National Travel Survey*.

U.S. Travel Service (Washington, D.C., U.S.A.) for its many publications.

World Tourism Organization (Madrid, Spain) for the *Compendium of Tourism Statistics* and many other publications.

Some sources of occupancy surveys of tourist accommodation, particularly hotels, are given below. Many national sources are listed and a selection of local ones to show the range of information available:

Denmark Statistics (Copenhagen, Denmark)

English Tourist Board (London, England)

Harris/Pannell Kerr Forster & Company (New York, U.S.A., or London, England)

Hong Kong Tourist Association (Hong Kong)

Horwath & Horwath International (New York, U.S.A)

Las Vegas Convention/Visitors Authority (Las Vegas, Nevada)

Mexican National Tourist Council (Washington, D.C., U.S.A.)

Newfoundland Department of Tourism (St. John's, Newfoundland)

New Zealand Tourist Department (Wellington, New Zealand)

Northern Ireland Tourist Board (Belfast, Ulster)

Nova Scotia Department of Tourism (Halifax, Nova Scotia)

Tourism Development Company of Puerto Rico (San Juan, Puerto Rico)

Scottish Tourist Board (Edinburgh, Scotland)

Wales Tourist Board (Cardiff, Wales)

There are many researches about particular types of enterprise in particular areas. They can be found in bibliographies of tourism research such as those published by the following:

Business Research Division, University of Colorado (Boulder, Colorado, U.S.A.)

Centre des Hautes Etudes Touristiques (Aix-en-Provence, France): Searches and lists are available from a computer-based index.

Commonwealth Agricultural Bureaux (Oxford, England): Leisure Recreation and Tourism Abstracts; searches and lists are available from a computer-based index.

The Travel and Tourism Press, Jeanne Gay (Santa Cruz, California, U.S.A.)

Particular sources named in the text are:

Goeldner, Charles R., and Karen Dicke (1984), *Travel Trends in the United States and Canada*, Boulder: University of Colorado.

Pizam, A., and J. Pokela, (1980), *The Benefits of Farm Tourism to Rural Communities: The Massachusetts Case*, Massachusetts Agricultural Experiment Station.

APPENDIX 1   THE MINI-SURVEY

Example of a self-completion questionnaire, handed personally to one guest in each tourist party, for return anonymously in a sealed envelope before departure.

The questions are designed for an enterprise providing overnight accommodation and meals. They could easily be adapted to other needs. All unnecessary questions should be deleted: the shorter a questionnaire the better.

It is vital to try out an experimental version on a dozen or so guests to see if any aspects of the questionnaire need improvement, such as the wording or the layout or the way it is issued to or collected from customers.

The "Lake" Hotel Customer Quiz

PLEASE ANSWER BY CHECKING THE BOX OR WRITING IN THE SPACE

Q. For what reason are you staying here?

on business   ☐
on holiday/vacation   ☐
visiting friends or relatives   ☐
a mixture, or other, please say _____

Q. About how frequently do you stay here?

three or more times a year   ☐
twice a year   ☐
once a year   ☐
most years   ☐
less often   ☐
first stay   ☐

Q. What was the main method of transport you used to get here?

Auto ☐   Train ☐   Plane ☐   Coach ☐   Other ☐

Q. Did you set out meaning to come here?   ☐

or decide during the journey?   ☐
or just stopped when you saw us?   ☐

Q. Can you remember how you first got to know about us?

saw your advertisement ☐   if so please say where _____
just chanced to stop by   ☐
mentioned by friends or relatives   ☐
mentioned by business colleagues   ☐
other, please say _____

Q. Did you have any difficulties on the journey? for instance

heavy traffic on the way   yes   ☐   no   ☐
finding us was   difficult ☐   easy   ☐
somewhere to park   difficult ☐   easy   ☐
public transport or taxi   scarce   ☐   plenty   ☐

Q. How big is the party staying here together with you?

just me ☐   two ☐   three ☐   four ☐   five or more ☐
The party is...   all adults ☐   adults and children ☐

Q. Have you found things to do and see during your stay?

plenty, some left for next time   ☐
enough for a good holiday/vacation   ☐
sometimes short of things in bad weather ☐
sometimes short of things in the evening ☐
not really enough   ☐

Q. Could you list the three highlights of your stay?

  1. _____
  2. _____
  3. _____

Q. Have you found enough choices in our dining menu?*

  great variety, things left to try next time   ☐
  enough for a good meal   ☐
  rather restricted starting courses   ☐
  rather restricted main courses   ☐
  rather restricted final courses   ☐
  not really enough variety   ☐

  *Other wording could be used for wine lists, displays, entertainments, sports facilities, or other features of competitive importance.

Q. Could you list your three favorite things about eating here?

  1. _____
  2. _____
  3. _____

Q. Please write down the total charges on your bill _____ which covered this number of people _____. Are there any other things or services that you think should be provided? If so, please describe, and say how much extra, if any, you would be willing to pay for them. _____

_____

Q. Please describe anything at all we ought to have done better to improve your stay.

_____

_____

Q. Have you read our brochure?

  No, didn't know there was one   ☐
  No, not truly interested in brochures   ☐
  Yes, but I don't remember much about it   ☐
  Yes, and I would have liked written description   more ☐   less ☐   OK ☐
  pictures   more ☐   less ☐   OK ☐
  maps   more ☐   less ☐   OK ☐
  details about the surroundings   more ☐   less ☐   OK ☐
  details about the place itself   more ☐   less ☐   OK ☐
  Any other comments on the brochure?_____

_____

Q. Please, would you record some personal details?

  age under 16   ☐   female   ☐
  16 to 24   ☐   male   ☐
  25 to 34   ☐
  35 to 44   ☐   paid employment   ☐
  45 to 54   ☐   homemaker or
  55 to 64   ☐   unpaid work only   ☐
  65 or over   ☐   retired   ☐
                           student or other   ☐
  If you have paid work, what is your job? _____

_____

Q. Where do you live?

  Country _____
  Province/County/State _____
  Town _____
  Date of Departure _____
  THANK YOU FOR YOUR HELP, PLEASE COME AGAIN. THERE IS NO NEED TO WRITE YOUR NAME ON THIS FORM. PLEASE SEAL IT IN THE ENVELOPE PROVIDED, AND RETURN TO THE RECEPTION DESK.

APPENDIX 2   THE OCCUPANCY SURVEY

An enterprise offering tourist accommodation can carry out its own occupancy survey in a way comparable with most published occupancy results. Actual occupancy of the enterprise is recorded on the form shown on the next page, which is completed daily. In a small hotel, the items recorded are:

- The number of new arrivals that day
- The number of rooms let that night
- The number of beds let that night

At the end of the month, those items are added to give *total arrivals*, *total rooms let*, and *total beds let*. The month's Room Occupancy percent is calculated as:

$$\frac{\text{total rooms let} \quad \times \quad 100}{\text{rooms in the hotel} \times \text{nights in the month}}$$

Taking the example given on the next page the calculation is:

$$\text{Room Occupancy} = \frac{634 \times 100}{28 \times 30} = 75.48\%$$

A similiar calculation is made for bed occupancy, which will nearly always be lower than room occupancy because double or family rooms are sometimes occupied by fewer people than the beds could accommodate.
  The month's Bed Occupancy percent is calculated as:

$$\frac{\text{total beds let} \quad \times \quad 100}{\text{bed-spaces in the hotel} \times \text{nights in the month}}$$

Taking the example given on the next page, the calculation is:

$$\text{Bed Occupancy} = \frac{1024 \times 100}{52 \times 30} = 65.64\%$$

The month's Average Duration of Stay is calculated as:

$$\frac{\text{total beds let}}{\text{total arrivals}}$$

Taking the example given on the next page the calculation is:

$$\text{Duration of Stay} = \frac{1024}{125} = 8.19 \text{ nights}$$

The occupancy of camp sites or chalets may be simply calculated each week as: the total number of pitches/units let that week divided by the total capacity of the site and multiplied by 100 to give the percent.

RECORD FORM FOR MONTHLY OCCUPANCIES AND ARRIVALS

This hotel, for example, has 10 single rooms (10 bed-spaces) plus 15 double- or twin-bed rooms (30 bed-spaces) plus 3 family rooms (12-bed spaces). Total capacity is, therefore, 28 rooms (10 + 15 + 3) with 52 bed-spaces (10 + 30 + 12). You can see the hotel has a weekly cycle of customers.

Hotel Capacity _____ 28 rooms   52 bed-spaces

June / date	daily ARRIVALS	ROOMS filled	BEDS filled
1	0	9	12
2	4	10	16
3	4	11	16
4	0	11	16
5	0	10	14
6	16	15	24
7	3	18	27
8	0	18	27
9	0	18	27
10	6	24	33
11	0	24	33
12	0	24	33
13	15	18	31
14	5	23	36
15	0	23	36
16	0	23	36
17	3	26	39
18	0	26	39
19	0	23	36
20	31	22	41
21	6	25	47
22	0	25	47
23	3	28	50
24	0	28	50
25	0	28	50
26	0	25	44
27	24	23	40
28	0	22	38
29	5	27	43
30	0	27	43
31	not applicable	not applicable	not applicable
TOTAL	125	634	1024

Part Six

ASSESSING THE IMPACTS OF TOURISM

Part Six of the Handbook focuses on a number of different research approaches having one common underlying theme, namely, the measurement of tourism impacts. Those impacts included are economic, employment, social, environmental, and those related to tourism events. In total, seven chapters are involved.

Of the seven chapters, three are devoted to the assessment of economic impacts. The importance accorded to this area is related both to the traditional importance of economic impacts to tourism planners and to the willingness of one of the industry's leading experts in this area to contribute extensively to the Handbook. The first of the three chapters authored by Douglas Frechtling provides readers with an introduction to travel impact estimation. In this introduction, Dr. Frechtling examines the nature of direct and indirect economic repercussions related to travel and tourism expenditures. In doing so, he briefly reviews the role of economic models in tourism impact analysis as well as the need for definitional clarity when conducting research in this area. The chapter subsequently discusses four approaches commonly used for estimating economic impacts, namely, direct observation, controlled experiments, analysis through economic models, and statistical analysis of traveler survey data. It then provides some guidelines concerning the criteria to be used for judging the utility of these alternative approaches. The chapter concludes by providing an overview of the nature of the economic benefits and costs associated with travel and tourism as well as the uses to which economic impact studies can be put.

Chapter 32, "Assessing the Impacts of Travel and Tourism—Measuring Economic Benefits," provides the reader with a much more in-depth review of the various approaches to measuring economic benefits and of the difficulties encountered in doing so. This discussion will be particularly valuable to managers and researchers who have an active interest in the estimation of economic impacts of travel and tourism. Dr. Frechtling, in presenting his material, first reviews a number of methods and models used to provide the estimates of travel expenditures on which impact analysis is based. He then discusses how these expenditure estimates are translated into impact assessments through economic simulation models. Dr. Frechtling subsequently devotes a significant portion of this lengthy chapter to a very thorough and updated examination of a large integrated model (the Travel Economic Impact Model) developed by the U.S. Travel Data Center to produce detailed estimates of the economic benefits of travel on the U.S. economy as well as on the economies of state and local areas. The chapter concludes with a very helpful review of the nature of tourism impact multipliers and how they relate to, and are used in, tourism impact assessments.

The final of the three chapters authored by Dr. Frechtling addresses the issue of economic costs associated with tourism and the means of measuring these costs. After pointing out the need to measure such economic costs, the author provides an in-depth discussion of both the fiscal and quality of life costs that may be incurred as a result of tourism development. In doing so, Dr. Frechtling reviews and provides examples of the distinction between direct and indirect costs associated with tourism. The chapter then focuses on a number of issues related to the measurement of these costs. While some readers may find certain parts of the discussion somewhat technical, the editors believe that this chapter is an important contribution to increasing the rigor of tourism research and tourism management. Taken together, these first three chapters of Part Six have become a benchmark in the field and a constant source of reference for tourism planners and researchers.

Next to the measurement of expenditures on tourism, it is the study of the employment impacts of tourism that has traditionally attracted the greatest degree of interest on the part of researchers and, particularly, on the part of policymakers and politicians. In Chapter 34, Randyl Elkin and Randall Roberts examine this important area and the nature of research that is required. This research falls into two major categories, human resource requirements and employment impact studies. Accordingly, the first part of the chapter reviews human resource requirements research, which, in turn, includes two main categories of enquiry. The first is methods of job analysis, which involves the collection and analysis of data about jobs within a tourism organization with a view to job restructuring, training-program development, standards development, performance evaluation, employee counseling, and salary administration, among others. The second category is that of projecting and forecasting labor demand and labor supply. The purpose here is to provide some understanding of the kinds of programs that will be needed to meet the employment requirements of the tourism industry of the future. In the latter part of the chapter, the authors discuss research designed to estimate the employment impacts of travel expenditures. In this case, the authors refer back directly to the Travel Economic Impact Model developed by the U.S. Travel Data Center and its ability to predict employment impacts as part of its overall estimation procedures.

A related and yet distinctively different examination of the social impacts of tourism, particularly as they relate to developing rather than developed regions, is presented in Chapter 35 by Louise Crandall. In the first part of her chapter, Ms. Crandall provides a comprehensive overview of the social impacts that can potentially affect developing nations. For purposes of discussion, these impacts are reviewed under the rubric of socioeconomic impacts and sociocultural impacts. In the second part of her chapter, the author turns to an examination of the methodologies appropriate to social impact assessment. While a number of the techniques discussed are familiar (such as surveys and Delphi studies), others are not traditionally included in the tourism research repertoire. Such approaches as the use of key informants/community leaders and the participant-observation approach, while well known in the field of sociology, have not received widespread attention in tourism. It is anticipated that Ms. Crandall's explanation of the use of these techniques will encourage their further application in tourism. This may also be true to a lesser degree of the use of secondary sources for estimating social impacts that may result from the examples provided by Ms. Crandall. The approaches discussed are the content analysis of newspapers and the analysis of government records and other public documents. In brief, Ms. Crandall provides the reader with another perspective on the measurement of social impacts that, because it has been conceived in relation to developing countries, is substantially different from that outlined by Dr. Frechtling.

Chapter 36 concerns the evaluation of environmental impacts of tourism, particularly as these pertain to the physical carrying capacity of a region. The chapter, authored by Peter Williams, provides a framework for conducting research and for assessing and managing the environmental impacts of tourism. As the author indicates, his focus is specifically upon the impacts of tourism on the physical environment in general and ecological impacts in particular. The chapter starts with a discussion of the nature of environmental impacts and how they may be classified and defined so as to permit meaningful research to be undertaken. An important follow-up to this initial discussion is a review of the various methodological constraints that must be faced by researchers who wish to systematically explore or measure the extent of environmental impacts. Having identified these constraints, Dr. Williams proceeds to outline a functional classification of environmental assessment approaches, how they may be used in different settings, and how the data resulting from them can or should be analyzed. For readers who are interested, a detailed example of the environmental impact of one type of tourism example is provided. The chapter concludes with an in-depth discussion of the concept of carrying capacity, a key but controversial concept associated with the physical planning of tourism areas.

The final chapter in Part Six is concerned with a more specialized yet increasingly important area of development, namely "Event Tourism." In this chapter, Donald Getz provides detailed insights into the many unique aspects of research designed to measure and evaluate the impacts of festivals and special events. Attention first focuses on a brief discussion of different approaches commonly used to assess the impacts of such festivals/events. This section is followed by a very insightful review of a number of commonly held presumptions regarding festivals and events that frequently lead to incorrect or inappropriate research in the area. One of the most critical of these concerns relates to the use of income multipliers in the assessment of the economic impacts of events. Because of this importance, the author provides an in-depth review of the use and abuse of such multipliers as they pertain to festival/event research. Finally, Dr. Getz concludes the chapter by providing the reader with a very comprehensive framework for the conduct of impact evaluation studies in the field.

31

Assessing the Economic Impacts of Travel and Tourism—Introduction to Travel Economic Impact Estimation

DOUGLAS C. FRECHTLING
Associate Professor of Tourism
George Washington University
Washington, D.C.

*E*conomic impact, the direct and secondary costs and benefits of travel, and the travel industry are defined. General methods of approaching travel and tourism impact estimation are presented, along with criteria for evaluating alternative approaches. Uses of tourism economic impact studies are also discussed.

Economic impact studies in travel and tourism are undertaken to determine specific activities' effects on the income, wealth, and employment of the residents of a given geographic area. The studies are conducted for cities, counties, towns, states, provinces, and nations, and for individual facilities (e.g., museums) and events (e.g., Olympic games). They often relate to an annual period, although seasonal and event impact studies are not unknown. The results indicate the contribution or cost of tourism activity to the economic well-being of residents of an area, usually in monetary terms.

In the broadest sense, economic impact studies can indicate the gross increase and the gross decrease in resident wealth resulting from the activity and the net of the two influences. The wealth effects are traced through household or personal activity, such as employment and income, and through the business and government sectors serving the area.

While implicit in economic impact studies, explicit consideration of the wealth effects of tourism is seldom found. Rather, measurement is limited to the impact on income. Since wealth is created primarily through income, it is clear that concentrating on the latter is consistent with the objectives of economic science.

As discussed here, economic impact studies are understood to include objective analyses of travel activity's impact on resident wealth or income in a defined area. On the benefit side, this normally means the study provides estimates of travel spending and the impact of this spending on employment, personal income, business receipts and profits, and government revenue. On the cost side, this means estimating the costs, sometimes nonmonetary, to government and residents of travel activity in the area.

A great number of studies have been limited to estimating travel spending in an area, often through direct surveys of travelers. No attempt is made in these studies to track the effects of this spending on area employment, income, or other economic variables.

Such travel expenditure studies are specifically excluded from this discussion. However, the broader impact studies that are considered here include the essential elements of the limited expenditure studies, so the reader will gain an understanding of them in what follows here.

The reason for this exclusion is that travel expenditures tend to obscure the impact on resident wealth and income. Although such expenditures may be substantial in an area, they often have little to do with resident earnings and employment. The extreme case is represented by a hotel in an underdeveloped economy, owned by nonresidents, staffed with nonresident employees who send their earnings home, and serviced by imported goods and services. Travelers may spend millions of dollars in the hotel each year, but the contribution to the wealth or income of the residents is virtually nonexistent.

A similar case can be found in the developed economy. Consider a popular self-service gasoline service station in a resort area. Visitors purchase gasoline and oil provided by nonresident suppliers. The station itself is owned by an oil company headquartered elsewhere. The employees may be residents, but it takes only one to oversee the sale of several hundred thousand dollars of petroleum products a year. The dollars spent are a poor guide to the impact on resident wealth or income.

The point is that travel expenditures can be quite misleading in evaluating the economic benefits or the economic costs of travel and tourism in an area. They are best viewed as merely the initial monetary activity that stimulates the production process and initiates realistic measurement of economic impact.

DIRECT AND OTHER IMPACTS

Economic impact should be understood to include both direct or primary costs and benefits and also secondary costs and benefits. The former occur as a direct consequence of travel activity in the area. Travel expenditures become business receipts that, in turn, are used to pay wages and salaries and taxes, the direct benefits of tourism. Visitor use of recreation areas requires expenditures on services for the visitors as well as on redressing any environmental damage: these are direct costs. These benefits and costs are directly related to the travel activity.

In addition to these primary impacts, there are secondary effects of travel activity. On the benefit side, entrepreneurs spend part of their receipts on goods and services they require to serve customers, including investment in new equipment and structures. In turn, their suppliers must purchase certain items from others. As this chain continues in an area, income and employment are produced indirectly.

The other type of secondary benefit is induced. Here, the consumption spending of the wage and salary income, directly generated by the travel expenditures in the area, is tracked. Secondary costs of travel can also be mentioned: These are related to the public goods and services required to serve those businesses and employees that are impacted at the secondary level. Very little work has been done in this area, probably due to its complex nature.

ECONOMIC MODELS

The world of tourism is quite complex. Economists develop theories that abstract the most powerful relationships in order to deal with such complexities. An *economic model* is a "representation of a theory or a part of a theory, often for the purpose of illuminating cause-and-effect relationships" (Baumol and Blinder 1988:14). Economic models come in all shapes and sizes, each reflecting a particular theory to be

tested or applied. Chapter 43, by James Rovelstad, describes the modeling process in detail.

Models are used widely in tourism economic impact analysis. Chapters 32 and 33 discuss a number of these.

DEFINITIONS AND DATA

At first glance, travel economic impact estimation appears quite arcane. This is due to the heterogeneous nature of what is called *travel demand* and the *travel industry*. The travel industry cannot be defined the way industries normally are; for example, U.S. industries are generally understood as collections of business firms or establishments with the same "primary activity, which is determined by its principal product or group of products produced or distributed, or services rendered" (Office of Management and Budget 1987:15).

This type-of-product classification system is not consistent with the definition of *travel and tourism* as "end-use" activities, that is, defined by the purpose of the purchase. Travel expenditures are viewed as those made by people traveling away from home. They cut across many type-of-product industries and only occasionally account for the bulk of such an industry's output. More often, travelers purchase a minority portion of a type-of-product industry's output.

It is difficult to square the end-use definition of *travel* with the type-of-product statistics available from government. Government data indicate total restaurant sales, for example, but not those attributable to travelers. Consequently, travel economic impact studies are confronted by an unusual challenge at the outset: to determine the impact of an end-use activity in a world of product-type data. That this is not easy is readily indicated by the number and complexity of current approaches to measuring the economic impact of travel.

This chapter and the two following are designed to cover all major aspects of travel's economic impact, including measures of both costs and benefits. The discussion reflects a broad range of studies and other literature on the economic impact of travel. The following pages discuss the major approaches to economic impact measurement, criteria for judging them, purposes of economic impact measurement in tourism studies, appropriate impact measures, estimation methods, and secondary measures of travel's impact.

As the discussion notes, there is a great deal more basic and applied research required in travel economic impact estimation to resolve significant issues. It is hoped these chapters will provide both a guide to what researchers have learned and a stimulus to others to teach more.

TRAVELERS AND VISITORS

It is important to clarify whether the study objective is to measure the economic impact of travelers or of visitors. At the national level, the comprehensive measurement of tourism's economic impact is based on *travelers*, that is, all people traveling away from home, and the industry that serves them. Sometimes, a study will concentrate on visitors to a country from other countries, to highlight foreign exchange or balance of payments consequences of tourism.

However, studies conducted on smaller geographic areas usually concentrate solely on *visitors*, that is, nonresidents entering the area on a trip away from home. Because researchers are interested solely in the economic contribution of outsiders to the community, they are not concerned with travel expenditures by residents, such as purchase of common carrier tickets and other items preparatory to taking a trip.

This distinction is vital because it determines the expenditure categories and travel-industry components to be included in an impact model. If the area of concern is the impact of visitors to an area, then air tickets purchased by that area's residents traveling to outside destinations should be excluded. The employment and payroll of travel agencies in the area are generally not included in a visitor impact study, for example, since they primarily service resident consumers and businesses.

In developing an economic impact model or reviewing someone else's, it is important to keep this distinction in mind. Two impact models may produce different estimates of tourism impact for a given area solely because of the way they treat resident travel spending.

IMPACT ESTIMATION APPROACHES

There are four major techniques that can be applied in attempting to measure tourism's economic impact (Samuelson and Nordhaus 1989:5–6):

- Observation
- Experiments, where the researcher controls the conditions under which two or more groups of people make economic decisions
- Analysis, based on prior assumptions about how individuals and firms act and relate to one another
- Statistical analyses, through sample surveys and secondary data

Observation has major drawbacks as a method of economic impact analysis in tourism. It is difficult to determine by watching whether an individual spending money is a tourist. Moreover, the logistics of observing the behavior of a tourist over time are formidable.

Direct observation approaches are apt to be partial in scope; that is, they virtually always focus on one measure of impact, usually travel expenditures, rather than consistently following the impact of this activity on income and employment down through the primary and secondary links in the impact chain.

It is conceivable that someone could observe employees in travel-related establishments, account for how much work time they spend serving travelers, and then apportion their compensation accordingly. It is also possible to observe how much of retail sales taxes collected are generated by travelers for an indicator of total retail sales tax revenue attributable to this activity. However, it is obvious that this is a cumbersome and costly approach. Moreover, it tends to break down

in estimating secondary impact on suppliers and the effects of travel-related employees spending their income in the area under study.

Attempts have been made to survey business operators to obtain their estimates of travel-generated receipts as a proportion of total receipts (West Virginia University 1981; Division of Tourism 1974). However, this has not proved a viable method in examples available to date. The businesses and agencies involved cannot distinguish activity attributable to travelers from that produced by local residents unless they conduct valid sample surveys of their customers. This appears to seldom be done, or it is done without releasing the results for public analysis.

Controlled experiments appear not to have been attempted for estimation of tourism's economic impact. The difficulty comes in isolating two or more groups or geographic areas so that they are not affected by any force except those under the researcher's control. There is, however, a growing literature in laboratory experiments in other areas of economic study (e.g., Plott 1986).

Analysis has been employed in economic impact studies through the construction of economic models. The usual approach is to build a model incorporating the major relationships at work among consumers and businesses and governments. The model is necessarily a simplification embodying only the most important relationships. What is deemed most important varies among those building the models, depending upon their perceptions of the world and their analyses of existing data available to them describing travel activity and impact.

These models vary between being simple and complex, explicit and implicit, and partial and integrated. Explicit models are comprised of clearly stated relationships, usually in the form of equations. Implicit models lack comprehensive statements of relationships and are often judgmental; that is, they reflect the views and experiences of the researcher regarding travel magnitudes rather than mathematical relationships among objective variables. Partial models estimate only one element of economic impact, usually traveler expenditures. Integrated models, on the other hand, use expenditures to derive estimates of employment, income, tax revenue, and other economic variables. This approach is elaborated on in the following chapter (Chapter 32).

By far, the most popular method of estimating traveler spending has been through *statistical analysis*. The favored method is to draw a sample of travelers and administer a survey to it asking for expenditure data. Then, means are computed for the various expenditure items, and these are multiplied by estimates of the traveler population. The strengths and weaknesses of this approach are detailed in the following chapter.

CRITERIA FOR EVALUATING ECONOMIC IMPACT METHODS

Methods of estimating travel's economic impact are numerous and vary widely in their approaches and output. It is important to judge the approaches by some formal criteria that permit the objective evaluation of the quality of a model because there are so few independent measures of travel's impact that can be used to assess an estimation effort.

It is vital to judge an approach used for travel economic impact estimates as objectively as possible. Researchers should be especially interested in the relevance, coverage, efficiency, accuracy, and transferability of the approach suggested for use.

RELEVANCE

The approach should measure tourism's economic impact and not that of some other activity. A study of the economic effects of restaurants in a community, for example, would not accurately represent travel's impact because most of the business could be derived from local residents; or an approach that uses data on recreation activity as input would include purely local-origin effects as well as those of travelers.

Specific attention should be directed to ensuring that an impact estimation method and the data used in it represent the community, city, state, region, or other area under study. Estimated economic benefits should truly accrue to the residents of the area, and these residents should truly bear any costs estimated from travel. Three aspects of the approach should be of particular interest in terms of relevancy: Does it relate to travel alone? Does it fairly represent the area under study and only that area? and Does it cover the time period under study?

COVERAGE

The approach should also cover all of travel away from home and related activities. On the economic-benefit side, the impact of purchases in anticipation of a trip as well as those during the trip should be included in a tourism impact study. Anticipatory purchases include major consumer durables, such as recreational vehicles and vacation homes, and minor items, such as tennis rackets and camping equipment. Expenditures during the trip should cover all types of transportation, accommodation, food consumption, entertainment and recreation, and incidental purchases, such as souvenirs. But again, the distinction between visitors and travelers should be observed, and expenditures measured should truly occur in the area under study.

EFFICIENCY

Since funds available for economic impact estimation are generally limited, the approach should make maximum use of existing data commensurate with satisfying the other criteria. Primary-data collection is costly and difficult to do well. It should be avoided whenever possible in favor of relevant, comprehensive, and accurate secondary data.

ACCURACY

The approach should also be judged on the basis of its accuracy: Are the input or survey data accurate measures of travel activity? Does the approach accurately reflect real relationships? Are the results reasonable? This involves investigating the techniques used to generate primary or secondary data. It also includes comparing the results with other, independent measures of travel impact wherever possible. Since these other measures generally do not pass these five evaluation criteria themselves, a good deal of judgment is often required to assess the accuracy of an approach and its output.

TRANSFERABILITY

The approach should be applicable to different geographic areas and different time periods, rather than requiring data unique to one particular case. It should also be sensitive to differences in travel patterns, industry structure, and prices in different places and times. The main objective here is an approach that is feasible in different areas for different time periods and that produces consistent results in varying contexts. This permits valid comparisons across time and space and provides a broader track record on which to assess the model.

These five criteria should be applied to the structure of the estimation procedure, the input data, and the results. They should also be applied to sample design, questionnaires, interview models, expansion factors, and weighting in surveys. If so desired, the user can weight the criteria based on his or her own requirements as to relative importance.

ECONOMIC BENEFITS OF TRAVEL AND TOURISM

An *economic benefit* is best understood as a gross increase in the wealth or income, measured in monetary terms, of people located in an area over and above the levels that would prevail in the absence of the activity under study, *ceteris paribus*.

Of interest here are *gross* increases because the costs of the activity will be estimated separately. Subtracting the gross costs from the gross benefits produces a measure of net economic benefit, either positive or negative.

This chapter concentrates here on the economic benefits (or costs) for the sake of convenience, not because other, nonmonetary benefits are insignificant. Most economic benefits are measured in terms of money (employment is the major exception) and are amply documented in data available. It is far more difficult to measure the psychic benefits of travel, such as a relaxed feeling, lower blood pressure, or enjoyment of beautiful surroundings. Techniques to measure these nonmonetary benefits are beyond the scope of these chapters. Indeed, little work has been done in this area. This does not mean these nonmonetary benefits are insignificant, only that there are few objective means of measuring them at the current time.

It is important to understand that economic benefits should actually accrue to the people located in the area under study. If the purpose of the study is to estimate the economic benefits of tourism to the people who live or work in Missouri, for example, the economic benefits should actually redound to the Missourians.

This analysis assumes the absence of these benefits if travel did not occur in the area, *ceteris paribus*. One could argue that with the cessation of tourism in an area, other industries would spring up to provide the same amounts of employment and income. However, this is by no means assured. Employees and proprietors skilled in tourism services could not necessarily find immediate employment in a manufacturing plant, for example. The study seeks to know what travel is contributing to the economy of an area under certain conditions. Analysis of alternative industries that could replace tourism, should tourism disappear, is beyond the scope of the study of travel's economic benefits.

Finally, a word about terms used to represent economic benefits. The one most often found in economic discussions of travel is *travel expenditures*. However, a little thought reveals expenditures imply little in themselves to the income and wealth of a community.

If travelers purchase all their goods and services from residents who employ labor and supplies originating solely in the area, then travel expenditures represent income to the community. However, it is far more common for travel-related businesses to purchase most of the supplies they need, and often labor as well, from sources outside the community. The gasoline station operator must buy gasoline from a supplier usually refining oil many miles away. Expenditures on an airline ticket do not remain in the community for long, but rather are remitted to some central office to pay for salaries, depreciation, fuel, and other items not found in the community where the ticket was bought.

Many of the goods purchased by travelers are likely to have high import content, that is, to consist primarily of intermediate goods produced outside the community. Even services, especially common carrier transportation, may have few linkages with the local economy. Consequently, to focus on travel expenditures as the measure of economic benefits to an area's residents is to grossly misstate the actual benefits generated in the area in many cases.

For a more accurate view, the labor income, corporate profits, and rents generated by travel spending must be calculated. Employment as an important economic-policy objective can also be viewed. Government revenue generated by travel expenditures is a valuable measure as well, for it helps convince governments to include tourism in public economic-development strategies and to treat tourism fairly in energy, regulatory, and other public policies.

Travel expenditures are an initial cause of economic benefits but should not be confused with these effects. Table 1 provides a comprehensive outline of the major types of economic benefits derived from travel and tourism.

ECONOMIC COSTS OF TRAVEL AND TOURISM

The *costs of travel* are normally thought of as the explicit prices the traveler pays for a trip, the "private costs." The

Table 1 Economic Benefits of Travel and Tourism

I. Primary or Direct Benefits
   A. Business receipts
   B. Income
      1. Labor's and proprietor's income
      2. Dividends, interest, and rent
      3. Corporate profits
   C. Employment
      1. Private employment
      2. Public employment
   D. Government receipts
      1. National
      2. State or province
      3. Local
II. Secondary Benefits
   A. Indirect benefits generated by primary business outlays, including investment
      1. Business receipts
      2. Income
         a. Labor's and proprietor's income
         b. Dividends, interest, and rent
         c. Corporate profits
      3. Employment
      4. Government receipts
   B. Induced benefits generated by spending of primary income
      1. Business receipts
      2. Income
         a. Labor's and proprietor's income
         b. Dividends, interest, and rent
         c. Corporate profits
      3. Employment
      4. Government receipts

traveler purchases transportation, lodging, food, entertainment, and numerous other goods and services, all at explicit prices in the marketplace.

However, it is important to recognize that all of the costs associated with a trip are not paid explicitly by the traveler or the traveler's employer, in the case of a business-related trip. Some are paid explicitly and implicitly by others. These costs borne by others but related to the traveler's activities fall in the general class economists call *spillover costs* or *detrimental externalities* (Baumol and Blinder 1988:251). The distinction is between the private costs of the trip, those paid explicitly by the traveler for goods and services in the marketplace, and incidental costs, which represent other resources that are sacrificed in the process: all the disutility generated by the production process that is not recompensed by traveler purchases (Baumol and Blinder 1988:251; Samuelson and Nordhaus 1989:770).

To the extent that all incidental costs can be made explicit and included in the traveler's costs, welfare will be maximized. The traveler then faces higher costs that reflect all the costs of the trip and, on this basis, chooses whether to purchase travel or not. The higher costs are also a signal to industry that competitive advantage can be gained by producing at lower than the prevailing costs, through greater efficiency either in directly serving the traveler or mitigating the detrimental externalities generated by the traveler. However, in practice, there will always be uncompensated incidental costs resulting from tourism.

As Table 2 indicates, a useful distinction can be made between the private costs of visiting a community and the incidental costs, depending upon whether the visitor explicitly pays the market prices for travel goods and service or the costs are borne by the residents of the community as a result of the visit.

Frequently, other distinctions are made in discussing the overall costs of tourism: economic costs, social costs, environmental costs, fiscal costs, and life-quality costs. These distinctions are valid if the purpose of the study is to find who initially bears the burden or what is initially sacrificed. They are also useful for actually measuring the costs associated with tourism. However, it should be recognized that these distinctions are not very useful for determining who finally bears the burden of visitation to a community. Instead, they reflect how a given community has decided to allocate the social costs of visitors at a given point in time.

The term *economic costs* covers all costs, both private and incidental, explicit and implicit, and refers to the value that must be sacrificed (called the *opportunity cost* by economists) in order to provide the visitor experience. It must be remembered that the subject of interest is the sacrifice of scarce goods and services to provide the experience. The fact that a visitor breathes air or absorbs the sun is not a cost to the community because the residents are not giving up anything scarce that they own and value.

Like economic costs, the term *social costs* is used to cover all costs of the visitor experience. It is the sum of private costs and incidental costs, emphasizing the total cost to the society (Baumol and Blinder 1988:251; Samuelson and Nordhaus 1989:745). *Environmental costs* are reductions in the quality of air, water, land, flora, and fauna in the area. These are initially imposed upon residents of the host area. *Fiscal costs* are those imposed by government on residents or visitors through taxes, user fees, license fees, fines, and admission charges. *Life-quality costs* are those that reduce the standard of living in some nonmonetary way; for example, highway congestion increases the time a resident

Table 2   Outline of the Costs of Travel and Tourism

I. Private costs
II. Incidental costs
  A. Direct incidental costs
    1. Life-quality costs
      a. Congestion
      b. Pollution
      c. Danger to life, health, and property
    2. Fiscal costs
      a. Public services
      b. Public investment
  B. Indirect incidental costs
    1. Life-quality costs
    2. Fiscal costs

must spend commuting to and from work—since the worker does not enjoy the time spent commuting, this is a reduction in the quality of life. Virtually all environmental costs are life-quality costs, but not all life-quality costs are environmental costs.

Environmental costs, fiscal costs, and reduction in resident standards of living or quality of life are all incidental costs and denote which group or entity is initially bearing the cost at the current time. They do not designate who finally sacrifices value.

An example will make this clear. Tourists crowd a park that a resident enjoys visiting in his or her town. If nothing is done, then the resident bears the burden as a reduction in the quality of life. The resident does not enjoy visiting the park as much as he or she would in the absence of the visitors. The visitors may also pollute the stream running through the park, again reducing the quality of life for the residents. If nothing is done about this, the residents directly bear these costs and the visitors do not.

However, residents have several options. For one, they can persuade the government to impose admission fees for the park. This will not only limit visitor demand somewhat and reduce crowding, but will also provide funds for cleaning up the stream and hiring park attendants to prevent pollution. If the admission fees now reduce crowding of the park to its previsitor level and provide funds for returning the environment to its previsitor state, then the environmental life-quality costs have become private costs and have been shifted to the visitors and residents who use the park. (In actual practice, it is unlikely that admission fees will both reduce visitor demand significantly and provide enough funds for cleaning up the park, since these are conflicting objectives: fewer visitors are achieved at the expense of revenue.)

There is another option. The residents can vote to spend public funds on enlarging the park and fencing in the stream. If successful in returning the park to its previsitor level of congestion and environmental quality, this tactic has turned one type of incidental cost (quality of life) into another (fiscal). However, in the absence of higher admission fees, the residents run the danger of attracting even more visitors than before, and there is no guarantee that the taxes required to pay for the park enlargement will be generated by the visitors or local users. The fact that the costs are now fiscal instead of life quality does not indicate who finally pays them. It may be that the residents have just transformed these costs into higher property taxes and still bear them on behalf of the visitors.

Residents can also attempt to reduce congestion and other ill effects of tourism by treating visitors in a repellent manner. In this way, travelers may be dissuaded from returning. It is not clear that negative resident attitudes are effective in reducing visitation, but the resident may not approach this issue in a rational manner (Pizam 1977:7–11).

Measuring the economic costs of tourism and comparing them to the economic benefits are discussed in Chapter 33.

USES OF ECONOMIC IMPACT STUDIES

Measurement of the economic benefits and costs of travel and tourism can help meet a variety of objectives for both marketers and planners.

These studies can inform public officials and business managers of the net benefits of investing in travel promotion or tourism and recreation facilities. The studies can also show how the costs and benefits are distributed geographically and among residents.

Economic impact studies can help tourism marketers evaluate the effectiveness of marketing efforts and the effects of additional facilities on demand for current ones.

Estimates of tourism's economic impact can educate travel-related employees about their role in economic and business development and about how their services contribute to the economic health of their communities.

By displaying the net returns to promotional and facility investment, these studies can encourage both business and government to seek out cooperative ventures with other organizations for mutual benefit.

By demonstrating the effects of travel development to the general public, economic impact studies can help citizens rationally choose whether to encourage or resist additional tourism marketing or development efforts.

Economic impact studies also aid public officials in developing laws and policies that best promote the economic, social, and cultural health of their citizens and in avoiding decisions that would threaten this health.

In short, the estimation of the economic benefits and costs of travel and tourism activities permits consumers, business, and government to make efficient and effective marketing and development decisions.

REFERENCES

Baumol, William J., and Alan S. Blinder (1988), *Economics, Principles and Policy: Microeconomics*, 4th ed., San Diego: Harcourt Brace Jovanovich, Inc.

Division of Tourism, California (1974), *Tourism Employment Study*, Sacramento: State of California Department of Commerce.

Fleming, William R., and Lorin Toepper (1990), "Economic Impact Studies: Relating the Positive and Negative Impacts to Tourism Development," *Journal of Travel Research* XXIX (Summer), 35–42.

Pizam, Abraham, and Ernest J. Acquaro (1977), *Some Social Costs and Benefits of Tourism to Rural Communities, The Cape Cod Case*, Amherst, MA: Massachusetts Agricultural Experiment Station.

Plott, Charles R. (1986), "Laboratory Experiments in Economics: The Implications of Posted-price Institutions," *Science* 232 (May 9) 732–738.

Samuelson, Paul A., and William D. Nordhaus (1989), *Economics*, 13th ed., New York: McGraw-Hill Book Company.

U.S. Office of Management and Budget (1987), *Standard Industrial Classification Manual*, Washington, D.C.: U.S. Government Printing Office.

West Virginia University (1981), *Creating Economic Growth and Jobs through Travel and Tourism*, Washington, D.C.: U.S. Government Printing Office.

32

Assessing the Impacts of Travel and Tourism—Measuring Economic Benefits

DOUGLAS C. FRECHTLING
Associate Professor of Tourism
George Washington University
Washington, D.C.

*E*ight approaches to estimating travel expenditures in an area are explained and evaluated. Sample surveys and respondent-recall bias are discussed in detail. Simulation models of economic impact are presented, with the Travel Economic Impact Model evaluated by the criteria established in Chapter 31. Measuring secondary benefits is also discussed, including alternative techniques for estimating multipliers.

The economic benefits of travel and tourism in an area are the gross contributions to resident income and wealth resulting from the presence of travelers. Normally, this income will result from traveler expenditures in the area. One could conceive of increased resident wealth in the absence of any visitors, say through construction of a tourist facility by a nonresident in anticipation of visitors who never arrive, but this is an unlikely exception that tests the rule.

Resident individuals' wealth may be augmented through labor earnings, rising real property values, or returns on capital invested in tourist facilities. Corporations are residents, too, and their wealth increases with profits and rising asset values. As a practical matter, economic benefit studies have focused on labor income and generally ignored the other measures. This is primarily due to the difficulty of estimating increases in real property values from tourists (indeed, values may *decline* with rising visitor volume), corporate profits of tourism facilities, and returns on tourism capital investment. Moreover, these wealth increases often accrue to nonresidents of the area as absentee owners.

There is an implicit consensus in economic benefit studies that their purpose is to determine the benefits accruing to residents. These are the people needing employment if tourism is viewed as an economic stimulant, and they are the people who choose the area's political leaders and representatives. While tourism development projects sometimes end up benefiting absentee owners more than residents, it is

unlikely the residents and local government originally had this objective in mind.

Measures of the direct benefits of travel spending in an area normally comprise business receipts or gross sales of establishments in the area visited, personal income (usually limited to forms of compensation paid to employees, such as wages, salaries, commissions, bonuses, vacation allowances, tips, etc.), employment in terms of total jobs or full-time equivalent jobs, and national, state, and local tax revenue (e.g., U.S. Travel Data Center 1991a).

The following pages discuss difficulties and methods of estimating the direct economic benefits of tourism in an area, and evaluation by the criteria established in Chapter 31. Methods of quantifying secondary benefits are introduced and evaluated as well.

No single chapter can exhaustively discuss measuring the economic benefits of travel and tourism. Indeed, at least one *book* has been devoted to estimating the impact of a single facility (Johnson and Thomas 1991). It is hoped that the reader will explore the individual references listed at the end of this chapter for further treatment of the issues.

TRAVEL EXPENDITURE ESTIMATION METHODS

Tourism's economic impact on an area is a flow process. Snapshots of the flow over any chosen time period can be taken and the resulting estimates called the *economic impact of tourism*. The objects in the snapshot will usually include measures of benefits: traveler expenditures, business receipts, labor earnings, jobs, and government revenue. Sometimes, changes in real property and other asset values, and fixed capital investment will be included. Far less often, the picture will include some measure of costs (see Chapter 33).

The presence of the traveler in the area, or his or her advance reservations and payments, begins the impact process. Most studies of economic benefits begin with the traveler's expenditures. Estimating the expenditures of individuals while traveling away from home is a formidable task, and, judging from the extensive literature on travel impact estimation, there is no consensus on the best approach at this time. In the literature on the subject, there are at least eight major recognized approaches to estimating tourism expenditures in a geographic area:

1. Direct observation
2. Sample surveys
3. Bank returns
4. Residual receipts models
5. Seasonal difference models
6. Supply-side judgmental models
7. Expenditure ratio models
8. Cost factor models

Each of these approaches is discussed in turn in the following sections, and then each will be evaluated by the established criteria.

DIRECT OBSERVATION

The simplest way to obtain estimates of traveler expenditures would appear to be to actually observe the traveler purchasing food, gasoline, lodging, and other items, either by following him or her around or by asking the seller to record purchases by local versus nonlocal customers. It would, of course, be quite expensive to follow the traveler even if he or she would allow this. Moreover, this method could distort travel spending patterns that would occur in the absence of an observer.

The sellers of air, bus, rail, and cruise transportation can estimate sales to travelers with a high degree of reliability due to the nature of their business. However, it is unlikely that restaurateurs, gas station operators, or entertainment and recreation facility managers can do so. Even hotel and motel operators do not have an easy time making such estimates. In a study conducted by the State of California in the San Diego area, hotel/motel operators were asked to estimate the percentage of their business arising from tourism. The responses ranged from 40 percent to 100 percent (California Division of Tourism 1974:21). It seems fair to conclude that following the traveler is not feasible, and business operators do not know distribution of their receipts between visitors and local residents (West Virginia University 1981:52).

Similarly, the *end-use* focus of travel impact studies prohibits valid application of the direct-observation approach for measures of tourism impact other than expenditures and

business receipts. If business operators cannot estimate accurately the proportion of their receipts due to tourists, employers or employees cannot be expected to correctly assess how many jobs are attributable to tourism. And there is no direct way to determine travel-generated profits, tax revenue, or income, except in a few cases of industry sectors or individual business establishments where it can be documented that virtually all receipts are attributable to travelers or visitors.

This group is small relative to the universe of businesses and items affected by travel and tourism. It includes Amtrak (although some studies suggest a significant proportion of receipts are derived from daily commuters), air passenger service (when it can be separated from cargo and other nonpassenger airline activities), commercial lodging guest-room rentals (distinct from food-and-beverage service activity), intercity bus service (if passenger revenue can be separated from that of other services), cruise lines, and arrangers of passenger transportation (travel agents, tour operators, etc.). Information can be derived on travel's economic contributions from tax, business, and employment data through the application of direct observation for these travel industry sectors.

However, the focus should not be on one segment just because it is easy to measure. A far more comprehensive and accurate picture of travel's economic benefits must come from examination of all business types, goods, and services affected by travel demand.

SAMPLE SURVEYS

The most popular travel expenditure estimation method in the literature is to survey a probability sample of travelers, either while traveling or in their homes. The results from questions on expenditures can then be projected to produce estimates of business receipts in various types of businesses. Surveys can be conducted as travelers enter an area (entry surveys), as they leave the area (exit surveys), or while in the area under study (visitor surveys). In addition, *en route* surveys can be conducted while passengers are traveling on an airplane, train, bus, or ship.

Among these, entry surveys are the least satisfactory because they cannot obtain information on actual expenditures in the area, only amounts intended, or "budgeted," to be spent.

Recall Bias

Exit surveys are superior to visitor surveys if one assumes no decay in respondent ability to recall spending amounts as the time elapsed between expenditure and interview increases. The recall issue is the most crucial in travel-generated business receipt estimation and has received substantial research attention. If there is little or no loss of recall as a function of the time lapse between expenditure and interview, then it makes little difference when the interview is conducted. Travel expenditure estimates derived from household surveys conducted months after the trip are just as accurate as those done in transit. However, if recall declines significantly as the duration between expenditure and interview increases, then the most accurate direct-observation results are obtained by reducing the time lapsed to a minimum: interviewing travelers while traveling.

A number of researchers have found that respondents cannot recall expenditures accurately after the fact (Burd 1991:6; Bureau of Management Consulting 1975a:41; Church 1969; Haynes 1975; Lansing and Morgan 1971:123–126; Mak, Moncur, and Yonamine 1977; Meyberg and Brog 1981:47; Ritchie 1975:3, 5; Steel 1981; Stynes and Mahoney 1989; Woodwise 1990:6, quoting Davidson.) One reason is the myriad of items a traveler may purchase on his trip. Moreover, currency may not change hands when the purchase is made, as the traveler may pay by personal checks, traveler's checks, vouchers, or credit card. It is difficult to believe the traveler can remember each of the cash or noncash purchases made and the amount as well.

In addition to problems with the human memory, the traveler may never know what some of his or her expenses were. Many expenses of business travel, convention trips, and incentive travel are paid directly by an employee's firm. This type of travel spending produced the lowest response rates among the expenditure questions in the U.S. Census Bureau's 1977 National Travel Survey (U.S. Bureau of the Census 1979).

There is one last difficulty in obtaining reliable expenditure information from travelers. Package tours provide transportation, accommodations, meals, entertainment, or any combination of these for a single price. The traveler cannot usually tell how much of the tour price is attributable to items provided in a given locale and, consequently, cannot give the interviewer reliable information on expenditures in the area under study.

Some objective evidence on the scope of recall decay in obtaining travel spending estimates is available. In the 1977 National Travel Survey, respondents who took trips involving public transportation, commercial accommodations, or a package tour were asked to report their expenditures for each of the categories. The elapsed time between the trip and the interview was as long as three months. Among those who took package tours, the tabulated data suggest only 70 percent could respond with any cost estimate at all. The response rates were higher for public transportation and lodging: 85 percent and 92 percent, respectively. These rates only indicate the proportion of those with eligible trips who reported some expenditures. They do not suggest the degree of underreporting of expenditures that may have taken place (U.S. Bureau of the Census 1979:54, 59).

Tourism Canada has concluded that travel expenditure estimates from surveys "are of low quality, expensive, and untimely" (Chau 1988:3). This matches the conclusion by the British Columbia Ministry of Trade, Development and Tourism that visitor surveys "cannot provide the necessary time-series economic data needed to determine the economic impact of the industry" (Burd 1991:13).

In another case, comparison of visitor expenditure estimates in Hawaii derived from diaries kept by visitors and

from questionnaires sent to former visitors one month after they returned home found "relative to the diary method, visitors who recall their vacation spending some time after returning home generally underestimate their expenditures" (Mak, Moncur, and Yonamine 1977). The same conclusion was reached in a similar study in British Columbia (Burd 1991:13). There, tourism expenditures reported by diary respondents were 30 percent higher than those who responded to a survey based on recall. The diary approach to traveler spending estimation has been applied elsewhere, but response rates in the 15 to 25 percent range raise serious concerns about respondent bias (Woodside 1981; Hunt and Cadez 1981; Burke and Gitelson 1990).

A study of delegates to a national conference found that posttrip recall of expenditures while attending were 20 percent less than estimates provided by respondents during the conference (Stynes and Mahoney 1989).

Howard, Lankford, and Havitz (1991:19) attempted to determine "how accurately travelers report trip expenditures" by gaining cooperation of participants in a track-and-field competition and their companions. One member of each of 40 couples recorded expenditures during the competition, while the other was asked to estimate travel spending just before departure from the event. Comparing the mean daily expenditures reported by each indicated that reported trip expenses were 8 percent lower than the recorded expenditures (ibid.:21). However, subsequent analyses of the significance test indicated there was no significant difference in the expenditures reported by the two groups (Roehl 1992; Howard et al. 1992).

The Fish and Wildlife Service of the U.S. Department of the Interior sponsored an exhaustive study to determine whether one-year recall periods produced a "serious systematic bias" in survey estimates of hunting and fishing activities (Westat, Inc. 1989). The study compared recall of these activities and related expenditures over annual, six-month, one-month, and two-week recall periods. The study found that recall bias increased with the length of the recall period. However, in contrast to other recall studies, here the longer recall periods resulted in *overreporting* of the number of hunting and fishing trips. The researchers speculated that telescoping (including trips that were not actually taken during the recall period) and prestige bias (respondent tendency to overestimate based on the social desirability or status of an activity) were contributing factors. In addition, counter to other recall-bias studies, this survey's respondents were asked to summarize experiences rather than itemize each event (ibid.:7.3). Results on expenditure estimation were mixed. Some fishing expenditures were significantly higher with annual recall than with two-week recall, but there were no significant differences for hunting expenditures (ibid.:7.2). These estimates proved to be extremely variable, especially for hunting.

Other studies have also found that the length of the respondent recall period can bias estimates of real travel activity. A comparison of the volumes of person-trips, for example, recorded in two different surveys of residents of the province of Ontario, Canada, found that the three-month recall method recorded only about 40 percent of the volume found in the one-month recall survey (Rogers 1991:7–8). The same study found a mail survey of U.S. residents where the three-month recall volume of same-day or one-night trips was about 80 percent of the one-month recall level (ibid.:9).

In a study of the impact of the amount of elapsed time between an intercity trip and the report of the trip on reported trip volume, Meyberg and Brog (1981) found that the longer the elapsed time, the smaller the proportion of actual trips reported; for example, more than 4 percent of actual intercity trips were unreported six to nine months later, and 13 percent were unreported nine to twelve months after they occurred (ibid.:48).

In 1992, Statistics Canada and Tourism Canada revised the biennial Canadian Travel Survey to reduce the respondent recall period from three months to one month, anticipating that "the suspected undercount of overnight trips should be significantly reduced" (Statistics Canada 1992). They noted this change should also diminish the undercount of same-day trips, "but not to the extent possible using an even shorter recall period."

More objective evidence is needed before handing down a final verdict on this important issue. However, the research that is available strongly supports the view that estimates of travel expenditures suffer as the elapsed time between purchase and interview increases. Moreover, for some types of travel, such as business or package tours, the respondent may never have knowledge of actual travel expenses in an area. In addition, recall of other trip events is also biased as the recall period increases.

Various methods have been tried to reduce recall bias in traveler surveys. During the years 1974–1981, the Florida Division of Tourism conducted exit surveys that included questions on out-of-state visitor expenditures during the previous 24 hours and was satisfied with the results (Haynes 1975; Schultz and Stronge 1980a). Subsequently, however, the question was changed to "a typical day," and then to requesting respondents' estimates of all expenditures in selected categories (Pitegoff 1992).

Researchers in Utah and Idaho have asked travelers to complete diaries as they travel through their respective states, but low response rates cast doubt on the validity of the information collected (Harris, Tynon, and McLaughlin 1990; Hunt and Cadez 1981).

This author believes recall decay substantially biases downward travel expenditure estimates derived from interviews more than a day or two after the purchase. Consequently, exit, visitor, or en route surveys in which the expenditure recall period is limited to the previous 24 hours appear better choices than entry surveys (e.g., Murphy and Carmichael 1991).

Other Estimation Issues

Visitor surveys can also suffer from "length-of-stay" bias. If visitors are interviewed while they are in an area rather than when they enter or leave, the probability of being selected increases with the length of stay. A visitor staying 10 days in Washington, D.C. has 10 times the probability of being interviewed than does a visitor staying one day, *ceteris paribus*. Adjustments should be made for this in en route surveys, or multiplying length of stay by daily travel expenditures is likely to produce estimates significantly biased upward (Archer and Shea 1975).

Like most sample surveys, traveler surveys require an estimate of the population size to which the sample results can be projected. If the survey is conducted among passengers on an airline or visitors to an amusement park, this estimate is straightforward. However, if the population being sampled is defined as visitors to a geographic area without controlled access, then the population cannot be estimated with much confidence.

Researchers may encounter at least one other problem in estimating spending through traveler surveys. Sometimes the estimates are distorted by a few travelers who make unusually large purchases while in the area and bias the results of a small-sample survey substantially upward. The motorist forced to buy a new set of tires while at his or her destination is one such case. A traveler who requires hospital care for an unexpected illness is another. This can be accounted for by asking both actual expenses during the previous 24-hour period and which of these were atypical. However, it would be unwise to remove completely the atypical expenditures because they do indeed constitute traveler spending. Rather, samples over time can yield the correct probability of encountering these, and this is used to adjust the survey results for these expenses (Haynes 1975).

Household Surveys

The conduct of surveys in the household have been discussed at length elsewhere (Lansing and Morgan 1971; Babbie 1973; Ferber 1978; Alreck and Settle 1985). The recall problem regarding travel expenditures as discussed earlier is a prime weakness of this approach. One strength is that sound sampling frames for household surveys are readily available, and it is a simple matter to project sample results to the total population for absolute estimates, something traveler surveys do not readily permit.

There is an analog to the length of stay bias in household surveys. Those people who travel the most are, by definition, least likely to be home to be interviewed. Repeated callbacks and adjusting for probability of being at home can be used to reduce this potential source of bias.

Another drawback of the household survey is that it misses travelers in an area who do not belong to the population being sampled. A survey using a probability sample of the U.S. population, for example, cannot provide information on foreign visitors in a locality. This requires either surveys among foreign-resident populations or surveys of travelers (e.g., U.S. Travel and Tourism Administration 1991).

Mail, Personal, and Telephone Interviews   There are three basic modes of household surveys: mail, personal interview, and telephone interview.

Mail surveys are the least expensive, allow the largest

sample size within a given budget, avoid not-at-home bias, eliminate interview bias, permit longer questionnaires, and allow respondents to consider their answers carefully, perhaps checking with other household members to insure accurate information (Bullen 1988). On the other hand, mail surveys are the slowest of the three modes, often adding four weeks or more to the survey process. Moreover, they permit the least control over question completion, are subject to loss in the postal system, do not permit interviewer probing for detailed recall, permit too much respondent self-selection, and produce the lowest response rates (Alreck and Settle 1985:43–46; Rappaport 1988). The last caused the U.S. Bureau of the Census to switch from mail to personal interviews in its last National Travel Survey (U.S. Bureau of the Census 1979:xxi).

Low response rates in mail surveys are likely to produce nonresponse bias, as those who take part in the activity being studied are more likely to respond than those who do not (Alreck and Settle 1985:45,78; Murray 1991:20). There is evidence that nonrespondents to mail traveler surveys tend to be less mobile in terms of trip frequency than respondents (Hunt and Dalton 1983; Woodside and Ronkainen 1984). This bias cannot be easily removed by adjusting sociodemographic weighting procedures (Brog and Meyberg 1980). The U.S. Travel Data Center noted similar evidence in mail surveys conducted in 1974 through 1976 (U.S. Travel Data Center 1975, 1976, 1977). In sum, the low response rates found in mail surveys argue against using the results to generalize to any population (Turco and Kelsey 1992: 20–21).

Personal interviews have the virtues of shorter elapsed time between interview and processing relative to mail and of higher response rates either through repeated call-backs or by substituting similar households. The drawbacks of this mode are the high cost of interviewing, the difficulty of obtaining interviews in some areas due to crime or exclusivity, heavy training and field-supervision requirements, and poor interviewer supervision (Alreck and Settle 1985:40–42). In some cases, interviewers have been known to falsify interview records to achieve interview quotas (Ferber 1978:426).

Compared to personal interviews, telephone surveys are considerably less costly, produce results more quickly, provide for direct supervision of interviewers, and offer respondent anonymity that may improve response rates (Alreck and Settle 1985; Westat, Inc., 1989:4.10–4.12). Response rates are similar to home interviews and can be higher through increased ease and lower cost of repeated call-backs.

Telephone surveys cannot be easily or accurately conducted among populations relatively inaccessible to the instrument. In the United States, it is estimated that 93.6 percent of all households have telephone service, making this an effective interview mode (U.S. Bureau of the Census 1992:551). Another drawback is that telephone surveys do not permit lengthy interviews or questions with many choices or with exhibits.

Compared to mail surveys, telephone interviews are more costly. However, they are superior in minimizing lag between interview and processing, in maximizing response rates, and in providing control over the interview.

When considering an interview mode, it is important to determine whether the interviews will be conducted among a probability sample of the chosen population or among a preselected *panel* of potential respondents.

Panel surveys are frequently found in the mail mode because they produce high response rates. These panels are large files of households that have agreed to be included in consumer surveys conducted by research firms (Alreck and Settle 1985:46). When a survey is to be conducted, a sample of necessary size is drawn to reflect the characteristics, usually demographic, of the population as a whole. This approach generally produces significantly higher response rates than a "cold" probability sample.

The failure of this approach is due to the basically upscale nature of the preselected panel. People interested in participating in surveys are apt to be more active in many aspects of life than those who are not, regardless of income or level of education (Lansing and Morgan 1971:59–62). The U.S. Travel Data Center's 1974 and 1975 National Travel Surveys were conducted among mail panels and found a considerably higher incidence of travel among nearly all groups than the Census Bureau's probability sample (U.S. Travel Data Center 1975, 1976).

Moreover, since all households in the population do not have a known, nonzero chance of participating in the panel, techniques for estimating sampling variability cannot be applied. Confidence intervals at different numbers of standard deviations from the mean cannot be computed, so this guide to the reliability of the survey in reflecting actual population behavior is not available (Alreck and Settle 1985:69–70; Dommermuth 1975:19; Cochran 1977:135).

In summary, among the sample survey methods of estimating travel expenditures, exit surveys are the best at limiting recall bias. However, the difficulty in projecting sample results to the total population is not resolved in any of the three kinds of traveler surveys.

Household surveys solve the projection problem but fall short on the recall-bias issue. If a household survey is the chosen direct-observation method, telephone surveys with minimum recall periods (one month at most) among national probability samples are the preferred mode.

This author believes none of the interview methods just discussed can provide reasonably accurate travel expenditure information, with the possible exception of the exit survey limited to 24-hour recall. Fortunately, there are other techniques available for estimating travel expenditures.

BANK RETURN ESTIMATES OF TRAVELER SPENDING

A number of countries measure foreign-visitor expenditures within their borders through accounting for foreign-exchange purchases by these visitors (World Tourism Organization 1986:195–196). The central bank attempts to compute the amount of national currency sold to visitors each period through reports from agencies making such currency sales.

The validity of this method is dependent on all entities selling currency to visitors reporting these sales accurately, making sure to exclude any nonrelated sales. In practice, this method fails because of the multitude of ways tourists can obtain national currency outside of this system: the black market; from hotels, shops, and other unofficial commercial sources; through advance or deferred payments for services; bringing currency in from previous visits; and purchases through tour operator and travel agencies (World Tourism Organization 1986:198).

These, and the fact that the bank-return method can only suggest total foreign-visitor spending but not categories of this spending or domestic spending volume severely limit the usefulness of this method in most studies of tourism economic impact.

RESIDUAL RECEIPTS MODELS

A model for estimating total visitor expenditures in a county using secondary data has been suggested by Kreutzwiser (Smith 1989:280–288). It is based on the assumption that total receipts of retail and service establishments in a county are greater than the expenditures by county residents in these establishments. By rearranging the identity that total establishment receipts equal sales to residents plus sales to nonresidents, the method subtracts resident spending from the total to leave visitor spending as a residual.

The method begins by multiplying total household income in a county by the percent of this income spent on retail goods and services. Both of these numbers can be obtained from public economic development agencies. Then, this total is subtracted from the sales of retail and service establishments in the county, and this residual is the amount attributable to visitors to the county.

To compute visitor expenditures to a collection of counties ("region"), the process is more complex. Spending by residents of one county in the region in another county must be subtracted. Kreutzwiser uses the geographic circulation patterns of all of the newspapers in the major city or metropolitan area in the region to suggest such resident purchase patterns. The percent of total newspaper circulation outside the city but within the region is used to calculate how much city residents spend outside the city but within the region. This is subtracted from the first residual to obtain a second residual, the retail and service receipts attributable to visitors from outside the region.

The drawbacks of this approach include the fact that it is applicable only to a single city or county or a small collection of adjacent counties and that it cannot break out expenditures by type of goods or services purchased, type of establishment patronized by visitors, or by type of traveler (business versus leisure; overnight versus day trip, domestic versus international, etc.). In the case of single-county studies, it defines a *visitor* as anyone who travels into the county from outside and makes a retail or service purchase. This might involve a trip of 1 mile or 100 miles.

Moreover, there are cases of a rural county that lacks a major retail center, causing residents to spend *more* of their income outside the county than within it. In such a case, subtracting an estimate of residents' purchases from county sales produces a negative number, suggesting visitors are being paid by businesses to visit the county.

Finally, the method is flawed from a measurement standpoint. Residuals are notoriously volatile: witness corporate profits from year to year. Measurement errors, as well as underlying behavior, are likely to produce estimates showing large swings that are not related to visitor activity.

SEASONAL DIFFERENCE MODELS

Another expenditure estimation method, which was suggested by Mueller (1977), requires looking at the monthly distribution of the receipts of a type of travel-related business (e.g., hotels/motels, eating and drinking places, amusement and recreation services) over a year's time to determine the month with the lowest total. This monthly total is assumed to represent average monthly sales to local residents. This amount is subtracted from the totals for each of the other months, and the residual is visitor or traveler spending.

This method is not used much today because of its structural flaws. It tends to *underestimate* traveler spending to the extent that the low-month receipts include some traveler spending. A summer resort area's hotel/motel receipts in February, for example, surely include the spending of some business travelers. When these receipts are subtracted from the receipts of other months, the difference does not account for this February spending.

This method tends to *overestimate* traveler spending to the extent that receipts in the peak months are inflated by nonvisitor purchases. Amusement and recreation service receipts, for example, are higher in the summer in many areas because local residents spend more time out of doors then or take their vacations at home. Sales of restaurants and other establishments may be higher in July than February because of nontourist, weather-related business activity, such as construction or water transportation. Construction employment often soars in the summer, and this would provide a boost to restaurant sales that is not tourism related.

The method also ignores the impact of trend on the monthly distribution of receipts. If the local economy is growing over time, then July sales of many businesses will be somewhat higher than February's due to more local activity rather than tourism.

Finally, the method works best in areas with clearly defined tourist seasons. The theory cannot apply in areas that have both summer and winter seasons, such as many major ski resorts in the United States.

SUPPLY-SIDE JUDGMENTAL MODELS

The British Columbia Ministry of Development, Trade and Tourism has developed a *Tourism Satellite Account* to measure economic impact (Burd 1991). Satellite accounts are basically sets of supplementary information tied to the main set of a nation's economic accounts (called the *system of national accounts*, or SNA) that are organized to display the stocks and flows that comprehensively characterize a national or regional economy (Carson and Grimm 1991). They feature data for a whole field of economic activity in more detail than can be shown in the main SNA. A transactor or transaction is included only if it is linked to the field. While they present information in ways different from the main accounts, they contain at least one measure that is also in the main accounts. A number of organizations are working on tourism satellite accounts, most notably Statistics Canada and the Organization for Economic Co-operation and Development (Lapierre et al. 1991; Tourism Committee 1991).

The British Columbia model is a separate input-output model specifically designed to display tourism's contributions to the province but related to the overall provincial input-output model (see discussion of input-output models on pages 384 and 385). It embodies three steps to determine the economic impact of the tourism industry: (1) identify the types of businesses comprising the tourism industry; (2) measure the output, GDP, and other measures of economic impact of these businesses; (3) estimate the proportion of these measures for each business type that can be attributed to tourism expenditures (Burd 1991:13).

The first two steps are straightforward and follow commonly accepted principles of definition and input-output model data collection. The third step, however, relies on the *judgment* of experts. Apparently, such a panel has developed a set of ratios of tourist-attributable business revenues to total revenues for each type of business (Burd 1991:15). These tourism ratios are then applied to the supply-side measures of output (value added, taxes, wages paid, etc.) for each type of business and summed to derive the total direct impact of tourism spending.

This adds a large element of subjectivity to what is basically an objective enumeration process. It is impossible to assess the accuracy of these estimates at the national level. If it were possible, the *actual* tourism ratios would be used rather than the judgmental ones. Moreover, a different panel of experts might arrive at significantly different ratios. Finally, these ratios can be expected to differ considerably among areas; for example, a larger proportion of restaurant sales in Las Vegas are attributable to tourists than is true in Minneapolis.

Apparently, the World Travel and Tourism Council similarly uses judgment in developing its estimates of global tourism expenditures and impact (Burd 1991). The Council's tourism ratios differ markedly from the Canadian ones, but there is no way to determine which set is more applicable to an area.

The six methods of *estimating* visitor expenditures discussed above rely on observing the traveler spend (direct observation), on asking the traveler to recount his expenditures (sample surveys) or on using secondary data (bank return estimates; Kreutzwiser, or residual receipts; seasonal difference; judgmental estimates). There are two other approaches that *simulate* expenditures by employing logic and algebra. They use a combination of survey data, secondary data, and common sense to derive measures of traveler or visiting spending. These models may be called *expenditure ratio models* and *cost factor models*.

EXPENDITURE RATIO MODELS

These expenditure estimation models rest on a foundation of certain expenditure-related data, which are readily available and relatively sound. To this is added a superstructure of travel expenditure relationships that build up to a total of all travel spending in an area.

The simplest version of this approach comprises four steps. The first step is to gather data on hotel/motel room receipts in an area, such as a county or metropolitan area. This can often be obtained from state or local tax agencies, particularly if the jurisdiction imposes a special sales tax on these receipts. The second step is to conduct a survey among visitors to the area to obtain estimates of the total amount spent in the area and expenditures on lodging at hotels and motels. In the third step, the ratio is computed by total visitor spending, as taken from the survey, to the survey estimate of spending on hotel/motel rooms. Finally, the fourth step is to multiply this ratio by the hotel/motel room receipts gathered in step one, and the product is the total spending by visitors in the area.

The leverage associated with this naive approach can be quite high. U.S. Travel Data Center estimates for traveler spending in Tennessee for 1990, for example, suggest total traveler spending is 7.6 times hotel/motel room receipts in the state. This indicates that every dollar of estimated spending on hotel/motel rooms translates into $7.60 of total traveler spending in the state. Should the estimate of hotel/motel receipts and the ratio of total spending to these receipts each erroneously be 5 percent too high, this would add $580 million in unwarranted expenditures to the state total.

In order to reduce this leverage, researchers develop expenditure ratios for each type of accommodation. One example is the set of ratios developed by Dean Runyan Associates for the following accommodation categories in its Regional Travel Impact Model (Dean Runyan Associates 1992):

Hotel, motel, resort, bed-and-breakfast establishments
Commercial campgrounds
Public campgrounds
Homes of friends/relatives
Day visitors

Where receipts data are not available, they are estimated by multiplying measures of annual daily occupancies by estimates of daily expenditures from traveler surveys (ibid.).

Another problem occurs when the survey respondent does not accurately report hotel/motel room expenses (Runyan 1988:211–212). If respondents tend to understate or overstate these costs, the resulting estimates of total traveler spending in the area will be overestimated or underestimated, respectively.

Other models embodying the expenditure ratio approach include the T-Map-I model operated by Davidson-Peterson Associates since 1988 and the TRAITS-II model developed by Dr. J. Rovelstad (West Virginia University 1981). They differ in how they gather the foundational data and how they handle the particularly difficult estimation problems of day visitors and of visitors staying in homes of friends and relatives. It is difficult to evaluate these two models because few details on their structures and input data have been published.

The validity and estimation accuracy of this approach for local areas are improved if the following criteria are satisfied:

1. The survey sample is large enough to produce relatively accurate estimates of the total-expenditure-to-lodging-receipts ratio for individual areas.
2. The survey response rate exceeds 70 percent (Burke 1987:300; Ellerbrock 1981:39; Hunt and Dalton 1983:16; Woodside and Ronkainen 1984:35).
3. Survey-respondent recall bias does not distort this ratio.
4. Surveys are conducted annually rather than assuming the ratio remains stable over time.
5. The hotel/motel-room-receipts data are accurate for a particular year and not distorted by payment of past taxes and penalties for previous periods, or by underreporting.
6. Survey respondents only report what they spent in the area rather than total trip expenditures or spending in other areas.

COST FACTOR MODELS

The cost factor model for estimating travel expenditures has a long history. It was first proposed by Church in 1969. Frechtling reported on the U.S. Travel Data Center's National Travel Expenditure Model in 1973; and the structure of the model, now termed the "Travel Expenditure Component of the Travel Economic Impact Model" (TEIM), was published in 1975 (Frechtling 1973; Frechtling et al. 1975a, b). About the same time, Tourism Canada announced the outline of its own cost factor model, called the "Tourism Expenditure Model" (Chau 1988). In 1991, the U.S. Travel Data Center completed a major revision of the TEIM under contract to the U.S. Department of Commerce. This revision extended the Travel Expenditure Component's expenditure categories and incorporated current functional relationships and more reliable and timely data (U.S. Travel Data Center 1991b).

A *travel expenditure* is assumed to take place in the Component wherever a person on a qualifying trip, a *traveler*, consumes a travel-related good or service. In most cases, this is where he or she exchanges money or executes a credit transaction for the product. This is also where the product is produced, since the production and consumption of most tourism services are inseparable (Morrison 1989). A "qualifying trip" occurs when a U.S. resident travels to a place 100 miles or more away from home within the United States or stays one or more nights in paid accommodations regardless of the distance away from home.

Travel expenditures are estimated for 19 different items in 6 basic expenditure categories: public transportation, auto transportation, lodging, food, entertainment/recreation, and incidental purchases. Total travel expenditure is the sum of all expenditure categories (Table 1).

Table 1   Travel Expenditure Categories in the Travel Expenditure Component

A. Public transportation
  1. Air, both commercial and general aviation
  2. Intercity bus and motorcoach
  3. Intercity rail (Amtrak)
  4. Cruise ship
  5. Taxi/limousine service
B. Auto/truck/RV transportation
  1. Own vehicle
    a. Operating costs
    b. Attributable fixed costs
  2. Rental vehicle
C. Lodging
  1. Hotels, motels, motor hotels, resort hotels
  2. Rented condominiums and vacation homes
  3. Camper, trailer, or recreational vehicle (RV)
  4. Own second home
D. Food
  1. Prepared food from restaurants, etc.
  2. Unprepared food from grocery stores, etc.
E. Entertainment/recreation
  1. Admission fees at theme and amusement parks
  2. Snow-ski lift tickets and lessons
  3. Casino gaming
  4. Other entertainment and recreation expenditures
F. Incidentals, such as medicine, cosmetics, clothing, personal services, and souvenirs.

The Travel Expenditure Component (TEC) can be thought of as a set of equations for each state where the independent variables are the levels of various travel activities (e.g., miles traveled by automobile, nights spent in hotels), the coefficients are the costs per unit of each activity (called "per-unit cost factors"), and the dependent variables are travel expenditures for certain categories of travel-related goods and services ("expenditure items").

Here is an example: The Travel Expenditure Component of the TEIM estimates what each traveler spends on meals in restaurants and other food-service establishments and on groceries in each state. This is defined to be the product of the number of days the traveler spends in each state and the average cost per day of food in the state, as shown in the following equations:

$$TFSS_s = TRLPN_s \cdot fscf_s \tag{1}$$
$$TGSS_s = TOLPN_s \cdot gscf_n \tag{2}$$
$$TMS_s = TFSS_s + TGSS_s \tag{3}$$

s = one of the 50 states or the District of Columbia
n = nationwide
$TFSS$ = traveler spending in food-service establishments
$TRLPN$ = traveler person-nights spent lodging in hotels, motels, and rental vacation homes and condominiums
$fscf$ = average cost per person per day of three meals
$TGSS$ = traveler spending in grocery stores
$TOLPN$ = traveler person-nights spent with friends/relatives, in campgrounds, and in own second homes

gscf = average cost per day of groceries on trips away from home

TMS = total traveler spending on meals

Equation (1) states that traveler spending in a state on meals in food-service establishments (i.e., eating and drinking places) equals the product of person-nights spent in the state in rental accommodations and the average cost of three meals in the state. The person-night estimates are derived from the U.S. Travel Data Center's National Travel Survey. The average cost for three meals in each state is obtained from Runzheimer International. The number of days each traveler remains in a given state is assumed equal to the number of person-nights (one person spending one night on a trip in a state).

Equation (2) indicates that traveler spending in a state for food in grocery stores equals the number of person-nights spent in the state in the homes of friends and relatives, in campground, and in own second homes multiplied by the average expenditure per person per day of U.S. residents traveling away from home as estimated by the U.S. Department of Labor Consumer Expenditure Survey.

Equation (3) simply sums the two estimates of meal spending to derive total expenditures on food in a state.

Similar equations simulate travel spending in 14 of the expenditure items. For five of the expenditure items, direct estimates of annual traveler spending in each state are available and are incorporated directly in the model. These include hotel/motel room revenue, Amtrak passenger sales, cruise ship passenger sales, admission fees at theme and amusement parks, and casino gaming expenditures.

The model allocates travel expenditures to states by simulating where the exchange of money for goods or services actually took place. According to their nature, some travel expenditures are assumed to occur at the traveler's origin, some at the destination, and some en route. Table 2 summarizes the allocations for the individual expenditure categories.

The Travel Expenditure Component also produces estimates of traveler spending for individual counties and cities in a state. The statewide estimate for each expenditure item is allocated to a county based on a relevant indicator of travel activity in the county; for example, traveler spending on meals in food-service facilities in a county is that proportion of statewide spending on these meals equal to the county's proportion of receipts from hotel/motel rental of rooms and vacation-home rentals.

The Travel Expenditure Component estimates are constrained by the definition of a trip, the individual expenditure categories included, and by the nature of the National Travel Survey. This latter limits expenditures to those by U.S. residents while traveling in the United States. However, the last revision of the TEIM added a foreign visitor expenditure component based on the U.S. Travel and Tourism Administration's annual surveys of foreign visitors. These surveys ask visitors, as they are returning home, what they spent while in the United States, thus keeping expenditure recall decay to a minimum.

Table 2 Allocation of Travel Expenditures by Category in the Travel Expenditure Component

A. To the origin state
1. Auto/truck/RV fixed costs
2. Air transportation fares and expenses (part)
3. Taxi/limousine fares (part)
4. Intercity bus/motorcoach fares (part)
5. Intercity rail fares (part)
6. Cruise ship fares
7. Auto rental expenses (part)

B. To the destination state
1. Air transportation fares and expenses (part)
2. Taxi/limousine fares (part)
3. Intercity bus/motorcoach fares (part)
4. Intercity rail fares (part)
5. Auto rental expenses (part)

C. To states visited (including destination state)
1. Auto/truck/RV variable costs
2. Hotel/motel lodging expenses
3. Campground rental and hook-up expenses
4. Own second home imputed rent
5. Food expenses
6. Entertainment/recreation expenses
7. Incidentals purchases

SIMULATION MODELS OF TRAVEL'S ECONOMIC BENEFITS

Travel expenditures by themselves tell relatively little about the economic benefits of tourism to an area. One reason is that businesses may use most of their receipts generated by visitor expenditures to purchase goods from outside the area, leaving little impact on the local economy. Another reason is that traveler expenditures tell little about the employment produced; for example, the U.S. Travel Data Center's 1987 TEIM estimates indicated that $1 million spent by travelers on meals directly generated 29 jobs in food-service facilities, but the same expenditure on auto transportation supported fewer than 5 jobs. Along with the fewer jobs in the latter go fewer dollars of income attributable to the traveler spending.

Once traveler expenditure estimates are produced by the appropriate expenditure model, the economic impact the expenditures generate can be simulated. The essence of building a model for estimating the economic benefits of tourism in an area is to abstract the major relationships operating among travel expenditures, employment, labor earnings, profits, and tax revenue. Most of these relationships are straightforward and vary only by the quality of the input data. One example is that a given amount of travel-generated employment in a business in an area will produce a certain amount of wage-and-salary income. The objective is to obtain the best data quantifying the relationship.

INTEGRATED VERSUS PARTIAL MODELS

Methods can be developed to estimate one aspect of economic impact, such as travel expenditures or travel-generated employment. These may be called *partial* models. Alternatively, *integrated* models can be developed that simulate the linkages among travel spending and a number of its economic effects, including employment, income, and tax revenue.

Compared to integrated models, partial models have the advantage of being simple and inexpensive: fewer input data are required, fewer interrelationships among variables need to be simulated, and a fixed amount of time and money can produce higher quality estimates.

The major disadvantage of partial models, and it is a large one, is that the one economic magnitude estimated is emphasized at the expense of other aspects of impact. Partial models are most frequently built to estimate travel spending and less frequently to estimate travel-generated employment. Travel expenditures tell very little about the economic contribution travel makes to an area, as noted previously. In an extreme case, such as small island economies that import nearly all productive goods, services, and capital, travel expenditures produce little or no economic benefit for the residents.

Travel-generated employment is a useful measure of economic contributions of travel to a community. There is an explicit commitment at all levels of government to fostering employment opportunities for residents. This commitment has spawned several partial models aimed at estimating only the employment attributable to travel and tourism (Mueller 1977; Ellerbrock and Hite 1980).

It is a mistake to raise this measure above others that characterize travel's economic benefits. In the final analysis, the interest in the jobs generated should not be for their own sake, but for the earnings these jobs provide. Community leaders should prefer 1,000 travel-generated jobs paying $10,000 each to 2,000 jobs paying $4,000 each.

Jobs generated by travel and tourism run the gamut from among the lowest hourly wages (eating and drinking places in the United States) to the highest (air transportation). Knowing how many jobs are attributable to tourism may well be a highly misleading indicator of the actual income earned by those holding them, and it is income that is the more revealing measure of travel's contribution to economic well-being, although not sufficient in itself.

Integrated models, admittedly more difficult to construct and more expensive to operate, have the advantage of simulating a number of relationships in the economic world. Relationships among the important economic measures of travel's contributions—business receipts, employment, earnings, profits, tax revenue—are specified in a logically consistent framework. There are then a number of measures of travel's economic benefits to work with in evaluating the importance of this activity to the residents of an area, with all measures consistent with one another. Moreover, all of the relationships in the model can be examined for validity.

TRAVEL ECONOMIC IMPACT MODEL

The Travel Economic Impact Model (TEIM) is a large integrated model developed by the U.S. Travel Data Center to produce detailed estimates of the economic benefits of travel

away from home by U.S. residents on the U.S. economy, as well as state and local areas. It is an attempt to satisfy the five evaluation criteria discussed in the previous chapter.

Development of the TEIM began in 1972 when the Data Center assembled a team of researchers to design the National Travel Expenditure Model. This model, later renamed the Travel Expenditure Component (TEC) of the TEIM, aimed to provide annual estimates of U.S. domestic traveler spending on a consistent basis for each state and the nation.

In 1975, the Data Center added the Economic Impact Component and the Fiscal Impact Component to the TEIM and extended it to produce estimates for counties and cities. This work was initially done under a contract with the Bureau of Land Management, U.S. Department of the Interior (Frechtling et al. 1975a, b). In 1991, the Data Center completed a major revision of the TEIM, adding expenditure components, updating impact relationships, and utilizing improved input data then available (U.S. Travel Data Center 1991a).

The TEIM has four components:

1. Travel Expenditure Component (TEC)—provides estimates of U.S. travel spending in each state or local area.
2. Economic Impact Component (EIC)—provides estimates of the business receipts, employment, and payroll income generated by travel spending in each state.
3. Fiscal Impact Component (FIC)—provides estimates of federal, state, and local tax revenue generated by travel spending in each state.
4. City/county Impact Component (CIC)—provides estimates of travel spending and the employment, payroll, and tax revenue generated by this spending in individual cities or counties.

TEIM estimation starts with the travel expenditure estimates of the TEC, as discussed above. U.S. tourists can travel by air, bus, rail, ship, personal motor vehicle, or some combination of these. They can spend the night in the homes of friends or relatives, hotels/motels, campgrounds, their own second or vacation homes, or en route. They can take taxicabs, rent cars, purchase meals, go skiing, and buy gifts and other incidentals. All of these activities are incorporated in the 19 categories of travel expenditures included in the TEIM.

Table 3 shows how these 19 travel expenditure items are directly related to 15 types of businesses, or the *tourism industry*. The U.S. Standard Industrial Classification (SIC) codes, designed to classify establishments by the type of activity in which they are engaged, are shown in parentheses (U.S. Office of Management and Budget 1987).

Several advantages arise from relating travel expenditures to individual SIC codes. One is that there is a wealth of data published by national and state agencies on the size, operations, and other characteristics of businesses by SIC code. This permits direct comparison of tourism-generated business receipts in, say, the eating and drinking place indus-

Table 3   Expenditure Categories and Related Types of Business Included in the Travel Economic Impact Model

EXPENDITURE CATEGORY	TYPES OF BUSINESS (SIC CODE*)
Transportation	
1. Air	Air Transportation (45)
2. Taxicab/limousine	Local and suburban passenger transportation and taxicab companies (411+412)
3. Auto/truck/RV operation	Gasoline service stations (554)
4. Auto/truck/RV fixed costs	Automotive dealers (55, except 554 and 555)
5. Auto rental	Passenger car and recreational vehicle
rental (7514+7519)	
6. Bus/motorcoach	Intercity and rural bus transportation and bus charter service, except local (413+4142)
7. Rail	Amtrak
8. Cruise ship	**
Lodging	
9. Hotels/motels, etc.	Hotels and motels (701)
10. Rented vacation homes	Hotels and motels (701)
11. Camper/trailer	Recreational vehicle parks and campsites (703)
12. Own second home	Building materials, hardware, garden supply, and mobile home dealers (52)
Food	
13. Prepared meals	Eating and drinking places (58)
14. Unprepared food	Grocery stores (54)
Entertainment/recreation	
15. Theme, amusement parks	Amusement and recreation services (79)
16. Snow skiing	Amusement and recreation services (79)
17. Casino gaming	Amusement and recreation services (79)
18. Other entertainment/recreation	Amusement and recreation services (79)
19. Incidental purchases	General merchandise and miscellaneous retail stores (53+59)
20. ***	Arrangement of passenger transportation (472)

*Standard Industrial Classification codes, as established by the U.S. Office of Management and Budget, 1987.
**The impact of this spending in the average state is included in arrangement of passenger transportation (472).
***No separate expenditures are identified with this category, since these establishments act as agents for air transportation, cruise ship transportation, hotel/motel lodging, and other types of businesses already listed.

try (SIC 58) to total receipts of this industry within a city or state.[1] Another advantage is that SIC data assist in constructing integrated travel impact models, as illustrated in the discussion of the TEIM that follows. Finally, relating travel spending to SIC codes is vital to national and international recognition of tourism as an important social and economic activity. Most national economic statistics in the world are based on supply-side reporting (Pisarski 1991:3). This requires an industrial classification system to insure exhaustive coverage. Indeed, the World Tourism Organization has submitted its design for a "Standard International Classification of Tourism Activities" to the United Nations Statistical Commission for endorsement as "essential to the proper and effective statistical representation of tourism" (World Tourism Organization 1991:9).

Economic Impact Component

TEIM procedures for estimating business receipts, payroll, and employment income are standard across most expenditure categories and types of businesses and are termed the *Economic Impact Component* (EIC).

Business receipts generated by U.S. travel spending as estimated in the TEIM follow the U.S. Bureau of the Census definition for service establishments, excluding sales, occupancy, admission, and other taxes collected from customers (U.S. Bureau of the Census 1989:A-3).

The standard equation for computing business receipts generated by travel in a state for a type of tourism business is as follows:

$$TBR_{i,s} = TES_{i,s} - TRST_{i,s} \qquad (4)$$

[1]For example, every year ending with a "2" or a "7," the U.S. Bureau of the Census conducts a large-scale census of business, including retail trade, service, and selected transportation establishments. Estimates of business receipts, payroll, and employment are provided down to the city and county level (e.g., U.S. Bureau of the Census, 1991, 1990).

i	=	one of the types of travel-related businesses
s	=	one of the 50 states or the District of Columbia
TBR	=	business receipts generated by U.S. traveler spending
TES	=	expenditures by U.S. travelers
TRST	=	retail sales taxes generated by U.S. traveler spending

Equation (4) indicates that a state's receipts generated by traveler spending for a specific type of business are equal to the travel expenditures affecting that business less the retail sales taxes generated by that spending. These taxes are estimated in the Fiscal Impact Component of the TEIM, as indicated on page 379.

Business receipts for air transportation (SIC 45) are estimated in a different manner because the relationship between travel expenditures (ticket purchase) and airline business receipts is geographically much more complex. In common carrier transportation, the service is consumed across as many geographic boundaries as the traveler passes. It is not feasible to allocate this spending over all such areas. Instead, the travel expenditure is assumed to take place where the ticket is purchased in the TEIM. Since most common carrier tickets are for round-trip travel, most of this spending occurs at the traveler's origin, and a minority is allocated to the destination in recognition of one-way return tickets purchased.

While this particular convention works reasonably well for expenditures, its applicability to the other measures of impact is not so clear. When a traveler purchases a round-trip ticket in Washington, D.C., for a trip on United Airlines to San Francisco, this gives rise to employment and income in Washington, D.C., San Francisco, the Chicago area where United's headquarters are, and other cities housing the airline's maintenance facilities, flight personnel, training centers, and regional offices. Equation (4a) attempts to deal with these complexities:

$$TATR_s = \frac{ATPR_n}{ATR_n} \cdot \frac{ATP_s}{atec_s} \qquad (4a)$$

s	=	one of the 50 states or the District of Columbia
n	=	nationwide
TATR	=	air transportation business receipts generated by traveler spending
ATPR	=	U.S. airline passenger revenue
ATR	=	total U.S. airline operating revenue
ATP	=	total air transportation (SIC 45) payroll
atec	=	earnings coefficient for air transportation from RIMS II

The first term on the right side of equation (4a) (i.e., $ATPR_n/ATR_n$) removes nonpassenger revenue from U.S. airline total operating receipts. The second term divides payroll earnings in the airline sector by the RIMS II earnings coefficient for the state to obtain a measure of business receipts actually generated in the state. RIMS II is an interindustry model maintained by the U.S. Department of

Commerce, and its earnings coefficient for an industry represents the ratio of labor earnings (payroll income) to business receipts for the industry. The estimate of annual payroll income for air transportation in each state is obtained from the U.S. Department of Labor.

Consequently, equation (4a) decouples traveler spending on air transportation from the business receipts generated by them in a state. It summarizes all of the relationships extant in the country between airline ticket purchases and air transport receipts, employment, and payroll in the states.

The estimation of economic benefits continues by estimating the payroll earnings attributable to travel spending in each category in each state. Payroll in the Economic Impact Component is defined as the U.S. Bureau of the Census defines it, including all forms of employee compensation and before deductions of payroll taxes (U.S. Bureau of the Census 1989:A-3). However, the TEIM adds a measure of the compensation of proprietors or partners of unincorporated businesses in its travel-generated payroll estimates.

The standard equation for computing payroll income generated by travel in a state for a type of tourism business is as follows:

$$TP_{i,s} = TBR_s^i \cdot \frac{PR_{i,s}}{BR_{i,s}} \qquad (5)$$

i	=	one of the types of travel-related businesses
s	=	one of the 50 states or the District of Columbia
TP	=	travel-generated payroll
TBR	=	travel-generated business receipts
PR	=	total payroll
BR	=	total business receipts

Equation (5) defines travel-generated payroll for an industry in a state as equal to travel-generated business receipts multiplied by the ratio of payroll to business receipts for that industry in that state as published by the U.S. Bureau of the Census or other sources.

Next, employment generated by travel spending is estimated by relating jobs to payroll. In effect, the proportion of a job supported by a dollar of payroll is estimated for each industry in a state and multiplied by the travel-generated payroll estimated in the previous component, as indicated in equation (6):

$$TE_{i,s} = TP_{i,s} \cdot \frac{EM_{i,s}}{PR_{i,s}} \qquad (6)$$

i	=	one of the types of travel-related businesses
s	=	one of the 50 states or the District of Columbia
TE	=	travel-generated employment (jobs)
TP	=	travel-generated payroll
EM	=	total employment (jobs)
PR	=	total payroll

Equation (6) states that travel-generated employment in one of the travel-related industries in a state is equal to travel-generated payroll for the industry in the state multiplied by the ratio of total employment to total payroll for that industry in the state. The data for statewide payroll and employment for each type of business are obtained from the U.S. Department of Labor.

Employment is defined as the Census Bureau defines it in its censuses of business: all full-time and part-time employees, including salaried officers and executives of corporations who were on the company payroll. The TEIM adds a measure of the salaries of the proprietors and partners of unincorporated businesses who owe their jobs to tourism-generated receipts.

Fiscal Impact Component

The Fiscal Impact Component of the TEIM estimates the tax revenue generated for national, state, and local governments by travel expenditures in the United States. Considerable amounts may be generated for local governments. Indeed, one study found the tax burden on residents was considerably lower in counties where tourism development was high (Perdue et al. 1991:200).

This component considers the income, sales, excise, and property tax implications of dollars spent in each of the expenditure categories or earned in each of the industry categories. The taxes covered are:

Federal
    Individual income and employment taxes
    Corporate income tax
    Gasoline excise tax
    Air transportation excise tax

State
    Individual income tax
    Corporate income tax
    Gasoline excise tax
    Sales and gross receipts taxes

Local (includes counties and municipalities)
    Individual income tax
    Sales and gross receipts taxes
    Property tax

The rates prevailing for these taxes in each state, locality, and the industry sectors to which they apply are obtained through surveys of governments and entered into this component. The following details the general approach for the major taxes estimated in the model (U.S. Travel Data Center 1991b): For excise, sales, and gross receipts taxes, the standard equation for an industry subsector subject to this tax is:

$$TSST_{i,s,g} = TES_{i,s} \cdot \frac{t_{i,s,g}}{1 + \Sigma\, t_{i,s,g}} \qquad (7)$$

where
i = one of the types of travel-related businesses
s = one of the 50 states or the District of Columbia
g = federal, state, or local government
$TSST$ = excise, sales, or gross receipts tax revenue attributable to travel spending

TES = travel spending
t = applicable tax rate

The denominator of the final term in equation (7)—$(1 + \Sigma\, t_{i,s,g})$—removes tax payments included in the travel expenditure so the rate is applied to the purchase price, not to the price plus the sales tax.

At this point, business receipts attributable to travel spending can be computed, as they are defined to be net of sales taxes, one component of the taxes estimated here.

Travel-generated individual income and employment tax revenue is estimated by developing the average rate of these taxes as a percent of personal income in the state and applying this to travel-generated payroll. The equation for the hotel/motel sector is

$$TIIT_{s,g} = TP_{a,s} \cdot \frac{IIT_{s,g}}{PY_s} \qquad (8)$$

where
s = one of the 50 states or the District of Columbia
g = federal, state, or local government
a = total for all industries
$TIIT$ = individual income tax and employment tax revenue generated by payroll attributable to travel spending
TP = payroll attributable to travel spending
IIT = total individual income tax and employment tax collections
PY = personal income

Equation (8) is used to estimate federal, state, or local income taxes attributable to traveler spending in the state. Total travel-generated payroll in a state is multiplied by the ratio of federal, state, or local individual income tax receipts to personal income in the state—the implicit average tax rate.

To estimate corporate income tax revenue attributable to travel spending, data are collected from the U.S. Internal Revenue Service and the states on the relationship of corporate income tax payments to business receipts, by type of business. Equation (9) presents the method used for a single type.

$$TCIT_{i,s,g} = TR_s \cdot \frac{CIT_{i,s,g}}{BR_{i,s}} \qquad (9)$$

where
i = one of the types of travel-related businesses
s = one of the 50 states or the District of Columbia
g = federal, state, or local government
$TCIT$ = corporate income tax revenue attributable to travel spending
TR = business receipts attributable to travel spending
CIT = corporate income tax collections
BR = total business receipts

Local governments generally rely most heavily on property taxes for revenue. Property taxes are normally paid by residents out of personal income. The income earned by residents in a location enables them to pay their annual property taxes. It is assumed that the amount of property tax a resident pays is proportionate to his income, including that earned in a job attributable to travel spending.

Equation (10) details the estimation technique for a state:

$$TPT_s = TP_{a,s} \cdot \frac{\sum_g PT_{s,g}}{PY_s} \qquad (10)$$

where

s	=	one of the 50 states or the District of Columbia
g	=	state or local government
a	=	total for all industries
TPT	=	property tax revenue attributable to travel spending
TP	=	payroll attributable to travel spending
PT	=	property tax revenue
PY	=	personal income

The state and local property tax revenue in a state attributable to travel spending is set equal to the product of total travel-generated payroll and ratio of the implicit tax rate to personal income.

This completes the TEIM estimates of travel's economic contributions at the state and national level. To produce county or city estimates of travel impact, the state totals in each impact category are distributed to a particular locality based upon available measures of business activity in the area; for example, for travel expenditures on hotel/motel lodging, the relevant expenditure equation is

$$THLS_l = THLS_s \cdot \frac{HLR_l}{HLR_s} \qquad (11)$$

where

l	=	any locality in the state
s	=	one of the 50 states or the District of Columbia
$THLS$	=	traveler spending on hotel/motel lodging
HLR	=	total hotel/motel receipts

Data are not generally available on the relationships among business receipts, payroll, and employment by industry at the local level. Consequently, the statewide relationships are assumed to hold, and equations similar to equation (11) are used to distribute travel-generated payroll and employment by industry among the localities.

Federal and state tax revenue attributable to travel are similarly distributed among the localities. However, local sales, use, excise, gross receipts, individual and corporate income, and property tax rates are entered for each locality and estimated directly.

EVALUATION OF THE TEIM

The evaluation criteria developed in the previous chapter can be applied to assess the quality of the Travel Economic Impact Model.

Relevance

The TEIM was developed to provide estimates of travel or visitor impact alone. It is based upon surveys of travel activity, rather than receipts of travel-related businesses. Some studies have begun with explicit estimates of the proportions of hotel/motel, restaurant, entertainment services, and other business receipts attributable to travelers. These proportions are generally subjective and often approach pure conjecture. In the TEIM, such proportions can be implicitly derived from the output but are not input assumptions in the model.

Insuring that the economic impact estimates actually relate to the geographic area under study is difficult in travel research. Some travel expenditures are made at home in anticipation of the trip, some are made en route, and some may even occur after the trip (e.g., developing photographs of the trip). Moreover, travelers may pay for their trip at home or en route by currency, check, or credit card. Determining where travel expenditures should be allocated requires special research effort.

The primary rule or convention for travel spending in the TEIM is that the expenditure takes place where the goods or services are actually consumed. If this rule cannot be applied, then the expenditure is assumed to take place where the service is purchased. Table 2, on page 375, indicates these assumptions embodied in the TEIM.

The primary rule works well for all items except common carrier transportation. Hotel expenditures are assumed to take place where the traveler spends the night. Gasoline purchases are made where traveler visits by car, truck, or recreational vehicle. Meals, amusement and recreation, and incidentals are similarly handled.

In common carrier transportation, the service is consumed across as many geographic boundaries as the traveler passes. It is not feasible to allocate this spending and its impact over all such areas. Instead, the travel expenditure is assumed to take place where the ticket is purchased in the TEIM. In the absence of the research that would trace the geographic impact of airline ticket purchases over all of these areas, the TEIM assumes (equation 4a) impact follows the geographic presence of payroll and employment, not ticket purchases.

Care is taken in the TEIM to specify whether the local estimates are of *traveler* impact or of *visitor* impact. If the latter, state-level travel expenditures for each industry sector are adjusted to represent the amount attributable to nonresidents entering a state or local area. This is particularly important for common carrier expenses, auto ownership costs, and travel agency services.

Coverage

This criterion is applied to determine how comprehensive a model is in providing estimates of all economic impacts of travel. A partial model will necessarily provide incomplete coverage of benefits. An integrated model may fail to treat certain classes of impact, and this can be due to either lack of necessary input data or deficiencies in the model's structure.

The TEIM produces travel expenditure estimates for 19 categories of goods and services (Table 3). However, two important classes of travel-related expenses are not estimated in the model due to lack of sufficient data. Consumers purchase certain goods and services in anticipation of a trip away from home. These include sports equipment (tennis racquets, skis, scuba gear, etc.), clothing (tennis clothes, ski togs, bathing wear, etc.), travel books and guides, and services such as language lessons and lessons for participatory sports (tennis, skiing, underwater diving, etc.). Although the magnitude of these purchases in preparation for a trip cannot now be quantified, it is probably significant, particularly in major urban centers and states.

The second type of spending not covered due to lack of sound, relevant data is the purchase of major consumer durables generally related to outdoor recreation on trips. While recreational vehicles (campers, motor homes, trailers, and mobile homes) are covered, spending for boats and boating supplies and off-road recreational vehicles, such as trail bikes, dune buggies, and snowmobiles, are not. Further research is required in this area to estimate the average spending on items such as these by travelers.

The TEIM records travel expenditures only for those states where travelers spend the night, originate, or are destined. Due to the nature of the National Travel Survey, expenditures cannot be allocated to states passed through in a single day. It is believed these expenditures may be significant in certain bridge states between major population concentrations and major destinations, with relatively little destination or stopover expenditures.

Among the benefit measures, the TEIM does not provide estimates of travel-generated profits, dividends, or interest payments in an area. Rent, the other component of personal income, is partially covered. The rent paid by travelers to owners of second homes, vacation condominiums, and like properties is included. However, the rent paid by a travel-related business to the owner of the structure housing it is not. Again, the lack of data is the problem.

The smaller the area under study, the less of a problem exclusion of dividend, interest, and rent payments attributable to travel may be. Travel may generate this income, but it is unlikely to accrue to residents of a small area. A hotel operator may borrow money from a bank in another city, and pay interest income that does not accrue to any resident of his or her area. Vacation-home owners are virtually all nonresidents of the area where the home is located, and their rental income should not show up in the area being studied.

Until 1984, little was known about the types and geographic distribution of foreign-visitor expenditures in the United States. However, the U.S. Travel and Tourism Administration's (USTTA) survey of international air travelers now provides a sound basis for estimating these expenditures by state and expenditure category (U.S. Travel and Tourism Administration 1991). Utilizing this data base and similar data on Canadian visitors from Statistics Canada and the TEIM, the U.S. Travel Data Center has prepared estimates for USTTA of the economic impact of foreign visitors on each of the 50 states and the District of Columbia for a number of years (e.g., U.S. Travel Data Center 1988). Future

editions of these estimates are anticipated, subject to funding availability.

The TEIM does not include a module for estimating public or government employment attributable to travel and tourism. This is because the relationship between travel activity and government employment is not evident. If there is no stable, discernible relationship, then employment in these agencies may not be related to travel activity and, therefore, does not belong in a model designed to estimate the economic impact of travel and tourism activity.

Perhaps relationships could be established between travel activity and employment in regulatory agencies and in government programs for constructing and maintaining travel-related facilities and rights of way. It is more difficult to speculate on the links between tourism promotion agency employment and travel activity, however.

It may be that firm relationships cannot be established at all. Governments frequently cut back on employment in travel-related agencies for budget considerations even while travel is rising. In any event, the appropriate research on the link between travel and government employment has not been conducted.

The TEIM measures tax revenue generated by travel for federal, state, and local governments. It does not similarly measure travel's contribution to other government revenues. These include user fees, license fees, and fines.

Travelers pay park entrance fees, purchase hunting and fishing licenses, and pay traffic and other fines. These are all government revenues attributable to travel. However, accounting for these in a national model is a difficult task. It requires examination of detailed revenue data for each level of government, to determine the appropriate relationships. The U.S. Travel Data Center conducted such a study for the State of Delaware, but the cost makes it prohibitive for comprehensive application across all states (U.S. Travel Data Center and Fothergill/Beekhuis Associates 1979:69–104).

The TEIM covers most U.S. travel away from home overnight and day trips to places 100 miles or more away. It does not measure the impact of travel to destinations less than 100 miles from the traveler's home with a return within the same day. While there may be a great number of trips of this type that may be of interest to the travel industry and others, the average expenditure per traveler is likely to be quite low, since no overnight lodging is purchased, little common carrier transportation is consumed, and other expenditures are likely to be small, being confined to a period less than one day. It is likely, therefore, that for most areas, excluding day trips of less than 100 miles will bias the economic impact estimates little, if at all (West Virginia University 1981:54).

The TEIM does not produce estimates of tourism-related investment and its impact on area employment, payroll, and tax revenue. Tourism Canada's Travel Impact Model does cover these expenditures through an application of the Keynesian accelerator concept, which assumes investment the present period is a function of the rate of change of related demand in the last period (Chau 1988:9). In the United States, such a stable relationship has not been demonstrated. On the contrary, investment in hotel and resort facilities since 1983 has been influenced more by the tax treatment of this spending than underlying demand conditions.

In summary, the TEIM fails to cover certain positive impacts due to lack of the necessary input data or a sound conceptual base. However, it does provide estimates of the major elements of travel's economic contribution to an area: travel-generated payroll income, employment, and tax revenue for most types of businesses serving the traveler while away from home.

Transferability

The TEIM was designed to provide estimates of travel's economic impact for any state, county, or significant city in the United States for 1977 and subsequent years. The same approach has been adapted for use in Canada by federal and provincial governments and in New Orleans (Chau 1988; Crawford and Nebel 1977). This suggests the model can be applied in different geographic areas.

Being quite complex, adapting the model to a certain country or other area is a difficult task. Moreover, it requires a good deal of input data that may not be readily available, particularly in lesser-developed countries.

In short, the TEIM has been used throughout the United States since 1975, either through the U.S. Travel Data Center or an adaptation of the original model. It is the only tourism impact model producing consistent annual estimates for all states. However, applicability in other countries, particularly lesser-developed ones, is questionable.

Efficiency

The TEIM was designed to be efficient. It does not require extensive primary data collection but rather uses information available from existing government and industry data-gathering projects. It is flexible in accepting alternative sources of input data when necessary.

It has been the Data Center's experience that the Travel Economic Impact Model provides annual economic benefit estimates for states, cities, and counties at costs considerably lower than alternative models.

Accuracy

The accuracy of an approach's estimates may be judged by examining the structure and input data of the approach and by comparing the estimates produced with independent estimates.

The TEIM structure is consistent and logical. The input data include survey results that are subject to sampling and nonsampling errors. However, survey-based data constitute a part of the input, not the whole. Other input data are derived from administrative records and complete censuses. It is difficult, therefore, to assess accuracy in terms of statistical reliability.

There are few independent estimates of travel impact to which reference can be made in judging the validity of the output. The TEIM was developed precisely because travel

economic impact data did not exist. In the few cases where valid comparisons can be made, the TEIM appears to be somewhat conservative in its estimates, reflecting its basic assumptions.

SECONDARY ECONOMIC BENEFITS

When purchasing goods and services, the traveler produces the direct economic benefits detailed in the preceding sections. These direct or *primary* impacts produce *secondary* economic effects as well that add to the community's economic well-being (Fletcher and Archer 1991:29–30).

The secondary economic benefits of travel activity include *indirect* benefits and *induced* benefits. The indirect benefits occur as the travel-related business operator (e.g., a restaurateur) purchases goods (e.g., food) and services (e.g., electricity) in order to serve patrons. These purchases generate economic output by food wholesalers and electric utility. In order to supply the restaurateur, the wholesalers and utility must, in turn, purchase goods and services from *their* suppliers. This chain of purchasing goods and services in order to produce continues in an area until the amount of the restaurateur's initial purchase leaks out of the area through taxes, purchases from suppliers outside the area (imports), business savings, distributed profits, and payments to employees. The faster the initial spending leaks out of the community's respending process, the smaller will be this indirect impact.

The measures of indirect impact of travel activity in an area are the output, transactions, income, employment, and tax revenue generated as businesses purchase from suppliers in order to support the initial sale to the traveler.

The other type of secondary impact is the induced economic impact of the travel expenditure. This results as the employees of the travel-related businesses, and those of suppliers along the chain of indirect impact, spend a part of their earnings in the area under study. This spending itself generates output and additional induced and indirect effects throughout the area.

The sum of indirect and induced effects constitutes the total secondary impact of travel activity.

TOURISM IMPACT MULTIPLIERS

The concept of the *multiplier* as used in recent tourism impact studies derives from a desire to summarize the amount of change in some economic benefit variable (output, income, employment, etc.) generated by a given amount of tourism spending in an area (Fletcher and Archer 1991:30–37). There are a number of different types of tourism multipliers and three main methods for computing them. Confusion over these different multipliers has limited the usefulness of a number of secondary impact studies (Archer 1982); for example, Fletcher and Archer (1991:37–39) distinguish the following:

- *Transactions multiplier*—One of the most common forms

of multiplier, it is the ratio of the total change in business sales in an area to the initial tourism expenditure that generated the sales.

• *Output multiplier*—Often confused with transactions multipliers, this is the ratio of the total productive output generated to the tourism expenditures; output in this sense is equivalent to sales less change in business inventories.

• *Income multiplier*—Perhaps the most useful of all multipliers, it is the ratio of income (labor income, business profits, dividends, interest, and rent) to the traveler spending that generated them; most often, the numerator is limited to wages and salaries (Fletcher and Archer 1991:37).

• *Employment multiplier*—This is the ratio of jobs, either actual or full-time equivalent, produced by tourism spending to the amount of the spending; it is expressed in small decimal numbers, such as the U.S. Travel Data Center's estimate of the employment multiplier for all travel spending in the United States as .0000393, or 39.3 jobs for every $1 million spent (U.S. Travel Data Center 1991b).

In addition, there could be computed a *government revenue multiplier* that would indicate the total amount of tax, fee, fine, license, public enterprise, and other such revenue generated by one dollar in tourist spending, either for all governments in an area or some subset (Fletcher 1989:526). And Bull (1991:141) suggests an *asset multiplier*, which indicates the increases in an economy's stock of productive assets.

The multipliers described above are all *normal* multipliers: they relate the measure of total impact to the initial tourism expenditure. Researchers should beware of *ratio* multipliers, or the ratio of a primary plus secondary measure of impact to the primary measure of that same impact; for example, a ratio employment multiplier would equal all employment in an area, both primary and secondary, generated by travel spending divided by employment generated directly. In the U.S. Travel Data Center (1991b) example quoted earlier, the ratio employment multiplier would be 2.18, since 1.18 jobs are produced by secondary impact for every 1 job generated directly. These are magnitudes larger than the normal employment multiplier and of little use other than to confuse the unwary (Archer 1982:238–239).

Archer (1989:128–132) notes that economic theory suggests six factors that affect the size of tourism's impact on an area:

1. The initial volume of tourism expenditure
2. Supply constraints in the area economy (If there is insufficient capacity to meet the tourism demand, the expenditure will generate local inflation and a rise in imports.)
3. The size of the area economy
4. Value added in the first round (The more of the initial expenditure that is translated into income for area residents, the higher the multiplier should be.)
5. Tourism industry linkages with the area economy (The more industry requirements to meet tourist demand that

can be met by area businesses, the higher the multiplier impact.)
6. Leakages (The less that leaves the area economy in each round of transactions, the higher the multiplier.)

As a practical matter, Archer has found that only supply constraints (item 2) and linkages (item 5) correlate closely with size of the income multiplier (ibid.). However, items (3) through (6) represent the interdependence of the area economy: the degree to which area businesses and employees/consumers buy and sell from one another rather from outside the area. Each of the items is only an incomplete representation of this characteristic and may not individually indicate multiplier size.

Archer's factors suggest it is a mistake to think of the "tourist" or the "tourism industry" as monolithic. Different types of tourists may have different impacts on an area economy (Bull 1991:141; Fletcher 1989:518,521). This is most likely related to the items they purchase and where they purchase them, because different subsectors of the tourism industry will have different linkages to the local economy. The extremes might be tourist purchases of gasoline for a rental car (gasoline service stations import their product and contribute little value added) and restaurants specializing in local cuisine (low import content and high value added). This can be summarized by noting that the size of the multiplier is dependent on the traveler's "bill of goods," as well as the linkages of the tourism subsectors within the area economy.

TURNOVER VERSUS THE MULTIPLIER

In speaking of transactions multipliers, it is common to discuss the *turnover* of the travel dollar. This term refers to the process by which the dollar spent by the traveler becomes a receipt to a business and a portion of it is, in turn, respent for goods and services. The suppliers of these goods and services, both businesses and employees, also respend part of the receipts they receive, and this continues until leakages reduce the original dollar to near zero.

There is a definite relationship between the transactions multiplier and the number of times the original dollar spent turns over before disappearing from the area. An example can make this clear. If 50 percent of the dollar disappears in leakages each time it is respent, then the initial dollar expenditure would produce $1.00 in transactions directly, $0.50 in the first round of the indirect impact, $0.25 in the second round, $0.125 cents in the third round, and continue in this manner until it disappears. The equation for the total impact transactions multiplier is:

$$TM = 1 + \sum_i (1-L)^i \qquad (12)$$

which is equivalent to

$$TM = \frac{1}{L} \qquad (13)$$

where
TM = transactions multiplier
L = average leakage per round of spending as a percent of spending
t = number of the round

Applying equation (12) to the 50 percent leakage example and working it out for each round reveals that the amount of the dollar left to be respent drops below one-half of one cent after the eighth round; that is, it effectively disappears.

Consequently, a multiplier of 2.0 (1/0.5) is equivalent to eight rounds of dollar turnover. Unfortunately, the terms are sometimes confused, and someone might state that for every dollar spent by tourists, a total of eight dollars is generated by turnover in the area, when the correct estimate is two dollars (e.g., Archer 1982:239).

REPRESENTATIVE MULTIPLIERS

Table 4 presents a number of tourism income multipliers covering a variety of geographic areas. These indicate the ratio of income generated by tourism expenditures to the expenditures themselves for each area noted. They were derived from a variety of models, most of which were input-output models. While a comprehensive measure of income includes wages and salaries, proprietors' income, corporate profits, dividends, interest, and rent, it is not known how income was defined for these estimates.

These examples suggest that the smaller the area, and, by extension, the less developed it is, the smaller the multiplier tends to be. National income multipliers are unlikely to exceed 2.0, and regional ones will always be smaller. Tourism income multipliers are very specific, and a value derived for one area should not be applied to another, even if the areas appear to have similar economies. However, these values can be a good reality check for researchers developing multiplier estimates for other areas.

MULTIPLIER ESTIMATION METHODS

There are three basic techniques available for estimating the secondary and total impact of travel spending. These are the input-output model, the economic base model, and what Archer calls the "ad hoc" model (Archer 1973:44).

INPUT-OUTPUT MODELS

The input-output model, or what the U.S. Department of Commerce calls the "input-output accounts," is a means of analyzing interindustry relationships in the production process in an area's economy (Interindustry Economics Division 1990:41). It permits analysis of the flow of goods and services from one producer to another and from the final producer to the final buyer, such as consumers. It covers all production, both final and intermediate, and provides a detailed understanding of the linkages among industries that

Table 4 Tourism Income Multipliers for Selected Areas of the World

DEVELOPED COUNTRIES	MULTIPLIER
Turkey	1.96
United Kingdom	1.73
Republic of Ireland	1.72
Egypt	1.23
ISLAND NATIONS	
Jamaica	1.23
Dominican Republic	1.20
Cyprus	1.14
Bermuda	1.09
Hong Kong	1.02
Mauritius	0.96
Antigua	0.88
Bahamas	0.79
Fiji	0.72
Cayman Islands	0.65
Iceland	0.64
British Virgin Islands	0.58
Republic of Palau	0.50
Solomon Islands	0.52
Western Samoa	0.39
LARGER REGIONS	
Hawaii	0.90–1.30
Missouri	0.88
Walworth County, WI	0.78
Grand County, CO	0.60
Door County, WI	0.55
Sullivan County, PA	0.44
Southwestern Wyoming	0.39–0.53
SMALLER REGIONS/CITIES	
Victoria metro area, Canada	0.50
City of Carlisle, United Kingdom	0.40
Gwynedd, United Kingdom	0.37
Cumbria, United Kingdom	0.35–0.44
East Anglia, United Kingdom	0.34
Isle of Skye, United Kingdom	0.25–0.41
City of Winchester, United Kingdom	0.19

Source: Fletcher 1989:527; Archer 1982:240–241.

cannot be obtained from analysis of the value of final production sold to final buyers alone (Ritz 1979).

Input-output analysis starts with the development of a direct requirements or transactions table. This table shows the sales in dollars of the total output of an industry to all other industries in the economy and to final demand, usually comprising households (consumption), businesses (investment), government, and exports (Fletcher 1989:522). By convention, the rows of the table show the sales by each industry—listed at the left—to every other industry and to the final-demand sectors listed at the top of the columns. By reading down the column, one can see how much input every industry requires from every other industry.

From the transactions table is developed the direct requirements, or technical coefficients, table. Each column in the direct requirements table shows the inputs required by the industry listed at the head from the industries listed at the beginning of each row to produce one dollar of the column-industry's output. Reading down the 1985 U.S. input-output direct requirements table for eating and drinking places, one can see that for every dollar of output, these establishments buy 23 cents worth of food and kindred products, 5 cents of trade services, 5 cents of business services, and almost 4 cents of real estate and rental services (Interindustry Economics Division 1990:47). Eating and drinking places buy 15 cents worth per dollar of their own output from each of 46 other industries. They pay 49 cents to their employees and other sources of value added. Each of these values is an input coefficient for the eating-and-drinking-place industry.

By manipulating the direct requirements table through matrix algebra, one obtains the total requirements, or inverted technology, table, which can be used to obtain indirect output multipliers and, ultimately, to estimate total secondary impact (Fletcher and Archer 1991:36).

The total requirements table shows the output required, both directly and indirectly, from each industry and primary input listed in the rows by the industry at the head of the column to deliver a dollar of output to final demand. It summarizes all of the intermediate output required for an industry to produce for retail, including employee consumption effects. Consequently, by summing the coefficients in the columns, one obtains an indirect output multiplier that can be applied to industry sales at producers' prices to obtain the total output required.

As indicated, total primary and secondary output and payroll generated by travel spending is produced through the input-output process. Employment can be added by developing ratios of employment to earnings, as in the Travel Economic Impact Model, for all of the industries with substantial impact. The TEIM approach to estimating direct travel-generated profits and tax revenue can be similarly applied to the total output and payroll estimates to obtain the appropriate multipliers.

Fletcher notes a number of advantages of using input-output models to estimate total economic benefits of tourism compared to alternative methods listed below (Fletcher 1989:515–516):

1. Provides policymakers with a comprehensive view of an economy.
2. Focuses attention on the interindustry linkages in an economy.
3. Researchers can customize the model to provide more detail on individual industries.
4. Every industry and sector is treated in a uniform manner.
5. Allows investigation of individual direct, indirect, and induced impacts.

The method has its disadvantages as well (Fletcher 1989). Archer has discussed the following limitations of input-output multiplier analysis (1977a):

1. Input-output assumes linear production functions; that is, any additional final demand will be met by an industry through purchasing inputs in the same proportion from the same suppliers: this may particularly be a problem where the supply of a certain input, such as qualified labor, is limited.

2. All additional income resulting from additions to final demand will be spent in the same proportions on the same consumption items, with the same split between intraregional purchases and imports: this is analogous to the assumption of a linear production function in limitation 1; while this can be overcome by disaggregating resident purchases in an area, this is quite expensive.

3. Interindustry relationships change considerably over a period of perhaps five years, yet most input-output data are older than this.

4. Travel spending items may not be consistent with the industry or with commodity groups in the input-output tables.

5. Most input-output models are static in nature and do not explicitly recognize time lags that may operate between initial expenditure and full multiplier effects.

All five of these are serious considerations in applying the input-output model to estimating the total impact of travel expenditures in an area. However, it should be noted that the first two limit the usefulness of the ad hoc and economic-base models as well. Fletcher and Archer present ways of dealing with the input-output model drawbacks (1991: 41–43).

ECONOMIC BASE MODELS

Once commonly used to estimate regional impact multipliers, the economic base approach divides the local economy into two sectors: (1) firms serving markets outside the region and (2) firms serving markets within the region (Archer 1977a:14–16; Tiebout 1962; Krikelas 1992).

The goods and services that firms sell outside area boundaries are considered exports and are assumed to be the prime mover of the local economy. If sales and employment serving this export market rise, sales and employment of firms serving the regional market are presumed to grow as well, stimulated by the injection of "new" spending; for example, the more a hotel can sell to nonresident visitors, the greater the employment of residents and the more money will be spent by these employees and by the hotel operator in the local economy.

This approach recognizes that industries and firms within industries may sell their products in both regional and extraregional (export) markets. For each industry in the area, output, payroll, or employment is divided between basic (export) and nonbasic (local) markets. Ratios are then developed of total employment or earnings in a region to basic employment or earnings to estimate the multiplier.

To develop these multipliers, data from sources such as the U.S. Census Bureau's censuses of business are used to divide sales, employment, and payroll between basic and nonbasic markets by industry sector in an area (U.S. Bureau of the Census 1989, 1990). The amounts allocated to basic markets are summed and used as the denominator, with the total for the area magnitude (output, employment, or earnings) as the numerator. The resulting multiplier is then applied to the direct tourism expenditures in the area to obtain the total of primary and secondary impact.

The advantage of this approach is that it is simple and straightforward, employing data generally available even for small areas such as counties. Its disadvantages include the often subjective nature of allocating industry activity between basic and nonbasic markets, the assumption that all types of export sales to basic markets have the same multiplier effect regardless of their industry source, and the assumption that the growth in an area economy is attributable primarily or totally to export sales. Other variables that affect regional growth and not explicitly recognized in the economic base model include interregional capital flows, technological changes, demographic shifts, and state/local tax-law changes (Krikelas 1991:18).

For these reasons, base-theory multipliers are seldom found in tourism impact studies today, reflecting the conclusion that "the findings on economic base models are conclusive. . . . The literature would need to be much more convincing than it has been hitherto for a disinterested observer to resist the conclusion that economic base models should be buried, and without prospects for resurrection" (Richardson 1985, quoted in Krikelas 1992:17).

THE AD HOC MODEL

Archer and Owen (1972) first adapted the Keynesian multiplier model to estimating the total impact of tourism expenditures in an area. They termed their adaptation *ad hoc models* because they are developed individually for each area studied.

The ad hoc model concentrates on the income generated in an area from the initial travel expenditure through the consumption patterns of its residents. The simple ad hoc model is (Fletcher and Archer 1991:40):

$$AHM = \frac{A}{1-BC} \qquad (14)$$

where
AHM = value of the ad hoc multiplier
A = proportion of tourism expenditure remaining in the economy after first-round leakages
B = proportion of residents' income spent in the area economy
C = proportion of expenditure by residents that accrues as income in the area economy

The more developed form actually used for individual areas is (ibid.):

$$AHM_{i,j} = \frac{\sum_j \sum_i Q_j K_{i,j} V_i}{1-c \sum_i X_i Z_i V_i} \qquad (15)$$

where
AHM = value of the ad hoc multiplier
j = types of travelers
i = types of business establishment directly serving travelers
Q = proportion of total tourist expenditure spent by each type of tourist
K = proportion of total tourist expenditure spent in each type of business establishment
V = direct and indirect income generated per dollar spent by each type of business
c = residents' marginal propensity to consume
X = proportion of total residents' consumption expenditures in each type of business
Z = proportion of X that is spent within the study area

The ad hoc model traces the impact of expenditures of different types of travelers (e.g., business, leisure) in different types of tourism-related business establishments (e.g., hotels, restaurants) through the direct and indirect income generated by each. The sum of these incomes for each type of business is divided by a measure of leakage that takes into account the marginal propensity to spend this income on consumption in the study area.

The ad hoc model requires a substantial amount of data to be collected through surveys: In addition to estimates of income generated per dollar of travel expenditure for each type of travel-related business (V), the distribution of resident consumer spending among types of businesses (X) must be developed, as well as the proportion of income spent in the area by residents (Z). Moreover, additional structures need to be specified to develop the other types of multipliers, such as employment and income multipliers.

Finally, it is not clear from the literature how the indirect income generated by expenditures in each type of business for V is estimated. This can be a formidable task. Liu (1986) solved this problem by employing estimates of direct and indirect income from an input-output matrix. But if the researcher has access to an adequate input-output model, why ignore it in favor of following the ad hoc model approach? On the other hand, the ad hoc multiplier appears suitable for areas where building individual input-output models is too expensive or impractical.

Given the inherent flaws in the base-theory model, the researcher's choice is between the ad hoc model and the input-output approach, depending on the budget available and the expertise of the researchers. Fletcher and Archer (1991:44) maintain that the advantages of the input-output model are "overwhelming" from an analytical standpoint. Mathieson and Wall (1982:71) agree input-output analysis produces more accurate results than ad hoc models. The major drawback is the extensive data-collection requirements. Recent developments, however, have all but eliminated this disadvantage in the United States and Canada.

Many state and provincial (Canada) economic development agencies and state universities have developed input-output tables for individual areas (e.g., Burd 1991). Moreover, the appropriate tables are available at the national, regional, and local levels for most areas on a periodic basis through the U.S. Department of Commerce's RIMS II regional input-output modeling system (U.S. Bureau of Economic Analysis 1984). And the U.S. Department of Agriculture IMPLAN system can be used to develop input-output estimates for individual cities and counties in the United States (Turco and Kelsey 1992:64). Given the relatively modest cost of accessing these models, they can provide a cost-effective way to develop measures of total tourism impact on an area's economy.

OTHER ISSUES

The preceding has been limited to the economic benefits of tourism spending to the area visited. Bull (1992:136) reminds readers that the generating area may well benefit from outbound travel, too:

*Very few researchers have attempted to analyze the value, if any, of tourism to generating economies. . . . However, **mass tourism generation**, at least, is likely to produce:*

- *employment in travel agencies, tour operators, transport undertakings, and enterprises engaged in marketing destinations;*
- *investment by carriers and tour operators, and the possibility of developing multinational tourism enterprises;*
- *a possible fall in seasonal price levels whilst tourists are away and demand is slacker;*
- *increases in short-term saving as people "put by" for trips, or businesses hold prepayments on money markets;*
- *a source of taxation revenue on those items purchased before or on departure.*

To this can be added the business receipts, income, and employment produced by purchases in anticipation of the trip, from golf balls to a yacht. Through additional questions added to the National Travel Survey, the TEIM could include several of these impacts. Other models might as well. However, there appears to be little interest in this impact at this time.

There is no discussion here of nonmonetary benefits that can accrue to an area as a result of tourists. Tourist demand may stimulate ethnic pride and encourage preservation of cultural heritage and may aid preservation of local arts and crafts (Long 1991:205–206). The quality of health care may

also rise as tourism develops (Perdue et al. 1991:196). These are enhancements to residents' quality of life, enhancements that have value but are difficult to quantify. The researcher seeking a full disclosure of tourism's benefits in an area would do well to at least enumerate such positive effects to supplement the monetary ones.

CONCLUSION

If there were any doubts about the importance of measuring tourism's economic impact, the myriad of studies available on the topic should remove them. But there have been too many divergent techniques employed owing more to the imagination of the designer than to the reality they attempt to measure. Reading descriptions of them reminds this author of a recent commentary on the field of risk analysis:

Risk analysis begins with scientific studies, usually performed by academics or government agencies, and sometimes incomplete or disputed. The data from the studies are then run through computer models of bewildering complexity, which produce results of implausible precision (Davis 1992).

But perhaps some useful conclusions can be drawn from comparing and contrasting efforts so far.

1. Tourism contributes significantly to the economy of virtually any geographic area where people live or work.
2. It is impossible to distinguish all of tourism's contributions by observation alone or solely by use of secondary data.
3. Expert judgment is no substitute for sound, objective research techniques in deriving quantitative estimates.
4. Recall bias significantly affects measures of trips and expenditures, and this bias grows with the length of the recall period.
5. Recall decay is a substantially greater problem in estimating expenditures than in determining measures of real travel activity, such as trips and nights away from home.
6. There are few independent secondary measures that can be used to judge the accuracy of a given tourism-impact model.
7. Tourism multiplier analyses based on input-output models are superior to those dependent on other techniques of measuring total economic impact of tourism in an area.

Two consequences result from these conclusions:

A. In order to evaluate a given model, considerable efforts must be directed toward examining its structure, that is, its assumptions, relationships, and output and its input data; this means carefully applying the criteria for model evaluation presented in Chapter 31 and employed in this chapter.

B. Application of several different models to estimating

impact in a given area and at a given time would contribute considerably to the assessment of this impact and of the accuracy of individual models.

Point B commends the use of "convergent validity" in estimating impact and evaluating alternative models (Easterby-Smith et al. 1991:121; WTO 1988:206). If two or more ways of measuring a phenomenon agree, than there is a high likelihood that this measurement is accurate. Occasionally, such comparisons are found in the literature (e.g., Runyan 1988), but they are often plagued by different definitions and scopes, preventing a true appraisal. More research involving parallel estimates of economic impact could be quite rewarding.

Additional research is also required on the size and variability of respondent recall decay, especially with regard to travel expenditures. The publication of now-hidden structures of tourism impact models would also add considerably to the understanding of the economic effects of tourism and their measurement.

Most studies of the economic contribution of tourism to date have focused on measuring its volume and on simple analyses of its relative size. This analysis needs to be extended to larger issues faced by public agencies; for example, Kottke (1988) has suggested using linear-programming models to assess the land, labor, and capital consequences of expanding tourism demand in an area. And more research on the varying economic contributions of different types of tourists would be quite productive (Frechtling 1992; Fletcher 1989:518; Moisey and McCool 1990; Tyrrell 1989; Liu 1986; Tatzin 1978). Expanding tourism satellite accounts beyond their input-output model linkages offers great promise here. Such studies could better guide public agencies in the allocation of scarce marketing funds in order to maximize returns to their constituent communities.

In short, it is time for tourism researchers to progress beyond measurement issues and begin to draw conclusions that can be applied broadly to public marketing, planning, and development decision making. This can help ensure that world tourism continues to grow on terms congenial to residents, tourists, and the environment.

REFERENCES

Alreck, Pamela L., and Robert B. Settle (1985), *The Survey Research Handbook*, Homewood, IL: Richard D. Irwin, Inc.

Archer, Brian (1973), *The Impact of Domestic Tourism*, Bangor, Wales: University of Wales Press.

Archer, Brian (1977a), "Input-Output Analysis: Its Strengths, Limitations and Weaknesses," *Eighth Annual Conference Proceedings*, Salt Lake City, UT: The Travel Research Association.

Archer, Brian (1977b), *Tourism Multipliers: The State of the Art*, Bangor, Wales: University of Wales Press.

Archer, Brian (1982), "The Value of Multipliers and Their Policy Implications," *Tourism Management* 3(December), 236–241.

Archer, Brian (1991), "Tourism and Island Economies: Impact Analyses," *Progress in Tourism, Recreation and Hospitality Management*, Volume 1, C. P. Cooper, ed., 125–134, London: Belhaven Press.

Archer, Brian, and Christine B. Owen (1972), "Towards a Tourist Regional Multiplier," *Journal of Travel Research* XI (Fall), 9–13.

Archer, Brian, and Sheila Shea (1975), "Length of Stay Problems in Tourism Research," *Journal of Travel Research* XII (Winter), 8–10.

Babbie, Earl R. (1973), *Survey Research Methods*, Belmont, CA: Wadsworth Publishing Company.

Brog, Werner, and Arnim H. Meyburg (1980), "Nonresponse Problems in Travel Surveys: An Empirical Investigation," *Transportation Research Record, Travel Demands Models: Application, Limitations and Quantitative Methods* (775), 34–38.

Bull, Adrian (1991), *The Economics of Travel and Tourism*, New York: John Wiley & Sons, Inc.

Bullen, Joan M. (1988), "Pushing Proficiency—Making Better Use of Existing Research Tools," *Tourism Research: Expanding Boundaries, Proceedings of the Nineteenth Annual Conference of the Travel and Tourism Research Association*, 319–321, Salt Lake City, UT: Travel and Tourism Research Association.

Burd, Martha (1991), "The Economic Impact of Tourism Industries in B.C., draft," unpublished manuscript, British Columbia Ministry of Development, Trade and Tourism, Canada, September 27.

Burke, James F. (1987), "Conversion Study Methods, Improving Accuracy and Usefulness," *Travel and Tourism: Thrive or Survive?, Proceedings of the Eighteenth Annual Conference of the Travel and Tourism Research Association*, 297–304, Salt Lake City, UT: Travel and Tourism Research Association.

Burke, James F., and Richard Gitelson (1990), "Conversion Studies: Assumptions, Applications, Accuracy and Abuse," *Journal of Travel Research* XXVII (Winter), 46–51.

California Division of Tourism (1974), *Tourism Employment Study*, Sacramento: State of California Department of Commerce.

Canadian Bureau of Management Consulting (1975a), *Tourism Expenditures Model, A Functional Planning and Policy Making Tool*, Ottawa: Department of Supply and Services.

Canadian Bureau of Management Consulting (1975b), *Tourism Impact Model*, Ottawa: Department of Supply and Services.

Carson, Carol S., and Bruce T. Grimm (1991), "Satellite Accounts in a Modernized and Extended System of Economic Accounts," *Business Economics* XXVI (January), 58–63.

Chau, Peter (1988), "The Canadian Tourism Economic Impact

System," paper prepared for Tourism Canada, Ottawa, Canada, August 1, 1988.

Church, Donald E. (1969), "A Proposed Model for Estimating and Analyzing Travel Expenditures," *Western Council for Travel Research Bulletin* VIII (Summer), 1–6.

Cochran, William G. (1977), *Sampling Techniques*, 3rd ed., New York: John Wiley & Sons, Inc.

Crawford, William D., and E.C. Nebel III (1977), "The Importance of Travel Activity to the New Orleans Economy," *Louisiana Business Survey* (July), 1–5.

Davis, Bob (1992), "Risk Analysis Measures Needed for Regulation, But It's No Science," *Wall Street Journal*, August 6, 1.

Dean Runyan Associates (1992), *Travel-related Economic Impacts and Visitor Volume in Oregon: 1990*, Portland, OR: Dean Runyan Associates.

Dommermuth, William P. (1975), *The Use of Sampling in Marketing Research*, Chicago: American Marketing Association.

Easterby-Smith, Mark, Richard Thorpe, and Andy Lowe (1991), *Management Research, An Introduction*, London: Sage Publications.

Ellerbrock, Michael (1981), "Improving Coupon Conversion Studies: A Comment," *Journal of Travel Research* XIX (Spring), 37–38.

Ellerbrock, Michael J., and James C. Hite (1980), "Factors Affecting Regional Employment in Tourism in the United States," *Journal of Travel Research* XVIII (Winter), 26–32.

Ferber, Robert (ed.) (1978), *Readings in Survey Research*, Chicago: American Marketing Association.

Fjelsted, Boyd L., and Frank C. Hachman (1991), "Estimating the Economic Impact of Non-resident Skiers on a State Economy," *Tourism: Building Credibility for a Credible Industry, Proceedings of the Twenty-second Annual Conference of the Travel and Tourism Research Association*, 461–472, Salt Lake City, UT: Travel and Tourism Research Association.

Fleming, William R., and Lorin Toepper (1990), "Economic Impact Studies: Relating the Positive and Negative Impacts to Tourism Development," *Journal of Travel Research* XXIX (Summer), 35–42.

Fletcher, John E. (1989), "Input-Output Analysis and Tourism Impact Studies," *Annals of Tourism Research* 16(4), 514–529.

Fletcher, J. E., and B. H. Archer (1991), "The Development and Application of Multiplier Analysis," *Progress in Tourism, Recreation and Hospitality Management*, Volume 3, 28–47, C. P. Cooper, ed., London: Belhaven Press.

Frechtling, Douglas C. (1973), "The United States Travel Data Center," *Research for Changing Travel Patterns: Interpretation and Utilization* (Fourth Annual Conference Proceedings) The Travel Research Association, 159–163, Salt Lake City, UT.

Frechtling, Douglas C. (1974), "A Model for Estimating Travel Expenditures," *Journal of Travel Research* XII (Spring)

Frechtling, Douglas C., (1978), "A Brief Treatise on Days and Nights," *Journal of Travel Research* XVIII (Fall), 18–19.

Frechtling, Douglas C. et al. (1975a), *Travel Economic Impact Model, Volume I, Final Economic Analysis Methodology*, Washington, D.C.: U.S. Travel Data Center.

Frechtling, Douglas C. (1975b), *Travel Economic Impact Model, Volume II, Final Demonstration Report*, Washington, D.C.: U.S. Travel Data Center.

Frechtling, Douglas C. (1992), "World Marketing and Economic Research Priorities for Tourism," *Tourism Partnerships and Strategies: Merging Vision with New Realities, Proceedings of the Twenty-third Annual Conference of the Travel and Tourism Research Association*, Denver, CO.

Harris, Charles C., Joanne F. Tynon, and William J. McLauglin (1990), "A Comprehensive Method for Studying Leisure Travel," *Journal of Travel Research* XXIX (Spring), 39–44.

Haynes, Landon G. (1975), "A Known and Equal Chance", *Sixth Annual Conference Proceedings*, 95–97, Salt Lake City, UT: The Travel Research Association.

Howard, Dennis R., Samuel V. Lankford, and Mark E. Havitz (1991), "A Method for Authenticating Pleasure Travel Expenditures," *Journal of Travel Research* XXIX (Spring), 19–23.

Howard, Dennis R., Samuel V. Lankford, and Mark E. Havitz (1992), "A Response to Roehl's 'A Comment Concerning "A Method for Authenticating Pleasure Travel Expenditures"'," *Journal of Travel Research* XXX (Spring), 68–69.

Hunt, John D., and Gary Cadez (1981), *Utah Tourism Motor Vehicle Travel: Annual Report 1980–81*, Logan, UT: Utah State University.

Hunt, John D., and Michael J. Dalton (1983), "Comparing Mail and Telephone for Conducting Coupon Conversion Studies," *Journal of Travel Research* XXI (Winter), 16–18.

Interindustry Economics Division (1990), "Annual Input-Output Accounts of the U.S. Economy, 1985," Survey of Current Business 70 (January), 41–56.

Johnson, Peter, and Barry Thomas (1991), *Tourism, Museums and the Local Economy*, Aldersshot, England: Edward Elgar Publishing Limited.

Kottke, Marvin (1988), "Estimating Economic Impacts of Tourism," *Annals of Tourism Research* 15(1), 122–133.

Krikelas, Andrew C. (1992), "Why Regions Grow: A Review of Research on the Economic Base Model," *Federal Reserve Bank of Atlanta Economic Review* 77 (July-August), 16–29.

Lansing, John B., and James N. Morgan (1971), *Economic Survey Methods*, Ann Arbor, MI: Institute for Social Research.

Lapierre, Jocelyn, Stewart Wells, Kishori Lal, Kathleen

Campbell, and John Joisce (1991), "A Proposal for a Satellite Account and Information System for Tourism," presented at the World Tourism Organization's International Conference on Travel and Tourism Statistics, Ottawa, Canada, June 26.

Liu, Juanita C. (1986), "Relative Economic Contributions of Visitor Groups in Hawaii," *Journal of Travel Research* XXVI (Summer), 2–9.

Mak, James, James Moncur, and David Yonamine (1977), "How or How Not to Measure Visitor Expenditure," *Journal of Travel Research* XVI (Summer), 1–4.

Mathieson, Alister, and Geoffrey Wall (1982), *Tourism: Economic, Physical and Social Impacts*, New York: Longman, Inc.

Meyberg, Arnim H., and Werner Brog (1981), "Validity Problems in Empirical Analyses of Non-Home-Activity Patterns," *Transportation Research Record 807: Travel Demand Forecasting and Data Considerations*, 46–50.

Moisey, Neil M., and Stephen F. McCool (1990), "The Benefit Segmentation-Expenditure Connection: The Case of Snowmobiles," *The Tourism Connection: Linking Research and Marketing, Proceedings of the Twenty-first Annual Conference of the Travel and Tourism Association*, 375–381, Salt Lake City, UT: Travel and Tourism Research Association.

Morrison, Alastair M. (1989), *Hospitality and Travel Marketing*, Albany, NY: Delmar Publisher, Inc.

Mueller, Raymond W. (1977), "When Is a Job a Job?," *Journal of Travel Research* XVI (Winter), 1–5.

Murray, John (1991), "Applied Tourism Economic Impact Analysis: Pitfalls and Practicalities," *Tourism: Building Credibility for a Credible Industry, Proceedings of the Twenty-second Annual Conference of the Travel and Tourism Research Association*, 19–31, Salt Lake City, UT: Travel and Tourism Research Association.

Murphy, Peter E., and Barbara A. Carmichael (1991), "Assessing the Tourism Benefits of an Open Access Sports Tournament: The 1989 B.C. Winter Games," *Journal of Travel Research* XXIX (Winter), 32–36.

Office of Business and Economic Development, District of Columbia Government (1981), *District of Columbia Tourism Development Policy Study Report*, Washington, D.C.

Perdue, Richard R., and Larry D. Gutske (1991), *Tourism: Building Credibility for a Credible Industry, Proceedings of the Twenty-second Annual Conference of the Travel and Tourism Research Association*, 191–201, Salt Lake City, UT: Travel and Tourism Research Association.

Pisarski, Alan E. (1991), *Draft Standard International Classification of Tourism Activities (SICTA)*, Madrid, Spain: World Tourism Organization, October.

Pitegoff, Barry (1992), Tourism Research Administrator, Florida Department of Commerce, personal conversation on July 13.

Rappaport, Michael (1988), "Telephone, Personal and Mail—The Elements of Deciding on Survey Approach," *Travel and Tourism: Thrive or Survive, Proceedings of the Eighteenth Annual Conference of the Travel and Tourism Research Association*, 167–171, Salt Lake City, UT: Travel and Tourism Research Association.

Richardson, Harry W. (1985), "Input-Output and Economic Base Multipliers: Looking Backward and Forward," *Journal of Regional Science* 25 (4), 607–661.

Ritchie, J. R. Brent (1975), "Some Critical Aspects of Measurement Theory and Practice in Travel Research," *Journal of Travel Research* XIV (Summer), 1–10.

Ritz, Philip M. (1979), "The Input-Output Structure of the U.S. Economy," *Survey of Current Business* (February), 34–72.

Roehl, Wesley S. (1992), "A Comment Concerning 'A Method for Authenticating Pleasure Travel Expenditures'," *Journal of Travel Research* XXX (Spring), 67–68.

Rogers, Judy (1991), *A Review of Provincial Resident Travel Studies & the CTS: A Discussion Paper*, Toronto, Canada: Ruston/Tomany & Associates, Ltd., August.

Runyan, Dean (1988), "Measuring the Economic Impacts of Travel in California," *Tourism Research: Expanding Boundaries, Proceedings of the Nineteenth Annual Conference of the Travel and Tourism Research Association*, 209–216, Salt Lake City, UT: Travel and Tourism Research Association.

Schultz, Ronald R., and William B. Stronge (1980a), "Social and Economic Effects of Tourism in Florida," *Business & Economic Dimensions* (2), 5–13.

Schultz, Ronald R. and William B. Stronge (1980b), "Tourism's Impact Is Not All Positive," *Business & Economic Dimensions* (2), 14–21.

Smith, Stephen L. J. (1989), *Tourism Analysis, A Handbook*, New York: John Wiley & Sons, Inc..

Statistics Canada (1992), "Canadian Travel Survey, Changes Between 1992 and 1990," May.

Steel, Brian F. (1981), "Measuring Tourist Expenditures—A Discussion Paper," unpublished manuscript, New Zealand Tourist and Public Department.

Stynes, Daniel J., and E. Mahoney (1989), "Measurement and Analysis of Recreational Travel Spending," *Abstracts 1989 Symposium on Leisure Research*, Alexandria, VA: National Recreation and Park Association.

Tatzin, Don (1978), "A Methodological Approach to Estimating the Value of Public Services Consumed by Tourists," *Using Travel Research for Planning and Profits, Proceedings of the Ninth Annual Conference of The Travel Research Association*, 53–60, Salt Lake City, UT: The Travel Research Association.

Tiebout, Charles M. (1962), *The Community Economic Base Study*, Washington, D.C.: Committee for Economic Development.

Tourism Committee, *Manual on Tourism Economic Accounts*, Paris, France: Organization for Economic Co-operation and Development.

Turco, Douglas M., and Craig W. Kelsey (1992), *Conducting Economic Impact Studies of Recreation and Parks Special Events*, National Recreation and Parks Association.

Tyrell, Timothy (1989), "Economic Frameworks for Tourism Development: Economic and Environmental Tradeoffs," *Travel Research: Globalization, the Pacific Rim and Beyond, Proceedings of the Twentieth Annual Conference of the Travel and Tourism Research Association*, 221–225, Salt Lake City, UT: Travel and Tourism Research Association.

U.S. Bureau of Economic Analysis (1977), *Industry Specific Gross Output Multipliers for BEA Economic Areas*, Washington, D.C.: U.S. Government Printing Office.

U.S. Bureau of Economic Analysis (1984), U.S. Department of Commerce, "RIMS II, Regional Input-Output Modeling System, A Brief Description," May.

U.S. Bureau of the Budget (1969), *Household Survey Manual*, Washington, D.C.: U.S. Government Printing Office.

U.S. Bureau of the Census (1979), *1977 Census of Transportation, National Travel Survey, Travel During 1977*, Washington, D.C.: U.S. Government Printing Office.

U.S. Bureau of the Census (1989), *1987 Census of Service Industries, Geographic Area Series* (various states), page A-3, Washington, D.C.: U.S. Government Printing Office.

U.S. Bureau of the Census (1990), *1987 Census of Transportation, Geographic Area Series: Selected Transportation Industries, Summary*, Washington, D.C.: U.S. Government Printing Office.

U.S. Bureau of the Census (1991a), *1987 Census of Service Industries, Subject Series: Hotels, Motels, and Other Lodging Places*, Washington, D.C.: U.S. Government Printing Office.

U.S. Bureau of the Census (1991b), Statistical Abstract of the United States 1991, Washington, D.C.: U.S. Government Printing Office.

U.S. Office of Management and Budget, U.S. (1987), *U.S. Industrial Classification Manual*, 1987, Washington, D.C.: U.S. Government Printing Office.

U.S. Travel and Tourism Administration (1991), *In-flight Survey of International Air Travelers, Overseas Travelers to the United States, January-December, 1990*, Washington, D.C.: U.S. Government Printing Office.

U.S. Travel Data Center (1975), 1974 *National Travel Survey Full Year Report*, Washington, D.C.: U.S. Travel Data Center.

U.S. Travel Data Center (1976), 1975 *National Travel Survey Full Year Report*, Washington, D.C.: U.S. Travel Data Center.

U.S. Travel Data Center (1977), 1976 *National Travel Survey Full Year Report*, Washington, D.C.: U.S. Travel Data Center.

U.S. Travel Data Center (1978), "An Analysis of Data on Travel Expenditures," unpublished manuscript submitted to the U.S. Travel Service, U.S. Department of Commerce.

U.S. Travel Data Center (1980), *The Economic Impact of Foreign Visitor Spending in the United States*, Washington, D.C.: U.S. Travel Service.

U.S. Travel Data Center (1988), *Impact of Foreign Visitors' Spending on State Economies, 1985–86*, Washington, D.C.: U.S. Travel Data Center.

U.S. Travel Data Center (1991a), *Impact of Travel on State Economies, 1989*, Washington, D.C.: U.S. Travel Data Center.

U.S. Travel Data Center (1991b), *Revision of the Travel Economic Impact Model: Final Report to the U.S. Travel and Tourism Administration*.

U.S. Travel Data Center, and Fothergill/Beekhuis Associates (1979), *Delaware Tourism Policy Study*, Dover, DE: Delaware State Travel Service.

Westat, Inc. (1989), *Investigation of Possible Recall/Reference Period Bias in National Surveys of Fishing, Hunting and Wildlife-Associated Recreation, Final Report*, Washington, D.C.: U.S. Department of the Interior, December.

West Virginia University (1981), *Creating Economic Growth and Jobs Through Travel and Tourism*, Washington, D.C.: U.S. Government Printing Office.

Woodside, Arch G. (1981), "Measuring the Conversion of Advertising Coupon Inquiries into Visitors," *Journal of Travel Research* XIX (Spring), 38–41.

Woodside, Arch G. (1990), "Measuring Advertising Effectiveness in Destination Marketing Strategies," *Journal of Travel Research* XXIX (Fall), 3–8.

Woodside, Arch G., and Ilkka A. Ronkainen (1984), "How Serious Is Nonresponse Bias in Advertising Conversion Research?," *Journal of Travel Research* XXII (Spring), 34–37.

World Tourism Organization (1988), *Guidelines for Tourism Statistics (First draft)*, Madrid. Spain: World Tourism Organization.

World Tourism Organization (1986), *Measurement of Travel and Tourism Expenditures*, Madrid, Spain: World Tourism Organization.

World Tourism Organization (1991), "International Conference on Travel and Tourism Statistics, Ottawa, Canada, 24–28 June 1991, Resolutions," Madrid, Spain: World Tourism Organization.

33

Assessing the Impacts of Travel and Tourism—Measuring Economic Costs

DOUGLAS C. FRECHTLING
Associate Professor of Tourism
George Washington University
Washington, D.C.

*T*he relationship of two kinds of incidental costs of tourism, fiscal costs and life quality costs, to a community are discussed. Methods of estimating the direct and secondary fiscal costs are presented, as well as comparing these costs to benefits. The role and method of discounting future costs and benefits are also detailed.

In a world where resources are scarce, measuring the economic benefits of tourism in an area without measuring the associated costs risks wasting limited public funds. Moreover, such an approach may also produce serious damage to the environment, which rapidly escalates public-service costs to support visitors, and significant declines in the quality of life for residents. This is true whether the project is a new facility, such as a hotel, additional infrastructure, such as a new airport, or a marketing program to attract visitors.

Public officials cannot survive many projects that cost their constituents more than they return. Nor can the tourism industry maintain its credibility after promoting such projects to residents. Beyond the increased efficiency in using scarce resources, it is a wise policy for public officials and tourism-industry operators to estimate the economic costs as well as the benefits of tourism projects.

There appears to be two main cases where researchers should apply cost analysis to travel and tourism. One is to examine the current situation to determine how much additional cost visitors are imposing on the community relative to conditions without visitors. When combined with benefits estimates, such information can guide officials in deciding whether and how to stimulate or restrict visitor volume. The other is to estimate the additional costs imposed by more visitors to a community, either from natural growth or produced by a prospective development, such as a new park, additional transportation capacity, or new marketing pro-

grams. It is the second case that has received the most attention, especially in public water-resource-development projects, where the costs and recreational benefits of a proposed project are estimated as part of the determination whether to proceed with the project (Waters and Valderrama 1984). Marketers in the public sector who are considering programs to increase visitor volume should consider the costs imposed by these additional tourists on local residents, both individuals and businesses.

INCIDENTAL COSTS

It is helpful to get the terminology right at the outset of cost analysis. One of the major failures of the marketplace economists recognize is that many economic activities indiscriminately impose costs on others for which no corresponding compensation is paid (Baumol and Blinder 1988:250; Bull 1991:161-165). Tourists give rise to such costs when they produce air pollution, trash, noise, and traffic congestion in a community. This is a cost to residents or government for which tourists pay no compensation.

Economists call such effects *detrimental externalities* (Bull 1991) or *external diseconomies* (Samuelson and Nordhaus 1989:771), and the costs they impose are called *incidental costs* (Baumol and Blinder 1988:251). The sum of incidental costs of an activity and its *private costs*, those paid for by

393

whoever generates the cost, is called the *social cost* of an activity, the total cost to society of the activity.[1]

Tourism imposes incidental costs on an area. The residents of the area (the *community*) affected by the incidental costs of tourism can choose to deal with them in one of three ways: (1) they may accept a lower quality of life than they enjoyed without tourists; (2) they may redress the decline in their life quality through public expenditures for which the residents tax themselves; or (3) they may directly impose monetary costs on the tourists through taxes and fees. The latter two solutions comprise *fiscal costs* and differ by who bears the public or government costs: residents or tourists.

Table 1 lists a number of categories of incidental costs that can be considered in tourism impact studies. The table makes clear that any type of incidental cost can fall on residents (life-quality costs) or on government (fiscal costs). Residents can decide whether to bear the fiscal costs through higher taxes on themselves or shift them to the tourist through specific taxes, through fees and fines on the activity, or through general taxes, such as on lodging, meals, and rental cars.

Study of the costs of travel and tourism should consider all of the direct incidental costs indicated in Table 1. It may well be that the nature and volume of the visitors will not produce any costs in several of the categories listed; for example, visitors to New York City will not impose costs on residents related to regulation of hunting and fishing or forestry management. And if an area is developing a facility or service that would attract few additional visitors, then the contribution to incidental costs in many of the categories may be negligible. However, the point is that the potential cost of visitors in each category should be explicitly examined if a study of the incidental costs of tourism is to be comprehensive.

SECONDARY INCIDENTAL COSTS

So far, the costs of visitors have been described only at the primary level, that is, those costs directly attributable to visitors. However, there are also indirect or secondary cost effects that can operate, as indicated in Table 2.

If the development of a new tourism facility attracts enough additional visitors, there may be an increase in the number and size of business establishments in the community, which require an increase in the labor force and, thus, the resident population. A resident-population increase imposes additional fiscal and life-quality costs on the community. Some of the costs of additional residents will be similar

[1]There is confusion over the meaning of the term *social cost*. Baumol and Blinder (1988) explicitly define it as the sum of private and incidental costs, while Samuelson and Nordhaus (1989:771–772) implicitly do so. This makes sense because the costs of an economic activity, such as tourism, to *society* is equal to its compensated plus uncompensated costs. However, Bull (1991:120) uses *social costs* to refer only to the uncompensated costs imposed on residents, and such terminology is loosely used elsewhere in tourism impact studies.

to those imposed by additional visitors and can be categorized as in Table 1. Then the same measurement techniques can be used for assessing their impact.

Often, some of the costs imposed by the additional residents needed to serve a larger visitor volume may not appear to residents to be travel related; for example, the children of the additional residents will require an increase in educational expenses in the community and may also require additional hospital facilities as well (Baumol et al. 1970:161–177).

One of the most troublesome areas of indirect costs is in welfare or income-maintenance programs. It has been alleged that tourism in certain regions provides highly seasonal job opportunities, attracting a work force that settles in and requires unemployment compensation and other income-transfer programs during off-peak seasons (Cournoyer 1975:205–227); for example, the opening of Florida's Walt Disney World attracted a surplus of unskilled migrant labor that forced the city of Orlando to hire additional police and to expand shelters (Zehnder 1975 quoted in Murphy 1985:99).

Table 2 details the indirect life-quality costs and the corresponding indirect fiscal costs that might be imposed on a community by an increase in the work force to serve an increase in visitor volume. They differ from those costs identified in Table 1 in that they are not generated directly by visitors, but indirectly. The two tables are intended to be exhaustive, but additional costs may be identified by others.

The larger resident population will impose an increased burden on education and hospital facilities. If these are not expanded, the community as a whole deteriorates somewhat as the ignorant and sick threaten to increase in number. The additional population may put increased pressure on already declining neighborhoods and require more urban renewal to prevent an increase in crime and street congestion, with concomitant declines in property values and the visual aesthetics of the community.

If the work force expands to take on additional, highly seasonal jobs, welfare payments and counseling costs may increase; otherwise, crime and disease may well grow. Finally, the population increase may expand the work force considerably more than the additional jobs produced by visitors, as the spouses and children of the travel-related employees look for work. In the absence of economic development programs, long-term residents may experience declines in opportunities for employment and income growth available to them.

The presence of visitors gives rise to indirect incidental costs, as the business and labor population expands to meet increased demand. These indirect costs may be fiscal or life quality, depending on how the residents decide to handle them. There is an additional set of public expenditure programs, however, that do not have direct counterparts on the life-quality side. These might be termed *fiscal overhead expenditures* and relate to the operation and management of government. They include financial administration, general control, and interest on the general debt.

It is not immediately evident whether these government expenditures should be included among travel-generated fis-

Table 1 Direct Incidental Costs of Tourism to a Community—Alternative Life-Quality Costs and Fiscal Costs

LIFE-QUALITY COSTS	FISCAL COSTS
Traffic congestion	Highway construction, police services, public transportation, port and terminal facilities
Crime	Police services, justice system
Fire emergencies	Fire protection
Water pollution	Water supply and sewage treatment
Air pollution	Police services, public transportation
Litter	Solid waste disposal, police services
Noise pollution	Police services, zoning
Destruction of wildlife	Police services, park and recreation facilities, forestry maintenance, fish and game regulation
Destruction of scenic beauty	Park and recreation facilities, police services
Destruction of social/cultural heritage	Maintenance of museums and historic sites, police services
Disease	Hospital and other health maintenance facilities, sanitation facilities, food-service regulation
Vehicular accidents	Police services, justice system

cal costs. On the one hand, it could be argued that fiscal overhead costs are sensitive to the size of government and that part of government is attributable to servicing travel and tourism activity. On the other hand, it could be argued that government primarily exists to serve its citizens and that these overhead costs should not be allocated to nonresident visitors: they would continue unabated in the absence of visitors. Moreover, public officials are occasionally able to cut back on these overhead expenses while the costs of servicing visitors is rising.

If it is decided to include fiscal overhead costs in the accounting of travel-generated fiscal costs, they can be allocated by the proportion that travel-related fiscal costs bear to total budget net of overhead costs; for example, if an exhaustive study of fiscal costs attributable to tourists indicates that one-third of the government's nonoverhead expenditure items are attributable to them, then one-third of the fiscal overhead costs can be attributed to visitors as well.

There is another area where it is unclear whether additional incidental costs for the community as a whole are

Table 2 Indirect Incidental Costs of Tourism to a Community Generated by Labor Inflow—Alternative Life-Quality Costs and Fiscal Costs

LIFE-QUALITY COSTS	FISCAL COSTS
Crime	Police services, justice system, education, employment services
Vehicular accidents	Police services, justice system
Disease, other threats to health	Hospital and other health maintenance facilities, sanitation facilities, public housing
Vagrancy, homelessness	Public housing, urban renewal, housing subsidies, public welfare
Traffic congestion	Police services, highway construction, public transportation
Uneducated electorate	Education

involved. This includes the redistribution effects of tourism projects. A new highway or transportation terminal located far from the old one may well cause a decline in the receipts of those businesses established near the obsolete facilities. However, businesses near the new road or terminal will thrive.

As another example, the hotels located in a community may be enjoying very high occupancy rates. Then a government program (low interest loans, loan guarantees, special infrastructure) stimulates additional hotel construction. After the new property opens, the original hotels suffer declines in occupancy and in return on investment.

As a final example, the additional visitors generated by a new public visitor-related facility may push up wage rates and property values in the community. Now employers must pay their workers more, and those wishing to buy property must pay more to those who already own it.

DISTRIBUTIONAL EFFECTS

These are distributional aspects of increased visitor demand. Income or wealth is transferred from one group in the community to another as the result of visitors. There are five major groups that may be differentially affected by the presence of tourists in a community (after Pearce 1989:215):

1. Tourism-related businesses—owners, operators, employees
2. Non-tourism-related businesses
3. Public authorities
4. Residents
5. Tourists

Most of the cost impacts on tourism-related businesses and tourists are covered under private costs, that is, are expressed through exchange transactions in the market place. However, uncompensated costs, especially to tourists, can be imagined where crowding reduces the quality of the *tourists'* lives. And there are subgroups within these who may be affected differently from other subgroups: residents living near the most popular tourist centers will suffer more than those living well away.

Since there is no objective way of determining whether the community is better or worse off as a result of intracommunity transfers related to tourists, and no additional output has been produced by the transfer, it is recommended that this be excluded from cost analysis (Prest and Turvey 1967:160).

One judgment can be made here, however. If it can be shown that a tourism program primarily benefits nonresidents at the expense of residents through shifting benefits to the former away from the latter, then the project is clearly costly from the residents' point of view. This can happen, for example, if locally owned and staffed hotels lose business to properties owned by absentee owners, staffed by imported labor, and operated with imported goods and services. It is clear here that the gross economic benefits of the project are

not benefits to the residents, and some are actually costs in terms of lost jobs and income.

It is important that the range of costs of tourism that are examined are consistent with the spectrum of benefits. It is not correct to calculate the indirect costs of additional visitors without recognizing the indirect benefits in terms of additional income and tax revenues in the community. It may be that the study of the costs and benefits of a given tourism project must be limited, due to available funds, to the direct implications to the community. In such a case, the researchers must make sure that the cost and benefit implications are consistent and that the scope of one side is not expanded beyond the scope of the other.

It should be clear that the optimum scope of cost analysis of tourism-related projects can be summarized as broad, deep, and long: *broad* in covering all incidental costs in the community; *deep* to include the indirect costs from population increases from an expanded work force to meet enlarged visitor demand; and *long* to cover the distant as well as the near future. This last aspect will be covered more fully in a succeeding section on the appropriate social rate of discount.

MEASUREMENT

It is difficult to measure the direct incidental costs of travel and tourism (Bull 1991:164). Many simplifying and, sometimes, subjective assumptions are made to arrive at final cost estimates. As the state of the art progresses, the subjective content can be reduced to produce the reliable objective estimates that are most useful.

Measuring the indirect costs is even more difficult, requiring an additional analytical step. First, assumptions must be made about the link between visitor demand and the resident businesses and individuals who service this demand. Once this is established, there must then be determined the relationship between those servicing visitors and the incidental costs of their activities. This two-step process may increase the subjective content of the estimates and reduce their accuracy.

Little work appears to have been done in measuring the indirect costs of travel and tourism (Zehnder 1975 is the only study of which this author is aware). This subject needs more serious attention before it can be considered as accurate as the measurement of secondary benefits.

The incidental-cost-measurement problem is facilitated to the extent residents have chosen to translate life-quality costs into fiscal costs, particularly, public expenditures.

FISCAL COSTS

Measurement of the fiscal costs of visitors to the community involves apportioning some of each category listed in Table 1 to visitors. The final estimates of visitor-related fiscal costs will be quite sensitive to the measurement method employed, so special care should be taken to develop objective and accurate techniques.

Looking at the direct fiscal costs of visitors, there are two basic issues. One is how to measure the *net* fiscal costs of visitors. Many of the program costs listed in Table 1 are at least partially offset by user charges in the community. Street and highway construction and maintenance programs are funded by motor gasoline taxes. The costs of developing and operating museums, historic sites, parks, and recreation areas may be offset by admission or user fees. The cost of fish and game regulation may be financed entirely by license fees. The question is, should the revenue from user charges be subtracted and only the net costs of each program be dealt with, or should user charges paid by visitors be addressed on the benefit side and the *gross* costs of each program attributable to visitors be dealt with on the cost side?

If the only interest is in the cost side, the former approach might be preferable. This gives the net costs of visitors that must be picked up by the residents. However, in doing so, the risk is run of neglecting to include travel-generated fiscal revenue not directly attributable to specific programs, such as sales and gross receipts taxes. Since these taxes are usually not earmarked for offsetting specific costs (i.e., are a general benefit), they are apt to be excluded in calculating the net costs of each visitor-related public service.

It seems far more advisable to maintain a strict distinction between costs and benefits. All of the fiscal costs generated by visitors should be totaled on one side, and all of the fiscal receipts derived from visitors should be summed on the other, and then comparisons made. This has the advantage of including all revenue items, whether related to a specific service or not, on the benefit side with other benefits. Similarly, gross fiscal costs can be compared with other social costs. All is laid out explicitly, with no "off balance-sheet accounting" to worry about.

Table 3 indicates the units of measurement suggested for apportioning public-service costs between visitors and residents. In each case, both total use and visitor use need to be estimated. Then the total program costs in each category are distributed to visitors according to the proportion of use generated by visitors.

It should be understood that in many cases the measurement units suggested are imperfect indicators of actual visitor consumption of public services. However, they have the virtue of being readily available from visitor surveys and resident-population data. Further research is required on better indicators of visitor use of public services.

The fiscal-cost categories are drawn from Table 1. While most of the units of measurement are self-explanatory, a few words about the *daily census* measure are required. The *daily census* is the average number of people present each day in the area under study for some period, usually a year. If the area studied is a local community, commuters from outside the community boundaries should be included along with residents and visitors. If the area is a state, it is unlikely commutation will add much relative to the total of residents and visitors.

The average daily census measure is an estimate of the average number of people present in the community for one year and is computed as follows:

$$ADC_{c,y} = \frac{VD_{c,y} + (RP_{c,y} \cdot 365 \text{ days}) + \dfrac{CP_{c,y} \cdot 236 \text{ days}}{3}}{365 \text{ days}} \quad (1)$$

where

c	=	community
y	=	year
ADC	=	average daily census
VD	=	annual visitor-days produced by tourists
RP	=	average annual resident population
CP	=	average daily commuters from outside the community

This is the sum of the number of visitor-days spent in the area for the year plus the product of resident population and 365 days in the year, plus a measure of commuter-days, divided by 365 days. Average daily commuter population is

Table 3 Suggested Units of Measurement for Direct Fiscal Costs of Tourists

FISCAL-COST CATEGORY	UNIT OF MEASUREMENT
Highway construction and maintenance	Vehicle-miles
Fish and game regulation	Licenses sold
Park and recreation facilities	Site visitor-days or visits (admissions)
Museums and historic sites	Site visits (admissions)
Port and terminal facilities	Arrivals and departures
Forestry maintenance	Site visitor-days or visits
Public transportation	Passengers
Police services	Daily census
Fire protection	Daily census
Hospital and health care facilities	Daily census
Environmental regulation	Daily census
Health and sanitation services	Daily census
Water supply and sewage treatment	Daily census
Trash and litter disposal	Daily census

represented by the number of daily commuters multiplied by the one-third of a day they spend in the community each day, the product multiplied by 236 days as an average work year, recognizing weekends, holidays, and vacations as nonwork days without commuting.

The daily census approach assumes that the cost of a given public service is a function of the number of people present in the area daily. The costs of the service can then be apportioned between visitors and others in the same proportion that the daily census is composed, that is (Baumol et al. 1970:149-160):

$$VP_{s,c,y} = \frac{VD_{c,y}}{365 \cdot ADC_{c,y}} \qquad (2)$$

where

s	=	given public service
c	=	community
y	=	year
VP	=	tourist proportion of the service's costs
VD	=	annual visitor-days produced by tourists
ADC	=	average daily census

It is attractive to the researcher to apply the daily census approach to estimating all or nearly all public program costs (Office of Business and Economic Development 1981). However, this tendency should be resisted in favor of measures that more accurately represent actual visitor usage of the program or facility. This allows for valid estimation of public costs related to visitors even if visitor-activity patterns change but visitor volume does not.

While a very simple concept, the daily census approach appears well suited for a number of public services (U.S. Travel Data Center et al. 1979). It was used, for example, to apportion costs of police protection and sewage treatment between visitors and others in the state of Delaware (ibid.). Tatzin (1978), however, has applied a different approach to estimating the tourist-related costs of "public goods," that is, those services supplied by public agencies that are not depleted by an additional user and for which it is generally difficult to exclude people from its benefits (Baumol and Blinder 1988:255).

Tatzin developed "probability of use" coefficients for each public service. These represented the likelihood that the average tourist would use the given service. Such coefficients were easy to develop for certain public services analogous to private businesses, such as the zoo. Here, tourist-days visiting the zoo were divided by total visitor-days to obtain the coefficient. For public goods, such as police protection, Tatzin relied on the judgment of knowledgeable officials.

Then Tatzin developed "relative cost coefficients," which represent the intensity with which tourists consume a public service. This, too, is based on informed judgment; for example, he found that police officials indicated that tourists place demand largely on patrol services, while residents use these as well as juvenile, investigative, and other police services (Tatzin 1978:55). Finally, he combined these coef-

ficients with the total budgets for each service to obtain public expenditures per visitor-day for each service for each type of tourist.

The two methods share the same objective—to estimate the public services costs per visitor-day—but differ in concept. The average daily census method assumes that the tourists' intensity of consuming most public goods cannot accurately be determined. Tatzin's approach assumes that informed judgment provides sound estimates of this intensity. It is interesting to note that he concludes (1978:60), "The public costs of tourism result largely from the mere presence of tourists." This suggests the average daily census method is equal to Tatzin's model in accuracy, although it is far less demanding in terms of researchers' time and costs.

Tatzin appears to have disregarded the overhead costs of administration, financial control, debt service, and other programs that support the public services that tourists consume. The U.S. Travel Data Center (1979) prorated these expenditures based on the proportion of certain fiscal costs shared between visitors and residents/commuters.

One other attempt to measure tourists' costs to local government used a limited number of public expenditure categories but attributed all of their costs to tourists (Yochum and Agarwal 1987:143). However, important categories were excluded, such as fire protection, which suggests that this cost-estimation procedure was incomplete.

LIFE-QUALITY COSTS

Putting actual dollar values on the life-quality costs is quite difficult. One conceptual approach is to estimate what residents would be willing to pay to return to their previsitor level of risk of destruction of flora, fauna, human life and health, natural and scenic beauty, historical and cultural heritage sites, and amount of crowding and congestion. However, the residents cannot actually be asked such hypothetical questions because what they say they would pay and what they would actually pay for reducing each visitor-related life-quality cost are likely to be quite different.

Moreover, the cost categories require trade-offs since residents have fixed budgets and visitor-related costs would have to be accommodated within them, along with maintenance, nurture, recreation, and other expenses. Finally, the residents have an incentive to understate the amount they would be willing to pay for collective goods such as police protection and pollution control. Since the amount of these services each consumes is equal and unrelated to the cost each would pay, each resident would hope to get someone else to pay more than he or she does by understating the value put on it (Prest and Turvey 1967:167-168; Waters and Valderrama 1984).

The measurement of life-quality costs associated with travel and tourism in a community has not been adequately addressed in past research. Some investigators have tried to estimate relative life-quality costs of alternative activities. These have generally been limited to environmental consequences of visitation and suggest that certain classes of visitors pursuing certain activities have lower benefit-cost ratios than others (Northeast Markets et al. 1974:155–174). However, these studies incorporate large subjective components in the estimation methods.

It could be argued that the residents have the ability to redress life-quality costs of visitors by transferring them as fiscal costs through taxes and fees on the visitors. If they do not choose to do so, this reasoning goes, then the life-quality costs cannot be significant to the residents. Therefore, the calculation of fiscal costs is sufficient to cover incidental costs.

A counter argument to this one is that individual residents do the benefit-cost calculus on their own and a majority decide that the life-quality reduction suffered is more than offset by personal economic benefits attributable to visitors. But this does not resolve the issue of whether the community is collectively better off with additional visitors or without them. It may be that the majority of voters feel they are better off, but that the minority, which may well bear most of the cost burden or value the quality of their environment most highly, bears net costs large enough to offset the majority's net benefits.

Further study of such reasoning and its implications and of methods of quantifying life-quality costs of tourism is required before this issue can be settled.

OTHER ISSUES

There are additional issues in analyzing the costs of travel and tourism that deserve study. However, so little attention has been given them so far that it is difficult to suggest even conceptual solutions at this time.

It was mentioned previously that the redistributional aspects of a development project in a community can be ignored since income and wealth would be transferred among community members. However, if it could be shown, for example, that the construction of a new terminal would benefit absentee property owners while demolition of the old terminal would hurt resident owners, then the community would experience a net cost from this aspect of the project.

Moreover, in some communities, there may be a broad consensus that all public projects should help the poor rather than the rich. In such a community, if a project reduced the business and employment opportunities of the poor, say around an old terminal, and increased those of the more advantaged around the proposed site for new construction, then it would have unfavorable redistributional costs from the community's standpoint.

As another issue, it has been assumed that the fiscal costs of redressing certain effects of visitation do not exceed the life-quality costs the resident would endure in the absence of these fiscal costs. The amount a community is willing to tax itself or its visitors to limit congestion or protect the environment is assumed to be fairly representative of the life-quality costs that would be imposed on the residents. However, this may not always be true. Inefficient public programs could cost the community or its visitors far more than they return in redressing life-quality costs.

One point has not been addressed: that certain kinds of visitors are more costly to service than others; for example, one study has found that convention visitors to a city produced some of the highest costs among visitor types (Tatzin 1978). Such information is crucial for the community deciding whether to attract new visitors or dissuade current ones.[2] One wonders how many scarce public resources have been spent to attract market segments that cost the community more than they return.

This chapter has sometimes discussed the additional costs to a community of attracting additional visitors. Optimally, this should be in terms of the *marginal* costs of these visitors, that is, how much additional social cost would be imposed by 1,000 more visitors. Usually, this question is answered by assuming that the marginal cost of serving 1,000 more visitors would be the same as the *average* cost of serving 1,000 current ones. This may not be true. If visitors, such as convention delegates, are served by a project with a large fixed cost, such as a convention center, then the marginal cost of servicing an extra 1,000 visitors could actually be less than the average cost. In other cases, the marginal cost could exceed the average cost because a facility has reached its service capacity. Far more study is required before researchers can be completely comfortable with their projections of the cost implications of additional visitors.

This discussion has ignored the concept of *opportunity costs*, that is, the value of the lost opportunity to the economy of using financial or other resources in the alternative activity with the highest returns (Bull 1991:159; Murphy 1985:103). There are always alternative ways of employing public funds, labor, land, and capital to investing them in tourism promotion and development. Returns on the highest-valued alternative use should be subtracted from the tourism benefits to obtain a sound economic measure of the benefits to the economy. However, measuring the opportunity cost of a tourism project or program requires the researcher to determine the value of what might have been: jobs that might have been produced, wages that might have been paid, financial returns that might have accrued. This requires a great deal of subjectivity and speculation, activities that the researcher is not comfortable in applying and that are subject to abuse by those wanting to prove tourism programs are or are not wise uses of scarce resources. This probably explains why little work has been done in this area (see Bryden 1973 quoted in Murphy 1985:103, for one example).

Another area of costs not specifically addressed is the phenomenon of rising prices in a community experiencing an influx of tourists (Bull 1991:135–136; Pearce 1989:212–213). This is most apt to occur in relatively undeveloped

[2]In 1985, Fort Lauderdale, Florida, determined, at least qualitatively, that the community's costs of hosting 350,000 college-age visitors every spring was greater than the visitor's expenditures. The community embarked on a marketing campaign to discourage such visitors and encourage new visitor markets, such as families, seniors, and convention delegates. By 1991, the number of young spring visitors had fallen below 15,000, yet total visitor volume and revenues were far greater than in 1985.

areas where the tourists add considerably to the average daily census (e.g., Long 1991:212). Land and housing prices, in particular, may rise rapidly, pricing many residents out of the market. Food prices may show extreme seasonal fluctuations, reflecting the ebb and flow of tourists.

This is certainly a cost to residents. However, quantifying costs to the community is hindered by increased revenue of some residents who are able to capitalize on the situation. In addition, dual markets may arise, where locals pay lower prices for food and other items than are charged the tourists (Bull 1991:136). Additional study is required to map out the dynamics of this phenomenon and to determine the distributional consequences and the net impact on the residents.

Finally, further research is required on more accurate ways to measure the incidental costs of tourism. Much is conjectural at this point. Better measurement techniques will help ensure better decisions.

COMPARING BENEFITS AND COSTS

Once the economic benefits and the economic costs of travel have been computed on a sound and consistent basis, then researchers are in a position to determine whether a given tourism project or program is good for an area in economic terms or whether it costs residents more than they gain. Similarly, researchers can analyze whether additional visitor promotion provides net benefits and what direction this promotion should take (U.S. Travel Data Center et al. 1979).

Estimation of the ratio of benefits to costs is straightforward, once these two magnitudes have been measured. Researchers must be clear about how they are measuring each, however. One British study compared tourism-related public-service costs in a local area to total visitor expenditures and found the ratio to be quite low (Heely quoted in Murphy 1985:102). This finding is irrelevant to determining whether tourism benefits the community. Visitor expenditures are not a good measure of tourism benefits to the community, nor do public service costs include all visitor-imposed costs. Rather, this finding helps local authorities to determine how much to invest in developing the visitor market. Certainly, local authorities in this case should not spend anything to stimulate tourism if the £3.1 million they spent servicing visitors was not recouped in public revenues.

There is one additional issue that relates to the timing of costs and returns from public investment projects designed to serve travelers that must be resolved.

THE SOCIAL RATE OF DISCOUNT

When residents through their government contemplate investing public funds in a travel-related development project, such as a park or recreation area, a highway, or a visitor-information facility, they should examine the total construction, operation, and maintenance costs of the project. These costs, as well as benefits from the project, stretch out over the useful life of the facility.

The total costs of the project stretch out in time over its useful life. However, the time stream of costs cannot be simply totaled because a dollar's worth of cost five years from now is not worth the same as a dollar's worth of cost today. A factor is needed that will put all costs, no matter in what year they occur, in terms of a consistent "present value." Benefits should be similarly treated.

A great deal has been written on devising a "discount rate" for valuing the streams of benefits and costs of a public investment project (Mikesell 1977). The debate has been quite technical and is not settled to the satisfaction of all. However, there is a strong case to be made for adopting a single approach for determining a public agency's *social rate of discount*, the interest rate for collapsing all of the costs and benefits of a project over time into a consistent current value.

Government should be interested in maximizing efficiency in the use of the area's total economic resources. Specifically, this means that a dollar's worth of resources withdrawn from the private sector for public investment should earn the same rate of return as it would in the private sector. If the dollar earns less in the public project, then society is worse off after the public investment than before because a less productive alternative has been implemented.

Consequently, in evaluating the cost stream, government should determine the *opportunity cost of capital* in the private sector, that is, what the investment funds required for the public project would have earned if left in the private sector. This interest rate is then used to discount future benefits and to compound present and future costs.

On the benefit side, a dollar's worth of some benefit, say income, in the future is worth less than a dollar received today (Samuelson and Nordhaus 1989:733-735). There are several ways of justifying this position, but one of the most lucid is to consider that a dollar received today can be invested in the private sector and earn a return, such as interest or dividends. So a dollar received today is worth 5 percent more than a dollar received one year from now because today's dollar can be invested and earn 5 percent in a year. The other side of this coin is that the dollar received one year from now is worth 5 percent less than the dollar received today.

In the general case, if the interest rate of return is r and the number of years that must be waited to receive the dollar's worth of income is n, then a dollar's worth of benefit received today is worth $\$(1+r)^n$ at the end of n years. This is also a measure of the return foregone by waiting until year n to receive the dollar's worth of benefit; that is, a dollar's worth of benefit in year n is worth $\$1/(1+r)^n$ today.

The resulting general equation for computing the present value of future benefits is,

$$PVB = \qquad\qquad\qquad\qquad (3)$$

$$= B_0 + \frac{B_1}{(1+r)} + \frac{B_2}{(1+r)^2} + \ldots + \frac{B_n}{(1+r)^n} + \frac{S_l}{(1+r)^n}$$

where
PVB = present value of benefits

B_t = dollar value of benefits in time period t
r = opportunity cost of capital or some other social discount rate
n = life of the project in years
S = salvage value at end of the project's life

While there is some debate over how to estimate the present value of future costs, the popular approach is to discount the current and future costs of a project in the same manner that benefits are discounted (see Mikesell 1977 for discussion of alternatives):

$$PVC = C_0 + \frac{C_1}{(1+r)} + \frac{C_2}{(1+r)^2} + \ldots + \frac{C_n}{(1+r)^n} \quad (4)$$

where:
PVC   = present value of costs
C_t = dollar value of costs in time period t
r = opportunity cost of capital
n = life of project in years

Finally, the present value of benefits is divided by the present value of costs; and if the ratio is higher than for any alternative use of the investment funds, then the project should be undertaken.

The comparison of the costs and benefits of a public investment project is quite sensitive to the discount rate employed. Most of the costs are incurred early in the project's life, so the present value of the costs does not vary much with the discount rate employed. On the other hand, the benefits flow over the life of the project rather than at the front end, many accruing far into the future. Thus, the present value of benefits *declines* rapidly as the discount rate increases.

It has been a common practice in some public investment areas to keep the discount rate low to maximize the ratio of benefits to costs and ensure project acceptance (Mikesell 1977:3-6). All this ensures is that investment resources are wasted as they are taken from their higher return uses in the private sector to be used in lower-return projects by government.

In order to determine the opportunity cost of capital in the private sector relevant to a given project, it must be first determined whether the project has private-sector counterparts. Campgrounds, resorts, transportation terminals, and several other types of public investment projects are often financed by the private sector. In this case, the appropriate social rate of discount is the comparable real before-tax rate of return for the same project in a similar risk class.

If there is no private-sector counterpart to the project being studied, then it is suggested that the average real rate on long-term U.S. government bonds be used, with additional premiums to account for the risk of the investment and the average corporate tax rate on total returns to private capital investment.

This approach will help ensure that the social rate of discount is not set too low, distorting the flow of investment funds in the private sector and reducing economic welfare in general.

When all is said and done, benefit-cost analysis is just one fairly blunt tool in the decision-maker's kit. In wielding this tool, it would be well to note the following perspective:

Cost-benefit analyses can seldom provide complete answers. They are intended primarily to provide more information to decision makers concerning the major trade offs and implications existing among the alternatives considered. This information would then be available for use by decision makers, along with any other information available—e.g., that pertaining to political, psychological, and other factors which may not have been included in the cost-benefit study (U.S. Senate Committee on Government Operations 1967:4).

CONCLUSIONS

These three chapters have attempted to address the nature, classification, and measurement of the economic benefits and costs of tourism in a comprehensive manner. This broad coverage of issues and alternatives necessarily prohibits detailed examination of any one topic. However, the sources used are amply documented for those who wish to learn more about a single subject.

More attention has been devoted to the benefit side of tourism than the cost side. This is not because determining benefits is more important than understanding costs; rather it reflects the amount of research resources that have gone into the two areas (Murphy 1985:78). Future efforts are best directed at developing better techniques to measure costs in an objective manner, for it is here that knowledge is weakest. This ignorance gives rise to radical attacks on tourism as an activity and an industry from time to time, attacks that are ill-founded but capture the public's attention. The public would all be better served by objective cost measurement rather than the speculation that has characterized many cost discussions so far.

The greatest rewards in terms of better public tourism development decisions will come with associating reliable estimates of economic benefits and costs with individual market segments. If agencies know which segments produce the greatest ratios of benefits to costs, they can invest their marketing dollars in attracting these segments and their investment dollars in building the facilities that appeal to them.

This author hopes that the future will bring a stronger interest in identifying the costs of tourism programs and that this field will develop in stature and respectability. A field of study such as tourism impact best develops by building research upon research. The field will develop faster and to the greater good of the public and the industry to the extent that researchers share their findings and substitute sound quantitative techniques for judgment. It is disturbing to see today a number of tourism impact studies relying on the judgment of experts as they did 20 years ago. This is partly in response to the frustrations of trying to grasp the elusive concepts and practices of tourism, tourists, and the tourism industry.

But no field of study develops without diligence, perseverance in the face of difficulty, vision, and refusing to settle for second best. It is the author's hope that tourism economic impact research will prove this rule again in the next 20 years.

REFERENCES

Baumol, William J., et al. (1970), *The Visitor Industry and Hawaii's Economy: A Cost-Benefit Analysis*, Princeton, NJ: Mathematica, 30.

Baumol, William J., and Alan S. Blinder (1988), *Economics Principles and Policy: Microeconomics*, 4th ed., San Diego, CA: Harcourt Brace Jovanovich, Publishers.

Bryden, J.M. (1973), *Tourism and Development*, Cambridge, UK: Cambridge University Press.

Bull, Adrian (1991), *The Economics of Travel and Tourism*, New York: John Wiley & Sons, Inc.

Cournoyer, Norman G., et al. (1975), *Travel and Tourism in Massachusetts*, 1975, Amherst, MA: University of Massachusetts.

Heeley, J. (1980), "Tourism and Local Government with Special Reference to the County of Norfolk" (2 vols.), unpublished Ph.D. dissertation, University of East Anglia, Norwich, England.

Long, Veronica H. (1991), "Government-Industry-Community Interaction in Tourism Development in Mexico," in *The Tourism Industry: An International Analysis*, M. Thea Sinclair and M. J. Stabler, eds., 205–222, Wallingford, UK: C.A.B. International.

Mikesell, Raymond F. (1977), *The Rate of Discount for Evaluating Public Projects*, Washington, D.C.: American Enterprise Institute.

Murphy, Peter E. (1985), *Tourism, A Community Approach*, New York: Routledge.

Northeast Markets, Arthur D. Little, and William Fothergill (1974), *Tourism in Maine: Analysis and Recommendations*, Yarmouth, ME: Northeast Markets, Inc.

Office of Business and Economic Development, District of Columbia Government (1981), *District of Columbia Tourism Development Policy Study Report*, Washington, D.C.

Pearce, Douglas (1989), *Tourism Development*, 2nd ed., Harlow, England: Longman Scientific & Technical.

Prest, A.R., and R. Turvey (1967), "Cost-Benefit Analysis: A Survey," *Surveys of Economy Theory, Volume III, Resource Allocation*, 155–207, New York: St. Martin's Press.

Samuelson, Paul A., and William D. Nordhaus (1989), *Economics*, 13th ed., New York: McGraw-Hill Book Company.

Tatzin, Donald L. (1978), "A Methodological Approach to Estimating the Value of Public Services Consumed by Tourists," *Using Travel Research for Planning and Profits, Ninth Annual Conference Proceedings*, 53–60, Salt Lake City, UT: The Travel Research Association.

Tyrrell, Timothy J., William K.B. Emerson, and David E. Molzan (1982), *The Economic Impact of Tourism on Westerly, Rhode Island*, Kingston, RI: University of Rhode Island Agricultural Experiment Station.

U.S. Senate Committee on Government Operations, (1967), *Criteria for Evaluation in Planning State and Local Programs*, Washington, D.C.: U.S. Government Printing Office.

U.S. Travel Data Center, and Fothergill/Beekhuis Associates (1979), *Delaware Tourism Policy Study*, Dover, DE: Delaware State Travel Service.

Waters, Robert C., and Ramiro Valderrama (1984), "Derivation of Unit-Day-Values for Recreation Benefit Valuation in Water Resource Planning Based on a Comprehensive Theoretical Framework," technical completion report prepared for the Geological Survey, U.S. Department of the Interior, Washington, D.C., July.

Yochum, Gilbert R., and Vinod B. Agarwal (1987), "An Economic Evaluation of Advertising Expenditures for the City of Virginia Beach," *Travel & Tourism: Thrive or Survive, Eighteenth Annual Conference Proceedings*, 131–145, Salt Lake City, UT: Travel and Tourism Research Association.

Zehnder, L.E. (1975), *Florida's Disney World: Promises and Problems*, Tallahassee, FL: Peninsular Publishing.

34

Evaluating the Human Resource (Employment) Requirements and Impacts of Tourism Developments[1]

RANDYL D. ELKIN[2]
Chairman and Professor
Department of Industrial and Labor Relations
West Virginia University
Morgantown, West Virginia

RANDALL S. ROBERTS
Employee Relations Manager
Louie Glass Company, Inc.
Weston, West Virginia

Human resources research in travel and tourism falls broadly into two categories: human resource requirements and employment impact studies. Human resources requirements research done internal to the firm often deals with problem and planning areas. This in-house research includes job restructuring to eliminate dead-end jobs and redundant tasks; turnover analysis to reduce recruiting, screening, and training costs; and training development programs to reduce turnover and to meet future human resource needs. Research done external to the travel firm is generally done for planning purposes. Industry trade associations, government agencies, and, in particular, those private and public units charged with providing training and education services plan classes and programs according to industry needs. They project or forecast the number and skills of employees both needed and available for future industry growth. Projected skills shortages are moderated through education and training programs.

Employment impact studies are used to determine past, current, and possible future effects of travel and tourism on employment and earnings. They are usually done by trade associations, universities, and government agencies. They are usually too complex and costly for an individual firm to undertake. Uses include planning for industry expansion (e.g., identifying viable markets with a readily available labor supply), substantiating applications for loans and government grants, and most commonly for travel promotion and public relations. The results can generate funding from government agencies (to provide training programs or development money), elicit community and resident support, and attract new businesses to the travel industry.

[1]**Editor's Note:** This chapter appeared in the first edition of the publication and is reprinted here substantially without change as the authors were unable to revise it. The reader will note that the salary information is woefully out of date; however, the procedures outlined are still sound and provide useful information on human resource requirements research.

[2]The authors wish to thank Dr. Paul Baktari for his technical assistance in the preparation of this manuscript.

INTRODUCTION

THE NATURE OF THE LABOR MARKET

Economists view the labor market as the arena of interaction between demand and supply. The labor-supply side of the market consists of people. Conceptually, it is the quantity of work hours individuals are willing to work at specific wage rates. For travel research purposes, studies usually seek to determine the number of people available to work who have the skills demanded by the travel industry. The quantity dimension of labor supply is the number of people and the wage for which they will work. The quality component relates to their skills and abilities.

On the demand side of the labor market are the firms that employ or wish to hire labor. The demand for labor is a derived demand; that is, firms hire labor because there is a demand for the firms' product. The demand for labor, then, is a reflection of the demand by the public for travel goods and services. The quantity dimension of labor demand is the number of workers that employers are willing to employ at the various wage rates they are willing to pay. The quality dimension relates to the skills and abilities required to do the job. Demand and supply interact to produce employment. Labor cost to the firm is income to its employees.

When examining labor at the firm level, the idea of the internal labor market (ILM) will prove useful. Jobs internal to the firm are relatively isolated from the external (outside) labor market. According to the theory, jobs are often related to one another as a progression of skills requirements. Employers employ new hires only for selected entry-level jobs. Vacancies in positions other than entry level are filled internally by promoting and transferring employees already on the payroll. In a unionized setting, these movements are often controlled by a posting-and-bidding contract clause whereby the positions are filled by current employees on the basis of seniority and ability. The employee assuming the open position is already partially trained for the job via on-the-job training (OJT).

The firm, then, is pictured as mobility clusters of jobs linked together by technology and custom. An employee starts at the entry-level job and progresses through OJT to better jobs (higher pay, more security) in the cluster. The internal labor market exists more or less in almost all firms. It is a matter of degree. Businesses characterized by many entry-level jobs and short promotion ladders have a stronger external and less internal market orientation. Enterprises that have few entry-level jobs and that have lengthy promotion ladders filled from within are more nearly internal labor markets.

CHOOSING THE RIGHT METHOD

Human resource requirements research falls broadly into two categories: methods of (1) job analysis and (2) projections and forecasts.

The choice of the appropriate research method depends upon the goal of the research; the amount of money available to finance it; the time allotted to do the study; the expertise available to design, conduct, and analyze it; and the will of the buyer of the results to do something with them.

The primary problem faced by those who conduct human resource research is a lack of a well-defined goal. All too often, consultants are hired by managers who have only hazily defined goals for research. The managers know they have a problem or an interest but cannot set concrete goals for research. The first step is to define the problem at hand; for example, "Our problem is excessive turnover. Our costs of turnover are too high. What can we do to decrease the costs of turnover?" The more specific the statement, the better. Such general statements as "Our labor costs are excessive" are not very helpful to the person assigned the research. "We're faced with a cutback in government support for travel bureaus. We need to determine what impact travel has on community wages and employment. We need credible research to have clout politically." This is a succinct goal statement for impact research.

The more general statement can be honed to specific research goals after examining the other parameters of the decision, such as available money and methods; for example, after a review of finances and research resources, a trade association might conclude, "We want a range of projected demand for chefs under varying industry-growth assumptions for each year over the next decade. We have $10,000 to put into the study and will have to contract with a consultant who has computer services available." Further discussion with the researcher can delineate the specifics of estimation.

The ends must be defined with an eye toward the means to achieve them. Research has a cost associated with it, and the decision to do or not to do research is no different from any other business decision. The key consideration is still the bottom line. Do the benefits of the proposed analysis outweigh the costs? Most travel businesses do not have the resources for pure research—knowledge for knowledge's sake. Thus, the more specifically the goals and means can be determined the greater is the likelihood that the research will pay off.

Research takes money, but it also has a time cost. A schedule for conducting the study and receiving the results should be included in the proposal. Information after a budgeting or other decision-making date is like old news. If the study is to be done in-house, the time of the person doing the research must be considered as should the time required of management and the employees who may be the targets of the effort. Whether the study can be done in-house will also depend upon resident expertise. Most small businesses and agencies simply do not have employees skilled in research methods or the sophisticated computer hardware needed to do extensive research projects.

Here are three rules of thumb on costs of research. First, there is a trade-off between accuracy and cost. General estimates are less costly than very close estimates. For public relations purposes, it may be sufficient to know the provincial or state employment impact within the nearest 1,000. Knowing to the nearest 10 is a waste of resources.

Second, primary sources of information are much more

costly than secondary sources. Do not reinvent the wheel. The information needed may already be available at little or no cost. Impact and human resources requirements studies are done constantly by government agencies, universities, trade associations, banks, and large businesses. The problem with secondary information is that it may be too general to be of much value. In that case, gathering primary data may be necessary. Very often, research internal to the firm requires primary data collection and analysis. Turnover analysis at firm A and at firm B will very likely use the same method, but the data and analysis will be unique to the firm. Primary research is much more costly when measured in time and money.

Finally, without the managerial will to use the research results, research is a waste of money. Knowledge is not a panacea in and of itself. It is only a tool. A turnover analysis forced by higher management on lower levels will neither be successfully conducted nor properly implemented.

JOB ANALYSIS

Job analysis is merely the collection and analysis of data about jobs within the firm. Its applications include job restructuring, training program development, qualifications standards development, test development, performance evaluation, employee counseling, safety and hazards identification, and wage and salary administration, among others. The focus here is on job content and worker-skills uses.

There are numerous systems of job analysis (Rohmert and Landau 1983). Consultants, often managers or industrial engineers, sell systems of job analysis. One method suitable for small businesses is readily available (U.S. Department of Labor, *A Handbook for Job Restructuring*, 1972b). Other methods use similar techniques.

Jobs are viewed as a hierarchical collection of positions, tasks, and elements. The basic building block is the element or smallest step into which work can be divided. Tasks are combinations of elements that are steps in performing work. A position is the total of tasks that constitute a work assignment. A job is composed of positions that are identical in most tasks.

Jobs are analyzed according to five categories of information: (1) worker functions; (2) work fields; (3) machines, tools, equipment, and work order; (4) materials, products, subject matter, and service; and (5) worker traits. Worker functions are used to identify the complexity of jobs on the belief that all jobs involve some level of relationship to data, people, and things. Worker functions in the *data* area include such items as synthesizing and compiling. *People* relationships include negotiating, supervising, and serving, for example. The *things* functions vary from handling to setting up.

Work fields are methods of production that have either a technological basis (e.g., characteristic of machines) or a socioeconomic one (e.g., providing a service). Materials, products, subject matter, and services refer to the raw materials, final goods, types of specialized knowledge (e.g., math),

and services associated with the job. Machines, tools, equipment, and work aids are self-explanatory.

One of the most useful categories is worker traits. These are requirements the job demands of the employee. They include training time, aptitudes, temperaments, interests, and physical demands. Training time has a "General Education Development" (GED) component, which refers to an employee's learned ability to reason and to follow directions and knowledge of such tools as language and mathematical skills. The "Specific Vocational Preparation" (SVP) component specifies the amount of vocational learning time required to do the job. Aptitudes are composed of such individual capacities as verbal, spatial, numerical, manual dexterity, and others.

Job restructuring, education and training analyses, and turnover studies illustrate several uses of job analysis.

JOB RESTRUCTURING

By using job analysis, comprehensive job descriptions can be produced and logical job interrelationships identified. This has the virtue of regularizing pay and progression schedules; it relates to employment and affirmative action in that hiring standards can be directly related to occupational requirements, and it provides a basis for human resources planning (e.g., training and recruitment).

The U.S. Department of Labor method for job restructuring consists of four steps (U.S. Department of Labor 1972b). The system makes extensive use of both the worker functions (data, people, and things) and the worker traits (GED, SVP, aptitudes) to rate job complexity and to identify occupational patterns. First, the occupations are examined for their task composition and are rated on the appropriate worker-function scales. There usually tends to be a layering of occupations by complexity scores. Then, the patterns that evolve are modified to take into account work flow, plant layout, plant technology, and other considerations relating to the firm's production process and organizational goals. Finally, the system is revisited to establish an internal mobility structure that will facilitate training on the job. What emerges is a system of effective job descriptions ordered in a logical fashion.

EDUCATION AND TRAINING ANALYSES

Associated with each job structure is a training-and-education structure. Using the GED, SVP, and aptitudes information on each occupation, it is possible to develop a human resource program. Career ladders emerge as a set of related jobs at progressively higher levels in the same occupational category. Dead-end jobs can be identified, and logical transfers from one mobility cluster to another can be seen. It should become apparent that recruiting, screening, and training costs can be decreased by relying on OJT to prepare employees for movement internal to the firm. Knowledge of the productivity and track record of the individuals already employed cuts down the expense and uncertainty of recruiting new hires from the outside for positions that can better be filled internally. Entry-level jobs can be identified, and training programs can be devised for use on a regular basis for new hires.

A survey of job analysis techniques and applications identified common problems with job analysis (Wilson 1974). Both the conduct and implementation of job analysis are hampered if the goals of the analysis are not well defined. Where the goal is lower turnover and absenteeism or increased mobility, it should be made as specific as possible from the start and modified if necessary as the study is conducted. The study and its implementation must have the support of management, employees, and, in a union setting, the labor organization. Where management itself is not of one mind as to the utility of the research, it is doomed to failure. Some managers may resent job analysis for reasons of indifference (it's a gimmick), insecurity (endangers their job), or prestige (dilutes authority). Some management attitudes are incompatible with job analysis. Managers may believe in use of the stick, not the carrot to improve productivity. Others may fear loss of quality employees to better jobs, and empire builders see mobility as a threat. Finally, lack of managerial support is likely to result in insufficient funding, time, and expertise to do the job right.

TURNOVER ANALYSES

High absenteeism and turnover are both costly and disruptive. Professors Cawsey and Wedley (1979), in a study of Canadian manufacturing firms, estimated partial turnover costs from $400 to $3,732. The average for production workers was in excess of $1,000 per turnover. As a proportion of the total wage bill, turnover cost varied from 3.3 percent for low turnover firms to 31.4 percent for high turnover firms. Turnover costs for professional employees may be in the five- and six-figure range.

Cawsey and Wedley suggest a method for turnover analysis. The five steps include: (1) define turnover, (2) identify the relevant cost components, (3) determine measurable and unmeasurable costs, (4) determine controllable and uncontrollable turnover, and (5) calculate total turnover cost.

The definition of *turnover* should take into consideration the expansion or contraction of the firm, student employees, and part-time employees. The cost components include the cost of exiting (severance pay), recruiting and screening, orientation and training, equipment under-utilization, and lost production and lost productivity due to training (managerial and trainee). Lost production and productivity are the most difficult to estimate because they are an opportunity cost. Dollar estimates for the first categories are usually visible, measurable, direct costs retrievable from business records. Controllable turnover includes separation due to taking another job, returning to school, or the nature of the work, working conditions, and wages. Uncontrollable turnover may be due to retirement or for health, death, or family reasons. Discharge, personal reasons, and turnover for other reasons might be classified in either category, depending upon the situation. Calculation of the total cost of turnover is confined to summing up the costs of avoidable turnover.

Armed with the knowledge of turnover cost and the reasons for controllable turnover (Thompson and Terpeniay 1983), management can devise a policy or continue to research a method (job restructuring) for cost reduction. Cawsey and Wedley (1979) suggest an accounting budgeting system that makes first line supervisors responsible for a turnover budget.

PROJECTIONS AND FORECASTS

Projections and forecasts of labor demand, supply, and employment are done by a variety of public and private entities. The primary use of these is for planning purposes. The Canadian and American governments pump millions of dollars into education, training, and other human resource programs each year. Private businesses and trade associations do so as well. The nature of most education and training is such that the education itself as well as the payoff are long term. Efficient use of resources mandates projections of the demand for and supply of trained and educated people in the future.

Before considering the common techniques, a distinction is appropriate. From data, projections and forecasts are made. Data may include historical employment by occupation, number in the labor force, business receipts, and so on. Projections are "if . . . , then . . ." statements. The "if" part states the assumptions that have to be made to do the projection (e.g., If we assume that there will be an occupancy rate of 80 percent capacity, . . .). The "then" part is the projection (. . . hotel and motel restaurants will hire 200 short-order cooks). Forecasts, in contrast to projections, state that the estimates will actually occur; for example, "Business conditions will be such that over the next four years grocery stores will hire 150 check-out trainees."

SURVEYS

Surveys are a commonly used method for gathering primary data. They neither project nor forecast, but provide the data to make projections and forecasts. They are usually expensive. Methodologically, a survey requires statement of a goal, selection of the target population, choice of a sample or census of the population, derivation of a questionnaire, administration of the questionnaire, and analysis of it.

The problems and pitfalls of obtaining useful survey data are many. Avoiding the problems and pitfalls usually requires the services of an expert. To do a survey of employment in the travel industry, one would first have to identify travel employers. The industry cuts across many types of employers who attribute varying proportions of their sales revenues to travel. Added to that problem is the fact that most travel businesses are small businesses. A sample of businesses is usually required. If a reasonably complete list of travel and tourism businesses can be had, it then becomes necessary to sample to save on cost. The scientific selection of the sample calls for the skills of a statistician to be sure that the data obtained are accurate. Questionnaire length, exact wording of the questions, and the layout to facilitate computer coding are matters best handled by experts. The same must be said for questionnaire administration. Often a pilot survey, or minisurvey, is used to get the bugs out of the questionnaire and the technique. Questionnaires may be administered by mail, telephone, or personal interview. Questionnaire analysis usually requires statistical methods and the use of a computer.

If possible, survey data should be obtained from secondary sources skilled in all aspects of survey methodology. Area-skills surveys are generally available from national, provincial, and state government agencies. In the United States, the Occupational Employment Statistics (OES) program provides useful survey data. Systematic surveys of nonfarm establishments collect wage and salary information by occupation. The system surveys 20 percent of the universe of establishments on a three-year cycle. From the surveys come total employment estimates by occupation and industry for state and substate area for over 2,000 occupations. These are available in the OES *Occupational Staffing Patterns and Occupational Employment Statistics* publications.

The authors did a survey and analysis that illustrate one application of the methodology. This was part of a larger study to assess the potential held by development of the travel industry for employing the hardcore unemployed (Elkin and Roberts 1981). The goal of the survey was to provide data on the internal mobility clusters in travel and tourism businesses. The target population were all travel-related employers in a specific labor-market area in West Virginia. A sample was drawn by industry classification and by size of employer. The population from which the sample was drawn was garnered from local travel association records, the telephone yellow pages, and trade listings. Because each person to be interviewed was a busy personnel manager or person in charge of employment, the questionnaire had to be short. All the information that could be gathered from secondary sources (especially the OES *Staffing Patterns*) was obtained before the interview. The interview was used to close information gaps. Trial interviews were conducted. A letter from the area Chamber of Commerce and travel association preceded a telephone call to schedule the on-site interview. The interviews were completed in an orderly and timely fashion.

Table 1 is a typical research summary generated by the survey. The design complements the purpose of the interview—to generate data on mobility clusters and associated entry-level occupations and their training requirements.

ORGANIZING THE BASIC DATA

The hotel/motel/lodging industry is very closely tied to the travel industry. It also characterizes much of the nature of employment in travel. The first column in Table 1 lists the major occupations. The Employment column has two figures: the first indicates the percentage of total industry employment in that occupation (e.g., 20% of the people employed in the hotel/motel industry are maids); the second indicates how many persons are predicted to be in each occupation—total industry employment (243)

multiplied by the percentage figure in the preceding column (for maids, 48 = 243 x 0.20). The Wages column also has two figures: the first is starting pay ($2.65 for maids), and the second is pay after being on the job one year ($3.00 for maids). Seasonality of employment is indicated next: maid employment is seasonal. The Recruitment column shows maids to be both recruited externally (from the Job Service, walk-ins, want-ads) and by promotion from within (internally); so the entry reads "Both." The Growth column shows actual employment change from one year ago—for maids growth was "stable" (no appreciable change over the year).

Promotion affords an application of the internal labor market concept. As noted earlier, a firm characterized by an internal labor market has mobility clusters or job ladders of promotability connected by on-the-job training. These clusters are insulated from outside (external) labor market pressures. Jobs beyond the entry level within a cluster are filled by promotion from within. Pay, skills, and responsibility increase with progression up the job ladders—maids are promotable to housekeepers. The Employer's Perception of Available Jobs column is a measure of the employer's perception of the ease with which vacancies can be filled in the current labor market—the market supply of maids is "adequate."

Entry Requirements has three columns. The first is what the employer requires by way of Education for an employee taking the job whether recruited externally or promoted from within—employers require a high school education or less for maids. The next column shows prior Experience an entrant must possess—becoming a maid requires none (0). The last column under Entry Requirements is an indication of typical, average on-the-job training put into those people becoming maids.

The last two columns are blank but could be filled in by users of the matrix. The entry would indicate the type of training program recommended, if any, and training time.

The individual subindustry occupational matrices provide thumbnail sketches per industry, but they are also the fundamental building blocks for more extensive analysis useful both for job development and human resource planning activities. Table 2 shows the mobility clusters derived from Table 1 for the hotel/motel industry.

Entry-level positions are numerous, tend to be near the minimum wage for unskilled and semiskilled jobs, and, for these workers, require 12 years of education or less and little or no experience. Employer training time is short—a few weeks. The more skilled workers, such as a chef, have much longer training times, are salaried, and require a higher educational attainment. Few are hired. Look further at the mobility cluster. Except for the busboy/busgirl cluster with five occupations, the rest are short. The numbers in the parentheses indicate the relatively low probability of promotion and upward mobility. Pay starts near the minimum wage and for unskilled and semiskilled jobs progresses somewhere but remains relatively low. The survey results suggest to employers that job restructuring and turnover analysis might decrease employment costs. To training and education planners, it suggests occupations for potential training classes

Table 1   Survey Results

Industry Occupation SIC 70 Hotel/Motel	Employment (Industry) (243)		Wages		Seasonality	Recruitment and Sources
	%	#	Start	After 1 Yr.		
Manager	2.8	7	Salary	Salary		External
Accountant/Auditor	2.8	7	3.50	9.00	None	Both
Housekeeper	2	5	4.50	7.00	None	Internal
Maid	20	48	2.65	3.00	None	Both
Janitor	6.2	15	3.00	N/A	Yes	Both
Bartender	6.2	15	3.00	N/A	None	Internal
Busboy	2.8	17	2.65	N/A	None	External
Kitchen Helper	6.2	15	2.65	3.00	None	External
Waiter/Waitress	27.6	67	1.50	1.75	Yes	Both
Cook-S.O.	4.8	12	3.00	N/A	Yes	Internal
Cook-Rest.	4.1	10	3.00	7.50	None	Both
Maintenance Person	2.1	5	4.00	4.50	None	Both
Cashier	2.1	5	3.00	N/A	None	Internal
Bookkeeper	1.3	3	4.50	5.00	None	Both
Hostess	1.3	3	3.50	N/A	None	Internal
Chef	0.7	2	Salary	Salary	None	External

and others to which training moneys should not be allocated (Connor and Pelletier 1981).

PROJECTIONS VERSUS FORECASTS

Most of the analyses of elements of future labor demand and supply are projections, not forecasts. Forecasts contain a judgment factor as to what actually will happen in the future. Rather than commit to a specific forecast, most analysts use an "if-then" format and leave it to the user to select the most likely "if." Problems for users of projections arise when either the analyst does not clearly specify the assumptions made (the "if") to get the projection or when the user treats the projection as a forecast.

Projections and forecasts are made up mechanically of a data base and a method for extrapolating that base into a future time period. So it is true that a projection is only as good as its data, and all projection methods must rely on the stability of some relationship between the phenomenon to be projected and the data used as a predictor.

Projections are either direct or derived. *Direct projections* include surveys and curve-fitting techniques. There are no intermediate variables between the base data and the projected results; for example, past employment is used to project future employment. *Derived projections* include an intermediate variable; for example, output would first be projected, and then future employment would be derived from the output estimate. Derived projection methods include the use of econometric models, input-output models, and industry-occupation models.

| | | | ENTRY REQUIREMENTS | | | PROGRAMS |
| | | EMPLOYER'S PERCEPTION OF AVAIL. | REQUIREMENTS | | EMPLOYEE TRAINING | |
GROWTH OCCUPATION	PROMOTION	JOBS	EDUCATION	EXPERIENCE	TIME	OJT CT
Stable	Regional Director	Adequate	12–16	6 mos.	8 wks.	
Stable	Asst. Mgr.	Adequate	12–14	1 yr.	3 wks.–1 yr.	
Stable	None	Adequate	12	6 mos.	3 wks.–6 mos.	
Stable	Housekeeper	Adequate	0–12	0	3 days–4 wks.	
Stable	Maintenance	Adequate	0	0	3 days–4 wks.	
Stable	None	Adequate	12	0	10 days	
Stable	Waiter/Front Desk	Adequate	0	0	2 days	
Stable	Cook	Adequate	0–12	3 mos.	2 days–2 mos.	
Stable	Hostess	Adequate	0–12	0	10 days–2 mos.	
Stable	None	Adequate	0	3 mos.	3 wks.	
Stable	Supervisor	Adequate	0	3 mos.	3 wks.–1 yr.	
Stable	Regional Maintenance	Adequate	0	5 yrs.	5 days–1 yr.	
Stable	Front Desk	Adequate	12	0	4 days	
Stable	Operational	Adequate	12	0	6 wks.–3 mos.	
Stable	Front Desk	Adequate	N/A	N/A	2 wks.	
Stable	None	Adequate	16	0	4 yrs.	

Surveys and Curve Fitting

As mentioned earlier, surveys are really data-collection devices. They become projections by asking respondents what they believe the future holds for the phenomenon in question. This type of analysis is subject to the greatest error because few employers plan far ahead when it comes to employment and because their expectations are overly pessimistic or optimistic depending upon the current business situation.

Curve-fitting techniques take historic data and literally fit a curve to the data and extend that curve out into a future time period. There are several methods for fitting the curve to the data (Morton 1968). Two methods are eyeballing a straight line between data points and regression models,

which minimize the square of the distance between the fit curve and the data points.

The hidden assumption that underlies this type of projection is one of historical constancy. As the OPEC (Organization of Petroleum Exporting Countries) experience has shown, this may not be an adequate long-term assumption. Projections of this sort are most useful for short-run decision making. Longer-term planning requires a more sophisticated methodology.

Econometric Models

Econometric models use either a single-equation or multiequation format. The equation postulates a stable relationship between what is to be projected and some interme-

Table 2 Mobility Clusters in the Hotel/Motel Industry

Cluster	Entry Level	Promotion To	Promotion To
One	Maid (20%/$2.65)[1]	Housekeeper (3%/$4.50)	
Two	Janitor (6.2%/$3.00)	Maintenance Person (2%/$4.00)	Regional Maintenance N/A
Three	Busboy/Busgirl (2.8%/$2.65)	Waiter/Waitress (2.8%/$1.50)	Host/Hostess (1.3%/$3.50)
		Desk Clerk (6%/$3.25)	Desk Superintendent N/A
Four	Kitchen Helper (6.2%/$2.65)	Cook (4%/$3.00)	Supervisor N/A
Five	Chef (1%/Salary)		
Six	Accountant/Auditor (2.8%/$3.50)	Assistant Manager	
Seven	Manager (2.8%/Salary)	Regional Director	

[1](Percentage of employees in the occupation, starting pay.)

diary economic variables; for example, long-term labor-supply projections often assume some type of stable relationship between the labor force and population; long-run demand projections postulate a relationship between output and employment.

A common single-equation model uses a production function. The production function has many possible forms but, in each case, makes the production of final goods and service (output) a function of resource inputs such as labor and capital. By making assumptions about the likely future levels of production and assuming the relationship estimated from historic data holds into the future (the "if"), then future levels of labor required to produce the output can be projected (the "then").

Multiequation models build systems of equations that are supposed to represent the workings of the economy. They may consist of a few equations or hundreds of them, as does the Brookings econometric model of the U.S. economy. Whether they are single-equation or multiequation models, most econometric projections require the use of a computer and knowledge of economics and regression analysis. The travel employer would do well to obtain these projections as secondary information and be very careful to understand the assumptions upon which the projections are made.

Input-Output Model

The advantage of input-output models is that they provide both direct and indirect estimates of human resource requirements; that is, they allow for interindustry economic actions and reactions. And they can be used to disaggregate employment into occupations changes and requirements. On the other hand, this type of model assumes a static economic structure. It assumes that there is one production method in each industry, that there is no change in the prices of resources, one relative to another; that each industry produces only one output; and that the method of production does not change.

Input-output analysis subdivides the economy into industries. Each industry uses resources (inputs) to produce a single industry output. What emerges is a table with industries (outputs) across the top and inputs along the side. The cells of this *transaction* matrix show what dollar amount of the total revenue generated by an industry is spent on each input. This transaction matrix is then divided out by the total revenue figure to yield a *coefficient* matrix that shows the percentage of a dollar of output that can be attributed to an input. The coefficient matrix is then manipulated to obtain its inverse. The inverse shows the direct and indirect requirements placed on all inputs to produce and support a final demand of one unit of output from each industry. The matrix indicates the direct input needs from its own industry and the indirect needs from other industries. These needs can then be transformed into a *human resources needs* matrix given knowledge of the occupational composition of the industries in the table.

Input-output models present a more realistic view of the interrelatedness of the sectors in the economy. They can provide direct and indirect estimates of total human resource requirements by occupation by industry. They assume, however, that the input-output coefficients in the table will not change, that is, that the economy is in a steady state. Changes in productivity, production methods, and hours of work that violate those assumptions can make the coefficients and the derived estimates in need of revision. Travel employers should obviously treat input-output estimates as a secondary-information source.

Industry-Occupation Analyses

Industry-occupation matrices are used widely by themselves or as a step in other models (e.g., the input-output approach just discussed). Each industry is decomposed into its occupational structure. The first column of Table 1 was a type of industry-occupation matrix. Industries run across the top of the table to head up columns of occupations, which run down the side of the table. Coefficients show either the number or percentage composition of employees in a particular occupation in a particular industry.

Publications such as *Tomorrow's Manpower Needs* (BLS) use a national industry-occupation matrix. They first estimate national output for the future. Then the total GNP is disaggregated into expenditures by type of demand and from there, in a process similar to input-output analysis, into future national occupational requirements.

These national figures are frequently used to make state and local estimates. A local-area base-period industry-occupation matrix is developed. The change factors from the national matrix are applied to the local matrix out to some future period. The matrix is then multiplied by base-period employment figures by occupation to get estimates of future local employment by industry and occupation. The greatest leap of faith required by this method is that the assumption made to get the national estimates will be valid in the subnational area.

TRAVEL EMPLOYMENT IMPACT MODELS

Travel has an impact on business receipts as travelers and tourists buy final goods and services. Travel also has an impact on the employment and wages of those who work in travel and travel-related industry as a result of the labor demand generated by travel demand. The focus of this section is on the estimation of the impact travel has on wages and employment.

The results of such studies are used for planning for the effects of travel on human resources when the industry contracts or expands. They are the meat of public relations and promotion campaigns. Requests for loans and government support are supported by a credible impact study.

The methods for assessing the employment impact of travel are the same methods used to determine the human resources requirements. The difference is one of outlook. The human resource requirements perspective is on the quantity and quality of labor that travel businesses need *to produce*. The employment impact model uses the same set of figures to view the employment *produced by* the travel industry.

Travel impact models generally have a scope of inquiry beyond employment. Other sections of this research Handbook address the more general types of studies (see Chapter 31). A U.S. Department of Commerce (1981) manual *Creating Economic Growth and Jobs Through Travel and Tourism* assesses the research methods for determining impact. It also critiques the various methods and details methods for household, traveler, and travel-business surveys.

The same input-output models that generate requirements information also provide impact estimates. Once again, the advantage of input-output models is their ability to use the economic interrelationships to generate direct and indirect travel effects. These indirect effects can be substantial. In the absence of a method of estimating these, travel impacts on employment can be severely understated; for example, a West Virginia study cited in the manual mentioned earlier (U.S. Department of Commerce 1981) found the direct economic impact of travel to be $579,119,000. The indirect figure was $197,651,000. The total impact would have been understated by 25 percent without a measure of indirect effects.

THE TRAVEL ECONOMIC IMPACT MODEL

The travel economic impact model (TEIM) was developed by the U.S. Travel Data Center (1974) to estimate the impact that travel has on the national, state, and local economies in the United States. It is a basic econometric model with input-output features that allow estimates of the impact of travel on business receipts, taxes of all kinds, employment, personal consumption, and personal income. It generates both primary and secondary effects.

The estimation process takes several steps. First, survey data on the number and types of travel trips are combined with average cost data to yield a national travel expenditure model. The results include expenditures on 15 categories by state. Then these figures are augmented with short-trip data to correspond with a more generally accepted definition of travel than was used by the initial survey. The result is a data set of total travel spending by state (or county), which is then categorized to become business receipts for 13 travel industries.

By using coefficients that show the number of jobs generated in each industry per dollar of business receipts, the business receipts figures can be multiplied to obtain the primary (direct) effect on employment. Knowing the blue collar, white collar, and service occupation distribution of each industry, the employment estimates yield direct occupational employment figures.

The secondary (indirect) effects of travel on employment are found by using a secondary economic impact component. This is done by separating earnings and employment into categories: basic and nonbasic. Basic employment is one that services entirely local consumption. Nonbasic employment generates goods and services that are exported out of the local economy. Employment multipliers are calculated that relate employment to travel earnings. The multipliers are used to generate the secondary employment impacts.

Obviously such involved calculations of travel employment impacts are beyond the resource availability of most travel entrepreneurs. The results of impact studies such as the TEIM model are best treated as secondary information. They can be purchased or are otherwise available from the researchers.

The impact models are mirror images of the human resource requirement models. Therefore, all of the caveats about the human resource requirements methodologies apply to the same types of impact research models. The admonitions regarding the costs and uses of research apply equally to both human resources requirements and uses of research.

REFERENCES

Cawsey, Thomas F., and William Wedley (1979), "Labor Turnover Costs: Measurement and Control," *Personnel Journal* (February), 90–95.

Connor, Samuel R., and May Beth Pelletier (1981), *The Handbook for Effective Job Development: Placing the Hard-to-Employ in the Private Sector*, Work in America Institute.

Elkin, Randyl D., and Randall S. Roberts (1981), "A Study of the Potential for Economic Development in the Travel and Tourism Industry to Provide New Employment Opportunities for the Chronically Unemployed," Economic Development Administration, U.S. Department of Commerce, Employment and Training Administration, U.S. Department of Labor, Washington, D.C.

Morton, J.E. (1968), "On Manpower Forecasting," The W.E. Upjohn Institute for Employment Research, 300 South Westnedge Avenue, Kalamazoo, Michigan 49007.

Rohmert, Walter, and Kurt Landau (1983), *A New Technique for Job Analysis*, New York: International Publications Service.

Thompson, Kenneth R., and Willbunn D. Terpeniay (1983), "Job-Type Variations and Antecedents to Intention to Leave: A Content Approach to Turnover," *Human Relations* (July), 655–681.

U.S. Department of Commerce, Economic Development Administration (1981), *Creating Economic Growth and Jobs Through Travel and Tourism: A Handbook for Community and Business Developers*, Washington, D.C.

U.S. Department of Labor, Bureau of Labor Statistics (1972a), *A Handbook for Analyzing Jobs*, Washington, D.C.

U.S. Department of Labor, Bureau of Labor Statistics (1972b), *A Handbook for Job Restructuring*, Washington, D.C.

U.S. Department of Labor, Bureau of Labor Statistics (1972c), *Tomorrow's Manpower Needs*, Washington, D.C.

U.S. Department of Labor, Bureau of Labor Statistics (Yearly), *Occupational Outlook Handbook*, Washington, D.C.

U.S. Department of Labor, Bureau of Labor Statistics (1980), *Methodology for Projection of Industry Employment to 1990*, Washington, D.C.

U.S. Department of Labor, Employment and Training Administration, Bureau of Labor Statistics, Research and Statistics Section (Yearly), *Occupational Employment Statistics*, Washington, D.C.

Wilson, Michael (1974), "Job Analysis for Human Resource Management: A Review of Selected Research and Development," National Technical Information Service, Springfield, Virginia 22151.

35

The Social Impact of Tourism on Developing Regions and Its Measurement

Corporate Planning Analyst
National Capital Commission
Ottawa, Ontario

Tourism affects the society and culture of a receiving country as well as its economy and environment. This is especially true of developing countries that are reliant on the tourism industry as a mainstay of their economies. This chapter presents an overview of the various types of social impacts that could be found in a tourism destination area and describes a number of methodologies that can be used to examine them.

As a tourism industry develops and grows, it usually has an impact on a number of sectors of society. A tourism industry or, on a smaller scale, tourism attractions such as beach resorts and theme parks are often developed with two main thoughts in mind: to attract as many tourists as possible and to maximize revenues. This is sometimes especially true of developing countries, with few resources, that are seeking to diversify their economies. These countries are generally islands or are small in size and rely on the export of one or two primary products for foreign exchange earnings. They often have little to sell except these products and their sun and sand. Tourism is, therefore, seen as a viable economic alternative. In many instances governments, having heard about the potential economic returns from tourism, jump into tourism development wholeheartedly with little analysis of potential impacts on their economies, on their environment, or on their people. Tourism can, however, be a major agent for change in the social, political, and cultural system of a destination area as well as in the economy and environment.

For years, tourism was accepted as a boon to local economies, and there was little realization on the part of government and residents that it leads to social change and, sometimes, to social problems. This social change can be gradual or rapid and large scale. Some governments are now starting to realize that tourism's contradictory impacts on the welfare of the public should be considered along with the needs of tourists and investors. In the 1960s and 1970s, riots and civil disturbances erupted in formerly peaceful countries. In many of these countries, such as St. Croix, Trinidad, Bermuda, and Jamaica, in the West Indies, the tourism industry acted as a catalyst in the disturbances (Turner and Ash 1975). Tourism is generally developed to meet one or more of the objectives of society, usually economic growth. When, after a number of years of disruption in their way of life, residents see few improvements except that a small minority has grown richer, questioning and frustration can erupt. Social stress and disorganization could already have developed through changes in the structure of local society. This is especially prevalent in traditional societies that have been forced to adapt rapidly to modern ideas, values, and technologies.

Rarely is an effort made to determine social as well as economic costs and benefits when the performance of tourism is being evaluated or when new developments are planned. The assessment of social impacts is very complex because one cannot quantify social impacts, subtract costs from benefits, and arrive at a conclusion, as in an economic cost/benefit analysis. It is also sometimes difficult to differentiate between social and economic costs and benefits, since they are so intertwined. Furthermore, the tourism industry will not have the same impacts on the economy and society of any two countries, no matter how similar they might appear. The potential impacts of the tourism industry depend on a large number of criteria, not only on the numbers of tourists, but on the historical, social, cultural, economic, and political background of the host country.

The first part of this paper presents a broad overview of the various negative and positive social impacts one could potentially find in a country with a developed tourism industry. They are divided into socioeconomic and sociocultural. The main focus is on small, developing countries where, for many reasons, negative impacts are more prevalent than in large developed regions with a mature and stable economy. The second part of the paper presents a discussion of some of the various methodologies that can be used to assess the social impact of tourism on a receiving area.

THE POTENTIAL SOCIAL IMPACTS OF TOURISM ON DEVELOPING NATIONS

SOCIOECONOMIC IMPACTS

While the tourism industry has definite effects on the economy of a country in terms of job creation, increased foreign exchange earnings, or a growth in the import bill, there are also indirect socioeconomic impacts, many that have both positive and negative aspects to them (as set out in Exhibit A). One should also remember that what is a cost to one segment of society is a benefit to another, in many cases.

Economic Independence

In most tourism areas, the majority of jobs, particularly the unskilled ones, will be filled by women and young people, many of whom are earning money for the first time. This can reinforce upward mobility but can also cause conflict in traditional societies where higher levels of power or status have always been held by parents and/or husbands who sometimes find it hard to accept the fact that family members have both economic independence and exposure to new and threatening ideas. This can lead to breakdown in family cohesion. Studies have shown this to be the case in areas like Malta, Cyprus, and the Seychelles (de Kadt 1979a; Boissevain 1977; Cleverdon 1979).

Labor Force Displacement

In many countries, especially those limited in size, local populations have been displaced by tourism developments that are often built in the more scenic areas (i.e., a type of competition for resources). Migration could occur because of the razing of a squatter townsite to build a resort or because of the flooding by tourists of a beach formerly used by fishermen; and as a result family and economic patterns can be broken. Examples of this occurred in western Mexico when resorts such as Ixtapa and Zihuatanejo were developed in the 1970s on the sites of small undeveloped villages (de

Kadt 1979a). The opposite phenomenon can also occur. In Cancun, in the Yucatan, the pattern of migration was towards the development rather than away, and many of the people working in the hotels are probably earning their first salaries. Labor force migration can, therefore, have both positive and negative effects. In undeveloped regions, it can mean paid employment; in urban areas, such as Acapulco, it can lead to further crowding, higher rates of unemployment, and the growth of slums.

Changes in Forms of Employment

A frequent impact in areas with growing tourism developments is that local residents will leave traditional forms of employment, such as agriculture and fishing, to work in the hotels and restaurants. While they might become wage earners for the first time and learn new skills, the primary sector of the economy may be adversely affected by a loss of labor. In the Seychelles, a shift from jobs in the agriculture sector to those in the tourism and construction industries eventually resulted in higher food prices (de Kadt 1979a). Second, many jobs in the tourism industry are seasonal, so that the worker must either remain unemployed throughout a number of months of the year or find supplementary work, which is often hard to do. These same people can also find themselves permanently unemployed if demand for their destination area shifts, a frequent occurrence, and there is overdependence in tourism.

Changes in Land Values and Ownership

A common occurrence in areas beginning to develop a tourism industry is the skyrocketing of land values, which can cause competition for natural resources, conflict over land use, and displacement of local residents from land that often goes into the hands of a group of powerful nationals or foreigners (Perez 1974; Cleverdon 1979). This is especially true where a tourism development is planned in a formerly untouched area. In parts of Barbados, the price of land rose almost 50 percent annually in the early 1970s (Crandall 1976).

Improved Standard of Living

A major beneficial impact of tourism is that local residents can take advantage of enhancements in community infrastructure; for example, improvements made in health services, airports, water and sewage systems, and recreational facilities that might have been built primarily with the tourist in mind or that are paid for by local governments with the surplus from tourism revenues. Another example is new roads, which can facilitate access to markets for local farmers. A frequent cost of tourism growth, however, is that prices of housing, food, and other goods and services are often driven up as a result of tourists who are willing to pay more for many items. While a two-price system may be in effect, more often prices remain at the higher tourist level. This inflation can sometimes negate the positive impact of flows of tourism revenue into a region.

Exhibit A   Potential Social Impacts of Tourism

IMPACT	POSITIVE ASPECTS	NEGATIVE ASPECTS
Socioeconomic		
Individual economic independence	Wages; upward mobility	Conflict in traditional societies
Labor force displacement	Migration to tourism region for employment	Forced migration of residents from region
Changes in employment	Employment in tourism sector; acquisition of new skills	Seasonal unemployment; abandonment of traditional forms of employment
Changes in land value	Increased value of land	Higher land prices; conflict over land use; competition for natural resources
Improved living standards	Improved services, facilities, and infrastructure	Inflation generated by tourism
Changes in political-economic system	Growth of new elite; growth of depressed regions	Splits in national unity
Sociocultural		
Growth in undesirable activities	—	Growth in crime, drugs, gambling, and prostitution
Social dualism	Cross-cultural exchange; widened dimensions	Conflicts in values and life-styles
Demonstration effect	Stimulation to improve living standards	Frustration; increased spending; growth in import bill
Culture as a commercial commodity	Preservation of cultural heritage; revival of traditional art forms; growth of pride	Culture loses meaning as it is commercialized for tourists; stereotypes and artificial products develop
Growth of resentment and hostility	—	Growth of servile attitude, violence, and conflict

Changes in the Political-Economic System

The development of tourism on a large scale can sometimes help to shift political and economic power from traditional groups to a new elite of businessmen who own the resources needed by the industry. Tourism growth can also lead to development of previously economically depressed regions, such as Mexico's Yucatan and certain Caribbean islands. This can have beneficial economic and social impacts or can lead to splits in national unity as one region gets precedence over another in terms of resource allocation (de Kadt 1979a; Cleverdon 1979; Butler 1975).

SOCIOCULTURAL IMPACTS

Growth of Undesirable Activities

Many people in tourism destination areas believe that tourism will bring in or help facilitate undesirable activities, such as gambling, drug use, and prostitution, which will result in changes in the local system of sexual values (Young 1973). One phenomenon that the industry has brought to many

countries is growth in the number of "beachboys," young men who do not look for jobs because they know that they can be supported by the female visitors in the area (Turner and Ash 1975). The church and many local residents in developing countries are especially bothered by this and place much of the blame on the tourists. Local residents are also often offended at the brief attire of tourists, women wearing shorts into town or bathing suits in the street. (However, this varies region by region and even city by city.) Another fear is that crime will increase as the tourism industry grows and affluent tourists are envied by poor residents. Studies carried out in Mexico and Hawaii have shown this to be the case (Jud 1975; Fujii, Mak, and Nishimura 1978).

Social Dualism

Another social cost of tourism is what has been called the "premature departure to modernization" (Jafari 1973). Foreign values, ideologies, and life-styles come to be accepted by and influence the lives and behavior of local residents. Some may copy tourist behavior and attitudes and ignore cultural and religious traditions. There may be abrupt and disruptive changes in social customs and patterns, for example, women leaving their homes for the first time to work in the hotels as maids or cooks. Studies in Hawaii have linked this occurrence to a sharp increase in the rate of divorce (Lundberg 1974). This can interrupt the slow, normal, and unique process of development, and it is claimed that social dualism can result in a person who is partly westernized and partly holding onto traditional values. Disruptions in societies and split families can often occur as a result (Cowan 1977).

Demonstration Effect

The demonstration effect is basically the adoption by local residents, especially the young, of tourist behavior and attitudes, consumption patterns, and even language. (In theory, cultures can borrow from each other, but, in fact, the weaker culture normally assimilates into the stronger (Mathieson and Wall 1982).) It can be beneficial when locals might see what else is available in the world and might be stimulated to work harder and get a better education in order to improve their living standards. However, this is only a social benefit when the opportunities for upward mobility are there to be exploited, such as the existence of jobs and schools. Otherwise, the result will be increased frustration as young people go to school or move to the city in the expectation of a better life but find a lack of employment opportunities. The demonstration effect can also lead to spending on diverse items, such as blue jeans, fast-food items, and sunglasses, even though the means to do so are not there. Some locals adopt the marks of affluence, wear foreign fashions, eat imported food, and drink imported liquor. Not only do they live beyond their means, but the consumption of imported goods is further increased (Turner and Ash 1975; de Kadt 1979a; Cleverdon 1979).

Culture as a Commercial Commodity

Another potential impact of tourism is that art, ceremonies and rituals, religious sites, music, and traditions can become marketable commodities and lose relevance and symbolic meaning to the local people (e.g., Haitian voodoo ceremonies, Balinese religious ceremonies, Hawaiian fire dances, and Canadian Indian rain dances put on mainly for the benefit of visitors). Moreover, remnants of the colonial past, such as forts and plantations, become tourism attractions. As well as lowering the dignity of the people and their culture, a deterioration of the standard of local arts and crafts and a watering down of local music, crafts, and ceremonies for mass tourist consumption can result. Pseudotraditional art forms (i.e., cheap, portable souvenirs) develop. Ceremonies and rituals, which once had great importance for a native people, now become meaningless and are used primarily to attract tourists who feel no respect for the local beliefs or traditions. In other words, a phoney folk culture develops (de Kadt 1979a; Perez 1975; Cleverdon 1979; Mathieson and Wall 1982).

On the more positive side, however, the tourist industry is also credited with helping to revive or preserve the cultural heritage of a destination area—monuments, ceremonies, arts and crafts, and traditions that otherwise might have been forgotten or died out (e.g., Inuit carvings). A sense of inferiority can be alleviated and a sense of pride in one's country promoted as tourists seek things not found elsewhere (Cowan 1977).

Growth of Hostility to Tourists

A major phenomenon seen in many tourist destination areas, but especially in the developing regions, is growth of resentment and hostility towards the tourist on the part of the local resident. One author wrote "the poorer the host country, the greater irritants (such as arrogant displays of wealth and disregard of the host's values and sensitivities) are likely to be" (Grey 1970). Two other factors influence relationships between the people of developing countries and the tourist: the fact that the former are often ex-colonies of the tourist-generating countries and, second, that the people are of different racial backgrounds (Turner and Ash 1975; Perez 1975). Fears have been expressed by West Indian writers that a form of neocolonialism has developed as former "slaves" serve former "white masters," and that a servile attitude or negative self-image could grow on the part of black, newly independent populations (Theuns 1973); for example, one author stated: "We find in the Caribbean predominantly colored people recently emerged from a colonial status, seeking an identity free from the legacy of slavery, colonial dependency and the plantation economy, who are suddenly thrust into having to serve rich, white tourists who either intentionally or unintentionally begin to dictate the shape of the environment to meet their leisure needs" (Doxey 1973).

Resentment, hostility, and violence against tourists can also grow as hordes of people descend on regions with limited space, thus leading to strains on infrastructure, such as roads and water and sewage systems. Services such as health clinics and police can be overtaxed; beaches become crowded and polluted; traffic jams become common, as do litter, noise, and long lines in stores. These phenomena are especially prevalent in areas that are tourism "ghettos" (i.e., where tourism is the major activity) or those with a short tourism season (Theuns 1973).

Irritation at these occurrences is a major sign that the saturation point (or social carrying capacity) of a destination area has been reached. The saturation point in most host countries is a vague undetermined point of diminishing returns at which the benefits from tourism start to be outweighed by the socioeconomic costs (Mathieson and Wall 1982; Getz 1983; Cook 1982). The saturation point is extremely hard to measure and depends on many variables, of which volume of tourists is just one. It is usually evident when euphoria with the tourism industry develops into antagonism, and eventually xenophobia. The following factors were identified by Butler (1975) as the major ones which influence the tourism saturation point of a country:

Visitor Characteristics

1. *Volume*: A major factor is volume of tourists. A small number of visitors to a country with a large population will have little effect, while a large number of tourists visiting a small island or resort town, especially over a short season, will have a major impact.

2. *Length of stay*: The longer the visitors stay, the greater will be their contact with the host population and their socio-economic penetration.

3. *Racial characteristics*: The greater the differences between the tourists and locals in terms of color, language, and culture, the greater will be their impact.

4. *Economic characteristics*: The greater the difference in levels of affluence, the stronger will be the resentment and desire for equality on the part of local residents.

5. *Activities of tourists*: Their activities determine the amount of contact, i.e., visiting local hangouts versus spending a week on the beach and in "tourist only" bars. The type of tourist is also a factor: the institutionalized mass tourist—seeks familiarity, does not stray from what has been called his "environmental bubble," and has superficial contacts with locals—versus the "explorer" or "drifter" (according to Cohen's typology, 1972)—who wishes to experience other cultures fully.

Characteristics of a Destination Area

1. *Economic development*: A general rule is that the more developed the local economy, the less the dependence on the tourism industry and the less its impact.

2. *Spatial characteristics*: This includes size of the destination area, size of population, location of resorts (i.e., close to or distant from local settlements), capacity of facilities, number of hotels, area of beach, miles of roads, and other physical variables. Ratios are then calculated between visitor arrivals and the population and land area (including total and peak arrivals), and between tourist-nights and land area, beach areas, road mileage, and restaurant capacity. Obviously, the higher the ratios, the more likely it is that friction will occur. (The concept involved here is the absorptive capacity of the host country.)

3. *Degree of local involvement*: The amount of contact is also a function of whether tourist enterprises are run and owned by local or foreign companies. (The former situation is better for the economy, of course.)

4. *Strength of local culture*: The stronger the local culture (i.e., unique, clear traits) and language, the better the ability to withstand the impact of a foreign culture.

5. *Other*: This can include the political attitudes and degree of nationalism in the host country, as well as its historical background (i.e., a long, stable history versus recent independence and a market of former "colonizers"). It can

also include the stage of development of the tourism industry, the length of its existence, and the rapidity of its development.

All these factors affect the penetration and pressure on the daily life of the local inhabitants of a resort area and the demand tourism has on their habitat. The physical saturation point, whether it be a tourist/resident ration of 1:1 or 10:1, is different in every destination area because psychological attitudes are difficult to quantify. The point of physical saturation can perhaps be determined, but, equally important, social attitudes must also be taken into account, since what one person finds irritating often might not bother someone else.

METHODOLOGIES OF SOCIAL IMPACT ASSESSMENT

The preceding pages presented an overview of the various types of social impacts and unwanted consequences one could find in a country that has a fairly advanced tourism industry, especially a country that is undergoing the process of development. These impacts can be examined or assessed in many ways, and a brief description of a number of nonstatistical methodologies follows. The majority are derived from social science and, more specifically, from social impact assessment methodology. Most social impact assessments, however, deal with natural resource developments and are carried out before the fact, with the aim of forecasting potential impacts and recommending mitigative measures. Although many of the initial processes in a social impact assessment are relevant to a study of the tourism industry, the latter is usually done *after* the fact, that is, when tourism has been in place a number of years and negative impacts are starting to be evident. Ideally, a government would carry out a social impact assessment (SIA) when the industry, or a particular development, was in the planning stages.

A *social impact assessment* has been defined as any study that attempts to determine the impacts of a particular physical development on the day-to-day quality of life of persons whose environment is affected by the development, other than those whom the development is expressly designed to serve; such a study may be prospective or retrospective (Boothroyd 1975).

There are many approaches that can be used to examine social impacts; no one way is best. To carry out a proper study, two points are important: the research should be carried out within the sociocultural context of the impacted group, and more than one methodology should be used. Exhibit B indicates some of the primary methodologies that can be used to collect data on each of the social impacts discussed previously. Since social impact assessment is an area in which much of the data available is qualitative, it is important to develop multiple lines of evidence with which to examine each potential impact. The researcher will undoubtedly face a number of problems, among them: (1) the difficulty in defining or quantifying the subject mat-

Exhibit B   Primary-Data Collection Methods for Potential Impacts

IMPACT	SURVEYS/INTERVIEWS				SECONDARY SOURCES	
	SURVEYS	KEY INFORMANTS	DELPHI	PARTICIPANT OBSERVATION	DATA ANALYSIS	CONTENT ANALYSIS
Socioeconomic						
Economic independence	X	X			X	
Labor force displacement		X			X	
Employment changes	X	X	X		X	
Change in land values		X	X		X	
Improved living standards	X	X			X	
Changes in political-economic system		X	X		X	
Sociocultural						
Undesirable activities	X	X		X	X	X
Social						
Dualism	X	X	X	X		X
Demonstration effect	X	X		X		
Commercialism of culture	X	X	X	X		
Hostility	X	X	X	X		X

ter; (2) the wide variety of methodologies available; (3) the question of validity of qualitative data, (4) the lack of complete, adequate data; (5) the problems posed by potentially conflicting interests, values, and perceptions of the impacted population, the government, and those in the industry; and (6) the difficulty in isolating the direct attributions to tourism and examining cross impacts. As a result, social research on tourism often tends to focus on one community, on one topic area, or on more measurable (economic) items (Mathieson and Wall 1982).

SURVEYS/INTERVIEWS

Surveys and interviews are key methods for collecting information about a community. Specific techniques that can be useful in assessing the social impact of tourism include attitude surveys, use of key informants, use of the Delphi technique, and (while not technically a survey) participant observation.

Design of Surveys of the Public

Since many potential impacts of tourism are only negative if so perceived by the local residents, it is important to discover their attitudes and perceptions towards tourism. Depending on the stage at which it is carried out, a survey can either serve as a benchmark for a later assessment of change or as a measure of current perceptions. The survey should test the researcher's theories on the impacts that tourism may have had, but it is also important that it be designed with the values of the impacted area in mind, that is, what is important to the community.

Surveys are especially relevant for studying all the sociocultural impacts, as well as economic independence, changes in employment, and improvements in living standards. They can be carried out by telephone, mail, or in person. In-person interviews have the highest response rate but also have the highest cost. Mail surveys are relatively less expensive, but have a low response rate. Telephone surveys can have a high response rate and cost less than in-person interviews. Another fairly low-cost method consists of surveys that are hand delivered and picked up, but are self-administered. Local residents to be surveyed can be chosen randomly to be representative of the population or selected in a purposefully biased way if only a particular group is to be surveyed. Different questionnaires can be administered to local residents and to employees in the tourism industry, since their involvement and perceptions will vary. It is believed that attitudes to tourism may vary with dependency on the industry, and there is evidence to suggest that those who work in tourism or benefit from it will likely identify more positive than negative impacts (Long, Perdue, and Allen 1990; Caneday and Zeiger 1991; Brougham and Butler 1981; Pizam 1978; Rothman 1978). There is also a belief that sensitivity of nonindustry employees to the impacts of tourism increases with education. It is also important to note that surveys measure perceived impacts, which can be different from actual impacts (Pizam 1978; Belisle and Hoy 1980).

A number of researchers have carried out surveys of attitudes of local residents to assess tourism impacts (Pizam 1978; Murphy 1981; Thomason, Crompton, and Kamp 1979; Allen, Long, Perdue, and Kielelback 1988; Long, Perdue, and Allen 1990). A minority of these attitude surveys have been carried out in developing countries—Sethna in the Caribbean (1977), Doxey in Barbados (1972), and Belisle and Hoy in Colombia (1980). The survey methodology is quite similar in all of the studies. The first step is usually to devise a questionnaire based on the hypotheses to be tested. Hypotheses should be based on the types of social impacts that may be present in the host country. Data with which to examine the relationship between the social impacts and various socioeconomic and demographic characteristics of residents (income, age, sex, language, education, etc.) can also be built into the survey; for example, the Belisle and Hoy study (1980) hypothesized that perceptions of tourism impacts vary with the distance from the tourist zone and with socioeconomic status. (The first hypothesis was judged to be proven while the second was not.) Hypotheses from which questions can be formed may also be derived from unstructured, open-ended interviews with residents. These can provide a range of attitudinal concepts, perhaps in the form of frequently repeated phrases (Knox 1978; Thomason, Crompton, and Kamp 1979).

The actual questionnaire may have a number of sections. If desired, the first section can elicit opinions on such things as perceived benefits or disadvantages of tourism using open-ended questions. In this way, factors that might have been overlooked in the survey design will be picked up. A survey carried out by the English Tourist Board (Report 1978) contained a number of probes such as "What in your opinion are the most important benefits/disadvantages to London/yourself from tourism?" and "Precisely what problems do you suffer from tourists in London?" Open-ended questions, though, may not elicit negative, complete, and/or relevant comments and responses, and they also are difficult to quantify.

A second section of the questionnaire can contain a survey of attitudes. This entails close-ended questions to be answered on a scale. (Bipolar scales, using adjective pairs with opposite meanings, are called *semantic differentials* and are a common method of measuring perceptions.) Attitude surveys can be used alone but are especially useful in getting indirectly at information that could be asked directly in a probe of opinions. One common technique is to set out statements that are to be rated on a scale, somewhere between "strong agreement" to "strong disagreement." (For a list of 100 attitudinal questions that can serve as a starting point in an attitude survey, see Knox 1978.) The attitudinal statements can be grouped into a number of topic areas. An attitude survey carried out on seven Caribbean islands (Sethna 1980) contained 56 attitudinal statements grouped into seven topics: financial, moral, religious, social, physical, human, and cultural. Respondents were asked to rate a typical attitudinal statement on a 5-point scale; for example, "Local people working in the luxury hotels or big shops do not treat the local people as nicely as they do tourists."

A third method that can also be used is to set out a list of potential developments such as "an increase in the cost of seafood" (Belisle and Hoy 1980) or "occurrence of prostitution" (Pizam 1978). The responses to this type of statement can be rated on an 11-point scale ranging from –5 to +5 (or a five-point scale ranging from –2 to +2), with 0 equating to "no impact from tourism." A fourth method is to use a semantic differential scale but vary the possible responses according to the item; for example, "Winter visitors are beneficial-harmful" and "Their presence results in crowded-uncrowded hotels/beaches/restaurants" (Thomason, Crompton, and Kamp 1979).

The last section can contain socioeconomic and demographic data on the respondent and should identify his/her contact with tourists. This data is useful for categorizing residents and later correlating perceived impacts with different variables. However, there is some evidence that sociodemographic characteristics have little impact on attitudes to tourism, at least in the developed world (Long, Perdue, and Allen 1990).

The next step in the survey is to pretest the questionnaire for reliability and validity and, if necessary, to modify questions to make them more relevant. The questionnaire is then administered to the sample of respondents selected. The data collected can be analyzed very simply using means, medians, or percentages, for example, or with any one of various statistical data analysis techniques, such as multiple regression (Pizam 1987), discriminant analysis (Murphy 1981), Thaid technique (Brougham and Butler 1981), analysis of variance (Thomason, Crompton, and Kamp 1979), common factor analysis, stepwise regression, or chi-square analysis (Belisle and Hoy 1980).

Use of Key Informants/Community Leaders/Expert Opinion

Interviews of key informants and experts can be used to elicit factual data, as well as opinions and attitudes towards tourism. The same questionnaire as used for the survey of the public can be administered, although a slightly more focused questionnaire would probably be more useful. *Key informants* are defined as people who work in the tourism industry, in the government, or in key jobs in the area (e.g., the police, mayor, local businessmen, etc.). Key informants can also be used to identify those people they think represent the community. (Each person is asked to identify community leaders, and those people who are mentioned a number of times are chosen to be interviewed.) While the responses are likely to be similar to those of the residents interviewed in the public survey, they can probably provide relevant information on all the potential impacts caused by the growth of tourism in their regions.

Delphi Study

A Delphi study is another way in which to gather information that is factual and/or attitudinal. It is a method of polling experts in order to arrive at a consensus of informed opinion on current or, more usually, future occurrences. In a Delphi study, a panel of experts is assembled who can be community leaders, tourism industry employees, government employees, or academics. They are often first given background information on possible tourism impacts and statistics on the tourism industry in the area. The panel members are then sent a questionnaire in which the various hypotheses to be tested are formed into questions, for example, "Has hostility to tourists increased in the past two years with the recent growth in tourism?" The Delphi technique would probably provide the most relevant information on changes in land values, employment and the political-economic system, social dualism, commercialization of culture, and hostility to tourists. Unstructured opinions and factual data can also be elicited. Responses are analyzed and synthesized and then sent back to respondents, who are given a chance to reconsider and change their answers if desired on the basis of this feedback. Answers are once again analyzed, and a third round of mailouts is sometimes carried out before the final analysis.

Participant Observation

Participant observation is a useful technique when carrying out a case study, especially when it is utilized along with surveys and data analysis. It can provide first-hand data on various ideas or theories the researcher wishes to study (especially sociocultural impacts of tourism), while allowing access to participants (often anonymously in a casual, social situation) who might not be represented in a survey. Participant observation uses an intuitive approach. The researcher, either overtly or covertly, observes a social system in order to (1) explore the society to look for possible predetermined social impacts, (2) develop new ideas and hypotheses, and (3) look for new data to test those ideas and hypotheses. It is especially useful if the researcher has detailed knowledge of an area before tourism developed, either through a baseline study or, preferably, through first-hand experience. In this way, a type of longitudinal (i.e., before and after) study can be carried out, and the intensity and impacts of change can be examined.

The data collected are usually somewhat subjective, however, which is why other techniques that provide more objective information should also be used. The problems with participant observation are that there are no checks on possible bias or distortion on the part of the researcher, there is no sampling design, and the introduction of an observer can, in itself, affect what is being studied (called the control effect).

ANALYSIS OF SECONDARY SOURCES

Two of the ways in which analysis of secondary sources can be carried out are (1) content analysis of newspapers and (2) analysis of quantifiable data found in government records and other public documents.

Content Analysis

Content analysis of newspaper articles, news items, advertisements, photos, and letters to the editor can provide a very good picture of developments in an area over time. It is possible to compare information over a period of years or decades, in other words, to "reconstruct" a community or region, identify changes over time, and determine their content. Content analysis can also serve to check the validity of other types of data, especially information related to social attitudes and behavior patterns (for example, social dualism, hostility, and the growth of undesirable activities).

Information collected by content analysis can be analyzed descriptively (i.e., thematic analysis) or quantitatively (i.e., using frequency counts of symbols or items). The main problem is that data can be biased, fragmented, and incomplete.

The first step is to identify questions to be answered and types of information sought. Categories must be devised to record the information for later analysis. The second step is to determine the best newspaper(s), the time period to be covered, and the number of issues to be reviewed. The newspapers are then examined for references to tourism and especially to its social impacts. It might be necessary to classify certain items as having equivalent meaning in order to fit them into the predetermined categories. All mentions of social impacts are then recorded as a frequency count (i.e., as a check in the appropriate category box) or as a quote for later thematic analysis. If certain potential social impacts are referred to a number of times, it is often possible to draw inferences as to when and why they developed and to compare them to quantitative data, such as annual tourist arrivals.

Data Analysis

Analysis of various types of statistics usually collected by governments can provide excellent information on past trends. A review of these statistics often provides useful insights on the impacts of a growth in tourism, assuming the statistics are available at the level of the region studied. Results from analysis of statistics can quantitatively reinforce results of qualitative research methodologies, such as participant observation. It is especially relevant for looking at the socioeconomic impacts of tourism discussed previously, although somewhat less so for examining most of the sociocultural impacts.

The first step in statistical analysis should be to analyze tourism arrivals (including cruise ship arrivals, if relevant) by year and month to chart their growth. These figures can be compared with population and land area (including roads, beaches, number of facilities, water supply, etc.) to determine the tourism density by month and, thereby, the pressure on both local people and infrastructure. The average length of stay and daily expenditure of tourists should also be calculated. (These are some of the factors that help determine the saturation point of tourism.) Other factors, such as racial characteristics, activities of tourists, and strength of local culture, can usually be determined through participant observation and surveys. In this way, a number of quantitative and qualitative lines of evidence can be utilized to estimate the saturation point of tourism. As already stated, however, it is a rather indefinite concept and cannot be exactly pinpointed.

Once arrival trends have been established, they should be compared with a number of other types of statistics in order to draw inferences and, perhaps, conclusions about the impact of tourism on the society and economy of the destination area. The growth of undesirable activities, for example, can be analyzed statistically through crime figures usually available in local police headquarters. They should be examined to see if crime has increased in certain categories that can involve tourists, such as indecent assault, prostitution, break-ins, drug use, theft, rape, and robbery. Although figures do not differentiate between crimes against tourists and those against locals, it would be surprising if the majority of break-ins in some regions, for example, did not involve tourist hotels and apartments, since they are often accessible and apt to contain valuables. If a number of observations are available, statistical analysis (regression analysis, etc.) can be used to determine the relationship between crime- and tourism-growth rates.

It is similarly possible to examine socioeconomic impacts through the analysis of directly relevant statistics or, if necessary, proxies. Changes in land values as a result of tourism developments may be estimated by analyzing the amount of development or redevelopment and land sale figures. These are usually available in local planning and tax assessment offices. Such statistics may also indicate whether migration into or out of an area has taken place.

Government labor-force-distribution statistics by sector can indicate growth of employment in the tourism sector, and, if it is the only industry in the area, these may be used as a proxy to ascertain economic independence for youth and women and overall improvements in standards of living. These figures can also indicate if other forms of employment have been abandoned (e.g., agriculture or fishing) or if workers have jobs only a few months a year. They can also show the growth of a newly wealthy elite or a middle class that formerly did not exist.

The retail price index is a good indication of how tourism growth might have affected the cost of living in a destination area, after inflation has been taken into account. On the more positive side, statistics on government spending for social services, such as health and education, should also be analyzed. Revenues from tourism can enable the government to accelerate spending on social services, which improve the standard of living of local residents. In this case, it would be useful to compare changes in expenditure levels for all categories to determine the government's priorities and areas of greatest impact.

Through analysis of statistical data, over half of the social impacts discussed previously can be examined, and, in some cases, conclusions may be drawn. Where evidence is less conclusive or where it is not possible to extract factors unrelated to tourism that also influence these indexes, inferences can often be made. These, however, should be tested against other sources of data to better estimate their validity.

SUMMARY AND CONCLUSION

The first section of this paper described briefly many of the potential social impacts that tourism can have on the society of a destination area, particularly one that is a developing country. These can be socioeconomic—economic independence, labor force displacement, changes in employment, changes in land values, improvement in living standards, and changes in the political-economic system—or sociocultural—growth in undesirable activities, social dualism, demonstration effect, commercialization of culture, and growth of hostility. Most of the social impacts contain both negative and positive aspects, which might or might not balance each other.

The second part of the paper examined various social science methodologies that can be used to look at the impacts of tourism. They are divided into surveys—attitude surveys, public surveys, key informants, Delphi studies, and participant observation—and analysis of secondary sources—content analysis and statistical analysis. Since the concept of social impact is still fairly subjective and nebulous, it is difficult to arrive at concrete conclusions. Therefore, a combination of a number of methodologies (i.e., multiple lines of evidence) should be used to assess social impacts. Most of the methodologies provide somewhat qualitative information (even the results of surveys and content analysis contain fairly subjective data); therefore, they can best be used as aids in attempts to define and understand the social impacts of tourism.

REFERENCES

Allen, L., P. Long, R. Perdue, and S. Kielelbach (1988), "The Impact of Tourism Development on Resident's Perceptions of Community Life," *Journal of Travel Research* 27 (Summer), 16–21.

Belisle, F., and D. Hoy (1980), "The Perceived Impacts of Tourism by Residents, A Case Study of Santa Marta, Colombia," *Annals of Tourism Research* 7(1), 84–100.

Boissevain, J. (1977), "Tourism and Development in Malta," *Development and Change*, 39.

Boothroyd, P. (1975), *Review of the State of the Art of Social Impact Research in Canada*, Ottawa, Ontario: Ministry of State for Urban Affairs.

Brougham, J.E., and R.W. Butler (1981), "A Segmentation Analysis of Residents' Attitudes to the Social Impact of Tourism," *Annals of Tourism Research* 8(4), 568–587.

Bryden, J. (1973), *Tourism and Development: A Case Study of the Caribbean*, Cambridge, U.K.: Cambridge University Press.

Butler, R. (1975), *Tourism as an Agent of Social Change*, Occasional Paper No. 4, Peterborough, Ontario: Department of Geography, Trent University.

Caneday, L., and J. Zeiger (1991), "The Social, Economic and Environmental Costs of Tourism to a Gaming Community as Perceived by its Residents," *Journal of Travel Research* 30 (Fall), 45–49.

Cleverdon, R. (1979), *The Economic and Social Impact of International Tourism on Developing Countries*, E.I.U. Special Report No. 60, London: Economist Intelligence Unit Ltd.

Cohen, E. (1972), "Toward a Sociology of International Tourism," *Social Research*, 39.

Collins, C. (1979), "Site and Situation Strategy in Tourism Planning," *Annals of Tourism Research* 6 (July/Sept.), 351–366.

Cooke, K. (1982), "Guidelines for Socially Appropriate Tourism Development in British Columbia," *Journal of Travel Research* 21, 22–28.

Cowan, G. (1977), "Cultural Impact of Tourism with Particular Reference to the Cook Islands," in *A New Kind of Sugar*, B. Finney and K. Watson, eds., Honolulu: East-West Center.

Crandall, A.L. (1976), "The Impact of Tourism on Developing Countries—A Case Study of Barbados," unpublished M.A. thesis, Ottawa, Ontario: Faculty of International Affairs, Carleton University.

D'Amore, L.J., and Associates (1977), *Tourism in Canada-1986*, Montreal: for the Canadian Government Office of Tourism.

Doxey, G. (1972), *The Tourist Industry in Barbados*, Kitchener, Ontario: Dusco Graphics.

Doxey, G. (1973), *Ensuring a Lasting Tourist Industry*, Fiji: PATA Research Seminar.

Doxey, G. (1975), *The Impact of Tourism*, Sixth Annual Travel Tourism Research Association Conference.

Farrell, B., ed. (1977), *The Social and Economic Impact of Tourism on Pacific Communities*, Santa Cruz, CA: Center for South Pacific Studies.

Finney, B., and K. Watson, eds. (1977), *A New Kind of Sugar*, Honolulu: East-West Center.

Finsterbusch, K., and C. Wold, eds. (1977), *Methodology of Social Impact Assessment*, Philadelphia: Dowden, Hutchison and Ross, Inc.

Fleming, W., and L. Toepper (1990), "Economic Impact Studies: Relating the Positive and Negative Impacts to Tourism Development," *Journal of Travel Research* 29 (Summer), 35–42.

Fujii, E., J. Mak, and E. Nishimura (1978), *Tourism and Crime*, Tourism Research Project, Occasional paper No. 2, Honolulu: University of l'awaii.

Getz, D. (1983), "Capacity of Absorb Tourism: Concepts and Implications for Strategic Planning," *Annals of Tourism Research* 10, 239–266.

Goodrich, J. (1977), "Differences in Perceived Similarity of Tourism Regions: A Spatial Analysis," *Journal of Travel Research* 16 (Summer), 10–13.

Gray, H. (1970), *International Travel-International Trade*, Boston: Heath Lexington Books.

Haywood, L. (1975), *Criteria for Evaluating the Social Performance of Tourism Development Projects*, Guelph, Ontario: Department of Geography, University of Guelph.

Hiller, H. (1976), *Some Basic Thoughts about the Effects on Tourism of Changing Values in Receiving Societies*, Seventh Annual Travel Tourism Research Association Conference.

Hills, T., and J. Lundgren (1977), *The Impacts of Tourism in the Caribbean*, Working Paper, Montreal: McGill University.

Hudman, L. (1980), "Proposed System Analysis Model for Assessing the Potential Impact of Tourism," *Tourism Marketing and Management Issues*, Washington, D.C.: George Washington University.

Jafari, J. (1973), "Role of Tourism in the Socio-Economic Transformation of Developing Countries," published M.A. thesis, Ithaca, NY: Cornell University.

Jud, G. (1975), "Tourism and Crime in Mexico," *Social Science Quarterly*, 56.

Jud, G., and W. Krause (1976), "Evaluating Tourism in Developing Areas," *Journal of Travel Research* 15 (Fall), 1–9.

de Kadt, E. (1979a), *Tourism, Passport to Development*, Washington, D.C.: Oxford University Press.

de Kadt, E. (1979b), "Social Planning for Tourism in the Developing Countries," *Annals of Tourism Research* 6 (Jan/March), 36–48.

Knox, J. (1978), *Classification of Hawaii Residents' Attitudes towards Tourists and Tourism*, Honolulu: University of Hawaii.

Laflamme, A. (1979), "The Impact of Tourism, A Case Study from the Bahamas," *Annals of Tourism Research* 6 (April/June), 137–147.

Linton, N. (1972), *Proceedings, Caribbean Travel Association Seminar*, San Juan, Puerto Rico.

Long, P., R. Perdue, and L. Allen (1990), "Rural Resident Tourism Perceptions and Attitudes by Community Level of Tourism," *Journal of Travel Research* 28 (Winter), 3–9.

Lundberg, D. (1974), "Caribbean Tourism," *Cornell H.R.A. Quarterly* (February/May), 30–45, 82–86.

MacCannell, D. (1973), *The Tourist*, New York: Schocken Books.

Mathieson, A., and G. Wall (1982), *Tourism Economic, Physical and Social Impacts*, London: Longman.

Murphy, P. (1981), "Community Attitudes to Tourism," *International Journal of Tourism Management* (September), 189–195.

Nettleford, R. (1975), "Regional Seminar on Tourism and Its Effects; Cultural Impact," *The Cultural and Environmental Impact of Tourism with Reference to the Caribbean*, Barbados, W.I.: Caribbean Tourism Research Centre.

Perez, L. (1973/1974), "Aspects of Underdevelopment: Tourism in the West Indies," *Science and Society* 37(4), 473–480.

Perez, L. (1975), "Tourism in the West Indies," *Journal of Communications* 25(2), 136–143.

Pizam, A. (1978), "Tourism's Impacts: The Social Costs to the Destination Community as Perceived by Its Residents," *Journal of Travel Research* 16 (Spring), 8–12.

Report on Survey of London Residents' Opinions on Tourism, (1978), London: English Tourist Board Market Research Department and N.O.P. Market Research Ltd.

Robinson, H. (1976), *A Geography of Tourism*, London: MacDonald and Evans Ltd.

Rothman, R. (1978), "Residents and Transients: Community Reaction to Seasonal Visitors," *Journal of Travel Research* 16 (Winter), 8–13.

Sethna, R. (1977), "The Caribbean Tourism Product—An Appraisal," *Inside Barbados* (October).

Sethna, R. (1980), "Social Impact of Tourism in Selected Caribbean Countries," *Tourism Planning and Development Issues*, Washington, D.C.: George Washington University.

Smith, V. (1977), *Hosts and Guests, An Anthropology of Tourism*, Philadelphia: University of Pennsylvania Press.

Theuns, H. (1973), "Conditions and Effects of International Tourism," *Tourist Review*, No. 3.

Thomason, P., J. Crompton, and D. Kamp (1979), "A Study of the Attitudes of Impacted Groups within a Host Community Toward Prolonged Stay Tourist Visitors," *Journal of Travel Research* 17 (Winter), 2–6.

Turner, L., and J. Ash (1975), *The Golden Hordes*, London: Constable.

Waiten, C. (1981), *A Guide to Social Impact Assessment*, Ottawa, Ontario: Department of Indian and Northern Affairs, Canada.

Wu, C. (1982, "Issues of Tourism and Socioeconomic Development," *Annals of Tourism Research* 9(3), 317–329.

Young, G. (1973), *Tourism, Blessing or Blight*, Middlesex, U.K.: Pelican.

Zehnder, L. (1978), *Tourism and Social Problems*, Ninth Annual Travel Tourism Research Association Conference.

36

Frameworks for Assessing Tourism's Environmental Impacts

PETER W. WILLIAMS
Director
Centre for Tourism Policy and Research
Simon Fraser University
Burnaby, British Columbia

This chapter examines frameworks for conducting research with respect to assessing and managing the environmental impact of tourism. Rather than addressing assessment techniques associated with all spheres of environmental impact (e.g., economic, social, cultural, political, etc.), the focus is specifically upon the impacts of tourism on the physical environment in general and the ecological impacts in particular. The first part briefly describes the nature of tourism's impact on the physical environment. The second segment suggests the methodological problems inherent in most physically based impact assessment research. The third part describes alternative research assessment frameworks suited to studying the physical impact of tourism. The fourth segment discusses the concept of carrying capacity and the inherent research requirements associated with it in a physical impact context. The final section provides an example of how carrying capacity methodologies can be applied in a lake environment setting.

INTRODUCTION

Tourism development has experienced tremendous expansion over the past three decades. It now touches most parts of the world, and its penetration into the social, economic, and environmental fabric of host regions continues to intensify. Few geographic regions have not experienced tourism's influence.

Little doubt exists that tourism is a powerful agent of change. Its strength in this respect is expressed in a wide variety of impacts ranging from those that are economic and/or sociocultural in character to those that are environmental in nature. This chapter focuses on approaches for assessing the environmental impacts of tourism development. It examines issues that are essentially physical in character; that is, it includes assessment concerns related to both natural and built dimensions of the physical environment. Land, air, water, vegetation, and wildlife represent the key components of the natural environment influenced by tourism. Built elements of the physical environment include tourism development's infrastructure and superstructure.

While the overall environmental effect of tourism is probably less than that of most other industries developed on a similar scale, the significance of its impacts lies in the fact that it frequently impinges on the most fragile, sensitive, and/or interesting segments of an area's landscape. What in absolute terms would normally represent a minor environmental disturbance could be of considerable significance because of where it occurs. With the escalating growth in the number of large-scale year-round resort developments, as well as the expansion in demand for nature-based tourism to natural places, it is quite conceivable that the environmental consequences of tourism projects could rival those of other industries.

As concern over environmental quality rises amongst both travel markets and destination residents, an appreciation of the potential impacts of tourism development becomes a necessity for planning, development, and management. As this need for an understanding of tourism's environmental impact becomes increasingly recognized and, in some instances, legally required, so does the need for information on the environmental effects of tourism. Credible frameworks and techniques for conducting such research are becoming critical management tools for many tourism destinations and development organizations.

TOURISM AND ENVIRONMENTAL IMPACT

Because tourism is such a highly differentiated phenomenon that occurs in a wide variety of environments, it is dangerous to refer to the physical effects of tourism in general terms. It is more appropriate to isolate those factors peculiar to the tourism situation and then evaluate the impact of each. Considerable research related to the physical impact of tourism exists. Most of the initial investigations flag the necessity of addressing environmental concerns in tourism development planning (Dasman et al. 1973; Bosselman 1980; Pigram 1980). Other initiatives have sought to integrate the findings of past research efforts and offer guidelines for future environmental research, planning, development, and management activities (Cohen 1978; OECD 1981; Mathieson and Wall 1982; Innskeep 1991; Pearce 1989). In most situations, the environmental impact of tourism appears to be primarily related to such factors as the resiliency of the ecosystem, the intensity of site development and use, the commitment and involvement of local stakeholders, and the transformational character of tourism operations.

ECOSYSTEM RESILIENCY

Not all physical environments can equally withstand tourism influxes. Urban centers are normally more resilient than are seminatural or natural settings. The worst environmental effects of tourism typically occur in the least resilient ecosystems. The most sensitive ecosystems tend to be associated with:

- Coastal systems, such as sand dunes, reef areas, and marshes, which represent early and very vulnerable ecosystem successional stages with unstable strata (Salm 1986)
- Montane habitats where growth and self-recovery capability is reduced by climatic influences and steep slopes (Mosimann 1985)
- Landscapes with shallow, nutrient-deficient (e.g., lowlands), and/or excessively wet soils (Jones 1989)

Such locations are often intensively developed for tourism because of their innate attractiveness as well as their limited capability for other forms of economic development.

SITE-USE INTENSITY

Tourist-flow levels (Lindsay 1986), length of stay (Cohen 1978), activity patterns (Edington and Edington 1986), and type of facility development (Jenkins 1991) all represent intensity factors that influence tourism's environmental effects. Generally, the need for tourism infrastructure grows with increases in the volume of tourism traffic and the intensity of site use (Pearce 1987). As time passes, the central areas of these intensively developed tourist centers become transformed. Similarly, the peripheral staging areas that are used to accommodate those persons visiting the core of the destination are also changed (Gunn 1988). Unless planned and managed in an integrated and coordinated fashion, such development activity can create many undesirable aesthetic and infrastructure concerns (Priestley 1986). It can eventually infringe upon less resilient seminatural and natural areas that surround many of these destinations (OECD 1981).

DEVELOPMENT MOTIVATION

Much of the rationale for tourism development is based on the economic use of natural and heritage-based resources. In many cases, these resources represent either the backdrop or the actual draw for tourism enterprises. It would seem reasonable to assume that developers would be concerned with maintaining these resources in sustainable ways. However, tourism proponents have frequently possessed only a limited awareness of the potential ramifications of their developments on the environment. As well, competition for the most attractive sites has often forced them into development strategies that, in the long run, were detrimental to not only the environment but also their own long-term interests (Holder 1988).

Tourism projects driven by proponents with a commitment to the long-run viability of the business are more apt to show a greater sensitivity to environmental concerns than will those with short-run profits in mind. In this context, development projects that incorporate local participation in the planning, construction, management, and monitoring of their activities are generally considered to be more sustainable (World Commission on Environment and Development 1987). Areas where speculative tourism projects have occurred reveal considerable disdain for environmental concerns (Williams 1978).

SITE TRANSFORMATION

It is doubtful that a natural environment can be completely preserved without any transformation and still be intensively used for tourism. Some changes of the environment occur even when care is taken to minimize the effects of human activity (Goudie 1981). Whether associated with the planning-and-design phase (e.g., the impact of uncertainty and speculation associated with theme/resort-park development upon surrounding land-use practices (Cameron and Bordessa 1981)), the construction phase (e.g., the effects of dredging and breakwater, pier, and wharf construction associated with marina development (Baines 1987)), direct facility operation (e.g., hiking and horse-riding effects in alpine areas (Price 1985)), or indirect impacts associated with the operation of a facility (e.g., macrophyte dispersal associated with boating (Johnstone et al. 1985)), an element of environmental transformation is found in most tourism developments. From a research and management perspective, the key is to be able to identify what changes are actually happening and what actions can be taken to manage their effects.

METHODOLOGICAL CONSTRAINTS

While the broad types and rates of environmental change caused by tourism can be related to many recognizable influences, specific impacts associated with any kind of environmental assessment are difficult to clearly specify. This situation is attributable to methodological problems associated with the determination of base points for comparative change analysis, man-environment entanglements, spatial and temporal discontinuities, and environmental interaction complexities.

BASE LEVEL DETERMINATION

To assess environmental impact, it is important to compare what the effects of tourism are or will be against some point of reference. In many cases, other land uses and their associated environmental impacts have existed well before the introduction of tourism development. This makes the determination of tourism-induced environmental impacts particularly difficult to disentangle from other influencing factors (Goudie 1981). Increased nutrient buildup in a lake environment, for example, may be due to tourist resort development, to other land uses (such as agriculture and fishing) or to a combination of all of these (Edington and Edington 1986). Tourism's contribution to lake eutrophication in such an instance is difficult to isolate.

MAN-NATURE ENTANGLEMENTS

Natural environments are in perpetually changing states. Determination of a base assessment level is at best hazardous under such conditions. From an environmental-impact perspective, this problem is compounded because tourism impacts frequently correspond with the flow of normal environmental processes. Tourism development might only hasten what was bound to occur naturally. Wave erosion is a natural process in lake environments, but it can be accentuated by the presence of tourism-related boating operations (Racey and Euler 1983). The processes may remain the same, but the rate at which they occur may be altered radically.

SPATIAL AND TEMPORAL DISCONTINUITIES

Environmental impact associated with tourism projects is hampered by spatial and temporal differences between "cause and effect" (Wall and Wright 1977); for instance, seemingly harmless melt-water runoff associated with artificial snowmaking practices in large ski-area developments may result in the destruction of key elements of aquatic-life habitat several miles downstream from the resort site (Jerome 1977). From a temporal viewpoint, considerable time may pass before the full impact of an activity is apparent; the impact of tourism on coral reef ecology may take years to develop (Dahl 1981).

ENVIRONMENTAL COMPLEXITY

The complexity of interactions between different components of the environment makes tourism's unique impact almost impossible to measure. Changes in water quality due in part to boating activity may lead to changes in aquatic vegetation, which in turn may generate changes in fish habitat, causing adjustments to sport fisheries' capability (Hansmann et al. 1974). In such cases, primary impacts sometimes generate secondary and tertiary effects that may cause several successive repercussions throughout the ecosystem. Such complexities in ecosystem interaction make the assessment of cause-and-effect relationships particularly difficult (Pearce 1985).

METHODOLOGICAL APPROACHES

Despite the aforementioned difficulties associated with assessing the environmental impacts of tourism, a variety of useful analytical techniques are available (Lee 1983). The approaches can be categorized according to either their analytical function (Dickert 1974) or the techniques of analysis that they employ (Warner and Bromley 1974).

ANALYTICAL FUNCTIONS

Analytical functions associated with environmental assessment can be separated into three categories. They are: identification, prediction, and evaluation. Each function has its own methodological thrust and utility in impact assessment. These are described in Table 1.

Identification functions assist in specifying the range, spatial distribution, and duration of impacts that might occur because of a proposed project. They seek to clarify the components of the project as well as what environmental elements may be affected by it. Tourism projects have three broad components (planning and design, construction, and operation) that create direct and indirect environmental impacts. The elements of the natural environment that can be influenced include the physical characteristics of the land (Stroud 1983), air (Kirkpatrick and Reeser 1976), water (Smith and Jenner 1989), flora (Candela 1982), fauna (Western 1986), surrounding land use (Singh and Kaur 1982), and more complex ecological relationships (Speight 1973).

There are essentially two types of identification methods. They are checklists and matrices/networks (Mitchell 1989). Checklists contain environmental factors that are useful to consider with respect to impact of developments. From a master list of environmental factors associated with typical development projects, researchers can select and evaluate those impacts expected from a particular type of tourism project under consideration. These checklists of factors encourage systematic consideration of the potentially wide array of effects associated with tourism development in a particular area. However, they fail to describe interactions between effects (e.g., the influence of reductions of water quality caused by boating on fishing) or the significance of

Table 1 Functional Classification of Environmental Assessment Approaches

FUNCTION	METHODOLOGICAL THRUST
Identification	Description of the existing environmental system
	Determination of the components of the project
	Definition of the environment modified by the project (including all components of the project)
Prediction	Identification of environmental modifications that may be significant
	Forecasting of the quantity and/or spatial dimensions of change in environment identified
	Estimation of the probability that the impact (environmental change) will occur (time period)
Evaluation	Determination of the incidence of costs and benefits to user groups and populations affected by the project
	Specification and comparison of the trade-offs (costs or effects being balanced) between various alternatives

Source: Adapted from Cantor 1977.

the impact (e.g., the extent to which reduced water quality will reduce sport-fish populations). Computer-aided identification systems are available to assist researchers in summarizing the key impacts identified through the use of such checklists (Strand et al. 1983).

Matrices are two-dimensional checklists that identify normal project-component actions and their potential impacts on environmental elements. In a tourism context, they might identify, for instance, the indirect influence of the construction of access channels to beach areas on coral-reef ecology (Archer 1985). Networks assist in recognizing interrelationships between affected environmental elements. They might flag interrelations between tourism-related trampling of soil and vegetation on flora and fauna numbers and species (Cole 1987).

Predictive methodologies are designed to forecast the quantity and/or spatial dimensions of environmental impact, as well as the probability of impact occurrence. They involve the greatest application of technology. Using "controlled" environments for testing purposes and technological aids (e.g., artificial tramplers, stream tables, wind-current tunnels, computer-simulation models, etc.), they attempt to simulate the influence of visitor traffic and facility development on proposed development areas (Mathews 1984).

Evaluative methodologies seek to determine the costs and benefits of proposed developments on local environments. They attempt to specify and compare the trade-offs between various forms of development. Evaluative techniques might be applied to tourism situations in which competing development strategies associated with a relatively fragile region can be assessed on a common basis (Fedler 1985). Two particularly well-documented approaches to this type of assessment are the Battelle environmental system (Dee 1972) and the optimum pathway matrix (Odum and Odum 1976). Using systematic analytical procedures, they both provide aggregate indexes of environmental impact for each alternative under investigation.

TECHNIQUES OF ANALYSIS

Five main techniques of environmental impact analysis are identifiable for tourism-related studies. They are ad hoc procedures, overlay techniques, checklists, matrices, and

networks. Information collected by all five techniques is valuable in signaling the magnitude and importance of tourism's environmental impact as well as potential areas of future research.

AD HOC

Ad hoc procedures involve assembling a team of specialists to identify impacts in their areas of expertise. Normally, such teams are given minimal guidance beyond the parameters as established by related environmental authorities. Typically, such an approach is evident in those regions possessing neither the incentive nor the human and economic resources to undertake extensive investigations.

OVERLAY

Overlay approaches involve the use of well-established techniques frequently employed in land-use planning and landscape architecture (McHarg 1969). They use a series of overlay maps to depict environmental elements or other land-resource factors that may be sensitive to development schemes. The overlay process provides a visual means of filtering through the natural environment of an area in order to separate environmentally durable from ecologically sensitive areas (Gunn 1988). In a tourism context, overlay techniques involving manual mapping procedures (Laventhol and Horwath 1982), computerized digital-mapping techniques (Gunn 1989), and more sophisticated geographic information systems (DPA 1990) have been employed to identify areas most appropriate for tourism development.

CHECKLISTS

Checklist approaches involve the use of master lists of different types of environmental impacts typically associated with various kinds of physical developments. Each type of development project normally carries its own peculiar set of environment-stressing activities (Jenkins 1982). They typically include a range of events associated with such things as permanent environmental restructuring, generation of waste residuals, shifts in land use, and changes in population dynamics (Table 2).

They can be expressed in the form of master checklists

Table 2   Environment-Stressing Tourism Events and Typical Associated Responses

STRESSOR EVENT	PRIMARY ENVIRONMENTAL RESPONSE
1. **Environmental restructuring** • Residential/commercial expansion • Transportation network expansion • Tourist facility development	• Change in habitat • Change in biological species • Change in visual quality • Change in health standards
2. **Waste residual generation** • Air pollution emission increase • Effluent discharge increases • Solid waste disposal increases • Noise level increases	• Change in natural resource pollution loadings • Change in health of biological organisms • Change in human health
3. **Tourist activity intensification** • Activity spatial distribution • Activity temporal patterns • Activity resource use	• Change in habitat • Change in biological species • Change in visual quality
4. **Shifting population structures** • Population growth • Population density • Population resource use • Population sociocultural mix	• Congestion increases • Changes in land-use demand • Changes in water demand • Changes in energy demand

Source: Adapted from OECD 1981.

that act as a guide in investigating the environmental effects of a proposed development. An example of an environmental checklist for a tourism project involving the creation of an artificial lake could include but need not be limited to the factors listed in Table 3.

The master list for a ski area development would probably be quite different. However, comprehensive lists of a multitude of environmental factors that are generally considered when conducting any impact assessment are available from most government agencies dealing with environmental matters (Warner and Preston 1973). From such lists, a project checklist suited to a particular form of tourism development can be established. Such checklists can be structured in a variety of ways. Essentially, they can be simple, descriptive, scaling, or scaling-weighting in character.

Simple checklists (Table 3) provide a basic list of assessment parameters. They can be organized by category of impact, temporal phase, spatial boundaries, or a combination of any or all of these. The structure of Table 3, for instance, focuses solely on categories of impact. On the other hand, Table 4 provides a checklist organized not only by category of impact but also temporally as to the phase of the project's development. This project checklist could be associated with the assessment of the impact of a proposed shoreline-oriented marina/resort complex. However, none of these checklists provides guidelines concerning how each checklist item is to be measured and interpreted with respect to environmental elements being assessed.

Descriptive checklists include both identification of environmental elements and guidelines concerning how each type of environmental impact is to be assessed. Using Section V.B of Table 4 as an example, a descriptive checklist might require the researcher to assess the impact of the

marina/resort development impact on local fauna. The descriptive checklist guidelines might also necessitate the researcher to identify important wildlife species in and immediately adjacent to the site; to indicate the habitat distribution and relationship to other species; to note rare or endangered species that exist in or near the site; to discuss the current degree of ecological succession in terms of its impacts upon current and future wildlife production; and to outline any other preexisting environmental stresses (e.g., surrounding land uses) that might influence the future fauna characteristics of the area.

Scaling checklists are similar to descriptive lists except for the addition of a subjective rating of environmental impact values. A scaling approach involving the comparative analysis of alternative transportation projects (Adkins and Burke 1974) provides a prototype for the analysis of tourism developments. It entails scaling the impact of alternative tourism-project actions such as those described in Table 4. Scaling in this instance would be conducted on a relative scale ranging from –5 to +5. The summary of the overall evaluation would be based on the number of plus and minus ratings, as well as their algebraic rating.

Scaling-weighting checklists are similar to scaling checklists except that they provide researchers with information concerning how to subjectively evaluate each potential environmental-impact parameter with respect to every other factor. They also suggest how to express these weighted factors in equivalent units for comparative purposes. In Table 4, for example, a scaling-weighting checklist would subjectively indicate that the weighting of this form of tourism development impact on III.A (i.e., groundwater elements) should be considered three times as significant as its influence upon III.B (i.e., surface water elements). The application of this

Table 3 Potential Tourism-Related Environmental Impact Elements Associated with Water Impoundments

I. Changes in land use and/or productivity
  A. Specified land uses
    1. Agricultural or grazing land
    2. Forests or timberland
    3. Wetlands or marshes
  B. Commercial productivity
    1. Mineral resources (gravel, limestone, oil, gas, etc.)
    2. Commercial fisheries
II. Modifications or relocations of built structures and other archeological or historical sites
  A. Archeological or historical sites
  B. Homes or villages
  C. Highways, railroads, and other transportation facilities
  D. Cemeteries
  E. Recreation facilities
III. Changes in wildlife habitat
  A. Specification of habitat type
  B. Change in hunting opportunities
IV. Aesthetic impact modification
  A. Decreased aesthetics
  B. Increased aesthetics
V. Natural stream-related environmental impacts
  A. Loss of stream fishery
  B. Loss of recreation and tourism potential
VI. Lake-related environmental impacts
  A. Substitution of a lake environment for a stream environment
  B. Creation of a warm-water fishery
  C. Change of wildlife habitat
VII. Water quality impacts
  A. Thermal stratification
  B. Growth of algae
  C. Impoundment of nutrients and wastes
    1. Decrease in water quality
    2. Increase in rate of eutrophication
VIII. Dam-related impacts
  A. Increased sediment deposition
  B. Loss of anadromous fish runs
IX. Spillway-related impacts
X. Downstream impacts
  A. Decreased silt or sediment in downstream channel
    1. Increased erosion downstream
    2. Increased water quality downstream
  B. Downstream fishery impacts
  C. Flow regulation effects
    1. Improvement of water quality downstream
    2. Improvement of downstream aesthetics
    3. Improvement of recreation and tourism downstream
    4. Reduction of mosquito problems downstream
XI. Effects of groundwater recharge
XII. Effects of fluctuating shorelines
  A. Adverse effects on wildlife
  B. Adverse effects on vegetation
  C. Decreased aesthetics at low-water-level stages

Source: Adapted from Warner and Bromley 1974.

methodology is well documented (Dee 1972) and has considerable applicability in a tourism context.

MATRICES

Matrix approaches to environmental impact assessment incorporate both a list of project activities and a checklist of potentially impacted environmental elements (Leopold 1971). The matrix is usually composed of project actions along one axis and environmental elements along the other axis. Where an impact on an environmental element (e.g., alteration of drainage on a ski slope) is anticipated because of a proposed action (e.g., construction of ski-area cables and lifts), the matrix is normally marked with a diagonal line in the interacting matrix cell (Figure 1).

The interactions between actions and the environment in terms of their magnitude and importance are assessed and recorded within the matrix. The magnitude of an interaction refers to its extensiveness or scale. It is described by the assignment of a relative numerical value ranging from 1 to 10, with 10 representing the largest impact in terms of scale or extensiveness. The development of Florida's Walt Disney World would probably receive a high score in terms of its scale, while many of the resort developments within North America's national park systems would rate scores of lesser magnitude because of their smaller areal extent.

The importance of an interaction is related to the significance of the subsequent relationship. Relative importance ratings range from a high of 10 to a low of 1. The extreme transformation of marine environments by tourism development in Hawaii (Clark and MacDonald 1991) might receive a high importance rating, while tourism's impact on local coastal plant communities in Great Britain (Edwards 1987) might be significantly less important. The numerical value is normally based upon subjective judgment.

Summation of the values assigned to those interacting cells within rows and columns of the matrix can offer insights into tourism's impact and the interpretation of that impact from a development perspective. Matrix procedures can be structured like simple checklists designed to identify impacts temporally and spatially. They can also be organized like scaling checklists to note detrimental impacts. This involves the use of positive and negative symbols or scribed notations (e.g., high, medium, and low significance) rather than ratio designations.

NETWORKS

Unlike their purely matrix approach counterparts, network approaches to environmental assessment examine the secondary and tertiary effects associated with project actions. This usually involves a stepped process in which primary and direct impacts are depicted as leading to other secondary and tertiary indirect impacts (Sorenson 1971). The direct action of dredging a coastal submerged shoreline for the development of a marina/resort complex can be assessed from an impact perspective using this technique. The dredging operation may lead to the primary impact of increasing water depth. This in turn may lead to the secondary impact

Table 4 Environment Checklist for Potential Environmental Impact of a Proposed Marina/Resort Complex

		PROJECT PHASE
CATEGORY OF IMPACT	PLANNING AND DESIGN	CONSTRUCTION OPERATION

I. Noise impacts
  A. Public health
  B. Land use

II. Air quality impacts
  A. Public health
  B. Land use

III. Water quality impacts
  A. Ground water
    1. Flow and water-table alteration
    2. Interaction with surface drainage
  B. Surface water
    1. Shoreline and bottom alteration
    2. Effects of flooding and dredging
    3. Drainage and flood characteristics
  C. Water-quality changes
    1. Effect of effluent loading
    2. Implication of other actions such as
      a. Disturbance of benthic layers
      b. Alteration of currents
      c. Changes in flow regime
      d. Saline intrusion in groundwater
    3. Land use
    4. Public health

IV. Soil erosion impacts
  A. Economic and land use changes
  B. Pollution and siltation effects

V. Ecological impacts
  A. Flora
  B. Fauna (other than humans)

VI. Aesthetic and visual impacts
  A. Scenic resources
  B. Urban design
  C. Noise
  D. Air quality
  E. Water quality

of inhibiting normal aquatic vegetation growth. This action could create such tertiary impacts as the destruction of fish habitat and the loss of a significant commercial sport fishery crucial to the long-run viability of development (Joliffe and Patman 1986). An example of a network analysis framework for dredging projects that might be related to tourism projects is described in Figure 2.

SUMMARY

The preceding discussion has described the primary methods and research starting points for assessing the environmental impact of tourism projects. Given the typical kinds of methodological constraints associated with such research, each technique must be used with care. Critical judgment must guide both their application to particular situations and the interpretation of the information that they generate. This judgment requires a thorough appreciation of the strengths

and weakness of the impact information on which the decisions are to be made and the sensitivities of the methodology employed to collect it (Whitney and Maclaren 1985). Assessment decisions often boil down to a matter of degree rather than to a single correct or wrong decision.

CARRYING CAPACITY

Changes in environment due to tourism development are inevitable and environmental impact research can provide an appreciation of these consequences. However, the determination of optimum levels of development can help to plan and manage the degree and direction of environmental change. Establishing the appropriate level of development and associated activity evolves around the concept of carrying capacity. In theory, once a carrying capacity for an area has been established, management policies (WTO 1989) and control systems (Innskeep 1987, 1991) can be enacted to help re-

Action Causing Impact

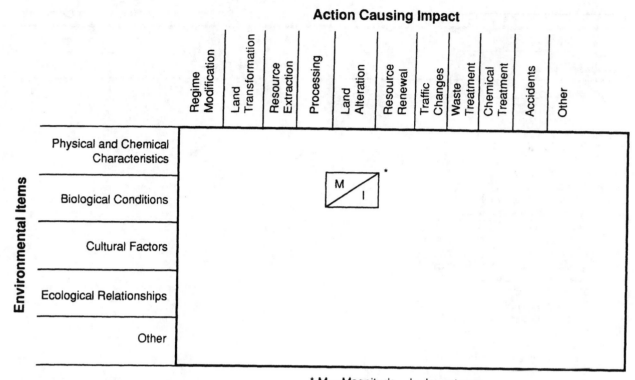

* M = Magnitude   I = Importance

FIGURE 1 Environmental assessment matrix format. *Source:* Adapted from Leopold 1971.

strict unhampered growth. The concept of carrying capacity and its determination in tourism are discussed in the following paragraphs.

Carrying capacity is a key but controversial concept associated with the physical and sociocultural management of tourism areas (Stankey and Manning 1986). The controversy focuses on the value judgments and the subjective decisions that characterize the concept (Shelby and Heberlein 1984). Carrying-capacity calculations for a site involve determining a continuum of use intensities that may be suited to an area. The polarities of the continuum range from virtually no direct tourism use, as exemplified by tourism management strategies for sensitive marine reserves in the Turks and Caicos Islands (Mitchell and Barborak 1991), to seemingly unlimited and environmentally destructive tourism use, as exemplified by coastal developments in some parts of the Mediterranean (Pearce 1987).

Carrying-capacity statements have both prescriptive and descriptive characteristics. In a prescriptive context, they can be used to assign a preferred type and amount of use to a tourism site. A carrying-capacity statement might indicate, for instance, the type of ski market most appropriate for a landscape and the number of skier-days suited to that environment given the capability and preferences of the skiers. From a descriptive perspective, carrying capacity guidelines might describe the relationships between the quantity (e.g., number of novice skiers) and the quality (e.g., length of ski-

lift-line waiting time) of use in an area (Lawson and Baud-Bovy 1977).

The common theme associated with most carrying-capacity statements concerns its role in establishing the level of use possible within a given environment without environmental deterioration and use-quality losses. A corollary to that theme is that carrying capacity-statements reflect decisions concerning the environmental degradation and use quality deemed acceptable as the cost for the use of a site. In any tourism development, there is no single carrying-capacity figure, but rather a range of use intensities and use-type management alternatives, each with its own consequences on the environment and the tourist. As well, for each alternative use, separate carrying-capacity continuums apply. To complicate matters further, the dynamics of constantly changing environmental conditions as well as shifting consumer preferences dictate the need for periodic reviews of previously established use-intensity levels.

Carrying-capacity statements can establish acceptable use intensities from a variety of different perspectives. Physical/biological carrying-capacity methods attempt to determine the attributes of a physical environment that will be affected by tourism use and the amount of use that can be withstood without significant degradation (Frissel and Duncan 1965). They have been used to examine acceptable water-quality changes that occur with changing intensities of accommodation development in lake environments (Michalski and Conroy

Project Causing Action	Primary Impacts	Secondary Impacts	Tertiary Impacts

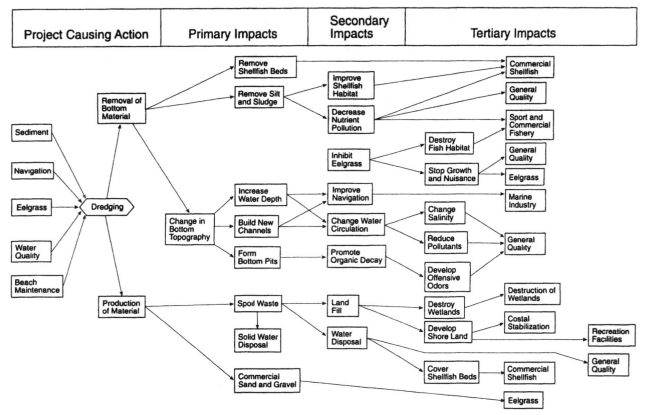

FIGURE 2 A network analysis framework for coastal dredging projects. *Source:* Sorenson 1971.

1972). Management-based carrying-capacity statements seek to determine a level of tourist use for a site that is efficient and safe for users, given the human and fiscal resources available to the management organization (Schreyer 1976). Social carrying-capacity estimates try to determine the most acceptable and psychologically satisfying intensity of site use as perceived by both tourists and their hosts. Carrying-capacity-related studies with a strong sociopsychological focus have been conducted in both natural and built tourism environments (Liu et al. 1987). All of these approaches to establishing the appropriate use intensity for a tourism environment have their own merit. Any defensible policy decision prescribing a certain carrying-capacity level for an area should consider all three approaches. Unfortunately, few examples of carrying-capacity guidelines based on information gained from the use of all three approaches exist. For the most part, carrying-capacity determinations tend to be based upon the use of a single approach rather than any integrative strategy.

One of the more integrative techniques for establishing carrying-capacity estimates is associated with lake environments. This approach is particularly valuable because so much of tourism development is associated with the use of water resources. The approach uses four capacity-estimation equations, combines this information, and then expresses the results as a spectrum of planning alternatives. It incorporates estimates based on the physical availability of the shoreline

for tourism use, the perceived appropriate boat density preferred by recreationists, and the managerial appropriateness of existing use levels. The suitability of each carrying-capacity estimate varies with the water body under investigation. Consequently, the relative significance of the various carrying-capacity measures employed should be weighted according to the water body under study (Jaakson 1979). This procedure makes it possible to consider a range of capacity estimates based upon the particular circumstances of the environment being used for tourism.

FUTURE CARRYING-CAPACITY RESEARCH DIRECTIONS

The preceding approaches provide valuable contributions to the understanding of carrying capacity and the management of visitor use. However, they have met with limited application in a tourism context. This situation exists primarily because of:

- Unrealistic expectations (i.e., a technique exists that can provide a "magic number" that identifies "how much is too much")
- Untenable assumptions (i.e., a direct relationship between visitor use and impact exists)
- Inappropriate value judgments (i.e., conflicts between

the views of experts as opposed to other stakeholders concerning what constitutes appropriate conditions for an area)
- Insufficient legal support (i.e., the unavailability of a formally recognized institutional process to ensure that management objectives are achieved)

Despite the rhetoric concerning tourism-use limits, ceilings, and thresholds, difficulties with developing typical rule-of-thumb numerical carrying-capacity ceilings exist. As in the case for recreation, little evidence exists that by simply lowering or raising a specific carrying-capacity standard, predictable changes in an area's ability to handle tourist use will occur. Instead, the key appears to lie in how change associated with tourism is managed. Research suggests that planning and development agencies must develop indicators and associated standards that clearly identify when preferred or desired conditions are being threatened by tourism. As encroachment on these standards occurs, action in the form of direct or indirect management strategies can be implemented. Such a focus for research centers more on identifying approaches for monitoring and managing growth towards specified goals, rather than identifying an illusive and questionable index of carrying capacity (Williams and Gill 1991).

CONCLUSION

The preceding discussion has focused on research methods for assessing and assisting in the management of tourism's environmental impacts. The impact methodologies presented provide a means of systematically filtering through the complex interactions that typify tourism-environment relationships. They describe these interactions in relative terms. All of the methods require credible information for their application and interpretation. Knowledge of tourism's potential impacts is growing but is still limited in both scope and comprehensiveness. Tourism research dealing with environmental impact as discussed here requires the involvement of many disciplines so that a better appreciation of its influence on natural and physical environments can be more clearly understood.

Carrying-capacity research techniques are equally limited in their development and application. Given the relative futility experienced by planning organizations in developing defensible carrying-capacity ceilings, research might be better focused in more useful directions. In particular, research should focus more on developing the indicators of tourism's environmental impacts so that management strategies designed to guide tourism's growth can be better measured and appreciated.

REFERENCES

Adkins, W.G., and D. Burke (1974), *Interim Report: Social, Economic and Environmental Factors in Highway Deci-*sion-making, Research Report 148–4, Texas Transportation Institute, Austin, Texas: Texas A&M University.

Archer, E. (1985), "Emerging environmental problems in a tourist zone: the case of Barbados," *Caribbean Geography* 2(1):45–55.

Baines, G.B. (1987), "Manipulation of islands and men: sandcay tourism in the South Pacific," in *Ambiguous Alternative: Tourism in Developing Countries*, S. Britton and W.C. Clarke, eds., 16–24, Suva: University of the South Pacific.

Bosselman, Fred, ed. (1978), *In the Wake of the Tourist, Managing Special Places in Eight Countries*, Washington, D.C.: The Conservation Foundation.

Cameron, J.M., and R. Bordessa (1981), *Wonderland Through the Looking Glass*, Maple, Ontario: Belstein Publishing.

Candela, R.M. (1982), "Piste de ski et erosion anthropique dans les Alpes du Sud," *Mediterranee* (3–4):51–55.

Canter, L. (1977), *Environmental Impact Assessment*, New York: McGraw-Hill.

Clark, A.M., and C.D. MacDonald (1990), "Hawaii's Experience in Managing the Expanding Use of Scenic Coastal Resources," in *Proceedings of the 1990 Congress on Coastal and Marine Tourism: A Symposium and Workshop on Balancing Conservation and Economic Development*, M. Miller and J. Auyong, eds., Volume I, 149–158, Newport, OR: National Coastal Resources Research and Development Institute.

Cohen, E. (1978), "The Impact of Tourism on the Physical Environment," *Annals of Tourism Research* 5(2):215–237.

Cole, D.N. (1987), "Effects of Three Seasons of Experimental Trampling on Five Mountain Forest Communities and a Grassland in Western Montana, U.S.A.," *Biological Conservation* 40:219–244.

Dahl, A.L. (1981), *Coral Reef Monitoring Handbook*, Noumea: South Pacific Commission.

Dasman, R.F., J.P. Milton, and P.H. Freeman (1973), *Ecological Principles for Economic Development*, New York: John Wiley & Sons, Inc.

Dee, N. (1972), *Environmental Evaluation System for Water Resource Planning*, report prepared by Battelle-Columbus for Bureau of Reclamation, U.S. Government, Washington, D.C.

Dickert, T.G. (1974), "Methods for Environmental Impact Assessment: A Comparison," in *Environmental Impact Assessment: Guidelines and Commentary*, T.G. Dickert and K.R. Domeny, eds., 127–143, Berkeley, CA: University of California.

DPA Group (1990), *Sustainable Development and GIS Technology: A Demonstration Project*, Government of British Columbia.

Edington, J.M., and M.A. Edington (1986), *Ecology, Recreation and Tourism*, Cambridge, U.K.: Cambridge University Press.

Edwards, J.R. (1987), "The U.K. Heritage Coast: An Assessment of the Ecological Impacts of Tourism," *Annals of Tourism Research* 14(1):71–87.

Fedler, A.J. (1985), "Consequences of Coastal Population Growth: Conflicts with Recreational Uses of the Coastal Zone," in *Proceedings: 1985 National Outdoor Recreation Trends Symposium II*, Atlanta, GA: Department of the Interior, National Parks Service, Southeast Regional Office.

Frissell, S.S., and D.P. Duncan (1965), "Composite Preference and Deterioration in the Quetico-Superior Canoe Country," *Journal of Forestry* 65:256–260.

Goudie, A. (1981), *The Human Impact: Man's Role in Environmental Change*, 187–238, Oxford: Basil Blackwell.

Gunn, C.A. (1988), *Vacationscape: Designing Tourist Regions*, New York: Van Nostrand Reinhold.

Gunn, C.A. (1989), *Tourism Planning*, 2nd ed., New York: Taylor and Francis.

Hansmann, E.W., D.E. Kid, and E. Gilbert (1974), "Man's Impact on a Newly Formed Reservoir," *Hydrobiologia* 45:185–197.

Holder, J.S. (1988), "Pattern and Impact of Tourism on the Environment of the Caribbean," *Tourism Management*, June, 119–127.

Innskeep, E. (1987), "Environmental Planning for Tourism," *Annals of Tourism Research* 14(1):118–135.

Innskeep, E. (1991), *Tourism Planning: An Integrated and Sustainable Development Approach*, New York: Van Nostrand Reinhold.

Jaakson, R. (1979), "A Spectrum Model of Lake Recreation Carrying Capacity Estimation," in *Water-Based Recreation Problems and Progress*, J. Marsh, ed., Occasional Paper 8, 62–83, Peterborough, Ontario: Department of Geography, Trent University.

Jenkins, C.L. (1982), "The Effects of Scale in Tourism Projects in Developing Countries," *Annals of Tourism Research* 9(2):229–249.

Jerome, J. (1977), "Skiing and the Environment," *EPA Journal* 3:11–14.

Johnstone, I.M., B.T. Coffey, and C. Howard-Williams (1985), "The Role of Recreational Boat Traffic in Interlake Dispersal of Macrophytes: a New Zealand Case Study," *Journal of Environmental Management* 20(3):263–279.

Joliffe, I.P., and G.R. Patman (1986), "Roses Bay, Northeast Spain: The Impact of Tourism on a Mediterranean Coastal Landscape," *Contemporary Ecological-Geographical Problems of the Mediterranean*, 113–128, International Geographical Union/UNESCO, Palma de Mallorca.

Jones, R.T. (1989), "Use of Wetlands in Golf Course Design," *Golf Course Management*, July, 7, 10, 12, 16.

Kirkpatrick, L.W., and W.K. Reeser (1976), "The Air Pollution Carrying Capacities of Selected Colorado Mountain Ski Valley Communities," *Journal of the Air Pollution Control Association* 26(10):992–994.

Laventhol & Horwath (1982), *Tourism Development Strategy for the Peterborough-Haliburton Tourism Zone*, report prepared for the Ontario Ministry of Industry and Tourism.

Lawson, F., and M. Baud-Bovy (1977), *Tourism and Recreation Development, A Handbook of Physical Planning*, London: The Architectural Press.

Lee, N. (1983), "Environmental Impact Assessment: A Review," *Applied Geography* 3:5–28.

Leopold, L.B. (1971), "A Procedure for Evaluating Environmental Impact," *U.S. Geological Survey Circular*, 645, Washington, D.C.: U.S. Government Printing Office.

Lindsay, J.J. (1986), "Carrying Capacity for Tourism Development in National Parks of the United States," *Industry and Environment* 9(1):17–20.

Liu, J.C., P.S. Sheldon, and T. Var (1987), "Resident Perceptions of the Environmental Impacts of Tourism," *Annals of Tourism Research* 14:17–37.

Mathews, P. (1984), "Planned by Computer," *Ski Area Management* 23(5):61–62, 94–95.

Mathieson, A., and G. Wall (1982), *Tourism: Economic, Physical and Social Impacts*, Essex, U.K.: Longman.

McHarg, I.L. (1969), *Design with Nature*, Garden City, NJ: Doubleday.

Michalski, M.F., and N. Conroy (1972), *Water Quality Evaluation*, Lake Alert Study, Toronto: Ontario Ministry of the Environment.

Mitchell, B. (1989), *Geography and Resource Analysis*, 2nd ed., Essex, England: Longman Scientific and Technical.

Mitchell, B.A., and J.B. Barborak (1991), "A New System of Marine Parks and Protected Areas in the Turks and Caicos Islands, BWI," in *Proceedings of the 1990 Congress on Coastal and Marine Tourism: a Symposium and Workshop on Balancing Conservation and Economic Development*, M. Miller and J. Auyong (eds.), Volume 1, 225–235, Newport, OR: National Coastal Resources Research and Development Institute.

Mosimann, T. (1985), "Geo-ecological Impacts of Ski Piste Construction in the Swiss Alps," *Applied Geography* 5(1):29–37.

OECD (1981), *The Impact of Tourism on the Environment*, Paris: Organization for Economic Cooperation and Development.

Odum, H.T., and E.C. Odum (1976), *Energy Basis for Man and Nature*, New York: McGraw-Hill.

Pearce, D.G. (1985), "Tourism and Environmental Research: A Review," *International Journal of Environmental Studies* 25(4):247–255.

Pearce, D.G. (1987), *Tourism Today: A Geographical Analysis*, Essex, England: Longman Scientific and Technical.

Pearce, D.G. (1989), *Tourist Development*, 2nd ed., Essex, England: Longman Scientific and Technical.

Pigram, J.J. (1980), "Environmental Implications of Tourism Development," *Annals of Tourism Research* 7(4):554–583.

Price, M.F. (1985), "Impacts of Recreational Activities on Alpine Vegetation in Western North America," *Mountain Research and Development* 5(3):263–277.

Priestley, G.K. (1986), *El turismo y la transformacion del territorio: un estudio de Tossa*, Lloret de Mar y Blanes a traves de la fotografia aerea 1956–81, in Fornades Tecniques Sobre Turisme, Mediambient Sant Feliu de Guixols-Costa Biava, Barcelona, 88–106.

Racey, G.D., and D. Euler (1983), "An Index of Habitat Disturbance for Lakeshore Cottage Development," *Journal of Environmental Management* 16:173–179.

Salm, R.V. (1985), "Integrating Marine Conservation and Tourism," *International Journal of Environmental Studies* 25:229–238.

Salm, R.V. (1986), "Coral Reefs and Tourist Carrying Capacity: The Indian Ocean Experience," *Industry and Environment* 9(1):11–15.

Schreyer, R. (1976), "Sociological and Political Factors in Carrying Capacity Decision-making," paper presented at Visitor Capacity Conference, Fort Worth, TX: National Park Service.

Shelby, B., and T.A. Heberlein (1984), "A Conceptual Framework for Carrying Capacity Determination," *Leisure Sciences* 6(4):487–496.

Singh, T.V., and J. Kaur (1986), "The Paradox of Mountain Tourism: Case References from the Himalaya," *UNEP Industry and Environment*, January, February, March, 21–26.

Smith, C., and P. Jenner (1986), "Tourism and the Environment," *EIU Travel and Tourism Analyst* 5:68–86.

Sorenson, J.C. (1971), *A Framework for Identification and Control of Resource Degradation and Conflict in the Multiple Use of the Coastal Zone*, Berkeley: University of California.

Speight, M.C.D. (1973), "Outdoor Recreation and Its Ecological Effects: A Bibliography and Review," *Discussion Papers in Conservation*, 4, London: University College.

Stankey, G.H, and R.E. Manning (1986), "Carrying Capacity of Recreational Settings," in *A Literature Review: The President's Commission on American Outdoors*, 47–57, Washington, D.C.: U.S. Government Printing Office.

Strand, R.H., M.P. Farrell, J.C. Goyert, and K.L. Daniels (1983), "Environmental Assessments Through Research Data Management," *Journal of Environmental Management* 16:269–280.

Stroud, H.B. (1983), "Environmental Problems Associated with Large Recreational Subdivisions," *Professional Geographer* 35(3):303–313.

WTO (1989), *Tourism Carrying Capacity Study—Goa, India*, Madrid: World Tourism Organization.

Wall, G., and C. Wright (1977), *The Environmental Impact of Outdoor Recreation*, Publication Series No. 11, 1–3, Waterloo, Ontario: Department of Geography, University of Waterloo.

Warner, M.L., and E.H. Preston (1973), *A Review of Environmental Impact Assessment Methodologies*, report prepared by Batelle-Columbus for the U.S. Environmental Protection Agency, Washington, D.C.

Warner, M.L., and D.W. Bromley (1974), *Environmental Impact Analysis: A Review of Three Methodologies*, Technical Report, Madison: University of Wisconsin, Wisconsin Water Resources Center.

Western, D. (1986), "Tourist Capacity in East African Parks," *UNEP Industry and Environment*, January, February, March, 14–16.

Whitney, J.B.R., and V.W. Maclaren (1985), *Environmental Impact Assessment: Current Approaches in the Canadian Context*, Toronto: Institute for Environmental Studies, University of Toronto.

Williams, P.W. (1978), "Retirement Community Impacts," *Utah Tourism and Recreation Review* 7(3):1–4.

Williams, P.W., and A. Gill (1991), *Carrying Capacity Management in Tourism Settings: A Tourism Growth Management Process*, Edmonton: Alberta Tourism.

World Commission on Environment and Development (1987), *Our Common Future*, Oxford University Press.

37

Event Tourism: Evaluating the Impacts

DONALD GETZ[1]
Associate Professor
Tourism and Hospitality Management
The University of Calgary
Calgary, Alberta

*M*easuring and evaluating the impacts of festivals and special events presents a number of unique issues and challenges, particularly with respect to economic effects. General approaches to assessing event tourism impacts are presented, followed by discussion of common misleading presumptions about event impacts. Special attention is given to multipliers, their uses, and abuses. Finally, a step-by-step guide to event tourism evaluation is given.

INTRODUCTION

Event tourism is the systematic planning, development, and marketing of festivals and special events as tourist attractions, image makers, catalysts for infrastructure and economic growth, and animators of built attractions (Getz 1991a). Growth in the number of tourist-oriented events has been spectacular, but the immature state of this field has been marked by exaggerated claims of economic impact, weak research methodology, and inadequate attention to the evaluation of costs and benefits.

In this chapter, a recommended process for measuring and evaluating event impacts is presented, emphasizing costs and benefits from the perspective of a destination. Readers are advised to first cover background material contained in the three chapters in this Handbook written by Douglas Frechtling (Chapters 31 to 33), as many of the issues pertaining to the impacts of event tourism are a special case of economic impact assessment.

General approaches to examining the effects of events are summarized first, followed by discussion of a number of common misleading presumptions about event impacts. Separate sections are devoted to the many issues and pitfalls surrounding the use of multipliers and conducting cost-benefit evaluations. A step-by-step guide to undertaking impact

evaluations is then provided, including a point-form listing of rules and recommendations.

APPROACHES TO ASSESSING EVENT IMPACTS

Table 1 (based on Getz 1991b) summarizes this discussion, showing approaches, related goals, and commonly employed measures for each. The approaches are arranged in order from least to most complex and, therefore, also in order of easiest to most difficult to implement.

BREAK-EVEN OR PROFIT/LOSS ASSESSMENT

For many events, merely surviving from year to year is a challenge. Organizers tend to look at the bottom line of their own financial statements at year end to determine their solvency or to measure their efficiency and effectiveness in achieving goals within their budget. This is a short-term approach, and the only impacts addressed are those affecting the organization's financial performance. Direct costs and revenues will be examined, and the exercise might include a statement of how surplus revenues or operating costs were spent; but wider economic impacts are not covered.

[1]Acknowledgement: I am very grateful for comments and advice from three experts: Brian Archer, University of Surrey; Douglas Frechtling, George Washington Univesity; and Trevor Mules, University of Adelaide. All opinions and any errors are the author's alone.

Table 1 Approaches to Event Impact Assessment

APPROACHES	GOALS	COMMONLY USED MEASURES
BREAK-EVEN OR PROFIT/LOSS	• Short-term assessment of financial efficiency or solvency	• Measure direct costs and revenues to organizers • Determine surplus or deficit (profit or loss)
RETURN ON INVESTMENT	• Show the benefits of grants or sponsorship • Calculate ROI for private investors or owners	• Determine the relationship between grants/sponsorships and levels of visitation or economic benefits • Use standard ROI accounting practices
ECONOMIC SCALE	• Determine the economic scale of one or more events from the destination perspective	• Measure total attendance and expenditure of event consumers, plus organizers' expenditures
ECONOMIC IMPACT	• Determine the macroeconomic benefits to the destination area	• Estimate direct and indirect income and employment benefits • Often uses multipliers or econometric models
COSTS AND BENEFITS	• Evaluate the costs and benefits from the perspective of the host community and environment • Determine the net work or value of the event	• Compare tangible and intangible costs and benefits short- and long-term • Assess opportunity costs of investments • Examine the distribution of impacts • Judge the net worth and acceptability of the event(s)

A profit, or surplus revenue, is not necessarily an economic benefit for the destination, depending on the sources of revenue; for example, an event-producing organization might generate a surplus, but only because of local government grants—in which case the "surplus" does not represent new income for the area.

RETURN ON INVESTMENT

Sponsors and grant-givers may wish to know if their investment in events is paying off. Most sponsors will be interested in sales, public relations, and other marketing goals (requiring a very specialized impact assessment not considered in this chapter). Public agencies giving grants to events will be more interested in how the event achieved certain goals, ranging from qualitative evaluations of changes in public attitudes to full economic impact assessments.

Some private investors or event organizers will want to calculate their ROI (return on investment) using standard accounting practices, but this, too, is not a measure of economic impact on the destination, only of financial performance.

When calculating a return on investment, it should be kept in mind that money earned today can be reinvested, and money spent on events could be invested elsewhere. Hence, the use of *net present value* calculations is recommended.

ECONOMIC SCALE

Some researchers set out to measure economic impact, but their methods and estimates fall short. Instead, they end up with a crude measure of economic scale—the total size of expenditures associated with an event. An example of a study that took this approach has been examined in Getz (1991b), but major problems are mentioned in the following paragraph and discussed further in ensuing sections of this chapter.

Problem one is that of including all event-goer expenditure in the calculation of economic benefit. In fact, little or none of the expenditure of area residents should be included. Problem two is that of failing to account for the reasons people attend events—if they were motivated to travel to an area because of an event, it results in new, or incremental, income for the area; if they were already in the area, the impact is much less, or even negated entirely. Problem three is that of including grants and sponsorships in the calculation of impact while failing to determine if the amounts are simply internal allocations as opposed to new money for the area. Problem four is the failure to note that much leakage is associated with tourist expenditure—that is, much of it leaves the area immediately, without creating local income or profit.

A valid way to express the economic scale of an event is to say how many tourists it attracted and how much the tourists spent in the area. This is very legitimate and probably all that most event organizers can and should attempt. It does, however, require careful explanation of how the measure of economic scale was determined and what assumptions have been made—particularly noting that gross visitor expenditure is not the same as net income created for the area.

ECONOMIC IMPACT

To validly measure or estimate the economic impacts of an event or events on the destination area requires more rigorous research methods. The specific goals are to determine the local income and employment created for residents of the area, and sometimes long-term, indirect impacts—such as improved ability to attract investment—are also considered. Promotion and image enhancement of the destination area might also be covered but are much more difficult to measure (see Ritchie and Smith 1991 for an evaluation of the impact of Calgary's 1988 winter Olympics on the city's image).

Major reliability and validity problems are inevitably encountered, often resulting in the making of unwarranted assumptions and the use of inappropriate techniques, especially with regard to the application of multipliers. These are discussed fully in the ensuing sections.

COSTS AND BENEFITS

Far too many economic impact studies have ignored the economic costs of producing events, or the indirect and external costs imposed on the community or environment. The development of cost-benefit evaluation methods can overcome this serious limitation by comparing economic costs with economic benefits and by comparing intangibles. Some progress has been made in quantifying intangibles such as social problems or psychological benefits.

Employing cost-benefit evaluation has the advantage of focusing attention on the value or worth of the event or project, rather than merely highlighting supposed profits, income, and job creation. Social, cultural, and environmental effects are considered alongside economic factors, yielding a more balanced evaluation.

COMMON MISLEADING PRESUMPTIONS ABOUT EVENT IMPACTS

A number of misleading presumptions persist about event impacts, presumably because of the immaturity of event-related research. Many organizers and researchers have done studies for the wrong reasons, using invalid or unreliable methods. Communication among those interested in events has been slow to develop, but this is being addressed through publication of the *Sports Economics* newsletter (published by The Centre for South Australian Economic Studies, P.O. Box 125, Rundle Mall, South Australia 5000) and

Festival Management and Event Tourism: An International Journal (published by Cognizant Communication Corp., 90 Fairview Park Drive, Elmsford, New York 10523, USA).

PRESUMPTION 1

To justify events, or to obtain grants, it is necessary to prove their economic benefits. Organizers and supporters of festivals and special events want to obtain grants from public agencies, and they feel that development-minded officials must have proof that events create economic benefits. This presumption is still true in many places, but increasingly these officials will want to hear less about multipliers and more about which types of events are worthy of support in order to meet specific goals, such as spreading tourism more widely or seasonally, or which ones to avoid because of the problems they cause; they will want to know which events will yield the best returns on public investment. And sometimes officials will sanction money-losing events that generate broader economic, political, social, or environmental gains for the area.

To answer these questions does not necessarily require the kind of impact assessment that typically employs multipliers or econometric models to generate estimates of income or employment creation. Rather, it requires careful analysis of individual events and their ability to attract high-yield tourists or to hold tourists longer, along with evaluation of their costs and benefits from economic, social, and environmental perspectives.

PRESUMPTION 2

All festivals and special events create economic benefits. The evidence strongly suggests that many events have little direct economic impact on their community or region, largely because they cater mostly to residents. Only when events attract out-of-region visitors do they start to create economic benefits. Events can also have a significant cumulative impact by improving the destination's image and overall attractiveness, which can be evaluated through studies of perception and trip motivation within target market areas.

Careful attention to the purpose of trips, spending patterns of tourists, and even the definition of *tourists* versus *residents* is necessary in event-impact evaluation. These points are discussed later, but it should be noted here that economic benefits are created only by attracting new tourists to the destination or by encouraging others to stay longer or spend more. Some studies count as benefits the expenditures of area residents, but most experts agree that it is a bad practice.

It is also wise to evaluate the potential displacement of economic activity caused by events; for example, spending at and around event venues might cause lowered spending elsewhere. This can only be assessed by surveys of businesses, but with the caution that the perception of managers is not a particularly reliable source.

PRESUMPTION 3

Construction of new facilities for mega-events is a benefit. For mega-events like world's fairs and Olympics, and sometimes smaller special events, new facilities or community infrastructure are required. Proponents of the event might claim these additions as benefits to the community, but they are usually costs. The benefit would exist only if capital for the construction is new money to the area, such as one-time grants from central governments.

Also, once the facilities are built—especially cultural and recreational ones—operating costs must be taken into account. Even if the new facilities are considered to be benefits, the permanent operating costs are borne by the host community. But some of these costs can be discounted if the facilities are able to attract new events and new tourist expenditure in the future.

Murray (1991) also advises that impacts are realized in stages, commencing with planning and bidding, and proceeding through construction, production, and wrap-up stages. Some impacts might not become apparent for years, while others will be extremely difficult to measure.

Where cities host multiple events, some annual and some occasional, cumulative and reinforcing impacts might become indistinguishable from general tourism impacts—in which case the application of traditional economic impact studies to single events might be meaningless.

PRESUMPTION 4

Festivals are for everyone; all visitors are alike. Many event organizers like to believe this, especially if they have a mandate to promote community development and foster leisure or the arts. However, numerous event-visitor surveys have revealed that event customers, and particularly event tourists, are a highly segmented market. This has major implications for event-impact evaluation and related demand-forecasting or feasibility studies. Some events attract more and higher-spending tourists than others, and, as reported for the Adelaide Festival (The Centre for South Australian Economic Studies 1990), event tourists spent more per day than average tourists, even when excluding festival ticket sales. The attraction of high-yield tourists, defined in the context of tourism goals for the area, should take higher priority than mass marketing and complex impact measurements.

A good example is the annual festival in Galveston, Texas, called "Dickens on the Strand." Ralston and Crompton (1988) conducted visitor surveys and found that adults attending without children accounted for 33 percent of visitors but 47 percent of expenditures. Families with children accounted for 22 percent of visitors but only 10 percent of expenditures. This fact was employed by organizers to improve their marketing and to obtain sponsors interested in the high-spending adult market, such as gasoline companies. Of course, there are other reasons for attracting families, so a total preoccupation with tourist yield should be avoided.

PRESUMPTION 5

Events create lots of employment. Another unfortunate consequence of the use of multipliers is the frequent estimate of employment generated by events. The assumption made by using multipliers or other impact models is that so many units of "new" or "incremental" income, created by tourist expenditure, will in turn create employment. Usually this supposed benefit is expressed as full-time job equivalents.

In reality, festivals and special events create few full-time jobs. Successful event organizations typically have small numbers of all-year or part-time staff, and most labor at events is done by volunteers. Economists are very reluctant to assign an economic benefit to the contribution of volunteers (*Sports Economics* No. 2, 1991, p. 2–3) because they create no new income for the area. Under some circumstances, volunteer labor might even be considered a cost, such as a case where people work on events for free instead of taking paid employment.

As to the income generated by tourist expenditure, it will usually be dispersed widely among suppliers, accommodation and dining establishments, retail shops, and so on. It helps sustain jobs, and that is very important, but the assumption that tourist expenditure at small events can create new jobs is largely wishful thinking.

PRESUMPTION 6

All the expenditures of all event-goers can be counted as economic benefits. This can be called the attribution question, or: Of all the money spent by event-goers, how much can be attributed validly to the event as its economic benefit to the area? It is a very complex question to answer, and there is no consensus among experts as to exactly what can be counted as benefits. The major questions to be addressed are: (a) Should expenditure of area residents be counted as benefits, or is it simply money that would otherwise be spent locally on other things? (b) Can tourist expenditure be counted as a benefit if the tourist would have visited the area regardless of the event? (c) Do events have cumulative and intangible impacts?

What Is *Incremental Income?*

To determine how much of the spending at events and on event-related trips can be considered *incremental* (i.e., new money for the area), a number of assumptions are typically made concerning the appropriate portion of resident and tourist expenditure. Some economists argue that only the expenditure of true tourists should be counted, while residents' spending must be ignored; yet frequently, studies include a percentage of resident spending on the assumption that the events acted to retain money that would otherwise be spent elsewhere or generated resident spending over and above normal levels.

In the study of eight festivals in Canada's Capital Region (Coopers and Lybrand 1989), the consultants asked area residents if they spent more than usual during the time of the events they attended, leading them to include a proportion of residents' expenditures. In a study of the Adelaide Festival (The Centre for South Australian Economic Studies 1990), residents attending the festival were asked if they stayed at home, rather than taking a vacation out of the state, because of the event. Researchers in Adelaide concluded that 10.3 percent of resident visitors were "holidaying at home" and 75 percent of those would have otherwise traveled outside the state. They also concluded that another 7,000 residents would have traveled outside South Australia more if it was not for the festival. Accordingly, a proportion of resident expenditures was counted as a benefit for the state.

Researchers who decide to include resident expenditure in the calculation of incremental income should think very carefully about the validity of this practice. First, inclusion of any resident spending is considered to be invalid by most experts (e.g., *Sports Economics*, 3, 1992, p. 2, recommends against it), and this researcher believes all resident expenditure to be merely an internal transfer—like taking in each others' laundry. Opportunity costs can occur because spending at an event likely decreases resident spending elsewhere in the area. It is also difficult to measure, requiring a separate survey or set of questions just for residents, resulting in higher research costs and more complex methods of survey and analysis. Respondents cannot be expected to give reliable answers to such questions as "Did you holiday at home because of the event?" or "Did you spend more than usual because of the festival?" And if it is assumed that residents would have spent equal amounts outside the area if it were not for the event, this has the effect of raising the induced income multiplier by reducing leakages—so if this resident expenditure is counted as new money and a multiplier is then applied that includes this reduced leakage, the residents' expenditure gets double-counted. Most importantly, the object of all such impact evaluation should be visitor oriented. The key questions pertain to the event's ability to attract outsiders and to generate revenue from tourism.

What Are *Social Benefits?*

An event's *social benefits*—its value as a leisure or cultural phenomenon—are legitimate, but that is an entirely different field of inquiry. As an example, Ellis (1990) conducted an evaluation of the Halifax, Nova Scotia, Buskers Festival and concluded that it had a great return on investment for the city because of the large entertainment value generated for residents. Coopers and Lybrand (1989) estimated the "social worth" of festivals by asking respondents about their willingness to pay for free events or to pay more for events having a charge. Burns, Hatch, and Mules (1986) described a technique to estimate the "psychic benefit" of an event by assigning monetary value to estimated costs of noise and disruption that residents were willing to bear. These are all useful methods to be included in cost-benefit evaluation, but they have little to do with event tourism.

Taking Visitor Motivation into Account

Tourists visiting an area because of an event (or any other kind of attraction) typically spend money getting there and back, some of which is within the destination area being studied, as well as at the event itself. It is tempting to consider all tourist expenditure at the event (usually admission fees, tickets to performances, parking, shopping, dining, and drinking) as a benefit to the area—minus, of course, the amounts lost to the area, such as: the costs of all goods and services that were imported; costs of bringing in talent or staff from outside; and organizational and marketing expenditures outside the area. But to do so ignores several issues.

What should be done about the expenditure of a tourist who happened to be in town for a convention and incidentally spent money at a festival? It is quite possible that the tourist would have spent money somewhere else if the event was not occurring, so that all the convention-goer's spending in town should be counted as a benefit of the meeting, not the festival. Attributing the expenditure to both the conference and the event would be double-counting, so some sort of allocation is required. The best way to determine the allocation is by asking all visitors a set of questions about their reasons for visiting the destination and what proportion of their spending in the area—including at the event—was due to the attraction of the event itself.

The types of questions commonly employed to solve the attribution problem are twofold: (1) "What proportion of your trip to this area is attributable to the event?" and (2) "Would you say that this event was the only (or the main, an important, a somewhat important, not at all an important) reason for your trip here?" From the answers, the proportion of tourist expenditure attributed to a given event or attraction can be estimated. In the example of Winterlude in Canada's Capital region (Coopers and Lybrand 1989), respondents were asked to give the proportion of their trip motivated by the festival, leading to an estimate that 75 percent of tourist expenditure could be considered incremental. In contrast, the Festival of Arts attracted only 8 percent of tourists in attendance, and it was deemed to have no incremental benefit at all (partly because residents attending it said they spent less than normal). Because Winterlude was the dominant tourist attraction of all eight festivals studied, it accounted for $40.6 million of the total $61 million in contribution to the region's gross domestic product.

For the Adelaide Festival (The Centre for South Australian Economic Studies 1990) it was estimated that 900 tourists extended their stay because of the festival, and only the portion of their spending that occurred during the extended stay was included as incremental.

There is a certain arbitrariness in these attribution procedures that might best be handled by doing a "sensitivity" analysis. Such an approach was taken in the study of nine festivals in Edinburgh (Scotinform Ltd. 1991), where the consultants used different attribution weightings (e.g., from 79% to 100% of the expenditure of residents and from 10% to 27% of day-tripper expenditure was excluded) before concluding that the results were not affected in a major way.

Time switching (Burns, Hatch, and Mules 1986) is another complication. Some tourists attending events might have simply rescheduled a planned visit to the area, while others might have stayed away because of perceived congestion or expense associated with an event. As well, some residents might actually be tempted to leave town while a major event is held, thereby generating an economic loss for the area. Researchers will find it difficult to take these considerations into account, but, at a minimum, visitors should be asked if their visit to the area would have been made at another time (say, within a 12-month surrounding period) and had merely been rescheduled to take in the event. The expenditure of time-switchers should be deleted completely from calculations of incremental income.

Cumulative and Intangible Effects

It can be argued that because festivals and events enhance the tourist image of an area, there is a "background" economic benefit attributable to events from tourists attracted by this enhanced image. An earlier study of Winterlude (Ekos Research Associates Inc. 1985) found that tourists believed their visit to the event heightened their image of the Capital region. This image-enhancing factor could have long-term, positive effects on tourism, but actual measurement of benefits would be very difficult. Some researchers have asked event-goers if they plan to return to an area or would recommend the event or the area to others.

A related line of questioning would be to assess the value of media coverage, either in qualitative terms or by assigning monetary value to free publicity. Even more subjective is the notion that special events make residents feel proud (confirmed by Burns, Hatch, and Mules 1986, in their study of the Adelaide Grand Prix) and that heightened civic spirit will have tangible benefits for the area.

PRESUMPTION 7

Multipliers and/or econometric models must be used to estimate the secondary impacts of events. Although accurate multiplier analysis can add to the evaluation process, multipliers have been greatly abused in economic-impact assessments, usually by misappropriating multipliers intended for quite different purposes, larger regions, or other areas (Archer 1982; Fleming and Toepper 1990; Murray 1991). Tourism-specific multipliers do not exist, and they are not generally calculated for local areas; so researchers are tempted to apply a general income multiplier for a country or a region without actually measuring the direct and indirect local/regional impacts of incremental spending generated by events. To overcome this problem, some researchers have employed econometric models, as with the Coopers and Lybrand (1989) study, but these also have limitations.

Unfortunately, it appears that the use of multipliers or other models in calculating secondary benefits is often for the purpose of exaggerating the estimate of economic ben-efits. Multipliers are really intended for use in comparing the economic performance of various sectors of the economy (Archer 1982).

Because of the importance of this topic and the confusion surrounding multipliers, the ensuing section provides a detailed examination of the applications and pitfalls researchers will encounter. (For a technical discussion of multipliers and input-output models, see Fletcher and Archer 1991.)

USE AND ABUSES OF MULTIPLIERS

According to Archer (1982), *income multipliers* are coefficients that express the amount of income (i.e., wages, profits, dividends, interest, and rent) generated in an area by an incremental unit of tourist expenditure. Thus, if $100 of new money creates $50 of income (after subtracting leakages and taking into account secondary and induced impact), then the income multiplier is 0.5. In small and undeveloped economies, income multipliers are much lower than in large and developed economies. In fact, small local areas might have insignificant multipliers that are not worth calculating (Hughes 1982).

The *direct income* for the area is that amount of tourist expenditure that remains locally after taxes, profits, and wages are paid outside the area and after imports are purchased (these are called *leakages*). As internal businesses buy and sell with each other in response to the initial expenditures, *indirect income* is generated. Again, much leakage from the area occurs, so this round of spending creates much less income. As employees and their households spend the resultant wages, *induced income* is created. The indirect effects continue through further rounds of business activity in the area, and these are supplemented by further induced income generated by the re-spending of households of money earned either directly or indirectly from tourism. Indirect and induced income are often lumped together and called *secondary local-area income*.

A source of much confusion is the use of different types of multipliers and different ways of expressing them. The multiplier usually used in tourism impact studies is the *income multiplier*, but sometimes a very similar value-added multiplier is used. *Transaction multipliers*, which measure the total change in business sales created by new spending, and *output multipliers*, which measure total productive output (i.e., sales minus changes in business investment), are useful economic planning tools but should not be employed in event impact assessments because they do not measure income for the area.

Income multipliers also come in three basic types (Fletcher and Archer 1991). Some economists prefer to include only direct and indirect income generated by initial tourist expenditure, while others include changing consumer-consumption patterns as income levels in the area rise. The most common type (which Frechtling has said is the most useful) includes direct, indirect, and induced income.

Sectors of the economy have different multipliers, which is why detailed input-output tables are used to calculate income multipliers. In their study of the Adelaide Grand Prix (Burns, Hatch, and Mules 1986), the researchers employed different multipliers for the various types of income: food and beverages; accommodation; entertainment; transport; personal services; and "other." An aggregate multiplier was then calculated from these individual multipliers, yielding a more reliable estimate of secondary income.

Employment multipliers are also commonly cited in tourism studies and can be expressed as the number of jobs created per unit of tourist expenditure (e.g., 1 job created for every $100,000) or as the ratio of total jobs created by incremental tourist spending to the jobs created directly in the tourism sector. Tourist expenditure in commercial accommodation creates many service-sector jobs, but day-trippers and tourists staying with friends and relatives have a much lesser impact. In general, events create few permanent jobs, and a local economy is probably able to absorb event-related income without new job creation. Therefore, it is potentially misleading to apply employment multipliers to event-related incremental expenditures.

EXAMPLES OF MULTIPLIERS

Archer (1982) cited a number of income multipliers from various studies: for small island countries, they ranged from 0.58 to 1.30; for counties and states in the United States, they were 0.88 to 1.30; for counties in the United States, they ranged from 0.39 to 1.30. Small town, county, and regional tourism income multipliers in Great Britain ranged from 0.18 to 0.47. These examples show clearly that the size of the area is an important factor in shaping the multiplier. The same applies for underdeveloped economies—a great deal of leakage occurs owing to imports and other outbound monetary flows.

Vaughan (1979) studied the Edinburgh Festival in Scotland and worked out income multipliers for different types of visitor. He calculated that each pound sterling of tourist spending yielded 29 pence of local income. In other words, the aggregated multiplier was 0.29. But spending by Scottish visitors resulted in a higher multiplier (0.32), owing to different spending patterns. Overseas tourists generated more expenditure per day, even though the resultant multiplier was slightly less, owing to greater use of commercial accommodation. More recent research concerning the impact of nine festivals in Edinburgh (Scotinform Ltd. 1991) borrowed a multiplier from a study of the impact of arts in Glasgow. The income multiplier (0.2087) was applied to the estimate of direct, incremental expenditures, yielding an estimate of 9.154 million pounds of local/regional income derived from approximately 43.864 million pounds of expenditure. This study also concluded that the Edinburgh festivals created significant income for Scotland as a whole by attracting tourists who also visited other areas. About 40 percent of the total impact of the festivals was judged to occur outside the Edinburgh region.

Hatten (1987) applied a "value-added" multiplier of 1.215 for off-site spending and one of 0.882 for on-site spending at Vancouver's Expo '86. It was assumed that 10 percent of the spending by Vancouver residents and 50 percent of the spending by other residents of British Columbia was incremental to the provincial economy, compared to 100 percent of the spending of out-of-province visitors. These multipliers were derived from an input-output model for the provincial economy that measures all the linkages and leakages that relate to each sector of the economy. Why should the multiplier be higher for off-site tourist spending? It depends a lot on the event, and, in the case of Expo '86, the on-site consumption of souvenirs, food, and other services resulted in a lot of leakage to U.S. companies.

OTHER LIMITATIONS OF THE MULTIPLIER

Using multipliers to estimate secondary impacts of incremental spending requires several assumptions about how much of the expenditure actually enters the local economy (as opposed to instant leakage) and the capacity of the economy to use the income for increased output. Multipliers are of no value in estimating long-term impacts (Archer 1982). To overcome this problem, consultants for the study of eight festivals in Canada's Capital Region (Coopers and Lybrand 1989) employed an econometric model that took into account the actual capacity of the regional economy to absorb related expenditures and converted them into indirect and induced income, tax revenue, and employment over a five-year period.

The way in which multipliers have been used suggests that all impacts are benefits to the economy, when in fact there might be hidden opportunity costs; that is, increased output in one sector might be at the expense of output in another. Tourism can generate opportunity costs by diverting economic activity from primary and secondary industries to the service sector. There is also a tendency to use the multiplier to demonstrate only macroeconomic benefits without consideration of economic costs and without evaluation of intangibles and noneconomic items. That makes the multiplier a tool for generating misleading conclusions.

Reliable studies have demonstrated that the economic benefits of events are predominantly the direct result of incremental tourist expenditure (i.e., new money for the area), not secondary effects stemming from the respending of this money and resultant creation of new income and jobs. A major study of eight festivals in Canada's Capital Region (Coopers and Lybrand 1989) concluded that only 10 percent of regional income benefits were "secondary" in nature, with 90 percent created by direct tourist expenditure. This occurs because event tourism leads to spending on services that have few backward linkages in the economy. The low level of secondary impacts was also due to the fact that the economy was in recession and additional tourist spending would not necessarily lead to new jobs.

It is rather pointless to use elaborate multipliers or econometric models to estimate scant secondary benefits, especially when doing so requires many assumptions and raises questions of validity. However, when not using a multiplier, it must be stressed that total incremental expenditure is not all economic benefit to the area.

EMPLOYING KNOWLEDGE OF MULTIPLIERS IN TOURISM PLANNING

Knowledge of the multiplier effect is most important in the planning stage of event tourism because it can be applied to increasing local economic linkages and decreasing leakages. Events should buy local, use local employees, and foster consumption and promotion of local goods and services. Marketing events to high-yield tourists—those who travel specifically for events or who stay longer and spend more—has a similar positive impact.

RECOMMENDED IMPACT EVALUATION PROCESS

Based on the foregoing discussion, a step-by-step process of impact evaluation for event tourism is provided below. In each step, a number of rules and recommendations are included. Rules must be followed if reliability and validity mistakes are to be avoided. Recommendations reflect this author's preference.

Step 1: Formulate Precise Research Goals

Care in formulating rescarch goals will help in avoiding many of the problems and pitfalls discussed in the preceding section. The researcher or manager must first decide what is of principal interest: for example, knowing that the event attracted a high proportion of out-of-region tourists is extremely important to most event organizers, but estimating regional income and employment benefits is likely to be of interest mainly to tourism agencies.

Rules

- Define the study area within which costs and benefits are to be calculated.
- Delimit the scope of the evaluation (which costs and benefits to measure; quantitative and qualitative evaluation techniques to be used).
- Define tourists and residents.
- Set criteria for attribution of incremental expenditure (i.e., should resident spending be included?).
- Formulate precise research and evaluation questions.

Recommendations

- A great deal of trouble and expense can be saved by avoiding multipliers and other models and by keeping the whole evaluation process as simple as possible.
- Aim the research at determining the number and types of tourists attracted to the area, with emphasis on high yield; if necessary, and a reliable methodology is available, estimate incremental expenditure.
- Exclude the spending of area residents.

Step 2: Determine Data Needs and Appropriate Methods

Rules

- Specify types of data needed to answer the research questions.
- Determine the measures needed and the appropriate methods to collect and analyze the data.

Recommendations

- Keep it simple!

Step 3: Determine Attendance at the Event— Calculate Total Number of Tourists and Tourist-Visits

The most basic piece of information needed is attendance at events; the measures can be of visitors, visitor parties, total gate, or number of visitations. Total attendance can be calculated by adding attendance at individual sites and attractions, but this is not the same as total person-visits.

The turnover rate (i.e., how long people stay) and peak attendance (the maximum number at the event at one point in time) might have to be calculated to get an estimate at events lacking gates or other controls on entrance and egress. Methods used to obtain these measures include gate counts, crowd estimates, vehicle counts, and random household surveys within target market areas (see Getz 1991a for a fuller discussion). No method of estimating event attendance is 100 percent reliable unless there is complete control of entrances and exits, and even then a visitor survey will be needed to determine the extent of multiple visits.

Rules

- Whenever possible, use controlled access and/or ticket sales to estimate attendance.
- For open events, use a systematic observation method that avoids double-counting by applying weightings derived from visitor surveys (asking: How many visits have you made, on how many days?).
- Take into account the difference between total number of visitors and total person-visits and between tourist and resident visits (feasible only if a visitor survey is undertaken).

Recommendations

- Avoid gross estimates based on casual observation (e.g., police guesses).
- Do not include estimates of mass audiences, such as parades and free fireworks displays, as these will be dominated by locals.

Step 4: Conduct Visitor Surveys

Because of the uniqueness of special events, there is generally no viable substitute for visitor surveys. Surveys are required to determine the proportion and number of tourists and their trip motivations, activity, and spending patterns. Separate surveys of performers, competitors, officials, and visiting suppliers or merchants might also be required. Additional information pertinent to marketing and program development are usually added. For a useful discussion of pertinent survey methodology, see Alreck and Settle (1985).

On-site surveys are most common, but alternatives exist. If the primary market area is known from previous visitor surveys, or can be assumed, a post-event random household survey, most easily undertaken by telephone, can be used to estimate total attendance, tourist volumes, and spending. Respondents must be asked who in the household attended what events, when, and how many times. The problems are twofold: (1) Long-distance tourists might be ignored and will have to be estimated by some other means—namely an on-site visitor survey that can determine the proportion of customers drawn from different market areas. (2) Telephone-based sample frames might contain errors because of unlisted numbers and households that have no phones.

Data could be taken from regional exit or travel surveys, but these seldom ask questions specific enough to assist in event impact evaluation. One possible use of general tourist surveys is the estimation of expenditures by typical visitors to the subject area. However, it is unwise to assume that event tourists are the same as others—most studies of events have revealed that they differ in a number of ways, including demographics, length of stay, and expenditure levels. Also, long-distance tourists are likely to be different from day-trippers.

Choosing the sample frame is a crucial decision, and, once it is determined, the survey staff must faithfully adhere to it. Volunteers must be trained, and all participants in the visitor survey must have the right attitude if bias is to be avoided. In a *turnstile sample*, every nth person (say, 1 of every 10 or 100) through the gate can be given a questionnaire or interviewed. This guarantees absolute randomness of individuals, but not necessarily of groups (see Latham 1991), and care must be taken to avoid coverage of the same person twice if people are allowed to leave and return. It must also be decided if only adults are to be covered or if one member of each family or party is to be covered. It is possible to estimate statistical levels of confidence for the sample only if it is known what proportion of the total attendance was sampled, and then only if there was no response bias (such as only certain types of people completing the forms).

Because of the nonresponse problem, interviews are often preferred. The interviewer can determine what types of people refuse to participate and can generally get a higher response rate than from impersonal questionnaires. However, interviews are restricted by the number of available interviewers, and, at peak times, the turnstile-interview sample might break down due to the sheer volume of arrivals.

An alternative to the turnstile method is to intercept visitors as they move about an open site or where they congregate on the site. Wherever people line up, surveyors have a good chance to systematically select every nth person. It is important to avoid arbitrary selection of respondents or a selection bias can occur (i.e., there might be a natural tendency to approach people of a certain type). Line-ups are particularly good because the people are waiting anyway and might not mind filling out a form. The alternative is to select every nth person past a given point, such as the entrance to a building or area.

The big problem is to ensure that the whole site and all activities are covered over the duration of the whole event. Keep in mind that the composition of the crowd will vary over time and over the site, depending on the attraction, services, and accessibility. To overcome this problem requires the following:

- Time sampling: instruct interviewers to conduct the survey during specified times throughout the event.
- Spatial sampling: ensure that surveyors are assigned specific sectors that cover the whole site.

Because these on-site intercept methods do not ensure a truly random sample but do apply strict selection criteria, they are called *systematic*. In terms of reliability, they are not as good as random samples but can potentially be better than quota samples.

Some evaluators, given the daunting problems of obtaining a random or systematic sample, might choose a quota sample instead. If 200 respondents are desired, interviewers can be told to collect 10 or 20 each, subject to getting a balance between the genders, along with an age spread. Other characteristics such as race or ethnicity might be important to specific events and can be incorporated in the quotas.

While this is a simple and useful approach, there is no basis for estimating the characteristics of the whole crowd from a quota sample. And there is no guarantee that a large number of respondents is more representative than a small one if a flawed sampling design is employed (Fleming and Toepper 1990).

Of course, none of the nonrandom methods can be used for estimating the characteristics of the whole crowd, at least according to strict statistical practices. The evaluator must try to get the most representative sample possible, then qualify the final estimates by noting the limitations of the sample and resulting response bias.

An example reveals some of the complications and possible approaches. For the Adelaide Festival (The Centre for South Australian Economic Studies 1990), two separate self-completion questionnaires were distributed to visitors and residents as audiences entered a sample of venues with stratification by type of performance, time of day, and day of week (results were weighted to reflect actual distributions based on ticket sales). Mail or drop-off returns were possible, with an incentive offered. The researchers assumed a 30 percent response rate (they obtained about 40 percent in both samples), then estimated that 2,000 questionnaires for each of the visitor and resident samples had to be distributed in order to obtain at least 600 responses, thereby allowing for a 5 percent standard error when statistically analyzing the data. Another complication was their assumption that 10 percent of the audience would be visitors, but they had to revise this to 20 percent.

Rules

- An on-site visitor survey is necessary for estimating the number and proportion of tourists at events, their motivations, spending patterns, and whether or not visits were extended or expenditures increased due to the event.
- Ensure that a systematic sample of individuals is taken.
- Include performers, officials, competitors, and so on.
- Stratify the sample by applicable factors such as venue, time, and day; use weightings to reflect the true distribution of attendance.
- Guard against sampling bias caused by length of stay and multiple-site visits by ensuring that individuals are not mistakenly counted twice; make estimates of average length of stay and number of visits, and weight the results to reduce the effect of length-of-stay bias.
- Use past experience or educated guesses to derive a sample size that will yield high confidence limits for statistical analysis, especially ensuring a large enough sample of tourists.

Recommendations

- Try to apply the principles of triangulation by employing more than one measure and method (e.g., combine visitor surveys with direct observation and selected interviews).
- Avoid recall bias by conducting surveys on-site or by combining on-site with take-home surveys.
- Offer incentives to obtain higher response rates.

Step 5: Estimate Total Expenditure by Tourists

Frechtling (Chapters 31 to 33) mentions eight different ways to make estimates of tourist expenditure, most of which are not applicable to events. Direct observation could be used at event sites, such as recording sales, admissions, and service fees, but this tells nothing of off-site expenditure. Post-event household surveys could measure event-related expenditure, but only in sampled market areas and with the added problem of recall bias. Whatever technique is used, the researchers must pay particular attention to the business traveler, who might not know all related trip expenses, and to the package tourist, who might not be able to assign the accurate portion of trip expenses to the study area. For these special cases, a number of additional questions are needed, or special subsamples will have to be taken to probe more deeply.

Regardless of the survey technique or sample frame, recall bias is a major problem. A number of studies have demonstrated that tourists often underestimate their expenditures, especially after some time has passed (Sheldon 1990; Howard, Lankford, and Havitz 1991). Consequently, on-site and exit surveys are likely to yield the best estimates of daily expenditure, and measurement of expenditure for the entire trip is best taken immediately upon completion of the visit. A combination of on-site interviews and self-completed, take-home questionnaires can also be used to good effect (Ralston and Crompton 1988).

For the purposes of estimating tourist expenditure, an average amount per tourist-visit can be calculated, and then multiplied by an estimate of total tourist-visits; or an average amount per tourist can be estimated and multiplied by the estimated number of tourists. In the case of a study of the Barossa Wine Festival (Tourism South Australia 1991), respondents were asked to itemize their spending on the day of the interviews only. Daily expenditure was divided by the number of adults covered in the sample, then multiplied by the total number of planned visitor-days. This yielded an estimate of visitor spending per adult.

Sports Economics (2, 1992:4) warns of the problems of using mean versus median tourist expenditure visits. If the sample is random and sufficiently large, there is no worry; but in inadequate samples, a few large outliers will distort the estimate of total incremental expenditure. Use of medians will result in bias, but lower statistical error. If the large outliers are a characteristic of the population as a whole, as well as the sample, use of the mean is proper. Otherwise, the median should be used to enumerate from the sample, but with outlier values added separately.

A special problem occurs when more than one event occurs simultaneously, as in the case of Edinburgh's festival season every August. The researchers (Scotinform Ltd. 1991) found that many tourists and residents went to several events during their stay, giving rise to a serious risk of double-counting. To overcome this problem, they invented a separate category for the "multiple event visitor" and avoided attribution of their expenditures to specific events. One interesting result was the conclusion that the Tattoo generated the most income for the area (45% of incremental expenditure) because it attracted more tourists who spent more and tended to visit no other event.

Normal expenditure categories are: food and beverage; recreation and entertainment; travel; accommodation; retail shopping; and admission fees. These should be disaggregated geographically (i.e., on-site; off-site within area; outside the subject area) and possibly by time (before, during, and after the event). If sector-specific multipliers are going to be applied, the expenditure categories must match the definitions of each sector.

Rules

- Determine average spending per visitor-day, separating on-site from off-site and within the study area from outside the study area (if total trip expenditure is estimated, the on-site, within-area amounts must be distinguished).
- Include spending by performers, officials, and so on, but also account for wages, profits, and so on, that they remove from the area.
- Avoid double-counting when events overlap; create a multiple-event category of visitor.

- In small, nonrandom samples, avoid using expenditure means if large outliers occur.
- Use expenditure categories that match available classes of multiplier.
- Take into account the special estimation problems associated with package tours (knowing what portion to allocate to the area) and business or related trips (the traveler might not have paid).
- Minimize recall bias by conducting surveys on-site or as soon after the event as possible.

Recommendations

- Use a combination of on-site exit interviews, diaries, and take-home questionnaires to get reliable estimates of expenditure per day and for the whole trip.

Step 6: Estimate Expenditure Attributable to Tourists

From questions on trip motivation, timing, and spending, an estimate can be made of new or incremental income derived from tourists. Only the spending of tourists who traveled because of the event and who would not have visited the region otherwise can be counted totally. The spending of time-switchers has to be discounted or eliminated, as does that of multiple-purpose travelers. For those staying longer or spending more because of the event, a portion of their expenditure can be included.

Rules

- Determine the importance of the event in motivating the trip, an extended stay, or increased spending.
- Subtract time-switchers, who would have visited the area anyway (say, during the same year).
- Do not confuse total incremental expenditure with economic impact.

Recommendations

- Ask several motivational questions to obtain a valid measure of the importance of the event.
- Do not include the expenditure of residents.
- Use a sensitivity analysis to see if different weights significantly affect the estimate of incremental expenditure.

Step 7: Calculate Net Income and Macroeconomic Impacts

Rules

- Gross visitor expenditure attributed to the event (i.e., the incremental income) does not equal net income for the area, because of leakage.
- Apply a value-added or income multiplier WITH CAUTION to account for all the direct and secondary effects of incremental expenditure.

- An econometric model can be used instead of multipliers to account for macro impacts over time.
- Government revenue, in the form of taxes at all levels, is usually taken into account when value-added multipliers are applied; otherwise it must be estimated separately.

Recommendations

- Yield should be emphasized, rather than macro impacts, by examining the number of tourists attracted and their spending patterns.

Step 8: Do a Cost-Benefit Evaluation

Cost-benefit analysis has the added advantage of being able to draw conclusions about the net benefit of the event after costs have been subtracted and of incorporating intangibles and noneconomic measures. It can be used in post-event evaluations or in feasibility studies to help determine the overall worthiness of a proposal. Full-scale cost-benefit studies can be time-consuming and expensive (which is one reason why multipliers are popular), but simplified evaluations can be done that still have the advantage of going beyond economic benefit estimates.

It is not a method without difficulties. Several general problems always arise:

- How to measure or compare tangibles, such as revenue, with intangibles such as psychological benefits?
- How to subtract intangible costs from tangible benefits?
- Determining the parameters of the calculations: What area to cover? What time period? Measure benefits and costs for the whole community or just the public sector?

Primary benefits include: receipts and profits; wages and salaries; employment; and taxes and other government revenue. Secondary benefits are the indirect and induced levels of income, profit, taxes, and investment stimulated by primary income. Costs must be allocated among public and private sectors and among fiscal and life-quality categories; they may be direct or induced (see the Frechtling chapters, Chapters 31 to 33, for details).

The Adelaide Grand Prix researchers (Burns, Hatch, and Mules 1986) had to wrestle with the very definition of *costs* as applicable to an event like the Grand Prix, and they decided to take the perspective of the state of South Australia. Typical of many mega-events, different levels of government were involved. Grants from the Commonwealth of Australia were counted as benefits to the state, as they brought new revenue made available only because of the event; but grants by the state to the event were counted as costs, because that money could have been used for other State purposes (i.e., it had an "opportunity cost" stemming from the opportunities foregone in order to assist the event). If the city of Adelaide had been the area for which the cost-benefit evaluation was undertaken, then State grants might have been considered benefits—if they were not simply diverted from some other payments to the city.

The Grand Prix costs were of the following types:

- Grants from within the state that could have been used for other purposes
- Construction and demolition expenditure (minus applicable grants)
- Amounts written off as depreciation
- Planning, marketing, and operating costs (minus applicable grants)
- Cost of borrowing (interest payments)
- Externalities: costs to other government agencies (police, fire, health, transport, waste disposal, etc.) that can be attributed to the event as being above and beyond the norm; costs of damage to private property caused by the event; economic losses to businesses adversely impacted by the event

One could also include the costs of crime associated with events, inflationary costs to housing, property, food, and so on if caused by the event and related development.

Benefits of the Grand Prix attributed to the State of South Australia included:

- Grants received from outside the area to construction or event operations
- Private investment attracted by the event (most events by themselves lack the ability to attract new hotels, etc., but might have the effect of accelerating developments; any development boom might also result in a subsequent glut with weaker businesses experiencing actual losses)
- Tourist expenditure attributable to the event (the value-added multipliers were used to estimate total impact on the state).

Value-added multipliers (similar to income multipliers) were derived from state input-output tables for various industry sectors. These ranged from 1.109 for expenditures in the food sector to 1.212 for transport, with a weighted average for all sectors of 1.192. This approach is more accurate than using a gross regional or national multiplier. The calculations were: 9.6 million dollars of visitor expenditure, minus 1.3 million dollars attributed to time-switchers, generated a net incremental expenditure of 8.3 million; this was multiplied by the aggregate value-added multiplier of 1.192, yielding an estimate of 9.8 million of income for the state. An upper and lower benefit-to-cost ratio was calculated, with the range being 3.1:1 to 3.8:1—a healthy return for the state's investment.

INTANGIBLE COSTS AND BENEFITS

Several intangible costs were dealt with in the Australian Grand Prix research. Traffic congestion and parking problems experienced by the general population were serious at times. A household survey of residents attempted to measure time lost by residents, and a monetary value was given to this time. Noise disturbances from the races were actually measured (in decibels), and the household surveys determined the degree of public inconvenience caused by noise in several zones around the racecourse. The public was also asked to measure its level of inconvenience arising from crowding.

A disturbing intangible cost of the races was an increase in motor accidents.

Giving surrogate monetary value to the intangible costs is useful but fraught with problems. It is also hard to argue that intangible costs are sufficient to neutralize the economic benefits. This line of cost-benefit assessment can only be done in a political forum where values are explicitly stated and weighted; for example, whether a motor-race can be justified if it leads to riots, crime, accidents, or deaths.

A major intangible benefit was also considered in the case of the Australian Grand Prix. Surveys revealed a very high level of support for the event, stemming from the excitement, entertainment value, and pride the races generated for Adelaide residents. The researchers called this a psychic benefit and tried to measure its value in monetary terms. The calculations were based on the fact that even those people who complained of noise or traffic delays were strongly in favor of the Grand Prix—as much in favor as the population as a whole. From this fact, an hypothesis was formulated: that the monetary value of the psychic benefit was at least equal to the estimated monetary costs of noise and traffic congestion.

THE DISTRIBUTION OF COSTS AND BENEFITS

The question of WHO benefits and WHO pays the costs is often more important than determining and measuring the actual costs and benefits. It is partially an issue of scale, as tourism is often promoted by senior levels of government and by the industry, with local governments and communities picking up many of the costs. And it is an issue of values, as in the case where the severity of some costs is seen to outweigh anticipated benefits. Unfortunately, these distributional questions are often not asked in impact assessments or in feasibility studies that forecast the costs and benefits of a proposal.

Regarding festivals and events, some of the key distributional issues have already been listed in the earlier discussion of the multiplier concept. There, it was argued that the multiplier is a planning tool to be used to help maximize benefits to the host community. By tracing the linkages and leakages that determine the multiplier, the evaluator can learn where the costs and benefits lie and then take measures to correct problems or realize opportunities. The goal should be to modify the event or its organization to achieve widespread benefits for the community and to minimize costs and disruptions.

Externalities are the most difficult problem. Is it justifiable for event organizers to attain their goals/profits at the expense of property damage, noise, traffic congestion, or other disruptions to uninvolved residents? And can ecological damage or pollution be accepted? What about changes in the social fabric of a community as a result of annual exposure to large influxes of tourists? The tourism industry gains, but the community is forced or encouraged to change. These are not easy issues to resolve, but they should be considered and debated.

Rules

- Define costs and benefits to be measured and what quantitative and qualitative measures will be applied.
- Determine the level (local, regional, national) at which costs and benefits will be evaluated, and the time-frame.
- Include externalities, intangibles, and distributional issues; consider displacement effects; evaluate cumulative, long-term effects.
- Calculate the benefit-to-cost ratio in economic terms, while evaluating the net worth of the event in qualitative terms.

Recommendations

- A good evaluation will require a team of experts, rigorous research, and a good budget; at a minimum, balance any estimate of economic benefits with reliable data on capital and operating costs, and a discussion of intangibles.
- Incorporate public input, such as attitude surveys.
- Cover the business community and public sector.
- In most cases it is not worthwhile to estimate indirect employment benefits.

CONCLUSION

In this chapter, many of the issues surrounding event-impact assessment have been addressed, including some of the presumptions that are made, problems and pitfalls encountered, and basic methodological challenges. A process has been recommended for undertaking event-impact evaluations, with the emphasis on determining tourism yield and cost-benefit evaluation.

Given the reliability and validity problems associated with the use of multipliers or other models in estimating macroeconomic benefits, it is strongly recommended that they not be used. The most important questions are not addressed by such estimates, and they are often abused. As the field of event tourism matures, officials and researchers will become less and less interested in the so-called macroeconomic impacts and more concerned about factors influencing tourist attractiveness, ways to encourage higher yield tourists (i.e., those who travel for events and spend a lot in the destination), the balance between costs and benefits, and the distribution of impacts.

REFERENCES

Alreck, Pamela L., and Robert B. Settle (1985), *The Survey Research Handbook*, Homewood, IL: Richard D. Irwin, Inc.

Archer, B. (1982), "The Value of Multipliers and Their Policy Implications," *Tourism Management* 3(4): 236–241.

Burns, J., J. Hatch, and T. Mules, eds. (1986), *The Adelaide Grand Prix: The Impact of a Special Event*, Adelaide: Centre for South Australian Economic Studies.

Centre for South Australian Economic Studies, The (1990), *The 1990 Adelaide Festival: The Economic Impact* (Vol. 1: Summary; Vol. 2: Methodology and Results: Details), Adelaide.

Coopers and Lybrand Consulting Group (1989), *NCR 1988 Festivals Study*, Final Report, for the Ottawa-Carleton Board of Trade.

Ekos Research Associates Inc. (1985), Ekos Report on Winterlude for the National Capital Commission, Ottawa.

Ellis, J. (1990), The Application of Cost-benefit Analysis: The 1987 Busker Festival—A Case Study, Master's Thesis in Development Economics, Dalhousie University, Halifax.

Fleming, W., and Toepper, L. (1990), "Economic Impact Studies: Relating the Positive and Negative Impacts to Tourism Development," *Journal of Travel Research* 29(1): 35–42.

Fletcher, J., and B. Archer (1991), "The Development and Application of Multiplier Analysis" in *Progress in Tourism, Recreation and Hospitality Management*, Vol. 3, 28–47, C. Cooper, ed., University of Surrey and London: Belhaven Press.

Getz, Donald (1991a), *Festivals, Special Events, and Tourism*, New York: Van Nostrand Reinhold.

Getz, Donald (1991b), "Assessing the Economic Impacts of Festivals and Events: Research Issues," *Journal of Applied Recreation Research* 16(1): 61–77.

Hatten, A. (1987), *The Economic Impact of Expo '86*, Victoria: British Columbia Tourism and Provincial Secretary.

Howard, D., S. Lankford, and M. Havitz (1991), "A Method for Authenticating Pleasure Travel Expenditures," *Journal of Travel Research* 29(4): 19–23.

Hughes, G. (1982), "The Employment and Economic Effects of Tourism Reappraised," *Tourism Management* 3(3): 167–176.

Latham, J. (1991), "Bias Due to Group Size in Visitor Surveys," *Journal of Travel Research* 29(4): 32–35.

Murray, J. (1991), "Applied Tourism Economic Impact Analysis: Pitfalls and Practicalities," in *Building Credibility for a Credible Industry*, 19–31, proceedings of the TTRA 23rd annual conference, Long Beach, CA.

Ralston, L., and J. Crompton (1988), Motivations, Service Quality and Economic Impact of Visitors to the 1987 Dickens on the Strand Emerging From a Mail-Back Survey, for the Galveston Historical Society.

Ralston, L., J. Hamilton, and J. Awang (1991), "A Methodological Perspective of Multiple Festival Research Studies," presented to the Leisure Research Symposium, National Parks and Recreation Association.

Ritchie, B., and B. Smith (1991), "The Impact of a Mega-event on Host Region Awareness: A Longitudinal Study," *Journal of Travel Research* 30(1): 3–10.

Scotinform Ltd. (1991), *Edinburgh Festivals Study 1990–91: Visitor Survey and Economic Impact Assessment*, Final Report, Edinburgh: Scottish Tourist Board.

Sheldon, P. (1990), "A Review of Tourism Expenditure Research," in *Progress in Tourism, Recreation and Hospitality Management*, Vol. 2, C. Cooper, ed., University of Surrey and London: Belhaven Press.

South Australian Department of Tourism (1986), *Report on a Survey of Visitors to the 1985 Australian Formula 1 Grand Prix*, Adelaide.

Sports Economics, published by The Centre For South Australian Economic Studies, Adelaide.

Tourism South Australia (1991), *Barossa Valley Vintage Festival Visitor Survey*, April 1991, Research Report, Adelaide.

Vaughan, R. (1979), *Does A Festival Pay? A Case Study of the Edinburgh Festival in 1976*, Working Paper No. 5, Tourism Recreation Research Unit, University of Edinburgh.

Part Seven

DATA COLLECTION METHODS OF PARTICULAR RELEVANCE

Part Seven of the Handbook contains a total of eight chapters dealing with data collection methods that have achieved particular prominence or are considered especially useful in the field of travel and tourism. The first of these, "En Route Surveys," Chapter 38, has been authored by Fred Hurst. As those in the travel industry are aware, the en route survey provides a data collection context that is unique. Starting from this perspective, Mr. Hurst first examines the characteristics of en route surveys as compared with other data collection approaches. He subsequently provides an overview of the methodology underlying the en route survey and the characteristics of common users. Recognizing that there is a bewildering array of possible en route survey methods, Mr. Hurst then examines some of the methodological difficulties likely to be encountered in executing en route surveys and provides guidelines for dealing with these difficulties. His discussion of "sleuthing for bias" provides particularly helpful examples of the kinds of errors that can creep into research data in this area unless great care is taken to understand such data thoroughly. The chapter concludes with a very detailed example of an application of the en route survey method. Individuals who are interested in developing their own en route surveys will find the details provided by Mr. Hurst in this example to be extremely useful.

Chapter 39 deals with a methodology that, while not developed for or unique to tourism, has proven to be particularly relevant to the field. As a result, it has received fairly widespread application and is likely to continue to be a basic methodological approach for tourism planners. The methodology in question is the Delphi technique, an approach that attempts to provide planners with forecasts of probable states of the future. The Handbook chapter describing the Delphi technique has been authored by George Moeller and Ed Shafer. The chapter first reviews the value of attempting to forecast the future and identifies some of the difficulties associated with attempting to do so. Following these introductory remarks, the authors review other forecasting techniques that have been used to predict the future prior to their discussion of the Delphi technique itself. In this discussion, the authors provide a description of the Delphi technique as well as a critical review of its strengths and weaknesses. The latter part of the chapter provides a specific example of an application of Delphi in the area of recreation planning. Again, it is expected that readers will find this example extremely helpful should they actually be required to undertake a Delphi study.

In Chapter 40, Wilbur LaPage examines another research methodology that has been developed outside the field of tourism but that has been found to be particularly relevant for the collection of certain kinds of data—the use of panels for travel and tourism research and their particular value for trend monitoring, test marketing, impact assessment, and future assessment. The author then discusses the relative advantages and disadvantages of this approach as compared with other methods that might be employed. The chapter concludes by providing guidelines for prospective panel developers concerning the factors that need to be considered in the design and maintenance of such a panel.

The fourth chapter in this section of the Handbook continues with the theme of adapting general research approaches to travel and tourism. In this chapter, Karen Peterson reviews the use of qualitative research methods as an aid to understanding consumer behavior in the field. Ms. Peterson first examines the general characteristics of qualitative research and the particular research situations for which it is best suited. In doing so, she takes care to provide readers with an understanding of the limitations of the method. The remainder of the chapter provides a brief overview of the variations that exist in qualitative research methods and then discusses in some depth the steps that researchers can take to enhance the quality of this kind of research.

Chapter 42 introduces readers to a research technique that has been widely utilized in the fields of planning and consumer behavior but that has received relatively little attention in tourism until recently. Authored by Brent Ritchie, this chapter describes the nominal group technique (NGT) with an emphasis upon its role as a tool for assisting in policy formulation. The chapter first describes NGT as it is normally employed. This general discussion is followed by an example describing the manner in which the method was applied in one case of consensus planning. This example includes an examination of some of the data analysis issues that are peculiar to this type of research. Subsequently, a discussion is presented concerning the potential applications of NGT in other areas of tourism and research planning. The chapter concludes with an assessment of the relative strengths and weaknesses of NGT compared to other commonly used planning/research approaches.

Chapter 43 continues the transition from qualitative to quantitative research techniques that started in the previous chapter on NGT. In this chapter, James Rovelstad examines the use of model building and simulation as research tools for assisting managers and government officials in analyzing and understanding their markets, the travel consumer, and the facilities and resources for which they are responsible. As Dr. Rovelstad points out, both qualitative and quantitative models are available to assist such individuals. It is from this perspective that the author reviews the scope, nature, and range of uses of models in the field of tourism. The chapter starts out by examining the nature of modeling itself and discussing the different types of models that can be employed. These include physical and economic impact models, input-output models, and behavioral models. The chapter next provides two examples designed to provide a more substantive understanding of the applications and benefits related to modeling in tourism. The chapter concludes with a brief discussion of the relationship between models and the process of management.

The next chapter in Part Seven again describes how a general research technique developed in other fields has been adapted to tourism. In this case, however, the technique described, namely conjoint measurement, is highly quantitative in nature. Chapter 44, which has been authored by John Claxton, presents conjoint measurement as a technique for assessing the trade-offs that travelers make when choosing among alternative destinations, travel modes, accommodation, and so on. After positioning conjoint measurement as a tool that can help researchers understand consumer trade-offs, Dr. Claxton describes in some detail the specific nature of conjoint measurement by use of an example drawn from the field of transportation. He also summarizes a number of other examples where conjoint measurement has been applied to enhance understanding of travel-related behavior. The chapter concludes by providing managers with a general appreciation of the major issues involved in the use of conjoint measurement as a research approach as well as an understanding of the manager's role when employing the technique.

The concluding chapter reviews yet another methodology that is now well established in the general marketing research literature but that has not been used as extensively in the field of tourism. In Chapter 45, Fenton and Pearce first describe the origins and nature of multidimensional scaling (MDS). They then discuss the characteristics of the measures that are required for its use. In this discussion, a clear distinction is drawn between the nature of direct and indirect measures of proximity that serve as the basis of input for subsequent analysis. The following section provides the reader with an overview as to how MDS actually works using different variations of the basic model. In the final section of the chapter, the authors review a number of applications of MDS in the field of tourism. These examples involve studies of Mediterranean destinations, highways in Australia, and perceptions of Finland as a tourist destination. They also discuss briefly how current descriptive uses of MDS might be extended to include more formal hypothesis testing.

38

En Route Surveys

FRED HURST
Port Authority of New York & New Jersey
New York, New York

*T*his chapter reviews the growing use of en route survey methods, who uses them, and why. Key factors to consider in the design and implementation of en route surveys are described. The significance of control over the sample selection procedures is described insofar as it relates to the quality of the survey product. Additionally, some guidance is offered in assessing the value of en route survey research to the travel manager, particularly with regard to the three most important parameters of any survey plan: cost per interview, sampling error, and control. The interrelationships among these values reveal that low cost per interview does not necessarily represent the best value to a travel manager; on the contrary, it is sometimes a symptom of poor quality.

INTRODUCTION

Travel industry managers must have timely information about their changing travel markets in order not to be left behind by their rapidly growing industry. Some of this information is obtained from:

1. Financial reports: reflecting the health of the industry, such as annual reports from airlines, hotel chains, and railroads
2. Traffic reports: such as vehicle and passenger counts
3. Economic indicators: past, present, and forecast
4. Population surveys: household and telephone surveys of people in their homes
5. En route surveys: surveys of travelers at various stages of their trips away from home; riding in planes, automobiles, buses, autos, or ships; visiting attractions or stopping over at hotels or motels

Financial reports top the list of critical information sources for measuring and maintaining the viability of the travel business, followed closely by traffic reports and economic indicators.

Population surveys usually provide basic demographics on a national and worldwide scale. Generally, they are extensive and, therefore, expensive. Surveys of people while they are away from home on their travels provide a sharper and less expensive time/place focus on travel industry factors

such as: air travel, highway travel, cruises, hotels/motels, sightseeing, and amusement attractions. Taken together, en route and household-population surveys can provide powerful tools for effective management of growth and development in the travel industry.

En route surveys are a cost-effective and, therefore, popular travel-industry tool used by travel managers everywhere. This chapter will describe how en route surveys have been used and by whom.

SURVEY COSTS

Unlike financial reports, traffic statistics, economic indicators, and household surveys, which are often available with relatively small cost from travel industry and government sources, en route surveys are more likely to be locally funded for local interests. Being sample surveys of the travel population, however—not a complete census—the costs of en route surveys can be controlled by careful design of the sample-selection procedures and efficient gathering of only the information that is most cogent to filling the information void that gives rise to the need for the survey. The samples may be small and relatively simple while still being adequate to solve big problems. Costs are minimized, and timely results are achieved.

Nevertheless, there are times when the problems cannot be brought within budget, and decisions will continue to be made on a trial-and-error basis with its attendant, probably higher, risks. As the competition for the travelers' dollar intensifies, reliable information from an en route survey might become more likely to be judged cost effective. Only travel management can decide whether a given en route survey proposal is cost effective or not, of course, but the scientific design of en route surveys provides for the consideration of a wide range of alternatives that can minimize costs at given levels of confidence in the results. These options have frequently been enough to choose one and proceed with an investment in en route survey methodology.

HOUSEHOLD SURVEYS VS. EN ROUTE SURVEYS

Household surveys are probably more familiar to the public than en route surveys, in part because almost everyone has a chance of being included in a household survey, while en route surveys are encountered only by that part of the population that makes significant trips each year.

The selection of people for inclusion in a household survey proceeds through various stages of sampling. For a survey of households in the United States, for example, the area of the country is first mapped into small areas that are manageable to administer. A sample of these areas is then drawn at random to provide the first stage of selection. Then a sample of households within those selected areas is drawn. Finally a sample of people from within the selected households is drawn for inclusion in the sample. The sample-selection process goes through three stages of sampling before a respondent is chosen.

The people selected for inclusion in a household survey may be interviewed by a survey representative. This, of course, involves the complex administration of a widespread corps of interviewers. It is most expensive.

In some applications, costs have been reduced by mailing questionnaires to the households in the sample, but experience reveals that many of the intended respondents fail to complete and mail back the questionnaires. The response rates are considerably lower than when an interviewer confronts the respondent. As a result, the specter of bias looms large; that is, the sample may not be representative of the whole population as intended—it may be significantly skewed.

Another cost-reduction alternative for a survey of the nation's population is a telephone survey. The potential for success of this method is enhanced by the fact that almost all households in the United States today have at least one phone. While this method is obviously less expensive, response rates are still lower than that yielded by a personal interview in the home—particularly for long questionnaires of the type often used in major household surveys. A wide variety of supplemental sampling schemes have been created in efforts to control the bias that can result from low initial-response rates in telephone surveys.

For travel industry purposes, household and telephone surveys are particularly flawed because travelers are, of course, the most apt to be "not at home" when the inter-

viewer appears or when the phone rings. While this problem has been addressed by call-backs using sophisticated strategies, it nevertheless does increase the cost of these surveys.

Another problem with these surveys, from the travel-industry point of view, occurs when respondents are asked for past-trip details they find they have forgotten. This kind of response error has been shown to increase with the length of time elapsed between the trip and the survey interview. This problem has not been ignored either. Respondents may be asked, for example, for details of only the "most recent" trip, thus increasing the likelihood that they will be remembered. This kind of questioning can be structured so that the results can be interpreted in proper perspectives. Again, however, these procedures add costs to the survey effort.

En route survey methodology has proliferated because it is the first method that comes to mind when addressing a particular segment of the travel market at a particular time and place. When the en route survey results are in hand, they can sometimes be enhanced by referencing them to broad results from the more expensive national population surveys and censuses.

EN ROUTE METHODOLOGY

En route survey plans often proceed, like household surveys, through two or three stages of selection. The first stage is usually a sample drawn from a time/place domain, for example, an airport for a year. The second stage involves a selection of "schedules" within the selected time/place domains. The third, and last, stage might be a selection of passengers (i.e., people in vehicles such as planes, trains, or buses). These concepts can also embrace survey solutions to problems in auto travel, cruise-ship patronage, hotel usage, and attendance at sightseer attractions. Again, the information might be obtained from self-completion questionnaires collected by a survey representative or mailed back. The information might also be collected by interviewers at the en route site. The telephone option is not available, of course, to the en route survey yet—maybe when cellular phones are carried by vacationers. Combinations of these alternatives give rise to a wide variety of en route surveys. The most successful combinations of these factors are probably best revealed by a review of how the principal users of en route surveys have conducted these studies.

USERS OF EN ROUTE SURVEYS

En route surveys have been used by the airlines for more than 30 years. En route surveys helped them to develop their markets during those early days when "fear of flying" seemed to be the biggest obstacle to growth. Population surveys helped to identify the potentials for growth and to identify the most basic factors to generating new customers, such as education. They also used en route methods to evaluate inflight services and to identify market segments among their various routes.

The airlines selected a sample of their flight schedules within a certain time frame and route context. Then they supplied the cabin crews on these flights with questionnaires to distribute to all passengers as they boarded the flights or after they were seated and comfortably indulged by the stewardesses. The crews used the inflight public address system to alert their passengers to the survey and instruct them as to where and when they would collect the questionnaires. The crews also asked the passengers to complete the questionnaires while en route. The passengers responded with outstandingly high response rates.

As the air passenger market continued to grow, so did the size of the aircraft and the number of flight crew serving a given flight. In the very successful early days, there were typically two stewardesses to serve a plane full of passengers, and response rates were very high. By the end of the 1970s, there were as many as a dozen or so cabin personnel needed to attend to the much larger passenger loads, and response rates were much lower.

The survey results were losing some credibility because of low response rates. One transatlantic airline chose the option of selecting a random sample of passengers from within these huge aircraft in an effort to restore control. They recognized that while it was not statistically necessary to have more questionnaires than, say, 20 percent from each flight, the real threat was that those few passengers who were becoming part of the sample under the old system might not be "representative" of the flight. Using a random discipline assured that the new system would be representative in the long run. Under the new system, nonresponse was considerably reduced because it was measured among only those passengers who did, in fact, receive questionnaires.

As others sought to cope with low response rates and the administrative problems with big aircraft, mailback questionnaires were tried. The low response rates to mailbacks in household surveys was also encountered in en route surveys—with the further problem that neglected questionnaires cluttered the aircraft interiors, impacting severely on inflight service standards.

Another alternative system used to improve the response rate from large planes was to distribute questionnaires to passengers as they boarded—and pick them up from those passengers as they left the plane down the line. This relieved the cabin crews of much of the involvement that might have distracted them from their prime mission of full attention to their passengers. Many other alternatives were tried.

The airlines have also cooperated with airport administrations by allowing their cabin crews to do inflight surveys on small flight samples of their operations in the past. An outstanding example of such cooperation has been between the Port Authority of New York & New Jersey and the airlines serving LaGuardia, JFK International, and Newark International airports. As a result of this cooperation, there exists a long documented history of inflight surveys at the New York/New Jersey airports. Yearlong inflight surveys were conducted at approximately six-year intervals since 1954 when only 9 million passengers were handled at these three airports. Traffic grew until, by 1991, these airports handled a peak of almost 79 million passengers in one year (1987).

The Port Authority of New York & New Jersey adminis-

tered the New York/New Jersey airports and other regional transportation facilities that were essentially of an interstate nature. It found en route survey methods to be a valuable tool in a number of these other contexts.

The Port Authority of New York & New Jersey used en route survey methods to monitor the characteristics of the automobile travel market using its trans-Hudson tunnels and bridges.

During a designated year, a sample of work shifts was selected at each of the toll plazas in its system of trans-Hudson crossings—a sample of a "time/place domain." Then a sample of autos, "every nth car," was selected and the driver engaged for a very brief interview yielding origin, destination, passenger load (by observation), residence, purpose of trip, and frequency of usage. Response rates were high, and the quality of the results was excellent. For a number of years, these surveys were continued on a nonstop basis with no impact on traffic flow.

The Port Authority of New York & New Jersey also used en route methods for studying its bus terminal patronage. In 1992, for example, a sample of bus schedules was selected from an appropriate time frame. A survey representative in New York was assigned to board each of the buses selected for inclusion in the sample and invite the passengers to participate in the survey. The survey representative distributed questionnaires that were designed to be completed by each of the passengers, and the representative collected them from the the passengers as they left the bus in New Jersey. The survey representatives were trained to elicit good cooperation from the passengers, and, as a result, the response rates averaged a high 72 percent.

The Port Authority of New York & New Jersey also used en route survey methods in the passenger train market in cooperation with the (then) New York Central Railroad. Although the Port Authority administered no railroad terminals, it cooperated with regional planning commissions to help fill gaps in identifying regional passenger flows. In this case, a survey representative boarded a sample of trains scheduled out of Grand Central Terminal, invited participation in the survey, distributed self-completion questionnaires, and collected the completed forms, sometimes as the passengers left the train at their destination stations.

En route survey methods were also used by the Port Authority to identify some characteristics of the cruise-ship passenger market using passenger terminal piers in New York City.

Many other airport administrations have used en route survey methods, and some of them used inflight survey methods. The Baltimore/Washington, D.C., Metropolitan Area Council used inflight survey methods extensively at their Washington National, Dulles, and Baltimore airports in highly successful efforts to supply parameters for their airports' development plan for their region. Other airport administrations using en route survey methodology in the past are those of Boston's Logan International airport and the airports serving Chicago, Atlanta, Los Angeles, San Francisco, Dallas, Toronto, and Munich.

Inflight surveys have been used by many other government and industry organizations throughout the Western world. The U.S. Travel and Tourism Association of the United States Department of Commerce has for many years commissioned inflight surveys on most international airlines serving the United States. In Europe, the International Association of Transatlantic Airlines conducted frequent inflight surveys of international travelers.

The list of users of en route survey technology is obviously very large. This technology has been used to measure the characteristics of the automobile travel market by highway administrators and to identify the origin and destination of traffic. It has also been used by state and local tourist commissions to measure key characteristics of their tourist markets. En route techniques have also been used to survey visitors to national parks and attractions. En route surveys have been applied in such a bewildering array of circumstances as to defy documentation, particularly since most of them have been done for parochial purposes. That still leaves a vast store of publicly available reports describing methods and their performance that may be accessed by diligent and patient research.

CONSIDERING A FIRST SURVEY

Travel managers, who must make difficult decisions on the basis of fuzzy information, might consider the possibilities of improving their batting averages by using the more definitive information that can be generated with en route survey technology. The very process of considering a survey would inevitably bring into focus some factors that had only been vaguely perceived before the effort is made to get a better fix on the marketplace. One of the first things to do is define the *population* of interest and do it rather rigorously. Is the population all previous customers—present customers—and/or potential customers—or who? The next step might then be to describe the *characteristics* that provide the leverage needed to sway the market—or to sway the management of the travel facilities to better accommodate the market. These are the things that are critical to the travel managers' plans to grow and prosper. It could be expected that consideration for a survey would pass back and forth between these two realms and eventually converge into a coherent integration of both factors—survey population and characteristics. Together, these two factors are the cornerstones of an en route survey proposal. As the planning of a survey moves further along towards an active proposal, it can be expected that the original problem(s) will become clearer and the alternative solutions better defined.

Some travel managers have the personnel resources to develop their own sampling plans and perform the analyses. Most can do it better with the help of professionals who have demonstrated expertise in market studies. Sometimes, travel managers solicit proposals from a number of different suppliers in order to select the best value.

Judging the value of an en route survey proposal is based on cost, of course, as well as on the prospects that a proffered plan will satisfy the need. These are seldom easy judgments

to make. Some unfamiliar language would probably enter the considerations: terms such as *sampling error* and, perhaps, *bias*. These are discussed in the following subsections.

SAMPLING ERROR

Sampling error, as commonly used in the literature of survey technology, describes a mathematical concept that relates the size of error in estimates from samples to the size of those samples. These estimates of error are based on the assumption that the sample is drawn at random; it is a random sample. It is expressed, for example, in language such as: All estimates of percentages of people with certain attributes are within two percentage points of the true value—with a confidence level of 95 percent. The "true value" is intended to mean the value that would be obtained if all elements of the population were observed rather than just a sample. The "confidence level of 95 percent" is based on the idea that as many as, say, 100 samples of the size of the one in question could be drawn according to exactly the same random process and only 5 of them would yield estimates that were further than two percentage points from the true value. So, of course, you are persuaded to believe you have one of the 95 good samples. In practice, the sampling-error estimate is much more useful as a relative measure of what happens as the size of the sample goes up, and as the costs increase. It points the way to getting the most value from the survey investment.

Of course, the sampling error is expected to go down as the size of the sample goes up. But what one might not expect to find is how fast the error goes down, as revealed in Figure 1. In this chart, the percentage points of error are plotted along the y axis and the sample size is measured on the x axis. A logarithmic scale is used in order to "fit" a wide range of sample sizes on the chart and show that the shape of the curve is such that, after a certain point, further observations are not at all effective in reducing the error in the estimates. Two curves are plotted: one for estimates of 50% and the other for estimates of small values, 10%. These two points, that is, 10% and 50%, encompass the range of all practical values to expect from a survey sample because anything over 50% has the same error as its complement; for example, an estimate of 70% has the same error as 30%.

In Figure 1, sample sizes in excess of 1,000 or 2,000 yield virtually no improvement in the precision of the sample estimates. In practice, however, the samples are not drawn quite as simply as those assumed as a basis for the graph. The sampling in Figure 1 is assumed to be simple random sampling, for example, drawing colored balls from an urn. Furthermore, the errors for percentages, that is, proportions, is smaller than for variables like "average dollars spent." As mentioned earlier, most en route surveys (as well as population surveys) are based on samples selected according to a design that passes through two or three stages of selection before emerging with the final sampling observation. The sampling errors for these practical designs are estimated by more complex formulations. They yield a multiplier to use on the simple estimates such as those plotted in Figure 1.

PERCENT POINTS

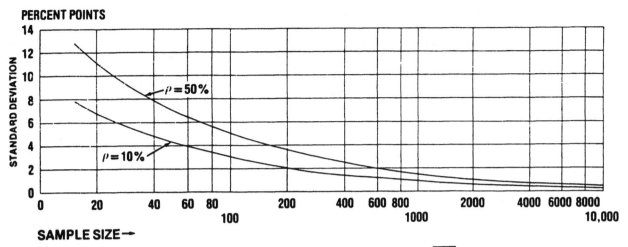

FIGURE 1 Standard deviation as function of sample size (SRS for proportions $\sigma = \sqrt{pq/n}$).

These multipliers are usually in the range of two or maybe three. Thus, the essential message of the charting is hardly lost; it is simply displaced by a multiple of two or three. In other words, practical samples of size greater that 3,000 to 6,000 are at the outer limit of the need for protection from sampling errors. Nevertheless, there may still be survey designs where even this criteria might be exceeded because there are subpopulations within the overall sampling scheme from which good estimates are sought. These are the cases where expertise in sample design is particularly useful in obtaining an efficient sampling plan.

BIAS

The crux of any population survey is the design of the sample, that is, the plan for selecting the ultimate sample of people of whom observations will be made—questions will be asked. It starts with the definition of the population. The uniqueness of en route surveys is determined by the fact that the study population is usually targeted at a component of the travel system: planes, hotels, sightseeing attractions, resorts, national parks, and so on. Thus, the population might be all people using a particular travel accommodation over a specific period of time. How the information is to be obtained from the sample elements/people will have a bearing on the selection plans. Whether a self-completion questionnaire is to be the "survey instrument" or whether an interviewer is to engage the chosen respondent in an information-producing dialogue is important to the ultimate design. Of course, the observations may also be simply to make visual observations of select characteristics or visual observations as well as interviews on each respondent. The complex pathway to these ultimate sampling units will result in a schedule of work for the personnel forces required to carry out the survey. It is probably the most significant element of variable cost in the program, followed by the data processing, analysis, and report production.

Inherent in the schedule of personnel assignments are sample-selection procedures to be followed by the survey personnel. The selection procedures are designed to assure that random choices are made at each stage of the selection process—that the sampling is done objectively and bias does not creep into the sample. During the implementation phase of the survey, it is necessary to keep careful records of the shifts actually worked and the details of how the selection procedures performed during the full course of the survey. There will be failures, of course, but there will also be instructions in the design on how to handle them. These alternatives will be largely judgment types developed by the survey experts.

As the survey progresses, the quality of the work will probably be controlled by constant scrutiny of the various failure rates, for example, the number of shifts that had to be rescheduled or the number of selectees who refused to participate in the survey. As long as these failures remain "small," the possibility of significant bias in the estimates is also small. But when they are "large," they provide a bias alert.

A biased sample can be flagged by high nonresponse rates, but not all samples with high nonresponse rates are biased. One way to derive some measure of comfort that the sample is indeed unbiased is to find an element of information derived from the sample that can be compared with extraneous statistics of exactly the same sort—and find no significant difference. Of course, the information from the sample is usually collected because it is available from no other source. Thus, it is rare that such comparisons can be made. It is obviously a difficult problem to resolve. Low nonresponse rates (high response rates) then are highly desirable.

Unfortunately, "sampling error" has no value in determining whether or not there exists significant bias in the estimates. If by some quirk of the sampling procedures females were never selected for observation, the sampling error would not yield any hint that this egregious error had occurred. Although, in reality, such a case would be easy to detect by simply scanning the survey results, there are many more subtle biases that can enter into the sample-selection process that are not so easily detected. Nor are they revealed by sampling error.

Another more insidious type of bias can enter into the survey estimates if the questionnaire contains questions that evoke biased answers or inadvertently invite wrong answers.

QUESTIONNAIRE

The choice of a survey instrument—a record sheet for observations, a self-completion questionnaire, or a questionnaire administered by an interviewer—depends on the specifics of the survey objectives and the environment at the time of making the observations. A few general remarks will lend some perspective to this process.

A self-completion questionnaire will probably yield the most thoughtful responses so long as it is administered under conditions that are relatively free of distractions and stressful aggravations. It should be carefully constructed so as to flow smoothly to the respondent. Simple, factual questions should dominate the questionnaire, and they should be organized in a way that will emphasize the logical ordering that the respondent could be expected to have (not necessarily that of the researcher's). Subject labeling of the various sectors of inquiry could help to ease the respondent through the questionnaire. Certainly it should be as short as practicable, but not at the expense of being cryptic and ambiguous. If there must be questions evoking critical judgments, it is probably best to relegate them to the last sections of the questionnaire because the respondent may prefer to reject such questions rather than expend the effort to make a difficult choice. Any questions that follow difficult questions that may have caused the respondent to stop would probably be given little or no further consideration.

A questionnaire to be used by an interviewer who engages the respondent in a dialogue shifts some of the burden of structure and phrasing to the training program for interviewers. The inquiry can be more intricately structured so that the interviewer can answer some questions simply by observation and omit others based on a series of earlier questions. There can exist a questioning tree to follow that relieves the respondent of having to deal with irrelevant questions as might be the case in self-completion questionnaires. However, the respondent does not get the chance to review the completed questionnaire for accuracy as is the case in self-completion questionnaires.

In either case, the principal focus is on presenting the questions in a way that is most satisfactory to the respondent. It requires a lot of careful preparation, review, and maybe some testing. A judicious amount of redundancy is sometimes appropriate to enhance the ability to edit the responses so that errors do not slip through. The value of the information obtained can sometimes be substantially increased by using two or more different questionnaires (more on that later in the "Example" at the end).

RANDOMNESS

When the elements drawn at each stage of the survey design are selected with known probabilities, the result is a random sample. There are many methods for drawing probability samples, all of which are characterized by objective selection procedures at each stage. Frequently, a random-number series is used to discipline the selection procedures, or perhaps a random matrix is used for some stage of the selection. Sample estimates, then, are simply derived for each of the elements included in the sample by cumulating the reciprocals of the probabilities for inclusion of each element through each of the stages of sampling. The estimates of sampling error, then, are conclusive sources of confidence in the results.

Nonresponse rates quantify the departures from strict control of the random process of selection and, if too large, might signal the possibility of more error in the estimates due to significant bias. High nonresponse rates are found in many good surveys using selection methods that are, based on the experience of the expert survey designer, free of bias, even though not strictly disciplined by what could be unnecessarily expensive sample-selection procedures. Such a judgment made in good faith by the experienced expert has frequently been admissible.

SLEUTHING FOR BIAS

One way to unveil a hidden bias in surveys with high nonresponse rates is to take an estimate or a set of estimates from the survey, and compare it to like statistics from an extraneous source. Surveys, however, are usually devoted to collecting information that is available from no other source, so finding comparable parameters from someplace else is not easy. Nevertheless, the following case illustrates that it can be done and that the effort can yield some tantalizing results with value on their own merits.

The Port Authority of New York & New Jersey made such a test of the results from the last in their 30-year series of inflight surveys: the 1985 survey. But first a brief review of five ways in which the 1985 survey differed from its predecessors:

1. Instead of a first-stage sampling of work shifts, one flight per day was selected at random for the year-long survey at each airport.

2. Because 1985 was a year in the pace-setting People Express explosion, the Newark International Airport flight sampling was divided into two parts—two "airports"—People Express and all other airlines combined. Thus, the flight-sample size was four "airports" (La Guardia, JFK, Newark except People Express, and People Express) multiplied by 365 days in the year to yield 1,480 flights in all.

3. Instead of rescheduling surveyed flights that "failed" because their response rates were less than 20 percent, these flights were matched, that is, carried in the statistical weighting of, like flights already in the sample.

4. Instead of hiring extra people for the field work, regular airport employees were found who could absorb the task of equipping one flight each day for the survey. By the end of the survey, the share of the flight selections that failed to yield a response rate as high as 20 percent was 40 percent. THIS IS A

HAZARDOUS STATISTIC! There is lots of room for bias to skew the results.

5. And, finally, only one questionnaire was used instead of two or three in tandem.

The flight sample was obviously jeopardized by the fragmentation incurred from poor inflight performance. To check for bias in the flight sample, the survey results from past inflight surveys were compared with results from the Department of Transportation's massive origin/destination analysis of their 10 percent ticket sample from all U.S. airlines. With response rates from within flights much more into the danger zone in the 1985 survey, a more intense test was also in order. Thus, the subject of this test was airport parking—because comparable data for checking this survey were available from an independent source.

The number of cars parked at the Port Authority's airports is known from parking-lot accounting records. It was also estimable from inflight survey results because the survey was designed to yield parameters for planning facilities (e.g., parking) to accommodate the growing need for easy airport access by ground modes.

The survey estimate was intricately entwined with the whole air-passenger profile. The number of travel groups using a car to access the airports and leaving it in the airport parking lots while away on a trip was the survey statistic. In addition to the simple total number of cars (assumed equal to the number of groups), the number of nights such groups spent away was also taken from their questionnaires. This created a more robust test using the likeness of two SERIES of statistics. The result was two statistical series of absolute values: not shares or percentages but variables; a tougher hurdle for the survey estimates. The series were the number of cars parked per day during the survey year 1985 according to number of days parked—one series from the survey and one series from the parking lot accounting records. To make the test even more robust, it was done separately for each of the three airports—four "airports" when treating People Express and "Other airlines" at Newark International Airport

like two other airports. These series could be plotted and the resulting curves examined casually to see whether there was a good resemblance between the two at each of the airports. For whichever among the four comparisons of the two curves a reasonable match was found, it might be concluded that this was persuasive evidence that survey sector was unbiased.

The subsample used for the test represented only 10 percent of all the air passengers in the survey, and virtually all of them were residents of the NY/NJ/CT metropolitan area, not visitors to the area: less than 2,000 questionnaires from long-term parkers out of about 17,000 questionnaires in all.

A glance at Figures 2, 3, and 4, portraying the results for La Guardia, JFK, and Newark airports, respectively, immediately reveals that the two curves are so close in EACH case as to be barely distinguishable. "Which curve is which?" hardly matters. What does matter is that each of the three airports obviously had unique patterns of long-term parking patronage according to length of parking and that those patterns were faithfully reproduced in the 1985 inflight survey. The surveys were taking "pictures" of the same phenomenon and producing four unique portraits. Figures 5 and 6 yielded the same kind of support when Newark Airport was done separately for People Express vs. All Other airlines; the curves were unique and well approximated by the survey. This was probably a good place to stop. So far—no glaring evidence of bias.

Comparing the curves had provided supportive results. It is apparent that the data can stand up under closer scrutiny. A simple test of the total number of cars parked long-term at each of the airports, for example, may pose a more intense challenge to the survey estimates.

The four basic airport cases provide a pool of data for isolating oddities. Perhaps the most obvious departure from a complete correspondence between the two series is the fact that the number of air-passenger groups from the surveys on one-day trips who left their car at the airport until their return was considerably less than the number recorded in the park-

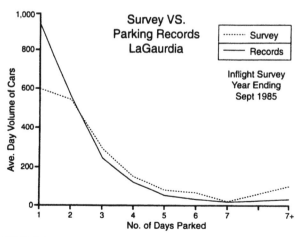

FIGURE 2

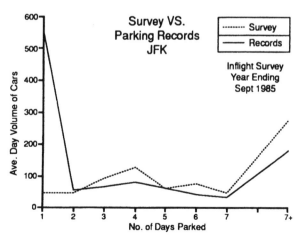

FIGURE 3

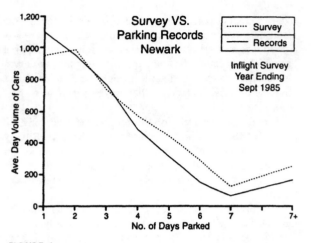

FIGURE 4

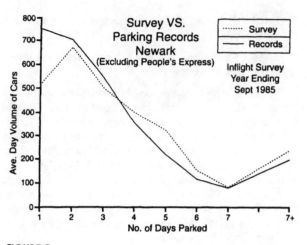

FIGURE 5

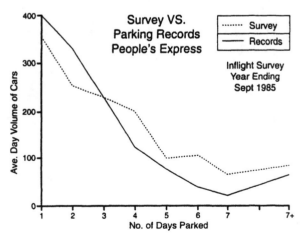

FIGURE 6

ing lot reports in three out of the four tests. At People Express they were virtually equal.

Other parking lot studies indicated that a significant number of employees parked in this 5-to-24-hour interval at some of the airports. Thus, the volumes from the survey and the parking lot records for one-day parkers could not be expected to match. A more sensitive test of total volumes should be made excluding one-dayers.

Another observation to be made is the fact that the survey estimates of over-7-day parking invariably exceed the record values—rather considerably. This may be symptomatic of other problems with the record sources that might cloud the comparison between survey estimates of long-term parking activity and the accounting records.

Omitting both extreme end points from the series, then, would seem to improve the sensitivity of the check of the survey results.

The support data for Figures 2 through 6 are given in Table 1. These data describe the number of cars entering an airport parking lot on an average day in 1985—to park for 1 day, 2 days, . . ., up to a week or more as yielded by the two

sources: the inflight-survey estimates and the parking lot reports. The total long-term parking is also given in each case, and it reveals considerably different levels of this activity at each of the three airports: roughly 1,000 per day at Kennedy; 2,000 at LaGuardia; and 4,000 per day at Newark. The table also provides the totals stripped of their two end points: the total cars parked 2 through 7 days—a "core" group with which to compare the two independent sources.

If the four survey estimates varied by only a few percentage points above or below the results abstracted from the parking lot reports, the results could have been interpreted as substantial "proof" that there was no bias in the survey estimates. The test would have ended there with a very positive level of endorsement for the integrity of the survey.

The survey estimates, however, were all greater than the report values. Furthermore, the next line—of percentage differences—seems to indicate two distinct levels of overestimation.

There are two airports with small overestimates of less than 10 percent and two airports with large overestimates of over 30 percent: JFK and People Express at Newark. Why should these two "airports" be so severely overestimated? This pattern of overestimation is also found in another set of simple estimates from the survey.

The survey also yielded estimates of the shares of air passengers who used the airports only to connect with another flight. These air passengers do not reside in the airport's local service area. The survey estimates of transfer-passenger shares at each of the four airports have also been appended to the data presented in Table 1. The pattern of survey excesses exhibits much the same pattern as found in the transfer-passenger shares at each of the four airports. Could this correspondence be rationalized?

The self-completion questionnaires used in the inflight survey for 1985 made it immediately clear to the prospective respondent that The Port Authority of NY/NJ was sponsoring the study. Transfer passengers might have been more prone to neglect the questionnaire if they had the attitude "The Port Authority couldn't really care too much about me; I am only passing through": that is, they could have had an

TABLE 1 Number of Cars Left at an Airport for the Duration of an Air Trip

INFLIGHT-SURVEY ESTIMATES COMPARED WITH PARKING LOT REPORTS (AVERAGE DAY—1985)

PORT AUTHORITY OF NEW YORK & NEW JERSEY

DAYS AWAY	LaGuardia		JFK		People Express		Other Airlines		Total Newark	
	SURVEY	REPORTS	SURVEY	REPORTS	SURVEY	REPORTS	SURVEY	REPORTS	SURVEY	REPORTS
1	573	940	20	554	375	347	451	750	826	1090
2	516	523	45	64	321	256	664	710	985	962
3	283	270	111	74	220	229	491	543	711	767
4	116	107	147	84	206	131	388	360	594	482
5	74	57	71	74	98	76	310	222	408	304
6	55	25	89	39	120	36	191	105	311	147
7	3	10	42	29	62	23	52	32	114	79
7+	60	16	267	210	133	49	219	196	352	255
TOTAL	1,680	1,948	792	1,128	1,535	1,147	2,766	2,918	4,301	4,086
TOTAL: 2–7	1,047	992	505	364	1,027	751	2,096	1,972	3,123	2,741
% SUR/RPTS	5%		39%		36%		6%		14%	
% TRANSFERS	4%		32%		38%		4%		20%	

NOTE: Survey estimates do NOT include the small volumes of parking in the off-airport periphery lots.

attitudinal difference from others on the flight that made non-response from that group greater than from the others—significantly greater. If the foregoing was true, the transfers would be underrepresented in the sample and lead to an underestimate of the number of passengers who were transferring—and, as a consequence, lead to an overestimate of the other kinds of air passengers. It would lead to overestimates of the air passengers who resided in the NY/NJ/CT metropolitan area. The local residents may well have been more prone to complete their questionnaires because they cared more about what happened to their airports. And if residents were overestimated, then so were the estimates of the volumes of long-term-parking patronage.

If all the foregoing conjectures were true, the answer would be YES, the surveys were biased—skewed away from transfer-passenger activity. The next item on such an investigatory agenda would be to devise tests of the various "if" clauses in the plausible inference chain developed in the preceding sections and, if substantiated, to introduce corrective procedures—either in the field work or in the survey-results processing programs—or in the parking statistics.

This part of the sleuthing for bias did not prove the survey to be unbiased. Instead, it led to the suggestion that transfer passengers may be particularly nonresponsive to Port Authority of NY/NJ surveys. In this way, the investigation goes on until the doubts raised by the test are reconciled: bias is identified and corrected.

The preceding example makes it clear that careful planning of the survey and continuous efforts during the survey to maximize response rates might save some vexing problems later in the ultimate analysis of the survey results.

The deliberate introduction of one or more "checkable" statistics in the survey design, if possible, might also be a valuable feature of the planning for an important survey.

It might also be noted that the foregoing demonstration is some testimony to the fact that survey problems can rarely be solved by increasing the size of the survey. Very substantial leverage was obtained from this test based primarily on about 2,000 questionnaires. Increasing the sample size would probably not help to solve the perceived problem of overestimates at airports with high transfer rates.

A POSTSCRIPT

The Port Authority of New York & New Jersey in their latest air-passenger survey abandoned the inflight method and reverted to an intercept method (last used in 1948) where enplaning air passengers were selected by interviewing teams as the air passengers passed through the security gates and down the fingers to board their flights. This yearlong survey ended in March 1991 and yielded a 67 percent response rate; that is, 33 percent refused to be interviewed. The airlines' cabin crews were not involved at all, and almost 14,000 interviews were successfully completed, which is pretty close to the 17,000 completed in the next most recent air-passenger survey in 1985.

SUMMARY

The travel manager who is considering the use of en route surveys wants estimates of market characteristics to confirm something that is already suspected and/or to learn something that is not known. A survey sampling plan and its analysis provide the basis for evaluating the feasibility of getting this information from an en route survey. The cost is a prime determinant of the feasibility, of course. The quality of the survey product is specified by an acceptable level of sampling error together with the expected size of the sample and its method of controlling bias.

One of the most common errors in survey design is probably the assumption that quality of the estimates and size of the sample go hand in hand. Many surveys have been conducted with sample sizes that were much too large, resulting in ponderous administrative problems, complex data processing systems that are fraught with the hazard of large-scale undetected errors, and an air of detachedness that desensitizes a more meaningful interpretation of the results. The sample size and the sampling plan need to be carefully developed to just meet reliability standards and stay within established cost parameters. A rich variety of en route survey methods have been used by a great many managers in the travel industry. Some of the successful methods used for en route surveys have been highlighted in the foregoing text. Some attention was also directed towards the type of users who have benefited from en route survey technology.

The role of "Sampling Error" and "Bias" in interpreting the quality of an en route survey proposal was also clarified. Particular attention was given to the importance of monitoring the extent to which the quality of the original sampling plan is maintained in the conduct of the survey as measured by the response rates. Low response rates raise the specter of bias, a question that must be answered either by the judgment of an expert and/or by testing. Monitoring response rates during survey pretests and during the conduct of an en route survey focuses attention on where corrective procedures could be introduced while there might still be time to modify the design and protect the ultimate results from the risk of bias.

Details of the planning and design of an en route survey are brought out in the example appended to this chapter. It uses an inflight survey as a model because that application illustrates most of the main points that can be expected in the broad range of en route survey types. It utilizes a multistage sampling scheme as might be expected in most applications.

AN EXAMPLE OF THE EN ROUTE SURVEY METHOD

This section describes how an en route survey is conducted. It does this by example. A model is developed from applications in the airline industry. The airline model is chosen because inflight surveys provide the richest background for gaining a broad perspective on the methodology that can be useful for interpreting the results from completed en route surveys or for considering the feasibility of further applications. An inflight survey for an airport is used.

THE MODEL—AIRPORT X

Airport X has reached a stage of growth at which the need is recognized for a more intense understanding of the passenger-traffic flows to enhance the ability of management to plan and coordinate the development of their facilities more effectively. About a million passengers are enplaned on about 10,000 scheduled flight departures per year. The airport is served by five or six scheduled airlines. The use of an inflight survey is being considered. The following is a detailed development of a practical proposal for an inflight survey that provides the necessary flexibility for negotiating its implementation under highly variable conditions.

INFLIGHT SURVEYS: A SCALAR MODEL

Airport operating and planning problems generally have two significant facets: physical and economic. Physical problems generally emphasize peak-hour flows, while economic problems depend on round-the-clock traffic activity and revenue generation. An inflight survey will give results in both these areas by providing a model of the total operations with a scalar factor about equal to the sampling rate. Peak hours will come into the model with the same significance they have in the population, and peak-hour measurements will derive their strength from repeated observations over the time span of the survey.

AIRLINE COOPERATION

A successful inflight survey program requires the cooperation of virtually every airline serving Airport X. Accordingly, the proposal must be prepared so as to minimize the impact on any airline's ongoing operations and yet be specific enough to clearly describe the extent of the airline's involvement under the simplest conditions. At the same time, the proposal must be flexible enough to adapt to variable procedures insofar as they are unique to each airline. Some airlines have their own inflight survey programs. Some are conducted periodically and systemwide, others on an ad hoc basis. Some airlines do not do inflight surveys.

For those airlines that do not conduct inflight surveys, the services of a survey representative to meet the flight crew of selected flights and supply them with questionnaire kits, which include addressed pouches for returning completed questionnaires to the originating airport via airline company mail services, are almost a necessity. Some airlines could not participate unless this service was provided. The survey field representative is also needed to instruct the chief cabin crew member on the method—most simply, to distribute a questionnaire to everyone aboard the plane as it leaves Airport X, ask for cooperation on the PA system, and be responsive to questions about the survey.

The representative then collects the load statistics for the flight—the number of throughs, enplaned revenue, and nonrevenue passengers—for response-rate analysis and weighting completed questionnaires. The representative also picks up kits from the airline ticket counter that have been returned from earlier flight selections. Flight crew cooperation is improved if their airline management provides advance notice that their flight has been included in the sample selection for Airport X's inflight survey. For this reason, the airline must receive notice of the flight selections as much in advance of the contact date as possible; by the middle of the month preceding a month's selections is a practical schedule for flight-sample selections and clearing with the airlines.

Airlines with inflight survey programs of their own may participate in Airport X's inflight program with the proviso that their own inflight selections have precedence. They may still, however, welcome the services of a field representative to reduce the extent of their participation in Airport X's survey. Others among them may prefer to board Airport X's survey kits themselves without the intervention of a field representative. Still others may have their own inflight passenger-sampling schemes that they are willing to extend for Airport X's program, again without the intervention of a field representative.

Airline cooperation, then, may take various forms. One way to approach the problems this might create is to prepare a proposal consistent with the lowest common denominator before soliciting airline cooperation. A basic proposal would include the services of a field representative, a completely designed questionnaire, and a specific plan for selecting flights for inclusion in the sample, with the time span and total flight-sample size clearly specified together with an estimate of the number of flights needed from each airline. Then when it comes to soliciting each airline's cooperation, the basic proposal can be modified to accommodate individual airline requirements. The following is a development of such a basic proposal for an airport with a million passenger enplanements per year on 10,000 scheduled flight departures operated by six airlines.

OUTBOUND FLIGHTS ONLY

Providing a field person as an integral part of a basic inflight design limits the feasibility of survey coverage to flights outbound from Airport X only; otherwise, delivering survey kits to all upline airports for inbound flights involves additional costs that are not usually commensurate with the value of the information added. Since virtually all passengers found at Airport X use it at least twice on each trip—once in and once out—the amount of unique information provided by inbound passengers may be only hour of arrival and expected mode of egress.

TIME FRAME

An inflight-survey program can be thought of as a "model" of Airport X's passenger market that can be used for both short- and long-term analysis. Its utility is enhanced if the sample covers all seasons, days of the week, and hours of the day so as to minimize the amount of projection and extrapolation that will be necessary in applying the results to real problems. The simplest survey-design assumption is that the survey shall span a full year. This provides results that are reasonably free from otherwise unknown seasonality. It also allows the necessary amount of sampling to be done at the lowest level of ongoing activity, thus minimizing the interruption of normal operations and maximizing control over the field work. It also reduces the number of different people who must be trained to work on the survey while providing optimum conditions for ongoing feedback in a wide range of survey-operating characteristics—flight crew cooperation, inflight response rates, and questionnaire design—as well as yielding interim results on a timely basis. The design can be made in building blocks of time that can be assimilated for full-year coverage or that can be truncated at a half, third, or even quarter year without inordinately jeopardizing the quality of the results. The damage done to the estimates by not finishing a full year can be limited to little more than the damage that arises from incomplete control over seasonality.

QUESTIONNAIRE DESIGN

The model questionnaire given on page 465 illustrates some of the problems encountered with self-completion inflight surveys. It is structured on the assumption that it will be given to all passengers aboard a selected flight after it leaves Airport X, but it is not limited to that condition.

The easiest questions are put first in order to encourage response. "Where did you board this airplane?" seems obvious, but some flights contain "through" passengers who stayed aboard the aircraft while it stopped at Airport X to enplane passengers. This question provides the information necessary to segregate them from analyses of Airport X enplanements. It is also protection against distributions that occur after the flight has made another stop and new enplanees erroneously receive questionnaires.

Question #3 "Where will you leave this airplane?" is almost as simple. Some transfer passengers will give their ultimate destination and forget about a change of planes en route. For some purposes, this ultimate destination today is more important. It depends, for example, on whether or not the adequacy of through service is being evaluated. Question #4 elicits this information.

Together, questions #2 and #3 provide the basic means for identifying the population being studied.

Question #5 "Where do you live?" is vital to a meaningful analysis of airport-access modes. Generally the passenger has a car available for the trip to the airport nearest to home and more often uses public modes at the other end of the trip. The clarification addenda are not necessary for most of the passengers. Question #6, home ZIP code, gives adequate geography in easy-to-code numerics that are known by virtually all passengers who live in the USA.

Question #7 is a simple purpose question liable to some ambiguity, but, used in conjunction with Question #8, nights away, it provides a qualitative basis for market analysis.

Other types of survey research may require more detail in this question.

Question #9, travel-group composition, is liable to more response error than the foregoing questions because of the many possibilities for travel-group arrangements and because it is not altogether unreasonable to suppose that each passenger is "traveling with" everyone else on the flight. It is also somewhat ambiguous: some people travel "alone" in a group tour and some travel with their spouses in a group tour. It is structured to provide a basis for qualitative classification.

Question #10, mode of airport access and local origin, are also difficult concepts to communicate in a self-completion questionnaire; for example, business visitors with a number of stops do not know where to say their trip to the airport "originated"; some visitors on personal trips do not know the ZIP code of the home they visited and are reluctant to give street address. Part C is useful for converting passengers into the number of different people using Airport X.

Questions #11, #12, and #13 are common ingredients of almost all population surveys. When age is open-ended instead of multiple-choice (as herein presented), it encounters a little more nonresponse but provides a more definitive distribution. The incremental nonresponse has not been found to be localized in any particular age brackets.

Question #14, occupation, is structured to identify nonrevenue passengers and to classify passengers on broad occupation bases of particular significance in travel studies.

Question #15, household income, generally has the most nonresponse, about 15 percent, but it is usually localized among females and students, while the response from male business travelers is high. Open-ended income questions increase the nonresponse to 20 percent or 25 percent but expedite the handling of comparisons with other distributions. Again, the incremental nonresponse has not been found to be localized in any particular categories.

In any effort to shorten the model questionnaire, there are some obvious candidates for omission because they are not of interest to the majority of passengers. The appended remarks to Question #5 (residence) are directed towards passengers who are moving or going to or from school. The last box for Question #8 (nights away) is only for people who are changing residence. Questions #9A and #9B are primarily directed towards passengers traveling in groups, while about half the travelers are generally found to be traveling alone. If these questions are dropped, the people who need them may be annoyed by this apparent ambiguity. As a result, they may not complete the questionnaire. On the other hand, those who do not need these questions may fail to respond because of the clutter introduced by having the questions included.

Dilemmas of the above sort are common in the design of self-completion questionnaires. Explanations, clarifying remarks, and other extraneous notations on self-completion questionnaires add to the complexity of the instrument and consequently increase nonresponse, perhaps significantly.

Sometimes pretesting the questionnaire provides enough reliable information to permit rational decisions in these problem areas. Often, however, the pretest is not sensitive enough, the sample size is inadequate, and/or the selection of pretest "groups" misses some important components of the population or includes too many of another group.

Another way to handle problems of this sort is to use more than one questionnaire type. Half the questionnaires can be produced in ultimate simplicity—the other half could be produced with technical precision. The two questionnaires can then be collated on an every-other-one basis so that half the respondents get one questionnaire and the other half get the other. Since reliability of the sample estimates is about as good from half the respondents as it is from the two combined, one questionnaire result can be used for very sensitive corrections to the other, and best estimates can be obtained from their interaction if significant defects in population coverage are discovered. A technique like this together with careful attention to original questionnaire design and survey goals can sometimes yield detailed results while still protecting the ultimate estimates from significant response bias. An open-ended income question, for example, can be run with a multiple-choice income question. The multiple-choice questionnaires would maximize response while the open-ended questionnaires would provide fine detail for alternative income groupings. The former provides protection against response bias while the latter provides details for better comparisons of the results with other information sources. Open-ended age against multiple-choice is another example for applying this technique.

AIRPORT INFLIGHT SURVEY—SELF-COMPLETION (OUTBOUND FLIGHTS ONLY)

1. WHERE DID YOU BOARD THIS AIRPLANE? _____ _____ _____

                                                                 Airport/City   State/Prov.   Country

2. Airport/City above is ☐ Where you live—or the nearest suitable airport

                                      ☐ Where you visited—or the nearest suitable airport

                                      ☐ An airport that you used only to change from a plane boarded in another city; which city?

                                                Airport/City   State/Prov.   Country

3. WHERE WILL YOU LEAVE THIS AIRPLANE? _____ _____ _____

                                                Airport/City   State/Prov.   Country

4. Airport/city above is ☐ Where you live—or the nearest suitable airport

                                      ☐ Where you will visit—or the nearest suitable airport

                                      ☐ An airport that you will use only to change to another plane going to another city; which city?

                                            City   State/Prov.   Country

5. WHERE DO YOU LIVE? _____ _____ _____

                                          City   State/Prov.   Country

        Note: If you are changing residence, check here and give last address above

        If you are making a temporary change of residence (school or extended work assignment), check here and give permanent address above.

6. If you live in USA, give home ZIP code. ☐ ☐ ☐ ☐ ☐

7. IS THIS A BUSINESS TRIP? Yes ☐   No ☐

8. HOW MANY NIGHTS WILL YOU HAVE BEEN AWAY by the time this trip is completed?

                    ☐ No nights—a one-day trip

Number of nights: _____

                    ☐ A one-way trip; a permanent change of residence, moving

9.A. Are you traveling in a charter or tour group today?   Yes ☐   No ☐

    If Yes: About how many in the group? 20 or less ☐   21 or more ☐

B. Your PERSONAL travel party—you are making this trip:

   ☐ With your spouse   ☐ With friends or business associates

   ☐ With other relatives   ☐ Alone

C. If you are *not* making this trip alone—How many others are in your PERSONAL travel party   _____ _____ _____ _____

                                 (adults)   (teenagers)   (children)   (infants)

10. If you boarded this flight at Airport X, answer A, B, and C below; if you didn't, check here ☐ and go on to Question #11

   A. IN WHAT KIND OF TRANSPORTATION DID YOU ARRIVE AT THE AIRPORT TODAY?

   ☐ Private CAR   ☐ Taxi

   ☐ Company CAR   ☐ Bus

   ☐ Rent-a-CAR   ☐ Limousine

   Other, please specify: _____

   B. Where did you board the above transportation—or, if you used more than one mode—WHERE DID YOU START YOUR TRIP TO AIRPORT X TODAY?

   ☐ Your home   ☐ An office

   ☐ Another private house ☐ A hotel/motel

   Other, please specify: _____

   ZIP CODE OF STARTING POINT: ☐ ☐ ☐ ☐ ☐

   Or, if you don't know ZIP code,

   Street Address: _____
                   (or name of hotel, nearest street intersection, etc.)

   City/Town: _____

   C. How many times did you *board* a flight at Airport X during the past 12 months?

   ☐ Once, just this flight. OR   ☐ Number of other flights boarded at Airport X.

11. AGE: ☐ 12–21   ☐ 22–39   ☐ 40–64   ☐ 65+

12. SEX: ☐ Male   ☐ Female

13. MARRIED: Yes ☐   No ☐

14. WHAT IS YOUR MAIN OCCUPATION?

   ☐ Student   ☐ Travel agent

   ☐ Military   ☐ Self-employed

   ☐ Housewife/Homemaker   ☐ Employed by government

   ☐ Retired   ☐ Employed by industry

   ☐ Airline employee or family thereof   ☐ Employed by nonprofit organization

   Other, please specify: _____

15. What is your approximate HOUSEHOLD INCOME?

   Yours plus that of your spouse, parents, etc., in U.S. dollars.

   ☐ to $5,000   ☐ to $25,000

   ☐ to $10,000   ☐ to $50,000

   ☐ to $15,000   ☐ to $75,000

   ☐ to $20,000   ☐ $75,000 plus   ☐ Don't know.

THANK YOU!

SAMPLING PLAN

One of the basic sampling elements in a manned inflight survey is a field representative's working shift. During a selected work shift, the field survey representative would be expected to contact the flight crews from a selection of six or so flights. Any day's outbound schedules at Airport X, for example, will probably all fall easily within two eight-hour shifts: 6 AM to 2 PM, or 2 PM to 10 PM. The definition of the two shifts hinges on the choice of afternoon hours—2 PM or 3 PM—whichever divides the schedules into most nearly equal parts. The other end of the shifts is determined by the fact that activity between 10 PM and 6 AM is usually nil. For any shift, then, all scheduled flight departures will be listed in chronological order, and a random-start systematic selection of six flights for inclusion in the sample will be made.

If flight schedules are fairly evenly distributed over the shift period from 6 AM to 2 PM, the interval between sampled flights will be about an hour or so. If they are not, listing them in chronological order before making the sample selection assures maximum intervals between flight selections. If the schedules are highly clustered, it may be necessary to reduce the flight sample size in the shifts or use a more complicated sampling scheme.

Thus, two shifts cover a day's flights at Airport X; 14 shifts cover 7 days' flights in any given week. Since Saturday and Sunday activity before 2 PM or 3 PM is usually weakest, these shifts might be pooled and covered by one field work shift scheduled on either Saturday or Sunday— alternately as the sampling plan is replicated. This is one way to draw a sample of shifts—stratify first by day types. Schematically, the resultant 13 day-types can be depicted as follows:

Thirteen Day-Type Strata

	MON	TUE	WED	THURS	FRI	SAT	SUN
Day (to 2 PM)	1	3	5	7	9	———11———	
Night (from 2 PM)	2	4	6	8	10	12	13

Since there are 13 weeks in a quarter year, a reasonable shift-sampling scheme would be to schedule a different day-type shift each week, thus covering all day-types in a quarter. If they were scheduled in the order numbered in the diagram—day-type #1 (Monday day shift) in week #1; day-type #2 (Monday night shift) in week #2; and so on—weekends would not be covered until the last month of the quarter year. One way to reduce risks inherent in selecting a shift sample this way is to introduce an element of random sampling for the quarter by using a permutation of the numbers 1 through 13.

WORKING SHIFT SAMPLE

A shift schedule for one full year based on one such random permutation is given below. It selects one shift per week.

Full Year's Shift Schedule

		(Q1 = First Quarter, Q2 = Second Quarter, etc.)										
	MON		TUES		WED		THURS		FRI		SAT/SUN	SAT	SUN
WEEK	D	N	D	N	D	N	D	N	D	N	D	N	N
1			Q4				Q1			Q2			Q3
2	Q4				Q1			Q2			Q3		
3	Q3			Q4				Q1			Q2*		
4		Q3			Q4				Q1			Q2	
5	Q1			Q2			Q3			Q4			
6		Q2			Q3			Q4				Q1	
7			Q1			Q2			Q3			Q4	
8	Q2			Q3			Q4				Q1		
9			Q1			Q2			Q3				Q4
10			Q3			Q4			Q1				Q2
11		Q1			Q2			Q3			Q4*		
12		Q4				Q1			Q2			Q3	
13			Q2			Q3			Q4				Q1

* = Scheduled on Sunday; other two on Saturday

If it was necessary to reduce the span of the survey to a half year, the same array could be adapted in the following way: for two shifts per week (a half-year survey) quarter #1 and #2 could be collapsed to read as quarter #1 and quarters #3 and #4 could be collapsed to read as quarter #2. It also follows that to reduce the survey to only a 13-week period (one quarter) the four shifts for each week could all be done in one calendar week. For practical purposes, it is usually appropriate to change holiday shifts to the same day-type in an adjoining week so that holidays are not covered in the sample. This is usually a tolerable omission because holidays are relatively few and are especially light air-travel days.

The fact that Saturday and Sunday day-types are pooled into one day-type implies that results from these shifts are doubled at some point during the ultimate weighting procedures. Otherwise each shift result is multiplied by 13, simply because there is one shift selected of each day-type in each 13-week period (assuming the survey extends for the full year). The SAT/SUN day-type then is multiplied by 26.

FLIGHT SAMPLE

Each flight scheduled to depart during a shift selected for inclusion in the shift sample is listed in chronological order of departure time. Each month's schedules are usually listed in the month prior to contact so that problems with schedule changes are kept to a minimum. A random-start systematic selection of six flights is made from these schedules; for example, if there are 12 flights scheduled, divide 12 by 6 and find that every second flight will be selected for inclusion in the flight sample. To select the first one, a random source for selecting the first or second flight is used. The results obtained from the six flights are multiplied by two (or whatever the sampling faction was in each shift) in the ultimate weighting procedures to bring the statistics up to full shift level. Because the flight sample is selected from schedules, cancellations are not failures. The basic survey design is intended to describe what happens to flight schedules, and cancellations are a real consequence of some schedules. Replacing them would bias the results. In an analogous sense, extra sections to a flight schedule should also be covered as well as the original flight section.

PASSENGER SAMPLE

Although it assumed that each passenger receives a questionnaire, completed questionnaires are not received from each passenger on a flight. Some passengers never receive a questionnaire from the flight crew; some do not fill them out when they get them; and some completed questionnaires are not returned. The ratio of the number of completed questionnaires received to the number of passengers on the flight can be called the *response rate*, but it includes coverage as well as response gaps. The reciprocal of this ratio yields a weight that can be given to each questionnaire to bring it up to the full flight load.

In that sense, it may be said that there is sampling within flights. The term *sampling* is, in theory however, associated with an objective process of selection that is made under controlled conditions. A controlled random sample can rarely be generated without the interjection of a random-numbers generator (book or computer) at one point or another in the design. The sampling within flights as herein described is not under control and, therefore, its objectivity is not assured. Initially, however, it might be assumed that the results produced are not significantly different from a random sample. Subsequent audits of field procedures can be used thereafter to identify departures from this assumption and corrections introduced.

The risk that biased selection of respondents within a flight will have a significant effect on estimates is a function of response rates; higher, more response rates give rise to greater risk of significant bias. A lower limit for acceptable flights can be implemented in order to protect resulting estimates from damage introduced by extremely bad flights. If that standard is set at a minimum of 20 percent response, experience indicates that about two-thirds of the flights selected will meet the standard—more if they are domestic flights, less if international; more if short haul, less if long haul; more on small aircraft, less on large aircraft.

WEIGHTING

Each questionnaire processed is assigned a weight that is calculated as the product of sampling at three stages: shifts, flights, and passengers within flights. If, for example, questionnaires were completed by 50 passengers on a flight of 100 passengers selected from a weekday day shift of 12 scheduled departures, where 4 out of 6 selected flights met the 20 percent response standard, each questionnaire would be given a weight of 78; that is, the product of the shift weight—13—times the flight weight—3 (12 schedules divided by 4 "successful" flights)—times the ratio of completed questionnaires to passengers on the flight—2: 13 x 3 x 2 = 78. A similar questionnaire obtained from a flight sampled during a Saturday/ Sunday shift would be weighted with twice that value, e.g., 156. The sum of the weights on all the questionnaires will provide an estimate of the number of passengers enplaned at Airport X during the time spanned by the survey. The actual number of passengers enplaned at Airport X is generally known from traffic statistics. The first meaningful statistic then is the enplaned passenger total. If it compares reasonably well with the traffic statistics, the two sources are compatible; if not, one or the other is measuring different things, and a problem of reconciling the estimates is created.

SAMPLE SIZE

The foregoing design yields a sample of one shift per week; 52 for a year. Each shift yields a selection of six schedules or 312 departure schedules for the year. With a minimum standard of 20 percent response within flights, this might result in about 200 successful flights yielding an average of about 50 percent response. With an average plane load of 100 passengers enplaned at Airport X, the total number of completed questionnaires could be expected to reach about 10,000. Of course, the same sample-size results would also hold if the schedules were condensed to just one quarter.

Adequacy of the sample size is normally evaluated on the basis of sampling theory formulae. Most are based on the assumption that the sample is randomly generated. The validity of this assumption depends on the adequacy of control over field work.

Since the sample design is implemented in three stages—shifts, flights, and passengers—the error in the estimates has components attributable to time, flight schedules, and people. The quality of an estimate of the proportion of Airport X's passengers destined for City Y is largely determined by the flight sample size, assuming almost all the passengers on a given flight depart at a given city. In the extreme case, the sample need include only one passenger from each flight going to City Y, together with the flight load, to estimate route volume. Local access mode, however, can depend on whether or not the passenger lives around Airport X or is visiting the area, not so much on the destination. In this sense, the number of respondents within each flight is important and the hour of departure is significant; residents tend to enplane in the morning, visitors in the evening. It is apparent, then, that the quality of destination estimates depends on flight-sample size while the quality of local-access-mode estimates might depend more on sample size within flights.

Simple random sampling is more efficient for many classes

of estimates than the sampling design put forth here for Airport X. The Airport X inflight design contains cluster effects that can result in errors two and three times as big as graphed in the chart. The importance of the chart, however, is in depicting the extent to which large sample sizes are not productive in reducing error—particularly when field-control problems probably increase nonlinearly with very large sample sizes. The chart may be interpreted, then, as evidence that effort spent in editing the questionnaires and in the field control of inflight surveys as herein depicted is likely to be more cost-effective than expenditures to increase the sample size.

NONRESPONSE PROBLEMS

Nonresponse as used in the preceding development encompasses all of the departures from random sampling encountered in implementing the design. There are many. The quality of a sample is determined by the extent to which these departures are minimized. Sample size, in practice, is a relatively small consideration in generating estimates that can be used with confidence. Large sample sizes cannot correct the damage that can be done when control of the field work is weak or ineffective.

Failures to maintain the integrity of a random sample can result in bias, or wrong estimates. At the first stage of selection, for example, the field representative might fail to cover some shifts. If there are many such failures, they might tend to be weekend shifts—or rainy days. One might try to correct this by rescheduling, in another week, for the same type of shift lost but the replacement schedule will be different—hopefully, not significantly.

At the second stage of selection—flights within shifts—there can be errors in the source flight listing or in the record of flights selected. If the schedule is not found when the field representative looks for the flight, a departure from random sampling is encountered. Intensive control over the flight-selection procedure is necessary to minimize this problem.

In practice, the third stage of selection—passengers—is where control is the weakest. The successful return of a completed questionnaire depends on a chain of events fraught with frail links, any one of which can result in the failure to complete an observation on a randomly selected element. Thus, the sample that results—the final collection of completed questionnaires—becomes the result of a "selection" process that has many nonrandom elements. This is where the most important sources of possible bias can be encountered, where wrong estimates are born.

The field rep meets the chief cabin attendant before flight departure time to deliver enough questionnaires for each seat on the flight (in order to assure that there are enough for all enplaned passengers) in a return-addressed envelope or pouch designed to survive the return trip to Airport X and remain there until the rep retrieves the kit at a later date. The chief cabin attendant must be contacted because there can be 13 or more cabin attendants involved, and good supervision of the inflight phase is critical to proper coverage. Although the contact is brief, it is obviously important that the communi-

cation be effective. It is most effective if the time and place of meeting are carefully coordinated with airline procedures. Nevertheless, some flight crews will refuse to accept the survey kit, and a contribution to nonresponse is encountered. While rescheduling the same flight a week or so later is clearly desirable, it may not be practical.

Even after accepting the survey, the flight crew may not choose to implement the inflight phase—because of bad weather, a full flight, or other reasons; and more nonresponse is encountered. Again, rescheduling might be desirable, but at best, it would be delayed a few weeks until the absence of the returned flight kit gave evidence of the failure to perform the inflight phase. It might still not be practical to reschedule.

Inflight distributions may fall short, far short, of the intended 100 percent for a variety of reasons that are rarely documented. The only evidence available is the number of completed questionnaires finally received versus the load statistics. The questionnaires may have been given only to passengers in aisle seats, who might tend to be experienced business travelers; or they might have been given only to passengers in window seats, who might tend to be new travelers on vacation. These are just two of the obviously many possibilities for bias in an undisciplined selection of passengers on the flight. Similarly there may be gaps in the collection of completed questionnaires adding further to the nonresponse problems. Numbering the questionnaires provides information for evaluating problems of these kinds.

The last level at which nonresponse is encountered is from the passenger. This, too, can be importantly influenced by the flight crew—by whether or not response is solicited on the PA system and, if an announcement is made, the quality of the appeal. Again, numbering the questionnaires provides information that can be used to identify the contributions to nonresponse from passengers themselves.

SOME PERSPECTIVES ON RESPONSE RATES

Some qualitative inferences about the relative significance of these various components of nonresponse accumulated over years of inflight surveys may be useful to someone contemplating an inflight survey (or using results from one). Domestic inflight surveys during the late 1950s produced a 96 percent success rate on flight contacts; 96 percent of the flights selected for inclusion in the sample came back with a 50 percent or better response rate from within the flight. The response rate within successful flights was 92 percent. Overseas (transatlantic and western hemisphere) inflight surveys were weaker: 78 percent of the flight contacts came back with a 50 percent response rate or better, and the response rate from within successful flights averaged 80 percent (with multilingual questionnaires).

Ten years later, in the late 1960s, domestic-inflight-success rates were down to 80 percent of the flights coming back with 50 percent or better response—and response within successful flights (having 50 percent or better) was 80 percent. Among transatlantic flights, the success rate went down to 68 percent of the sampled flights coming back with 50 percent or better response, and down to 63 percent response within successful flights.

Another 10 years later, in the late 1970s, performance criteria had been further eroded. The standard for an acceptable flight had to be lowered from 50 percent to 20 percent, and rescheduling of flight failures completely abandoned. Only 40 percent of domestic flight contacts were "successful" under the old standard of yielding a 50 percent or better within-flight response, while only about 20 percent of the overseas flight selections met the same standard. By reducing the standard to a 20 percent for within-flight response, the successful flights became 67 percent in domestic and 55 percent in overseas.

In summary, the increasing problem with inflight survey response can be described by the following table describing the share of all flights drawn into the sample yielding a 50 percent or better response rate from passengers within the flight:

Proportion of Flights Contacted Yielding 50% or Better Response

	DOMESTIC	OVERSEAS
1958	96%	78%
1968	80%	68%
1978	40%	20%

It has been shown that the nonresponse problem is a function of the increasing size of aircraft. The administrative problems of distributing and collecting questionnaires on jumbo aircraft are formidable. Airlines are coping with this problem in a variety of ways. One approach taken is to designate a specific cabin crew member to deliver questionnaires to an occupant of a preselected random sample of 8 to 10 seats instead of attempting 100 percent coverage.

Other methods of improving control of the inflight phase of these surveys will no doubt appear as problems with the old methods are further amplified. The most likely improvements will probably hinge on the fact that quality is more effective than quantity—that more effort put towards the selection and inclusion of a few carefully chosen passengers or flights will lead to estimates commanding more confidence than dissipating effort in the accumulation of large samples of doubtful origin. In any case, it is rather clear that a designated survey representative is necessary in each selected flight.

SAMPLING ERROR

Among the theoretical implications of a well-founded random sample is the ability to describe confidence intervals around the estimates. A wide variety of estimating functions for error due to sampling are available. The simplest are the replicated sample type that are best accommodated in the early stages of sample design. The plan described herein can be adapted to these formulae with relatively modest constraints, but added complication, nonetheless. It is beyond the scope of this elemental exposition to give adequate atten-

tion to sampling error or attendant considerations for efficiency. It may suffice to state that the design as herein proposed could yield estimates within a few percentage points of true values for the sample universe.

EXTENSIONS

The model inflight-survey proposal developed in the foregoing can be easily extended to encompass another airport, say Airport Y, if there is sufficient community of interest to support a cooperative inflight-survey program for two airports—or three or four airports. Cooperative programs among airports can produce efficiencies that will lead to lower unit costs and enhance the value of the information derived.

REFERENCES

Kish, Leslie (1965), *Survey Sampling*, New York: John Wiley & Sons, Inc.

Kish, Leslie, and Martin R. Frankel (1970), "Balanced Repeated Replication for Standard Errors," *Journal of the American Statistical Association* 65, 1071–1094.

Kish, Leslie, and Martin R. Frankel (1974), "Inference from Complex Samples," *Journal of the Royal Statistical Society* B36, 1–37.

The Port Authority of New York & New Jersey (1965), *New York's Domestic Air Passenger Market*. A report of a one-year survey conducted April 1963 through March 1984.

The Port Authority of New York & New Jersey (1970), *New York's Domestic Air Passenger Market*. A report of a one-year survey conducted June 1967 through May 1968.

The Port Authority of New York & New Jersey (1980), *Airport Access Survey*. A report of a one-year survey conducted among all scheduled airline passengers at La Guardia, J.F. Kennedy, and Newark Airports during the calendar year 1978 in collaboration with the FAA.

The Port Authority of New York & New Jersey (1987), *Inflight Survey Results*. A report of a one-year survey conducted during the year ending September 1985.

The Port Authority of New York & New Jersey (1991a), *Customer Attitude Tracking Study*, Port Authority Bus Terminal. Prepared for The Interstate Transportation Department, Office of Business Development, August.

The Port Authority of New York & New Jersey (1991b), *Air Passenger Survey 1990*, Four volumes; one for each of the airports and a collected volume with all airports combined: La Guardia Airport, Newark International Airport, and John F. Kennedy International Airport. Reports on a survey conducted during the year ending March 1991.

The Port Authority of New York & New Jersey (1991c), *Aviation Air Passenger Survey*, specifications for an intercept survey of all air passengers using LaGuardia, J. F. Kennedy International, and Newark International Airports during the full year ending March 1991.

New York's Air Travelers (1956)—(88 pages) "Forward."

This survey was conducted by The Port of New York Authority with the collaboration of all domestic air carriers serving New York City airports and Air France. It is probably the first of its kind conducted in this country.

Because of its uniqueness and informative nature, it could well be the forerunner of other profitable studies of all carriers and other major transportation areas. It is published with the permission of The Port of New York Authority.

The Eno Foundation extends its kindest appreciation for the privilege of publishing it.

ENO FOUNDATION (1956), The Eno Foundation for Highway Traffic Control, Saugatuck; this Eno report marks one of the first public efforts to evaluate the quality of a survey by comparing some of its estimates with "known" values from other (independent) sources—thus combining both sampling error and the possibility of bias in the quality evaluation of survey statistics.

39

The Delphi Technique: A Tool for Long-Range Travel and Tourism Planning

GEORGE H. MOELLER
Deputy Station Director
Pacific Northwest Research Station
U.S. Forest Service
Portland, Oregon

ELWOOD L. SHAFER
Professor of Environmental Management & Tourism
School of Hotel, Restaurant & Institutional Management
The Pennsylvania State University
University Park, Pennsylvania

Travel and tourism planning and management require looking to the future for events that are likely to influence current decisions. The rapid change that underlies future tourism and related travel activities is frequently attributed to advancing technology. This paper examines the state-of-the-art methodologies to forecast future travel and tourism activities as they may be impacted by oncoming technology and discusses the results of a study that uses some of these methodologies. Future events in this study are catalogued in five categories: natural resource management, wildland recreation management, environmental controls, population—work force—leisure, and urban environments.

WHY STUDY THE FUTURE?

The future was once a kind of never-never land that had nothing to do with practical matters like earning a living, making a success of one's life, or managing an organization. But, today, events are occurring rapidly, and the future has become part of the present! If measured by the time between events, time is actually speeding up. To cope with this accelerated rate of time, one needs to plan to meet anticipated change. Tourism planning and management require looking to the future for events that are likely to influence current decisions, as well as to evaluate future impacts of current decisions. To cope, attention must be focused on the future, not on the present or the past, because these are beyond being changed. Never in history have human beings been subjected to so many changes in so short a time. Few agree on where

all this change is leading or what its ultimate result may be. But it is clear that a hurricane of change is sweeping through all human institutions—particularly in the fields of recreation and tourism. If planners and managers are to cope, they must focus on the future and plan to meet it through today's program decisions.

The rapid change that underlies future states of travel and tourism is frequently attributed to advancing technology. People often think of technology as consisting of such things as machinery and chemicals. But, in a broader sense, it includes practical knowledge as well as the social and political arrangements found effective to implement developing technology.

Advancing technology has greatly intensified an ancient problem: the unintended consequences of any action or plan. Every action radiates forward in time and outward in space,

473

eventually affecting almost everything else. Recent technology influencing travel and tourism has convincingly demonstrated that the consequences of a new technology are often far different and far greater than the users of that technology may have first dreamed. The automobile, for example, did much more than just provide people with a way to travel rapidly, easily, and inexpensively from their homes to their places of business. The social and economic changes brought about by the automobile form a long list—effects on the family, on jobs, on entertainment, on the landscape, and, obviously, on travel and tourism. What are the implications of other emerging changes on the future of travel and tourism? Is there anything that can be done about this—and, what approaches can be taken to assessing future change and its impact on travel and tourism?

It is not possible for anyone to come up with a neat, effective master plan for the future of tourism; and if anyone tried, it would be either farcical or dangerous. Changes in tourism systems take place on so vast a scale that they cannot be easily controlled by a handful of experts or politicians. The process of change occurs at a million points at once—in transportation systems, in businesses, in communities, as well as in government—and it involves millions of ordinary people, as well as specialized or elite groups. Nevertheless, futurism can make a significant contribution to solving tourism planning and management challenges in the next decade and beyond.

THE UNCERTAINTY BARRIER

There is a period of time, perhaps three years, beyond which the ability to understand and suggest future events become extremely hazy and uncertain. How uncertain? More uncertain than people care to admit! More uncertain than people can afford to be in making some of the decisions they must make! The world is faced, for instance, with committing to energy conservation (10- to 20-year commitments) while lacking the ability to foresee the effects of related government policy (or lack of it) on tourism activities even two years ahead.

Future studies give some comfort, but not much. Experience suggests that such studies substantially understate future uncertainties. For one thing, there are few experts to call on in gauging future political compromises or in assessing public sentiment, which is whipsawed so erratically, sometimes by modern media. Additionally, growing world interdependence and intercommunication have grossly complicated the models and the number of parameters involved in the study of future tourism business environments. This complexity alone presents a barrier to how far insight can reach into the future.

Admittedly, there are limits imposed by a type of "uncertainty principle" applied to planning for the future of tourism. This might be stated as a trade-off between time and detail. In other words, the further ahead one tries to look, the less discrimination there is in understanding. Is this a hopeless situation? No. But it is a very tough one—one that

should compel the rethinking of tourism planning methods and objectives.

FUTURES METHODOLOGIES

The time-honored way to deal with change has been to take it as it comes and then adjust to its impact. Under today's conditions of rapid change, however, the time available for such evaluation and adjustment has decreased. But scientists have started to develop methods for investigating the future that do not require the future to merge with the present before action programs can be developed.

TREND EXTRAPOLATION

The most common way to make projections is to extrapolate historical experience or past trends. Such projections are based on the assumption that the future will be a logical extension of the past. The approach has severe limitations (Rescher 1967). The effects of technological innovation and predictable future political-social events cannot be incorporated into extrapolations. Extrapolation techniques are based on the restrictive assumption that causal relationships that have produced past trends will continue to operate in the future. Yet, it is reasonably certain that the future will be nothing like the past. This method of forecasting is used not only by people in their everyday lives but also by city planners, economists, demographers, and all the other specialists who first identify a trend and then make a projection suggesting where that trend will lead.

SCENARIOS

A *scenario* is simply a series of events intertwined to form a concept of the future. Everyday thinking continuously takes ventures into the mysterious world of next week's or even next year's scenario. Someone may begin a scenario by asking, "What would happen if I went to the theater on Saturday night?" With the question posed, the person can begin to imagine the various consequences of the action. First, it would require certain preparations: for example, transportation to the theater would be needed. Then, if the event did occur, further consequences might arise, such as missing a relative who might drop in unexpectedly for a visit.

A scenario awakens one to potential problems that might accompany a proposed action. A scenario can help people to decide whether they want to do something and how to do it. Many policy analysts working for various governments now use scenarios to explore alternative policies that their governments might pursue. In effect, a scenario provides a way to shape futures more intelligently.

ANALYTICAL MODELS

A host of analytical approaches to projections of the future have developed with the advent of rapid data-processing and associated improvements in mathematical and systems-modeling techniques. Analytical models are based on mathematical relationships between relevant elements that are thought to produce or influence the outcome of the process of interest. Although based largely on past relationships, analytical models are flexible so that relationships between modeled elements and the absolute levels of elements themselves can be changed for estimating the effect on the performance of a system. Such analytical models provide a powerful tool for investigating the future and evaluating outcomes of alternative courses of action.

EXPERT OPINION

When someone considers taking an important course of action, he or she usually solicits the advice of other people—often people who have some special knowledge of the proposed venture. These people will give their judgments of what will likely happen in response to the actions. In effect, these "consultants" make forecasts based on their own special insights and knowledge. Their counsel helps one to understand what may be encountered in the future and how the future can be dealt with. Top leaders in business and government use this forecasting technique; for example, the President of the United States may describe a number of alternative courses of action to his or her cabinet and get their views on the consequences of each.

Scholars in research institutes ("think tanks") use the methods mentioned, plus others, to explore the future. In recent years, they have made many improvements in the naive methods of forecasting that most people use. Yet the basic principles remain the same.

THE DELPHI TECHNIQUE

Any or all of the aforementioned techniques can be used to predict the future of travel and tourism. But whatever the method used, judgment is required, even in sophisticated analytical models where expert opinion is needed to specify future levels of the model components. Judgment must be based on knowledge, opinion, or speculation. Knowledge, of course, provides information on which to make a firm judgment. Opinion is informed judgment based on limited evidence or a thought process that can be opened to discussion. Thus, opinion can be altered as new evidence becomes available. Speculation does not provide a valid basis for judgment, because it is not based on knowledge or other tangible evidence (Dalkey 1968b). Thus, without knowledge, opinion is the next best insight on which to base futures evaluations.

DESCRIPTION

The Delphi technique is a method used to systematically combine expert knowledge and opinion to arrive at an informed group consensus about the likely occurrence of future events. The technique derives its importance from the realization that projections of future events, on which decisions must often be based, are formed largely through the insight of informed individuals, rather than through predic-

tions derived from well-established theory (Helmer and Rescher 1960).

The Delphi technique is based on the assumption that although the future is uncertain, its probabilities can be approximated by individuals who are able to make informed judgments about future contingencies. It is intended to provide a general perspective on the future rather than a sharp picture.

Instead of the traditional approach to achieve consensus of opinion through face-to-face discussion, the Delphi technique ". . . eliminates committee activity altogether, thus . . . reducing the influence of certain psychological factors, such as specious persuasion, unwillingness to abandon publicly expressed opinions, and the bandwagon effect of majority opinion" (Helmer and Rescher 1960).

The Delphi technique encourages individual input by maintaining anonymity among those who take part in the process. Information relevant to the development of consensus is systematically fed back to participants by the Delphi study director. Several rounds of rethinking the problem, with information feedback provided after each round, usually result in a convergence of a group opinion (Dalkey 1968a).

The Delphi technique replaces direct open debate with a series of questionnaires sent to a selected panel of experts. The general procedures used to conduct a Delphi investigation are outlined in Table 1. Successive questionnaires contain opinion-feedback summaries from previous panel responses (Weaver 1969). Feedback information includes summaries of reasons given by individuals for their responses about the probability, desirability, interaction, or impact of future events. This information serves to stimulate further thought about points that other panel members may have overlooked and allows them the opportunity to reconsider arguments they may have at first thought to be unimportant.

Delphi study results are summarized graphically to show the interquartile range of predictions (Figure 1). The median is most often used as the most probable year of occurrence because half the predictions fall above and half below that point. Independent events are then often woven together to form an abstract concept of the future or to develop scenarios.

CRITIQUE

The Delphi technique has been subjected to much criticism (Weaver 1972). Identification of panel experts and evaluation of their expertise present problems. Experts are usually busy people, and it is difficult to get them to serve on a Delphi panel for an extended period of time. Panel attrition can be severe. The effect of dropout has not been evaluated.

The Delphi study director can have a strong effect on study results. The events he or she chooses to include in the study and the way in which event statements are phrased can easily lead to misinterpretation (Salanick et al. 1971). The study director can also influence results by editing panel response-feedback information.

The Delphi technique has been criticized because it usu-

TABLE 1 Steps in Conducting a Delphi Study

STEP	PROCEDURE	
Identify relevant events.	Determine events from theoretical models, futures scenarios, or literature. Panel members may also suggest events.	
Prepare event statements.	Statements must be clear and precise.	
Select and establish panel of experts.	Select panelists from area of expertise suggested by the problem—expertise based on contributions to the literature and peer recognition.	
Mail Delphi questionnaire.	Questions asked of panel members.	Summary information sent to panel members.
Round 1 questionnaire	Assign probabilities and dates to events. Add events to list. Solicit information on ambiguous statements.	Edit event statements. Prepare response summary distributions showing individual responses.
Round 2 questionnaire	Ask individuals to reevaluate their round-1 responses based on summary distributions. Ask panelists to provide reasons for changing or not changing their responses if they remain outside interquartile range.	Prepare interquartile response summaries for round-2 questionnaire. Edit reasons given by those outside interquartile range.
Round 3 questionnaire	Ask individuals to evaluate their round-2 responses based on summary information. Ask panelists to provide reasons for changing or not changing their responses if they remain outside interquartile range.	Prepare summaries of interquartile distribution of round-3 questionnaire responses. Edit reasons given by those outside interquartile range.
Round 4 questionnaire	Give individuals final chance to reevaluate their round-3 responses based on summary information. Ask panelists to rate their expertise, evaluate desirability of each event, evaluate interactions between events, and evaluate social impact of each event.	
Other rounds	Questionnaires should continue until a consensus prediction begins to emerge.	
Data analysis	Prepare event summaries showing event distribution, probabilities, impacts, desirabilities, and interactions. Use median prediction as most probable year of event occurrence. Prepare summaries of interquartile distributions. Prepare futures scenarios.	

ally treats events as independent of one another (Dalkey 1968a). It does not provide a way to evaluate the interaction between events. As well, an event's probability of occurrence depends largely on the general perspective assumed by panel members when they make their evaluations. If panel members do not share common perspectives, resulting predictions of events will be based on different criteria.

The Delphi technique has not been extensively tested in predicting events other than those directly related to technol-

ogy. It has been shown to be most accurate in predicting technological events related to space and medical developments and in forecasting political alliances. The technique has had limited application for predicting events that involve human interaction.

Although based on many restrictive assumptions, the Delphi technique is useful where decisions have to be made quickly with limited knowledge. Indeed, in such situations, there may be no alternative. The need to make decisions

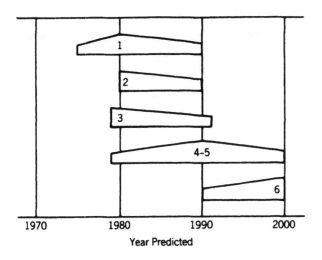

Key to Events:

1. Different recreation activities allocated specific time periods for the same recreation-management area.
2. Computers used to advise recreationists where to go for recreation.
3. Tax credits to industries that practice pollution control.
4. Consumers accept major cost of pollution control.
5. Most homes have videotape systems.
6. Five hundred miles is a reasonable one-way distance to travel for a weekend.

FIGURE 1 Example, graphic summary of Delphi results: medians and interquartile ranges of panel predictions.

today to meet tomorrow's leisure needs provides an example. It is easy for professionals in recreation to get tied up with everyday problems. Seldom can they see beyond next year's operating budget. But, if changing leisure needs are to be met, they must take a longer look into the future. The Delphi technique can help focus their thinking.

AN EXAMPLE—APPLICATION OF DELPHI TO RECREATION EVALUATION

Following is an example of how the Delphi technique was used in a study to probe for social, managerial, and technological events that are likely to shape the future of park and recreation management to the year 2000. Although study results are somewhat dated, they have strong implications for future travel and tourism planning and management.

In 1974, 900 experts in the biological sciences, ecology, conservation, and fields related to population dynamics, recreation resource management, and environmental technology were asked to take part in the study. Selection of panel members was based on their contributions to the current literature on environment and technology.

The panel of experts were asked to list events that they felt had a fifty-fifty chance of occurring by the year 2000. They were instructed to consider only those events that

related to their own areas of expertise. Responses were summarized and resubmitted to the panel through four rounds of questionnaires (Table 1). Each time, panel members were given the opportunity to reevaluate their previous predictions in light of these summaries.

Results were summarized by grouping events by the median year of prediction—the year falling at the midpoint of the distribution of panel predictions—50 percent of the experts felt that the event would occur on or before the median year, and 50 percent felt it would occur on or after the median year or never. Descriptive information returned to panel members in each round included the median and interquartile distribution of panel responses for each event.

Events fell into five categories: Natural Resource Management, Wildland Recreation Management, Environmental Controls, Population—Work Force—Leisure, and Urban Environments. More detailed results of this study have been reported elsewhere (Shafer and Moeller 1974).

NATURAL RESOURCE MANAGEMENT

The panel predicted an expanding role of government in directing natural resource management. It forecast that, by 1980, economic incentives would be offered to private landowners who manage for fish and wildlife. Although not precise, it appears that this panel prediction was reasonably accurate. Several states have enacted laws that allow tax revenues to be diverted directly toward fish-and-game management activities. Federal cost-sharing has also been made available to support fish and wildlife habitat-improvement projects. The panel further predicted that these programs would broaden by 1985 to include tax incentives for providing scenic amenities.

The panel anticipates that the federal role in coordinating natural resource planning will expand from establishing the first land, water, and air-use plan in 1990 to a comprehensive national land-use zoning plan in 2000. By 2000, environmental planning will be effectively coordinated among all levels of government and private interests. Also by 2000, land-use patterns will stabilize, and land preempted for one use will be replaced with comparable land. All land resources, including marine and estuarine areas, will be under intensive management.

WILDLAND RECREATION MANAGEMENT

In this area, it was forecast that, by 1980, restrictions would be placed on recreational use of wildland areas. Again, this prediction was relatively accurate. Permits are now required for use of many remote recreation areas. It is also a common wildland recreation management practice to restrict and allocate particular kinds of recreation use to specific areas and times and to allow use of only certain kinds of recreation equipment. The panel also predicted that, by 1980, computers would be used to advise people on where to go for resource-based outdoor recreation. Such computerized information systems are now commonly available.

By 1985, it was predicted that limits would be placed on the number of people allowed to use all wilderness and remote recreation areas and that maximum noise levels would be established for recreation vehicles. It was further forecast that the outdoor recreation experience would change: that facilities such as cable TV hookups would be available at most campgrounds. Also by 1985, it was expected that economic incentives would be offered to private landowners who open their land for public recreation.

Growing demand will require further restrictions on recreation use by 1990. Restrictive management techniques will be employed to reinforce heavily used recreation sites and to direct use patterns. Public recreation areas will be assigned maximum carrying capacities, and use will be kept at or below these levels. Reservations will be required for use of developed public recreation facilities. Maximum sizes will be established for boat motors used on public water bodies. Licenses will be required for all types of saltwater fishing.

By 2000, wilderness management policy will change to allow for more intensive recreational development. Permits, used to control all forms of wildland recreation, will also require certification for certain user groups. The wildland recreation area of 2000 will be vastly different from that of today. Only transportation systems that have a minimum physical and visual impact on the natural environment will be allowed, and only recreation vehicles that employ nonpolluting propulsion systems will be permitted in wildland recreation areas. Heavily used areas will be serviced by air, and parks will be aesthetically improved by underground placement of utility lines.

Technology will aid the park manager of 2000: Artificial lighting will extend use of recreation facilities, and remote-sensing devices will be used to monitor park use. Waste-disposing bacteria will be incorporated into recreation area equipment to reduce sanitary disposal problems. Extensive irrigation of arid regions will broaden and enhance recreational opportunities.

Technology will also create challenging management problems; for example, the experts felt that, by 2000, small private recreational submarines, hovercraft, jet-powered backpacks, and one-man helicopters will be in common use.

The wildlife manager will utilize captive rearing to raise endangered species for release and will monitor wildlife migrations by satellite. Controls will be placed on hunting, and motorized vehicles will be excluded from all public hunting areas during hunting seasons. But, by 2000, wildlife resources will be used primarily for nonconsumptive purposes such as photography.

ENVIRONMENTAL CONTROLS

Most experts felt that, by 1980, tax credits would be available to industries that meet pollution-control standards. Indeed, many kinds of tax credits have become available to industries to retrofit plant and equipment for pollution abatement. But, the panel felt that by 1990, standards will be strongly enforced and companies that do not comply will be closed.

It was expected that concern for landscape aesthetics would lead to half the states passing legislation to control

outdoor advertising by 1985. Also by that year, experts foresaw that effective controls would be placed on auto and airplane exhaust emissions and that all consumer products judged to have adverse impacts on the environment would be banned from production.

By 1990, data collected through a nationwide monitoring system will be incorporated into models that accurately simulate the environmental effects of pollutants. Consumers will accept the major costs of effective pollution controls. By 1995, all consumer products will be packaged in biodegradable containers.

By 2000, strict international pollution-control standards will be established, and an international environmental monitoring agency will be organized. Although predictions varied considerably among panel members, other events predicted for the turn of the century include: setting exact human-tolerance limits for various pollutants; allowing only biodegradable chemicals to be discharged directly into the environment; and restricting federal reserve chartered banks from financing companies that are known polluters.

POPULATION—WORK FORCE—LEISURE

A growing population with changing attitudes toward leisure will have a major impact on recreation programs. By 1985, experts predicted that there would be an average 4-day, 34-hour work week and that most employers would provide leisure counseling services. By 1990, data on leisure activities and interests will be a regular part of the U.S. decennial population census. In response to changing leisure patterns, public schools will operate year-round, with staggered vacation periods. Most homes will be equipped with videotape systems for entertainment and education.

By 2000, panel members felt that 500 miles would be a reasonable one-way distance to travel on weekend recreation trips. Tax incentives will be available to employers who include recreation facilities in the design and construction of new plants.

By 2000, "weekends" will be distributed throughout the week. With an average retirement age of 50 years, more total leisure time will be available during retirement. In response to this abundant leisure, the role of public schools will expand further to serve the recreation needs of the entire community. Middle-income families will vacation as commonly on other continents as they now vacation in the United States. Panel members also felt that, by 2000, the work ethic would have assumed a lesser role in society and leisure would become an acceptable life-style. An attempt will be made to control population growth through tax incentives, but panel members felt that a mandatory population-control program would eventually be established.

URBAN ENVIRONMENT

Improved planning and technology will combine to make future urban environments much more enjoyable than they are today. It was predicted that, by 1985, more emphasis would be placed on providing recreation services for specific urban-population groups; for example, experts predicted that most urban areas will have special fishing areas for the handicapped, elderly, and children.

By 1990, private aircraft will be excluded from all metropolitan airports. Ten years later, only non-air-polluting vehicles will be allowed in downtown urban areas. Computers will be used to control the movement of individual vehicles. More urban land will be provided for leisure enjoyment; cemeteries, water reservoirs, and planned open space will be available for recreation. Facilities, like city parks and play fields, will be covered with artificial turf to sustain heavy recreation pressure, and some will be covered with transparent domes to allow year-round use. Natural environments will be simulated inside manmade structures to provide urban residents with recreation opportunities now available only in the outdoors.

SUMMARY OF STUDY RESULTS

Results of the example Delphi study should not be taken as indisputable fact. Individual items may be grossly inaccurate. But taken as a whole, the predictions represent a future perspective, with clearly identified underlying trends. This future perspective and the trends on which it is based are perhaps the most valuable product of a Delphi.

What are the trends in these Delphi predictions? Action will be taken at all levels of government to face environmental pressures brought about by increasing demands of a growing population with more time and money. Rational resource planning will be coupled with rigid, enforced controls. How much controls will affect individual freedom cannot easily be determined.

Taken as a whole, the panel of experts predict an optimistic future. The events are certainly possible and even probable; some have already occurred. But whether they occur will depend on the route that is selected along the road to the future. People cannot suddenly be expected to become more rational than they have been in the past. But, through better understanding, people can become more aware of the consequences of their decisions and can choose their own future.

IMPLICATIONS OF FUTURES PERSPECTIVES

Everyone working in the rapidly changing field of travel and tourism faces hundreds of problems, each demanding more than they can possibly give. Pressed by the urgent tasks of the moment, people often feel a little impatient with anyone who suggests that they should think about the future. The person might naturally reply, "How can you ask me to think about the future when I'm trying to deal with a crisis right now?"

Yet, the fact that the world is experiencing a crisis today offers one of the best reasons for thinking about the future. Almost always, the crisis has resulted from a failure to deal with a problem before it became a crisis. In retrospect, it is generally easy to see how a modest amount of thought and

effort—if invested earlier—could have forestalled a crisis and saved the subsequent money and grief.

Identifying the potential crises of the future in order to avert them is one important function of the study of the future. In effect, the systematic exploration of future possibilities serves as an early warning system, permitting people to deal with problems before they become disasters.

A study of the future of travel and tourism can help provide reasonable assumptions about what the future may hold. At the same time, it can help identify future dangers and opportunities, giving planners and managers a set of perspectives with which they can respond to a rapidly changing world. The futures perspective should be reinforced through an understanding that:

1. The future is not fixed but consists of a variety of alternatives to choose from in order to meet goals.
2. Choice is unavoidable; refusing to choose is itself a choice.
3. Small changes today can become major changes through time.
4. The future world of travel and tourism will be drastically different from the present one.
5. Planners and managers in travel and tourism are largely responsible for the travel and tourism of the future; that future will not just happen to them, they will create it!
6. Methods successful in the past probably will not work in the future.

In an era when momentous long-term decisions about humans and their environment must be made, similar attention should be given to the underlying prediction process upon which all tourism planning must be based; for example, the United States government staked $20 billion on inventing a future that included placing a man on the moon by 1970. Similarly, many other potential futures are open to humankind.

Short-term (two-to-five-year) analysis—upon which many of today's tourism management decisions are based—has the advantage of being able to extrapolate from existing trends. But in many tourism systems, long-range analyses are needed that consider future breakthroughs in technology that may appear and interact before a specific future event occurs. Thus, the variables and contingencies of most futures beyond five years from now can only be assessed intuitively. The use of intuitive "forecasting" as a basis for long-range tourism planning is unavoidable.

The Delphi technique, along with the other futures forecasting methods reviewed here, provides a useful tool with which to probe the future so that individuals, organizations, and public agencies concerned with travel and tourism can work together in a framework of cooperation and desired progress.

REFERENCES

Dalkey, Norman C. (1968a), "Experiments in Group Prediction," Paper P-3820, Santa Monica, CA: Rand Corp.

Dalkey, Norman C. (1968b), "Predicting the Future," Paper P-3948, Santa Monica, CA: Rand Corp.

Helmer, Olaf, and Nicholas Rescher (1960), "On the Epistemology of the Exact Sciences," Paper R-353, Santa Monica, CA: Rand Corp.

Rescher, Nicholas (1967), "The Future as an Object of Research," Paper P-3593, Santa Monica, CA: Rand Corp.

Salanick, J.R., William Wenger, and Ellen Helfer (1971), "The Construction of Delphi Event Statements," *Technology Forecasting and Social Change* 3:65–73.

Shafer, Elwood L., Jr., and George H. Moeller (1974), "Through the Looking Glass in Environmental Management," *Parks and Recreation* 9(2):20–23, 48, 49.

Toffler, Alvin (1971), *Future Shock*, New York: Bantam Books, Inc.

Weaver, Timothy W. (1969), "Delphi as a Method for Studying the Future: Testing Some Underlying Assumptions," Syracuse, NY: Syracuse University, School of Education Policy Research Center.

Weaver, Timothy W. (1972), "Delphi: a critical review," Syracuse, NY: Syracuse University, School of Education Policy Research Center, Research Report 7.

40

Using Panels for Travel and Tourism Research

WILBUR F. LaPAGE
Director
Division of Parks and Recreation
State of New Hampshire
Concord, New Hampshire

While relatively little use has been made of panels for travel and tourism research, this method offers enormous potential for improved understanding of travel market trends and tourism promotion analysis. Panels of consumers and of producers of travel experiences are discussed from four specific research objectives: trend monitoring, test marketing, impact assessment, and future assessment. The advantages and disadvantages of panels are discussed, and several examples are cited. Considerations for the design and maintenance of panels are presented and references included for a variety of panel studies and analysis techniques.

Consumer panels have played an important role in studies of consumer purchasing patterns, including such leisure interest trends as television viewing and dining out. Less well known are the numerous industry panels of dealers, agents, retailers, and various professionals that also are valuable sources of market trend insight.

Although panels are usually viewed as a longitudinal survey technique, they do have important uses other than trend monitoring. Many new products arriving on the market, for example, have received extensive testing by panels. Because of their stand-by capability, panels also are valuable for assessing the social impacts of unforeseen events. And voter panels as well as panels of specialists have been used effectively for short-term predictions. Each of these uses has potential applications for travel and tourism research.

PANELS FOR TREND MONITORING

Reliable facts and figures on trends in tourism are surprisingly scarce in light of the high values placed on such data by planners and investors. While available indicators such as park visits, passports issued, commercial lodging, vacation trips, airline travel, and gasoline consumption provide gross estimates of tourism trends, their value for planning purposes is limited. Questions of travel market shifts, interactivity substitutions, changing travel interests and frequencies, planned equipment purchases, and travel intentions reflect a more ideal level of detail for corporate planning. This kind of data, along with documented trends in tourism developments and profitability, could spell the difference between sound planning and superficial planning. Such trend data can best be generated by longitudinal studies of specific populations.

Longitudinal studies of tourists can be classified broadly as: (1) independent samples (resurveys) of a given population at two or more points in time, or (2) repeated measurements of the same sample (panels) over time. Both approaches have distinct applications for the study of travel and tourism depending on the specific research objectives. In general, resurveys are best for monitoring gross changes in large populations over extended time intervals; panels tend to be more commonly used for sensitive monitoring and in-depth studies of the factors (attitudes, interests, etc.) that may have contributed to those changes.

Most commonly, longitudinal studies take the form of periodic resurveys in which a new sample of the population is drawn for each survey. The National Boating Surveys (U.S. Coast Guard), The National Hunting and Fishing Surveys (U.S. Fish and Wildlife Service), The National Camping Market Surveys (USDA Forest Service), and The National Outdoor Recreation Participation Surveys (U.S. Department of the Interior) are federally sponsored resurveys conducted at approximately five-year intervals. A number of states, industries, and nonprofit research centers also conduct periodic travel and tourism surveys. The U.S. Travel Data Center, for example, conducts a telephone survey of 1,500 adults each month to gather information on travel behavior. The Commerce Department's periodic Surveys of National Travel, Retail Trade, Purchase of Durables, and Consumer Expenditures all provide opportunities for analysis of tourism-related trends. While obviously better than the available indicators, population resurveys are still basically descriptive and have a limited capability for explaining trends and shifts in leisure-related travel.

For longitudinal studies with greater explanatory capability, it is sometimes desirable to periodically recontact the same sample of respondents. Panels are superior for providing in-depth answers to questions of why market shifts and trends are taking place. An eight-year-long travel-oriented panel study conducted by the USDA Forest Service (LaPage and Ragain 1979) to document trends in camping participation showed clear relationships between family life-cycle stages and styles of camping participation. The study also documented the impacts of crowding on camping frequencies and destinations.

Panels of tourist businesses are more common than panels of tourists and have provided useful indexes of changes in business volume and profitability. One of the longest such series (23 years) is the Economic Analysis of North American Ski Areas conducted by the University of Colorado's Graduate School of Business Administration. This survey uses essentially the same sample of respondents each year (Goeldner et al. 1992). A similar commercial campground industry survey that has been in operation since 1979 provides a biweekly occupancy index (National Campground Owners' Association 1981).

A number of long-term market research panels are in use by industries, university research groups, and government agencies. The Census Bureau's Consumer Buying Expectation Survey, The University of Michigan Index of Consumer Sentiment, and the *Chicago Tribune* Panel are well-known and proven tools for monitoring changes in consumer behavior and attitudes. Several large companies such as General Electric (Carman 1974) maintain their own national panels to monitor such items of consumer behavior as brand loyalty, which can influence their market share. A number of independent research organizations (e.g., Market Facts, Inc.; Market Research Corp. of America; J. Walter Thompson; and National Family Opinion) maintain large consumer panels to provide their clients with up-to-date information about consumer purchases, purchase intentions, product recognition, and the likely acceptance of new products, services, packaging, and

delivery modes. The 10,000 member CREST (Chain Restaurant Eating-Out Share Trend) panel, using diaries, has monitored market shares and regional and seasonal purchasing changes among patrons of the nation's chain restaurants since 1975.

PANELS FOR TEST MARKETING

The availability of existing consumer panels, whose primary purpose is to track changes in purchasing patterns or in television viewing, provides an ideal opportunity for the test marketing of new products. Pilot television shows are evaluated in just this way to determine their potential for development into a continuing series. Comparisons of competing household products are frequently made by panels of homeowners who receive unidentified product samples for blind testing. Such panels can require intensive researcher-client interaction, including lengthy interviews, diary records of expenditures and use of time, and even the installation of recording instrumentation in the home, such as television audiometers.

While most panels exist with the full knowledge of the panel members, it is also possible, in fact highly likely, that most people have served on informal test marketing panels without knowing it. Mailing lists of credit card holders or college alumni, for example, may be sent brochures offering "discount" rates for vacation tours. The response rates are analyzed and, if favorable, the list becomes targeted for additional promotions—a de facto panel whose responses are purchases instead of opinions! In a similar fashion, buyers of chainsaws, garden tractors, television sets, guns, campers, snowmobiles, and so on, are often provided with a warranty containing a brief questionnaire that must be returned to the manufacturer for validation. The buyer gets his warranty and the sales department gets a mailing list, a purchaser profile, and a test-marketing panel.

The possibilities for establishing both formal and informal panels of travelers and tourists are clearly unlimited—every reservation, registration, and most equipment purchases and travel tickets can contribute to a potential master list for sampling and promotional targeting. The advantages of these informal panels are that they are already "in the market" and are inexpensive to establish. The disadvantage is that they can tell the researcher little about the market's potential size and distribution—critical facts for large-scale test marketing.

While the emphasis on panel research has been in the realm of long-term trend monitoring, the value of panels for short-term studies and experimental uses should not be overlooked: Entry and exit surveys at recreation areas or on cruise ships constitute a form of short-term panel ideally suited to matching visitor expectations and satisfactions. Short-term panels using diaries have been effective in studying seasonal changes in leisure behavior (Moeller 1975). Club memberships, subscription lists, and visitor registration afford outstanding opportunities for experimental panels to test the effectiveness of different promotional strategies. In terms of available sampling frames, the opportunities for using short-term panels to assess consumer acceptance of new travel products and tour-promotion packages have too often gone unrecognized.

Panels are ideally suited for a true before-after experimental design and, therefore, are capable of generating some of the strongest cause-effect data available to the social scientist. Once a panel's levels of travel expenditures, travel behavior, and travel attitudes have been determined, the panel can be subjected to stimuli in the form of promotional materials, price incentives, or new information, and then the panel's response can be determined. Sophisticated, split-sample designs can introduce the elements of control and of multivariate analysis. In this way, the images of various tourist destinations and travel modes can be determined and the effectiveness of a variety of measures to enhance those images can be assessed. Or the effectiveness of different tourism promotions might be assessed by first determining a base level of interest among the panel, distributing different brochures in a randomized block design, and subsequently recontacting the panel to determine new interest levels, trip plans, or actual trips taken. Obviously, subjecting a panel to this type of experimental use may compromise the future use of that same panel for trend monitoring purposes, or even for further experiments.

The stand-by capability of a panel to assess the impact of unforeseen events is often a case of "planned serendipity"! Voter panels established for the sole purpose of charting changing voter sentiment during an election campaign are frequently used to provide instant impact assessment of potentially significant turning points in the campaign. Since every campaign has its share of blunders, good and poor speeches, perceived ethnic slurs, and surprising revelations, today's astute political analyst will have a panel poised and ready for rapid feedback. Travel and tourism panels could provide the same type of impact analysis for such unforeseen (but highly probable) events as a series of airplane crashes, labor disputes at tourist attractions, hotel fires, bear attacks in national parks, or volcano eruptions!

In addition to assessing the impacts of real events, research on the effect of assumed or imagined events could prove useful in demonstrating the real costs to a tourist economy of erroneous news reporting or faulty weather forecasting. Again, the panel with its known behavior patterns provides a superior analytic model to the "what if" approach of an ad hoc survey.

Using panels for impact assessment is clearly a variation of the experimental design in which the intervening stimulus in the before-after sequence is not induced by the experimenter. This means that inferences from the data may be questionable. Specifically, all of the panel members are unlikely to have had equal exposure to the stimulus. Some may have been totally unaware of it, others may have received biased second- and third-hand accounts of it. The imaginative researcher may, however, be able to partially account for some of these sources of variation by careful questioning of the panel.

PANELS FOR FUTURE ASSESSMENT

Although the use of expert panels to provide a window on the future is discussed elsewhere in this Handbook, it is important to recognize that formal Delphi techniques are but one panel approach to developing probable future scenarios. An excellent model study of future leisure environments that uses the Delphi method has important implications for travel and tourism planners (Shafer et al. 1974).

At least two major national surveys have used panels to estimate future consumer impacts on the economy: The Consumer Buying Expectations Survey (U.S. Bureau of the Census) and the Index of Consumer Sentiment (University of Michigan). Both surveys include two to four panel contacts per year for assessing expectations of major consumer purchases and consumer confidence in the economy. Planned purchases of cars, campers, and boats, along with probability estimates for taking vacation trips, are important indicators for the travel and tourism industries. To the extent that these expectations can be correlated with actual past consumer behavior (via a trend-monitoring panel), their utility and reliability can be greatly extended.

In addition to panels of experts and panels of consumers, important future insights can be generated through the imaginative use of producer panels. Panels composed of equipment dealers, travel agents, park managers, airline stewardesses, and almost any group having constant contact with the traveling public are potential sources of information about tourists' unmet needs and dissatisfactions. It is safe to assume that there is a direct link between unmet needs and future market declines or shifts in market shares. The front line is an information source that is so obvious that it is all too often ignored by many market researchers and most managers!

ADVANTAGES AND DISADVANTAGES OF PANELS

The decision of whether to use a panel for travel and tourism research is a complex one. The panel approach must be appropriate to the objectives of the research and must be viewed in terms of organizational commitment. For trend-monitoring purposes, a simple listing of panel advantages and disadvantages is not very helpful to the researcher who must choose between a panel and periodic resurveys. The kind of detail desired in trend monitoring is far more important to the decision than the possibility that a panel, once established, might be useful for test marketing or for its stand-by potential.

Panels are often credited with being more economical than resurveys because sampling is only done once, and secondary contacts are often by mail. In fact, to be representative, the panel's composition must be constantly monitored, and procedures must be established for introducing replacements to the panel. Even if the follow-up contacts are by mail, the costs of panel maintenance may well offset that economic advantage. It is increasingly common for panel members to be paid for their services. Because of their continuing relationship, panel members often request follow-up information from the researcher. Unless one responds promptly to these requests, the panelists may lose interest and drop out.

Panels do provide a distinct advantage over other types of surveys in that they can tell the researcher a great deal about the nonrespondent. As members drop out of the panel over time, they leave behind a useful file of their characteristics and predropout purchasing/ participation patterns. And if budget restrictions require a mail survey rather than personal interviews, panels do tend to produce very high rates of mail response. In the Forest Service camper-panel study, 65 percent of the initial panel members continued to respond to the annual survey after five years. After eight years (and a three-year lapse between contacts), 53 percent of the panelists responded.

Panels are, of course, ideally suited to minimizing the error in social surveys that result from faulty memory recall. And where the study objectives require detailed responses about quantities purchased, prices paid, dates, brands, expectations, and satisfactions, carefully designed panel procedures can serve to shorten the gap between the event and its reporting. Waves of questionnaires can be timed to follow seasonal fluctuations in travel, for example, rather than using one survey to cover a full year. Frequent participants, such as a panel of skiers, may be asked to record their activities in a specially prepared diary format. And the simple fact of being a panel member can make the subjects more alert to remembering the kinds of travel facts being asked of the panel.

Because panels are expected to provide detailed data, there is a concern that the panel may lose its representivity as it becomes sensitized to the objectives of the survey. Panelists may assume that their price reactions might help to lower prices. They may fine-tune their comparisons, becoming far more discriminating than normal, as their awareness and analytic abilities are tested. Panels of hotel owners may overreport their occupancy, and panels of restaurants may overreport meals served if they assume that the data might be interpreted as a gain in their market share. In fact, underreporting, by consumer panels at least, is more of a problem than overreporting. No matter how carefully the researcher designs his study, humans forget. In general, the bias from underreporting due to forgetfulness is a constant and will have little impact on trend findings. It does, however, become important in the case of test marketing, and procedures are available for estimating its impact (Hyett and McKenzie 1976).

Because panels are considered sensitive social-measurement instruments, undetected errors can have serious consequences. So it is essential to undertake panel research only with a strong organizational commitment to the method to ensure awareness of the many potential error sources. By understanding the potential problems of panels, the researcher may be able to compensate for them, rather than discard the method. Concern relative to sensitization of the subjects, for example, can be countered by a panel design that includes

"controls" of different question wording and small-sample validity checks. Any survey contact produces a degree of sensitization to the study objectives and may generate bias due to the respondent trying to please the researcher. As a suspected limitation of panels, sensitization to the study objectives is probably exaggerated. In the case of the Forest Service camper panel, increasingly large numbers of campers were reporting that they were dissatisfied with conditions and planned to drop out of the market. Sensitization was suspected; however, in comparing panel responses with those of a national market survey conducted during the eighth year of the panel's existence, there were no significant differences in camper attitudes or participation patterns between panel members and nonmembers.

If sensitization is the most overrated source of bias in panel studies, selective dropout is probably the most underrated. Panel mortality is often related to the factors under study. Camper-panel members would sometimes report that they had lost interest in camping and would no longer be responding. In assuming that their contribution to the panel was now unimportant, they seriously compromised the panel's potentially most significant findings regarding the nature and duration of market dropout. Similarly, those panelists who are most interested and involved are also more likely to be panel losses simply because they may be too busy to participate. In a panel of travelers, these may be the most important and most difficult panel members to retain.

While incentives and compensation may help to avoid potential panel losses, they are likely to do so not because of value received but because that value convinces them that their contribution is important. Stressing that importance, for example with telephone follow-ups to nonrespondents, is probably the single most important guideline for panel maintenance.

Panels are clearly useful devices for travel and tourism research, both for long-term trend monitoring and short-term experimental testing. Long-term panels require considerable maintenance effort on the part of the researcher and are subject to a variety of sources of error from selective mortality, nonresponse, panel conditioning, initial selection bias, and underreporting. The potential effects of these errors on the survey results must be carefully considered in deciding whether to use panels or population resurveys. Despite the problems associated with them, panels are an effective and efficient way of developing indicators of change. There are many instances where consistency of bias is a reasonable trade-off for representivity, particularly when complete sampling frames are nonexistent, making representivity an impossible objective.

DESIGN AND MAINTENANCE OF PANELS

Panels are a powerful technique for understanding the process of social change and should be designed to take maximum advantage of that power. If only the volume of change and its mathematical time-series description were obtained, the panel approach would be underutilized and probably inappropriate. In designing panel studies, it is essential to consider: (1) the kinds of changes that may be taking place, (2) the measurement units of change that are appropriate to describe that change, (3) the factors that can affect change, (4) the period of time in which it is realistic to expect the change to occur, and (5) the natural variation that exists within the population. A panel designed to monitor changing leisure-travel patterns, for example, must consider, at a minimum:

1 Kinds of Changes
   a. Increasing, decreasing, or constant travel levels
   b. Longer or shorter trips
   c. Shifting modes of travel
   d. Expanding or shrinking range of destinations
   e. More business and vacation combinations
   f. Greater use of travel agents and information services
2 Measurement Units
   a. Trips, days in travel, dollars spent, number of destinations
   b. Total miles traveled, average miles per trip, states or countries visited
   c. Incidence and frequency of travel by auto (owned or rented), plane, ship, train, or bus, organized tours, and types of accommodations
   d. Number, types, and distances of destinations considered/visited per time unit
   e. Frequency of personal/household trips per time unit; conventions/convention centers visited; use of time while away from home
   f. Incidence, frequency, and nature of contacts with travel bureaus, tourism promotional offices, and so on; travel mailings (information units) received/requested
3 Change Factors
   a. Personal influences such as financial, family, occupational, and residential limitations
   b. Opportunity influences, such as improved residential location, availability of business trips, and personal invitations to visit or use another's facilities
   c. Social influences, such as the travel experiences of friends and relatives
   d. Informational/incentive influences, such as specialized media exposure and the availability of free or low-cost travel and/or accommodations
4 Time Periods
   a. Are there normal cycles involved in personal travel, such as a major trip in alternative years?
   b. To what extent do annual business cycles (conventions, etc.) affect personal travel patterns?
   c. Are there seasonal cycles at work: spring fishing, summer camping, fall hunting, winter skiing?
   d. What is a realistic recall period for the type of data being collected: daily exposure to promotional materials; weekly participation in recreation travel; monthly purchases of travel magazines and travel

related clothing/equipment; annual vacations; biennial foreign travel?
5 Normal Variation
   a. How much variation around a long-term trend line is normal? How many units of difference produce a significant increase or decrease?
   b. How many consecutive time periods of declining travel are necessary to conclude that a real decline exists?
   c. What shifts, alternations, and substitutions occur that may tend to obscure or exaggerate a real trend?

Obviously, not all of the above questions can be answered in advance; if they could, research might be unnecessary. To the extent that the researcher designs his panel procedures around such questions, his analysis will be easier and his conclusions more defensible. Suggestions for the analysis of panel data are provided in a number of references cited at the end of this chapter (Ahl 1970; Carman 1974; Hyett and McKenzie 1976; Parfitt and Collins 1968).

Ignoring any one of the four Ms of panel design—methods, measures, meaning, and maintenance (LaPage and Ragain 1979)—will clearly compromise the panel's utility. Problems of panel maintenance are most likely to be overlooked. Panels are somewhat more difficult to establish than normal population surveys. Special-populations lists, for example, travelers, may not exist and will have to be developed through a screening phase of a general-population survey. The recurring nature of the panel needs to be carefully explained to prospective panelists—and even then many will agree to cooperate without realizing what is involved or will agree with little or no commitment to actually cooperate. Incentives to encourage cooperation commonly used include commemorative stamps, coins, raffles, samples, discounts, free information, and monetary compensation.

Since much is usually known about panel member's backgrounds, it is often possible to develop a sense of panel cohesiveness and loyalty by the use of occasional newsletters, birthday cards, "anniversary" specials, and other discount offers. If the panel is supplying information that is potentially critical to the success of corporate decisions, a commitment to invest in that panel is appropriate.

SUMMARY AND CONCLUSIONS

Panels are neither inexpensive nor an alternative way of engaging in longitudinal research on changing behavior patterns of large populations. They are an extremely potent means for understanding social change, for test marketing new services and products, for assessing the impact of unforeseen events, and for short-term forecasting. However, these are their uses, not their advantages, and no one panel could logically be used to monitor naturally occurring changes, to react to experimentally induced changes, or to provide in-depth understanding of the factors producing changes.

Initiation of panel research requires a substantial commitment on the part of the researcher. Maintenance of a panel's representivity and response rates requires careful planning and, often, a substantial investment in time and incentives. Analysis of panel data requires an exceptional degree of advance planning and study design—particularly if the panel is to be used for explanatory or experimental purposes.

Despite the costs, complexity, and commitment associated with panels, they are distinctly appropriate to the problems of travel, tourism, and leisure research. The magnitude of change in people's leisure-behavior patterns, and their receptivity to new leisure opportunities, appear to be far greater than would be true for household purchases—a field where panel research has been most conspicuous.

Panels of repeat visitors to popular tourist attractions could provide a sensitive measure of trends in the quality of service and its impacts on visit length and repeat visitation. Panels of purchasers of expensive hunting and fishing equipment could be used for test marketing of remote sporting lodges. Panels of motor home buyers could provide a sensitive monitor of new features for which prospective buyers are looking. A panel of former visitors to Spirit Lake Lodge at Mt. Saint Helens could have provided unique information on the dispersal of clientele when their favorite vacation spot was no longer available. And panels of campground owners could provide immediate feedback on the impacts of gasoline shortages and price increases. The monitoring, stand-by, marketing, and forecasting opportunities for travel and tourism research are limitless. And because of the relatively large changes that are possible in discretionary leisure spending, there is a distinct opportunity for travel and tourism panels to make a major contribution to the understanding of the processes of social change.

REFERENCES

Ahl, D.H. (1970), "New Product Forecasting Using Consumer Panels," *Journal of Marketing Research* 12 (May), 160–167.

Carman, J.M. (1974), "Consumer Panels," in *Handbook of Marketing Research*, Robert Ferber, ed., New York: McGraw-Hill.

Churchill, G.A. (1992), *Basic Marketing Research*, Orlando, FL: The Dryden Press.

Hyett, G.P., and J.R. McKenzie (1976), "Effect of Under-reporting by Consumer Panels on Level of Trial and Repeat Purchasing of New Products," *Journal of Marketing Research* 13, 80–86.

Goeldner, C.R., T.A. Buchman, C.E.D. Persio, and G.S. Hayden (1992), *Economic Analysis of North American Ski Areas 1990–91 Season*, Boulder, CO: University of Colorado, Graduate School of Business Administration.

Kinnear, T.C., and J.R. Taylor (1991), *Marketing Research—An Applied Approach*, New York: McGraw-Hill.

LaPage, W.F., and D.P. Ragain (1974), "Family Camping Trends—an Eight-Year Panel Study," *Journal of Leisure Research* 6 (Spring), 101–112.

LaPage, W.F., and D.P. Ragain (1979), "Research Problems in Monitoring Recreation Trends," in *Dispersed Recreation and Natural Resource Management Symposium Proceedings*, Joan Shaw, ed., Logan, UT: Utah State University, College of Natural Resources.

Moeller, G.H. (1975), "Identifying Leisure Behavior Patterns of Onondaga County Adult Residents," Ph.D. thesis, State University of New York.

National Campground Owners' Association (1981), *American Campground Industry 1979 Economic Analysis and 1980 Occupancy Data*, Washington, D.C.: NCOA.

Parfitt, J.H., and B.J.K. Collins (1968), "Use of Consumer Panels for Brand Share Prediction," *Journal of Marketing Research* 5 (2) (May), 131–145.

Shafer, E.L., G.H. Moeller, and R.E. Getty (1974), *Future Leisure Environments*, Broomall, PA: USDA Forest Service.

41

Qualitative Research Methods for the Travel and Tourism Industry

KAREN IDA PETERSON
Principal
Davidson-Peterson Associates, Inc.
York, Maine

*T*he methods of qualitative, exploratory, and developmental research widely used in the general marketing world are today underutilized in travel and tourism marketing research. There are steps in the marketing research process for travel and tourism for which qualitative research methods are uniquely suited. The purpose of this chapter is to review five basic questions: What is qualitative research? What purposes does it serve? What are its limitations? What are the techniques of qualitative research? What is good qualitative research?

WHAT IS QUALITATIVE RESEARCH?

Qualitative research is the foundation on which strong, reliable research programs are based. It is most often the first step in a research program—the step designed to uncover motivations, reasons, impressions, perceptions, and ideas that relevant individuals have about a subject of interest. Unlike more quantitative methods of research, qualitative research involves talking in depth and detail with a few individuals. The goal is to develop extensive information from a few people.

With the quantitative types of research, the goal is to develop important—but limited—information from each individual and to talk with a sizable number of individuals in order to draw inferences about the population at large. The characteristics of qualitative research, on the other hand, include small samples, extensive information from each respondent, and a search for meaning, ideas, and relevant issues to quantify in later steps of the research program.

WHAT PURPOSES DOES QUALITATIVE RESEARCH SERVE?

Qualitative research is used to address a number of different types of objectives in the research process. Some are pur-

poses related to using qualitative research as the first step in a research program.

PURPOSES RELATED TO RESEARCH

To Develop Hypotheses Concerning Relevant Behavior or Attitudes

Qualitative research is used very often to generate hypotheses to suggest solutions to marketing problems when a travel researcher is faced with a marketing problem such as: Why are a hotel's/resort's rooms not full? Why has occupancy in this resort been declining over the past two years? What are the primary reasons for visiting a resort's destination area? These questions may trigger the decision to do a research project. The travel marketer may well have some hypotheses, some possible answers. However, before proceeding to do a major quantitative work to address those hypotheses, the researcher may suggest doing some qualitative work to search for additional hypotheses and new consumer-based ideas to address the problem.

To Identify the Full Range of Issues, Views, and Attitudes that Should be Pursued

Qualitative research serves often to broaden the researcher's views and to uncover issues and topics that should be considered in quantitative evaluations. Since the small samples used in qualitative research are in no way projectable to the population at large, an idea expressed by one individual may be critically important to the success of the final study. Thus, the purpose of the qualitative work is to explore the full range of views, developing the range of issues that need to be addressed in the final study.

To Suggest Methods for Quantitative Inquiry

Qualitative research can also direct the methodological decisions that will be made for quantitative studies. If in-depth conversations with travelers suggest the importance of the role of the travel agent in a particular decision, for example, the research design might be adjusted to include a sample of travel agents where none had been planned. Or in-depth discussions may indicate that a new product is so difficult to understand that the study to project market size cannot be done on the telephone but rather must use a personal interview. Or if, in individual discussions, those who have taken a particular vacation trip find it extremely difficult to reconstruct the decision process they went through prior to taking that particular trip, it may be necessary to interview decision makers for the confirmatory study during the time period after the decision is made but before the trip has been taken. All such inputs from qualitative research guide the selection of specific quantitative methods.

To Identify Language Used to Address Relevant Issues

In the travel industry, the specific language used by operators, travel agents, and travelers to describe the same phenomenon is quite different. One cannot talk with a travel agent using the traveler's language, and vice versa. Thus, qualitative research is an important way of learning just how the relevant groups talk about the issues, what language they use to describe their understanding of the topics.

To Understand How a Buying Decision Is Made

In any marketing task, one of the key issues is how to influence a competitive buying decision. Unless the marketer understands how the buyer makes the decision, he or she is unlikely to be able to influence that decision maker. Thus, qualitative research contributes through understanding in depth and detail what steps are undertaken, allowing the marketer to quantify that process and direct his or her strategies toward influencing a particular segment of the market.

PURPOSES RELATED TO MARKETING

To this point, the purposes of qualitative work have been seen as a first step in the research process. In those situations, the qualitative work is generating issues, attitudes, language, and hypotheses for later confirmation, rejection, or use in quantitative survey methods.

In addition, however, qualitative research methods may be used to guide the marketing efforts for a company or

destination in the travel industry. The purposes that qualitative research can fill in this area include the following.

To Develop New Product, Service, or Marketing-Strategy Ideas

For a travel-related company anxious to broaden its market share or enter new fields, qualitative research can contribute importantly to developing new products or services that the company might consider. Even in qualitative research, however, no consumer or travel trade professional can create the new product alone. What needs to be done is to explore in-depth problems, dissatisfactions, dreams, wishes, concerns, and so on. Then, the analyst can create new product/service opportunities based on expressed consumer needs.

To Provide an Initial Screening of New Product, Service, or Strategy Ideas

Once new product/service ideas are developed, qualitative research is often used to explore the strengths and weaknesses of alternate ideas, to cull out those ideas that offer the least opportunity, and to suggest which ideas ought to be developed further or pursued in further quantitative assessments. Qualitative research should not be used to select the single alternate that will be marketed, but rather to eliminate the least interesting and suggest a group of ideas or concepts that should be subjected to further modification and evaluation.

To Learn How Communications are Received—What is Understood and How

Qualitative research is used extensively in the development of advertising strategies and approaches by learning what messages intended recipients take from proposed advertising in order to suggest how wordings and approaches might be improved. Again, however, qualitative research should not be used to judge which of several alternatives is best, but rather to explore what each communicates. In addition, qualitative research can shed no light on the intrusiveness of advertising, its attention-getting values, among others. Qualitative research makes its contribution in what the advertising or promotional material communicates, not in whether it will gain attention from the intended audience.

Clearly, then, there are a number of specific purposes that may be addressed by qualitative research in the travel tourism market.

WHAT ARE THE LIMITATIONS OF QUALITATIVE RESEARCH?

The findings from a qualitative research effort must be regarded as informed hypotheses, not as proven facts. The samples that are used are quite small and usually selected in a purposive rather than a probability-sampling procedure. Thus, the inferences that are made based on qualitative research are normally subjected to evaluation using quantitative procedures at a subsequent time. Hypotheses, issues, ideas for new product/services, or communications strategies need to be confirmed on more reliable samples before major decisions are made.

In addition, qualitative findings may be limited by the skill, experience, and understanding of the individual gathering the information. Thus, the skill of a group-session moderator to draw out all participants, to reduce domination by some members of the group, and to develop sufficient rapport to gain truthful information from participants must be assessed in judging the value of a group-session study. Additionally, when individual interviews are used in a qualitative research effort, the interviewers asking the questions and probing responses may also influence responses and perhaps bias the results. A number of interviewers each doing a small number of interviews helps to control for this potential bias.

WHAT ARE THE TECHNIQUES OF QUALITATIVE RESEARCH?

Two basic methods of data collection are used in qualitative research: the individual interview and the focused group discussion. The advantages and limitations of each will now be examined.

FOCUSED GROUP DISCUSSIONS

In a focused group discussion, eight to ten relevant individuals are gathered together to discuss a topic under the leadership of a trained moderator. One key benefit of this approach is the interaction among respondents. Each individual is free to argue, disagree, question, and discuss the issues with others in the room. Thus, the group session becomes the most useful when exploring a broad range of attitudes and views, when searching for a variety of responses, and when interaction is a plus for the study.

Additionally, group sessions in most locations can be done in professional facilities with one-way mirrors and sound systems so that the discussion can be observed by others. So, if observation by one or members of the management or research team is desirable, focused group discussions would be suggested. Care must be taken, however, to ensure that hearing a few customers discuss a topic does not lead management to make premature decisions on the subject.

On the liability side, the major drawback to using groups in the qualitative research process is that despite the efforts of a trained moderator, some individuals may dominate the discussion, leaving open to question whether the views obtained are biased or prejudiced in any way because of the group dynamics or the group leader. Concern with biasing of this type is most important in studies designed to screen out products/services that offer limited opportunities for development. In cases where the goal is to develop a range of views or attitudes, the problem is not so serious, though it may mean that one or more groups have been less productive than should have been true.

INDIVIDUAL INTERVIEWS

Individual interviews are used most often in qualitative research when the interaction of a group is not desirable, when the goal of the research effort is to understand a process or an event in which each individual must talk at length about how he or she went about doing something. Individual interviews are particularly useful in travel research when the goal is to understand, for example, how travelers go about making a decision to take one vacation trip versus another. To gather that information, it is necessary to delve into each person's decision process at length—to learn where the idea originated, what information was gathered, who was consulted, whose views were sought out, and, finally, what led the individual to make a choice for one opportunity and to reject the others.

Where this type of information is sought from each individual, the group process breaks down. It is reasonably boring and uninteresting for each participant in a group to sit and listen to the decision process through which another participant went. Interaction is of little importance in these types of studies, and, therefore, groups are replaced with a series of individual interviews.

On the limitation side, individual interviews require that a reasonably careful topic guide be written prior to the start of interviewing. Since a number of interviewers will conduct the interviews, the process has to be well defined prior to the start of interviewing.

Each interviewer uses the general questions posed and probes with his or her own additional questions to gather more meaning. Thus, with a number of interviewers, the probing questions may differ, and each may get slightly different information. In a qualitative study, such variations are often beneficial since they bring to light a broad range of views and insights.

In comparison with groups, it is much more difficult for interested marketers and researchers to observe such individual interviews, and these interviews can frequently be quite costly. Interviewers must be specifically trained to conduct these interviews, and that training cannot be amortized over too many interviews since each interviewer does only a small number.

WHAT MAKES GOOD QUALITATIVE RESEARCH STUDIES?

The criteria for successful qualitative research differ somewhat for focused group discussions and for individual interviews. The following sections point out some of the key elements in the assessment of each type of qualitative research.

FOCUSED GROUP DISCUSSIONS

Several steps are key to having a successful focused group discussion:

First, all respondents must be *relevant* to the topic under discussion. It is critical that prospective participants be selected using a screening questionnaire that establishes their relevance to the topic; for example, should the study be designed to understand the full range of attitudes toward and impressions of a destination area, it is likely that all participants should have visited that area in the recent past.

To the extent possible, the screening questionnaire should be a *blind questionnaire*—that is, the respondent should not be able to detect just exactly who is sponsoring the study, what behavior is being explored, and what attitudes will be sought. Naturally, it will be clear to respondents that the concern is with travel, but the specific destination or property should not be easily identifiable by the respondent during the screening process.

Additionally, there should be *exclusion of potentially biased people*: Anyone with special knowledge of or interest in the topic or the technique should be excluded. Those involved in advertising, market research, or any aspect of travel should not qualify as participants in a traveler group. Similarly, those who have participated in a group session or been interviewed individually in the past six months should be eliminated.

Second, to permit good information exchanges, good interaction and a lively discussion, all participants must feel comfortable presenting their views during the discussion. People are simply more comfortable discussing topics with "their own kind." Thus, one goal should be to *do separate groups* in most cases—younger apart from older people; white collar families apart from blue collar families; experienced international travelers apart from inexperienced ones; and so on. Such homogeneity is important in establishing psychological comfort for the respondents. This psychological comfort can be achieved with people of different demographic backgrounds if they have shared similar experiences recently that are relevant to the subject of interest to the researcher.

In designing a focused group discussion study, one group session with any population subgroup is seldom, if ever, sufficient. While a second session with the same subgroup may not be identical in content, if there are signs of consistency and commonality, researchers can confirm that neither is truly aberrant or deviant and, thus, be comfortable with inferences from the groups. In addition, should there be a need to conduct more than eight or ten groups (four or five different population groups) then it would appear that another, perhaps more quantitative research approach should be used. Upon completion of a group discussion study, the researcher still has only informed hypotheses, judgments, and ideas—not confirmed facts. Thus, spending time and dollars to conduct more than eight or ten focused groups and still not having facts on which to base a marketing decision is usually wasteful.

Third, the role of the *moderator* is critical in producing a good focused group discussion. The moderator is a director, but also a facilitator. He or she must develop rapport with the group participants, help them to relax and speak freely with each other, draw out the reluctant contributors, and keep natural leaders from dominating the conversation. The

moderator's job is also to guide the discussion so that all important topics are covered and to probe and question (usually in a nonthreatening manner) to elicit the broadest range of information and views.

The moderator's topic guide should be thoroughly and completely worked out prior to the beginning of the session. The outline of questions should include the researcher's best thinking on the topics that must be addressed and the likely order in which they will emerge during the discussion.

The moderator, however, must be fully cognizant of the goals and objectives of the research, knowing which topic areas are most critical to cover in depth and which may be treated more lightly. In addition, the moderator must be sensitive to the emergence of unexpected information, ideas not anticipated at all by the research team, and must decide if and how to pursue those issues. One of the benefits of focused group research is that the moderator is free to gather new ideas, pursue new directions, and achieve new insights during the course of the session itself.

Fourth, the *physical comfort of respondents* in the group discussion should be of primary concern. Comfortable chairs and a well-ventilated room at the appropriate temperature are often as important in setting the tone of the session as are proper recruiting procedures and a good moderator. When appropriate, serving light refreshments also contributes to the development of the relaxed and informal atmosphere that is essential. Since most group discussions will last from one and a half to just over two hours, respondents need to be comfortable physically as well as psychologically.

Finally, the *analysis and interpretation* of the focused group sessions contribute importantly to the assessment of a successful study. The way in which the findings are approached and interpreted depends, of course, on the purpose for which the study was designed. Thus, it is not possible to suggest rules of interpretation that would apply to all analyses.

In reviewing the report on a focused group session study, however, the research/marketer should probably note whether the objectives have been addressed, whether the analysis covers the broad range of issues and ideas that emerged in the discussions, whether generalizations and conclusions are based soundly on the session input, and so on. The key assessment criteria should probably be: How useful are the results? How well do they guide and inform further steps in the research and development process?

INDIVIDUAL INTERVIEWS

In designing a qualitative study that includes individual interviews, several steps are important to a successful study.

First, as with groups, the *participants need to be carefully selected* so as to be relevant to the problem under study; for example, should the issue be learning about the vacation decision process, then all participants should have taken the appropriate vacation, been involved in the decision process, and should have done so recently enough to remember the steps through which they went.

The screening questionnaire designed to identify these

individuals should be carefully constructed to find only appropriate individuals and to eliminate those who could contribute only marginally to the study objectives. When only a few interviews will be conducted (15 to 30 is often an appropriate sample size), it is clearly critically important that each one contribute to the overall study goal.

Additionally, since studies in which qualitative research is accomplished through individual interviews usually seek to gain an understanding of behavior or decision making from a variety of points of view, it is often important to include individuals with a variety of demographic characteristics to ensure that all population subgroups of importance are included in the qualitative research.

Second, the *development of the interview guide* is critically important. The careful assessment of all issues likely to arise in the conversation, ordering of topics into a likely sequence, and listing of possible probe questions are critical to the success of an individual-interview qualitative project.

Third, the *selection and thorough training of the interviewers* who will conduct the interviews form a crucial step in the individual-interview study. It is likely that the professional researcher who will ultimately analyze the responses to these interviews should conduct at least some of the interviews.

Interviewers being trained to conduct the interviews should observe the initial interview by professional researchers and be further trained in the goals and objectives of the project. They will need to ask additional questions and probes as they proceed through the interview as ideas emerge and are discussed.

Finally, *interpreting the results* of individual interviews is likely to be as varied as the purposes for which they were conducted. If the goal is to understand a decision process, then the results should include the variety of typologies that seem to occur in the process. If it is to understand motivations and reasons for particular behaviors, again, the interpretation should include the array of ideas gathered from the individuals who are included in the study.

Again, however, the interpretation and analysis are best judged on the basis of how useful the findings and recommendations are to the study as it progresses.

ASSESSING QUALITATIVE RESEARCH

The following series of questions may be used by a travel researcher/marketer in assessing the quality and effectiveness of qualitative research conducted. For the most part, the questions can be used for studies employing either focused group sessions or individual interviews.

- Are the objectives for the qualitative research clearly stated, appropriate for the techniques used, and targeted toward the marketing/research needs of the study?
- Is the number of groups and/or interviews appropriate for the problem? Are the population segments under study carefully delineated?
- Is the screening questionnaire tightly designed to eliminate all who will not be relevant to the project and who might create bias?

- Does the moderator's guide/interviewer's guide show clear and careful thinking about the issues to be explored and the logical flow of questioning?
- Is each group session conducted in facilities and with accoutrements that will generate both physical and psychological comfort for the respondents?
- Is the moderator/interviewer well versed in the goals and objectives of the study? Is he or she well trained and experienced in the professional skills required?
- Are the respondents comfortable with and able to talk with each other, and is the moderator without pretense?
- Are the topics of interest covered in sufficient depth and detail in each session/interview?
- Do the analysis and report reflect the full range of views expressed and generalize to the level of meaningful conclusions for further steps in the research effort or the marketing strategy development?
- Are all elements of the qualitative research effort handled in a professional manner?

If travel researcher/marketer can answer these questions in the affirmative, the qualitative research study should have contributed importantly to the solution of research and marketing problems.

REFERENCES

Axelrod, Myril D. (1975a), "Marketers Get an Eyeful When Focus Groups Expose Products, Ideas, Images, Ad Copy, etc., to Consumers," *Marketing News*, February 28, 6–7.

Axelrod, Myril D. (1975b), "10 Essentials for Good Qualitative Research," *Marketing News*, March 14, 10–11.

Bellenger, Danny N., Kenneth L. Bernhardt, and Jac L. Goldstucker (1976), "Qualitative Research Techniques: Focus Group Interviews," 7–18, Chicago, IL: American Marketing Association.

Calder, Bobby J. (1977), "Focus Groups and the Nature of Qualitative Marketing Research," *Journal of Marketing Research*, 14(3, August), 353–364.

Dichter, Ernest (1964), "Depth Interviewing," in *Handbook of Consumer Motivations*, 413–417, New York: McGraw-Hill Book Co.

Goldman, Alfred E. (1962), "The Group Depth Interview," *Journal of Marketing*, 26(3, July), 61–68.

Merton, Robert K., Marjorie Fiske, and Patricia Kendall (1956), "The Group Interview," in *The Focused Interview*, Glencoe, IL: The Free Press.

Payne, Melanie S. (1976), "Preparing for Group Interview," in *Advances in Consumer Research*, 434–436, Beverlee Anderson, ed., Ann Arbor, Michigan: University of Michigan.

Sampson, Peter (1972), "Qualitative Research and Motivation Research," in *Consumer Market Research Handbook*, 7–27, Robert M. Worchester, ed., Maidenhead, England: McGraw-Hill Book Co. (U.K.), Ltd.

Smith, Joan Macfarlane (1972), "Group Discussions," in *Interviewing in Market and Social Research*, London and Boston: Routledge and Kegan Paul.

Wells, William D.(1974), "Group Interviewing," in *Handbook of Marketing Research*, 133–146, Robert Ferber, ed., New York: McGraw-Hill Book Co.

42

The Nominal Group Technique—
Applications in Tourism Research[1]

J.R. BRENT RITCHIE
Chairman
World Tourism Education and Research Centre
The University of Calgary
Calgary, Alberta

The purpose of this chapter is to introduce tourism researchers and policymakers to a group planning and research process that has achieved considerable recognition in other fields while being largely ignored in tourism. This procedure, termed the nominal group technique (NGT), was originally developed by Delbecq, Van de Ven, and Gustafson (1971) as an organizational planning technique. Although the developers indicated that NGT may be useful in a wide variety of planning tasks, no applications were found in relation to tourism. Accordingly, this chapter describes the use of NGT as a tool for consensus planning at the regional level with a view to demonstrating its strengths as a research procedure within this and other areas of tourism.

The discussion that follows is divided into five major sections. The first section describes the nominal group technique (NGT) as it is normally employed. This general discussion is followed in the next section by a description of the manner in which the method was applied in the case of consensus planning by the Tourism Industry Association of Alberta (TIAALTA). The third section focuses on issues of data analysis peculiar to this type of research. Subsequently, a discussion is presented concerning the potential applications of NGT in other areas of tourism research and planning. The final section provides an assessment of the relative strengths and weaknesses of NGT compared to other commonly used planning/research approaches.

NOMINAL GROUP TECHNIQUE

The NGT procedure, as used for program planning, is normally implemented in six stages. Participants are first presented by the session moderator with an initial statement of the topic area to be discussed. Top management of a corpo-

ration might be asked to indicate what directions future diversification would take, for example. Once it is clear that participants understand the issue, further discussion is halted.

Participants are then directed to reflect individually on the topic and to record their personal responses on a worksheet containing a written statement of the issue being addressed. This period of individual reflection and recording of responses usually lasts from 5 to 20 minutes, depending on the complexity of the topic under discussion.

The group moderator subsequently asks a participant, chosen at random, to state one of the responses she or he has arrived at individually. This response is written in a concise yet complete manner on a large flipchart. At this point, the participant is allowed to explain his or her response briefly, so that its meaning is clear to other participants. This process is repeated in round-robin fashion until all participants have had a chance to express a response. Second and third rounds may follow, depending on the number of ideas identified by members. Participants are allowed, and even encouraged, to express additional ideas that have been stimulated by the remarks of others.

[1]Material in this chapter was originally published in *Tourism Management* Vol. 6, No. 2, 1985. Permission to reprint is gratefully acknowledged.

The next stage involves consolidation and review of the complete set of ideas. At this point, all flipchart sheets are posted so that all responses are visible. The moderator reviews the responses recorded on the flipcharts to eliminate duplications and to ensure that all responses are clearly understood by participants. Each response is then assigned an identifier code, such as a letter of the alphabet.

Participants are subsequently requested to establish the relative importance that should be accorded to each of the response ideas. This importance may reflect, for example, the desirability of a given idea for corporate diversification. Although various approaches may be employed to establish the importance of each response (Delbecq et al. 1975), a commonly used method is to instruct each individual first to select a certain number of responses (e.g., eight)[2] that he considers to be most important. The participant then writes each of these responses on a 3 x 5 card, along with the alphabetic identifier, and is asked to rank the eight responses in terms of their relative order of importance.

The final stage is compilation of the results. In this stage, the rankings accorded to the various ideas by each participant are aggregated to provide a measure of overall importance. As per the Delphi technique (Linstone and Turoff 1975), these results may be presented to participants, and a second round of ranking undertaken to permit individuals to adjust their judgments in the light of the earlier evaluations. However, this round is not essential unless the initial judgments were highly variable or unless the purpose is to achieve a reasonable level of group consensus.

To summarize, the NGT process is a systematic approach designed to provide two specific types of output: first, it provides a list of ideas relevant to the topic in question; and second, the technique provides quantified individual and aggregate measures of the relative desirability of the ideas raised in the session.

AN APPLICATION OF NGT TO TOURISM RESEARCH AND PLANNING

THE RESEARCH/PLANNING CONTEXT

The private sector of the tourism industry in Alberta is composed of a broad range of firms and organizations dispersed geographically throughout the province. While each of these firms and organizations has its own goals, they all share in and benefit from one common objective—the growth and development of tourism to and within Alberta.

For the growth and development of tourism in the province to be successful, it is essential that the efforts of the private sector be complemented by the activities of government. Indeed, the partnership that exists between the public and private sectors is an important characteristic of tourism in Alberta and in Canada as a whole. As in any such relation,

it is important that each partner fulfills its role effectively and contributes equitably to the partnership.

From an operational standpoint, the public/private sector partnership roles in tourism at the provincial level in Alberta are formally carried out, respectively, by Travel Alberta and the Tourism Industry Association of Alberta (TIAALTA). In the past, this partnership has functioned reasonably well. However, several trends have indicated that significant modifications to the management of provincial tourism may be required to meet the challenges of the future. These trends include:

- A stabilization and even a decline in tourism to Canada and to Alberta. Among the reasons for this situation is a dramatic increase in competition from other international destinations.
- A movement towards increased privatization of numerous functions previously carried out by governments in response to growing pressures on public expenditures.
- A recognition of the need to develop and expand the tourism industry in the province as part of an overall industrial strategy aimed at providing a broader range of employment opportunities for Albertans (Government of Alberta 1984).

As a result of these trends and other factors, TIAALTA concluded in 1983 that the private sector in Alberta must accept a greater role in developing and managing tourism in the province. To do this, however, it was essential that the association formulate a coherent statement of its views concerning the directions that tourism development in the province should take. While it was recognized that the size and diversity of the private sector would never permit the preparation of the type of unanimous report that is possible from a government agency, TIAALTA saw the need to develop a consensus of its members' views, which would serve to focus association efforts and to prioritize its actions. It was with this need in mind that TIAALTA undertook a three-phase program designed to set out the views of the private sector concerning provincial tourism development and promotion. The contents of each phase were defined as follows:

- **Phase I**   Definition of priority issues and problems facing tourism in the province.
- **Phase II** Identification of initiatives, actions, and programs to deal with the priority issues and problems facing Alberta Tourism.
- **Phase III** Monitoring of recommendations concerning initiatives, actions, and programs for tourism development to ensure timely and effective implementation.

This chapter describes Phase I of the program, which undertook to identify those issues and problems that private operators view as most seriously affecting the future development of tourism in the province (TIAALTA 1984). The process involved, which is subsequently discussed, was one in which an overall consensus was derived from inputs obtained from

[2]Delbecq et al., (1975) suggest having respondents select and rate (7±2) preferred ideas.

the many tourism regions (zones) and industry-sector associations that constitute TIAALTA.

In Phase II of the program, TIAALTA will be undertaking to identify solutions to the most serious issues facing the industry, to determine how those solutions can be most effectively implemented, and to define what individual group or organization should assume responsibility for solution implementation.

Finally, in Phase III of the program, TIAALTA will establish a process to assist in monitoring the degree of progress and the level of success in relation to its recommendations for actions and programs to further develop tourism in Alberta. The intent here is to actively work with government to ensure timely and effective implementation of those initiatives judged most critical to the success of tourism in the province.

SPECIFIC OBJECTIVES OF PHASE I

While the objectives of Phase I of the study are implied in the foregoing discussion, they may be explicitly stated as follows:

1. To identify the most significant issues, problems, and concerns currently facing the development of Alberta tourism:
   a. at the provincial level
   b. within the various zones
   c. within various industry sectors
2. To establish the relative priority which members of TIAALTA attach to the seriousness of the identified issues, problems, and concerns.

STUDY PARTICIPANTS

Participants in the study were drawn from among members of the Boards of Directors of the Zone and Industry Sector associations that make up TIAALTA. A total of 16 sessions were conducted during the period June 1983 to June 1984. Of this total, 11 sessions involved zone organizations, and 5 sessions obtained inputs from industry-sector associations. The size of the groups ranged from a minimum of 6 to a maximum of 19, with the average number of participants per session being between 9 and 10. As such, data for the study were obtained from a total of 153 active leaders from the private sector of tourism in Alberta.

DATA BASE

The raw data obtained from each NGT session were of three types:

- A list of problems, concerns, and issues facing Alberta tourism as identified by session participants
- A list of the problems, concerns, and issues facing tourism within the zone or industry sector as identified by session participants
- A selection and ranking by each participant of the 10 problems, issues, and concerns that he or she judged to

be most significant at both the provincial and zone/industry-sector level

As might be anticipated, the number, the nature, and the wording of the concerns emanating from each of the 16 sessions varied across the different NGT groups. The number of provincial issues identified per session ranged from a minimum of 12 to a maximum of 29, with the average being 18 (for a total of 288 issues). An example of actual problem statements resulting from an individual session is given in Table 1. For purposes of the present study, the detailed analysis reported below focuses only on data related to the 288 provincial tourism issues.

ANALYSIS OF NGT DATA

Analysis of data obtained from the NGT process involves a combination of qualitative and quantitative procedures requiring four basic steps:

- Categorization of initial problem statements into problem themes
- Regrouping of problem themes within a conceptual model to form major problem dimensions
- Calculation of a score or index reflecting the importance of each problem theme
- Ranking of problem themes according to their importance index

TABLE 1 Example of Provincial Problems/Issues Resulting from a Zone Session

A. Provincial campsites are too small and overcrowded.
B. Government regulations, e.g., Sunday liquor laws.
C. Government red tape discourages development.
D. Less than desirable quality of hospitality by front-line staff.
E. Need for higher wages/more qualified people for interpretive staff in provincial parks.
F. Need for business in general to understand the importance of the tourism industry.
G. Difficulties in identifying the most important market targets.
H. Lack of liaison and continuity among zones—need for more exchange of information.
I. Shortage of professionally trained people in the tourism industry—need for additional educational programs and greater industry input to programs.
J. Better signage on highways for facilities and attractions.
K. Need for more rest stops.
L. Need by public in general to understand financial impact of tourism on their communities.
M. Lack of key destination areas in the province—too much reliance on Banff, need for "nonmajor" destination areas.
N. Too much competition between government and the private sector (e.g., golf courses; standards for campsites).
O. High level of taxation has made Alberta/Canada noncompetitive with the United States.

IDENTIFICATION AND CLASSIFICATION OF PROBLEM THEMES

The purpose of the first step was to identify ideas or themes that were common across the statements obtained from each of the group sessions. These themes were subsequently regrouped according to a framework describing major managerial functions in tourism. The framework employed in this case corresponded to the various areas of functional responsibility within TIAALTA.

It is useful at this point to note the difference between identifying problem themes and the subsequent classification of these themes according to the TIAALTA managerial framework of Figure 1. The purpose in identifying themes is to aggregate across group sessions statements that express essentially the same idea, a process conceptually similar to content analysis (Holsti 1969; Kassarjian 1977). On the other hand, the classification according to the dimensions of the managerial framework is done with a view to providing a structure relating the themes, a process similar to taxonomic analysis (Green and Wind 1973).

The foregoing analysis resulted in the identification of 35 problem themes, which were subsequently classified within the four major components of the TIAALTA management model. Of this total, the majority of the themes identified from the problem statements of the private sector participants (13 of 35) were found to be related to tourism development issues. Nine themes concerned difficulties involving overall policy issues, while eight themes pertained to perceived shortcomings in the area of marketing and promotion. Finally, six themes addressing concerns in the area of human resource development were identified. The original report (TIAALTA 1984) contains a detailed listing by management function of each of the 35 themes as well as the individual problem statements falling under each of the themes. Table 2 provides a selected example of one problem theme and associated problem statements.

INDEX OF THEME IMPORTANCE

The Index of Theme Importance that was developed was designed to reflect two different measures of importance,

namely the *frequency* with which a problem had been mentioned across the 16 sessions and the *priority* accorded to it when it was mentioned in a session. Thus, a theme that had been identified in most sessions and that had been ranked highly by most participants would receive a high index score; one mentioned frequently but considered less important, or mentioned less frequently but judged important by certain participants, would receive an intermediate index score; and, finally, a theme mentioned infrequently and accorded little importance would receive a low index score. In the present study, the Index of Importance for each theme was developed according to the procedure described in Exhibit 1.

RANKING AND PRIORITIZING OF THEME IMPORTANCE

Based on the Index of Theme Importance, it was possible to rank the 35 themes in order of perceived priority as rated by the entire sample. Because this overall ranking was somewhat too detailed for managerial purposes, the themes were further classified into two levels of priority. The classification was made after examining both the distribution of the Indexes of Importance for all 35 themes and the characteristics of the themes judged most significant. This classification, which is partially summarized in Table 3, was carried out according to the following criteria:

- **Priority 1**   Includes 15 themes that identify the most serious problems currently facing tourism in Alberta. As seen from Table 3, each of these themes tended to address fundamental issues affecting virtually all aspects of provincial tourism. As such, it is these concerns that are the object of further in-depth review and study within Phase II and the resolution of which provides the focus for TIAALTA's ongoing efforts.

- **Priority 2**   Involves the remaining 22 themes. These themes were identified as important, but not as critical as those categorized as Priority 1. In general, these themes tended to involve more specific issues. Problems related to these themes will receive attention by TIAALTA to the extent that time and resources permit. In particular, an effort will be made to resolve a given problem in cases for which an opportunity for substantial progress within a reasonable time frame appears possible.

OTHER APPLICATIONS OF NGT

The foregoing discussion has provided one detailed example as to how NGT can be used as a consensus formulation tool at the initial or problem-definition stage of the planning process. The potential tourism applications of NGT, however, go far beyond the single example described in this

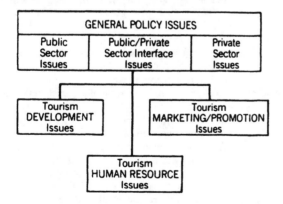

FIGURE 1   Structure of the managerial areas of responsibility within TIAALTA used as classification framework for problem themes.

TABLE 2   Human Resources

Theme:
Lack of Education and Training Programs Necessary to Improve Professionalism and Effectiveness of the Tourism Industry

11 mentions	3 x 5	= 15
	2 x 3	= 6
	2 x 2	= 4
	4 x 1	= 4
Index of Theme Importance		= 29

SESSION RANK	SESSION SCORE/ AVERAGE	PROBLEM/ISSUE	ZONE/ ASSOCIATION
3	51/9=5.7	Service industry staff not properly trained to handle public—need more educational programs.	Z7
3	49/10=4.9	Need for provincial subsidies to educational system to train people in hospitality industries (need to return some of the revenues).	AR/E
4	54/11=4.9	Shortage of professionally trained people in the tourism industry— need for additional educational programs and greater industry input to programs.	Z4
5	53/16=3.3	Lack of qualified private-sector manpower to develop and sell tourism.	Z5
7	20/8=2.5	Lack of training/tourism studies program for province. No return business because of poor attitudes and service.	AHA
9	24/7=3.4	Need for improved training and educational facilities for industry at provincial level.	AR/C
11	30/13=2.3	Lack of education/training programs to raise quality of staff and service in industry.	Z9
12	25/11=2.3	Need for higher wages/more qualified people for interpretive staff in provincial parks.	Z4
13	19/10=1.9	Need for industry training programs for staff and management.	H
15	27/13=2.1	Tourism operators/businesses not sufficiently educated on how to deal with wholesalers.	Z9

paper. These applications may be categorized as other planning situations and more general research uses.

OTHER PLANNING SITUATIONS

At least two other planning tasks lend themselves to the application of the nominal group technique. The first of these relates to *organizational goal setting*. In this context, the process serves first as a means of eliciting a set of statements defining the mission and the objectives of the organization. In the case of a private sector tourism operator, these goals would normally relate to the overall direction of the firm and the specific achievements it hopes to realize within a specific time frame. For a public sector organization, the process would normally involve attempting to specify the economic and social contributions it is hoped will be achieved through tourism development. In both cases, once the organizational

goals have been defined, the NGT process provides a mechanism for determining the relative priority the top management wishes to accord to the various goal statements that have been proposed.

A further area of application relates to the *identification and evaluation of alternative courses of action* for resolving a management issue. In this situation, NGT can first be used to generate a range of possible solutions to the problem or opportunity facing a management team and then can be subsequently employed to rate the perceived effectiveness or desirability of the options generated. It is this approach that, in fact, will be used in Phase II of the present planning process. In this context, special task forces have been formed to identify initiatives, actions, and programs that might contribute to the resolution of the priority problems or issues that were defined in Phase I. The judgments of task force members concerning the desirability and feasi-

EXHIBIT 1   Procedure for Developing Index of Theme Importance

Step 1: Session Score
  Calculation of average importance ranking of each statement within total set of statements from a single session.

Step 2: Session Rank
  Ranking of each statement within a session from most to least important as determined by session score.

Step 3: Statement Index Score
  Assignment of points to the relevant theme in which a statement was classified according to the following scale:

Session rank of	1–4	5 points
	5–7	3 points
	8–10	2 points
	11 or more	1 point

Step 4: Theme Index Score
  Calculation of total points assigned to all problem statements with a given theme.

bility of the ideas proposed will serve to determine which initiatives, actions, and programs will be endorsed by TIAALTA for implementation.

RESEARCH APPLICATIONS OF NGT

In addition to being employed as an internal tool for organizational planning, NGT can be very effectively employed in *consumer research* as an alternative means of data collection. In this regard, NGT provides a methodology that falls between unstructured focus group techniques and structured survey methods. Examples of the kinds of consumer research that might be addressed by NGT would include:

• Studies to identify and establish the relative importance of factors that consumers view as critical in determining the quality of service in a hotel, a ski resort, or other tourism facility.

• Studies to identify and establish the relative importance of information sources used by consumers when choosing among alternative types of tour packages.

• Studies to identify the dimensions that are important in defining the images of different countries as travel destinations.

By extension, it is seen that NGT can be adapted for use in the study of most research questions in which individuals are required to generate ideas and, subsequently, to provide some rating of the ideas' relative desirability.

A second research application of NGT is an alternative to the Delphi technique (Linstone and Turoff 1975) when attempting to obtain *expert consensus* on a given research topic. While the Delphi method is effective when respondents are geographically dispersed, it is somewhat cumbersome and time-consuming unless it can be conducted in an electronic format. In contrast, in situations where experts can be physically brought together, NGT provides a very effective data collection approach. Examples of potential applications in this area include:

• Research to identify and determine the relative importance of factors influencing the choice of meeting and convention sites.

• Research to examine how wholesalers assess the attractiveness of proposals submitted by different travel destinations and suppliers when assembling their tour packages.

• Research to identify those regulations and laws that are most severely impacting on the success of private tourism operators.

Again, as in the case of consumer research, NGT is appropriate in situations where it is required to gather and structure information from a defined group of respondents who can be brought together for a limited period of time.

STRENGTHS AND WEAKNESSES OF NGT AS A PLANNING AND RESEARCH METHODOLOGY

To this point, the discussion has described the nature of NGT and has provided a number of examples of its use or potential uses. As for any methodology, however, NGT has its limitations. The remainder of this chapter will assess the relative strengths and weaknesses of NGT as a tool for tourism planning and research and will attempt to show where NGT fits relative to other data collection procedures.

Several strengths can be identified. First, although a group method, NGT provides structured output that can be analyzed at an individual level. The term *nominal group technique* is intended to suggest that the method is *nominally* viewed as group based although, for the most part, the activities and output focus on individual efforts. The early stages of the process provide respondents with the opportunity to hear the views of others as they are thinking through the topic under discussion—similar to other group methods. On the other hand, the final stages require respondents to sort and rank the items generated in earlier stages. Thus, the data output is more structured than is usual with group methods.

TABLE 3   Prioritization of Tourism Problems Themes—Priority 1

Index of Theme Importance	Overall Ranking	Theme Description	TIAALTA Area of Responsibility
50	1	The high cost of travel in Alberta/Canada has crippled our ability to compete in tourism markets.	Development
46	2	The present structure for managing Alberta's tourism system does not involve the private sector adequately or early enough in the planning process. The result is a perceived lack of cooperation, coordination, and effectiveness.	Policy—Public/Private Interface
44	3	Despite some recent progress, governments are still perceived as failing to acknowledge the current or the potential importance of the tourism industry to the well-being of the province.	Policy—Public
42	4	Lack of appreciation on the part of supervisors and front-line staff of the critical role that positive attitudes, hospitality, and quality service play in the success of the tourism industry—and a pressing need to rectify the situation.	Human Resources
37	5	Lack of adequate funding for the promotion of Alberta as a tourism destination.	Marketing/Promotion
36	6	Government legislation, regulation, and bureaucracy are perceived as major deterrents to the successful development and functioning of the tourism industry in Alberta.	Marketing/Promotion Policy—Public
32	7	Lack of adequate funding and funding mechanisms for tourism development.	Development
31	8	Need to substantially improve the level of cooperation, liaison, and communication among all tourism zones and industry sector associations.	Policy—Private
29	9	Lack of education and training programs necessary to improve the professionalism and effectiveness of the tourism industry.	Human Resources
29	9	Lack of public awareness of the importance and significance of tourism to the socioeconomic well-being of Alberta.	Human Resources
27	11	Ineffective and inappropriate expenditure of those funds that are available for the promotion of tourism to Alberta.	Marketing/Promotion
27	11	Need to upgrade the quality of information, particularly road signage, available to visitors to Alberta.	Marketing/Promotion
24	13	Need to develop additional facilities, attractions, events, and activities in the province so as to make Alberta a more viable and competitive tourism destination.	Development
24	13	Need for a greater degree of creativity and innovation in marketing and promotional efforts that will result in a well-focused, recognized image/ theme for Alberta as a tourism destination.	Marketing/Promotion
20	15	Government is perceived as having access to a disproportionate share of tourism planning and development resources, thus placing the private sector in a disadvantage position.	Policy—Public/Private Interface

Second, the NGT process results in high respondent involvement and commitment. This commitment develops as respondents express their views to others in the group and realize that they are sharing in the identification of items to be evaluated. This advantage can be particularly useful when participants need time to think through their responses. This is not to imply that they are thinking up new ideas in a creative sense. Rather, when asked to recall behavioral experience, it is probable that respondents have had little experience identifying the various steps that were involved in the behavior. In other words, although the behavior of interest may be current or even habitual, the process of articulation requires time and commitment to recall the various components.

Third, the process of identifying and scoring problem themes, as developed in this application, makes it possible to study both intra- and intergroup differences.

The major disadvantage of NGT relates to sampling. Because participants have to agree to come to a central meeting location, attempts at probability sampling are met by a serious level of nonresponse, as discussed further in the following sections.

COMPARISON WITH FOCUS GROUP INTERVIEWS

A number of authors provide reviews of qualitative research methods (Bellenger, Bernhardt, and Goldstucker 1976; Bogdan and Taylor 1975; Higginbotham and Cox 1979). One of the most insightful of these reviews has been presented by Calder (1977) in which he distinguishes among the exploratory, clinical, and phenomenological dimensions of qualitative research. Although NGT possesses some characteristics of each of these dimensions, it is perhaps closest to what Calder defines as exploratory research. As he points out, a major strength of exploratory methods is the ability to identify major issues or attributes associated with a particular research problem. However, there are several characteristics of standard focus groups that restrict this method to exploratory applications. First, the output of the session is relatively unstructured. Although the session can provide an extensive list of attributes, the process does not facilitate establishing attribute priorities. Second, a small subset of the participants may be outspoken and dominate or intimidate the rest of the group. Third, to minimize this potential domination and to ensure the desired depth of coverage, a highly trained session leader is required. Finally, the necessity to bring participants to a meeting room virtually precludes the use of probability sampling procedures. However, the quota sampling methods usually adopted are entirely consistent with the exploratory nature of the focus group process.

Nominal group technique shares with exploratory focus groups the facility for identifying issues relevant to target consumers and also adds a number of other very useful features. First, in addition to providing an extensive listing of issue or attributes, NGT enables the researcher to identify priorities for each individual session participant. Second, an advantage of NGT is that the structuring and establishing of priorities makes it possible to analyze similarities and differences across multiple NGT sessions. Third, because of the procedural rules established at the outset of the session, the NGT session leader is able to ensure that all participants have an equal voice in the session. Fourth, the author's experience indicates that the added structure of NGT sessions simplifies the process of training session leaders. In other words, session leadership is somewhat less of an art than appears to be the case with focus group sessions. Despite these advantages, it must be remembered that NGT shares with focus groups the need to assemble participants in the meeting room, and hence, the need to adopt quota sampling procedures.

COMPARISON WITH STRUCTURED SURVEY METHODS

Although NGT is not seen as a substitute for structured survey methods, it is useful to draw several contrasts. A summary of the major strengths of structured research methods would be: (1) ability to cover a large number and range of items, (2) use of probability sampling, and (3) structured output that facilitates analysis. The difficulties associated with these methods include: (1) problems inherent in establishing questions or items that are relevant to intended respondents, and (2) maintaining control of the interview setting. The former problem is handled by careful exploratory research and pretesting. However, despite methodical preliminary efforts, most researchers have experienced studies in which some aspect of the research problem has been undermeasured. The second problem mentioned, controlling the interview setting, is related to the use of a large number of interviewers. In a field situation, interviewers often feel a pressure to hurry the interview and, as a result, respondents are not encouraged to think out their answers. Further, as the questionnaire length increases, the interviewer has increasing difficulty maintaining respondent interest and commitment.

The strengths and weaknesses of NGT methods are almost the mirror image of those associated with survey methods. The advantage of probability sampling is not available with NGT. Although both methods provide structured output, the range of topics that can be covered is reduced with NGT. On the other hand, the problem of establishing items that are relevant to the intended respondents is enhanced. Furthermore, the control of the interview setting is simplified by the highly structured NGT process. This latter point can be emphasized by noting that in the application discussed earlier, each session lasted a total of three hours. At the end of the sessions, respondents continued to express a keen interest in the research and felt a strong sense of achievement for their efforts.

To restate an earlier comment, the intention is not to suggest NGT methods as a substitute for structured surveys. However, the added structure of NGT, not normally available in group methods, together with the judicious use of multiple quota-based groups, may provide an opportunity to go considerably beyond the usual exploratory research.

COMPARISON WITH THE DELPHI METHOD

As indicated earlier, NGT and the Delphi method may be viewed as alternatives when gathering information from industry experts is required. While both approaches are often referred to as "consensus planning" techniques, the nature of the process associated with each provides different benefits and limitations.

The most obvious difference pertains to the need to physically assemble NGT participants. In contrast, the Delphi method usually assumes that experts are geographically dispersed. Since such dispersion is not unusual when dealing with a select group of experts, the Delphi method may be the only option available. Increasingly, however, professional groups are finding that it is very effective to schedule what are effectively different types of research sessions as part of national or international conferences, which by their nature attract experts in sharply defined fields. One example is a recent focus group sponsored by the Marketing Science Institute that attempted to identify the key success factors for organizations involved in the marketing of services (Schmalensee et al. 1983). In this type of context, NGT might prove to be a useful alternative to either focus groups or the Delphi method for reasons outlined earlier.

Another advantage of the Delphi method is that, by its nature, it allows for more information to be provided to respondents and for more time to consider and reflect upon that information prior to making judgments. Conversely, there is no control over respondents and, thus, no guarantee that judgments across respondents will be made with the same degree of care. In this regard, NGT data are gathered under more controlled conditions with the opportunity for discussion and direct explanations. As such, a reasonable argument can be made that the judgments underlying NGT data are at least as considered and reliable as those available from the Delphi approach.

Another advantage of both NGT and Delphi is that they lend themselves to phased research and planning programs in which data are gathered sequentially. This approach enables planners/researchers to benefit from respondent learning and to develop a cumulative knowledge base on which to formulate policy and make decisions. While this benefit is theoretically available from focus groups and structured surveys, the reality appears to be that respondent commitment is more difficult to obtain using these approaches.

CONCLUSION

The quality of research and planning activities is no better than the quality of information on which these activities are based. In turn, the quality of this information depends upon the use of methods of data collection that provide appropriate, reliable inputs that can be analyzed and interpreted so as to provide meaningful insights and conclusions. This paper has attempted to familiarize readers with one technique that the author has found to be extremely useful and that it is believed deserves wider recognition and use by those involved in tourism research, tourism planning, and tourism management. In addition, it is hoped that the contents of this article will stimulate greater levels of interest and debate concerning the relative merits of different planning and research techniques as tools for improving management effectiveness in tourism.

REFERENCES

Bellenger, Danny N., Kenneth L. Bernhardt, and Jac L. Goldstucker (1976), *Qualitative Research in Marketing*, Chicago: American Marketing Association.

Bogdan, R., and S.J. Taylor (1975), *Introduction to Qualitative Research Methods*, New York: John Wiley & Sons, Inc.

Calder, Bobby J. (1977), "Focus Groups and the Nature of Qualitative Marketing Research," *Journal of Marketing Research* 14, 353–364.

Delbecq, Andre L., and Andrew H. Van de Ven (1971), "A Group Process Model for Problem Identification and Program Planning," *Journal of Applied Behavioral Science* 7, 4.

Delbecq, Andre L., Andrew H. Van de Ven, and David H. Gustafson (1975), *Group Techniques for Program Planning*, Glenview, IL: Scott, Foresman and Co.

Government of Alberta (1984), *Proposals for an Industrial Strategy for Albertans*, 1985 to 1990, Edmonton, Alberta, Canada.

Green, Paul E., and Yoram Wind (1973), *Multiattribute Decisions in Marketing*, Hinsdale, IL: The Dryden Press.

Higginbotham, James B., and Keith K. Cox (1979), *Focus Group Interviews: A Reader*, Chicago: American Marketing Association.

Holsti, Ole R. (1969), *Content Analysis for the Social Sciences and Humanities*, Reading, MA: Addison-Wesley Publishing Co.

Kassarjian, Harold H. (1977), "Content Analysis in Consumer Research," *Journal of Consumer Research* 4, 8–18.

Linstone, Harold A., and Murray Turoff, eds. (1975), *The Delphi Method*, Reading, MA: Addison-Wesley Publishing Co.

Schmalensee, Diane H., Kenneth Bernhardt, and Nancy Gust (1983), "Focus Group Examines Keys to Services Success," Marketing Science Institute, Cambridge, MA.

Tourism Industry Association of Alberta (1984), *A Program for Furthering Tourism Development in Alberta—Phase I*, Calgary, Alberta, Canada.

43

Model Building and Simulation

JAMES M. ROVELSTAD

Director
Center for Survey & Marketing Research
University of Wisconsin-Parkside
Kenosha, Wisconsin

*T*he use of models and simulation has grown rapidly. Both qualitative and quantitative models are available to assist managers and government officials analyzing and understanding their markets, the travel consumer, and the facilities and resources for which they are responsible. This chapter provides an overview of the scope, nature, and range of uses of models in tourism. Several examples are provided to suggest the diversity and value of models available. However their ultimate value to the individual firm or agency depends on management's interest, understanding, and acceptance.

Many of the chapters in other sections and most in this section directly or implicitly incorporate models in some form or another. This chapter describes some of the concepts employed in model building and a rationale for their development and use. It is not the purpose here to provide a comprehensive and definitive guide for the design of models or their use. But it is hoped that this discussion will provide the reader with an understanding of what models are, ways that they can be used in general and by tourism related organizations in particular, and their roles and relationships vis-à-vis management.

SCOPE AND LIMITATIONS

The following sections provide an overview of the major types of models being used in the travel industry and in other related fields and describe some of the uses of models in the travel and tourism field. The role of models in the management process is defined, with special attention on the interface and balance between theory and quantitative analysis on the one hand and managerial judgment on the other. Finally, two models developed by the author are described in some detail, including both the methods employed in their construction and their uses.

As noted earlier, this chapter is dedicated to the user, or potential user, of models—not to the model builder. Its purpose is to encourage an awareness and interest among those who may have had little exposure and/or are skeptical, or even cynical, about the value of investing time and resources in what appear to them to be theoretical exercises.

Only a few of the relevant examples of the models from travel and its component functional fields, such as economics, marketing, finance, and the other management sciences, can be included here. However, the interested reader will find some useful references for further study at the end of the chapter. Some of the examples described come from industries not specifically confined to travel, but these models have significant application potential for travel related organizations.

The final caveat is that (through a heroic effort in restraint and self-control on the part of the author) no attempt is made to offer value judgments as to which of similar modeling concepts is better. This is really dependent on many external factors including, but not limited to, the availability of resources, the pressure of time, and the level of expertise to which the organization has access.

WHAT IS MODELING?

DEFINITION OF A *MODEL*

The term *model* as used here is defined as a simplified representation of a more complex process or condition

(Markin 1974:78–79). It may be quantitative or qualitative, normative or descriptive, and may range from simple to very complex.

Moreover, a model may be static and serve primarily to aid the understanding of the user; it may be dynamic and interactive, permitting manipulation of its components to test alternative actions or predict future conditions; or it may synthesize a whole from an incomplete set of component parts, as is the case in one of the examples in the latter part of this chapter.

Although the design and use of models is a science that has a long history, especially at the theoretical level and in the physical sciences, it is of much more recent vintage in its broad use for practical business applications. This usage is a phenomenon that corresponds roughly with the growth in the population of professionally trained managers and the increased availability of electronic data processing—a development mainly of the 1960s and 1970s. This explosion of knowledge and capability also produced a gap between many of the younger managers and the decision makers in higher management.

GENERAL TYPES OF MODELS

While all models do not fit neatly into one category or incorporate cleanly defined attributes, it is helpful to know what some of the possible dimensions might be. Perhaps the broadest division can be made between the qualitative and the quantitative.

Qualitative

Qualitative models commonly are employed in the analysis and prediction of consumer behavior. These might, for example, describe the ways that individual personality characteristics relate to purchase behavior. One notable research study disclosed that in sales situations the level of a person's self-confidence is inversely related to his or her persuasibility,

that is, the degree to which the salesperson will be able to influence a change in choice of competitive product purchased (Cox and Bauer 1971).

Personality has been combined with other variables to form complex models of purchase behavior to provide a conceptual basis for understanding the process and variables involved for a consumer in making the ultimate decision, say, to take a trip, to where, by what means, and including which components. With nearly all of these models, the user of the model is aided in design of marketing strategy, but not delivered a set of quantitative criteria—how much to spend on advertising, what the price should be, and the resulting sales volume. One of the more comprehensive and well developed of these is the Howard-Sheth model of consumer behavior (Howard and Sheth 1969). Table 1 illustrates the nature and scope of variables incorporated in this model.

Quantitative

Quantitative models have the capability of providing the user with numerical outputs. These might be measurements of traveler flows and expenditures, forecasts of return on investment, or estimates of changes in market share and the like.

Quantitative models generally are more limited than the behavioral or qualitative models in the range of situations in tourism for which they can be constructed. This is due to the difficulty in quantifying many of the variables relating to human behavior and to the fact that statistical data for the travel and tourism industry have not been thoroughly and systematically collected and maintained; these historical data often form the basis for designing and/or evaluating a model.

These models often are designed around or with general statistical or mathematical models such as linear programming, probability theory, regression, Markov chains, Bayesian theory, factor analysis, and many others. The use of these theories and tools at the model design stage does require persons with relatively high levels of technical training and

TABLE 1   Variables Involved in Consumer Purchase Decision

MARKET INPUTS	ENVIRONMENTAL	CONSUMPTION

Variety of brands available
  Quality
  Price
	Importance of purchase
	
	Personality
		Information search
		
		Sensitivity to information

Distinctiveness Availability Service Warranties	Social class Culture	Perceptual bias Evoked set

Commercial information
  Advertising
  Personal sales
  Publicity
	Organization
	
	Time pressure
	
	Financial status
		Predisposition
		
		Prior satisfaction and experience

Source: Adapted from Howard and Sheth (1969).

experience, which, for many potential users of models, presents a barrier. But with the wide availability of computer services and specialized consultants, this should not be a significant deterrent.

Other model attributes may be described under one or more of the following dichotomies (Markin 1974:85):

- Partial/comprehensive: Represents only a part of the situation, say, the role of personality; or focuses on the complete process.
- Normative/descriptive: Provides a prescriptive guide to optimal action; or a picture or measurement.
- Macro/micro: Describes a group; or an individual situation.
- Static/dynamic: Provides a "snapshot" at one point in time; or indicates interactive relations or flows over time.
- Hypothetical/concrete: Based on theoretical vs. empirical evidence or data.

Simulation is a special type of quantitative modeling that may incorporate several of the types of modeling concepts already discussed. However, it includes the additional feature that a number of variables can be examined under differing dynamic conditions over simulated periods of time, with the outcome, say, profits, determined through the process rather than providing a single solution.

Simulation seeks to develop a realistic model of a real world system or process rather than just a problem solving procedure. Simulation models differ from mathematical models in that simulation abandons the requirement that an (unique) analytical solution for the mathematical structure must exist (Day and Parsons 1971:635).

It is a reasonable generalization to state that nearly all simulation models are computer dependent tools. This is due to the volume of numerical computation that typically is required. They also require a high level of technical sophistication in their initial construction.

However, once developed and programmed for the computer, simulation models often can be used readily by those having little technical background. Some of the types of simulation models useful in tourism include:

Economic systems
Intraorganizational, communication, decision making
Competitive markets
Group dynamics
Distribution/location strategy

USES OF MODELS IN TRAVEL

The potential applications of models in travel are infinite in variety and in type of user. Probably the heaviest users are government agencies and the larger private corporations. This no doubt is due more to the availability of persons in the

organizations with training and familiarity with models and their value than it is to size or scale as a precondition for utility. Internal access to a computer is another enabling—*but not prerequisite*—factor.

It is true that the design and implementation of some of the more complex specialized quantitative models require the commitment of substantial time and resources. But much of the work in model building that has been published, say, in the marketing field can be of great value to even the smaller entrepreneur with limited or no further investment in original research or data collection. This is particularly true in the use of models as a basis for designing and implementing consumer-oriented marketing strategies.

Some of the more common areas of application include market measurement and analysis, process or project monitoring and control, communications, consumer behavior analysis and prediction, management-decision analysis, and training of personnel. The following examples are only suggestive of the range of possibilities.

Physical and economic impact models of tourism flows provide estimates of the size and composition of tourism activity within, and to and from, the specified jurisdiction. These models may also measure changes in size, traveler origin/destination, and the like, in order to evaluate promotional efforts and/or assess changes in the demand in different markets.

The U.S. Government (Bureau of Economic Analysis) has used a model based on a sample drawn from international visitors to estimate the total and net impact of travel on the U.S. balance of payments (Wynegar 1980). The quinquennial U.S. *National Travel Survey*, discontinued in 1982, used a statistical model of the U.S. population to translate a sample survey of households into a measure of the size, nature, and distribution of domestic travel in the United States. Similar information is developed in the intervening years by a statistical model using a different statistical approach designed and implemented by the U.S. Travel Data Center (U.S. Travel Data Center *National Travel Survey*).

State governments also make use of the outputs from these models. In addition, the federal government and many states have need for models to estimate the economic impact of tourism. Several different models, generally based on one or more types of survey research, have been developed (Rovelstad 1974; U.S. Travel Data Center 1975). Each has some limitations in comprehensiveness or accuracy but provides data that are of great value in assessing the role of tourism in the economy, justifying support for tourism-developmental appropriations in legislative bodies, and providing essential basic market data for potential private-sector developers. Such information also has great importance in generating the support of the residents of host communities.

Input/output models of an economy also are used by government agencies to estimate the impacts of tourist expenditures on various sectors of an economy. It is possible, for example, to show how a dollar spent in a hotel is respent in wages and with supplier firms, such as food suppliers, and to estimate the multiplier effect. Such models may be developed as general models of all economic activity for a country, state, or region (Seastrand 1963) or for tourism specifically (Archer 1977).

Generally, input/output (I/O) models have been developed by government agencies for purposes of economic planning and development. The level of detail in breaking down individual component sectors—hotels and motels, automobile services, eating and drinking places, and so on—varies from state to state in the United States. Also these models need to be updated from time to time as the relative mix of businesses sector productivity and other factors change. However, the use of I/O tables is relatively simple and permits tracing of, say, one dollar of tourist expenditure through the various types of businesses affected, state and local taxes created, wages paid, labor hours required and payments (leakages) to out-of-region recipients.

Behavioral models developed specifically for tourism, or derived from other consumer research, provide important insights for the design of marketing strategies for all sectors of the travel industry. These may be very general or highly specific as to application.

One general model of long standing is the motivational model specified by A.H. Maslow. He postulated that behavior is the result of five basic needs. In order of decreasing importance they are physiological, safety, love, esteem, and self-actualization. But once the more basic needs (physiological and safety) have been *adequately* satisfied, they cease to be important motivators, and the "higher" needs predominate (Maslow 1954).

Maslow's model does not help to produce numbers—estimates of profits, market share, and so on. It does provide important insight as to what factors to look for in marketing a discretionary product such as pleasure travel to an affluent population. Of course, it also shows why an unusual situation such as political unrest and violence in a destination area creates such intractable short-run market problems.

A *transactional analysis* model has been proposed to explain the underlying reason why people decide to travel and the process that promotional efforts must undertake in order to motivate a decision to take a pleasure trip. This starts, it suggests, by "hooking" the "I want" child ego state (Kennedy 1977). This model does not conflict with Maslow's but provides further insight as to how the higher level needs can be aroused.

The Howard-Sheth model mentioned earlier has been applied as a basis for determining how travelers choose among alternative, competitive destinations, once they have decided to travel. This model helps those with the responsibility to promote a destination to understand the differing promotion needs as a function of traveler awareness level vis-à-vis the destination. It suggests levels of "evoked sets" of consumer awareness that a travel destination must pass through in order to achieve market success and also the most feasible targets for each stage (Woodside and Ronkainen 1980).

A further aspect of the Howard-Sheth model is the grouping of purchasing behavior into three patterns: *extensive problem solving* (EPS)—the buyer seeks a great deal of information as in the case of a product where the buyer has little or no prior similar experience; *limited problem solving*

(LPS)—the buyer is considering a new product that is comparable to previous experience and the buyer, therefore, knows the information and criteria for decision making; and *routinized response behavior* (RRB)—the buyer repeats previous product choice(s), selecting the same product or one of a small group of products based on price, availability, or even whim. Two points are salient: A person/household in RRB with respect to a particular product, say, vacation destination choice, will require a very strong cue from the market, a new destination, to revert to LPS or EPS. And the extent and persuasibility of the information will have to be high. It has been shown that, while there always is a potential for a change, the tendency for most people is to go to and stay in the behavioral pattern that involves the least effort and perceived risk, that is, RRB (Lehman, Moore, and Elrod 1982).

The idea of evoked set might be the basis of specific individual studies by destinations, hotel chains, airlines, and so on, to measure the level of specific consumer awareness and determine appropriate market segmentation strategies. As an example, a state may learn that in many parts of the nation it has no significant image or awareness. In general, no reasonable level of general mass media promotion will be effective. However, tightly targeted efforts on small segments could be.

International tourism is increasingly viewed as a vital element in a country's trade account. A family of mathematical models for foreign travel expenditures in the United States was derived that shows the relative importance of such factors as price levels, per capita incomes, exchange rate, and unique special events (e.g., Olympic Games). The models also show how these factors' influence varies for different countries of origin (Loeb 1982). Models such as these not only aid governments in policy and economic areas, but also provide guidance to private businesses as to where they may expect their marketing efforts to be most effective at any given time and which factors will have the greatest promotional impact.

Some models have been designed for highly specific uses, for example, casino gaming. Planning, equipping, and staffing a casino, especially deciding which games and how many positions of each, are critical to the business's success. Dandurand (1982) has suggested a modeling approach that could be useful in projecting the demand for each.

The models described collectively as Multidimensional Scaling and Conjoint Measurement are among the newer tools in marketing and have been used for tourism applications. In brief, these methods provide a means of product positioning vis-à-vis specific markets and market segments. They also can be used to predict which combination of product attributes are most likely to be preferred by various segments. Bjorklund and King (1982) designed a model for determination of the best mix of hotel facilities for a new resort area.

A conjoint model has even been applied to evaluation of restaurant menus. This model included such variables as menu mix—appetizers, entrees, and desserts—and prices, in the context of consumer background variables—place of residence, demographics, general food preferences, frequency of eating out, and even whether on a weight-reducing program or not (Green and Wind 1973).

Most of the preceding discussion of uses for models has centered on marketing. Other travel-related applications include recreational land management/development optimization (Gunderman 1980), determining trends in demand for different types of recreational activity (O'Leary and Dottavio 1980), and demand forecasting for international tourism (Edgell and Seely 1980). The list is much longer and covers nearly every facet of tourism activity.

Simulation models designed specifically for tourism applications are not yet numerous. Of course, many of the general business and economic simulation models are directly applicable to travel-industry needs. A few of the existing travel-specific simulators are described here.

Before doing so, it may be useful to note the most important value of simulation models, that is, that they allow the user to conduct a "laboratory experiment" with differing mixes and types of decisions and actions under varying environmental conditions (e.g., consumer, competition, economic conditions, etc.) to learn probable business outcomes. This can be done without the market cost or risk required by a real market test, with no time cost, and without exposing future strategies to competitors.

One of the most difficult problems for major portions of the travel industry has been and continues to be designing strategies to deal with deregulation in the U.S. transportation industry. A simulation model has been developed that permits airline management to evaluate alternative actions with regard to fleet composition and to route and schedule changes, and also provides a tool for executive training. This model, called CASS (Competitive Airline Strategy Simulation), also has been used by the FAA to study slot-allocation problems for capacity-limited airports (Archer 1980).

Simulation also is used by recreation and park system planners to evaluate prospective development and resource management strategies. In this application, changes in such factors as visitor density can be "tested" without substantial cost or exposing the natural resources involved to perhaps irreversible environmental damage (Shecter and Lucas 1980).

EXAMPLES OF MODELING APPLICATIONS

The preceding review of some of the models in or related to the travel industry provides a sense of the range of types and uses of models in the travel and tourism industry. Following are two examples, both developed by the author, that are presented to provide a more substantive understanding of the applications and benefits in modeling.

VACATION DESTINATION CHOICE— A QUALITATIVE EXAMPLE

The most important factors in marketing discretionary, or vacation travel are those that affect the choice of a place to

go. From these derive the development of destination facilities, transportation systems and routes, and the marketing efforts and support of the trade channels—wholesalers and retailers.

One of a continuing series of research studies conducted for the state of West Virginia yielded useful insights as to why vacationers choose a particular destination and led to a conceptual model of this process. This model was derived by grouping survey respondents' answers to the open-ended question, "What three factors do you consider most important in choosing a vacation spot?" The factors fell into four groups, which were identified as "Facilities," "Aesthetics," "Time/Cost," and "Quality of Life" (Rovelstad 1975).

While this is a qualitative rather than quantitative model, it can be expressed in mathematical form as:

$$V = f(F, A, C, Q)$$

where

V = number of vacation or pleasure travelers to a destination

F = quality and quantity of facilities (lodgings, attractions/activities, outdoor facilities, roads, etc.)

A = perceived aesthetic qualities, perhaps also including those encountered en route (scenery, historical sites, weather, atmosphere of isolation, relaxation)

C = travel time and costs to reach and stay at destination

Q = perceived quality of life at the destination (people/residents, lack of pollution)

Moreover, in terms of the relative importance of these factors, it was found that:

$$F > A > C > Q$$

For each person or household, there would be some maximum or minimum threshold for each of the factors that, if exceeded (or unmet), would make that factor an absolute barrier, regardless of its relative importance when within the range of acceptability. Thus, for a person with only two weeks for vacation, a trip/destination requiring more than this is eliminated no matter how well it rates in the other three areas. This model also will explain why attractions with a strong facilities image may bring visitors in spite of high costs, relatively poor aesthetic qualities, and quality-of-life factors that are perceived to be poor.

The model provides substantial insight for tourism planners and marketers, even though it does not yield precise numerical answers; for example, when applied to West Virginia in conjunction with a field survey of travelers, the strengths and deficiencies of the state become apparent. Figure 1 shows these results, which led to reorientation of the state travel development agency's marketing plan. The importance of improved facilities spurred new development, and market targets were geographically revised.

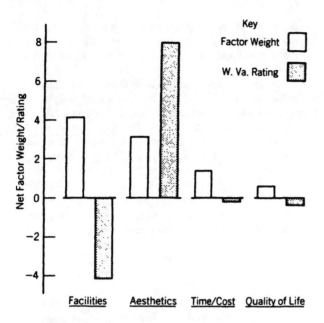

FIGURE 1   Evaluation of West Virginia on vacation choice factors. (*Source:* Adapted from James M. Rovelstad *Behavior Based Marketing Strategies for Travel and Tourism.* (Morgantown: Bureau of Business Research, West Virginia University 1975).

ECONOMIC IMPACT MEASUREMENT— A QUANTITATIVE EXAMPLE

Accurate measures of the economic impacts of visitors to an area are important for planning, evaluation of strategy, gaining government support, and many other reasons. The direct impacts include the jobs and wages created for community residents; the profits received by local businesses from sales to travelers; the direct net revenues received by local, state, or federally owned facilities such as state parks or beaches; and the taxes paid to local, state, and federal governments from wages and sales created by travelers' purchases.

The direct impacts (sales, profits, jobs, and taxes) also create indirect impacts, which themselves can be very significant. A hotel employee, for example, uses the after-tax wages earned to purchase goods and services from businesses, government agencies, and other organizations, as does the business owner with his or her profits. Also, the hotel purchases goods and services to support its sales to travelers. The size of these indirect effects varies from community to community, depending on the local availability of merchants and suppliers. They can total several times the size of the original tourism sale, especially if the effects of the repeated recycling of the travel-sales dollar are considered; for example, the purchases made by the sales clerk whose wages come from the store that sold products to the hotel employee.

The model described here was designed originally for the state of West Virginia to obtain measures of the size and dynamics of its travel and tourism industry. The principal goal was a model to be used on a statewide basis, but the outputs provide useful information down to the county level.

This approach has been in use in West Virginia since 1972 and has been one of the principal planning and evaluation criteria used by that state's travel industry (Rovelstad 1974). An improved version of the model is now being used in New York and Wisconsin.

Obtaining data to measure either potential or actual travel-market performance is especially difficult because of the fragmented nature of the industry and a variety of definitional problems. Indeed, the industry is a collage of various size firms from many industries. The types of businesses involved include hotels, motels, tourist courts, and campgrounds, which receive nearly all of their revenues from travel and tourism, and gasoline stations, movie theaters, and liquor stores, which receive only part of their income from travel and tourism.

Three criteria were central factors in development of the model:

1. *Reliability and continuity*—The measurement should be made in a way that can be repeated in successive periods and reliably show the changes that have occurred in the amount and type of travel in the area.
2. *Comprehensiveness*—Measurements should cover all relevant and significant kinds of travel activity.
3. *Community/Area Sensitivity*—Since the interests of the planners are assumed to be in a relatively small geographic area, the method employed should make disaggregation to this level possible.

The West Virginia model incorporates:

1. A model of traveler expenditures as a function of lodgings choice and a model of lodging choice as a function of trip purpose, both developed primarily by means of traveler surveys
2. A lodging model based on an annual survey of private and publicly operated lodging places and campgrounds
3. A distributive model derived from secondary sources that provides an estimate of the impact of day trips, visits with friends and relatives, and trips using other types of lodgings (sleeping in car or in owned or rented vacation home) as a percentage of commercial lodging sales

These serve as inputs to determine total travel-industry sales revenues, and from these are projected indirect impacts, employment, and tax receipts using an input/output model plus actual tax rates.

The model is used to project responses from an annual survey of lodging facilities (hotels, motels, resorts, and state park cabins and lodges) and campgrounds (privately and publicly owned) into a measure of total overnight-space-sales revenues by class of lodging. It also serves as an input to the TRavel Industry Analysis and InformaTion System (TRAITS).

There are two versions of the lodging model: one for campgrounds and one for hotels, motels, and state-owned accommodations. They are very much alike, and input variables for the hotel/motel sector are:

Number of units (rooms, cabins, etc.)
Average single rental rate ($)
Average double rental rate ($)
Charge per additional person above two ($)
Average occupancy rate (%)
Average party size, or number of guests per unit per night when a unit is occupied (person-nights/unit-nights)
Number of nights open for business per year
Percentage of out-of-state guests (%)

A special computer program, TRAITS, was designed for this application. It was possible to incorporate the SPSS software package for some of the tabular reporting program. Thus, TRAITS is, in fact, a hybrid that consists of, in large part, specialized routines for state-travel-data analysis and, in part, the standard routines from SPSS.

Table 2 is a sample of one of the types of tabularized reports produced by the TRAITS program. A table is provided for each type of establishment (hotel, camp, park) for each county and travel region and for the entire state.

Some of the general uses of this impact information include the following:

Planning and implementation

- identification of markets and potential markets
- benefit/cost and business forecasts
- assessing results of development process
- early identification of changes in traveler behavior

Promotion and public relations

- gaining attention and support from government agencies and elected officials
- gaining community business and resident support
- attracting potential new travel industry entrepreneurs and investors

Basis for credibility

- obtaining debt capital from lending institutions
- obtaining grants from regional, state, and federal agencies

- gaining support for improvement/development of public infrastructure
- influencing legislation favorable to travel industry operations

Information is organized and presented in different forms and levels of detail for each of these uses. Table 3 is an example of a presentation included in an eight-page color brochure summarizing the annual measurement in West Virginia and designed primarily to serve the third category—especially with the state legislators.

The brochure also serves secondarily as a promotion and public relations piece. But more impact is gained by selecting specific figures, such as total sales, employment, or taxes collected, and using these in press releases or documented interviews. It is important in communicating the desired message that the major points do not become lost among too many less directly meaningful bits of information.

MODELS AND MANAGEMENT

The growth in variety and quality of business/management models over the past two decades has been great, but this has not been accompanied by proportionate growth in their acceptance and use. Some of the reasons for this include the normal lags between theory and practical application, inadequate communications to potential users, and lack in some organizations of personnel trained to use these techniques. Time may ultimately narrow these gaps to some extent.

But the relatively limited use appears to have additional causes that might be remedied more quickly. Among these is the reluctance of many in senior management to accept these ideas because they do not understand them—and may even view them as a threat. This probably is more true for the smaller business and for those having less intrinsic involvement with advanced technology of other kinds. Frequently, these managers have little or no advanced formal education themselves.

A related factor is reluctance to invest time and resources

TABLE 2   Sample TRAITS Report

WEST VIRGINIA TRAVEL INDUSTRY QUARTERLY REGIONAL SUMMARY
LODGING
ENTIRE STATE
SECOND QUARTER, 19XX

	THIS PERIOD	LAST PERIOD	1 YEAR AGO	CUMULATIVE AVERAGE[1]
Occupancy rate	73%	77%	76%	66%
Average guest per unit	1.55	1.23	1.43	1.01
Revenue (thousands)	$98,765	$87,654	$76,543	$65,432
Out of state	98%	97%	96%	95%
Average room rate	$55.00	$54.00	$53.00	$52.00
Person-nights	98,765	87,654	76,543	65,432

[1]Calculated for 27 samples.
Source: Rovelstad (1975).

TABLE 3 Travel Council Area Sales, Employment, and Wages and Salaries

TRAVEL COUNCIL	TOTAL SALES (MILLION $)	EMPLOYMENT	WAGES AND SALARIES (MILLION $)
Country Roads	42.3	2,247	11.5
Eastern Gateway	5.2	2,772	11.5
Mountainaire	192.8	10,255	52.6
Mountaineer Country	90.2	4,798	24.6
Nine Valley	209.7	11,153	57.2
Potomac Highland	77.9	4,144	21.3
Upper Ohio	49.8	2,649	13.6
State Total*	715.0	38,017	195.0

*Totals may not add due to rounding.

TRAVEL SALES BY COUNTY

COUNTY	SALES (MILLION $)	COUNTY	SALES (MILLION $)	COUNTY	SALES (MILLION $)
Barbour	3.2	Jackson and Roane	6.7	Pleasants	1.1
Berkeley	30.1	Jefferson	15.1	Pocahontas	9.8
Boone	1.4	Kawawha and Clay	127.0	Preston	3.6
Braxton	6.3	Lewis	2.3	Putnam	4.3
Brooke	5.1	Lincoln	0.1	Raleigh	32.9
Cabell	51.2	Logan	8.8	Randolph	25.0
Calhoun	0.8	McDowell	4.1	Ritchie	2.9
Clay—see Kanawha		Marion	12.5	Roane—see Jackson	
Doddridge—see Harrison		Marshall	4.3	Summers	13.3
Fayette	8.1	Mason	6.2	Taylor	4.9
Gilmer	0.8	Mercer	41.1	Tucker	17.2
Grant	4.6	Mineral	3.3	Tyler	1.5
Greenbrier	84.0	Mingo	7.5	Upshur	10.6
Hampshire	9.7	Monogalia	32.3	Wayne	3.2
Hancock	7.5	Monroe	0.3	Webster	2.0
Hardy	1.4	Morgan	6.9	Wetzel	4.3
Harrison and Doddridge	20.8	Nicholas	5.1	Wirt and Wood	22.0

in "soft" projects (or personnel), which in themselves do not produce a profit. It may appear more attractive to devote whatever resources are available to activities that, however risky, *can* produce a direct return.

While there are many other potential reasons for management reluctance to make use of appropriate modeling and simulation techniques, perhaps one of the more significant is that the wide availability of low-cost data processing is not fully comprehended. This probably is simply because of the rapid growth in supply and the substantial decline in costs for service and equipment over a very short time. This has made it possible for even the small business to own its own computer for not much more than the cost of an electric typewriter.

Barriers such as these will best be resolved by understanding what modeling techniques can do and where their limits are. Perhaps the most important point to note is that models do not make management decisions; they only help to organize the available knowledge and information and, therefore, to permit better focus on those facets of problem solving and decision making where judgment and experience are most needed.

This chapter started with a definition of *models*, noting that they are simplifications of reality. Given this, no model can fully incorporate all of the variables and dynamics of the real world. What they can do is help management to understand and deal with complex situations more effectively and thoroughly. It is just as vital, in fact, that management not be lulled into overreliance on cranking out numbers and accepting them on blind faith.

Benefits from the use of models in the planning, monitoring, and evaluation process include the following:

- Forces early organization of information, identification of potential problems, and location of information gaps and needs.
- Enables management to reduce the number of factors of uncertainty on which subjective judgment must be used.
- Increases understanding of the operational environment(s).
- Reduces risk and probability of wrong decision.

Caveats to the use of modeling and simulation methods have been identified in this and earlier sections and, with some additions, include the following:

- Management acceptance is imperative.
- Limitations of the models must be identified and understood in interpretation of results.
- Models, especially quantitative, are derived from empirical information, and therefore have to be updated and revalidated as environments change.
- Limitations in data, especially in the travel industry, may be difficult to overcome.
- The simplest *useful* model probably is best—level of complexity should increase as problem is more fully defined.

CONCLUSION

This chapter has provided an overview of the nature, uses, and concepts of models used for the travel and tourism industry. Simulation is a special type of modeling concept and was described as a valuable tool for planning, evaluation, and training.

While *modeling* may require persons with special and highly technical skills, the *use* of models does not. In some applications, access to computers is needed, but this should not be considered a barrier with the wide availability and low cost of using such services today.

One of the biggest barriers is likely to be gaining the interest and acceptance of management. The rapid growth of modeling knowledge and technology appears to have opened a gap that serves to inhibit the use of these tools. It is, therefore, important for senior management to become aware of and receptive to the potential that modeling and simulation offer for increased tourism revenues and profits.

REFERENCES

Archer, Brian (1977), "Input-Output Analysis: Its Strengths, Limitations and Weaknesses," *The 80's—Its Impact on Travel and Tourism Marketing*, Proceedings of the Eighth Annual Conference, 89–108, Salt Lake City, UT: The Travel Research Association.

Archer, Brian (1980), "CASS, Competitive Airline Strategy Simulation," an unpublished descriptive summary by Flight Transportation Associates Inc., Cambridge, MA.

Bjorklund, Richard A., and Barry King (1982), "A Consumer-Based Approach to Assist in the Design of Hotels," *Journal of Travel Research* XX, 4 (Spring), 45–52.

Cox, Donald F., and Raymond A. Bauer (1971), "Self Confidence and Persuasability in Women," in *Marketing Models: Behavioral Science Applications*, Ralph L. Day and Thomas E. Ness, eds., 62–76, Scranton, PA: Intext Educational Publishers.

Dandurand, Lawrence (1982), "Incorporating Casino Game Preference Market Segmentation Data into Marketing Plans," *Journal of Travel Research* XX, 4 (Spring), 15–19.

Day, Ralph L., and Leonard J. Parsons, eds. (1971), *Marketing Models: Quantitative Applications*. Scranton, PA: Intext Educational Publishers.

Edgell, David, and Richard Seely (1980), "A Multi-Stage Model for the Development of International Tourism Forecasts for States and Regions," in *Tourism Planning and Development Issues*, Donald E. Hawkins, Elwood L. Shafer, and James M. Rovelstad, eds., 407–410, Washington D.C.: George Washington University.

Green, Paul E., and Yoram Wind (1973), *Multiattribute Decision Making in Marketing: A Measurement Approach*. Hinsdale, IL: The Dryden Press.

Gunderman, Habil Egon (1980), "The Question of Optimal Densities of Forest Land in the Tourist Regions of Central Europe," in *Tourism Planning and Development Issues*, Donald E. Hawkins, Elwood L. Shafer, and James M. Rovelstad, eds., 3–22, Washington, D.C.: George Washington University.

Howard, John A., and Jagdish N. Sheth (1969), *The Theory of Buyer Behavior*. New York: John Wiley & Sons, Inc.

Kennedy, John L. (1977), "A Transactional Analysis Model for Understanding Travel Decisions," *The 80's—Its Impact on Travel and Tourism Marketing*, Proceedings of the Eighth Annual Conference, Salt Lake City, UT: The Travel Research Association.

Lehman, Donald R., William L. Moore, and Terry Elrod (1982), "The Development of Distinct Choice Process-Segments Over Time: A Stochastic Modeling Approach," *Journal of Marketing* 46, 2 (Spring), 48–59.

Loeb, Peter D. (1982), "International Travel to the United States: An Econometric Evaluation, *Annals of Tourism Research* 9 (1), 7–20.

Markin, Ron J., Jr. (1974), *Consumer Behavior: A Cognitive Orientation*, New York: MacMillan Publishing Co., Inc.

Maslow, Abraham H. (1954), *Motivation and Personality*, New York: Harper and Row.

O'Leary, Joseph L., and F. Dominic Dottavio (1980), "Recreation Activity Clusters in Resource Settings: A First Approximation," in *Tourism Planning and Development Issues*, Donald E. Hawkins, Elwood L. Shafer, and James M.

Rovelstad, eds., 161–178, Washington, D.C.: George Washington University.

Rovelstad, James M. (1974), *Analytical Measures of Travel and Tourism: The West Virginia Model*, Morgantown, West Virginia: Bureau of Business Research, West Virginia University.

Rovelstad, James M. (1975), *Behavior Based Marketing Strategies for Travel and Tourism: The West Virginia Model*, Morgantown, West Virginia: Bureau of Business Research, West Virginia University.

Seastrand, Frans (1963), "New York State Economic System: The Interindustry Structure of the New York State Economy," Albany, NY: Data and Systems Bureau, Office of Planning Services.

Schecter, Mordechai, and Robert Lucas (1980), "A Park Visitor Travel Simulation Model as a Management Tool," in *Tourism Marketing and Management Issues*, Donald E. Hawkins, Elwood L. Shafer, and James M. Rovelstad, eds., 379–390, Washington, D.C.: George Washington University.

U.S. Department of Commerce, *U.S. Travel* (periodical), "Summary and Analysis of International Travel to the U.S." Washington, D.C.: U.S. Travel Service.

U.S. Travel Data Center (1975), "Travel Expenditure Impact Model," Washington, D.C.: U.S.Travel Data Center.

U.S. Travel Data Center (annual), *National Travel Survey*, Washington, D.C.: U.S. Travel Data Center.

Woodside, Arch G., and Ilkka A. Ronkainen (1980), "Tourism Management Strategies for Competitive Vacation Destinations," in *Tourism Marketing and Management Issues*, Donald E. Hawkins, Elwood L. Shafer, and James M. Rovelstad, eds., 3–22, Washington, D.C.: George Washington University.

Wynegar, Don (1980), "International Outlook," *Proceedings: 1981 Travel Outlook Forum*, 157–174, Washington, D.C.: U.S. Travel Data Center.

44

Conjoint Analysis in Travel Research: A Manager's Guide

JOHN D. CLAXTON

Professor
Faculty of Commerce
University of British Columbia
Vancouver, British Columbia

*C*onjoint analysis has been put forward as a procedure for evaluating the relative importance that buyers place on the various components of a product or service. This chapter discusses the advantages and pitfalls associated with the application of these procedures and highlights manager versus researcher roles in this type of study.

A traveler wanting to go from the airport to downtown may be faced with a number of public transport options: a local bus that costs $2.00, makes many stops, and takes 60 minutes; an express bus that costs $5.00, is nonstop, and takes 45 minutes; or a helicopter service that costs $25.00, and takes 10 minutes. The trip characteristics that might be considered by travelers choosing one of these options include waiting time until next service, travel time, comfort en route, cost, baggage handling, sights en route, and possibly many others. Each traveler weighs the pros and cons and makes a choice. Since all three services attract customers, the implication is that all travelers do not make the same trade-offs—each traveler makes the *trade-offs* that suit individual values and preferences.

In 1973, a research paper titled "Forecasting Traffic on STOL" (Short Takeoff and Landing) introduced conjoint analysis as a method of evaluating transportation user trade-offs (Davidson 1973). Since then conjoint analysis has become widely used with numerous applications in the travel and transportation field. The purpose of this chapter is to describe some of these applications, with a view to helping research *users* assess the merits of this research approach. In other words, this chapter is not written for researchers, but rather for managers who use research to guide decisions and are interested in understanding the potential strengths and pitfalls of conjoint analysis.

The discussion is presented in the following sequence.

First, there is a discussion of the range of travel-related situations where user trade-offs are of interest. Second, a conceptual description of conjoint analysis is presented. Third, a number of travel-related applications of conjoint analysis are reviewed. And finally, a number of suggestions are presented for managers when working with research specialists on the design and evaluation of user trade-off studies.

USER TRADE-OFFS

THE TRADE-OFF VIEW OF USER CHOICES

The purpose of this section is: (1) to provide a conceptual description of user choice as a trade-off process and (2) to suggest examples of travel situations where user trade-offs are of concern. First, to introduce the idea of trade-offs consider the following examples:

- Why do some people drive to work, even though parking is expensive and a bus stops a block from their home?
- Why do some people make their own travel arrangements, while their neighbors use a travel agent?
- Why do travelers have individual preferences for one airline over another?
- Why does one municipal government decide on a bus system and another opt for rail rapid transit?
- How do travelers decide on one hotel over another?

- Why does one tour operator decide on a fleet of GM vehicles rather than Ford?
- How does a department of tourism decide whether to emphasize low-cost camping holidays or luxury resort vacations?

At the root of each of these decisions is the issue of attribute trade-offs. In some sense, the decision maker must give up one attribute (or characteristic) in order to gain another—give up low price to gain flexibility, give up convenience to gain satisfaction, give up frequent departure times to gain better meals, give up shorter travel times to gain low capital costs, give up convenient location to gain quieter surroundings, give up fuel economy to gain better dealer service, give up attracting tourists to cities to gain tourists in rural regions. Although each of these is hypothetical, jointly they indicate that attribute trade-offs are of concern in a broad range of travel-related situations.

The second point to be made is that trade-off decisions can usefully be viewed as a process where *a decision maker implicitly sums up the value (or utility) of various parts of each alternative and then selects the alternative with the greatest net utility*. Returning to the situation of the traveler wishing to travel from the airport to downtown, it is clear that some travelers place a very high utility on speed of service. These travelers are willing to spend five times the price to shorten the trip from 45 to 10 minutes. At the other extreme, some travelers consider it extremely important to minimize their travel costs. Between these extremes there are those who are willing to pay an extra $3.00 to reduce the trip time from 65 to 45 minutes, but are not willing to pay an increment of $20.00 to shorten the trip an additional 35 minutes.

The implication of this example is that users can be viewed as having certain values or utilities for various levels of each attribute and that, for each alternative, the utilities of the parts (the "part-worths") are in some manner combined. The alternative chosen will be the one with the highest net utility. Table 1 provides a simple numerical illustration of part worths and net utilities. This example does not imply that users explicitly keep score cards on each alternative being considered, rather this summing up of pros and cons is done in a very implicit fashion. Further, this summing up is equivalent to making a series of trade-offs, giving up less import aspects to gain more important ones.

The third point to be made regarding user trade-offs is to reinforce the view that faced with one particular set of alternatives *different users have different utility profiles and, thus, make different decisions*. As was pointed out with the airport to downtown example, the value placed on the various attributes differs from one traveler to another. As a result, the net utility for the alternatives will differ and, therefore, so will the alternatives selected. The implication of this for trade-off research is the importance of identifying user segments with various attribute preferences, that is, various utility profiles. In the airport to downtown example, the size of the segment that has very high utility for short travel time will determine the feasibility of a helicopter service.

In summary, user trade-offs are of concern in a broad range of travel-related situations. User trade-off can be viewed as a process whereby users consider the value of the various parts of each alternative, in some manner combine these "part-worths," and select the alternative with the greatest net value (utility). Finally, because users differ in terms of the trade-offs they would prefer to make, segmentation on this basis can be used to assess the viability of specific travel services.

USER TRADE-OFF SITUATIONS

Before leaving the discussion of user trade-offs, it is important to emphasize the range of travel- and leisure-related situations in which this type of information can be of importance to management decisions. As outlined in Table 2, both private- and public-sector managers might be faced with situations in which user trade-offs are of concern. Further, the focus could be either trying to increase market share within a particular mode or trying to shift travelers from one mode to another.

An intramode (market share) example would be a hotel manager considering whether a discount price, a room-meals-entertainment package, or some other alternative would be the most effective way to improve his share of the weekend-guest market. An intermode (market growth) example would be a government program to switch commuters from private autos to public transit. In both of these examples, a clear understanding of user trade-offs with respect to various mode characteristics is of critical importance to the mode manager. As noted in Table 2, *mode* is used in this discussion to refer to any particular travel product or service.

CONJOINT ANALYSIS

The discussion of this point has not considered how to obtain information on user trade-offs, rather it has only argued that this type of information can be useful. This section discusses the use of conjoint analysis for the evaluation of user trade-offs.

Conjoint analysis was first developed in the field of mathematical psychology (Luce and Tukey 1964). It was introduced to consumer research in 1971 (Green and Rao) with the first transportation-related study being reported by Davidson in 1973. An example is used here to explain the nature of conjoint analysis. The example was selected because it dealt with a transportation issue, the purchase of an electric vehicle, and because the conjoint analysis utilized two different data-collection procedures.

ATTRIBUTE TRADE-OFFS BETWEEN ELECTRIC AND CONVENTIONAL VEHICLES

It is clear that even when an electric vehicle could meet usage requirements, a consumer may not switch from a conventional vehicle. Several additional attributes come into consideration: Electric vehicles represent a new propulsion system—consumers who enjoy innovation may consider this

TABLE 1 The Concept of Part-Worth and Net Utilities: Airport to Downtown Example[a]

PART-WORTH UTILITIES

	ATTRIBUTE 1: TRIP TIME			ATTRIBUTE 2: COST		
	SLOW (60 MIN.)	MODERATE (45 MIN.)	FAST (10 MIN.)	LOW ($2.00)	MODERATE ($5.00)	HIGH ($25.00)
Traveler A: (placing high value on speed)	2[b]	3	10	6	5	4
Traveler B: (placing high value on low cost)	4	5	6	9	6	0
Traveler C: (placing value on both)	2	6	7	8	5	2

NET UTILITIES

	LOCAL BUS (SLOW-LOW)	EXPRESS BUS (MODERATE-MODERATE)	HELICOPTER (FAST-HIGH)
Traveler A: (will go by helicopter)	8[c]	8	14
Traveler B: (will go by local bus)	13	11	6
Traveler C: (will go by express bus)	10	11	9

[a]In this example, it is assumed that only two attributes, travel time and cost, influence user choice.
[b]Entries indicate the value between 0 (low value) and 10 (high value) that Traveler A places on each possible attribute level.
[c]It is assumed that part worths are simply added to obtain net utilities. Other combinational approaches such as multiplication could have been assumed.

desirable, but consumers who prefer to stay with the tried and true may be deterred. Electric vehicles, at least initially, will be priced at premium. On the other hand, electrics will have lower operating costs and will offer very low levels of air-noise pollution, both desirable attributes. The study of interest here (Hargreaves, Claxton, and Siller 1976) used conjoint measurement to assess the relative importance of these attributes.

Table 3 describes both a conventional and an electric vehicle in terms of five major attributes. The research issue is to assess the relative importance of these five attributes on consumers' vehicle preferences. Unfortunately, simply ask-

ing consumers to choose between a conventional versus an electric would not indicate which attribute(s) influenced preference most. However, if hypothetical vehicles were specified with various combinations of the five attributes, consumer preferences for these hypothetical vehicles would reveal attribute importance.

In the electric vehicle study, each of the five attributes was specified by two levels. All combinations would result in 2 x 2 x 2 x 2 x 2 = 32 hypothetical vehicles. Since conjoint analysis requires only rank-preference data, consumers would be asked to rank 32 vehicles if all alternatives were included. Clearly, as the number of attributes and number of levels

TABLE 2 Examples of Travel and Leisure Situations in Which Information About User Trade-offs Can Have Impact on Management Decisions

	INTRAMODE[a]	INTERMODE
Private Sector	• An airline trying to improve its service relative to other airlines • A bus manufacturer trying to interest a city in its model of buses • A hotel attempting to increase its share of the weekend market	• A train system attempting to attract auto travelers • A boat manufacturer association trying to increase the number of families that buy boats • A symphony company attempting to attract a broader cross-section of attendees
Public Sector	• A municipal bus company trying to decide on the price of an express bus service • A "miles per gallon" campaign attempting to shift car owners to energy efficient vehicles	• A subsidy program to facilitate the introduction of a rapid transit system • Grants to enable the operation of a cultural organization

[a]*Mode* is used in a general sense to refer to any particular travel product or service.

TABLE 3   Attribute-Level Specification: Electric Vehicle Study

Attribute	Level A	Level B	Conventional Vehicle	Electric Vehicle
Speed and range	40 miles and 40mph	Unlimited	[B][a]	[A]
Operating costs	10 cents/mile	5 cents/mile	[A]	[B]
Initial price	$8,000	$5,000	[B]	[A]
Air and noise Pollution	"normal"	"zero"	[A]	[B]
Propulsion system	"gas engine"	"new system"	[A]	[B]

Attribute-Level Combinations Use in Electric Vehicle Study[b]

	1	2	3	4	5	6	7	8	9	10	11	12	13	14	15	16
Speed and Range	B	B	B	B	A	B	B	B	B	A	A	A	A	A	A	A
Operating Costs	B	B	B	A	B	B	A	A	A	B	B	B	A	A	A	A
Initial price	B	B	A	B	B	A	B	A	A	B	A	A	B	B	A	A
Pollution	B	A	B	B	B	A	A	B	A	A	B	A	B	A	B	A
Propulsion	A	B	B	B	B	A	A	A	B	A	A	B	A	B	B	A

[a]The attribute-level combination for a conventional vehicle is: level B on speed and range, level A on operating costs, level B on initial price, level A on pollution, and level A on propulsion.
[b]For example, "Card 1" was specified as: Unlimited speed and range, 5 cents/mile, $5,000, zero air and noise pollution, and a gasoline engine.

increases, the ranking of all alternatives becomes onerous. However, the use of a balanced subset reduces the respondent task and still allows evaluation of attribute importance (Green 1974). As indicated in Table 3, the electric vehicle study had consumers rank a subset of 16 hypothetical vehicles. The selection of the 16 was based on an experimental design referred to as an orthogonal array.

The method employed to obtain consumers' preferences was to prepare sets of 16 cards, each card containing one of the attribute-level combinations. Consumers were asked to sort the set from most to least preferred.

Analysis of the rank-preference data was done using MONANOVA (Kruskal 1965). This computer program searches for values (utilities) for each of the 10 attribute levels such that when the utilities are added together, the net utilities for each of the 16 combinations will correspond to the original preference rankings. This analysis can be based on either the rankings of individual consumers or the composite ranking of a group of respondents.

For the electric vehicle study, analysis of the composite rankings of all respondents produced the part-worth utilities of the 10 attribute levels indicated in Table 4. Also indicated are the net utilities resulting when the part-worth utilities are combined for conventional and electric vehicles.

The net utilities indicate that electric vehicles capable of only 40 miles and 40 miles per hour, and priced at $3,000 premium will be seen as inferior to conventional vehicles, even when operating costs are reduced by 50 percent and pollution eliminated. However, the part-worth utilities also indicate that only one of the electric vehicles' impediments need to be eliminated for consumer preferences to be reversed.

AN ALTERNATIVE DATA-COLLECTION APPROACH

The foregoing study indicates a data-collection approach referred to as *full profile* or *concept evaluation*; that is, the

TABLE 4   Part-Worth Utilities of Attribute Levels

Attribute	Level A	Level B	Conventional Vehicle	Electric Vehicle
Speed and range	−1.43	+1.43	+1.43	−1.43
Operating costs	−0.93	+0.93	-0.93	+0.93
Initial price	−0.90	+0.90	+0.90	−0.90
Air and noise Pollution	−0.54	+0.54	−0.54	+0.54
Propulsion system	−0.02	+0.02	−0.02	+0.02
NET[a]			+0.84	−0.84

[a]Comparison of conventional and electric vehicles indicates the attribute levels of conventional have a high net utility.

respondent compares alternatives specified in terms of all of the attributes of interest. A second conjoint-measurement approach involves evaluating two attributes at a time and is referred to as *trade-off matrix* approach. An example of this is also provided by electric vehicle study.

When the importance of operating capacity became apparent, further attention was directed to this characteristic. Electric propulsion technology limited operating capacity in terms of speed, range, and number of stop-start cycles. However, technology did make possible various combinations of these three characteristics. Thus, it was important to assess consumers' preferences in this regard.

Figure 1 indicates the trade-off matrices used to evaluate the three capacity attributes. With this approach, consumers were asked to rank the nine cells of each of the 3 x 3 matrices from one (most preferred) to nine (least preferred). Analysis similar to the earlier example was then used to assess the part-worth utilities for the three levels of each of the three attributes.

CONJOINT ANALYSIS SUMMARY

The assessment of consumer trade-offs via conjoint analysis can be divided into five steps. The first, and most critical, is the careful identification of the attributes that are important to consumers; for example, assessment of consumers' trade-offs when selecting a resort hotel will only be valid if the measurement process asks about attributes of concern in the actual choice situation.

The second step is to specify the levels to be evaluated for each attribute. Again, the criterion should be specification that is consistent with the actual choice situation; for example, if air travel choices were being evaluated and an attribute of concern was price, the price levels used for trade-off assessment should be consistent with feasible price levels on the route of interest.

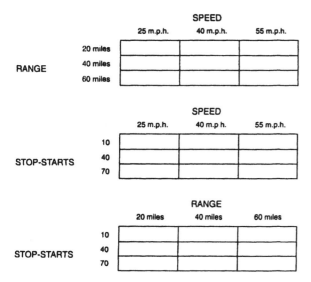

FIGURE 1 Trade-off matrix approach—consumers respond by ranking the 9 cells from 1 (most preferrred) to 9 (least preferred).

The third step is the design of a data-collection approach. As indicated earlier, the research can be based on full-profile or trade-off matrices. The trade-offs can be presented in a verbal or pictorial format. Consumers can be asked to respond by using a paper-and-pencil approach or by means of an interactive computer display. These and other design issues are discussed further in a later section of the paper.

The fourth step is the data-collection process. It is clear that this process is influenced by the choice of trade-off measurement procedures. Sorting of full profiles from most to least preferred places two constraints on the data-collection process. Use of full profiles requires careful explanation by the interviewer and a flat surface to spread out the concept cards. Similarly, use of computer display places a restriction on interview location.

The final step in conjoint analysis applications is parameter estimation. In the electric vehicle study, attribute-level utilities were estimated using monatonic analysis of variance. As discussed later, other procedures, including regression analysis, can also be applied.

TRAVEL-RELATED APPLICATIONS

A study sponsored by the Research Branch of the Canadian Transport Commission provided several examples of the application of conjoint analysis in travel-related applications (Strachan 1978). The purpose of the study was to interview managers who had used conjoint analysis. The applications reviewed included four studies of air traveler trade-offs and three studies of rail traveler trade-offs. These are summarized here to indicate the approaches utilized and some of the problems encountered.

The Appendix indicates for each of the seven studies: the study objectives, the method of attribute specification, the sampling method, the measurement approach, and the attributes evaluated. As the Appendix indicates, the critical decisions as to which attributes to include and which attribute levels to evaluate were based on a combination of in-depth group interviews with consumers and group discussions by industry professionals. Future studies will continue to require careful attention to this phase of study design, and these group approaches continue to provide a most fruitful approach (Claxton, Ritchie, and Zaichkowsky 1980).

The Appendix also indicates that the seven studies each evaluated the importance of from 11 to 27 attributes and estimated from 35 to 71 attribute-level parameters. The most ambitious study, the Service Design Study done by Air Canada, divided 27 air-trip attributes into four major groups (Ground service, In-flight service, Aircraft decor, and Other) and asked respondents to evaluate the trade-offs associated with each group. Even with this subdivision into four groups, the number of potential trade-offs is very large; for example, each of the seven "other" attributes was specified at three levels; if respondents were asked to rank all combinations they would be faced with 3^7, or 2187, alternatives. Fortunately, the use of carefully selected subsets of these alternatives makes it possible to estimate the 21 attribute-level parameters without burdening the respondent with an impossible task (Green 1974).

The final observations to be made regarding the seven example applications are directed at the nature of attribute-level specification (Table 5 provides an example taken from Study II, the Rail Corridor Study). First, a major criterion in the selection of attribute levels is that they encompass alternatives that are representative of marketplace possibilities; for example, the Rail Corridor Study considered travel times ranging from 1 to 9 hours, consistent with the modes and the route being evaluated. Second, it can be noted that the attribute levels can be expressed in a qualitative manner, as in the case of "quality of ride," or in a quantitative manner, as in the case of "door-to-door travel time."

In summary, the applications presented here serve to identify some of the major issues facing users of conjoint analysis. The following sections discuss these issues in greater detail and highlight the areas where user-researcher interaction is critical to the success of a conjoint analysis study.

A MANAGER'S PERSPECTIVE

For managers to be able to make effective use of conjoint analysis, there must be (1) a general appreciation of the major issues involved in the implementation in this type of research study and (2) an understanding of the manager's role in this process. These two topics are discussed in the final sections of this paper. Prior to this, other reference papers on conjoint analysis are suggested.

REFERENCE DOCUMENTS

A thorough discussion of conjoint analysis was first provided by Green and Wind in their book *Multiattribute Deci-*

sions in Marketing (1973). There also have been a number of journal articles that provide overview discussions (for example, Johnson 1974a; Green and Wind 1975). Green and Srinivasan (1978) discussed research concerns that have emerged since the introduction of conjoint analysis methods.

Papers specifically addressing tourism and travel have also utilized conjoint analysis. A paper in *Traffic Quarterly* (Ross 1975) discussed these methods. A paper in *Harvard Business Review* (Green and Wind 1975) indicated the use of conjoint analysis in a transatlantic air-traveler study. Papers have also been published that indicate the application of conjoint analysis in applications dealing with the performing arts (Currim, Weinberg, and Wittink 1981) and with urban transportation (Srinivasan, Flachsbart, Dajani, and Hartley 1981).

The references just indicated were selected to provide an overview of conjoint analysis methods and applications. References in the following sections address specific aspects of conjoint analysis research.

MAJOR ISSUES IN CONJOINT ANALYSIS

The major issues involved in the application of conjoint analysis can be divided into three phases: attribute generation, data collection, and parameter estimation. These three phases are discussed next.

Attribute Generation

The identification of attributes that consumers will be asked to evaluate is part of the problem-definition process, the cornerstone of research design. What product/service attributes do consumers consider when making their purchase choices? What attributes can managers modify to achieve a

TABLE 5   Attribute-Level Specification Examples from Study II

ATTRIBUTE	ATTRIBUTE LEVELS
1. On-time reliability	1. Usually arrives on time. 2. Does not usually arrive on time.
2. Personal comfort	1. Room to stretch out when you are sitting. 2. Not much room to stretch out when you are sitting.
3. Ride quality	1. Smooth enough to be able to read or write. 2. Not smooth enough to be able to read or write.
4. Baggage arrangements	1. Baggage may be checked. 2. Baggage may be stored in a special area near the entrance of the vehicle.
5. Mobility during trip	1. You can leave your seat to go to another area, such as a lounge. 2. You cannot get up and move around during the trip.
6. Door-to-door travel time	Nine attribute levels specified as 1 hour through 9 hours, inclusive.
7. Mode	1. Car 2. Bus 3. Train

more desirable product/service? These questions are clearly a central focus for many research studies.

A survey of 698 applications of conjoint analysis (Cattin and Wittink 1981) indicated that all applications used "expert judgment" to identify relevant attributes and that a large majority also used in-depth group interviews. It is absolutely critical that methods such as these be used to generate attributes that are relevant to consumers. Further, because of the somewhat intuitive nature of attribute generation, there is a danger that this phase of the research will be given second place to more technical aspects of conjoint analysis, whereas the opposite should be the case.

Data Collection

The purpose here is not to describe the variety of data-collection procedures in detail, rather to indicate the range of available alternatives. As indicated earlier, the data-collection *format* may be either full profile or concept evaluation (Green 1974). Another alternative involves pairwise comparisons of partial profiles (Johnson 1975). A second data-collection consideration is the method of *stimulus communication* with the major alternatives being to describe the stimuli in prose, to use pictures, or to show respondents' actual products. In addition, Johnson (1974b) has introduced the use of interactive computer terminals.

A third consideration is the nature of *response information* to be collected. Respondents can be asked their degree of liking, preferences, and/or intentions to buy. Finally, a related consideration is *respond format* with alternatives being paired choice, rankings, or ratings (Carmone, Green, and Jain 1978).

Parameter Estimation

Accompanying the initial introduction of conjoint analysis procedures for data collection, computer programs were developed for data analysis. Probably the most well known, MONANOVA was based on monatonic analysis of variance (Kruskal 1965); another, LINMAP, was based on linear programming (Srinivasan and Schocker 1973).

Researchers have applied a variety of procedures including ordinary least squares regression (OLS), monatone regression, and logit analysis (Cattin and Wittink 1981; Jain, Acito, Malhotra, and Mahajan 1979). A paper by Wittink and Cattin (1981) compared alternative estimation methods and argued in favor of OLS on the basis of robustness and ease of interpretation.

THE MANAGER'S ROLE IN RESEARCH DESIGN

The following section raises a series of questions that should be raised by a manager when a conjoint analysis study is being designed. The reader will recognize that similar questions could be asked when evaluating a study that was already completed.

• Is conjoint analysis appropriate? Whenever consumer trade-offs are a serious concern, conjoint analysis presents a major research option. In parallel with conjoint analysis, respondents should be asked to provide a direct rating of the importance of each attribute. Such parallel measures will provide a useful indication of research validity. Managers would be well advised to ensure that direct measures accompany conjoint analysis methods.

• What attributes should be measured? As discussed earlier, this is a critical question in the research design process. Further, it is the area where the manager rather than the researcher should provide research leadership.

• Do the data-collection methods seem reasonable? One aspect of this question is the extent to which the response task simulates real-world decisions. In other words, the attribute-level combinations should represent alternatives that respondents will consider realistic. The second aspect of this question is the complexity of the response task. Care must be taken not to overtax respondents by asking them to evaluate an onerous set of attribute-level combinations. Careful pilot testing of the data-collection methods can provide important insights in this area. A manager's major concern when evaluating data-collection methods should be to insure that consumers will consider the response task to be realistic and not tiring and/or confusing.

• Will the analysis produce results that are readily understood? This question can be divided into four subsidiary questions:

1. Does the parameter-estimation procedure provide an indication of goodness-of-fit for the overall model? In other words, is it possible to assess how well the attribute utilities derived by the analysis capture the information contained in the respondent data? In a regression analysis, for example, R^2 provides this indication of variance accounted for.

2. Does the analysis provide an indication of the statistical significance for each attribute utility or only for the overall model? The overall results may be highly significant when consumers consider a few of the attributes to be very important and other attributes to be irrelevant. Again, using regression as an example, the statistics provide an indication of the significance of individual attributes.

3. Will the analysis facilitate the evaluation of differences across consumers? Although an overall indication of consumers' attribute utilities is an important starting point, it is frequently equally important to be able to identify groups of consumers with common values for purposes of market segmentation.

4. Will the analysis attempt to provide some indication of the validity of the findings? As indicated earlier, use of direct measures of attribute importance in parallel with conjoint analysis methods is one validation approach, with converging results providing confidence in the findings. Looking for similar results across split-sample analyses is another approach. A third approach that has been used with conjoint analysis is to predict market share of existing prod-

ucts based on the derived-attribute utilities and then to compare predicted with actual market-share figures.

It is clear that managers faced with attempting to understand relatively complex analytical techniques must draw on the expertise of their research associates. Looking for answers to the four questions outlined should provide a useful framework for this interaction.

Since introduced in 1971, conjoint analysis has gained widespread acceptance as a method for evaluation of customer trade-offs. Cattin and Wittink (1981) surveyed commercial usage in the United States and found 698 applications prior to 1981. As with any new technique, potential users are faced with assessing the merits of the new approach and deciding whether or not it is appropriate for their needs. The purpose of this paper has been to provide potential users in the field of tourism and travel with an overview of conjoint analysis and to suggest key issues to consider when a study using these procedures seems appropriate.

APPENDIX   Applications of Conjoint Analysis

STUDY I: INTERCITY SHORT TAKEOFF AND LANDING (STOL) SERVICE
(BY THE TRANSPORTATION DEVELOPMENT CENTER)

1. Study objectives—to develop a model for forecasting traffic on a new STOL service and to predict the effect of changing the levels of service offered.
2. Attribute specification—in-depth group interviews with business travelers used to identify 13 attributes of concern and to specify each at 2 to 4 levels.
3. Sampling—random telephone calls to quality potential users of service, followed by personal interviews.
4. Measurement approach—21 trade-off matrices supported with sketches to convey some of the attributes.
5. Attributes—(levels in brackets)

Trip time (3)	Reliability (2)
Trip cost (4)	Reading comfort (2)
Transfers (3)	Ride comfort (3)
Departure (3)	Refreshments (4)
Reservations (3)	Seat width (3)
Baggage (3)	Credit (2)
Other travelers (3)	

6. Outcomes—aided in decision regarding number of aircraft needed for the introduction of new STOL service.

STUDY II: RAIL CORRIDOR STUDY
(BY THE TRANSPORTATION DEVELOPMENT CENTER)

1. Study objectives—to compare alternative intercity travel modes and to determine how to increase passenger rail traffic.
2. Attribute specification—in-depth group interviews used to identify 13 attributes and to specify each at 2 to 14 levels.
3. Sampling—random telephone calls to qualify corridor travelers, followed by personal interviews.
4. Measurement approach—69 paired choices specified by sets of 3 attributes (Johnson 1975).
5. Attributes—(levels in brackets)

On-time reliability (2)	Food and beverage (3)
Reservations (3)	Travel time (9)
Personal comfort (2)	Cost (14)
Mobility en route (2)	Mode (4)
Departure times (3)	Terminal convenience (3)
Ride quality (2)	Peace and quiet (2)
Baggage (2)	

6. Outcome—indicated that it would be extremely difficult to switch travelers from auto to rail.

STUDY III: INDEX OF AIR SERVICE QUALITY
(BY THE CANADIAN TRANSPORT COMMISSION)

1. Study objectives—to develop a measure of quality of air service as perceived by business and pleasure travelers.
2. Attribute specification—in-depth group interviews used to identify 13 attributes and to specify each at 3 to 5 levels.
3. Sampling—random selection of households with respondents qualified for travel patterns.
4. Measurement approach—60 trade-off matrices.
5. Attributes—(levels in brackets)

Reservations (3)	Seat width (3)
Ticketing wait (3)	Airport access (3)
Flight time (3)	Food service (3)

Reliability (3)   Stops (3)
Airplane size (3)   Airport crowds (3)
Frequency (3)   Fare (5)
Baggage service (3)

6. Outcome—provided a general description of consumer interests with respect to air travel (for example, on-time service was found to be more important than in-flight time).

STUDY IV: TRANSCONTINENTAL RAIL STUDY
(BY THE CANADIAN TRANSPORT COMMISSION)

1. Study objectives—to study service preferences of rail travelers.
2. Attribute specification—based on expert opinion, 11 attributes identified and specified at 2 to 5 levels.
3. Sampling—on-board interviews with random sample of rail travelers.
4. Measurement approach—concept evaluation.
5. Attributes—(levels in brackets)

Sleeping accommodation (4)   Reliability (3)
Accommodation space (2)   Trip time (3)
Toilet facilities (4)   Food quality (3)
Fare supplement (5)   Meal service (3)
Departures (3)   Meal price (4)
Arrivals (3)

6. Outcome—used to guide the modification of passenger service.

STUDY V: MARITIME RAIL SERVICE
(BY THE CANADIAN TRANSPORT COMMISSION)

This study was very similar to Study IV.

STUDY VI: SERVICE DESIGN STUDY (AIR CANADA)

1. Study objectives—to determine the relative importance of air-trip components.
2. Attribute specification—group sessions involving industry professionals used to identify four groups of air-trip attributes—9 ground service, 4 in-flight, 7 aircraft decor, and 7 others—and to specify each at 2 to 5 levels.
3. Sampling—random telephone screening from passenger list resulting in subjects qualified by route and business/pleasure, personal interviews conducted with qualified subjects.
4. Measurement approach—concept evaluation with pictures used to represent the various combinations of attribute levels for each of the four main groups of air-trip attributes.
5. Attributes—(levels in brackets)

GROUND SERVICE   AIRCRAFT DECOR
Telephone answer speed (2)   Leg room (30
Telephone voice (2)   Seat width (2)
Telephone info (2)   Overhead racks (2)
Check-in line (2)   Carry-on room (2)
Check-in personnel (2)   Interior color (2)
Ground hostess (2)   Seat adjustments (2)
Personal grooming (2)   Lavatory line-up (2)
P/A announcements (2)
Baggage wait (2)
IN-FLIGHT SERVICE   OTHER
Attendant grooming (3)   Attendant groomin g (3)
Reading material (5)   Reading material (5)
Refreshments (5)   Refreshments (5)
Entertainment (5)   Entertainment (5)

6. Outcome—indicated areas of emphasis for service improvement (for example, baggage handling needed more attention than in-flight snacks and newspapers).

STUDY VII: TRANSATLANTIC AIR TRAVEL STUDY
(I.A.T.A.)

1. Study objectives—to assess consumers' perceptions of transatlantic airfare packages for nonbusiness travel.

2. Attribute specification—group discussions involving international representatives of I.A.T.A. used to identify 12 attributes and to specify each at 2 to 8 levels.

3. Sampling—random telephone screening from passenger lists to qualify respondents who had traveled across the North Atlantic; personal interviews were conducted with qualified subjects in 6 countries.

4. Measurement approach—matrix trade-offs.

5. Attributes—(levels in brackets)

Length of stay (8)	Seasons (5)
Advanced booking (6)	Stand-by (5)
In-flight service (4)	Group flights (5)
Land accommodation (5)	Dropovers (4)
Flexible booking (4)	Day of week (4)
Airfare (8)	Flight type (2)

6. Outcome—provided general guidelines for the design and promotion of new transatlantic fare packages.

REFERENCES

Carmone, Frank J., Paul E. Green, and Arun K. Jain (1978), "Robustness of Conjoint Analysis: Some Monte Carlo Results," *Journal of Marketing Research* 15 (May), 300–303.

Cattin, Philippe, and Dick R. Wittink (1981), "Commercial Use of Conjoint Analysis: A Survey," Research Paper No. 596, Graduate School of Business, Stanford University.

Claxton, John D., J.R. Brent Ritchie, and Judy Zaichkowsky (1980), "The Nominal Group Technique: Its Potential for Consumer Research," *Journal of Consumer Research* 7 (December), 308–313.

Currim, Imran S., Charles B. Weinberg, and Dick R. Wittink (1981), "The Design of Subscription Programs for a Performing Arts Series: Issues in Applying Conjoint Analysis," *Journal of Consumer Research* 8 (June), 67–75.

Davidson, J.D. (1973), "Forecasting Traffic on STOL," *Operation Research Quarterly* 24, 561–569.

Green, Paul E. (1973), "On the Analysis of Interactions in Marketing Research Data," *Journal of Marketing Research* 10 (November), 410–419.

Green, Paul E. (1974), "On the Design of Choice Experiments Involving Multifactor Alternatives," *Journal of Consumer Research*, 1 (September), 61–68.

Green, Paul E., and Vithala R. Rao (1971), "Conjoint Measurement for Quantifying Judgment Data," *Journal of Marketing Research* 8 (August), 355–363.

Green, Paul E., and V. Srinivasan (1978), "Conjoint Analysis in Consumer Research: Issues and Outlook," *Journal of Consumer Research* 5 (September), 103–123.

Green, Paul E., and Yoram Wind (1973), *Multiattribute Decisions in Marketing: A Measurement Approach*, Hinsdale, IL: The Dryden Press.

Green, Paul E., and Yoram Wind (1975), "New Way to Measure Consumers' Judgments," *Harvard Business Review* (July), 107–117.

Hargreaves, George, John D. Claxton, and Fred H. Siller (1976), "New Product Evaluation: Electric Vehicles for Commercial Applications," *Journal of Marketing* (January), 74–77.

Jain, Arun K., Franklin Acito, Naresh K. Malhotra, and Vijay

Mahajan (1979), "A Comparison of the Internal Validity of Alternative Parameter Estimation Methods in Decomposition Multiattribute Preference Models," *Journal of Marketing Research* 16 (August), 313–322.

Johnson, Richard M. (1974a), "Trade-off Analysis of Consumer Values," *Journal of Marketing Research* 11 (May), 121–127.

Johnson, Richard M. (1974b), "Measurement of Consumer Values Using Computer Interactive Techniques," in *Market Measurement and Analysis*, David B. Montgomery and Dick R. Wittink, eds., 271–277, Cambridge, MA: Marketing Science Institute.

Johnson, Richard M. (1975), "Beyond Conjoint Measurement: A Method of Pairwise Trade-off Analysis," in *Advances in Consumer Research*, Volume 3, B.B. Anderson, ed., 353–358, Proceedings Association of Consumer Research.

Kruskal, J.B. (1965), "Analysis of Factorial Experiments by Estimating Monotone Transformations of the Data," *Journal of the Royal Statistical Society*, Series B, 27 (No. 2), 251–263.

Luce, R. Duncan, and John W. Tukey (1964), "Simultaneous Conjoint Measurement: A New Type of Fundamental Measurement," *Journal of Mathematical Psychology* 1 (February), 1–27.

Ross, Richard B. (1975), "Measuring the Influence of Soft Variables on Travel Behavior," *Traffic Quarterly* (July), 336–346.

Srinivasan, V., and Alan D. Shocker (1973), "Linear Programming Techniques for Multi-Dimensional Analysis of Preferences," *Psychometrica* 38, 337–369.

Srinivasan, V., Peter G. Flachsbart, Jarir S. Dajani, and Rolfe G. Hartley (1981), "Forecasting the Effectiveness of Work-Trip Gasoline Policies through Conjoint Analysis," *Journal of Marketing* 45 (Summer), 157–172.

Strachan, Morley B. (1978), "Conjoint Measurement-Transport Model Choice," Research Paper, Center for Transportation Studies, University of British Columbia.

Wittink, Dick R., and Philippe Cattin (1981), "Alternative Estimation Methods for Conjoint Analysis: A Monte Carlo Study," *Journal of Marketing Research* 18 (February), 101–106.

45

Multidimensional Scaling and Tourism Research[1]

MARK FENTON
Curtin University of Technology,
Bentley, WA, Australia

PHILIP PEARCE
Head, Department of Tourism
James Cook University
North Queensland, Australia

Multidimensional scaling (MDS) is a form of analysis which permits the relationships among a set of elements to be represented as inter-element distances in spaces. It is suitable for data collected according to a number of different formats. This article describes a number of the formal and technical features of MDS analysis and its variants. The main purpose of MDS approaches lies in their capacity to explore the structure underlying a set of judgements. Existing and potential uses of the multidimensional scaling procedure in tourist studies are discussed. It is concluded that the multidimensional scaling approach can provide more than a complex technique for simplifying data sets. It is also argued that the technique can be used to test hypotheses and conceptual arguments in the tourist literature.

INTRODUCTION

Imagine that a map of Australia lies across a desk. Recorded in kilometers are the distances among all major cities in Australia, resulting in a triangular data set which represents all the intercity distances. With this data set of all intercity distances, it would be possible to construct, on the basis of these distances, a map showing the location of each of these cities. Now this could take some time since each city would have to be positioned on the map in such a way that the map of distances represent the data matrix of distances among cities. Rather than developing the map by hand, the data could be subjected to a multidimensional scaling analysis (MDS), the result of which would be a map of Australian cities, where the mapped intercity distances would be identical to the matrix.

Multidimensional scaling began primarily as a variant of factor analysis within the field of psychophysics in the late 1930s (Eckart and Young 1936; Richardson 1938; Young and Householder 1938). Later, through the papers of Shepard (1962; 1972), Kruskal (1964), and Carroll and Chang (1970), it was expanded into a broad family of scaling techniques. While it was initially developed within the area of psychology, it has been usefully applied to a number of areas outside the general scope of psychology, including marketing (Green and Carmone 1972), political science (Easterling 1984), and archaeology (Hodson, Kendall, and Tautu 1971).

The twofold aim of MDS is to reduce data so as to make them more manageable and meaningful, and at the same time to identify whether there is any inherent underlying structure within the data. Both aims of MDS are related, as the recovery of underlying structure usually means the reduction of

[1]This article was originally published in *The Annals of Tourism Research*, Vol. 15, No. 2, 1988. Permission to reprint is gratefully acknowledged.

the entire data set to a manageable and limited number of dimensions, clusters, or groupings.

Multidimensional scaling has many elements in common with factor analysis, but it differs from it in three important respects. First, while factor analysis, like MDS, attempts to identify the inherent structure within data, factor analysis requires that the variables to be analyzed must be measured on at least an interval scale. MDS does not necessarily require this assumption as it determines inherent structure on the ordered relations existing among elements. Second, an MDS solution is usually easier to interpret than a factor analysis solution, as the MDS model is based on the distance between points in a multidimensional space. In factor analysis, the model which is generated is based on the angles between vectors. A third important difference between MDS and factor analysis, which is related to the interpretation of the final configuration, is that the researcher using MDS usually finds relatively fewer dimensions than would occur if the data were analyzed through factor analysis. As Shepard (1972:3) has noted "the high dimensionality characteristic of factor-analytic results is in part a consequence of the rigid assumptions of linearity upon which the standard factor analytic methods have been based," and, as such, one would expect a solution of lower dimensionality when the assumptions of linearity are removed.

The data on which the MDS analysis is based consists of a series of "proximities" which indicate the degree of similarity or dissimilarity *among elements within a defined set.* The proximity measures may be either "direct" or "derived" measures of proximity. If the measures are direct, then the subject has usually provided a direct estimate of the degree of (dis)similarity between any pair of elements, either through a rating or classification task. Derived proximities, on the other hand, usually consist of some measure of association among elements within a set which are not made directly by a subject.

MEASURES OF PROXIMITY

DIRECT MEASURES OF PROXIMITY

One of the most common measures of direct proximity is paired comparisons. Through pairwise judgments, the subject indicates the degree to which two elements are similar or different. In this task, a bipolar rating scale of which the endpoints are anchored with the verbal labels of "very similar" and "very different" is used to record the judgment. While the use of the rating scale is the most common form of eliciting direct measures of proximity from subjects, Schiffman, Reynolds and Young (1981) have suggested that it is sometimes a difficult and somewhat ambiguous task to perform in terms of assigning a specific meaning to the numeric points on the scale. For this reason, Schiffman et al. (1981) have suggested that rather than making judgments of similarity with reference to a numeric scale, a less ambiguous and more effective procedure is to have subjects simply place a mark on a line of which the endpoints of the line are

anchored with the verbal labels "exact same" and "most different". The length of the line is then measured in millimeters from the verbal label up to and including the mark, and as such represents a direct measure of proximity between elements.

A second method of obtaining direct measures of proximity is to have subjects sort a large pool of elements into a number of smaller groups which are perceived as being alike on some attribute of interest. The number of groupings can be predetermined by the researcher or determined during the sorting by the subject. After completion, a matrix is constructed of binary values representing the degree of similarity between elements, where a 1 might indicate that the elements were sorted into the same group with a 0 indicating that the elements were sorted into different groups.

A third method of obtaining some index of similarity among elements is to have subjects rank order the elements on a particular attribute. Alternatively, elements may be rank-ordered in terms of how similar they are to a predefined standard. The completed matrix represents a rectangular matrix of elements by attributes, or elements by standards, where the values in the body of the matrix represent the ranking of the element in relation to the attribute or standard.

While there are a number of other variants of the three procedures for obtaining direct measures of proximity (see Coxon 1982: Ch. 10), the rating, grouping, and ranking procedures are the most common within the behavioral sciences literature. Examples of obtaining direct proximities through the use of rating scales include research on the perception of natural settings (Fenton 1985) and the perception of nations (Wish 1971), while examples of the use of grouping procedures include the perception of tourist highways (Pearce and Promnitz 1984), urban settings (Nassar 1980), and music (Halpern 1984). The ranking procedure is not as common as either the rating or grouping methods, but has been used by Harshman and De Sarbo (1984) in the context of marketing research.

One important consideration which is often overlooked in planning a study, which uses MDS and is based on direct measures of proximity, is the number of elements that are going to be used and the time required to obtain direct measures of proximity among all elements. For example, if the researcher who decides to use the paired comparisons procedure wishes to know what the underlying dimensions are that subjects use in discriminating among four elements, then in order to form a complete proximity matrix six paired comparisons will have to be completed; with eight elements 28 paired comparisons will be required; with 12 elements 66 comparisons; and with 20 elements 190 comparisons. Clearly, as the number of elements increases, there is a corresponding and rapid increase in the number of paired comparisons required. In addition, Schiffman et al. (1981) indicate that while the time required to complete a paired comparisons task depends upon the type of elements used, paired comparisons among all possible pairs of 20 elements, with no readaption or rest intervals, could take upwards of $1\frac{1}{2}$ hours

In order to partly reduce the time required to complete a set of paired comparisons, MacCallum (1979:69) has suggested the use of an incomplete data design, where only a certain percentage of the proximity matrix is completed by any one individual. Monte Carlo studies, which have compared analyses based on different percentages of incomplete data, have shown that very accurate recovery of true distances, stimulus coordinates, and weight vectors could be achieved with as much as 60% missing data as long as sample size was sufficiently large and the level of random error was low.

INDIRECT MEASURES OF PROXIMITY

Indirect measures of proximity usually consist of some index of association, such as a correlational index, as in Pearson's r; a contingency measure, such as Cramer's V or Phi; or a distance measure as usually found in Euclidian, City Block, or Minkowski distances. Given that such indexes of proximity are normally based on aggregated data either across individuals, stimuli, or replications on the variable of interest, then the resulting spatial configuration may simply be an artifact of the process of aggregation.

One of the most valuable reference sources for identifying the different types of indirect measures of proximity available is the SPSSx Users Guide (1986). Not only are the measures identified and the defining formulae supplied, but the SPSSx proximities program module will generate selected proximities on the basis of either the rows or columns of a square or rectangular matrix.

HOW MDS WORKS

MDS consists of a broad family of scaling techniques, where the selection of any one procedure is dependent on the type of data to be analyzed, decisions as to how the data are to be treated during the analysis, and which end result is required. As such, the following discussion applies only to the most common elementary form of MDS, which will be referred to as classical multidimensional scaling (CMDS). Many of the other MDS procedures are simply an extension of this basic model.

Given a triangular matrix of either derived or direct proximities produced through any of the procedures previously discussed, the objective of MDS is to take the proximities among elements and represent them as distance in a space of minimal dimensionality so that the distances approximate as best as possible the proximities among elements. This is accomplished through an interactive cycle and begins with an estimated or random starting configuration of distances among elements. The distances in the starting configuration are then compared to the original proximity values among elements and a "goodness of fit" function computed, which in most MDS procedures is usually identified as "stress." Once this function has been computed the starting configuration is adjusted so that it more closely approximates the original proximity values with a goodness of fit function being computed. This iterative cycle continues until

the maximum number of iterations specified by the user has been reached or the improvement in fit or stress is less than a critical interval, which leads to the completion of the iterative cycle.

The process of locating elements in a space, where the distances among elements corresponds as much as possible to the proximities, may be undertaken in a space of any dimensionality as specified by the user prior to the analysis. Solutions will normally be obtained in a number of dimensions, beginning with a one-dimensional solution. As for the maximum dimensionality for the data set, Kruskal and Wish (1978:34), as a rule of thumb, have indicated that in order for the solution to be statistically stable, the number of elements minus one should be greater than four times the proposed dimensionality. Once a series of dimensional solutions is obtained for a data set, the researcher is then faced with the problem of selecting the most appropriate dimensionality and interpreting the dimensional solution.

INTERPRETING THE MDS SOLUTION

It must be emphasized that there is no one index that will identify the correct dimensional representation for the data. Although the goodness of fit function for each configuration may partially answer this question, consideration must also be given to the interpretability of the dimensional space. When using stress to identify the appropriate dimensionality, it is usual to construct a plot showing the relationship between stress levels and dimensional solutions (i.e., Kruskal and Wish 1978, Fig. 16; Schiffman et al. 1981, Fig. 1.6). When inspecting the plot, the dimensionality after which there is little or no substantial improvement in stress is usually selected as the most appropriate dimensional solution.

In addition to an evaluation of the stress value, careful consideration must be given to the interpretation of the dimensional solution. It may well be that the solution with the optimum stress value is not necessarily the most interpretable and meaningful solution, and solutions in a higher or lower dimensionality may also need to be considered.

DATA THEORY

A number of schemes have been developed for classifying the broad range of MDS procedures, the earliest of which was probably that developed by Shepard (1972). However, the most recent non-mathematical overview of MDS, which at the same time attempts a partial taxonomy of MDS models in terms of a general data theory, is that proposed by Schiffman et al. (1981).

The concepts embedded within the data theory proposed by Schiffman et al. (1981) attempt to link attributes of the data with the model being used to understand the data. As such, three organizing concepts are used to define the data theory proposed: the shape of the data, the number of "ways" of the data, and the nature of the MDS model.

SHAPE OR MODE OF THE DATA

The data for an MDS analysis can be in the form of a rectangular or square matrix. A rectangular data matrix is sometimes also referred to as two-mode data since the proximities within a rectangular matrix emphasize the degree of relationship between two distant sets of elements. For instance, the columns of a rectangular matrix may represent specific objects, places, or people, while the rows may consist of the rating scales on which the column elements are judged. This is a common type of data matrix collected in behavioral science research, and is in fact the type of matrix that is most often analyzed through factor analysis.

By contrast, the second data shape common to MDS data is the square data matrix which is also sometimes identified as consisting of one mode data. In this matrix, the proximities denote the degree of relatedness among one set of elements, rather than two, as in the case of rectangular data. If the square matrix is symmetrical (i.e., where there is no substantive difference between asking the degree of similarity between element A and B and element B and A), then a special case of the square matrix can be developed known as the triangular or offdiagonal data matrix. Such a triangular data matrix is the most common form of data matrix to be analyzed by MDS.

In some circumstances, it may not be possible to assume symmetry in proximity measures. For example, asymmetric proximity measures may be found in interpersonal perception research, where person A may regard himself as similar to person B, but person B may regard himself as very dissimilar to person A. While it is possible to use a specific MDS program to analyze such data (ALSCAL-AMDS), it is possible under some circumstances to consider the asymmetry as noise, and to average the two proximity measures and form a triangular data matrix. A second alternative in dealing with this situation is to analyze upper and lower triangles of the original square matrix separately and compare the resulting solutions.

THE "WAY" OF THE DATA

The way of the data simply represents the dimensionality of the original data matrix to be analyzed. Any data matrix must in the first instance be two-way data representing the columns and rows of either a square or rectangular matrix. Three-way data usually takes the form of several matrices, where the third way is usually represented by either three-way or even three mode data (cf. Law, Snyder, Hattie and McDonald 1984 for a review of such approaches), and there are MDS programs which will analyze such data (i.e., CANDECOMP and PARAFAC). However, the procedure is extremely rare. As Coxon (1982:187) indicates, users are advised to proceed beyond three-way data with considerable caution. They are in largely uncharted territory.

It is appropriate when discussing data suitable for MDS analysis to use both the number of modes and number of ways to define the original data matrix. For instance, a triangular data matrix of averaged proximity measures across

subjects which represents the degree of dissimilarity among a number of countries recently visited could be defined as one mode (countries), two-way data. If, on the other hand, one did not average across subjects but wished to include individual subjects data matrices in the MDS analysis, one would then have two mode (countries, subjects), three-way data. Alternatively, the researcher might ask subjects to complete a rectangular matrix consisting of ratings given to countries on a number of predefined scales. If the researcher does not aggregate across subjects but includes each individual subjects rectangular matrix in the analysis, then there would be three mode (countries, rating scales, subjects), three-way data.

MDS MODELS

There are two broad classes of MDS models that can be defined as either unweighted MDS or weighted MDS. Only the first of these two will be reviewed here. The most significant difference between the two types of MDS procedures is that weighted MDS specifically examine the variation among matrices that might occur in three-way data. In this case, *and* if individuals are represented by different matrices, *then* it is possible to examine the weighting given by individuals to the averaged spatial configuration.

UNWEIGHTED MDS

The most common unweighted MDS model is Classical Multidimensional Scaling (CMDS). This model attempts to identify the underlying structure of one mode two-way data (i.e., proximity data represented in a lower triangular matrix). In this model, the proximities, which usually represent the degree of dissimilarity between elements, are represented as distances in a multidimensional space.

There are a number of MDS programs which will analyze data of this type including MINISSA from within the MDS(X) set of programs, KYST, POLYCON, MULTISCALE, and ALSCAL. ALSCAL is perhaps the most appropriate MDS program, as apart from it also being an integral part of the SPSSx statistical package, it has theoretically no limit to the size of the data which can be analyzed, although system memory will ultimately determine this. In addition, ALSCAL has a large number of options available through which the data can be analyzed. For instance, data can be analyzed assuming any level of measurement, as continuous or discrete, and with missing data.

Of course, it must be emphasized that while a CMDS program will analyze one mode two-way data, and hopefully produce an interpretable dimensional solution, this may well be that due to some a priori theoretical reason, the researcher is not interested in identifying the underlying dimensional structure, but wishes to know if there is any clustering or grouping of the elements. In this case, rather than a dimensional analysis being most appropriate, a cluster analysis should be used, such as the program CLUSTER or QUICK CLUSTER from within the SPSSx package, or the clustering algorithm HICLUS (Johnson 1967) which is available from within the MDS(X) program set.

The second type of unweighted MDS is perhaps more appropriately referred to as multidimensional unfolding (MDU), and is used to analyze two mode two-way data. Data suitable for this type of analysis typically consists of a rectangular data matrix, comprising ratings which have been given to a number of elements on the basis of a series of predefined rating scales. MINIRSA from within the MDS(X) program series will perform a MDU analysis, but perhaps the most appropriate program is again ALSCAL from the SPSSx package.

The MDU analysis produces a multidimensional solution which is very different from that achieved in classical MDS, since one is now identifying a spatial solution which represents the interrelationships between two sets of elements or data modes and not one. Given two sets of elements are represented in the derived spatial configuration, it is often referred to as a joint space solution. For instance, if individuals record their preference for visiting a number of different countries, then a MDU analysis of this two mode data (individuals, countries) would provide a spatial solution where both the individuals and countries were identified in a joint space, with some points in the space representing individuals and some points representing countries. Whenever MDU is used, care should be taken when interpreting the dimensional solutions that emerge as they are notoriously uninterpretable or degenerate (Purcell 1984; Schiffman et al. 1981). This instability is a result of the mathematical procedures in transforming joint proximities to joint distances.

There are, however, a number of alternatives to the analysis of rectangular, two mode two-way data, and since such data matrices are common in behavioral science research, such alternatives are worth identifying. First, if a large rectangular data matrix needed to be analyzed, principal components or factor analysis could be used in preference to MDS, where the factor loadings could be used to interpret one mode of the data, while the factor scores could be used to identify the relationship of the second data mode to the first. Of course, as mentioned earlier, there are a number of drawbacks to the use of factor analysis.

The second alternative is to perform two CMDS analyses on the data matrix. In this case, derived proximities would be obtained for both sets of elements and each derived proximity matrix analyzed by CMDS. While this solution appears to be straightforward, the most obvious shortcoming is that it is very difficult to relate one MDS solution to another, although a program such as PINDIS, which may be found in the MDS(X) series may be useful in this context.

A third procedure which has been used, and which has provided a meaningful interpretation of two mode data, is the external MDS analysis. This procedure initially obtains derived proximity measures for elements within one mode of the data, and subsequently analyzes them through CMDS. In the next phase of the analysis, the second mode of data is regressed or located into the first. For example, Fenton and Hills (1987), in exploring the perception of animals between animal liberationists and hunters, had subjects rate animal categories on a number of elicited constructs, resulting in a two-way mode matrix consisting of animal categories by constructs. One objective of this study was to identify the most salient dimensions individuals used to discriminate among the animal categories. In order to accomplish this, a CMDS was performed on a matrix of derived proximity measures which consisted of Euclidian distances among the animal categories across all constructs. Following the identification of space of suitable dimensions, each of the constructs representing the second mode of the data was then regressed into the space through the use of a property fitting program, PROFIT, from the MDS(X) program series. Those constructs which were highly correlated with specific orientations in the space were then used to identify the way in which individuals appeared to discriminate among the animal categories.

MDS STUDIES IN TOURISM RESEARCH

There are a number of examples of multidimensional scaling procedures employed in the existing tourism literature. In an early application of the technique, Anderssen and Colberg (1973) studied the similarity of would-be travelers' perceptions of Mediterranean destinations. This kind of work is closely allied to market research approaches to the image of one's product compared to its competitors and affords the possibility of diachronic studies of product image. For example, if one destination is marketed intensively as offering an exclusive and expensive style of holiday experience, then a series of MDS analyses should be able to follow the success of the image making over time.

Similarly, the choice of route to a destination is sometimes of interest. Pearce and Promnitz (1984) demonstrated that highways in Australia were judged to be very different in their tourist appeal. This study also indicated that the perceptions people hold about tourist products and services can be clearly linked to their choices and behavior patterns. In this study, the researchers found one cluster of highways which was simply seen as undesirable, unattractive, and to be avoided at holiday times. The traffic flow figures for these highways supported the perceptual data. It would be valuable in many other image studies (including MDS studies) if the perceptions and cognitions of tourists could be linked more frequently to their behaviors in regard to those settings (Figure 1).

In an attempt to refine and extend an earlier article on tourist roles by Cohen (1974), Pearce used multidimensional scaling techniques to provide a picture of how a student sample saw 15 travel related roles (Pearce 1982; 1985) (See Figure 2). In a recent extension of this approach, Smithson (1986) noted that the MDS picture provided contrasting degrees of fuzziness, as defined by fuzzy set theory. Those roles in the center of the space were rated as clearer and less confused than roles towards the periphery. Despite the fact that the behavioral ratings were organized to assess tourism related roles, the *core role* of tourist is the fuzziest in the whole set.

Smithson's interpretation of the original MDS data with fuzzy set theory methods raises the possibility of other inter-

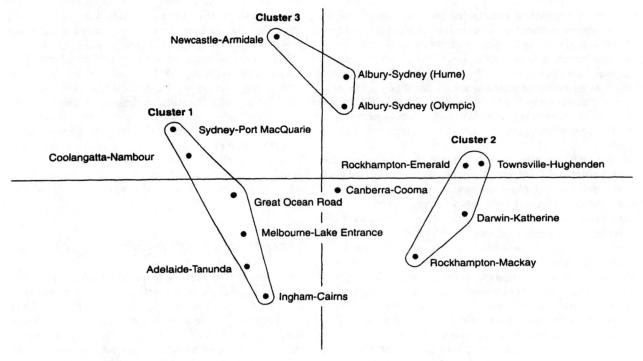

FIGURE 1 MDS (Minnisa) spatial configuration of 14 highway journeys, illustrating three main clusters.
Cluster 1: Short distances; scenic recreational areas; usually coastal.
Cluster 2: Hot, arid, long, inland routes; not scenic.
Cluster 3: High volume; inland; NSW; medival distance; somewhat scenic.

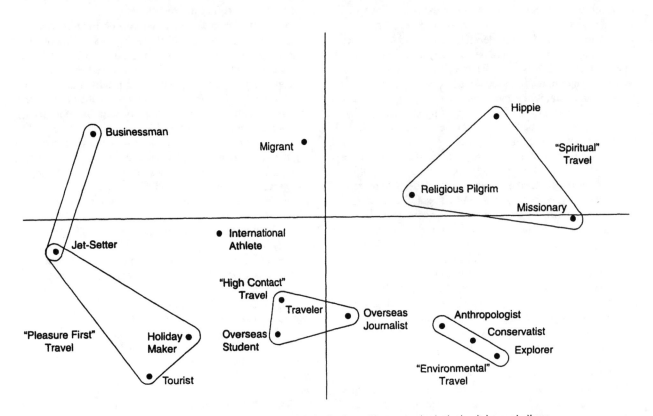

FIGURE 2 A multidimensional scaling analysis of travel-related roles with suggested cluster interpretations.

pretive and statistical approaches adding on to MDS procedures. Recently, Canter has proposed the extensive use of facet theory to interpret, comment on, and organize basic MDS solutions (Canter 1985).

Moscardo and Pearce (1986) used archival material as the input for their multidimensional scaling analysis of the similarity of 17 visitor centers in Britain. The data consisted of ratings of the centers on a number of dimensions and these ratings were converted into similarity scales as discussed earlier in this article. The resulting map of the visitor centers revealed several types of centers which appeared to function in different ways. One cluster of centers provided little more than pamphlets and a booking service, while another group offered the visitor detailed ecological and environmental interpretations of the surrounding area. In general, the more detailed visitor centers were those with which the visitors were most satisfied (Figure 3).

A further study employing the MDS technique was conducted at Green Island, one of the most popular destinations on Australia's Great Barrier Reef. In this study, the perceptions of tourists and national park staff were compared, and MDS results reflecting the views of each group were obtained. It can be seen that the national park staff not only groups the activities differently to the tourists, but indeed uses different dimensions or scales to organize their clusters of activities. National park staff emphasize management related issues in its mental maps of the activities (e.g., safe-dangerous, well promoted-not well promoted), while the

tourists appear to focus on the experiential dimensions of the activities (how close they get to the reef, the enjoyment level of the activity, and its physical location) (Figures 4 and 5).

Other research efforts using the technique have profitably explored tourists' perceptions of Finland as a destination (Haahti 1986) using a two mode, two-way PREF MAP analysis of the rectangular matrix of countries by attributes data. This study is allied to the correctional marketing use of MDS research and is functionally similar to the earlier Anderssen and Colbey (1973) analysis and use. A more creative use of the procedure is offered by Kemper, Roberts and Goodwin (1983). They employed a card sorting technique to explore the cultural perceptions of a New Mexico community from an anthropological perspective. They used 50 items relating to cultural interests, activities, or services in the card sorting task (e.g., fishing, weaving, pottery) and provided a dimensional solution of the 89 subjects' perceptions. Their analysis revealed a culture-nurture dimension in the data, an active/passive classification of the activities, and a local/widespread identity to the activities. Interestingly, the latter two dimensions are somewhat similar to those reported on the other side of the world in the Green Island study of tourists' perceptions.

Within the wider domain of leisure research applications of the MDS, techniques have included a classification of leisure activity types (Becker 1976; Hirschman 1985; Ritchie 1975), the relationship between public and private recreational systems (Lovingood and Mitchell 1978), an explora-

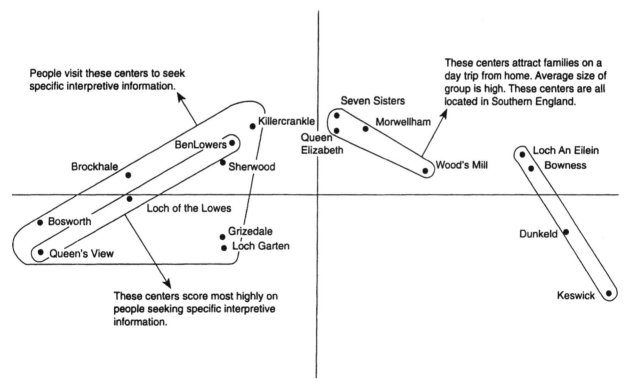

FIGURE 3   Similarity of visitor centers emphasizing visitor characteristics and purposes; the results of a multidimensional scaling analysis.

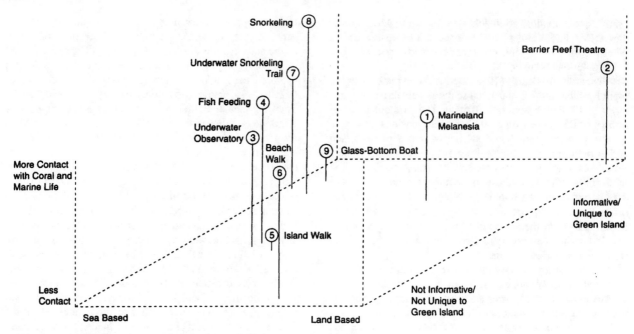

FIGURE 4 Multidimensional scaling plot of activities as seen by tourists.

tion of the kinds of psychological benefits which a recreational park can produce (Uluch and Addoms 1981), and a test of Maslow's theory of motivation (Mills 1985).

ADDITIONAL USES

In addition to the studies cited, the multidimensional scaling procedures outlined above provide an exciting methodology for a host of tourism studies. One of the core areas of interest in contemporary tourism studies is how tourists perceive and classify the visited setting (Iso-Ahola 1980; Mayo and Jarvis 1981; Stringer and Pearce 1984). MDS procedures provide a technique for investigating the ways in which tourists rate and organize such stimuli as countries, cities, national parks, theme parks, museums, tourist sites, and information centers. Tourist services, too, can be examined with this approach and target stimuli might include airline companies, restaurants, package tours, destination resorts, and travel agents. If a large number of these studies were to be conducted by tourism researchers, one's knowledge of tourists'

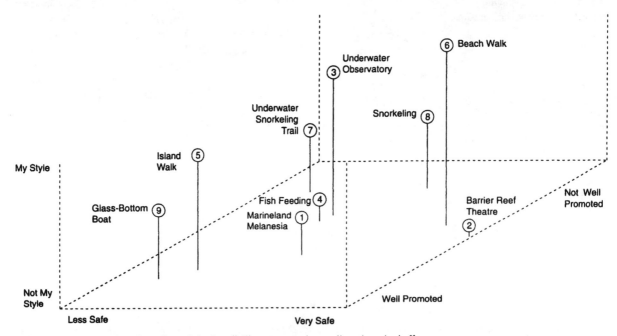

FIGURE 5 Multidimensional scaling plot of activities as seen by national park staff.

preferences and judgments would be substantially enhanced and could permit the investigation of cross-national and sampling differences in tourists' perceptions.

Some researchers have argued that descriptive research is perhaps less sophisticated and less desirable than hypothesis testing approaches. Initially it might appear that the multidimensional scaling approach will only provide a plethora of descriptive information. It is possible, however, to use the approach to facilitate the testing of theoretical perspectives in tourism studies. For example, one might hypothesize that certain elements should be seen as closer together than others in the final MDS solution. For example, in the study of tourist roles, one might have argued that tourists should be seen more as businessmen than conservationists. The MDS picture obtained from 100 students would have supported this perspective. A sample of conservationists might also have been studied and their mental arrangement of tourist roles could also have been explored. One could then test the proposal that conservationists would see the tourist roles as even more like that of businessmen and other exploitative groups than the cluster of roles which include conservationists, explorers, and scientists. The basis for such a prediction could lie in the assumed value differences of the conservationist group and this difference could in fact be measured with a scale of values test (e.g., the Rokeach scale) or a measure such as the Environmental Response Inventory (McKechnie 1974). If one were to find the anticipated pattern of similarity with the MDS results, then the predictive power of these personality and individual difference measures for tourism related material would be enhanced. It is in fact surprising how little of the conventional psychological testing material has been used in evaluating tourists' behavior and responses.

Therefore, one theoretical use of the MDS approaches is to specify the pattern of anticipated results according to a theoretical perspective and inspect the final structure for its adherence to this pattern. Additionally, one can compare the perceptions of two or more groups of people which could be two different types of tourists, tourists and locals, or tourists and the providers of tourist services. It is argued here that this hypothesis testing or exploring function of multidimensional scaling has much to offer tourism research. It is hoped that the future use of the procedure will follow some of these exciting possibilities for research integration and conceptual development.

REFERENCES

Anderssen, P., and R. Colberg (1973), "Multivariate Analysis in Travel Research: A Tool for Travel Package Design and Market Segmentation," The Travel Research Association, Fourth Annual Conference Proceedings.

Becker, B.W. (1976), "Perceived Similarities Among Recreational Activities," *Journal of Leisure Research* 8:112-122.

Canter, O. (1985), *Facet Theory: Approaches to Social Research*, New York: Springer-Verlag.

Carroll, J.D., and J.J. Chang (1970), "Analysis of Individual Differences in Multidimensional Scaling via an N-way Generalization of Eckart-Young Decomposition," *Psychometrika*, 35:283-319.

Cohen, E. (1974), "Who is a Tourist? " *Sociological Review* 22(4): 527-553.

Coxon, A.P.M. (1982), *The Users Guide to Multidimensional Scaling*, London: Chaucer Press.

Easterling, D.V. (1984), "Ideological Shifts in the U.S. Senate between 1971 and 1978: A Principal Directions Scaling of Roll Call Votes," In *Theory and Applications of Multidimensional Scaling*, F.W. Young and R.M. Hamer, eds. Hillsdale NJ: Erlbaum.

Eckart, C., and C. Young (1936), "The Approximation of one Matrix by Another of a Lower Rank," *Psychometrika* 1: 211-218.

Fenton, D.M. (1985), "Dimensions of Meaning in the Perception of Natural Settings and their Relationship to Aesthetic Response," *Australian Journal of Psychology* 37(3):325-339.

Fenton, D.M., and A.M. Hills (1987), "The Perception of Animals Amongst Animal Liberationists and Hunters: A Multidimensional Scaling Analysis," (Under review).

Green, P.E. and F.J. Carmone (1972), "Marketing Research Applications of Nonmetric Scaling Methods," In *Multidimensional Scaling: Theory and Applications in the Behavioral Sciences*, Vol 2: pp. 183-210, A.K. Romney, R.N. Shepard, and S.B. Nerlove, eds. New York: Seminar Press.

Haahti, A.J. (1986), "Finland's Competitive Position as a Destination," *Annals of Tourism Research* 13:11-26.

Halpern, A.R. (1984) "Organization in Memory for Familiar Songs," *Journal of Experimental Psychology: Learning, Memory, and Cognition* 10(3): 496-512.

Harshman, R.A., and W.S. De Sarbo (1984), "An Application of PARAFAC to a Small Sample Problem, Demonstrating Preprocessing, Orthogonality Constraints, and Split-half Diagnostic Techniques," In *Research Methods for Multimode Data Analysis*, pp. 602-642, H.G. Law, C.W. Snyder, J.A. Hattie, and R.P. McDonald, eds. New York: Praeger.

Hirschman, E.C. (1985), "Multdimensional Analysis of Content Preferences for Leisure time Media," *Journal of Leisure Research* 17:14-28.

Hodson, F.R., D.C. Kendall and P. Tautu eds. (1971), *Mathematics in the Archaeological and Historical Sciences*, Edinburgh: University Press.

Iso-Ahola, S.E. (1980), *The Social Psychology of Leisure and Recreation*, Dubuque, Iowa: William C. Brown.

Johnson, S.C. (1967), "Hierarchical Clustering Schemes," *Psychometrika* 32:241-254.

Kemper, R.V., J.M. Roberts, and R.D. Goodwin (1983), "Tourism as a Cultural Domain," *Annals of Tourism Research* 10:149-171.

Kruskal, J.B. (1964), "Nonmetric Multidimensional Scaling: A Numerical Method," *Psychometrika* 29:115-129.

Kruskal, J.B. and M. Wish (1978), "Multidimensional Scaling," Sage University Paper Series on Quantitative Applications in the Social Sciences, 7-11. Beverly Hills: Sage Publications.

Law, H.G., C.W. Snyder, J.A. Hattie, and R.P. McDonald eds. (1984), *Research Methods for Multimode Data Analysis.* New York: Praeger.

Lovingood, P.E., and L.S. Mitchell (1978), "The Structure of Public and Private Recreational Systems: Columbia, South Carolina," *Journal of Leisure Research* 10:21-36.

MacCallum, R.C. (1979), "Recovery of Structure in Incomplete Data by ALSCAL," *Psychometrika* 44:69.

Mayo, E.J., and Jarvis, L.P. (1981), *The Psychology of Leisure and Travel,* Boston: CBI Publishing.

McKechnie, G.E. (1974), *Manual for The Environmental Response Inventory,* Palo Alto, California: Consulting Psychologists Press.

Mills, A.S. (1985), "Participation Motivations for Outdoor Recreation: A Test of Maslows Theory, *Journal of Leisure Research* 17:184-199.

Moscardo, G., and P.L. Pearce (1986), "Visitor Centres and Environmental Interpretation: An Exploration of the Relationships Among Visitor Enjoyment, Understanding and Mindfulness," *Journal of Environmental Psychology* 6:89-108.

Nassar, J. (1980), "On Determining Dimensions of Environmental Perception," In *Optimizing Environments: Research, Practice, and Policy,* R.P. Stough and A. Wandersman, eds. Environmental Design and Research Association.

Pearce, P.L. (1982), *The Social Psychology of Tourist Behavior.* Oxford: Pergamon.

Pearce, P.L. (1985), "A Systematic Comparison of Travel-related Roles," *Human Relations* 38:1001–1011.

Pearce, P.L., and J. Promnitz (1984), "Research for Tourist Highways," *Australian Road Research* 14(3):156-160.

Purcell, A.T. (1984), "Multivariate Models and the Attributes of the Experience of the Built Environment," *Environment and Planning* 11:193-212.

Richardson, M.W. (1938), "Multidimensional Psychophysics," *Psychological Bulletin* 35:659-660.

Ritchie, J.R.B. (1975), "On the Derivation of Leisure Activity Types: A Perceptive Mapping Approach," *Journal of Leisure Research* 7 :128-164 .

Shepard, R.N. (1962), "Analysis of Proximities: Multidimensional Scaling with an Unknown Distance Function (part 1)," *Psychometrika* 27(1):125-139.

Shepard, R.N. (1972), "Taxonomy of Some Principal Types of Data and of Multidimensional Methods of their Analysis," In *Multidimensional Scaling: Theory and Applications In The Behavioral Sciences,* Vol 1:21-47, R.N. Shepard, A.K. Romney, and S.B. Nerlove, eds. New York: Seminar Press.

Schiffman, S.S., M.L. Reynolds, and D.F.W. Young (1981), *Introduction to Multidimensional Scaling: Theory, Methods, and Applications.* New York: Academic Press.

Smithson, M. (1986), *Fuzzy Set Analysis for Behavioural and Social Sciences.* New York: Springer Verlag.

SPSS Inc. (1986), *SPSSx: Users Guide* (2nd ed.) New York: McGraw-Hill.

Stringer, P.F., and Pearce, P.L. (1984), "Toward a symbiosis of Social Psychology and Tourism Studies," *Annals of Tourism Research* 11: 5-17.

Uluch, R.S., and Addoms, D.L. (1981), "Psychological and Recreational Benefits of a Recreational Park," *Journal of Leisure Research* 13: 43-56.

Wish M. (1971), "Individual Differences in Perceptions and Preferences Among Nations," In *Attitude Research Reaches New Heights* (pp 312-318), C.W. King and D. Tigert, eds. Chicago: American Marketing Association.

Young, C., and A.S. Householder (1938), "Discussion of a Set of Points in Terms of Their Mutual Distances," *Psychometrika* 3: 19-22.

Part Eight

SPECIAL MARKETING APPLICATIONS

This final part of the Handbook contains seven chapters that describe the application of particular research approaches to increasing understanding of two important marketing problems commonly facing managers in the travel and tourism industry. The first concerns the evaluation of the effectiveness of advertising and promotion; the second relates to the determination of the potential size and nature of demand in international tourism markets.

The first of these topics has received considerable attention over the past five years. As a consequence, it is reviewed in considerable depth and from several perspectives. In Chapter 46, Tom Davidson provides an overview concerning how managers can assess the effectiveness of advertising or other forms of persuasive communications targeted to the travel/tourism/entertainment/hospitality marketplace. The initial part of the chapter clarifies what is meant by research designed to evaluate advertising and emphasizes that both technical and managerial dimensions are involved. Davidson then briefly notes some exceptional characteristics of advertising related to conversion studies, a topic covered in greater depth in subsequent chapters. The author goes on to review the key questions that a marketing manager must answer when attempting to assess advertising effectiveness. These questions involve ensuring that the objectives of the advertising are clear, defining when research should be conducted, ensuring that the correct factors are being studied, determining the most appropriate measurement method, and being clear on the appropriate sampling frame. The chapter concludes by reminding readers that it is critical for managers to keep clearly in mind the purpose of research related to their advertising activities. A brief addendum highlights recent efforts to better measure advertising effectiveness that were commissioned by the United States Travel and Tourism Administration (USTTA) Task Force on Accountability Research. Selected aspects of these efforts are presented in greater detail in Chapters 48 and 49.

In Chapter 47, Woodside and Ronkainen present a first perspective on the use of conversion research as an aid to assessing the effectiveness of tourism promotion. The initial section of the chapter provides an extensive review of the purpose as well as the strengths and weaknesses of previous conversion studies that have been reported in advertising, marketing, and tourism literature. Based on this review, the authors reach several important conclusions regarding the validity and usefulness of previous conversion studies. They subsequently offer a number of guidelines for the proper conduct of research in this area. These guidelines are accompanied by a plea for their adoption on the part of destination marketing executives. In the second half of the chapter, Woodside and Ronkainen examine the different research approaches that may be used to gather data for conversion studies and discuss the kinds of samples used, the response rates obtained, and the kind of data gathered. They subsequently provide examples concerning the types of data analysis commonly employed and the nature of the findings obtained.

In Chapter 48, Siegel and Ziff-Levine provide their views concerning the relative merits of both the conversion model and an alternative advertising-tracking model as means of assessing the effectiveness of tourism-related advertising. Towards this end, the authors review and discuss each of these two approaches, arguing that the advertising-tracking model is more appropriate in most cases. They subsequently provide the reader with a framework for carrying out an advertising-tracking study. Advice is also given concerning the analysis and interpretation of data from such studies. Finally, Siegel and Ziff-Levine offer a number of guidelines for those who are considering the possibility of carrying out tracking research in tourism.

The second chapter that draws on the efforts of the USTTA Task Force is by Perdue and Pitegoff (Chapter 49). These authors adopt the tourism destination as the primary focus of efforts to evaluate the extent to which advertising efforts have been successful. Towards this end, they first review the role of marketing communications carried out by destination marketing organizations (DMOs). Second, they identify a set of generic guidelines for research efforts intended to evaluate the effectiveness of such communications. The latter half of the chapter addresses the evaluation of three alternative forms of tourism promotion having distinctly different purposes. The first of these concerns promotional efforts designed to influence the consumer prior to leaving home. Such efforts most commonly include media advertising, familiarization tours, trade missions, travel writer tours, consumer travel shows, and direct mail. The second type of promotion discussed by Perdue and Pitegoff is one that seeks to influence the traveler while he/she is en route to the destination area. Again, the authors briefly describe such promotional techniques (which include welcome centers and outdoor advertising) and then suggest possible research methods that are appropriate to the assessment of their effectiveness. The third and final promotional type is addressed in a similar manner. Approaches in this category are defined as those that aim to influence visitors after they have arrived at the destination area: They include information conveyed through visitor centers, media programs that inform visitors of local attractions and events, and hospitality training designed to enhance the quality of service provided by industry employees

Chapter 50, by Abraham Pizam, examines in greater detail the evaluation of the effectiveness of the first category of promotional efforts identified by Perdue and Pitegoff. More specifically, Dr. Pizam provides the reader with a comprehensive review of approaches for assessing the effectiveness of travel trade shows and related sales-promotion techniques. Towards this end, the chapter first documents the current prevalence and nature of sales promotion in the tourism industry based on a survey of state tourism agencies in the United States. The survey also identifies the relative importance of different methods currently used to measure the effectiveness of the most commonly used promotion techniques. Because existing evaluation methods tend to be unsystematic, Dr. Pizam goes on to propose a more rigorous series of methods for determining the relative effectiveness of a number of the most popular types of sales promotion in tourism. The types of promotion examined include trade shows, consumer travel shows, familiarization trips, sales blitzes, and educational seminars. For each of the types of promotional activities, the author recommends up to ten different methods of evaluation. The concluding section of the chapter describes these methods of evaluation and provides guidelines for their use.

In a manner designed to parallel Part One, which introduced this Handbook, this final section also concludes with a recognition of the growing importance of the internationalization of tourism. In Chapter 51, Geoffrey Crouch presents an in-depth treatise on the study of international tourism demand using regression analysis. Dr. Crouch first provides a summary of existing literature in the field with a particular focus on the methodology employed in various studies. He then examines a number of considerations to be kept in mind when choosing among different regression techniques. It is thought that readers will find Dr. Crouch's subsequent discussion of the selection and definition of variables for use in international regression studies to be extremely helpful. Finally, the author concludes the chapter by alerting the potential researcher to the many shortcomings of international tourism data.

The final chapter in Part Eight and the Handbook, which has been prepared by Don Wynegar, again emphasizes the ongoing globalization of tourism. The chapter, entitled "Estimating the Potential of International Markets," complements the previous one by providing a more managerial focus on research designed to understand the international marketplace. Mr. Wynegar, who has considerable experience in the international field, provides readers with a very thorough and systematic framework for analyzing the potential and relative importance of international markets. Towards this end, the author presents a model providing a step-by-step approach to the analysis of international travel market potential. This model incorporates measures of both existing size and incremental market potential. In addition to these quantitative factors, the model includes several qualitative variables that can affect the marketability of a country in its travel markets. By incorporating a system of weighted indices into his model, the various factors are aggregated to form a Cumulative Market Evaluation Index. This index provides a measure of the relative marketing viability of each country and, thus, serves as one basis for resource allocation. Readers responsible for undertaking the analysis of international markets will very much appreciate the rigor of the model presented by Mr. Wynegar and the level of detail he has provided.

46

Assessing the Effectiveness of Persuasive Communications in Tourism

THOMAS LEA DAVIDSON
Principal
Davidson-Peterson Associates, Inc.
York, Maine

This chapter is directed to the manager who, in the course of discharging his or her marketing responsibilities, must fund, commission, and use the results of research efforts designed to evaluate the effectiveness of advertising or other forms of persuasive communications targeted to the travel/ tourism/entertainment/hospitality marketplace. The comments are intended to help such a manager make decisions concerning advertising/communications research that will lead to more effective and cost-efficient marketing efforts. It is emphasized that the ultimate goal of evaluating advertising is to contribute to future sales and profits by increasing the effectiveness and the cost efficiency of future marketing efforts.

WHAT IS ADVERTISING EVALUATION RESEARCH?

Advertising evaluation research can be defined in two ways—technical and managerial.

• *Technical:* Advertising evaluation research is that body of systematic, scientific procedures employed to ISOLATE, DEFINE, MEASURE, and UNDERSTAND the relationship between advertising efforts and the influence of such advertising on the marketplace. These advertising efforts are usually specific as to copy, layout, artwork, media, timing, weight, and/or frequency.

• *Managerial:* Advertising evaluation research includes those procedures and techniques that may be employed to provide knowledge about the effect of advertising—which knowledge can be used by managers to make better decisions. The researcher or evaluator is attempting to replace opinion and guess with fact and, thereby, reduce risk.

Both definitions focus on cause-and-effect studies in which advertising is the cause and some marketplace change is the effect.[1] The direct effect or influence of advertising is viewed as being a change in the mind-set of the potential buyer—that is, in attitudes, opinions, perceptions, image, desires, expectations, knowledge, awareness, or inclination to act (buy). The marketing manager anticipates that these changes in mind-set will, in turn, lead to favorable changes in buying behavior that will mean more sales of the advertiser's travel products and, hence, will increase his or her profits. To influence sales, advertising must be exposed to the buyer, a message must be communicated, and a change in the buyer's thinking must occur.

Although profitable sales are the ultimate objective, advertising evaluation research has opted most of the time to study the changes in mind-set rather than actual sales performance. There are several reasons for this choice.

• Because sales are influenced by many factors besides advertising, it is frequently difficult to isolate the influence of

[1] For simplicity, the term *advertising* will be used herein to refer broadly to all forms of persuasive marketing efforts whereby the marketer wishes to communicate a given sales message to a specific customer audience regardless of the medium used. Such activities include point-of-purchase promotions, as well as print, direct mail, broadcast, billboard, or outdoor, etc., advertising. And the broad category of research that can be used to study any or all of these forms will be referred to as *advertising evaluation research*.

advertising alone. There are strong influences on tourism outside the realm of advertising. Word-of-mouth discussions, currency values, the development of a destination as an "in" place, cost changes (such as airline discounts), tour packages, or the influence of terrorism may have more effect on tourism decisions than does advertising.

• The decision to buy a travel product is often not an impulse purchase that can be triggered by a single advertisement. Rather, travel buying is generally considered and planned over a period of time. The length of the lead may be shortening considerably as shorter trips become the dominant form of leisure travel. Still, the target of much advertising is the considered travel decision. Whether it should be is another question.

• Furthermore, sales effect—a decision to visit a given hotel, for example—may be far removed in time and place from the advertising that influenced it, and marketing needs to know effectiveness now. It cannot wait for future studies.

In essence, the science of predicting human behavior—of which advertising evaluation research is a branch—is at best imprecise. The relationship between message and a change in mind-set is more direct and easier to study; and if the effect of advertising begins in the potential customer's mind then advertising evaluation research should also begin in the potential customer's mind.

Thus, the remainder of these comments will focus on research whose primary concern is studying changes in mind-set such as attitudes, opinions, perceptions, images, desires, expectations, knowledge, awareness, or inclinations to buy—changes that are influenced by advertising.

This focus should not imply that advertising evaluation research is in practice isolated from other forms of marketing research.

• Any study that provides information on what motivates travelers, who they are, and what they want or will buy will help management improve advertising effectiveness. Knowledge of the consumer will help create concepts and provide benchmarks against which future change can be assessed.

• And what is being called advertising evaluation research here can contribute to understanding of other areas of marketing as well. Advertising evaluation research is merely a cause-and-effect-focused portion of all marketing research efforts.

In the final analysis, the effectiveness of advertising evaluation research may depend on the degree to which it is seen as part of and coordinated with the entire research program.

In essence, advertising is both very expensive and very fragile. Advertising dollars are often a major portion of the marketing budget, and they should be held accountable for their performance. Advertising can be detrimental to sales efforts if it is not believed, if it confuses the traveler, or if it conveys the wrong message. Improperly done, advertising may even sell competitive products more than the sponsor's. Managing advertising involves making many decisions, and the more the manager knows, the better those decisions will be. Besides, well-executed advertising evaluation research works; it helps managers spend advertising dollars more

effectively. Identifying ways to make even small improvements in communications impact or preventing the repetition of mistakes can lead in the long run to substantial gains in sales and profits.

Because of the lack of precision in predicting human behavior, some marketing managers tend to question the value of doing any advertising evaluation research. It seems to this author that this is somewhat like questioning the value of a flashlight because it is not a floodlight. A small bulb that at least guides one in the general direction in which one wants to go and prevents stumbling may not show all that is happening, but is better than traveling in total darkness.

CONVERSION STUDIES: AN EXCEPTION

There is one common exception to the focus of advertising evaluation research on mind-set rather than on actual behavior. This exception involves direct-response advertising wherein the intent is to stimulate prospects to request travel information by returning a coupon, calling an 800 number, or mailing a bingo card to the print media that carried the advertising. Upon receiving the request, material such as a lure piece, a travel planner, or other brochures are sent to the requestor.

Because the name and address of the requestors are known, it is possible to conduct a conversion study wherein a sample of these requestors are interviewed by mail or by telephone to see whether they have visited or plan to visit the advertiser in the near future. Given the total number of requests and the projected number of visits, it is then possible to determine the "cost per inquiry" or the "return on investment" of the dollars spent for advertising and fulfillment.

However, a number of recent studies have raised serious questions about the validity of most conversion research. The findings of these studies suggest that neither the number of requests nor the data on subsequent visits (conversion) are an accurate evaluation of advertising effectiveness. In fact, these conversion-study results may be very misleading. Surveys that probe the character and attitude of travel-information requestors have shown that:

• Many—in fact, as many as 80 percent in one study—of those requesting travel information have already made the decision to visit and may even have made travel or accommodations reservations before they actually requested information from their destination. They are looking for help in planning what to do, not help in deciding where to go.

• Furthermore, many of those who requested information as the result of a given campaign had done so several times in the recent past. In fact, they had also visited the same destination enough to be classified as frequent visitors (three or four times per year) as well as frequent requestors (two or more times per year from the same destination).

Thus, many travelers who visit a destination after requesting and receiving travel information from that destination cannot be considered to have visited as a result of either the advertising or the brochure. Including those who already decided their visits and the dollars they spent greatly distorts (overstates) the actual sales impact and, hence, the effectiveness of the advertising-fulfillment program.

This phenomenon suggests a need to consider the difference between deciding to travel, selecting a destination, and planning the trip. The information needs of each differ, all of which makes the issue of assessing communications effectiveness much more complicated.

WHAT DOES THE MARKETING MANAGER NEED?

In order to fulfill responsibilities to fund, commission, and use effectively the results of advertising evaluation research, the marketing manager needs the answers to several key questions.

• For some of these questions—such as defining the advertising objectives—the burden of providing answers is the manager's. The research professional has the right to expect and the marketing manager has the obligation to provide specific advertising objectives against which the research can be planned.

• For other questions, the manager's responsibility is to ask the question of a research professional and to understand the answer and the implications of that answer for the study. (Thus, if someone else does not raise these questions or provide answers that are satisfactory to the manager, he or she should pursue them until satisfactory answers are obtained.) Only with these answers will the manager be able to judge fairly the potential gain in advertising effectiveness that will result from the spending of research dollars.

There are three ways that asking and answering these questions will contribute to the potential effectiveness of advertising evaluation research:

• They will help design the "best" study. Deciding on answers to the key questions and the discussion leading to those answers will ensure that the proposed research effort will provide the most effective, efficient, and relevant method for assessing the advertising efforts. However, it must be kept in mind that seldom is there any absolutely right or absolutely wrong answer. There is, at best, an optimum answer that combines compromise with judgment. Nevertheless, the critical issue is to be sure the answers are carefully thought out and agreed to by both research professional and marketing manager before the fieldwork begins.

• They will ensure that the manager understands the research process and is confident that the results can be used. The manager needs to be part of the evaluation process, not merely the recipient of "scores" once the study is completed— "scores" that he or she may or may not believe. Being part of the planning process generates in the marketing manager an association with the results that will help him or her to be comfortable with their use.

• They will determine before the research begins that all the data to be generated can, in fact, be used. The evaluation study needs to produce data that will have direct use and meaning in planning future advertising, not simply nice-to-know facts.

To reinforce these benefits and to be sure that the key questions have been satisfactorily answered, it may be useful to hold a mock presentation before the actual fieldwork begins, but after the study has been designed. In this mock presentation, hypothetical results are offered and the manager is asked to discuss how such data might be used. Assume, for example, that a study shows that the number of people considering a cruise vacation in the next six months and who mention Cruise Line "A" unaided when asked to list all cruise lines they were considering goes from 20 percent to 25 percent. The manager might then be asked what actions he or she would take if that finding does indeed result. The answer and the subsequent discussion will clearly point out the value of the data and any concerns or questions the manager has, and they can be a considerable aid in improving the entire study. No amount of sophisticated analysis can compensate for a study that fails to provide useful data or that contains what the manager views as critical design faults.

WHAT ARE THE KEY QUESTIONS FOR THE MARKETING MANAGER?

The following pages provide a detailed description of the eight key questions to include.

WHAT ARE THE OBJECTIVES OF THE ADVERTISING?

The first task in any advertising evaluation research project is to establish clearly stated, specific objectives against which the advertising's performance, or effectiveness, can be measured. These objectives are the basis for selecting the research approach, defining the sample, designing the questionnaire, and establishing the criteria for tabulation and analysis.

Advertising objectives are best set if they are based on some underlying theory or model that expresses the laws or principles by which advertising works. Several such general theories exist that, while neither the final answer nor universally accepted, do offer a beginning. Briefly, they include:

• AIDA—Attention–Interest–Desire–Action. This sequence purports to indicate how advertising affects consumers.
• DAGMAR (Defining Advertising Goals for Measured Advertising Results) uses the order Awareness–Comprehension–Conviction–Action.
• Some work the author has done suggests that for a tourist destination there is a consideration set through which the destination must move before a visit is planned. This sequence might be summarized as Awareness–Association–Conviction–Perceived Value–Action.

If a theoretical construct is lacking, then objectives need to be based on a sound analysis of the marketing task being undertaken. Reference to previous research can guide the selection of changes in mind-set that should improve the predisposition to want the advertiser's travel product.

To set advertising objectives, the manager needs to understand the concept of the potential buyer's continuum from ignorance to purchase. In establishing objectives, it is important to keep several guidelines in mind:

A. The objective must state who is to be affected by the advertising—essentially the target market. The target market might be defined as those in a geographic area; those with particular past vacation habits; those of a certain age, level of affluence, or other demographic characteristics; or those who read a particular publication—or some combination of those characteristics. Essentially, the research purpose of this definition is to decide who will be interviewed when the purpose is to learn if the advertising has been effective. The more precise the definition of the target market, the more precise the measure of effectiveness can be.

B. The objectives must state clearly and precisely what the advertising is designed to do. The ultimate goal of the tourism-marketing effort might be to increase the number of visitor-days at a destination. That could mean the same number of guests who stay longer, new guests who visit for the first time, or previous guests whose frequency of visit is increased. The goal has been stated in terms of sales. It is unlikely that advertising can be measured directly in terms of sales.

Thus, the objective for the advertising—one that can be measured—must be more limited and more specific and stated in terms of the mind-set change desired; for example, the objective for a campaign might be stated as:

- To increase awareness of the destination/hotel/carrier as an option for the next decision.
- To increase the number in the target market who hold favorable attitudes toward the destination/hotel/carrier (but favorable attitudes need more precise definition).
- To broaden knowledge of the specifics of the destination/hotel/carrier and what it offers the vacationer.
- To increase the number in the target market who say they will seriously consider the destination/hotel/carrier the next time the vacation decision arises.

Consideration of the anticipated or hoped for gain can help the researcher determine the degree of precision required, the sample size, and, hence, cost.

C. The objective must be stated in terms that allow measurement—essentially numeric. Without some numeric statement of objectives, it is not possible to measure advertising effectiveness. Research can provide a statistically reliable measure of whether an objective has been achieved only if that objective is stated in measurable terms, for example, if the objective is stated as "Increase the proportion of the target market who say they will definitely consider vacationing with us from 20% to 30%." Research cannot provide an assessment of whether a campaign has achieved its goal if that goal was stated as "Get more people to think well of us."

In sum, the objectives of the advertising must then include who is to be addressed and what is to be achieved in a way that can be measured. Once the objectives have been established, then a research program can be designed to measure whether these objectives have been achieved.

WHEN IN RELATION TO THE ADVERTISING WILL THE RESEARCH OCCUR?

Any given advertising can be viewed as having a life cycle lasting from the generation of the original concept to the end of the campaign. Evaluation research can occur at any time during this cycle. Research done early in the cycle will be more predictive in nature and will be designed to make the expenditure of current advertising dollars as productive as possible, that is, improve the campaign being tested. Research done toward the end of the campaign will focus more on the measurement of actual results that have occurred already in the marketplace. Here, the intent should be more oriented toward making the next advertising effort more productive.

Concept Testing

Concept tests are usually small-scale, qualitative studies that occur as soon as the idea of an ad or campaign has been created. The concept or concepts being studied are usually presented as a statement, possibly with rough sketches. The intent is to make some initial judgments regarding whether to proceed with development of the concept(s) and to suggest directions for improvement. Results should usually be viewed as tentative. Focused group discussions or small-sample one-on-one interviews are usually employed.

Pretesting

Pretests are studies that are more rigorous than concept tests and usually involve more rigorous sampling. Travelers from the target audiences are exposed to preliminary (or finished) versions of the proposed advertisements, and are asked a battery of questions to measure potential response. Such research is done before the advertisements are exposed to the market using a regular media schedule.

The purpose of pretesting is to attempt to predict the actual performance, identify problems, select from among alternative versions, and provide guidance for fine-tuning the advertisements themselves.

Most exposure is "artificial" in that the potential travelers are aware that they are research subjects. The extent of realism can range, however, from showing a prototype ad to employing cable television in one city as a test for the entire campaign.

Testing During the Campaign

In many respects, tests conducted during the time the advertising is actually being exposed in the marketplace are merely early posttests. The intent of during-the-campaign studies is usually to provide an early indication of what the total impact will be. Such information can help the marketer decide whether to extend a successful campaign or to cut short one that is not working well.

These studies can also help assess wear-out—that is, how much repetition it takes before a given advertisement begins to lose effectiveness.

Methods and procedures are similar to those in posttesting.

Posttesting

Posttests are studies conducted after or almost after the advertising has run its course, and the scheduled media are finished. Hopefully, posttesting results will be compared with some benchmark measurements developed before the advertising began to run. The intent is to score the advertising by measuring how the potential travelers' mind-sets have changed.

Sampling procedures and questionnaires are designed to disguise the advertising nature of the study.

WHAT IS BEING STUDIED OR MEASURED?

The issue here is to select just which components of the advertising are being studied. Is the research to focus on some component of the advertising—headline, copy, layout, use of color, media selection, or frequency; is it to focus on a single ad in its entirety; or is the research to focus on an entire campaign? Each can be a meaningful and valid focus for a research effort. The determinant is what management needs to know to improve advertising effectiveness and what questions exist that need to be settled in planning advertising.

WHAT MEASUREMENT METHODS WILL BE EMPLOYED?

Another way to restate this question is, "What (types of) questions will be asked and how will they be worded?" Or, "How will the questionnaire be designed?" Basically, questionnaire design is better left to the research professional and will not be discussed here in any detail. There is too much to say, and there are many excellent and lengthy references that say it well. However, several comments are in order.

First, the determination of the subject matter of the questionnaire and the wording of the questions come directly from the statement of advertising objectives. When the questionnaire is written, the relationship between it and the objectives should be clear. It may be useful to go so far as to write a rationale in which the reason for each question is shown by relating the question to the objective it addresses and, conversely, each objective is related to the relevant questions. Then it is known that the relationship is complete and all the data will be relevant and all the objectives measured.

Second, there is really no limit on the type of questionnaire nor on the type of measurement method that may be employed. Interviews can be done in person, by mail, over the telephone, or even self-administered with groups of people who congregate at one spot. Each technique has, of course, its own strengths, weaknesses, and peculiarities.

Questionnaires can be highly structured and direct, or they can call for discursive answers. Frequently, they rely on the subject's memory as when recall, recognition, or association questions are asked. They can use scales to measure opinions and attitudes, or they can make use of projective techniques.

The content of a typical sequence of questions might include:

1. Awareness of and preference for the travel product being advertised and key competitors. This would include intent to visit each if appropriate. These questions are asked early in the interview so that responses will not be biased by specific questions to be asked later.
2. Image of the travel product and key competitors.
3. Registration and comprehension of the message being delivered. This could include factual questions about the advertising or the travel product itself as well as measures of comprehension, believability, and clarity of message.
4. Specific buying/shopping behavior, including previous travel patterns.
5. Demographic and psychographic (attitudes, intent, opinion, and life-style) characteristics.
6. Exposure to media. Because memory is fragile, it is not possible to develop accurate measures of previous media exposure. It is, however, possible to develop an index of impact by combining two measures: (1) a ranking of perceived exposure relative to competitive advertising possibly factored by relative dollars spent and (2) a "test" including specific questions on format and/or message content.

Some techniques employ electronic or mechanical aids to assist in understanding buyer response. These aides include eye cameras (optical devices that track eye movement), a tachistoscope to control exposure time, the use of voice analysis to determine when the respondent is telling the truth, commercial lie detectors, and other devices that provide a means whereby a respondent can indicate interest or attention. The artificial nature of the test situation and an apparent lack of acceptance by many advertising executives limit the use of mechanical devices.

Finally, the author's experience suggests that the use of one or more indexing procedures can be very beneficial. Consider, for example, measures of exposure to advertising. Generally, people cannot recall accurately how much advertising they have seen or where they saw or read the ads. Asking them does not generate accurate measures. However, if a series of questions are asked about relative frequency, advertising content, use of information learned, and perceived level of exposure, it is possible to construct an index that, for each respondent, provides a relative measure. This is not a measure of exposure. It is a relative measure of the extent to which the advertising message was received. As said, it is a useful measure to equate with attitude and/or behavior when assessing a given campaign.

Another useful index can be constructed to measure how a given destination is positioned along a spectrum from a dream destination that will someday be visited, a place requiring special planning, to a frequently visited—often on impulse—destination. Combining the response to several questions into a single index number for each respondent provides a more sensitive value, a value that can be related to other answers, and a more accurate measure than any single answer can provide.

WHO IS BEING INCLUDED IN THE SAMPLE?

The basic issue here is to be sure of two things: first, that the sample and screening criteria reflect the target audience as specified in the objectives, and, second, that the manager clearly understands who is being interviewed.

WILL THE ASSESSMENT BE MADE IN A REAL-LIFE SITUATION, OR WILL IT BE IN A LABORATORY SETTING?

A number of services are available that offer laboratory, or artificial, settings for conducting advertising evaluation research. They include:

- Cable television systems where ad exposure can be directed to specific households, allowing for split-run testing of two commercials simultaneously
- Theaters where groups of people see films interspersed with commercial material
- Minimarkets where consumers see commercials and then shop for items including those for which commercials were shown

These laboratory settings offer more control. Real-life testing occurs when the advertising is run on a limited basis such as in a single test city on one television station or in a limited number of copies of a limited edition of a magazine.

IS THE STUDY AD HOC, OR WILL SOME EXISTING SYSTEM OR OMNIBUS TECHNIQUE BE EMPLOYED?

A number of firms offer special techniques for testing advertising in either television or print. The usual procedure is to expose the advertising by means of some predetermined procedure; a series of questions usually related to awareness, intention to buy, or comprehension may be asked. The result is often a score that can then be compared to norms for the category developed from previous comparable studies. The cost is usually less than that for ad hoc studies.

One problem for the tourism marketer is much the same for existing systems as for laboratory procedures. Most of these were designed for the package goods/supermarket business and, thus, may be less effective when the advertising is for travel or tourism. Thus, the tourism marketer may be forced to employ more ad hoc procedures wherein the study is specifically designed and implemented.

ARE WE KEEPING SCORE OR DEVELOPING A GAME PLAN?

In some ways, this can be one of the most critical questions. Too frequently, research wastes effort documenting where a

company has been in the past—documentation that often takes on the appearance of a report card or a scorecard that offers little value as a guide to how to improve. The thrust of the scorecard assessment is to tell management what they bought with their advertising dollars. Furthermore, scorekeeping research can lead to antagonism as it is used to rate the performance of the advertising agency or creative media or the account staffs. This antagonism leads to ill will, defensive reactions, and reduced performance.

Another danger of "single-number" or scorecard research is that the goal becomes one of getting a better score, not necessarily of creating more effective advertising. Unfortunately, a better score and more effective advertising are not necessarily synonymous.

Advertising evaluation research that will contribute to future sales should focus on developing data and analyses that help advertising/marketing decide where they should be going and how to get there. The future should be viewed as an opportunity for achievement. Game-plan development based on sound diagnosis of past performance should be the hallmark of effective and contributing advertising evaluation research. Game-plan research helps the marketer learn what works and what does not work so that this new knowledge can be used to make future advertising more effective. This is constructive research designed to provide creative guidance for developing advertising that is increasingly more effective.

CONCLUSION

This chapter has attempted to suggest three ideas:

- One key to the success of advertising evaluation research is the active involvement of the marketing manager in the evaluation process. The manager must provide clear, precise advertising objectives, must understand the method being employed, and must be prepared to use the results in planning future advertising efforts. Lacking these commitments, the ultimate value of this type of research is questionable.

- There are a great many techniques that can be employed to assess advertising effectiveness—each with its strengths and weaknesses. A marketing manager should get competent professional research guidance to select that mix of techniques that will optimize each individual study.

- Done well, advertising evaluation research can offer continuing assistance in improving the performance of advertising. A modest increase in advertising effectiveness—generated by the intelligent use of research findings—can almost always result in sales and profits that are larger than the cost of doing the research.

AN ADDENDUM

Since this chapter was prepared for the original edition of this Handbook (1987), three developments have occurred that are worth noting:

• First, there is an increasing focus on accountability, especially among the public sector of tourism. In this use, *accountability* can be defined as providing evidence that the dollars provided to public tourism agencies, such as state tourism offices or convention and visitor bureaus, were spent well. This evidence is needed to justify future spending for tourism. With the tight budgets currently confronting governments at all levels, continued funding requires sound accountability.

Often, half or more of these funds are spent on advertising. Hence, measuring advertising effectiveness is a key component of accountability. The other key component is measuring economic impact. Thus, the issue of how to assess effectiveness in an accurate and believable manner has become an issue of greatly added importance.

• Second, in response to this increased recognition of the importance of accurate measures of effectiveness and to the growing discontent with the obvious error of some existing studies, the U.S. Department of Commerce (USTTA) sponsored a Task Force on Accountability Research. The mission of this group was to provide guidance on how to improve this type of research.

The results of the Task Force's efforts were published by the Travel and Tourism Research Association (TTRA) in a monograph entitled Accountability Research: Getting the Right Numbers and Getting the Numbers Right. This document should be required reading for anyone interested in accurate, believable measures of the effectiveness of marketing efforts.

• Third, the author's firm has developed a new procedure to measure accountability. This new procedure combines a study using inquirers or information requestors with a matched, random sample of neighbors (general population). Telephone interviewing is employed. The questionnaire includes information on behavior and attitude. A tracking study of market penetration and communications effectiveness is combined with the visiting behavior of requestors to develop a more in-depth look at what is happening in the marketplace. When economic impact measures are added, the result is a sound report card on the marketing dollars spent.

REFERENCES

While a number of journal articles have been written on assessing advertising, almost nothing has been published on assessing tourism advertising. Probably the best general bibliography can be found in the *Handbook of Marketing Research* edited by Robert Ferber (McGraw-Hill Book Company). Certainly the *Journals of Marketing, Marketing Research*, or *Advertising* are also good sources. The only other text the author has found that stands the test of use and time is *Measuring Advertising Effectiveness* by Lucas and Britt (McGraw-Hill Book Company).

47

Improving Advertising Conversion Studies

ARCH G. WOODSIDE
The Malcolm S. Woldenberg Professor of Marketing
Tulane University
New Orleans, Louisiana

ILKKA A. RONKAINEN
Associate Professor of Marketing
School of Business Administration
Georgetown University
Washington, D.C.

*F*or travel and tourism destination marketers, the principal purpose of doing conversion research studies has been to learn whether or not advertising and marketing campaigns to attract visitors and profits actually do cause visitors and profits more than would have occurred anyway, that is, without using the advertising and marketing campaigns. Unfortunately, the conversion research studies in the literature were designed inadequately to answer this issue, that is, most reported conversion studies employ one-group designs and all violate the requirements for valid, scientific design to assess cause-and-effect relationships. The good news is that the published conversion studies do provide useful answers to other important strategy issues for destination marketers. These issues, as well as when and how to do conversion research studies, will be addressed in this chapter.

IMPROVING ADVERTISING CONVERSION STUDIES

Destination marketing executives responsible for designing and implementing strategies for attracting visitors to their destinations are asked annually to give concrete answers to four hard questions. First, how many people did the marketing strategy influence over the number that would have acted anyway without the marketing strategy? Second, how much income net of the marketing campaign costs resulted from implementing the marketing campaign versus the income that would have resulted without the campaign? Third, what specific elements in the marketing campaign worked well, and what worked poorly: advertisement A versus B, C, D, or E; ads in newspapers versus television versus magazines; ads

in specific media vehicles; general versus specific-activity-fulfillment literature? Fourth, what are the demographic, life-style, and travel behavior profiles of inquirers and visitors associated with the marketing campaign?

To answer these questions in the travel and tourism industry, advertising conversion research studies are used most often by destination marketing executives (DMEs), for example, by directors of U.S. state and Canadian province travel and tourism departments, by DMEs of regional and city tourism offices, and by DMEs for theme parks and event marketing programs. Such conversion research studies are conducted to answer the questions of how many inquirers from travel ads convert to visitors and what are the convertors' demographic and travel-behavior characteristics, including length of stay, travel-party size, destination activities, and destination expenditures. Thus, equation 1 is the basic equation used in advertising conversion research studies:

$$\text{Conversion} = \frac{\text{Visitors}}{\text{Inquirers}} \quad (1)$$

Thus, governors, legislative bodies, and CEOs annually expect detailed accountability reports from DMEs on the impact of advertising and marketing campaigns on causing visitors and net income. Advertising conversion research studies have been used as the primary research method for such accountability studies.

Much has been written in the 1980s and 1990s on the strengths and weaknesses of advertising conversion studies in the advertising, marketing, and tourism literatures (see Woodside and Motes 1981; Yochum 1985; Silberman and Klock 1986; Ronkainen and Woodside 1987; Wynegar 1989; Davidson and Wiethaupt 1989; Burke and Lindblom 1989; Perdue and Pitegoff 1990; Woodside and Soni 1988, 1990, 1991; Woodside 1990; Burke and Gitelson 1990; Perdue and Merrion 1991; Perdue and Gustke 1992).

Several insights and important conclusions can be offered from these literatures—the principal insight being that most advertising conversion research studies are designed and implemented inadequately to provide valid answers if the principal issue posed is whether an advertising and marketing campaign causes visitors and positive net income for the destination above the number of visitors and net income that would have occurred without the campaign.

Scientific methods to assess cause-and-effect relationships are well developed and have been applied extensively in advertising and marketing, as well as other disciplines (e.g., agriculture, medicine, psychology). For a review of some of this literature, see Woodside (1990) and Banks (1965). The two basic requirements for scientific testing of cause-and-effect relationships are: (1) including two groups of subjects (e.g., magazine subscribers), one group to be the treatment group and one group to be a control group, to be able to make valid comparisons of impact of the treatment-versus-no-treatment conditions on dependent variables; and (2) before implementing the advertising and marketing campaign, using random assignment to place each subject in either a treatment group to be exposed to an ad message (or other marketing variable) or the control group that is not exposed to the ad message, and to create two groups not significantly different from one another statistically before running the treatment-versus-no-treatment condition with both groups being exposed to unmeasured influences taking place during the advertising campaign period.

To control for all other possible influences on the dependent variables of interest (e.g., number of visitors and net income for the destination), two groups need to be designed to be as equal as possible in every way before the treatment is administered. Random assignment of each subject to either the treatment group or the control group accomplishes

this task. Internal research-design validity is achieved by using such a two-group, true-experimental method (see Banks 1965; Caples 1974).

High external validity is achieved by random selection; for example, selecting a sample of 1,000 inquirers randomly from a population of 10,000 inquirers. Thus, random selection and random assignment are two separate research steps that are used to accomplish two worthwhile aims: random selection to generalize the results of the study from a sample to a population, and random assignment to achieve internal research-design validity. Both of these steps can, and should, be used in the same study to assess the cause-and-effect relationship of advertising on visitors and income.

Hundreds of scientific tests of cause-and-effect relationships of advertising and marketing variables on causing new customers and net income have been done (see Caples 1974 and journal issues of *Marketing Science*). Such true experiments can be applied easily and with little increase in expenditures already planned for advertising and marketing campaigns by destination marketing executives.

For destination ads planned for placement in magazines and newspapers, for example, samples of subscribers of several of these media vehicles can be **selected** randomly by household or ZIP codes and **assigned** randomly to a treatment group to receive the vehicle issue containing the ad or to the control group to receive the vehicle issue excluding the ad (or to receive ad A versus ad B, if two ads are being tested). Such scientific true tests of cause-and-effect are known as split-run tests in advertising.

After the ad schedule is run, then a conversion research study on all subjects (treatment and control) can be used to learn how many subjects recall requesting literature about the destination, how many report visiting the destination, and how much they report spending at the destination. Substantial differences in the averages between the treatment and control groups for each of these dependent variables can be attributed to the treatment received (exposure versus nonexposure).

Two hypotheses are likely to be supported by the findings when such scientific cause-and-effect advertising conversion studies in destination marketing are done. First, most advertising and marketing campaigns have a small but important influence in causing additional customers—small, because most people are likely to have already made the commitment for the trip to the destination before being exposed (and not exposed) to the ad; however, the ad is likely to cause some meaningful increase in number of party-visits because the fulfillment literature received does convert some undecideds into visitors. Second, most advertising and marketing campaigns have a large impact on increasing the net income from visitors to the destination (e.g., a state or province) because reading and carrying the fulfillment literature on the trip to the destination increases the knowledge of things to do, and ways to spend money, at the destination.

These two propositions are developed from insights from the conversion research literature. Pitegoff (1991) reports,

With the traditional broad targeting of the advertisements for Florida's Vacation Guide (fulfillment literature), we would expect many of those requesting it to have been there before and to have a relatively low traditional conversion rate as a result. Indeed, we would expect the Vacation Guide to do far more than just attract first-time (or repeat) visitors. Finally, the traditional Conversion Study assumes inherently that a vacation to convert prospects into first-time visitors. Something else might be operating (Pitegoff 1991:441).

In fact, many other factors might be operating that are not controlled for in traditional conversion studies. Factors other than being exposed to the advertisement and receiving the fulfillment literature (such as word-of-mouth advertising among family and friends, weather reports, and hallmark and other special events) are collectively identified as sources of internal invalidity (see Campbell and Stanley 1963; Banks 1965).

Some researchers maintain that traditional conversion studies can and should be improved by including questions in the conversion survey that ask if the sampled inquirers had already decided to visit the destination before inquiring and requesting the fulfillment literature (see Ballman, Burke, Korte, and Blank 1983, 1984; Burke and Gitelson 1990; Siegel and Ziff-Levine 1990). Such an improvement is of dubious value for several reasons. First, such a question assumes that an individual respondent can report accurately the amount of impact of the combination of noticing the ad, requesting the fulfillment literature offered, and examining the fulfillment literature received versus other potential influences; a major reason for using true-experimental designs in consumer psychological research is to overcome the limitations of self-reports of relative influence of independent variables.

Second, the question is a leading one and reminds the inquirers that they responded to an advertising offer; many inquirers who are sent fulfillment literature that they request fail to report requesting such literature when asked rather than informed, that they made such requests (see Woodside and Soni 1991).

Third, no doubt the destination ad campaign likely causes many inquiries from households that would not otherwise have inquired if the ad had not been run, but most of these people have already planned to visit the destination; thus, the real issue is unlikely to be whether the advertising and marketing campaign (fulfillment literature) caused a substantial increase in visitors. The explained variances of number of visits caused by advertising and marketing campaigns are likely to be significant statistically but to be low (vary between 2 and 8 percent) in well-designed and -implemented, scientific conversion studies. The major cause-and-effect impact of the advertising and marketing campaign is likely to be the increase in expenditures by inquirers who make use of the fulfillment literature for planning and visiting the destination.

In a traditional conversion study, including a decrease in the conversion rate to reflect when the destination-choice decision was reported to have been made does not provide for a scientific comparison of the treatment-versus-control conditions of being exposed-versus-not-exposed to the advertising. Also, even if a scientific conversion research design is used and the finding made that an advertising and marketing campaign delivers a low conversion rate (visitors/inquirers), attention should be directed to where the campaign likely caused the biggest impacts: increases in the numbers of activities and dollars spent at the destination among households using the fulfillment literature.

To test the cause-and-effect impact of only the fulfillment literature on increasing the number of visits, visitors, activities, and money spent at the destination, a sample of inquirers (e.g., $n = 2,000$) should be randomly assigned to two equal-sized groups, a treatment group and a control group ($n = 1,000$ each), with only the treatment group receiving the literature requested and the control group receiving nothing. Then, after the end of the relevant tourism season, all sampled members of both groups would be studied in a conversion research study to measure the dependent variables, including number of visits, visitors, activities, money spent at the destination, and tax revenues generated. For each dependent variable, the difference between the treatment group versus the control group is the effect of the fulfillment literature in causing changes in the dependent variable.

Such a study may seem insane and unethical, yet can be justified just as medical research (using randomly assigned treatment and placebo groups) on life-saving drugs is justified: scientific proof is required that the new drug (or fulfillment literature) is an effective treatment versus not receiving the drug (or causes increases in visits, activities, revenues); and only after successful results are found from carefully executed true experiments does such proof exist.

However, such drastic action need not be taken to scientifically estimate the cause-and-effect impact of an advertising and marketing campaign on several dependent variables (e.g., conversion rate, number of destination activities, and expenditures at the destination). If the DME wants to learn the combined impact of users of the media vehicle possibly being exposed to the campaign and sending for the fulfillment literature, then a scientific conversion study would be to do a split-run test of media vehicle subscribers. One example would be if 5,000 media vehicle subscribers are exposed to the ad and fulfillment-literature offer and another 5,000 media vehicle subscribers are not exposed (or 10 ZIP-code markets are exposed and 10 are not exposed). Then, a conversion research study is conducted on members of both groups.

Such a split-run study does not enable the DME to separate the influence of the ad from the fulfillment literature; the cause-and-effect of the ad and the fulfillment literature on the dependent variables are confounded. However, the major question can be answered from such scientific conversion studies: Did the combined use of the ad and fulfillment literature cause increases in the dependent variables (e.g., visit and visitor conversion rates, number of destination activities, and expenditures at the destination)?

Why do DMEs fund traditional but not do scientific (i.e., true-experiments; e.g., split-run ad tests) conversion studies, given that such scientific research methods have been used, and extra ads do not have to be run for such tests since the tests can be planned into advertising and marketing campaigns that will be implemented anyway? Several reasons are likely responsible: (1) no applications of split-run tests in the destination marketing literature have appeared, and the telling shortcomings of traditional conversion research studies are only beginning to receive widespread attention (thanks, in part, to the U.S. Department of Commerce Task Force on Accountability Research; see: Wynegar 1989; Davidson and Wiethaupt 1989; Burke and Gitelson 1990; Siegel and Ziff-Levine 1990; Erdmann 1991); (2) not planning ahead of running the advertising and marketing campaign, for example, split-run tests have to be coordinated with cooperating media executives before running the ads, and usually a two-year planning cycle is needed to start up split-run tests; (3) a lack of skills and knowledge of scientific research methods among DMEs and CEOs (how many are familiar with Banks 1965, the classic report on true experiments in marketing?); (4) and possibly, a general bias against cause-and-effect assessments by advertising agency account managers (e.g., "the results might be negative and our agency could get canned because the results do not meet expectations").

Given: (1) the low quality of all reported conversion research studies for answering the principal question of whether the advertising and marketing campaign causes net increases in visits, visitors, number of activities by visitors at the destination, and revenues, and (2) the fact that many applications of high-quality, cause-and-effect studies are available and that how to do such studies is reported in the marketing literature, how can DMEs be motivated to do scientific conversion research studies? Hopefully, examples of scientific conversion studies will be available sometime in the 1990s and serve as models for learning, designing, and implementing better research designs by DMEs; also, the continued absence of scientific evidence of cause-and-effect, advertising-to-sales relationships and resulting continued threats to cut and eliminate tourism advertising and marketing budgets made by state and provincial legislators will motivate DMEs to move up to scientific conversion research studies.

THE RESEARCH PROCESS

DATA COLLECTION MODES

Three primary, conversion research, data collection methods are available: personal interviews, telephone interviews, and mail interviews. Personal interviews have not been reported as a primary mode mainly because of their cost and staff requirements. Typically, a questionnaire is mailed to (or a

phone call made to) a sample of inquirers 6 to 10 months after receiving the inquiries.

In comparing and contrasting the telephone and mail methods, the advantages of one are often the disadvantages of the other. While a general comparison (such as the one provided in Table 1) can be made, a major caveat should be emphasized: The choice of a mode is situation specific, that is, factors such as time constraints, budget, sample size, and information requirements determine a particular mode's advantages and disadvantages in a given situation (Peterson 1982; Churchill 1983).

The per-contact cost of the mail questionnaire is generally low; for example, Hunt and Dalton (1983) found that the cost per usable questionnaire was estimated to run approximately 40 percent more for the telephone method ($1.33 versus $2.05). However, if nonresponse is substantial, the cost per return can end up being high.

The introduction of computer-controlled cathode-ray terminals (CRT) has had a significant impact on the conduct of telephone interviews. In addition to assisting in sequencing of questions, results are available at a moment's notice since all replies are stored in memory. Depending on the number of follow-up mailings required, the total time needed to conduct a good mail survey can be substantial. However, as the number of required contracts increases, the attractiveness of the telephone mode decreases (with additional staff requirements and escalating costs).

Although the mail questionnaire mode allows little speed control, it represents a standardized stimulus. With telephone interviews, interviewer-induced variance can be reduced through proper selection, training, and supervision during the data collection.

The types of questions that can be asked as well as the amount and the accuracy of the information needed will influence the choice of the mode. Telephone interviews, although they usually do not allow the same quantity of data collection as mail, will enable flexibility in terms of probing respondents' comments further as well as the use of open-ended questions to a greater extent. Since respondents to a mail questionnaire are able to work at their own pace, a better thought-out response may result. The appropriateness of these responses, however, is a function of the adequacy of the questionnaire.

Mail questionnaires permit data collection from a wide geographic dispersion of individuals since the mode is relatively time and cost insensitive. With sample sizes of 5,000 to 10,000 (e.g., Woodside and Reid 1974; Woodside and Motes 1980), mail interviews become the only feasible mode of data collection.

SAMPLING

Since the number of inquirers is usually quite high, for example, 73,831 inquirers from black-and-white ads placed in magazines as reported by Woodside and Ronkainen (1982), sampling is one of the major problem areas to be encountered. Random sampling in some form is the generally accepted method. Ballman et al. (1983) provide a thorough

TABLE 1   Comparisons of Data Collection Methods[a]

	Mode	
Characteristic	Telephone	Mail
Unit cost	Moderate	Low
Speed	Fast	Slow
Control of data collection environment	Good	None
Refusal, nonresponse problems	Moderate	Substantial
Control of data collection process	Good	Very good
Size of staff required	Moderate	Small
Quantity of data possible	Limited	Considerable
Diversity of questions possible	Limited	Moderate
Interviewer-interviewee bias	Slight	None
Flexibility in data collection	Moderate	Low
Geographical reach	Good	Very good
Perceived anonymity by subject	Moderate	High

[a]For more information consult Peterson (1982) and Churchill (1983).

discussion on incorporating sampling precision to improve the quality of management decisions based on conversion studies.

Given total inquiry numbers above 50,000 (and above 500,000 in many annual destination advertising/marketing campaigns), a serious issue is how big a sample should be used in the conversion study. The answer depends on several important issues including: (1) the desired precision level in estimating a principal dependent population parameter (such as the conversion rate) (for example, assume that a sample estimate within 5 percent of the population value is desired); (2) the confidence level desired in estimating the population parameter (for example, assume a 95 percent confidence level is desired so that the estimated conversion rate be within 5 percent of the population value); and (3) the total number of inquiries for each inquiry population desired to be examined.

Two principal mistakes are made often in selecting sample sizes in conversion studies: (1) given a large population of inquirers (e.g., 25,000), using a too-large sample (e.g., 3,000 inquirers); and (2) given a small population of inquirers (e.g., 250), using a too-small sample (e.g., only 50 or 100 inquirers).

Given a desired precision level of plus-or-minus 5 percent, and a 95 percent confidence level, practical and helpful rules of thumb in destination conversion research studies include the following points: Set the sample size between 300 and 500 inquirers for **each** population of inquirers to be studied. Thus, if a travel profile and conversion rate are to be estimated for each population of inquirers from 20 different magazines and magazine ads—with each magazine generating 300 or more inquirers, then about 6,000 inquirers should be included in the study (300 by 20). The important point here is that the sample size is not dependent much on the population size to achieve useful information; an inquiry population of 25,000 versus 5,000 does not translate into substantially different sample sizes.

For small numbers of inquirers (e.g., 100, 200, or 300

inquirers) for a given media vehicle that a DME wants to study, include all the inquirers in the study; do not take a sample of the inquirers.

A conversion study that includes achieving a 75 percent survey response rate among 300 sampled households from an inquiry population of 5,000 households is superior in quality to the conversion study that includes achieving a 40 percent survey-response rate among 2,000 sampled households of 5,000 households. Unlike the buying of pizza by a college freshman, quality is more important than quantity in the combination of sample size and response rates; and quality goes way down if a large sample is used without also using multiple methods to insure for high response rates (above 70 percent).

However, adequate sample sizes need to be selected for each population of interest in a conversion study. Thus, if the conversion rate, inquiry profile, and destination revenue performance of each of 10 radio stations, 20 magazines, and 30 newspapers are to be examined, a total of 60 samples of 300 each should be selected to achieve reasonable precision and confidence levels to permit conclusions about the performance of each ad media vehicle. Consequently, trade-offs between answers desired and research budgets usually result in the performances of only a handful (e.g., 5 to 10) of media vehicles being examined adequately in any one year.

RESPONSE RATE

Typically, the response rates produced from an initial mailing range from 20 percent to 40 percent. If a second mailing to nonrespondents to the first mailing is used, the response rates usually range between 30 percent to 50 percent; response rates after a third mailing have been reported at 40 percent to 80 percent. Only one study reported by Wettstein (1982) had a single mailing. The results of this study after a 40 percent response rate should be treated with suspicion, especially when no further sampling of nonrespondents was reported.

Ellerbrock (1981) points out that people who actually visit are more likely to respond to a survey due to the feeling that their answers are more valuable to the state than those who did not visit. It is, therefore, clear that failure to correct for nonresponse bias leads to inflated conversion estimates. Hunt and Dalton (1983) calculated that not correcting for nonresponse bias would have resulted in a 44 percent overstatement of conversion. Woodside and Ronkainen (1983) found that conversion rates of inquirers were substantially lower for second- versus first-mailing respondents, while rates were similar for third- versus second-mailing respondents. While demographics were found to be similar across respondent categories, travel behavior was found to differ between first-, second-, and third-mailing respondents.

Two approaches have been proposed to correct for the nonresponse problem. Response rates above 70 percent should be achieved. Hunt and Dalton (1983) suggest that telephone survey methods (probably) give more accurate results than mail surveys composed of only one or two mailings. Telephone surveys are, however, subject to bias resulting from the exclusion of households without telephones and not having the telephone numbers of unlisted households who are in the initial sampling pool of households. Of the 498 households selected by Hunt and Dalton (1983), for instance, 100 did not list a telephone number, and not including these 100 households as nonrespondents is underreporting the nonresponse rate. Furthermore, an additional 62 could not be located, and another 81 had been disconnected or would not cooperate. Recommendation: sampled households for a telephone conversion study with unlisted telephone numbers who cannot be reached by telephone should be contacted by mail or otherwise included in the proportion of nonrespondents to the study.

A number of studies report the use of incentives to increase response rates. These incentives have usually been posters of the region sponsoring the study (not recommended because of the likely bias created in identifying the sponsor of the study) or a promise to send the respondent the summary results of the study once completed (a recommended incentive to help increase response rates; about 50 percent of the respondents will ask for the summary).

Both mail and telephone methods are likely to suffer from low response rates of the initial pool of sampled households (below 50 percent should be considered low and a serious weakness) unless several attempts are made to reach nonrespondents. Hunt and Dalton (1983) and Woodside and Ronkainen (1984) have advocated achieving response rates above 70 percent. Several actions are effective for increasing the response rate: making two or more additional attempts to reach nonrespondents of the first attempt is the most effective tool for increasing response rates; personalizing each cover letter with the name and address of the sampled household member and hand-signing each cover are useful steps to increase response rates.

The single, most useful source of how to do high-quality and useful mail and telephone surveys continues to be Dillman (1978). His work should be consulted for more detailed recommendations. Dillman's "total design method" includes the use of multiple attempts to reach nonrespondents to the initial survey contact. See Perdue and Gustke (1992) for a destination conversion research application of Dillman's recommendations.

EXPENDITURES

Respondents are typically asked how much they spent while in the location under study. Muha (1976) and Mak, Moncur, and Yonamine (1977) have attacked conversion studies with respect to the accuracy of expenditures reported by respondents. Mak et al. (1977) empirically tested the relationship between data from recall surveys and diaries and found that survey respondents tend to underestimate their expenditures. Ellerbrock (1981) proposes the use of diary techniques at the minimum as a control group from which to weigh the expenditure figures reported by a large group of survey respondents. However, the diary technique is not recommended as the primary data collection method. Less than 20 percent of the persons approached agree to participate in such endeavors, but this initial contact problem is inadequately discussed (i.e., usually not described) by its advocates. Of these, less than 50 percent return their diaries. Also, daily and accurate entries are doubtful (Woodside 1981). The additional costs and nonresponse problems incurred by using a diary panel should not be acceptable for most state and province tourism offices.

Travelers do accurately respond to questions on expenditures if broad expenditure categories are used. Typically, 9 to 12 categories are used (e.g., $0, $1–$50, $51–$100, etc.). Vehicles, media, ads, and campaigns can be evaluated and decisions made based on revenue projections using such expenditure categories.

SPONSOR IDENTITY

The identification of a state or location as the sponsor of the study should be avoided. To desensitize respondents, the questionnaire should be used to collect data on travel behavior with respect to competing travel destinations. Furthermore, the letter accompanying the questionnaire should not refer to the fact that the respondent is known to have written for travel information. Recent conversion studies have been conducted by independent research agencies identified as the sponsor of the study. However, no direct test has been reported to substantiate this proposition.

ASSESSING MULTIPLE TRIPS

Some portion of inquirers from an advertising and marketing campaign who do visit the destination are likely to make more than one trip. The impact of multiple trips associated with the advertising and marketing campaign should be estimated (Perdue and Gustke 1992). In a meta-analysis of five high-quality conversion studies done for Tennessee and North Carolina, for example, Perdue and Gustke (1992) found that 17 percent of the survey respondents reported making multiple trips to the destination areas after receiving the travel information packet and during the calendar year of the inquiry. Of those individuals who visited the destination, an average of 30 percent made more than one trip. Across the five studies, the estimated number of total trips increased an average of 38 percent, estimates of total visitor-nights increased 39 percent, and estimates of total visitor expenditures increased 37 percent (Perdue and Gustke 1992).

EXAMPLE OF A SURVEY FORM

A sample questionnaire from a conversion study (Woodside and Soni 1988, 1990, 1991) is provided in Exhibit 1. This questionnaire incorporates most of the recommendations made in this chapter.

DATA ANALYSIS

REVENUES

In calculating the average revenue per inquiry (RPI), the total number of parties actually visiting has to be estimated. The total number of inquiries (e.g., 4,135) is multiplied by the percentage of those respondents who visited (e.g., 44%—0.44 x 4,135 = 1,836), it is estimated that 1,836 inquirers visited as a result of the advertisement. Woodside and Reid (1974) have noted that this estimate may be inflated since the calculations are based on the assumption that the percentage of inquirers who visited is identical to that indicated by the results. This, of course, can be remedied by a high response rate.

Ellerbrock (1981) and Ballman et al. (1983) point out the need to use net versus gross conversion rates. They propose that a true conversion rate is one in which inquirers who decide to visit the destination before ad exposure are not included. Ballman et al. (1983) suggest that gross conversion rates may be overestimating conversion by 50 percent; in their study, the gross conversion rate was 33 percent, while the net rate was 22 percent. Their results are based on answers to the following question: "Did you request information from us before or after you decided to vacation in X?" The literature received may, in some cases, cause the final decision, although the respondent will most likely indicate that the decision had been made before the request.

Woodside (1981) calls for the use of a true experiment to meaningfully answer the question of whether the advertising and the literature influenced visits. Cities could be used for such research along with regional editions of magazines; or split-run tests could be used that include every other household subscriber's issue including or not including the test ad.

For a true experiment done on geographic basis for a specific magazine or newspaper, some ZIP code areas, or cities, would include an advertisement (i.e., treatment) while some would not (i.e., control). Random samples of all subscribers in all cities could be drawn, and information on their travel behavior collected. The travel behavior of the treatment versus the control groups could be compared.

The average expenditure per part (e.g., $432) is then multiplied by the estimated number of visitors (1,836) to arrive at an estimate for total revenue ($793,000). Estimated total revenue divided by the total number of inquirers results in RPI: $793,000/4,135 = $192.

The more specific the destination for which the conversion study is performed (e.g., state versus specific location), the more careful the definition of the barriers of the region to the respondents needs to be. Misunderstanding or misconception may lead to unnecessary inflation of the results.

COSTS

Average cost per inquiry (CPI) is obtained by dividing the total cost of the advertising campaign (e.g., $128,000) by the number of inquiries (4,135): $128,000/4,135 = $31. It is important that all relevant campaign costs be assigned, including production and insertion charges and inquiry handling costs (e.g., postage, brochure printing, etc.). It is even appropriate to add conversion study costs to the overall costs of the campaign.

The ratio of CPI as a percentage of RPI ($31/$192 = 16%) provides a means of comparing the effectiveness of different campaigns, media vehicles, or ads. The interesting criterion for a state agency is to see if taxes as a percentage of revenue generated are greater than the cost per inquiry as a percentage of revenue per inquiry (CPI/RPI). In a study on South Carolina's advertising tourism campaign, CPI as a part of RPI for five advertising campaigns was less than the estimated 9.9% tax rate (Woodside and Motes 1981).

In Table 2, some conversion studies are summarized in terms of important research-design dimensions.

APPLICATIONS

Although conversion studies are designed primarily to estimate rates of conversions of inquirers into visitors, applications can, should, and have been extended well beyond this purpose. Woodside and Motes (1981), for example, studied five distinct advertising strategies—with different creative approaches, different media schedules, and different direct-mail literature—that were used to affect vacation behavior of five market segments. Substantial differences in estimated total revenues, costs, and net revenues produced from each market and advertising strategy were detected. The findings resulted in the advertiser's reallocation of advertising efforts for the following year.

Woodside and Motes (1980) compared image versus direct-response advertising and found no significant demographic profile differences between direct-response and image-ad inquirers; but data showed significant differences in cost and net revenue. The findings resulted in the reduction of the advertiser's use of image-only advertisements.

Woodside and Ronkainen (1982) compared the performance of black-and-white and color ads placed in

Exhibit 1 Vacation and Pleasure Travel in 1987

Your help is appreciated in completing this survey on vacation and pleasure travel in 1987.

1. Your city of residence: _____ state: _____

2. In 1987, did you (will you) or members of your household travel for vacation or pleasure in or through Alabama, Arkansas, Florida, Georgia, Louisiana, Mississippi, or Texas?

   Yes ( )   No ( )   Not sure ( )

   If yes, which states did you (will you) visit or pass through in 1987? Please check all that apply:

   Alabama ( )   Arkansas ( )   Florida ( )   Georgia ( )

                Louisiana ( )   Mississippi ( )   Texas ( )

3. In 1987, did you or members of your households write for travel-related information to any of the following states? Please check all the states to which you wrote for information:

State	If you did write, to whom did you write?
Alabama	( ) _____
Arkansas	( ) _____
Florida	( ) _____
Georgia	( ) _____
Louisiana	( ) _____
Mississippi	( ) _____
Texas	( ) _____

   Anyone else?   Yes ( )   No ( )   If yes, whom? _____

   If you did write for information on travel in the States mentioned, please check any of the following that apply:

   Please mention source from which you requested the information.

   I did not receive information/material   ( ) _____
   Information received was not helpful   ( ) _____
   Information received was helpful   ( ) _____
   Information received was taken on trip   ( ) _____
   Additional comments about information?   ( ) _____

4. If you did not (will not) travel or pass through one of the following four states (Alabama, Arkansas, Louisiana, or Texas) in 1987, please skip the following question, but mail this questionnaire at your earliest convenience. Thank you for your help.

5. In 1987 how many separate vacation or pleasure trips did (will) you or members of your household take in or through the following states? Please count each day-trip (7 hours or longer away from home) and each overnight as separate trips:

   Number of Trips in 1987

State	0	1	2	3	4	5	6+
Alabama	( )	( )	( )	( )	( )	( )	( )
Arkansas	( )	( )	( )	( )	( )	( )	( )
Louisiana	( )	( )	( )	( )	( )	( )	( )
Texas	( )	( )	( )	( )	( )	( )	( )

6. For your longest trip (in nights away from home) in 1987 in or through Alabama, Arkansas, Louisiana, or Texas, what was (will be) your major destination away from home?

   City/Location:_____State:_____

7. The number of persons in your travel party for this trip:

   Adults: _____   Children under 16 years of age: _____

8. How many nights, if any, did (will you) stay in each of the following states during this trip?

   Number of nights in: Alabama _____ Arkansas _____ Louisiana _____ Texas _____

   If you stayed overnight, in what city/location did you stay in each state?

Alabama   _____

Arkansas   _____

Louisiana   _____

Texas   _____

From the following list, please identify by letter the type of accommodations used, if any, in each state of your 1987 trip:

M = Motel/Hotel

F = Friends/Relatives' Home

S = State Park Campground

C = Commercial/Private Campground

R = Rental House/Cabin

O = Other, please identify:

_____

Alabama   _____

Arkansas   _____

Louisiana   _____

Texas   _____

9. Which of the following best describes your activity in each of the four states in 1987? Please check one activity for each state:

Activity	Alabama	Arkansas	Louisiana	Texas
Did not visit or pass through this state in 1987	( )	( )	( )	( )
Just passing through	( )	( )	( )	( )
Visiting friends/relatives	( )	( )	( )	( )
Attending a sporting event (football, basketball game, etc.)	( )	( )	( )	( )
Attending a festival or special event (tour of homes, State Fair, Pope's visit, museum exhibits, Mardi Gras, etc.)	( )	( )	( )	( )
Beaches	( )	( )	( )	( )
Scenery/natural attractions	( )	( )	( )	( )
Camping	( )	( )	( )	( )
Historical attractions	( )	( )	( )	( )
Business meeting	( )	( )	( )	( )
Convention/conference	( )	( )	( )	( )
Golfing	( )	( )	( )	( )
Fishing/boating	( )	( )	( )	( )
Racetrack (auto, dogs, horse, etc.)	( )	( )	( )	( )
Other _____ (please specify)	( )	( )	( )	( )

If you did travel to one or more of these four states in 1987, please share with us the names of cities, attractions, events, or special activities that you and members of your travel party experienced on this longest trip:

_____

_____

10. If you visited or passed through **Alabama** in 1987, please check your party's total expenditures (including lodging, food, use of car, recreation, gifts, etc.) while in **Alabama**:

$0	( )	$101–$300	( )	$901–$2,000	( )
$1–50	( )	$301–$600	( )	$2,001–$4,000	( )
$51–100	( )	$601–$900	( )	Over $4,000	( )

If you visited or passed through **Arkansas** in 1987, please check your party's total expenditures (including lodging, food, use of car, recreation, gifts, etc.) while in **Arkansas**:

$0	( )	$101–$300	( )	$901–$2,000	( )
$1–50	( )	$301–$600	( )	$2,001–$4,000	( )
$51–100	( )	$601–$900	( )	Over $4,000	( )

If you visited or passed through **Louisiana** in 1987, please check your party's total expenditures (including lodging, food, use of car, recreation, gifts, etc.) while in **Louisiana**:

$0 ( )	$101–$300 ( )	$901–$2,000 ( )
$1–50 ( )	$301–$600 ( )	$2,001–$4,000 ( )
$51–100 ( )	$601–$900 ( )	Over $4,000 ( )

If you visited or passed through **Texas** in 1987, please check your party's total expenditures (including lodging, food, use of car, recreation, gifts, etc.) while in **Texas**:

$0 ( )	$101–$300 ( )	$901–$2,000 ( )
$1–50 ( )	$301–$600 ( )	$2,001–$4,000 ( )
$51–100 ( )	$601–$900 ( )	Over $4,000 ( )

11. How likely/unlikely are you to visit each of the states for a pleasure or vacation trip in 1988?

State	Very Likely	Likely	Not Sure	Unlikely	Very Unlikely
Alabama	( )	( )	( )	( )	( )
Arkansas	( )	( )	( )	( )	( )
Louisiana	( )	( )	( )	( )	( )
Texas	( )	( )	( )	( )	( )

12. If you would like a copy of the summary of the study, please provide your name, address, and complete ZIP Code below:

Name: _____

Address: _____

City _____ State: _____ ZIP Code: _____

Thank you for your help. Please mail in the post-paid envelope.

---

newspapers versus magazines. Although substantially more national, city, and state tourism advertising expenditures are allocated to magazines, newspapers were found to outperform magazines in revenue-generating power. Similar findings and conclusions were reached by Yochum (1985).

Using the questionnaire shown in Exhibit 1, Woodside and Soni (1990) profiled the net destination revenue (and other dependent variables) performances of 10 magazine vehicles, including *Southern Living, National Geographic Traveler, Family Circle,* and *Gourmet,* for one conversion study.

CONCLUSION

Conversion studies, since their introduction, have been developed with respect to controlling factors that may inflate conversion rates estimated to be associated with (read: caused by) the advertising and marketing campaign. The following improvements have been suggested:

1. Using scientific research methods (i.e., true experiments, such as split-run tests) to estimate cause-and-effect relationships between the advertising/marketing campaign and dependent variables, such as number of households visiting caused by the campaign, number of total visits caused by the campaign, expenditures and net revenues for the destina-

tion marketing organization (e.g., state or province) caused by the campaign.

2. Controlling for nonresponse bias by ensuring response rates of 70 percent or better. This can be achieved by following standard methods of increasing response propensity (e.g., Kanuk and Berenson 1975; Heberlein and Baumgartner 1978; Dillman 1978), such as individualizing the letters, providing postage-paid envelopes, providing incentives, and, most importantly, making multiple attempts to convert nonrespondents into respondents.

3. Not identifying the real sponsor (nor the economic impact reason) of the study by using an independent research agency. This avoids unnecessary sensitizing of the respondents and allows for collection of data on competing vacation destinations.

4. Examining the dependent variables for four groups of respondents: Group A, persons not reporting asking (nor receiving) the fulfillment literature requested by them and sent to them; Group B, persons finding the fulfillment literature not to be helpful in their travel planning; Group C, persons finding the fulfillment literature to be helpful; and Group D, persons finding the fulfillment literature to be helpful and taking the materials on their trip(s). The sponsor-bias problem included the fact that the size and travel behavior of Group A cannot be learned if the fact is divulged to the sampled households in the conversion study that they are known to

TABLE 2 Conversion Studies and Their Critical Dimensions

MAIL	TOTAL No. OF INQUIRERS	SAMPLE SIZE[a]	MAILING Second	MAILING Third	RESPONSE RATE[a]	PERCENTAGE OF INQUIRERS WHO VISITED[a]	SPONSOR IDENTIFIED	INDUCE-MENT[b]	DATA COLLECTION ON COMPETITIVE DESTINATION	STATE INVOLVEMENT
Woodside and Reid (1974)	39,502	42%	No	No	28%	53%	Yes	No	Yes	SC
Wettstein (1982)	10,000	5%	No	No	40%	50%	Yes	Yes	No	AZ
Woodside and Motes (1980)	14,075–95,664	14–16%	Yes	No	31–34%	62%	Yes	No	Yes	SC
Woodside and Motes (1981)	682–11,234	8–100%	Yes	Yes	62–65%	47–58%	Yes	Yes	Yes	SC
Woodside and Ronkainen (1982)	4,135–73,831	1–2%	Yes	Yes	74–80%	43–61%[c]	No	Yes	Yes	NC,SC,VA
Hunt and Dalton (1983)	67,000	1%	Yes	No	68%	33%	Yes	No	No	UT
Perdue and Merrion (1991)	62,591	320	No	No	65%	NR	Yes	Yes	No	CO
Pitegoff (1991)	N.R.[f]	6,500	No	No	22%	83%[g]	Yes	No	No	FL
Woodside and Soni (1988)	43,404	2,040	Yes	No	44%	11–47%	No	Yes	Yes	LA

TELEPHONE	TOTAL No. OF INQUIRERS	SAMPLE SIZE[a]	FOLLOW-UP CALLS	RESPONSE RATE[a]	PERCENTAGE OF INQUIRERS WHO VISITED[a]	SPONSOR IDENTIFIED	INDUCEMENT	DATA COLLECTION ON COMPETITIVE DESTINATION	STATE INVOLVEMENT
Ballman et al. (1983)	2,353	31%	Yes	NR[d]	22%	Yes	No	Yes	MN
Hunt and Dalton (1983)	67,000	1%	Yes	66%	23%	Yes	No	Yes	UT
Yochum (1985)	1,830–19,140	3%	NR[e]	77%	19–26%	No	No	NR[f]	Virginia

[a]The range of answers is provided for studies with comparisons (e.g., of one medium against another).
[b]Inducements ranged from posters to promising respondents the results of the completed study.
[c]Percentage given is for total number of visits; the State was the major destination for 21–35% of respondents.
[d]A total of 750 completed interviews.
[e]Given the high response rate, most likely two or more attempts were made to reach sampled households.
[f]Not reported.
[g]Planning to visit FL.

have responded to the advertising/marketing campaign (see Woodside and Soni 1991).

5. Including all relevant costs, not only inquiry-generating costs, that can be directly allocated to the project, such as postage for mailing material to inquirers.

6. Clearly defining the area(s) of vacation, especially in the case of individual locations, to avoid possibility of misinterpretation and subsequent inflation of results.

7. Striving for an accurate estimate of the expenditures incurred by the respondents. Remedial actions include using broad expenditure classification categories.

8. Estimating the impact of the advertising/marketing campaign on both total number of visits as well as number of households visiting the destination, as well as many other dependent variables.

Given the approach's intuitive appeal and relative simplicity of the methodology, conversion studies enjoy widespread popularity. However, if the conversion study is conducted poorly, the results can lead to interpretive errors based on inflated results. Hopefully, DMEs will become converts themselves to the use of scientific versus traditional conversion research studies. If executed as an integral part of an advertising campaign (i.e., planning for a conversion study starts with the planning of a campaign), scientific conversion studies can provide invaluable input in decision making with regard to improving travel destination marketing.

Given the widespread use of conversion research studies to estimate the cause-and-effect impact of tourism advertising/marketing campaigns, two final suggestions are offered. (1) State travel and tourism marketing directors, and their counterparts in Canada and in other countries (as well as city and other regional destination marketing and research managers), need to increase their skills, knowledge, and insights to conversion research methods; and they need to become more questioning and demanding that high-quality, scientific conversion studies are planned and implemented. (2) Adequate conversion research budgets should be planned up front, within the initial advertising/marketing plan; most conversion research studies are likely to have been underfunded for meeting the intended research objectives. Recommended conversion research budgets should be 3 to 7 percent of total direct-media-placement costs for each media vehicle examined in the conversion study.

REFERENCES

Advertising Age (1982), "Alaska Goes after Tourists in a Big Way," 4 (January), 10.

Ballman, Gary, Jim Burke, Uel Blank, and Dick Korte (1983), "Real Conversion Rates of Regional Advertising Programs: Working from Gross to Net Rates," *Proceedings of the 13th Annual Meeting of the TTRA*, 244–245, Salt Lake City, UT: TTRA.

Ballman, Gary, Jim Burke, Uel Blank, and Dick Korte (1984), "Toward Higher Quality Conversion Studies: Refining the Numbers Game," *Journal of Travel Research* 22 (Spring), 28–33.

Banks, Seymour (1965), *Experimentation in Marketing*, New York: McGraw-Hill.

Burke, James F., and Lisa A. Lindbloom (1989), "Strategies for Evaluating Direct Response Tourism Marketing," *Journal of Travel Research* 27 (Fall), 33–38.

Burke, James F., and Richard Gitelson (1990), "Conversion Studies: Assumptions, Applications, Accuracy and Abuse," *Journal of Travel Research* 28 (Winter), 46–51.

Campbell, Donald T., and Julian Stanley (1963), "Experimental and Quasi-Experimental Designs for Research in Teaching," in *Handbook on Research on Teaching*, N. L. Gage, ed., Chicago: Rand-McNally.

Caples, John (1974), *Tested Advertising Methods*, 4th ed., Englewood Cliffs, NJ: Prentice-Hall.

Churchill, Gilbert A. (1983), *Marketing Research*, Hinsdale, IL: The Dryden Press.

Davidson, Thomas Lea, and Warren B. Wiethaupt (1989), "Accountability Marketing Research: An Increasingly Vital Tool for Travel Marketers," *Journal of Travel Research* 26 (Spring), 42–45.

Dillman, Don A. (1978), *Mail and Telephone Surveys: The Total Design Method*, New York: Wiley Interscience.

Erdmann, Ron (1991), "Back to Basics: Accountability of Tourism Market Research," *Tourism: Building Credibility for a Credible Industry, Proceedings of the 22nd Annual Travel and Tourism Research Association Annual Conference*, 433–434, Salt Lake City, UT: Bureau of Economic and Business Research, Graduate School of Business, University of Utah.

Ellerbrock, Michael J. (1981), "Improving Coupon Conversion Studies," *Journal of Travel Research* 19 (Spring), 37–38.

Goeldner, Charles R., and Karen P. Dicke (1981), *Travel Trends in the United States and Canada*, 44–50, Boulder, CO: Business Research Division, University of Colorado.

Heberlein, T.A., and R.A. Baumgartner (1978), "Factors Affecting Response Rates to Mailed Questionnaires: A Quantitative Analysis of the Published Literature," *American Sociological Review* 43 (August), 447–462.

Hunt, John D., and Michael J. Dalton (1983), "Comparing Mail and Telephone for Conducting Coupon Conversion Studies," *Journal of Travel Research* 21 (Winter), 16–18.

Kanuk, Leslie, and Conrad Berenson (1975), "Mail Surveys and Response Rates: A Literature Review," *Journal of Marketing Research* 12 (November), 440–453.

Mak, James, James Moncur, and David Yonamine (1977), "How or How Not to Measure Visitor Expenditures," *Journal of Travel Research* 16 (Summer), 1–4.

Mok, Henry M. K. (1990), "A Quasi-Experimental Measure of the Advertising Effectiveness of Destinational Advertising: Some Evidence from Hawaii," *Journal of Travel Research* 29 (Summer), 30–34.

Muha, S.L. (1976), "Evaluating Travel Advertising: A Survey of Existing Studies," paper presented at the Fifth Annual Educational Seminar for State Travel Officials, Lincoln, Nebraska, October 4, 1976.

Peterson, Robert A. (1982), *Marketing Research*, Plano, TX: Business Publications, Inc.

Perdue, Richard R., and Barry E. Pitegoff (1990), "Methods of Accountability Research for Destination Marketing," *Journal of Travel Research*, 28 (Spring), 45–49.

Perdue, Richard R., and Don Merrion (1991), "Developing Low Cost, But Improved Conversion Methodologies," *Tourism: Building Credibility for a Credible Industry, Proceedings of the 22nd Annual Travel and Tourism Research Association Annual Conference*, 435–440, Salt Lake City, UT: Bureau of Economic and Business Research, Graduate School of Business, University of Utah.

Perdue, Richard R., and Larry D. Gustke (1992), "The Influence of Multiple Trips on Inquiry Conversion Research Results," *Journal of Travel Research* 30 (Spring), 27–30.

Pitegoff, Barry E. (1991), "Accountability Research: Florida Tourism Examples," *Tourism: Building Credibility for a Credible Industry, Proceedings of the 22nd Annual Travel and Tourism Research Association Annual Conference*, 441–444, Salt Lake City, UT: Bureau of Economic and Business Research, Graduate School of Business, University of Utah.

Ronkainen, Ilkka A., and Arch G. Woodside (1987), "Advertising Conversion Studies," in *Travel, Tourism, and Hospitality Research—A Handbook for Managers and Researchers*, J.R. Brent Ritchie and Charles R. Goeldner, eds., 481–488, New York: John Wiley & Sons, Inc.

Siegel, William, and William Ziff-Levine (1990), "Evaluation of Tourism Advertising Campaigns: Conversion vs. Advertising Tracking Studies," *Journal of Travel Research* 28 (Winter), 46–50.

Silberman, Jonathan, and Mark Klock (1986), "An Alternative to Conversion Studies for Measuring the Impact of Travel Ads," *Journal of Travel Research* 24 (Spring), 12–16.

U. S. Travel Data Center (1983), *Survey of State Travel Offices*, Washington, D.C.: U.S. Travel Data Center.

Wettstein, Earl (1982), "Agency's Business Reply Card Survey Elicits 40% Response; Results Valuable," *Marketing News* 15 (22 January), 20.

Woodside, Arch G. (1981), "Measuring the Conversion of Advertising Coupon Inquirers into Visitors," *Journal of Travel Research* 19 (Spring), 38–41.

Woodside, Arch G. (1990), "Measuring Advertising Effectiveness in Destination Marketing Strategies," *Journal of Travel Research* 29 (Fall), 3–8.

Woodside, Arch G., and David M. Reid (1974), "Tourism Profiles versus Audience Profiles: Are Upscale Magazines Really Upscale?" *Journal of Travel Research* 12 (Spring), 17–23.

Woodside, Arch G., and William H. Motes (1980), "Image versus Direct-Response Advertising," *Journal of Advertising Research* 20 (April/May), 31–39.

Woodside, Arch G., and William H. Motes (1981), "Sensitivities of Market Segments to Separate Advertising Strategies," *Journal of Marketing* 45 (Winter), 63–73.

Woodside, Arch G., and Ilkka A. Ronkainen (1982), "Travel Advertising: Newspapers versus Magazines," *Journal of Advertising Research* 22 (June/July), 39–43.

Woodside, Arch G., and Ilkka A. Ronkainen (1983), "How Serious is Non-response Bias in Advertising Conversion Research?" *Journal of Travel Research* 21 (Spring), 34–37.

Woodside, Arch G., and Ilkka A. Ronkainen (1984), "Principles of Pretesting Travel Advertising," *Proceedings of the 14th Annual Meeting of the TTRA*, Salt Lake City, UT: TTRA.

Woodside, Arch G., and Praveen K. Soni (1988), "Assessing the Quality of Advertising Inquirers by Mode of Response," *Journal of Advertising Research* 20 (August), 31–37.

Woodside, Arch G., and Praveen K. Soni (1990), "Performance Analysis of Advertising in Competing Media Vehicles," *Journal of Advertising Research* 30 (February/March), 53–66.

Woodside, Arch G., and Praveen K. Soni (1991), "Direct-Response Advertising Information: Profiling Heavy, Light, and Nonusers," *Journal of Advertising Research* 31 (December), 26–36.

Wynegar, Don (1989), "U.S. Department of Commerce Task Force on Accountability Research," *Journal of Travel Research* 27 (Spring), 41.

Yochum, Gilbert (1985), "The Economics of Travel Advertising Revisited," *Journal of Travel Research* 24 (Fall), 9–12.

48

Evaluating Tourism Advertising Campaigns: Conversion vs. Advertising Tracking Studies[1]

WILLIAM SIEGEL

President
Longwoods International Inc.
Toronto, Ontario

WILLIAM ZIFF-LEVINE

Managing Director
Data Management Counsel Inc.
Radnor, Pennsylvania

This article is the fourth in a series of articles prepared by the U.S. Department of Commerce Task Force to examine the issues of accountability and evaluation in travel research. The chapter compares advertising tracking studies and conversion studies in an effort to measure the effectiveness of tourism advertising.

In the spring of 1988, the U.S. Department of Commerce invited interested professionals to participate in a task force to examine the issues of accountability and evaluation in travel research. Of particular concern was the growing misuse or abuse of research to provide justification to funding bodies for tourism marketing programs, using misleading or inflated statistics.

It should be made clear at the outset that:

1. Justification of marketing budgets is a natural and reasonable requirement of those holding the purse strings, and researchers have a clear-cut role and responsibility in this area.
2. Requests for justification are likely to increase, particularly when marketing budgets are large or increased.
3. Research methodologies will come under increased scrutiny and must reflect high standards of rigor and integrity if research professionals are to maintain credibility with their clients and political masters.

While all aspects of evaluation research are subject to occasional abuse and potential criticism, many task force members pointed to one particular type of research as most likely to mislead users—namely, the conversion study.

Indeed, despite the heavy reliance placed on the conversion study for justification purposes by many destinations, some members of the task force were prepared to adopt the extreme position that this technique be torpedoed and sunk. Others expressed the opinion that the conversion study has its purpose and can be used to evaluate advertising if conducted and analyzed correctly.

Burke has attempted to provide a balanced point of view on the role of the conversion study and its use and abuses in two papers in this series (Burke and Gitelson 1990; Burke

[1]This chapter was originally published in *Journal of Travel Research* 29 (1), 1990. Permission to reprint is gratefully acknowledged.

and Lindblom 1989). He argues that, when appropriate care is taken with regard to study design, analysis, and interpretation, the conversion study can provide useful diagnostic information to the destination marketer and to those who approve marketing budgets. He cautions, however, that the use of conversion studies to provide a "golden number" of payout (return on investment) to justify advertising expenditures is both misleading and misguided.

In order to be able to assess the relative merits of the conversion study as a vehicle for evaluating the effectiveness of tourism advertising campaigns, the industry must have an understanding of how advertising works. Once a model of advertising impact has been agreed upon, it becomes much easier to achieve consensus as to the research paradigms that are required to assess its impacts.

In the following sections, two alternative models of advertising impacts, the conversion model and the advertising tracking model, are outlined and contrasted.

THE CONVERSION MODEL

The conversion model is applied to advertising campaigns with a direct-response component the major goal of which is to generate inquiries, usually via a print coupon or a toll-free number.

Implicit in the conversion model is a "funnel" process (Figure 1)—advertising is assumed to lead the consumer through a series of stages, each of which moves him or her ever closer to the final goal of conversion, that is, visiting the destination as a result of seeing or hearing the advertising. The process is linear and sequential, involving an ever smaller group of consumers as they get closer to final conversion, hence, the funnel analogy.

According to the conversion model, advertising is assumed to work as follows:

1. A subset of target audience is exposed to advertising and can remember seeing or hearing it (*advertising awareness*).
2. Among those aware of advertising, a subset will become spontaneously aware of the destination advertised (*unaided awareness of destination*) as a place to visit.
3. Among those made aware of the destination, a subset will have their image of that destination enhanced by the advertising (*positive image of destination*).
4. The combination of awareness and positive imagery will result in a subset of consumers inquiring about the destination and receiving a fulfillment piece (*inquiry/ fulfillment*).
5. After receiving the fulfillment piece, a further subset of consumers will be interested in visiting the destination in the immediate future (*motivation*).
6. A subset of these will then finally visit the destination during a defined time period (*conversion*).

It should be noted that the funneling process assumes that both advertising and the fulfillment process move the consumer through a series of stages over time. Movement through

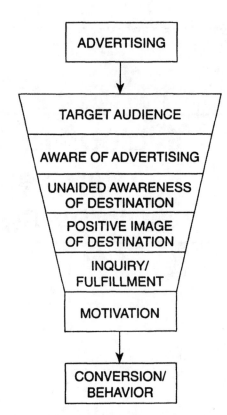

FIGURE 1   The conversion model.

each stage in sequence is necessary before the next stage can be reached. Therefore, inquiry is a necessary step in the selling of a destination and must occur prior to visitation, according to the conversion model.

The conversion model therefore assumes that *all* advertising-driven visitations depend upon the inquiry/fulfillment process.

While the conversion study is a commonly used paradigm for evaluating the effectiveness of tourism advertising campaigns, in the authors' experience, its use is idiosyncratic to the tourism industry and is not typically applied to other product categories.

A possible rationale is that the tourism industry is somehow unique, requiring a customized approach for campaign evaluation. An alternative hypothesis is that tourism advertising works analogously to other product advertising and that many tourism marketers are simply unaware of the standard approaches that have been developed for other industries.

THE ADVERTISING TRACKING MODEL

There is a standard approach for measuring advertising effectiveness that is commonly used by advertisers and their agencies and that cuts generally across product categories— namely, the advertising tracking study. The underlying model for the advertising tracking study is shown in Figure 2.

According to the advertising tracking model, the main

goals of advertising are to: (1) generate advertising awareness among the target audience; (2) generate awareness of the destination as a place to visit, that is, get it on the shopping list of acceptable destinations; (3) create a positive image of the destination versus competition; (4) motivate consumers to travel to that destination in the near future, through (2) and (3) above; and (5) influence travel behavior, by converting those motivated by advertising to actually visit the destination.

Note that, unlike the conversion model, the advertising tracking model shows a dotted line between motivation, the generation of an inquiry, and behavior. This represents the key point that inquiries may or may not have a pivotal determining role to play with regard to the ultimate purchase decision.

In other words, the advertising tracking model assumes that consumers may be converted by advertising solely on the basis of awareness and image-building impacts. The inquiry fulfillment process *may facilitate* conversion, but it is *not a necessary condition* for advertising-driven visitation.

It is proposed that, in general, the advertising tracking model is more realistic than the conversion model for destination advertising. The reasoning is as follows:

1. Inquiries usually represent a small percentage of those visiting a destination.
2. Conversion studies usually show inquirers to be dramatically different demographically and otherwise from the typical visitor to a destination. Often they are repeat visitors, whose main goal is to get detailed planning information for their next visit. Since many are already "converted" when they inquire, the use of *net* conversion statistics is mandatory (see Burke and Gitelson 1990); that is, a valid measure of conversion should include only those people who visited the destination as a result of receiving the fulfillment piece and must exclude those who had already decided to visit the destination before inquiring.
3. Advertising tracking studies typically show that a *much*

larger group of consumers is impacted upon by campaigns than just those who inquire.

Therefore, while a number of biases are inherent in conversion studies that inflate advertising impact (Burke and Gitelson 1990), it is noted that, even with a direct-response campaign, inquirers may be only a small subset of those impacted upon by advertising. Because of this, conversion studies in many cases underestimate the real impact of a campaign.

In summary, the main value of a conversion study would appear to be the ability to get diagnostic information on a fulfillment piece, not to provide hard numbers on the bottom-line return-on-investment of a campaign. Moreover, by placing such major emphasis on inquiries, the conversion model typically downplays the importance of such critical impacts as awareness and image shifts. For all these reasons, it is the authors' belief that the advertising tracking model is a more realistic and comprehensive approach for assessing the full range of advertising impacts than the conversion model.

This is particularly the case when the advertising objectives involve changing the image of a destination (repositioning) or building awareness; for example, when Longwoods International Inc. conducted a major survey of the U.S. market for Tourism Canada in 1985, it was found that Canada suffered from two major problems with regard to its largest external market:

1. A stereotyped image of "moose, mountains, and Mounties," and
2. A lack of familiarity and spontaneous awareness of Canada and its tourism products.

As a result, a major new campaign was developed to position Canada as "The World Next Door," foreign but friendly and close at hand.

The Canadian government uses tracking research on an ongoing basis to assess shifts in awareness and imagery attributable to the new campaign. Beginning in 1986, Tourism Canada has conducted a number of telephone tracking probes in four major U.S. markets. The results have tracked progress on such key measures as:

- Recall of the "World Next Door" slogan
- Advertising awareness
- Likelihood of visiting Canada in the next 2 years, by trip type
- Canada's image on a number of important dimensions

According to Tourism Canada:

> . . . the research does more than simply corroborate that the campaign is well-directed. It also points out where certain elements could work harder or a new emphasis should be considered.
>
> In 1987, new television production was undertaken, and a new composite format adopted when tracking data suggested that even greater play be given to our foreign flavors.
>
> In 1988, the magazine format was similarly ad-

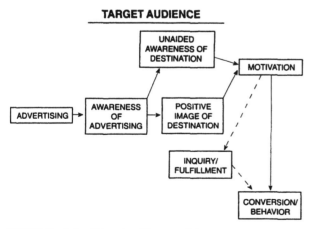

TARGET AUDIENCE

FIGURE 2 Advertising tracking model.

justed, in response to both escalating space costs and research findings.

In the final analysis, tracking only matters if it helps build traffic; if image changes affect attitudes and thus intentions, and these in turn translate to actual trips—"The World Next Door" campaign has had a positive, pronounced and measurable impact on the American traveling public. (Tourism Canada 1989).

THE ADVERTISING TRACKING STUDY

The advertising tracking study typically has the following features:

1. A prewave consisting of interviews with a large, representative sample of respondents within the campaign's target group. This is typically conducted immediately prior to the launch of the campaign.
2. A postwave consisting of the same questionnaire administered to a large, representative sample of respondents drawn from the same sample frame immediately after a major flight of advertising. Normally, in order to prevent sensitization effects attributable to the research, independent samples are drawn for the prewave and postwave probes.

Usually tracking research is conducted by telephone for reasons of cost and timing. When accurate measures of aided campaign recall are required, personal interviews are employed because this technique allows for forced exposure of campaign materials. Mail surveys are generally more economical but are often avoided for tracking studies because of their inability to provide accurate unaided recall measures.

While there is some variation and customization possible within the format of an advertising tracking study, the following represent a set of core measures that are commonly included.

Advertising Awareness

- Unaided (spontaneous mentions)
- Aided (partially or fully cued mentions)

Source of Advertising Awareness

- Mentions by medium, where seen or heard

Brand Awareness

- Destinations of which one is aware (for a particular type of trip)
- Unaided (spontaneous) mentions vs. aided awareness

Message Recall

- What one remembers seeing or hearing in the advertising for a specific destination (open-ended)

Main Point Communication

- The main point or message that the advertising was trying to get across

Campaign Diagnostics

- Overall evaluation/rating of the campaign
- Specific likes and dislikes
- Adjective checklist (interesting, boring, irritating, believable, etc.)

Destination Imagery

- Ratings of destination vs. competition on a battery of image items (typically 15 to 30 scales)

Motivation

- Intention to visit destination (time-frame specified)

Behavior

- Inquiry via coupon or toll-free number as a result of the advertising
- Visit to the destination (time-frame specified)

Demographics

- Age
- Sex
- Education
- Occupation
- Income

ANALYSIS AND INTERPRETATION OF TRACKING STUDIES

Fundamental to the analysis of the tracking study are two types of comparisons: First, there are pre/post differences in advertising awareness, brand awareness, message recall, main-point communication, imagery, motivation, behavior, and diagnostics. Note that a "false alarm" problem with unaided measures makes the prewave benchmark imperative for comparison purposes. However, because other factors besides advertising may have changed between the pre- and postwaves of the tracking study, great care should be undertaken in interpreting any shifts; for example, with foreign destinations, currency changes, changes in government, and catastrophic events (such as terrorism, earthquakes, or hurricanes) can all have much more impact on consumer awareness and perceptions than advertising.

Second, there are differences between those aware versus unaware of advertising on key measures. These differences control for time, unlike pre/post differences. However, biases can creep in if, for example, those predisposed to visit a destination are more attuned to its advertising, leading to self-selection of respondents.

It should be noted that neither pre/post measures or aware/

unaware measures are perfectly clean. When the two sets of measures align and give consistent results, the interpretation can be relatively conclusive and straightforward. When, as is often the case, the results of the two sets of comparisons are not completely consistent, the experience and judgment of the researcher become paramount.

The interpretation function can only properly be served by an experienced researcher assessing *all* the performance measures and coming to conclusions based on an accumulated body of related knowledge. A mere mechanical analysis of numbers will not work.

The following are important points to consider when interpreting tracking data:

• None of the typical measures used in tracking research are perfectly clean; all are subject to uncontrolled influences other than advertising.

• Measures most directly related to advertising itself (awareness, recall) are the most interpretable.

• Changes in brand awareness, attitudes/imagery, knowledge, and purchase intention can be attributed to advertising if: large, significant shifts are obtained; the pattern of results (e.g., pre vs. post/aware vs. unaware of advertising) are consistent; and, since the prewave, no other major changes have occurred in the marketplace that could explain the shifts.

It is more difficult to attribute bottom-line behavioral changes (e.g., visitations, ROI) directly to advertising using a tracking study (or any other form of survey research for that matter). What is being dealt with here are correlational data that can be affected by a number of factors other than advertising; "control" groups are usually not available.

In evaluating the effectiveness of an advertising campaign, a number of issues should be considered, for example, campaign strategy and objectives; media weight; media mix; duration; the category (high vs. low interest); competitive advertising expenditures; and other factors affecting awareness, imagery, intention, and behavior, factors such as major events, currency rates, terrorism, and so on.

Once these factors have been taken into account, the "evaluating" can be done. However, it is only rarely that definitive conclusions can be drawn about the impact of advertising on travel behavior. Instead, tracking research is far more valuable, from a diagnostic perspective, in pinpointing the strengths and weaknesses of a campaign for the fine-tuning of creative development and media buying.

SOME TIPS IN CONDUCTING AN ADVERTISING TRACKING STUDY

The following are some pointers for those considering conducting tracking research:

1. Interview prospective customers—those who are at least potentially in the market for your destination. The advertising agency's definition of the target audience is the best starting point.

2. Keep an accurate record of calls to track incidence levels.
3. A probability sample is desirable, or at least coverage of key markets.
4. Large samples are desirable in order to track changes in key measures.
5. A minimum sample size of 100 to 150 is required for any subsample to be analyzed (e.g., markets, demographic groups, those aware of advertising, etc.) in order to ensure reasonable levels of statistical precision.
6. Independent samples should be conducted for each wave.
7. Postwaves should be conducted as soon as possible after the campaign.

CONCLUSION

The conversion study and the advertising tracking study are both commonly used techniques for evaluating the effectiveness of tourism advertising. Because many tourism campaigns include a direct-response component, the conversion study has tended to gain favor among destination marketers as the paradigm of choice because, taken at face value, it can appear to generate a relatively simple measure of bottom-line impact, namely, return on investment.

Burke and Gitelson (1990) have provided a thorough critique of the conversion study that argues that no magic formula exists for deriving a simple "golden number" from conversion studies.

In this article, the proposition has been put forward that the advertising tracking study is the standard paradigm for evaluating advertising across a wide range of industries. Unfortunately, tracking research also fails to provide the elusive "golden number." The only approach that can accurately allow measuring return on investment is a controlled field experiment.

In the real world, such controls are seldom available, and so short-of-sales measures of advertising impact and directional estimates of behavioral change must usually be lived with.

Given a choice between two imperfect techniques, what then is the authors' recommendation? The answer lies in the marketer's advertising objectives and his or her faith in the models underlying each approach. If the main objective of the campaign is to generate inquiries, and the focus is purely direct response, then the conversion approach has its merits if the cautions advocated by Burke and Gitelson are carefully noted and applied. Again, it is important to note the key assumption of the conversion model that all advertising-driven visitations are the result of the inquiry/fulfillment process, an assumption that many professionals would view as dubious.

If the advertising objectives include the building of awareness or positive imagery for the destination, then the advertising tracking study is the appropriate choice. Furthermore, tracking research assesses the impact of advertising on the entire target group, not just inquirers.

Both the conversion study and the advertising tracking study are better at providing diagnostic measures of advertising effectiveness than a measure of return on investment. However, because of the wider range of key short-of-sales measures typically included in the tracking study, along with its broader definition of the target audience, tracking research deserves consideration as the paradigm of choice for the majority of campaigns.

From a purely marketing perspective, the advertising tracking study has proven its value to advertisers and their agencies over the years. Directionally, the tracking study also can have value in assessing the impact of advertising on bottomline sales.

For the purposes of justification, however, the research community must admit to those who provide funding that definitive answers are seldom available, as much as it would be delighted to be able to provide them.

REFERENCES

Burke, James F., and R. Gitelson (1990), "Conversion Studies: Assumptions, Applications, Accuracy and Abuse," *Journal of Travel Research* 28(3), 46–51.

Burke, James F., and Lisa A. Lindblom (1989), "Strategies for Evaluating Direct Response Tourism Marketing," *Journal of Travel Research* 28(2), 33–37.

Tourism Canada (1989), *Changing Opinions: The Marketing of Canada, The World Next Door*, Ottawa, Canada: Industry, Science and Technology Canada.

49

Methods of Accountability Research for Destination Marketing[1]

RICHARD R. PERDUE
Professor of Marketing
Tourism Management Program
Boulder, Colorado

BARRY E. PITEGOFF
Tourism Research Administrator
Office of Marketing Research
Florida Division of Tourism
Tallahassee, Florida

The purpose of this article is to discuss the types of persuasion tools commonly used in destination marketing and the types of accountability methods that may be suitable for those tools. Tourism persuasion activities are aimed at influencing the consumer at three times: prior to leaving home; while en route to the destination; and after arriving in the destination area. The article shows that a variety of different accountability methods exist depending upon the particular persuasion technique.

This article on marketing research in the travel industry is the fifth in a series of articles written under the auspices of the U.S. Department of Commerce Task Force on Accountability Research and authored by marketing and research professionals in the travel industry in North America. This task force was formed because of widespread concern that inquiry conversion research methodologies are being overemphasized in the evaluation of destination marketing. As discussed in this article, inquiry conversion methodologies are one means of evaluating one specific type of destination marketing, media advertising. Obviously, many other types of destination marketing exist. The goal here is to show that accountability research can play a role across the board in destination marketing, helping to assess the effectiveness of all types of marketing activities.

MARKETING COMMUNICATIONS IN TOURISM

Marketing, as defined by the American Marketing Association, is "the process of planning and executing the conception, pricing, promotion, and distribution of ideas, goods, and services to create exchanges that satisfy individual (consumer) and organizational objectives." Tourism marketing typically involves an array of organizations jointly representing or offering the product, which is the travel experience.

A typical travel experience may involve lodging purchased at several different properties, food purchased from a variety of food services, recreation activities from a variety of attractions, and transportation from several different car-

[1]This article was originally published in the *Journal of Travel Research* 28 (4), 1990. Permission to reprint is gratefully acknowledged.

riers. Due to the complex nature of the travel experience and the difficulty it presents to the consumer seeking information on a destination area, a variety of tourism marketing organizations have been formed. These organizations, hereafter generically termed *destination marketing organizations* (DMOs), include local, regional, and state convention and visitor bureaus; tourism development authorities; and offices of travel and tourism. The role of DMOs is to enhance the efficiency of the transaction between those offering goods and services to travelers and the traveler who desires to possess or to acquire information about those goods and services. For the most part, DMOs have historically focused their activities on marketing communications, the promotion and diffusion of information about the destination area. DMOs also fulfill the primary leadership role in tourism market research. For that reason, this article focuses on the most common promotional activities of DMOs and alternative means of evaluating those activities.

In Exhibit 1, what the authors consider the 10 most common or frequently utilized promotional activities of DMOs are identified. These activities are organized into three general types: (1) those activities aimed at influencing the potential consumer before she/he leaves home, (2) those aimed at influencing the consumer while en route from her/his home to the destination area, and (3) those aimed at influencing the consumer after she/he arrives in the destination area. The following discussion will focus on the evaluation of each of these activities.

OVERALL GUIDELINES FOR ACCOUNTABILITY RESEARCH

It is important, however, to first establish some generic guidelines for accountability research in tourism marketing. Four basic guidelines are suggested. First, and most importantly, *the focus is on change*. The objectives of a marketing plan focus on bringing desirable changes in the target market. These changes may be increased consumer awareness of the destination, improved image, or increased visitation. The fact that 40 percent of a target market, for example, is aware of a destination is relatively unimportant or, at least, tells

very little about the success or failure of a marketing campaign. However, if as a result of the campaign, it can be documented that the percentage of the target-market aware of the destination has increased from 15 to 25 percent, then there exists specific evidence of the change brought about by the campaign. In order to assess change, it is imperative that the marketing research include both before and after measures. Just as marketing is a continuous effort, marketing research is also a continuous effort involving periodic measures of the target.

Second, *market segmentation is an essential component for the evaluation of tourism marketing*. At a minimum, target markets are defined on a geographical basis. Markets are also typically defined on the basis of trip purpose (business vs. pleasure), group type (individual vs. tour group), and predisposition toward travel to that destination. And, finally, for the past several years, a continuing body of research has emphasized the merits of alternative psychographic and life-style segmentation techniques; for example, much of the current services marketing literature emphasizes the merits of "benefit" segmentation, wherein the consumers are grouped on the basis of similarities in the benefits they are seeking from the purchases. If segmentation is utilized, then accountability research necessarily must focus on the changes brought about in the target market, not overall changes.

Third, *measures of success exist other than economic return on investment*. To say that it is myopic to focus on economic return on investment as the measure of success would be an understatement. While the political motivations for accountability research are recognized, it is still essential to broaden the measures of success in tourism advertising, particularly in those campaigns that focus on information dissemination to both potential and actual consumers. The concept of visitor satisfaction, for example, may be a very valuable evaluation measure. Over the past decade, numerous studies have reported the sources of information used by tourists when making their travel decisions. In virtually every case, previous experience and word of mouth from friends and relatives have far and away dominated the response. Working on the premise that trip satisfaction is the key contributor to both return visitors and positive word-of-mouth

EXHIBIT 1 Common DMO Promotional Methods

TIMING OF PROMOTION	PROMOTIONAL TECHNIQUE
At home, prior to trip	Media advertising Familiarization trips Sales blitz and trade mission Travel writer tours Consumer shows Direct mail
While en route to the destination	Interstate welcome centers Outdoor advertising
After arriving at the destination	Visitor centers Media programs Hospitality training

publicity, it is astonishing that so little accountability research has examined the contribution of travel information packets, hospitable employees, and so on, to visitor satisfaction. Given the continuing finding that 60 to 70 percent of the people who request a state travel information packet have already made their trip decision, why has research not been conducted to examine the contribution of that information packet to visitor satisfaction?

The fourth guideline is that *accountability research must be designed to adequately measure the projected change.* The change that occurs as a result of a marketing campaign may be relatively small; for example, a .05 percent increase in market share may reflect a very successful campaign and a very significant improvement in a region's industry. In many cases, however, accountability research is not sensitive to small changes. Consequently, the research does not provide a clear understanding of the campaign's results. Obviously, the measure of success must be sensitive to the level of expected change. However, there is a direct correlation between measurement precision and research costs. During the research design phase, it is imperative to determine the level of precision (accuracy) necessary to adequately evaluate the marketing effort and, then, to design the research accordingly.

In summary, all accountability research should address the following four questions:

1. Is the campaign bringing about the desired change(s)?
2. Is the campaign changing the target market?
3. Is the appropriate measure of change being used?
4. Is the measure of change sufficiently precise to adequately measure the projected campaign results?

Further, efforts to evaluate tourism promotional campaigns need to more effectively examine not only the overall campaign, but also the various aspects of the campaign. Evaluation of a television campaign, for example, needs ideally to include both an overall assessment of the campaign and assessments of different commercial formats and media schedules. Similarly, evaluation of a travel-show booth should consider not only overall effectiveness, but also the effects of different staffing and display formats. Careful experimental design and coordinated promotion and evaluation planning are necessary to accomplish this level of evaluation.

EVALUATING PROMOTIONAL EFFORTS AIMED AT INFLUENCING THE CONSUMER PRIOR TO LEAVING HOME

As previously noted, efforts to influence consumer travel decision prior to leaving home commonly include the promotional techniques of media advertising, familiarization trips, sales blitz and trade missions, travel writer tours, consumer shows, and direct mail. The following briefly describes each of these promotional techniques and then suggests possible accountability and evaluation methods.

MEDIA ADVERTISING

As a general rule of thumb, media advertising in an origin area is conducted with five goals: (1) to increase the target market's awareness of the destination; (2) to improve the destination's image; (3) to encourage new tourists to visit the destination area; (4) to remind previous tourists to return to the area; and/or (5) to inform about changes in the tourism product at the destination. In many cases, media advertising is a two-stage process, with the advertisement encouraging requests for a travel information packet. However, destination advertising varies widely in the extent to which the message directs attention to the availability of the travel information packet.

Inquiry conversion research has been the dominant accountability research tool for evaluating media advertising. In recent years, several authors have criticized inquiry conversion methodologies, primarily on the substantiated argument that most people have already decided to visit the destination area prior to requesting the information packet. While this criticism is valid, it is important to recognize that inquiry conversion research can make a valid contribution to campaign evaluation efforts. As noted earlier, the focus of the evaluation effort is to assess the changes that result from the marketing campaign. If a goal of the campaign is to improve conversion rates, then the conversion study may be the appropriate methodology. If an evaluation determined that conversion rates were low because of high predisposition to visit the destination, then changing the media placement schedules and the targeted segments could improve the resulting conversion rates.

An inquiry conversion study can also be used to determine if the advertising is reaching its target market. Specific media placements are commonly purchased on the basis of user profile information provided by the media salesperson. Whether this profile information is in the form of a print media "readership" study or a television "viewer" study, it is important to test its accuracy. Most profile studies are based on relatively poor survey-research methodologies. In many cases, the survey response rate is in the 20 to 25 percent range, creating the potential for very significant nonresponse bias. Thus, testing the accuracy of the profile information is a potentially important step in determining advertising effectiveness.

Finally, inquiry conversion research can assess the quality of the travel information packet and its contribution to visitor satisfaction. An inquiry conversion study will not, however, address the advertising goals of increasing awareness, improving image, or encouraging visitation. The obvious value of the inquiry conversion study is its relatively low cost and ease of implementation.

A far more accurate means of evaluating media advertising is to conduct before surveys and after surveys in the primary market regions or simulated test markets These surveys allow the DMO to examine awareness, image, visitation, and persuasiveness as a result of the advertising campaign. Similarly, ad recall is a very valuable postcampaign means of evaluating media advertising. While ad recall does not address awareness, image, or visitation, it still provides a means of examining whether the DMO's efforts are being seen and remembered. It is most valuable for examining ad content and media selection.

FAMILIARIZATION TOURS/SALES BLITZES AND TRADE MISSIONS

For the purpose of this article, a *familiarization tour* is defined as a promotional effort wherein intermediary travel buyers (travel agents, corporate booking agents, tour packagers, etc.) are invited on a complimentary tour of the destination area with the purposes of (1) improving their image of the area and, ultimately, (2) increasing their recommendations and bookings of travelers to the area. For the most part, formal evaluations are not conducted of familiarization tours. In many cases, the measure of success has been the number of agents visiting the destination area. Obviously, the number of attendees does not address either of the stated goals. The appropriate measure of success is the number of additional bookings generated by the attendees over some specified time period. Consequently, some method of monitoring the level of bookings by intermediary buyer and some method of qualifying the potential of the invited travel intermediaries are needed. Such monitoring programs typically focus on lodging properties. Specifically, the lodging properties must monitor their number of reservations by type, comparing those that are made directly by the traveler and those made by the intermediary buyer. Changes in the level of intermediary-directed bookings may then be used to assess the effectiveness of the familiarization tour. Obviously, the DMO needs the cooperation of the local lodging properties to effectively evaluate these efforts.

The sales blitz or trade mission also focuses primarily on influencing intermediary buyers of travel services. However, the sales blitz or trade mission involves traveling to the origin area and meeting with the various intermediary buyers at their office or place of work. As with the familiarization tour, the best measure of success from a sales blitz is the number of additional bookings generated.

TRAVEL WRITER TOURS

As with the familiarization tour, the travel writer tour is a promotional effort involving a complimentary tour of the destination area. However, in the travel writer tour, the invited individuals are not direct or intermediary buyers of the destination's product. Rather, they are individuals, typically members of the American Society of Travel Writers, who write travel-related articles for magazines and newspapers. The promotional effort is to encourage publicity about the destination's attractions, events, and facilities. The goals of the writer tour are the same as those of media advertising: to increase awareness, improve image, and encourage visitation to the destination. An additional advantage of the article is the credibility given by the third-party travel writer as opposed to the paid advertisement. On the other hand, a disadvantage of the travel writer tour is that often the destination has little if any assurance if and when a published article will result from the tour.

As with the familiarization tour, there has traditionally been very little effort to formally evaluate travel writer tours. The traditional measure of success is the number of resulting articles, in some cases supplemented by a measure of the size of the audience exposed to those articles. Given the lack of control over the timing, media, and audience of most travel writer articles, it is not feasible to conduct a pre/post measure of success for a travel writer tour. There are, however, possibilities for improving the measure of success. Virtually all travel writer articles include the DMO's phone number under "sources of additional information." It would be relatively easy to instruct the telephone operators to inquire as to where the inquirer got the number of the DMO and to record those that resulted from each article. Of course, this misses those who act on information in the articles without the need to request additional information.

CONSUMER TRAVEL SHOWS

An increasingly popular travel promotional technique, consumer shows involve exhibiting at travel, outdoor recreation, and similar exhibitions in target market regions. Like the sales blitz, consumer shows involve traveling to an origin area and talking directly with potential consumers. In this case, the potential consumers are individual travelers. Due to the nature of individual travel decisions, it is very difficult to evaluate a consumer show. The more innovative techniques that have been observed involve the distribution of coupons for special services or rate reductions at properties in the destination area and the subsequent monitoring of redemption rates for those coupons. To be effective, the coupons must be individualized so that they cannot be given away or traded, and the value from their use should meet or exceed a desired relationship with the investment needed to participate in the consumer show. Obviously, coupon systems also require considerable cooperation from the local property owners.

DIRECT MAIL

Over the past five years, DMOs have become much more active with direct-mail promotion of their attractions and facilities, focusing almost exclusively on tour packagers/operators and meeting managers. To date, very little evaluation of these activities has occurred. Given that tours and meetings are relatively easy to track, the authors are of the opinion that direct-mail promotional activities are best evaluated by monitoring the changes in the number of group bookings in the destination area, while monitoring changes in other potentially significant external variables.

EVALUATING PROMOTIONAL EFFORTS AIMED AT INFLUENCING THE CONSUMER WHILE EN ROUTE TO THE DESTINATION AREA

As previously noted, efforts to influence consumer travel decisions while en route to the destination commonly include use of both interstate welcome centers and outdoor advertising. The following briefly describes each of these promotional techniques and then suggests possible accountability and evaluation research methods.

INTERSTATE WELCOME CENTERS

Next to media advertising, the operation of interstate welcome centers is the second highest promotional expense of most state tourism DMOs. Essentially, the purpose of these centers is to distribute information to visitors as they enter the state with the goals of (1) encouraging them to extend their stay in the state, (2) encouraging them to expand their list of tourism products enjoyed at the destination, and (3) enhancing their satisfaction with their visit to the state. Existing efforts to evaluate the effectiveness of welcome centers have focused on visitor surveys at the time of the visit. The obvious difficulty with these surveys is that the measurement occurs prior to the visit to the state. Thus, while they provide good information on the profiles and characteristics of welcome-center visitors, they cannot provide accurate information on the effects of the welcome-center visit on the respondents' visit to the state.

Florida has been distributing survey cards at its welcome centers with a request of visitors to complete and mail back the card after the Florida stay in exchange for a state pin. While this provides insight into the marginal tourism trip experience related to stopping at the welcome center, it does present a traditional difficulty with the representativeness of the sample returning the survey.

Several authors have argued that the only way to effectively evaluate welcome centers is to compare the behaviors of welcome-center users to nonusers. Although this article's authors do not have any evidence to support their opinion, they feel this is incorrect for two reasons. First, a research design comparing welcome-center users and nonusers assumes they are essentially similar on all other characteristics. No evidence has been seen to support or refute that assumption. Differences in the behaviors of welcome-center users and nonusers can be a function of (1) whether or not they visited a welcome-center and/or (2) other personal and behavioral characteristics. Second, the pragmatic problems of stopping people on interstate highways, particularly the safety of both visitors and surveyors, outweigh the research benefits in almost all cases. While visitor surveys using roadblocks have been conducted in some western states, it is pragmatically not possible in most states due to heavier traffic volumes and the potential liability problems.

One means of evaluating welcome centers would be to include questions on planned length of stay and intended activities in an on-site survey at the time of the welcome-center visit. A follow-up telephone or mail survey could then be conducted to determine actual length of stay. This follow-up survey could also include questions on the attractions visited and the influence of the welcome center on the selection of those attractions. Another possibility would be to interview out-of-state visitors at major attractions, asking them the sources of information involved in their decision to visit the attraction. It would be relatively easy to monitor the changes in the percentage of attraction visitors influenced by the welcome centers.

OUTDOOR ADVERTISING

The primary value of outdoor advertising is its potential to influence impulse decisions to visit various attractions and facilities. Therein lies the most effective means of evaluation. Given the focus on impulse behavior that occurs within a very short time of being exposed to the outdoor advertising, the most effective means of evaluation is to simply cover the signs and/or displays on random dates and monitor the changes in business levels. Additionally, laboratory testing techniques also exist to evaluate outdoor advertising content and persuasiveness in a focus-group-type environment.

EVALUATING PROMOTIONAL EFFORTS AIMED AT INFLUENCING THE CONSUMER AFTER ARRIVING IN THE DESTINATION AREA

As previously noted, efforts to influence consumer travel decision after arriving in the destination area commonly include use of visitor centers, media programs, and hospitality training. The following briefly describes each of these promotional techniques and then suggests possible accountability and evaluation research methods.

VISITOR CENTERS

The primary purpose of visitor centers is to disburse information to visitors and answer their questions about the attractions and facilities in the area. While visitor centers may not immediately influence the level of business at local attractions/facilities, they serve a very valuable role in enhancing visitor satisfaction. Hence, any evaluation of visitor centers should focus on their effectiveness in distributing information. Both the ability to answer questions correctly and the hospitality of the visitor center staff should be included as components of the evaluation. Two general research designs are appropriate. The first and most common is a user survey, essentially asking visitor-center users their impressions of the center and its staff. The problem with this methodology is that it is very difficult to assess the accuracy of the information received by the users. They do not know if the answers they received are correct, only that they received an answer. The second research design involves disguising the researcher as a visitor. The researcher or team of researchers then ask the visitor center staff a series of questions and rate the answers received both in terms of accuracy and hospitality.

MEDIA PROGRAMS

For the purpose of this article, *media programs* are being defined as the television programs produced by many DMOs with the purpose of informing visitors of local attractions and special events. Much like outdoor advertising for the en route traveler, these programs are essentially geared to influencing impulse decisions to visit particular attractions and events. Similarly, the most effective evaluation procedure is to not offer the programs on random dates and monitor the changes, if any, in attraction visitation.

HOSPITALITY TRAINING

The primary purpose of hospitality training is to enhance the quality of service provided to visitors by industry employees. The premise underlying this promotional effort is that visitor satisfaction will improve with better quality service, thereby creating greater return visitation and improved word-of-mouth publicity. As with visitor center staff, it is very difficult to define a short-term correlation between level of hospitality training and level of business. Consequently, the best means of evaluating hospitality training programs is by disguising the research team as visitors. These individuals rate the hospitality staff on a quality of service. As with the visitor center evaluation, this rating involves both the ability to answer questions correctly and the quality of hospitality. Unfortunately, for the research perspective, hospitality staff members are frequently aware that an evaluation of their performance is being conducted. In fact, rewards are commonly offered to those achieving exceptional levels of performance, creating a competition among employees. Thus, the rating process itself influences behavior, resulting in a classical Hawthorne effect.

CONCLUSION

The purpose of this article was to discuss the types of persuasion tools more commonly used in destination marketing and the accountability methods that may be suitable for those tools. In so doing, it should appear evident that a variety of different accountability methods exist and that different methods are appropriate for different types of persuasion. Unlike many of the articles that have been published recently, the authors are not advocating total dismissal of inquiry conversion research methodologies. Rather, the goal is to suggest that a body of accountability methodologies exists, of which inquiry conversion techniques are only one possible approach. As stated by the previous authors in this

series, the appropriate accountability methodology depends upon the objectives of the marketing effort.

The discussion in this article has tended toward being a cookbook of "these are the techniques for these various promotional efforts." It is critical to recognize that the real world of destination marketing requires an integrated accountability assessment plan as a component of the overall marketing plan. In addition to the specific methodologies discussed in this article, the DMO should constantly monitor indicators of its tourism industry. Examples of such indicators may include lodging receipts (particularly in those areas with an accommodations tax), gasoline tax receipts, traffic volumes, out-of-state fishing and hunting licenses sales, state and national park visitation, and so on. Through its research, the DMO should begin to understand the relationship between these industry indicators and the actual level of tourism and, of perhaps more importance, the likely future level of tourism.

REFERENCES

Aaker, D.A., and G.S. Day (1986), *Marketing Research,* 3rd ed., New York: John Wiley & Sons, Inc.

Burke, J.F., and L.A. Lindblom (1989), "Strategies for Evaluating Direct Response Tourism Marketing," *Journal of Travel Research* 28 (2), 33–37.

Blomstrom, R.L., ed. (1983), *Strategic Marketing Planning in the Hospitality Industry,* East Lansing, MI: The Educational Institute of the American Hotel and Motel Association.

Davidson, T.L., and W.B. Wiethaupt (1989), "Accountability Marketing Research: An Increasingly Vital Tool for Travel Marketers," *Journal of Travel Research* 27 (4), 42–44.

Gartrell, R.B. (1988), *Destination Marketing for Convention and Visitor Bureaus,* Dubuque, IA: Kendall Hunt Publishing.

Kotler, P. (1988), *Marketing Management,* 6th ed., Englewood Cliffs, NJ: Prentice Hall, Inc.

Lovelock, C.H. (1984), *Services Marketing,* Englewood Cliffs, NJ: Prentice Hall, Inc.

McIntosh, R.W., and C.R. Goeldner (1986), *Tourism Principles, Practices, Philosophies,* New York: John Wiley & Sons, Inc.

Morrison, A.M. (1989), *Hospitality and Travel Marketing,* Albany, NY: Delmar Publishing.

Ritchie, J.R.B., and C.R. Goeldner, eds. (1987), *Travel, Tourism and Hospitality Research,* New York: John Wiley & Sons, Inc.

Sheth, J.N., and D.E. Garrett, eds. (1986), *Marketing Management: A Comprehensive Reader,* Cincinnati, OH: Southwestern Publishing.

Smith, S.L.J. (1989), *Tourism Analysis: A Handbook,* New York: John Wiley & Sons, Inc.

Tourism Canada (1986), *Tourism Is Your Business: Marketing Management,* Toronto: MacLean Hunter Ltd.

Tull, D.S., and D.I. Hawkins (1987), *Marketing Research: Measurement and Method,* New York: Macmillan Publishing Co.

Witt, S.F., and L. Moutinho, eds. (1989), *Tourism Marketing* *and Management Handbook,* Englewood Cliffs, NJ: Prentice Hall, Inc.

Wynegar, D. (1989), "U.S. Department of Commerce Task Force on Accountability Research," *Journal of Travel Research* 27 (4), 41.

50

Evaluating the Effectiveness of Travel Trade Shows and Other Tourism Sales-Promotion Techniques[1]

ABRAHAM PIZAM
University of Central Florida
Orlando, Florida

This article analyzes the uses of sales-promotion programs in the tourism industry and proposes a number of quantitative and qualitative methods for evaluating their effectiveness. It is based on a study conducted by Dr. Pizam for the Florida Department of Commerce Division of Tourism. Dr. Pizam greatly appreciated the Division's support and sponsorship of the study. Inquiries on the 78-page study can be directed to the Florida Department of Commerce Division of Tourism.

Each year the travel and tourism industry spends billions of dollars on a variety of sales-promotion techniques intended to lure tourists or travel retailers to buy tourism products and services or visit tourist destinations. These techniques include participation in consumer and trade shows, conducting sales blitzes, educational seminars, and familiarization trips, and they are used by both private tourism enterprises and public agencies involved in the promotion of tourism to local, regional, or national destinations. The question, however, is whether the huge sums spent on these sales-promotion techniques produce any serious results and, more importantly, whether these results can be measured at all.

PREVALENCE OF SALES PROMOTION IN THE INDUSTRY

Although quantitative data on the use of sales-promotion techniques by private enterprises in the tourism industry are not publicly available, data do exist on the use of these methods in the public sector. A study conducted in 1985 on

46 state tourism agencies by the Dick Pope, Sr., Institute for Tourism Studies at the University of Central Florida found that an absolute majority of state agencies regularly used a variety of sales-promotion techniques. However, despite the high costs involved in using such techniques, only a minority of state agencies took the trouble to evaluate their effectiveness relative to the costs.

Table 1 lists the methods used by these agencies and the extent of measuring their effectiveness. Of the state travel offices that responded (85% of the population) most have used familiarization trips, and almost all of them participated in trade shows. A large proportion also participated in consumer shows organized by others and conducted their own sales blitzes. The least popular promotional activities were found to be self-organized consumer shows and educational seminars.

However, evaluation measurements were applied mainly to familiarization trips, followed by trade shows and sales blitzes. None of the travel offices measured self-organized consumer shows, and only a few offices measured the effectiveness of their educational seminars. Further examination

[1]This chapter was originally published in the *Journal of Travel Research* 29(1), 1985. Permission to reprint is gratefully acknowledged.

TABLE 1   Types of Promotion Participation and Percentage Using Measurement Methods

	PARTICIPATE		MEASURE	
TYPES OF PROMOTION	N[a]	%	N[a]	%
Trade shows				
Organized by others	43	94%	26	61%
Self-organized	5	11	3	60
Consumer travel shows				
Organized by others	35	76	13	37
Self-organized	3	7	0	0
Sales blitzes	26	57	12	46
Familiarization trips	45	98	30	67
Educational seminars	20	44	5	25

[a]Multiple responses

of the methods used in measuring the effectiveness of the promotion techniques showed that these methods were simple and rudimentary.

As Table 1 shows, 26 agencies used at least one method to measure the effectiveness of trade shows organized by others.

The distribution of methods used for trade shows organized by others is listed in Table 2. Twelve types of methods were mentioned, the most widely used being that of measuring the number of inquiries and leads. This usually involves counting the number of information-request cards at the show. The next most popular methods were counting the number of contacts made at the show and the number of new expanded tours and group bookings that resulted from the show. Only one office reported that it set objectives before participating in a show and measured their attainment afterwards.

As to the types of measurements used in consumer travel

TABLE 2   Methods Used to Measure the Effectiveness of Participation in Trade Shows Organized by Others

TYPES OF METHODS USED	N[a]	%
Amount of literature distributed	1	2.7%
Tracking active bookings	1	2.7
Number of contacts	7	19.0
Inquiries/leads	10	27.0
New/expanded tours	5	13.5
Staff evaluation	2	5.4
Show history	1	2.7
Attendance at show	1	2.7
Number of group bookings	4	10.8
Room-occupancy levels	1	2.7
Surveys	3	8.1
Set objectives	1	2.7
Total	37	100%

[a]Multiple responses

shows organized by others, the data in Table 1 show that 35 state travel offices participated in these shows, and only 13 of these offices used a variety of methods to measure their effectiveness. As shown in Table 3, eight categories of methods were used, the most prevalent being those of counting the number of inquiries or leads received at the show and conducting conversion studies. Conversion studies included responses indicating that surveys were conducted to determine the number of tourists that visited the state and the amount of influence that the consumer show had on their decision making. The next most popular method was determining the amount of literature distributed at the show. Some offices evaluated this further by determining the cost of distribution per brochure. The tracking category referred to sampling welcome centers or state-park reservation centers to determine the number of tourists arriving from the area in which the promotion was held.

Table 4 lists six methods used to measure the effectiveness of sales blitzes. The most widely used method, tracking, was a broad category that included conducting studies on the surrounding area where the promotion was held. It also included efforts to track actual bookings by keeping in close

TABLE 3   Methods of Measurement Used When Participating in Consumer Travel Shows Organized by Others

TYPES OF METHODS USED	N[a]	%
Inquiries/leads	7	26.9%
Attendance at show	2	7.6
Amount of literature distributed	4	15.3
Number of articles published	1	3.8
Tracking	1	3.8
Staff evaluations	3	11.5
Quality contacts	1	3.8
Conversion studies	7	26.9
Total	26	99.6%

[a]Multiple responses

TABLE 4 Methods Used to Measure the Effectiveness of Organizing Sales Blitzes

Types of Methods Used	N[a]	%
Inquiries/leads	1	6.6%
Tracking	4	26.6
Survey (attendees and/or participants)	2	13.3
Number of articles published	4	26.6
New/expanded tours	1	6.6
Number of contacts	3	20.0
Total	15	99.7%

[a]Multiple responses

contact with the suppliers who participated in the sales blitz. The next most popular method was evaluating the number of articles published as a result of the promotion. The remaining four methods were mentioned by only one or two offices with the exception of number of contacts which was mentioned by three offices.

With respect to measuring the effectiveness of familiarization trips, it is worthwhile to note that 45 state travel offices responding to the survey participated in familiarization trips for the travel trade as can be seen in Table 5. Thirty of these offices said they used one or more methods of measurement to determine the effectiveness of these programs. The most widely used method was to evaluate the number of articles published as a result of these trips, followed by continued contact with the suppliers to determine an increase in sales. Next was the number of new and expanded tours, and the remaining four categories were mentioned by only one to three offices.

In conclusion, this study found that the majority of state travel offices participated and used rather rough methods of measuring the effectiveness of familiarization trips and trade shows organized by others. Familiarization trips were frequently measured by the number of articles published as a result of the trip, the creation of new or expanded tours, and surveying attendees.

All offices except one participated in trade shows. How-

TABLE 5 Methods of Measurement Used in Familiarization Trips

Types of Methods Used	N[a]	%
Inquiries/leads	3	7.5%
Cost evaluation of article space	2	5.0
Number of articles published	21	52.5
New/expanded tours	4	10.0
Number of group bookings	1	2.5
Survey (attendees)	2	5.0
Follow-up with suppliers	7	17.5
Total	40	100%

[a]Multiple responses

ever, no consensus seems to exist on how to measure the effectiveness and efficiency of these programs. The types of methods used to measure trade shows were the most diversified. The most widely used method was counting the number of inquiries.

Finally, fewer than half of the state travel offices measured consumer travel shows, sales blitz campaigns, or educational seminars.

PROPOSED METHODS OF MEASURING PROMOTION EFFECTIVENESS

A review of the literature regarding the existing methods used in evaluating the effectiveness of sales-promotion programs in nontourism industries resulted in very little published material (Alles 1973; Barasch 1973; Konikow 1983; Swandby 1982; Trade Show Bureau 1980, 1982). Most of the articles and booklets published in this area were restricted to the evaluation of trade shows. Despite this limitation, it was still possible to apply some of these methods not only to travel trade shows but also to the other types of tourism sales-promotion techniques described earlier.

The remainder of this article is a summary of proposed methods for measuring the effectiveness of sales-promotions. These proposals are based on a review of practices in both tourism and nontourism industries, on observations, and on the author's own opinions. They are by no means restricted to the activities of public state agencies; these methods seem to be valid for any tourism enterprise, private or public, that is engaged in such sales-promotion activities as participation in shows, familiarization trips, sales blitzes, and trade educational seminars.

This part of the article is divided into three sections. Section one enumerates the proposed methods of evaluation for each sales-promotion activity; section two describes these methods and explains their correct uses; and section three makes some general recommendations related to other aspects that influence the effectiveness of sales promotions in the tourism industry.

PROPOSED METHODS OF EVALUATION

Table 6 is a summary of proposed methods of evaluations as applied to the seven most popular promotional activities in the tourism industry. For each of the promotional activities, a combination of no fewer than six methods of evaluation is recommended and in some cases even ten. Sometimes not all of these methods would be possible to administer owing to budgetary and other constraints, but in each activity no fewer than four methods of evaluation should be used. These would be one in each of the categories of objective-setting, preactivity, during activity, and postactivity.

The following describes in detail the methods of evaluating effectiveness that are proposed for each of the seven promotional activities.

TABLE 6 Summary of Proposed Methods of Evaluating the Effectiveness of Tourism Sales-Promotional Activities

METHOD OF EVALUATION	ACTIVITY[1]						
	A	B	C	D	E	F	G
Selection of events/participant	X	X	X	X	X	X	X
Objective-setting	X	X	X	X	X	X	X
Show audits	X		X				
Exhibit efficiency	X	X		X			
Inquiry/leads	X	X	X	X	X	X	X
Competition analysis	X		X				
Staff evaluation	X	X	X	X		X	X
Tracking of leads	X	X		X	X	X	X
Cost per inquiry/participant	X	X	X	X	X		X
Audience survey	X	X	X	X	X		

[1]A = trade shows organized by others
B = self-organized trade shows
C = consumer shows organized by others
D = self-organized consumer shows
E = familiarization trips
F = sales blitzes (i.e., telephone solicitation)
G = educational seminars

Trade Shows Organized by Others

TIMING	METHOD	FREQUENCY
Yearly	Selection of shows	Yearly
Preactivity	1. Objective-setting	Every show
	2. Show audit	Yearly (if data are available from show organizers)
	3. Exhibit efficiency	Every third year (for large shows only)
During activity	1. Inquiry/leads	Every show
	2. Competition analysis	Every show
Postactivity	1. Staff evaluation	End of each show
	2. Tracking of leads	6–9 months after every show
	3. Cost per inquiry	Every show
	4. Audience survey	Every fifth year (for large shows only)

Self-Organized Trade Shows

The following proposals relating to self-organized trade shows apply only to public agencies or enterprises that organize their own trade shows. Industry participants in these shows should use the methods described in the previous section (Trade Shows Organized by Others).

TIMING	METHOD	FREQUENCY
Yearly	Selection of shows	Yearly
Preactivity	1. Objective-setting	Every show
	2. Exhibit efficiency	Every third year (for large shows only)

During activity	Inquiry/leads	Every show
Postactivity	1. Staff evaluation 2. Tracking of leads 3. Cost per inquiry 4. Audience survey	End of each show 6–9 months after every show Every show Every fifth year (for large shows only)

Consumer Travel Shows Organized by Others

TIMING	METHOD	FREQUENCY
Yearly	Selection of shows	Yearly
Preactivity	1. Objective-setting 2. Show audit	Every show Yearly (if data are available from show organizers)
During activity	1. Inquiry/leads 2. Competition analysis	Every show Every show
Postactivity	1. Staff evaluation 2. Cost per inquiry 3. Audience survey	End of each show Every show Every fifth year (for large shows only)

Self-Organized Consumer Travel Shows

The following proposals relating to self-organized consumer travel shows apply only to public agencies or enterprises that organize their own consumer shows. Industry participants in these shows should use the methods described in the previous section (Consumer Travel Shows Organized by Others).

TIMING	METHOD	FREQUENCY
Yearly	Selection of shows	Yearly
Preactivity	1. Objective-setting 2. Exhibit efficiency	Every show Every third year
During activity	Inquiry/leads	Every show
Postactivity	1. Staff evaluation 2. Tracking of leads 3. Cost per inquiry 4. Audience survey	End of each show 6–9 months after every show Every show Every fifth year (for large shows only)

Familiarization Trips

TIMING	METHOD	FREQUENCY
Yearly	Selection of participants	Yearly
Preactivity	Objective-setting	Every trip
During activity	Inquiry/leads	Every trip
Postactivity	1. Tracking of leads 2. Cost per participant	6–9 months after every show Every trip

Sales Blitzes

TIMING	METHOD	FREQUENCY
Yearly	Selection of location	Yearly
Preactivity	Objective-setting	Every blitz
During activity	Inquiry/leads	Every blitz
Postactivity	1. Tracking of leads 2. Staff evaluation	6–9 months after every blitz Every blitz

Educational Seminars

TIMING	METHOD	FREQUENCY
Yearly	Selection of locations and participants	Yearly
Preactivity	Objective-setting	Every seminar
During activity	Inquiry/leads	Every seminar
Postactivity	1. Staff evaluation 2. Tracking of leads 3. Cost per participant	Every seminar 6–9 months after every seminar Every seminar

DESCRIPTION OF EVALUATION METHODS

Selection of Events

Each year, both private and public tourism enterprises face the difficult task of deciding in which promotional activities to participate. This decision is often made on gut feelings or biased opinions when a systematic and quantifiable method is preferable. The following quantitative method is a modification of a technique proposed by Alles (1973).

Step 1. Define a set of marketing objectives for participation, and assign a relative weight of importance of 1 to 5 (where 1 = little importance and 5 = high importance) to each objective. In the case of trade shows organized by others, for example, the following five marketing objectives (coded as M1, M2, etc.) might be assigned these appropriate weights:

M1: Contacts with new travel agents and tour operators—5
M2: Marketing of new products—4
M3: Increase awareness of destination/firm—5
M4: Renew contacts with previous clients—3
M5: Preserve destination/firm image—5

Step 2. List all the events that will take place in the next 12 months. The following four trade shows (coded as E1, E2, etc.) illustrate how this method can be used:

E1: Travel Market Place
E2: ARTA Trade Show
E3: MITA Trade Show
E4: ASTA Central Region

Step 3. Give each of shows E1 to E4 an "impact rate" based on the extent to which it fulfills each of the marketing objectives by assigning a number of 1 to 3 (where 1 = low and 3 = high). In the hypothetical example, this will take the following form:

OBJECTIVE	IMPACT OF SHOW			
	E1	E2	E3	E4
M1	3	2	2	3
M2	3	3	2	1
M3	2	2	2	2
M4	3	2	3	2
M5	3	3	1	3

Step 4. Multiply each of the weights of the marketing objectives (from Step 1) by the impact rates (from Step 3), and compute totals for each show. In the hypothetical example, this will take the form shown in Table 7.

Step 5. List a group of qualitative criteria that events ought to have, and rate the extent to which they exist in each show by assigning a number from 1 to 5 (where 1 = low and 5 = high). Then compute the totals for each show. In this hypothetical example, the following qualitative criteria, coded Q1, Q2, and Q3, would be computed as follows:

CRITERION	RATING			
	E1	E2	E3	E4
Q1: Visitor quality	5	4	3	3
Q2: Show quality (aesthetic, size, etc.)	4	3	4	1
Q3: Geographic sphere of influence	5	4	1	1
TOTAL	14	11	8	5

TABLE 7   Step 4 of Hypothetical Example

Objective	Weight	Impact Rate x Weights			
		E1	E2	E3	E4
M1	5	3 x 5 = 15	2 x 5 = 10	2 x 5 = 10	3 x 5 = 15
M2	4	3 x 4 = 12	3 x 4 = 12	2 x 4 = 8	1 x 4 = 4
M3	5	2 x 5 = 10	2 x 5 = 10	2 x 5 = 10	2 x 5 = 10
M4	3	3 x 3 = 9	2 x 3 = 6	3 x 3 = 9	2 x 3 = 6
M5	5	3 x 5 = 15	3 x 5 = 15	1 x 5 = 5	3 x 5 = 15
	Totals	61	53	42	50

Step 6. Add the total points from Step 4 to the points from Step 5. In the hypothetical example, the final ratings of the four shows will be as shown in Table 8.

The shows with the highest number of points will be selected. Reliability required the method to be conducted separately by several persons and the results averaged.

Objective Setting

The first step in developing any promotional plan is to set objectives. Without objectives, effectiveness cannot be measured. All objectives have to be specific, clearly defined, and, above all, quantifiable.

Because of the differential nature of the promotional activities in which a tourism enterprise is involved, universally applicable objectives cannot be set. Therefore, it would be necessary to determine separate objectives for each activity or event that is being planned. The following are a few examples of possible objectives for trade shows:

- To increase awareness of the destination or product by 10 percent
- To contact 70 percent of the potential audience
- To make 50 follow-up appointments
- To distribute 1,000 brochures
- To increase by 5 percent the number of wholesalers or tour operators representing the product

Experience shows that the more specific the goals of an event are, the more effective the sales personnel will be. They will know exactly what is expected of them and will spend their time more efficiently by concentrating their efforts on the target market specified.

The objectives also dictate the measurement methods needed to evaluate effectiveness. If, for example, a show's main objective is to increase awareness about a product or a product feature, two audience surveys would be needed. The

TABLE 8   Final Ratings of Four Shows

Trade Shows	Code	Total Points
Travel Market Place	E1	14 + 61 = 75
ARTA Trade Show	E2	11 + 53 = 64
MITA Trade Show	E3	8 + 42 = 50
ASTA Central Region	E4	5 + 50 = 55

first would be taken as visitors enter the show, to verify the base percentage of awareness. The second survey would be taken as visitors exit the show, to measure any change in awareness. The surveys of both entering and exiting visitors would include the same set of questions, with one exception: exiting viewers would also be asked a question that would indicate whether they have seen the relevant exhibit.

On the other hand, if a show's main objective is to generate a specific number of editorial articles, its success would be measured after the exhibit, by monitoring trade journals to gauge the amount of press coverage resulting from the show.

Other examples applicable to familiarization trips, educational seminars, or sales blitzes are:

- To receive 10 editorial coverages from the trade press in the next 12 months
- To increase business from travel agents participating in familiarization trips by 10 percent
- To book five new conferences in a given sales blitz

Show Audits

Show audits contain information on past attendance and characteristics of the audience. The audits normally are prepared by an independent professional organization at the request of the show organizers. This information is sent to all prospective exhibitors and is used as an input to the show-selection process.

Since the practice of preparing such audits is not yet fully acceptable in travel trade shows, it is recommended that whenever possible, the participating tourist enterprises require that such data be made available to them. If a large group of exhibitors got together and insisted that such data be made available to them, the organizers of the travel trade shows could be "convinced" to adopt this practice, which is widely available in nontourism trade shows.

Exhibit Efficiency

An exhibitor's *exhibit efficiency* is defined as "the percentage of the potential audience that receives person-to-person contact at the exhibit." *Potential audience* is defined as "the percentage of the audience with a high interest in seeing an exhibitor's products."

Obviously, to compute exhibit efficiency, one needs to

know the potential audience. To arrive at this information, an audience survey needs to be taken (a description of audience surveys appears later). When such surveys are not available, it is recommended that the potential audience be estimated— from discussions with a variety of exhibitors at travel trade shows, the author estimates a range of between 40 and 60 percent.

The efficiency level of a show has to be determined as an objective in advance and measured appropriately. If a show has a total attendance of 2,000 visitors and the potential audience is 50 percent, for example, then the total number of visitors with high interest in the exhibitor's products is 1,000. If an efficiency level of 70 percent is set in advance as an objective, the booth attendants will have to contact 700 visitors (presumably of the 1,000 in the high-interest group). To eliminate any possible miscounting, an objective method of documenting the counts (such as the one described in the next paragraph) should be employed.

Inquiries and Leads

The most prevalent system of inquiry or leads used in travel trade shows is collecting business cards for follow-up. If each card is qualified according to some predetermined scheme when it is received, this system can be very helpful. There are many ways to qualify a contact. If special inquiry cards are designed for exhibiting, the firm can decide what information it wants. Some exhibitors, for example, put on the front of the inquiry card the name, title, and address of the contact, leaving the back of this card for any necessary notes. It is possible to develop a shorthand coding system that identifies type of contact and indicates what type of follow-up is necessary. A contact may require a sales call, a phone call, special literature, or investigation of a complaint.

Many exhibitors have found that even separating the cards according to immediacy of follow-up helps delineate the quality of contacts made. Some exhibitors put their cards into one of three boxes, according to the urgency of follow-up. One box is for contacts requiring immediate response; the second box includes contacts requiring follow-up within two weeks; and the third box is for such typical follow-up as inclusion on the mailing list.

In smaller and less crowded shows, it is possible to have special inquiry cards printed and ask the visitors to fill them out. Under no circumstances should business cards be directly deposited in a basket by the visitors.

Competition Analysis

While the show is in progress, the exhibit staff should take a tour of the premises to analyze the competition. This analysis should be recorded on a simple one-page questionnaire listing the competitor's name, location, products, exposition theme, aesthetic aspects, staff behavior, and the like. These analyses should be carefully reviewed by management on a periodic basis, and the conclusions drawn from them should be incorporated in future promotional plans.

Staff Evaluation

Immediately following a show, the exhibit staff should have a debriefing meeting for the purpose of formally evaluating the show. The evaluation can be conducted by completing a simple form that lists subjective information on the quality of contacts, functional and aesthetic attributes of the exhibit and the show, and the overall quality and success of the show.

Tracking of Leads

Most private exhibitors participating in travel trade shows and sales blitzes track their newly established leads on a regular basis for the purpose of making sales. However, public exhibitors usually do not. Public exhibitors such as state tourism offices, tourism development corporations, convention and visitor bureaus, chambers of commerce, and so on, are not involved in direct sales and, therefore, are not able to track potential customers.

Since most private exhibitors maintain accurate records of sales, public exhibitors must collect from the private exhibitors the sales data relevant to the shows in which they participated. The data can be collected through a questionnaire sent about six to nine months after the show to all the state (or national) participants in a given show. The sales data to be reported should include such items as estimated volume of sales generated by the show and estimated value of new business.

Cost per Inquiry

Cost per inquiry can be calculated by dividing the direct costs of exhibiting by the number of visitors who were contacted at the exhibit. Items to be included in direct costs include:

- Cost of show
- Shipping/freight
- Phone
- Building the exhibit
- Literature
- Models (if used)
- Set-up personnel (if hired)
- Hospitality suite, food and beverages, and entertainment for VIP customers
- Incidentals

If audience surveys are conducted, then cost per inquiry should be substituted with cost per visitor reached (CVR), which is a more accurate measure of effectiveness. CVR is a three-year average, calculated by dividing the direct costs of exhibiting by the number of visitors who stopped to talk to a salesperson or acquire literature, remembered doing so 8 to 10 weeks after the show, and indicated an interest in the exhibitor's products. Suppose, for example, that the total direct cost of a show is $15,000 and 500 attendees were reached. Then the CVR would be $30 ($15,000/500). A three-year average is taken in order to eliminate misleading fluctuations that occur in annual computation.

A high CVR does not necessarily mean that the expenditure in the show should be reduced. Instead of spending less, it may be more advantageous to improve efficiency by adding one or two additional booth personnel in order to increase the number of visitor contacts. This would require a very small increase in exhibit cost but would result in a lower CVR because the exhibit efficiency would be increased. A high exhibit efficiency means a high percentage of the potential audience is being contacted. Therefore, if a large number of prospects are being contacted, but the CVR is still high, then this indicates the expenditures are excessive. In this case, an examination of the expenditures is required to identify the problem, correct the situation, and lower the CVR. This is not an easy task because a high CVR may be the result of a combination of factors.

Audience Survey

Audience surveys are intended to measure the increase in visitors' awareness and interest resulting from visiting an exhibit. These surveys are conducted in two phases: (1) before entering the show and (2) a few weeks after visitation. In a majority of cases, these surveys are conducted by independent organizations who are commissioned by several exhibitors to conduct a cooperative study. Audience surveys are necessary elements for determining exhibit efficiency and CVR.

OTHER FACTORS AFFECTING EFFECTIVENESS

To increase the effectiveness of participation in promotional events and to boost attendance, participants should employ a variety of preshow promotion techniques. Some suggested techniques include:

- Stuffer or sticker on mail
- Quantity direct mailing
- Promotion in routine correspondence (e.g., "See you at Berlin ITB" rubber stamp)
- Mailing invitations with exhibitors' names and booth numbers
- News releases to trade and industry publications
- Advertising in a show's city

Employee performance standards are also essential, and all exhibitors that regularly participate at travel shows should establish a set of trade-show-performance standards for their employees. These standards, which should be written and well publicized, should cover such issues as work assignments, hours of operation, breaks, grooming and dress code, and improper behavior (smoking, eating, talking, etc.), as well as any other issues of concern. Finally, the physical and aesthetic aspects of the exhibit should be addressed in order to increase the impact of the exhibit on the visitors. These aspects include location, size, furniture, decor, general theme, and anything else that might be emphasized.

CONCLUSION

Using the methods outlined in this article can provide a more complete and objective assessment of a given sales-promotion effort than usually results after an effort is finished. Fundamental to any assessment is the setting of clear and measurable objectives, which can then be evaluated for the degree to which they were reached in any given promotion. Weighting the factors that apply to the objectives lends a degree of objectivity to the assessment and allows comparison of the effectiveness of various efforts. Since sales promotion requires sizable dollar investments, applying a measure of effectiveness can result in more objective and economically justifiable expenditures.

REFERENCES

Alles, Alfred (1973), *Exhibitions Universal Marketing Tools*, New York: John Wiley & Sons, Inc.

Dick Pope, Sr., Institute of Tourism Studies (1985), "Measuring the Effectiveness of Tourism Sales-Promotions," Orlando: University of Central Florida.

Barasch, Kenneth L. (1973), *Marketing Problem Solver*, 8–41, Fullerton, CA: Cochrane Chase.

Konikow, Robert B. (1983), *How to Participate Profitably in Trade Shows*, Chicago, IL: Dartnell.

Swandby, Richard K. (1982), " Selecting Space . . . How Much and Where," *Exhibitor, 1, 4.*

Trade Show Bureau (1980), "Study Number 6, How Shows Influence Sales," New Canaan, CT: Trade Show Bureau.

Trade Show Bureau (1982), "Study Number 13, How to Boost Your Exhibit's Prospect Appeal," New Canaan, CT: Trade Show Bureau.

Trade Show Bureau (1983), "Study Number 19, The Exhibitors. Their Trade Show Practice," New Canaan, CT: Trade Show Bureau.

51

Guidelines for the Study of International Tourism Demand Using Regression Analysis

GEOFFREY I. CROUCH
Associate Professor
Tourism and Hospitality Management
The University of Calgary
Calgary, Alberta

The pattern of international tourism flows is quite distinct. The determinants of this pattern, however, are not as clear. As evidenced by the large number of empirical studies over the last three decades, a knowledge of these determinants is of considerable interest to the industry and governments. Regression analysis is a particularly useful tool in this endeavor.

The purpose of this chapter is to provide some guidelines for the application of regression analysis to the study of international tourism demand. There are numerous books and other sources that explain the general application of regression analysis, so this chapter does not seek to repeat such information. Rather, the chapter focuses on the problems of applying regression analysis to the phenomenon of international tourism. In this regard, it draws heavily from the experience of previous studies.

UNDERSTANDING THE DEMAND FOR INTERNATIONAL TOURISM

THE NEED

International travel and tourism has grown rapidly since the end of the Second World War. Total worldwide international tourism receipts now total over US$250 billion. The battle for a share of this market has become highly competitive. An understanding of international tourism demand is, therefore, of considerable importance.

As a commercial and economic activity, international tourism has been attracting increasing attention (Edgell 1990:19). Balance-of-payments issues, forecasting and strategic planning of the tourism industry, resource allocation, and the marketing programs of national tourist offices hinge on an appreciation of factors influencing the demand for international tourism. Other concerns include demands on infrastructure, future needs of transportation carriers, accommodation requirements, and demands on suppliers to the tourist industry.

THE USE

Understanding the determinants of demand, particularly those that can be controlled or influenced by governments and tourism enterprises (such as promotion, exchange rates, air fares, and the price and quality of tourist services), will be critical in this competitive environment.

Almost all managerial decisions, whether directly or indirectly, explicitly or implicitly, somewhere along the line depend somehow on demand expectations. The decision may vary from a short-term concern, such as how to stimulate demand during the off-peak seasonal trough, to a long-term concern, such as the type of building controls necessary in a resort area to meet demand and facilitate growth of the tourism industry whilst preserving the intrinsic qualities of the region. The problem of demand is ubiquitous.

THE SUITABILITY OF REGRESSION ANALYSIS

The development of an understanding of the demand for international tourism could be approached in a variety of ways. Fundamentally, the choice is between descriptive research or experimental research. Descriptive research would include literature searches of other demand studies, focus groups of tourists, case analyses, surveys, and longitudinal or cross-sectional studies of observed tourist behavior. On the other hand, experimental research, which tests certain hypotheses in such a way that the effects can be observed objectively and distinguished from the influence of other variables, might be employed to draw stronger conclusions. The study of demand at the micro- (i.e., individual or household) or macro- (i.e., national) level provides a further research dimension.

In the context of international tourism, descriptive research is favored since experimental research is highly problematic, particularly at the macrolevel. Statistical data on tourism at the macrolevel is also normally readily available. Hence, descriptive studies at the macrolevel have been popular. Although other analytical techniques could be employed, regression analysis generally provides the most suitable, rigorous method for the estimation of the relationship between several variables (i.e., determinants) and a single dependent variable (i.e., a measure of demand).

PREVIOUS APPLICATIONS

A review of previous empirical studies that have attempted to estimate the relationship between the demand for international tourism and its determinants (Table 1) demonstrates the dominance of regression analysis techniques. Ordinary least-squares multivariable regression analysis has been the most widely used approach. Witt and Martin (1989:12, 13) discuss some of its principal advantages and disadvantages. Morely (1991:40) notes that is is unlikely "that the widespread use of multiple regression for estimating tourism-demand functions will diminish, given its widely perceived advantages over other ways of forecasting demand." The use of regression analysis is not, however, without its critics (e.g., Summary 1987:317; Uysal 1983:51).

The majority of studies have applied regression analysis to the estimation of parameters in single-equation models. A small number of studies, however, have examined the application of simultaneous equations. Bakkalsalihoglu (1987:4) argued that such an approach is theoretically more flexible. Fujii, Khaled, and Mak (1985:161) noted that single-equation models are inefficient in their use of information and are deficient in their analysis of crossprice elasticities. They argued for the application of a systems approach favoring the application of the Almost Ideal Demand System (AIDS) of Deaton and Muelbauer (1980) over the Linear Expenditure System (LES) of Stone (1954). On the other hand, users, of single-equation models generally justify their decision on the basis that, with regard to the modeling of international tourism demand, the explanatory variables can be assumed to be predetermined; that is, the analyst can ignore the problem of simultaneity of supply and demand because supply is largely perfectly elastic since the demand by foreigners for tourism services is usually small compared to the demand by nationals.

The results of the previous studies vary considerably. However, many of the hypothesized determinants of international tourist flows have been found to be significant under a variety of conditions. However, the magnitude of the influence of each variable appears to vary considerably as a function of both the substantive and methodological characteristics of each study.

CHOOSING A REGRESSION TECHNIQUE

REGRESSION METHODS

Regression modeling has been generally of three types. Econometric models have focused on the analysis of the impact of economic influences on demand. Gravity models adopt a geographic perspective with an emphasis on mass (i.e., population) and distance considerations. Trip generation models are more of a hybrid between the other two types. The three types, however, differ more in their origin than in their method, with gravity models being expressed in a more rigid form (Archer 1980:8; Anastasopoulos 1984:63).

Ordinary least-squares (OLS) regression offers the most straight-forward application. For this reason, most previous empirical studies have adopted this method. However, a number of potential problems may arise in its application. The most serious problem in studies of international tourism demand relates to the incidence of multicollinearity. Multicollinearity occurs when two or more independent variables are significantly correlated. The effect is to make it difficult to isolate the separate effect of each of the independent variables on the dependent variable, and spurious results are possible. This problem has been commonly handled by omitting certain independent variables. The risk, however, is that biased results may occur. Ridge regression (e.g., Fujii and Mak 1981; Uysal 1983) and constrained or Bayesian regression (Straszheim 1969) offer alternative solutions to the multicollinearity problem.

A further problem occurs when adjacent error terms are found to be serially correlated (as evidenced by the Durbin-Watson statistic). In these circumstances, one of the assumptions underlying the OLS method is violated. The Chochrane-Orcutt method can then be applied on these occasions.

Other analysts (e.g., Kanafani 1983; Mak, Moncur, and Yonamine 1977; Askari 1973) have also advocated the use of two-stage least-squares regression in situations when the simultaneity problem, discussed earlier, is evident.

The best approach, in general, is to start by using OLS regression. The data and results should then be checked to see whether any of the OLS assumptions are violated and the results are plausible. Other regression methods might then be tried if any problems are identified.

TABLE 1   Methodologies of Previous Studies

Study	1	2	3	4	5	6	7	8	9	10	11	12	13	14	15	16	17*
Anastasopoulos 1984		*															
Anastasopoulos 1989a		*															
Artus 1970		*															
Artus 1972		*															
Askari 1973	*									*							
A.T.R.I., Australia 1988	*																
Barry and O'Hagan 1972	*																
Bechdolt 1973	*																
Blackwell 1970	*	*															
Bond 1979		*															
Bond and Ladman 1972	*																
B.T.C.E., Australia 1988	*	*													*		
Chadee et al. 1987	*																
Cigliano 1980	*																
Clarke 1978	*																
Cline 1975		*															
Crampon and Tan 1973	*																
Crouch 1992a	*																
Diamond 1977	*																
Edwards 1976	*																
Edwards 1979	*																
Edwards 1985	*																
Edwards 1987														*			
Fujii and Mak 1981	*						*	*									
Gerakis 1965			*														
Gray 1966		*															
Gray 1970		*															
Guthrie 1961	*																
Haitovsky et al. 1987														*			
Hanlon 1976	*																
Hiemstra 1991	*																
Hollander 1982		*															
I.A.C., Australia 1989a		*															
Jud 1971	*																
Jud 1974	*																
Jud and Joseph 1974[1]		*															
Kanellakis 1975	*																
Kliman 1981	*																
Kwack 1972	*																
Laber 1969		*															
Lin and Sun 1983		*				*											
Little 1980		*															
Loeb 1982		*	*														
Mak et al. 1977						*											
Martin and Witt 1987		*	*														
Martin and Witt 1988		*	*														
Moncur 1978	*																
Moshirian 1989	*	*															
Mutti and Murai 1977		*															
Noval 1975		*															
O'Hagan and Harrison 1984a																	*
O'Hagan and Harrison 1984b																	*
Oliver 1971	*																
Papadopoulos 1985	*	*															
Paraskevopoulos 1977		*															
Poole 1988			*														
Quayson and Var 1982	*																
Rojwannasin 1982	*																

TABLE 1 *(continued)*

STUDY	1	2	3	4	5	6	7	8	9	10	11	12	13	14	15	16	17*
Rugg 1971	*																
Rugg 1973	*																
Schulmeister 1979	*																
Smeral 1988	*				*												
Smith and Toms 1978		*															
Straszheim 1969	*												*	*			
Straszheim 1978		*															
Stronge and Redman 1982	*																
Summary 1987	*					*											
Sunday 1978	*																
Tremblay 1989	*																
Truett and Truett 1982	*																
Truett and Truett 1987	*																
Uysal 1983	*	*															
Uysal and Crompton 1984	*	*															
Uysal and O'Leary 1986											*						
Var et al. 1990	*																
White 1985				*													
White and Walker 1982								*									
Witt 1980a	*																
Witt 1980b	*																
Witt and Martin 1987a	*	*															
Number of studies:	67	14	1	1	1	3	1	1	1	1	1	1	1	1	1	2	1
Percentage of studies:	84	18	1	1	1	4	1	1	1	1	1	1	1	1	1	3	1

[1]See also Krause et al. (1973)

*LEGEND:
1. Ordinary least-squares multiple regression
2. Multiple regression using the Cochrane-Orcutt procedure
3. Quasi-experimental static group comparison (ex post facto design)
4. Almost Ideal Demand System (AIDS) of demand equations solved by maximum likelihood estimation
5. Ordinary least-squares multiple regression using residuals
6. Two-stage least-squares estimation
7. Generalized least-squares estimation
8. Ridge regression
9. Regression with a first-order autocorrelation correction procedure using the SHAZAM computer program
10. Maximum likelihood estimation using the Hildruth-Lu transformation for serial correlation correction
11. Canonical correlation analysis
12. Constrained regression
13. Bayesian regression
14. Variance component modeling of pooled data
15. Ad hoc procedure involving fitting an S-curve to market share and relative price data by regression analysis where the two variables are expressed in percent annual change to derive elasticities
16. Version of AIDS system of demand equations solved using Zellner's generalized least-squares method for seemingly unrelated regressions
17. Single-equation estimation using Zellner's seemingly unrelated regressions

TIME-SERIES STUDIES

Individual researchers or organizations interested in studying the demand for international tourism frequently do so from the perspective of a particular country or region. Typically, travel from a single origin country to single destination country has been modeled using data in the form of a time series. On occasions, aggregate inbound (outbound) travel from (to) either the rest of the world or specific regions of the world has also been modeled.

Time-series studies estimate the relationship between demand and its hypothesized determinants by comparing the variation in demand over time with the variation in the presumed determinants over time. The principle advantage of the time-series approach is that it enables the modeling of trends (Armstrong 1972:118), and the results are suited to forecasting purposes if it is reasonable to assume that the estimated structural relationship between the variables is likely to remain largely unchanged over the forecast period. The time-series approach also explicitly recognizes that the structural relationship is likely to vary as a function of origin and destination countries involved.

Time-series studies, however, suffer from five important limitations. First, sample sizes are often severely limited by the period of available data. As a consequence, the number of explanatory variables that may be studied can be quite restricted. Second, there are reasons to believe that the structural relationships change over time. Hence, the estimated demand coefficients reflect averages over the time period studies. Third, certain demand determinants (such as the effect of population and cultural differences) are largely irrelevant in time-series studies as they do not usually change significantly over time. Fourth, the problem of multicollinearity is more prevalent since independent variables often covary in time. Last, serial correlation of the error term is common in time-series studies.

CROSS-SECTIONAL STUDIES

Partly in response to the limitations of time-series studies, a number of researchers have examined the pattern of demand cross-sectionally. This approach involves the estimation of relationships by comparing the variation in demand from country to country with the variation in the presumed determinants from country to country. Because a potentially large number of origin-destination pairs is available, the regression analysis does not suffer, to the same extent, from limited data. A larger set of independent variables can, therefore, be investigated. Although time trends cannot be investigated and results are less useful for forecasting purposes, cross-sectional analysis can be used to investigate different types of factors. Hanlon (1976:48) has noted that "the parameters of cross-sectional models generally reflect a different kind of behavior than that which is examined in time-series analyses. Basically, the main difference is that cross-section parameters measure long-term adjustments, whereas time-series relationships are affected by short-term fluctuations. In many cases, this may mean that time-series estimates of demand elasticities are smaller than cross-section estimates."

The problem of multicollinearity is also likely to be reduced as independent variables are less likely to covary across countries. Also, the fact that the variation in the independent variables is likely to be much greater across countries than over time enhances the analysis in terms of its ability to estimate relationships. The problem of serial correlation, too, disappears since there is no sequential pattern in cross-sectional data.

The main problem with most cross-sectional studies is that they assume that the structural relationships are constant across origin and destination countries. This is often not a reasonable assumption since, for example, origin countries may differ in their sensitivity to prices. The use of dummy variables to account for the effect of origin and/or destination countries provides a means around this limitation.

ANALYSIS OF POOLED DATA

Time-series and cross-sectional studies, therefore, each possess certain advantages and disadvantages. In order to miti-gate the limitations of either approach, a small number of researchers have recommended the use of pooled data (i.e., a combination of time-series and cross-sectional data). Tremblay (1989), for example, used pooled data to study the demand for international tourism in Western Europe. Country dummy variables were used to allow both the regression intercepts and slopes to vary. It has been argued, however, that pooling might violate the assumption of equal-error variances assumed by regression analysis (Uysal 1983:9; Clarke 1978:9).

MODEL FORM

ADDITIVE (LINEAR) FORM

Selecting an appropriate form for the regression model is also an important decision. One approach is to specify demand as an additive (linear) function of the independent variables as follows:

$$D = \beta_0 + \beta_1\beta_1 + \beta_2\beta_2 + \ldots + \beta_n\beta_n + \varepsilon \qquad (1)$$

where D = demand
β_0 = regression constant (intercept)
$\beta_1, \ldots, \beta_n$ = regression coefficients (slopes)
$V_1, \ldots, V_n$ = independent variables
ε = error term

The parameters of principal interest are the regression coefficients. The value of the regression coefficients estimated for the additive model form depends upon the units of measurement for the dependent and independent variables.

The elasticity of demand, with respect to each of the independent variables, can be calculated by multiplying the respective value of B by the average value of the independent variable and dividing by the average value of the dependent (demand) variable. Hence, the implied elasticities of demand resulting from the additive (linear) model vary as a function of the level of the dependent and independent variables.

MULTIPLICATIVE (LOG-LINEAR) FORM

In this situation, demand is specified as a multiplicative function of the independent variables, as follows:

$$D = \gamma_0 \cdot V_1{}^{\beta_1'} \cdot V_2{}^{\beta_2'} \ldots V_n{}^{\beta_n'} \cdot \varepsilon' \qquad (2)$$

Taking logarithms of both sides of the equation yields:

$$\log D = \log\gamma_0 + \log V^{\beta_1'} + \log V^{\beta_2'} + \ldots + \log V^{\beta_n'} + \log\varepsilon'$$

$$(3)$$

$$= \beta_0 + \beta_1' \log V_1 + \beta_2' \log V_2 + \ldots + \beta_n' \log V_n + \varepsilon'$$

Equation 3 is linear in the logarithms. As such, the parameters can be estimated again using linear regression. The advantage of the multiplicative form is that the resulting estimated regression coefficients provide an explicit estimate of the demand elasticities. Kanafani (1983:245) and Bakkalsalihoglu (1987:93) point out, however, that the constant elasticity structure of the multiplicative functional form can produce absurd results in forecasting when the independent variables are extended well beyond their original range. As long as the regression results are not misapplied, then, the multiplicative form has some practical advantages over the additive form.

Leaving aside the issue of which functional form is more useful, among the past studies of international tourism demand there appears to be almost universal agreement that the multiplicative form is superior to the additive form. Those studies that have attempted to fit both model forms to the data almost invariably find the multiplicative form to be preferable based on the proportion of the variance in the dependent variable explained by the model. The two models, however, will not necessarily estimate the same value of the demand elasticity. Assmus, Farley, and Lehmann (1984:67) note that "for elasticities near unity, the constant elasticity estimate [from log-linear models] and the average computed elasticity [from linear models] may not differ, though individual values will differ for all but one point. For values of elasticities substantially less than unity . . . the additive [linear] model is likely to produce a higher average elasticity than the multiplicative [log-linear] model."

OTHER FORMS

Previous studies have, at times, tried other ad hoc forms. Most other forms are not particularly useful either because they generally do not perform as well in terms of fit or because the parameter values have no direct meaning.

Edwards (1976, 1979, 1985), however, estimated demand elasticities by modeling, in linear form, percentage changes in the dependent and independent variables.

TESTING AND SELECTION

Apart from the possibility of testing the performance of different functional forms, most of the regression analysis will involve the testing of potentially significant independent (explanatory) variables. The analyst should avoid the temptation of going on a "fishing expedition." Doing so increases one's chances of finding statistically significant relationships that arise purely by chance rather than by there being any sort of causal relationship.

The selection of the most suitable model should be a subjective judgment based on the following considerations:

1. The amount of variance explained by the model
2. The statistical significance of the parameters, both individually and as a set
3. The plausibility of parameter magnitudes and signs
4. The extent of multicollinearity and serial correlation
5. The testing of the assumptions of linearity and homogeniety of variance, and the independence of error
6. The purpose for which the results are to be used

SELECTING AND DEFINING VARIABLES

THE RESEARCH OBJECTIVE

The study must begin with a clear understanding of the research objectives so that the regression-model specification matches the analyst's needs. The decision will influence the type of regression technique to be used, the form the model will take, and the variables and their definition to be included in the model. A national tourist office wishing to evaluate, for example, the effectiveness of its promotional activities in certain origin markets will likely find a time-series approach, with promotional spending expressed in terms that adjust for variations in exchange rates and inflation over time, to be useful. On the other hand, if the purpose of the study is to understand how destination promotion impacts on the global distribution of international tourism, a cross-sectional study might be more appropriate with the promotional expenditure of each country expressed in terms of a common currency. The use of dummy variables may be necessary to model supply constraints where the number of hotel rooms may limit the volume of inbound tourism. A clear understanding of the research problem to be addressed, and how the results are to be used, must be achieved before the regression model can be specified.

A WIDE SELECTION OF POTENTIAL VARIABLES

The dependent variable, *demand*, is normally defined in economic studies as the **quantity** of the product purchased. In the study of international tourism, however, it is difficult to measure quantity in the usual way. This can be illustrated as follows:

$$\text{Total Tourist Expenditure} = \text{number of tourists} \times \text{average length of stay} \times \text{average daily expenditure}$$

$$\text{Total Tourist Nights} = \text{number of tourists} \times \text{average length of stay}$$

In the study of tourism, "the dependent variable is an aggregate of several separate activities definable in money terms and not a quantity as in the conventional way of estimating such coefficients" (Kanellakis 1975:17). Hence, the matter of selecting an appropriate measure of demand is problematic. It is further compounded by the fact that tourism demand in real money terms represents both an amount of expenditure as well as the quality of consumption (Smeral 1988:40).

Most previous studies have relied upon data on the number of tourist arrivals/departures as this is often the only type of demand data available. Approximately half of all studies have investigated demand in terms of expenditures/receipts. The number of tourist-nights and the average length of stay have also been studied in a few cases.

Demand measured in real-money terms is preferable, but reliable data is often not available (Anastasopoulos 1984:97;

O'Hagan and Harrison 1984a:921). Data on tourist numbers is generally more reliable (Barry and O'Hagan 1972:147) but is likely to be less responsive to determinants as tourists are able to alter both their length of stay or daily expenditure as they adjust to changing circumstances. Hence, demand measured in terms of tourist numbers is likely, in general, to be less elastic (Noval 1975:161; Uysal 1983:76, 95; Economist Intelligence Unit 1975:34). Paraskevopoulos (1977:31) suggested that the night-stay is the basic commodity purchased by tourists. Such a measure is superior to tourist numbers as it accounts for changes in the average length of stay but does not allow for changes in average daily expenditure.

A further consideration in the selection of an appropriate dependent variable concerns the intended use of the results. Mak et al. (1977:5) point out that transportation carries, for example, are primarily interested in tourist numbers. Lodging establishments, on the other hand, have a particular interest in the length of stay. Merchants are interested in the level of spending by tourists, and governments are interested in all measures of demand.

With regard to the independent or explanatory variables, the number of potential-demand determinants is very large indeed (Keintz 1968:59). Selection of appropriate variables will depend on a number of factors, including whether a time-series or cross-sectional study is to be attempted, the countries to be examined, the time period to be investigated, and the type of tourism involved (e.g., business travel, "sunlust" or "wanderlust" pleasure travel, travel for the purpose of visiting friends and relatives, etc.).

Mikulicz (1983:8) has isolated three groups of independent variables. These include factors that determine *market volume* (e.g., population, income, leisure time, education, occupation, etc.), the *cost of travel* (e.g., travel cost, distance, and time; the cost of tourist services, including the impact of inflation and exchange rates), and *utility image* (such as tourist appeal, publicity, information, weather, language, ancestry, etc.).

Vanhove (1980:2) defined four mutually exclusive groups of explanatory variables: The *market element* represents factors determining the overall number of trips; the *destination element* includes attributes of the destination itself that would attract or deter tourists; the *location element* defines the geographic relationship between the destination and the market; and the *ties element* includes factors that represent business, cultural, and other links between countries.

Six classes of variables were defined by Noval (1975:141), namely *tendency to generate* travel, *tendency to receive/ attract* travel, *impediments* to travel, *interaction* between pairs of countries, *interdependence* factors (e.g., the influence of third countries), and *stochastic* disturbances.

Measures of income (employed in 89 percent of studies), the price of tourist goods and services (70 percent), the cost of transportation (58 percent), and exchange rates (33 percent) dominate the research history. This reflects the fact that the majority of studies have adopted an econometric approach to the phenomenon. A little more than half of all studies (54 percent) have included dummy variables to ac-

count for various disturbances that might have biased the estimated parameters had they been ignored. Typically, such disturbances include political factors (e.g., political unrest, terrorism), various travel restrictions (e.g., limits on foreign spending), special events (e.g., Olympic Games, Expo), and other transitory disturbances that are difficult to quantify. A number of the time-series studies (54 percent of studies) also included a trend term in order to account for changing travel tastes and to deal with multicollinearity, particularly between the decrease in the real cost of air transportation, the increase in real incomes, and the increasing propensity to travel over the study period.

Other independent variables of particular interest have included measures of marketing effort, population, ethnic attraction/cultural ties, and distances/travel time. Some studies in particular have specifically focused on the impact of marketing effort in terms of total promotional spending, advertising spending, or other spending by national governments designed to facilitate development of their own tourism industries. Travel distance is also an interesting factor as distance can both deter and attract tourists (Mayo and Jarvis 1986; Beaman 1974; Smith 1983).

Variables that have been the object of minor interest include measures of weather/climate (Mieczkowski 1985), supply factors (Stroombergen, Jackson, and Miller 1991; Summary 1987; Truett and Truett 1982), the introduction of direct flights (Fujii, Im, and Mak 1989), trade/business links, tourist appeal, barriers to travel, demographic factors, and the extent of previous visitation. A number of studies have also considered the temporal aspect of causal relationships by introducing lagged variables into the regression equations. Income, prices, exchange rates, transportation costs, and marketing expenditure have each been examined in this way. Anticipatory effects (e.g., anticipation of future income) has also been evaluated by specifying lead variables in the model. Other similar attempts have included moving averages, quadratic lag structures, and the definition of "permanent" income. Habit/persistence has been investigated by introducing a lag in the dependent variable as an explanatory variable for the next time period. This approach also allows for the explicit evaluation of short- and long-term demand elasticities.

VARIABLE DEFINITIONS

A further important consideration associated with the selection of independent variables concerns their definition. There are a multitude of ways in which factors such as income, price, travel costs, and so on, could be defined. Should they be represented in real or nominal terms? Should they be expressed in per capita terms or should population be included as a separate explanatory variable? Would an absolute or relative price definition be more effective? If price is to be defined in relative terms, to what should it be related—prices in the origin country, prices in alternative destinations, or some other alternative? How should changes in exchange rates be modeled? Would it be best to adjust prices for changes in exchange rates, or do tourists respond differently to exchange-rate changes than they do to price changes?

An examination of the past research reveals a wide variety of decisions on these issues. There appears to be more disagreement than consensus. Income definitions, for example, have varied as a function of the income measure used (e.g., total income, disposable income, permanent income, consumption expenditure, various production indexes, etc.), and whether it was deflated by changes in population (i.e., expressed in per capita terms). Percentage changes in discretionary income are greater than corresponding changes in total income. Hence, estimated discretionary income elasticities of demand should be lower. Increases in per capita income will be lower than corresponding increases in total national income. Per capita elasticities should, therefore, be higher.

STATISTICAL CONSIDERATIONS

Modeling constraints, particularly with regard to considerations of sufficient degrees of freedom, multicollinearity, and reliability of data, have usually governed the selection of independent variables. Paraskevopoulos (1977:23) noted that, in applied econometric work, efficiency of estimation is not always compatible with the inclusion of all relevant variables. Kanafani (1983:246) argued that about 10 degrees of freedom are required in travel-demand research after the number of independent variables has been chosen. It is likely that many analysts would suggest that a much higher figure is desirable.

Numerous studies have recognized that estimated demand coefficients might be biased if relevant explanatory variables are omitted from demand models (e.g., Allen, Stevens, and Barrett 1981; Horowitz 1981; Jung and Fujii 1976; Paraskevopoulos 1977; Tellis 1988; Assmus et al. 1984; Morley 1991). "The size of the bias in the estimated coefficient of a particular explanatory variable included in the equation is given by the product of two regression coefficients: (1) the coefficient of the omitted variable, and (2) the auxiliary regression coefficient of that particular explanatory variable in the regression equation of the omitted variable on all the included explanatory variables (auxiliary regression equation)" (Paraskevopoulos 1977:48).

As previously noted, there are numerous alternatives available for defining each of the respective explanatory variables (Hollander 1982:3). It is, therefore, likely that the estimated demand coefficients will vary depending on the particular definition in each study. A particularly important issue concerns the fact that, in many instances, explanatory variables are expressed as a composite of several factors. Price, for example, was typically expressed in relative terms as a ratio between destination and origin prices. Correlations between ratios do not permit unambiguous inferences about the variables from which the results are formed (McCuen 1974). In a small number of cases, transportation prices were added to the price of tourism services in the destination country. The resulting estimated demand elasticities, therefore, represent an average sensitivity to both transportation and tourism

service prices (Paraskevopoulos 1977:27). Allen et al. (1981) point out that the combining of collinear variables to reduce the extent of multicollinearity reduces precision. Considerable care is, therefore, required in interpreting elasticities depending on the definition used (Kanafani 1983:247; White and Walker 1982:41).

LOCATING DATA

DEMAND

Depending on the nature of the intended study, several data sources are available that publish information on international tourism flows. For the analyst interested in studying travel to or from one particular country, the most useful source is likely to be the relevant travel-data-collecting institutions in that country. Typically these institutions include the national social and economic statistical office as well as a national organization set up to guide the development and promotion of the tourism industry in that country. Sometimes, a separate institution has been created, as an arm of the government and or industry, to collect tourism data that augments that collected by the national statistical office.

When the study is to investigate demand across several or many countries it will generally be more convenient to turn to the publications of one or more of the international agencies such as the World Tourism Organization (a United Nations affiliate based in Madrid), the Organization for Economic Cooperation and Development (located in Paris), and the Pacific Asia Travel Association (headquartered in San Francisco). Each of these bodies produces an annual publication of international tourism statistics covering its area of interest.

Other useful information on demand may be found in the *World Travel and Tourism Review* (published by CAB International, Wallingford, UK), *The Big Picture* (published by Child and Waters Inc., New York), and the *Travel & Leisure's World Travel Overview* (published by the American Express Publishing Company).

DEMAND DETERMINANTS

Gathering data on the potential detriments of demand is usually a much more difficult task than gathering demand data. The fact that there exists a potentially large number of determinants is only part of the story. Some of the more frequently cited international sources of data are listed in Table 2. Apart from these sources, other sources, too numerous to list here, have been cited among the previous demand studies. Most other sources, however, concern national institutions. However, some authors have managed to track down some more obscure data sources on a variety of factors that they have found to be useful; such as, Pick's *Currency Yearbook Black Market Rates*, *Transnational Terrorism: A Chronology of Events*, UN's *Cost of Living of United Nations Personnel in Selected Cities as Reflected by Indices of Retail Prices*, and *A System of International Comparisons of Gross Product and Purchasing Power* (Kravis, Kennessay,

TABLE 2   International Data Sources—Demand Determinants

International Monetary Fund (IMF) Balance of Payments Yearbook
IMF International Financial Statistics
IMF Annual Reports on Exchange Restrictions
United Nations (UN) Yearbook of National Account Statistics
UN Statistical Yearbook
UN Demographic Yearbook
UN Yearbook of International Trade Statistics
Organization for Economic Cooperation and Development (OECD) Economic Indicators
OECD National Account Statistics
OECD Consumer Price Indices Special Issue
Official Airline Guide
ABC World Airways Guide
International Air Transport Association (IATA) World Air Transport Statistics
IATA Annual Report
IATA Agreeing Rates and Fares
IATA Tabulation of Great Circle Distances
International Civil Aviation Organization (ICAO) Statistical Yearbook
ICAO Digest of Statistics
Official Steamship Guide
ABC Shipping Guide
UNESCO Statistical Yearbook
World Handbook of Political and Social Indicators
European Airlines Research Bureau
International Labor Office, Holidays with Pay

Heston, Summers 1975). Data of a general economic nature, such as incomes, prices, exchange rates, and so on, can normally be obtained without too much difficulty. However, data on climate, promotional expenditure, tourist attractions, tourist infrastructure and supply, and so on, is normally very difficult to obtain, and only the intrepid typically venture that far. Most people presume that data on the cost of air transportation should be easy to obtain and compile. However, many analysts have given up on this variable, too, upon finding that no convenient, comprehensive source of information exists and what does exist is patchy and complicated by the vast array of airfare types in existence. But, for the those who have staying power, proxy measures for each of the principal factors can usually be constructed somehow.

INTERPRETING RESULTS

RELIABILITY

A healthy dose of realism is always called for when interpreting the results of empirical studies, and, in this respect, it is important to point out that data on international tourism demand is far from perfect. Inaccuracies and the inability to compare data result when countries use different definitions and methodologies for gathering international tourism data. Some countries collect data only at airports, for example, while other countries collect statistics only from international visitors staying in hotels. Also, some countries use sample surveys, while other countries survey all international visitors. Definitions tend to vary between countries as well, and many do not differentiate between visitors, excursionists, and tourists.

White and Walker (1987:37) examined many of the problems that occur in trying to collect information on international travel. They concluded that "often the quality of the data is low. In fact, it is likely that some countries are not able to tell whether they have a surplus of deficit on travel accounts."

Inconsistencies in international trade statistics have long been observed. Parniczky (as reported by White and Walker) noted that world imports surprisingly exceed world exports by 3 percent to 5 percent. Measured imports by country A from country B rarely equal measured exports by country B to country A. Apart from smuggling and losses, the difference is due to a number of factors, including tariffs, exchange conversions, transport costs, different definitions, and so on. Estimation error is also an important source of error. The largest inconsistencies in travel statistics occur in the estimation of expenditure and receipts. The inconsistencies tend to be greatest between neighboring countries due to the large amount of traffic and smuggling. White and Walker found reported receipts and expenditures in international tourism to differ by as much as 100 percent or more.

ASSOCIATION AND CAUSE-EFFECT

It is common to refer to regression analysis as a causal technique as it implies a causal relationship between the dependent variable (demand) and the set of independent variables. However, unless the data analyzed has been obtained through experimental manipulation and control, a cause-effect relationship cannot be proven. Rather, it is more correct to say that the variation in demand *is associated with* variations in certain factors. Hence, as experimentation in international tourism is not practical, regression analysis measures only *association* and not *causation*. The regression analysis results should, therefore, be treated as *prima facie* evidence of a cause-effect relationship and not as *conclusive proof*. Consider estimated marketing elasticities, for example. It is reasonable to infer that a positive relationship found between marketing and inbound-tourism demand represents the effect of marketing on demand if the variation in marketing expenditure over the period of study is independent of the variation in inbound tourism. It is quite possible that this is not entirely the case. Many economic, marketing, and political considerations probably influence marketing expenditure, and one input to the decision-making process is probably the historical pattern of inbound tourism. Hence, a positive relationship probably represents, to a degree, both the effect of marketing on inbound tourism as well as the effect of inbound tourism on marketing expenditure.

SOURCES OF BIAS

Estimated demand coefficients depend not only upon the data used in their estimation, but also upon the way in which the regression model is specified. As noted earlier under **Selecting and Defining Variables**, the independent variables included in, and omitted from, the model, as well as their definition, are likely to have an effect on the estimated coefficient. Hence, considerable care is required in the interpretation of the results. Consider, for example, the situation of estimated price elasticities of demand. Suppose one study uses the total number of tourist-nights as the measure of demand. As the price of tourism in the destination increases, normally one would expect the total number of tourist-nights to decline as tourists switch to less expensive destination. The effect on tourist receipts, however, assuming average daily expenditure remains unchanged, will depend on the price elasticity of demand. If the price elasticity of demand is unity, the effect on total tourist receipts will remain unchanged as the decline in the number of tourist nights would be equal and opposite the increase in price per night. If, however, demand had been measured in terms of total receipts, a price elasticity of zero in this situation would be approximately equivalent to a price elasticity of unity in the previous situation.

MATCHING RESULTS WITH EXPECTATIONS

It is generally argued that an estimated regression model should, in part, be evaluated by comparing the sign and magnitude of the estimated demand coefficients with theoretical expectations; for example, one would expect income elasticity to be positive and exceed unity to the extent that international tourism is a luxury. Some analysts have dropped variables from a model where results and expectations do not match. However, considerable caution is necessary if this practice is to be adopted; for example, it is theoretically possible for income elasticity to take a negative sign. It can also be shown that price elasticities can be positive or negative as a function of (1) the particular price definition employed, (2) the degree to which alternative destination(s)

compete with or complement the destination under consideration, and (3) the circumstances causing a variation in the relative price ratio that would determine the relative magnitudes of the substitution and income effects (Crouch 1992b).

CHECKING ASSUMPTIONS

The decision to use linear multiple regression analysis involves the acceptance of certain underlying assumptions, as follows:

1. *Linearity:* The variable relationships are linear.
2. *Equality of Variance:* The error components of the model have equal variance.
3. *Independence of Error:* The error components of the model are uncorrelated.
4. *Normality:* The error components of the model are normally distributed.

It is surprising how few regression studies appear to check whether these assumptions turn out to be valid.

STATISTICAL INDICATORS

Regression analysis provides a number of statistical indicators that assess the quality of the model. In summary, the most important indicators include:

1. *T-statistic* or *standard error* of the regression coefficient, which indicates whether an independent variable is statistically significant
2. *F-statistic*, which indicates whether the set of independent variables, as a whole, are statistically significant
3. The *coefficient of determination* adjusted for the number of degrees of freedom, which indicates the proportion of variation in the dependent variable explained by the model (Most studies on international tourism have generally found values above 0.8.)
4. The *tolerance* of each independent variable, which indicates the extent to which multicollinearity is a problem
5. The *Durbin-Watson statistic*, which indicates the extent of serial correlation
6. A *scatterplot of residuals* to search for violation of underlying assumptions

It may also be appropriate to fit the model to a subset of the data and apply the model to the balance of data as an independent test of its performance. If the model performs satisfactorily, the parameters may then be estimated for the data set as a whole.

CONCLUSION

Regression analysis is a very useful tool for the study of international tourism demand. It is a technique of which many people have some knowledge, and, for this reason, it receives widespread use. However, a little knowledge can be a bad thing. It can be a very easy tool to use, which hides the fact that there are numerous pitfalls in its application. It behooves all users to fully understand the method so that these pitfalls can be avoided and the results interpreted and used correctly.

REFERENCES

Allen, P. Geoffrey, Thomas H. Stevens, and Scott A. Barett (1981), "The Effects of Variable Omission in the Travel Cost Technique," *Land Economics* 57 (2), 173–180.

Anastasopoulos, Petros G. E. (1984), *Interdependencies in International Travel: The Role of Relative Prices. A Case Study of the Mediterranean Region*, Ph.D. dissertation, New School for Social Research, New York.

Anastasopoulos, Petros G. E. (1989a), "Italy's Importance in the Development of Tourism in the Mediterranean, "*Annals of Tourism Research* 16 (4), 570–574.

Anastasopoulos, Petros G. E. (1989b), "The U.S. Travel Account: The Impact of Fluctuations of the U.S. Dollar," *Hospitality Education and Research Journal* 13 (3), 469–481.

Archer, Brian H. (1980), "Forecasting Demand—Quantitative and Intuitive Techniques," *International Journal of Tourism Management* 1 (1), 5–12.

Armstrong, C. W. G. (1972), "International Tourism: Coming or Going, the Methodological Problems of Forecasting," *Futures* 4 (2), 115–125.

Artus, Jacques R. (1970), "The Effect of Revaluation on the Foreign Travel Balance of Germany," *International Monetary Fund Staff Papers* 17, 602–619.

Artus, Jacques R. (1972), "An Econometric Analysis of International Travel," *International Monetary Fund Staff Papers* 19 (3), 579–614.

Askari, Gholam Hossein (1973), "Demand for Travel to Europe by American Citizens," *Economia Internazionale* 26 (May), 305–317.

Assmus, Gert, John U. Farley, and Donald Lehmann (1984), "How Advertising Affects Sales: A Meta-Analysis of Econometric Results," *Journal of Marketing Research* 21 (1), 65–74.

Australian Tourism Research Institute (1988), "Potential Tourism Demand in Australia: A Review of the Lessons of History," published as attachment 2 to *Submission to Industries Assistance Commission Inquiry into Travel and Tourism*, Australian Tourism Industry Association.

Bakkalsalihoglu, I. (1987), *Analysis of Demand for International Tourism in Northern Mediterranean Countries*, Ph.D. dissertation, Northern Illinois University.

Barry, Kevin, and John O'Hagan (1972), "An Econometric Study of British Tourist Expenditure in Ireland," *Economic and Social Review* 3 (2), 143–161.

Beaman, Jay (1974), "Distance and the 'Reaction' to Distance as a Function of Distance," *Journal of Leisure Research* 6 (3), 220–231.

Bechdolt, Burley V. (1973), "Cross-Sectional Travel Demand Functions: U.S. Visitors to Hawaii 1961–1970," *Quarterly Review of Economics and Business* 13 (4), 37–47.

Blackwell, John (1970), "Tourist Traffic and the Demand for Accommodation: Some Projections," *Economic and Social Review* 1 (3), 323–343.

Bond, Marian E. (1979), "The World Trade Model: Invisibles," *International Monetary Fund Staff Papers* 26, 257–333.

Bond, Marian E., and Jerry R. Ladman (1972), "International Tourism and Economic Development: A Special Case for Latin America," *Mississippi Valley Journal of Business and Economics* 8 (Fall), 43–55.

Bureau of Transport and Communications Economics (1988), *Trends and Prospects for Australian International Air Transport*, Bureau of Transport and Communications Economics, Occasional Paper No. 88, Canberra.

Chadee, D., and Z. Mieczkowski (1987), "An Empirical Analysis of the Effects of the Exchange Rate on Canadian Tourism," *Journal of Travel Research* 26, (1), 13–17.

Cigliano, J. M. (1980), "Price and Income Elasticities for Airline Travel: The North Atlantic Market," *Business Economics* 15 (4), 17–21.

Clarke, Carl D. (1978), *An Analysis of the Determinants of Demand for Tourism in Barbados*, Ph.D. dissertation, Fordham University.

Cline, Roger S. (1975), "Measuring Travel Volumes and Itineraries and Forecasting Future Travel Growth to Individual Pacific Destinations," in *Management Science Applications to Leisure Time Operations*, 134–145, New York: North Holland.

Crampon, L. J., and K. T. Tan (1973), "A Model of Tourism Flow into the Pacific," *Revue de Tourisme* 28, 98–104.

Crouch, Geoffrey I. (1992a), "Marketing International Tourism to Australia: A Regression Analysis," *Tourism Management* 13 (2), 196–208.

Crouch, Geoffrey I. (1992b), "Effect of Income and Price on International Tourism," *Annals of Tourism Research* 19 (4), 643–664.

Deaton, Angus, and John Muellbauer (1980), "An Almost Ideal Demand System," *American Economic Review* 70 (3), 312–326.

Diamond, J. (1977), "Tourism's Role in Economic Development: The Case Reexamined," *Economic Development and Cultural Change* 25 (3), 539–553.

Edgell, David L. (1990), *International Tourism Policy*, New York: Van Nostrand Reinhold.

Edwards, Anthony (1976), *International Tourism Development Forecasts to 1985*, The Economist Intelligence Unit Ltd., Special Report No. 33, London.

Edwards, Anthony (1979), *International Tourism Development Forecasts to 1990*, The Economist Intelligence Unit Ltd., Special Report No. 62, London.

Edwards, Anthony (1985), *International Tourism Forecasts to*

1995, The Economist Intelligence Unit, Special Report No. 188, London.

Edwards, Anthony (1987), *Choosing Holiday Destinations: The Impact of Exchange Rates and Inflation*, The Economist Intelligence Unit, Special Report No. 1109, London.

Economist Intelligence Unit (1975), "Currency Changes, Exchange Rates and Their Effects on Tourism," *International Tourism Quarterly*, Special Article No. 18, 4, 34–45.

Fujii, Edwin T., Eric I. Im, and James Mak (1989), *The Impact of Direct Flights on Consumer Choice of Travel Destinations: An Interrupted Time Series Analysis*, Working Paper No. 89–19, Department of Economics, University of Hawaii.

Fujii, Edwin T., Mohammed Khaled, and James Mak (1985), "An Almost Ideal Demand System for Visitor Expenditures," *Journal of Transport Economics and Policy* 19 (2), 161–171.

Fujii, Edwin T., and James Mak (1981), "Forecasting Tourism Demand; Some Methodological Issues," *Annals of Regional Science* 15 (2), 72–82.

Gerakis, Andreas S. (1965), "Effects of Exchange-Rate Devaluations and Revaluations on Receipts from Tourism," *International Monetary Fund Staff Papers* 12 (3), 365–384.

Gray, H. Peter (1966), "The Demand for International Travel by the United States and Canada," *International Economic Review* 7 (1), 83–92.

Gray, H. Peter (1970), *International Travel—International Trade*, Lexington, MA: D.C. Heath and Company.

Guthrie, Harold W. (1961), "Demands for Tourists' Goods and Services in a World Market," *Papers and Proceedings of the Regional Science Association* 7, 159–175.

Haitovsky, Y., I. Salomon, and L. A. Silman (1987), "The Economic Impact of Charter Flights on Tourism to Israel: An Econometric Approach," *Journal of Transport Economics and Policy* 21 (2), 111–134.

Hanlon, James Patrick (1976), *Econometric Estimates of the Demand for Air Travel; Analysis of Business Travel over Routes to the United Kingdom*, University of Birmingham, Department of Transportation and Environmental Planning, Department Publication No. 49.

Hiemstra, Stephen J. (1991), "Projections of World Tourist Arrivals to the Year 2000," in *World Travel and Tourism Review: Indicators, Trends and Forecasts*, Donald E. Hawkins, J.R. Brent Ritchie, Frank Go, Douglas Frechtling, eds., Vol. 1, CAB International.

Hollander, G. (1982), *Determinants of Demand for Travel to and from Australia*, Bureau of Industry Economics, Australia, Working Paper No. 26.

Horowitz, Joel L. (1981), "Sources of Error and Uncertainty in Behavioral Travel-Demand Models," in *New Horizons in Travel-Behavior Research*, Peter R. Stopher, Arnim H. Meyburg, and Werner Brog, eds., 543–558, Lexington, MA: Lexington Books.

Industries Assistance Commission (1989a), *Some Economic Implications of Tourism Expansion*, Inquiry into Travel and Tourism, Discussion Paper No. 2, Australian Government Publishing Service, Canberra.

Industries Assistance Commission (1989b), *Travel and Tourism*, Industries Assistance Commission, Report No. 423, Australian Government Publishing Service, Canberra.

Jud, G. Donald (1971), *The Demand for Tourism: The Case of Latin America*, Ph.D. dissertation, University of Iowa.

Jud., G. Donald (1974), "Tourism and Economic Growth in Mexico Since 1950," *Inter-American Economic Affairs* 28 (1), 19–43.

Jud, G. Donald, and Hyman Joseph (1974), "International Demand for Latin American Tourism," *Growth and Change* 5 (1), 25–31.

Jung, J. M., and E. T. Fujii (1976), "The Price Elasticity of Demand for Air Travel: Some New Evidence," *Journal of Transport Economics and Policy* 10 (3), 257–262.

Kanafani, Adib (1983), *Transportation Demand Analysis*, New York: McGraw-Hill, Inc.

Kanellakis, Vassilios (1975), *International Tourism: Its Significance and Potential as an Instrument for the Economic Development of Greece*, Ph.D. dissertation, Department of Economics, Kansas State University.

Keintz, Rita M. (1968), "A Study of the Demand for International Travel to and from the United States," *Proceedings of the 10th Conference, Western Council for Travel Research*, 59–69.

Kliman, M. L. (1981), "A Quantitative Analysis of Canadian Overseas Tourism," *Transportation Research* 15A (6), 487–497.

Krause, Walter, G. Donald Jud, and Hyman Joseph (1973), *International Tourism and Latin American Development*, Austin, TX: Bureau of Business Research, Graduate School of Business, The University of Texas at Austin.

Kravis, I. B., Z. Kenessey, A. Heston, and R. Summers (1975), *A System of International Comparisons of Gross Product and Purchasing Power*, Baltimore, MD: Johns-Hopkins University Press.

Kwack, Sung Y. (1972), "Effects of Income and Prices on Travel Spending Abroad 1960 III—1967 IV," *International Economic Review* 13 (2), 245–256.

Laber, Gene (1969), "Determinants of International Travel Between Canada and the United States," *Geographical Analysis* 1 (4), 329–336.

Lin, Tzong-Biau, and Yun-Wing Sun (1983), "Hong Kong," in *Tourism in Asia: The Economic Impact*, Elwood A. Pye and Tzong-Biau Lin, eds., 1–100, Singapore: Singapore University Press.

Little, Jane Sneddon (1980), "International Travel in the U.S. Balance of Payments," *New England Economic Review* (May/June), 42–55.

Loeb, Peter D. (1982), "International Travel to the United States:

An Econometric Evaluation," *Annals of Tourism Research* 9 (1), 7–20.

Mak, James, James Moncur, and Dave Yonamine (1977), "Determinants of Visitor Expenditures and Visitor Lengths of Stay: A Cross-Section Analysis of U.S. Visitors to Hawaii," *Journal of Travel Research* 15 (3), 5–8.

Martin, Christine A., and Stephen F. Witt (1987), "Tourism Demand Forecasting Models: Choice of Appropriate Variable to Represent Tourists' Cost of Living," *Tourism Management* 8 (3), 223–245.

Martin, Christine A., and Stephen F. Witt (1988), "Substitute Prices in Models of Tourism Demand," *Annals of Tourism Research* 15 (2), 255–268.

Martin, Christine A., and Stephen F. Witt (1989), "Accuracy of Econometric Forecasts of Tourism," *Annals of Tourism Research* 16 (3), 407–428.

Mayo, Edward J., and Lance P. Jarvis (1986), "Objective Distance Versus Subjective Distance and the Attraction of the Far-Off Destination," in *Tourism Services Marketing: Advances in Theory and Practice*, W. B. Joseph, L. Moutinho, and I. R. Vernon, eds., 43–52, Academy of Marketing Science, University of Miami.

McCuen, Richard H. (1974), "Spurious Correlation in Estimating Recreation Demand Functions," *Journal of Leisure Research* 6 (3), 232–240.

Mieczkowski, Zbigniew (1985), "The Tourism Climatic Index: A Method of Evaluating World Climates for Tourism," *The Canadian Geographer*, 29 (3), 220–233.

Mikulicz, Hans (1983), "Determinants of Tourism Flows in Europe," in *Seminar on the Importance of Research in the Tourism Industry*, Helsinki, Finland, 8–11 June 1983, European Society for Opinion and Marketing Research, 7–16.

Moncur, James E. T. (1978), *Thailand's Tourism: An Analysis of Visitor Length of Stay and Expenditures*, Discussion Paper Series, No. 69, Faculty of Economics, Thammasat University, December 1978.

Morley, Clive (1991), "Modeling International Tourism Demand: Model Specification and Structure," *Journal of Travel Research* 30 (1), 40–44.

Moshirian, Fariborz (1989), International Trade in Services, Ph.D. dissertation, Department of Economics, Monash University.

Mutti, John, and Yoshitaka Murai (1977), "Airline Travel on the North Atlantic. Is Profitability Possible?" *Journal of Transport Economics and Policy* 11 (1), 45–53.

Noval, Stanley (1975), *The Demand for International Tourism and Travel: Theory and Measurement*, Ph.D. dissertation, Princeton University.

O'Hagan, J. W., and M. J. Harrison (1984a), "Market Shares of U.S. Tourist Expenditures in Europe: An Econometric Analysis," *Applied Economics* 16 (6), 919–931.

O'Hagan, J. W., and M. J. Harrison (1984b), "U.K. and U.S. Visitor Expenditure in Ireland: Some Econometric Findings," *The Economic and Social Review* 15 (3), 195–207.

Oliver, F. R. (1971), "The Effectiveness of the UK Travel Allowance," *Applied Economics* 3, 219–226.

Papadopoulos, Socrates I. (1985), *An Economic Analysis of Foreign Tourism to Greece 1960–1984, With a Planning Model and Marketing Policy Recommendations*, Ph.D. dissertation, University of Bradford, UK.

Paraskevopoulos, George N. (1977), *An Economic Analysis of International Tourism*, Athens: Center of Planning and Economic Research, Lecture Series 31.

Poole, Michael (1988), *Forecasting Methodology*, Occasional Paper No. 3, Bureau of Tourism Research, Australia.

Quayson, Jojo, and Turgut Var (1982), "A Tourism Demand Function for the Okanagan, BC," *Tourism Management* 3 (June), 108–115.

Rojwannasin, Bang-Ornrat (1982), *Determinants of International Tourist Flows to Thailand*, Ph.D. dissertation, Faculty of Economics, Thammasat University, Bangkok, Thailand.

Rugg, Donald D. (1971), *The Demand for Foreign Travel*, Ph.D. dissertation, University of California, Los Angeles.

Rugg, Donald D. (1973), "The Choices of Journey Destination: A Theoretical and Empirical Analysis," *Review of Economics and Statistics* 55 (1), 64–71.

Schulmeister, Stephen (1979), *Tourism and the Business Cycle; Econometric Models for the Purpose of Analysis and Forecasting of Short-term Changes in the Demand for Tourism*, Austrian Institute for Economic Research, Vienna.

Smeral, Egon (1988), "Tourism Demand, Economic Theory and Econometrics: An Integrated Approach," *Journal of Travel Research* 26 (4), 38–42.

Smith, A. B., and J. N. Toms (1978), *Factors Affecting Demand for International Travel to and from Australia*, Bureau of Transport Economics, Australian Government Publishing Service, Canberra, Australia.

Smith, Stephen L. J. (1983), "A Method for Estimating the Distance Equivalence of International Boundaries," *Journal of Travel Research* 22 (3), 37–39.

Straszheim, Mahlon R. (1969), *The International Airline Industry*, Washington, D.C.: The Brookings Institution.

Straszheim, Mahlon R. (1978), "Airline Demand Functions in the North Atlantic and Their Pricing Implications," *Journal of Transport Economics and Policy* 12 (2), 179–195.

Stroombergen, A. H., G. M. Jackson, and J. Miller (1991), *The Economic Determinants of International Visitor Arrivals to New Zealand*, Economic Research Series 1991/3, New Zealand Tourism Department, Wellington.

Stone, J. R. N. (1954), "Linear Expenditure Systems and Demand Analysis: An Application to the Pattern of British Demand," *Economic Journal* 65 (Sept), 511–527.

Stronge, William B., and Milton Redman (1982), "U.S. Tourism in Mexico: An Empirical Analysis," *Annals of Tourism Research* 9 (1), 21–35.

Summary, Rebecca (1987), "Estimation of Tourism Demand by

Multivariable Regression Analysis: Evidence from Kenya," *Tourism Management* 8 (4), 317–322.

Sunday, Alexander A. (1978), "Foreign Travel and Tourism Prices and Demand," *Annals of Tourism Research* 5 (2), 268–273.

Tellis, Gerard J. (1988), "The Price Elasticity of Selective Demand: A Meta-Analysis of Econometric Models of Sales," *Journal of Marketing Research* 25 (4), 331–341.

Tremblay, Pascal (1989), "Pooling International Tourism in Western Europe," *Annals of Tourism Research* 16 (4), 477–491.

Truett, Lila J., and Dale B. Truett (1982), "Public Policy and the Growth of the Mexican Tourism Industry 1970–1979," *Journal of Travel Research* 20 (3), 11–19.

Truett, Dale B., and Lila J. Truett (1987), "The Response of Tourism to International Economic Conditions: Greece, Mexico and Spain," *The Journal of Developing Areas* 21 (2), 177–190.

Uysal, Muzaffer (1983), *Construction of a Model Which Investigates the Impact of Selected Variables on International Tourist Flows to Turkey*, Ph.D. dissertation, Texas A & M University.

Uysal, Muzaffer, and John L. Crompton (1984), "Determinants of Demand for International Tourist Flows to Turkey," *Tourism Management* 5 (4), 288–297.

Uysal, Muzaffer, and Joseph T. O'Leary (1986), "A Canonical Analysis of International Tourism Demand," *Annals of Tourism Research* 13 (4), 651–655.

Vanhove, N. (1980), "Forecasting in Tourism," *Revue de Tourisme* 3, 2–7.

Var, Turgut, Golam Mohammad, and Orhan Icoz (1990), "Factors Affecting International Tourism Demand for Turkey," *Annals of Tourism Research* 17 (4), 606–638.

White, Kenneth J. (1985), "An International Travel Demand Model: US Travel to Western Europe," *Annals of Tourism Research* 12 (4), 529–545.

White, Kenneth J., and Mary B. Walker (1982), "Trouble in the Travel Account," *Annals of Tourism Research* 9 (1), 1–24.

Witt, Stephen F. (1980a), "An Abstract Mode-Abstract (Destination) Node Model of Foreign Holiday Demand," *Applied Economics* 12 (2), 163–180.

Witt, Stephen F. (1980b), "An Econometric Comparison of UK and German Foreign Holiday Behavior," *Managerial and Decision Economics* 1 (3), 123–131.

Witt, Stephen F., and Christine A. Martin (1987a), "Econometric Models for Forecasting International Tourism Demand," *Journal of Travel Research* 25 (3), 23–30.

Witt, Stephen F., and Christine A. Martin (1987b), "Deriving a Relative Price Index for Inclusion in International Tourism Demand Estimation Models: Comment," *Journal of Travel Research* 25 (3), 38–40.

Witt, Stephen F., and Christine A. Martin (1989), "Demand Forecasting in Tourism and Recreation," *Progress in Tourism, Recreation, and Hospitality Management* 1, 4–32.

52

Estimating the Potential of International Markets

DON WYNEGAR
Deputy Assistant Secretary
United States Travel and Tourism Administration
Washington, D.C.

This chapter provides a structured approach to analyzing the potential and relative importance of international travel markets. A model is developed, utilizing a weighted indexing system for evaluating the cumulative significance of pertinent variables for countries under study. The model's output provides decision makers with an indication of the relative marketing viability of each country.

A national tourism office, other federal, state, and regional tourism agencies, and private industry concerned with promoting international travel are faced with the need for allocating often relatively minimal resources in the most cost-effective and productive manner. To accomplish an optimum distribution of marketing efforts, it is essential that an organization employ a systematic approach for objectively determining the importance and relative attractiveness of various international travel markets for the host country.

Before a government agency or, for that matter, a private business organization can accurately gauge the resource level necessary to compete effectively in a given market, some measure of the total potential of that market must be ascertained (Munsinger and Hansen 1974). Determination of this measure not only entails study of current market performance and/or historical trend analyses of travel patterns, but also evaluation of factors that provide indications of possible market demand and facility of promotional efforts. In analyzing these factors, the potential for growth, or incremental market development, can be determined.

The model outlined in this chapter provides a step-by-step approach to the analysis of international travel market potential. It incorporates measures of both existing market size and realized performance and total and incremental market potential. In addition to these quantitative factors, several qualitative variables that affect the marketability of respective country travel markets are evaluated. By incorporating a system of weighted indexes, these factors are aggre-

gated to form a Cumulative Market Evaluation Index, providing a measurement of the relative marketing viability of each country and a basis for resource allocation.

Other market-potential models have been developed that address specific travel market segments, such as the Market Potential Index developed by Drs. Munsinger and Hansen of the University of Arizona for the United States Travel Service in 1971. This current model is considerably disparate in its coverage, in the variables included in the model, and in the methods of indexing utilized. An effort has been made to make this model as straightforward and easily applied as possible by research practitioners and market analysts.

In addition to providing a structural approach for estimating the potential of international markets, a brief section is provided addressing other factors that an organization should take into consideration when studying the feasibility of establishing and funding programs/offices in foreign countries. Analysis of these "cost-of-doing-business" indicators can provide additional quantitative data for decision makers in allocating resources in international travel markets.

As an illustration, the United States is considered as the host country in the following analysis, and the country travel markets of Canada, Mexico, Japan, the United Kingdom, Germany, and France—the six countries in which the USTTA currently maintains offices—are included for evaluation. The model is, however, designed for possible application in other host countries and, with appropriate modifications, could be used by bodies concerned with domestic markets. Finally, as each input variable is introduced into the model, the availability and limitations of the data are also discussed.

DEFINITIONS

Two terms that are used throughout this chapter should be defined at the outset. *Potential* as employed in a marketing context refers to the sales, measured in dollars or units, that could be attained from a given market, within a certain period of time, under optimal conditions. Performance should never exceed potential, although theoretically, it is possible for the two to be equal. Potential differs from a *forecast* in that the latter represents what is expected to happen, based on an analysis of demand factors coupled with the effort the organization plans to expend. Potential is not effected by company plans. Rather, it can be thought of as a quantity of which a part can be purchased through marketing efforts. In general, the greater the potential realized, the more difficult it becomes to capture the potential remaining. As a firm or agency strives to increase the share of potential it attracts, the ratio of sales to effort applied tends to decrease; for example, the first 70 percent can in all probability be realized more efficiently than the next 20 percent (Munsinger and Hansen 1974:6).

The term *index* as used in this text should also be clarified. For each variable or factor considered for the six countries in the illustration, an index base of 100.0 is assigned to the country displaying the most favorable rating. The remaining five countries receive index ratings that are derived by dividing each country's factor value by that of the country that has the most favorable factor value. If Canada, for example, with some 10.7 million tourists visiting the United States, ranks highest in this category, Canada would be assigned an index value of 100.0. Japan, with some 1.1 million arrivals, would achieve an index rating of 10.2 (derived by dividing the number of Japanese arrivals by the number of Canadian arrivals and multiplying the quotient by 100). An index sequence is thus determined for the six countries, which provides a direct relative ranking of each for the variable under consideration.

QUANTITATIVE FACTORS INDEX

While this model attempts to provide an objective process for determining aggregate international travel market potentials, the selection of the variables that are to be used as input factors is, at best, a subjective procedure. This chapter does not attempt to provide exhaustive "cookbook" inclusion of all pertinent variables that could possibly be used, and in that sense, this particular combination should be viewed as exemplificative. Another analyst employing this method could easily substitute other variables into the model, should other factors be deemed more appropriate to a particular host country.

The variable "financial capability for travel to the host country" is not included in this model, although it has been used as a measure of the overall potential of a market population for international travel in other models. This factor is excluded because use of this characteristic produces an exaggerated estimate of the true market potential. Not all persons possessing the economic capacity for international travel are inclined to venture abroad. The incidence of nontravelers in all socioeconomic categories is unavoidable. Furthermore, measurements of this financial capacity cannot be arbitrarily linked to a singular, specific economic criterion, such as the proportion of a country's population classified in certain income groupings. It is reasonable to assume that, due to factors such as market contiguity and varying modes/costs of transportation used in travel to the host country, this financial capability would not necessarily be linked to the same economic criteria for each country; for example, the economic determinants affecting capacity for travel to the United States would not be the same for Canada (a contiguous, auto-oriented travel market) as it would be for Germany (a long-haul, air-oriented travel market).

An attempt is made to include input variables that more closely reflect the actual market population that has potential for travel to the United States—by taking into account the tendency and inclination of the populations under study for international/long-haul travel. The quantitative travel-potential determinants used here are grouped as follows:

A. Travel Volume Potential
   1. Competitive market potential
   2. Competitive market travel as proportion of total population travel
   3. Current travel to host country
   4. Potential incremental trips to host country
   5. Potential for further marketing penetration
B. Travel Receipts Potential
   1. Current travel receipts
   2. Per capita travel receipts
   3. Total potential travel receipts
   4. Potential incremental travel receipts.

TRAVEL VOLUME POTENTIAL

In this section, the quantitative input variables that deal with numbers of potential travelers/trips to the host country are discussed and developed for use in the evaluative model.

Competitive Market Potential

Marketers concerned with promoting international tourism to a host country are most likely to concentrate their efforts on that market segment that is most inclined to travel abroad and, therefore, more receptive to promotional stimuli. The input variable used here as a quantitative indication of a population's marketing potential is simply the number of "competitive trips" taken by the respective populations—trips that in distance or time spent away from home or by their international nature approximate the competitive potential market for travel to the United States.

Differing measures of competitive trips are used here because of inclusion of Canada and Mexico in the country inventory. Due to the proximity of these nations to the United States, certain categories of domestic trips taken by their residents must be included as part of the competitive market that has real potential for travel to the United States. For the four overseas countries under study, only certain international trips taken by their residents are evaluated as indicators of the competitive market for travel to the United States. Table 1 provides a comparative ranking and index rating of this market potential variable for the six country travel markets.

As indicated by the various types of information used in estimating the competitive market potential and by the various sources referenced, strict comparability of the data between countries is clearly impossible. This nonconformity need not be a prohibitive drawback provided the researcher exercises care in relying only on official sources and carefully utilizes data that more closely approximates that market in which the host country must realistically compete for international travelers. In this sense, the standard of competitive market does provide comparability for the purposes of this analysis.

For the most reliable and up-to-date information on this market factor, the official national tourist offices of the respective countries should be referenced whenever possible. A limited amount of country departure information on a country-by-country basis is available in reports published by the World Tourism Organization (WTO) and the Organization for Economic Cooperation and Development (OECD), although these data are usually not current and are of insufficient detail for studies of this type.

Competitive Market Travel as Proportion of Total Population Travel

As an indication of market penetration and the incidence and preference of the population of each country for possible international tourism, travel by the competitive potential market should be compared to all travel by the residents of each nation. The resulting proportion sheds light on the general receptivity and accessibility of the target market in each country's populace. This input variable (Competitive Market Share) is derived simply by division of Variable A, competitive trips taken by population (see Table 1), by the total number of domestic and international trips taken by the residents of each country. The results of this exercise, along with comparative index ratings for this factor for the six country travel markets, are shown in Table 2.

As with the previous input data, information on total trips (domestic plus international) taken by a country's residents should be obtained either directly or indirectly from the national tourist office of that country. Domestic tourism data will likely be incomparable between countries since each national tourist office usually incorporates its own set of definitions designed to meet its individual needs in gathering and reporting statistics on intracountry travel by residents. Many countries, such as Germany, report domestic trips as tourist arrivals at all accommodation establishments, excluding stays with friends and relatives. Other nations, such as Canada, provide domestic tourism information based on all travel exceeding a certain distance away from home (e.g., 50 miles) and/or overnight or longer. The limitations of comparisons made between such data should be taken into account in this analysis.

Current Travel to Host Country

Existing arrivals from a given country to the host nation are, of course, an important factor which a promotional organization should include in an evaluation of marketing potential. Current market performance in supplying international trips to the United States from each of the six countries is

TABLE 1 Variable A—Competitive Market Potential

Country	Competitive Trips Taken by Population (Year X) (Thousands)	Ranking	Index Rating (I_a)
Canada	23,900[a]	1	100.0
Mexico	17,600[b]	2	73.6
Japan	4,038[c]	5	16.9
United Kingdom	7,175[d]	3	30.0
Germany	5,100[d]	4	21.3
France	2,310[d]	6	9.7

[a]Estimated interprovincial domestic (excluding business trips) and international person-trips taken by Canadians in reference year; derived from data from the Canadian Government Office of Tourism.
[b]Estimated number of international and domestic (air) person-trips taken by Mexican residents in reference year; derived from data from the Mexican Ministry of Tourism and the Bank of Mexico.
[c]Total number of international person-trips taken by Japanese residents in reference year; Source: Japan National Tourist Office.
[d]Estimated international holiday trips (person-trips) taken by air transportation by residents in reference year; Sources: British Tourist Authority, Statistisches Bundesamt, Wiesbaden (Germany), and Secretariat d'Etat au Tourisme (France).

TABLE 2 Variable B—Competitive Market Travel as Proportion of Total Population Travel

COUNTRY	COMPETITIVE MARKET SHARE	RANKING	INDEX RATING (I_b)
Canada	19.3	2	64.8
Mexico	29.8	1	100.0
Japan	2.0	6	6.7
United Kingdom	14.7	3	49.3
Germany	11.0	4	36.9
France	4.5	5	15.1

outlined in Table 3, as are resultant market rankings and relative index ratings.

Potential Incremental Trips to Host Country

This measurement refers to the arithmetic difference between the total competitive market trips taken and the number of tourist trips taken to the host country, or Variable A minus Variable C. The resulting increment reflects that market that remains to be tapped—in other words, potential incremental trips. The results of this computation for the sample countries under evaluation are illustrated in Table 4.

Potential for Further Market Penetration

In defining the term *potential* at the outset of this chapter, it was noted that potential should be thought of as a quantity of which a part can be attained through marketing efforts. Additionally, it was pointed out that as a firm or agency attempts to increase its share of potential, an increasing amount of marketing effort is required; in other words, the first 50 percent of potential is much easier to achieve than the next 50 percent.

Based on the theory of decreasing marginal returns, it is logical to assume that the greater the ratio of as-yet unattained market potential to the total market potential, the more attractive the market would be in terms of facilitating efficient penetration through promotional efforts. In the parameters of this mode, this ratio may be determined by dividing Variable D, potential incremental trips to the United States, by Variable A, total competitive trips by population (see Tables 1 and 4). The higher the proportion obtained, the more favorable the country market appears in terms of marketing viability. Table 5 provides the results of this exercise for the six major international travel markets to the United States.

While not included in this model, another input variable that might be considered by a host country is historical growth in travel. Aggregate or average annual growth in arrivals during the past five years, for example, might be analyzed as an indicator of the trend in market demand. A country market exhibiting a pattern of strong growth in arrivals may appear more attractive as a potential market than a country displaying only marginal expansion. Conversely, marketers may prefer to stimulate latent growth in a particular marketplace that has not undergone rapid growth but, due to other influencing factors, may be ready for development.

TABLE 3 Variable C—Current Travel to Host Country

COUNTRY	TOURIST TRIPS TO THE UNITED STATES (YEAR X) (THOUSANDS)	RANKING	INDEX RATING (I_c)
Canada	10,716[a]	1	100.0
Mexico	8,770[b]	2	81.8
Japan	1,089[c]	3	10.2
United Kingdom	930[c]	4	8.7
Germany	608[c]	5	5.7
France	303[c]	6	2.8

[a]Source is Statistics Canada; reflects the number of Canadians returning from the United States after a stay of at least one night.
[b]Estimate of Mexican travelers spending at least 24 hours in the United States. For technical reasons associated with documentation, the United States has historically counted only a portion of the Mexican tourist and excursionist trips to this country. Consequently, the true number of Mexican tourist arrivals has been understated. A USTS survey of Mexican travel to the U.S. border zone, for example, indicates that the existing data system may be excluding over six million *tourists* in U.S. tabulations of annual nonimmigrant arrivals from Mexico. This inadequacy results from a lack of data concerning the actual length of stay in the United States by total visitors. The figure for Mexican tourist trips shown here was derived for purposes of this study only and should not be confused with the arrival data generated by the existing U.S. arrival data system.
[c]U.S. Travel and Tourism Administration estimates.

TABLE 4 Variable D—Potential Incremental Trips to Host Country

Country	Potential Incremental Trips to U.S. (Var. A - Var. C) (Thousands)	Ranking	Index Rating (I_d)
Canada	13,184	1	100.0
Mexico	8,830	2	67.0
Japan	2,949	5	22.4
United Kingdom	6,245	3	47.4
Germany	4,492	4	34.1
France	2,007	6	15.2

TRAVEL RECEIPTS POTENTIAL

The desired end results of an agency's or firm's marketing effort are, naturally, sales. The economic purpose of encouraging increased international tourism is to increase the amount of foreign exchange earnings that flow into the host country's economy as a result of spending by international visitors. The importance of these travel receipts was highlighted by a study sponsored by the U.S. Travel Service that indicated that in 1978, foreign tourist spending in the United States directly and indirectly supported some 571,000 U.S. jobs while generating 5.1 billion dollars in payroll (U.S. Travel Service and U.S. Travel Data Center 1980). In analyzing possible foreign tourism markets, it is necessary to look closely at those variables that provide indications of a market's potential economic contribution. The quantitative factors that deal with potential travel receipts from the foreign traveler are developed and discussed in this section.

Current Travel Receipts

The amount that travelers from individual countries currently spend in the host country should be analyzed in a straightforward comparison of total travel receipts. These data usually reflect spending while in the destination country and do not include amounts paid by foreign travelers for international transportation. A single source that provides comparable country-by-country spending estimates should be used—usually an agency in the government of the host country charged with gathering and reporting these data for purposes of balance payments accounting. In the United States, the Bureau of Economic Analysis, U.S. Department of Commerce, carries out this function. A comparison of international travel receipts and the resultant index ratings for Canadian, Mexican, Japanese, British, German, and French visitors to the United States are illustrated in Table 6.

Per Capita Travel Receipts

Spending patterns of visitors from different countries vary considerably, and it is necessary to take these variances into account. The average German tourist, for example, in the United States may spend three or four times as much as would the average Canadian visitor. Consequently, the marginal economic impact of the German's expenditures would be greater. It follows that the marginal return from an agency's or firm's marketing efforts would likely be greater if concentrated on the visitor market displaying tendencies for higher per capita spending. (This is, of course, only one consideration.)

Per capita trip-spending estimates may be derived either directly from market-survey results or indirectly by dividing total current foreign travel receipts (Variable F) by the current tourist trips to the host country (Variable C) for each of the country markets under consideration. Due to limitations in the U.S. systems that generate tourist arrival and spending

TABLE 5 Variable E—Potential for Further Market Penetration

Country	Potential Incremental Trips as Share of Total Market Potential (Var. D+Var. A) (%)	Ranking	Index Rating (I_e)
Canada	55.2	5	62.7
Mexico	50.2	6	57.0
Japan	73.0	4	82.9
United Kingdom	87.0	2	98.8
Germany	88.1	1	100.0
France	86.9	3	98.6

TABLE 6   Variable F—Current Travel Receipts

Country	Travel Spending in the U.S. (Year X) (Millions)	Ranking	Index Rating (I_f)
Canada	$2,092[a]	1	100.0
Mexico	1,869[a]	2	89.3
Japan	699	3	33.4
United Kingdom	375	5	17.9
Germany	440	4	21.0
France	180	6	8.6

Source: Bureau of Economic Analysis, U.S. Department of Commerce.
[a]Receipt data for Canada and Mexico includes spending by excursionists (staying less than 24 hours).

data, both methods are used in this case study. Table 7 provides the comparative ratings for this input variable.

Total Potential Travel Receipts

The third quantitative variable dealing with travel receipts is the total amount of international tourism receipts a host country could possibly receive, should its potential for achieving full competitive market penetration (monopoly) be realized. These total potential travel receipts are tabulated in this model by multiplying current per capita travel receipts (Variable G) by the number of competitive trips taken by the population (Variable A). The results of this exercise for the United States are outlined in Table 8.

Potential Incremental Travel Receipts

The arithmetic difference between total potential travel receipts (Variable H) and current travel receipts (Variable F) provides an indication of the incremental amount of potential foreign travel receipts that remain to be tapped from the competitive marketplace. This helps determine which country travel markets possess the greater potential for further economic contribution to the host country. (This input factor may also be generated by multiplying per capita travel re-

ceipts, Variable G, by potential incremental trips to the host country, Variable D.) For the six country travel markets to the United States under consideration, potential incremental travel receipts are ranked and indexed in Table 9.

CUMULATIVE QUANTITATIVE FACTORS INDEX

Upon determination of these sets of indexes for the nine quantitative input variables, A–I, the next step is development of a cumulative index for the quantitative factors. A series of weights are applied to the individual variable indexes, and the resulting products are aggregated to formulate overall quantitative factors index ratings. This procedure may be notated as follows:

$$I_{qti} = W_a I_{ai} + \ldots W_i I_{ii}$$

where

I_{qti} = cumulative quantitative index rating for country i
$w_a, w_b, \ldots, w_i$ = weights assigned to country i's index ratings in indices $I_a, I_b, \ldots, I_i$
$I_{ai}, I_{bi} \ldots I_{ii}$ = country i's index ratings in indices $I_a, I_b, \ldots, I_i$

TABLE 7   Variable G—Per Capita Travel Receipts

Country	Expenditures in the U.S. Per Tourist Trip (U.S. $)	Ranking	Index Rating (I_g)
Canada	$155[a]	5	21.4
Mexico	101[b]	6	14.0
Japan	642[c]	2	88.7
United Kingdom	403[c]	4	55.7
Germany	724[c]	1	100.0
France	595[c]	3	82.0

[a]Spending per Canadian person-trip (one night or longer) to the United States in reference year; Statistics Canada.
[b]Estimated spending per Mexican person-trip (one night or longer) to the United States in reference year; unofficial estimate based on USTS market survey results.
[c]Derived by dividing total travel receipts by total tourist trips to the United States (Variable F÷Variable C).

TABLE 8 Variable H—Total Potential Travel Receipts

Country	Total Potential Travel Receipts (Var. G x Var. A)	Ranking	Index Rating (I_h)
Canada	$4,136[a]	1	100.0
Mexico	2,761[a]	4	66.8
Japan	2,592	5	62.7
United Kingdom	2,892	3	69.9
Germany	3,692	2	89.3
France	1,372	6	33.2

[a]Receipt figures for Canada and Mexico have been adjusted to include expenditures by excursionists (staying less than 24 hours), since total travel spending data for these two countries reported by the Bureau of Economic Analysis, U.S. Department of Commerce, currently include these sums.

The determination of the individual weights (w_a, w_b, ...) is one of the most critical steps in this system. A country travel market's final quantitative factors index rating is directly dependent on the weights assigned to the individual variable indexes (I_a, ...,I_{ii}). Unfortunately, a degree of subjectivity comes into play at this stage since these weights must be derived from opinions concerning the respective importance of the nine different quantitative-input variables. The most appropriate method to overcome this subjectivity, to the extent possible, is to utilize a modified Delphi technique in which a series of "expert opinions" may be obtained and averaged to achieve the distribution of index weights.

These factors' weights should be applied as proportions of 1, or unity. In other words, the arithmetic sum of the weights should be 100.0. (This value could only be obtained if the country market had achieved individual index ratings of 100.0 for each of the variables A through I.)

For the nine quantitative input variables, the corresponding index weights derived for this example are as follows:

w_a = 0.12 (Competitive market potential, I_a)
w_b = 0.07 (Competitive market share, I_b)
w_c = 0.13 (Current travel to the United States, I_c)
w_d = 0.08 (Potential incremental trips to the United States, I_d)
w_e = 0.12 (Potential for further market penetration, I_e)
w_f = 0.15 (Current travel receipts, I_f)
w_g = 0.11 (Per capita travel receipts, I_g)
w_h = 0.09 (Total potential travel receipts, I_h)

w_i = 0.13 (Potential incremental travel receipts, I_i)

$\overline{1.00}$

For illustrative purposes, the following is the application of Equation (1) in deriving the cumulative quantitative factors index rating for the Canadian travel market to the United States:

$$I_{qt} = (0.12)(100.0) + (0.07)(64.8) + (0.13)(100.0) \\ + (0.08)(100.0) + (0.12)(62.7) + (0.15)(100.0) \\ + (0.11)(21.4) + (0.09)(100.0) + (0.13)(62.9) \\ = 12.0 + 4.5 + 13.0 + 8.0 + 7.5 + 15.0 + 2.4 \\ + 9.0 + 8.2 = 79.6$$

Summary Table Qt provides the completed listing of cumulative quantitative factors index ratings for the six country travel markets to the United States.

QUALITATIVE/REFINING FACTORS INDEX

Quantitative factors, such as outlined in the foregoing section, are quite important in analyzing the potential of international tourism markets. However, they must not be considered the sole indicator of marketing viability. Other qualitative factors that directly affect demand in the marketplace

TABLE 9 Variable I—Potential Incremental Travel Receipts

Country	Potential Incremental U.S. Travel Receipts (Var. H – Var. F) (Millions)	Ranking	Index Rating (I_i)
Canada	$2,044	3	62.9
Mexico	892	6	27.4
Japan	1,893	4	58.2
United Kingdom	2,517	2	77.4
Germany	3,252	1	100.0
France	1,192	5	36.6

TABLE Qt Cumulative Quantitative Factors Index

COUNTRY	CUMULATIVE QUANTITATIVE FACTORS INDEX RATING (I_{qt})	RANKING
Canada	79.6	1
Mexico	63.1	2
Japan	43.5	5
United Kingdom	49.1	4
Germany	55.8	3
France	33.8	6

must be considered in the evaluation process. In this model, these qualitative variables are applied as refining factors that, when taken together with the cumulative quantitative factors index, result in a final Market Evaluation Index.

As with quantitative input variables, the selection of the refining factors for inclusion in the study is a subjective matter. Those appearing here were chosen as important inputs for consideration of the competitive marketplace for travel to the United States and should be thought of as illustrative. Throughout this chapter, it is the *method* of analysis that should be focused on; other input variables considered more appropriate by a particular host country or analyst can be easily incorporated into the model.

The qualitative input factors used here are:

1. Cost and distance of travel to host country—Cost and distance affect/effect existing commercial transportation infrastructure, fare structures, trip itineraries, type of transportation utilized by visitors, purpose of trips, and length of stay.

2. General political/social attitude toward host country—This affects tendencies/propensities of population to consider the host country as a possible trip destination.

3. Competitive environment—The degree to which other destinations are competing for potential travelers in the marketplace affects the host country's likelihood of achieving further market penetration.

4. Market concentration—The more concentrated the potential market (i.e., in a single major urban area), the greater the ease in reaching that market with promotional messages; marketing efforts can be more tailored and more effectively targeted and delivered.

5. Trade structure—The extent to which the market country's travel industry infrastructure (airlines, travel agencies, tour operators, etc.) is organizationally equipped to handle the type of travel that is to be promoted affects the host country's facility for success in that market.

A single refining index is developed for these five qualitative variables. A scaled grading system is first used to assign a numerical rating (from 1, representing the least favorable situation in the market for a particular variable, to 10, the most favorable rating) to an individual country for each qualitative factor. A modified Delphi procedure of

averaging gradings given by a panel possessing firsthand experience in or knowledge of the individual country travel markets is suggested. For each variable under consideration, graders should attempt to assign ratings based on relativity between country markets.

Canada, for example, due to its proximity to the United States (nine of ten Canadians live within 100 miles of the U.S. border) and the high incidence of relatively low-cost auto travel to the United States, would likely receive a numerical rating of 10 for the input variable of "cost and distance of travel to host country." European countries would naturally receive lower marks for this variable. For the six subject travel markets to the United States, Table 10 provides the averaged gradings achieved for the individual qualitative refining factors.

Next, a series of weights must be applied to the five variable gradings achieved for each country, and the resulting products must be aggregated to formulate respective refining factors index ratings. In order to produce a qualitative index comparable to that achieved for the quantitative variables, with a maximum possible rating of 100.0, these weights must be five numbers that total 10.0. (If a country market should receive perfect ratings of all 10s for the five refining factors, its final index rating would be 100.0) A modified Delphi technique may also be used to determine these weighting values.

This procedure of applying weights to the refining factor's scalar gradings and the subsequent summation of the products to formulate the qualitative/refining factors index is notated as follows:

$$I_{qli} = w_1 g_{ci} + w_2 g_{ai} + w_3 g_{ei} + w_4 g_{mi} + w_5 g_{ti} \qquad (2)$$

where

I_{qli} = qualitative/refining factor index rating for country i

$w_1 - w_5$ = respective weights assigned to the five refining factors

g_{ci} = averaged grade achieved by country i for the variable "cost and distance of travel to host country"

g_{ai} = averaged grade achieved by country i for the variable "general political/social attitude toward host country"

TABLE 10 Qualitative/Refining Factors—Grading Results

COUNTRY	COST AND DISTANCE OF TRAVEL TO U.S.	POLITICAL/ SOCIAL ATTITUDE TOWARD U.S.	COMPETITIVE ENVIRONMENT	MARKET CONCENTRATION	TRADE STRUCTURE
Canada	10.0	9.2	6.8	7.2	5.6
Mexico	8.8	5.2	7.2	7.6	5.2
Japan	4.4	8.0	5.2	8.0	10.0
United Kingdom	5.6	8.8	4.0	7.6	8.0
Germany	5.6	8.0	4.0	4.8	9.6
France	5.2	5.2	4.0	8.4	5.2

NOTE: Grading Scale: 1 (most unfavorable) to 10 (most favorable)

g_{ei} = averaged grade achieved by country i for the variable "competitive environment"

g_{mi} = averaged grade achieved by country i for the variable "market concentration"

g_{ti} = averaged grade achieved by country i for the variable "trade structure"

For the five qualitative/refining factors, the corresponding grading weights derived for this example are:

w_1 = 4.5 (cost and distance of travel to U.S.)
w_2 = 1.0 (political/social attitude toward U.S.)
w_3 = 2.5 (competitive environment)
w_4 = 1.0 (market concentration)
w_5 = 1.0 (trade structure)
     10.0

For purposes of illustration, following is the application of Equation (2) for deriving the qualitative/refining factors index rating for the Canadian travel market:

$$I_{ql} = (4.5)(10.0) + (1.0)(9.2) + (2.5)(6.8) + (1.0)(7.2)$$
$$+ (1.0)(5.6)$$
$$= 45.0 + 9.2 + 17.0 + 7.2 + 5.6$$
$$= 84.0$$

Summary Table QL provides the completed refining factors index ratings for the six country travel markets to the United States under study here.

CUMULATIVE MARKET EVALUATION INDEX

In order to formulate a single set of numerical country ratings, the Cumulative Quantitative Factors Index (I_{qt}) and the Qualitative/Refining Factors Index (I_{ql}) must be combined. By again applying appropriate weights to each country's I_{qt} and I_{ql} ratings and aggregating the results, a cumulative market evaluation index can be produced.

The equational notation for this combination of the two major indices is:

$$I_{mei} = w_{qt}I_{qti} + w_{ql}I_{qli} \tag{3}$$

where

I_{mei} = cumulative market evaluation index rating for country

w_{qt} = weight assigned to index ratings in I_{qt}
w_{ql} = weight assigned to index ratings in I_{ql}
I_{qti} = country i's index rating in I_{qt}
I_{qli} = country i's index rating in I_{ql}

For the example used in this model, the two index weights, w_{qt} and w_{ql}, are assigned values of 0.75 and 0.25, respectively.

Using Equation (3) for the Canadian travel market, the following results are obtained:

TABLE QL Qualitative/Refining Factors Index

COUNTRY	QUALITATIVE/ REFINING FACTORS INDEX RATING (I_{ql})	RANKING
Canada	84.0	1
Mexico	76.0	2
Japan	58.8	4
United Kingdom	59.6	3
Germany	57.6	5
France	50.5	6

TABLE ME Cumulative Market Evaluation Index

Country	Cumulative Market Evaluation Index Rating (I_{me})	Final Ranking
Canada	80.7	1
Mexico	66.3	2
Japan	47.3	4
United Kingdom	51.7	3
Germany	56.3	5
France	38.0	6

$$I_{me} = (0.75)(79.6) + (0.25)(84.0)$$
$$= 59.7 + 21.0$$
$$= 80.7$$

Carrying out this tabulation for the six principal country travel markets to the United States results in the series of cumulative market evaluation index ratings shown in summary Table ME.

This final index provides a means for comparison of international tourism markets, in terms of market potential and overall viability for market development. In essence, this index provides an agency or firm concerned with allocating resources in the most productive and cost-efficient manner with a decision-making tool on which to base distribution of those resources among international tourism markets.

OTHER EVALUATIVE FACTORS

The output of the foregoing model yields measurements on relative market importance and potential, providing a basic system for determination of appropriate target country markets. After these choices are made, decisions concerning promotional, budgetary, and resource requirements are necessarily affected by other external variables that are inherent in the marketplace operations.

These factors, which involve "cost-of-doing-business" considerations, must be systematically included in any evaluation concerning resource allocation in international tourism markets. While this text does not attempt to develop specific quantitative data on these factors, a brief listing of the major variables to be considered is provided.

When studying the feasibility of establishing field marketing offices and/or allocating resources for marketing programs in foreign countries, an organization should quantitatively analyze the following costing variables:

1. *Cost of Advertising/Promotion*—Cost of air time and print space varies considerably from country to country.

2. *Cost of Public Relations Efforts*—Costs incurred in providing public relations materials and familiarization and product inspection tours to foreign travel writers, travel agents, and tour operators vary, due to disparate competitive environments, cost of travel, and so on.

3. *Cost of Consumer Information System*—Ongoing provision of detailed travel information, either promotional or descriptive, directly to the public can vary by market, involving costs and logistical considerations for supply of informational materials, translation requirements, location and costs of facilities, and so on.

4. *Cost of Trade Liaison and Support*—Market development efforts with the travel trade in the competitive marketplace involve sales calls, educational seminars, supplying promotional support materials, financial support for tour development, and so on. The amount of personal budgetary resources required to carry out comparable functions of this type varies by country market.

5. *Cost of Field Office Maintenance*—Varying expenses are incurred in renting/leasing appropriately located field office space, in maintaining employee staff support, and in meeting fixed and variable costs associated with office operations.

These variables, along with the characteristics of the marketplace and the target audience, will influence an organization's mix of marketing programs, as well as the ultimate commitment of resources to support these programs.

REFERENCES

Burkart, A.J., and S. Medlik (1974), *Tourism—Past, Present, and Future*, London: Heinemann.

Crampon, L.J., L.M. Rothfield, and Salah Wahab (1976), *Tourism Marketing*, London: Tourism International Press.

Economic Development Administration, U.S. Department of Commerce (1981), *Creating Economic Growth and Jobs Through Travel and Tourism*, Washington, D.C.

Gearing, C.E., W.W. Swart, and T. Var (1976), *Planning for Tourism Development*, New York: Praeger Publishers.

Munsinger, Gary M., and Richard W. Hansen (1974), *A Market Potential Index*, Washington, D.C.: United States Travel Service, U.S. Department of Commerce.

Schmoll, G.A. (1977), *Tourism Promotion*, London: Tourism International Press.

U.S. Travel Service (1978), *Tourism USA, Volume II—Development, Assessing Your Product and the Market*, Washington, D.C.

U.S. Travel Service and U.S. Travel Data Center (1980), *The Economic Impact of Foreign Visitor Spending in the United States*, Washington, D.C.

Index